USING THE THEORY

D1416708

ECONOMICS

PRINCIPLES AND APPLICATIONS

THIRD EDITION

Robert E. Hall
Department of Economics
Stanford University

Marc Lieberman
Department of Economics
New York University

THOMSON

SOUTH-WESTERN

Australia · Canada · Mexico · Singapore · Spain · United Kingdom · United States

THOMSON

SOUTH-WESTERN

Economics: Principles and Applications, 3e

Robert E. Hall and Marc Lieberman

Vice President / Editorial Director:
Jack W. Calhoun

Vice President / Editor-in-Chief:
Michael P. Roche

Publisher of Economics:
Michael B. Mercier

Acquisitions Editor:
Michael W. Worls

Sr. Developmental Editor:
Susanna C. Smart

Executive Marketing Manager:
Janet Hennies

Sr. Marketing Coordinator:
Jenny Fruechtenicht

Production Editor:
Daniel C. Plofchan

Manufacturing Coordinators:
Sandee Milewski, Rhonda Utley

Sr. Media Technology Editor:
Vicky True

Media Developmental Editor:
Peggy Buskey

Media Production Editor:
Pam Wallace

Compositor:
Pre-Press Company, Inc.
East Bridgewater, MA

Sr. Design Project Manager:
Michelle Kunkler

Cover and Internal Designer:
Ramsdell Design, Cincinnati

Cover Image:
© Getty Images, Inc.

Printer:
QuebecorWorld
Versailles, KY

COPYRIGHT © 2005
by South-Western, a division of
Thomson Learning. Thomson
Learning™ is a trademark used herein
under license.

Printed in the United States of America

1 2 3 4 5 06 05 04 03

For more information
contact South-Western,
5191 Natorp Boulevard,
Mason, Ohio 45040.
Or you can visit our Internet site at:
hyyp://www.swlearning.com

ALL RIGHTS RESERVED.
No part of this work covered by the
copyright hereon may be reproduced
or used in any form or by any
means—graphic, electronic, or
mechanical, including photocopying,
recording, taping, Web distribution or
information storage and retrieval
systems—without the written
permission of the publisher.

For permission to use material from this
text or product, contact us by
Tel (800) 730-2214
Fax (800) 730-2215
http://www.thomsonrights.com

Library of Congress Control Number:
2003114589

Package ISBN: 0-324-26034-2

Book ISBN: 0-324-29064-0

International Student Edition Package
ISBN: (Not for Sale in the United
States) 0-324-22548-2

International Student Edition Book
ISBN: (Not for Sale in the United
States) 0-324-22549-0

Preface

Economics: Principles and Applications is about economic principles and how economists use them to understand the world. It was conceived, written, and for the third edition, substantially revised to help your students focus on those basic principles and applications

We originally decided to write this book because we thought that existing books often confused students about economics and what it is all about. In our view, the leading texts can be divided into three categories. In the first category are the encyclopedias—the heavy tomes with a section or a paragraph on every topic or subtopic you might possibly want to present to your students. These books are often useful as reference tools. But because they cover too many topics—many of them superficially—the central themes and ideas are lost in the shuffle.

The second type of text we call the "scrapbook." In an effort to elevate student interest, these books insert multicolored boxes, news clippings, interviews, cartoons, and whatever else they can find to jolt the reader on each page. While these special features are often entertaining, there is a trade-off: these books sacrifice a logical, focused presentation of the material. Once again, the central themes and ideas are lost.

Finally, the third type of text, perhaps in response to the first two, tries to do less in every area—a *lot* less. But instead of just omitting the extraneous or inessential details, these texts attempt to redefine introductory economics by throwing out key ideas, models and concepts. Students who use these books may think that economics is overly simplified and unrealistic. After the course, they may be unprepared to go on in the field, or to think about the economy on their own.

A DISTINCTIVE APPROACH

Our approach is very different. We believe that the best way to teach principles is to present economics as a coherent, unified subject. This does not happen automatically. On the contrary, principles students often miss the unity of what we call "the economic way of thinking." For example, they are likely to see the analysis of goods markets, labor markets, and financial markets as entirely different phenomena, rather than as a repeated application of the same methodology with a new twist here and there. So the principles course appears to be just "one thing after another," rather than the coherent presentation we aim for.

CAREFUL FOCUS

Because we have avoided encyclopedic complexity, we have had to think hard about what topics are most important. As you will see:

We avoid nonessential material. When we believed a topic was not essential to a basic understanding of economics, we left it out. However, we have strived to include core material to *support* an instructor who wants to present special topics in class. So, for example, we do not have comprehensive treatments of environmental economics, agricultural economics, urban economics, health care economics, or comparative systems *as separate subject matter*. But instructors should find in the text a good foundation for building any of these areas—and many others—into their course. And we have included examples from each of these areas as *applications* of core theory where appropriate throughout the text.

We avoid distracting features. This text does not have interviews, news clippings, or boxed inserts with only distant connections to the core material. The features your students *will* find in our book are there to help them understand and apply economic theory itself, to help them avoid common mistakes in applying the theory (the Dangerous Curves feature), and to help them explore sources of information on their own using the Internet.

We explain difficult concepts patiently. By freeing ourselves from the obligation to introduce every possible topic in economics, we can explain the topics we *do* cover more thoroughly and patiently. We lead students, step-by-step, through each aspect of the theory, through each graph, and through each numerical example. In developing this book, we asked other experienced teachers to tell us which aspects of economic theory were hardest for their students to learn, and we have paid special attention to the trouble spots.

We use concrete examples. Students learn best when they see how economics can explain the world around them. Whenever possible, we develop the theory using real-world examples. You will find numerous references to real-world corporations and government policies throughout the text. When we employ hypothetical examples because they illustrate the theory more clearly, we try to make them realistic. In addition, each chapter ends with a thorough, extended application (the "Using the Theory" section) focusing on an important real-world issue.

FEATURES THAT REINFORCE

To help students see economics as a coherent whole, and to reinforce its usefulness, we have included some important features in this book.

The Three-Step Process

Most economists, when approaching a problem, begin by thinking about buyers and sellers, and the markets in which they come together to trade. They move on to characterize a market equilibrium, then give their model a workout in a comparative statics exercise. To understand what economics is about, students need to understand this process, and see it in action in different contexts. To help them do so, we have identified and stressed a "three-step process" that economists use in analyzing problems. The three key steps are:

1. **Characterize the Market.** Decide which market or markets best suit the problem being analyzed, and identify the decision makers (buyers and sellers) who interact there.
2. **Find the Equilibrium.** Describe the conditions necessary for equilibrium in the market, and a method for determining that equilibrium.
3. **Determine What Happens When Things Change.** Explore how events or government policies change the market equilibrium.

A full statement of each key step appears toward the end of Chapter 3. Thereafter, when one or more of the three steps plays an important part in a section of a future chapter, you'll often see a "steps symbol" as shown above. (It will be up to the student to determine which step or steps are applied in a particular section.) Through the use of the three-step process, students learn how to think like economists, and in a very natural way. And they come to see economics as a unified whole, rather than as a series of disconnected ideas.

Dangerous Curves

Anyone who teaches economics for a while learns that, semester after semester, students tend to make the same familiar errors. In class, in office hours, and on exams, students seem pulled, as if by gravity, toward certain logical pitfalls in thinking about, and using, economic theory. We've discovered in our own classrooms that merely explaining the theory properly isn't enough; the most common errors need to be *confronted*, and the student needs to be shown *specifically* why a particular logical path is incorrect. This was the genesis of our "Dangerous Curves" feature—boxes that anticipate the most common traps in economics, and warn students just when they are most likely to fall victim to them. We've been delighted to hear from instructors how effective this feature has been in overcoming the most common points of confusion for their students.

Using the Theory

 This text is full of applications that are woven throughout the narrative. In addition, virtually every chapter ends with an extended application ("Using the Theory") that pulls together several of the tools learned in that chapter. These are not news clippings or world events that relate only tangentially to the material. Rather, they are step-by-step presentations that help students see how the tools of economics can explain things about the world—things that would be difficult to explain without those tools.

Capstone Chapters

Another way we stress the unity of economics is through two capstone chapters. These chapters pull together the tools learned in *several* of the micro- or macroeconomics chapters, and apply them to a single real-world issue.

In microeconomics, the capstone chapter is titled, **Using *All* the Theory: The Microeconomics of Domestic Security.** In it we show how the three-step process can help us understand the reallocation of resources toward domestic security in the years following the terror attacks of September 11, 2001. We revisit key ideas about production possibilities frontiers, product and resource markets, the government's role in the economy, and international trade, and apply them in this new and important context.

In macroeconomics, the capstone chapter is **Using *All* the Theory: The Stock Market and the Macroeconomy.** This chapter utilizes a variety of macro tools learned in earlier chapters, and applies them to an issue that students find intriguing—the stock market. More specifically, the chapter pulls together material on GDP, unemployment, inflation, the aggregate expenditure model, the money market, and Federal Reserve policy, while focusing on the two-way relationship between the stock market and the macroeconomy.

Internet References

HTTP:// Throughout the book, we've included very brief Internet References where students can look at data, or explore topics further.

Content Innovations

In addition to the special features just described, you will find some important differences from other texts in topical approach and arrangement. These, too, are designed to make the theory stand out more clearly, and to make learning easier. These are not pedagogical experiments, nor are they innovation for the sake of innovation. The differences you will find in this text are the product of years of classroom experience.

Innovations In Microeconomics

Scarcity, Choice, and Economic Systems (Chapter 2): This early chapter, while covering standard material such as opportunity cost, also introduces some central concepts much earlier than other texts. Most importantly, it introduces the concept of *comparative advantage*, and the basic principle of *specialization and exchange*. We have placed them at the front of our book because we believe they provide important building blocks for much that comes later. For example, comparative advantage and specialization *within* the firm help explain economies of scale (Chapter 6). International trade (Chapter 15) can be seen as a special application of these principles, extending them to trade between nations.

How Firms Make Decisions: Profit Maximization (Chapter 7): Many texts introduce the theory of the firm using the perfectly competitive model first. We believe this is an unfortunate choice, because it forces students to simultaneously master the logic of profit maximization *and* the details of a rather special kind of market at the same time. Students quite naturally think of firms as facing *downward*-sloping demand curves—not horizontal ones. We have found that they have an easier time learning the theory of the firm with the more familiar, downward-sloping demand curve.

Further, by treating the theory of the firm in a separate chapter, *before* perfect competition, we can separate concepts that apply in *all* market structures (the shapes of marginal cost and average cost curves, marginal cost equals marginal revenue, the shut-down rule, etc.), from concepts that are unique to perfect competition (horizontal demand curve, marginal revenue the same as price, etc.). This avoids confusion later on.

Monopolistic Competition and Oligopoly (Chapter 10): Two features of our treatment are worth noting.

First, we emphasize advertising, a key feature of both of these types of markets. Students are very interested in advertising, and how firms make decisions about it. Second, we have omitted older theories of oligopoly that raised more questions than they answered, such as the kinked demand curve model. Our treatment of oligopoly is strictly game theoretic, but we have taken great care to keep it simple and clear. Here, as always, we provide the important tools to *support* instructors who want to take game theory further, without forcing every instructor to do so by including too much.

Capital and Financial Markets (Chapter 13): This chapter focuses on the common theme of these subjects: the present value of future income. Moreover, it provides simple, principles-level analyses of the stock and bond markets—something that students are hungry for, but that few principles textbooks address.

Description vs. Assessment (Chapters 8–10 and 14): In treating product market structures, most texts switch back and forth between the *description and analysis* of different markets on the one hand, and their *efficiency* properties on the other.

Our book collects the material on efficiency into a single chapter (Chapter 14). This has several advantages. First, it permits you to focus on *description* and *prediction* when teaching about market structures—a full plate, in our experience. Second, a chapter devoted to efficiency allows a more comprehensive treatment of the topic than we have seen elsewhere. Finally, our approach—in which students learn about efficiency *after* they have mastered the four market structures—allows them to study efficiency with the perspective needed to really understand it. This chapter—which also covers market failures and government's role—includes what we believe to be a core topic that is often missing from introductory texts: the economic role of the legal system.

Comparative Advantage and the Gains from International Trade (Chapter 15): We've found that international trade is best understood through clear numerical examples, and we've developed them carefully in this chapter. We also try to bridge the gap between the economics and politics of international trade with a systematic discussion of winners and losers.

Innovations in Macroeconomics

Long-Run Macroeconomics (Chapters 19 and 20): Our text presents long-run growth before short-run fluc-

tuations. Chapter 19 develops the long-run, classical model at a level appropriate for introductory students, mostly using supply and demand. Chapter 20 then *uses* the classical model to explain the causes—and costs—of economic growth in both rich and poor countries.

We believe it is better to treat the long run before the short run, for two reasons. First, the long-run model makes full use of the tools of supply and demand, and thus allows a natural transition from the preliminary chapters (1, 2, and 3) into macroeconomics. Second, we believe that students can best understand economic fluctuations by understanding *how* and *why* the long-run model breaks down over shorter time periods. This, of course, requires an introduction to the long-run model first.

Economic Fluctuations (Chapter 21): This unique chapter provides a bridge from the long-run to the short-run macro model, and paves the way for the short-run focus on *spending* as the driving force behind economic fluctuations.

Aggregate Demand and Aggregate Supply (Chapter 25): One of our pet peeves about other introductory texts is the too-early introduction of aggregate demand and aggregate supply curves, *before* teaching where these curves come from. Students then confuse the *AD* and *AS* curves with their microeconomic counterparts, requiring corrective action later. In this text, the *AD* and *AS* curves do not appear until Chapter 25, where they are fully explained. Our treatment of aggregate supply is based on a very simple mark-up model that our students have found easy to understand.

Exchange Rates and Macroeconomic Policy (Chapter 28): Many students find international macroeconomics the most interesting topic in the course, especially the material on exchange rates and what causes them to change. Accordingly, you will find unusually full coverage of exchange rate determination in this chapter. This treatment is kept simple and straightforward, relying exclusively on supply and demand. And it forms the foundation for the discussion of open-economy macro policy that ends the chapter.

ORGANIZATIONAL FLEXIBILITY

We have arranged the contents of each chapter, and the table of contents as a whole, according to our recommended order of presentation. But we have also built in flexibility.

In microeconomics: *Chapter 5 develops consumer theory with both marginal utility and (in an appendix) indifference curves, allowing you to present either method in class. (Instructors will find it even easier to make their choice in this edition—see below.) If you wish to highlight international trade or present comparative advantage earlier in the course, you could assign Chapter 15 immediately following Chapter 3. An instructor who feels strongly that economic efficiency should be interwoven with market structure can assign the relevant sections of Chapter 14 with Chapters 8, 9, and 10. (Again, easier to do in this edition.) Similarly, the relevant parts of the capstone chapter (Using* All the Theory: The Microeconomics of Domestic Security*) can be assigned with Chapters 3, 8, 11, 13, 14 and 15.*

In macroeconomics: *Once the core chapters (16–25) have been taught, the remaining chapters (26–28) can be presented in any order. Some instructors may want to assign selections from Chapter 27 (Fiscal Policy) along with Chapter 22 (The Short-Run Macro Model). Similarly, parts of the capstone chapter (Using All the Theory: The Stock Market and the Macroeconomy) can be assigned with Chapters 22, 25, and 26.*

Finally, we have included only those chapters that we thought were both essential and teachable in a year-long course. But not everyone will agree about what is essential. While we—as authors—cringe at the thought of a chapter being omitted in the interest of time, we have allowed for that possibility. Nothing in Chapter 12 (economic inequality), Chapter 13 (capital and financial markets), Chapter 14 (economic efficiency and government's role), Chapter 15 (international trade), Chapter 21 (economic fluctuations), Chapter 26 (monetary policy), Chapter 27 (fiscal policy and the budget), or Chapter 28 (international macro) is required to understand any of the other numbered chapters in the book. Skipping any of these should not cause continuity problems.

In many cases, a chapter can be assigned selectively. For example, in Chapter 11 (labor markets), an instructor who feels rushed could focus on the equilibrium and comparative statics results in labor *markets*, and skip the analyses of the firm as a demander of labor. And in macroeconomics, an instructor who is anxious to get to the short-run macro model could freely select among the sections in Chapter 20 (economic growth and rising living standards) and Chapter 21 (economic fluctuations).

NEW TO THE THIRD EDITION

For this third edition, we've incorporated many excellent suggestions from reviewers and adopters. We've also conducted lengthy interviews with several adopters to refine their suggestions further. While the overall approach and philosophy of the book remain unchanged, you'll find that every chapter has been affected by the revision.

For example, we've worked hard to clarify and simplify figures, and we've increased the use of caption boxes that enable students to work their way through diagrams more easily. We've replaced examples and made adjustments in the narrative on every page, recognizing that often a more apt example or a slight change in phrasing can vastly improve clarity. We've added a few dozen new Dangerous Curves boxes, in response to some great suggestions from instructors. About a third of the end-of-chapter "Using the Theory" sections are either entirely new or substantially expanded from previous editions. And, of course, we've updated all tables and figures with new data, and adjusted content to reflect the rapid economic changes that have taken place over the past few years.

In addition, we've made some major changes that all instructors should know about in preparing their course.

- *Chapter 2 (Scarcity, Choice, and Economic Systems):* We've revised the discussion of opportunity and incorporated "the opportunity cost of college" as a running example. We've also added a new section on technological change and the PPF.
- *Chapter 3 (Supply and Demand):* We've added an entirely new appendix covering supply and demand equations that teaches students how to solve for equilibrium algebraically. We've also replaced "productive capacity" (as a shift variable for supply curves) with the simpler "number of firms."
- *Chapter 4 (Working with Supply and Demand):* We've reorganized the chapter, with a more careful motivation for the elasticity approach. And we've added new sections on supply elasticity and tax incidence.
- *Chapter 5 (Consumer Theory):* The chapter has been reorganized to allow a genuine choice between the marginal utility approach (in the body) and the indifference curve approach (in an expanded appendix). Instructors wishing to cover the indifference curve approach should assign all sections of the chapter except "The Marginal Utility Approach," substituting the appendix for this section. This substitution now

results in a seamless fit with the rest of the chapter. Those who prefer the marginal utility approach can simply skip the appendix.

- *Chapter 7 (Theory of the Firm: Profit Maximization):* We've removed the material on the principal-agent problem from this chapter, and included a briefer discussion of this concept in the new "Using the Theory" at the end of Chapter 12 (on CEO pay).
- *Chapters 11 and 12 (Labor Markets and Economic Inequality):* These chapters now include appendices on monopsony, and how it can change conclusions about the minimum wage and union wage setting. We've also emphasized the increase in inequality of the 1990s and early 2000s.
- *Chapter 13 (Capital and Financial Markets):* The chapter now motivates the need for present value calculations in an entirely new way (see the section, "A First Simple Approach").
- *Chapter 14 (Efficiency and Government's Role):* This is a thoroughly rewritten chapter, combining material in the previous edition's chapters 14 and 15. While the chapter is still based on Pareto improvements, welfare is now measured with consumer and producer surplus. We've also added a principles-level explanation of the Coase theorem and its implications.
- *Chapter 15 (International Trade and Comparative Advantage):* We've included the ideas of the Heckscher-Ohlin model (without using the term) in explaining the origins of comparative advantage, and paid more attention to the power politics of protectionism.
- *Chapter 20 (Economic Growth and Rising Living Standards):* The chapter is organized around an entirely new framework for understanding growth, leading to a new emphasis on the role of productivity.
- *Chapter 21 (Economic Fluctuations):* This chapter has been vastly simplified by removing the more technically difficult material on disequilibrium and the adjustment to the long run, while retaining and improving the material on why the classical model cannot explain fluctuations.
- *Chapters 22, 24, and 25 (Short-Run Model, The Money Market, and Aggregate Demand and Aggregate Supply):* The "Using the Theory" sections at the ends of these chapters are now organized around the theme of the 2001 recession and its aftermath. With each presentation, the analysis is deepened and extended, taking advantage of the new tools presented in each chapter.
- *Chapter 26 (Monetary Policy):* This chapter includes a new, integrated discussion of the Taylor rule.
- *Chapter 27 (Fiscal Policy):* We've thoroughly rewritten the section on the long-run consequences of large budget deficits, and included a new "Using the Theory" on the Bush tax cuts.

Finally, to make the switch from the previous edition to this one as easy as possible, we have posted a more extensive list of chapter-by-chapter changes on our Web site at http://hall-lieb.swlearning.com.

TEACHING AND LEARNING AIDS

To help you present the most interesting principles courses possible, we have created an extensive set of supplementary items. Many of them can be downloaded from the Hall/Lieberman Web site (http://hall-lieb.swlearning.com). The list includes:

For the Instructor

- An *Instructor's Manual*, by Jane Himarios of the University of Texas, Arlington. The manual provides chapter outlines, teaching ideas, Experiential Exercises for many chapters, suggested answers to the end-of-chapter questions, solutions to all problems, and answers to the e-con @pps (Economic Applications) exercises.
- *Instructor's Resource CD-ROM.* This easy-to-use CD allows quick access to instructor ancillaries from your desktop. It also allows you to review, edit, and copy exactly the material you need. Or, you may choose to go to *Instructor Resources* on the *Product Support Web Site.* This site at http://hall-lieb.swlearning.com features the essential resources for instructors, password-protected, in downloadable format: the *Instructor's Manual* in Word, the Test Banks in Word, and PowerPoint® Lecture and Exhibit Slides.
- *Microeconomics and Macroeconomics Test Banks,* revised by Dennis Hanseman, University of Cincinnati. These contain over 4,000 multiple-choice questions. The test questions have been arranged according to chapter headings and subheadings, making it easy to find the material needed to construct examinations.
- Two supplemental test banks, created for Microeconomics and Macroeconomics: *Supplemental Test Bank for Microeconomics,* by Douglas Kinnear of Colorado State University, and *Supplemental Test*

Bank for Macroeconomics, by Jeffrey Johnson, Sullivan University. Each includes approximately 1,500 new Multiple Choice and True/False questions, arranged by chapter headings.

- *ExamView® Computerized Testing Software.* ExamView is an easy-to-use test creation package compatible with both Microsoft Windows and Macintosh client software, and contains all of the questions in all of the printed test banks. You can select questions by previewing them on the screen, selecting them by number, or selecting them randomly. Questions, instructions, and answers can be edited, and new questions can easily be added. You can also administer quizzes online—over the Internet, through a local area network (LAN), or through a wide area network (WAN).

- *Full-Color Transparency Acetates.* Acetates are available in both a micro and a macro version and consist of many key graphs and illustrations from the text.

- *PowerPoint® Lecture and Exhibit Slides.* Available only on the Web site and the IRCD are two versions of the PowerPoint presentations. The first, prepared by John F. Hall, is a comprehensive and user-friendly *Lecture* outline presentation for use in the classroom, consisting of speaking points in chapter outline format, accompanied by numerous graphs and tables from the main text. The second version, *Exhibit Slides*, provides the instructor with key graphs from the text, many with animation, which may be printed for use as transparency masters.

- *Principles of Economics Videotape.* *Principles of Economics* is a 40-minute videotape that offers students an insightful overview of ten common economic principles: Trade-offs, Opportunity Cost, Marginal Thinking, Incentives, Trade, Markets, Government's Role, Productivity, Inflation, and the Phillips Curve. *Principles of Economics* shows viewers how to apply economic principles to their daily lives. This video is filled with interviews from some of the country's leading economists, includes profiles of real students facing economic choices, and shows the economy's impact on U.S. and foreign companies. The video can be used at the beginning of a term to give students a general overview of economics, or used one section at a time prior to teaching each of these principles.

- *CNN Video with Integration Guide.* Professors can bring the real world into the classroom by using the CNN Principles of Economics Video Updates. This video provides current stories of economic interest.

The accompanying integration guide provides a summary and discussion questions for each clip. The video is produced in cooperation with Turner Learning, Inc.

- *Favorite Ways to Learn Economics: Instructor's Edition.* Authors David Anderson of Centre College and Jim Chasey of Homewood-Flossmoor High School use experiments to bring economic education to life. This is a lab manual for the classroom and for individual study that contains experiments and problem sets that reinforce key economic concepts. The Instructor's Edition provides you the guidance and tips to ensure that these experiments are facilitated successfully.

- *MarketSim.* MarketSim, by Tod Porter at Youngstown State University, is an online simulation designed to help students in microeconomics classes better understand how markets work, by taking on the roles of consumers and producers in a simulated economy. In the simulations, students "make" and "accept" offers to buy and sell labor and goods asynchronously via the Internet. The goal of MarketSim is to provide instructors with a flexible teaching tool that can be used to motivate students to better understand a wide variety of microeconomic concepts.

- *TextChoice.* TextChoice is a custom format of Thomson Learning's online digital content. TextChoice provides the fastest, easiest way for you to create your own learning materials. You may select content from hundreds of best-selling titles, choose material from our numerous databases, and add your own material. Contact your South-Western/Thomson sales representative for more information at http://thomsoncustom.com.

- *eCoursepacks.* Create a customizable, easy-to-use, online companion for any course with eCoursepacks, from Thomson companies South-Western and Gale. eCoursepacks give educators access to current content from thousands of popular, professional, and academic periodicals, including NACRA and Darden cases, and business and industry information from Gale. You also have the ability to easily add your own material—even collecting a royalty if you choose. Permissions for all eCoursepack content are already secured, saving you the time and worry of securing rights. eCoursepacks online publishing tools also save you time and energy by allowing you to quickly search the databases and make selections, organize all your content, and publish the final outline product in a clean, uniform, and full-color format. eCoursepacks are the best ways to provide your audience with current information easily, quickly, and inexpensively. http://ecoursepacks.swlearning.com.

- *WebTutor Advantage.* *WebTutor Advantage* is an interactive, Web-based, student supplement on WebCT and/or BlackBoard that harnesses the power of the Internet to deliver innovative learning aids that actively engage students. The instructor can incorporate WebTutor as an integral part of the course, or the students can use it on their own as a study guide. Benefits to students include automatic and immediate feedback from quizzes and exams; interactive, multimedia-rich explanation of concepts; online exercises that reinforce what students have learned; flashcards that include audio support; and greater interaction and involvement through online discussion forums. Visit WebTutor to see a demo and for more information at http://webtutor.swlearning.com.

- *WebTutor Toolbox.* WebTutor™ ToolBox provides instructors with links to content from the book companion Web site. It also provides rich communication tools to instructors and students, including a course calendar, chat, and e-mail. For more information about the WebTutor products, please contact your local Thomson sales representative.

For the Student

- The *Active Learning Guide*, by Geoffrey A. Jehle of Vassar College. This guide provides numerous exercises and self-tests for problem-solving practice. It is a valuable tool for helping students strengthen their knowledge of economics.

- Answers to even-numbered end-of-chapter Questions and Problems can be found on the text Web site at http://hall-lieb.swlearning.com.

- The *Hall/Lieberman Xtra!* at http://hallxtra. swlearning.com. Xtra! provides students with access to the robust set of additional online learning tools found at the site. Here is a tour through some of the study support features you will find there:

  - **Diagnostic Pretests.** These innovative quizzes offer students diagnostic self-assessment of their comprehension of each chapter and an individualized plan for directed study based on the areas in which they are found to have a weaker understanding.

  - **Master the Learning Objectives.** Each chapter's Master the Learning Objectives gives step-by-step instructions associated with each learning objective to guide students systematically through all the activities that will deepen their understanding of that particular concept.

- **The Graphing Workshop.** The Graphing Workshop is a one-stop learning resource for help in mastering the language of graphs, which is one of the more difficult aspects of an economics course for many students. It enables students to explore important economic concepts through a unique learning system made up of tutorials, interactive drawing tools, and exercises that teach how to interpret, reproduce, and explain graphs.

- **"Using the Theory" Applications.** Activities and exercises are available that ask students to use the three key steps to analyze unique and real world questions.

- **CNN Video Clips.** CNN video segments bring the "real world" right to students' desktops. The accompanying CNN video exercises help to illustrate how economics is an important part of their daily lives, and help them learn the material by applying it to current events.

- **Ask the Instructor Video Clips.** Via streaming video, difficult concepts from each chapter are explained and illustrated by an economics instructor, Dr. Peter Olson from Indiana University. These video clips can be extremely helpful review and clarification tools if a student had trouble understanding an in-class lecture or is more of a visual learner.

- **Economic Applications.** (e-con @pps). Econ-News Online, EconDebate Online, EconData Online, and EconLinks Online features help to deepen students' understanding of theoretical concepts through hands-on exploration and analysis of the latest economic news stories, policy debates, and data.

- NEW to this edition—and in conjunction with these Xtra! features: **Economic Applications exercises** at the end of every chapter. Prepared by Brian J. Peterson (Manchester College) and Hamid Azari-Rad (SUNY–New Paltz), the exercises direct students to one or more of the applications to solve problems through brief research. These exercises help students to understand the relationship of current issues to the theories studied in the chapters. Xtra! is available as an optional package with the text.

- *InfoTrac® College Edition.* Students can receive anytime, anywhere, online access to a database of full-text articles from hundreds of scholarly and popular periodicals such as *Newsweek, Fortune, American Economist,* and the *Quarterly Journal of Economics.* The InfoTrac subscription card is good for four months, and is a great way to practice online research using academically-based and reliable sources.

- The *Hall/Lieberman Web site* (http://hall-lieb. swlearning.com). The site contains a wealth of useful teaching and learning resources. Important features available at the Web site include:
  - *Interactive Quizzes* with feedback on answers. Completed quizzes can be e-mailed directly to the instructor.
  - Links to the Internet addresses referred to in the text.
  - PowerPoint slides for review and note-taking.
  - A sample chapter from the *Active Learning Guide*.
- *Economics: Hits on the Web.* This resource booklet supports your students' research efforts on the World Wide Web. The manual covers materials such as: introduction to the World Wide Web, browsing the Web, finding information on the World Wide Web, e-mail, e-mail discussion groups, newsgroups, and documenting Internet sources for research. It also provides a listing of the hottest economic sites on the Web.
- *Favorite Ways to Learn Economics.* In *Favorite Ways to Learn Economics,* authors David Anderson of Centre College and Jim Chasey of Homewood-Flossmoor High School use experiments to bring economic education to life. This is a lab manual for the classroom and for individual study that contains experiments and problem sets that reinforce key economic concepts.
- *9/11: Economic Viewpoints.* The shape, pace, and spirit of the global economy have been greatly impacted by the events that occurred on September 11, 2001. With *9/11: Economic Viewpoints,* South-Western offers a collection of essays that provides a variety of perspectives on the economic effects of this event. Each essay is written by one of South-Western's economics textbook authors, all of whom are highly regarded for both their academic and professional achievements. This unique collaboration results in one of the most cutting-edge resources available to help facilitate discussions of September 11's impact within the context of economics courses.
- *The Economist's Handbook: A Research and Writing Guide,* 2nd Edition. This reference book, by Thomas Wyrick of Southwest Missouri State University, is designed to help students develop skills in conducting and interpreting economic research. *The Economist's Handbook* provides commonsense explanations, relevant examples, and focused assignments, as well as an extensive glossary of economic terms, information about economics careers, and other useful reference materials.

- *Economics Alive! CD-ROMs.* These interactive multimedia study aids provide a high-tech, fun way to study economics. Through a combination of animated presentations, interactive graphing exercises, and simulations, the core principles of economics come to life in an upbeat and entertaining way. Available as both Macroeconomics Alive! and Microeconomics Alive!. Visit the Economics Alive! Web site at http://econalive.swlearning.com.
- *The Wall Street Journal.* The Hall and Lieberman texts are available with a special 15-week *Wall Street Journal* subscription offer. Have your instructor contact your South-Western/Thomson Learning sales representative for package pricing and ordering information.

ACKNOWLEDGMENTS

Our greatest debt is to the many reviewers who carefully read the book and provided numerous suggestions for improvements. While we could not incorporate all their ideas, we did carefully evaluate each one of them. To these reviewers, we are most grateful:

Ljubisa Adamovich	Florida State University
Brian A'Hearn	Franklin and Marshall College
Rashid Al-Hmoud	Texas Tech University
David Aschauer	Bates College
Richard Ballman	Augustana College
Chris Barnett	Gannon University
Sylvain Boko	Wake Forest University
Mark Buenafe	Arizona State University
Steven Call	Metropolitan State College
Kevin Carey	American University
Steven Cobb	Xavier University
Dennis Debrecht	Carroll College
Selahattin Dibooglu	Southern Illinois University
John Duffy	University of Pittsburgh
Stephen Erfle	Dickinson College
James Falter	Mount Marty College
Sasan Fayazmanesh	California State University, Fresno
Sarmila Ghosh	University of Scranton
Satyajit Ghosh	University of Scranton
Scott Gilbert	Southern Illinois University–Carbondale
Michael Gootzeit	University of Memphis

John Gregor	Washington and Jefferson University	Khosrow Doroodian	Ohio University
Rik Hafer	Southern Illinois University	Debra S. Dwyer	SUNY, Stony Brook
Andrew Hildreth	University of California, Berkeley	Sasan Fayazmanesh	California State University, Fresno
Thomas Husted	American University	Lehman B. Fletcher	Iowa State University
David Kaun	University of California, Santa Cruz	James R. Gale	Michigan Technological University
Philip King	San Francisco State University	Arunee C. Grow	Mesa Community College
Kate Krause	University of New Mexico	Dennis Hanseman	
Viju Kulkarni	San Diego State University	Roger Hewett	Drake University
Nazma Latif-Zaman	Providence College	Shahruz Hohtadi	Suffolk University
Teresa Laughlin	Palomar College	Jeffrey Johnson	Sullivan University
Judith Mann	University of California, San Diego	Jacqueline Khorassani	Marietta College
		Frederic R. Kolb	University of Wisconsin, Eau Claire
Shahruz Mohtadi	Suffolk University		
Chris Niggle	University of Redlands	Brent Kreider	Iowa State University
Farrokh Nourzad	Marquette University	Bruce Madariaga	Montgomery College
Jim Palmieri	Simpson College	Mark McCleod	Virginia Tech University
Yvon Pho	American University	Steve McQueen	Barstow Community College
Teresa Riley	Youngstown State University	William R. Melick	Kenyon College
William Rosen	Cornell University	Paul G. Munyon	Grinnell College
Thomas Sadler	Pace University	Rebecca Neumann	University of Wisconsin, Milwaukee
Jonathan Sandy	University of San Diego		
Ramazan Sari	Texas Tech University	Emmanuel Nnadozie	Truman State University
Ghosh Sarmila	University of Scranton	Zaohong Pan	Western Connecticut State University
Edward Scahill	University of Scranton		
Mary Schranz	University of Wisconsin, Madison	Gregg Pratt	Mesa Community College
Alden Shiers	California Polytechnic State University	Alannah Orrison Rosenberg	Saddleback Community College
Kevin Siqueira	Clarkson University	Robert F. Schlack	Carthage College
Kevin Sontheimer	University of Pittsburgh	Pamela M. Schmitt	U.S. Naval Academy
Richard Steinberg	Indiana University–Purdue University Indianapolis	John Vahaly	University of Louisville
		Mikayel Vardanyan	Oregon State University
Martha Stuffler	Irvine Valley College	Michael F. Williams	University of St. Thomas
Mohammad Syed	Miles College	Dirk Yandell	University of San Diego
Thomas Watkins	Eastern Kentucky University	Petr Zemcik	Southern Illinois University, Carbondale
Glen Whitman	California State University, Northridge		
Robert Whaples	Wake Forest University		

To help us with improvements to this third edition, we went through a number of special reviews, surveys, and phone conversations. We would like to thank the following instructors for their thoughtful comments and insights:

Parantap Basu	Fordham University
Tibor Besedes	Rutgers University
Gautam Bhattacharya	University of Kansas
James E. Dietz	California State University, Fullerton

We also wish to acknowledge the talented and dedicated group of instructors who helped put together a supplementary package that is second to none. Geoffrey A. Jehle of Vassar College cowrote the *Active Learning Guide* and created numerous improvements to this edition, making it even more user-friendly *active*. Jane Himarios of the University of Texas, Arlington, revised the *Instructor's Manual*, the Test Banks were carefully revised by Dennis Hanseman, and the new Supplemental Test Banks were created by Douglas Kinnear of Colorado State University, and Jeffrey Johnson of Sullivan University. We appreciate the contributions of Hamid Azari-Rad of SUNY–New Paltz and Brian J. Peterson of

Manchester College, both of whom created the new Economic Applications exercises for this edition. And we are grateful to Mark Karscig of Central Missouri State University for his contributions to the "Using the Theory" exercises for the Web site. In addition, we appreciate the work of the three people who contributed to the Web site's Online Quizzes: Brian Peterson, Jeffrey Johnson, and Douglas Kinnear. Our thanks go also to John and Pamela Hall (Western Washington University), who thoroughly revised and improved the PowerPoint slides for this edition. Finally, special thanks go to Dennis Hanseman, who was our development editor for the first edition; his insights and ideas are still present in this third edition, and his continued assistance has proved invaluable.

The beautiful book you are holding would not exist except for the hard work of a talented team of professionals. Book production was overseen by Dan Plofchan, Production Editor at South-Western, and undertaken by Pre-Press Company. At Pre-Press, all things are possible because of the dedicated work of Gordon Laws. Dan and Gordon showed remarkable patience, as well as an unflagging concern for quality throughout the process. We couldn't have asked for better production partners. A team of NYU students helped to locate and fix the few remaining errors. They included Leslie Miller, Abigail Trainer, Martin Paredes, and Wen-Jyh Chao.

The overall look of the book and cover was planned by Michelle Kunkler and executed by Craig Ramsdell of Ramsdell Design. John Hill managed the photo program, and Sandee Milewski and Rhonda Utley made all the pieces come together in their roles as Manufacturing Coordinators.

Finally, we are especially grateful for the hard work of the dedicated and professional South-Western editorial, marketing, and sales teams. Mike Worls, Acquisitions Editor, has once again shepherded this text through publication with remarkable skill and devotion. Lisa Lysne and Janet Hennies, Executive Marketing Managers, have done a first-rate job getting the message out to instructors and sales reps. Susan Smart, Senior Development Editor, delved into every chapter and contributed to their improvement; her patience, flexibility, and skill went far beyond the call of duty. Vicky True, Senior Media Technology Editor; Peggy Buskey, Media Development Editor; and Pam Wallace, Media Production Editor, have put together a wonderful package of media tools. And the South-Western sales representatives have been extremely persuasive advocates for the book. We sincerely appreciate all their efforts!

A Request

Although we have worked hard on the first three editions of this book, we know there is always room for further improvement. For that, our fellow users are indispensable. We invite your comments and suggestions wholeheartedly. We especially welcome your suggestions for additional "Using the Theory" sections and Dangerous Curves. You may send your comments to either of us care of South-Western.

Bob Hall
Marc Lieberman

About the Authors

Robert E. Hall is a prominent applied economist. He is the Robert and Carole McNeil Professor of Economics at Stanford University and Senior Fellow at Stanford's Hoover Institution where he conducts research on inflation, unemployment, taxation, monetary policy, and the economics of high technology. He received his Ph.D. from MIT and has taught  there as well as at the University of California, Berkeley. Hall is Director of the research program on Economic Fluctuations of the National Bureau of Economic Research, and Chairman of the Bureau's Committee on Business Cycle Dating, which maintains the semiofficial chronology of the U.S. business cycle. He has published numerous monographs and articles in scholarly journals, and coauthored a popular intermediate text. Hall has advised the Treasury Department and the Federal Reserve Board on national economic policy, and has testified on numerous occasions before congressional committees.

Marc Lieberman is Clinical Associate Professor of Economics at New York University. He received his Ph.D. from Princeton University. Lieberman has presented his extremely popular Principles of Economics course at Harvard, Vassar, the University of California, Santa Cruz, and the University of Hawaii, as well as at NYU, where he won the university's Golden  Dozen teaching award and also the Economics Society Award for Excellence in Teaching. He is coeditor and contributor to *The Road to Capitalism: Economic Transformation in Eastern Europe and the Former Soviet Union*. Lieberman has consulted for the Bank of America and the Educational Testing Service. In his spare time, he is a professional screenwriter. He co-wrote the script for *Love Kills*, a thriller that aired on the USA Cable Network, and he teaches screenwriting at NYU's School of Continuing and Professional Studies.

Brief Contents

Contents

PART II: MICROECONOMIC DECISION MAKERS

PART III: PRODUCT MARKETS

PART IV: LABOR, CAPITAL, AND FINANCIAL MARKETS

PART V: EFFICIENCY, GOVERNMENT, AND THE GLOBAL ECONOMY

PART VII: LONG-RUN MACROECONOMICS

PART VIII: SHORT-RUN MACROECONOMICS

USING *ALL* THE THEORY: THE STOCK MARKET AND THE MACROECONOMY   961

What Is Economics?

Economics. The word conjures up all sorts of images: manic stock traders on Wall Street, an economic summit meeting in a European capital, a somber television news anchor announcing good or bad news about the economy. . . . You probably hear about economics several times each day. What exactly *is* economics?

First, economics is a *social science,* so it seeks to explain something about *society.* In this sense, it has something in common with psychology, sociology, and political science. But economics is different from these other social sciences, because of *what* economists study and *how* they study it. Economists ask fundamentally different questions, and they answer them using tools that other social scientists find rather exotic.

ECONOMICS, SCARCITY, AND CHOICE

A good definition of economics, which stresses the difference between economics and other social sciences, is the following:

> *Economics is the study of choice under conditions of scarcity.*

Economics The study of choice under conditions of scarcity.

1

This definition may appear strange to you. Where are the familiar words we ordinarily associate with economics: "money," "stocks and bonds," "prices," "budgets," . . . ? As you will soon see, economics deals with all of these things and more. But first, let's take a closer look at two important ideas in this definition: scarcity and choice.

Scarcity and Individual Choice

Think for a moment about your own life—your daily activities, the possessions you enjoy, the surroundings in which you live. Is there anything you don't have that you'd *like* to have? Anything you'd like *more* of? If your answer is "no," congratulations! You are well advanced on the path of Zen self-denial. The rest of us, however, feel the pinch of limits to our material standard of living. This simple truth is at the very core of economics. It can be restated this way: We all face the problem of **scarcity**.

Scarcity A situation in which the amount of something available is insufficient to satisfy the desire for it.

At first glance, it may seem that you suffer from an infinite variety of scarcities. There are so many things you might like to have right now—a larger room or apartment, a new car, more clothes . . . the list is endless. But a little reflection suggests that your limited ability to satisfy these desires is based on two other, more basic limitations: scarce *time* and scarce *spending power*.

> *As individuals, we face a scarcity of time and spending power. Given more of either, we could each have more of the goods and services that we desire.*

HTTP://

To make good use of the Internet, you will need the Adobe Acrobat Reader. It can be downloaded from http://www.adobe.com/products/acrobat/readermain.html. An economic question is: Why does Adobe give the Reader away free?

The scarcity of spending power is no doubt familiar to you. We've all wished for higher incomes so that we could afford to buy more of the things we want. But the scarcity of time is equally important. So many of the activities we enjoy—seeing a movie, taking a vacation, making a phone call—require time as well as money. Just as we have limited spending power, we also have a limited number of hours in each day to satisfy our desires.

Because of the scarcities of time and spending power, each of us is forced to make *choices*. We must allocate our scarce *time* to different activities: work, play, education, sleep, shopping, and more. We must allocate our scarce *spending power* among different goods and services: housing, food, furniture, travel, and many others. And each time we choose to buy something or do something, we also choose *not* to buy or do something else.

Economists study the choices we make as individuals and also the *consequences* of those choices. For example, in 2002 and 2003, large numbers of consumers in the United States decided to spend less on air travel, due to concerns about safety and increased delays at airport security checkpoints. Many shifted their vacation spending toward home-improvement projects. Collectively, these decisions led to a contraction and layoffs in the airline industry, and in businesses associated with air travel (e.g., hotels and car rental firms). At the same time, businesses associated with home improvement (e.g., lumber mills, contractors, hardware stores) expanded, and hired additional workers.

Economists also study the more subtle and indirect effects of individual choice on our society. Will most Americans continue to live in houses or—like Europeans—will most of us end up in apartments? Will we have an educated and well-informed citizenry? Will traffic congestion in our cities continue to worsen or is there relief in sight? These questions hinge, in large part, on the separate decisions of millions of people. To answer them requires an understanding of how individuals make choices under conditions of scarcity.

Scarcity and Social Choice

Now let's think about scarcity and choice from *society*'s point of view. What are the goals of our society? We want a high standard of living for our citizens, clean air, safe streets, good schools, and more. What is holding us back from accomplishing all of these goals in a way that would satisfy everyone? You already know the answer: scarcity.

In society's case, the problem is a scarcity of **resources**—the things we use to make goods and services that help us achieve our goals. Economists classify resources into four categories:

1. **Labor** is the time human beings spend producing goods and services.
2. **Capital** is something produced that is long-lasting, and used to make *other* things that we value. Note the word *long-lasting*. If something is used up quickly in the production process—like the flour a baker uses to make bread—it is generally *not* considered capital. A good rule of thumb is that capital should last at least a year, although most types of capital last considerably longer.

    It's useful to distinguish two different types of capital. **Physical capital** consists of things like machinery and equipment, factory buildings, computers, and even hand tools like hammers and screwdrivers. These are all long-lasting *physical* goods that are used to make other things.

    Human capital consists of the skills and knowledge possessed by workers. These satisfy our definition of capital: They are *produced* (through education and training), they help us produce *other* things, and they last for many years, typically through an individual's working life.[1]

    The **capital stock** is the total amount of capital at a nation's disposal at any point in time. It consists of all the physical and human capital made in previous periods that is still productively useful.
3. **Land/Natural resources** are the preexisting "gifts of nature" in a country. This includes land—the physical space on which production takes place—as well as useful materials found under it or on it, such as crude oil, iron, coal, or fertile soil.
4. **Entrepreneurship** is an individual's ability (and the willingness to *use* this ability) to combine the *other* resources into a productive enterprise. An entrepreneur may be an *innovator* who comes up with an original idea for a business or a *risk taker* who provides her own funds or time to nurture a project with uncertain rewards.

Anything *produced* in the economy comes, ultimately, from some combination of these resources. Think about the last lecture you attended at your college. You were consuming a service—a college lecture. What went into producing that service? Your instructor was supplying labor. Many types of capital were used as well. The physical capital included desks, chairs, a chalkboard or transparency projector, the classroom building itself, and the computer your instructor may have used to

Resources The labor, capital, land and natural resources, and entrepreneurship that are used to produce goods and services.

Labor The time human beings spend producing goods and services.

Capital Something produced that is long-lasting and used to produce other goods.

Physical capital The part of the capital stock consisting of physical goods, such as machinery, equipment, and factories.

Human capital The skills and training of the labor force.

Capital stock The total amount of capital in a nation that is productively useful at a particular point in time.

Natural resources Land as well as the naturally occurring materials that come with it.

Entrepreneurship The ability and willingness to combine the *other* resources—labor, capital, and natural resources—into a productive enterprise.

---

[1] An individual's human capital is ordinarily supplied along with his labor time. (When your instructor lectures or holds office hours, she is providing both labor time and her skills as an economist and teacher.) Still, it's often useful to distinguish the *time* a worker provides (her labor) from any skills or *knowledge* possessed (human capital).

compose lecture notes. In addition, there was human capital—your instructor's specialized knowledge and lecturing skills. There was a natural resource—land—the property on which your classroom building sits. And some individual or group had to play the role of innovator and risk taker in order to combine the labor, capital, and natural resources needed to create and guide your institution in its formative years. (If you attend a public college or university, this entrepreneurial role was largely filled by the state government and the risk takers were the state's taxpayers.)

The scarcity of resources like these causes the scarcity of all goods and services produced from them.

> *As a society, our resources—land and natural resources, labor, capital, and entrepreneurship—are insufficient to produce all the goods and services we might desire. In other words, society faces a scarcity of resources.*

This stark fact about the world helps us understand the choices a society must make. Do we want a more educated citizenry? Of course. But that will require more labor—construction workers to build more classrooms and teachers to teach in them. It will require more natural resources—land for classrooms and lumber to build them. And it will require more capital—cement mixers, trucks, and more. These very same resources, however, could instead be used to produce *other* things that we find desirable, things such as new homes, hospitals, automobiles, or feature films. As a result, every society must have some method of *allocating* its scarce resources—choosing which of our many competing desires will be fulfilled and which will not be.

Input Anything (including a resource) used to produce a good or service.

Many of the big questions of our time center on the different ways in which resources can be allocated. The cataclysmic changes that rocked Eastern Europe and the former Soviet Union during the early 1990s arose from a very simple fact: The method these countries used for decades to allocate resources was not working. Closer to home, the never-ending debates between Democrats and Republicans in the United States about tax rates, government services, and even foreign policy reflect subtle but important differences of opinion about how to allocate resources. Often, these are disputes about whether the private sector can handle a particular issue of resource allocation on its own or whether the government should be involved.

DANGEROUS CURVES

The term *resources* is often confused with another, more general term—**inputs.** An input is *anything* used to make a good or service—including (but not limited to) a resource. *Resources,* by contrast, are the *special* inputs that fall into one of four categories: labor, natural resources (including land), capital, and entrepreneurship.

What's so special about resources? They are the ultimate source of everything that is produced. If you think about any good or service that you use—say, an automobile—it is made from the four resources and *other* inputs (such as steel). But any of these *other* inputs can be traced back to the resources used to produce it (steel is made from iron ore, labor, capital, etc.). Goods and services, and the inputs used to make them, are all made from resources. This is why a nation's capacity to produce goods and services is limited by the amounts of the four resources at its disposal.

Scarcity and Economics

The scarcity of resources—and the choices it forces us to make—is the source of all of the problems you will study in economics. Households have limited incomes for satisfying their desires, so they must choose carefully how they allocate their spending among different goods and services. Business firms want to make the highest possible profit, but they must pay for their resources; so they carefully choose *what* to produce, *how much* to produce, and *how* to produce it. Federal, state, and local government agencies work with limited budgets, so they must carefully choose which goals to pursue. Economists study these decisions made by households, firms, and governments to explain how our economic system operates, to forecast the future of our economy, and to suggest ways to make that future even better.

THE WORLD OF ECONOMICS

The field of economics is surprisingly broad. It extends from the mundane—why does a pound of steak cost more than a pound of chicken?—to the personal and profound—how do couples decide how many children to have? With a field this broad, it is useful to have some way of classifying the different types of problems economists study and the different methods they use to analyze them.

Microeconomics and Macroeconomics

The field of economics is divided into two major parts: microeconomics and macroeconomics. **Microeconomics** comes from the Greek word *mikros,* meaning "small." It takes a close-up view of the economy, as if looking through a microscope. Microeconomics is concerned with the behavior of *individual* actors on the economic scene—households, business firms, and governments. It looks at the choices they make and how they interact with each other when they come together to trade *specific* goods and services. What will happen to the cost of movie tickets over the next five years? How many management-trainee jobs will open up for college graduates? How would U.S. phone companies be affected by a tax on imported cell phones? These are all microeconomic questions because they analyze individual *parts* of an economy rather than the *whole.*

Macroeconomics—from the Greek word *makros,* meaning "large"—takes an *overall* view of the economy. Instead of focusing on the production of carrots or computers, macroeconomics lumps all goods and services together and looks at the economy's *total output.* Instead of focusing on employment of management trainees or manufacturing workers, it considers *total employment* in the economy. Instead of asking why credit card loans carry higher interest rates than home mortgage loans, it asks what makes interest rates *in general* rise or fall. In all of these cases, macroeconomics focuses on the big picture and ignores the fine details.

Microeconomics The study of the behavior of individual households, firms, and governments; the choices they make; and their interaction in specific markets.

Macroeconomics The study of the behavior of the overall economy.

Positive and Normative Economics

The micro versus macro distinction is based on the level of detail we want to consider. Another useful distinction has to do with our *purpose* in analyzing a problem. **Positive economics** deals with *how* the economy works, plain and simple. If someone says, "Recent increases in spending for domestic security have slowed the growth rate of the U.S. economy," she is making a positive economic statement. A statement need not be accurate or even sensible to be classified as positive. For example, "Government policy has no effect on our standard of living" is a false, but positive, statement. Whether true or not, it's a statement about how the economy works and its accuracy can be tested by looking at the facts—and just the facts.

Normative economics concerns itself with what *should be.* It is used to make judgments about the economy, identify problems, and prescribe solutions. Rather

Positive economics The study of how the economy works.

Normative economics The study of what *should be;* it is used to make value judgments, identify problems, and prescribe solutions.

DANGEROUS CURVES

Be alert to statements that may *seem* positive but are actually normative. Here's an example: "If we want to reduce pollution, our society will have to use less gasoline." This may *sound* positive, because it seems to refer only to facts about the world. But it's actually normative. Why? Cutting back on gasoline is just *one* policy among many that could reduce pollution. To say that we *must* choose this method makes a value judgment about its superiority to other methods. A purely positive statement on this topic would be, "Using less gasoline—with no other change in living habits—would reduce pollution."

Similarly, be alert to statements that use vague terms with hidden value judgments. An example: "All else equal, the less gasoline we use, the better our quality of life." Whether you agree or disagree, this is *not* a positive statement. Two people who agree about the facts—in this case, the consequences of using less gasoline—might disagree over the meaning of the phrase "quality of life," how to measure it, and what would make it better. This disagreement could not be resolved just by looking at the facts.

than limiting its concerns to just "the facts," it goes on to say what we should *do* about them and therefore depends on our values.

If an economist says, "We should cut total government spending," she is engaging in normative economic analysis. Cutting government spending would benefit some citizens and harm others, so the statement rests on a value judgment. A normative statement—like the one about government spending above—cannot be proved or disproved by the facts alone.

Positive and normative economics are intimately related in practice. For one thing, we cannot properly argue about what we should or should not do unless we know certain facts about the world. Every normative analysis is therefore based on an underlying positive analysis. But while a positive analysis can, at least in principle, be conducted without value judgments, a normative analysis is always based, at least in part, on the values of the person conducting it.

Why Economists Disagree. The distinction between positive and normative economics can help us understand why economists sometimes disagree. Suppose you are watching a television interview in which two economists are asked whether the United States should eliminate all government-imposed barriers to trading with the rest of the world. The first economist says, "Yes, absolutely," but the other says, "No, definitely not." Why the sharp disagreement?

The difference of opinion may be *positive* in nature: The two economists may have different views about what would actually happen if trade barriers were eliminated. Differences like this sometimes arise because our knowledge of the economy is imperfect or because certain facts are in dispute.

More likely, however, the disagreement will be *normative*. Economists, like everyone else, have different values. In this case, both economists might agree that opening up international trade would benefit *most* Americans, but harm *some* of them. Yet they may still disagree about the policy move because they have different values. The first economist might put more emphasis on benefits to the overall economy, while the second might put more emphasis on preventing harm to a particular group. Here, the two economists have come to the same *positive* conclusion, but their *different values* lead them to different *normative* conclusions.

In the media, economists are rarely given enough time to express the basis for their opinions, so the public hears only the disagreement. People may then conclude that economists cannot agree about how the economy works, even when the *real* disagreement is over goals and values.

WHY STUDY ECONOMICS?

Students take economics courses for all kinds of reasons.

To Understand the World Better

Applying the tools of economics can help you understand global and cataclysmic events such as wars, famines, epidemics, and depressions. But it can also help you understand much of what happens to you locally and personally—the worsening traffic conditions in your city, the raise you can expect at your job this year, or the long line of people waiting to buy tickets for a popular concert. Economics has the power to help us understand these phenomena because they result, in large part, from the choices we make under conditions of scarcity.

Economics has its limitations, of course. But it is hard to find any aspect of life about which economics does not have *something* important to say. Economics cannot explain why so many Americans like to watch television, but it *can* explain how TV networks decide which programs to offer. Economics cannot protect you from a robbery, but it *can* explain why some people choose to become thieves and why no society has chosen to eradicate crime completely. Economics will not improve your love life, resolve unconscious conflicts from your childhood, or help you overcome a fear of flying, but it *can* tell us how many skilled therapists, ministers, and counselors are available to help us solve these problems.

To Gain Self-Confidence

Those who have never studied economics often feel that mysterious, inexplicable forces are shaping their lives, buffeting them like the bumpers in a pinball machine, determining whether or not they'll be able to find a job, what their salary will be, whether they'll be able to afford a home, and in what kind of neighborhood. If you've been one of those people, all that is about to change. After you learn economics, you may be surprised to find that you no longer toss out the business page of your local newspaper because it appears to be written in a foreign language. You may no longer lunge for the remote and change the channel the instant you hear "And now for news about the economy. . . . " You may find yourself listening to economic reports with a critical ear, catching mistakes in logic, misleading statements, or out-and-out lies. When you master economics, you gain a sense of mastery over the world, and thus over your own life as well.

To Achieve Social Change

If you are interested in making the world a better place, economics is indispensable. There is no shortage of serious social problems worthy of our attention—unemployment, hunger, poverty, disease, child abuse, drug addiction, violent crime. Economics can help us understand the origins of these problems, explain why previous efforts to solve them have failed, and help us to design new, more effective solutions.

To Help Prepare for Other Careers

Economics has long been a popular college major for individuals intending to work in business. But it has also been popular among those planning careers in politics, international relations, law, medicine, engineering, psychology, and other professions. This is for good reason: Practitioners in each of these fields often find themselves confronting economic issues. For example, lawyers increasingly face judicial

HTTP://

The Federal Reserve Bank of Minneapolis asked some Nobel Prize winners how they became interested in economics. Their stories can be found at http://www.minneapolisfed.org/pubs/region/int.cfm.

rulings based on the principles of economic efficiency. Doctors will need to understand how new technologies or changes in the structure of health insurance will affect their practices. Industrial psychologists need to understand the economic implications of workplace changes they may advocate, such as flexible scheduling or on-site child care.

To Become an Economist

Only a tiny minority of this book's readers will decide to become economists. This is welcome news to the authors, and after you have studied labor markets in your *microeconomics* course you will understand why. But if you do decide to become an economist—obtaining a master's degree or even a Ph.D.—you will find many possibilities for employment. Of 16,780 members of the American Economic Association who responded to a recent survey,[2] 62 percent were employed at colleges or universities. The rest were engaged in a variety of activities in the private sector (19 percent), government (8 percent), and international organizations (3 percent). Economists are hired by banks to assess the risk of investing abroad; by manufacturing companies, to help them determine new methods of producing, marketing, and pricing their products; by government agencies, to help design policies to fight crime, disease, poverty, and pollution; by international organizations, to help create aid programs for less developed countries; by the media, to help the public interpret global, national, and local events; and even by nonprofit organizations, to provide advice on controlling costs and raising funds more effectively.

THE METHODS OF ECONOMICS

One of the first things you will notice as you begin to study economics is the heavy reliance on *models*. Indeed, the discipline goes beyond any other social science in its insistence that every theory be represented by an explicit, carefully constructed *model*.

You've no doubt encountered many models in your life. As a child, you played with model trains, model planes, or model people—dolls. In a high school science course, you probably saw a model of an atom—one of those plastic and wire contraptions with red, blue, and green balls representing protons, neutrons, and electrons. You may have also seen architects' cardboard models of buildings. These are physical models, three-dimensional replicas that you can pick up and hold. Economic models, on the other hand, are built not with cardboard, plastic, or metal but with words, diagrams, and mathematical statements.

What, exactly, is a model?

Model An astract representation of reality.

> *A **model** is an abstract representation of reality.*

The two key words in this definition are *abstract* and *representation*. A model is not supposed to be exactly like reality. Rather, it *represents* the real world by *abstracting* or *taking from* the real world that which will help us understand it. In any model, many real-world details are left out.

---

[2] *American Economic Review,* Table of Employment, 2003 (*http://www.vanderbilt.edu/AEA/Tbl. Employ.htm*).

The Art of Building Economic Models

When you build a model, how do you know which details to include and which to leave out? There is no simple answer to this question. The right amount of detail depends on your purpose in building the model in the first place. There is, however, one guiding principle:

A model should be as simple as possible to accomplish its purpose.

This means that a model should contain only the *necessary* details.

To understand this a little better, think about a map. A map is a model—it represents a part of the earth's surface. But it leaves out many details of the real world. First, maps are two-dimensional, so they leave out the third dimension—height—of the real world. Second, maps always ignore small details, such as trees and houses and potholes. Third, a map is much smaller than the area it represents. But when you buy a map, how much detail do you want it to have?

Let's say you are in Boston, and you need a map (your *purpose*) to find the best way to drive from Logan Airport to the downtown convention center. In this case, you would want a very detailed city map, with every street, park, and plaza in Boston clearly illustrated and labeled. A highway map, which ignores these details, wouldn't do at all.

But now suppose your purpose is different: to select the best driving route from Boston to Cincinnati. Now you want a highway map. A map that shows every street between Boston and Cincinnati would have *too much* detail. All of that extraneous information would only obscure what you really need to see.

Although economic models are more abstract than road maps, the same principle applies in building them: The level of detail that would be just right for one purpose will usually be too much or too little for another. When you feel yourself objecting to a model in this text because something has been left out, keep in mind the purpose for which the model is built. In introductory economics, the purpose is entirely educational. The models are designed to help you understand some simple, but powerful, principles about how the economy operates. Keeping the models simple makes it easier to see these principles at work and remember them later.

Of course, economic models have other purposes besides education. They can help businesses make decisions about pricing and production, help households decide how and where to invest their savings, and help governments and international agencies formulate policies. Models built for these purposes will be much more detailed than the ones in this text, and you will learn about them if you take more advanced courses in economics. But even complex models are built around very simple frameworks—the same frameworks you will be learning here.

Assumptions and Conclusions

Every economic model begins with *assumptions* about the world. There are two types of assumptions in a model: simplifying assumptions and critical assumptions.

A **simplifying assumption** is just what it sounds like—a way of making a model simpler without affecting any of its important conclusions. The purpose of a simplifying assumption is to rid a model of extraneous detail so its essential features can stand out more clearly. A road map, for example, makes the simplifying assumption, "There are no trees," because trees on a map would only get in the way. Similarly, in

These maps are models. *But each would be used for a different purpose.*

© SUSAN VAN ETTEN

Simplifying assumption Any assumption that makes a model simpler without affecting any of its important conclusions.

an economic model, we might assume that there are only two goods that households can choose from or that there are only two nations in the world. We make such assumptions *not* because they are true, but because they make a model easier to follow and do not change any of the important insights we can get from it.

A **critical assumption**, by contrast, is an assumption that affects the conclusions of a model in important ways. When you use a road map, you make the critical assumption, "All of these roads are open." If that assumption is wrong, your conclusion—the best route to take—might be wrong as well.

Critical assumption Any assumption that affects the conclusions of a model in an important way.

In an economic model, there are always one or more critical assumptions. You don't have to look very hard to find them, because economists like to make these assumptions explicit right from the outset. For example, when we study the behavior of business firms, our model will assume that firms try to earn the highest possible profit for their owners. By stating this assumption up front, we can see immediately where the model's conclusions spring from.

The Three-Step Process

As you read this textbook, you will learn how economists use economic models to address a wide range of problems. In Chapter 2, for example, you will see how a simple economic model can give us important insights about society's production choices. And subsequent chapters will present still different models that help us understand the U.S. economy and the global economic environment in which it operates. As you read, it may seem to you that there are a lot of models to learn and remember . . . and, indeed, there are.

But there is an important insight about economics that—once mastered—will make your job easier than you might think. The insight is this: There is a remarkable similarity in the types of models that economists build, the assumptions that underlie those models, and what economists actually *do* with them. In fact, you will see that economists follow the same *three-step process* to analyze almost any economic problem. The first two steps explain how economists *build* an economic model, and the last explains how they *use* the model.

What are these three steps that underlie the economic approach to almost any problem? Sorry for the suspense, but you'll have to wait a bit—until the end of Chapter 3—for the answer. By that time, you'll have learned a little more about economics, and the three-step process will make more sense to you.

Math, Jargon, and Other Concerns . . .

HTTP://

An online introduction to the use of graphs can be found at http://syllabus.syr.edu/cid/graph/book.html.

Economists often express their ideas using mathematical concepts and a special vocabulary. Why? Because these tools enable economists to express themselves more precisely than with ordinary language. For example, someone who has never studied economics might say, "When used textbooks are available, students won't buy new textbooks." That statement might not bother you right now. But once you've finished your first economics course, you'll be saying it something like this: "When the price of used textbooks falls, the demand curve for new textbooks shifts leftward."

Does the second statement sound strange to you? It should. First, it uses a special term—a *demand curve*—that you haven't yet learned. Second, it uses a mathematical concept—a *shifting curve*—with which you might not be familiar. But while the first statement might mean a number of different things, the second statement—

as you will see in Chapter 3—can mean only *one* thing. By being precise, we can steer clear of unnecessary confusion.

If you are worried about the special vocabulary of economics, you can relax. All of the new terms will be defined and carefully explained as you encounter them. Indeed, this textbook does not assume you have any special knowledge of economics. It is truly meant for a "first course" in the field.

But what about the math? Here, too, you can relax. While professional economists often use sophisticated mathematics to solve problems, only a little math is needed to understand basic economic *principles*. And virtually all of this math comes from high school algebra and geometry.

Still, you may have forgotten some of your high school math. If so, a little brushing up might be in order. This is why we have included an appendix at the end of this chapter. It covers some of the most basic concepts—such as interpreting graphs, the equation for a straight line, and the concept of a slope—that you will need in this course. You may want to glance at this appendix now, just so you'll know what's there. Then, from time to time, you'll be reminded about it when you're most likely to need it.

HOW TO STUDY ECONOMICS

As you read this book or listen to your instructor, you may find yourself following along and thinking that everything makes perfect sense. Economics may even seem easy. Indeed, it *is* rather easy to *follow* economics, since it's based so heavily on simple logic. But *following* and *learning* are two different things. You will eventually discover (preferably *before* your first exam) that economics must be studied actively, not passively.

If you are reading these words lying back on a comfortable couch, a phone in one hand and a remote control in the other, you are going about it in the wrong way. Active studying means reading with a pencil in your hand and a blank sheet of paper in front of you. It means closing the book periodically and *reproducing* what you have learned. It means listing the steps in each logical argument, retracing the cause-and-effect steps in each model, and drawing the graphs that represent the model. It means *thinking* about the basic principles of economics and how they relate to what you are learning. It does require some work, but the payoff is a good understanding of economics and a better understanding of your own life and the world around you.

Summary

Economics is the study of choice under conditions of scarcity. As individuals, and as a society, we have unlimited desires for goods and services. Unfortunately, the *resources*—land and natural resources, labor, capital, and entrepreneurship—needed to produce those goods and services are scarce. Therefore, we must choose which desires to satisfy and how to satisfy them. Economics provides the tools that explain those choices.

The field of economics is divided into two major areas. *Microeconomics* studies the behavior of individual households, firms, and governments as they interact in specific markets. *Macroeconomics,* by contrast, concerns itself with the behavior of the entire economy. It considers variables such as total output, total employment, and the overall price level.

Economics makes heavy use of *models*—abstract representations of reality. These models are built with words, diagrams, and mathematical statements that help us understand how the economy operates. All models are simplifications, but a good model will have *just enough detail for the purpose at hand.*

When analyzing almost any problem, economists follow a three-step process in building and using economic models. This three-step process will be introduced at the end of Chapter 3.

Key Terms

Capital	Input	Natural resources
Capital stock	Labor	Physical capital
Critical assumption	Macroeconomics	Positive economics
Economics	Microeconomics	Resources
Entrepreneurship	Model	Scarcity
Human capital	Normative economics	Simplifying assumption

Review Questions

Answers to even-numbered Questions and Problems can be found on the text Web site at http://hall-lieb.swlearning.com.

1. What is a *resource*? What are the four different types of resources?

2. What determines the level of detail that an economist builds into a model?

3. What is the difference between a simplifying assumption and a critical assumption?

4. Would each of the following be classified as microeconomics or macroeconomics? Why?
   a. Research into why the growth rate of total production increased during the 1990s.
   b. A theory of how consumers decide what to buy.
   c. An analysis of Dell Computer's share of the personal computer market.
   d. Research on why interest rates were unusually high in the late 1970s and early 1980s.

5. What is the difference between an input and a resource?

Problems

1. Come up with a list of critical assumptions that could lie behind each of the following statements. Discuss whether each assumption would be classified as normative or positive.
   a. The United States is a democratic society.
   b. European movies are better than American movies.
   c. The bigger the city, the higher the quality of the newspaper.

2. Discuss whether each statement is an example of positive economics or normative economics or if it contains elements of both:
   a. An increase in the personal income tax will slow the growth rate of the economy.
   b. The goal of any country's economic policy should be to increase the well-being of its poorest, most vulnerable citizens.
   c. Excess regulation of small business is stifling the economy. Small business has been responsible for most of the growth in employment over the last 10 years, but regulations are putting a severe damper on the ability of small businesses to survive and prosper.
   d. The 1990s were a disastrous decade for the U.S. economy. Income inequality increased to its highest level since before World War II.

3. For each of the following, state whether economists would consider it a *resource*, and if they would, identify which of the four types of resources the item is.
   a. A computer used by an FBI agent to track the whereabouts of suspected criminals.
   b. The office building in which the FBI agent works.
   c. The time that an FBI agent spends on a case.
   d. A farmer's tractor.
   e. The farmer's knowledge of how to operate the tractor.
   f. Crude oil.
   g. A package of frozen vegetables.
   h. A food scientist's knowledge of how to commercially freeze vegetables.
   i. The ability to bring together resources to start a frozen food company.
   j. Plastic bags used to buy a frozen food company to hold its product.

 These exercises require access to Hall/Lieberman Xtra! If Xtra! did not come with your book, visit http://hallxtra.swlearning.com to purchase.

1. Use your Xtra! password at the Hall and Lieberman Web site (http://hallxtra.swlearning.com), select Chapter 1, and under Economic Applications, click on EconDebates. Choose Economic Fundamentals; Scarcity, Choice and Opportunity Cost; and scroll down to find the debate, "Are Americans Overworked?" Read the debate, and use the information to answer the following questions.

   a. Is the question in the title of this debate an example of positive or normative economics? Why?
   b. Why is leisure time becoming scarcer over time?
   c. Identify three statements of positive economics in this debate.

APPENDIX

GRAPHS AND OTHER USEFUL TOOLS

TABLES AND GRAPHS

A brief glance at this text will tell you that graphs are important in economics. Graphs provide a convenient way to display information and enable us to immediately *see* relationships between different variables.

Suppose that you've just been hired at the advertising department of Len & Harry's—an up-and-coming manufacturer of high-end ice cream products, located in Texas. You've been asked to compile a report on how advertising affects the company's sales. It turns out that the company's spending on advertising has changed repeatedly in the past, so you have lots of data on monthly advertising outlays and monthly sales revenue, both measured in thousands of dollars.

Table A.1 shows a useful way of arranging this data. The company's advertising outlays in different months are listed in the left-hand column, while the right-hand column lists total sales revenue ("sales" for short) during the same month. Notice that the data here is organized so that spending on advertising increases as we move down the first column. Often, just looking at a table like this can reveal useful patterns. Here, it's clear that higher spending on advertising is associated with higher monthly sales. These two variables—advertising and sales—have a **positive relationship**.[3] A rise in one is associated with a rise in the other. If higher advertising had been associated with *lower* sales, the two variables would have a **negative** or **inverse relationship:** A rise in one would be associated with a fall in the other.

We can be even more specific about the positive relationship between advertising and sales: Logic tells us that the association is very likely *causal*. We'd expect that sales revenue *depends on* advertising outlays, so we call sales our **dependent variable** and advertising our **independent variable**. Changes in an independent variable cause changes in a dependent variable, but not the other way around.

To explore the relationship further, let's graph it. As a rule, the *independent* variable is measured on the *horizontal* axis and the *dependent* variable on the *vertical* axis. In economics, unfortunately, we do not always stick to this rule, but for now we will. In Figure A.1, monthly advertising outlays—our independent variable—are measured on the horizontal axis. If we start at the *origin*—the corner where the two axes intersect—and move rightward along the horizontal axis, monthly advertising outlays increase from $0 to $1,000 to $2,000 and so on. The vertical axis measures monthly sales—the dependent variable. Along this axis, as we move upward from the origin, sales rise.

The graph in Figure A.1 shows six labeled points, each representing a different pair of numbers from our table. For example, point *A*—which represents the

TABLE A.1 **Advertising and Sales at Len & Harry's**	Advertising ($1,000 per Month)	Sales ($1,000 per Month)
	2	46
	3	49
	6	58
	7	61
	11	73
	12	76

---

[3] Key Terms found in this appendix are defined at the end of the appendix and in the glossary.

numbers in the first row of the table—shows us that when the firm spends $2,000 on advertising, sales are $46,000 per month. Point *B* represents the *second* row of the table, and so on. Notice that all of these points lie along a *straight line*.

Straight-Line Graphs

You'll encounter straight-line graphs often in economics, so it's important to understand one special property they possess: The "rate of change" of one variable compared with the other is always the same. For example, look at what happens as we move from point *A* to point *B*: Advertising rises by $1,000 (from $2,000 to $3,000), while sales rise by $3,000 (from $46,000 to $49,000). If you study the graph closely, you'll see that anywhere along this line, whenever advertising increases by $1,000, sales increase by the same $3,000. Or, if we define a "unit" as "one thousand dollars," we can say that every time advertising increases by one unit, sales rise by three units. So the "rate of change" is three units of sales for every one unit of advertising.

The rate of change of the *vertically* measured variable for a one-unit change in the *horizontally* measured variable is also called the **slope** of the line. The slope of the line in Figure A.1 is three, and it remains three no matter where along the line we measure it. For example, make sure you can see that from point *C* to point *D*, advertising rises by one unit and sales rise by three units.

What if we had wanted to determine the slope of this line by comparing points *D* and *E*, which has ad-

vertising rising by four units instead of just one? In that case, we'd have to calculate the rise in one variable *per unit* rise in the other. To do this, we divide the change in the vertically measured variable by the change in the horizontally measured variable.

$$\text{Slope of a straight line} = \frac{\text{change in vertical variable}}{\text{change in horizontal variable}}.$$

We can make this formula even simpler by using two shortcuts. First, we can call the variable on the vertical axis "Y" and the variable on the horizontal axis "X." In our case, Y is sales, while X is advertising outlays. Second, we use the Greek letter Δ ("delta") to denote the words "change in." Then, our formula becomes:

$$\text{Slope of straight line} = \frac{\Delta Y}{\Delta X}.$$

Let's apply this formula to get the slope as we move from point *D* to point *E*, which causes advertising (*X*) to rise from 7 units to 11 units. This is an increase of 4, so $\Delta X = 4$. For this move, sales rise from 61 to 73, an increase of 12, so $\Delta Y = 12$. Applying our formula,

$$\text{Slope} = \frac{\Delta Y}{\Delta X} = \frac{12}{4} = 3.$$

This is the same value for the slope that we found earlier. Not surprising, since it's a straight line and a straight line has the same slope everywhere. The particular pair of points we choose for our calculation doesn't matter.

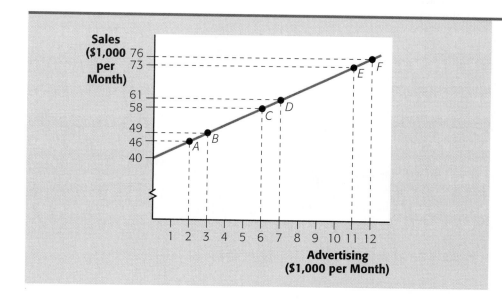

FIGURE A.1
A Graph of Advertising and Sales

FIGURE A.2
Measuring the Slope of a Curve

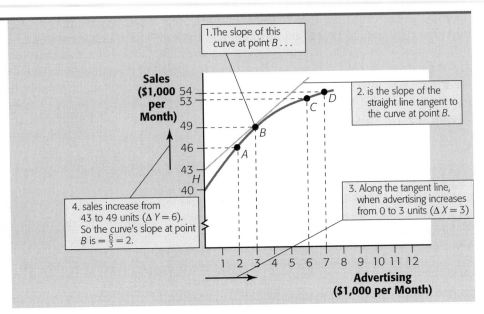

Curved Lines

Although many of the relationships you'll encounter in economics have straight-line graphs, many others do not. Figure A.2 shows *another* possible relationship between advertising and sales that we might have found from a different set of data. As you can see, the line is curved. But as advertising rises, the curve gets flatter and flatter. Here, as before, each time we spend another $1,000 on advertising, sales rise. But now, the rise in sales seems to get smaller and smaller. This means that the *slope* of the curve is *itself changing* as we move along this curve. In fact, the slope is getting smaller.

How can we measure the slope of a curve? First, note that since the slope is different at every point along the curve, we aren't really measuring the slope of "the curve" but the slope of the curve *at a specific point along it*. How can we do this? By drawing a **tangent line**—a straight line that touches the curve at just one point and that has the same slope as the curve at that point. For example, in the figure, a tangent line has been drawn for point *B*. To measure the slope of this tangent line, we can compare any two points on it, say, *H* and *B*, and calculate the slope as we would for any straight line. Moving from point *H* to point *B*, we are moving from 0 to 3 on the horizontal axis ($\Delta X = 3$) and from 43 to 49 on the vertical axis ($\Delta Y = 6$). Thus, the slope of the tangent line—which is the same as the slope of the curved line at point *B*—is:

$$\frac{\Delta Y}{\Delta X} = \frac{6}{3} = 2.$$

This says that, at point *B*, the rate of change is two units of sales for every one unit of advertising. Or, going back to dollars, the rate of change is $2,000 in sales for every $1,000 spent on advertising.

The curve in Figure A.2 slopes everywhere upward, reflecting a positive relationship between the variables. But a curved line can also slope downward to illustrate a negative relationship between variables, or slope first one direction and then the other. You'll see plenty of examples of each type of curve in later chapters and you'll learn how to interpret each one as it's presented.

LINEAR EQUATIONS

Let's go back to the straight-line relationship between advertising and sales, as shown in Table A.1. What if you need to know how much in sales the firm could expect if it spent $5,000 on advertising next month? What if it spent $8,000, or $9,000? It would be nice to be able to answer questions like this without having to pull out tables and graphs to do it. As it turns out, anytime the relationship you are studying has a straight-line graph, it is easy to figure out an equation for the entire relationship—a *linear equation*. You then can use the equation to answer any such question that might be put to you.

All straight lines have the same general form. If *Y* stands for the variable on the vertical axis and *X* for the variable on the horizontal axis, every straight line has an equation of the form

$$Y = a + bX,$$

where *a* stands for some number and *b* for another number. The number *a* is called the vertical *intercept*, because it marks the point where the graph of this equation hits (intercepts) the vertical axis; this occurs when *X* takes the value zero. (If you plug $X = 0$ into the equation, you will see that, indeed, $Y = a$.) The number *b* is the slope of the line, telling us how much *Y* will change every time *X* changes by one unit. To confirm this, note that as *X* increases from 0 to 1, *Y* goes from *a* to $a + b$. The number *b* is therefore the change in *Y* corresponding to a one-unit change in *X*—exactly what the slope of the graph should tell us.

If *b* is a positive number, a one-unit increase in *X* causes *Y* to *increase* by *b* units, so the graph of our line would slope upward, as illustrated by the red line in panel (a) of Figure A.3. If *b* is a negative number, then a one-unit increase in *X* will cause *Y* to *decrease* by *b*

units, so the graph would slope downward, as the blue line does in panel (a). Of course, *b* could equal zero. If it does, a one-unit increase in *X* causes no change in *Y*, so the graph of the line is flat, like the black line in panel (a).

The value of *a* has no effect on the slope of the graph. Instead, different values of *a* determine the graph's position. When *a* is a positive number, the graph will intercept the vertical *Y*-axis above the origin, as the red line does in panel (b) of Figure A.3. When *a* is negative, however, the graph will intercept the *Y*-axis *below* the origin, like the blue line in panel (b). When *a* is zero, the graph intercepts the *Y*-axis right at the origin, as the black line does in panel (b).

Let's see if we can figure out the equation for the relationship depicted in Figure A.1. There, *X* denotes advertising and *Y* denotes sales. Earlier, we calculated that

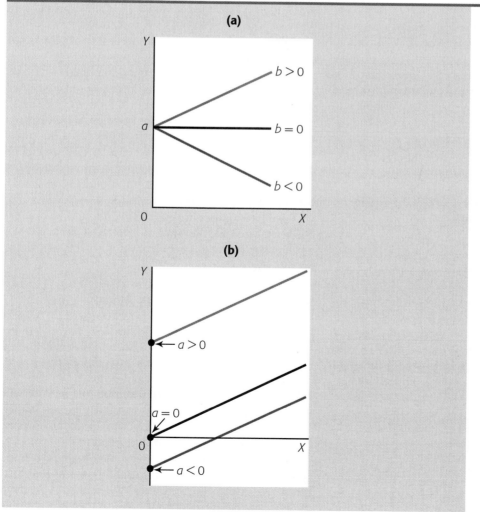

FIGURE A.3
Straight Lines with Different Slopes and Vertical Intercepts

the slope of this line, *b*, is 3. But what is *a*, the vertical intercept? On the graph, you can see that when advertising outlays are zero, sales are $40,000. That tells us that $a = 40$.[4] Putting these two observations together, we find that the equation for the line in Figure A.1 is

$$Y = 40 + 3X.$$

Now if you need to know how much in sales to expect from a particular expenditure on advertising, you'd be able to come up with an answer: You'd simply multiply the amount spent on advertising by 3, add $40,000, and that would be your sales. To confirm this, plug in for *X* in this equation any amount of advertising in dollars from the left-hand column of Table A.1. You'll see that you get the corresponding amount of sales in the right-hand column.

HOW STRAIGHT LINES AND CURVES SHIFT

So far, we've focused on relationships where some variable *Y* depends on a single other variable, *X*. But in many of our theories, we recognize that some variable of interest to us is actually affected by more than just one other variable. When *Y* is affected by both *X* and some third variable, changes in that third variable will usually cause a *shift* in the graph of the relationship between *X* and *Y*. This is because whenever we draw the graph between *X* and *Y*, we are holding fixed every other variable that might possibly affect *Y*.

> *A graph between two variables X and Y is only a picture of their relationship when all other variables affecting Y are held constant.*

But suppose one of these other variables *does* change? What happens then?

Think back to the relationship between advertising and sales. Earlier, we supposed sales depend only on advertising. But suppose we make an important discovery: Ice cream sales are *also* affected by how hot the weather is. What's more, all of the data in Table A.1 on which we previously based our analysis turns out to have been

from the month of June in different years, when the average temperature in Texas is 80 degrees. What's going to happen in July, when the average temperature rises to 100 degrees?

In Figure A.4 we've redrawn the graph from Figure A.1, this time labeling the line "June." Often, a good way to determine how a graph will shift is to perform a simple experiment like this: Put your pencil tip anywhere on the graph labeled June—let's say at point *C*. Now ask the following question: If I hold advertising constant at $6,000, do I expect to sell more or less ice cream as temperature rises in July? If you expect to sell more, then the amount of sales corresponding to $6,000 of advertising will be *above* point *C*, at a point such as *C'* (pronounced "C prime"), representing sales of $64,000. From this, we can tell that the graph will *shift upward* as temperature rises. In September, however, when temperatures fall, the amount of sales corresponding to $6,000 in advertising would be less than it is at point *C*. It would be shown by a point such as *C''* (pronounced "C double-prime"). In that case, the graph would shift downward.

The same procedure works well whether the original graph slopes upward or downward and whether it is a straight line or a curved one. Figure A.5 sketches two examples. In panel (a), an increase in some third variable, *Z*, increases the value of *Y* for each value of *X*, so the graph of the relationship between *X* and *Y* shifts upward as *Z* increases. We often phrase it this way: "An increase in *Z* causes an increase in *Y*, *at any value of X*." In panel (b), an increase in *Z* *decreases* the value of *Y*, at any value of *X*, so the graph of the relationship between *X* and *Y* shifts *downward* as *Z* increases.

You'll notice that in Figures A.4 and A.5, the original line is darker, while the new line after the shift is drawn in a lighter shade. We'll use this convention—a lighter shade for the new line after a shift—throughout this book.

Shifts versus Movements Along a Line

If you look back at Figure A.1, you'll see that when advertising increases (say, from $2,000 to $3,000), we *move along* our line, from point *A* to point *B*. But you've just learned that when average temperature changes, the entire line *shifts*. This may seem strange to you. After all, in both cases, an independent variable changes (either advertising or temperature). Why should we move *along* the line in once case and *shift* it in the other?

The reason for the difference is that in one case (advertising), the independent variable is *in our graph*, measured along one of the axes. When an independent variable in the graph changes, we simply move along

---

[4] We could also use direct logic to find the vertical intercept. In the figure, locate any point—we'll use point *A* as our example, where $X = 2$ and $Y = 46$. From this point, to get to the vertical intercept, we'd have to decrease *X* by two units. But with a slope of 3, a two-unit decrease in *X* will cause a six-unit decrease in *Y*. Therefore, *Y* will decrease from 46 to 40. Summing up, we've found that when $X = 0$, $Y = 40$, so our vertical intercept is 40.

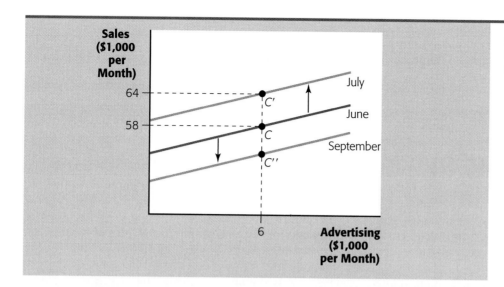

FIGURE A.4
Shifts in the Graph of Advertising and Sales

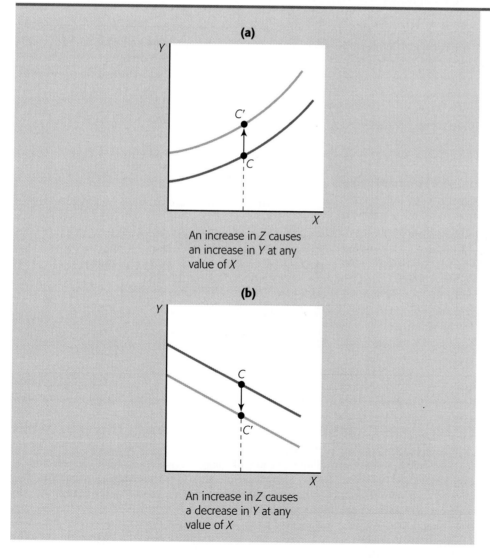

FIGURE A.5
Shifts of Curved Lines and Straight Lines

(a)

An increase in *Z* causes an increase in *Y* at any value of *X*

(b)

An increase in *Z* causes a decrease in *Y* at any value of *X*

the line. In the other case (temperature), the independent variable does *not* appear in our graph. Instead, it's been in the background, being held constant.

Here's a very simple—but crucial—rule:

> *Suppose* Y *is the **dependent** variable, which is measured on one of the axes in a graph. If the independent variable **measured on the other axis** changes, we **move along** the line. But if **any other** independent variable changes, the **entire line shifts.***

Be sure you understand the phrase "any other independent variable." It refers to any variable that actually *affects* Y but is *not* measured on either axis in the graph.

This rule applies to straight lines as well as curved lines. And it applies even in more complicated situations, such as when *two different* lines are drawn in the same graph, and a shift of one causes a movement along the other. (You'll encounter this situation in Chapter 3.) But for now, make sure you can see how we've been applying this rule in our example, where the three variables are total sales, advertising, and temperature.

SOLVING EQUATIONS

When we first derived the equation for the relationship between advertising and sales, we wanted to know what level of sales to expect from different amounts of advertising. But what if we're asked a slightly different question? Suppose, this time, you are told that the sales committee has set an ambitious goal of $64,000 for next month's sales. The treasurer needs to know how much to budget for advertising, and you have to come up with the answer.

Since we know how advertising and sales are related, we ought to be able to answer this question. One way is just to look at the graph in Figure A.1. There, we could first locate sales of $64,000 on the vertical axis. Then, if

we read over to the line and then down, we find the amount of advertising that would be necessary to generate that level of sales. Yet even with that carefully drawn diagram, it is not always easy to see just exactly how much advertising would be required. If we need to be precise, we'd better use the equation for the graph instead.

According to the equation, sales (Y) and advertising (X) are related as follows:

$$Y = 40 + 3X.$$

In the problem before us, we know the value for sales, and we need to solve for the corresponding amount of advertising. Substituting the sales target of $64,000 for Y, we need to find that value of X for which

$$64 = 40 + 3X.$$

Here, X is the unknown value for which we want to solve.

Whenever we solve one equation for one unknown, say, X, we need to *isolate* X on one side of the equals sign and everything else on the other side of the equals sign. We do this by performing identical operations on both sides of the equals sign. Here, we can first subtract 40 from both sides, getting

$$24 = 3X.$$

We can then divide both sides by 3 and get

$$8 = X.$$

This is our answer. If we want to achieve sales of $64,000, we'll need to spend $8,000 on advertising.

Of course, not all relationships are linear, so this technique will not work in every situation. But no matter what the underlying relationship, the idea remains the same:

> *To solve for X in any equation, rearrange the equation, following the rules of algebra, so that X appears on one side of the equals sign and everything else in the equation appears on the other side.*

Key Terms

Dependent variable A variable whose value depends on the value of some other variable.

Independent variable A variable that causes changes in some other variable (the dependent variable).

Negative or inverse relationship A relationship between two variables that move in opposite directions to each other (when one increases the other decreases).

Positive relationship A relationship between two variables that move in the same direction (when one increases so does the other; when one decreases so does the other).

Slope The rate of change of one variable with respect to another variable. In a graph, the change in the vertical-axis variable divided by the change in the horizontal-axis variable.

Tangent line A straight line that touches a curve at just one point, and has the same slope as the curve at that point.

Scarcity, Choice, and Economic Systems

CHAPTER OUTLINE

The Concept of Opportunity Cost
Opportunity Cost for Individuals
Opportunity Cost and Society
Production Possibilities Frontiers
The Search for a Free Lunch
Economic Systems
Specialization and Exchange
Resource Allocation

Resource Ownership
Types of Economic Systems
Using the Theory: Are We Saving Lives Efficiently?

What does it cost you to go to the movies? If you answered eight or nine dollars, because that is the price of a movie ticket, then you are leaving out a lot. Most of us are used to thinking of "cost" as the money we must pay for something. A Big Mac costs $2.70, a new Toyota Corolla costs $16,000, and the baby-sitter costs $8.00 an hour. Certainly, the money we pay for a good or service is a *part* of its cost. But economics takes a broader view of costs, recognizing monetary as well as nonmonetary components.

THE CONCEPT OF OPPORTUNITY COST

The total cost of any choice we make—buying a car, producing a computer, or even reading a book—is everything we must *give up* when we take that action. This cost is called the *opportunity cost* of the action, because we give up the opportunity to have other desirable things.

> The **opportunity cost** of any choice is what we must forego when we make that choice.

Opportunity cost What is given up when taking an action or making a choice.

Opportunity cost is the most accurate and complete concept of cost—the one we should use when making our own decisions or analyzing the decisions of others.

21

HTTP://

Is college worth the opportunity cost for you? Find out by trying Professor Jane Leuthold's COLLEGE CHOICE program at http://courses.atlas.uiuc.edu/econ/econ214/Choice/choice.htm.

Opportunity Cost for Individuals

Virtually every action we take as individuals uses up scarce money, scarce time, or both. This money or time *could* have been used for other things that you value. Thus, the true cost of any choice you make—the *opportunity cost*—is everything you actually sacrifice in making the choice.

Suppose, for example, it's 8 P.M. on a weeknight and you're spending a couple of hours reading this chapter. As authors, that thought makes us very happy, especially because we know there are many other things you could be doing: going to a movie, having dinner with friends, playing ping pong, earning some extra money tutoring high school students, watching TV. . . . Some of these alternatives might be more fun than reading your economics text. But, assuming you're still reading—and you haven't just run out the door to do something else—let's relate this to opportunity cost.

What *is* the opportunity cost of reading this chapter? Is it *all* of those other possibilities we've listed? Not really, because if you weren't reading for these two hours, you'd probably have time to do only *one* of them. And you'd no doubt choose whichever one among these alternatives you regarded as best. So, by reading, you sacrifice the best choice among the alternatives that you could be doing instead.

> The opportunity cost of a choice is the best among the available alternatives to that choice.

For many choices, a large part of the opportunity cost is the money sacrificed. If you spend $15 on a new DVD, you have to part with $15, which is money you could have spent on something else (whatever the best choice among the alternatives turned out to be). But for other choices, money may be only a small part, or no part, of what is sacrificed. If you walk your dog a few blocks, it will cost you time but not money. Still, economists often like to attach a monetary value even to costs that *don't* involve money. By translating such sacrifices into a dollar value, we can express opportunity cost as a single number, albeit a roughly estimated one. That, in turn, enables us to compare the cost of a choice with its benefits, which are also often expressed in dollars.

An Example: The Opportunity Cost of College. Let's consider an important choice you've made for this year: to attend college. What is the opportunity cost of this choice? A good starting point is to look at the actual monetary costs—the annual out-of-pocket expenses borne by you or your family for a year of college. Table 1 shows the College Board's estimates of these expenses for the average student. For example, the third column of the table shows that the average in-state resident at a four-year state college pays $4,081 in tuition and fees, $786 for books and supplies, $5,582 for room and board, and $2,394 for transportation and other expenses, for a total of $12,843 per year.

So, is that dollar figure the opportunity cost of a year of college for the average student at a public institution? Not really. Even if the entries are what you or your family actually pays out for college, there are two problems with using these figures to calculate the opportunity cost.

First, the table includes some expenses that are *not* part of the opportunity cost of college. For example, room and board is something you'd need no matter *what* you choose to do. That's obvious if, as part of your best choice among the alterna-

Type of Institution	Two-year Public	Four-year Public	Four-year Private
Tuition and fees	$ 1,735	$ 4,081	$18,273
Books and supplies	$ 727	$ 786	$ 807
Room and board	$ 5,430	$ 5,582	$ 6,779
Transportation and other expenses	$ 2,566	$ 2,394	$ 1,820
Total out-of-pocket costs	$10,458	$12,843	$27,679

TABLE 1

Average Cost of a Year of College, 2002–2003

Source: *Annual Survey of Colleges*, The College Board, New York, NY, 2003.

Notes: Averages are enrollment-weighted by institution, to reflect the average experience among students across the United States. Average tuition and fees at public institutions are for in-state residents only. Room and board charges are for students living on campus at four-year institutions, and off-campus (but not with parents) at two-year institutions.

tives, you'd have lived in an apartment and paid rent. But even living in your old room at home doesn't eliminate this cost: Your family *could* have rented out the room to someone else, or used it for some other valuable purpose. Either way, something is sacrificed. Let's suppose, for simplicity, that if you weren't in college, you or your family would be paying the same amount for room and board as your college charges. Then, that room and board expense should be excluded from opportunity cost. And the same applies to transportation and other expenses, at least the part that you would have spent anyway even if not in college.

Now we're left with payments for tuition and fees, and for books and other school supplies. For an in-state resident going to a state college, this averages $4,867 per year. Since these dollars are paid only when you attend college, they represent something sacrificed for that choice and are part of its opportunity cost. Costs like these—for which dollars are sacrificed through actual payments—are called **explicit costs,** and they are *part* of the opportunity cost.

But college also has **implicit costs**—sacrifices for which no money changes hands. The biggest sacrifice in this category is *time*. But what is that time worth? That depends on what you *would* be doing if you weren't in school. For many students, the alternative would be working full-time at a job, something most students can't manage while attending college. If you are one of these students, attending college requires the sacrifice of the income you *could* have earned at a job—a sacrifice we call *foregone income*.

How much income is foregone when you go to college for a year? In 2001, the average total income of an 18- to 24-year-old high school graduate who worked full-time was $21,650. If we assume that only nine months of work must be sacrificed to attend college, and that you could still work full-time in the summer, then foregone income is about 9/12 of $21,650, or $16,237.

Summing the explicit and implicit costs gives us a rough estimate of the opportunity cost of a year in college. For a public institution, we add $4,867 in explicit costs and $16,237 in implicit costs, giving us a total of $21,104 per year. Notice that this is significantly greater than the total charges estimated by the college board, which—in addition to including some expenses that are not part of opportunity cost—excludes the largest cost of all: foregone income. When you consider paying this opportunity cost for four years, its magnitude might surprise you. Without

Explicit cost The dollars sacrificed—and actually paid out—for a choice.

Implicit cost The value of something sacrificed when no direct payment is made.

financial aid in the form of tuition grants or other fee reductions, the average in-state resident will sacrifice about $80,000 to get a bachelor's degree at a state college and about $145,000 at a private one.

Our analysis of the opportunity cost of college is an example of a general, and important, principle:

> *The opportunity cost of a choice includes both* **explicit costs** *and* **implicit costs.**

A Brief Digression: Is College the Right Choice? Before you start questioning your choice to be in college, there are a few things to remember. First, in addition to its high cost, college has substantial *benefits*, including financial ones. In fact, over a 40-year work life, the average college graduate will make about $2.5 million, which is about a million dollars *more* than the average high school graduate.[1] So, even when we properly add the foregone income into our measure of opportunity cost, attending college appears to be one of the best *financial* investments you can make.

Second, remember that we've left out of our discussion many important aspects of this choice that would be harder to estimate in dollar terms, but could be very important to you. Do you *enjoy* being at college? If so, it would be difficult (although not impossible) to value that enjoyment in dollars. But your enjoyment should still be considered—along with the more easily measured financial rewards—as part of your benefits. (Of course, if you *hate* college and are only doing it for the financial rewards or to satisfy your parents, that's an implicit cost—which is part of your opportunity cost—that we haven't included.)

Time Is Money. Our analysis of the opportunity cost of college points out a general principle, one understood by economists and noneconomists alike. It can be summed up in the expression, "Time is money." Those three words contain a profound truth: The sacrifice of time often means the sacrifice of money—in particular, the money that *could* have been earned during that time.

As a rule, economists have a simple technique to estimate the dollar value of time. First, we assume that working additional hours for pay is the best among the alternatives to the choice being considered. Then, each hour sacrificed for the choice is multiplied by the individual's hourly wage. (Even someone paid a monthly salary has an implied hourly wage: their total monthly income divided by the total monthly hours of work.)

For example, suppose Jessica is a freelance writer who decides to see a movie. The ticket price is $8, and the entire activity—including getting there and back—will take three hours out of her evening. What is the opportunity cost of seeing this

---

[1] Jennifer C. Day and Eric C. Newburger, "The Big Payoff: Educational Attainment and Synthetic Estimates of Work-Life Earnings," in *Current Population Reports* (U.S. Census Bureau), July 2002. There are two provisos. First, part of the additional earnings of college graduates may be due to the type of person that goes to college, rather than the degree itself. Second, remember that much of the additional income you'll earn with a college degree is postponed far into the future, which reduces its value to you right now. (If you are using the hardcover or the Microeconomics paperback version of this book, you'll learn—in a later chapter—some special techniques for estimating the value of postponed income.) These two provisos reduce the benefits of attending college. But even when economists account for these reductions in benefits, a college degree still appears to be one of the best financial investments you can make.

movie? Let's say Jessica earns an annual income of $40,000 by working 2,000 hours per year, giving her an implied hourly wage of $40,000 / 2,000 hrs = $20 per hour. Then for Jessica, the opportunity cost is the sum of the explicit costs ($8 for the ticket) and the implicit costs ($20 × 3 hrs = $60 in foregone income), giving her a total opportunity cost of $68.

The idea that a movie "costs" $68 might seem absurd to you. But if you think about it, $68 is a much better estimate than $8 of what the movie costs for Jessica. After all, Jessica gives up three hours that *could* have been spent working on an article that, on average, would provide her with another $60. Thus, in a very real sense, Jessica sacrifices $68 for the movie.[2]

Our examples about the cost of college and the cost of a movie point out an important lesson about opportunity cost:

> *The explicit (direct money) cost of a choice may only be a part—and sometimes a small part—of the opportunity cost of a choice.*

Indeed, the higher an individual's income, the less important is the direct money cost, and the more important the time cost of an activity. For example, suppose that Samantha is an attorney who bills out her time at $100 per hour. For her, the opportunity cost of the same movie—which entails three hours and the ticket—would be $308 dollars!

You might wonder if Samantha would ever see a movie at such a high cost. The answer for Samantha is the same as for Jessica or anyone else: yes, as long as the benefits of the movie are greater than the explicit and implicit costs. It's easy to see why Samantha might decide to see a movie. Imagine that she begins taking on more and more clients, working longer and longer hours, and earning more and more income. At some point, she will realize that leisure activities like movies are very important, while earning more income will seem less important. And at some point, the enjoyment of taking time off to see a movie might be well worth sacrificing the $308 that she could have had.

Once you understand the concept of opportunity cost and how it can differ among individuals, you can understand some behavior that might otherwise appear strange. For example, why do high-income people rarely shop at discount stores like Kmart or Target and instead shop at full-service stores where the same items sell for much higher prices? It's not that high-income people *like* to pay more for their purchases. But discount stores are generally understaffed and crowded with customers, so shopping there takes more time. While discount stores have lower *money* cost,

---

[2] In using the wage rate to measure the opportunity cost of time, we are assuming (1) that Jessica *could* work three additional hours and earn an additional $20 per hour; and (2) that among all the alternatives to the movie, working for pay is the best. Any violations of these assumptions would make our measure of opportunity cost less accurate. For example, suppose Jessica would *like* to work longer hours for additional pay, but her job doesn't permit this. Then she may already be diverting her nonwork time into an alternative she values at *less* than $20 per hour—say, $15 per hour. In this case, when Jessica considers a new choice, any time sacrificed would be worth only $15 an hour to her, so using her $20 hourly wage would *overestimate* the opportunity cost of the new choice.

On the other hand, if Jessica *could* work more hours but has chosen *not* to, she must already be doing other things that she values *more highly* than $20 per hour—say, at $25. In this case, a new choice would require giving up time worth $25 per hour, and using her $20 wage would *underestimate* the opportunity cost of the new choice.

they impose a higher *time cost*. For high-income people, discount stores are actually more costly than stores with higher price tags.

We can also understand why the most highly paid consultants, entrepreneurs, attorneys, and surgeons often lead such frenetic lives, doing several things at once and packing every spare minute with tasks. Since these people can earn several hundred dollars for an hour of work, every activity they undertake carries a correspondingly high opportunity cost. Brushing one's teeth can cost $10, and driving to work can cost hundreds! By combining activities—making phone calls while driving to work, thinking about and planning the day while in the shower, or reading the morning paper in the elevator—the opportunity cost of these routine activities is reduced.

And what about the rest of us? As our wages rise, we all try to cram more activities into little bits of free time. Millions of Americans now carry cell phones and use them while waiting for an elevator or walking their dogs. Books on tape are becoming more popular and are especially favored by runners. (Why just exercise when you can also "read" a book?) And for some, vacations have become more exhausting than work, as more and more activities are crammed into shorter and shorter vacation periods. These trends can be partly explained by the increasing opportunity cost of time.

Opportunity Cost and Society

For an individual, opportunity cost arises from the scarcity of time or money. But for society as a whole, opportunity cost arises from a different source: the scarcity of society's *resources*. Our desire for goods is limitless, but we have limited resources to produce them. Therefore,

> *virtually all production carries an opportunity cost: To produce more of one thing, society must shift resources away from producing something else.*

For example, we'd all agree that we'd like better health for our citizens. What would be needed to achieve this goal? Perhaps more frequent medical checkups for more people and greater access to top-flight medicine when necessary. These, in turn, would require more and better-trained doctors, more hospital buildings and laboratories, and more high-tech medical equipment such as positron emission tomography (PET) scanners and surgical lasers. In order for us to produce these goods and services, we would have to pull resources—land, labor, capital, and entrepreneurship—out of producing other things that we also enjoy. The opportunity cost of improved health care, then, consists of all the other goods and services we would have to do without.

Production Possibilities Frontiers

Let's build a simple model to help us understand the opportunity cost we must pay for improved health care. To be even more specific, we'll measure production of health care by the *number of lives saved*. This variable is plotted along the horizontal axis in Figure 1. To measure the opportunity cost of health care, we'll make a simplifying assumption: that all goods *other* than lifesaving health care can be lumped into a single category, and that we can measure how many units of these "other goods" we're producing. In Figure 1, the quantity of "other goods" is measured on the vertical axis.

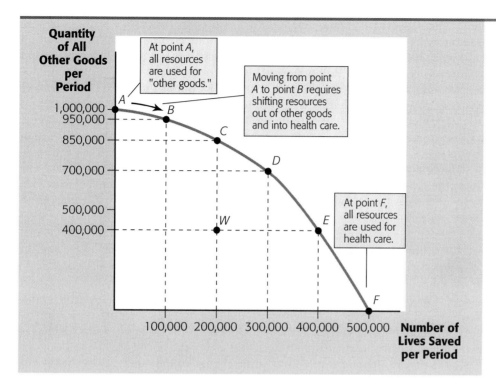

FIGURE 1
The Production Possibilities
Frontier

Now look at the curve drawn in Figure 1. It is society's **production possibilities frontier (PPF)**, *giving the different combinations of goods that can be produced with the resources and technology currently available.* More specifically, this PPF tells us the *maximum quantity* of all other goods we can produce for each number of lives saved and the maximum number of lives saved for each different quantity of other goods. Positions outside the frontier are unattainable with the technology and resources at the economy's disposal. Society's choices are limited to points *on* or *inside* the PPF.

Let's take a closer look at the PPF in Figure 1. Point *A* represents one possible choice for our society: to devote all resources to the production of "other goods" and none to health care. In this case, we would have 1,000,000 units of other goods, but we would have to forego every opportunity to save lives. Point *F* represents the opposite extreme: all available resources devoted to lifesaving health care. In that case, we'd save 500,000 lives, but we'd have no other goods.

If points *A* and *F* seem absurd to you, remember that they represent two *possible* choices for society but choices we would be unlikely to make. We want lifesaving health care to be available to those who need it, but we also want housing, clothing, entertainment, cars, and so on. So a realistic choice would include a *mix* of health care and other goods.

Suppose we desire such a mix, but the economy, for some reason, is currently operating at the undesirable point *A*—no health care but maximum production of everything else. Then we need to shift some resources from other goods to health care. For example, we could move from point *A* to point *B*, where we'd be saving 100,000 lives. But as a consequence, we'd have to cut back on other goods, producing 50,000 fewer units. The opportunity cost of saving 100,000 lives, then, would be 50,000 units of all other goods.

Production possibilities frontier (PPF) A curve showing all combinations of two goods that can be produced with the resources and technology currently available.

Increasing Opportunity Cost. Suppose we are at point *B* and now we want to save even more lives. Once again, we shift enough resources into health care to save an additional 100,000 lives, moving from point *B* to point *C*. This time, however, there is an even *greater* cost: Production of other goods falls from 950,000 units to 850,000 units, or a sacrifice of 100,000 units. The opportunity cost of saving lives has risen. You can see that as we continue to save more lives—by increments of 100,000, moving from point *C* to point *D* to point *E* to point *F*—the opportunity cost of producing other goods keeps right on rising, until saving the last 100,000 lives costs us 400,000 units of other goods.

The behavior of opportunity cost described here—the more health care we produce, the greater the opportunity cost of producing still more—applies to a wide range of choices facing society. It can be generalized as the *law of increasing opportunity cost.*

Law of increasing opportunity cost The more of something that is produced, the greater the opportunity cost of producing one more unit.

> *According to the **law of increasing opportunity cost**, the more of something we produce, the greater the opportunity cost of producing even more of it.*

The law of increasing opportunity cost causes the PPF to have a *concave* shape, becoming steeper as we move rightward and downward. To understand why, remember (from high school math) that the slope of a line or curve is just the change along the vertical axis divided by the change along the horizontal axis. Along the PPF, as we move rightward, the slope is the change in the quantity of other goods divided by the change in the number of lives saved. This is a negative number, because a positive change in lives saved means a negative change in other goods. The absolute value of this slope is the opportunity cost of saving another life. Now—as we've seen—this opportunity cost increases as we move rightward. Therefore, the absolute value of the PPF's slope must rise as well. The PPF gets steeper and steeper, giving us the concave shape we see in Figure 1.[3]

Why should there be a law of increasing opportunity cost? Why must it be that the more of something we produce, the greater the opportunity cost of producing still more?

Because most resources—*by their very nature*—are better suited to some purposes than to others. If the economy were operating at point *A*, for example, we'd be using all of our resources to produce other goods, including resources that are much better suited for health care. A hospital might be used as a food cannery, a surgical laser might be used for light shows, and a skilled surgeon might be driving a cab or trying desperately to make us laugh with his stand-up routine.

As we begin to move rightward along the PPF, say from *A* to *B*, we shift resources out of other goods and into health care. But we would *first* shift those resources *best suited to health care*—and *least* suited for the production of other things. For example, the first group of workers we'd use to save lives would be those who already have training as doctors and nurses. A surgeon—who would probably not make the best comedian—could now go back to surgery, which he does very well. Similarly, the first buildings we would put to use in the health care industry would be those that were originally built as hospitals and medical offices,

---

[3] You might be wondering if the law of increasing opportunity cost applies in both directions. That is, does the opportunity cost of producing "other goods" increase as we produce more of them? The answer is yes, as you'll see when you do Problem 1 at the end of this chapter.

and weren't really doing so well as manufacturing plants, retail stores, or movie studios. This is why, at first, the PPF is very flat: We get a *large* increase in lives saved for only a *small* decrease in other goods.

As we continue moving rightward, however, we shift away from other goods to those resources that are less and less suited to lifesaving. As a result, the PPF becomes steeper. Finally, we arrive at point *F*, where all resources—no matter how well suited for other goods and services—are used to save lives. A factory building is converted into a hospital, your family car is used as an ambulance, and comedic actor Jim Carrey is in medical school, training to become a surgeon.

The principle of increasing opportunity cost applies to all of society's production choices, not just that between health care and other goods. If we look at society's choice between food and oil, we would find that some land is better suited to growing food and some land to drilling for oil. As we continue to produce more oil, we would find ourselves drilling on land that is less and less suited to producing oil, but better and better for producing food. The opportunity cost of producing additional oil will therefore increase. The same principle applies in choosing between civilian goods and military goods, between food and clothing, or between automobiles and public transportation: The more of something we produce, the greater the opportunity cost of producing still more.

The Search for a Free Lunch

This chapter has argued that every decision to produce *more* of something requires us to pay an opportunity cost by producing less of something else. Nobel Prize–winning economist Milton Friedman summarized this idea in his famous remark, "There is no such thing as a free lunch." Friedman was saying that, even if a meal is provided free of charge to someone, society still uses up resources to provide it. Therefore, a "free lunch" is not *really* free: Society pays an opportunity cost by not producing other things with those resources. Therefore, some members of society will have to make do with less.

The same logic applies to other supposedly "free" goods and services. From society's point of view, there is no such thing as free Internet service, free broadcast television, or free medical care, even if those who enjoy these things don't pay for them as individuals. Providing any of these things requires us to sacrifice *other* things, as illustrated by a movement along society's PPF.

But there are some situations that seem, at first glance, to violate Freidman's dictum. Let's explore them.

Operating Inside the PPF. What if an economy is not living up to its productive potential, but is instead operating *inside* its PPF? For example, in Figure 1, suppose we are currently operating at point *W*, where the health care system is saving 200,000 lives and we are producing 400,000 units of other goods. Then we can move from point *W* to point *E* and save 200,000 more lives with no sacrifice of other goods. Or, starting at point *W*, we could move to point *C* (more of other goods with no sacrifice in lives saved) or to a point like *D* (more of *both* health care *and* other goods).

But why would an economy ever be operating inside its PPF? There are two possibilities.

Productive Inefficiency. One reason an economy might be operating inside its PPF is that resources are being wasted. Suppose, for example, that many people who could be outstanding health care workers are instead producing other goods, and many who would be great at producing other things are instead stuck in the health care industry. Then switching people from one job to the other could enable us to have more of *both* health care *and* other goods. That is, because of the mismatch of workers and jobs, we would be *inside* the PPF at a point like *W*. Creating better job matches would then move us to a point *on* the PPF (such as point *E*).

Economists use the phrase *productive inefficiency* to describe the type of waste that puts us inside our PPF.

Productive inefficiency A situation in which more of at least one good can be produced without sacrificing the production of any other good.

> *A firm, an industry, or an entire economy is **productively inefficient** if it could produce more of at least one good without pulling resources from the production of any other good.*

The phrase *productive efficiency* means the absence of any productive *ine*fficiency. For example, if the computer industry is producing the maximum possible number of computers with the resources it is currently using, we would describe the computer industry as productively efficient. In that case, there would be no way to produce any more computers except to use more resources and shift them from the production of some other good. For an entire *economy* to be productively efficient, there must be no way to produce more of *any* good except by pulling resources from the production of some other good.

Although no firm, industry, or economy is ever 100 percent productively efficient, cases of gross inefficiency are not as common as you might think. When you study microeconomics, you'll learn that business firms have strong incentives to identify and eliminate productive inefficiency, since any waste of resources increases their costs and decreases their profit. When one firm discovers a way to eliminate waste, others quickly follow.

For example, empty seats on an airline flight represent productive inefficiency. Since the plane is making the trip anyway, filling the empty seat would enable the airline to serve more people with the flight (produce more transportation services) without using any additional resources (other than the trivial resources of the in-flight meal). Therefore, more people could fly without sacrificing any other good or service. When American Airlines developed a computer model in the late 1980s to fill its empty seats by altering schedules and fares, the other airlines followed its example very rapidly. And when—in the late 1990s— Priceline.com enabled airlines to auction off empty seats on the Internet, several airlines jumped at the chance and others quickly followed. As a result of this—and similar efforts to eliminate waste in personnel, aircraft, and office space—many cases of productive inefficiency in the airline industry were eliminated.

The same sorts of efforts have eliminated some easy-to-identify cases of productive inefficiency in all types of industries: banking, telephone service, Internet service providers, book publishers, and so on. There are certainly instances of inefficiency that remain (a possible example appears at the end of this chapter). But on the whole, if you search the economy for a free lunch due to productive inefficiency, you won't find as many hearty meals as you might think.

Recessions. Another reason an economy might operate inside its PPF is a *recession*—a slowdown in overall economic activity. During recessions, many resources are idle. For one thing, there is widespread *unemployment*—people *want* to work but are unable to find jobs. In addition, factories shut down, so we are not using all of our avail-

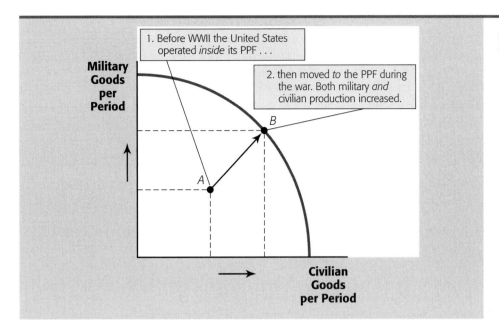

FIGURE 2
Production and Unemployment

able capital or natural resources either. An end to the recession would move the economy from a point *inside* its PPF to a point *on* its PPF—using idle resources to produce more goods and services without sacrificing anything.

This simple observation can help us understand an otherwise confusing episode in U.S. economic history. During the early 1940s, after the United States entered World War II and began using massive amounts of resources to produce military goods and services, the standard of living in the United States did *not* decline as we might have expected but actually improved slightly. Why?

Figure 2 helps to solve this puzzle. The PPF in Figure 2 is like the PPF in Figure 1. But this time, instead of pitting "health care" against "all other goods," we look at society's choice between *military* goods and *civilian* goods. When the United States entered the war in 1941, it was still suffering from the Great Depression—the most serious and long-lasting economic downturn in modern history, which began in 1929 and hit most of the developed world. For reasons you will learn when you study macroeconomics, joining the allied war effort helped end the Depression in the United States and moved our economy from a point like *A, inside* the PPF, to a point like *B, on* the frontier. Military production increased, but so did the production of civilian goods. Although there were shortages of some consumer goods, the overall result was a rise in the material well-being of the average U.S. citizen.

An economic downturn, such as the Great Depression of the 1930s, does seem to offer the possibility of a free lunch. And a war is only one factor that can reverse a downturn. In fact, no rational nation would ever *choose* war as an economic policy designed to cure a recession, since there are alternative policies that virtually everyone would find preferable. Still, eliminating a recession is not *entirely* cost-free. When you study macroeconomics, you will learn that policies to cure or avoid recessions can have risks and costs of their own. Of course, we may feel it is worth the possible costs, but they are costs nonetheless. Once again, a truly free lunch is hard to find.

Economic Growth. If the economy is already operating *on* its PPF, we cannot exploit the opportunity to have more of everything by moving *to* it. But what if the PPF itself were to change? Couldn't we then produce more of everything? This is exactly what happens when an economy's productive capacity grows.

Many factors contribute to economic growth, but they can be divided into two categories. First, the quantities of available *resources*—especially capital—can increase. An increase in physical capital—more factories, office buildings, tractors, or high-tech medical equipment—enables the economy to produce more of *everything* that uses these tools. The same is true for an increase in human capital—the skills of doctors, engineers, construction workers, software writers, and so on. In thinking about growth from greater resources, economists focus mostly on capital because, over time, increases in the capital stock have contributed more to higher living standards than other resources.

The second main factor behind economic growth is *technological change,* which enables us to produce more from a *given* quantity of resources. For example, the development of the Internet has enabled people to retrieve information in a few seconds that used to require hours of searching in a library. As a result, teachers, writers, government officials, attorneys, and physicians can produce more without working longer hours.

These two main causes of economic growth—increases in capital and technological change—often go hand in hand. In order for the Internet (a technological change) to be widely used, the economy had to produce and install servers, Internet-capable computers, and fiber-optic cable (increases in capital). In any case, both technological change and increases in the capital stock have the same type of effect on the PPF.

Let's explore a specific example that affects the PPF: body scanners that use PET. This technology enables doctors to quickly view every organ system in the body, and diagnose tumors, brain anomalies, cancers, and even potential heart problems more rapidly and accurately than previous scanning systems like magnetic resonance imaging (MRI). As this is being written (late 2003), PET scanners are being installed in hospitals around the country. Once they're widely distributed, we'll be able to save thousands more lives every year even if we use unchanged quantities of *other* resources (doctors, nurses, hospitals, lab technicians, etc.).

What is the impact on the economy's PPF, like the one in Figure 3? First look at point *F*, where we assume *all* of our resources are devoted to lifesaving, with 500,000 lives saved per period. Under this assumption, having PET scanners would enable us to save even *more* lives—say, a total of 600,000 per period. Thus, the horizontal intercept of the PPF moves rightward, from *F* to *F'*.

Now consider point *A*, where we assume *none* of our resources would be devoted to lifesaving, and we'd produce 1,000,000 units of other goods. The new PET scanners have no productive use other than lifesaving, so having them would *not* change the vertical intercept, *A*.

As you can see, the impact of PET scanners is to stretch the PPF outward along the horizontal axis. Our society can then choose any point along the *new* PPF. For example, we could move from point *D* on the original PPF to point *H* on the new one. For this move, we'd be using all of the benefits of the new technology to save lives, with *unchanged* production of other goods. Or we could choose to move from point *D* to point *J* where, as you can verify, we produce more of *both* things that we value: more lives saved *and* more of other goods.

You may be wondering: How can a technological change in lifesaving enable us to produce more goods in *other* areas of the economy? The answer is: Society can

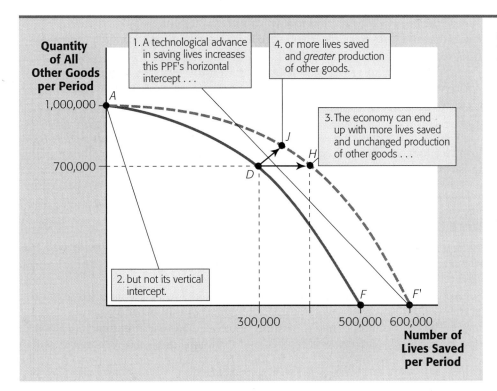

FIGURE 3
The Effect of a New Medical Technology

The figure shows a graph with y-axis labeled "Quantity of All Other Goods per Period" and x-axis labeled "Number of Lives Saved per Period."

1. A technological advance in saving lives increases this PPF's horizontal intercept . . .

2. but not its vertical intercept.

3. The economy can end up with more lives saved and unchanged production of other goods . . .

4. or more lives saved and *greater* production of other goods.

Points labeled: A at 1,000,000; J; H; D at 700,000; F at 500,000; F' at 600,000; with 300,000 marked on x-axis.

choose to use *some* of the increased lifesaving potential to shift other resources *out* of the medical care and into the production of other things. Because of the technological advance and the new capital, we can shift these resources without sacrificing lives.

We'd get a similar result from a technological change, or an increase in capital, that directly affected only *non*medical production. For example, the development and distribution of new assembly-line robots for the mass-production of automobiles, televisions, and home furniture would shift the *vertical* intercept of the PPF but leave its *horizontal* intercept unchanged. But once again, we could choose to save more lives *and* produce more of other goods. (You may want to draw the old and new PPFs for this case, and find a point that illustrates this choice.)

In general,

> *a technological change or an increase in the capital stock, even when the direct impact is to increase production of just one type of good, allows us to choose greater production of all types of goods.*

This conclusion certainly *seems* like a free lunch. After all, if we can produce more of the things that we value, without having to produce less of anything else, haven't we escaped from paying an opportunity cost?

Yes . . . and no. Figure 3 tells only *part* of the story, because it leaves out the steps needed to *create* this shift in the PPF in the first place. For example, technological innovation doesn't just "happen." Rather, resources must be used to create it—mostly by the research and development (R&D) departments of large corporations. In 2002, these corporations used $300 billion worth of resources on R&D, resources that *could* have been used to produce other things that we'd like right now—cars, apartments, entertainment, or even more *unimproved* medical services that can save lives in the present. The same is true when we produce and install new capital equipment; this, too, uses resources that could have been used for some other purpose.

> In order to produce more goods and services **in the future**, we must shift resources toward R&D and capital production, and away from the production of things we'd enjoy right now.

We must conclude that although economic growth—at first glance—*appears* to be a free lunch, someone ends up paying the check. In this case, the bill is paid by those members of society who will have to make do with less in the present.

ECONOMIC SYSTEMS

As you read these words—perhaps sitting at home or in the library—you are experiencing a very private moment. It is just you and this book; the rest of the world might as well not exist. Or so it seems. . . .

Actually, even in this supposedly private moment, you are connected to the rest of the world in ways you may not have thought about. In order for you to be reading this book, the authors had to write it. Someone had to edit it, to help make sure that all necessary material was covered and explained as clearly as possible. Someone else had to prepare the graphics. Others had to run the printing presses and the binding machines, and still others had to pack the book, ship it, unpack it, put it on a store shelf, and then sell it to you.

And there's more. People had to manufacture all kinds of goods: paper and ink, the boxes used for shipping, the computers used to keep track of inventory, and so on. It is no exaggeration to say that thousands of people were involved in putting this book in your hands.

And there is still more. The chair or couch on which you are sitting, the light shining on the page, the heat or the air conditioning in the room, the clothes you are wearing—all these things that you are using right now were *produced by somebody else*. So even now, as you sit alone reading this book, you are economically linked to others in hundreds—even thousands—of different ways.

Take a walk in your town or city, and you will see even more evidence of our economic interdependence: People are collecting garbage, helping schoolchildren cross the street, transporting furniture across town, constructing buildings, repairing roads, painting houses. Everyone is producing goods and services for *other people*.

Why is it that so much of what we consume is produced by other people? Why are we all so heavily dependent on each other for our material well-being? Why doesn't each of us—like Robinson Crusoe on his island—produce our own food, clothing, housing, and anything else we desire? And how did it come about that *you*—who did not produce any of these things yourself—are able to consume them?

These are all questions about our *economic system*—the way our economy is organized. Ordinarily, we take our economic system for granted, like the water that runs out of our faucets. But now it's time to begin looking at the plumbing—to learn how our economy serves so many millions of people, enabling them to survive and prosper.

Specialization and Exchange

If we were forced to, many of us could become economically *self-sufficient*. We could stake out a plot of land, grow our own food, make our own clothing, and build our own homes. But in no society is there such extreme self-sufficiency. On the contrary, every economic system over the past 10,000 years has been characterized by two features: (1) **specialization,** in which each of us concentrates on a limited number of productive activities, and (2) **exchange,** in which most of what we desire is obtained by trading with others rather than producing for ourselves.

> *Specialization and exchange enable us to enjoy greater production, and higher living standards, than would otherwise be possible. As a result, all economies exhibit high degrees of specialization and exchange.*

Specialization A method of production in which each person concentrates on a limited number of activities.

Exchange The act of trading with others to obtain what we desire.

There are three reasons why specialization and exchange enable us to enjoy greater production. The first has to do with human capabilities: Each of us can learn only so much in a lifetime. By limiting ourselves to a narrow set of tasks—fixing plumbing, managing workers, writing music, or designing Web pages—we are each able to hone our skills and become experts at one or two things instead of remaining amateurs at a lot of things. It is easy to see that an economy of experts will produce more than an economy of amateurs.

A second gain from specialization results from the time needed to switch from one activity to another. When people specialize, and thus spend more time doing one task, there is less unproductive "downtime" from switching activities.

Adam Smith first explained these gains from specialization in his book *An Inquiry into the Nature and Causes of the Wealth of Nations*, published in 1776. Smith explained how specialization within a pin factory dramatically increased the number of pins that could be produced there. In order to make a pin . . .

> *One man draws out the wire, another straightens it, a third cuts it, a fourth points it, a fifth grinds it at the top for receiving the head; to make the head requires three distinct operations; to put it on is a [separate] business, to whiten the pins is another; it is even a trade by itself to put them into the paper; and the important business of making a pin is, in this manner, divided into about eighteen distinct operations, which, in some manufactories, are all performed by distinct hands.*

HTTP://

Economics is a subject that has benefited from specialization and the division of labor. To get a feel for the many different subjects that economists investigate, take a look at the *Journal of Economic Literature's* classification system at http:// www.econlit.org/ subject_descriptors.html.

Smith went on to observe that 10 men, each working separately, might make 200 pins in a day, but through specialization they were able to make 48,000! What is true for a pin factory can be generalized to the entire economy: Total production will increase when workers specialize.

Notice that the production gains from specialization we've been discussing—and that Adam Smith described so well—do *not* depend on any differences in individuals' capabilities. Even in a society where initially everyone is *identical* to everyone else, specialization would still yield gains for the two reasons we've discussed: People would develop expertise over time and there would be less downtime from switching tasks.

Of course, in the real world, workers are *not* identically suited to different kinds of work. Nor are all plots of land, all natural resources, or all types of capital equipment identically suited for different tasks. This observation brings us to the *third* source of gains from specialization—one based on individual differences.

Further Gains to Specialization: Comparative Advantage. Imagine a shipwreck in which there are only two survivors—let's call them Maryanne and Gilligan—who wash up on opposite shores of a deserted island. Initially they are unaware of each other, so each is forced to become completely self-sufficient.

| TABLE 2 | | Labor Required for: | |
Labor Requirements for Berries and Fish		1 Cup of Berries	1 Fish
	Maryanne	½ hour	1 hour
	Gilligan	2 hours	6 hours

On one side of the island, Maryanne finds that it takes her half an hour to pick one cup of berries and an hour to catch one fish, as shown in the first row of Table 2. On the other side of the island, Gilligan—who is less adept at both tasks—requires two hours to pick a cup of berries and six hours to catch one fish, as listed in the second row of the table. Since both castaways would want some variety in their diets, we can assume that each would spend part of the week catching fish and part picking berries.

Suppose that, one day, Maryanne and Gilligan discover each other. After rejoicing at the prospect of human companionship, they decide to develop a system of production that will work to their mutual benefit. Let's rule out any of the gains from specialization that we discussed earlier (minimizing downtime or developing expertise). Will it still pay for these two to specialize? The answer is yes, as you will see after a small detour.

Absolute Advantage: A Detour. When Gilligan and Maryanne sit down to figure out who should do what, they might fall victim to a common mistake: basing their decision on *absolute advantage*. An individual has an **absolute advantage** in the production of some good when he or she can produce it using *fewer resources* than another individual can. On the island, the only resource being used is labor time, so the reasoning might go as follows: Maryanne can pick a cup of berries more quickly than Gilligan (see Table 2), so she has an *absolute advantage* in berry picking. It seems logical, then, that Maryanne should be the one to pick the berries.

But wait! Maryanne can also catch *fish* more quickly than Gilligan, so she has an absolute advantage in fishing as well. If absolute advantage is the criterion for assigning work, then Maryanne should do *both* tasks. This, however, would leave Gilligan doing nothing, which is certainly *not* in the pair's best interests. What can we conclude from this example? That absolute advantage is an unreliable guide for allocating tasks to different workers.

Comparative Advantage. The correct principle to guide the division of labor on the island is comparative advantage:

> *A person has a **comparative advantage** in producing some good if he or she can produce it with a smaller opportunity cost than some other person can.*

Notice the important difference between absolute advantage and comparative advantage: You have an *absolute* advantage in producing a good if you can produce it using fewer *resources* than someone else can. But you have a *comparative* advantage if you can produce it with a smaller *opportunity cost*. As you'll see, these are not necessarily the same thing.

Absolute advantage The ability to produce a good or service, using fewer resources than other producers use.

Comparative advantage The ability to produce a good or service at a lower opportunity cost than other producers.

Let's see who has a *comparative* advantage in fishing, by calculating—for each of the castaways—the opportunity cost of catching one fish. For Maryanne, catching a fish takes an hour. This is time that could instead be used to pick *two* cups of berries. Thus, we can write

Maryanne: opportunity cost of 1 fish = 2 cups of berries

It takes Gilligan *six* hours to catch a fish, time with which he could pick *three* cups of berries. Thus,

Gilligan: opportunity cost of 1 fish = 3 cups of berries

Comparing the two results, we see that the opportunity cost of one fish is *lower* for Maryanne than it is for Gilligan. Therefore, *Maryanne has a comparative advantage in fishing.*

Now let's determine who has a comparative advantage in berries by determining the opportunity cost of one cup of berries for both castaways. For Maryanne, one cup of berries takes half an hour, time that could be used to catch half a fish. Thus, we can write

Even castaways do better when they specialize and exchange with each other, instead of trying to be self-sufficient.

Maryanne: opportunity cost of 1 cup berries = ½ fish

Of course, no one would ever catch *half* a fish, unless they were fishing with a machete. But it's still useful to know the *rate* of trade-off of one good for the other. It tells us, for example, that Maryann's opportunity cost for *two* cups of berries would be *one* fish—which is easier to imagine.

It takes Gilligan *two* hours to pick a cup of berries, time that could get him ⅓ fish instead. Thus,

Gilligan: opportunity cost of 1 cup berries = ⅓ fish

Comparing these results, we see that for berries, it's *Gilligan* who has the lower opportunity cost. Therefore, Gilligan—who has an absolute advantage in nothing—has a *comparative* advantage in berry picking.

Let's see what happens as the two decide to move toward *specializing* according to their comparative advantage. Let's have Gilligan catch *three fewer fish* each week, freeing up 18 hours that he can use to pick *nine* more cups of berries:

Gilligan: Fish ↓ 3 ⇒ Berries ↑ 9

Since Maryanne has the comparative advantage in fish, let's have her catch *four more fish* each week. This requires that she shift eight hours out of berry picking, sacrificing eight cups of berries:

Maryanne: Fish ↑ 4 ⇒ Berries ↓ 8

Now, what happens to *total* production as a result of these moves? As you can see, Maryanne *more* than makes up for the fish that Gilligan is no longer catching, and Gilligan *more* than makes up for the berries that Maryanne isn't picking. Taken together, the pair is producing one more fish *and* one more cup of berries, without requiring either to work more hours.

Since—by producing according to comparative advantage—total production on the island increases, total *consumption* can increase, too. Gilligan and Maryanne can figure out some way of trading fish for berries that makes each of them come out ahead. In the end, each of the castaways can enjoy a higher standard of living when they specialize and exchange with each other, compared to the level they'd enjoy under self-sufficiency.

What is true for our shipwrecked island dwellers is also true for the entire economy:

> *Total production of every good or service will be greatest when individuals specialize according to their comparative advantage. This is another reason why specialization and exchange lead to higher living standards than does self-sufficiency.*

When we turn from our fictional island to the real world, is production, in fact, consistent with the principle of comparative advantage? Indeed, it is. A journalist may be able to paint her house more quickly than a housepainter, giving her an *absolute* advantage in painting her home. Will she paint her own home? Except in unusual circumstances, no, because the journalist has a *comparative* advantage in writing news articles. Indeed, most journalists—like most college professors, attorneys, architects, and other professionals—hire house painters, leaving themselves more time to practice the professions in which they enjoy a comparative advantage.

Even comic book superheroes seem to behave consistently with comparative advantage. Superman can no doubt cook a meal, fix a car, chop wood, and do virtually *anything* faster than anyone else on the earth. Using our new vocabulary, we'd say that Superman has an absolute advantage in everything. But he has a clear comparative advantage in catching criminals and saving the known universe from destruction, which is exactly what he spends his time doing.

Specialization in Perspective. The gains from specialization, whether they arise from developing expertise, minimizing downtime, or exploiting comparative advantage, can explain many features of our economy. For example, college students need to select a major and then, upon graduating, to decide on a specific career. Those who follow this path are often rewarded with higher incomes than those who dally. This is an encouragement to specialize. Society is better off if you specialize, since you will help the economy produce more, and society rewards you for this contribution with a higher income.

The gains from specialization can also explain why most of us end up working for business firms that employ dozens, or even hundreds or thousands, of other employees. Why do these business firms exist? Why isn't each of us a *self-employed* expert, exchanging our production with other self-employed experts? Part of the answer is that organizing production into business firms pushes the gains from specialization still further. Within a firm, some people can specialize in working with their hands, others in managing people, others in marketing, and still others in keeping the books. Each firm is a kind of minisociety within which specialization occurs. The result is greater production and a higher standard of living than we would achieve if we were all self-employed.

Specialization has enabled societies everywhere to achieve standards of living unimaginable to our ancestors. But, it can have a downside as well. Adam Smith himself—while lauding specialization for raising living standards—worried that it could be taken too far, narrowing the range on an individual's interests and abilities, and damaging his character.

Of course, maximizing our material standard of living is not our only goal. In some instances, we might be better off *increasing* the variety of tasks we do each day, even if this means some sacrifice in production and income. For example, in many societies, one sex specializes in work outside the home and the other specializes in running the home and taking care of the children. Might families be better off if children had more access to *both* parents, even if this meant a somewhat lower family income? This is an important question. While specialization gives us material gains, there may be *opportunity costs* to be paid in the loss of other things we care about. The right amount of specialization can be found only by balancing the gains against these costs.

Resource Allocation

It was only 10,000 years ago—a mere blink of an eye in human history—that the Neolithic revolution began and human society switched from hunting and gathering to farming and simple manufacturing. At the same time, human wants grew beyond mere food and shelter to the infinite variety of things that can be *made*. Ever since, all societies have been confronted with three important questions:

1. *Which* goods and services should be produced with society's resources?
2. *How* should they be produced?
3. *Who* should get them?

Together, these three questions constitute the problem of **resource allocation**. The way a society chooses to answer these questions—that is, the method it chooses to allocate its resources—will in part determine the character of its economic system.

Resource allocation A method of determining which goods and services will be produced, how they will be produced, and who will get them.

Let's first consider the *which* question. Should we produce more health care or more movies, more goods for consumers or more capital goods for businesses? Where on its production possibilities frontier should the economy operate? As you will see, there are different methods societies can use to answer these questions.

The *how* question is more complicated. Most goods and services can be produced in a variety of different ways, each method using more of some resources and less of others. For example, there are many ways to dig a ditch. We could use *no capital at all* and have dozens of workers digging with their bare hands. We could use *a small amount of capital* by giving each worker a shovel and thereby use less labor, since each worker would now be more productive. Or we could use *even more capital*—a power trencher—and dig the ditch with just one or two workers. In every economic system, there must always be some mechanism that determines how goods and services will be produced from the infinite variety of ways available.

Finally, the *who* question. Here is where economics interacts most strongly with politics. There are so many ways to divide ourselves into groups: men and women, rich and poor, workers and owners, families and single people, young and old . . . the list is endless. How should the products of our economy be distributed among these different groups and among individuals within each group?

Determining *who* gets the economy's output is always the most controversial aspect of resource allocation. Over the last half-century, our society has become more sensitized to the way goods and services are distributed, and we increasingly ask whether that distribution is fair. For example, men get a disproportionately larger share of our national output than women do, whites get more than African-Americans and Hispanics, and middle-aged workers get more than the very old and the very young. As a society, we want to know *why* we observe these patterns (a positive economic question) and *what* we should do about them (a normative economic question). Our society is also increasingly focusing on the distribution of particular goods and services. Should scarce donor organs be rationed to those who have been waiting the longest so that everyone has the same chance of survival? Or should they be sold to the highest bidder so that those able to pay the most will get them? Should productions of Shakespeare's plays be subsidized by the government to permit more people—especially more poor people—to see them? Or should the people who enjoy these plays pay the full cost of their production?

The Three Methods of Resource Allocation. Throughout history, every society has relied primarily on one of three mechanisms for allocating resources. In a **traditional economy,** resources are allocated according to the long-lived practices of the past. Tradition was the dominant method of resource allocation for most of human history and remains strong in many tribal societies and small villages in parts of Africa, South America, Asia, and the Pacific. Typically, traditional methods of production are handed down by the village elders, and traditional principles of fairness govern the distribution of goods and services.

> **Traditional economy** An economy in which resources are allocated according to long-lived practices from the past.

Economies in which resources are allocated mostly by tradition tend to be stable and predictable. But these economies have one serious drawback: They don't grow. With everyone locked into the traditional patterns of production, there is little room for innovation and technological change. Traditional economies are therefore likely to be stagnant economies.

In a **command economy,** resources are allocated mostly by explicit instructions from some higher authority. *Which* goods and services should we produce? The ones we're *ordered* to produce. *How* should we produce them? The way we're *told* to produce them. *Who* will get the goods and services? Whoever the authority *tells* us should get them.

> **Command or centrally planned economy** An economic system in which resources are allocated according to explicit instructions from a central authority.

In a command economy, a government body *plans* how resources will be allocated. That is why command economies are also called **centrally planned economies.** But command economies are disappearing fast. Until about 15 years ago, examples would have included the former Soviet Union, Poland, Rumania, Bulgaria, Albania, China, and many others. Beginning in the late 1980s, all of these nations began abandoning central planning. The only examples left today are Cuba and North Korea, and even these economies—though still dominated by central planning— occasionally take steps away from it.

The third method of allocating resources—and the one with which you are no doubt most familiar—is "the market." In a **market economy**, neither long-held traditions nor commands from above guide most economic behavior. Instead, people are largely free to do what they want with the resources at their disposal. In the end, resources are allocated as a result of individual decision making. *Which* goods and services are produced? Whichever ones producers *choose* to produce. How are they produced? However producers *choose* to produce them. *Who* gets these goods and services? Anyone who *chooses* to buy them.

Market economy An economic system in which resources are allocated through individual decision making.

Of course, in a market system, freedom of choice is constrained by the resources one controls. And in this respect, we do not all start in the same place in the economic race. Some of us—like the Rockefellers and the Kennedys—have inherited great wealth; some—entrepreneur Bill Gates, the novelist Toni Morison, and the model Gisele Bündchen—have inherited great intelligence, talent, or beauty; and some, such as the children of successful professionals, are born into a world of helpful personal contacts. Others, unfortunately, will inherit none of these advantages. In a market system, those who control more resources will have more choices available to them than those who control fewer resources. Moreover, every market economy imposes limits on freeedom of choice. Some restrictions are imposed by government to ensure an orderly, just, and productive society. We cannot kill, steal, or break contracts—even if that is our desire—without suffering serious consequences. And we must pay taxes to fund government services. Still, in spite of the limitations imposed by government and the constraints imposed by limited resources, the market relies heavily on individual freedom of choice to allocate resources.

But wait . . . isn't there a problem here? People acting according to their own desires, without the firm hand of command or tradition to control them? This sounds like a recipe for chaos! How, in such a free-for-all, are resources actually *allocated*?

The answer is contained in two words: *markets* and *prices*.

The Nature of Markets. The market economy gets its name from something that nearly always happens when people are free to do what they want with the resources they possess. Inevitably, people decide to specialize in the production of one or a few things—often organizing themselves into business firms—and then sellers and buyers *come together to trade*. A **market** is a collection of buyers and sellers who have the potential to trade with one another.

Market A group of buyers and sellers with the potential to trade with each other.

In some cases, the market is *global*; that is, the market consists of buyers and sellers who are spread across the globe. The market for oil is an example of a global market, since buyers in any country can buy from sellers in any country. In other cases, the market is local. Markets for restaurant meals, haircuts, and taxi service are examples of local markets.

Markets play a major role in allocating resources by forcing individual decision makers to consider very carefully their decisions about buying and selling. They do so because of an important feature of every market: the *price* at which a good is bought and sold.

The Importance of Prices. A **price** is *the amount of money a buyer must pay to a seller for a good or service*. Price is not always the same as *cost*. In economics, as you've learned in this chapter, cost means *opportunity cost*—the *total* sacrifice needed to buy the good. While the price of a good is a *part* of its opportunity cost,

Price The amount of money that must be paid to a seller to obtain a good or service.

it is not the only cost. For example, the price does not include the value of the time sacrificed to buy something. Buying a new jacket will require you to spend time traveling to and from the store, trying on different styles and sizes, and waiting in line at the cash register.

Still, in most cases, the price of a good is a significant part of its opportunity cost. For large purchases such as a home or automobile, the price will be *most* of the opportunity cost. And this is why prices are so important to the overall working of the economy: They confront individual decision makers with the costs of their choices.

Consider the example of purchasing a car. Because you must pay the price, you know that buying a new car will require you to cut back on purchases of other things. In this way, the opportunity cost to *society* of making another car is converted to an opportunity cost *for you*. If you value a new car more highly than the other things you must sacrifice for it, you will buy it. If not, you won't buy it.

Why is it so important that people face the opportunity costs of their actions? The following thought experiment can answer this question. Imagine that the government passed a new law: When anyone buys a new car, the government will reimburse that person for it immediately. The consequences would be easy to predict. First, on the day the law was passed, everyone would rush out to buy new cars. Why not, if cars are free? The entire stock of existing automobiles would be gone within days—maybe even hours. Many people who didn't value cars much at all, and who hardly ever used them, would find themselves owning several—one for each day of the week or to match the different colors in their wardrobe. Others who weren't able to act in time—including some who desperately needed a new car for their work or to run their households—would be unable to find one at all.

Over time, automobile companies would drastically increase production to meet the surge in demand for cars. So much of our available labor, capital, natural resources, and entrepreneurial talent would be diverted to the automobile industry that we'd have to sacrifice huge quantities of all other goods and services. Thus, we'd end up *paying* for those additional cars in the end, by making do with less education, less medical care, perhaps even less food—all to support the widespread, frivolous use of cars. Almost everyone—even those who love cars—would conclude that society had been made worse-off with the new "free-car" policy. By eliminating a price for automobiles, and severing the connection between the opportunity cost of producing a car and the individual's decision to get one, we would have created quite a mess for ourselves.

> *When resources are allocated by the market, and people must* pay *for their purchases, they are forced to consider the opportunity cost to society of their individual actions. In this way, markets are able to create a sensible allocation of resources.*

Resource Allocation in the United States. The United States has always been considered the leading example of a market economy. Each day, millions of distinct items are produced and sold in markets. Our grocery stores are always stocked with broccoli and tomato soup, and the drugstore always has Kleenex and aspirin—all due to the choices of individual producers and consumers. The goods that are traded, the way they are traded, and the price at which they trade are determined by the traders themselves. No direction from above is needed to keep markets working.

But even in the United States, there are numerous cases of resource allocation *outside* the market. For example, families are important institutions in the United

States, and many economic decisions are made within them. Families tend to operate like traditional villages, not like market economies. After all, few families charge prices for goods and services provided inside the home.

Our economy also allocates some resources by command. Various levels of government collect, in total, about one-third of our incomes as taxes. We are *told* how much tax we must pay, and those who don't comply suffer serious penalties, including imprisonment. Government—rather than individual decision makers—spends the tax revenue. In this way, the government plays a major role in allocating resources—especially in determining which goods are produced and who gets them.

There are also other ways, aside from strict commands, that the government limits our market freedoms. Regulations designed to protect the environment, maintain safe workplaces, and ensure the safety of our food supply are just a few examples of government-imposed constraints on our individual choice.

What are we to make, then, of resource allocation in the United States? Markets are, indeed, constrained. But for each example we can find where resources are allocated by tradition or command, or where government restrictions seriously limit some market freedom, we can find hundreds of examples where individuals make choices according to their own desires. The things we buy, the jobs at which we work, the homes in which we live—in almost all cases, these result from market choices. The market, though not pure, is certainly the dominant method of resource allocation in the United States.

Resource Ownership

So far, we've been concerned with how resources are allocated. Another important feature of an economic system is how resources are *owned*. The owner of a resource—a parcel of land, a factory, or one's own labor time—determines how it can be used and receives income when others use it. And there have been three primary modes of resource ownership in human history.

Under *communal* ownership, resources are owned by everyone—or by no one, depending on your point of view. They are simply there for the taking; no person or organization imposes any restrictions on their use or charges any fees. It is hard to find economies with significant communal ownership of resources. Karl Marx believed that, in time, all economies would evolve toward communal ownership, and he named this predicted system **communism**. In fact, none of the economies that called themselves Marxist (such as the former Soviet Union) ever achieved Marx's vision of communism. This is not surprising: Communal ownership on a broad scale can work only when individuals have no conflicts over how resources are used. Therefore, communism requires the end of *scarcity*—an unlikely prospect in the foreseeable future.

Communism A type of economic system in which most resources are owned in common.

Nevertheless, there are examples of communal ownership on a smaller scale. Traditional villages maintain communal ownership of land and sometimes cattle. In some of the cooperative farms in Israel—called *kibbutzim*—land and capital are owned by all the members. Conflicts may result when individuals differ over how these resources should be used, but these conflicts are resolved by consensus rather than by decree or by charging fees for their use.

Closer to home, most families operate on the principle of communal ownership. The house, television, telephone, and food in the refrigerator are treated as if owned jointly. More broadly, who "owns" our sidewalks, streets, and public beaches? No one does, really. In practice, all citizens are free to use them as much and as often as they would like. This is essentially communal ownership.

Socialism A type of economic system in which most resources are owned by the state.

Under **socialism,** the *state* owns most of the resources. The prime example is the former Soviet Union, where the state owned all of the land and capital equipment in the country. In many ways, it also owned the labor of individual households, since it was virtually the only employer in the nation and unemployment was considered a crime.

State ownership also occurs in nonsocialist economies. In the United States, national parks, state highway systems, military bases, public colleges and universities, and government buildings are all state-owned resources. Over a third of the land in the country is owned by the federal government. The military, even under our current volunteer system, is an example in which the state owns the labor of soldiers—albeit for a limited period of time.

Capitalism A type of economic system in which most resources are owned privately.

Finally, the third system. When most resources are owned *privately*—as in the United States—we have **capitalism.** Take the book you are reading right now. If you turn to the title page, you will see the imprint of the company that published this book. This is a corporation owned by thousands of individual stockholders. These individuals own the buildings, the land under them, the office furniture and computer equipment, and even the reputation of the company. When these facilities are used to produce and sell a book, the company's profits belong to these stockholders. Similarly, the employees of the company are private individuals. They are selling a resource they own—their labor time—to the company, and they receive income—wages and salaries—in return.

The United States is one of the most capitalistic countries in the world. True, there are examples of state and communal ownership, as we've seen. But the dominant mode of resource ownership in the United States is *private* ownership. Resource owners keep *most* of the income they earn from supplying their resources, and they have broad freedom in deciding how their resources are used.

Types of Economic Systems

We've used the phrase *economic system* a few times already in this book. But now it's time for a formal definition.

Economic system A system of resource allocation and resource ownership.

> *An **economic system** is composed of two features: a mechanism for allocating resources and a mode of resource ownership.*

HTTP://

The Center for International Comparisons at the University of Pennsylvania (http://pwt.econ.upenn.edu/) is a good source of information on the performance of economies around the world.

Let's leave aside the rare economies in which communal ownership is dominant and those in which resources are allocated primarily by tradition. That leaves us with four basic types of economic systems, indicated by the four quadrants in Figure 4. In the upper left quadrant, we have *market capitalism*. In this system, resources are *allocated* primarily by the market and *owned* primarily by private individuals. Today, most nations have market capitalist economies, including all of the countries of North America and Western Europe, and most of those in Asia, Latin America, and Africa.

In the lower right quadrant is *centrally planned socialism*, under which resources are mostly allocated by command and mostly owned by the state. This *was* the system in the former Soviet Union and the nations of Eastern Europe until the late 1980s. But since then, these countries' economies have gone through cataclysmic change by moving from the lower right quadrant to the upper left. That is, these nations have simultaneously changed both their method of resource allocation and their systems of resource ownership.

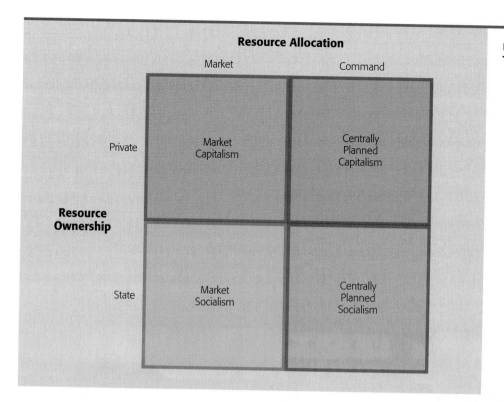

FIGURE 4
Types of Economic Systems

Although market capitalism and centrally planned socialism have been the two paramount economic systems in modern history, there have been others. The upper right quadrant represents a system of *centrally planned capitalism,* in which resources are owned by private individuals yet allocated by command. In the recent past, countries such as Sweden and Japan—where the government has been more heavily involved in allocating resources than in the United States—have flirted with this type of system. Nations at war—like the United States during World War II—also move in this direction, as governments find it necessary to direct resources by command in order to ensure sufficient military production.

Finally, in the lower left quadrant is *market socialism,* in which resources are owned by the state yet allocated by the market mechanism. The possibility of market socialism has fascinated many social scientists, who believed it promised the best of both worlds: the freedom and efficiency of the market mechanism and the fairness and equity of socialism. There are, however, serious problems—many would say "unresolvable contradictions"—in trying to mix the two. The chief examples of market socialism in modern history were short-lived experiments—in Hungary and the former Yugoslavia in the 1950s and 1960s—in which the results were mixed at best.

Economic Systems and This Book. In this book, you will learn how market capitalist economies operate. This means that the other three types of economic systems in Figure 4 will be, for the most part, ignored. Until 10 years ago, these statements would have been accompanied by an apology that would have gone something like this: "True, much of the world is characterized by alternative economic systems, but there is only so much time in one course . . ."

In the past decade, however, the world has changed dramatically: About 400 million people have come under the sway of the market as their nations have abandoned centrally planned socialism; another billion or so are being added as China changes course. The study of modern economies is now, more than ever before, the study of market capitalism.

Understanding the Market. The market is simultaneously the most simple and the most complex way to allocate resources. For individual buyers and sellers, the market is simple. There are no traditions or commands to be memorized and obeyed. Instead, we enter the markets we *wish* to trade in and we respond to prices there as we *wish* to, unconcerned about the overall process of resource allocation.

But from the economist's point of view, the market is quite complex. Resources are allocated indirectly, as a *by-product* of individual decision making, rather than through easily identified traditions or commands. As a result, it often takes some skillful economic detective work to determine just how individuals are behaving and how resources are being allocated as a consequence.

How can we make sense of all of this apparent chaos and complexity? That is what economics is all about. And you will begin your detective work in Chapter 3, where you will learn about the most widely used model in the field of economics: the model of supply and demand.

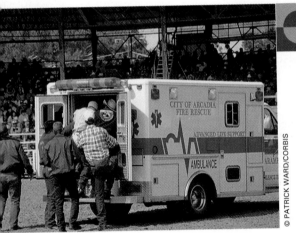
© PATRICK WARD/CORBIS

USING THE THEORY
Are We Saving Lives Efficiently?

In this chapter, you learned that if resources are being wasted, we will operate *inside* our PPF rather than on the PPF. For example, suppose "all other goods" are being produced inefficiently. Then, by eliminating the productive inefficiency, we would free up resources. Some of the resources could be used to save more lives and some to produce more of other goods. In Figure 1, this would move us from a point like W to a point like D, where we end up saving more lives *and* having more of other goods.

But there could also be productive inefficiency in the saving of human lives. If that is the case—if it is possible to save more lives without devoting any additional resources to doing so—then we would, once again, be operating inside our PPF. And once again, we could have a free lunch—save more lives *and* have more of other goods—by eliminating the inefficiency.

Some economists have argued that we do, indeed, waste significant amounts of resources in our lifesaving efforts. How have they come to such a conclusion?

The first thing to remember is that saving a life—no matter how it is done—requires the use of resources. Any lifesaving action we might take—putting another hundred police on the streets, building another emergency surgery center, or running an advertising campaign to encourage healthy living—requires certain quantities of resources. In a market economy, resources sell at a price. This allows us to use the dollar cost of a lifesaving method to measure the value of the resources used up by that method.

Moreover, we can compare the "cost per year of life saved" of different methods. For example, in the United States we currently spend about $253 million on heart transplants each year and thereby add about 1,600 years to the lives of heart patients. Thus, the cost per year of life saved from heart transplants is $253,000,000/1,600 = $158,000 (rounded to the nearest thousand).

Method	Cost per Life-Year Saved
Brief physician antismoking intervention:	
Single personal warning from physician to stop smoking	$150
Sickle cell screening and treatment for African-American newborns	$236
Replacing ambulances with helicopters for medical emergencies	$2,454
Intensive physician antismoking intervention:	
Physician identification of smokers among their patients; three physician counseling sessions; two further sessions with smoking-cessation specialists; and materials—nicotine patch or nicotine gum	$2,587
Mammograms: Once every three years, for ages 50–64	$2,700
Chlorination of water supply	$4,000
Next step after suspicious lung X-ray:	
PET Scan	$3,742
Exploratory Surgery	$4,895
Needle Biopsy	$7,116
Vaccination of all infants against strep infections	$80,000
Mammograms: Annually, for ages 50–64	$108,401
Exercise electrocardiograms as screening test:	
For 40-year-old males	$124,374
Heart transplants	$157,821
Mammograms: Annually, for age 40–49	$186,635
Exercise electrocardiograms as screening test:	
For 40-year-old females	$335,217
Seat belts on school buses	$2,760,197
Asbestos ban in automatic transmissions	$66,402,402

TABLE 3

The Cost of Saving Lives

Sources: Electrocardiograms: Charles E. Phelps, *Health Economics,* 2nd ed. (Reading, MA: Addison-Wesley, 1997). Regular exercise: L. Goldman, A. M. Garber, S. A. Grover, & M. A. Hlatky (1996). Task Force 6. Cost-effectiveness of assessment and management of risk factors (Bethesda Conference). *JACC,* 27(5), 1020–1030. Anti-smoking intensive intervention: *Journal of the American Medical Association,* Dec. 3, 1997. Anti-smoking brief intervention: Malcolm Law and Jin Ling Tang, "An Analysis of the Effectiveness of Interventions Intended to Help People Stop Smoking," *Archives of Internal Medicine,* 1995; 155: pp. 1933–1941, and authors' calculations to convert "per life saved" to "per year of life saved." Annual mammograms: Kent Jeffreys, "Progressive Environmentalism: Principles for Regulatory Reform (Policy Report No. 194), National Center for Policy Analysis, June 1995. Benzene emission controls: Tammy O. Tengs et al., "Five Hundred Life-Saving Interventions and Their Cost-Effectiveness," *Risk Analysis,* 1994. All other figures: Tammy O. Tengs, "Dying Too Soon: How Cost-Effectiveness Analysis Can Save Lives," School of Social Ecology, University of California, Irvine, NCPA Policy Report No. 204, May 1997. Replacing ambulances with helicopters: Peter A. Gearhart, Richard Wuerz, A. Russell Localio, "Cost Effectiveness Analysis of Helicopter EMS for Trauma Patients," *Annals of Emergency Medicine,* Oct. 1997, 30:500–506. Chlorination of water supply: Kent Jeffreys, "Guide to Regulatory Reform: The Cost Benefit Rule," National Center for Policy Analysis, *Brief Analysis,* No. 150, January 31, 1995. Strep Vaccination: "A Pound of Prevention," in *News from Harvard Medical, Dental and Public Health Schools,* March 24, 2000 (based on price of $232 for a four-dose vaccination series with Prevnar). Lung cancer screening: M. Ditelin, D. Modka, K. Weber, P. Theiseen, H. Schicha, "Cost Effectiveness of PET in the Management Algorithms of Lung Tumors: Comparison of Health Economic Data," *Nuklearmedizin,* 40(4), August 2001, pp. 122–128, viewed at *http://www.acor.org/cnet/710582.html* (May 2003). Euros have been converted to dollars.

Table 3 lists several of the methods we currently use to save lives in the United States. Some of these methods reflect legal or regulatory decisions (such as the ban on asbestos) and others reflect standard medical practices (such as annual mammograms for women over 50). Other methods are used only sporadically (such as seat belts in school buses). You can see that the cost per life saved ranges widely—from $150 per year of life saved for a physician warning a patient to quit smoking, to over $66,000,000 per year of life saved from the ban on asbestos in automatic transmissions.

The table indicates that some lifesaving methods are highly cost effective. For example, our society probably exhausts the potential to save lives from brief physician antismoking intervention. Most doctors *do* warn their smoking patients to quit.

But the table also indicates some serious productive *in*efficiency in lifesaving. For example, screening and treating African-American newborns for sickle cell anemia is one of the least costly ways of saving a year of life in the United States—only $236 per year of life saved. Nevertheless, 20 percent of African-American newborns do *not* get this screening at all. Similarly, intensive intervention to discourage smoking is far from universal in the U.S. health care system, even though it has the relatively low cost of $2,587 per year of life saved.

Why is the less than universal use of these lower cost methods *productively inefficient?* To answer, let's do some thought experiments. First, let's imagine that we shift resources from heart transplants to *intensive* antismoking efforts. Then for each year of life we decided *not* to save with heart transplants, we would free up $157,821 in medical resources. If we applied those resources toward intensive antismoking efforts, at a cost of $2,587 per year of life saved, we could then save an additional $157,821/$2,587 = 61 life-years. In other words, we could increase the number of life-years saved without any increase in resources flowing to the health care sector, and therefore, without any sacrifice in other goods and services. If you look back at the definition of productive inefficiency given earlier in this chapter, you'll see why this is an example of it.

But why pick on heart transplants? Our ban on asbestos in automobile transmissions—which requires the purchase of more costly materials with greater quantities of scarce resources—costs us about $66 million for each life-year saved. Suppose these funds were spent instead to buy the resources needed to provide women aged 40 to 49 with annual mammograms (currently *not* part of most physicians' recommendations). Then for each life-year lost to asbestos, we'd save $66 million/186,635 = 354 life-years from earlier detection of breast cancer.

Of course, allocating lifesaving resources is much more complicated than our discussion so far has implied. For one thing, the benefits of lifesaving efforts are not fully captured by "life-years saved" (or even by an alternative measure, which accounts for improvement in *quality* of life). The cost per life-year saved from mandating seat belts on school buses is extremely high—almost $3 million. This is mostly because very few children die in school bus accidents—about 11 per year in the entire United States—and, according to the National Traffic Safety Board, few of these deaths would have been prevented with seat belts. But mandatory seat belts—rightly or wrongly—might decrease the anxiety of millions of parents as they send their children off to school. How should we value such a reduction in anxiety? Hard to say. But it's not unreasonable to include it as a benefit—at least in some way—when deciding about resources.

Another difficulty in allocating our lifesaving resources efficiently—which has become profoundly more serious in the last few years—is uncertainty. Consider, for example, our efforts to prevent a terrorist attack via hijacked airliners. What is the cost per life-year saved? We cannot know. An earlier study of antiterrorist efforts in the mid-1990s had estimated the cost at $8,000,000 per life-year saved, which seems productively inefficient.[4] But this study made two critical assumptions to ar-

---

[4] "The Cost of Anti-terrorist Rhetoric," The Cato Review of Business and Government, Dec. 17, 1996, and authors' calculations to convert "per life saved" to "per year of life saved."

rive at that number. First, that—without the new procedures—37 people would perish each year from airline-related terrorist incidents—equal to the rate we had had in the late 1980s and early 1990s. Second, the study assumed that the safety procedures being evaluated would be 100 percent effective in eliminating attacks.

Both of these assumptions were proven wrong by the events of September 11, 2001. On that day, we discovered that airline hijacking could take many more lives than we had imagined, dramatically reducing the cost per-life-year saved of antiterrorist measures. On the other hand, we also realized that our efforts to prevent such attacks could not be entirely successful—*increasing* the cost per life-year saved.

We confront similar uncertainties in allocating resources to protect against potential bioterrorism. Should our government be stockpiling smallpox vaccine? Should it go further, and press for vaccination of the entire population? The expected cost per life-year saved under each of these policies can range from minuscule to exorbitant, depending on the likelihood of a smallpox attack and how many lives the policy would save—things we can't realistically know. Clearly, trying to gauge and improve our productive efficiency in saving lives—which was never an exact science—has become even *less* exact in the post-9/11 era.

Summary

One of the most fundamental concepts in economics is *opportunity cost*. The opportunity cost of any choice is what we give up when we make that choice. At the individual level, opportunity cost arises from the scarcity of time or money; for society as a whole, it arises from the scarcity of resources—land and natural resources, labor, capital, and entrepreneurship. To produce and enjoy more of one thing, we must shift resources away from producing something else. The correct measure of cost is not just the money price we pay, but the opportunity cost: what we must give up when we make a choice. The *law of increasing opportunity cost* tells us that the more of something we produce, the greater the opportunity cost of producing still more.

In a world of scarce resources, each society must have an economic system—its way of organizing economic activity.

All *economic systems* feature *specialization*, where each person and firm concentrates on a limited number of productive activities—and *exchange*, through which we obtain most of what we desire by trading with others. Specialization and exchange enable us to enjoy higher living standards than would be possible under self-sufficiency.

Every economic system determines how resources are owned and how they are allocated. In a market capitalist economy, resources are owned primarily by private individuals and allocated primarily through markets. Prices play an important role in markets by forcing decision makers to take account of society's opportunity cost when they make choices.

Key Terms

Absolute advantage	Exchange	Price
Capitalism	Explicit cost	Production possibilities frontier (PPF)
Centrally planned economy	Implicit cost	Productive inefficiency
Command economy	Law of increasing opportunity cost	Resource allocation
Communism	Market	Socialism
Comparative advantage	Market economy	Specialization
Economic system	Opportunity cost	Traditional economy

Review Questions   *Answers to even-numbered Questions and Problems can be found on the text Web site at http://hall-lieb.swlearning.com.*

1. "Warren Buffett is one of the world's wealthiest men, worth billions of dollars. For someone like Buffet, the principle of opportunity cost simply doesn't apply." True or false? Explain.

2. What are some reasons why a country might be operating inside its production possibilities frontier (PPF)?

3. Why is a PPF concave—that is, bowed out from the origin? Be sure to give an *economic* explanation.

4. What are three distinct reasons why specialization leads to a higher standard of living?

5. What is the difference between comparative advantage and absolute advantage? Which is more important from an economic viewpoint?

6. List the three questions any resource allocation mechanism must answer. Briefly describe the three primary methods of resource allocation that have evolved to answer these questions.

7. What are the three primary ways in which resources are *owned*? Briefly describe each of them.

8. Why can't the United States economy be described as a *pure market capitalist economy*?

9. True or false?: "Resource allocation and resource ownership are essentially the same thing. Once you know who owns the resources in an economy, you also know by what mechanism those resources will be allocated." Explain your answer.

Problems and Exercises

1. Redraw Figure 1, but this time identify a different set of points along the frontier. Starting at point F (500,000 lives saved, zero production of other goods), have each point you select show equal increments in the quantity of other goods produced. For example, point H should correspond to 200,000 units of other goods, point J to 400,000 units, point K to 600,000 units, and so on. Now observe what happens to the opportunity cost of "200,000 more units of other goods" as you move leftward and upward along this PPF. Does the law of increasing opportunity cost apply to the production of "all other goods"? Explain briefly.

2. Suppose that you are considering what to do with an upcoming weekend. Here are your options, from least to most preferred: (1) Study for upcoming midterms; (2) fly to Colorado for a quick ski trip; (3) go into seclusion in your dorm room and try to improve your score on a computer game. What is the opportunity cost of a decision to play the computer game all weekend?

3. How would a technological innovation in lifesaving—say, the discovery of a cure for cancer—affect the PPF in Figure 1?

4. How would a technological innovation in the production of *other* goods—say, the invention of a new kind of robot that speeds up assembly-line manufacturing—affect the PPF?

5. Suppose that one day, Gilligan (the castaway) eats a magical island plant that turns him into an expert at everything. In particular, it now takes him just half an hour to pick a quart of berries, and 15 minutes to catch a fish.
   a. Redo Table 2 in the chapter.
   b. Who—Gilligan or Maryanne—has a comparative advantage in picking berries? In fishing? When the castaways discover each other, which of the two should specialize in which task?

c. Can *both* castaways benefit from Gilligan's new abilities? How?

6. Suppose that two different castaways, Mr. and Mrs. Howell, end up on a different island. Mr. Howell can pick 1 pineapple per hour, or 1 coconut. Mrs. Howell can pick 2 pineapples per hour, but it takes her two hours to pick a coconut.
   a. Construct a table like Table 2 showing Mr. and Mrs. Howell's labor requirements.
   b. Who—Mr. or Mrs. Howell—has a comparative advantage in picking pineapples? In picking coconuts? Which of the two should specialize in which tasks?
   c. Assume that Mr. and Mrs. Howell had originally washed ashore on different parts of the island, and that they originally each spent 12 hours per day working, spending 6 hours picking pineapples and 6 hours picking coconuts. How will their total production change if they find each other and begin to specialize?

7. You and a friend have decided to work jointly on a course project. Frankly, your friend is a less than ideal partner. His skills as a researcher are such that he can review and outline only two articles a day. Moreover, his hunt-and-peck style limits him to only 10 pages of typing a day. On the other hand, in a day you can produce six outlines or type 20 pages.
   a. Who has an absolute advantage in outlining, you or your friend? What about typing?
   b. Who has a comparative advantage in outlining? In typing?
   c. According to the principle of comparative advantage, who should specialize in which task?

8. One might think that performing a mammogram once each year—as opposed to once every three years—would triple the cost per life saved. But according to Table 3, performing the exam annually raises the cost per life-year saved by about 40 times. Does this make sense? Explain.

9. Use the information on college costs shown in Table 1 to calculate the average opportunity cost of a year in college for a student at a four-year public institution under the following assumptions:
   a. The student receives free room and board at home at no opportunity cost to the parents.
   b. The student receives an academic scholarship covering all tuition and fees (in the form of a grant, not a loan or a work study aid).
   c. The student works half time while at school at no additional emotional cost.

10. Work the following problems.
   a. Use the information on college costs shown in Table 1 to compare the opportunity cost of attending a year of college at a two-year public college, a four-year public college, and a four-year private college.
   b. Consider Kylie, who has been awarded academic scholarships covering all tuition and fees at three different colleges. College #1 is a two-year public college. College #2 is a four-year public college, and College #3 is a four-year private college. Explain why, if the decision is based solely on opportunity cost, Kylie will turn down her largest scholarship offers.
   c. Given your calculations in part b, what nonmonetary considerations might induce Kylie to go to the college with the highest opportunity cost? How large (in dollar terms) must these nonmonetary benefits be to persuade Kylie to choose the most expensive college?

11. Suppose the Internet enables more production of other goods *and* helps to save lives (for simplicity, assume proportional increases).
   a. Show how the PPF would be affected.
   b. Does this affect any of the general conclusions about economic growth?
   c. Graphically show the conclusion that more lives could be saved if technological change occurred that enabled greater production of other goods, but that did not directly affect the number of lives saved.

Challenge Question

1. Suppose that an economy's PPF is a straight line, rather than a bowed out, concave curve. What would this say about the nature of opportunity cost as production is shifted from one good to the other?

 *These exercises require access to Hall/Lieberman Xtra! If Xtra! did not come with your book, visit http://hallxtra.swlearning.com to purchase.*

1. Use your Xtra! password at the Hall and Lieberman Web site (http://hallxtra.swlearning.com), select Chapter 2, and under Economic Applications, click on EconDebates. Choose *Economic Fundamentals; Scarcity, Choice and Opportunity Cost* and scroll down to find the debate, "Should There Be a Market for Human Organs?" Read the debate, and answer the following questions.
   a. How (if at all) would compensation for organ donation offset the opportunity cost of donation?
   b. Now click on EconNews. Choose *Economic Fundamentals; Scarcity, Choice and Opportunity Cost* and scroll down to find the article, "What Price for a Life?" Does this form of compensation eliminate the same opportunity cost as organ donation? Why or why not?

2. Use your Xtra! password at the Hall and Lieberman Web site (http://hallxtra.swlearning.com), select Chapter 2, and under Economic Applications, click on EconNews. Choose *Economic Fundamentals; Production Possibility Frontier* and scroll down to find the article, "The Federal Budget: What a Difference a Day Makes." Read the summary, and answer the questions below.
   a. Does the article imply that the economy is producing efficiently? Why or why not?
   b. Draw a PPF between military spending on the horizontal axis, and all other government spending on the vertical axis. Where on the PPF does this article suggest the economy is moving?
   c. Is it possible for government to simultaneoiusly increase both military spending and domestic spending?

Supply and Demand

Father Guido Sarducci, a character on the early *Saturday Night Live* shows, once observed that the average person remembers only about five minutes worth of material from college. He therefore proposed the "Five Minute University," where you'd learn only the five minutes of material you'd actually remember and dispense with the rest. The economics course would last only 10 seconds, just enough time for students to learn to recite three words: "supply and demand."

Of course, there is much more to economics than these three words. Still, Sarducci's observation had some truth. Many people *do* regard the phrase "supply and demand" as synonymous with economics. But surprisingly few people actually understand what the phrase means. In a debate about health care, poverty, recent events in the stock market, or the high price of housing, you might hear someone say, "Well, it's just a matter of supply and demand," as a way of dismissing the issue entirely. Others use the phrase with an exaggerated reverence, as if supply and demand were an inviolable physical law, like gravity, about which nothing can be done. So what does this oft-repeated phrase really mean?

First, supply and demand is just an economic model—nothing more and nothing less. It's a model designed to explain *how prices are determined in certain types of markets.*

Why has this model taken on such an exalted role in the field of economics? Because prices themselves play such an exalted role in the economy. In a market system, once the price of something has been determined, only those willing to pay that price will get it. Thus, prices determine which households will get which goods and services and which firms will get which resources. If you want to know why the cell phone industry is expanding while the video rental industry is shrinking, or why homelessness is a more pervasive problem in the United States than hunger, you need to understand how prices are determined. In this chapter, you will learn how the model of supply and demand works and how to use it. You will also learn about the strengths and limitations of the model. It will take more time than Guido Sarducci's 10-second economics course, but in the end you will know much more than just three little words.

MARKETS

Put any compound in front of a chemist, ask him what it is and what it can be used for, and he will immediately think of the basic elements—carbon, hydrogen, oxygen, and so on. Ask an economist almost any question about the economy, and he will immediately thinking about *markets.*

In ordinary language, a market is a specific location where buying and selling take place: a supermarket, a flea market, etc. In economics, a market is not a place, but rather a collection of *traders.* More specifically,

> *a market is a group of buyers and sellers with the potential to trade with each other.*

Economists think of the economy as a collection of individual markets. In each of these markets, the collection of buyers and sellers will be different, depending on what is being traded. There is a market for oranges, another for automobiles, another for real estate, and still others for corporate stocks, euros, and anything else that is bought and sold.

However, unlike chemistry—in which the set of basic elements is always the same—in economics, we can define a market in *different* ways, depending on our purpose. In fact, in almost any economic analysis, the first step is to define and characterize the market or collection of markets to analyze.

How Broadly Should We Define the Market?

Suppose we want to study the personal computer industry in the United States. Should we define the market very broadly ("the market for computers"), or very narrowly ("the market for ultra-light laptops"), or something in between ("the market for laptops")? The right choice depends on the problem we're trying to analyze.

For example, if we're interested in the price of equipment for connecting to the Internet, there would be no reason to divide computers into desktops and laptops, since the distinction would have nothing to do with e-mail access and would only get in the way. Thus, we'd treat all types of computers as if they were the same

Aggregation The process of combining distinct things into a single whole.

good. Economists call this process **aggregation**—combining a group of distinct things into a single whole.

But suppose we're asking a different question: Why do laptops always cost more than desktops with similar computing power? Then we'd aggregate all laptops together as one good, and all desktops as another, and look at each of these more narrowly defined markets.

The same general principle applies to the *geographic* breadth of the market. If we want to predict how instability in the Persian Gulf will affect gasoline prices around the world, we'd use the "global market for oil," in which the major oil producers in about 20 countries sell to buyers around the globe. But if we want to explain why gasoline is cheaper in the United States than in most of the rest of the world, we'd want to look at the "U.S. market for oil." In this market, global sellers choose how much oil to sell to U.S. buyers.

> *In economics, markets can be defined broadly or narrowly, depending on our purpose.*

How broadly or narrowly markets are defined is one of the most important differences between *macro*economics and *micro*economics. In macroeconomics, goods and services are aggregated to the highest levels. Macro models even lump all consumer goods—dishwashers, cell phones, blue jeans, and so forth—into the single category "consumption goods" and view them as if they are traded in a single, broadly defined market, "the market for consumption goods." Similarly, instead of recognizing different markets for shovels, bulldozers, computers, and factory buildings, macro models analyze the market for "capital goods." Defining markets this broadly allows macroeconomists to take an overall view of the economy without getting bogged down in the details.

In microeconomics, by contrast, markets are defined more narrowly. Instead of asking how much we'll spend on *consumer goods*, a microeconomist might ask how much we'll spend on *health care* or *video games*. Although microeconomics always involves some aggregation, the process stops before it reaches the highest level of generality.

Buyers and Sellers

A market is composed of the buyers and sellers that trade in it. But who, exactly, *are* these buyers and sellers?

When you think of a seller, your first image might be of a business. In many markets, you'd be right: The sellers *are* business firms. Examples are markets for restaurant meals, airline travel, clothing, and banking services. But businesses aren't the only sellers in the economy. For example, *households* are the primary sellers in labor markets, such as the markets for Web page designers, accountants, and factory workers. Households are also important sellers in markets for used cars, residential homes, and rare artworks. Governments, too, are sometimes important sellers. For example, state governments are major sellers in the market for education through state colleges and universities.

What about buyers? Your first thought may be "people" like yourself, or "households." Indeed, many goods and services are bought primarily by households: college education, movies, housing, clothing, and so on. But businesses and government agencies are the primary buyers in labor markets, and they are also important buyers of personal computers, automobiles, and airline transportation.

As you can see, the buyers in a market can be households, business firms, or government agencies. And the same is true of sellers. Sometimes, it's important to recognize that all three groups are on both sides of a market. But not always. Once again, it depends on our purpose.

Our purpose in this book—and your purpose in taking a college course in economics—is educational. We want to identify the major forces at work in the economy, the ones that cause prices to rise and fall, industries to expand and contract, and so on. Accordingly, we want to keep our models simple, so the important ideas stand out more clearly. This is why we'll usually (but not always) follow this guideline:

For the most part, in markets for consumer goods, we'll view business firms as the only sellers, and households as the only buyers.

Similarly, when we analyze markets for labor or capital in later chapters, we'll generally view business firms as the only buyers, and households as the only sellers. Of course, we'll make exceptions whenever decisions by *other* groups of buyers or sellers matter to the problem at hand.

One last simplification should be mentioned. In many of our discussions, we'll be leaving out the "go-between." When analyzing, say, the market for books, we'll view book publishers as selling directly to households, rather than using retailers like Barnes and Noble or Amazon.com to do the selling for them. And in labor markets—such as say, the market for business managers—we'll view business firms as hiring workers directly, rather than using headhunting firms as intermediaries. Except for special issues in which retailers, headhunters or other intermediaries are important, including them would add complexity but not much else.

Competition in Markets

A final issue in defining a market is how individual buyers and sellers view the price of the product. In many cases, individual buyers or sellers have an important influence over the price they charge. For example, in the market for cornflakes, Kellogg's—an individual *seller*—simply sets its price every few months. It can raise the price and sell fewer boxes of cereal or lower the price and sell more. In the market for windshield wiper motors, Ford Motor Company—an individual *buyer*—can influence the price by negotiating special deals or by changing the number of motors it buys. The market for breakfast cereals and the market for windshield wiper motors are examples of *imperfectly competitive* markets.

In imperfectly competitive markets, individual buyers or sellers can influence the price of the product.

But now think about the national market for wheat. Can an individual seller have any impact on the market price? Not really. On any given day there is a going price for wheat—say, $5.80 per bushel. If a farmer tries to charge more than that—say, $5.85 per bushel—he won't sell any wheat at all! His customers will instead go to one of his many competitors and buy the identical product from them for less. Each wheat farmer must take the price of wheat as a "given."

The same is true of a single wheat *buyer:* If he tries to negotiate a lower price from a seller, he'd be laughed off the farm. "Why should I sell my wheat to you for

HTTP://

The Inomics search engine is devoted solely to economics (http://www.inomics.com/cgi/show). Use it to investigate topics related to supply and demand.

Imperfectly competitive market A market in which a single buyer or seller has the power to influence the price of the product.

$5.75 per bushel, when there are others who will pay me $5.80?" Accordingly, each buyer must take the market price as a given.

The market for wheat is an example of a *perfectly competitive market.*

Perfectly competitive market
A market in which no buyer or seller has the power to influence the price.

> *In perfectly competitive markets (or just competitive markets), each buyer and seller takes the market price as a given.*

What makes some markets imperfectly competitive and others perfectly competitive? You'll learn the complete answer when you are well into your study of *microeconomics*, along with more formal definitions. But here's a hint: In perfectly competitive markets, there are many small buyers and sellers, each is a small part of the market, and the product is standardized, like wheat. Imperfectly competitive markets, by contrast, have just a few large buyers or sellers, or else the product of each seller is unique in some way.

Using Supply and Demand

Supply and demand is a versatile model. It can be applied to broadly defined goods (the market for food) or narrowly defined goods (the market for Granny Smith apples). Households, business firms, or government agencies can appear in any combination on the buying side or the selling side. The buyers and sellers can reside within a small geographic area or be dispersed around the world.

But there is one important restriction in using supply and demand: We are implicitly assuming that the market is perfectly competitive.

> *The supply and demand model is designed to explain how prices are determined in perfectly competitive markets.*

This suggests that the model isn't very useful. After all, perfectly competitive markets—in which an individual buyer or seller has *no* influence on the market price—are not that common in the real world. However, many markets come reasonably close—close enough, in fact, that we can choose to view them as perfectly competitive.

Think of the market for fast-food hot dogs in a big city. On the one hand, every hot dog stand is somewhat different from every other one in terms of location, quality of service, and so on. This means an individual vendor has *some* influence over the price of his hot dogs. For example, if his competitors are all charging $1.50 for a hot dog, but he sells in a more convenient location, he might be able to charge $1.60 or $1.70 without losing too many customers. In this sense, the market for sidewalk hot dogs does not seem perfectly competitive.

On the other hand, there are rather narrow limits to an individual seller's freedom to change his price. With so many vendors in a big city, who are not *that* different from one another, one who charged $2.00 or $2.25 might soon find that he's lost all of his customers to the other vendors who are charging the market price of $1.50. Since no single seller can deviate *too* much from the market price, we could—if we wanted to—view the market as more or less perfectly competitive.

How, then, do we decide whether to consider a market, such as the market for big-city hot dogs, as perfectly or imperfectly competitive? You won't be surprised to hear that it depends on the question we want to answer. If we want to explain why there are occasional price wars among hot dog vendors, or why some of them routinely charge higher prices than others, viewing the market as perfectly competitive would be counterproductive—it would hide, rather than reveal, the answer. For these questions, the supply and demand model would not work, so we'd choose a *different* model—one designed for a type of *im*perfectly competitive market. (If your current course is *micro*economics, you will soon learn about these models and how to use them.)

But if we want to know why hot dogs are cheaper than most other types of fast foods, the simplest approach is to view the market for hot dogs as perfectly competitive. True, each hot dog vendor does have *some* influence over the price. But that influence is so small, and the prices of different sellers are so similar, that our assumption of perfect competition works pretty well.

Perfect competition then, is a matter of degree, rather than an all-or-nothing characteristic. While there are very few markets in which sellers and buyers take the price as completely given, there are many markets in which a *narrow range* of prices is treated as a given (as in the market for hot dogs). In these markets, supply and demand often provides a good approximation to what is going on. This is why it has proven to be the most versatile and widely used model in the economist's tool kit. Neither laptop computers nor orange juice is traded in a perfectly competitive market. But ask an economist to tell you why the cost of laptops decreases every year, or why the price of orange juice rises after a freeze in Florida, and he or she will invariably reach for supply and demand to find the answer.

Supply and demand are like two blades of a scissors: To analyze a market, we need both of them. In this and the next section, we will be sharpening those blades, learning separately about supply and demand. Then, we'll put them together and put them to use. Let's start with demand.

DEMAND

It's tempting to think of "demand" as just a psychological phenomenon, a pure "want" or "desire." But that notion can lead us astray. For example, you *want* all kinds of things: a bigger apartment, a better car, nicer clothes, more and better vacations. The list is endless. But you don't always *buy* them. Why not?

Because in addition to your wants—which you'd very much like to satisfy—you also face *constraints*. First, you have to *pay*. And in most cases, you don't have any influence over the price of what you buy—you just have to pay up or do without. You also have limited total funds with which to buy things, so every decision to buy one thing is also a decision *not* to buy something else. As a result, every purchase confronts you with an opportunity cost. (Even if you don't spend all of your income during the year, you still face an opportunity cost: Every purchase is money you are not saving for later, so you sacrifice future spending power.) Your "wants," together with the real-world constraints that you face, determine what you will choose to buy in any market. Hence, the following definition:

> *A **household's quantity demanded** of a good is the specific amount the household would choose to buy over some time period, given (1) a particular price that must be paid for the good; (2) all other constraints on the household.*

Household's quantity demanded The specific amount a household would choose to buy over some time period, given (1) a particular price, (2) all other constraints on the household.

When we add up the buying behavior of all households in a market, we get a similar definition:

Market quantity demanded The specific amount of a good that *all* buyers in the market would choose to buy over some time period, given (1) a particular price, (2) all other constraints they face.

> *Market quantity demanded* (often just *quantity demanded*) *is the specific amount of a good that* all *buyers in the market would choose to buy over some time period, given (1) a particular price they must pay for the good; (2) all other constraints on households.*

Since this definition plays a key role in any supply and demand analysis, it's worth discussing briefly exactly what it means and doesn't mean.

Quantity Demanded Implies a *Choice*. Quantity demanded doesn't tell us the amount of a good that households feel they "need" or "desire" in order to be happy. Instead, it tells us how much households would like to buy *when they take into account the opportunity cost* of their decisions. The opportunity cost arises from the constraints households face, such as having to pay a given price for the good, limits on spendable funds, and so on.

Quantity Demanded Is *Hypothetical*. Will households actually be *able* to purchase the amount they want to purchase? Maybe yes, maybe no. There are special situations—analyzed in microeconomics—in which households are frustrated in buying all that they would choose to buy. But quantity demanded makes no assumptions about the availability of the good. Instead, it's the answer to a hypothetical question: How much would households *want* to buy, at a specific price, given real-world limits on their spending power?

Quantity Demanded Depends on *Price*. The price of the good is just one variable among many that influences quantity demanded. But because one of our main purposes in building a supply and demand model is to explain how prices are determined, we try to keep that variable front-and-center in our thinking. This is why for the next few pages we'll assume that all other influences on demand are held constant, so we can explore the relationship between price and quantity demanded.

The Law of Demand

How does a change in price affect quantity demanded? You probably know the answer to this already: When something is more expensive, people tend to buy less of it. This common observation applies to air travel, magazines, education, guitars, and virtually everything else that people buy. For all of these goods and services, price and quantity are *negatively related*: that is, when price rises, quantity demanded falls; when price falls, quantity demanded rises. This negative relationship is observed so regularly in markets that economists call it the *law of demand*.

Law of demand As the price of a good increases, the quantity demanded decreases.

> *The law of demand states that when the price of a good rises and everything else remains the same, the quantity of the good demanded will fall.*

Read that definition again, and notice the very important words, "everything else remains the same." The law of demand tells us what would happen *if* all the other influences on buyers' choices remained unchanged, and only one influence—the price of the good—changed.

This is an example of a common practice in economics. In the real world, many variables change *simultaneously*. But to understand changes in the economy, we must first understand the effect of each variable *separately*. So we conduct a series of mental experiments in which we ask: "What would happen if this one variable—and only this variable—were to change?" The law of demand is the result of one such mental experiment, in which we imagine that the price of the good changes, but all other influences on quantity demanded remain constant.

The Demand Schedule and the Demand Curve

To make our discussion more concrete, let's look at a specific market: the market for real maple syrup in the United States. In this market, the buyers are all U.S. residents, whereas the sellers (to be considered later) are maple syrup producers in the United States or Canada.

Table 1 shows a hypothetical **demand schedule** for maple syrup in this market. This is *a list of different quantities demanded at different prices, with all other variables that affect the demand decision assumed constant*. For example, the demand schedule tells us that when the price of maple syrup is $2.00 per bottle, the quantity demanded will be 60,000 bottles per month. Notice that the demand schedule obeys the law of demand: As the price of maple syrup increases, the quantity demanded falls.

Now look at Figure 1. It shows a diagram that will appear again and again in your study of economics. In the figure, each price-and-quantity combination in Table 1 is represented by a point. For example, point *A* represents the price $4.00 and quantity 40,000, while point *B* represents the pair $2.00 and 60,000. When we connect all of these points with a line, we obtain the famous *demand curve*, labeled with a *D* in the figure.

> The **market demand curve** (or just **demand curve**) *shows the relationship between the price of a good and the quantity demanded, holding constant all other variables that influence demand. Each point on the curve shows the total quantity that buyers would choose to buy at a specific price.*

Demand schedule A list showing the quantities of a good that consumers would choose to purchase at different prices, with all other variables held constant.

Notice that the demand curve in Figure 1—like virtually all demand curves—*slopes downward*. This is just a graphical representation of the law of demand.

> *The law of demand tells us that demand curves virtually always slope downward.*

Market demand curve The graphical depiction of a demand schedule; a curve showing the quantity of a good or service demanded at various prices, with all other variables held constant.

Shifts vs. Movements Along the Demand Curve

Markets are affected by a variety of events. Some events will cause us to *move along* the demand curve; others will cause the entire demand curve to *shift*. It is crucial to distinguish between these two very different types of effects.

Let's go back to Figure 1. There, you can see that when

Price (per Bottle)	Quantity Demanded (Bottles per Month)
$1.00	75,000
2.00	60,000
3.00	50,000
4.00	40,000
5.00	35,000

TABLE 1
Demand Schedule for Maple Syrup in the United States

FIGURE 1
The Demand Curve

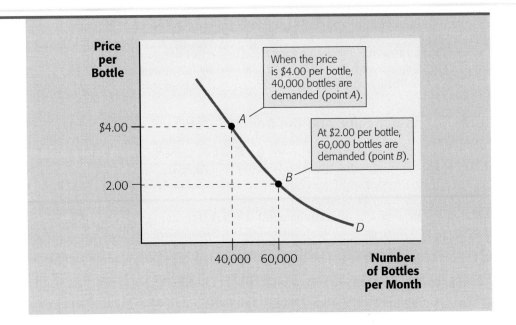

Price per Bottle

When the price is $4.00 per bottle, 40,000 bottles are demanded (point A).

$4.00 ---- A

At $2.00 per bottle, 60,000 bottles are demanded (point B).

2.00 ---- B

D

40,000   60,000

Number of Bottles per Month

the price of maple syrup rises from $2.00 to $4.00 per bottle, the number of bottles demanded falls from 60,000 to 40,000. This is a movement *along* the demand curve, from point A to point B. In general,

> *a change in the price of a good causes a movement* along *the demand curve.*

In Figure 1, a *fall* in price would cause us to move *rightward* along the demand curve (from point A to point B), and a *rise* in price would cause us to move *leftward* along the demand curve (from B to A).

Remember, though, that when we draw a demand curve, we assume all other variables that might influence demand are *held constant* at some particular value. For example, the demand curve in Figure 1 might have been drawn to give us quantity demanded at each price when average household income in the United States remains constant at, say, $40,000 per year.

But suppose average income increases to $50,000? With more income, we'd expect households to buy more of *most* things, including real maple syrup. This is illustrated in Table 2. At the original income level, households would choose to buy 60,000 bottles of maple syrup at $2.00 per bottle. But after income rises, they would choose to buy more at that price—80,000 bottles, according to Table 2. A similar change would occur at any other price for maple syrup: After income rises, households would choose to buy more than before. In other words, the rise in income *changes the entire relationship between price and quantity demanded.* We now have a *new* demand curve.

Figure 2 plots the new demand curve from the quantities in the third column of Table 2. The new demand curve lies to the *right* of the old curve. For example, at a price of $2.00, quantity demanded increases from 60,000 bottles on the old curve (point B) to 80,000 bottles on the *new* demand curve (point C). As you can see, the rise in household income has *shifted* the demand curve to the right.

Price (per Bottle)	Original Quantity Demanded (Bottles per Month)	New Quantity Demanded After Increase in Income (Bottles per Month)
$1.00	75,000	95,000
2.00	60,000	80,000
3.00	50,000	70,000
4.00	40,000	60,000
5.00	35,000	55,000

TABLE 2

Increase in Demand for Maple Syrup in the United States

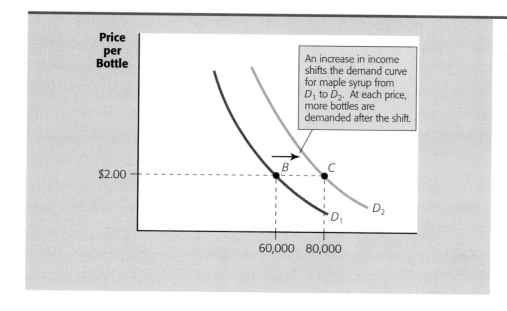

FIGURE 2

A Shift of the Demand Curve

More generally,

a change in any variable that affects demand—except for the good's price—causes the demand curve to shift.

If buyers choose to buy a greater quantity at any price, the demand curve shifts *rightward*. If they decide to buy a smaller quantity at any price, the demand curve shifts *leftward*.

Factors That Shift the Demand Curve

Let's take a closer look at what might cause a change in demand (a shift of the demand curve). Keep in mind that for now, we're exploring *one factor at a time*, always keeping *all other determinants of demand constant*.

Income. In Figure 2, an increase in income shifted the demand for maple syrup to the right. In fact, a rise in income has the same effect on the demand for *most* goods. We call these **normal goods**. Housing, automobiles, health club memberships, and

Income The amount that a person or firm earns over a particular period.

Normal good A good that people demand more of as their income rises.

DANGEROUS CURVES

"Change in Quantity Demanded" vs. "Change in Demand." Language is important when discussing demand. The term *quantity demanded* means a *particular amount* that buyers would choose to buy at a specific price. It's a number represented by a single point on a demand curve. *Demand*, by contrast, means the *entire relationship* between price and quantity demanded, and is represented by the entire demand curve.

For this reason, when a change in the price of a good moves us *along* a demand curve, we call it a **change in quantity demanded**. For example, in Figure 1, the movement from point *A* to point *B* is an *increase* in quantity demanded. This is a change from one number (40,000 bottles) to another (60,000 bottles).

When something *other* than the price changes, causing the entire demand curve to shift, we call it a **change in demand**. In Figure 2, for example, the shift in the curve would be called an *increase in demand*.

Change in quantity demanded A movement along a demand curve in response to a change in price.

Change in demand A shift of a demand curve in response to a change in some variable other than price.

Inferior good A good that people demand less of as their income rises.

Wealth The total value of everything a person or firm owns, at a point in time, minus the total value of everything owed.

Substitute A good that can be used in place of some other good and that fulfills more or less the same purpose.

real maple syrup are all examples of normal goods.

But not all goods are normal. For some goods—called **inferior goods**—a rise in income would *decrease* demand—shifting the demand curve *leftward*. Regular-grade ground chuck is a good example. It's a cheap source of protein, but not as high in quality as sirloin. With higher income, households could more easily afford better types of meat—ground sirloin or steak, for example. As a result, higher incomes would cause the demand for ground chuck to decrease. For similar reasons, we might expect that Greyhound bus tickets (in contrast to airline tickets) and single-ply paper towels (in contrast to two-ply) are inferior goods.

> *A rise in income will* increase *the demand for a* normal *good, and* decrease *the demand for an* inferior *good.*

Wealth. Your **wealth** at any point in time is the total value of everything you *own* (cash, bank accounts, stocks, bonds, real estate or any other valuable property) minus the total dollar amount you *owe* (home mortgage, credit card debt, auto loan, student loan, and so on). Although income and wealth are different (see the nearby Dangerous Curves box), they have similar effects on demand. Increases in wealth among buyers—because of an increase in the value of their stocks or bonds, for example—gives them more funds with which to purchase goods and services. As you might expect,

> *an increase in wealth will* increase *demand (shift the curve rightward) for a normal good, and* decrease *demand (shift the curve leftward) for an inferior good.*

Prices of Related Goods. A **substitute** is a good that can be used in place of another good and that fulfills more or less the same purpose. For example, many people use real maple syrup to sweeten their pancakes, but they could use a number of other things instead: honey, sugar, jam, or *artificial* maple syrup. Each of these can be considered a substitute for real maple syrup.

When the price of a substitute rises, people will choose to buy *more* of the good itself. For example, when the price of jam rises, some jam users will switch to maple syrup, and the demand for maple syrup will increase. In general,

> *a rise in the price of a substitute increases the demand for a good, shifting the demand curve to the right.*

Of course, if the price of a substitute falls, we have the opposite result: Demand for the original good decreases, shifting its demand curve to the left.

There are countless examples in which a change in a substitute's price affects demand for a good. A rise in the price of postage stamps would increase the demand for electronic mail. A drop in the rental price of videos would decrease the demand for movies at theaters. In each of these cases, we assume that the price of the substitute is the only price that is changing.

A **complement** is the opposite of a substitute: It's used *together with* the good we are interested in. Pancake mix is a complement to maple syrup, since these two goods are used frequently in combination. If the price of pancake mix rises, some consumers will switch to other breakfasts—bacon and eggs, for example—that *don't* include maple syrup. The demand for maple syrup will decrease.

Income vs. Wealth It's easy to confuse *income* with *wealth*, because both are measured in dollars and both are sources of funds that can be spent on goods and services. But they are not the same thing. Your income is how much you earn *over a period of time* (such as, $20 *per hour*, $3,500 *per month*, or $40,000 *per year*). Your wealth, by contrast, is the value of what you *own* minus the value of what you *owe* at a *moment in time*. (Such as, on December 31, 2005, the value of what you own is $12,000, but the value of what you owe is $9,000, so you have $3,000 in wealth.)

To help you see the difference: suppose you get a good job after you graduate, but you have very little in the bank, and you still have large, unpaid student loans. Then you'd have a moderate-to-high *income* (what you earn at your job each period), but your wealth would be negative (since what you would *owe* is greater than what you *own*).

DANGEROUS CURVES

> *A rise in the price of a complement decreases the demand for a good, shifting the demand curve to the left.*

Complement A good that is used *together with* some other good.

For this reason, we'd expect a higher price for automobiles to decrease the demand for gasoline. (To test yourself: How would a lower price for milk affect the demand for breakfast cereal?)

Population. As the population increases in an area, the number of buyers will ordinarily increase as well, and the demand for a good will increase. The growth of the U.S. population over the last 50 years has been an important reason (but not the only reason) for rightward shifts in the demand curves for food, rental apartments, telephones, and many other goods and services.

Expected Price. If buyers expect the price of maple syrup to rise next month, they may choose to purchase more *now* to stock up before the price hike, an increase in demand. If people expect the price to drop, they may postpone buying, hoping to take advantage of the lower price later.

> *In many markets, an expectation that price will rise in the future shifts the current demand curve rightward, while an expectation that price will fall shifts the current demand curve leftward.*

Expected price changes are especially important in the markets for financial assets such as stocks and bonds and in the market for real estate. People want to buy more stocks, bonds, and real estate when they think their prices will rise in the near future. This shifts the demand curves for these items to the right.

Tastes. Suppose we know the number of buyers in the United States, their expectations about the future price of maple syrup, the prices of all related goods, and the average levels of income and wealth. Do we have all the information we need to draw the demand curve for maple syrup? Not really. Because we do not yet know how consumers *feel* about maple syrup. How many of them eat breakfast? Of these, how many eat pancakes or waffles? How often? How many of them *like* maple syrup, and how much do they like it? And what about all of the other goods and services competing for consumers' dollars: How do buyers feel about *them*?

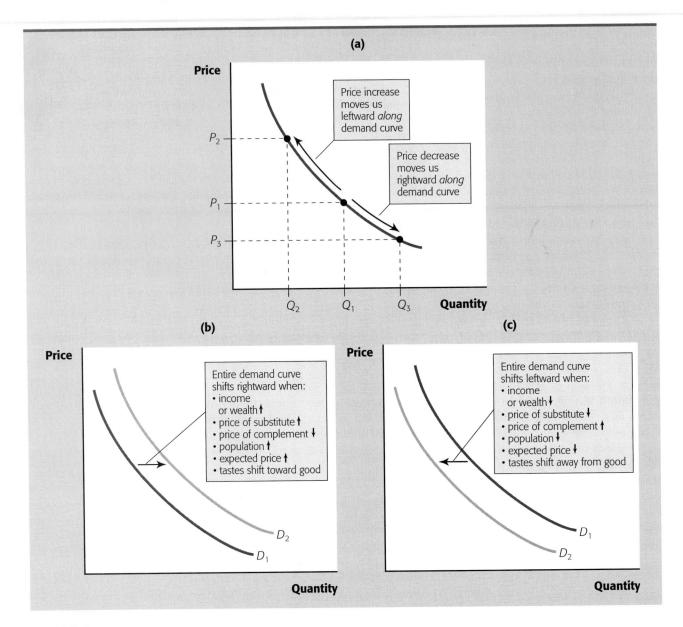

FIGURE 3
Movements Along and
Shifts of the Demand Curve

The questions could go on and on, pinpointing various characteristics about buyers that influence their attitudes toward maple syrup. The approach of economics is to lump all of these characteristics of buyers together and call them, simply, *tastes*. Economists are sometimes interested in where these tastes come from or what makes them change. But for the most part, economics deals with the *consequences* of a change in tastes, whatever the reason for its occurrence.

When tastes change *toward* a good (people favor it more), demand increases, and the demand curve shifts to the right. When tastes change *away* from a good, demand decreases, and the demand curve shifts to the left. An example of this is the change in tastes away from cigarettes over the past several decades. The cause may have been an aging population, a greater concern about health among people of *all* ages, or successful antismoking advertising. But regardless of the cause, the effect has been to decrease the demand for cigarettes, shifting the demand curve to the left.

Figure 3 summarizes the variables we've discussed that affect the demand side of the market, and how their effects are represented with a demand curve. Notice the important distinction between movements *along* the demand curve and *shifts* of the entire curve.

Does Supply Affect Demand? A troubling thought may have occurred to you. Among the variables that shift the demand curve in Figure 3, shouldn't we include the amount of syrup available? Or to put the question another way, doesn't supply influence demand?

No—at least not directly. The demand curve answers a series of hypothetical questions about how much buyers *would like* to buy at each different price. A change in the amount available would not affect the answers, and so can't shift the demand curve. As you'll see later, a change in supply *will* change the *price* of the good, but this causes a movement along—not a shift of—the demand curve.

DANGEROUS CURVES

Keep in mind that other variables, besides those listed in Figure 3, can influence demand. For example, weather can affect the demand for many goods: A rise in temperature can increase the demand for ice cream and decrease the demand for sweaters. Expectations other than the future price can matter too. If buyers expect a recession and fear their incomes may fall, demand may decrease for normal goods *now*, even though current income remains unchanged. Some of these other *shift-variables* for the demand curve will be discussed when they become relevant in a specific application. But we'll always use the same logic we used here: If an event makes buyers want to purchase more or less of a good *at any given price*, it causes the demand curve to shift.

SUPPLY

When most people hear the word *supply*, their first thought is that it's the amount of something "available," as if this amount were fixed in stone. For example, someone might say, "We can only drill so much oil from the ground," or "There are only so many apartments for rent in this town." And yet, the world's known oil reserves—as well as yearly production of oil—have increased dramatically over the last quarter century, as oil companies have found it worth their while to look harder for oil. Similarly, in most towns and cities, short buildings have been replaced with tall ones, and the number of apartments has increased. Supply, like demand, can change, and the amount of a good supplied in a market depends on the *choices* made by those who produce it.

What governs these choices? We assume that business firms' managers have a goal: to earn the highest profit possible. But they also face constraints. First, in a competitive market, the price they can charge for their product is a *given*—the market price. Second, firms have to pay the *costs* of producing and selling their product. These costs will depend on the production process they use, the prices they must pay for their inputs, and more. A firm's desire for profit, together with the real-world constraints that it faces, determines how much it will choose to sell in any market. Hence, the following definition:

> A **firm's quantity supplied** of a good is the specific amount its managers would choose to sell over some time period, given (1) a particular price for the good; (2) all other constraints on the firm.

Firm's quantity supplied The specific amount a firm would choose to sell over some time period, given (1) a particular price for the good; (2) all other constraints on the firm.

When we add up the selling behavior of all firms in a market, we get a similar definition:

Market quantity supplied The specific amount of a good that *all* sellers in the market would choose to sell over some time period, given (1) a particular price for the good; (2) all other constraints on firms.

> *Market quantity supplied (often just **quantity supplied**) is the specific amount of a good that* all *sellers in the market would choose to sell over some time period, given (1) a particular price for the good; (2) all other constraints on firms.*

Let's briefly go over the notion of quantity supplied to clarify what it means and doesn't mean.

Quantity Supplied Implies a *Choice*. We assume that the managers of firms have a simple goal—to earn the highest possible profit. But they also face constraints: the specific price they can charge for the good, the cost of any inputs used, and so on. Quantity supplied doesn't tell us the amount of, say, maple syrup that sellers would like to sell *if* they could charge a thousand dollars for each bottle, and *if* they could produce it at zero cost.

Instead, it's the quantity that gives firms the highest possible profits *when* they take account of the constraints presented to them by the real world. Thus, each firm's quantity supplied reflects a *choice* made by its managers. Adding up those choices for all sellers in the market gives us the market quantity supplied.

Quantity Supplied Is *Hypothetical*. Will firms actually be *able* to sell the amount they want to sell at the going price? At this point, we don't know. But the definition makes no assumptions about firms' *ability* to sell the good. Quantity supplied answers the hypothetical question: How much would firms' managers *want* to sell, given the price of the good and all other constraints they must consider.

Quantity Supplied Depends on *Price*. The price of the good is just one variable among many that influences quantity supplied. But—as with demand—we want to keep that variable foremost in our thinking. This is why for the next few pages we'll assume that all other influences on supply are held constant, so we can explore the relationship between price and quantity supplied.

The Law of Supply

How does a change in price affect quantity supplied? When a seller can get a higher price for a good, producing and selling it become more profitable. Producers will devote more resources toward its production—perhaps even pulling resources out of other types of production—so they can sell more of the good in question. For example, a rise in the price of laptop computers will encourage computer makers to shift resources out of the production of other things (such as desktop computers) and toward the production of laptops.

In general, price and quantity supplied are *positively related:* When the price of a good rises, the quantity supplied will rise as well. This relationship between price and quantity supplied is called the law of supply, the counterpart to the law of demand we discussed earlier.

> *The **law of supply** states that when the price of a good rises, and everything else remains the same, the quantity of the good supplied will rise.*

Law of supply As the price of a good increases, the quantity supplied increases.

Once again, notice the very important words "everything else remains the same." Although many other variables influence the quantity of a good supplied, the law of supply tells us what would happen if all of them remained unchanged and only one—the price of the good—changed.

The Supply Schedule and the Supply Curve

Let's continue with our example of the market for maple syrup in the United States. Who are the suppliers in this market? Maple syrup producers are located mostly in the forests of Vermont, upstate New York, and Canada. The market quantity supplied is the amount of syrup all of these producers together would offer for sale at each price for maple syrup in the United States.

Table 3 shows the **supply schedule** for maple syrup—a *list of different quantities supplied at different prices, with all other variables held constant.* As you can see, the supply schedule obeys the law of supply: As the price of maple syrup rises, the quantity supplied rises along with it. But how can this be? After all, maple trees must be about 40 years old before they can be tapped for syrup, so any rise in quantity supplied now or in the near future cannot come from an increase in planting. What, then, causes quantity supplied to rise as price rises?

Price (per Bottle)	Quantity Supplied (Bottles per Month)
$1.00	25,000
2.00	40,000
3.00	50,000
4.00	60,000
5.00	65,000

TABLE 3

Supply Schedule for Maple Syrup in the United States

Supply schedule A list showing the quantities of a good or service that firms would choose to produce and sell at different prices, with all other variables held constant.

Many things. First, with higher prices, firms will find it profitable to tap existing trees more intensively. Second, evaporating and bottling can be done more carefully, so that less maple syrup is spilled and more is available for shipping. Finally, the product can be diverted from other areas and shipped to the United States instead. For example, if the price of maple syrup rises in the United States but not in Canada, producers would shift deliveries away from Canada so they could sell more in the United States.

Now look at Figure 4, which shows a very important curve—the counterpart to the demand curve we drew earlier. In Figure 4, each point represents a price-quantity pair taken from Table 3. For example, point *F* in the figure corresponds to a price of $2.00 per bottle and a quantity of 40,000 bottles per month, while point *G* represents the price-quantity pair $4.00 and 60,000 bottles. Connecting all of these points with a solid line gives us the *supply curve* for maple syrup, labeled with an *S* in the figure.

> *The **market supply curve** (or just **supply curve**) shows the relationship between the price of a good and the quantity supplied, holding constant the values of all other variables that affect supply. Each point on the curve shows the quantity that sellers would choose to sell at a specific price.*

Supply curve A graphical depiction of a supply schedule; a curve showing the quantity of a good or service supplied at various prices, with all other variables held constant.

FIGURE 4
The Supply Curve

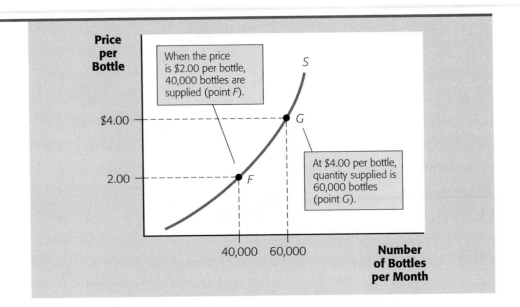

Notice that the supply curve in Figure 4—like all supply curves for goods and services—is *upward sloping*. This is the graphical representation of the law of supply.

> *The law of supply tells us that supply curves slope* upward.

Shifts vs. Movements Along the Supply Curve

As with the demand curve, it's important to distinguish those events that will cause us to *move along* a given supply curve for the good, and those that will cause the entire supply curve to *shift*.

If you look once again at Figure 4, you'll see that if the price of maple syrup rises from $2.00 to $4.00 per bottle, the number of bottles supplied rises from 40,000 to 60,000. This is a movement *along* the supply curve, from point F to point G. In general,

> *a change in the price of a good causes a movement* along *the supply curve.*

In the figure, a *rise* in price would cause us to move *rightward* along the supply curve (from point F to point G) and a *fall* in price would move us *leftward* along the curve (from point G to point F).

But remember that when we draw a supply curve, we assume that all other variables that might influence supply are *held constant* at some particular values. For example, the supply curve in Figure 4 might tell us the quantity supplied at each price when the cost of an important input—transportation from the farm to the point of sale—remains constant.

But suppose the cost of transportation drop. Then, at any given price for maple syrup, firms would find it more profitable to produce and sell it. This is illustrated in Table 4. With the original transportation cost, and a selling price of $4.00 per bottle, firms would choose to sell 60,000 bottles. But after transportation cost falls, they would choose to produce and sell more—80,000 bottles in our example—assuming they could still charge $4.00 per bottle. A similar change would occur for any other

Price (per Bottle)	Original Quantity Supplied (Bottles/Month)	Quantity Supplied After Decrease in Transportation Cost	TABLE 4
$1.00	25,000	45,000	**Increase in Supply of Maple Syrup in the United States**
2.00	40,000	60,000	
3.00	50,000	70,000	
4.00	60,000	80,000	
5.00	65,000	90,000	

price of maple syrup we might imagine: After transportation costs fall, firms would choose to sell more than before. In other words, *the entire relationship between price and quantity supplied has changed*, so we have a *new* supply curve.

Figure 5 plots the new supply curve from the quantities in the third column of Table 4. The new supply curve lies to the *right* of the old one. For example, at a price of $4.00, quantity supplied increases from 60,000 bottles on the old curve (point *G*) to 80,000 bottles on the *new* supply curve (point *J*). The drop in the transportation costs has *shifted* the supply curve to the right.

In general,

> *a change in any variable that affects supply—except for the good's price—causes the supply curve to shift.*

If sellers want to sell a greater quantity at any price, the supply curve shifts *rightward*. If sellers would prefer to sell a smaller quantity at any price, the supply curve shifts *leftward*.

"Change in Quantity Supplied" vs. "Change in Supply" As we stressed in our discussion of the demand side of the market, be careful about language when thinking about supply. The term *quantity supplied* means a *particular amount* that sellers would prefer to sell at a particular price. It's a number, represented by a single point on the supply curve. The term *supply*, however, means the *entire relationship* between price and quantity supplied, as represented by the entire supply curve.

For this reason, when the price of the good changes, and we move *along* the supply curve, we have a **change in quantity supplied.** For example, in Figure 4, the movement from point *F* to point *G* is an *increase* in quantity supplied.

When something *other* than the price changes, causing the entire supply curve to shift, we call it a **change in supply.** The shift in Figure 5, for example, would be called an *increase in supply.*

DANGEROUS CURVES

Change in quantity supplied A movement along a supply curve in response to a change in price.

Change in supply A shift of a supply curve in response to some variable other than price.

Factors That Shift the Supply Curve

Let's take a closer look at some of the *causes* of a change in supply (a shift of the supply curve). As always, we're considering *one* variable at a time, keeping all other determinants of supply constant.

Input Prices. In Figure 5, a drop in transportation costs shifted the supply curve for maple syrup to the right. But producers of maple syrup use a variety of other inputs, too: land, maple trees, evaporators, sap pans, labor, glass bottles, bottling machinery, and more. A lower price for any of these means a lower cost of producing and selling maple syrup, making it more profitable. As a result, we would expect producers to shift resources into maple syrup production, causing an increase in supply.

FIGURE 5
A Shift of the Supply Curve

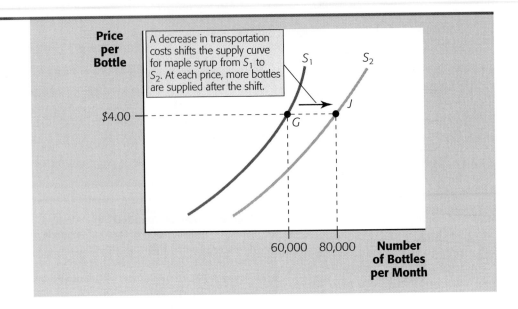

In general,

a fall in the price of an input causes an increase in supply, shifting the supply curve to the right. A rise in the price of an input causes a decrease in supply, shifting the supply curve to the left.

If, for example, the wages of maple syrup workers rose, the supply curve in Figure 5 would shift to the left.

Price of Related Goods. Many firms can switch their production rather easily among several different goods or services, all of which require more or less the same inputs. For example, a dermatology practice can rather easily switch its specialty from acne treatments for the young to wrinkle treatments for the elderly. An automobile producer can—without too much adjustment—switch to producing light trucks. And a maple syrup producer could dry its maple syrup and produce maple *sugar* instead. Or it could even cut down its maple trees and sell maple wood as lumber. Other goods that firms *could* produce are called **alternate goods.**

Alternate goods Other goods that a firm could produce, using some of the same types of inputs as the good in question.

For example, if the price of maple *sugar* rose, then at any given price for maple *syrup*, producers would choose to shift some production from syrup to sugar. This would be a decrease in the supply of maple syrup. Alternatively, if firms already are producing maple sugar, and its price *falls*, the supply of syrup would increase. Remember that we are assuming—as always—that every *other* determinant that affects the supply of maple syrup remains unchanged.

When the price of an alternate good rises, the supply curve for the good in question shifts leftward. When the price of an alternate falls, the supply curve for the good in question shifts rightward.

Technology. A *technological advance* in production occurs whenever a firm can produce a given level of output in a new and cheaper way than before. For example, the discovery of a surgical procedure called Lasik—in which a laser is used to reshape the interior of the cornea rather than the outer surface—has enabled eye surgeons to correct their patients' vision with fewer follow-up visits and smaller quantities of medication than were used with previous procedures. This example is a technological advance because it enables firms to produce the same output (eye surgery) more cheaply than before.

Does Demand Affect Supply? In the list of variables that shift the supply curve in Figure 6 we've left out the amount that buyers would like to buy. Is this a mistake? Doesn't demand affect supply?

The answer is no—at least, not directly. The supply curve tells us how much sellers *would* choose to sell at alternative prices. Buyers' decisions don't affect this hypothetical quantity, so they cannot shift the supply curve. But—as you'll soon see—buyers *can* affect the price of the good, which in turn affects quantity supplied. But this is a movement *along* the supply curve—not a shift.

DANGEROUS CURVES

In maple syrup production, a technological advance might be a new, more efficient tap that draws more maple syrup from each tree, or a new bottling method that reduces spillage. Advances like these would reduce the cost of producing maple syrup, making it more profitable, and producers would want to make and sell more of it at any price.

In general,

> *cost-saving technological advances increase the supply of a good, shifting the supply curve to the right.*

Number of Firms. A change in the number of firms in a market will change the quantity that all sellers together would want to sell at any given price. For example, if—over time—more people decided to open up maple syrup farms because it was a profitable business, the supply of maple syrup would increase. And if maple syrup farms began closing down, their number would be reduced and supply would decrease.

> *An increase in the number of sellers—with no other change—shifts the supply curve rightward, while a decrease in the number of sellers shifts it leftward.*

Expected Price. Imagine you're the president of Sticky's Maple Syrup, Inc., and you've determined that the market price of maple syrup—over which you, as an individual seller, have no influence—will rise next month. What would you do? You'd certainly want to postpone selling your maple syrup until the price is higher, and profit greater. Therefore, at any given price *now*, you might slow down production, or just slow down sales by warehousing more of what you produce. If other firms have similar expectations of a price hike, they'll do the same. Thus, an expectation of a *future* price hike will decrease supply *in the present.*

Suppose instead you expect the market price to *drop* next month. Then—at any given price—you'd want to sell more *now*, by stepping up production and even selling out of your inventories. Now, an expected future drop in the price would cause an increase in supply in the present. In terms of our supply curve:

> *In many markets, an expectation of a* future price hike *shifts the current supply curve* leftward. *Similarly, an expectation of a* future price drop *shifts the current supply curve* rightward.

Changes in Weather and Other Natural Events. Weather conditions are an especially important determinant of the supply of agricultural goods.

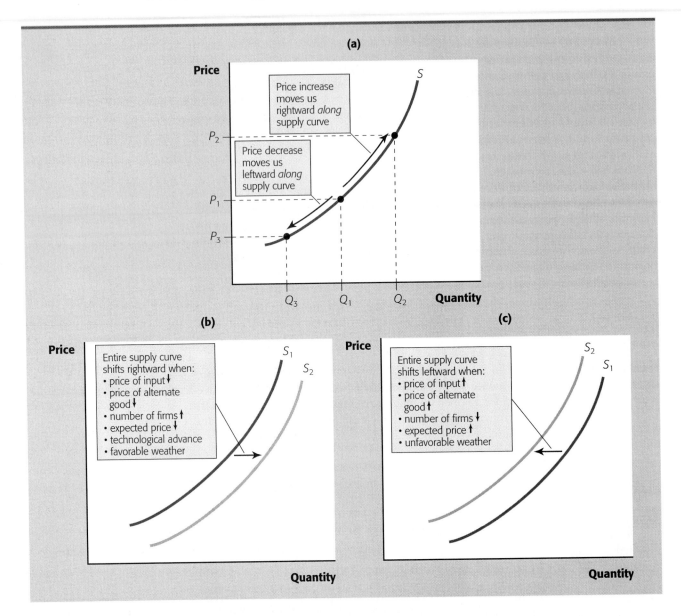

FIGURE 6
Changes in Supply and in Quantity Supplied

Favorable weather *increases crop yields, and causes a* rightward *shift of the supply curve for that crop.* Unfavorable weather *destroys crops and shrinks yields, and shifts the supply curve* leftward.

In addition to bad weather, natural disasters such as fires, hurricanes, and earthquakes can destroy or disrupt the productive capacity of *all* firms in a region. If many sellers of a particular good are located in the affected area, the supply curve for that good will shift leftward. For example, a sudden blight that destroyed many maple trees in Vermont would cause the supply curve to shift leftward in the market we've been analyzing.

Figure 6 summarizes the various factors we've discussed that affect the supply side of the market, and how we illustrate them using a supply curve. But the short list of *shift-variables* for supply is far from exhaustive. For example, a government tax on a good—or a government subsidy paid to producers—will shift the supply curve. So can other government policies, such as environmental and safety regulations. And man-made disasters, such as wars, riots, terrorist attacks, or epidemics, can have the same effects as natural disasters.

Even the *threat* of such events can seriously affect production. In mid-2003, in countries around the world, supply curves for children's toys shifted leftward. The reason? In China—where most of the world's toys are produced—tens of thousands of workers stayed away from their jobs for weeks, fearful of catching SARS (Severe Acute Respiratory Syndrome).

Some of the other shift-variables that shift supply curves will be discussed as they become relevant in future chapters. The basic principle, however, is always the same: Anything that makes sellers want to sell more or less *at any given price* will shift the supply curve.

PUTTING SUPPLY AND DEMAND TOGETHER

HTTP://

Try your hand at a Java-based supply and demand simulation. You can find it at **http:// openteach.com/economics/ microeconomics.html**.

What happens when buyers and sellers, each having the desire and the ability to trade, come together in a market? The two sides of the market certainly have different agendas. Buyers would like to pay the lowest possible price, while sellers would like to charge the highest possible price. Is there chaos when they meet, with buyers and sellers endlessly chasing after each other or endlessly bargaining for advantage, so that trade never takes place? A casual look at the real world suggests not. In most markets, most of the time, there is order and stability in the encounters between buyers and sellers. In most cases, prices do not fluctuate wildly from moment to moment, but seem to hover around a stable value. Even when this stability is short-lived—lasting only a day, an hour, or even a minute in some markets—for this short-time the market seems to be at rest. Whenever we study a market, therefore, we look for this state of rest—a price and quantity at which the market will settle, at least for a while.

Economists use the word *equilibrium* when referring to a state of rest. When a market is in equilibrium, both the price of the good and the quantity bought and sold have settled into a state of rest. More formally,

the **equilibrium price** *and* **equilibrium quantity** *are values for price and quantity in the market that, once achieved, will remain constant—unless and until the supply curve or the demand curve shifts.*

Equilibrium price The market price that, once achieved, remains constant until either the demand curve or supply curve shifts.

Equilibrium quantity The market quantity bought and sold per period that, once achieved, remains constant until either the demand curve or supply curve shifts.

What will be the price of maple syrup in the United States? And how much will people actually buy each month? We can rephrase these questions as follows: What is the *equilibrium* price of maple syrup, and what is the *equilibrium* quantity of maple syrup that will be bought and sold? These are precisely the questions that the supply and demand model is designed to answer.

Look at Figure 7, which combines the supply and demand curves for maple syrup. We'll use Figure 7 to find the equilibrium price in this market through the process of elimination.

Let's first ask what would happen if the price was $1.00 per bottle. At this price, buyers would want to buy 75,000 bottles each month, while sellers would offer to sell only 25,000. There would be an **excess demand** of 50,000 bottles. What would happen? Buyers would compete with each other to get more maple syrup than was

Excess demand At a given price, the excess of quantity demanded over quantity supplied.

FIGURE 7
Market Equilibrium

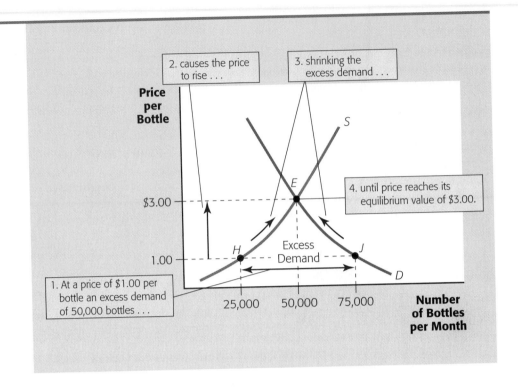

2. causes the price to rise . . .

3. shrinking the excess demand . . .

4. until price reaches its equilibrium value of $3.00.

1. At a price of $1.00 per bottle an excess demand of 50,000 bottles . . .

Price per Bottle

$3.00

1.00

E

S

H

Excess Demand

J

D

25,000   50,000   75,000

Number of Bottles per Month

available, and would offer to pay a higher price rather than do without. The price would then rise.

We conclude that a price of $1.00—or *any* price we might imagine that is less than $3.00—cannot be an equilibrium price. Why not? As we've just seen, if the price starts below $3.00, it would start rising—*not* because the supply curve or the demand curve had shifted, but from natural forces within the market itself. This directly contradicts our definition of equilibrium price.

At this point, we should ask another question: If the price were initially $1.00, would it ever *stop* rising? Yes. Since excess demand is the reason for the price to rise, the process will stop when the excess demand is gone. And as you can see in Figure 8, the rise in price *shrinks* the excess demand in two ways. First, as price rises, buyers demand a smaller quantity—a leftward movement along the demand curve. Second, sellers increase supply to a larger quantity—a rightward movement along the supply curve. Finally, when the price reaches $3.00 per bottle, the excess demand is gone and the price stops rising.

This logic tells us that $3.00 is an *equilibrium* price in this market—a value that won't change as long as the supply and demand curves stay put. But is it the *only* equilibrium price? We've shown that any price *below* $3.00 is not an equilibrium, but what about a price *greater* than $3.00? Let's see.

Suppose the price of maple syrup was, say, $5.00 per bottle. Figure 8 shows us that, at this price, quantity supplied would be 65,000 bottles per month, while quantity demanded would be only 35,000 bottles—an **excess supply** of 30,000 bottles. Sellers would compete with each other to sell more maple syrup than buyers wanted to buy, and the price would fall. Thus, $5.00 cannot be the equilibrium price.

Moreover, the decrease in price would move us along both the supply curve (leftward) and the demand curve (rightward). As these movements continued, the

Excess supply At a given price, the excess of quantity supplied over quantity demanded.

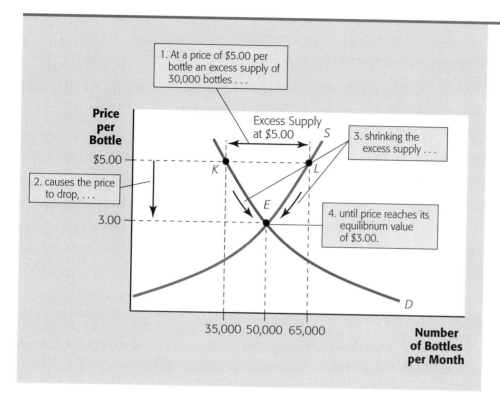

FIGURE 8
Excess Supply and Price Adjustment

The figure contains the following labels:

1. At a price of $5.00 per bottle an excess supply of 30,000 bottles . . .

2. causes the price to drop, . . .

3. shrinking the excess supply . . .

4. until price reaches its equilibrium value of $3.00.

Excess Supply at $5.00

Price per Bottle

$5.00

3.00

Number of Bottles per Month

35,000 50,000 65,000

excess supply of maple syrup would shrink until it disappeared, once again, at a price of $3.00 per bottle. Our conclusion: If the price happens to be above $3.00, it will fall to $3.00 and then stop changing.

You can see that is the equilibrium price—and the *only* equilibrium price—in this market. Moreover, at this price, sellers would want to sell 50,000 bottles—the same quantity that households would want to buy. So, when price comes to rest at $3.00, quantity comes to rest at 50,000 per month—the *equilibrium quantity*.

No doubt, you have noticed that $3.00 happens to be the price at which the supply and demand curves cross. This leads us to an easy, graphical technique for locating our equilibrium:

> To *find the equilibrium price and quantity in a competitive market, draw the supply and demand curves. The equilibrium price and equilibrium quantity can then be found on the vertical and horizontal axes, respectively, at the point where the supply and demand curves cross.*

This graphical insight helps make the logic of equilibrium even more apparent. In equilibrium, the market is operating on *both* the supply curve *and* the demand curve. Therefore, at the going price, quantity demanded and quantity supplied are equal. There are no dissatisfied buyers unable to find goods they want to purchase, nor are there any frustrated sellers unable to sell goods they want to sell. Indeed, this is why $3.00 is the equilibrium price. It's the only price that creates consistency between what buyers choose to buy and sellers choose to sell.

But we don't expect a market to stay at any particular equilibrium forever, as you're about to see.

WHAT HAPPENS WHEN THINGS CHANGE?

Remember that in order to draw the supply and demand curves in the first place, we had to assume particular values for all the other variables—besides price—that affect demand and supply. If one of these variables changes, then either the supply curve or the demand curve will shift, and our equilibrium will change as well. Let's look at some examples.

Income Rises, Causing an Increase in Demand

In Figure 9, point E shows an initial equilibrium in the U.S. market for maple syrup, with an equilibrium price of $3.00 per bottle, and equilibrium quantity of 50,000 bottles per month. Suppose that the incomes of buyers rise because the U.S. economy recovers rapidly from a recession. We know that income is one of the shift-variables in the demand curve (but not the supply curve). We also can reason that maple syrup is a *normal good*, so the rise in income will cause the demand curve to shift rightward. What happens then?

The old price—$3.00—is no longer the equilibrium price. How do we know? Because if the price *did* remain at $3.00, quantity demanded would exceed quantity supplied—an excess demand that would drive the price upward. The new equilibrium—at point E'—is the new intersection point of the curves *after* the shift in the demand curve. Comparing the original equilibrium at point E with the new one at point E', we find that the shift in demand has caused the equilibrium price to rise (from $3.00 to $4.00) and the equilibrium quantity to rise as well (from 50,000 to 60,000 bottles per month).

Notice, too, that in moving from point E to point E', we move *along* the supply curve. That is, a shift of the demand curve has caused a movement along he supply curve. Why is this? The demand shift causes the *price* to rise, and a rise in price always causes a movement *along* the supply curve. But the supply curve itself does not shift, because none of the variables that affect sellers—other than the price of the good—has changed.

In this example, the equilibrium price and quantity changed because income rose. But *any* event that shifted the demand curve rightward would cause both equilibrium price and quantity to rise. For example, if tastes changed in favor of maple syrup, or a substitute good like jam rose in price, or a complementary good like pancake mix became cheaper, the demand curve for

The Endless Loop of Erroneous Logic At some point, you might find yourself caught in an endless loop of erroneous logic about supply and demand. In our example in which income rises and demand increases, you might reason as follows: "The rise in income causes an increase in demand, which causes the price to rise. But a higher price increases supply. Higher supply, in turn, causes the price to fall. But then, when the price falls, demand will increase . . ." and so on. In this logic, the price bobs up and down and never stops moving.

What's the mistake here? The first sentence is indeed correct. But the second sentence—and all that follows from it—is wrong. The second sentence states that "a higher price increases supply," when it *should* say that a higher price increases *quantity supplied.*

This is more than just semantics. An "increase in supply" would be a rightward *shift* of the supply curve, which is what is implied in the incorrect statement. But look again at Figure 9. There is no supply shift, because none of the shift-variables for the supply curve have changed. Only *price* has changed, and that causes a movement *along* the supply curve. So a correct second sentence would be, "And the higher price increases quantity supplied until the new equilibrium is reached, at which point the price stops rising." End of story.

You can avoid this mistake by remembering that *a shift of one curve causes a movement along the other curve to the new equilibrium point.*

maple syrup would shift rightward, just as it did in Figure 9. So, we can summarize our findings as follows:

FIGURE 9

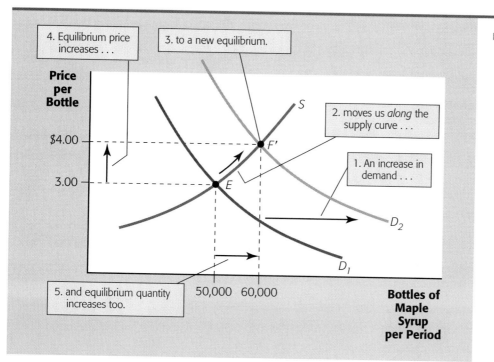

4. Equilibrium price increases . . .

3. to a new equilibrium.

Price per Bottle

2. moves us *along* the supply curve . . .

$4.00

F'

1. An increase in demand . . .

3.00

E

S

D₂

D₁

5. and equilibrium quantity increases too.

50,000   60,000

Bottles of Maple Syrup per Period

A rightward shift in the demand curve causes a rightward movement along the supply curve. Equilibrium price and equilibrium quantity both rise.

An Ice Storm Causes a Decrease in Supply

In January 1998, New England and Quebec were struck by a severe ice storm. Hundreds of thousands of maple trees were downed, and many more were damaged. In Vermont alone, 10 percent of the maple trees were destroyed. How did this affect the market for maple syrup?

As you've learned, weather is a shift-variable for the supply curve.

Figure 10 shows how the ice storm affected this market. Initially, the supply curve for maple syrup was S_1, with the market in equilibrium at Point E. After the ice storm, the supply curve shifted leftward— say, to S_2. The result: a rise in the equilibrium price of maple syrup (from $3.00 to $5.00 in the figure)

Do Curves Shift Up and Down? Or Right and Left? When describing an increase in demand or supply, it's tempting to substitute "upward" for "rightward," and to substitute "downward" for "leftward" when describing a decrease in demand or supply. But be careful! While this interchangeable language works for the demand curve, it does *not* work for the supply curve. To prove this to yourself, look at Figure 6. There you can see that a rightward shift of the supply curve (an increase in supply) is also a *downward* shift of the curve. In later chapters, it will sometimes make sense to describe shifts as upward or downward. For now, it's best to avoid these terms and stick with *rightward* and *leftward*.

DANGEROUS CURVES

and a fall in the equilibrium quantity (from 50,000 to 35,000 bottles).

In this case, it was an ice storm that shifted the supply curve leftward. But suppose, instead, that the wages of maple syrup workers had increased or that evaporators became more expensive or that some maple syrup producers went out of business and sold their farms to housing developers. Any of these changes would have

FIGURE 10
A Shift of Supply and a New Equilibrium

An ice storm causes supply to decrease from S₁ to S₂. At the old equilibrium price of $3.00, there is now an excess demand. As a result, the price increases until excess demand is eliminated at point E'. In the new equilibrium, quantity demanded again equals quantity supplied. The price is higher, and fewer bottles are produced and sold.

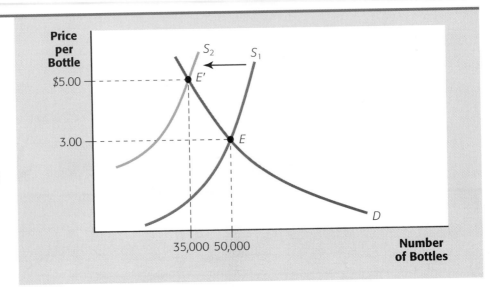

caused the supply curve for maple syrup to shift leftward, increased the equilibrium price, and decreased the equilibrium quantity.

More generally,

> *any change that shifts the supply curve leftward in a market will increase the equilibrium price and decrease the equilibrium quantity in that market.*

Handheld PCs in 2003: Both Curves Shift

Since shifts in supply and demand work the same way in any market, let's leave maple syrup for now and look at a different market: that for handheld computers like the Palm, HP Ipaq, and Sony Clie. In early 2003, prices for these devices dropped. For example, the price of both Palm's high-end Tungsten T model and Sony's new Clie NX60V dropped from $500 to $400. At the same time, the number of handheld PCs sold dropped—from 3.33 million (in the last quarter of 2002) to 2.45 million (first quarter of 2003). What explains these movements in price and quantity?

To answer this question, we'll use the supply and demand model. In doing so, we're assuming this is a perfectly competitive market, in which each producer sells a standardized product and treats the market price as a given. This is not too far off: Product differences among manufacturers are rather modest, and to stay in business, each producer must charge a price within a rather narrow *range*. Our assumption of perfect competition is, as in most cases, a useful approximation.

Figure 11 shows the market supply and demand curves for handheld PCs in late 2002, labeled S_{2002} and D_{2002}, respectively. Point E shows the equilibrium at that time, with an average price of $500 and a quantity of 3.33 million PCs per quarter.

Now, what happened in this market between late 2002 and mid-2003? Let's start with demand, where three factors combined to shift the demand curve leftward.

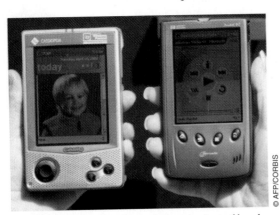

In 2001, a decrease in demand caused prices of handheld PCs to fall

© AFP/CORBIS

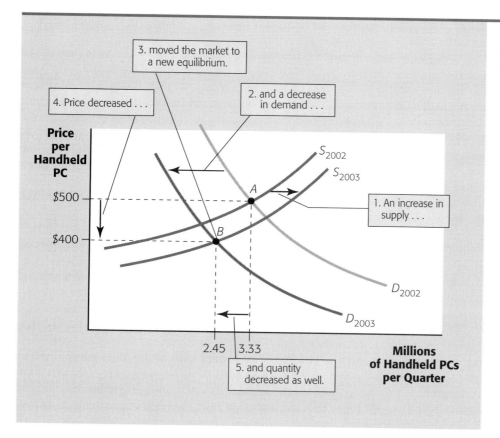

FIGURE 11

Changes in the Market for Handheld PCs

First, by early 2003, handheld PCs had already been on the market for a few years. Most of those who regarded them as useful had already bought one. Since these first-time buyers had been behind the high demand in earlier periods, their withdrawal from the market amounted to a decrease in demand. (*The shift-variable: a change in market preferences for new handhelds.*)

Second, uncertainties caused by continued slow growth in the U.S. and European economies, and a looming U.S. war with Iraq, caused consumers to worry about their future income. These kinds of worries especially decrease the demand for goods that are relatively expensive and not considered necessities, such as handheld PCs. (*Shift-variable: a change in expectations*, in this case, about future income.)

Finally, in early 2003, cell phones that incorporated some of the key features of handheld PCs were becoming cheaper. Many of those who *would* have bought a handheld PC decided to purchase a cell phone with limited PC-capabilities instead. (*Shift-variable: a decrease in the price of a substitute good.*)

Any one of these three factors, by itself, would have caused a leftward shift in the demand curve for handhelds. When they all occurred together, the result was an even *larger* shift to the left. This is illustrated in Figure 11 by the shift from D_{2002} to D_{2003}.

What about supply? Throughout the early 2000s, new firms—at least, new to handheld PCs—entered the market. And entry continued through 2003, as Dell, Gateway, and Matsushita brought their first handhelds to the market. The entry of new firms increased the number of handhelds that would be offered for sale at any price, shifting the supply curve rightward (from S_{2002} to S_{2003} in the figure). (*Shift-variable: an increase in the number of firms.*)

As you can see in Figure 11, the result of all these events was a change in the market equilibrium—from point A to point B. In our diagram, the equilibrium price has fallen—from $500 to $400. This should not surprise you: *Either* a leftward shift in the demand curve *or* a rightward shift of the supply curve, by itself, would cause the price to drop. When these two shifts occur together, price drops even more.

But what about equilibrium quantity? Here, the two shifts work in *opposite* directions. The leftward shift in demand works to decrease equilibrium quantity, while the rightward shift in supply tends to increase equilibrium quantity. Figure 11 illustrates what *actually* happened: a decrease in quantity from 3.33 million to 2.45 million units sold. So we know that, over this period, the demand shift was *greater* than the supply shift.

To prove this to yourself, draw a graph that shows a leftward demand shift that is *smaller* than a rightward supply shift. What happens to equilibrium quantity in your diagram? Then draw a graph that shows equilibrium quantity remaining unchanged. If you draw these cases, you'll see that while the price *must* fall when the curves shift in the directions shown in Figure 11, the quantity could either rise, fall, or remain the same; it's *ambiguous*, unless we know the relative *sizes* of the shifts.

This example involves just *one* possible combination of directions that the two curves could shift. But remember that a leftward or rightward shift of one curve can occur together with either a leftward or rightward shift of the other curve. Table 5 lists all the possible combinations. It also shows what happens to equilibrium price and quantity in each case, and when the result is ambiguous (a question mark). For example, the top left entry tells us that when both the supply and demand curves shift rightward, the equilibrium *quantity* will always rise, but the equilibrium price could rise, fall or remain unchanged, depending on the relative *size* of the shifts.

The most general conclusion we can draw from this table is the following:

> *When just one curve shifts, and we know the direction of the shift, we can determine the direction that both equilibrium price and quantity will move.*

> *When both curves shift, and we know the directions of the shifts, we can determine the direction for either price or quantity—but not both. The direction of the other will depend on which curve shifts by more.*

Do *not* try to memorize the entries in Table 5. Instead, remember the advice in Chapter 1: to study economics actively, rather than passively. This would be a good time to put down the book, pick up a pencil and paper, and see whether you can draw a graph to illustrate each of the nine possible results in the table. When you see a question mark (?) for an ambiguous result, determine which shift would have to be greater for the variable to rise or to fall.

THE THREE-STEP PROCESS

In this chapter, we built a model—a supply and demand model—and then used it to analyze price changes in several markets. You may not have noticed it, but we took three distinct key steps as the chapter proceeded. Economists take these same three steps to answer almost *any* question about the economy. Why? Because they are so

	Increase in Demand (Rightward Shift)	No Change in Demand	Decrease in Demand (Leftward Shift)
• **Increase in Supply** (Rightward Shift)	$P? \, Q\uparrow$	$P\downarrow \, Q\uparrow$	$P\downarrow \, Q?$
• **No Change in Supply**	$P\uparrow \, Q\uparrow$	No change in P or Q	$P\downarrow \, Q\downarrow$
• **Decrease in Supply** (Leftward Shift)	$P\uparrow \, Q?$	$P\uparrow \, Q\downarrow$	$P? \, Q\downarrow$

TABLE 5

Effect of Supply and Demand Shifts on Equilibrium Price (P) and Quantity (Q)

effective in cutting through the chaos and confusion of the economy and helping us see how things really work.

In this book, we'll focus on this *three-step process,* which forms the core of economists' unique methodology. And we'll start right now by listing and discussing all three steps.

Key Step 1—Characterize the Market: *Decide which market or markets best suit the problem being analyzed, and identify the decision makers (buyers and sellers) who interact there.*

In economics, we make sense of the very complex, real-world economy by viewing it as a collection of *markets.* Each of these markets involves a group of *decision makers*—buyers and sellers—who have the potential to trade with each other. At the very beginning of any economic analysis, we must decide which market or markets to look at and how these markets should be *defined.*

To define a market, we decide how to view (a) the thing being traded (such as maple syrup); (b) the decision makers in the market (such as maple syrup producers in New England and Canada selling to U.S. households); and (c) the trading environment (such as our decision in this chapter to view the markets for maple syrup and handheld PCs as perfectly competitive).

Often, especially in microeconomics, we may want to define the specific *goals* and *constraints* of those who trade in the market. In the supply and demand model, for example, we assume that the goal of sellers is to earn the highest possible profit, but they are constrained by the market price they can charge, and the costs of production they must pay. Buyers are assumed to maximize their utility—their well-being or satisfaction. But they too are constrained by the market price they must pay, and by the limited funds at their disposal.

In addition to having goals, decision makers also face constraints. Firms are constrained by their production technology, the prices they must pay for their inputs, and the price they can get for their output. Households are constrained by the prices they must pay for their purchases and by their limited incomes. Government agencies are constrained by the prices of the things they buy and by limited budgets. And even entire nations, as a whole, are constrained in their choices by the resources at their disposal.

Key Step 2—Find the Equilibrium: *Describe the conditions necessary for equilibrium in the market, and a method for determining that equilibrium.*

Once we've defined a market, and put buyers and sellers together, we look for the point at which the market will come to rest—the equilibrium. In this chapter, we used supply and demand to find the equilibrium price and quantity in a perfectly competitive market, but this is just one example of how economists apply Step 2.

Key Step 3—What Happens When Things Change: Explore how events or government policies change the market equilibrium.

Once you've found the equilibrium, the next step is to ask how different events will *change* it. In this chapter, for example, we explored how an ice storm affected the equilibrium price and quantity for maple syrup, and how several events altered the equilibrium price and quantity for handheld PCs.

Do economists really follow this same procedure to analyze almost *any* economic problem? Indeed they do. They use it to answer important *microeconomic* questions. Why does government intervention to lower the price of a good (such as apartment rents) often backfire and sometimes harm the very people it was designed to help? Why do some people earn salaries that are hundreds of times higher than others? How will resources be reallocated to enable the United States to fight the war on terrorism that it declared in September 2001? If you're studying *micro*economics, you'll soon see how the three-step process helps us answer all of those questions.

Economists also use the procedure to address important *macroeconomic* questions. What caused the recession that began in early 2001, and what can we do to prevent recessions in the future? Why has the United States experienced such low inflation in recent years, and how long can we expect our recent good fortune to continue? How will concern about domestic security affect our standard of living over the next year? . . . over the next decade?

In *macro*economics, the three steps help us answer once again.

In this book, we'll be taking these three key steps again and again, every time we want to understand an aspect of the economy. From now on, you'll recognize these steps, because we'll be calling them to your attention as we use them.

To help you keep track you'll sometimes see an icon in the margins of this book when one or more of the steps is being used. If you pay attention to them, you will soon find yourself thinking like an economist.

USING THE THEORY
College Administrators Make a Costly Mistake

In the late 1980s, several East Coast colleges purchased expensive equipment that would enable them to switch rapidly from oil to natural gas as a source of heat. The idea was to protect the colleges from a sudden rise in oil prices, like the one they had suffered a decade earlier.

Finally, an event occurred that gave the colleges a chance to put their new equipment to use: In the fall of 1990, Iraq invaded Kuwait. As oil prices skyrocketed, the colleges switched from burning oil to burning natural gas. The college administrators expected big savings on their energy bills. But they were in for a shock. When they received the bills from their local utilities, they found that the price of natural gas—like the price of oil—had risen sharply. As a result, they did not save much in energy costs at all, certainly not enough to justify the costly switching equipment they had purchased. Many of these administrators were angry at the utility compa-

© BOB KRIST/CORBIS

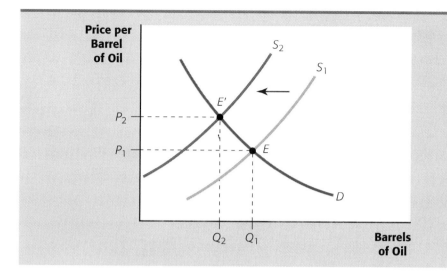

FIGURE 12
The Market for Oil

Before the Iraqi invasion of Kuwait, the oil market was in equilibrium at point E. The invasion and the resulting embargo on Iraqi oil decreased supply to S_2. Price increased to P_2, and the quantity exchanged fell to Q_2.

nies and accused them of price gouging. Iraq's invasion of Kuwait, they reasoned, had not affected natural gas supplies at all, so there was no reason for the price of natural gas to rise.

Were the college administrators right? Was this just an example of price gouging by the utility companies who were taking advantage of an international crisis to increase their profits? A simple supply and demand analysis will give us the answer. More specifically, it will enable us to answer two questions: (1) Why did Iraq's invasion of Kuwait cause the price of oil to rise, and (2) Why did the price of natural gas rise as well?

Figure 12 shows supply and demand curves in one of the markets relevant to our analysis: the market for crude oil. In this market, oil producers—including those in Iraq and Kuwait—sell to American buyers. Before the invasion, the market was in equilibrium at E with price P_1 and total output Q_1.

Then came the event that changed the equilibrium: Iraq's invasion and continued occupation of Kuwait—one of the largest oil producers in the world. Immediately after the invasion, the United States led a worldwide embargo on oil from both Iraq and Kuwait. As far as the oil market was concerned, it was as if these nations' oil fields no longer existed—a significant decrease in the oil industry's productive capacity. If you look back at Figure 6 you will see that a decrease in productive capacity shifts the supply curve to the left, and this is just what happened. The new equilibrium at E' occurred at a lower quantity and a higher price. This change in the oil market's equilibrium was well understood by most people—including the college administrators—and no one was surprised when oil prices rose.

But what has all this got to do with natural gas prices? Everything, as the next part of our analysis will show.

Figure 13 shows the next market relevant to our analysis: the market for natural gas. In this market, world producers (which did not include Iraq or Kuwait) sell natural gas to American buyers. In this market, the initial equilibrium—before the invasion and before the rise in oil prices—was at point F. How did the invasion affect the equilibrium?

Oil is a *substitute* for natural gas. A rise in the price of a substitute, we know, will increase the demand for a good. (Look back at Figure 3 if you need a reminder.) In this case, the increase in the price of oil caused the demand curve for natural gas to shift rightward. In Figure 13, the price of natural gas rose from P_3 to P_4.

FIGURE 13
The Market for Natural Gas

Oil is a substitute for natural gas. A rise in the price of oil increases the demand for natural gas. Here, demand for natural gas increases from D₁ to D₂ and the price rises from P₃ to P₄.

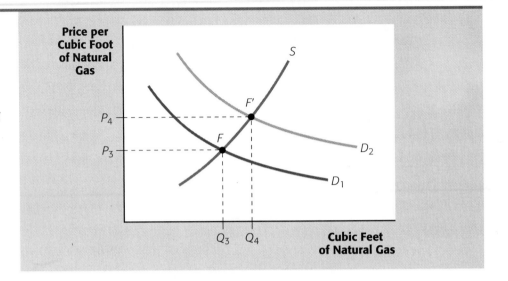

FIGURE 13
The Market for Natural Gas

Oil is a substitute for natural gas. A rise in the price of oil increases the demand for natural gas. Here, demand for natural gas increases from D_1 to D_2 and the price rises from P_3 to P_4.

The administrators were right that the invasion of Kuwait did not affect the supply of natural gas. What they missed, however, was the invasion's effect on the *demand* for natural gas. With a fuller understanding of supply and demand, they could have predicted—*before* investing in their expensive switching equipment—that any rise in oil prices would cause a rise in natural gas prices. Armed with this knowledge, they would have anticipated a much smaller savings in energy costs from switching to natural gas and might have decided that there were better uses for their scarce funds.

Summary

In a market economy, prices are determined through the interaction of buyers and sellers in *markets*. *Perfectly competitive* markets have many buyers and sellers, and none of them individually can affect the market price. If an individual, buyer, or seller has the power to influence the price of a product, the market is *imperfectly competitive*.

The model of *supply and demand* explains how prices are determined in perfectly competitive markets. The *quantity demanded* of any good is the total amount buyers would choose to purchase at a given price. The *law of demand* states that quantity demanded is negatively related to price; it tells us that the *demand curve* slopes downward. The demand curve is drawn for given levels of income, wealth, tastes, prices of substitute and complementary goods, population, and expected future price. If any of those factors changes, the demand curve will shift.

The *quantity supplied* of a good is the total amount sellers would choose to produce and sell at a given price. According to the *law of supply*, supply curves slope upward. The supply curve will shift if there is a change in the price of an input, the price of an alternate good, the number of firms, or expectations of future prices.

Equilibrium price and quantity in a market are found where the supply and demand curves intersect. If either of these curves shifts, price and quantity will change as the market moves to a new equilibrium.

Economists use a three-step process to answer questions about the economy. The three steps—taken several times in this chapter—are to (1) characterize the market or markets involved in the question; (2) find the equilibrium in the market; and (3) ask what happens when something changes. This three-step process will be used throughout the textbook.

Key Terms

Aggregation
Alternate goods
Change in demand
Change in quantity demanded

Change in quantity supplied
Change in supply
Complement
Demand schedule

Equilibrium price
Equilibrium quantity
Excess demand
Excess supply

Firm's quantity supplied
Household's quantity demanded
Imperfectly competitive market
Income
Inferior good
Law of demand

Law of supply
Market demand curve
Market quantity demanded
Market quantity supplied
Normal good
Perfectly competitive market

Substitute
Supply curve
Supply schedule
Wealth

Review Questions
Answers to even-numbered Questions and Problems can be found on the text Web site at http://hall-lieb.swlearning.com.

1. How does the way each of the following terms is used in economics differ from the way it is used in everyday language?
   a. market
   b. demand
   c. normal good
   d. inferior good
   e. supply

2. What is the difference between *demand* and *quantity demanded*?

3. List and briefly explain the factors that can shift a demand curve and the factors that can shift a supply curve.

4. What is the difference between substitutes and complements? Which of the following pairs of goods are substitutes, which are complements, and which are neither?
   a. Coke and Pepsi
   b. Computer hardware and computer software
   c. Beef and chicken
   d. Salt and sugar
   e. Ice cream and frozen yogurt

5. Rank each of the following markets according to how close you think it comes to perfect competition:
   a. Wheat
   b. Personal computer hardware
   c. Gold
   d. Airline tickets from New York to Kalamazoo, Michigan

6. Is each of the following goods more likely to be *normal* or *inferior?*
   a. Lexus automobiles
   b. Secondhand clothes
   c. Imported beer
   d. Baby-sitting services
   e. Recapped tires
   f. Futons
   g. Home haircutting tools
   h. Restaurant meals

7. What does the term *equilibrium* mean in economics?

8. Explain why the price in a free market will not remain above or below equilibrium for long, unless there is outside interference.

9. Determine whether each of the following will cause a change in demand or a change in supply, and in which direction:
   a. Input prices increase.
   b. Income in an area declines.
   c. The price of an alternate good increases.
   d. Tastes shift away from a good.

10. In the Using the Theory section at the end of this chapter, the three-step process is used.
    a. Identify and briefly describe *where* each step is used.
    b. For each step, carefully explain how it is used.

Problems and Exercises

1. In the late 1990s, beef—which had fallen out of favor in the 1970s and 1980s—became popular again. On a supply and demand diagram, illustrate the effect of such a change on equilibrium price and quantity in the market for beef.

2. In the late 1990s and through 2000, the British public became increasingly concerned about "Mad Cow Disease," which could be deadly to humans if they ate beef from these cattle. Fearing the disease, many consumers switched to other meats, like chicken, pork, or lamb. At the same time, the British government ordered the destruction of thousands of head of cattle. Illustrate the effects of these events on the equilibrium price and quantity in the market for British

beef. Can we determine with certainty the direction of change for the quantity? For the price? Explain briefly.

3. Discuss, and illustrate with a graph, how each of the following events will affect the market for coffee:
   a. A blight on coffee plants kills off much of the Brazilian crop.
   b. The price of tea declines.
   c. Coffee workers organize themselves into a union and gain higher wages.
   d. Coffee is shown to cause cancer in laboratory rats.
   e. Coffee prices are expected to rise rapidly in the near future.

4. The following table gives hypothetical data for the quantity of two-bedroom rental apartments demanded and supplied in Peoria, Illinois:

Monthly Rent	Quantity Demanded (Thousands)	Quantity Supplied (Thousands)
$ 800	30	10
$1,000	25	14
$1,200	22	17
$1,400	19	19
$1,600	17	21
$1,800	15	22

a. Graph the demand and supply curves.
b. Find the equilibrium price and quantity.
c. Explain briefly why a rent of $1,000 cannot be the equilibrium in this market.
d. Suppose a tornado destroys a significant number of apartment buildings in Peoria, but doesn't affect people's desire to live there. Illustrate on your graph the effects on equilibrium price and quantity.

5. The following table gives hypothetical data for the quantity of You-Snooze-You-Lose brand alarm clocks demanded and supplied per month.

Price per Alarm Clock	Quantity Demanded	Quantity Supplied
$ 5	3,500	700
$10	3,000	900
$15	2,500	1,100
$20	2,000	1,300
$25	1,500	1,500
$30	1,000	1,700
$35	500	1,900

a. Graph the demand and supply curves.
b. Find the equilibrium price and quantity.
c. Illustrate on your graph how a decrease in the price of wake-up services would affect the market for You-Snooze-You-Lose alarm clocks.
d. What would happen if there was a decrease in the price of wake-up services at the same time that the price of the plastic used to manufacture You-Snooze-You-Lose alarm clocks rose?

6. The following table gives hypothetical data for the quantity of electric scooters demanded and supplied per month.

Price per Electric Scooter	Quantity Demanded	Quantity Supplied
$150	500	250
$175	475	350
$200	450	450
$225	425	550
$250	400	650
$275	375	750

a. Graph the demand and supply curves.
b. Find the equilibrium price and quantity.
c. Illustrate on your graph how an increase in the wage rate paid to scooter assemblers would affect the market for electric scooters.
d. What would happen if there was an increase in the wage rate paid to scooter assemblers at the same time that tastes for electric scooters increased?

7. The following table gives hypothetical data for the quantity of gasoline demanded and supplied in Los Angeles per month.

Price per Gallon	Quantity Demanded (Millions of gallons)	Quantity Supplied (Millions of gallons)
$1.20	170	80
$1.30	156	105
$1.40	140	140
$1.50	123	175
$1.60	100	210
$1.70	95	238

a. Graph the demand and supply curves.
b. Find the equilibrium price and quantity.
c. Illustrate on your graph how a rise in the price of automobiles would affect the gasoline market.

8. How would each of the following affect the market for blue jeans in the United States? Illustrate each answer with a supply and demand diagram.
a. The price of denim cloth increases.
b. An influx of immigrants arrives in the United States. (Explicitly state any assumptions you are making.)
c. An economic slowdown in the United States causes household incomes to decrease.

9. Indicate which curve shifted—and in which direction—for each of the following. Assume that only one curve shifts.
a. The price of furniture rises as the quantity bought and sold falls.
b. Apartment vacancy rates increase while average monthly rent on apartments declines.
c. The price of personal computers continues to decline as sales skyrocket.

10. Consider the following forecast: "In 2004, we predict that the demand curve for handheld PCs will continue its shift leftward, which will tend to lower price and quantity. However, with a lower price, supply will decrease as well, shifting the supply curve leftward. A leftward shift of the supply curve will tend to raise price and lower quantity. We conclude that as 2004 proceeds, quantity will decrease but the price of handheld PCs may either rise or fall." There is a serious mistake of logic in this forecast. Can you find it? Explain.

11. Draw supply and demand diagrams for market A for each of the following. Then use your diagrams to illustrate the impact of the following events. In each case, determine what happens to price and quantity in each market.

a. *A* and *B* are substitutes, and the price of good *B* rises.
b. *A* and *B* satisfy the same kinds of desires, and there is a shift in tastes away from *A* and toward *B*.
c. *A* is a normal good, and incomes in the community increase.

d. There is a technological advance in the production of good *A*.
e. *B* is an input used to produce good *A*, and the price of *B* rises.

Challenge Questions

1. Suppose that demand is given by the equation $Q^D = 500 - 50P$, where Q^D is quantity demanded, and *P* is the price of the good. Supply is described by the equation $Q^S = 50 + 25P$, where Q^S is quantity supplied. What is the equilibrium price and quantity? (See Appendix)

2. While crime rates have fallen across the country over the past few years, they have fallen especially rapidly in Manhattan. At the same time, there are some neighborhoods in the New York metropolitan area in which the crime rate has remained constant. Using supply and demand diagrams for rental housing, explain how a falling crime rate in Manhattan could make the residents in *other* neighborhoods *worse off*. (Hint: As people from around the country move to Manhattan, what happens to rents there? If someone cannot afford to pay higher rent in Manhattan, what might they do?)

3. A Wall Street analyst observes the following equilibrium price-quantity combinations in the market for restaurant meals in a city over a four-year period:

Year	P	Q (Thousands of Meals per Month)
1	$12	20
2	$15	30
3	$17	40
4	$20	50

She concludes that the market defies the law of demand. Is she correct? Why or why not?

ECONOMIC *Applications*

These exercises require access to Hall/Lieberman Xtra! If Xtra! did not come with your book, visit http://hallxtra.swlearning.com to purchase.

1. Use your Xtra! password at the Hall and Lieberman Web site (http://hallxtra.swlearning.com), select Chapter 3, and under Economic Applications, click on Econ-News. Choose *Economic Fundamentals: Equilibrium*, and scroll down to find the article "Sweet Home Improvement Market." Read the article summary, and answer the questions below.
   a. Show graphically, using supply and demand curves, the impact of the increase in new home sales on the home improvement market.
   b. Now click on EconData. Under Hot Data, scroll down to find *Housing Starts*. Click on it, and read the definition of Housing Starts. Then click on *Diagrams/Data*, and see how the level of housing starts relates to the 30-year mortgage rate. What relationship should this variable have with the mortgage rate? Do you see this in the graph? Why or why not?
   c. Next click on EconNews again. Choose *Economic Fundamental: Supply and Demand* and scroll down to find the article, "PC Price Cuts." Read the article summary, and describe, using supply and demand curves, how the effects of computer price cuts impacts the market for home improvement described in part a.

2. Use your Xtra! password at the Hall and Lieberman Web site (http://hallxtra.swlearning.com), select Chapter 3, and under Economic Applications click on EconDebate.

Choose *Economic Fundamental: Supply and Demand*, and scroll down to find the debate, "Do slave redemption programs reduce the problem of slavery?" Read the debate and answer the questions below.
   a. What incentive problem is mentioned in the debate regarding slave redemption programs? Illustrate this using supply and demand curves.
   b. How could you modify the incentives of slave redemption programs to reduce the problem of increased slave raids?

3. Use your Xtra! password at the Hall and Lieberman Web site (http://hallxtra.swlearning.com), select Chapter 3, and under Economic Applications, click on Econ-News. Choose *Economic Fundamentals: Equilibrium*, and scroll down to find the article "Students Learn the Hard Way." Read the article summary, and answer the questions below.
   a. As the article points out, many schools are seeing an increase in costs as well as a reduction in state funds available. Illustrate, using a graph of supply and demand in the market for a college education, the effect of increasing costs of producing that education.
   b. Why would student government groups on college campuses with incentives like the ones described in the article be concerned about the quality of the education students were receiving?

APPENDIX

SOLVING FOR EQUILIBRIUM ALGEBRAICALLY

In the body of this chapter, notice that the supply and demand curves for maple syrup were *not* graphed as straight lines. This is because the data they were based on were not consistent with the straight-line graph. You can verify this if you look back at Table 2: When the price rises from $1.00 to $2.00, quantity demanded drops by 15,000 (from 75,000 to 60,000). But when the price rises from $2.00 to $3.00, quantity demanded drops by 10,000 (from 60,000 to 50,000). Since the change in the independent variable—price—is $1.00 in both cases, but the change in the dependent variable—quantity demanded—is different, we know that when the the relationship between quantity demanded and price is graphed, it will not be a straight line.

We have no reason to expect that demand or supply curves in the real world will be straight lines (to be *linear*). However, it's often useful to approximate a curve with a linear relationship that is reasonably close to the original curve. One advantage of doing this is that we can then express both supply and demand as simple equations, and solve for the equilibrium using basic algebra.

For example, suppose the demand for take-out pizzas in a modest-size city is represented by the following equation:

$$Q^D = 64,000 - 3,000\,P$$

where Q^D stands for the quantity of pizzas demanded per week. This equation tells us that every time the price of pizza rises by $1.00, the number of pizzas demanded each week *falls* by 3,000. As we'd expect, there is a negative relationship between price and quantity demanded. Moreover, since quantity demanded always falls at the same rate (3,000 fewer pizzas for every $1.00 rise in price), the equation is linear.[1]

Now we'll add an equation for the supply curve:

$$Q^S = -20,000 + 4,000\,P$$

where Q^S stands for the quantity of pizzas supplied per week. This equation tells us that when the price of pizza rises by $1.00, the number of pizzas supplied per week *rises* by 4,000—the positive relationship we expect of a supply curve.[2] And like the demand curve, it's linear: Quantity supplied continues to rise at the same rate (4,000 more pizzas for every $1.00 increase in price).

We know that if this market is in equilibrium, quantity demanded (Q^D) will equal quantity supplied (Q^S). So let's *impose* that condition on these curves. That is, let's require $Q^D = Q^S$. This allows us to use the definitions for Q^D and Q^S that have price as a variable, and set those equal to each other in equilibrium:

$$64,000 - 3,000\,P = -20,000 + 4,000\,P$$

This is one equation with a single unknown—P—so we can use the rules of algebra to isolate P on one side of the equation. We do this by adding 3,000 P to both sides, which isolates P on the right, and adding 20,000 to both sides, which moves everything that *doesn't* involve P to the left, giving us:

$$84,000 = 7,000\,P$$

Finally, dividing both sides by 7,000 gives us

$$84,000 / 7,000 = P$$

or

$$P = 12$$

We've found our equilibrium price: $12. What about equilibrium quantity? In equilibrium, we know quantity demanded and quantity supplied are equal, so we can *either* solve for Q^D using the demand equation, or solve for Q^S using the supply equation, and we should get the same answer. For example, using the demand equation, and using the equilibrium price of $12:

$$Q^D = 64,000 - 3,000\,(12)$$

or

$$Q^D = 28,000$$

To confirm that we didn't make any errors, we can also solve for quantity supplied at the same price:

$$Q^S = -20,000 + 4,000\,(12)$$

or

$$Q^S = 28,000$$

We've now confirmed that the equilibrium quantity is 28,000.

---

[1] If you try to graph the demand curve, don't forget that supply and demand graphs reverse the usual custom of graphing the independent variable on the horizontal axis and the dependent variable on the vertical. That is, quantity demanded is the dependent variable (it *depends* on price), and yet it's graphed on the *horizontal* axis.

[2] Don't be troubled by the negative sign ($-20,000$) in this equation. It helps determine a minimum price that suppliers must get in order to supply any pizza at all. Using the entire equation, we find that if price were $5.00, quantity supplied would be zero, and that price has to rise *above* $5.00 for any pizzas to be supplied in this market. But since a "negative supply" doesn't make sense, this equation is valid only for prices of $5.00 or greater.

Working with Supply and Demand

CHAPTER OUTLINE

In Chapter 3, you learned that supply and demand explain how prices are determined in competitive markets, and also how and why prices change. But this versatile model can do even more. We can use it to see what happens when governments intervene in markets to influence prices. We can add details to the model—such as measurements of buyers' and sellers' sensitivity to price changes—that will deepen our understanding of how markets work. And we can use it to gain insights into social policy issues, ranging from the war against illegal drugs to the design of an effective health care system. This chapter is all about *working with* supply and demand, and applying it in the real world.

GOVERNMENT INTERVENTION IN MARKETS

The forces of supply and demand deserve some credit. They force the market price to adjust until something remarkable happens: The quantity that sellers want to sell

FIGURE 1
**A Price Ceiling in the Market
for Maple Syrup**

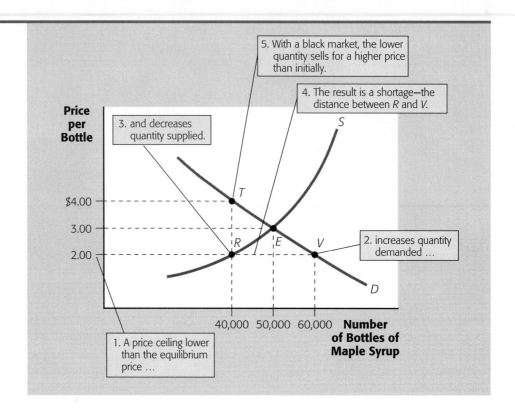

is also the quantity that buyers want to buy. Thus, no buyer or seller should have trouble turning his intentions into actual market trades.

So, three cheers for supply and demand! Or better make that *two* cheers. Because while everyone agrees that having prices is necessary for the smooth functioning of our economy, not everyone is happy with the prices that supply and demand give us. Apartment dwellers often complain that their rent is too high, and farmers complain that the price of their crops is too low.

Responding to this dissatisfaction, governments will sometimes intervene to *change* the price in a market. In this section, we'll look at two methods governments use to prevent a market price from reaching its equilibrium value.

Price Ceilings

Price ceiling A government-imposed maximum price in a market.

Figure 1 shows our familiar market for maple syrup, with an equilibrium price of $3.00 per bottle. Suppose that maple syrup buyers complain to the government that this price is too high. The government responds by imposing a **price ceiling** in this market—a regulation preventing the price from rising above the ceiling.

More specifically, suppose the ceiling is $2.00 per bottle, and it is strictly enforced. Then producers will no longer be able to charge $3.00 for maple syrup but will have to content themselves with $2.00 instead. In Figure 1, we will move down along the supply curve, from point E to point R, decreasing quantity supplied from 50,000 bottles to 40,000. At the same time, the decrease in price will move us along the demand curve, from point E to point V, increasing quantity demanded from 50,000 to 60,000. These changes in quantities supplied and demanded together create an *excess demand* for maple syrup of 60,000 − 40,000 = 20,000 bottles each month. Ordinarily, the excess demand would force the price back up to $3.00. But now the price ceiling prevents this from occurring. What will happen?

There is a practical observation about markets that helps us arrive at an answer:

> *When quantity supplied and quantity demanded differ, the **short side of the market**—whichever of the two quantities is smaller—will prevail.*

Short side of the market The smaller of quantity supplied and quantity demanded at a particular price.

This simple rule follows from the voluntary nature of exchange in a market system: No one can be forced to buy or sell more than they want to. With an excess demand, sellers are the short side of the market. Since we cannot force them to sell any more than they want to (40,000 units) the result is a **shortage** of maple syrup—not enough available to satisfy demand at the going price.

But this is not the end of the story. Because of the shortage, all 40,000 bottles produced each month will quickly disappear from store shelves and many buyers will be disappointed. The next time people hear that maple syrup has become available, everyone will try to get there first, and we can expect long lines at stores. Those who really crave maple syrup may have to go from store to store, searching for that rare bottle. When we include the *opportunity cost* of the time spent waiting in line or shopping around, the ultimate effect of the price ceiling may be a *higher* cost of maple syrup for many consumers.

Shortage An excess demand not eliminated by a rise in price, so that quantity demanded continues to exceed quantity supplied.

> *A price ceiling creates a shortage and increases the time and trouble required to buy the good. While the price decreases, the opportunity cost may rise.*

And there is still more. While the government may be able to prevent maple syrup *producers* from selling above the price ceiling, it may not be able to prevent enterprising individuals from buying maple syrup at the official ceiling price and then reselling it to desperate buyers for a profit. The result is a **black market**, where goods are sold illegally at prices higher than the legal ceiling.

Black market A market in which goods are sold illegally at a price above the legal ceiling.

Ironically, the black market price will typically exceed the original, freely determined equilibrium price—$3.00 per bottle in our example. To see why, look again at Figure 1. With a price ceiling of $2.00, sellers supply 40,000 bottles per month. Suppose all of this is bought by people—maple syrup scalpers, if you will—who then sell it at the highest price they can get. What price can they charge? We can use the demand curve to find out. At $4.00 per bottle (point *T*), the scalpers would just be able to sell all 40,000 bottles. They have no reason, therefore, to charge any less than this.

The unintended consequences of price ceilings—long lines, black markets, and, often, higher prices—explain why they are generally a poor way to bring down prices. Experience with price ceilings has generally confirmed this judgment, so in practice they are rare.

An exception, however, is **rent controls**—city ordinances that specify a maximum monthly rent on many apartments and homes. If you live in a city with rent control, you will be familiar with its consequences. In any case, you may want to reread this section with the market for apartments in mind. How are shortages and long lines manifested? Do rent controls always decrease the cost of apartments to renters? (Think: opportunity cost.) And who are the middlemen—the "apartment scalpers"—who profit in this market?

Rent controls Government-imposed maximum rents on apartments and homes.

Price Floors

Price floor A government-imposed minimum price in a market.

Sometimes, governments try to help sellers of a good by establishing a **price floor**—a minimum amount below which the price is not permitted to fall. The most common use of price floors around the world has been to raise prices (or prevent prices from falling) in agricultural markets. Price floors for agricultural goods are commonly called *price support programs.*

In the United States, price support programs began during the Great Depression, after farm prices fell by more than 50 percent between 1929 and 1932. The Agricultural Adjustment Act of 1933, and an amendment in 1935, gave the president the authority to intervene in markets for a variety of agricultural goods. Over the next 60 years, the United States Department of Agriculture (USDA) put in place programs to maintain high prices for cotton, wheat, rice, corn, tobacco, honey, milk, cheese, butter, and many other farm goods.

Things were supposed to change in 1996. In April of that year, Congress passed—and President Clinton signed—the Federal Agriculture Improvement and Reform Act. The new law eliminated many of the government's price support programs and dramatically scaled back others, leaving only three important exceptions: peanuts, sugar, and dairy products. But after several years of falling farm prices and emergency assistance, pressure built to return to some kind of permanent government aid to farmers. Finally, in May 2002, Congress passed—and President Bush signed—the Farm Security and Rural Investment Act. Although this bill improved in some ways on the design of the pre-1996 programs, it brought back price supports for many of the old crops and, once again, maintained support programs for peanuts, sugar, and dairy products.

To see how price floors work, let's look at the market for nonfat dry milk—a market in which the USDA has been supporting prices continually since 1933. Figure 2 shows that—before any price floor is imposed—the market is in equilibrium at point A, with an equilibrium price of 65 cents per pound and an equilibrium quantity of 200 million pounds per month.

Now let's examine the impact of the mid-2003 price floor of $0.81 per pound. At this price, producers want to sell 220 million pounds, while consumers want to purchase only 180 million pounds. There is an excess supply of 220 million − 180 million = 40 million pounds. Our short-side rule tells us that buyers determine the amount actually traded. They purchase 180 million of the 220 million pounds produced and producers are unable to sell the remainder. The excess supply of 40 million pounds would ordinarily push the market price down to its equilibrium value: $0.65. But now the price floor prevents this from happening. The result is a **surplus**—continuing extra production of nonfat dry milk that no one wants to buy at the going price.

Surplus An excess supply not eliminated by a fall in price, so that quantity supplied continues to exceed quantity demanded.

But what prevents the price from falling? Something more than just a government *declaration* of a price floor. After all, if the government merely *declared* that nonfat dry milk must be sold for $0.81 per pound, producers would have a strong incentive to sell some of their milk for less. Buyers, of course, would be happy to buy at the lower price. How, then, does the government *enforce* its price floor?

With a foolproof strategy. The government simply promises to buy nonfat dry milk from any seller at $0.81 per pound. With this policy, no supplier would ever sell at any price *below* $0.81, since it could always sell to the government instead. With the price effectively stuck at $0.81, private buyers buy 180 million pounds—point K on the demand curve in Figure 2. But since quantity supplied is 220 million,

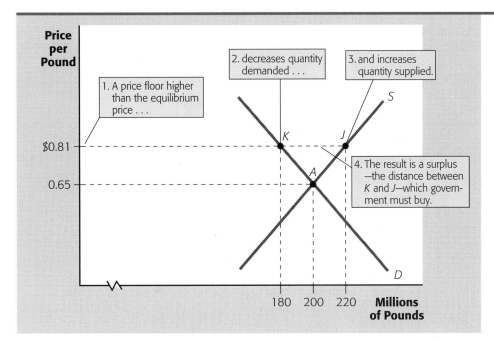

FIGURE 2
A Price Floor in the Market for Nonfat Dry Milk

at point *J*, the government must buy the excess supply of 40 million pounds each year. In other words, the government maintains the price floor by *buying up* the entire excess supply. This prevents the excess supply from doing what it would ordinarily do: drive the price down to its equilibrium value.

And, indeed, this is what the government has done in markets for many agricultural goods, including nonfat dry milk. In 2002, for example, the USDA had to purchase 619 million pounds of surplus nonfat dry milk at a cost of about $500 million. By the end of that year, the government owned more than 1 billion pounds of nonfat dry milk—purchases that it had made in previous years and still held.

> *A price floor creates a surplus of a good. In order to maintain the price floor, the government must prevent the surplus from driving down the market price. In practice, the government often accomplishes this goal by purchasing the surplus itself.*

However, purchasing surplus food is expensive, so price floors are usually accompanied by government efforts to *limit* any excess supplies. In the dairy market, for example, the U.S. government has developed a complicated management system to control the production and sale of milk to manufacturers and processors, which helps to limit the government's costs. In other agricultural markets, the government has ordered or paid farmers *not* to grow crops on portions of their land and has

Floor Above, Ceiling Below! It's tempting to draw a supply and demand diagram with a price floor set *under* the equilibrium price, or a price ceiling *above* the equilibrium price. After all, a floor is usually on the bottom of something, and a ceiling is on the top. Right? In this case, wrong! A price floor set *below* the equilibrium price would have no impact on a market, because the market price would *already* satisfy the requirement that it be higher than the floor. Similarly, a price ceiling set *above* the equilibrium price would have no impact (make sure you understand why). So remember: Always draw an effective price floor *above* the equilibrium price and an effective price ceiling *below* the equilibrium price.

DANGEROUS CURVES

imposed strict limits on imports of food from abroad. Many of these supply limitations are still in place. As you can see, price floors often get the government deeply involved in production decisions, rather than leaving them to the market.

Price floors have certainly benefited farmers and helped them in times of need. But this market intervention has many critics—including most economists. They have argued that the government spends too much money buying surplus agricultural products, and the resulting higher prices distort the public's buying and eating habits—often to their nutritional detriment. For example, the General Accounting Office has estimated that from 1986 to 2001, price supports for dairy products have cost American consumers $10.4 billion in higher prices. And this does not include the cost of the health effects—such as calcium and protein deficiencies among poor children—due to decreased milk consumption. The irony is that many of the farmers who benefit from price floors are wealthy individuals or large, powerful corporations that do not need the assistance.

Economists argue that assistance to farmers would be more cost-effective if given directly to those truly in need, rather than supporting all farmers with artificially high prices. But they also recognize that markets for agricultural goods have some special characteristics and that unchecked market forces are more of a threat to farmers than workers in most other industries. We'll discuss these special characteristics in the Using the Theory section at the end of this chapter.

PRICE ELASTICITY OF DEMAND

Imagine that you are the mayor of one of America's large cities. Every day, the headlines blare about local problems—poverty, crime in the streets, the sorry state of public education, roads and bridges that are falling apart, traffic congestion—and you, as mayor, are held accountable for all of them. Of course, you could help alleviate these problems, if only you had more money to spend on them. But where to get the money?

One day, an aide bounds into your office. "I've got the perfect solution," he says, beaming. "We raise mass transit fares." He shows you a sheet of paper on which he's done the calculation: Each year, city residents take 100 million trips on public transportation. If fares are raised by 50 cents, the transit system will take in an additional $50 million—enough to make a dent in some of the city's problems.

You stroke your chin and think about it. So many issues to balance: fairness, practicality, the political impact. But if you have taken the first week or two of introductory microeconomics, another thought will occur to you: Your aide has made a serious mistake! Public transportation—like virtually everything else that people buy—obeys the law of demand: A rise in price—with no other change—will cause a decrease in quantity demanded. If you raise fares, each *trip* will bring in more revenue, but there will be *fewer trips* taken. If the impact on the number of trips is small, mass transit revenue might rise. But if people begin to abandon mass transit in droves, the city will be much worse off, actually *losing* revenue, even as those continuing to ride pay higher fares. How can you determine the ultimate impact of the fare hike on the city's revenue?

To answer that question, you would need one more piece of information. And the same information is needed by anyone who needs to know how a change in price affects his or her revenue: a theater setting ticket prices, a cell phone company setting the price per minute for phone calls, or a doctor deciding on patients' fees. The information you need concerns something that economists call the *price elas-*

ticity of demand, which is a measure of how *sensitive* quantity demanded is to a change in price. But how to measure it?

The Problem with Rate of Change

You might think that the rate of change of quantity demanded compared to the change in price would be a good measure of price sensitivity. Unfortunately, it isn't. Suppose you have data showing that for a particular good when price rises by $1, quantity demanded falls by 500 units per period. That's a rate of change of 500 units per dollar.[1] Is demand for this product *sensitive* to price? *Insensitive*? Let's see.

Suppose this data refers to *chocolate bars purchased in the United States per year.* Then it suggests almost *no* price sensitivity for chocolate bars. After all, a $1 price increase is almost a doubling—or more—of price, and a drop of 500 units per year—in a market where millions of bars are sold each year—is hardly a drop in the ocean.

But now suppose this data refers to *private jets purchased in the United States per year.* Then this same rate of change of 500 units per dollar would suggest an astonishingly large price sensitivity. After all, less than a thousand private jets are produced every year; even the cheapest among them costs around $1 million. So a $1 price hike would be insignificant—hardly noticeable—while a 500-unit drop in quantity demanded would be considered huge.

As you've just seen, the change in quantity demanded for a $1 change in price doesn't tell us much about sensitivity. But why not? The problem with a rate of change is that it doesn't tell us whether a change in price (e.g., $1) or a change in quantity demanded (e.g., 500 units) is a *relatively large* or *relatively small* change. By *relative*, we mean compared to the value of price or quantity *before* the change. For example, a $1 rise in the price of chocolate bars is a relatively large change because it amounts to a doubling of the original price, while the same $1 change in the price of private jets would be a change of less than one-ten-thousandth of a percent. Logic tells us that demand for a good should be considered price-sensitive only when a *relatively small* price change causes a *relatively large* change in quantity demanded.

The Elasticity Approach

The elasticity approach solves the problems with rate of change by comparing the *percentage change* in quantity demanded with the *percentage change* in price. More specifically:

> The **price elasticity of demand** (E_D) for a good is the percentage change in quantity demanded divided by the percentage change in price:
>
> $$E_D = \frac{\%\ \text{Change in Quantity Demanded}}{\%\ \text{Change in Price}}.$$

Price elasticity of demand The sensitivity of quantity demanded to price; the percentage change in quantity demanded caused by a 1-percent change in price.

For example, if a 2 percent rise in the price of newspapers causes a 3 percent drop in the quantity of newspapers demanded, then $E_D = -3\%/2\% = -1.5$. We would say, "The price elasticity of demand for newspapers is minus 1.5."

---

[1] The rate of change we're discussing is $\Delta Q^D/\Delta P$, which is *not* the same as the slope of the demand curve in a graph. But they are closely related. Remember that for the demand curve, price is measured on the vertical axis and quantity on the horizontal. Thus, the graphical slope of the demand curve is $\Delta P/\Delta Q^D$, which is the reciprocal of the rate of change we're referring to. For example, when the rate of change is 500, the slope of the demand curve would be $1/500 = .002$.

There are a few things to keep in mind about a price elasticity of demand (or just *elasticity of demand*, for short). First, it will virtually always be a *negative* number: As long as the good obeys the law of demand, a positive change in price will cause a negative change in quantity demanded, so the ratio of the two must have a minus sign.

Second, an elasticity of demand has a straightforward interpretation: It tells us the percentage change in quantity demanded *for each 1-percent increase* in price. An elasticity of −2.5, for example, tells us that if price rises by 1 percent, quantity demanded falls by 2.5 percent. If price rises by 2 percent, quantity demanded falls by 5 percent, and so on. In general, the greater the *absolute value* of the number, the more sensitive quantity demanded is to price: An elasticity of −2.5 means greater price sensitivity than an elasticity of −1 or −0.5.

Finally, keep in mind that a demand elasticity tells us the response of quantity demanded to a price change *if all other influences on demand remain unchanged.* Thus, it measures price sensitivity for movements along an unchanging demand curve, holding constant buyers' incomes, the prices of all other goods, and so on. In other words,

> *a price elasticity of demand tells us the percentage change in quantity demanded caused by a 1 percent rise in price as we move along a demand curve from one point to another.*

Calculating Price Elasticity of Demand

A percentage change is *usually* defined as the change in a variable divided by its starting, or base, value. But this can create a problem when we use elasticities.

For example, look at Figure 3, which shows a hypothetical monthly demand curve for laptop computers in the United States. As we move from point *A* to point *B* on this curve, the price of an average laptop rises from $1,000 to $1,500. The corresponding *percentage* change in price—using our starting price of $1,000 as the base price—would be ($1,500 − $1,000)/$1,000 = 0.50 or 50 percent. But what if—instead of moving from *A* to *B*—we move from *B* to *A*? Then, instead of increasing from $1,000 to $1,500, the price would *decrease* from $1,500 to $1,000. In this case, our base price would be $1,500 and our percentage change in price would now become ($1,000 − $1,500)/$1,500 = −0.33, or −33 percent. So, if we use the starting value as the base, the percentage change in price between two points on the demand curve—and our measure of price elasticity that is based on it—would depend on which direction we were moving. The same would be true of the percentage change in quantity demanded.

But this would be problematic, especially when we want to say whether a particular segment of a demand curve is price-sensitive or price-insensitive, and to what degree. We'd like this to be a characteristic of the segment, rather than

Mistakes in Observing Elasticities It's tempting to calculate an elasticity from simple observation: looking at what actually happened to buyers' purchases after some price changed. But this often leads to serious errors. Elasticity of demand tells us the effect a price change would have on quantity demanded *if* all other influences on demand remain unchanged. But in the real world, it is unlikely that other influences will remain unchanged in the weeks or months after a price change.

Consider what happened in Baltimore in March 1996, when the city increased mass transit fares by 8 percent. Over the next six months, ridership *increased* by 4.5 percent. Does this mean that the elasticity of demand for mass transit in Baltimore is positive? Does mass transit violate the law of demand? Not at all. Around the time of the fare hike, the city also made improvements in service and advertised them heavily. This no doubt helped to change tastes in favor of mass transit, shifting the demand curve rightward. If all other influences on demand for mass transit had remained unchanged—so that we moved along a stable demand curve—ridership would have fallen when the price rose. Economists and statisticians have developed tools to isolate the effect of price changes on quantity demanded when other variables are changing at the same time.

DANGEROUS CURVES

Movement Along Demand Curve	%ΔQ^D	%ΔP	Elasticity of Demand
Point *A* to Point *B*	(500,000 − 600,000)/550,000	($1,500 − $1,000)/$1,250	−18.2%/40%
	= −0.182 or −18.2%	= 0.40 or 40%	= −0.46
Point *C* to Point *D*	(100,000 − 200,000)/150,000	($3,500 − $3,000)/$3,250	−66.7%/15.4%
	= −0.667 or −66.7%	= 0.154 or 15.4%	= −4.33

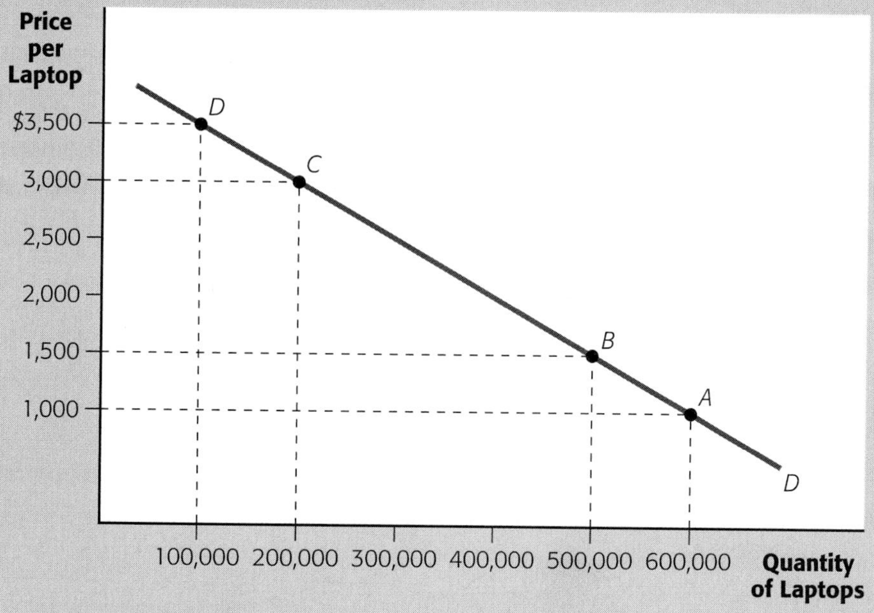

FIGURE 3
Calculating Price Elasticity of Demand

the direction we're moving along that segment. To accomplish this goal, we adopt a simple convention:

When calculating elasticity, the base value for percentage changes in price or quantity is always midway between the initial value and the new value.

Thus, if the price rises from $1,000 to $1,500, or falls from $1,500 to $1,000, we use as our base price the value midway between these two prices, found by calculating their simple average: ($1,000 + $1,500)/2 = $1,250. This way, we are using the same base value regardless of the direction that price changes.

More generally, when price changes from any value P_0 to any other value P_1, we define the percentage change in price as

$$\% \text{ Change in Price} = \frac{(P_1 - P_0)}{\left[\frac{(P_1 + P_0)}{2}\right]}$$

The term in the numerator is the change in price; the term in the denominator is the base price—the midpoint between the two prices. If you plug the preceding numbers into this formula, you'll see that if price rises from \$1,000 to \$1,500, the percentage change in price is (\$1,500 − \$1,000)/\$1,250 = 0.40 or 40 percent. If price falls from \$1,500 to \$1,000, the percentage change is (\$1,000 − \$1,500)/\$1,250 = −0.40 or −40 percent.

The percentage change in quantity demanded is calculated in a similar way. When quantity demanded changes from Q_0 to Q_1, the percentage change is calculated as

$$\% \text{ Change in Quantity Demanded} = \frac{(Q_1 - Q_0)}{\left[\frac{(Q_1 + Q_0)}{2}\right]}$$

Once again, we are using the number midway between the initial and the new quantity demanded as our base quantity.

An Example. Now let's calculate an elasticity of demand for laptop computers using the data in Figure 3. For now, we'll stick to the interval from point A to point B. As price rises from \$1,000 to \$1,500, quantity demanded falls from 600,000 to 500,000. We have

$$\% \text{ Change in Quantity Demanded} = \frac{(500,000 - 600,000)}{\left[\frac{(500,000 + 600,00)}{2}\right]} =$$

$$\frac{-100,000}{550,000} = -0.182, \text{ or } -18.2\%.$$

$$\% \text{ Change in Price} = \frac{(\$1,500 - \$1,000)}{\left[\frac{(\$1,500 + \$1,000)}{2}\right]} = \frac{\$500}{\$1,250} = 0.400, \text{ or } 40.0\%.$$

Finally, we use the percentage changes for price and quantity to calculate the price elasticity of demand (E_D):

$$E_D = \frac{-0.182}{0.400} = -0.46.$$

We find that, over the interval from point A to B in Figure 3, the quantity of laptops demanded falls by 0.46 percent (a little less than half a percent) for each 1 percent increase in price.

Elasticity and Straight-Line Demand Curves

In Figure 3, we drew the demand curve for laptops as a straight line. Along this demand curve, each time price rises by \$500, the quantity of laptops demanded decreases by 100,000 per month. This behavior remains constant regardless of the price at which we start. Does this mean that the price elasticity of demand for laptops is the same for any interval along this demand curve? Absolutely not!

To see why, let's compare what happens when the price of laptops rises by \$500 along two different intervals. If we move from A to B, the price rise of \$500 corresponds to a *percentage* price rise of \$500/\$1,250 = 0.40 or 40 percent. But if we move from C to D—another \$500 increase in price—the *percentage* rise in price is \$500/\$3,250 = 0.154 or 15.4 percent. In other words, the same *absolute* price increase corresponds to a smaller *percentage* increase. In general, as we move upward

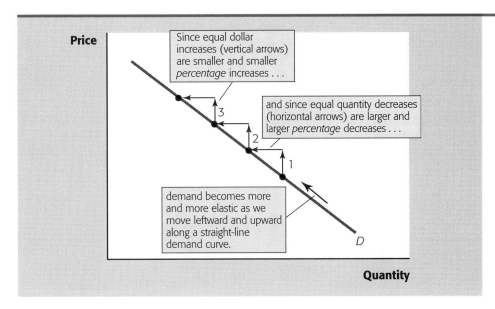

FIGURE 4
Elasticity and Straight-Line Demand Curves

and leftward along a straight-line demand curve, the same absolute increment in price will correspond to smaller and smaller percentage increments in price. Why? Because the base price used to calculate percentage changes keeps rising.

Something similar happens as quantity changes. Whether we move from A to B or from C to D quantity demanded falls by the same number: 100,000. But the *percentage* drop in quantity demanded is greater along the interval C to D because the base quantity there is smaller. In general, as we move upward and leftward along a straight-line demand curve, the same *absolute* decrease in quantity corresponds to larger and larger *percentage* decreases in quantity.

Figure 4 summarizes what we've just discovered about any straight-line demand curve. As we move upward and leftward by equal distances, the percentage change in quantity rises, while the percentage change in price falls. Together, this means that the price elasticity of demand must be getting larger.

> *Elasticity of demand varies along a straight-line demand curve. More specifically, demand becomes more elastic as we move upward and leftward.*

You can verify this by looking at the demand elasticity calculation for the interval from point C to point D (shown in Figure 3). As expected, demand is more elastic (−4.33) over this interval than it is over the interval from A to B that we calculated earlier (−0.46).

Categorizing Goods by Elasticity

When the numerical value of the price elasticity of demand is *between 0 and −1.0* (or the absolute value of elasticity $|E_D|$ is between 0 and 1), we say that demand is **inelastic**.

$$\text{Inelastic Demand} \Rightarrow \left| \frac{\%\text{ Change in Quantity Demanded}}{\%\text{ Change in Price}} \right| < 1.0.$$

$$\Rightarrow |\%\text{ Change in Quantity Demanded}| < |\%\text{ Change in Price}|$$

Inelastic demand A price elasticity of demand with absolute value between 0 and 1.

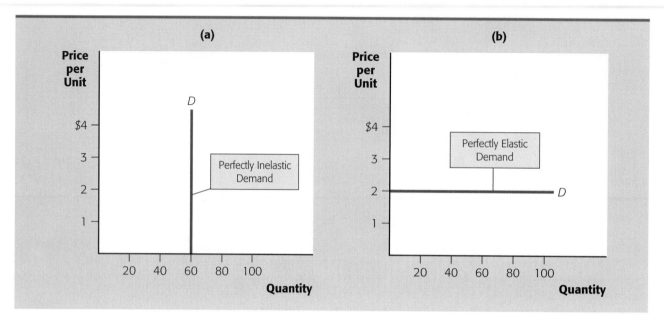

FIGURE 5
Extreme Cases of Demand

In words, inelastic demand means that the percentage change in quantity demanded will be *smaller* than the percentage change in price, ignoring the sign. For example, if price rises by 4 percent, quantity demanded will fall, but by *less* than 4 percent. When demand is inelastic, quantity demanded is *not* very sensitive to price.

An extreme case of inelastic demand occurs when a change in price causes no change in quantity demanded. Since

$$\% \text{ Change in Quantity Demanded} = 0,$$

Perfectly inelastic demand A price elasticity of demand equal to 0.

the elasticity will equal zero. We call this special case **perfectly inelastic** demand. Panel (a) of Figure 5 shows what the demand curve for a good would look like if demand were perfectly inelastic at every price. The demand curve is vertical: No matter what the price, quantity demanded is the same.

Perfectly inelastic demand is mostly interesting from a theoretical point of view; it is difficult to find examples of goods with zero elasticity of demand in the real world. With zero demand elasticity, the good would have to be one that consumers want only in a fixed quantity. One example might be insulin—the drug needed by diabetics to control their blood sugar. Insulin has no use other than in the management of diabetes. For diabetics, quantity requirements for insulin are quite rigid and there would be no substitutes for its use. A drop in price will not encourage diabetics to use more, nor will a modest rise in price cause diabetics to economize on its use.

Elastic demand A price elasticity of demand with absolute value greater than 1.

When E_D is less than -1.0, we say that demand is **elastic.** In this case, the *absolute value* of the elasticity will be *greater* than 1.0:

$$\text{Elastic Demand} = \left| \frac{\% \text{ Change in Quantity Demanded}}{\% \text{ Change in Price}} \right| > 1.$$

$$\Rightarrow |\% \text{ Change in Quantity Demanded}| > |\% \text{ Change in Price}|$$

When demand is elastic, the percentage change in quantity demanded is *larger* than the percentage change in price, ignoring the signs. For instance, if price rises by

4 percent, quantity demanded will fall by *more* than 4 percent. Elastic demand means that quantity demanded is *sensitive to price*.

An extreme case of price sensitivity occurs when demand is **perfectly** or **infinitely elastic**. Even the tiniest change in price causes a huge change in quantity demanded, so huge that, for all intents and purposes, we can call the response infinite. When demand is perfectly elastic over an interval, the demand curve will be a horizontal line—as shown in panel (b) of Figure 5. The demand for a single brand of salt may fall into this category. If the price of Morton salt rose a little, while other brands next to it on the supermarket shelf continued to cost the same, everyone might switch to the other brands, causing the quantity of Morton salt demanded to plummet.

Finally, when elasticity of demand is exactly equal to −1, we have **unitary elasticity**. In this case, % Change in Quantity Demanded = % Change in Price, and demand for the good is exactly at the boundary between elastic and inelastic. Many consumer products seem to have price elasticities near −1.0. In addition, a price elasticity of −1.0 is important as a benchmark case, as you will see a bit later.

Perfectly (infinitely) elastic demand A price elasticity of demand approaching minus infinity.

Unitary elastic demand A price elasticity of demand equal to −1.

Elasticity Along a Demand Curve You've seen that elasticity changes along a straight-line demand curve. But the result applies more generally as well. Except in special cases (such as those in Figure 5), elasticity can change along *any* demand curve, whether a straight line or a curve. For this reason, you should try to avoid two common mistakes. First, don't describe a "demand curve" as elastic or inelastic; while demand might be elastic along *part* of the demand curve, it might be inelastic along another part of the curve.

Second, don't equate the "flatness" or "steepness" of a demand curve with how elastic or inelastic it is. Slope and elasticity are not the same. A straight-line demand curve, for example, remains equally steep or flat along its entire length. Yet—as you've seen—the elasticity of demand changes as we move along it.

DANGEROUS CURVES

Elasticity and Total Revenue

When the price of a good increases, the law of demand tells us that people will demand less of it. But this does not necessarily mean that they will *spend* less on it. After the price rises, fewer units will be purchased but each unit will cost more. It turns out that whether a rise in a price will cause total spending on a good to rise or fall depends entirely on the price elasticity of demand for the good. And since total spending by buyers is also the total revenue of sellers, elasticity will tell us what happens to total revenue as well.

To see this more formally, note that the total revenue (TR) of all firms in the market is defined as

$$TR = P \times Q$$

where P is the price per unit and Q is the total quantity sold. Now, we can use a rule about percentage changes: *When two numbers are both changing, the percentage change in their product is (approximately) the sum of their individual percentage changes.* Applying this to total revenue, we can write

% Change in TR = % Change in Price + % Change in Quantity Demanded.

Now let's assume that P rises by 10 percent. What will happen to total revenue? If demand is *unitary elastic,* then Q will fall by 10 percent, so we will have

% Change in TR = 10% + (−10%) = 0.

The percentage change in total revenue is zero, meaning that total expenditure does not change at all! If demand is *inelastic,* a 10-percent rise in price will cause quantity demanded to fall by *less* than 10 percent, so we have

TABLE 1
Effects of Price Changes on Revenue

Where demand is:	A price increase will:	A price decrease will:
inelastic ($|E_D| < 1$)	increase revenue	decrease revenue
unitary elastic ($|E_D| = 1$)	cause no change in revenue	cause no change in revenue
elastic ($|E_D| > 1$)	decrease revenue	increase revenue

TABLE 2
Effects of Price Changes for Laptop Computers

Price per Laptop (P)	Quantity Demanded (per Month) (Q)	Total Monthly Revenue of Sellers ($P \times Q$)
$1,000	600,000	$600 million
$1,500	500,000	$750 million
$3,000	200,000	$600 million
$3,500	100,000	$350 million

$$\% \text{ Change in } TR = 10\% + (\text{something less negative than } -10\%) > 0.$$

The percentage change in total revenue is greater than zero, so total revenue rises. Finally, if demand is *elastic*, so that Q falls by more than 10 percent, TR will fall:

$$\% \text{ Change in } TR = 10\% + (\text{something more negative than } -10\%) < 0.$$

Of course, the results we just obtained for a price increase of 10 percent would hold for any price change—increase or decrease. Our conclusions about elasticity and total revenue are presented in Table 1. They can be summarized as follows:

> *Where demand is inelastic, total revenue moves in the same direction as price. Where demand is elastic, total revenue moves in the opposite direction from price. Finally, where demand is unitary elastic, total revenue remains the same as price changes.*

Let's check the statements in Table 1, using our hypothetical demand curve for laptop computers. The first two columns of Table 2 present familiar price and quantity pairs for laptops, taken from Figure 3. The third column lists total revenue of sellers.

Notice what happens to total revenue as we move along the demand curve. Demand for laptops, you recall, was inelastic ($E_D = -0.46$) when price rose from $1,000 to $1,500. According to the rules in Table 1, we expect a price rise to *increase* total revenue, and that is exactly what happens: The $500 rise in price causes total revenue to increase from $600 million to $750 million. When price rose from $3,000 to $3,500, however, demand was elastic ($E_D = -4.33$). Our rules tell us that a rise in price should decrease total revenue. Indeed, the $500 price hike causes total revenue to fall from $600 million to $350 million.

There is an easy way to see how a change in price changes the total revenue of firms (or the total spending of buyers), using a graph of the demand curve. Look at

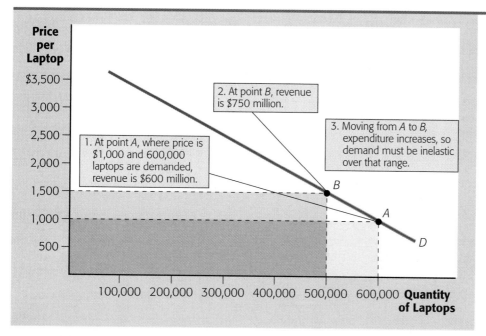

FIGURE 6
Elasticity and Total Revenue
Any point along a demand curve defines a rectangle whose area indicates total revenue from the good.

Figure 6. At point *A*, price is $1,000 per laptop and quantity demanded is 600,000 laptops. Total revenue is price × quantity = $1,000 × 600,000 = $600 million. But this is exactly equal to the *area* of the wider rectangle, which has a width of 600,000 and a height of $1,000. Thus, the area of this rectangle shows total revenue from the good when price is $1,000. More generally,

> *at any point on a demand curve, sellers' total revenue (buyers' total expenditure) is the area of a rectangle with width equal to quantity demanded and height equal to price.*

Now suppose that price rises from $1,000 to $1,500, so we move along the demand curve to point *B*, where quantity demanded drops to 500,000. Here, total revenue is $1,500 × 500,000 = $750 million, given by the area of the taller rectangle, with width equal to 500,000 and height equal to $1,500. You can see that the area of the total revenue rectangle drawn for price = $1,500 is larger than the area of the total revenue rectangle for price = $1,000. This confirms what we know already from Table 2: The rise in price from $1,000 to $1,500 causes total revenue to increase because demand is inelastic for that price change.

Determinants of Elasticity

Table 3 lists the price elasticity of demand for several goods and services. Keep in mind that these elasticities are calculated for a specific range of prices that have been observed in the past. If a large price change moved us out of the range of past observations, the elasticity might be very different. For example, although the elasticity of demand for gasoline is −0.20 when the price varies in a range from $1.00 to $2.00

	Specific Brands		Narrow Categories		Broad Categories	
TABLE 3	Tide Detergent	−2.79	Transatlantic Air Travel	−1.30	Recreation	−1.09
Some Short-Run Price Elasticities of Demand			Tourism in Thailand	−1.20		
	Pepsi	−2.08	Ground Beef	−1.02	Clothing	−0.89
	Coke	−1.71	Pork	−0.78	Food	−0.67
			Milk	−0.54	Imports	−0.58
			Cigarettes	−0.45	Transportation	−0.56
			Electricity	−0.40 to −0.50		
			Beer	−0.26		
			Eggs	−0.26		
			Gasoline	−0.20		
			Oil	−0.15		

Sources: Michael G. Vogt and Chutima Wittayakorn, "Determinants of the Demand for Thailand's Exports of Tourism," *Applied Economics*, Vol. 30, Issue 6, pp. 711–715. Sachin Gupta et al., "Do Household Scanner Data Provide Representative Inferences from Brand Choices? A Comparison with Store Data," *Journal of Marketing Research*, Fall 1996, pp. 383ff. F. Gasmi, J. J. Laffont, and Q. Vuong, "Econometric Analysis of Collusive Behavior in a Soft-Drink Market," *Journal of Economics and Management Strategy*, Summer 1992, pp. 277–311. Richard Blundell, Panos Pashardes, and Guglielmo Weber, "What Do We Learn about Consumer Demand Patterns from Micro Data?" *American Economic Review*, June 1993, pp. 570–597. Michael T. Maloney and Robert E. McCormick, "Setting the Record Straight: The Consumer Wins the Competition," *Citizens for a Sound Economy Foundation*, Issue Analysis No. 46, January 30, 1997. J. L. Sweeney, "The Response of Energy Demand to Higher Prices: What Have We Learned?" *American Economic Review*, May 1984, pp. 31–37. F. Chaloupka, "Rational Addictive Behavior and Cigarette Smoking," *Journal of Political Economy*, August 1991, pp. 722–742; J. M. Cigliano, "Price and Income Elasticities for Airline Travel," *Business Economics*, September 1980, pp. 17–21. M. D. Chinn, "Beware of Econometricians Bearing Estimates," *Journal of Policy Analysis and Management*, Fall 1991, pp. 546–557. M. R. Baye, D. W. Jansen, and Jae-Woo Lee, "Advertising Effects in Complete Demand Systems," *Applied Economics*, October 1992, pp.1087–1096. Dale M. Heien, "The Structure of Food Demand: Interrelatedness and Duality," *American Journal of Agricultural Economics*, May 1982, pp. 213–221. Gary W. Brester and Michael K. Wohlgenant, "Estimating Interrelated Demands for Meats Using New Measures for Ground and Table Cut Beef," *American Journal of Agricultural Economics*, November 1991, pp. 1182–1194. David R. Henderson, "Do We Need to Go to War for Oil?" *Cato Foreign Policy Briefing*, No. 4, October 24, 1990.

per gallon, the elasticity might be very different for price changes in a range from $10.00 to $15.00 per gallon, which have never been observed in the United States.

Notice that all of the price elasticities of demand are negative: Each of these goods obeys the law of demand. Even cigarettes—which are highly addictive—have an elasticity less than zero: A rise in price reduces the quantity of cigarettes demanded.

You can also see that the calculated elasticities vary widely. Why is it that demands for Tide detergent, Pepsi, and Coke are so elastic, while those for eggs and gasoline are so inelastic? More generally, what determines whether the demand for a good will be elastic or inelastic?

Availability of Substitutes. When the price of a good rises, we look for substitutes. If close substitutes are easy to find, we can cut back on our purchases of the good in question, and demand is more elastic. If close substitutes are difficult to find, we can't cut back as much, and so demand is less elastic.

This logic helps explain some of the differences in elasticity values found in Table 3. If the price of ground beef rises, it's not too difficult to substitute steak, pork, or chicken. (Remember: The prices of these substitutes are assumed to remain constant as the price of ground beef rises.) And, as you can see in the table, the elasticity for ground beef is very close to unitary. However, the available substitutes for *gasoline* are more distant: car pooling, mass transit, walking. . . . This is an important reason why the demand for gasoline is less elastic than the demand for ground beef.

Narrowness of Market. Remember that, in analyzing any problem, the first step of our three-step process is to characterize the market we are dealing with. You may also remember that we can choose to define a market narrowly or broadly, depending on the question we want to analyze. This choice has an important influence on elasticity of demand in the market:

> *The more narrowly we define a good, the easier it is to find substitutes, and the more elastic is the demand for the good. The more broadly we define a good, the harder it is to find substitutes and the less elastic is the demand for the good.*

The key is that different things are assumed constant when we use a narrow definition compared with a broader definition. Once we define the good in question, our elasticity calculations always assume that all "other" prices do not change. "Other" means any price *outside* the market we've defined. Pepsi has a large price elasticity because when the price of this particular soft drink rises, we consider the effect on quantity demanded, assuming that the prices of *all other soft drinks*, including Coke, are not changing. We therefore expect a strong quantity response as consumers switch to these other soft drinks that are now *relatively* cheaper. But suppose we had defined our good more broadly as *carbonated soft drinks*. Now, any price increase would apply to Pepsi, Coke, and *all* soft drinks at the same time. While it is still possible to substitute other drinks in place of soft drinks, it is not as easy as substituting one soft drink for another. So we expect the more aggregated item, soft drinks, to have a much lower price elasticity of demand. (Now look at the elasticity entry for Tide detergent. Suppose the good had instead been defined as "laundry detergent." Would you expect a larger or smaller elasticity value?)

Table 3 also shows that when markets are defined *very* broadly—food rather than ground beef, or transportation rather than transatlantic travel—elasticities of demand tend to be lower. There are very few substitutes for food in general. Although many people can eat less, it is not an easy adjustment to make. The same is true for other broad categories, such as recreation, transportation, and clothing.

Necessities versus Luxuries. The ability to find substitutes for goods also depends on our tastes. Goods that we think of as *necessities*—for example, medical care, food, and housing—are difficult to find substitutes for. Goods that we think of as *luxuries*—like a trip to Europe or recreation—can be substituted for more easily. We expect necessities to be less price elastic than luxuries, and Table 3 confirms this. The demand for food is less elastic than the demand for recreation, and the demand for milk is less elastic than the demand for transatlantic travel.

> *In general, the more "necessary" we regard an item, the harder it is to find substitutes, and the less elastic is demand for the good.*

	Short Run (a few months or less)	Long Run (a year or more)
TABLE 4 **Adjustments After a Rise in the Price of Gasoline**	Use public transit more often Arrange a car pool Get a tune-up Drive more slowly on the highway Eliminate unnecessary trips (use mail order instead of driving to stores; locate goods by phone instead of driving around; shop for food less often and buy more each time) If there are two cars, use the more fuel-efficient one	Buy a more fuel-efficient car Move closer to your job Switch to a job closer to home Move to a city where less driving is required

But here, too, how broadly or narrowly we define the good makes an important difference. Many goods we would consider necessities when broadly defined (e.g., medical care) become easy-to-substitute-for luxuries when more narrowly defined (e.g., visits to Dr. Hacker). When the price of *all medical care* rises, we expect a relatively small decrease in quantity demanded. But if the price of just *Dr. Hacker's medical care* rises, the quantity response should be much larger.

Time Horizon. The ease with which we can substitute one good for another will usually depend heavily on the *time horizon* of our analysis. The elasticities in Table 3 are all **short-run elasticities**—in which the quantity response is measured just a short time—say, a few months—after a price change. A **long-run elasticity** measures the quantity response after a year or more has elapsed. In study after study, we find that demand is more elastic in the long-run than in the short-run.

Short-run elasticity An elasticity measured just a short time after a price change.

Long-run elasticity An elasticity measured a year or more after a price change.

Why? Because it is easier for consumers to find substitutes when they have more time to do so. For example, while the *short-run* elasticity for gasoline is relatively low—about −0.2—most studies show a *long-run* elasticity at least three times as great. This is because some of the adjustments needed to substitute for gasoline—like buying a more fuel-efficient car—take some time. Table 4 lists some of the ways households would adjust to a significant rise in the price of gasoline over the short run and the long run. Notice that the options available in the long run have a greater potential impact on consumers' demand for gasoline than the options available in the short run.

Other goods show a similar pattern of greater elasticity in the long run than the short run. Estimates of long-run elasticities for cigarettes and electricity (−0.80 and −0.97, respectively) are each about twice the size of their short-run counterparts in Table 3.

> *It is usually easier to find substitutes for an item in the long run than in the short run. Therefore, demand tends to be more elastic in the long run than in the short run.*

Importance in the Buyer's Budget. When a good takes up a large part of your budget, a price change has a large impact on how much money you have left to spend on other goods. For example, most people spend a large fraction of their budget on housing. If the price of housing rises by, say, 10 percent, the impact on people's budgets would be substantial. As a result, people would try hard to economize on housing (move to a smaller apartment, or live with a roommate). We thus expect housing to have a large elasticity of demand.

In general,

> *the more of their total budgets that households spend on an item, the more elastic is demand for that item.*

For example, a trip to Europe would take a big bite out of most people's budgets. A rise in price will therefore make consumers think very carefully about substitutes—traveling to Canada or Mexico, perhaps. This is partly why the demand for transatlantic air travel is so elastic.

For the opposite extreme, consider the case of ordinary table salt. A family with an income of $50,000 per year will typically spend less than 0.005 percent of it on salt. The price of salt could double—even triple or quadruple or quintuple—and still have virtually no impact on that family's ability to afford other goods. Economically, there is little to be gained by cutting back on salt consumption when its price rises, so we expect it to be relatively price *inelastic*.[2]

Using Price Elasticity of Demand

Knowing the price elasticity of demand for a good and understanding the link between elasticity and total revenue or total expenditure is helpful in many different contexts. For example, producers of goods and services—doctors, bakers, theater owners, manufacturers, and others—can use price elasticity of demand to predict how a price change will affect their total sales revenue. And government policy makers can and do use demand elasticities to price many government services, to make tax policy, and to design programs to help the needy. The concept of demand elasticity is even at the center of the debate over the war on drugs in the United States and many other countries, as the next section shows.

The War on Drugs. Every year, the U.S. government spends about $20 billion intervening in the market for illegal drugs like cocaine, heroin, and marijuana. Most of this money is spent on efforts to restrict the *supply* of drugs. But many economists argue that society would be better off if antidrug efforts were shifted from the supply side to the demand side of the market. Why? The answer hinges on the price elasticity of demand for illegal drugs.

Look at Figure 7(a), which shows the market for heroin if there were no government intervention. The equilibrium would be at point A, with price P_1 and quantity Q_1. Total revenue of sellers—and total spending by buyers—would be the area of the shaded rectangle, $P_1 \times Q_1$.

Panel (b) of the figure shows the impact of a policy to restrict supply through any one of several methods, including vigilant customs inspections, arrest and stiff penalties for drug dealers, or diplomatic efforts to reduce drug traffic from

---

[2] Earlier, we argued that the demand for one brand of table salt should be perfectly *elastic*. Now, we're suggesting that the demand for salt should be *inelastic*. Is this a contradiction? Not at all. Can you explain why? (*Hint:* Are we defining our market the same way in both statements?)

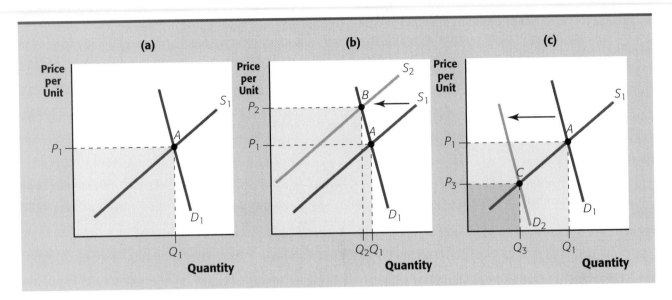

FIGURE 7
The War on Drugs

Panel (a) shows the market for heroin in the absence of government intervention. Total expenditures—and total receipts of drug dealers—are given by the area of the shaded rectangle. Panel (b) shows the effect of a government effort to restrict supply: Price rises, but total expenditure increases. Panel (c) shows a policy of reducing demand: Price falls, and so does total expenditure.

producing countries like Colombia, North Korea, and Thailand. The decrease in supply is represented by a leftward shift of the supply curve, establishing a new equilibrium at price P_2 and quantity Q_2. As you can see, supply restrictions, if they successfully reduce the equilibrium quantity of heroin, will also raise its equilibrium price.

But now let's consider the impact of this policy on the users' total expenditure on drugs. The demand for addictive drugs such as heroin and cocaine is price *inelastic*. As you've learned, when demand is inelastic, a rise in price will *increase* total expenditure. This means that a policy of restricting the supply of illegal drugs, if successful, will also increase the total expenditure of drug users on their habit. In panel (b), total expenditure rises from the area of the shorter rectangle to the area of the taller one.

The change in total expenditure has serious consequences for our society. Many drug users support their habit through crime. If the total expenditure needed to support a drug habit rises, they may commit more crimes—and more serious ones. And don't forget that the total expenditure of drug users is also the total *revenue* of the illegal drug industry. The large revenues—and the associated larger profits to be made—attract organized as well as unorganized crime and lead to frequent and very violent turf wars.

The same logic, based on the inelastic demand for illegal drugs, has led many economists to advocate a shift of emphasis from decreasing supply to decreasing demand. Policies that might decrease the demand for illegal drugs and shift the demand curve leftward include stiffer penalties on drug *users*, heavier advertising against drug use, and greater availability of treatment centers for addicts. In addition, more of the effort against drug sellers could be directed at retailers rather than those higher up the chain of supply. It is the retailers who promote drugs to future users and thus increase demand.

Panel (c) illustrates the impact these policies, if successful, would have on the market for heroin. As the demand curve shifts leftward, price *falls* from P_1 to P_3,

The war on drugs has focused on decreasing supply.

and quantity demanded falls from Q_1 to Q_3. Now, we cannot say whether the drop in quantity will be greater under a demand shift than a supply shift (it depends on the relative sizes of the shifts). But we *can* be sure that a demand-focused policy will have a very different impact on equilibrium price, moving it down instead of up. Moreover, the demand shift will decrease total expenditure on drugs—to the *inner* shaded rectangle—since both price and quantity decrease. This can contribute to a lower crime rate by drug users and make the drug industry less attractive to potential dealers and producers.

Mass Transit. Earlier in this section, you were asked to imagine that you were mayor of a large city considering an increase in mass transit fares. Your assistant advised you to do it, since you would collect more revenue on each commuter trip. But you were worried that raising fares might cause so many more people to stop using mass transit that your revenue would actually decline. Can elasticity help here?

Very much so. Studies show that the long-run demand for mass transit is inelastic, which tells us that raising the fare would *increase* revenue. More specifically, the long-run elasticity of demand in large cities (those with more than 1 million inhabitants) averages around −0.36. In words: A 1 percent increase in fares would decrease ridership by about a third of a percent.

Let's use this elasticity figure to analyze what would happen if New York City raised the price of its subway and bus rides from $2.00 to $2.50. Since this would be an increase of about 22 percent, we could expect ridership to change by 0.22 × −0.36 = −.079, or a decrease of about 8 percent. In the early 2000s, commuters took about 2 billion trips per year on New York buses and subways, for a total revenue of 2 billion × $2.00 = $4 billion. The price hike would decrease the total number of trips by 8 percent to about 1.85 billion, but also raise the revenue from each trip to $2.50. Thus, total revenue would be about 1.85 billion × $2.50 = $4.63 billion. Comparing $4 billion with $4.63 billion, we see that the fare hike would increase total revenue by more than half a billion dollars—a substantial increase.

Why, then, doesn't New York raise the mass transit fare to $2.50? In fact, why stop at $2.50? If the demand remains inelastic, why not continue to raise fares to $3.00, or $4.00, or even higher? In fact, why don't cities across the country raise *their* fares above present levels as well?

The answer is that generating revenue is only *one* goal that city governments consider in pricing mass transit. In addition to obtaining revenue, city officials want to provide an affordable means of transportation to low-income households, to manage traffic congestion on city streets, and to limit pollution of city air. To accomplish these other goals requires a large ridership. A fare increase, even if it would raise total revenue, would decrease total ridership and require the city to sacrifice these other goals. This is what keeps mass transit fares lower than the revenue-maximizing fare.

An Oil Crisis. For the past five decades, the Middle East has been a geopolitical hot spot. And the stakes for the rest of the world are high because the region produces about one-fifth of the world's oil supply. That is why the U.S. military is constantly asking "what if" questions and making contingency war plans to respond to hypothetical crisis situations.

Elsewhere in government, *economic* officials ask their own "what if" questions. One central question is this: If an event in the Middle East were to disrupt oil supplies, what would happen to the price of oil on world markets? Not surprisingly, elasticity plays a crucial role in answering this question.

As you can see in Table 3, the short-run elasticity of demand for oil is about -0.15. Since a political or military crisis is usually a short-run phenomenon, the short-run elasticity is what we are interested in. But for this problem, we need to use elasticity in a new way. Remember that elasticity tells us the percentage decrease in quantity demanded for a 1-percent increase in price. But suppose we flip the elasticity fraction upside down, to get

$$\frac{1}{E_D} = \frac{\% \text{ Change in Price}}{\% \text{ Change in Quantity Demanded}}.$$

This number—the inverse of elasticity—tells us the percentage rise in price that would bring about each 1-percent decrease in quantity demanded. For oil, this number is $1/-0.15 = -6.67$. What does this number mean? It tells us that to bring about each 1-percent decrease in world oil demand, oil prices would have to rise by 6.67 percent.

Now we can make reasonable forecasts about the impact of various events on oil prices. Imagine, for example, an event that temporarily removed half of the Middle East's oil from world markets. And let's assume a worst-case scenario: No other nation increases its production during the time frame being considered. What would happen to world oil prices?

Since the Middle East produces about 20 percent of the world's oil, a reduction by half would decrease world oil supplies by 10 percent. It would then require a price increase of $10 \times 6.67 = 66.7$ percent to restore equilibrium to the market. If oil were initially selling at $20 per barrel, we could forecast the price to rise by $20 \times 0.667 = 13.34 per barrel, for a final price of $33.34.

Why is it so important to forecast the price of oil that might result from a crisis? If you were a heavy industrial user of oil, you would know the answer. But the forecast is also of immense value to government economists, who would use it to help answer *other* questions. These would include macroeconomic questions, such as, How would a $13.34 per barrel rise in the price of oil affect the U.S. inflation rate? and microeconomic questions, such as, How would a $13.34 rise in the price of oil affect the number of flights offered by U.S. airlines, and the prices they'd charge for them?

OTHER ELASTICITIES

The concept of *elasticity* is a very general one. It can be used to measure the sensitivity of virtually *any* variable to any other variable. All types of elasticity measures, however, share one thing in common: They tell us the change in one variable caused by a 1-percent change in the other. But each different measure tells us something different and important about behavior in markets. Let's look at three additional elasticity measures, and what each of them tells us.

Income Elasticity of Demand

You learned in Chapter 3 that household income is one of the variables that influences demand. The *income elasticity of demand* tells us how *sensitive* quantity demanded is to changes in buyers' incomes. Economists often use the symbol "Y" to represent income (since "I" is reserved for investment in macroeconomics), so we'll use E_Y in the following definition:

> **The *income elasticity of demand* E_Y is the percentage change in quantity demanded divided by the percentage change in income, with all other influences on demand—including the price of the good—remaining constant.**
>
> $$E_Y = \frac{\% \text{ Change in Quantity Demanded}}{\% \text{ Change in Income}}$$

Income elasticity of demand The percentage change in quantity demanded caused by a 1-percent change in income.

More simply, we can interpret this number as *the percentage increase in quantity demanded for each 1-percent rise in income.* For example, if the income elasticity of demand for a certain good is 1.4, then a 1-percent rise in income will increase demand for the good by 1.4 percent, a 2-percent rise in income will increase demand by 2.8 percent, and so on.

Income elasticities and price elasticities of demand differ in several respects. First, a price elasticity of demand measures the effect of changes in the *price* of the good and assumes that other influences on demand, including income, remain unchanged. An income elasticity does just the reverse: It measures the effect on demand we would observe if income changed and all other influences on demand—including the price of the good—remained the same. In other words, instead of letting price vary and holding income constant, now we are letting income vary and holding price constant.

This leads to another difference between price and income elasticities of demand: A price elasticity measures the sensitivity of demand to price as we *move along the demand curve* from one point to another. An income elasticity, by contrast, tells us the relative *shift* in the demand curve—the increase in quantity demanded *at a given price.*

Finally, while a price elasticity is virtually always negative, an income elasticity can be positive or negative. This is because an increase in income will increase the demand for normal goods (a positive income elasticity) and decrease the demand for inferior goods (a negative income elasticity). If you look at the income elasticities in Table 5, you will see examples of both types of goods.

Notice that when we define goods by broad categories—food, housing, clothing, entertainment, energy, transportation—income elasticity is always positive because an increase in income will always increase demand in each of these categories, even if it decreases spending on particular goods *within* the category. For example, a rise in income may enable you to afford better-quality clothing—so you will buy more high-quality items and fewer low-quality items—but you almost certainly will end up buying *more clothing* in general. But even when we narrow our definition to specific goods and services—books, CDs, chicken, fresh vegetables, automobiles, and trips to Europe—income elasticities are usually positive. In Table 5, the first eight goods have positive income elasticities, as do all of the broad categories.

But there are some inferior goods in the list. While food is normal—as are steak, fresh fruit, and sushi—potatoes and ground beef are inferior. As income rises, many households will shift from these inferior goods to more expensive items. (Why do some studies show that tooth extraction is an inferior good? *Hint:* What are the substitutes for tooth extraction? How much do they cost?)

TABLE 5
Some Income Elasticities

Good or Service	Income Elasticity	Good or Service	Income Elasticity
Narrow Categories		*Broad Categories*	
Fresh Fruit	1.99	Imports	2.73
Computers	1.71		
Transatlantic Air Travel	1.40	Transportation	1.79
College Education	0.55		
Cigarettes	0.50	Recreation	1.07
Chicken	0.42	Clothing	1.02
Pork	0.34	Food	0.60 to 0.85
Fresh Vegetables	0.26		
Tooth Extraction	−0.13 to 0.47		
Ground Beef	−0.20		
Bread	−0.42		
Potatoes	−0.81		

Sources: Erik Brynjolfsson, "Some Estimates of the Contribution of Information Technology to Consumer Welfare," MIT Sloan School, Working Paper #161, Revised, January 1994. Trisha Bezmen and Craig A. Depken, II, "School Characteristics and the Demand for College," *Economics of Education Review*, Vol. 17, No. 2, 1998. F. Chaloupka, "Rational Addictive Behavior and Cigarette Smoking," *Journal of Political Economy*, August 1991, pp. 722–742. J. M. Cigliano, "Price and Income Elasticities for Airline Travel," *Business Economics*, September 1980, pp. 17–21. M. D. Chinn, "Beware of Econometricians Bearing Estimates," *Journal of Policy Analysis and Management*, Fall 1991, pp. 546–557. Willard G. Manning, Jr., and Charles E. Phelps, "The Demand for Dental Care," *Bell Journal of Economics*, Autumn 1979. Dale M. Heien, "The Structure of Food Demand: Interrelatedness and Duality," *American Journal of Agricultural Economics*, May 1982, pp. 213–221. M. R. Baye, D. W. Jansen, and Jae-Woo Lee, "Advertising Effects in Complete Demand Systems," *Applied Economics*, October 1992, pp.1087–1096. Gary W. Brester and Michael K. Wohlgenant, "Estimating Interrelated Demands for Meats Using New Measures for Ground and Table Cut Beef," *American Journal of Agricultural Economics*, November 1991, pp. 1182–1194.

Economic necessity A good with an income elasticity of demand between 0 and 1.

Normal goods can be further divided into two categories. An **economic necessity** has an income elasticity between zero and one. If you look again at the formula for income elasticity (% change in quantity demanded /% change in income) you can see that when $0 < E_Y < 1$, we must have % change in quantity demanded < % change in income. For an economic necessity, a given percentage increase in income causes a *smaller* percentage increase in quantity demanded. The broad category of food is certainly an economic necessity: A 10-percent rise in income will cause the quantity of food demanded to rise, but by less than 10 percent. In fact, using the lower estimate in Table 5, $(E_Y = 0.60)$, a 10-percent rise in income would increase the demand for food by only 6 percent.

Economic luxury A good with an income elasticity of demand greater than 1.

Goods whose income elasticity is greater than 1.0 are called **economic luxuries**. From the definition of income elasticity, if $E_Y > 1$, we must have % change in quantity demanded > % change in income. Thus, when income rises, the quantity demanded of these items will increase by a greater percentage than the rise in income. For example, transportation is an economic luxury: Using the income elasticity in Table 5 $(E_Y = 1.79)$, we see that a 10-percent rise in income will increase quantity of transportation demanded by about 18 percent.

An interesting implication follows from these definitions: As income rises, the proportion of income spent on economic necessities will fall, while the proportion of income spent on economic luxuries will rise. To see this more clearly, consider

Income	Spending on Food	Percent of Income Spent on Food	Spending on Transportation	Percent of Income Spent on Transportation
$10,000	$ 6,000	60%	$ 1,000	10%
$20,000	$ 9,600	48%	$ 2,800	14%
$40,000	$15,360	38%	$ 7,840	20%
$80,000	$24,576	30%	$21,952	27%

TABLE 6

Income and Spending on Economic Necessities and Economic Luxuries

Table 6, which shows what might happen to a particular family's spending on two goods—food and transportation—if its income were to double again and again. We'll use the income-elasticity estimates from Table 5: $E_Y = 0.60$ for food, and $E_Y = 1.8$ for transportation.

In the table, food is an economic necessity ($E_Y < 1$), so that each time income doubles, spending on food increases but by less than 100 percent. Transportation, by contrast, is an economic luxury ($E_Y > 1$), so that each time income doubles, spending on transportation more than doubles. Notice how the percentage of income spent on food continues to fall, while that spent on transportation continues to rise.

To some extent, our definitions of economic necessities and economic luxuries correspond to the more common notions of necessity and luxury. In common speech, people use the word *necessity* to mean the most basic requirements of living. Food, medical care, and housing all correspond to this common notion, and each has an income elasticity that is less than 1.0. A luxury is considered something desirable but not really necessary. Most of us would regard restaurant meals, ski trips, and certainly yachts and caviar as luxuries, and studies show that each of these items has an income elasticity greater than 1.0.

But it is important to remember that economic necessities and luxuries are categorized by actual consumer behavior and *not* by our judgment of a good's importance to human survival. People can certainly survive without cigarettes. But since cigarettes have an income elasticity between 0 and 1, they are categorized as an economic necessity. Similarly, some of us might think of a computer as a necessity in our lives, and yet—because studies show that the income elasticity of spending on computers is greater than 1.0—we categorize it as an economic luxury.

Cross-Price Elasticity of Demand

A cross-price elasticity relates the change in quantity demanded for one good to a price change in another. More formally, we define the **cross-price elasticity of demand** between good X and good Z as:

$$E_{x,z} = \frac{\%\text{ Change in Quantity of X Demanded}}{\%\text{ Change in Price of Z}}$$

In words,

a cross-price elasticity of demand tells us the percentage change in quantity demanded of a good for each 1-percent increase in the price of some other good, while all other influences on demand remain unchanged.

Cross-price elasticity of demand The percentage change in the quantity demanded of one good caused by a 1-percent change in the price of another good.

TABLE 7
Some Cross-Price Elasticities

Products	Cross-Price Elasticity
Margarine with price of butter	1.53
Pepsi with price of Coke	0.80
Coke with price of Pepsi	0.61
Ground beef with price of beef table cuts	0.41
Ground beef with price of poultry	0.24
Electricity with price of natural gas	0.20
Theater with price of all other lively arts	0.12
Entertainment with price of food	−0.72

Sources: F. Gasmi, J. J. Laffont, and Q. Vuong, "Econometric Analysis of Collusive Behavior in a Soft-Drink Market," *Journal of Economics and Management Strategy,* Summer 1992, pp. 277–311. Dale M. Heien, "The Structure of Food Demand: Interrelatedness and Duality," *American Journal of Agricultural Economics,* May 1982, pp. 213–221. Gary W. Brester and Michael K. Wohlgenant, "Estimating Interrelated Demands for Meats Using New Measures for Ground and Table Cut Beef," *American Journal of Agricultural Economics,* November 1991, pp. 1182–1194. E. T. Fuji et al., "An Almost Ideal Demand System for Visitor Expenditures," *Journal of Transport Economics and Policy,* May 1985. C. Hsiao and D. Mountain, "Estimating the Short-Run Income Elasticity of Demand for Electricity by Using Cross-Sectional Categorized Data," *Journal of the American Statistical Association,* June 1985, pp. 259–265.

For example, look at the cross-price elasticities reported in Table 7. The cross-price elasticity of Pepsi with the price of Coke is 0.8. This means that when the price of Coke rises by 10 percent, the quantity of Pepsi demanded increases by 8 percent, *all other influences on demand remaining unchanged.* Among the other influences that are assumed to remain unchanged are the price of the good itself (Pepsi), the prices of all related goods *except* Coke, and household income in the market.

As you can see in the table, a cross-price elasticity can be positive or negative, and the sign gives us valuable information about the relationship between the two goods. If $E_{x,z} < 0$, an increase in the price of good Z causes a *decrease* in quantity demanded for good X. As we know from Chapter 3, this means that goods X and Z are complements. For example, in Table 7, the cross-price elasticity between entertainment and food is negative: A 1-percent rise in the price of food causes a 0.7-percent decrease in the quantity of entertainment demanded. Entertainment and food are complements. This is not surprising: Many forms of entertainment—throwing a party, having a picnic in a state park, or even seeing a movie—are accompanied by spending on food. Similarly, we'd expect the cross-price elasticities between bread and butter, computers and Internet service, or sunblock lotion and trashy novels to be negative: A rise in the price of one item in the pair should decrease the quantity demanded of the other.

If $E_{x,z} > 0$, an increase in the price of good Z causes an increase in quantity demanded for good X. In this case, goods X and Z are *substitutes*. Most of the cross-price elasticities in Table 7 are positive, indicating that most of the pairs of goods are substitutes rather than complements. For example, the table tells us that margarine and butter are substitutes as are ground beef and poultry.

While the *sign* of the cross-price elasticity helps us distinguish substitutes and complements among related goods, its *size* tells us how *closely* the two goods are related. A large absolute value for $E_{x,z}$ suggests that the two goods are *close* substitutes or complements, while a small absolute value suggests a weaker relationship.

Butter and margarine seem to be very close substitutes—even closer than Pepsi and Coke. A 10 percent rise in the price of butter will increase the quantity of margarine demanded by about 15 percent. This makes sense, since either good can be substituted for the other in most recipes. While electricity and natural gas are substitutes, they are more distant substitutes than butter and margarine. This, too, makes sense: Natural gas and electricity are exchangeable only in certain uses, and even then, only when the proper equipment is available.

Price Elasticity of Supply

So far, we've talked only about elasticity as a measure of the responsiveness of quantity demanded to different variables. But we can apply the same principles to study the response of quantity supplied. The most important supply elasticity is the price elasticity of supply, which measures the sensitivity of market quantity supplied to the market price:

> The **price elasticity of supply** is the percentage change in the quantity of a good supplied that is caused by a 1-percent change in the price of the good, with all other influences on supply held constant.
>
> $$E_S = \frac{\% \text{ Change in Quantity Supplied}}{\% \text{ Change in Price}}$$

Price elasticity of supply The percentage change in quantity supplied of a good or service caused by a 1-percent change in its price.

The price elasticity of supply measures the sensitivity of quantity supplied to price changes as we move *along* the supply curve. The law of supply tells us that a rise in price—with everything else constant—will increase quantity supplied. This means that the numerator and denominator of E_S will have the same sign, so price elasticity of supply will be a *positive* number. A large value for the price elasticity of supply means that quantity supplied is very sensitive to price changes. For example, an elasticity value of 20 would imply that if price increased by 1 percent, quantity supplied would rise by 20 percent. Notice that, since this elasticity will virtually always be positive, there is no need for absolute-value signs.

When do we expect supply to be price elastic ($E_S > 1$), and when do we expect it to be price inelastic ($E_S < 1$)? A major determinant is the ease with which suppliers can find profitable activities that are *alternatives* to producing the good in question. In general, supply will tend to be more elastic when suppliers can switch to producing alternate goods more easily. For example, an easy alternative to selling whole oranges is to juice them and sell orange juice. As a result, if the price of whole oranges drops but the price of orange juice remains the same, we would expect a relatively large decrease in the quantity of whole oranges supplied. Thus, the supply of whole oranges should be rather elastic. But suppose there were a law preventing orange growers from juicing their oranges. Then we have closed off one of the most important alternatives for orange growers. A price drop would cause a much smaller quantity response, and supply would be more price inelastic as a result.

When can we expect suppliers to have easy alternatives? First, the nature of the good itself will be important. All else equal, the supply of envelopes should be more elastic than the supply of microprocessor chips. This is because envelope producers can more easily modify their production lines to produce alternative paper products. Microprocessor suppliers, however, would be hard-pressed to produce anything other than computer chips.

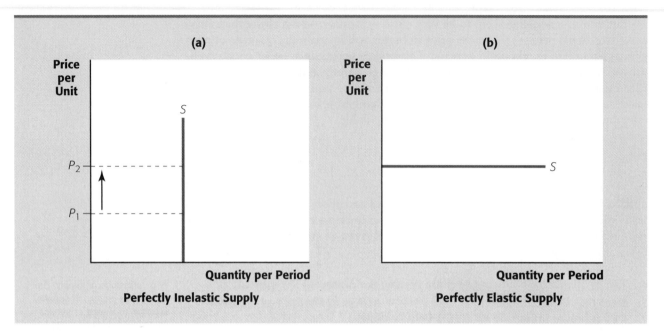

(a)

Price per Unit

P_2

P_1

S

Quantity per Period

Perfectly Inelastic Supply

(b)

Price per Unit

S

Quantity per Period

Perfectly Elastic Supply

FIGURE 8
Extreme Cases of Supply

The vertical supply curve of panel (a) represents the case of perfectly inelastic supply. At every price, the same quantity is supplied. The horizontal curve in panel (b) represents perfectly elastic supply. A small change in price would lead to an extremely large change in quantity supplied.

The narrowness of the market definition matters too—especially *geographic* narrowness. For example, in the market for oranges, the market for oranges in Illinois should be more supply-elastic than the market for oranges in the United States. In the former case, as the price of oranges decreased in Illinois, we'd be holding constant the price of oranges in *all other states*. This gives suppliers an easy alternative: They could sell their oranges in other states! Similarly, the supply of oranges to Chicago would be even more elastic than the supply of oranges to Illinois.

Finally, once again, the *time horizon* is important. The longer we wait after a price change, the greater the supply response to a price change. As we will see when we discuss the theory of the firm, there may be *some* response to a price change almost immediately, as firms simply speed up or slow down production with existing production techniques. But further responses might come about only as firms have time to change their plant and equipment.

There are two extreme cases of supply elasticity. The *perfectly inelastic* supply curve is a vertical line, as in panel (a) of Figure 8. This kind of supply behavior is not as rare as it might seem. In many markets *over very short periods of time,* we can expect a completely or almost completely inelastic supply curve. For example, over a time horizon up to a few months, the supply of new homes should be almost perfectly inelastic. The number of new homes available for sale *now* is determined by construction begun many months ago. If the price of new homes rises, there will not—at least for several months—be much increase in the number of new homes offered for sale. Similarly, the supply of fresh-caught tuna or of tickets to a Broadway play would be almost completely inelastic over a short period of time. Of course, in each case, supply will become more elastic as we lengthen the time horizon. (Can you identify what sorts of adjustments in each case might be possible in the long run but impossible in the short run?)

The other extreme is the *perfectly elastic* supply curve—a horizontal line, as shown in panel (b) of Figure 8. Here, even the tiniest change in price brings about a virtually infinite response in quantity supplied. Think of the market for shares of IBM stock at the Pacific Stock Exchange, a small stock market located in San Francisco. If the price of IBM shares in that market rises even the tiniest bit above the price in other markets, virtually *all* sellers of IBM stock will offer their shares in San Francisco. For all intents and purposes, the supply elasticity to the San Francisco market is infinite.

TAXES AND MARKET EQUILIBRIUM

In the United States and most other countries, governments tax household income, corporate profits, real estate holdings, inheritances, imports, goods and services in general, and specific goods and services. Taxes provide revenue to all levels of government, enabling them to provide public services. But there are other motives for taxes as well. For example, income and inheritance taxes are often viewed as a means to correct inequities in the distribution of income and wealth. Taxes are also levied on particular goods in order to raise their price and discourage their use. And these motives can overlap.

For example, state and local taxes on cigarettes are partly designed to discourage smoking, but many states and cities have become dependent on these taxes as a major source of revenue. Similarly, the gasoline tax originated to fund the building and maintaining of the national highway system. But in recent years, some have wanted to increase this tax to discourage the use of gasoline and thereby lessen U.S. dependence on foreign oil.

This section is our first look at how taxes affect markets, but not our last. In later chapters, we'll return to this topic, using new analytical tools that you'll have acquired along the way.

Example: The Tax on Airline Travel

A tax on a particular good or service is called an **excise tax.** One market affected by a variety of federal and local excise taxes is the market for air travel. Let's suppose you pay an airline a total of $300 for a round-trip ticket, with one stopover each way. Out of that $300, the airline pays $44.50 in taxes to the federal government (to support airport operations, air traffic control, and post-9/11 security costs). In addition, it pays as much as $18 to local governments to support airport projects. Thus, the total would be $62.50 in taxes—and if it's an international flight, total taxes could be triple that amount.

Excise tax A tax on a specific good or service.

In order to examine the impact of these taxes, the first step is to learn a new way of interpreting the market supply curve. Look at the left panel of Figure 9, which shows a supply curve labeled $S_{\text{Before Tax}}$. In our standard way of interpreting this curve, we choose a price along the vertical axis, read over to the supply curve, and then move down to the horizontal axis to find the corresponding quantity supplied. For instance, at a price of $260, 7 million tickets would be supplied.

But there is another, equally valid way to interpret this supply curve: It shows us the *minimum price* per ticket at which the airlines would be willing to sell any

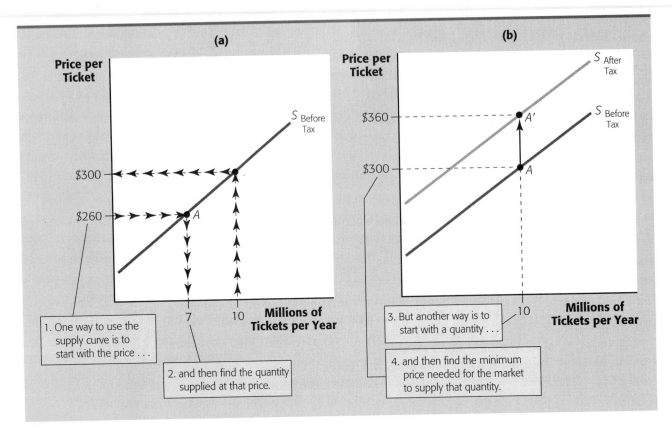

FIGURE 9
The Tax on Airline Travel

number of tickets. Under this interpretation, we choose a quantity—say, 10 million tickets in the figure—and read up to the supply curve and then over to the vertical axis to find the corresponding price per ticket. So, for example, airlines would be willing to supply 10 million tickets only if they are paid at least $300 per ticket. We know this because if the airlines were to receive any amount less than $300, they would supply *fewer* than 10 million tickets.

Now suppose that the government collects a tax of $60 per ticket from the airlines. The old supply curve will no longer represent their selling behavior in this market. Why not? Look at point A. Before the tax, this point told us that the airlines would sell 10 million tickets only if they received at least $300 per ticket. But now, $60 must be turned over to the government, so a price of $300 would leave only $240 for the airlines. This is not enough for the airlines to provide 10 million tickets.

How much *would* be enough? The answer is $360. At that price, they could pay the $60 tax to the government and keep $300 for themselves—just enough to induce them supply 10 million tickets.

The same argument could be applied to *every* quantity along the supply curve. Whatever the minimum price needed per ticket before the tax, it will be $60 *greater* after the tax. In other words, the tax creates a *new supply curve* in this market. The right panel of Figure 9 shows that the new supply curve (labeled $S_{\text{After Tax}}$) lies $60 above the original curve.

The new supply curve tells us the minimum price that the airlines must be *paid* to sell each quantity of tickets after the tax is imposed. This is the airlines' *gross price*—what they collect from travelers. But what is the airlines' *net price*—the amount they actually get to keep? To find that, we must deduct the tax—$60 per ticket—from the gross price. That is, at each quantity, the *original* supply curve, which lies $60 below the new one, tells us the net price—what airlines keep after paying the tax.

> *An excise tax shifts the market supply curve upward by the amount of the tax. For each quantity supplied, the new, higher curve tells us the firm's gross price, and the original, lower curve tells us the net price.*

Now let's see how this tax affects the market. Figure 10 shows the initial equilibrium at point A, with price at $300 and 10 million tickets bought and sold per year. When the tax is imposed, the supply curve shifts upward to $S_{\text{After Tax}}$. The tax moves the equilibrium to point B, where the new supply curve intersects the original demand curve at a price of $340.

How has the tax affected the airlines? With the new equilibrium at point B, their gross price is $340 on the new supply curve. But their net price—which is read off the old supply curve directly below B—is only $280. So the excise tax has reduced the airlines' net price from $300 before the tax to $280 after—a drop of $20.

What about travelers? Since no tax is collected from them directly, the total price they pay is the same as what the airlines charge them—the gross price. But this price has risen from $300 to $340, an increase of $40.

Now let's take a step back and think about what's happened. This tax is legally imposed on, and collected from, the airlines. They are the ones who actually send the check to the government. But who *really pays* the tax is a dif-

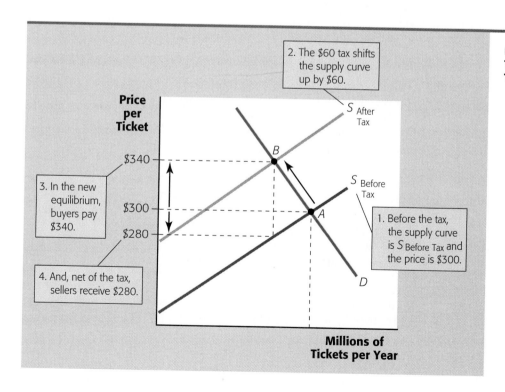

2. The $60 tax shifts the supply curve up by $60.

FIGURE 10
The Effect of an Excise Tax on Airlines

3. In the new equilibrium, buyers pay $340.

4. And, net of the tax, sellers receive $280.

1. Before the tax, the supply curve is $S_{\text{Before Tax}}$ and the price is $300.

120

Incidence The division of a tax payment between buyers and sellers, determined by comparing the new (after tax) and old (pretax) market equilibriums.

ferent question. Economists call the **incidence** of the tax. As we've seen, out of each $60 collected by the government, the airlines pay $20, because that is the decrease in their net price. And travelers pay $40—the increase in what they fork over to the airlines. Of course, the specific numbers in this example are arbitrary. But except in the most extreme circumstances, buyers and sellers will *share* in the payment of an excise tax, even though it's officially imposed on just the sellers.[3] We call this **tax shifting**—the process that causes some of the tax collected from one side of the market (here, the airlines) to be paid by the other side of the market (travelers).

Tax shifting The process by which some or all of a tax imposed on *one* side of a market ends up being paid by the *other* side of the market.

Are there any rules that determine *how much* of the burden of an excise tax on sellers will be shifted from sellers to buyers? The answer is yes. And these rules are based on a tool you've learned in this chapter: elasticity.

Tax Incidence and Demand Elasticity

Suppose that the demand for air travel was *perfectly inelastic*, as in the left panel of Figure 11. As always, a tax on air travel will shift the supply curve up by the amount of the tax—$60. But notice that this time, the equilibrium price—what travelers will pay—rises by the full $60 to $360. And when we subtract the tax to obtain the airlines' *net* price, we get $300—the same as before the tax. In this case, travelers pay the full amount of the tax and airlines pay none of it. The entire tax has been shifted from sellers to buyers.

What accounts for this result? In the figure, travelers want to buy 10 million tickets no matter what the price. Therefore, after the tax is imposed, equilibrium requires that the airlines want to *supply* the 10 million tickets that are demanded. But, as we know, the airlines require a *net* price of $300 to supply those 10 million tickets, which requires a gross price of $360. Thus, in equilibrium, the price will be $360. (To further prove this to yourself, imagine that the new gross price was *less* than $360. Then the net price would be less than $300 and the airlines would supply *fewer* than 10 million tickets. This would create an excess demand for tickets and cause the price to rise.)

Now look at the right-hand panel of Figure 11, which shows the opposite extreme: perfectly *elastic* demand. This time—when the tax shifts the supply curve upward by $60—the equilibrium price remains at $300. It does not change at all. Travelers pay *none* of the tax and the airlines pay all of it (their net price falls to $300 − $60 = $240, which is $60 less than before the tax). Here, *none* of the tax is shifted to travelers.

How can this be? This time, with perfectly elastic demand, travelers won't buy *any* tickets if the price is greater than $300. Therefore, in equilibrium, the airlines will have to charge travelers $300 per ticket. But with a gross price of $300, the net price is $240. Thus, with demand in equilibrium, the price must be $300. (To prove this further, imagine that part of the tax was shifted onto buyers, so their price rose

---

[3] In this chapter, we consider only one type of burden from a tax—changes in the *price* paid by buyers or receivd by sellers. But notice in Figure 10 that a tax also reduces the *quantity* bought and sold. Thus, buyers are harmed not only by paying a hgher price for each ticket, but also by enjoying *fewer* flights. And sellers are harmed not only by receiving a lower net price per ticket, but also by selling *fewer* of them. Chapter 14 presents a more comprehensive way of measuring the burden of a tax that takes account of changes in both price and quantity.

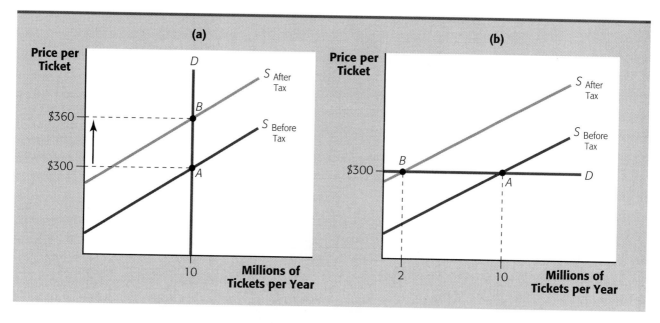

FIGURE 11
**Tax Incidence and Demand
Elasticity**

above $300. Then quantity demanded would fall to zero. This would create an excess supply and the price would drop.)

The two panels in Figure 11 show extreme cases, in which the *entire* tax is paid by either buyers or sellers. In most cases, though, the tax will be shared, as it is in Figure 10. But the extreme cases point to a general rule about *how* the tax payment will be shared:

> *For a given supply curve, the more* elastic *is demand, the more of an excise tax is paid by sellers. The more* inelastic *is demand, the more of the tax is paid by buyers.*

Tax Incidence and Supply Elasticity

Supply elasticity, just like demand elasticity, helps determine how a tax is shared. The left panel of Figure 12 shows what would happen if the supply of air travel was *perfectly inelastic*. Notice that in this case, the supply curve doesn't shift after the tax. Why not? In all the previous cases, the supply curve shifted because a minimum price was required to get the airlines to offer any given quantity. But in Fig-ure 12(a), the airlines will supply 10 million tickets no matter *what* the price. Therefore, when the tax is imposed, the airlines continue to supply 10 million tickets—so the price remains at $300. (Convince yourself, using the figure, that if the price rose or fell from $300, the result would be an excess demand or excess supply that would force the price back to $300.) But with travelers still paying $300 after the tax, the *net* price for the airlines falls from $300 to $240. In this case, the airlines pay the full amount of the tax and travelers pay none of it.

Now look at the right-hand panel of Figure 12, where the supply curve is perfectly *elastic*. In this case, the tax shifts the supply curve upward by $60, and in the new equilibrium, travelers pay $360, which is $60 more than before. But after the

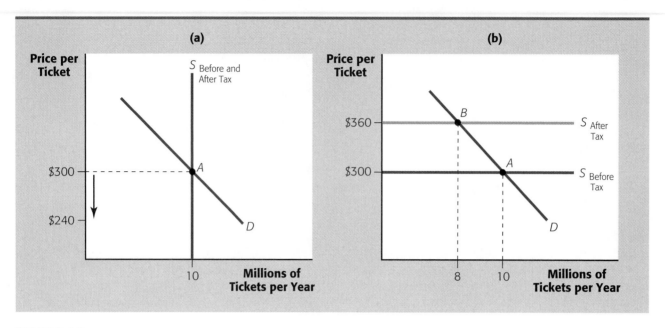

FIGURE 12
Tax Incidence and Supply Elasticity

airlines pay the tax out of that $360, they'll keep $300 per ticket—the same as before the tax. The entire tax is shifted onto travelers.

The logic may be familiar by now: With perfectly elastic supply, the airlines won't sell *any* tickets if they keep less than $300 per ticket. Therefore, in equilibrium, the airlines will have to charge travelers $360 per ticket; it's the only way the net price can be $300.

Although the two panels in Figure 12 show extreme cases of supply elasticity, in which the *entire* tax is paid by either buyers or sellers, they once again point to a general rule:

> *For a given demand curve, the more* elastic *is supply, the more of an excise tax is paid by buyers. The more* inelastic *is supply, the more of the tax is paid by sellers.*

Our discussion of tax shifting points to the importance of understanding how markets work and the meaning of elasticities. Whenever we impose a tax on sellers in a market, we must anticipate that some or even most of the tax may be shifted to buyers. This applies to taxes on specific goods—such as the taxes on airline travel or cigarettes—and also to broader taxes—such as state and city sales taxes that are applied to *all* goods and services. It also applies to taxes in markets for capital and labor. In all of these cases, who *really* ends up paying a tax depends on the elasticities of supply and demand in the market.

© TED STRESHINSKY/CORBIS

USING THE THEORY
The Story of Two Markets

The Market for Food

As we discussed earlier in this chapter, price floors are infrequent in market economies with one glaring exception: markets for agricultural goods. Almost every government in the world has, at one time or another, experimented with price floors to help keep food prices high. And many governments—including the U.S. government—still have them. What is so special about agricultural markets? Why do governments intervene there so often? What would happen if they did *not* intervene?

Agricultural markets have a rare combination of features affecting supply and demand. The best way to understand these features is to consider the market for food *as a whole*, rather than the market for one particular crop. Why? Because the market forces that affect one type of food product tend to affect virtually *all* food products at the same time. By combining all food products into one category, we can see more realistically the problems that affect agricultural markets as a whole.

What are the unique forces that affect the market for food? First, we find that the *supply* of food is subject to:

1. significant technological advance in the long run, and
2. extreme sensitivity to weather in the short run.

At the same time, the *demand* for food is characterized by another pair of forces:

3. a very low price elasticity, and
4. a very low income elasticity.

To see how farmers are plagued by these features in the long run, let's see how each affects the supply and demand curves. Property (1) tells us that the supply curve for food tends to shift rightward over time. To see this, think of the effects on output as farmers have shifted from hand plows to horse-drawn plows to tractors. Each of these innovations has caused a significant decrease in the cost per unit of virtually every kind of food, and farmers have been able to produce more food at any given price.

Over the past 50 years, mechanization in farming has led to steady rightward shifts in the supply curve of food. Because of these technological changes, food production has grown much faster than population. That is very good news for the human race, but bad news for the average farmer. When the supply curve for food shifts rightward, the equilibrium price will fall.

In order to prevent the price of food from falling, the demand curve would have to shift rightward by the same distance as the supply curve. We have already pointed out, however, that population growth—one cause of a rightward-shifting demand curve—has fallen short of food-production growth. Aside from population, the only other change that could shift the demand curve continuously rightward would be growth in the average income of the population. But farmers can expect no rescue here either. Notice property (4). Food is characterized by a very low

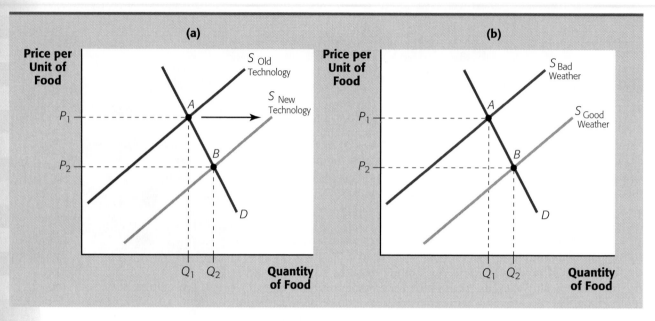

FIGURE 13
The Market for Food

Over the typical range of prices, the demand for food is inelastic. Panel (a) depicts the market over the long run. Over time, technological changes shift the supply curve to the right, lowering both price and total revenue of farmers. Panel (b) represents the market in the short run. If the weather is good, supply will be greater and price will be lower than when the weather is bad. Farmers' total revenue (and their incomes) are lower when the weather is good.

income elasticity; a 1-percent increase in income causes less than a 1-percent increase in the demand for food. Thus, income growth has only weak effects on the demand for food. Since technological change in farming has outpaced both the growth in population and the effects of rising incomes on the demand for food, the shifts in demand have not been able to keep up with the shifts in supply.

Since, in the long run, the rightward shifts in the supply curve seem to outpace the small shifts in the demand curve, let's simplify things by imagining that the demand curve does not shift at all. This is a close approximation to the long-run situation in agricultural markets, and it will enable us to see how elasticities shed light on the problem.

In Figure 13(a), we see that the market is initially in equilibrium at point A. When the supply curve shifts rightward, we move along the demand curve for food, from point A to point B. What happens to the total revenue of farmers as we make this move? You already have the tools to answer this question: Demand for food is price inelastic, as stated in property (3). Therefore, when price decreases, total expenditure on food (the total revenue of farmers) will *fall*. Now we see the ultimate effect of technological progress on farmers: As long as rapid technological progress continues (and as we enter the era of biotechnology, there is every reason to think it will accelerate) the farm sector is doomed to ever-decreasing total revenue. Since new technologies often require large-scale production, only the largest farms will enjoy a decrease in production costs. The result—for the typical small and medium-size farmer—is a squeeze on profits.

Now let's turn to the short run. Here, the problem is that crop harvests depend heavily on weather patterns, which are very unstable from year to year. If there is good weather, production will be high and the supply of food will be large. As shown in Figure 13(b), the supply curve shifts rightward. If there is bad weather, the supply of food will be much lower, and the supply curve shifts leftward. You can see that under good weather, we have a lower equilibrium price, but higher equilib-

	1996	1997	1998
Bushels produced	1.47 billion	1.84 billion	1.90 billion
Average price per bushel	$4.33	$3.52	$2.50
Total value of sales	$6.40 billion	$5.95 billion	$4.77 billion

TABLE 8
U.S Winter Wheat Production

Source: U.S. Department of Agriculture, *Marketing Year Average Prices and Value of Production, by States and United States, 1996, 1997, and 1998.* Production figures calculated by authors as total value of sales divided by average price.

rium quantity, of food. With bad weather, the equilibrium price is higher, but the equilibrium quantity is lower.

Since the demand for food is price inelastic, a leftward shift in the supply curve, which raises the price of food, will also increase total expenditure on food. So shifts in the supply curve have an ironic effect: Total revenue of farmers is greater when the weather is bad! As long as total costs of production do not differ too greatly under good and bad weather, farm profits will also be higher under bad weather. (This is why farmers actually hope for bad weather—it will create a scarcity of food, which will drive the price up and increase their profits—even with lower crop yields.) You can see, then, that farm profits—which depend on unstable and unpredictable weather patterns—will be highly unstable themselves.

Table 8 shows the impact that improving weather (and, to some extent, continuing technological progress) had on the U.S. winter wheat crop and the fate of winter wheat farmers during three years in the 1990s. Notice the large variations in prices and quantities. As winter weather changed from bad to good to even better, the supply curve shifted rightward: Production rose from 1996 to 1997 and again from 1997 to 1998. Notice also that each rise in output was associated with a fall in price. The price fell by about 20 percent from 1996 to 1997 and about 30 percent from 1997 to 1998. Finally, you can see that each price drop is associated with a decrease in the total sales revenue of winter wheat farmers. From its high in 1996 to its low in 1998, the value of sales decreased by $1.6 billion

Shrinking and unstable incomes are clearly problems for farmers, but are they problems for society? Under ordinary circumstances, the answer would be no. If there is something inherent in farming that makes it a risky or unrewarding type of work, then we would expect farm employment and farm production to shrink. This shrinkage would raise the price of food until those remaining on farms found the job attractive enough to stay. In other words, left to its own devices, the market for farm goods would reach an *equilibrium*—just like any other market.

But farming seems to be special. If the market were allowed to function on its own, the first to leave would be small family farmers, who could not compete against the large conglomerates, which are more technologically advanced and can bear the risk of unstable revenue more easily. And here lies the problem: The notion of the small family farm has tremendous political appeal. In addition, farmers have banded together to form powerful and effective government lobbies, to make sure that agricultural markets do not have to go through the same painful process of adjustment as other markets in the economy. The result has been continual government interference with supply and demand in agricultural markets around the world.

As you saw earlier in this chapter, such interference causes problems of its own—the price we pay to protect our farmers from the harsh realities of the market.

Health Insurance and the Market for Health Care

In 1990, health-related expenditures in the United States amounted to about $700 billion, or 12.2 percent of Gross Domestic Product (GDP). By the end of the decade, the figure had risen to about $1.3 trillion, or 14.3 percent of GDP. With this rapid rise in spending, the United States found itself devoting a larger share of its resources to health care than any other nation in the world. Why such rapid growth—with no end in sight? A variety of explanations have been offered.

On the supply side, scientific breakthroughs have made it possible to treat diseases and conditions that only a few years ago would have proved fatal. These technological changes enable us to live longer, but some of them also raise the cost of keeping a person healthy. On the demand side, as U.S. society ages, it is only natural that spending on health care will increase. After all, as individuals become older, they require more frequent visits to the doctor, have more operations, and may eventually need geriatric care.

Both of these reasons—our longer lives and the use of more expensive types of services—contribute to the rise in health care spending. But there is another reason as well—health insurance.

In the United States most—but by no means all—citizens have some form of health insurance. For the elderly and some of the poor, the insurance is provided by the federal and state governments through the Medicare and Medicaid programs. For others, health insurance comes as a fringe benefit provided by employers. Many of these insurance policies have a special feature called *coinsurance* in which patients share the cost of medical care with their insurance company. With 30 percent coinsurance, for example, the patient would pay 30 percent of a physician's or hospital bill, and the insurance company would pay the remaining 70 percent.

Let's look at the market for a specific type of health care—annual physical examinations in a large urban area. In this market, the buyers are patients, and the sellers are physicians and HMOs. In the absence of health insurance, there would be a demand for physical exams represented by demand curve $D_{\text{Before Insurance}}$ in Figure 14. There would also be a supply of exams provided by doctors and represented by supply curve S. At point A, the two curves intersect to determine an equilibrium price of $50 per examination and an equilibrium quantity of 100,000 examinations per year.

Now let's examine the effects of health insurance with a 50 percent coinsurance rate. Since consumers now pay only half the cost of any health services they utilize, the effect is to rotate their demand curve upward to $D_{\text{After Insurance}}$.

To understand why the demand curve rotates in this way, we just need to reinterpret the demand curve in a way analogous to our reinterpretation of the supply curve earlier, in Figure 9. Usually we think of the demand curve as telling us the quantity buyers will buy at each price. But it also tells us the maximum price that buyers can be charged and still have them buy a given quantity. For example, using the original demand curve $D_{\text{Before Insurance}}$, we see that to get consumers to buy 100,000 examinations, the most they could be charged would be $50 per exam. If the price is any higher than $50, people will buy fewer than 100,000 examinations.

Now, once consumers have a 50 percent coinsurance rate, they could be charged twice as much as before for any given quantity, and still end up paying out of their

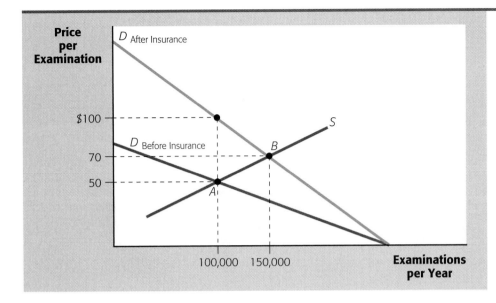

FIGURE 14
The Market for Health Care with Coinsurance

At point A, the market for physical examinations is in equilibrium with 100,000 exams provided each year at $50 each. The introduction of health insurance with a 50% coinsurance rate causes the demand curve to rotate upward from $D_{Before\ Insurance}$ to $D_{After\ Insurance}$. In the new equilibrium at point B, more exams are provided at a higher price, so that total expenditure on physical examinations has increased.

own pockets the same amount as before. Thus, coinsurance doubles the dollars they'd be willing to pay for any given quantity. This is why the demand curve rotates from $D_{Before\ Insurance}$ to $D_{After\ Insurance}$. At any quantity along the horizontal axis, the corresponding price along demand curve $D_{After\ Insurance}$ is twice the price along $D_{Before\ Insurance}$. For example, at a quantity of 100,000 examinations, the price along $D_{After\ Insurance}$ is $100 per exam, while the price along $D_{Before\ Insurance}$ is $50.

Once consumers are insured, the new market equilibrium is determined at point B where supply curve S and demand curve $D_{After\ Insurance}$ cross. The effect of insurance is to increase both the quantity of health care provided and the price per unit. In our example, total expenditure on physical examinations increases from $50 × 100,000 or $5,000,000, to $70 × 150,000 or $10,500,000.

The actual amount by which expenditure increases depends in part on the price elasticities of demand and supply. But it also depends on the effective coinsurance rate. For given demand and supply curves, the higher the coinsurance rate, the greater the increase in health care spending. You can see this by imagining the effect of a 10 percent coinsurance rate (which is much closer to reality than our hypothetical 50 percent rate was). With 10 percent coinsurance, each individual pays only one-tenth of the cost of a unit of health care. In that case, prices along the new demand curve will be *10 times* higher than on the original.

Health insurance has definite benefits to our society. Since most people are risk averse, they feel better off and more secure when they are insured. And since some operations and therapies can cost $100,000 or more, insurance coverage against catastrophic illness can mean the difference between prosperity and bankruptcy for some families. On the other hand, our current health insurance system keeps patients from facing the full opportunity costs of their health care decisions. This can cause people to *overconsume* health care. And some economists believe that health insurance encourages the development of high-cost, low-benefit technologies. At a minimum, health insurance reduces buyers' incentives to monitor their health care expenditures very closely or to shop around for high-quality, low-cost care. Concerns such as these lie at the heart of current debates about the nature of our health care system.

Summary

The model of supply and demand is a powerful tool for understanding all sorts of economic events. For example, governments often intervene in markets—either by creating *price ceilings* or *price floors*, or by imposing taxes or subsidies. Supply and demand enables us to predict how these interventions affect the price of a good and the quantity exchanged.

Another powerful tool is the *price elasticity of demand*, defined as the percentage change in quantity demanded divided by the percentage change in price that caused it. In general, price elasticity of demand varies along a demand curve. In the special case of a straight-line demand curve, demand becomes more and more elastic as we move upward and leftward along the curve. Along an elastic portion of any demand curve, a rise in price causes sellers' revenues and consumers' expenditures to fall. Along an *inelastic* portion of any demand curve, a rise in price causes sellers' revenues and consumers' expenditures to increase. Generally speaking, demand for a good tends to be more elastic: The more narrowly the good is defined, the easier it is to find substitutes for the good, and the greater the share of households' budgets that is spent on the good. And *long-run-elasticities* are almost always larger—in absolute value—than *short-run elasticities*.

The *income elasticity of demand* is the percentage change in quantity demanded divided by the percentage change in income that causes it. For *normal goods*, the income elasticity of demand is positive. For *inferior goods*, the income elasticity is negative.

The *cross-price elasticity of demand* measures the percentage change in the quantity demanded of one good as a result of a one percent increase in the price of some other good. If the cross-price elasticity is positive, we say that the two goods are *substitutes*. If the elasticity is negative, the two goods are said to be *complements*.

Key Terms

Black market
Cross-price elasticity of demand
Economic luxury
Economic necessity
Elastic demand
Excise tax
Incidence
Income elasticity of demand

Inelastic demand
Long-run elasticity
Perfectly inelastic demand
Perfectly (infinitely) elastic demand
Price ceiling
Price elasticity of demand
Price elasticity of supply
Price floor

Rent controls
Shortage
Short-run elasticity
Short side of the market
Surplus
Tax shifting
Unitary elastic demand

Review Questions

Answers to even-numbered Questions and Problems can be found on the text Web site at http://hall-lieb.swlearning.com.

1. What is the difference between the price elasticity of demand along a demand curve and the rate of change along the demand curve?

2. Price elasticity of demand is defined as

$$\frac{\% \text{ Change in Quantity Demanded}}{\% \text{ Change in Price}}.$$

   a. What formulas do economists use to calculate %Δ quantity demanded and %Δ price?
   b. Why do economists use these specific formulas?
   c. Suppose that the price elasticity of demand for a good is −0.4. Explain precisely what that means.

3. For each of the following pairs of goods or services, indicate which good you would expect to have the *smaller* (in absolute value) price elasticity of demand. In each case, explain why.
   a. ExxonMobil gasoline; gasoline in general
   b. Beauticians' services; plumbers' services
   c. Automobiles; color photocopies
   d. Coach-class airfare; business-class airfare

4. Give some examples of goods for which demand would be almost perfectly *inelastic*. Then give some examples of goods with almost perfectly *elastic* demands. In each case, justify your answers.

5. What is the relationship between the price elasticity of demand for a good and total expenditure on (or total revenue from) that good? Explain how this relationship arises.

6. Are short-run price elasticities of demand generally larger or smaller (in absolute value) than long-run elasticities? Why is this so?

7. What factors determine the size of the price elasticity of demand for a good? Specifically, how does each factor influence elasticity?

8. Which of the following goods are likely to be normal goods? Which are likely to be inferior goods? Defend your answers.
   a. Canned spaghetti
   b. Vacuum cleaners

c. Used books

d. Computer software

9. How are the words *necessity* and *luxury* used differently in economics than in everyday speech?

10. For each of the following pairs of goods, would you expect the cross-elasticity of demand to be positive or negative? Large (in absolute value) or small? Defend your answers.

a. Computer hardware and computer software

b. Antibiotics and over-the-counter decongestants

c. Gasoline and automobile repairs

11. Explain the "short side" rule of markets. What quantity would be traded if, at a price ceiling of $40, buyers wanted to buy 5,000 units and sellers wanted to sell 4,000 units?

12. Who would bear the burden of an excise tax if supply is perfectly elastic and demand is perfectly inelastic? What if the situation were reversed so that supply is perfectly inelastic and demand is perfectly elastic?

13. Answer the following questions.

a. Why might dentures have a negative income elasticity of demand?

b. What effect did the development of Lasik surgery to correct myopia have on the price elasticity of demand and the income elasticity of demand for prescription eyeglasses?

Problems and Exercises

1. The market for rice has the following supply and demand schedules:

P (per ton)	Q^D (tons)	Q^S (tons)
$10	100	0
$20	80	30
$30	60	40
$40	50	50
$50	40	60

To support rice producers, the government imposes a price floor of $50 per ton.

a. What quantity will be traded in the market? Why?

b. What steps might the government have to take to enforce the price floor?

2. The market for one-bedroom apartments in a city has the following supply and demand schedules:

Monthly Rent	Q^D (thousands)	Q^S (thousands)
$1,000	800	300
$1,200	600	350
$1,400	400	400
$1,600	200	450
$1,800	100	500

The government imposes a price ceiling (rent control) of $1,200.

a. With the price ceiling, is there an excess demand, excess supply, or neither? If there is an excess demand or excess supply, state which and give the numerical value.

b. What quantity of one-bedroom apartments will actually be rented?

c. Suppose, instead, that the price ceiling is set at $1,600. What quantity of one-bedroom apartments will be rented now? Is there an excess supply, excess demand, or neither?

3. The demand for bottled water in a small town is as follows:

P (per bottle)	Q_d (bottles per week)
$1.00	500
$1.50	400
$2.00	300
$2.50	200
$3.00	100

a. Is this a straight-line demand curve? How do you know?

b. Calculate the price elasticity of demand for bottled water for a price rise from $1.00 to $1.50. Is demand elastic or inelastic for this price change?

c. Calculate the price elasticity of demand for a price rise from $2.50 to $3.00. Is demand elastic or inelastic for this price change?

d. According to the chapter, demand should become less and less elastic as we move downward and rightward along a demand curve. Use your answers in *b.* and *c.* to confirm this relationship.

e. Create another column for total revenue on bottled water at each price.

f. According to the chapter, a rise in price should *increase* total revenue on bottled water when demand is inelastic, and *decrease* total revenue when demand is elastic. Use your answers in *b.* and *c.* above, and the new total revenue column you created, to confirm this.

4. The demand for rosebushes at Rosie's Nursery is as follows:

Price (per rosebush)	Quantity Demanded (rosebushes per week)
$3	230
$4	150
$5	90
$6	40

a. Is this a straight-line demand curve? How do you know?

b. Calculate the price elasticity of demand for roses for a price increase from $3 to $4. Is demand elastic or inelastic for this price change?

c. Calculate the pric elasticity of demand for roses for a price increase from $4 to $5. Is demand elastic or inelastic for this price change?

d. Use the determinants of price elasticity of demand to explain why this demand curve might exhibit the elasticity shown in parts *b*. and *c*.

5. Refer to Table 3 in this chapter and answer the following questions:

a. Which is more elastically demanded: cigarettes or pork? Does this make sense to you? Explain briefly.

b. If the price of milk rises by 5 percent, what will happen to the quantity demanded? (Be specific.)

6. Once again, refer to Table 3 in this chapter and answer the following questions:

a. Is the demand for recreation more or less elastic than the demand for clothing?

b. If 10,000 two-liter bottles of Pepsi are currently being demanded in your community each month, and the price increases from $0.90 to $1.00 per bottle, what will happen to quantity demanded? Be specific.

c. By how much would the price of ground beef have to increase (in percentage terms) in order to reduce quantity demanded by 5 percent?

7. From the information in the following table, calculate the income elasticity of demand for this good if income increases from $10,000 to $20,000, and if income increases from $40,000 to $50,000. (All the quantities were measured at a price of $10 per unit.)

Income	Quantity Demanded
$10,000	50
$20,000	60
$30,000	70
$40,000	80
$50,000	90

a. Is this a normal or an inferior good? How can you tell?

b. Does the proportion of household income spent on this good increase or decrease as income increases?

c. Is this good considered an economic luxury, an economic necessity, or neither? Why?

8. Consider the table and answer the following questions.

a. From the information in the following table, calculate the cross-price elasticity of demand between Good A and Good B as the price of Good A rises from $1 to $2.

P_A	Quantity of B Demanded
$1	1,000
$2	3,500
$3	7,000

b. What information does your answer give you about the relationship between these two goods?

9. Use the data in Table 5 of this chapter to answer the following questions:

a. Which is more income elastic: food or clothing?

b. If income rises from $30,000 to $32,000, what, specifically, will happen to the demand for chicken?

c. By what percentage would income have to rise to cause the demand for potatoes to fall by 10 percent?

10. Use the data in Table 7 of this chapter to answer the following questions:

a. If the price of entertainment increases by 2 percent, what will happen to the quantity of food demanded? Be specific.

b. If the price of electricity falls by 3 percent, what will happen to the quantity of natural gas demanded? Again, be specific.

c. If a shift in tastes increases the demand for poultry and drives up its price by 5 percent, what will happen to the quantity of ground beef demanded?

11. Three Guys Named Al, a moving company, is contemplating a price hike. Currently, they charge $20 per hour, but Al thinks they could get $30. Al disagrees, saying it will hurt the business. Al, the brains of the outfit, has calculated the price elasticity of demand for their moving services in the range from $20 to $30 and found it to be −0.5.

a. Should they do as Al suggests and raise the price? Why or why not?

b. Currently, Three Guys is the only moving company in town. Al reads in the paper that several new movers are planning to set up shop there within the next year. Twelve months from now, is the demand for Three Guys' services likely to be more elastic, less elastic, or the same? Why?

12. Suppose that the health care market is as depicted in Figure 14, except that the *supply* of health care is *perfectly inelastic*, and the supply curve passes through the initial equilibrium point *A*. If health insurance with a 50-

percent coinsurance rate is introduced into this market, what will be

a. the price doctors will charge;
b. the net price patients will pay (after deducting their insurance reimbursement)?

13. Suppose that the health care market is as depicted in Figure 14, except that the *supply* of health care is *perfectly elastic*, and the supply curve passes through the initial equilibrium point *A*. If health insurance with a 50-percent coinsurance rate is introduced into this market, what will be

a. the price doctors will charge;
b. the net price patients will pay (after deducting their insurance reimbursement)?

14. In February, 2003, Germany's patent office proposed a solution to reimburse copyright holders for illegal digital file sharing: personal computer manufacturers—charging a fee of $13 per computer go into a special fund to reimburse the copyright holders. Two computer makers—Fujitsu-Siemens and Hewlett-Packard—claimed that imposing the fee would do great injury cause them, because they would be *unable to pass any of the fee onto consumers*. Under what assumptions about the market would the computer-makers' claim be true? [Hint: there are two possibilities.] Is either assumption realistic?

Challenge Questions

1. As discussed in Chapters 3 and 4, price acts as an allocation mechanism, determining how the quantity produced is distributed among those who wish to consume the good. In the case of a price ceiling, the allocative mechanism is frustrated.

   Consider the market for rental housing. If a rent ceiling is set below the market price:
   a. Will there be a shortage or a surplus of rental housing?
   b. Since price can no longer allocate rental housing, what other mechanism might emerge?

2. Suppose that the health care market is as depicted in Figure 12, except that the *supply* of health care is *perfectly inelastic*, and the coinsurance rate is 20 percent instead of 50 percent. When health insurance with a 20-percent coinsurance rate is introduced into this market, what will be

   a. the price doctors will charge;
   b. the net price patients will pay (after deducting their insurance reimbursement); and
   c. the total revenue of doctors?
   d. the total net expenditure of patients? Compare with the original situation in Figure 12, and state whether each of these values has increased or decreased.

These exercises require access to Hall/Lieberman Xtra! If Xtra! did not come with your book, visit http://hallxtra.swlearning.com to purchase.

1. Use your Xtra! password at the Hall and Lieberman Web site (http://hallxtra.swlearning.com), select this chapter, and under Economic Applications, click on EconNews. Choose *Economic Fundamentals: Supply and Demand,* and scroll down to find the article, "A Tale of Two Countries: Hemp Farming." Read the article summary there.

   a. Suppose the U.S. government decriminalized the farming of hemp, and therefore the production of hemp-related products. What would that action do to the equilibrium price and quantity of hemp in the U.S. market? Use a price-quantity diagram to show the effect on the price and quantity of hemp.
   b. What impact might this have on the market for marijuana in the United States? Use a price-quantity diagram to show the effect on the price and quantity of marijuana following the decrimimalization of hemp production.
   c. Now click on EconDebate. Choose *Economic Fundamentals: Supply and Demand* and scroll down to find

   the debate, "Should Marijuana be Decriminalized?" Read the debate and answer the question, "How Does the Legalization of Hemp Fit into the Debate on Decriminalization of Marijuana?" Use your answer in part b. to help you answer the question.

2. Use your Xtra! password at the Hall and Lieberman Web site (http://hallxtra.swlearning.com), and click on Economic applications, EconNews. Choose *Economic Fundamentals: Supply and Demand,* and scroll down to find the article "Baseball Prices Cause Home run." Read the article summary there and answer these questions:

   a. What does the article suggest is the range of elasticity of demand for baseball game attendance? Why do you think this is?
   b. Given your response in a., would a slight decrease in ticket price (as well as related prices of game attendance) increase or decrease a baseball team's total revenue? Why?

Consumer Choice

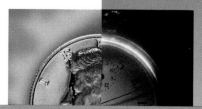

You are constantly making economic decisions. Some of them are rather trivial. (Have coffee at Starbucks or more cheaply at home?) Others can have a profound impact on your life. (Live with your parents a while longer or get your own place?) The economic nature of all these decisions is rather obvious, since they all involve *spending*.

But in other cases, the economic nature of your decisions may be less obvious. Did you get up early today in order to get things done, or did you sleep in? Which leisure activities—movies, concerts, sports, hobbies—do you engage in, and how often do you decline an opportunity to have fun for lack of time? At this very moment, what have you decided *not* to do in order to make time to read this chapter? All of these are economic choices, too, because they require you to allocate a scarce resource—your *time*—among different alternatives.

To understand the economic choices that individuals make, we must know what they are trying to achieve (their goals) and the limitations they face in achieving them (their constraints).

But wait. How can we identify the goals and constraints of *consumers* when we are all so *different* from each other?

Indeed, we *are* different from one another . . . when it comes to *specific* goals and *specific* constraints. But at the highest level of generality, we are all very much alike. All of us, for example, would like to maximize our overall level of *satisfaction*. And all of us, as we attempt to satisfy our desires, come up against the same constraints: too little income or wealth to buy everything we might enjoy, and too little time to enjoy it all.

We'll start our analysis of individual choice with constraints, and then move on to goals. In most of the chapter, we will focus on choices about *spending*: how people decide what to buy. This is why the theory of individual decision making is often called "consumer theory." Later, in the Using the Theory section, we'll see how the theory can be broadened to include decisions about allocating scarce *time* among different activities.

THE BUDGET CONSTRAINT

Virtually all individuals must face two facts of economic life: (1) They have to pay prices for the goods and services they buy, and (2) they have limited funds to spend. These two facts are summarized by the consumer's *budget constraint*:

> A consumer's **budget constraint** identifies which combinations of goods and services the consumer can afford with a limited budget, at given prices.

Budget constraint The different combinations of goods a consumer can afford with a limited budget, at given prices.

Consider Max, a devoted fan of both movies and the local music scene, who has a total entertainment budget of $150 each month. Each movie costs Max $10, while the average ticket price for local rock concerts is $30. If Max were to spend all of his $150 budget on concerts at $30 each, he could see at most five each month. If he were to spend it all on movies at $10 each, he could see 15 of them.

But Max could also choose to spend *part* of his budget on concerts and *part* on movies. In this case, for each number of concerts, there is some *maximum* number of movies that he could see. For example, if he goes to one concert per month, it will cost him $30 of his $150 budget, leaving $120 available for movies. Thus, if Max were to choose one concert, the *maximum* number of films he could choose would be $120/$10 = 12.

Figure 1 lists, for each number of concerts, the maximum number of movies that Max could see. Each combination of goods in the table is affordable for Max, since each will cost him exactly $150. Combination *A*, at one extreme, represents no concerts and 15 movies. Combination *F*, the other extreme, represents 5 concerts and no movies. In each of the combinations between *A* and *F*, Max attends both concerts and movies.

The graph in Figure 1 plots the number of movies along the vertical axis and the number of concerts along the horizontal. Each of the points *A* through *F* corresponds to one of the combinations in the table. If we connect all of these points with a straight line, we have a graphical representation of Max's budget constraint, which we call Max's **budget line.**

Note that any point below or to the left of the budget line is affordable. For example, two concerts and six movies—indicated by point *G*—would cost only $60 + $60 = $120. Max could certainly afford this combination. On the other

Budget line The graphical representation of a budget constraint, showing the maximum affordable quantity of one good for given amounts of another good.

FIGURE 1
The Budget Constraint

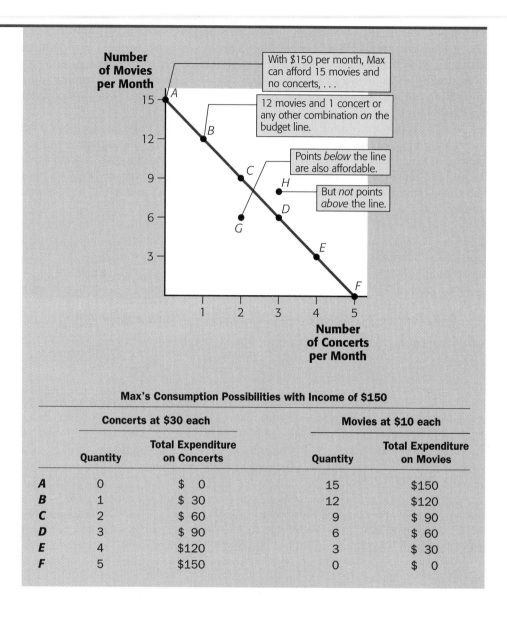

Max's Consumption Possibilities with Income of $150

	Concerts at $30 each		Movies at $10 each	
	Quantity	Total Expenditure on Concerts	Quantity	Total Expenditure on Movies
A	0	$ 0	15	$150
B	1	$ 30	12	$120
C	2	$ 60	9	$ 90
D	3	$ 90	6	$ 60
E	4	$120	3	$ 30
F	5	$150	0	$ 0

hand, he *cannot* afford any combination *above* and to the right of this line. Point *H*, representing 3 concerts and 8 movies, would cost $90 + $80 = $170, which is beyond Max's budget. The budget line therefore serves as a *border* between those combinations that are affordable and those that are not.

Let's look at Max's budget line more closely. The *vertical intercept* is 15, the number of movies Max could see if he attended zero concerts. Starting at the vertical intercept (point *A*), notice that each time Max increases one unit along the horizontal axis (attends one more concert), he must decrease 3 units along the vertical (see three fewer movies). Thus, the slope of the budget line is equal to –3. The slope tells us Max's *opportunity cost* of one more concert. That is, the opportunity cost of one more concert is 3 movies foregone.

There is an important relationship between the *prices* of two goods and the opportunity cost of having more of one or the other. The prices Max faces tell us how many dollars he must give up to get another unit of each good. If, however, we divide one money price by another money price, we get what is called a **relative price,** the price of one good *relative* to the other. Since $P_{concert}$ = \$30 and P_{movie} = \$10, the *relative price of a concert* is the ratio $P_{concert}/P_{movie}$ = \$30/\$10 = 3. Notice that 3 is the opportunity cost of another concert in terms of movies; and, except for the minus sign, it is also the slope of the budget line. That is, *the relative price of a concert, the opportunity cost of another concert, and the slope of the budget line* have the same absolute value. This is one example of a general relationship:

Relative price The price of one good relative to the price of another.

> *The slope of the budget line indicates the spending trade-off between one good and another—the amount of one good that must be sacrificed in order to buy more of another good. If P_y is the price of the good on the vertical axis and P_x is the price of the good on the horizontal axis, then the slope of the budget line is $-P_x/P_y$.*

Changes in the Budget Line

To draw the budget line in Figure 1, we have assumed given prices for movies and concerts, and a given income that Max can spend on them. These "givens"—the prices of the goods and the consumer's income—are always *assumed constant* as we move along a budget line; if any one of them changes, the budget line will change as well. Let's see how.

Changes in Income. If Max's available income increases from \$150 to \$300 per month, then he can afford to see more movies, more concerts, or more of both, as shown by the change in his budget line in Figure 2(a). If Max were to devote *all* of his income to movies, he could now see 30 of them each month, instead of the 15 he was able to see before. Devoting his entire income to concerts would enable him to attend 10, rather than 5. Moreover, for any number of concerts, he will be able to see more movies than before. For example, before, when his budget was only \$150, choosing 2 concerts would allow Max to see only 9 movies. Now, with a budget of \$300, he can have 2 concerts and *24* movies.

The Budget Line's Slope It's tempting to think that the slope of the budget line should be $-P_y / P_x$, with the price of the vertical axis good y in the numerator. But notice that the slope is the other way around, $-P_x / P_y$, with P_x in the numerator. If we write out the equation for the budget line, this is easy to see. Start by recognizing that the price of good y (P_y) times the quantity of good y consumed (Q_y) is the total amount *spent* on good y ($P_y \times Q_y$). Similarly, the total amount spent on good x is $P_x \times Q_x$. If we are *on* the budget line, the total amount spent on these two goods must equal the total budget (B), so $P_y \times Q_y + P_x \times Q_x = B$. Solving for Q_y gives us the equation for the budget line: $Q_y = (B - P_x \times Q_x)/P_y$. This can be rewritten as: $Q_y = (B/P_y) + [(-P_x/P_y) \times Q_x]$. The first term in parentheses (B/P_y) is the vertical intercept of budget line. The second term in parentheses ($-P_x/P_y$) is the slope. (See the mathematical appendix to Chapter 1 if you need to review slopes and intercepts.)

DANGEROUS CURVES

Notice that the old and new budget lines in Figure 2(a) are parallel; that is, they have the same slope of –3. This is because we changed Max's income but *not* prices. Since the ratio $P_{concert}/P_{movie}$ has not changed, the spending trade-off between movies and concerts remains the same. Thus,

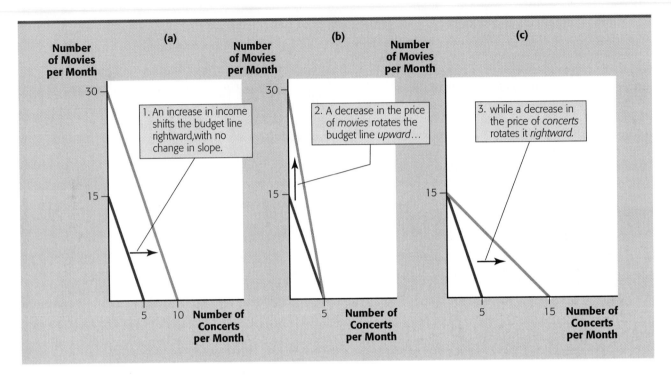

FIGURE 2
Changes in the Budget Line

HTTP://

The Bureau of Labor Statistics
Consumer Expenditure Survey will
give you a snapshot picture of the
consumption behavior of typical
U.S. households (http://stats.
bls.gov/news.release/cesan.
toc.htm).

an increase in income will shift the budget line upward (and rightward). A decrease in income will shift the budget line downward (and leftward). These shifts are parallel: Changes in income do not affect the budget line's slope.

Changes in Price. Now let's go back to Max's original budget of $150 and explore what happens to the budget line when a price changes. Suppose the price of a movie falls from $10 to $5. The graph in Figure 2(b) shows Max's old and new budget lines. When the price of a movie falls, the budget line rotates outward; that is, the vertical intercept moves higher. The reason is this: When a movie costs $10, Max could spend his entire $150 on them and see 15; now that they cost $5, he can see a maximum of 30. The horizontal intercept—representing how many concerts Max could see with his entire income—doesn't change at all, since there has been no change in the price of a concert. Notice that the new budget line is also *steeper* than the original one, with slope equal to $-P_{concert}/P_{movie} = -\$30/\$5 = -6$. Now, with movies costing $5, the trade-off between movies and concerts is 6 to 1, instead of 3 to 1.

Panel (c) of Figure 2 illustrates another price change. This time, it's a fall in the price of a *concert* from $30 to $10. Once again, the budget line rotates, but now it is the horizontal intercept (concerts) that changes and the vertical intercept (movies) that remains fixed.

We could draw similar diagrams illustrating a *rise* in the price of a movie or a concert, but you should try to do this on your own. In each case, one of the budget line's intercepts will change, as well as its slope:

> *When the price of a good changes, the budget line rotates: Both its slope and one of its intercepts will change.*

The budget constraint, as illustrated by the budget line, is one side of the story of consumer choice. It indicates the trade-off consumers *are able to* make between one good and another. But just as important is the trade-off that consumers *want to* make between one good and another, and this depends on consumers' *preferences*, the subject of the next section.

PREFERENCES

How can we possibly speak systematically about people's preferences? After all, people are different. They like different things. American teens delight in having a Coke with dinner, while the very idea makes a French person shudder. What would satisfy a Buddhist monk would hardly satisfy the typical American.

And even among "typical Americans," there is little consensus about tastes. Some read Jane Austen, while others pick John Grisham. Some like to spend their vacations traveling, whereas others would prefer to stay home and sleep in every day. Even those who like Häagen-Dazs ice cream can't agree on which is the best flavor—the company notices consistent, regional differences in consumption. In Los Angeles, chocolate chocolate chip is the clear favorite, while on most of the East Coast, it's butter pecan—except in New York City, where coffee wins hands down. (And economics instructors have different preferences about teaching consumer theory. More on this in a few pages).

In spite of such wide differences in preferences, we can find some important common denominators—things that seem to be true for a wide variety of people. In our theory of consumer choice, we will focus on these common denominators.

Rationality

One common denominator—and a critical assumption behind consumer theory—is that people *have* preferences. More specifically, we assume that you can look at two alternatives and state either that you prefer one to the other or that you are entirely indifferent between the two—you value them equally.

Another common denominator is that preferences are *logically consistent*, or *transitive*. If, for example, you prefer a sports car to a jeep, and a jeep to a motorcycle, then we assume that you will also prefer a sports car to a motorcycle. When a consumer can make choices, and is logically consistent, we say that she has **rational preferences**.

Notice that rationality is a matter of how you make your choices, and not what choices you make. You can be rational and like apples better than oranges, or oranges better than apples. You can be rational even if you like anchovies or brussels sprouts! What matters is that you make logically consistent choices, and most of us usually do.

Rational preferences Preferences that satisfy two conditions: (1) Any two alternatives can be compared, and one is preferred or else the two are valued equally, and (2) the comparisons are logically consistent or transitive.

More Is Better

Another feature of preferences that virtually all of us share is this: We generally feel that *more is better*. Specifically, if we get more of some good or service, and nothing else is taken away from us, we will generally feel better off.

This condition seems to be satisfied for the vast majority of goods we all consume. Of course, there are exceptions. If you hate eggplant, then the more of it you have, the worse off you are. Similarly, a dieter who says, "Don't bring any ice cream into the house. I don't want to be tempted," also violates the assumption. The model of consumer choice in this chapter is designed for preferences that satisfy the "more is better" condition, and it would have to be modified to take account of exceptions like these.

So far, our characterization of consumer preferences has been rather minimal. We've assumed only that consumers are rational and that they prefer more rather than less of every good we're considering. But even this limited information allows us to say the following:

> *The consumer will always choose a point on the budget line, rather than a point below it.*

To see why this is so, look again at Figure 1. Max would never choose point *G*, representing 2 concerts and 6 movies, since there are affordable points—on the budget line—that we know make him better off. For example, point *C* has the same number of concerts, but more movies, while point *D* has the same number of movies, but more concerts. "More is better" tells us that Max will prefer *C* or *D* to *G*, so we know *G* won't be chosen. Indeed, if we look at any point below the budget line, we can always find at least one point on the budget line that is preferred, as long as more is better.

Knowing what Max will not do—knowing he *will not* choose a point inside his budget line—is helpful. It tells us that we can narrow our search for the point he *will* choose to just the ones along the budget line *AF*. But how can Max find the one point along the budget line that gives him a higher utility than all the others?

This is where your *instructor's* preferences come in. There are two theories of consumer decision making, and they share much in common. First, both assume that preferences are rational. Second, both assume that the consumer would be better off with more of any good we're considering. This means the consumer will always choose a combination of goods *on*, rather than below, his budget line. Finally, both theories come to the same general conclusions about consumer behavior. However, to *arrive* at those conclusions, each theory takes a different road.

The next section presents the "Marginal Utility" approach to consumer decision making. If, however, your instructor prefers the "Indifference Curve" approach, you can skip the next section and go straight to the appendix. Then, come back to the section titled "Income and Substitution Effects, which is where our two roads converge once again.

One warning, though. Both approaches to consumer theory are *models*. They use graphs and calculations to explain how consumers make choices. While the models are logical, they may appear unrealistic to you. And in one sense, they *are* unrealistic: Few consumers in the real world are aware of the techniques we'll discuss, yet they make choices all the time.

Economists don't imagine that, when making choices, households or consumers actually *use* these techniques. Rather, the assumption is that people mostly behave *as if* they use them. Indeed, most of the time, in most markets, household behavior has proven to be consistent with the model of consumer choice. When our goal is to describe and predict how consumers are likely to behave in markets—rather than describe what actually goes on in their minds—our theories of consumer decision making can be very useful.

CONSUMER DECISIONS: THE MARGINAL UTILITY APPROACH

Economists assume that *any* decision maker—a consumer, the manager of a business firm, or officials in a government agency—tries to make the *best* out of any situation. Marginal utility theory treats consumers as striving to maximize their **utility**—an actual *quantitative* measure of well-being or satisfaction. Anything that makes the consumer better off is assumed to raise his utility. Anything that makes the consumer worse off will decrease his utility.

Utility A quantitative measure of pleasure or satisfaction obtained from consuming goods and services.

Utility and Marginal Utility

Figure 3 provides a graphical view of utility—in this case, the utility of a consumer named Lisa who likes ice cream cones. Look first at panel (a). On the horizontal axis, we'll measure the number of ice cream cones Lisa consumes each week. On the vertical axis, we'll measure the utility she derives from consuming each of them. If Lisa values ice cream cones, her utility will increase as she acquires more of them,

FIGURE 3
Total and Marginal Utility

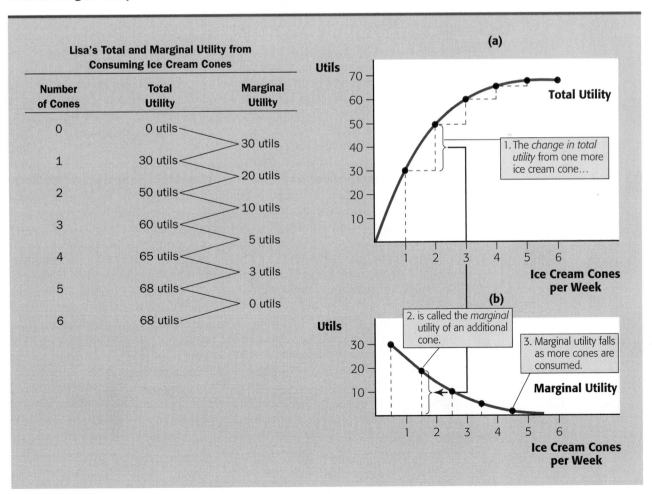

Lisa's Total and Marginal Utility from Consuming Ice Cream Cones

Number of Cones	Total Utility	Marginal Utility
0	0 utils	
		30 utils
1	30 utils	
		20 utils
2	50 utils	
		10 utils
3	60 utils	
		5 utils
4	65 utils	
		3 utils
5	68 utils	
		0 utils
6	68 utils	

(a)

1. The *change in total utility* from one more ice cream cone...

Total Utility

(b)

2. is called the *marginal utility* of an additional cone.

3. Marginal utility falls as more cones are consumed.

Marginal Utility

as it does in the figure. There we see that when she has one cone, she enjoys total utility of 30 "utils," and when she has two cones, her total utility grows to 50 utils, and so on. Throughout the figure, the total utility Lisa derives from consuming ice cream cones keeps rising as she gets to consume more and more of them.

But notice something interesting, and important: Although Lisa's utility increases every time she consumes more ice cream, the *additional* utility she derives from each *successive* cone gets smaller and smaller as she gets more cones. We call the *change in utility* derived from consuming an *additional unit* of a good the *marginal utility* of that additional unit.

Marginal utility The change in total utility an individual obtains from consuming an additional unit of a good or service.

> *Marginal utility is the change in utility an individual enjoys from consuming an additional unit of a good.*

What we've observed about Lisa's utility can be restated this way: As she eats more and more ice cream cones in a given week, her *marginal utility* from another cone declines. We call this the **law of diminishing marginal utility,** which the great economist Alfred Marshall (1842–1924) defined this way:

Law of diminishing marginal utility As consumption of a good or service increases, marginal utility decreases.

> *The marginal utility of a thing to anyone diminishes with every increase in the amount of it he already has.[1]*

According to the law of diminishing marginal utility, when you consume your first unit of some good, like an ice cream cone, you derive some amount of utility. When you get your second cone that week, you enjoy greater satisfaction than when you only had one, but the extra satisfaction you derive from the second is likely to be smaller than the satisfaction you derived from the first. Adding the third cone to your weekly consumption will no doubt increase your utility further, but again the marginal utility you derive from that third cone is likely to be less than the marginal utility you derived from the second.

Figure 3 will again help us see what's going on. The table summarizes the information in the total utility graph. The first two columns show, respectively, the quantity of cones Lisa consumes each week and the total utility she receives each week from consuming them. The third column shows the *marginal* utility she receives from each successive cone she consumes per week. As you can see in the table, Lisa's total utility keeps increasing (marginal utility is always positive) as she consumes more cones (up to five per week), but the rate at which total utility increases gets smaller and smaller (her marginal utility diminishes) as her consumption increases.

Marginal utility is shown in panel (b) of Figure 3. Because marginal utility is the change in utility caused by a change in consumption from one level to another, we plot each marginal utility entry between the old and new consumption levels.

Notice the close relationship between the graph of total utility in panel (a) and the corresponding graph of marginal utility in panel (b). If you look closely at the two graphs, you will see that for every one-unit increment in Lisa's ice cream consumption her marginal utility is equal to the change in her total utility. Diminishing marginal utility is seen in both panels of the figure: in panel (b), by the downward sloping marginal utility curve, and in panel (a), by the positive but decreasing slope (flattening out) of the total utility curve.

---

[1] *Principles of Economics,* Book III, Ch. III, Appendix notes 1 & 2. Macmillan & Co., 1930.

One last thing about Figure 3: Because marginal utility diminishes for Lisa, by the time she has consumed a total of five cones per week, the marginal utility she derives from an additional cone has fallen all the way to zero. At this point, she is fully satiated with ice cream and gets no extra satisfaction or utility from eating any more of it in a typical week. Once this satiation point is reached, even if ice cream were free, Lisa would turn it down ("Yechhh! Not more ice cream!!"). But remember from our earlier discussion that one of the assumptions we always make about preferences is that people prefer *more* rather than less of any good we're considering. So when we use marginal utility theory, we assume that marginal utility for every good is positive. For Lisa, it would mean she hasn't yet reached five ice cream cones per week.

Combining the Budget Constraint and Preferences

The marginal utility someone gets from consuming more of a good tells us about his *preferences*. His budget constraint, by contrast, tells us only which combinations of goods he can *afford*. If we combine information about preferences (marginal utility values) with information about what is affordable (the budget constraint), we can develop a useful rule to guide us to an individual's utility-maximizing choice.

To develop this rule, let's go back to Max and his choice between movies and concerts. Figure 4 reproduces Max's budget constraint from Figure 1. But now, we've added information about Max's preferences, in the table below the graph.

Each row of the table corresponds to a different point on Max's budget line. For example, the row labeled C corresponds to point C on the budget line. The second entry in each row tells us the number of concerts that Max attends each month, and the third entry tells us the marginal utility he gets from consuming the last concert. For example, at point C, Max attends two concerts, and the second one gives him an additional 1,200 utils beyond the first. Notice that as we move down along the budget line, from point A to B to C and so on, the number of concerts increases and the marginal utility numbers in the table get smaller, consistent with the law of diminishing marginal utility.

The fourth entry in each row shows something new: the marginal utility *per dollar* spent on concerts, obtained by dividing the marginal utility of the last concert by the price of a concert ($MU_{concerts}/P_{concerts}$). This tells us the gain in utility Max gets *for each dollar he spends* on the last concert. For example, at point C, Max gains 1,200 utils from his second concert during the month, so his marginal utility *per dollar* spent on that concert is 1,200 utils/$30 = 40 utils per dollar. Marginal utility per dollar, like marginal utility itself, declines as Max attends more concerts. After all, marginal utility itself decreases, and the price of a concert isn't changing, so the ratio of marginal utility to price must decrease as he sees more concerts.

The last three entries in each row give us similar information for movies: the number of movies attended, the marginal utility derived from the last movie, and the marginal utility per dollar spent on the last movie (MU_{movies}/P_{movies}). As we travel *up* this column, Max attends more movies, and both marginal utility and marginal utility per dollar decline—once again, consistent with the law of diminishing marginal utility.

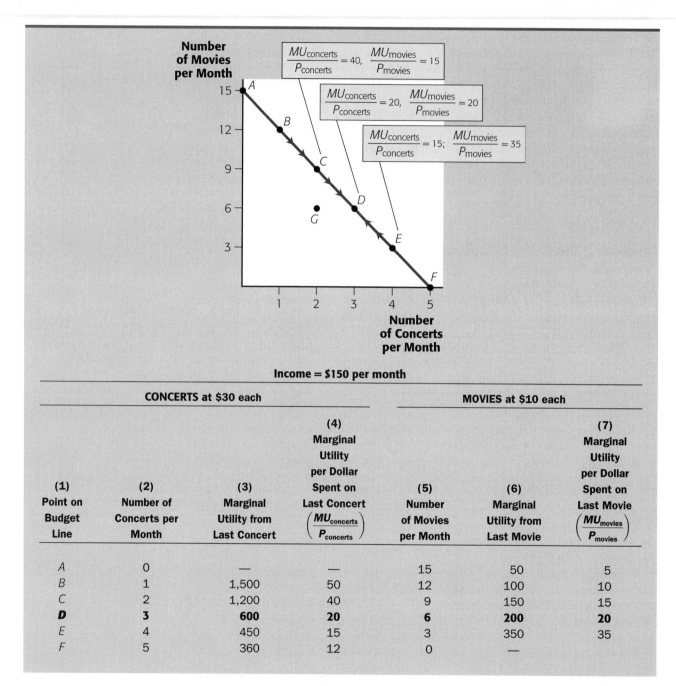

Income = $150 per month

	CONCERTS at $30 each				MOVIES at $10 each	
(1) **Point on** **Budget** **Line**	**(2)** **Number of** **Concerts per** **Month**	**(3)** **Marginal** **Utility from** **Last Concert**	**(4)** **Marginal** **Utility** **per Dollar** **Spent on** **Last Concert** $\left(\dfrac{MU_{concerts}}{P_{concerts}}\right)$	**(5)** **Number** **of Movies** **per Month**	**(6)** **Marginal** **Utility from** **Last Movie**	**(7)** **Marginal** **Utility** **per Dollar** **Spent on** **Last Movie** $\left(\dfrac{MU_{movies}}{P_{movies}}\right)$
A	0	—	—	15	50	5
B	1	1,500	50	12	100	10
C	2	1,200	40	9	150	15
D	**3**	**600**	**20**	**6**	**200**	**20**
E	4	450	15	3	350	35
F	5	360	12	0	—	

FIGURE 4
Consumer Decision Making

The budget line shows the maximum number of movies Max could attend for each number of concerts he attends. He would never choose an interior point like G because there are affordable points—on the line—that make him better off. Max will choose the point on the budget line at which the marginal utilities per dollar spent on movies and concerts are equal. From the table, this occurs at point D.

Now, Max's goal is to find the affordable combination of movies and concerts—the point on his budget line—that gives him the highest possible utility. As you are about to see, this will be the point at which *the marginal utility per dollar is the same for both goods*.

To see why, imagine that Max is searching along his budget line for the utility-maximizing point, and he's currently considering point *B*, which represents 1 concert and 12 movies. Is he maximizing his utility? Let's see. Comparing the fourth and seventh entries in row *B* of the table, we see that Max's marginal utility per dollar spent on concerts is 50 utils, while his marginal utility per dollar spent on movies is only 10 utils. Since he gains more additional utility from each dollar spent on concerts than from each dollar spent on movies, he will have a net gain in utility if he shifts some of his dollars from movies to concerts. To do this, he must travel farther down his budget line.

Next suppose that, after shifting his spending from movies to concerts, Max arrives at point *C* on his budget line. What should he do then? At point *C*, Max's *MU* per dollar spent on concerts is 40 utils, while his *MU* per dollar spent on movies is 15 utils. Once again, he would gain utility by shifting from movies to concerts, traveling down his budget line once again.

Now suppose that Max arrives at point *D*. At this point, the *MU* per dollar spent on both movies and concerts is the same: 20 utils. There is no further gain from shifting spending from movies to concerts. At point *D*, Max has exploited all opportunities to make himself better off by moving down the budget line. He has maximized his utility.

But wait . . . what if Max had started at a point on his budget line *below* point *D*? Would he still end up at the same place? Yes, he would. Suppose Max finds himself at point *E*, with 4 concerts and 3 movies. Here, marginal utilities per dollar are 15 utils for concerts and 35 utils for movies. Now, Max could make himself better off by shifting spending away from concerts and toward movies. He will travel *up* the budget line, once again arriving at point *D*, where no further move will improve his well-being.

As you can see, it doesn't matter whether Max begins at a point on his budget line that's above point *D* or below it. Either way, if he keeps shifting spending toward the good with greater marginal utility per dollar, he will always end up at point *D*. And because marginal utility per dollar is the same for both goods at point *D*, there is nothing to gain by shifting spending in either direction.

What is true for Max and his choice between movies and concerts is true for *any* consumer and *any* two goods. We can generalize our result this way: For any two goods *x* and *y*, with prices P_x and P_y, whenever $MU_x/P_x > MU_y/P_y$, a consumer is made better off shifting spending away from *y* and toward *x*. When $MU_y/P_y > MU_x/P_x$, a consumer is made better off by shifting spending away from *x* and toward *y*. This leads us to an important conclusion:

A utility-maximizing consumer will choose the point on the budget line where marginal utility per dollar is the same for both goods ($MU_x/P_x = MU_y/P_y$). At that point, there is no further gain from reallocating expenditures in either direction.

We can generalize even further. Suppose there are more than two goods an individual can buy. For example, we could imagine that Max wants to divide his

Why Use Marginal Utility *per Dollar*? In finding the utility-maximizing combination of goods for a consumer, why do we use marginal utility *per dollar* instead of just marginal utility? Shouldn't the consumer always shift spending wherever *marginal utility* is greater? The answer is no. The following thought experiment will help you see why. Imagine that you like to ski and you like going out for dinner. Further, given your current combination of skiing and dining out, your marginal utility for one more skiing trip is 2,000 utils, and your marginal utility for an additional dinner is 1,000 utils. Should you shift your spending from dining out to skiing? It might seem so, since skiing has the higher marginal utility.

But what if skiing costs $200 per trip, while a dinner out costs only $20? Then, while it's true that another ski trip will give you twice as much utility as another dinner out, it's also true that *skiing costs 10 times as much*. You would have to sacrifice 10 restaurant meals for 1 ski trip, and that would make you *worse* off. Instead, you should shift your spending in the other direction: from skiing to dining out. Money spent on additional ski trips will give you 2,000 utils/$200 = 10 utils per dollar, while money spent on additional dinners will give you 1,000 utils/$20 = 50 utils per dollar. Dining out clearly gives you "more bang for the buck" than skiing. The lesson: When trying to find the utility-maximizing combination of goods, compare marginal utilities *per dollar*, not marginal utilities of the two goods.

entertainment budget among movies, concerts, football games, and what have you. Or we can think of a consumer who must allocate her entire income among thousands of different goods and services each month: different types of food, clothing, entertainment, transportation, and so on. Does our description of the optimal choice for the consumer still hold? Indeed, it does. No matter how many goods there are to choose from, when the consumer is doing as well as possible, it must be true that $MU_x/P_x = MU_y/P_y$ for any pair of goods x and y. If this condition is *not* satisfied, the consumer will be better off consuming more of one and less of the other good in the pair.[2]

What Happens When Things Change?

If every one of our decisions had to be made only once, life would be much easier. But that's not how life is. Just when you think you've figured out what to do, things change. In a market economy, as you've learned, prices can change for any number of reasons. (See Chapter 3.) A consumer's income can change as well. He may lose a job or find a new one; she may get a raise or a cut in pay. Changes in our incomes or the prices we face cause us to rethink our spending decisions: What maximized utility before the change is unlikely to maximize it afterward. The result is a change in our behavior.

Changes in Income. Figure 5 illustrates how an increase in income might affect Max's choice between movies and concerts. As before, we assume that movies cost $10 each, that concerts cost $30 each, and that these prices are not changing. Initially, Max has $150 in income to spend on the two goods, so his budget line is the line from point A to point F. As we've already seen, under these conditions, Max would choose point D (three concerts and six movies) to maximize utility.

Now suppose Max's income increases to $300. Then his budget line will shift upward and outward in the figure. How will he respond? As always, he will search along his budget line until he finds the point where the marginal utility per dollar spent on both goods is the same. But where will this point be? There are several

---

[2] There is one exception to this statement: Sometimes the optimal choice is to buy *none* of some good. For example, suppose that $MU_y/P_y > MU_x/P_x$ no matter how small a quantity of good x a person consumes. Then the consumer should always reduce consumption of good x further, until its quantity is zero. Economists call this a "corner solution," because when there are only two goods being considered, the individual will locate at one of the end points of the budget line in a corner of the diagram.

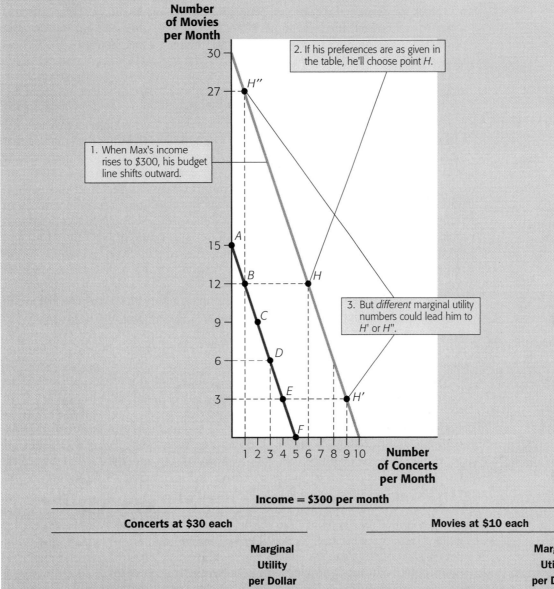

FIGURE 5
Effects of an Increase in Income

possibilities, and they depend on Max's preferences, as reflected in his marginal utility values for movies and concerts. Now that his income has increased, the points along Max's budget line have more movies for any number of concerts, or more concerts for any number of movies. Thus, we'll have to specify Max's preferences among these *new* combinations he can afford.

Let's start out with a simple assumption: that for Max, the marginal utility of any given movie depends only on the total number of movies per month, and *not* on the number of concerts. For example, the marginal utility of the *12th* movie per month would be 100 utils, regardless of whether that movie is enjoyed along with 1 concert per month (point *B*), or with 6 concerts (point *H*). Similarly, suppose that the marginal utility of any *concert* depends on only total concerts, and not on the number of movies that go with them. Then we can bring the marginal utility values for different numbers of movies and concerts from Figure 4 over to Figure 5. With our assumption that marginal utilities for one good are independent of amounts of the other, these marginal utility values will still apply to Max's new set of choices. Figure 5 also includes some additional marginal utility values for combinations that weren't affordable before, but are now. For example, the *sixth* concert—which Max couldn't afford in Figure 4—is now assumed to have a marginal utility of 300 utils.

With the preferences described by these marginal utility numbers, Max will search along his budget line for the best choice. This will lead him directly to point *H*, enjoying 6 concerts and 12 movies per month. For this choice, *MU/P* is 10 utils per dollar for both goods, so total utility can't be increased any further by shifting dollars from one good to the other.

Now let's take a step back from these calculations and look at the figure itself. We see that an increase in income has changed Max's best choice from point *D* on the old budget constraint to point *H* on the new one. In moving from *D* to *H*, Max chooses to buy more concerts (6 rather than 3) and more movies (12 rather than 6). As discussed in Chapters 3 and 4, if an increase in income (with prices held constant) increases the quantity of a good demanded, the good is *normal*. For Max, with the marginal utility values we've assumed in Figure 5, both concerts and movies would be normal goods.

But what if Max's feeling toward one good depends on the amount of the *other* good he's also enjoying? For example, the marginal utility of the 4th concert might *depend on* whether he's also seeing 3 movies that month, or 18 movies. In that case, when Max's income increases, we can't just "borrow" the marginal utility of the 4th concert from Figure 4, because the 4th concert was paired with the 3rd movie there, while in Figure 5, the 4th concert is paired with the 18th movie. And this will apply to *all* of the marginal utility numbers in Figure 5: They will be different than the numbers we've listed in the figure. When we allow for this possibility, Max's best choice in Figure 5 may be some point other than point *H*. Without more information—provided in a table like the one in Figure 5—we can't be certain which point will satisfy this condition. But we can discuss some of the possibilities.

Figure 5 illustrates two alternatives to point *H* that Max might choose, depending on his marginal utility values.

For example, Max's marginal utilities per dollar might now be equal at a point like *H'*, with 9 concerts and 3 movies. In this case, the increase in income would cause Max's consumption of concerts to increase (from 3 to 9), but his consumption of movies to *fall* (from 6 to 3). If so, movies would be an *inferior good* for Max—one for which demand decreases when income increases—while concerts would be a *normal* good.

Finally, let's consider another possible outcome for Max: point H". At this point, he attends more movies and fewer concerts compared to point D. If point H" is where Max's marginal utilities per dollar are equal after the increase in income, then *concerts* would be the inferior good, and movies would be normal. An end-of-chapter problem will provide some supporting details for these alternatives—examples of preferences (marginal utility numbers) that would induce Max to choose point H' or H", instead of H. But the fact that any of these outcomes are possible leads us to this general conclusion:

The Special Meaning of "Inferior" in Economics It's tempting to think that *inferior* goods are of lower quality than *normal* goods. But economists don't define normal or inferior based on the intrinsic properties of a good, but rather by the choices people make when their incomes increase. For example, Max may think that both movies and concerts are high-quality goods. When his income is low, he may see movies on most weekends because, being cheaper, they enable him to spread his budget further. But if his income increases, he can afford to switch from movies to concerts on some nights. If Max attends fewer movies with a higher income, then his *behavior* tells us that movies are inferior for him. If instead he chose to see fewer *concerts* when his income increased, then concerts would be the inferior good.

DANGEROUS CURVES

> *A rise in income—with no change in prices—leads to a new quantity demanded for each good. Whether a particular good is normal (quantity demanded increases) or inferior (quantity demanded decreases) depends on the individual's preferences, as represented by the marginal utilities for each good, at each point along his budget line.*

Changes in Price. Let's explore what happens to Max when the price of a concert decreases from $30 to $10, while his income and the price of a movie remain unchanged. The drop in the price of concerts rotates Max's budget line rightward, pivoting around its vertical intercept, as illustrated in the upper panel of Figure 6. What will Max do after his budget line rotates in this way? Again, he will select the combination of movies and concerts on his budget line that makes him as well off as possible. This will be the combination at which the marginal utility per dollar spent on both goods is the same.

Once again, we've taken some of Max's marginal utility values from Figure 4 and added some additional numbers to construct the table in Figure 6. This table extends what we already knew about Max's preferences to cover the new, expanded possibilities. As we did earlier, we've made an assumption in borrowing the numbers for Figure 6 from our earlier table: that for Max, the marginal utility for one good is independent of the amount of the other good.

With the preferences represented by these marginal utility numbers, Max will search along his budget line for the best choice. This will lead him directly to point J, where his quantities demanded are 7 concerts and 8 movies. Note that with each concert costing only $10 now, Max can afford this combination. Moreover, it satisfies our utility maximizing rule: Marginal utility per dollar is 18 for both goods.

What if we dropped the price of concerts again—this time—to $5? Then Max's budget line rotates further rightward, and he will once again find the utility-maximizing point. In the figure, Max is shown choosing point K, attending

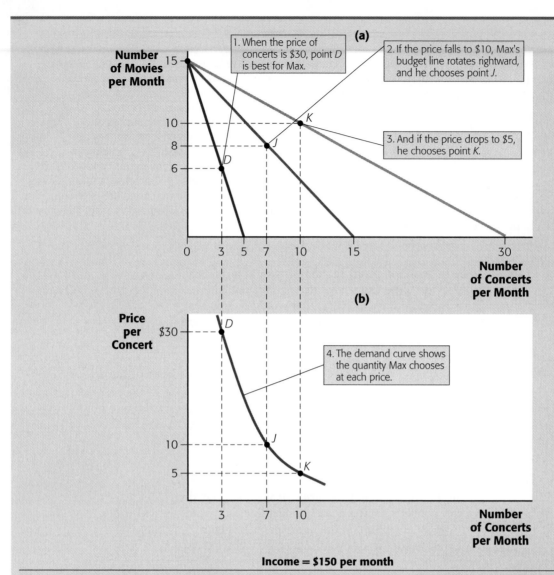

(a)

1. When the price of concerts is $30, point *D* is best for Max.

2. If the price falls to $10, Max's budget line rotates rightward, and he chooses point *J*.

3. And if the price drops to $5, he chooses point *K*.

(b)

4. The demand curve shows the quantity Max chooses at each price.

Income = $150 per month

	Concerts at $10 each			Movies at $10 each	
Number of Concerts per Month	Marginal Utility from Last Concert ($MU_{concerts}$)	Marginal Utility per Dollar Spent on Last Concert $\left(\dfrac{MU_{concerts}}{P_{concerts}}\right)$	Number of Movies per Month	Marginal Utility from Last Movie (MU_{movies})	Marginal Utility per Dollar Spent on Last Movie $\left(\dfrac{MU_{movies}}{P_{movies}}\right)$
3	600	60	12	100	10
4	450	45	11	120	12
5	360	36	10	135	13.5
6	300	30	9	150	15
7	**180**	**18**	**8**	**180**	**18**
8	150	15	7	190	19
9	100	10	6	200	20
10	67.5	6.75	5	210	21

FIGURE 6
Deriving the Demand Curve

10 concerts and 10 movies. (The table in the figure cannot be used to find point *K*, because the table assumes the price of concerts is $10.)

The Individual's Demand Curve

You've just seen that each time the price of concerts changes, so does the quantity of concerts Max will want to see. The lower panel of Figure 6 highlights this relationship by plotting the quantity of concerts demanded on the horizontal axis and the price of concerts on the vertical axis. For example, in both the upper and lower panels, point *D* tells us that when the price of concerts is $30, Max will see three of them. When we connect points like *D*, *J*, and *K* in the lower panel, we get Max's **individual demand curve**, which shows *the quantity of a good he demands at each different price*. Notice that Max's demand curve for concerts slopes downward—a fall in the price of concerts increases the quantity demanded—showing that Max's responses to price changes obey the law of demand.

But if Max's preferences—and his marginal utility values—had been different, could his response to a price change have *violated* the law of demand? The answer is yes . . . and no. Yes, it is theoretically possible. (As a challenge, try identifying points on the three budget lines that would give Max an *upward-sloping* demand curve.) But no, it does not seem to happen in practice.

To understand why and to gain other insights, the next section takes a deeper look into the effects of a price change on quantity demanded.

Individual demand curve A curve showing the quantity of a good or service demanded by a particular individual at each different price.

INCOME AND SUBSTITUTION EFFECTS

Whether you've studied about the marginal utility approach (the previous section) or the indifference curve approach (appendix), you've learned a logical process that leads directly to an individual's demand curve. But the demand curve actually summarizes the impact of *two* separate effects of a price change on quantity demanded. As you are about to see, these two effects sometimes work together, and sometimes oppose each other.

The Substitution Effect

Suppose the price of a good falls. Then it becomes less expensive *relative to* other goods whose prices have not fallen. Some of these other goods are *substitutes* for the now cheaper good—they are different goods, but they are used to satisfy the same general desire. When *one* of the ways of satisfying a desire becomes relatively cheaper, consumers tend to purchase more of it (and tend to purchase less of the substitute goods).

In Max's case, concerts and movies, while different, both satisfy his desire to be entertained. When the price of concerts falls, so does its relative price (relative to movies). Max can now get more entertainment from his budget by substituting concerts in place of movies, so he will demand more concerts.

This impact of a price decrease is called a **substitution effect**: the consumer substitutes *toward* the good whose price has decreased, and away from other goods whose prices have remained unchanged.

Substitution effect As the price of a good falls, the consumer substitutes that good in place of other goods whose prices have not changed.

© PHILIP JAMES CORWIN/CORBIS

Cheaper cell phone calls, and the substitution effect, may soon drive pay phones out of the market.

> *The **substitution effect** of a price change arises from a change in the relative price of a good, and it always moves quantity demanded in the opposite direction to the price change. When price decreases, the substitution effect works to increase quantity demanded; when price increases, the substitution effect works to decrease quantity demanded.*

The substitution effect is a powerful force in the marketplace. For example, while the price of cellular phone calls has fallen in recent years, the price of pay phone calls has remained more or less the same. This fall in the relative price of cell phone calls has caused consumers to substitute toward them and away from using regular pay phones. As a result, many private providers of pay phones are having financial difficulty.

The substitution effect is also important from a theoretical perspective: It is the main factor responsible for the law of demand. Indeed, if the substitution effect were the *only* effect of a price change, the law of demand would be more than a law; it would be a logical necessity. But as we are about to see, a price change has another effect as well.

The Income Effect

In Figure 6, when the price of concerts decreases from $30 to $10, Max's budget line rotates rightward. Max now has a wider range of options than before: He can consume more concerts, more movies, or *more of both*. The price decline of *one* good has increased Max's total purchasing power over *both* goods.

A price cut gives the consumer a gift, which is rather like an increase in *income*. Indeed, in an important sense, it *is* an increase in *available* income: Point D (3 concerts and 6 movies) originally cost Max $150, but after the decrease in the price of concerts, the same combination would cost him just $(6 \times \$10) + (3 \times \$10) = \$90$, leaving him with $60 in *available income* to spend on more movies or concerts or both. This leads to the second effect of a change in price:

Income effect As the price of a good decreases, the consumer's purchasing power increases, causing a change in quantity demanded for the good.

> *The **income effect** of a price change arises from a change in purchasing power over both goods. A drop in price increases purchasing power, while a rise in price decreases purchasing power.*

How will a change in purchasing power influence the quantity of a good demanded? That depends. Recall that an increase in income will increase the demand for normal goods and decrease the demand for inferior goods. The same is true for the *income effect* of a price cut: It can work to either *increase* or *decrease* the quantity of a good demanded, depending on whether the good is normal or inferior. For example, if concerts are a normal good for Max, then the income effect of a price cut will lead him to consume more of them; if concerts are inferior, the income effect will lead him to consume fewer.

Combining Substitution and Income Effects

Now let's look again at the impact of a price change, considering the substitution and income effects together. A change in the price of a good changes both the relative price of the good (the substitution effect) and the overall purchasing power of

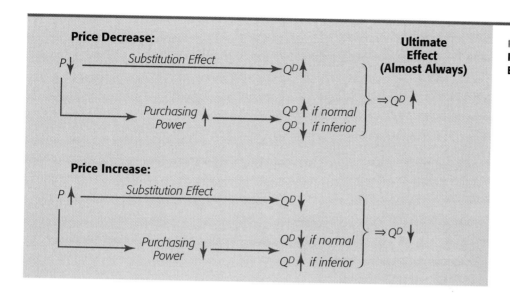

FIGURE 7
Income and Substitution Effects

the consumer (the income effect). The ultimate impact of the price change on quantity demanded will depend on *both* of these effects. For normal goods, these two effects work together to push quantity demanded in the same direction. But for inferior goods, the two effects oppose each other. Let's see why.

Normal Goods. When the price of a normal good falls, the substitution effect *increases* quantity demanded. The price drop will also increase the consumer's purchasing power—and for a normal good—*increase* quantity demanded even further. The opposite occurs when price increases: The substitution effect decreases quantity demanded, and the decline in purchasing power further decreases it. Figure 7 summarizes how the substitution and income effects combine to make the price and quantity of a normal good move in opposite directions:

> *For normal goods, the substitution and income effects work together, causing quantity demanded to move in the opposite direction of the price. Normal goods, therefore, must always obey the law of demand.*

Inferior Goods. Now let's see how a price change affects the demand for *inferior* goods. As an example, consider inter-city bus service. For many consumers, this is an inferior good: with a higher income, these consumers would choose quicker and more comfortable alternatives (such as air or train travel), and therefore demand *less* bus service. Now, if the price of bus service falls, the substitution effect would work, as always, to *increase* quantity demanded. The price cut will also, as always, increase the consumer's purchasing power. But if bus service is inferior, the rise in purchasing power will *decrease* quantity demanded. Thus, we have two opposing effects: the substitution effect, increasing quantity demanded, and the income effect, decreasing quantity demanded. In theory, either of these effects could dominate the other, so the quantity demanded could move in either direction.

In practice, however, the substitution effect almost always dominates for inferior goods.

Why? Because we consume such a wide variety of goods and services that a price cut in any one of them changes our purchasing power by only a small amount. For example, suppose you have an income of $20,000 per year, and you spend $500 per year on bus tickets. If the price of bus travel falls by, say, 20 percent, this would save you $100—like a gift of $100 in income. But $100 is only ½ percent of your income. Thus, a 20 percent fall in the price of bus travel would cause only a ½ percent rise in your purchasing power. Even if bus travel is, for you, an inferior good, we would expect only a tiny decrease in your quantity demanded when your purchasing power changes by such a small amount. Thus, the income effect should be very small. On the other hand, the *substitution* effect should be rather large: With bus travel now 20 percent cheaper, you will likely substitute away from other purchases and buy more bus travel.

> *For inferior goods, the substitution and income effects of a price change work against each other. The substitution effect moves quantity demanded in the opposite direction of the price, while the income effect moves it in the same direction as the price. But since the substitution effect virtually always dominates, consumption of inferior goods—like normal goods—will virtually always obey the law of demand.*

CONSUMERS IN MARKETS

Since the market demand curve tells us the quantity of a good demanded by *all* consumers in a market, it makes sense that we can derive it by adding up the individual demand curves of every consumer in that market.

Figure 8 illustrates how this can be done in a small local market for bottled water, where, for simplicity, we assume that there are only three consumers—Jerry, George, and Elaine. The first three diagrams show their individual demand curves. If the market price were, say, $2 per bottle, Jerry would buy 4 bottles each week (point *c*), George would buy 6 (point *c'*), and Elaine would buy zero (point *c"*). Thus, the market quantity demanded at a price of $2 would be 4 + 6 + 0 = 10, which is point *C* on the market demand curve. To obtain the entire market demand curve, we repeat this procedure at each different price, adding up the quantities demanded by each individual to obtain the total quantity demanded in the market. (Verify on your own that points *A, B, D,* and *E* have been obtained in the same way.) In effect, we obtain the market demand curve by summing horizontally across each of the individual demand curves:

> *The market demand curve is found by horizontally summing the individual demand curves of every consumer in the market.*

Notice that as long as each individual's demand curve is downward sloping (and this will virtually always be the case), then the market demand curve will also be downward sloping. More directly, if a rise in price makes each consumer buy fewer units, then it will reduce the quantity bought by *all* consumers as well. Indeed, the market demand curve can still obey the law of demand even when *some* individuals violate it. Thus, although we are already quite confident about the law of demand at the individual level, we can be even *more* confident at the market level. This is why we always draw market demand curves with a downward slope.

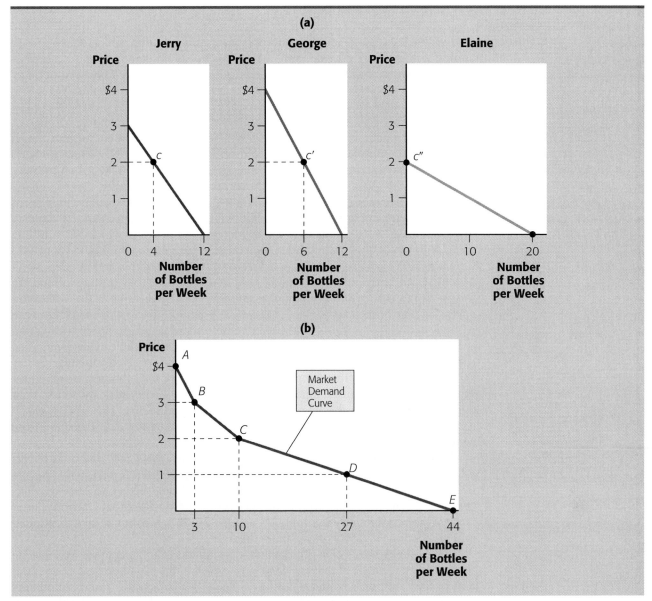

FIGURE 8
From Individual to Market Demand

The individual demand curves show how much bottled water will be demanded by Jerry, George, and Elaine at different prices. As the price falls, each demands more. The market demand curve in panel (b) is obtained by adding up the total quantity demanded by all market participants at different prices.

CONSUMER THEORY IN PERSPECTIVE

Our model of consumer theory—whether using marginal utility or indifference curves—may strike you as rather simple. Indeed, it was *purposely* kept simple, to bring out the "big ideas" more clearly. But can it explain and predict behavior in more complicated, real-world situations? In many cases, yes—with appropriate modification. In other cases, . . . no.

HTTP://

To get an insight into the economic forces driving a fad, read "Pokemon Economics" at
http://economics.about.com/
library/weekly/aa010900.htm.

Extensions of the Model

One problem our simple model ignores is *uncertainty*. In our model, the consumer knows with certainty the outcome of any choice—so many movies and concerts—and knows with certainty how much income is available for spending. But in many real-world situations, you make your choice and you take your chances. When you buy a car, it might be a lemon; when you pay for some types of surgery, there is a substantial risk that it will be unsuccessful; and when you buy a house, you cannot be sure of its condition or how much you will like the neighborhood. Income, too, is often uncertain. Employees risk being laid off, and self-employed lawyers, doctors, and small-business owners might have a good year or a bad year. When uncertainty is an important aspect of consumer choice, economists use other, more complex models. But even these models are based on the one you have learned in this chapter.

Another problem is *imperfect information*. In our model, consumers are assumed to *know* exactly what goods they are buying and the prices at which they can buy them. But in the real world, we must sometimes spend time and money to get this information. Prices can be different in different stores and on different days, depending on whether there is a sale, so we might have to make phone calls or shop around. To be sure of the quality of our purchases, we may have to subscribe to *Consumer Reports* magazine or spend time inspecting goods or getting advice from others. Over the past few decades, economists have been intensely interested in imperfect information and its consequences for decision-making behavior. And our simple model—modified to take account of the *cost* of acquiring information—has proven very useful.

A third problem is that people can spend more than their incomes in any given year, by borrowing funds or spending out of savings. Or they may spend less than their incomes because they choose to save or pay back debts. This, too, is easily handled by our model of consumer choice, for example, by defining one of the goods as "future consumption."

Finally, you might think that consumer theory always regards people as relentlessly selfish, concerned only about their own consumption. In fact, when people trade in impersonal markets this is mostly true: People *do* try to allocate their spending among different goods to achieve the greatest possible satisfaction. But in many areas of economic life, people act unselfishly. This, too, has been incorporated into the traditional model of consumer theory.

For example, Max's *own* utility might depend on the utility enjoyed by someone else—either a member of his own family, or others in his neighborhood or community, or even the average level of utility in the world. In fact, the "utility of others" can be treated as "another good" in the model. Useful analyses of charitable giving, bequests, and voting behavior have been based on this modification of the model.

Challenges to the Model

From our discussion, you can see that the model of consumer choice is quite versatile, capable of adapting to more aspects of economic behavior than one might think. But economists have long observed that certain types of behavior do not fit the model at all. For example, people will sometimes *judge quality by price*. Diamonds, designer dresses, men's suits, doctors' services, and even automobiles are sometimes perceived as being better if their prices are higher. This means that the consumer cannot choose among different combinations of goods by themselves; she must first know their prices. And when prices change, so will her preferences—violating our description of rational preferences.

Behavioral Economics. In recent years, a broader challenge has emerged from a new subfield of economics known as **behavioral economics.** Behavioral economists try to incorporate facts about actual human behavior—often pointed out by psychologists—that deviate from the standard assumptions of economic models. While economists—dating back to Adam Smith—have often reached outside the field for broader insights, behavioral economists do so in a more systematic and formal way. And while their models incorporate some of the traditional tools of economic analysis, others are conspicuously left out. Behavioral economists are represented on the faculties of the most prestigious universities, win major professional awards, and are the subject of much attention in the media.[3]

Behavioral economics A subfield of economics focusing on behavior that deviates from the standard assumptions of economic models.

To understand what's different about behavioral economics, let's take a broad look at the more standard approach of economics. As a rule, economists view decision makers as striving to achieve a well-defined goal: typically, the goal of *maximizing some quantity*. In this chapter, for example, consumers are viewed as trying to maximize their utility or well-being. In later chapters, business firms are striving to *maximize profit*. Even when households or firms are recognized as *groups* of individuals with different agendas, economists typically assume that maximization is involved. For example, while a firm's owners might want the firm to maximize profits, the managers might want to consider their own incomes, power, prestige, or job security. When the goals conflict, the behavior of the firm will depend on how the conflict is resolved. Still, each individual or group within the firm is depicted as trying to maximize something. Economists have often disagreed over *what* is being maximized, but have usually accepted the idea that *something* is.

Behavioral economists, however, point out that some human behavior is not consistent with *any* type of maximization. For example, stock market investors will often hold on to shares when the price has fallen, refusing to sell until the price rises enough to prevent any loss. They do so even when selling the stock and using the money for other purposes—such as buying a new car—would make them better off. Their desire to avoid regret over a past loss seems to get in the way of maximizing their current utility.

Another example: Dieters will often refuse to have ice cream in the house, to help them avoid temptation. This might seem innocuous, but it's inconsistent with our notion of the rational, utility-maximizing consumer. After all, if a consumer can select the utility-maximizing choice among all available options, he should never try to limit the options available. Or—more simply—a rational consumer should be able to say no, and not be harmed by the option of saying yes.

Indeed, there are many examples where emotion seems to trump narrowly defined rationality: procrastination, drug addiction, and even honesty—especially when telling the truth is costly and a lie would not be discovered. And how can it be rational to spend $3 on gas and wear and tear on your car when driving to a slightly less-expensive supermarket, where you'll save only $2 at checkout? Moreover, why would someone make this drive for groceries, but not to save $3 on a $1,000 personal computer?

Behavioral economists have offered explanations for these and other examples of economic behavior that wholly or partially abandon the idea of maximization. Instead, they incorporate notions about people's *actual thinking process* in making decisions. And they point out that such behavior by large groups of people can alter a market's equilibrium, or how we view the equilibrium.

---

[3] A brief summary of behavioral economics, and some of the controversy surrounding it, is in Roger Lowenstein's "Exuberance Is Rational," *New York Times Magazine,* February 11, 2001. For further insights, consult the list of behavioral economics and finance resources, compiled by the librarians at the University of California at Berkeley: *http://www.lib.berkeley.edu/BUSI/pdfs/behave.pdf.*

This can have important policy implications. For example, in Chapter 4, you learned that at least part of an excise tax will be shifted to buyers, raising their price and therefore harming them. But if buying cigarettes is an irrational addictive behavior rather than a choice, then a cigarette tax—if it encourages people to quit—can make them *better* off.[4]

However, before you start wondering why you've bothered to learn about the utility-maximizing consumer, or why you should go on to read about the profit-maximizing firm, a little perspective is in order. While we do, indeed, observe many cases where behavior is *not* rational, we observe far many more cases where it *is*. While the questions raised by behaviorists are fascinating, and their insights valuable, even its strongest proponents would *not* use behavioral models to explain why gasoline prices rise and fall, or how bad weather might affect Florida orange growers. In fact, they wouldn't use behavioral models to explain most of what happens in the vast majority of markets around the world, because the standard economic models work so much better for this purpose.

So while behavioral economics is often portrayed in the media as an "alternative" or even a "replacement" for traditional economic theory, few if any economists see it that way. Instead, behavioral economics is more commonly viewed as an addition to the existing body of economic theory—an extra limb that extends the theory's reach to some anomalous behavior.

© SUSAN VAN ETTEN

USING THE THEORY
Improving Education

So far in this chapter, we've considered the problem of a consumer trying to maximize utility by selecting the best combination of goods and services. But consumer theory can be extended to consider almost *any* decision between two alternatives, including activities that cost us time rather than dollars. In this section, we apply the model of consumer choice to an important issue: the quality of education.[5]

Billions of dollars have been spent over the past few decades trying to improve the quality of education in our schools, colleges, and universities. In 2003 alone, the U.S. Department of Education spent about $3 billion on research to assess and implement new educational techniques. For example, suppose it is thought that computer-assisted instruction might help students learn better or more quickly. A typical research project to test this hypothesis would be a *controlled experiment* in which one group of students would be taught with the computer-assisted instruction and the other group would be taught without it. Then students in both groups would be tested. If the first group scores significantly higher, computer-assisted instruction will be deemed successful; if not, it will be deemed unsuccessful. To the disappointment of education researchers, most promising new techniques are found to

[4] Jonathan Gruber and Botond Koszegi, "A Theory of Government Regulation of Addictive Bads: Optimal Tax Levels and Tax Incidence for Cigarette Excise Taxation," National Bureau of Economic Research Working Paper 8777, February 2002.

[5] This section is based on ideas originally published in Richard B. McKenzie and Gordon Tullock, *The New World of Economics*, 3d ed. (Burr Ridge, IL: Irwin, 1981).

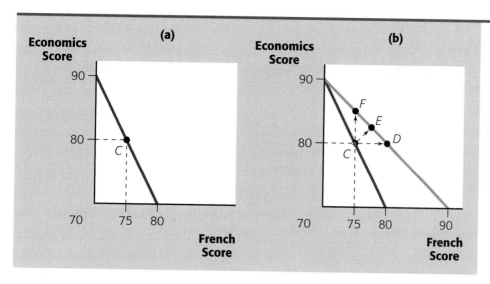

FIGURE 9
Time Allocation

Panel (a) shows combinations of French and economics test scores that can be obtained for a given amount of study time. The slope of −2 indicates that each additional point in French requires a sacrifice of 2 points in economics. The student chooses point C. Panel (b) shows that computer-assisted French instruction causes the budget line to rotate outward; French points are now less expensive. The student might move to point D, attaining a higher French score. Or she might choose F, using all of the time freed up in French to study economics. Or she might choose an intermediate point such as E.

be unsuccessful: Students seem to score about the same, no matter which techniques are tried.

Economists find these studies highly suspect, since the experiments treat students as passive responders to stimuli. Presented with a stimulus (the new technique), students are assumed to give a simple response (scoring higher on the exam). Where in this model, economists ask, are students treated as *decision makers,* who must make *choices* about allocating their scarce time?

Let's apply our model of consumer choice to a student's time allocation problem. To keep things simple, we'll assume a bleak world in which there are only two activities: studying economics and studying French. Instead of costing money, each of these activities costs *time,* and there is only so much time available. And instead of buying quantities of two goods, students "buy" points on their exams with hours spent studying.

Panel (a) of Figure 9 shows how we can represent the time allocation problem graphically. The economics test score is measured on the vertical axis and the French score on the horizontal axis. The straight line in the figure is the student's budget line, showing the trade-off between economics and French scores. Our student can achieve any combination of scores on this budget line with her scarce time.

A few things are worth noting about the budget line in the figure. First, the more study time you devote to a subject, the better you will do on the test. But that means *less* study time for the other subject and a lower test score there. Thus, the opportunity cost of scoring better in French is scoring lower in economics, and vice versa. This is why the budget line has a negative slope: the higher the score in French, the lower the score in economics. As our student moves downward along the budget line, she is shifting hours away from studying economics and toward studying French.

Second, notice that the vertical and horizontal axes both start at 70 rather than 0. This is to keep our example from becoming too depressing. If our student devotes *all* her study time to economics and none to French, she would score 90 in economics but still be able to score 70 (rather than zero) in French, just by attending class and paying attention. If she devotes all her time to French, she would score 80 in French and 70 in economics. (*Warning:* Do not try to use this example to convince your economics instructor you deserve at least a 70 on your next exam.)

Finally, the budget line in our example is drawn as a straight line with a slope of −2. So each additional point in French requires our student to sacrifice two points in economics. This assumption helps make the analysis more concrete. But none of our conclusions would be different if the budget line had a different slope, or even if it were curved so that the trade-off would change as we moved along it. But let's take a moment to understand what our example implies.

As you've learned, the slope of any budget line is $-P_x/P_y$, where x is the good measured on the horizontal axis and y is the good measured on the vertical axis. In our example, $-P_x/P_y$ translates into $-P_{\text{French point}}/P_{\text{econ point}}$. But what is the "price" of a test point in French or economics? Unlike the case of Max, who had to allocate his scarce *funds* between concerts and movies, our student must allocate her scarce *time* between the two "goods" she desires: test points in French and test points in economics. The *price* of a test point is therefore not a money price, but rather a *time price*: the number of study hours needed to achieve an additional point. For example, if it takes an additional two hours of studying to achieve another point in French, then the price per point in French is two hours. Moreover, in the figure, we assume that the price per point in economics is one-half the price per point in French, so if $P_{\text{French point}} = 2$, then $P_{\text{econ point}} = 1$. The slope of the budget line is therefore $-P_{\text{French point}}/P_{\text{econ point}} = -2$.

Now let's turn our attention to student decision making. Our student derives satisfaction of utility from both her economics score and her French score—the greater either score, the better off she is. But among all those combinations of scores on her budget line, which is the best choice? That depends on the student's preferences, whether characterized by the marginal utility approach or the indifference curve approach. Suppose that initially, this student's best choice is at point C, where she scores 80 in economics and 75 in French.

Now, let's introduce a new computer-assisted technique in the French class, one that is, in fact, remarkably effective: It enables students to learn more French with the same study time or to study less and learn the same amount. This is a *decrease* in the price of French points—it now takes fewer hours to earn a point in French—so the budget line will rotate outward, as shown in panel (b) of Figure 9. On the new budget line, if our student devotes all of her time to French, she can score higher than before—90 instead of 80—so the horizontal intercept moves rightward. But since nothing has changed in her economics course, the vertical intercept remains unaffected. Notice, too, that the budget line's slope has changed—to −1. Now, the opportunity cost of an additional point in French is one point in economics rather than two.

After the new technique is introduced in the French course, our *decision-making* student will locate at a point on her new budget line based once again on her preferences. Panel (b) illustrates some alternative possibilities. At point D, her performance in French would improve, but her economics performance would remain the same. This seems to be the kind of result education researchers have in mind when they design their experiments: If a successful technique is introduced in the French course, we should be able to measure the impact with a French test.

Point F illustrates a different choice: *Only* the economics performance improves, while the French score remains unchanged. Here, even though the technique in French is successful (it does, indeed, shift the budget line), none of its success shows up in higher French scores.

But wait: How can a new technique in the French course improve performance in economics but not at all in French? The answer is found by breaking down the impact of the new technique into our familiar income and substitution effects. The new technique lowers the student's time cost of getting additional points in French. The substitution effect (French points are relatively cheaper) will tend to improve her score in French, as she substitutes her time away from studying economics and toward studying French. But there is also an *"income"* effect: The "purchasing power" of her time has increased, since now she could use her fixed allotment of study time to "buy" higher scores in *both* courses. If performance in French is a "normal good," this increase in "purchasing power" will work to increase her French score, but if it is an "inferior good," it could work to *decrease* her French score. Point F could come about because French performance is *such* an inferior good that the negative income effect exactly cancels out the positive substitution effect. In this case, the education researchers will incorrectly judge the new technique a complete failure—it does not affect French scores at all.

Could this actually happen? Perhaps. It is easy to imagine a student deciding that 75 in French is good enough and using any study time freed up from better French instruction to improve her performance in some other course. More commonly, we expect a student to choose a point such as E, somewhere between points D and F, with performance improving in *both* courses. But even in this case, the higher French score measures just a *part* of the impact of the technique; the remaining effect is seen in a higher economics score.

This leads us to a general conclusion: When we recognize that students make *choices,* we expect only *some* of the impact of a better technique to show up in the course in which it is used. In the real world, college students typically take several courses at once and have other competing interests for their time as well (cultural events, parties, movies, telephone calls, exercising, and so on). Any time saved due to better teaching in a single course might well be "spent" on *all* of these alternatives, with only a little devoted to that single course. Thus, we cannot fully measure the impact of a new technique by looking at the score in one course alone. This suggests why educational research is conducted as it is: A more accurate assessment would require a thorough accounting for all of a student's time, which is both expensive and difficult to achieve. Nevertheless, we remain justified in treating this research with some skepticism.

Summary

Graphically, the budget constraint is represented by the *budget line.* Only combinations on or below the budget line are affordable. An increase in income shifts the budget line outward. A change in the price of a good causes the budget line to rotate. Whenever the budget line shifts or rotates, the consumer moves to a point on the *new* budget line. The consumer will always choose the point that provides the greatest level of satisfaction or *utility,* and this will depend on the consumer's unique preferences.

There are two alternative ways to represent consumer preferences, which lead to two different approaches to consumer decision making. The *marginal utility approach* is presented in the body of the chapter. In this approach, a utility-maximizing consumer chooses the combination of goods along her budget line at which the marginal utility per dollar spent is the same for all goods. When income or price changes, the consumer once again equates the marginal utility per dollar of both goods, resulting in a choice along the *new* budget line.

In the *indifference curve approach,* presented in the appendix, a consumer's preferences are represented by a collection of her *indifference curves,* called her *indifference map.* The highest level of utility or satisfaction is achieved at the point on the budget line that is also on the highest possible indifference curve. When income or price changes, the consumer moves to the point on the *new* budget line that is on the highest possible indifference curve.

Using either of the two approaches, we can trace the quantity of a good chosen at different prices for that good, and generate a downward sloping *demand* curve for that good. The downward slope reflects the interaction of the *substitution effect* and the *income effect*. For a normal good, both effects contribute to the downward slope of the demand curve. For an inferior good, we can have confidence that the substitution effect dominates the income effect, so—once again—the demand curve will slope downward.

Key Terms

Behavioral economics	Individual demand curve	Relative price
Budget constraint	Law of diminishing marginal utility	Substitution effect
Budget line	Marginal utility	Utility
Income effect	Rational preferences	

Review Questions   *Answers to even-numbered Questions and Problems can be found on the text Web site at http://hall-lieb.swlearning.com.*

1. What variables are assumed constant along a budget line?

2. What kinds of changes will shift or rotate the budget line?

3. [Uses the Marginal Utility Approach] Explain the relationship between a total quantity and a marginal quantity.

4. [Uses the Marginal Utility Approach] State and explain the law of diminishing marginal utility. Can you think of a good or service you consume that is not subject to this law? Could marginal utility be negative? Give an example.

5. Economists usually assume that consumer preferences are logically consistent. What does that mean? What are some other assumptions economists make about preferences?

6. Discuss the following statement: "Economists' assumption of consumer rationality is too strong. For example, anyone who smokes cigarettes is clearly being irrational."

7. What condition will be satisfied when a consumer has chosen the combination of goods that maximizes utility subject to a budget constraint? Use either the Marginal Utility Approach or Indifference Curve Approach.

8. What are income and substitution effects? How are they related to the law of demand?

9. "The demand curve for an inferior good is upward sloping." True or false? Explain.

10. How is a market demand curve derived?

Problems and Exercises

1. Parvez, a pharmacology student, has allocated $120 per month to spend on paperback novels and used CDs. Novels cost $8 each; CDs cost $6 each. Draw his budget line.
   a. Draw and label a second budget line that shows what happens when the price of a CD rises to $10.
   b. Draw and label a third budget line that shows what happens when the price of a CD rises to $10 *and* Parvez's income rises to $240.

2. [Uses the Marginal Utility Approach] Now go back to the original assumptions of problem 1 (novels cost $8, CDs cost $6, and income is $120). Suppose that Parvez is spending $120 monthly on paperback novels and used CDs. For novels, $MU/P = 5$; for CDs, $MU/P = 4$. Is he maximizing his utility? If not, should he consume (1) more novels and fewer CDs or (2) more CDs and fewer novels? Explain briefly.

3. [Uses the Marginal Utility Approach] Anita consumes both pizza and Pepsi. The following tables show the amount of utility she obtains from different amounts of these two goods:

Pizza		Pepsi	
Quantity	Utility	Quantity	Utility
4 slices	115	5 cans	63
5 slices	135	6 cans	75
6 slices	154	7 cans	86
7 slices	171	8 cans	96

Suppose Pepsi costs $0.50 per can, pizza costs $1 per slice, and Anita has $9 to spend on food and drink. What combination of pizza and Pepsi will maximize her utility?

4. Three people have the following individual demand schedules for Count Chocula cereal that show how many boxes each would purchase monthly at different prices:

Price	Person 1	Person 2	Person 3
$5.00	0	1	2
$4.50	0	2	3
$4.00	0	3	4
$3.50	1	3	5

   a. What is the market demand schedule for this cereal? (Assume that these three people are the only buyers.) Draw the market demand curve.
   b. Why might the three people have different demand schedules?

5. Suppose that 1,000 people in a market *each* have the same monthly demand curve for bottled water, given by the equation $Q^D = 100 - 25P$, where P is the price for a 12-ounce bottle in dollars.
   a. How many bottles would be demanded in the entire market if the price is $1?
   b. How many bottles would be demanded in the entire market if the price is $2?
   c. Provide an equation for the *market* demand curve, showing how the market quantity demanded by all 1,000 consumers depends on the price.

6. What would happen to the market demand curve for polyester suits, an inferior good, if consumers' incomes rose?

7. Larsen E. Pulp, head of Pulp Fiction Publishing Co., just got some bad news: The price of paper, the company's most important input, has increased.
   a. On a supply/demand diagram, show what will happen to the price of Pulp's output (novels).
   b. Explain the resulting substitution and income effects for a typical Pulp customer. For each effect, will the customer's quantity demanded increase or decrease? Be sure to state any assumptions you are making.

8. "If a good is inferior, a rise in its price will cause people to buy more of it, thus violating the law of demand." True or false? Explain.

9. Which of the following descriptions of consumer behavior violates the assumption of *rational preferences*? In each case, explain briefly.
   a. Joseph is confused: He doesn't know whether he'd prefer to take a job now or go to college full-time.
   b. Brenda likes mustard on her pasta, in spite of the fact that pasta is not meant to be eaten with mustard.
   c. Brewster says, "I'd rather see an action movie than a romantic comedy, and I'd rather see a romantic comedy than a foreign film. But given the choice, I think I'd rather see a foreign film than an action movie."

10. [Uses the Indifference Curve Approach] Howard spends all of his income on magazines and novels. Illustrate each of the following situations on a graph, with the quantity of magazines on the vertical axis and the quantity of novels on the horizontal axis. Use two budget lines and two indifference curves on each graph.
    a. When the price of magazines rises, Howard buys fewer magazines and more novels.
    b. When Howard's income rises, he buys more magazines *and* more novels.
    c. When Howard's income rises, he buys more magazines but *fewer* novels.

11. [Uses the Marginal Utility Approach] In Figure 5, we assumed that when Max's income rose, his marginal utility values for any given number of movies or concerts remained the same. But now suppose that when Max's income rises, and he can consume more movies and concerts, *an additional movie has less value* to Max than before. In particular, assume that Max's marginal utility values are as in the table below. Fill in the blanks for the missing values, and find Max's utility maximizing combination of concerts and movies. In Figure 5 in the chapter, at what point does Max end up?

Income = $300 per month

Concerts at $30 each			Movies at $10 each		
(1) Number of Concerts per Month	(2) Marginal Utility from Last Concert	(3) Marginal Utility per Dollar Spent on Last Concert	(4) Number of Movies per Month	(5) Marginal Utility from Last Movie	(6) Marginal Utility per Dollar Spent on Last Movie
3	600		21	4	
4	450		18	6	
5	360		15	10	
6	300		12	20	
7	180		9	30	
8	150		6	35	
9	120		3	40	

12. [Uses the Marginal Utility Approach] In Figure 5, we assumed that when Max's income rose, his marginal utility values for any given number of movies or concerts remained the same. But now suppose that when Max's income rises, having the ability to enjoy more concerts or movies makes the *last movie* and the *last concert less valuable* to him, so all the marginal utility numbers shrink. In particular, assume that Max's marginal utility values are as in the table below. Fill in the blanks for the missing values, and find Max's utility maximizing

combination of concerts and movies. In Figure 5 in the chapter, at what point does Max end up?

Income = $300 per month

(1) Number of Concerts per Month	(2) Marginal Utility from Last Concert	(3) Marginal Utility per Dollar Spent on Last Concert	(4) Number of Movies per Month	(5) Marginal Utility from Last Movie	(6) Marginal Utility per Dollar Spent on Last Movie
	Concerts at $30 each			**Movies at $10 each**	
1	450		27	150	
2	390		24	175	
3	300		21	200	
4	225		18	225	
5	180		15	250	
6	150		12	275	
7	90		9	300	
8	75		6	325	
9	60		3	350	

13. [Uses the Indifference Curve Approach]
    a. Draw a budget line for Cameron, who has a monthly income of $100. Assume that he buys steak and potatoes, and that steak costs $10 per pound and that potatoes cost $2 per pound. Add an indifference curve for Cameron that is tangent to his budget line at the combination of 5 pounds of steak and 25 pounds of potatoes.
    b. Draw a new budget line for Cameron, if his monthly income falls to $80. Assume that potatoes are an inferior good to Cameron. Draw a new indifference curve tangent to his new budget constraint that reflects this inferiority. What will happen to Cameron's potato consumption? What will happen to his steak consumption?

14. [Uses the Indifference Curve Approach]
    a. Draw a budget line for Rafaella, who has a weekly income of $30. Assume that she buys chicken and eggs, and that chicken costs $5 per pound while eggs cost $1 each. Add an indifference curve for Rafaella that is tangent to her budget line at the combination of 4 pounds of chicken and 10 eggs.
    b. Draw a new budget line for Rafaella, if the price of chicken falls to $3 per pound. Assume that Rafaella views chicken and eggs as substitutes. What will happen to her chicken consumption? What will happen to her egg consumption?

15. [Uses the Indifference Curve Approach]
    a. Draw a budget line for Lynne, who has a weekly income of $225. Assume that she buys food and clothes, and that food costs $15 per bag while clothes cost $25 per item. Add an indifference curve for Lynne that is tangent to her budget line at the combination of 3 items of clothing and 10 bags of food.
    b. Draw a new indifference curve for Lynne, showing what will happen if her tastes change, so that she gets more satisfaction from an extra item of clothing, and less satisfaction from an extra bag of food.
    c. Returning to the original tangency, what will happen if Lynne decides to join a nudist colony?

16. Use the numbers in the marginal utility columns of Figure 6 to figure out that point K is optimal after the price of concerts falls from $10 to $5.

Challenge Questions

1. The Smiths are a low-income family with $10,000 available annually to spend on food and shelter. Food costs $2 per unit, and shelter costs $1 per square foot per year. The Smiths are currently dividing the $10,000 equally between food and shelter. Use either the Marginal Utility Approach or Indifference Curve Approach.
    a. Draw their budget constraint on a diagram with food on the vertical axis and shelter on the horizontal axis. Label their current consumption choice. How much do they spend on food? On shelter?
    b. Suppose the price of shelter rises to $2 per square foot. Draw the new budget line. Can the Smiths continue to consume the same amounts of food and shelter as previously?
    c. In response to the increased price of shelter, the government makes available a special income supplement. The Smiths receive a cash grant of $5,000 that must be spent on food and shelter. Draw their new budget line and compare it to the line you derived in part a. *Could* the Smiths consume the same combination of food and shelter as in part a?
    d. With the cash grant and with shelter priced at $2 per square foot, *will* the family consume the same combination as in part a? Why, or why not?

2. When an economy is experiencing inflation, the prices of most goods and services are rising but at different rates. Imagine a simpler inflationary situation in which *all* prices, and all wages and incomes, are rising at the same

rate, say 5 percent per year. What would happen to consumer choices in such a situation? (*Hint:* Think about what would happen to the budget line.)

3. [Uses the Indifference Curve Approach] With the quantity of popcorn on the vertical axis and the quantity of ice cream on the horizontal axis, draw indifference maps to illustrate each of the following situations. (*Hint:* Each will look different from the indifference maps in the appendix, because each violates one of the assumptions we made there.)

    a. Larry's marginal rate of substitution between ice cream and popcorn remains constant, no matter how much of each good he consumes.

    b. Heather loves ice cream but hates popcorn.

    c. When Andy eats ice cream, he tends to get addicted: The more he has, the more he wants still more, and he's willing to give up more and more popcorn to get the same amount of additional ice cream.

4. [Uses the Indifference Curve Approach] The appendix to this chapter states that when a consumer is buying the optimal combination of two goods x and y, then $MRS_{y,x} = P_x / P_y$. Draw a graph, with an indifference curve and a budget line, and with the quantity of y on the vertical axis, to illustrate the case where the consumer is buying a combination on his budget line for which $MRS_{y,x} > P_x / P_y$.

ECONOMIC *Applications* *These exercises require access to Hall/Lieberman Xtra! If Xtra! did not come with your book, visit http://hallxtra.swlearning.com to purchase.*

1. Use your Xtra! password at the Hall and Lieberman Web site (http://hallxtra.swlearning.com), select this chapter, and under Economic Applications, click on EconNews. Choose *Microeconomics: Elasticity,* and scroll down to find the articles, "Health Maintenance Organizations Fail to Maintain Health Benefits" and "Higher Health-Care Costs: Who Pays?" Read the article summaries and answer the following questions:

    a. Construct a budget line for two goods: health care and all other goods, assuming the following information: you have an income level of $30,000, one unit of health care (office visits, for example) costs $100, one unit of all other goods costs $50. You currently have no health insurance. Be sure to label your axes and your intercept points.

    b. Now assume that you receive health care from your employer at a cost to you of $2,000 per year, but as a result of your purchase of health care, all costs are covered (you are 100% insured). How does your budget line change from that in a? (*Hint:* now that you are fully insured, what is the price of health care?) Draw a new budget line in the graph you made in part a.

    c. After reading the articles, it is clear that employers are taking steps to reduce the burden they assume in

covering employees' medical expenses. If the cost of coverage remained the same, but only 80% of medical costs were covered by insurance (in effect, you now have a 20% copayment), what would happen to your budget line in b? Draw this in the same graph as before.

    d. Did this have the effect desired by employers and health maintenance organizations? Why or why not?

2. Use your Xtra! password at the Hall and Lieberman Web site (http://hallxtra.swlearning.com), select this chapter, and under Economic Applications, click on EconNews. Choose *Microeconomics: Utility and Consumer Choice* and scroll down to find the article, "Does the Anti-sweatshop Movement Help or Harm Workers In Low-Wage Economies?" Read the debate and consider the following question: Much of the discussion, in economic terms, revolves around the relative differences in marginal utility of production and wage rates paid between developing and developed countries. According to the article, how does a firm use the *principle of marginal decision making* and maximize its own utility when deciding to move operations, for example, from the United States to a developing country?

APPENDIX

THE INDIFFERENCE CURVE APPROACH[6]

This appendix presents an alternative approach to consumer decision making, and can be read in place of the approach in the body of the chapter ("Consumer Decisions: The Marginal Utility Approach"). We're naming it the "Indifference Curve Approach" after a graph that you will soon encounter.

Let's start by reviewing what we've already discussed about preferences. We assume that an individual (1) can compare any two options and decide which is best, or that both are equally attractive, (2) makes choices that are logically consistent, and (3) prefers more of every good to less. The first two assumptions are summarized as rational preferences; the third tells us that a consumer will always choose to be *on* her budget line, rather than below it.

But now, we'll go a bit further.

AN INDIFFERENCE CURVE

In Figure A.1, look at point *G*, which represents 20 movies and 1 concert per month. Suppose we get Max to look at this figure with us, and ask him to imagine how satisfied he would be to have the combination at point *G*. Max thinks about it for a minute, then says, "Okay, I know how satisfied I would be." Next, we say to Max, "Suppose you are at point *G* and we give you *another* concert each month, for a total of 2. That would make you even *more* satisfied, right?" Since Max likes concerts, he nods his head. But then we ask, "After giving you this additional concert, how many movies could we *take away* from you and leave you no better or worse off than you were originally, at point *G*?" Obliging fellow that he is, Max thinks about it and answers, "Well, if I'm starting at point *G*, and you give me another concert, I suppose you could take away 9 movies and I'd be just as happy as I was at *G*."

Max has essentially told us that he is *indifferent between* point *G* on the one hand and point *H* on the other. We know this because starting at point *G*, adding 1 more concert and taking away 9 movies puts us at point *H*.

But let's keep going. Now we get Max to imagine that he's at point *H*, and we ask him the same question, and this time he answers, "I could trade 5 movies for 1 more concert and be equally well off." Now Max is telling us that he is indifferent between point *H* and *J*, since *J* gives him 1 more concert and 5 fewer movies than point *H*.

So far, we know Max is indifferent between point *G* and point *H*, and between point *H* and point *J*. So long as he is rational, he must be entirely indifferent among all three points—*G, H,* and *J*—since all three give him the same level of satisfaction. By continuing in this way, we can trace out a set of points that—as far as Max is

> An **indifference curve**[7] represents all combinations of two goods that make the consumer equally well off.

concerned—are equally satisfying. When we connect these points with a curved line, we get one of Max's *indifference curves*.

Notice two things about the indifference curve in Figure A.1. First, it slopes downward. This follows from our assumption about preferences that "more is better." Every time we give Max another concert, we make him better off. In order to find another point on his indifference curve, we must make him worse off by the same amount, *taking away* some movies.

Second, notice the *curvature* of the indifference curve. As we move downward and rightward along it, the curve becomes flatter (the absolute value of its slope decreases). Why is this?

---

[6] This section can be read in place of the section titled "Consumer Decisions: The Marginal Utility Approach" in the body of the chapter, if your instructor so chooses.

[7] Key Terms found in this appendix are defined at the end of the appendix and in the glossary.

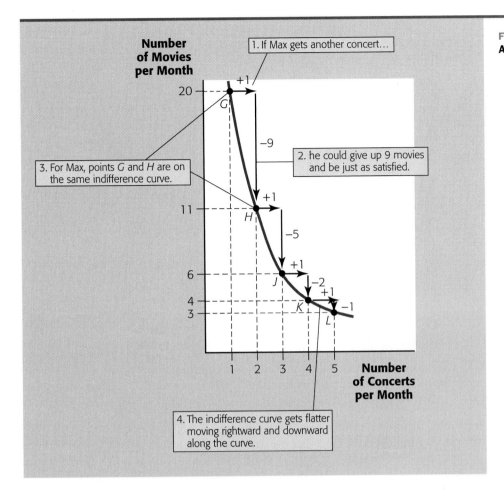

The Marginal Rate of Substitution

We can better understand the shape of the indifference if we first think a bit more about what its slope means. Think of the slope (without the minus sign) as the maximum number of movies that Max would *willingly trade* for one more concert. For example, going from point *G* to point *H*, Max gives up 9 movies for 1 concert and remains indifferent. Therefore, from point *G*, if he gave up *10* movies for 1 concert, he'd be *worse off*, and he would not willingly make that trade. Thus, at point *G*, the *greatest* number of movies he'd sacrifice for another concert would be 9.

This notion of "willingness to trade," as you'll soon see, has an important role to play in our model of consumer decision making. And there's a technical term for it: the *marginal rate of substitution of movies for concerts*. More generally, when the quantity of good *y* is

measured on the vertical axis, and the quantity of good *x* is measured on the horizontal axis,

> *the **marginal rate of substitution of good y for good x (MRS$_{y,x}$)** along any segment of an indifference curve is the absolute value of the slope along that segment. The MRS tells us the maximum amount of y a consumer would willingly trade for one more unit of x.*

This gives us another way of describing the shape of the indifference curve: As we move downward along the curve, the *MRS* (the number of movies Max would willing trade for another concert) gets smaller and smaller. To see why the *MRS* behaves this way, consider point *G*, high on Max's indifference curve. At this point, Max is seeing a lot of movies and relatively few concerts compared to points lower down, such as *J, K,* or *L*. With so

FIGURE A.2
An Indifference Map

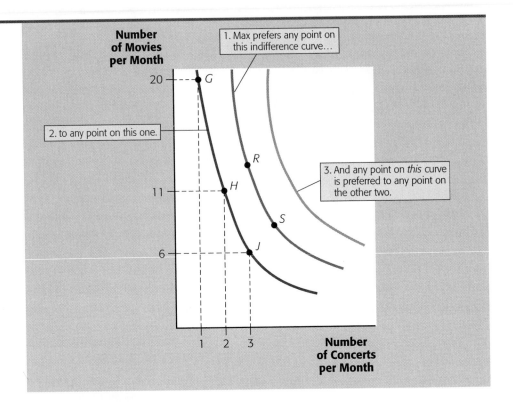

few concerts, he'd value another one very highly. And with so many movies, each one he gives up doesn't harm him much. So, at a point like G, he'd be willing to trade a large number of movies for even one more concert. His $MRS_{\text{movies, concerts}}$ is relatively large, and since the MRS is the absolute value of the indifference curve's slope, the curve is relatively steep at point G.

But as we continue traveling down his indifference curve, from G to H to J and so on, movies become scarcer for Max, so each one given up hurts him a bit more. At the same time, he's attending more and more concerts, so adding another one doesn't benefit him as much as before. At a point like K, then, Max is more reluctant to trade movies for concerts. To get another concert, he'd willingly trade fewer movies at point K than at point G. So at point K, the MRS is relatively small and the curve is relatively flat.

THE INDIFFERENCE MAP

To trace out the indifference curve in Figure A.1, we began at a specific point—point G. Figure A.2 reproduces that same indifference curve through G, H, and J. But

now consider the new point R, which involves more movies *and* more concerts than at point H. We know that point R is preferred to point H ("more is better"), so it is not on the indifference curve that goes through H. However, we can use the same procedure we used earlier to find a *new* indifference curve, connecting all points indifferent to point R. Indeed, we can repeat this procedure for any initial starting point we might choose, tracing out dozens or even hundreds of Max's indifference curves, as many as we'd like.

The result would be an **indifference map**, a set of indifference curves that describe Max's preferences, like the three curves in Figure A.2. We know that that Max would always prefer any point on a higher indifference curve to any point on a lower one. For example, consider the points H and S. S represents more concerts but fewer movies than H. How can we know if Max prefers S to H, or H to S? Max's indifference map tells us that he *must* prefer S to H. Why? We know that he prefers R to H, since R has more of both goods. We also know that Max is indifferent between R and S, since they are on the same indifference curve. Since he is indifferent between S and R, but prefers R to H, then he must also prefer S to H.

The same technique could be used to show that

> *any point on a higher indifference curve is preferred to any point on a lower one.*

Thus, Max's indifference map tells us how he ranks all alternatives imaginable. This is why we say that an indifference map gives us a complete characterization of someone's preferences: It allows us to look at any two points and—just by seeing which indifference curves they are on—immediately know which, if either, is preferred.

CONSUMER DECISION MAKING

Now we can combine everything you've learned about budget lines in the chapter, and what you've learned about indifference curves in this appendix, to determine the combination of movies and concerts that Max should choose. Figure A.3 adds Max's budget line to his indifference map. In drawing the budget line, we assume that Max has a monthly entertainment budget of $150, and that a concert costs $30 and a movie costs $10.

We assume that Max—like any consumer—wants to make himself as well off as possible (to "maximize his utility"). Max's optimal combination of movies and concerts will satisfy two criteria: (1) it will be a point on his budget line; and (2) it will lie on the highest indifference curve possible. Max can find this point by traveling down his budget line from A. As he does so, he will pass through a variety of indifference curves. (To see this clearly, you can pencil in additional indifference curves *between* the ones drawn in the figure.) At first, each indifference curve is higher than the one before, until he reachest the highest curve possible. This occurs at point D, where Max sees six movies and three concerts each month. Any further moves down the budget line will put him on lower indifference curves, so these moves would make him worse off. Point D is Max's optimal choice.

Two Mistakes with Indifference Curves First, don't allow the ends of an indifference curve to "curl up," like the curve through point B in the following figure, so that the curve slopes upward at the ends. This violates our assumption of "more is better." To see why, notice that point A has more of both goods than point B. So as long as "more is better," A must be preferred to B. But then A and B are not indifferent, so they cannot lie on the same indifference curve. For the same reason, points M and N cannot lie on the same indifference curve. Remember that indifference curves cannot slope upward.

Second, don't allow two indifference curves to cross. For example, look at the two indifference curves passing through point V. T and V are on the same indifference curve, so the consumer must be indifferent between them. But V and S are also on the same indifference curve, so the consumer is indifferent between them, too. Since rationality requires the consumer's preferences to be consistent, the consumer must then also be indifferent between T and S, but this is impossible because S has more of both goods than T, a violation of "more is better." Remember that indifference curves cannot cross.

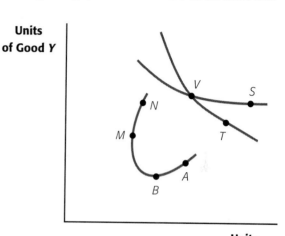

Notice something interesting about point D. First, it occurs where the indifference curve and the budget line are tangent—where they touch but don't cross. As you can see in the diagram, when an indifference curve actually crosses the budget line, we can always find some other point on the budget line that lies on a higher indifference curve.

Second, at point D, the slope of the indifference curve is the same as the slope of the budget line. Does this make sense? Yes, when you think about it this way: The absolute value of the indifference curve's slope—the *MRS*—tells us the rate at which Max would *willingly* trade movies for concerts. The slope of the budget line, by contrast, tells us the rate at which Max is *actually able* to trade movies for concerts. If there's any difference between the rate at which Max is *willing* to trade one good for another and the rate at which he is *able* to trade, he can always make himself better off by moving to another point on the budget line.

For example, suppose Max were at point B in Figure A.3. The indifference there is steeper than his budget

FIGURE A.3
Consumer Decision Making with Indifference Curves

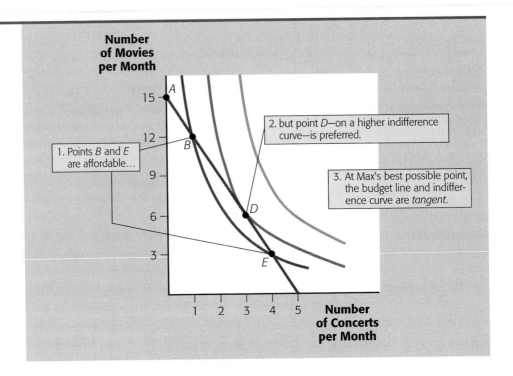

line. In fact, the indifference curve appears to have a slope of about −6, so Max's *MRS* there is about 6; he'd willingly give up 6 movies for 1 more concert. But his budget line—as you learned earlier in the chapter—has a slope of −3. Thus, at point *B*, Max would be *willing* to trade about 6 movies for one concert. But according to his budget line, he is *able* to trade just 3 movies for each concert. If trading 6 movies for a concert would leave him indifferent, then trading just 3 movies for a concert must make him better off. We conclude that when Max's indifference curve is steeper than his budget line, he should spend more on concerts and less on movies.

Using similar reasoning, convince yourself that Max should make the opposite move—spending less on concerts and more on movies—if his indifference curve is *flatter* than his budget line, as it is at point *E*. Only when the indifference curve and the budget line have the same slope—when they touch but do not cross—is Max as well off as possible. This is the point where the indifference curve is *tangent* to the budget line. When Max, or any other consumer, strives to be as well off as possible, he will follow this rule:

The optimal combination of goods for a consumer is the point on the budget line where an indifference curve is tangent to the budget line.

We can also express this decision-making rule in terms of the *MRS* and the prices of two goods. Recall that the slope of the budget line is $= -P_x / P_y$, so the absolute value of the budget line's slope is P_x / P_y. As you've just learned, the absolute value of the slope of an indifference curve is $MRS_{y,x}$. This allows us to state the decision-making rule as follows:

The optimal combination of two goods x and y is that combination on the budget line for which $MRS_{y,x} = P_x / P_y$

If this condition is not met, there will be a difference between the rate at which a consumer is *willing* to trade good *y* for good *x*, and the rate at which he is *able* to trade them. This will always give the consumer an opportunity to make himself better off.

WHAT HAPPENS WHEN THINGS CHANGE?

So far, as we've examined Max's search for the best combination of movies and concerts, we've assumed that Max's income, and the prices of each good, have remained unchanged. But in the real world, an individual's income, and the prices of the things they buy, *can* change. How would these changes affect a consumer's choice?

Changes in Income

Figure A.4 illustrates how an increase in income might affect Max's choice between movies and concerts. We assume that movies cost $10 each, concerts cost $30 each, and that these prices are not changing. Initially, Max has $150 to spend on the two goods, so his budget line is the lower line through point D. As we've already seen, under these conditions, the optimal combination for Max is point D (3 concerts and 6 movies).

Now suppose Max's income increases to $300. Then his budget line will shift upward and rightward in the figure. How will he respond? As always, he will search along his budget line until he arrives at the highest possible indifference curve, which will be tangent to the budget line at that point.

But where will this point be? There are several possibilities, and they depend on Max's preferences, as reflected in his indifference map. In the figure, we've used an indifference map for Max that leads him to point H, enjoying 6 concerts and 12 movies per month. As you can see in the figure, at this point, he has reached the highest possible indifference curve that his budget allows. It's also the point at which $MRS_{\text{movies, concerts}} = P_{\text{concerts}}/P_{\text{movies}} = 3$.

Notice that, in moving from D to H, Max chooses to buy more concerts (6 rather than 3) and more movies (12 rather than 6). As discussed in Chapters 3 and 4, if an increase in income (with prices held constant) increases the quantity of a good demanded, the good is *normal*. For Max, with the indifference map we've assumed in Figure A.4, both concerts and movies would be normal goods.

But what if Max's preferences, and his indifference map, had been different from the one in the figure? For example, suppose that after income increased, the

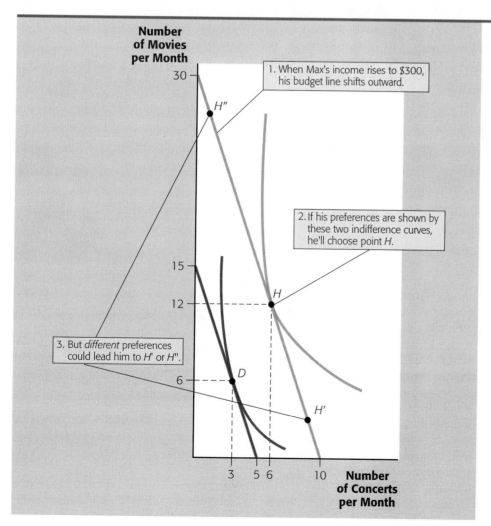

FIGURE A.4
An Increase in Income

Number of Movies per Month

1. When Max's income rises to $300, his budget line shifts outward.

2. If his preferences are shown by these two indifference curves, he'll choose point H.

3. But *different* preferences could lead him to H' or H".

Number of Concerts per Month

FIGURE A.5
Deriving the Demand Curve

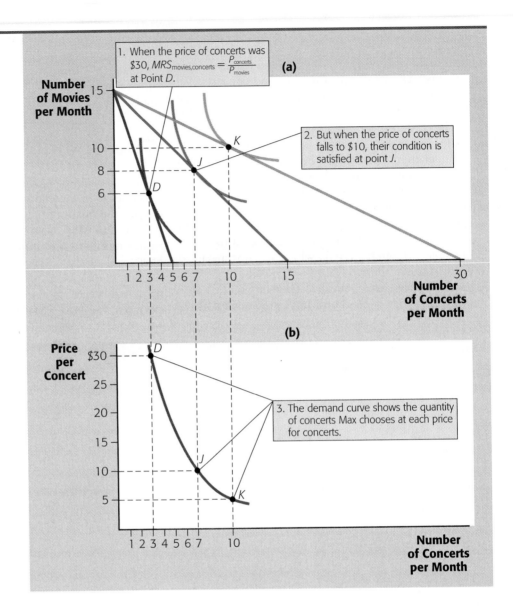

1. When the price of concerts was $30, $MRS_{movies, concerts} = \frac{P_{concerts}}{P_{movies}}$ at Point D.

(a)

2. But when the price of concerts falls to $10, their condition is satisfied at point J.

(b)

3. The demand curve shows the quantity of concerts Max chooses at each price for concerts.

tangency between his budget line and the hightest indifference curve he could reach occurred at a point like *H'*, with 9 concerts and 3 movies. In this case, the increase in income would cause Max's consumption of concerts to increase (from 3 to 9), but his consumption of movies to *fall* (from 6 to 3). If so, movies would be an *inferior good* for Max, one for which demand decreases when income increases, while concerts would be a normal good.

It's also possible for Max to have preferences that lead him to point *H"*—with more movies and fewer concerts compared to point *D*. In this case, *concerts* would be the inferior good and movies would be normal.

A rise in income, with no change in prices, leads to a new quantity demanded for each good. Whether a particular good is normal (quantity demanded increases) or inferior (quantity demanded decreases) depends on the individual's preferences, as represented by his indifference map.

Changes in Price

Let's explore what happens to Max when the price of a concert decreases from $30 to $10, while his income and the price of a movie remain unchanged. The drop in the price of concerts rotates Max's budget line rightward, pivoting around its vertical intercept, as illustrated in the upper panel of Figure A.5. What will Max do after his budget line rotates in this way? Based on his indifference curves—as they appear in the figure—he'd choose point *J*. This is the new combination of movies and concerts on his budget line that makes him as well off as possible (puts him on the highest possible indifference curve that he can afford). It's also the point at which $MRS_{movies, concerts} = P_{concerts}/P_{movies} = 1$, since movies and concerts now have the same price.

What if we dropped the price of concerts again, this time, to $5? Then Max's budget line rotates further rightward, and he will once again find the best possible point. In the figure, Max is shown choosing point *K*, attending 10 concerts and 10 movies.

THE INDIVIDUAL'S DEMAND CURVE

You've just seen that each time the price of concerts changes, so does the quantity of concerts Max will want to attend. The lower panel of Figure A.5 illustrates this relationship by plotting the quantity of concerts demanded on the horizontal axis and the *price* of concerts on the vertical axis. For example, in both the upper and lower panels, point *D* tells us that when the price of concerts is $30, Max will see three of them. When we connect points like *D*, *J*, and *K* in the lower panel, we get Max's **individual demand curve**, which shows the quantity of a good he demands at each different price. Notice that Max's demand curve for concerts slopes downward—a fall in the price of concerts increases the quantity demanded—showing that for Max, concerts obey the law of demand.

But if Max's preferences—and his indifference map—had been different, could his response to a price change have *violated* the law of demand? The answer is yes . . . and no. Yes, it is theoretically possible. (As a challenge, try penciling in a new set of indifference curves that would give Max an *upward-sloping* demand curve in the figure.) But no, it does not seem to happen in practice. To find out why, it's time to go back to the body of the chapter, to the section titled, "Income and Substitution Effects."

Key Terms

Indifference curve A curve representing all combinations of two goods that make the consumer equally well off.

Indifference map A set of indifference curves that represent an individual's preferences.

Individual demand curve A curve showing the quantity of a good or service demanded by a particular individual at each different price.

Marginal rate of substitution ($MRS_{y,x}$) The maximum amount of good *y* a consumer would willingly trade for one more unit of good *x*. Also, the slope of a segment of an indifference curve.

Production and Cost

On September 5, 2001, Hewlett Packard announced that it planned to buy one of its major competitors, Compaq Computer, for $25 billion—the largest merger in the history of the computer industry. The announcement ignited a firestorm of controversy. Although management at both companies and most of *Compaq*'s shareholders were enthusiastic about the plan, a group of influential Hewlett Packard shareholders was vehemently opposed. Each side had its eye on March 19, 2002—the official date of a yes-or-no vote among Hewlett Packard shareholders.

For the next six months, the two sides campaigned with full-page ads in major newspapers, daily appearances on CNBC, MSNBC, and CNN, and behind-the-scenes lobbying. As the vote neared, the conflict occasionally strayed into questions about motives, accusations of unethical conduct, and even personal attacks. But the debate always returned to one of the central issues: the effect of the proposed merger on *costs*. Specifically, Hewlett Packard's managers claimed that within a couple of years the merger would create annual cost savings of $2.5 billion for the two companies. The opposition did not believe them. In the end, the shareholders approved, and the two companies merged into one on May 3, 2002.

Although this particular transaction was unusually lively, mergers are anything but unusual. In a typical year, more than a thousand U.S. corporations—with a total value of close to $1 trillion—are acquired by other companies. Thousands more companies are acquired each year in Europe and Asia. In most cases, the stockholders of both firms end up favoring these deals. And in most cases, a major reason for the move—and the stockholders' approval—is the impact on costs.

This chapter is mostly about costs: how to think about them, how to measure them, and how business decisions cause them to change. By the time you've finished the chapter, you'll understand why costs play such an important role in mergers and acquisitions. But since this chapter also begins our study of business firms, some general but important questions will be addressed first. What *are* business firms? Why are they so prevalent in our economy—and in every market economy? Why do so many of us work for them, instead of striking out on our own? In the next section, we begin to answer these questions.

THE NATURE OF THE FIRM

What is a business firm? In the most general sense,

> *a business firm is an organization, owned and operated by private individuals, that specializes in* production.

Business firm An organization, owned and operated by private individuals, that specializes in production.

Your first image when you hear the word *production* may be a busy, noisy factory where goods are assembled, piece by piece, and then carted off to a warehouse for eventual sale to the public. Large manufacturers may come to mind—General Motors, Boeing, or even Ben & Jerry's. All of these companies produce things, but the word *production* encompasses more than just manufacturing.

> *Production is the process of combining* inputs *to make* outputs.

Some outputs are, indeed, physical *goods*, like automobiles, aircraft, or ice cream. But outputs can also be *services*. Indeed, many of America's largest corporations produce services. Think of Citicorp (banking services), American Airlines (transportation services), Verizon (telecommunications services), and Wal-Mart (retailing services).

Figure 1 illustrates the relationships between the firm and those it deals with. Notice that we have put the firm's management in the center of the diagram. It is the managers who must decide what the firm will do, both day-to-day and over a longer time horizon. When we refer to the firm as a *decision maker*, we mean the manager or managers who actually make the decisions.

As you can see in the figure, the firm must deal with a variety of individuals and organizations. It sells its output to *customers*—which can be households, government agencies, or other firms—and receives *revenue* from them in return. For example, Ford Motor Company sells its automobiles to households, to other firms (such as rental car companies), and to government agencies (such as local police departments). Ford earns revenue from all of these customers.

Where does the revenue go? Much of it goes to *input suppliers*. Ford must pay for labor, machinery, steel, rubber, electricity, factory buildings and the land underneath

FIGURE 1
The Firm and Its Environment

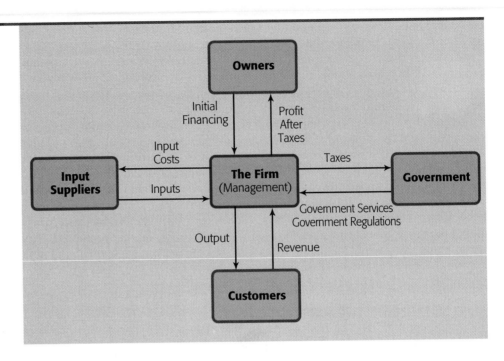

them, and much, much more. The total of all of these payments makes up the firm's *costs* of production.

When costs are deducted from revenue, what remains is the firm's **profit:**

$$\text{Profit} = \text{Revenue} - \text{Costs}.$$

Profit Total revenue minus total cost.

Figure 1 shows that the firm's profit (after taxes) accrues to the *owners* who provided the firm's initial financing.

Finally, every firm must deal with the government. On the one hand, it pays taxes to the government, and must obey government laws and regulations. On the other hand, firms receive valuable services from the government. These include the use of public capital, like roads and bridges, as well as the presence of a legal and financial system that help the economy run smoothly.

Types of Business Firms

There are more than 25 million business firms in the United States, and each of them falls into one of three legal categories, based on the rules and conditions of ownership. In a **sole proprietorship,** a single individual owns the firm and is entitled to all of the profit after taxes. In Figure 2, you can see that most business firms are sole proprietorships. This is not surprising, since they are the easiest form of business to start. In many cases, the owner just begins doing business. For tax purposes, the firm's profit is simply treated as part of the owner's personal income and is subject to the personal income tax.

Sole proprietorship A firm owned by a single individual.

In a **partnership,** responsibilities are shared among several co-owners. One advantage of a partnership is that the owners can often share many inputs—such as secretaries, advertising, and reception areas—reducing the costs for each partner. Of course, the profits must be shared with the co-owners as well. Partnerships are common among professionals, such as doctors, lawyers, and architects.

Partnership A firm owned and usually operated by several individuals who share in the profits and bear personal responsibility for any losses.

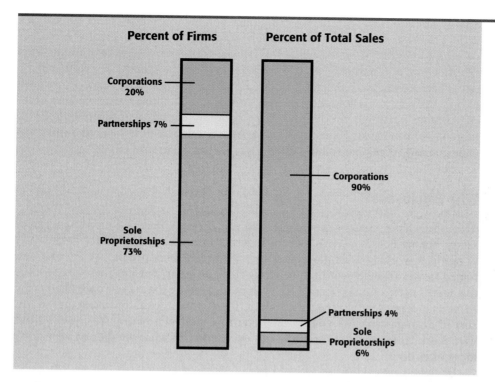

Percent of Firms

Corporations
20%

Partnerships 7%

Sole
Proprietorships
73%

Percent of Total Sales

Corporations
90%

Partnerships 4%

Sole
Proprietorships
6%

FIGURE 2
**Forms of Business
Organization**

Although sole proprietorships and partnerships are easy to create, they share two problems that ultimately make many owners decide against them. The first is *unlimited liability:* In either of these types of businesses, each owner is held personally responsible for the obligations of the firm. If the business runs up debts and closes down, or is successfully sued for a large sum of money, the owners will usually have to honor these obligations out of their own pockets.

A second, related problem is the difficulty of raising money to expand the business. In a sole proprietorship or partnership, owners must think very carefully before bringing in new partners—especially strangers—because each partner bears full responsibility for the poor judgment of any one of them. Thus, when owners need additional funds, they typically use their own money or borrow from a bank. In either case, the current owners bear substantial risk if the business fails.

These drawbacks lead many business firms to choose the third type of organization: a **corporation**. In this type of firm, ownership is divided among those who buy shares of *stock*. Each share of stock entitles its owner to a vote for the board of directors, which in turn hires the corporation's top managers. And each share of stock entitles its owner to a share of the corporation's profit, some of which is paid out as *dividends*. The corporate form of organization makes it easier to raise additional funds: The corporation simply sells additional shares of stock, thereby bringing in new owners. People are less hesitant to become co-owners of a corporation because of its other chief advantage: *limited liability*. The owners (stockholders) of a corporation can lose only what they have paid for the stock they own; they will never have to reach into their own pockets to honor the firm's obligations.

Why, then, doesn't every firm choose the corporate form? Because a corporation, in addition to its many advantages, also has its additional costs. To set up a corporation, government documents must be filed, and lawyers and accountants are

Corporation A firm owned by those who buy shares of stock and whose liability is limited to the amount of their investment in the firm.

usually hired to help with the job. And once you incorporate, you are subject to a variety of laws and regulations that apply only to corporations. Finally, owners of corporations suffer *double taxation*. First, the corporation pays taxes on its total profit. Then, households must pay income taxes on the portion of profit they receive as dividends. Each dollar of profits is thus taxed twice: once as corporate profits and again as household income. Still, for the largest firms, the advantages of incorporating outweigh the disadvantages. Although only a minority—about 20 percent—of businesses choose to be corporations, they tend to be large firms, producing about 90 percent of our national output (see Figure 2).

Why Employees?

Most firms have *employees*—people who work for the firm and receive a wage or salary, but are not themselves owners. Indeed, most of us will spend the greater part of our lives working as employees of firms owned by other people. We are so accustomed to this arrangement that we rarely think about it. But life doesn't have to be this way. There is no law to prevent each of us from operating our own one-person firms as independent contractors. Indeed, there would be many advantages to this sort of arrangement: We could each determine our own hours, we could set our own work rules, and no one could fire us, no matter what we did. So why don't more of us do it?

Imagine that each of us worked as independent contractors, specializing in a craft or profession and trading with each other, but working only for ourselves. If you wanted to buy a desk, you would go to an independent furniture maker. She, in turn, would buy her saw from an independent saw maker, her lumber from a lumber cutter, and so on throughout the economy. In this way, we would each operate on our own. We'd specialize according to our comparative advantage, enjoying the gains in living standards that specialization brings about. But we would not be enjoying the highest standard of living possible.

The Advantages of Employment. Suppose that, in this economy of independent contractors, someone got a brilliant idea: to set up a new organization, a *firm with employees*, to produce desks. In this firm, hundreds or even thousands of employees would promise to show up for work every day in exchange for an agreed-upon wage or salary. Would this kind of production have major advantages over production by independent contractors? Absolutely.

Further Gains from Specialization. One advantage of production by firms with employees is the possibility of further gains from specialization. When many people work within a single organization, assembly line methods—in which each worker specializes in *one aspect* of production—become feasible. Whereas the independent contractor must design the desk, make it, deal with customers, and advertise her services, at the furniture factory each of these tasks would be performed by different individuals who would work full-time at their activity. This increases the gains from specialization, giving the firm a competitive advantage over an unaffiliated group of individuals producing the same product.

Lower Transaction Costs. Another advantage for a firm with employees is lower **transaction costs**—a term economists use for the hassles of doing business. In a

Transaction costs The time costs and other costs required to carry out market exchanges.

world of independent contractors, business relationships would be more temporary and flexible, and each of us would spend a great deal of time searching for high-quality, reliable suppliers of raw materials and negotiating contracts with them. As a result, transaction costs would be high.

In a firm with employees, however, many supplies and services can be produced *inside* the organization. The firm's owners negotiate just *one* contract with each person—an employment contract—specifying the responsibilities and obligations of both sides. As long as employee turnover isn't too great, the firm can enjoy significant savings on transaction costs—a further competitive advantage over independent contractors supplying the same good.

Reduced Risk. Finally, the large firm with employees offers opportunities for everyone involved to reduce *risk*. When workers join firms and agree to work for a stable wage or salary, they receive a kind of insurance that protects them against fluctuations in their incomes. The protection is not complete; there is always the possibility of being laid off when times are bad. But it is understood by both firms and workers that those who remain on the job will continue to receive their regular wage or salary, regardless of business conditions. Many people—preferring not to gamble with the source of their livelihood—place a high value on this feature of employment contracts, a feature not available to the independent contractor.

But how can firms provide this kind of protection to employees? Doesn't offering stable wages, even when business is bad, increase the variability of the firm's profits? Won't this increase the risk faced by the firm's owners?

Perhaps. But large firms create opportunities for owners to reduce their risk, too, through **diversification.** To *diversify* is to spread the source of your income among several different alternatives, as suggested by the saying "Don't put all your eggs in one basket." With large firms, two kinds of diversification are possible. First, the firm itself can produce several different product lines, so that if one is selling poorly, another may be selling well. This is diversification *within* the firm.

Diversification The process of reducing risk by spreading sources of income among different alternatives.

Second, owners need not limit themselves to ownership of just one firm; instead, they can spread their investment, buying shares in a *portfolio* of firms. The portfolio can be chosen so that when some firms are doing poorly, others are likely to be doing well. This is diversification *among* firms, and it allows the income of each owner to be more stable than the profits at any one firm.

You can see that a large firm with employees offers several advantages over independent contractors. These advantages help it attract customers, workers, and potential owners. Since modern firms with employees have clear advantages for both owners and employees, and because they have a competitive advantage as suppliers in the market, it is not surprising that they produce so much of our output.

The Limits to the Firm

From all of this, you might be tempted to conclude that bigger is always better; the larger the firm, the greater will be the cost savings. But if that were true, there would be just one enormous firm in the economy and we'd all be working for it! In fact, there are limits to the gains from specialization, the savings on transaction costs, and opportunities for diversification. Bigger is *not always* better. Later in this chapter, we'll discuss some of the problems of "bigness," and the limits on firm expansion.

THINKING ABOUT PRODUCTION

When you think of production, it is quite natural to think of *outputs*—the things firms *make*—and *inputs*—the things firms *use* to make outputs. Inputs include resources (labor, capital, natural resources, and entrepreneurship), as well as other inputs. For example, to produce this book, South-Western used a variety of resources: *labor* (including that provided by the authors, editors, artists, printers, and company managers); *human capital* (the knowledge and skills possessed by each of the preceding workers); *physical capital* (including computers, delivery trucks, and a company headquarters building in Cincinnati); and *land* (under the headquarters). The company also used other inputs, including raw materials such as paper and ink, as well as the services of trucking companies, telephone companies, and Internet access providers.

Technology A method by which inputs are combined to produce a good or service.

A firm's **technology** refers to the variety of methods the firm can use to turn its inputs into goods and services. We leave it to engineers and scientists to spell out a firm's technology and to discover ways to improve it. When thinking about the firm, economists treat technology as a given, a constraint on the firm's production. This constraint is spelled out by the firm's *production function*:

Production function A function that indicates the maximum amount of output a firm can produce over some period of time from each combination of inputs.

> *For each different combination of inputs, the **production function** tells us the maximum quantity of output a firm can produce over some period of time.*

The idea behind a production function is illustrated in Figure 3. Quantities of each input are plugged into the box representing the production function, and the maximum quantity of goods or services produced pops out. The production function itself—the box—is a mathematical function relating inputs and outputs.

When a firm uses many different inputs, production functions can be quite complicated. This is true even of small firms. For example, the production function for a video and DVD rental store would tell us how many movies it could rent per day with different combinations of floor space, shelving, salesclerks, cash registers, movies in stock, lighting, air conditioning, and so on.

In this chapter, to keep things simple, we'll spell out the production function for a mythical firm that uses only two inputs: capital and labor. Our firm is Spotless Car Wash, whose output is a service: the number of cars washed. The firm's capital is the number of automated car-washing lines, and its labor is the number of full-time workers who drive the cars onto the line, drive them out, towel them down at the end, and deal with customers.[1]

The Short Run and the Long Run

When a firm alters its level of production, its input requirements will change. Some inputs, such as labor, can be adjusted relatively quickly. Other inputs—for example, capital equipment—may be more difficult to change. Why? Leases or rental agreements may commit the firm to keep paying for equipment over some period of time,

---

[1] Of course, a car wash would use other inputs besides just capital and labor: water, washrags, soap, electricity, and so on. But the costs of these inputs would be minor when compared to the costs of labor and capital. To keep our example simple, we ignore these other inputs.

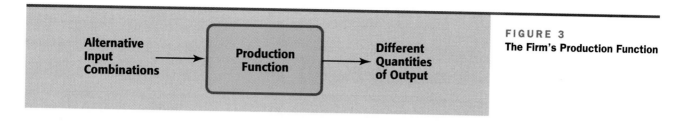

FIGURE 3
The Firm's Production Function

whether the equipment is used or not. Or there may be practical difficulties in adjusting capital, like a long lead time needed to acquire new equipment or sell off existing equipment. These considerations make it useful to categorize firms' decisions into one of two sorts: *long-run decisions* and *short-run decisions*.

> *The long run is a time horizon long enough for a firm to vary all of its inputs.*

Long run A time horizon long enough for a firm to vary all of its inputs.

The long run will be different for different firms. For a surgeon who would need several months to obtain a new surgical laser, to find a buyer for the one he has, or to find a larger or a smaller office, the long run is several months or more. At Spotless Car Wash, it might take a year to acquire and install an additional automated line or to sell the ones it already has. For Spotless, then, the long run would be any period longer than a year.

When a firm makes long-run decisions, it makes choices about *all* of its inputs. But firms must also make decisions over shorter time horizons, during which some of its inputs *cannot* be adjusted. We call these **fixed inputs**. Any input which is *not* fixed is called a **variable input**. Using this terminology, we can define the short-run planning horizon as follows:

Fixed input An input whose quantity must remain constant, regardless of how much output is produced.

Variable input An input whose usage can change as the level of output changes.

> *The short run refers to any time horizon over which at least one of the firm's inputs cannot be varied.*

Short run A time horizon during which at least one of the firm's inputs cannot be varied.

For Spotless Car Wash, the short run would be any period *less* than a year, the period during which it is stuck with a certain number of automated lines.

You can think of the short run and long run as two different lenses that a firm's managers must look through to make decisions. The short-run lens makes at least one of the inputs appear to be fixed, but the long-run lens makes all inputs appear variable. To guide the firm over the next several years, the manager must use the long-run lens; to determine what the firm should do next week, the short-run lens is best.

PRODUCTION IN THE SHORT RUN

When firms make short-run decisions, there is nothing they can do about their fixed inputs: They are stuck with whatever quantity they have. They can, however, make choices about their variable inputs. Indeed, we see examples of such short-run decisions all the time. Boeing might decide *this month* to cut its production of aircraft by 5 percent and lay off thousands of workers, even though it cannot change its factory buildings or capital equipment for another year or more. For Boeing (using a time

TABLE 1
Short-Run Production at Spotless Car Wash

Quantity of Capital	Quantity of Labor	Total Product (Cars Washed per Day)
1	0	0
1	1	30
1	2	90
1	3	130
1	4	161
1	5	184
1	6	196

horizon of less than a year) labor is variable, while its factory and equipment are fixed. Levi Strauss might decide to increase production of blue jeans over the next quarter by obtaining additional workers, cotton cloth, and sewing machines, yet continue to make do with the same factories because there isn't time to expand them or acquire new ones. Here, workers, cloth, and sewing machines are all variable, while only the factory buildings are fixed.

Spotless Car Wash uses only two inputs to produce its output, labor and capital. In the short run, we'll assume that labor is the variable input, and capital is the fixed input. The three columns in Table 1 describe Spotless's production function in the short run. Column 1 shows the quantity of the fixed input, capital (K); column 2 the quantity of the variable input, labor (L). Note that in the short run, Spotless is stuck with one unit of capital—one automated line—but it can take on as many or as few workers as it wishes. Column 3 shows the firm's *total product* (Q).

Total product The maximum quantity of output that can be produced from a given combination of inputs.

> *Total product is the maximum quantity of output that can be produced from a given combination of inputs.*

For example, the table shows us that with one automated line but no labor, total product is zero. With one line and six workers, output is 196 cars washed per day.

Figure 4 shows Spotless's *total product curve*. The horizontal axis represents the number of workers, while the vertical axis measures total product. (The amount of capital—which is held fixed at one automated line—is not shown on the graph.) Notice that each time the firm hires another worker, output increases, so the total product curve slopes upward. The vertical arrows in the figure show precisely *how much* output increases with each one-unit rise in employment. We call this rise in output the *marginal product of labor*.

Using the Greek letter Δ ("delta") to stand for "change in," we can define marginal product this way:

Marginal product of labor The additional output produced when one more worker is hired.

> *The **marginal product of labor** (MPL) is the change in total product (ΔQ) divided by the change in the number of workers employed (ΔL):*
>
> $$MPL = \frac{\Delta Q}{\Delta L}$$
>
> *The MPL tells us the rise in output produced when one more worker is hired.*

For example, if employment rises from 2 to 3 workers, total product rises from 90 to 130, so the marginal product of labor for *that* change in employment is calculated as $(130 - 90) / 1 = 40$ units of output.

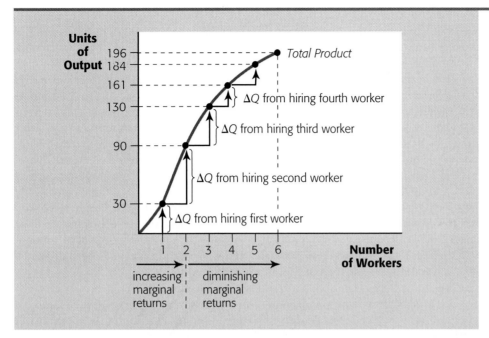

FIGURE 4
Total And Marginal Product

The total product curve shows the total amount of output that can be produced using various numbers of workers. The marginal product of labor (MPL) is the change in total product when another worker is hired. The MPL for each change in employment is indicated by the length of the vertical arrows.

Marginal Returns to Labor

Look at the vertical arrows in Figure 4, which measure the marginal product of labor, and you may notice something interesting. As more and more workers are hired, the *MPL* first increases (the vertical arrows get longer) and then decreases (the arrows get shorter). This pattern is believed to be typical at many types of firms, so it's worth exploring.

Increasing Marginal Returns to Labor. When the marginal product of labor rises as employment rises, there are **increasing marginal returns to labor.** Each time a worker is hired, total output rises by more than it did when the previous worker was hired. Why does this happen? One reason is that additional workers may allow production to become more specialized. Another reason is that at very low levels of employment, there may not be enough workers to properly operate the available capital. In either case, the additional worker not only produces some additional output as an individual, but also makes all other workers more productive.

Figure 4 tells us that Spotless Car Wash experiences increasing returns to labor up to the hiring of the second worker. While one worker *could* operate the car wash alone, he or she would have to do everything: drive the cars on and off the line, towel them down, and deal with customers. Much of this worker's time would be spent switching from one task to another. The result, as we see in Table 1, is that one worker can wash only 30 cars each day. Add a second worker, though, and now specialization is possible. One worker can collect money and drive the cars onto the line, and the other can drive them off and towel them down. Thus, with two workers, output rises all the way to 90 car washes per day; the second worker adds more to production (60 car washes) than the first (30 car washes) by making *both* workers more productive.

Increasing marginal returns to labor The marginal product of labor increases as more labor is hired.

Diminishing Returns to Labor. When the marginal product of labor is decreasing, we say there are **diminishing marginal returns to labor.** Output rises when another worker is added, so marginal product is positive. But the rise in output is smaller and smaller with each successive worker. Why does this happen? For one thing, as we keep adding workers, additional gains from specialization will be harder and harder to achieve. Moreover, each worker will have less and less of the fixed inputs with which to work.

Diminishing marginal returns to labor The marginal product of labor decreases as more labor is hired.

This last point is worth stressing. It applies not just to labor but to any variable input. In all kinds of production, if we keep increasing the quantity of any one input, while holding the others fixed, diminishing marginal returns will eventually set in. If a farmer keeps adding additional pounds of fertilizer to a fixed amount of land, the yield may continue to increase, but eventually the *size* of the increase—the marginal product of fertilizer—will begin to come down. If a small bakery continues to acquire additional ovens without hiring any workers or enlarging its floor space, eventually the additional output of bread—the marginal product of ovens—will decline. This tendency is so pervasive and widespread that it has been deemed a law, and economists have given that law a name:

Law of diminishing marginal returns As more and more of any input is added to a fixed amount of other inputs, its marginal product will eventually decline.

> The **law of diminishing (marginal) returns** states that as we continue to add more of any one input (holding the other inputs constant), its marginal product will eventually decline.

The law of diminishing returns is a physical law, not an economic one. It is based on the nature of production—on the physical relationship between inputs and outputs with a given technology.

At Spotless, diminishing returns set in after two workers have been hired. Beyond this point, the firm is crowding more and more workers into a car wash with just one automated line. Output continues to increase, since there is usually *something* an additional worker can do to move the cars through the line more quickly, but the increase is less dramatic each time.

This section has been concerned with *production*—the *physical* relationship between inputs and outputs. But a more critical concern for a firm is: What will it *cost* to produce any level of output? Cost is measured in dollars and cents, not in physical units of inputs or outputs. But as you are about to see, what you've learned about production will help you understand the behavior of costs.

THINKING ABOUT COSTS

HTTP://
Dwight Lee's "Opportunity cost and hidden invention" is an interesting debunking of the myth that corporations try to suppress inventions that make their products obsolete. (The location of Lee's essay changes frequently. To find the current page, go to http://www.google.com and enter both author and title.)

Talk to people who own or manage businesses, and it won't be long before the word *cost* comes up. People in business worry about measuring costs, controlling costs, and—most of all—reducing costs. This is not surprising: Owners want their firms to earn the highest possible profit, and costs must be subtracted from a firm's revenue to determine its profit. We will postpone a thorough discussion of profit until the next chapter. Here, we focus on just the *costs* of production: how economists think about costs, how costs are measured, and how they change as the firm adjusts its level of output.

Let's begin by revisiting a familiar notion. In Chapter 2 you learned that economists always think of cost as *opportunity cost*—what we must give up in order to do something. This concept applies to the firm as well:

> *A firm's total cost of producing a given level of output is the opportunity cost of the owners—everything they must give up in order to produce that amount of output.*

This notion—that the cost of production is its opportunity cost—is at the core of economists' thinking about costs. It can help us understand which costs matter— and which don't—when making business decisions.

The Irrelevance of Sunk Costs

Suppose that last year, Acme Pharmaceutical Company spent $10 million developing a new drug to treat acne that, if successful, promised to generate annual sales revenue many times that amount. At first, it seemed that the drug worked as intended. But then, just before launching production, management discovered that some early test results had been misinterpreted. The new drug, it turns out, doesn't cure acne at all—but it's remarkably effective in treating a rare underarm fungus. In this smaller, less lucrative market, annual sales revenue would be just $30,000. Now management must decide: Should they sell the drug as an antifungus remedy?

When confronted with a problem like this, some people will answer something like this: "Acme should *not* sell the drug. You don't sell something for $30,000 a year when it cost you $10 million to make it." Others will respond this way: "Of course Acme should sell the drug. If they don't, they'd be wasting that huge investment of $10 million." But neither approach to answering this question is correct, because both use the $10 million development cost to reach a conclusion. The $10 million is completely *irrelevant* to the decision.

The $10 million already spent on developing the drug is an example of a *sunk cost*. More generally,

> *a **sunk cost** is one that already has been paid, or must be paid*, regardless of *any future action being considered.*

In the case of Acme, the development cost has been paid already, and the firm will not get this money back, whether it chooses to sell the drug in this new smaller market, or *not* to sell the drug there. Since it's not part of the opportunity cost of either choice—something that would have to be sacrificed *for* that choice—it should have no bearing on the decision. For Acme, as for any business,

> *Sunk costs should not be considered when making decisions.*

What *should* be considered are the costs that *do* depend on the decision about producing the drug, namely, the cost of actually manufacturing it and marketing it for the smaller market. If the $30,000 Acme could earn in annual revenue exceeds these costs, Acme should produce it.

Any sunk costs of pharmaceutical development are irrelevant to the decision to market a new drug.

Sunk cost A cost that has been paid or must be paid, regardless of any future action being considered.

Look again at the definition of sunk cost and you'll see that even a *future* payment can be sunk, if an *unavoidable commitment to pay it has already been made.* Suppose, for example, Acme Pharmaceuticals has signed an employment contract with a research scientist, legally binding the firm to pay her annual salary for three years even if she is laid off. Although some or all of the payments haven't yet been made, all three years of salary are sunk costs for Acme because they *must* be made no matter what Acme does. As sunk costs, they are irrelevant to Acme's decisions.

Our insight about the irrelevance of sunk costs applies beyond the business sector, to decisions in general. For example, suppose that after completing two years of medical school, you've decided that you've made a mistake: You'd rather be lawyer than a doctor. You might be tempted to stay in medical school because of the money and time you've already spent there. But you can't get your time back. And since you can't sell your two years of medical training to someone else, you can't get your money back either. Thus, the costs of your first two years in medical school have either *been* paid or the *commitment* to pay them has already been made (say, future payments on a student loan). They are sunk costs and should have no influence on the decision. Only the costs that *depend* on your decision are relevant. If you choose to stay in medical school, you'll have to spend time, effort, and expense for your *remaining* years there. If you switch to law school, you'll sacrifice the time, effort, and expense of three years there. These are the costs you should consider (along with the benefits) for each choice.

Explicit Versus Implicit Costs

Explicit costs Money actually paid out for the use of inputs.

Implicit costs The cost of inputs for which there is no direct money payment.

In Chapter 2, in discussing the opportunity cost of education, you learned that there are two types of costs: **explicit** (involving actual payments) and **implicit** (no money changes hands). The same distinction applies to costs for a business firm.

Suppose you're thinking about opening up a restaurant in a building that you already own. You wouldn't have to pay any rent, so there's no explicit rental payment. Does this mean that using the building is free?

To an accountant—who focuses on actual money payments—the answer is yes. But to an economist—who thinks of opportunity cost—the answer is *absolutely not.* By choosing to use your own building for your restaurant, you would be sacrificing the opportunity to rent it to someone else. This *foregone rent* is an implicit cost, and it is as much a cost of production as the rent you would pay if you rented the building from someone else. In both cases, something is given up to produce your output.

Now suppose that instead of *borrowing* money to buy ovens, dishes, tables, chairs, and an initial inventory of food for your restaurant, you used your *own* money. You would then have no loans or interest to pay back. However, that money of yours *could* have been put in a bank account, lent to someone else, or invested elsewhere. With these options, you could earn investment income on your money. Economists measure the opportunity cost of funds you invest in a business as the income you *could* earn by investing the funds elsewhere. This *foregone investment income* is an implicit cost of doing business.

Finally, suppose you'd decide to manage your restaurant yourself. Have you escaped the costs of hiring a manager? Not really, because you are still bearing an opportunity cost: You *could* do something else with your time. We measure the value of your time as the income you *could* earn by devoting your labor to your next-best

TABLE 2
A Firm's Costs

Explicit Costs	Implicit Costs
Rent paid out	Opportunity cost of:
Interest on loans	Owner's land and buildings (rent foregone)
Managers' salaries	Owner's money (investment income
Hourly workers' wages	foregone)
Cost of raw materials	Owner's time (labor income foregone)

income-earning activity. This *foregone labor income*—the wage or salary you could be earning elsewhere—is an implicit cost of your business, and therefore part of its opportunity cost.

Table 2 summarizes our discussion by listing some common categories of costs that business firms face, both explicit (on the left) and implicit (on the right).

COSTS IN THE SHORT RUN

Managers must answer questions about costs over different time horizons. One question might be, "How much will it cost us to produce a given level of output *this year*?" Another might be, "How much will it cost us to produce a given level of output *three years from now and beyond*?" In this section, we'll explore managers' view of costs for a time horizon—perhaps a month, a few months, or a year—during which *at least one* of the firm's inputs is fixed. That is, we'll be looking at costs with a *short-run* planning horizon.

Remember that no matter how much output is produced, the quantity of a fixed input *must* remain the same. Other inputs, by contrast, can be varied as output changes. Because the firm has these two different types of inputs in the short run, it will also face two different types of costs.

The costs of a firm's fixed inputs are called, not surprisingly, **fixed costs**. Like the fixed inputs themselves, fixed costs must remain the same no matter what the level of output. Typically, we treat rent and interest—whether explicit or implicit—as fixed costs, since producing more or less output in the short run will not cause any of these costs to change. Managers typically refer to fixed costs as their *overhead costs,* or simply, overhead.

Fixed costs Costs of fixed inputs.

The costs of obtaining the firm's variable inputs are its **variable costs**. These costs, like the usage of variable inputs themselves, will rise as output increases. Most businesses treat the wages of hourly employees and the costs of raw materials as variable costs, since quantities of both labor and raw materials can usually be adjusted rather rapidly.

Variable costs Costs of variable inputs.

Measuring Short-Run Costs

In Table 3, we return to our mythical firm—Spotless Car Wash—and ask: What happens to *costs* as output changes in the short run? The first three columns of the table give the relationship between inputs and outputs—the production function—just as in Table 1 a few pages earlier. But there is one slight difference: In Table 3,

(1) Output (per Day)	(2) Capital	(3) Labor	(4) TFC	(5) TVC	(6) TC	(7) MC	(8) AFC	(9) AVC	(10) ATC
			Labor cost = $60 per day			Capital cost = $75 per day			
0	1	0	$75	$ 0	$ 75		—	—	—
						$2.00			
30	1	1	$75	$ 60	$135		$2.50	$2.00	$4.50
						$1.00			
90	1	2	$75	$120	$195		$0.83	$1.33	$2.17
						$1.50			
130	1	3	$75	$180	$255		$0.58	$1.38	$1.96
						$1.94			
161	1	4	$75	$240	$315		$0.48	$1.49	$1.96
						$2.61			
184	1	5	$75	$300	$375		$0.44	$1.63	$2.04
						$5.00			
196	1	6	$75	$360	$435		$0.41	$1.84	$2.22

TABLE 3
Short-Run Costs for Spotless Car Wash

we've reversed the order of the columns, putting total output first. We are changing our perspective slightly: Now we want to observe how a change in the quantity of *output* causes the firm's *inputs*—and therefore its *costs*—to change.

In addition to Spotless's production function, we need to know one more thing before we can analyze its costs: what it must *pay* for its inputs. In Table 3, the price of labor is set at $60 per worker per day, and the price of each automated car-washing line at $75 per day.

How do Spotless's short-run costs change as its output changes? Get ready, because there are a surprising number of different ways to answer that question, as illustrated in the remaining columns of Table 3.

Total Costs. Columns 4, 5, and 6 in the table show three different types of total costs. In column 4, we have Spotless's **total fixed cost** (TFC), the cost of all inputs that are fixed in the short run. Like the quantity of fixed inputs themselves, fixed costs remain the same no matter what the level of output.

Total fixed cost The cost of all inputs that are fixed in the short run.

For Spotless Car Wash, the daily cost of renting or owning one automated line is $75, so total fixed cost is $75. Running down the column, you can see that this cost—because it is fixed—remains the same no matter how many cars are washed each day.

Column 5 shows **total variable cost** (TVC), the cost of all variable inputs. For Spotless, labor is the only variable input. As output increases, more labor will be needed, so TVC will rise. For example, to wash 90 cars each day requires 2 workers, and each worker must be paid $60 per day, so TVC will be 2 × $60 = $120. But to wash 130 cars requires 3 workers, so TVC will rise to 3 × $60 = $180.

Total variable cost The cost of all variable inputs used in producing a particular level of output.

Finally, column 6 shows us that

Total cost The costs of all inputs—fixed and variable.

total cost (TC) *is the sum of all fixed and variable costs:*

$$TC = TFC + TVC.$$

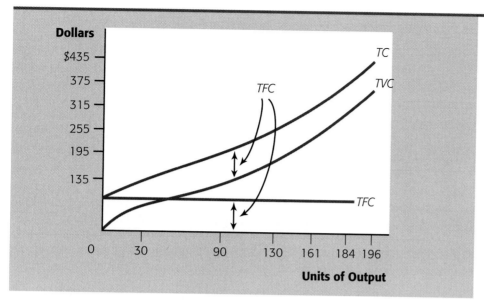

FIGURE 5
The Firm's Total Cost Curves

At any level of output, total cost (TC) is the sum of total fixed cost (TFC) and total variable cost (TVC).

For example, at 90 units of output, *TFC* = $75 and *TVC* = $120, so *TC* = $75 + $120 = $195. Because total variable cost rises with output, total cost rises as well.

Now look at Figure 5, where we've graphed all three total cost curves for Spotless Car Wash. Both the *TC* and *TVC* curves slope upward, since these costs increase along with output. Notice that there are *two* ways in which *TFC* is represented in the graph. One is the *TFC* curve, which is a horizontal line, since *TFC* has the same value at any level of output. The other is the *vertical distance* between the rising *TVC* and *TC* curves, since *TFC* is always the *difference* between *TVC* and *TC*. In the graph, this vertical distance must remain the same, at $75, no matter what the level of output.

Average Costs. While total costs are important, sometimes it is more useful to track a firm's costs *per unit* of output, which we call its *average cost*. There are three different types of average cost, each obtained from one of the total cost concepts just discussed.

*The firm's **average fixed cost** (AFC) is its total fixed cost divided by the quantity (Q) of output:*

$$AFC = \frac{TFC}{Q}.$$

Average fixed cost Total fixed cost divided by the quantity of output produced.

No matter what kind of production or what kind of firm, *AFC* will always fall as output rises. Why? Because *TFC* remains constant, so a rise in *Q* *must* cause the ratio *TFC/Q* to fall. Business managers often refer to this decline in *AFC* as "spreading their overhead" over more output. For example, a restaurant has overhead costs for its buildings, furniture, and cooking equipment. The more meals it serves, the lower will be its overhead cost per meal. Does *AFC* fall with output at Spotless Car Wash? Look at Table 3, column 8. When output is 30 units, *AFC* is $75/30 = $2.50. But at 90 units of output, *AFC* drops to $75/90 = $0.83. And *AFC* keeps declining as we continue down the column. The more output produced, the lower is fixed cost per unit of output.

Average variable cost Total variable cost divided by the quantity of output produced.

Average variable cost (**AVC**) *is the cost of the variable inputs per unit of output:*

$$AVC = \frac{TVC}{Q}.$$

AVC is shown in column 9 of the table. For example, at 30 units of output, *TVC* = $60, so *AVC* = *TVC*/*Q* = $60/30 = $2.00.

What happens to *AVC* as output rises? Based on mathematics alone, we can't be sure. On the one hand, a rise in *Q* raises the denominator of the fraction *TVC*/*Q*. On the other hand, *TVC* increases, so the numerator rises as well. Thus, it's possible for *AVC* to either rise or fall, depending on whether *TVC* or *Q* rises by a greater percentage. But if you run your finger down the *AVC* column in Table 3, you'll see a pattern: The *AVC* numbers first decrease and then increase. Economists believe that this pattern of decreasing and then increasing average variable cost is typical at many firms. When plotted in Figure 6, this pattern causes the *AVC* curve to have a U shape. We'll discuss the reason for this characteristic U shape a bit later.

Average total cost Total cost divided by the quantity of output produced.

Average total cost (**ATC**) *is the total cost per unit of output:*

$$ATC = \frac{TC}{Q}.$$

Values for *ATC* are listed in column 10 of Table 3. For example, at 90 units of output, *TC* = $195, so *ATC* = *TC*/*Q* = $195/90 = $2.17. As output rises, *ATC*, like *AVC*, can either rise or fall, since both the numerator and denominator of the fraction *TC*/*Q* rises. (See Table 3, column 10.) But we usually expect *ATC*, like *AVC*, to first decrease and then increase, so the *ATC* curve will also be U-shaped. However—as you can see in Figure 6—it is not identical to the *AVC* curve. At each level of output, the vertical distance between the two curves is equal to average *fixed* cost (*AFC*). Since *AFC* declines as output increases, the *ATC* curve and the *AVC* curve must get closer and closer together as we move rightward.

Marginal Cost. The total and average costs we've considered so far tell us about the firm's cost at a particular *level* of output. For many purposes, however, we are more interested in how cost *changes* when output *changes*. This information is provided by another cost concept:

Marginal cost The increase in total cost from producing one more unit of output.

Marginal cost (**MC**) *is the change in total cost* (Δ*TC*) *divided by the change in output* (Δ*Q*):

$$MC = \frac{\Delta TC}{\Delta Q}.$$

It tells us how much cost rises per unit increase in output.

For Spotless Car Wash, marginal cost is entered in column 7 of Table 3 and graphed in Figure 6. Since marginal cost tells us what happens to total cost when output *changes*, the entries in the table are placed *between* one output level and another. For example, when output rises from 0 to 30, total cost rises from $75 to

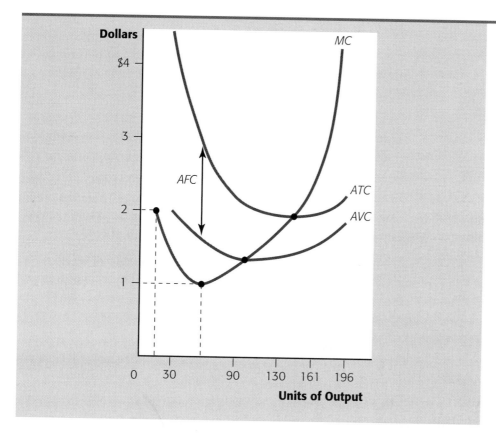

FIGURE 6
Average and Marginal Costs

Average variable cost (AVC) *and average total cost* (ATC) *are U-shaped, first decreasing and then increasing. Average fixed cost* (AFC), *the vertical distance between* ATC *and* AVC, *becomes smaller as output increases.*

The marginal cost (MC) *curve is also U-shaped, reflecting first increasing and then diminishing marginal returns to labor.* MC *passes through the minimum points of both the* AVC *and* ATC *curves.*

$135. For this change in output, we have $\Delta TC = \$135 - \$75 = \$60$, while $\Delta Q = 30$, so $MC = \$60/30 = \$2.00$. This entry is listed *between* the output levels 0 and 30 in the table.

Explaining the Shape of the Marginal Cost Curve

In Figure 6, where marginal cost is graphed. As in the table, each value of marginal cost is plotted *between* output levels. For example, the marginal cost of increasing output from 0 to 30 is $2, and this is plotted at output level 15—midway between 0 and 30. Similarly, when going from 30 to 90 units of output, the *MC* is plotted midway between 30 and 90. (For now, ignore the other bulleted points.)

The marginal cost curve has an important relationship to the total cost curve. As you can see in Figure 5, the total cost (*TC*) is plotted on the vertical axis, and quantity (*Q*) on the horizontal axis, so the slope along any interval is just $\Delta TC / \Delta Q$. But this is exactly the definition of marginal cost.

> *The marginal cost for any change in output is equal to the* slope *of the total cost curve along that interval of output.*

If you look carefully at the *TC* curve in Figure 5, you'll see that while its slope is always positive, it first decreases (the *TC* curve gets flatter), then increases (gets steeper). Correspondingly, in Figure 6, *MC* first declines and then rises. Why is this?

Here, we can use what we learned earlier about marginal returns to labor. At low levels of employment and output, there are increasing marginal returns to labor: $MPL = \Delta Q/\Delta L$ is rising. That is, each worker hired adds more to production than the worker before. But that means that *fewer additional workers are needed to produce an additional unit of output.* Now, since additional labor is this firm's only cost of increasing production, the cost of an additional unit of output (*MC*) must be falling. Thus, as long as *MPL* is rising, *MC* must be falling.

For Spotless, since *MPL* rises when employment increases from zero to one and then one to two workers, *MC* must fall as the firm's output rises from zero to 30 units (produced by one worker) and then from 30 to 90 units (produced by two workers).

At higher levels of output, we have the opposite situation: Diminishing marginal returns set in and the marginal product of labor ($\Delta Q/\Delta L$) falls. Therefore, additional units of output require *more* and *more* additional labor. As a result, each additional unit of output costs more and more to produce. Thus, as long as *MPL* is falling, *MC* must be rising.

For Spotless, diminishing marginal returns to labor occur for all workers beyond the second, so *MC* rises for all increases in output beyond the change from 30 to 90.

To sum up:

> *When the marginal product of labor* (MPL) *rises, marginal cost* (MC) *falls. When* MPL *falls,* MC *rises. Since* MPL *ordinarily rises and then falls,* MC *will do the opposite: It will fall and then rise. Thus, the MC curve is U-shaped.*

The Relationship Between Average and Marginal Costs

Although marginal cost and average cost are not the same, there is an important relationship between them. Look again at Figure 6 and notice that all three curves—*MC*, *AVC*, and *ATC*—first fall and then rise, but not all at the same time. The *MC* curve bottoms out before either the *AVC* or *ATC* curve. Further, the *MC* curve intersects each of the average curves *at their lowest points*. These graphical features of Figure 6 are no accident; indeed, they follow from the laws of mathematics. To understand this, let's consider a related example with which you are probably more familiar.

An Example: Average and Marginal Test Scores. Suppose you take five tests in your economics course during the term, with the results listed in Table 4. To your immense pleasure, you score 100 on your first test. Your total score—the total number of points you have received thus far during the term—is 100. Your marginal score—the *change* in your total caused by the most recent test—will also be 100, since your total rose from 0 to 100. Your average score so far is 100 as well.

Now suppose that, for the second test, you forget to study actively. Instead, you just read the text while simultaneously watching music videos and eavesdropping on your roommate's phone conversations. As a result, you get a 50. Your marginal score is 50. Since this score is lower than your previous average of 100, the second test will pull your average down. Indeed, whenever you score lower than your previous average, you will always decrease the average. In the table, we see that your average after the second test falls to 75.

Now you start to worry, so you turn off the TV while studying, and your performance improves a bit: You get a 60. Does the improvement in your score—from

Number of Tests Taken	Total Score	Marginal Score	Average Score
0	0		—
		100	
1	100		100
		50	
2	150		75
		60	
3	210		70
		70	
4	280		70
		80	
5	360		72

TABLE 4
Average and Marginal Test Scores

50 to 60—increase your *average* score? Absolutely not. Your average will decrease once again, because your *marginal* score of 60 is *still* lower than your previous average of 75. As we know, when you score lower than your average, it pulls the average down, even if you're improving. In the table, we see that your average now falls to 70.

For your fourth exam, you study a bit harder and score a 70. This time, since your score is precisely *equal* to your previous average, the average remains unchanged at 70.

Finally, on your fifth and last test, your score improves once again, this time to 80. This time, you've scored *higher* than your previous average, pulling your average up from 70 to 72.

This example may be easy to understand because you are used to figuring out your average score in a course as you take additional exams. But the relationship between marginal and average spelled out here is universal: It is the same for grade point averages, batting averages—*and* costs.

Average and Marginal Cost. Now let's apply our previous discussion to a firm's cost curves. Whenever marginal cost is below average cost, we know that the cost of producing *one more* unit of output is *less* than the average cost of all units produced so far. Therefore, producing one more unit will bring the average down. That is, when marginal cost is below average cost, average cost will come down. This applies to both average *variable* cost and average *total* cost.

For example, when Spotless is producing 30 units of output, its *ATC* is $4.50 and its *AVC* is $2.00 (see Table 3). But if it increases output from 30 to 90 units, the marginal cost of these *additional* units is just $1.00. Since *MC* is less than both *ATC* and *AVC* for this change, it pulls both averages down. Graphically, when the *MC* curve lies below one of the average curves (*ATC* or *AVC*), that average curve will slope downward.

Now consider a change in output from 90 units to 130 units. Marginal cost for this change is $1.50. But the *AVC* at 90 units is $1.33. Since *MC* is greater than *AVC*, this change in output will pull *AVC* up. Accordingly, the *AVC* curve begins to slope upward. However, *ATC* at 90 units is $2.17. Since *MC* is still *less* than *ATC*, the *ATC* curve will continue to slope downward.

Finally, consider what happens at higher levels of output, such as a change from 161 to 184 units. For this change in output, *MC* is \$2.61, which is greater than the previous values of both *AVC* (\$1.49) and *ATC* (\$1.96). If the firm makes this move, both *AVC* and *ATC* will rise.

Now, let's put together what we know about marginal cost and what we know about the relationship between marginal and average cost. Remember that marginal cost drops rapidly when the firm begins increasing output from low levels of production, due to increasing marginal returns to labor. Thus, *MC* will initially drop *below AVC* and *ATC*, pulling these averages down. But if the firm keeps increasing its output, diminishing returns to labor will set in. *MC* will keep on rising, until it *exceeds AVC* and *ATC*. Once this happens, further increases in output will *raise* both *AVC* and *ATC*.

> *At low levels of output, the* MC *curve lies below the* AVC *and* ATC *curves, so these curves will slope downward. At higher levels of output, the* MC *curve will rise above the* AVC *and* ATC *curves, so these curves will slope upward. Thus, as output increases, the average curves will first slope downward and then slope upward. That is, they will have a U shape.*

When we state this argument in terms of the curves graphed in Figure 6, we can finally understand why the *AVC* and *ATC* curves are U-shaped.

There is one more important observation to make before we leave the short run. We've just seen that whenever the *MC* curve lies *below* the *ATC* curve, *ATC* is falling. But when the *MC* curve crosses the *ATC* curve and rises *above* it, *ATC* will be rising. As a result, the *MC* curve must intersect the *ATC* curve at its *minimum* point, as it does in Figure 6. And the same is true of the *AVC* curve.

> *The* MC *curve will intersect the minimum points of the* AVC *and* ATC *curves.*

Time to Take a Break. By now, your mind may be swimming with concepts and terms: total, average, and marginal cost curves; fixed and variable costs; explicit and implicit costs. . . . We are covering a lot of ground here and still have a bit more to cover: production and cost in the *long run*.

As difficult as it may seem to keep these concepts straight, they will become increasingly easy to handle as you use them in the chapters to come. But it's best not to overload your brain with too much new material at one time. So if this is your first trip through this chapter, now is a good time for a break. Then, when you're fresh, come back and review the material you've read so far. When the terms and concepts start to feel familiar, you are ready to move on to the long run.

HTTP://

Examples of economies of scale can be found at http://bized.ac.uk/stafsup/options/notes/econ204.htm.

PRODUCTION AND COST IN THE LONG RUN

Most of the business firms you have contact with—such as your supermarket, the stores where you buy new clothes, your telephone company, and your Internet service provider—plan to be around for quite some time. They have a long-term planning horizon, as well as a short-term one. But so far, we've considered the behavior of costs only in the short run.

In the long run, costs behave differently, because the firm can adjust *all* of its inputs in any way it wants:

> *In the long run, there are no fixed inputs or fixed costs; all inputs and all costs are variable. The firm must decide what combination of inputs to use in producing any level of output.*

How will the firm choose? Its goal is to earn the highest possible profit, and to do this, it must follow the *least cost rule:*

> *To produce any given level of output, the firm will choose the input mix with the lowest cost.*

Let's apply the least cost rule to Spotless Car Wash. Suppose we want to know the cost of washing 196 cars per day. In the short run, of course, Spotless does not have to worry about how it would produce this level of output: It is stuck with one automated line, and the only way to wash 196 cars is to hire six workers (see Table 3). Total cost in the short run will be $6 \times \$60 + \$75 = \$435$.

In the long run, however, Spotless can vary the number of auto-

The Least Cost Rule When you read the *least cost rule* of production, you might think that the firm's long-run goal is to have the *least possible cost.* But this is not true. To convince yourself, just realize that the least possible cost would be zero, and in the long run this could be achieved by not using any inputs and producing nothing!

The least cost rule says that any *given* level of output should be produced at the lowest possible cost. The firm's goal is to maximize *profit,* and the least cost rule helps it do that. For example, if the firm is considering producing 10 units of output, and there are two ways to produce that number of units—one costing $6,000 and the other costing $5,000—the firm should always choose the latter way because it is cheaper. But notice that $5,000 is not the "lowest possible cost" for the firm; *it is the lowest possible cost for producing 10 units.*

DANGEROUS CURVES

mated lines as well as the number of workers. Its *long-run* production function will tell us all the different combinations of *both* inputs that can be used to produce any output level. Suppose four different input combinations can be used to wash 196 cars per day. These are listed in Table 5. Combination *A* uses the least capital and the most labor—no automated lines at all and nine workers washing the cars by hand. Combination *D* uses the most capital and the least labor—three automated lines with only three workers. Since each automated line costs $75 per day and each worker costs $60 per day, it is easy to calculate the cost of each production method. Spotless will choose the one with the lowest cost: combination *C*, with two automated lines and four workers, for a total cost of $390 per day.

Method	Quantity of Capital	Quantity of Labor	Cost
A	0	9	$540
B	1	6	$435
C	2	4	$390
D	3	3	$405

TABLE 5
Four Ways to Wash 196 Cars per Day

TABLE 6
Long-Run Costs for Spotless Car Wash

Output	LRTC	LRATC
0	$ 0	—
30	$ 100	$3.33
90	$ 195	$2.17
130	$ 255	$1.96
161	$ 315	$1.96
184	$ 360	$1.96
196	$ 390	$1.99
250	$ 650	$2.60
300	$1,200	$4.00

Retracing our steps, we have found that if Spotless wants to wash 196 cars per day, it will examine the different methods of doing so and select the one with the least cost. Once it has determined the cheapest production method, the other, more expensive methods can be ignored.

Table 6 shows the results of going through this procedure for several different levels of output. The second column, **long-run total cost** (*LRTC*), tells us the cost of producing each quantity of output *when the least-cost input mix is chosen*. For each output level, different production methods are examined, the cheapest one is chosen, and the others are ignored. Notice that the *LRTC* of zero units of output is $0. This will always be true for any firm. In the long run, all inputs can be adjusted as the firm wishes, and the cheapest way to produce zero output is to use *no* inputs at all. (For comparison, what is the *short*-run total cost of producing zero units? Why can it never be $0?)

Long-run total cost The cost of producing each quantity of output when all inputs are variable and the least-cost input mix is chosen.

The third column in Table 6 gives the **long-run average total cost** (*LRATC*), the cost per unit of output in the long run:

Long-run average total cost The cost of producing each quantity of output in the long run, when all inputs are variable.

$$LRATC = \frac{LRTC}{Q}.$$

Long-run average total cost is similar to average total cost, which was defined earlier. Both are obtained by dividing total cost by the level of output. There is one important difference, however: To calculate *ATC*, we used total cost (*TC*), which pertains to the short run, in the numerator. In calculating *LRATC*, we use *long-run* total cost (*LRTC*) in the numerator. Thus, *LRATC* tells us the cost per unit when the firm can vary *all* of its inputs and always chooses the cheapest input mix possible. *ATC*, however, tells us the cost per unit when the firm is stuck with some collection of fixed inputs.

The Relationship Between Long-Run and Short-Run Costs

If you compare Table 6 (long run) with Table 3 (short run), you will see something important: For some output levels, *LRTC* is smaller than *TC*. For example, Spotless can wash 196 cars for an *LRTC* of $390. But earlier, we saw that in the short run, the *TC* of washing these same 196 cars was $435. To understand the reason for this difference, look back at Table 5, which lists the four different ways of washing 196 cars per day. In the short run, the firm is stuck with just one automated line, so its only option is method *B*. In the long run, however, the firm can adjust *all* of its inputs, so it can choose any of the four methods of production, including method *C*, which is cheapest. In many cases, the freedom to choose among different production methods enables the firm to select a cheaper input mix in the long run than it can in the short run. Thus, in the long run, the firm may be able to save money.

But not always. At some output levels, the freedom to adjust all inputs doesn't save the firm a dime. To wash 130 cars, for example, the long-run cost—the cost when using the cheapest input mix—is the same as the short-run total cost (*LRTC = TC* ($255). For this output level, it must be that the *short-run* input mix is also the least-cost input mix. Thus, if Spotless wants to wash 130 cars per day, it would choose in the long run the same production method it is already using in the short run. At this output level, the firm could not save money by adjusting its capital in the long run. (There are other output levels listed in the tables for which *LRTC = TC*. Can you find them?)

What we have found for Spotless Car Wash is true for all firms:

> *The long-run total cost of producing a given level of output can be less than or equal to, but not greater than, the short-run total cost* (LRTC ≤ TC).

We can also state this relationship in terms of *average* costs. That is, we can divide both sides of the inequality by Q and obtain $LRTC/Q \leq TC/Q$. Using our definitions, this translates to $LRATC \leq ATC$.

> *The long-run average cost of producing a given level of output can be less than or equal to, but not greater than, the short-run average total cost* (LRATC ≤ ATC).

Average Cost and Plant Size. Often, economists refer to the collection of fixed inputs at the firm's disposal as its **plant.** For example, the plant of a computer manufacturer such as Dell would include its factory buildings and the assembly lines inside them. The plant of the Hertz car-rental company would include all of its automobiles and rental offices. For Spotless Car Wash, we've assumed that the plant is simply the company's capital equipment—the automated lines for washing cars. If Spotless were to add to its capital, then each time it acquired another automated line, it would have a different, and larger, plant. Viewed in this way, we can distinguish between the long run and the short run as follows: *In the long run, the firm can change the size of its plant; in the short run, it is stuck with its current plant.*

Now think about the *ATC* curve, which tells us the firm's average total cost in the short run. This curve is always drawn for a specific plant. That is, the *ATC* curve tells us how average cost behaves in the short run, *when the firm uses a plant of a given size.* If the firm had a different-size plant, it would be moving along a different *ATC* curve. In fact, there is a different *ATC* curve for each different plant the firm could have. In the long run, then, the firm can choose on which *ATC* curve it wants to operate. And, as we know, to produce any level of output, it will always choose that *ATC* curve—among all of the *ATC* curves available—that enables it to

Plant The collection of fixed inputs at a firm's disposal.

FIGURE 7
Long-Run Average Total Cost

*Average-total cost curves ATC$_0$,
ATC$_1$, ATC$_2$, and ATC$_3$ show
average costs when the firm has
zero, one, two, and three production lines, respectively. The
LRATC curve combines por-
tions of all the firm's ATC
curves. The firm will choose the
lowest-cost ATC curve for each
level of output.*

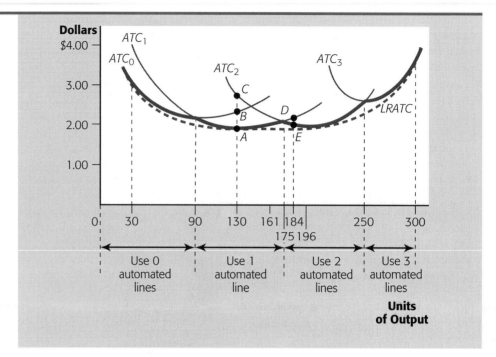

produce at lowest possible average total cost. This insight tells us how we can graph
the firm's *LRATC* curve.

Graphing the *LRATC* Curve. Look at Figure 7, which shows several different *ATC*
curves for Spotless Car Wash. There is a lot going on in this figure, so let's take it
one step at a time. First, find the curve labeled *ATC$_1$*. This is our familiar *ATC*
curve—the same one shown in Figure 6—which we used to find Spotless's average
total cost in the short run, when it was stuck with one automated line.

The other *ATC* curves refer to *different* plants that Spotless *might* have had instead. For example, the curve labeled *ATC$_0$* shows how average total cost would behave if Spotless had a plant with *zero* automated lines; *ATC$_2$* shows average total
cost with *two* automated lines, and so on. Since, in the long run, the firm can
choose which size plant to operate, it can also choose on which of these *ATC* curves
it wants to operate. And, as we know, in the long run, it will always choose the
plant with the lowest possible average total cost.

Let's take a specific example. Suppose that Spotless thinks that it might wash
130 cars per day. In the long run, what size plant should it choose? Scanning the
different *ATC* curves in Figure 7, we see that the lowest possible per-unit cost—
$1.96 per car—is at point *A* along *ATC$_1$*. The best plant for washing 130 cars per
day, therefore, will have just one automated line. For this output level, Spotless
would never choose a plant with zero lines, since it would then have to operate on
ATC$_0$ at point *B*. Since point *B* is higher than point *A*, we know that point *B* represents a larger per-unit cost. Nor would the firm choose a plant with two lines—operating on *ATC$_2$* at point *C*—for this would mean a still larger per-unit cost. Of all
the possibilities, only point *A* along *ATC$_1$* enables Spotless to achieve the lowest
per-unit cost for washing 130 cars. Thus, to produce 130 units of output in the

long run, Spotless would choose to operate at point A on ATC_1. Point A is the $LRATC$ of 130 units.

Now, suppose instead that Spotless wanted to produce 184 units of output in the long run. A plant with one automated line is no longer the best choice. Instead, the firm would choose a plant with *two* automated lines. How do we know? For an output of 184, the firm could choose point D on ATC_1, or point E on ATC_2. Since point E is lower, it is the better choice. At this point, average total cost would be $1.96, so this would be the $LRATC$ of 184 units.

Continuing in this way, we could find the $LRATC$ for *every* output level Spotless might produce. To produce any given level of output, the firm will always operate on the *lowest ATC curve* available. As output increases, it will move along an ATC curve until another, lower ATC curve becomes available—one with lower costs. At that point, the firm will increase its plant size, so it can move to the lower ATC curve. In the graph, as Spotless increases its output level from 90 to 175 units of output, it will continue to use a plant with one automated line and move along ATC_1. But if it wants to produce *more* than 175 units in the long run, it will increase its plant to *two* automated lines and begin moving along ATC_2.

Thus, we can trace out Spotless's $LRATC$ curve by combining just the lowest portions of all the ATC curves from which the firm can choose. In Figure 7, this is the thick, scallop-shaped curve.

A firm's $LRATC$ curve combines portions of each ATC curve available to the firm in the long run. For each output level, the firm will always choose to operate on the ATC curve with the lowest possible cost.

Figure 7 also gives us a view of the different options facing the firm in the short run and the long run. Once Spotless builds a plant with one automated line, its options in the short run are limited: It can only move along ATC_1. If it wants to increase its output from 130 to 184 units, it must move from point A to point D. But in the long run, it can move along its $LRATC$ curve—from point A to point E—by changing the size of its plant.

More generally,

in the short run, a firm can only move along its current ATC *curve. In the long run, however, it can move from one* ATC *curve to another by varying the size of its plant. As it does so, it will also be moving along its* LRATC *curve.*

Explaining the Shape of the *LRATC* Curve

In Figure 7, the $LRATC$ curve has a scalloped look because the firm can only choose among four different plants. But many firms—especially large ones—can choose among hundreds or even thousands of different plant sizes. Each plant would be represented by a different ATC curve, so there would be hundreds of ATC curves crowded into the figure. As a result, the scallops would disappear, and the $LRATC$ curve would appear as a smooth curve, like the dashed line in Figure 7.

In Figure 8, which reproduces this smoothed-out $LRATC$ curve, you can see that the curve is U-shaped—much like the AVC and ATC curves you learned about earlier. That is, as output increases, long-run average costs first decline, then remain constant, and finally rise. Although there is no law or rule of logic that requires an

FIGURE 8
The Shape of *LRATC*

If long-run total cost rises proportionately less than output, production reflects economies of scale, and LRATC *slopes downward. If cost rises proportionately more than output, there are diseconomies of scale, and* LRATC *slopes upward. Between those regions, cost and output rise proportionately, yielding constant returns to scale.*

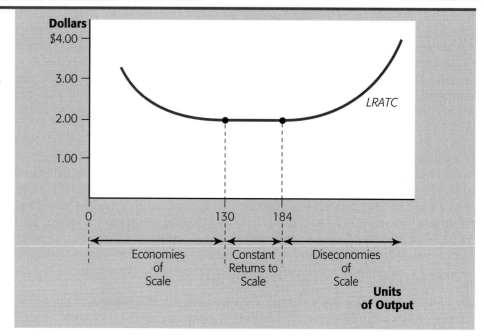

LRATC curve to have all three of these phases, in many industries this seems to be the case. Let's see why, by considering each of the three phases in turn.

Economies of Scale. When an increase in output causes *LRATC* to decrease, we say that the firm is enjoying **economies of scale:** the more output produced, the lower the cost per unit.

On a purely mathematical level, economies of scale mean that long-run total cost is rising by a smaller proportion than output. For example, if a doubling of output (Q) can be accomplished with less than a doubling of costs, then the ratio $LRTC/Q = LRATC$ will decline, and—voilà!—economies of scale.

> *When long-run total cost rises proportionately less than output, production is characterized by economies of scale, and the* LRATC *curve slopes downward.*

So much for the mathematics. But in the real world, *why* should total costs ever increase by a smaller proportion than output? Why should a firm experience economies of scale?

Gains from Specialization. One reason for economies of scale is gains from specialization. At very low levels of output, workers may have to perform a greater variety of tasks, slowing them down and making them less productive. But as output increases and workers are added, more possibilities for specialization are created. At Spotless, an increase in output and employment might permit one worker to specialize in taking cash from customers, a second to drive the cars onto the line, a third to towel them down, a fourth to work on advertising, and so on. Since each worker is more productive, output will increase by a greater proportion than costs.

Economies of scale Long-run average total cost decreases as output increases.

The greatest opportunities for increased specialization occur when a firm is producing at a relatively low level of output, with a relatively small plant and small workforce. Thus, economies of scale are more likely to occur at lower levels of output.

More Efficient Use of Lumpy Inputs. Another explanation for economies of scale involves the "lumpy" nature of many types of plant and equipment. **Lumpy inputs** are inputs that cannot be increased in tiny increments, but rather must be increased in large jumps.

Lumpy input An input whose quantity cannot be increased gradually as output increases, but must instead be adjusted in large jumps.

A doctor, for example, needs the use of an X-ray machine in order to serve her patients. Unless she can share with other doctors (which may not be possible), she must buy one or more *whole* machines; she cannot buy a half or a fifth of an X-ray machine. Suppose a single machine can service up to 500 patients per month and costs $2,000 per month (in interest payments or foregone investment income). Then the more patients the doctor sees (up to 500), the lower will be the cost of the machine per patient. For example, if she sees 100 patients each month, the cost per patient will be $2,000/100 = $20. If she sees 500 patients, the cost per patient drops to $2,000/500 = $4. If much of the doctor's plant and equipment are lumpy in this way, her *LRATC* curve might continue to decline over some range of output.

We see this phenomenon in many types of businesses: Plant and equipment must be purchased in large lumps, and a low cost per unit is achieved only at high levels of output. If you decide to start a pizza delivery business on campus, you will have to purchase or rent at least one pizza oven. If you can make 200 pizzas per day with a single oven, then your total oven costs will be the same whether you bake 1, 10, 50, 100, or 200 pizzas. The more pizzas you make, the lower will be your oven costs *per pizza.*

Other inputs besides equipment can also be lumpy in this way. Restaurants must pay a yearly license fee and are not permitted to buy part of a license if their output is small. An answering service must have a receptionist on duty at all times, even if only a few calls come in each day. A theater must have at least one ticket seller and one projectionist, regardless of how many people come to see the show. In all of these cases, an increase in output allows the firm to spread the cost of lumpy inputs over greater amounts of output, lowering the cost *per unit of output.*

Making more efficient use of lumpy inputs will have more impact on *LRATC* at low levels of output when these inputs make up a greater proportion of the firm's total costs. At higher levels of output, the impact is smaller. For example, suppose a restaurant must pay a yearly license fee of $1,000. If output doubles from 1,000 to 2,000 meals per year, license costs per meal served will fall from $1 to $0.50. But if output doubles from 10,000 to 20,000 meals, license costs per meal drop from $0.10 to $0.05—a hardly noticeable difference. Thus, spreading lumpy inputs across more output—like the gains from specialization—is more likely to create economies of scale at relatively low levels of output. This is another reason why the typical *LRATC* curve—as illustrated in Figure 8—slopes downward at relatively low levels of output.

A look back at Table 6 shows that there are, indeed, economies of scale for Spotless at low levels of output. It costs $100 to wash 30 cars and $195 to wash 90 cars. As output triples from 30 to 90, costs increase by only $95/$100, or 95 percent, so *LRATC* falls. Spotless is clearly enjoying economies of scale. Indeed, Figure 8 shows that it will experience economies of scale for all output levels up to 130 units.

Diseconomies of Scale. As output continues to increase, most firms will reach a point where bigness begins to cause problems. This is true even in the long run, when the firm is free to increase its plant size as well as its workforce. Large firms may require more layers of management, so communication and decision making become more time consuming and costly. Huge corporations like IBM, General Motors, and Verizon each have several hundred high-level managers, and thousands more at lower levels. Indeed, for much of the 1980s, IBM was criticized by its stockholders for the failure of its large, sluggish, managerial bureaucracy to keep up with rapid changes in the market for small computers. Large firms may also have a harder time screening out misfits among new hires and monitoring those already working at the firm, so there is an increase in mistakes, shirking of responsibilities, and even theft from the firm. These problems contribute to rises in *LRTC* as output increases, and work in the opposite direction to the forces helping to create economies of scale. When the firm reaches a certain size—and has exploited all major cost savings from "bigness"—these problems will start to dominate. And as the firm continues to grow larger, *LRATC* will rise.

More generally,

> *when long-run total cost rises more than in proportion to output, there are* ***diseconomies of scale****, and the* LRATC *curve slopes upward.*

Diseconomies of scale Long-run average total cost increases as output increases.

While economies of scale are more likely at low levels of output, *dis*economies of scale are more likely at higher output levels. In Figure 8, you can see that Spotless does not experience diseconomies of scale until it is washing more than 184 cars per day.

Constant Returns to Scale. In Figure 8, you can see that for output levels between 130 and 184, the smoothed-out *LRATC* curve is roughly flat. Over this range of output, *LRATC* remains approximately constant as output increases. Here, output and *LRTC* rise by roughly the same proportion:

> *When both output and long-run total cost rise by the same proportion, production is characterized by* ***constant returns to scale****, and the* LRATC *curve is flat.*

Constant returns to scale Long-run average total cost is unchanged as output increases.

Why would a firm experience constant returns to scale? We have seen that as output increases, cost savings from specialization and more efficient use of lumpy inputs will eventually be exhausted. But production may still have room to expand before the costly problems of "bigness" kick in. The firm will then have a range of output over which average cost neither rises nor falls as production increases—constant returns to scale. Notice that constant returns to scale, if present at all, are most likely to occur at some *intermediate* range of output.

In sum, when we look at the behavior of *LRATC*, we often expect a pattern like the following: economies of scale (decreasing *LRATC*) at relatively low levels of output, constant returns to scale (constant *LRATC*) at some intermediate levels of output, and diseconomies of scale (increasing *LRATC*) at relatively high levels of output. This is why *LRATC* curves are typically U-shaped.

Of course, even U-shaped *LRATC* curves will have different appearances for firms in different industries. And as you're about to see, these differences in *LRATC* curves have much to tell us about the economy.

USING THE THEORY
Long-Run Costs, Market Structure, and Mergers

If you want to buy a television, you can choose from among dozens of brands—Sony, Panasonic, Philips, JVC, Hitachi, and more—from among dozens of stores—Circuit City, Fry's, Best Buy, and other large chains, as well as a selection of small local stores. But if you want to hook up to cable, there will be only one company you can call: the one cable service provider in your area.

The same applies in many other markets in which you buy goods and services. For some purchases, you can choose from among many suppliers, such as manufacturers (of furniture, shoes, or computers) and retailers (of books, cars, and clothes). For other purchases, you've got only a few choices (such as cell phone service), and occasionally, just one (such as cross-country trains, regular mail delivery, and—in most areas—electricity).

The number of firms in a market is an important aspect of *market structure,* a general term for the environment in which trading takes place. What accounts for these differences in the number of sellers in the market? The shape of the *LRATC* curve plays an important role in the answer.

LRATC and the Size of Firms

Figure 9 shows how the *LRATC* curve might look for four different firms, each producing different types of goods in different markets. (For now, to make our analysis as general as possible, we won't name the specific goods.) Look first at panel (a) (ignore the demand curve for now). Notice that the *LRATC* curve for this firm displays economies of scale (slopes downward) up to an output level of 1,000 units per month, and then hits bottom before rising sharply. The output level at which the *LRATC* first hits bottom is known as the **minimum efficient scale (MES)** for the firm, the lowest level of output at which it can achieve minimum cost per unit. In the figure, if this firm were producing at its MES of 1,000 units, its long-run cost per unit would be $80. Moreover, if this *LRATC* curve is typical of *all* firms in the market, then $80 is the *lowest possible long-run price* in this market. We know this because if the price were any *less* than $80, the typical firm would eventually go out of business (it would be charging less for the good than the lowest possible cost of producing it).

Once we know the lowest possible price for this good, we can also determine the *maximum possible total quantity demanded* by using the market demand curve. In panel (a), for example, the market demand curve tells us that when price is $80, quantity demanded is 100,000 units. If the price can't be any lower than $80 in the long run, then market quantity demanded can't be any *greater* than 100,000 units.

Now let's apply these two curves—the *LRATC* for the *typical firm,* and the demand curve for the *entire market*—to market structure. When the MES is small relative to the maximum potential market as in panel (a), firms that are *relatively small* will have a cost advantage over relatively large firms. In the figure, a firm supplying just 1 percent of the maximum market (1,000 units out of 100,000) will put

Minimum efficient scale
The lowest output level at which the firm's *LRATC* curve hits bottom.

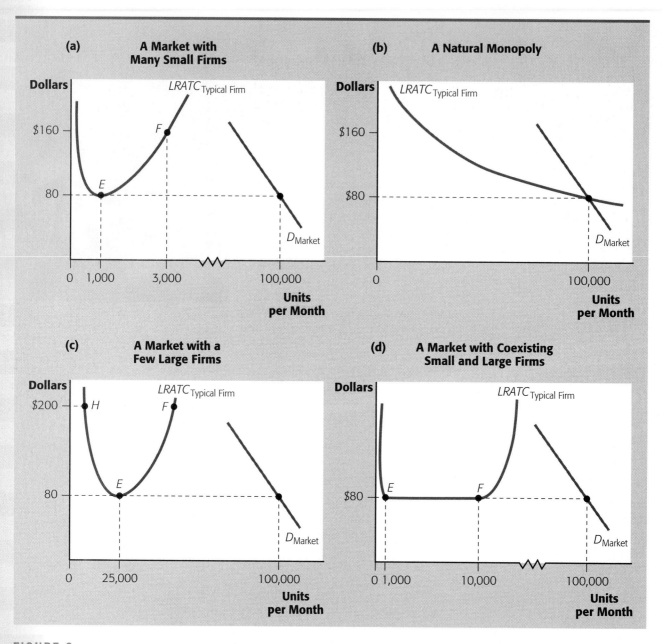

FIGURE 9
How *LRATC* Helps Explain Market Structure

In panel (a), the typical firm's MES occurs at an output level of 1,000—very small compared to the maximum potential market of 100,000. A small firm producing at point E has a cost advantage over a large firm producing at point F.

In panel (b), the typical firm's MES occurs beyond the maximum potential market. A single large firm producing at or near point E has a cost advantage over a smaller firm producing for just part of the market.

In panel (c), the typical firm's MES occurs at a relatively large fraction of the maximum potential market. A large firm producing at or near point E has a cost advantage over a smaller firm producing at point H, or an even larger firm producing at point F.

In panel (d), the MES occurs at a small fraction of the maximum potential market. But neither a small firm producing at point E nor a large firm producing at point F has a cost advantage over the other.

the firm at point E on its $LRATC$ curve, with cost per unit of $80. The cost per unit of a larger firm—say, one producing 3,000 units at point F—would be $160. A firm this large would be unable to compete with its smaller rivals.

Accordingly, we'd expect a market in which firms have this type of $LRATC$ curve to be populated by many small firms, each producing for only a tiny share of the market. In most cities, markets for personal services fit this pattern—haircuts, shoe repair, home remodeling, plumbing, lawn care, massages, and so on. For such businesses, economies of scale—from specialization and spreading lumpy inputs over more production—are exhausted rather rapidly, and then significant diseconomies of scale set in—perhaps from the difficulties of monitoring employees who are "in the field" performing services.

Panel (b) shows the opposite extreme: significant economies of scale that continue as output increases, even to the point where a typical firm is supplying the maximum possible quantity demanded. In such a market, a single, large firm enjoys a cost advantage over a smaller one. Once a single firm enters and expands production to reach most of the potential quantity demanded, it has already achieved a lower cost per unit than any new competitor could hope to achieve. Since this market will gravitate naturally toward *monopoly*, a market with just one seller, we call the market—as well as the single firm operating there—a **natural monopoly**. Regular mail delivery, cable television service, and city subway systems are all examples of natural monopolies, where the required lumpy inputs are so costly that even producing for the entire market does not exhaust economies of scale.

> **Natural monopoly** A market in which a single firm's production is characterized by economies of scale, even when its output expands to serve the entire market.

Panel (c) shows a third possibility. Here, the MES occurs at 25,000 units, which is 25 percent of the maximum potential market. In this type of market, we'd expect to see a few large competitors. Each of them would have a cost advantage over any single firm that tried to supply for the entire market on its own, but also have a cost advantage over a very small firm. This market has room for a few large competitors, but just a few. (Use the graph to prove to yourself that a smaller firm producing, say, just 5,000 units, or a larger firm producing, say, 50,000 units would have higher cost per unit than the 25,000-unit firm.) Examples of markets like this—where we'd expect to see (and do see) just a few firms—are manufacturers of passenger aircraft, airlines, pharmaceuticals, college textbook publishers, and online booksellers. In each of these cases, there are significant lumpy inputs that create economies of scale until each firm has expanded to produce for a relatively large share of the market.

Finally, look at panel (d). The MES of the typical firm in this market is 1,000 units, the lowest output level at which it reaches minimum cost per unit. But for firms in this market, diseconomies of scale don't set in until output exceeds 10,000 units. In between, firms experience constant returns to scale. Since both small and large firms can have equally low average costs, with neither having any advantage over the other, firms of varying sizes can coexist. Examples are orange producers (where large conglomerates coexist with small farmers), clothing stores (Macy's and the Gap coexist with the local men's and women's clothing shops), electronics retailers, law firms, and colleges. (More than half of all colleges and universities in the United States have fewer than 2,000 students. But they coexist with dozens of mega-universities, such as the University of Texas at Austin [the largest public] with 49,000 students, or New York University [the largest private] with 37,000 students.)

The Urge to Merge

Look again at panel (c), but now imagine that—for some reason—this market has 10 firms each with the *LRATC* shown there, and each is operating at point *H*, with cost per unit of $200. We'll assume that price is *at least* $200, so these firms can survive for the moment (which means that market quantity demanded must be *less* than its maximum potential of 100,000).

Each of these firms would want to expand in order to achieve the cost efficiencies that economies of scale makes possible. But they can't *all* expand to their MES of 25,000, because then market output would be $10 \times 25,000 = 250,000$, larger than the maximum potential quantity demanded. We'd expect to see cutthroat competition, with each firm trying to steal market share from the others. Eventually, some firms might expand, while others, seeing their market shrink further and their costs rise, might be forced out of business.

But something else might happen as well: Two of these small firms might realize that, by merging to form a larger, single firm with double the output, they could slide down the *LRATC* curve in the figure and enjoy a significant cost advantage over the other, still-smaller firms. This is a market that is ripe for a merger wave. In fact, any firm that *didn't* merge with another, or find some other way to expand, would likely be forced out of business, unable to compete with its larger and lower-cost rivals.

When market conditions are stable for long periods of time, we'd expect that firms would have already expanded to exploit economies of scale, through mergers or other means. So a sudden merger wave is usually set off by some *change* in the market. And recent history gives us some examples.

Consider the banking industry. For decades, commercial banks were prohibited from operating in more than one state. While estimates of the MES for banking have been controversial, it was likely that banks, especially in small states with smaller markets, were operating at output levels below their MES. Then, in the 1990s, a series of government policy changes, culminating in the Interstate Banking and Branching Efficiency Act of 1994, effectively ended the restrictions on interstate banking. The result was a wave of bank mergers that decreased the number of commercial banks by 30 percent—from 12,370 in 1990 to 8,698 in 1999. At the same time, the size of the average U.S. commercial bank almost doubled.

Another example is Hewlett Packard and Compaq, discussed at the beginning of this chapter. While these two firms make many products, and there were several benefits to be gained by a merger, we'll focus on just the personal computer market here.

Two major events shook the market for personal computers in 2001. One was a leftward shift in the market demand curve, largely caused by a souring economy. By itself, a shrinking market would affect all suppliers there, causing them to move leftward along their *LRATC* curves and raising cost per unit. But a second event was the determination of a nimble competitor, Dell Computer, to *gain* market share. Through cost-cutting innovations in taking orders and building machines, Dell succeeded: Its share of the world PC market rose from 9.7 percent in 1999 to 13.1 percent in early 2001. Much of this growth came at the expense of Hewlett Packard and Compaq, who each suffered a declining share of a shrinking total market. As these two firms moved leftward along their *LRATC* curves, they saw their cost per unit rising. Managers at both firms believed that a merger could reverse this move by creating one large firm with lower cost per unit.

Market structure in general, and mergers and acquisitions in particular, raise many important issues for public policy. Low-cost production can benefit consumers . . . *if* it results in lower prices. But when lower costs arise from mergers—which can reduce competition among the remaining firms—prices can rise even as costs fall. And in special markets, mergers often create special controversies. For example, in mid-2003, a Federal Communications Commission ruling made it easier for corporations to expand into local media markets, where significant, unexploited economies of scale may exist. The prospect of small, local television and radio stations being acquired by national media companies stirred a heated debate over access to diverse sources of news. We'll return to some of the public policy issues raised by different market structures in later chapters.

Summary

Business firms combine inputs to produce outputs. Compared to production by individual independent contractors, production through business firms with employees allows gains from specialization (each worker may specialize in one aspect of production), lower transaction costs, and reduced risk for employees.

A firm's *production function* describes the maximum output it can produce using different quantities of inputs. In the *short run,* at least one of the firm's inputs is fixed. In the *long run,* all inputs can be varied.

A firm's *cost of production* is the opportunity cost of its owners—everything they must give up in order to produce output. In the short run, some costs are *fixed* and independent of the level of production. Other costs—*variable costs*—change as production increases. *Marginal cost* is the change in total cost from producing one more unit of output. The *marginal cost curve* has a U shape, reflecting the underlying marginal product of labor. A variety of average cost curves can be defined. The *average variable cost curve* and the *average total cost curve* are each U-shaped, reflecting the relationship between average and marginal cost.

In the long run, all costs are variable. The firm's *long-run total cost curve* indicates the cost of producing each quantity of output with the least-cost input mix. The related *long-run average total cost (LRATC) curve* is formed by combining portions of different *ATC* curves, each portion representing a different plant size. The shape of the *LRATC* curve reflects the nature of returns to scale. It slopes downward when there are economies of scale, slopes upward when there are diseconomies of scale, and is flat when there are constant returns to scale. Variations in the shape of the typical firm's *LRATC* curve can help explain the number of firms and the average size of firms in different industries.

Key Terms

Average fixed cost
Average total cost
Average variable cost
Business firm
Constant returns to scale
Corporation
Diminishing marginal returns to labor
Diseconomies of scale
Diversification
Economies of scale
Explicit costs
Fixed costs
Fixed input

Implicit costs
Increasing marginal returns to labor
Law of diminishing marginal returns
Long run
Long-run average total cost
Long-run total cost
Lumpy inputs
Marginal cost
Marginal product of labor
Minimum efficient scale
Natural monopoly
Partnership
Plant

Production function
Profit
Short run
Sole proprietorship
Sunk costs
Technology
Total cost
Total fixed cost
Total product
Total variable cost
Transaction costs
Variable costs
Variable input

Review Questions
Answers to even-numbered Questions and Problems can be found on the text Web site at http://hall-lieb.swlearning.com.

1. What are the three types of business firm? Discuss the pros and cons of each type.

2. Why is most production activity carried out by firms, rather than by independent contractors?

3. A home builder incurs the following costs. Which are examples of transaction costs? Why?
   a. Cost of lumber
   b. Lawyer's fees for handling the legal work connected with the purchase of land
   c. Interest expense on a loan to buy new equipment
   d. Opportunity cost of time spent gathering bids from subcontractors

4. Given the advantages of larger firm size, why don't we expect firms to grow larger without limit?

5. Discuss the distinction between the short run and the long run as those terms relate to production.

6. Which of the following inputs would likely be classified as fixed and which as variable over a time horizon of one month? Why?
   a. Ovens to the Nabisco bakery
   b. Wood to the La-Z-Boy Chair Co.
   c. Oranges to Minute Maid Juice Co.
   d. Labor to a McDonald's hamburger franchise
   e. Cars to Hertz Rent-a-Car Co.

7. Explain the difference between the total output of a firm and the marginal product of labor (MPL) at that firm. How are they related?

8. Classify the following as fixed or variable costs for a time horizon of six months. Justify your categorization.
   a. General Motors' outlay for steel
   b. Pillsbury's rent on its corporate headquarters
   c. The cost of newsprint for the *New York Times*

9. Can long-run total cost ($LRTC$) ever be greater than short-run total cost (TC)? Why or why not?

10. Explain the U shape of a typical long-run average cost curve. Specifically, why is the curve downward sloping at lower levels of output and upward sloping at higher?

Problems and Exercises

1. The following table shows total output (in tax returns completed per day) of the accounting firm of Hoodwink and Finagle:

Number of Accountants	Number of Returns per Day
0	0
1	5
2	12
3	17
4	20
5	22

   Assuming the quantity of capital (computers, adding machines, desks, etc.) remains constant at all output levels:
   a. Calculate the marginal product of each accountant.
   b. Over what range of employment do you see increasing returns to labor? Diminishing returns?
   c. Explain why MPL might behave this way in the context of an accounting firm.

2. During the late 1990s, there were numerous mergers of firms. In some cases, these firms produced the same products. In other cases, the merger brought together firms that made totally different products. Explain a possible motive for the mergers in each case.

3. The following table gives the short-run and long-run total costs for various levels of output of Consolidated National Acme, Inc.:

Q	TC_1	TC_2
0	0	350
1	300	400
2	400	435
3	465	465
4	495	505
5	560	560
6	600	635
7	700	735

   a. Which column, TC_1 or TC_2, gives long-run total cost, and which gives short-run total cost? How do you know?
   b. For each level of output, find short-run TFC, TVC, AFC, AVC, and MC.
   c. At what output level would the firm's short-run and long-run input mixes be the same?
   d. Starting from producing two units, Consolidated's managers decide to double production to four units. So they simply double all of their inputs in the long run. Comment on their managerial skill.
   e. Over what range of output do you see economies of scale? Diseconomies of scale? Constant returns to scale?

4. In a recent year, a long, hard winter gave rise to stronger-than-normal demand for heating oil. The following summer was characterized by strong demand for gasoline by vacationers. Show what these two events might have done to the short-run *MC, AVC,* and *ATC* curves of Continental Airlines. (*Hint:* How would these events affect the price of oil?)

5. Ludmilla's House of Schnitzel is currently producing 10 schnitzels a day at point *A* on the following diagram. Ludmilla's business partner, Hans (an impatient sort), wants her to double production immediately.

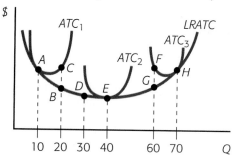

a. What point will likely illustrate Ludmilla's cost situation for the near future? Why?

b. If Ludmilla wants to keep producing 20 schnitzels, at what point does she want to be eventually? How can she get there?

c. Eventually, Ludmilla and company do very well, expanding until they find themselves making 70 schnitzels a day. But after a few years, Ludmilla discovers that profit was greater when she produced 20 schnitzels per day. She wants to scale back production to 20 schnitzels per day, laying off workers, selling off equipment, renting less space, and producing fewer schnitzels. Hans wants to reduce output by just cutting back on flour and milk and laying off workers. Who's right? Discuss the situation with reference to the relevant points on the diagram.

d. Does the figure tell us what output Ludmilla should aim for? Why or why not?

6. Clean 'n' Shine is a competitor to Spotless Car Wash. Like Spotless, it must pay $75 per day for each automated line it uses. But Clean 'n' Shine has been able to tap into a lower-cost pool of labor, paying its workers only $50 per day. Clean 'n' Shine's production technology is given in the table below. To determine its short-run cost structure, fill in the blanks in the table.

a. Over what range of output does Clean 'n' Shine experience increasing marginal returns to labor? Over what range does it experience decreasing marginal returns to labor?

b. As output increases, do average fixed costs behave as described in the text? Explain.

c. As output increases, do marginal cost, average variable cost, and average total cost behave as described in the text? Explain.

d. Looking at the numbers in the table, but without drawing any curves, is the relationship between *MC* and *AVC* as described in the text? What about the relationship between *MC* and *ATC*?

Short-Run Costs for Clean 'n' Shine Car Wash

(1) Output (per Day)	(2) Capital	(3) Labor	(4) TFC	(5) TVC	(6) TC	(7) MC	(8) AFC	(9) AVC	(10) ATC
0	1	0	$__	$__	$__		—	—	—
						$__			
30	1	1	$__	$__	$__		$__	$__	$__
						$__			
70	1	2	$__	$__	$__		$__	$__	$__
						$__			
120	1	3	$__	$__	$__		$__	$__	$__
						$__			
160	1	4	$__	$__	$__		$__	$__	$__
						$__			
190	1	5	$__	$__	$__		$__	$__	$__
						$__			
210	1	6	$__	$__	$__		$__	$__	$__

7. In Table 3, when output rises from 130 to 161 units, marginal cost is $1.94. For this change in output, marginal cost is greater than the previous *AVC* ($1.38) but less than the previous *ATC* ($1.96). According to the relationship between marginals and averages you learned in this chapter:
   a. What should happen to *AVC* due to this change in output? Does it happen?
   b. What should happen to *ATC* due to this change in output? Does it happen? (*Hint:* Calculate *ATC* to the third decimal place.)

8. A soft drink manufacturer that uses just labor (variable) and capital (fixed) paid a consulting firm thousands of dollars to calculate short-run costs at various output levels. But after the cost table (see below) was handed over to the president of the soft drink company, he spilled Dr Pepper on it, making some of the entries illegible. The consulting firm, playing tough, is demanding another payment to provide a duplicate table.
   a. Should the soft drink president pay up? Or can he fill in the rest of the entries on his own? Fill in as many entries as you can to determine your answer. (*Hint:* First, determine the price of labor.)
   b. Do *MC, AVC,* and *ATC* have the relationship to each other that you learned in this chapter? Explain.

9. "If a firm has diminishing returns to labor over some range of output, it cannot have economies of scale over that range." True or false? Explain briefly.

10. Use *LRATC* diagrams to graphically show the events (discussed in the "Using the Theory" section) that shook the market for personal computers in 2001 and led to the merger of Hewlett Packard and Compaq in 2002.

11. Down On Our Luck Studios has spent $100 million producing an awful film, *A Depressing Story About a Miserable Person.* If the studio releases the film, the most cost-effective marketing plan would cost an additional $5 million, bringing the total amount spent to $105 million. Box office sales under this plan are predicted to be $12 million, which would be split evenly between the theaters and the studio. Additional studio revenue from video and DVD sales would be about $2 million. Should the studio release the film? If no, briefly explain why not. If yes, explain how it could make sense to release a film that cost $105 million but earns only $12 million.

12. The term "orphan drug" refers to a product that treats a rare disease affecting fewer than 200,000 Americans. Given the high cost of developing drugs, and given the limited demand for orphan drugs, use *LRATC* and demand diagrams to show a situation in which an orphan drug will not be produced at all.

Output per day	Units of Capital	Number of Workers	TFC	TVC	TC	MC	AFC	AVC	ATC
0	10	0	$1,000	?	?		?	?	?
						?			
20,000	10	100	?	$9,000	?		?	?	?
						?			
40,000	10	?	?	?	?		?	?	$0.325
						?			
60,000	10	225	?	?	?		?	?	?
						?			
80,000	10	?	?	?	$27,000		?	?	?

Challenge Questions

1. Draw the long-run total cost and long-run average cost curves for a firm that experiences:
   a. Constant returns to scale over all output levels.
   b. Diseconomies of scale over low levels of output, constant returns to scale over intermediate levels of output, and economies of scale over high output levels. Does this pattern of costs make sense? Why or why not?

2. A firm has the strange *ATC* curve drawn below. Sketch in the marginal cost curve this firm must have. (*Hint:* Use what you know about the marginal-average relationship. Note that this *MC* curve does *not* have a standard shape.)

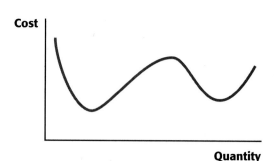

3. The following curve shows the *marginal* product of labor for a firm at different levels of output.

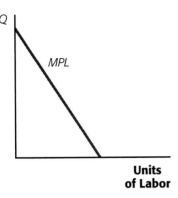

a. Show what the corresponding total product curve would look like.

b. Do the total and marginal product curves for this firm ever exhibit diminishing marginal returns to labor? Increasing marginal returns to labor?

 *Applications* *These exercises require access to Hall/Lieberman Xtra! If Xtra! did not come with your book, visit* http://hallxtra.swlearning.com *to purchase.*

1. Use your Xtra! Password at the Hall and Lieberman Web site (http://hallxtra.swlearning.com), select this chapter, and under Economic Applications, click on EconNews Online. Select *Microeconomics: Production and Costs,* and scroll down to find the articles, "Precision Plowing" and "Optimizing Operations." Read the summaries there.

   a. Is the utilization of GPS-guided tractors and wireless technologies examples of long-run production adjustments, or short-run production adjustment? Why?

   b. Are there any sunks, or unavoidable, costs incurred with these new technologies? If so, what are they?

   c. In what ways are GPS-guided tractors and wireless technologies similar forms of production advances?

2. Use your Xtra! Password at the Hall and Lieberman Web site (http://hallxtra.swlearning.com), select this chapter, and under Economic Applications, click on EconData

Online. Select *Microeconomics: Production and Costs,* and find the section on Labor Productivity. Click on this link, then on Labor Productivity, then on Updates, and select the February 21, 2003, *Economic Letter,* in the first line. Read the letter and answer the following questions.

   a. What does the article conclude had been the cause of productivity gains?

   b. Go back to the *Labor Productivity* page, and at the top, click on *Diagrams/Data.* Click on the link that shows the *relationship between labor productivity and real GDP* (national output). Scroll down to find the graph outlining this relation. Does the relationship in the Economic Letter reveal itself in the graph. Why or why not?

   c. Are these changes in productivity short run or long run? Why?

How Firms Make Decisions: Profit Maximization

In 2001, the managers of Nintendo America, Inc., knew that they had another winner on their hands: the Game Boy Advance handheld game machine. The new product ran 17 times faster than its predecessor (Game Boy Color), and displayed 32,768 colors on its 2.9 inch screen. It was sure to dazzle consumers, displaying images more spectacular and faster-moving than any competing product.

Then came the hard questions. Where should the new product be produced: Japan, the United States, or perhaps Hong Kong? How should the company raise the funds to pay the costs of production? When should it bring the product to market? How much should it spend on advertising, and in which types of media? And finally, what price should the company charge, and how many units should it plan to produce?

These last decisions—how much to produce and what price to charge—are the focus of this chapter. In the end, Nintendo planned to produce 23 million units for the first year, and decided to charge $99.95. But why didn't it charge a lower price that would allow it to sell more units? Or a higher price that would give it more profit on each unit sold?

Although this chapter concentrates on firms' decisions about price and output level, the tools you will learn apply to many other firm decisions. How much should MasterCard spend on advertising? How late should Starbucks keep its coffee shops open? How many copies should *Newsweek* give away free to potential subscribers? Should movie theaters offer Wednesday afternoon showings that only a few people attend? This chapter will help you understand how firms answer these sorts of questions.

THE GOAL OF PROFIT MAXIMIZATION

To analyze decision making at the firm, let's start with a very basic question: What is the firm trying to maximize?

Economists have given this question a lot of thought. Some firms—especially large ones—are complex institutions in which many different groups of people work together. A firm's owners will usually want the firm to earn as much profit as possible. But the workers and managers who actually run the firm may have other agendas. They may try to divert the firm away from profit maximization in order to benefit themselves. For now, let's assume that workers and managers are faithful servants of the firm's owners. That is,

> *we will view the firm as a single economic decision maker whose goal is to maximize its owners' profit.*

Why do we make this assumption? Because it has proven so *useful* in understanding how firms behave. True, this assumption leaves out the details of these other agendas that often are present in real-world firms. But remember that every economic model *abstracts* from reality. To stay simple and comprehensible, it leaves out many real-world details and includes only what is relevant for the purpose at hand. If the purpose is to explain conflict within the firm or deviations from profit-maximizing behavior, or even fraudulent accounting practices by management (such as the 2002 corporate scandals at Enron, WorldCom, and other firms), then the differing goals of managers and owners should be a central element of the model. Indeed, we'll look at some of these issues, and their implications, in Chapter 12.

But when the purpose is to explain how firms decide what price to charge and how much to produce, or whether to temporarily shut down the firm or continue operating, or whether to enter a new market or permanently leave a current one, the assumption of profit maximization has proven to be sufficient. It explains what firms actually do with reasonable—and sometimes remarkable—accuracy.

Why? Part of the reason is that managers who deviate *too* much from profit maximizing for *too* long are typically replaced. The managers may be sacked either by the current dissatisfied owners or by other firms that acquire the underperforming firm.

Another reason is that so many managers are well trained in the tools of profit maximization. This is in contrast to our model of consumer behavior, in which we asserted that consumers act *as if* they are using the model's graphs and calculations—although we recognize that most consumers never actually do. The basic economic model of the firm's behavior, however, is well understood *and used* by most managers, who have often taken several economics courses as part of their management education. In fact, economists' thinking about firm behavior has so permeated the language and culture of modern business that it's sometimes hard to distinguish where theory ends and practice begins.

UNDERSTANDING PROFIT

Profit is defined as the firm's *sales revenue* minus its *costs of production*. There is widespread agreement over how to measure the firm's revenue—the flow of money into the firm. But there are two different conceptions of the firm's costs, and each of them leads to a different definition of profit.

Two Definitions of Profit

One conception of costs is the one used by accountants. With a few exceptions, accountants consider only *explicit* costs, where money is actually paid out.[1] If we deduct only the costs recognized by accountants, we get one definition of profit:

Accounting profit = Total revenue − Accounting costs.

Accounting profit Total revenue minus accounting costs.

But economics, as you have learned, has a much broader view of cost—*opportunity cost*. For the firm's owners, opportunity cost is the total value of *everything* sacrificed to produce output. This includes not only the explicit costs recognized by accountants—such as wages and salaries and outlays on raw materials—but also *implicit costs,* when something is given up but no money changes hands. For example, if an owner contributes his own time or money to the firm, there will be foregone wages or foregone investment income—both implicit costs for the firm.

This broader conception of costs leads to a second definition of profit:

Economic profit = Total revenue − *All* costs of production

= Total revenue − (Explicit costs + Implicit costs)

Economic profit Total revenue minus all costs of production, explicit and implicit.

The difference between economic profit and accounting profit is an important one; when they are confused, some serious (and costly) mistakes can result. An example might help make the difference clear.

Suppose you own a firm that produces T-shirts and you want to calculate your profit over the year. Your bookkeeper provides you with the following information:

Total Revenue from Selling T-shirts	**$300,000**
Cost of raw materials	$ 80,000
Wages and salaries	150,000
Electricity and phone	20,000
Advertising cost	40,000
Total Explicit Cost	**290,000**
Accounting Profit	**$ 10,000**

---

[1] One exception is *depreciation*, a charge for the gradual wearing out of the firm's plant and equipment. Accountants include this as a cost even though no money is actually paid out.

From the looks of things, your firm is earning a profit, so you might feel pretty good. Indeed, if you look only at *money* coming in and *money* going out, you have indeed earned a profit: $10,000 for the year . . . an *accounting* profit.

But suppose that in order to start your business you invested $100,000 of your own money—money that could have been earning $6,000 in interest if you'd put it in the bank instead. Also, you are using two extra rooms in your own house as a factory—rooms that could have been rented out for $4,000 per year. Finally, you are managing the business full-time, without receiving a separate salary, and you could instead be working at a job earning $40,000 per year. All of these costs—the interest, rent, and salary you *could* have earned—are implicit costs that have not been taken into account by your bookkeeper. They are part of the opportunity cost of your firm, because they are sacrifices you made to operate your business.

Now let's look at this business from the economist's perspective and calculate your *economic* profit.

Total Revenue from Selling T-shirts		**$300,000**
Cost of raw materials	$ 80,000	
Wages and salaries	150,000	
Electricity and phone	20,000	
Advertising cost	40,000	
Total Explicit Costs	**$290,000**	
Investment income foregone	$ 6,000	
Rent foregone	4,000	
Salary foregone	40,000	
Total Implicit Costs	**$ 50,000**	
Total Costs		**$340,000**
Economic Profit		**−$ 40,000**

From an economic point of view, your business is not profitable at all, but is actually losing $40,000 per year! But wait—how can we say that your firm is suffering a loss when it takes in more money than it pays out? Because, as we've seen, your *opportunity cost*—the value of what you are giving up to produce your output—includes more than just money costs. When *all* costs are considered—implicit as well as explicit—your total revenue is not sufficient to cover what you have sacrificed to run your business. You would do better by shifting your time, your money, and your spare room to some alternative use.

Which of the two definitions of profit is the correct one? Either one of them, depending on the reason for measuring it. For tax purposes, the government is interested in profits as measured by accountants. The government cares only about the money you've earned, not what you *could* have earned had you done something else with your money or your time.

However, for our purposes—understanding the behavior of firms—economic profit is clearly better. Should your T-shirt factory stay in business? Should it expand or contract in the long run? Will other firms be attracted to the T-shirt industry? It is economic profit that will help us answer these questions, because it is economic profit that you and other owners care about.

The proper measure of profit for understanding and predicting the behavior of firms is economic profit. *Unlike accounting profit, economic profit recognizes all the opportunity costs of production—both explicit costs and implicit costs.*

Why Are There Profits?

When you look at the income received by households in the economy, you see a variety of payments. Those who provide firms with land receive *rent*—the payment for land. Those who provide labor receive a wage or salary. And those who lend firms money so they can purchase capital equipment receive interest. The firm's profit goes to its owners. But what do the owners of the firm provide that earns them this payment?

Economists view profit as a payment for two contributions of entrepreneurs, which are just as necessary for production as are land, labor, or machinery. These two contributions are *risk taking* and *innovation*.

Consider a restaurant that happens to be earning profit for its owner. The land, labor, and capital the restaurant uses to produce its meals did not simply come together magically. Someone—the owner—had to be willing to take the initiative to set up the business, and this individual assumed the risk that the business might fail and the initial investment be lost. Because the consequences of loss are so severe, the reward for success must be large in order to induce an entrepreneur to establish a business.

On a larger scale, Ted Turner risked hundreds of millions of dollars in the late 1970s when he created Cable News Network (CNN). Now that CNN has turned out to be so successful, it is easy to forget how risky the venture was at the outset. At the time, many respected financial analysts forecast that the project would fail and Turner would be driven into bankruptcy.

Profits are also a reward for *innovation*. Ted Turner was the first to create a 24-hour global news network, just as Pierre Omidyar—when he founded eBay in 1995—was the first to establish a commercially viable online auction market. These are obvious innovations.

But innovations can also be more subtle, and they are more common than you might think. When you pass by a successful laundromat, you may not give it a second thought. But someone, at some time, had to be the first one to realize, "I bet a laundromat in this neighborhood would do well"—an innovation. There can also be innovations in the production process, such as the improvement in mass production that made the disposable contact lens possible.

In almost any business, if you look closely, you will find that some sort of innovation was needed to get things started. Innovation, like taking on the risk of losing substantial wealth, makes an essential contribution to production. Profit is, in part, a reward to those who innovate.

THE FIRM'S CONSTRAINTS

If the firm were free to earn whatever level of profit it wanted, it would earn virtually infinite profit. This would make the owners very happy. Unfortunately for owners, though, the firm is not free to do this; it faces *constraints* on both its revenue and its costs.

The Demand Constraint

The constraint on the firm's revenue arises from a familiar concept: the demand curve. This curve always tells us the quantity of a good buyers wish to buy at different prices. But which buyers? And from which firms are they buying? Depending on how we answer these questions, we might be talking about different types of demand curves.

Market demand curves—like the ones you studied in Chapters 3 and 4—tell us the quantity demanded by *all* consumers from *all* firms in a market. In this chapter, we look at yet another kind of demand curve:

> The **demand curve facing the firm** *tells us, for different prices, the quantity of output that customers will choose to purchase from that firm.*

Notice that this new demand curve—the demand curve facing the firm—refers to only *one* firm, and to *all buyers* who are potential customers of that firm.

Let's consider the demand curve faced by Ned, the owner and manager of Ned's Beds, a manufacturer of bed frames. Figure 1 lists the different prices that Ned could charge for each bed frame and the number of them (per day) he can sell at each price. The figure also shows a graph of the demand curve facing Ned's firm. For each price (on the vertical axis), it shows us the quantity of output the firm can sell (on the horizontal axis). Notice that, like the other types of demand curves we have studied, the demand curve facing the firm slopes downward. In order to sell more bed frames, Ned must lower his price.[2]

The definition of the demand curve facing the firm suggests that once it selects a price, the firm has also determined how much output it will sell. But, as you saw a few chapters ago, we can also flip the demand relationship around: Once the firm has selected an output level, it has also determined the maximum price it can charge. This leads to an alternative definition:

> The demand curve facing the firm *shows us the maximum price the firm can charge to sell any given amount of output.*

Looking at Figure 1 from this perspective, we see that the horizontal axis shows alternative levels of output and the vertical axis shows the price Ned should charge if he wishes to sell each quantity of output.

These two different ways of defining the firm's demand curve show us that it is, indeed, a constraint for the firm. The firm can freely determine *either* its price *or* its level of output. But once it makes the choice, the other variable is automatically determined by the firm's demand curve. Thus, the firm has only *one* choice to make. Selecting a particular price *implies* a level of output, and selecting an output level *implies* a particular price. Economists typically focus on the choice of output level, with the price implied as a consequence. We will follow that convention in this textbook.

Demand curve facing the firm
A curve that indicates, for different prices, the quantity of output that customers will purchase from a particular firm.

© PHILIP GOULD/CORBIS

Like other firms, a furniture manufacturer must determine either its price for its products, or its level of output; once it chooses price, its level of output is determined, and vice versa.

[2] The downward-sloping demand curve tells us that Ned's Beds sells its output in an *imperfectly competitive market*, a market where the firm can *set* its price. Most firms operate in this type of market. If a manager thinks, "I'd like to sell more output, but then I'd have to lower my price, so let's see if it's worth it," we know he operates in an imperfectly competitive market. In a *perfectly competitive market*, by contrast, the firm would have to accept the market price as given. We assumed that markets were perfectly competitive in Chapter 3, and in the next chapter we'll examine them in more detail.

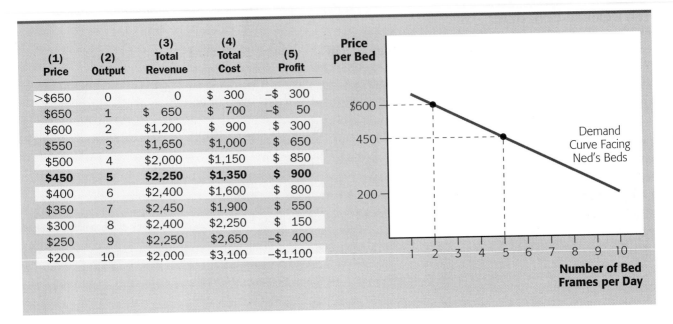

(1) Price	(2) Output	(3) Total Revenue	(4) Total Cost	(5) Profit
>$650	0	0	$ 300	–$ 300
$650	1	$ 650	$ 700	–$ 50
$600	2	$1,200	$ 900	$ 300
$550	3	$1,650	$1,000	$ 650
$500	4	$2,000	$1,150	$ 850
$450	**5**	**$2,250**	**$1,350**	**$ 900**
$400	6	$2,400	$1,600	$ 800
$350	7	$2,450	$1,900	$ 550
$300	8	$2,400	$2,250	$ 150
$250	9	$2,250	$2,650	–$ 400
$200	10	$2,000	$3,100	–$1,100

FIGURE 1
The Demand Curve Facing the Firm

The table presents information about Ned's Beds. Data from the first two columns are plotted in the figure to show the demand curve facing the firm. At any point along that demand curve, the product of price and quantity equals total revenue, which is given in the third column of the table.

Total revenue The total inflow of receipts from selling a given amount of output.

Total Revenue. A firm's **total revenue** is the total inflow of receipts from selling output. Each time the firm chooses a level of output, it also determines its total revenue. Why? Because once we know the level of output, we also know the highest price the firm can charge. Total revenue, which is the number of units of output times the price per unit, follows automatically.

The third column in Figure 1 lists the total revenue of Ned's Beds. Each entry is calculated by multiplying the quantity of output (column 2) by the price per unit (column 1). For example, if Ned's firm produces 2 bed frames per day, he can charge $600 for each of them, so total revenue will be 2 × $600 = $1,200. If Ned increases output to 3 units, he must lower the price to $550, earning a total revenue of 3 × $550 = $1,650. Because the firm's demand curve slopes downward, Ned must lower his price each time his output increases, or else he will not be able to sell all he produces. With more units of output, but each one selling at a lower price, total revenue could rise or fall. Scanning the total revenue column, we see that for this firm, total revenue first rises and then begins to fall. This will be discussed in greater detail later on.

The Cost Constraint

Every firm struggles to reduce costs, but there is a limit to how low costs can go. These limits impose a second constraint on the firm. Where do the limits come from? They come from concepts that you learned about in Chapter 6. Let's review them briefly.

First, the firm has a given production function, which is determined by its production technology. The production function tells us all the different ways in which the firm can produce any given level of output. In the long run, when all inputs are variable, the firm can use *any* method in its production function. In the short run, it is even more constrained: It can use only *some* of the methods in that production function, because one or more of its inputs are *fixed*.

Second, the firm must pay *prices* for each of the inputs that it uses, and we assume there is nothing the firm can do about those prices. Together, the production function and the prices of the inputs determine what it will cost to produce any given level of output. And once the firm chooses the *least cost* method available, it has driven the cost of producing that output level as low as it can go.

> *The firm uses its production function, and the prices it must pay for its inputs, to determine the least cost method of producing any given output level. Therefore, for any level of output the firm might want to produce, it must pay the cost of the "least cost method" of production.*

The fourth column of Figure 1 lists Ned's total cost—the lowest possible cost of producing each quantity of output. More output always means greater costs, so the numbers in this column are always increasing. For example, at an output of zero, total cost is $300. This tells us we are looking at costs in the short run, over which some of the firm's costs are *fixed*. (What would be the cost of producing 0 units if this were the long run?) If output increases from 0 to 1 bed frame, total cost rises from $300 to $700. This increase in total costs—$400—is caused by an increase in *variable* costs, such as labor and raw materials.

THE PROFIT-MAXIMIZING OUTPUT LEVEL

In this section, we ask a very simple question: How does a firm find the level of output that will earn it the greatest possible profit? We'll look at this question from several angles, each one giving us further insight into the behavior of the firm.

The Total Revenue and Total Cost Approach

At any given output level, we know (1) how much revenue the firm will earn and (2) its cost of production. We can then easily calculate profit, which is just the difference between total revenue (*TR*) and total cost (*TC*).

> *In the total revenue and total cost approach, the firm calculates* Profit = TR − TC *at each output level and selects the output level where profit is greatest.*

Let's see how this works for Ned's Beds. Column 5 of Figure 1 lists total profit at each output level. If the firm were to produce no bed frames at all, total revenue (*TR*) would be 0, while total cost (*TC*) would be $300. Total profit would be *TR* − *TC* = 0 − $300 = −$300. We would say that the firm earns a profit of negative $300 or a **loss** of $300 per day. Producing one bed frame would raise total revenue to $650 and total cost to $700, for a loss of $50. Not until the firm produces 2 bed frames does total revenue rise above total cost and the firm begin to make a profit. At 2 bed frames per day, *TR* is $1,200 and *TC* is $900, so the firm earns a profit of $300. Remember that as long as we have been careful to include *all* costs in *TC*—implicit as well as explicit—the profits and losses we are calculating are *economic* profits and losses.

In the total revenue and total cost approach, finding the profit-maximizing output level is straightforward: We just scan the numbers in the profit column until we

Loss The difference between total cost (*TC*) and total revenue (*TR*), when *TC* > *TR*.

find the largest value, $900, and the output level at which it is achieved, 5 units per day. We conclude that the profit-maximizing output for Ned's Beds is 5 units per day.

The Marginal Revenue and Marginal Cost Approach

There is another way to find the profit-maximizing level of output. This approach, which uses *marginal* concepts, gives us some powerful insights into the firm's decision-making process. Recall that *marginal* cost is the *change* in total cost per unit increase in output. Now, let's consider a similar concept for revenue.

Marginal revenue The change in total revenue from producing one more unit of output.

> *Marginal revenue* (MR) *is the change in the firm's total revenue* (ΔTR) *divided by the change in its output* (ΔQ):
>
> $$MR = \Delta TR/\Delta Q$$
>
> MR *tells us how much revenue rises* per unit *increase in output.*

Table 1 reproduces the *TR* and *TC* columns from Figure 1, but adds columns for marginal revenue and marginal cost. (In the table, output is always changing by one unit, so we can use ΔTR alone as our measure of marginal revenue.) For example, when output changes from 2 to 3 units, total revenue rises from $1,200 to $1,650. For this output change, *MR* = $450. As usual, marginals are placed *between* different output levels because they tell us what happens as output *changes* from one level to another.

Maximize Profit, Not Revenue You may be tempted to forget about profit and think that the firm should produce where its total revenue is maximized. As you can see in Figure 1 (column 3), total revenue is greatest when the firm produces 7 units per day, but at this output level, profit is not as high as it could be. The firm does better by producing only 5 units. True, revenue is lower at 5 units, but so are costs. It is the difference between revenue and cost that matters, not revenue alone.

There are two important things to notice about marginal revenue. First, when *MR* is *positive,* an increase in output causes total revenue to *rise.* In the table, *MR* is positive for all increases in output from 0 to 7 units. When *MR* is *negative,* an increase in output causes total revenue to *fall,* as occurs for all increases beyond 7 units.

The second thing to notice about *MR* is a bit more complicated: Each time output increases, *MR* is *smaller* than the price the firm charges at the new output level. For example, when output increases from 2 to 3 units, the firm's total revenue rises by $450—even though it sells the third unit for a price of $550. This may seem strange to you. After all, if the firm increases output from 2 to 3 units, and it gets $550 for the third unit of output, why doesn't its total revenue rise by $550?

The answer is found in the firm's downward-sloping demand curve, which tells us that to sell more output, the firm must cut its price. Look back at Figure 1 of this chapter. When output increases from 2 to 3 units, the firm must lower its price from $600 to $550. Moreover, the new price of $550 will apply to *all three* units the firm sells.[3] This means it *gains* some revenue—$550—by selling that third unit. But it also *loses* some revenue—$100—by having to lower the price by $50 on

---

[3] Some firms can charge two or more different prices for the same product. We'll explore some examples in Chapter 9.

Output	Total Revenue	Marginal Revenue	Total Cost	Marginal Cost	Profit
0	0		$ 300		–$300
		$650		$400	
1	$ 650		$ 700		–$50
		$550		$200	
2	$1,200		$ 900		$300
		$450		$100	
3	$1,650		$1,000		$650
		$350		$150	
4	$2,000		$1,150		$850
		$250		$200	
5	$2,250		$1,350		$900
		$150		$250	
6	$2,400		$1,600		$800
		$ 50		$300	
7	$2,450		$1,900		$550
		–$ 50		$350	
8	$2,400		$2,250		$150
		–$150		$400	
9	$2,250		$2,650		–$400
		–$250		$450	
10	$2,000		$3,100		–$1,100

TABLE 1
More Data for Ned's Beds

each of the two units of output it could have otherwise sold at $600. Marginal revenue will always equal the *difference* between this gain and loss in revenue—in this case, $550 − $100 = $450.

> *When a firm faces a downward-sloping demand curve, each increase in output causes a revenue gain, from selling additional output at the new price, and a revenue loss, from having to lower the price on all previous units of output. Marginal revenue is therefore less than the price of the last unit of output.*[4]

Using MR and MC to Maximize Profits. Now we'll see how marginal revenue, together with marginal cost, can be used to find the profit-maximizing output level. The logic behind the MC and MR approach is this:

> *An increase in output will always raise profit as long as marginal revenue is greater than marginal cost* (MR > MC).

[4] There is a connection between the behavior of total revenue, marginal revenue, and the price elasticity of demand you learned about in Chapter 4. When demand is elastic, a fall in price—and the associated rise in quantity—causes total revenue to rise. In Table 1, total revenue rises (marginal revenue is positive) for all changes in output between 0 and 7 units. Therefore, we know that demand is elastic along the interval of the demand curve between 0 and 7 units. Similarly, demand is *inelastic* along the interval of the demand curve between 7 and 10 units.

Notice the word *always*. Let's see why this rather sweeping statement must be true. Table 1 tells us that when output rises from 2 to 3 units, *MR* is $450, while *MC* is $100. This change in output causes both total revenue and total cost to rise, but it causes revenue to rise by *more* than cost ($450 > $100). As a result, profit must increase. Indeed, looking at the profit column, we see that increasing output from 2 to 3 units *does* cause profit to increase, from $300 to $650.[5]

The converse of this statement is also true:

> *An increase in output will always lower profit whenever marginal revenue is less than marginal cost* (MR < MC).

For example, when output rises from 5 to 6 units, *MR* is $150, while *MC* is $250. For this change in output, both total revenue and total cost rise, but cost rises *more*, so profit must go down. In Table 1, you can see that this change in output does indeed cause profit to decline, from $900 to $800.

These insights about *MR* and *MC* lead us to the following simple guideline the firm should use to find its profit-maximizing level of output:

> *To find the profit-maximizing output level, the firm should increase output whenever* MR > MC, *and decrease output when* MR < MC.

Let's apply this rule to Ned's Beds. In Table 1 we see that when moving from 0 to 1 unit of output, *MR* is $650, while *MC* is only $400. Since *MR* is larger than *MC*, making this move will increase profit. Thus, if the firm is producing 0 beds, it should always increase to 1 bed. Should it stop there? Let's see. If it moves from 1 to 2 beds, *MR* is $550, while *MC* is only $200. Once again, *MR* > *MC*, so the firm should increase to 2 beds. You can verify from the table that if the firm finds itself producing 0, 1, 2, 3, or 4 beds, *MR* > *MC* for an increase of 1 unit, so it will always make greater profit by increasing production.

Until, that is, output reaches 5 beds. At this point, the picture changes: From 5 to 6 beds, *MR* is $150, while *MC* is $250. For this move, *MR* < *MC*, so profits would decrease. Thus, if the firm is producing 5 beds, it should *not* increase to 6. The same is true at every other output level beyond 5 units: The firm should *not* raise its output, since *MR* < *MC* for each increase. We conclude that Ned maximizes his profit by producing 5 beds per day—the same answer we got using the *TR* and *TC* approach earlier.[6]

Profit Maximization Using Graphs

Both approaches to maximizing profit (using totals or using marginals) can be seen even more clearly when we use graphs. In Figure 2(a) and (b), the data from Table 1 have been plotted—the *TC* and *TR* curves in the upper panel, and the *MC* and *MR* curves in the lower one.

---

[5] You may have noticed that the rise in profit ($350) is equal to the difference between *MR* and *MC* in this example. This is no accident. *MR* tells us the *rise* in revenue; *MC* tells us the *rise* in cost. The difference between them will always be the *rise* in profit.

[6] It sometimes happens that *MR* is precisely equal to *MC* for some change in output, although this does not occur in Table 1. In this case, increasing output would cause *both* cost and revenue to rise by equal amounts, so there would be *no* change in profit. The firm should not care whether it makes this change in output or not.

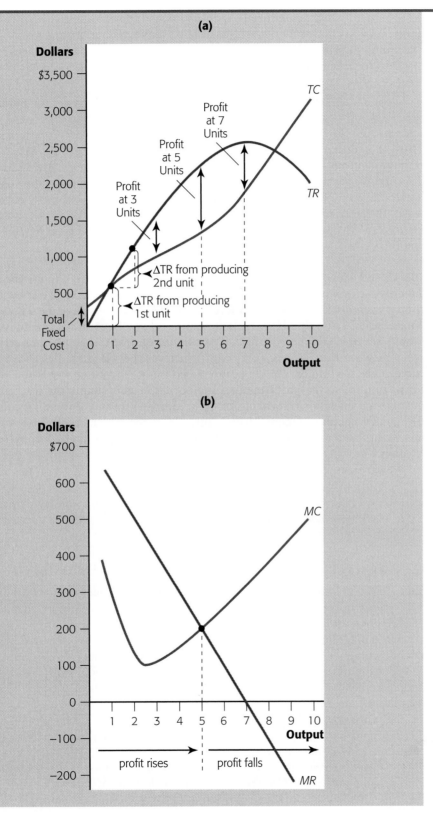

(a)

(b)

FIGURE 2
Profit Maximization

Panel (a) shows the firm's total revenue (TR) and total cost (TC) curves. Profit is the vertical distance between the two curves at any level of output. Profit is maximized when that vertical distance is greatest—at 5 units of output. Panel (b) shows the firm's marginal revenue (MR) and marginal cost (MC) curves. (As long as MR lies above the horizontal axis, the TR curve slopes upward.) Profit is maximized at the level of output closest to where the two curves cross—at 5 units of output.

The marginal revenue curve has an important relationship to the total revenue curve. As you can see in Figure 2(a), total revenue (*TR*) is plotted on the vertical axis, and quantity (*Q*) on the horizontal axis, so the slope along any interval is just $\Delta TR/\Delta Q$. But this is exactly the definition of marginal revenue.

> *The marginal revenue for any change in output is equal to the* slope *of the total revenue curve along that interval.*

Thus, as long as the *MR* curve lies above the horizontal axis *(MR > 0)*, *TR* must be increasing and the *TR* curve must slope upward. In the figure, *MR* > 0, and the *TR* curve slopes upward from zero to 7 units. When the *MR* curve dips below the horizontal axis (*MR* < *0*), *TR* is decreasing, so the *TR* curve begins to slope downward. In the figure, this occurs beyond 7 units of output. As output increases in Figure 2, *MR* is first positive and then turns negative, so the *TR* curve will first *rise* and then *fall*.

The *TR* and *TC* Approach Using Graphs. Now let's see how we can use the *TC* and *TR* curves to guide the firm to its profit-maximizing output level. We know that the firm earns a profit at any output level where *TR* > *TC* —where the *TR* curve lies *above* the *TC* curve. In Figure 2(a), you can see that all output levels between 2 and 8 units are profitable for the firm. The *amount* of profit is simply the *vertical distance* between the *TR* and *TC* curves, whenever the *TR* curve lies above the *TC* curve. Since the firm cannot sell part of a bed frame, it must choose whole numbers for its output, so the profit-maximizing output level is simply the whole-number quantity at which this vertical distance is greatest—5 units of output. Of course, the *TR* and *TC* curves in Figure 2 were plotted from the data in Table 1, so we should not be surprised to find the same profit-maximizing output level—5 units—that we found before when using the table.

We can sum up our graphical rule for using the *TR* and *TC* curves this way:

> *To maximize profit, the firm should produce the quantity of output where the vertical distance between the* TR *and* TC *curves is greatest and the* TR *curve lies above the* TC *curve.*

The *MR* and *MC* Approach Using Graphs. Figure 2 also illustrates the *MR* and *MC* approach to maximizing profits. As usual, the marginal data in panel (b) are plotted *between* output levels, since they tell us what happens as output changes from one level to another.

In the diagram, as long as output is less than 5 units, the *MR* curve lies above the *MC* curve (*MR* > *MC*), so the firm should produce more. For example, if we consider the move from 4 to 5 units, we compare the *MR* and *MC* curves at the midpoint between 4 and 5. Here, the *MR* curve lies above the *MC* curve, so increasing output from 4 to 5 will increase profit.

But now suppose the firm is producing 5 units and considering a move to 6. At the midpoint between 5 and 6 units, the *MR* curve has already crossed the *MC* curve, and now it lies *below* the *MC* curve. For this move, *MR* < *MC*, so raising output would *decrease* the firm's profit. The same is true for every increase in output beyond 5 units: The *MR* curve always lies below the *MC* curve, so the firm will decrease its profits by increasing output. Once again, we find that the profit-maximizing output level for the firm is 5 units.

Notice that the profit-maximizing output level—5 units—is the level closest to where the *MC* and *MR* curves cross. This is no accident. For each change in output that *increases* profit, the *MR* curve will lie above the *MC* curve. The first time that an output change *decreases* profit, the *MR* curve will cross the *MC* curve and dip below it. Thus, the *MC* and *MR* curves will always cross closest to the profit-maximizing output level.

With this graphical insight, we can summarize the *MC* and *MR* approach this way:

> *To maximize profit, the firm should produce the quantity of output closest to the point where* MC = MR—*that is, the quantity of output at which the* MC *and* MR *curves intersect.*

This rule is very useful, since it allows us to look at a diagram of *MC* and *MR* curves and *immediately* identify the profit-maximizing output level. In this text, you will often see this rule. When you read, "The profit-maximizing output level is where *MC* equals *MR*," translate to "The profit-maximizing output level is closest to the point where the *MC* curve crosses the *MR* curve."

A Proviso. There is, however, one important exception to this rule. Sometimes the *MC* and *MR* curves cross at two different points. In this case, the profit-maximizing output level is the one at which the MC curve crosses the MR curve *from below*.

Figure 3 shows why. At point A, the *MC* curve crosses the *MR* curve from *above*. Our rule tells us that the output level at this point, Q_1, is *not* profit maximizing. Why not? Because at output levels lower than Q_1, $MC > MR$, so profit *falls* as output increases toward Q_1. Also, profit *rises* as output increases *beyond* Q_1, since $MR > MC$ for these moves. Since it never pays to increase *to* Q_1, and profit rises when increasing *from* Q_1, we know that Q_1 cannot possibly maximize the firm's profit.

Misusing the Gap Between *MR* and *MC*   A common error is assuming that the firm should produce the level of output at which the difference between *MR* and *MC* is as large as possible, like 2 or 3 units of output in Figure 2. Let's see why this is wrong. If the firm produces 2 or 3 units, it would leave many profitable increases in output unexploited—increases where $MR > MC$. As long as *MR* is even a tiny bit larger than *MC*, it pays to increase output, since doing so will add more to revenue than to cost. The firm should be satisfied only when the difference between *MR* and *MC* is as *small* as possible, not as *large* as possible.

DANGEROUS CURVES

But now look at point B, where the *MC* curve crosses the *MR* curve from below. You can see that when we are at an output level lower than Q^*, it always pays to increase output, since $MR > MC$ for these moves. You can also see that, once we have arrived at Q^*, further increases will reduce profit, since $MC > MR$. Q^* is thus the profit-maximizing output level for this firm—the output level at which the *MC* curve crosses the *MR* curve *from below*.

What About Average Costs?

You may have noticed that this chapter has discussed *most* of the cost concepts introduced in Chapter 6. But it has not yet referred to *average* cost. There is a good

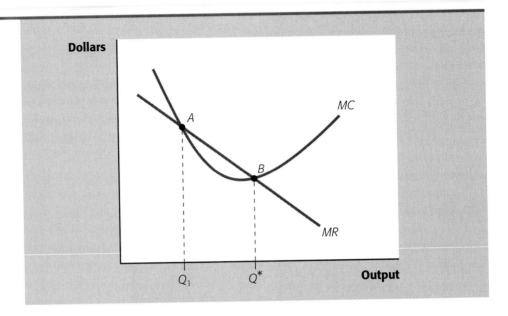

FIGURE 3
Two Points of Intersection

Sometimes the MR *and* MC
*curves intersect twice. The
profit-maximizing level of output is always found where* MC
crosses MR *from below.*

reason for this. We have been concerned about how much the firm should produce
if it wishes to earn the greatest possible level of profit. To achieve this goal, the firm
should produce more output whenever doing so *increases* profit, and it needs to
know only *marginal* cost and *marginal* revenue for this purpose. The different types
of average cost (*ATC*, *AVC*, and *AFC*) are simply irrelevant. Indeed, a common error—sometimes made even by business managers—is to use *average* cost in place of
marginal cost in making decisions.

For example, suppose a yacht maker wants to know how much his total cost
will rise in the short run if he produces another unit of output. It is tempting—*but
wrong*—for the yacht maker to reason this way: "My cost per unit (*ATC*) is currently $50,000 per yacht. Therefore, if I increase production by 1 unit, my total cost
will rise by $50,000; if I increase production by 2 units, my total cost will rise by
$100,000, and so on."

There are two problems with this approach. First, *ATC* includes many costs
that are *fixed* in the short run—including the cost of all fixed inputs such as the
factory and equipment and the design staff. These costs will *not* increase when
additional yachts are produced, and they are therefore irrelevant to the firm's decision making in the short run. Second, *ATC changes* as output increases. The
cost per yacht may rise above $50,000 or fall below $50,000, depending on
whether the *ATC* curve is upward or downward sloping at the current production
level. Note that the first problem—fixed costs—could be solved by using *AVC* instead of *ATC*. The second problem—changes in average cost—remains even when
AVC is used.

The correct approach, as we've seen in this chapter, is to use the *marginal cost*
of a yacht and to consider increases in output one unit at a time. The firm should
produce the output level where its *MC* curve crosses its *MR* curve from below. Average cost doesn't help at all; it only confuses the issue.

Does this mean that all of your efforts to master *ATC* and *AVC*—their definitions, their relationship to each other, and their relationship to *MC*—were a waste

of time? Far from it. As you'll see, average cost will prove *very* useful in the chapters to come. You'll learn that whereas marginal values tell the firm *what* to do, averages can tell the firm *how well* it has done. But average cost should *not* be used in place of marginal cost as a basis for decisions.

The Marginal Approach to Profit

The *MC* and *MR* approach for finding the profit-maximizing output level is actually a very specific application of a more general principle:

> The *marginal approach to profit* states that a firm should take any action that adds more to its revenue than to its costs.

Marginal approach to profit
A firm maximizes its profit by taking any action that adds more to its revenue than to its cost.

In this chapter, the action being considered is whether to increase output by 1 unit. We've learned that the firm should take this action whenever $MR > MC$.

But the same logic can be applied to *any other decision* facing the firm. Should a restaurant owner take out an ad in the local newspaper? Should a convenience store that currently closes at midnight stay open 24 hours instead? Should a private kindergarten hire another teacher? Should an inventor pay to produce an infomercial for her new gizmo? Should a bank install another ATM? The answer to all of these questions is yes—*if* the action would add more to revenue than to costs. In future chapters, we'll be using the marginal approach to profit to analyze some other types of firm decisions.

DEALING WITH LOSSES

So far, we have dealt only with the pleasant case of profitable firms and how they select their profit-maximizing output level. But what about a firm that cannot earn a positive profit at *any* output level? What should it do? The answer depends on what time horizon we are looking at.

The Short Run and the Shutdown Rule

In the short run, the firm must pay for its fixed inputs, because there is not enough time to sell them or get out of lease and rental agreements. But the firm can *still* make decisions about production. And one of its options is to *shut down*—to stop producing output, at least temporarily.

At first glance, you might think that a loss-making firm should always shut down its operation in the short run. After all, why keep producing if you are not making any profit? In fact, it makes sense for some unprofitable firms to continue operating.

Imagine a firm with the *TC* and *TR* curves shown in the upper panel of Figure 4 (ignore the *TVC* curve for now). No matter what output level the firm produces, the *TC* curve lies above the *TR* curve, so it will suffer a loss—a negative profit. For this firm, the goal is still profit maximization. But now, the highest profit will be the one with the *least negative value*. In other words, profit maximization becomes *loss minimization*.

FIGURE 4
Loss Minimization

The firm shown here cannot earn a positive profit at any level of output. If it produces anything, it will minimize its loss by producing where the vertical distance between TR and TC is smallest. Because TR exceeds TVC at Q*, the firm will produce there in the short run.

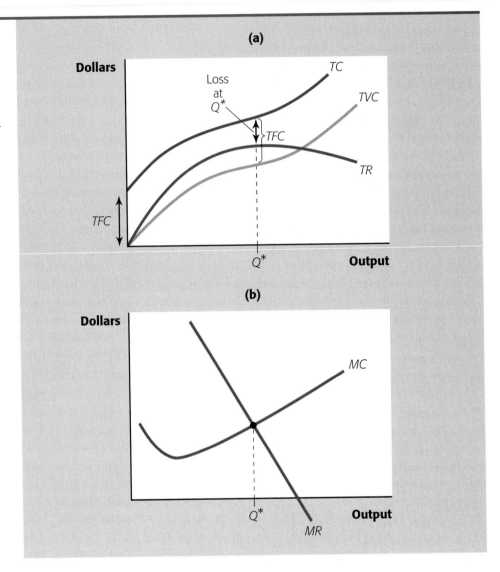

If the firm keeps producing, then the smallest possible loss is at an output level of Q^*, where the distance between the *TC* and *TR* curves is smallest. Q^* is also the output level we would find by using our marginal approach to profit (increasing output whenever that adds more to revenue than to costs). This is why, in the lower panel of Figure 4, the *MC* and *MR* curves must intersect at (or very close to) Q^*.

The question is: Should this firm produce at Q^* and suffer a loss? The answer is yes—*if* the firm would lose even *more* if it stopped producing and shut down its operation. Remember that, in the short run, a firm must continue to pay its total fixed cost (*TFC*) no matter what level of output it produces—even if it produces nothing at all. If the firm shuts down, it will therefore have a loss equal to its *TFC*, since it will not earn any revenue. But if, by producing some output, the firm can cut its loss to something *less* than TFC, then it should stay open and keep producing.

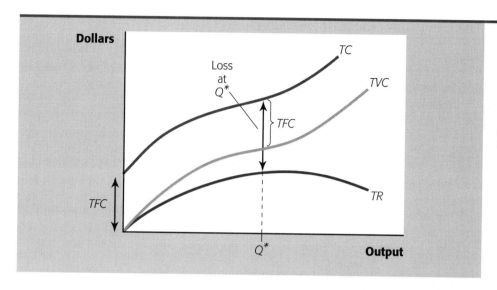

Dollars

Loss at Q*

TFC

TC

TVC

TFC

TR

Q*

Output

FIGURE 5
Shut Down

At Q*, this firm's total variable cost exceeds its total revenue. The best policy is to shut down, produce nothing, and suffer a loss equal to TFC in the short run.

To understand the shutdown decision more clearly, let's think about the firm's total variable costs. Business managers often call *TVC* the firm's *operating cost,* since the firm only pays these variable costs when it continues to operate. If a firm, by staying open, can earn *more* than enough revenue to cover its operating costs, then it is making an *operating profit* (*TR* > *TVC*). It should not shut down because its operating profit can be used to help pay its fixed costs. But if the firm cannot even cover its operating cost when it stays open—that is, if it would suffer an *operating loss* (*TR* < *TVC*)—it should definitely shut down. Continuing to operate only *adds* to the firm's loss, increasing the total loss beyond fixed costs.

This suggests the following guideline—called the **shutdown rule**—for a loss-making firm:

> *Let* Q* *be the output level at which* MR = MC. *Then, in the short run:*
> *If* TR > TVC *at* Q*, *the firm should keep producing.*
> *If* TR < TVC *at* Q*, *the firm should shut down.*
> *If* TR = TVC *at* Q*, *the firm should be indifferent between shutting down and producing.*

Shutdown rule In the short run, the firm should continue to produce if total revenue exceeds total variable costs; otherwise, it should shut down.

Look back at Figure 4. At *Q**, the firm is making an operating profit, since its *TR* curve is above its *TVC* curve. This firm, as we've seen, should continue to operate.

Figure 5 is drawn for a different firm, one with the same *TC* and *TVC* curves as the firm in Figure 4, but with a lower *TR* curve. This firm *cannot* earn an operating profit, since its *TR* curve lies below its *TVC* curve everywhere—even at *Q**. This firm should shut down.

The shutdown rule is a powerful predictor of firms' decisions to stay open or cease production in the short run. It tells us, for example, why some seasonal businesses—such as ice cream shops in summer resort areas—shut down in the winter, when *TR* drops so low that it becomes smaller than *TVC*. And it tells us why producers of steel, automobiles, agricultural goods, and television sets will often keep producing output for some time even when they are losing money.

The Long Run: The Exit Decision

The shutdown rule applies only in the short run, a time horizon too short for the firm to escape its commitments to pay for fixed inputs such as plant and equipment. In fact, we only use the term *shut down* when referring to the short run.

Exit A permanent cessation of production when a firm leaves an industry.

But a firm can also decide to stop producing in the long run. In that case, we say the firm has decided to **exit** the industry.

The long-run decision to exit is different than the short-run decision to shut down. That's because in the long run, there *are* no fixed costs, since all inputs can be varied. Therefore, a firm that exits, by reducing all of its inputs to zero, will have *zero* costs (an option not available in the short run). And since exit also means zero revenue, a firm that exits will earn zero profit. When would a firm decide to exit and earn zero profit? When its only other alternative is to earn *negative* profit.

> *A firm should exit the industry in the long run when—at its best possible output level—it has any loss at all.*

We will look more closely at the exit decision and other long-run considerations in the next chapter.

© GEORGE HALL/CORBIS

USING THE THEORY
Getting It Wrong and Getting It Right

Today, almost all managers have a good grasp of the concepts you've learned in this chapter, largely because microeconomics has become an important part of every business school curriculum. But if we go back a few decades—to when fewer managers had business degrees—we can find two examples of how management's failure to understand the basic theory of the firm led to serious errors. In one case, ignorance of the theory caused a large bank to go bankrupt; in the other, an airline was able to outperform its competitors because *they* remained ignorant of the theory.

Getting It Wrong: The Failure of Franklin National Bank

In the mid-1970s, Franklin National Bank—one of the largest banks in the United States—went bankrupt. The bank's management had made several errors, but we will focus on the most serious one.

First, a little background. A bank is very much like any other business firm: It produces output (in this case a service, making loans) using a variety of inputs (including the funds it lends out). The price of the bank's output is the interest rate it charges to borrowers. For example, with a 5 percent interest rate, the price of each dollar in loans is 5 cents per year.

Unfortunately for banks, they must also *pay* for the money they lend out. The largest source of funds is customer deposits, for which the bank must pay interest. If a bank wants to lend out *more* than its customers have deposited, it can obtain funds from a second source, the *federal funds market,* where banks lend money to one another. To borrow money in this market, the bank will usually have to pay a higher interest rate than it pays on customer deposits.

In mid-1974, John Sadlik, Franklin's chief financial officer, asked his staff to compute the average cost to the bank of a dollar in loanable funds. At the time, Franklin's funds came from three sources, each with its own associated interest cost:

Source	Interest Cost
Checking Accounts	2.25 percent
Savings Accounts	4 percent
Borrowed Funds	9–11 percent

What do these numbers tell us? First, each dollar deposited in a Franklin *checking* account cost the bank 2.25 cents per year,[7] while each dollar in a *savings* account cost Franklin 4 cents. Also, Franklin, like other banks at the time, had to pay between 9 and 11 cents on each dollar borrowed in the federal funds market. When Franklin's accountants were asked to figure out the average cost of a dollar in loans, they divided the total cost of funds by the number of dollars they had lent out. The number they came up with was 7 cents.

This average cost of 7 cents per dollar is an interesting number, but, as we know, it should have *no relevance to a profit-maximizing firm's decisions*. And this is where Franklin went wrong. At the time, all banks, including Franklin, were charging interest rates of 9 to 9.5 percent to their best customers. But Sadlik decided that since money was costing an *average* of 7 cents per dollar, the bank could make a tidy profit by lending money at 8 percent—earning 8 cents per dollar. Accordingly, he ordered his loan officers to approve any loan that could be made to a reputable borrower at 8 percent interest. Needless to say, with other banks continuing to charge 9 percent or more, Franklin National Bank became a very popular place from which to borrow money.

But where did Franklin get the additional funds it was lending out? That was a problem for the managers in *another* department at Franklin, who were responsible for *obtaining* funds. It was not easy to attract additional checking and savings account deposits, since, in the 1970s, the interest rate banks could pay was regulated by the government. That left only one alternative: the federal funds market. And this is exactly where Franklin went to obtain the funds pouring out of its lending department. Of course, these funds were borrowed not at 7 percent, the average cost of funds, but at 9 to 11 percent, the cost of borrowing in the federal funds market.

To understand Franklin's error, let's look again at the average cost figure it was using. This figure included an irrelevant cost: the cost of funds obtained from customer deposits. This cost was irrelevant to the bank's lending decisions, since *additional* loans would not come from these deposits, but rather from the more expensive federal funds market. Further, this average figure was doomed to rise as Franklin expanded its loans. How do we know this? The *marginal* cost of an additional dollar of loans—9 to 11 cents per dollar—was greater than the *average* cost—7 cents. As you know, whenever the marginal is greater than the average, it pulls the average up. Thus, Franklin was basing its decisions on an average cost figure that not only included irrelevant sunk costs but was bound to increase as its lending expanded.

More directly, we can see Franklin's error through the lens of the marginal approach. The *marginal revenue* of each additional dollar lent out at 8 percent was 8 cents, while the *marginal cost* of each additional dollar—since it came from the federal funds market—was 9 to 11 cents. MC was greater than MR, so Franklin was actually losing money each time its loan officers approved another loan! Not

[7] This cost was not actually a direct interest payment to depositors, since in the 1970s banks generally did not pay interest on checking accounts. But banks *did* provide free services such as check clearing, monthly statements, free coffee, and even gifts to their checking account depositors, and the cost of these freebies was computed to be 2.25 cents per dollar of deposits.

surprisingly, these loans—which never should have been made—caused Franklin's profits to *decrease,* and within a year the bank had lost hundreds of millions of dollars. This, together with other management errors, caused the bank to fail.

Getting It Right: The Success of Continental Airlines

In the early 1960s, Continental Airlines was doing something that seemed like a horrible mistake. All other airlines at the time were following a simple rule: They would offer a flight only if, on average, 65 percent of the seats could be filled with paying passengers, since only then could the flight break even. Continental, however, was flying jets filled to just 50 percent of capacity and was actually expanding flights on many routes. When word of Continental's policy leaked out, its stockholders were angry, and managers at competing airlines smiled knowingly, waiting for Continental to fail. Yet Continental's profits—already higher than the industry average—continued to grow. What was going on?

There *was,* indeed, a serious mistake being made, but by the *other* airlines, not Continental. This mistake should by now be familiar to you: using average cost instead of marginal cost to make decisions. The "65 percent of capacity" rule used throughout the industry was derived more or less as follows: The total cost of the airline for the year (TC) was divided by the number of flights during the year (Q) to obtain the average cost of a flight ($TC/Q = ATC$). For the typical flight, this came to about $4,000. Since a jet had to be 65 percent full in order to earn ticket sales of $4,000, the industry regarded any flight that repeatedly took off with less than 65 percent as a money loser and canceled it.

As usual, there are two problems with using ATC in this way. First, an airline's average cost per flight includes many costs that are irrelevant to the decision to add or subtract a flight. These *sunk costs* include the cost of running the reservations system, paying interest on the firm's debt, and fixed fees for landing rights at airports—none of which would change if the firm added or subtracted a flight. Also, average cost ordinarily *changes* as output changes, so it is wrong to assume it is constant in decisions about *changing* output.

Continental's management, led by its vice-president of operations, had decided to try the marginal approach to profit. Whenever a new flight was being considered, every department within the company was asked to determine the *additional* cost they would have to bear. Of course, the only additional costs were for additional *variable* inputs, such as additional flight attendants, ground crew personnel, in-flight meals, and jet fuel. These additional costs came to only about $2,000 per flight. Thus, the *marginal* cost of an additional flight—$2,000—was significantly less than the marginal revenue of a flight filled to 65 percent of capacity—$4,000. The marginal approach to profits tells us that when $MR > MC$, output should be increased, which is just what Continental was doing. Indeed, Continental correctly drew the conclusion that the marginal revenue of a flight filled at even 50 percent of capacity—$3,000—was *still* greater than its marginal cost, and so offering the flight would increase profit. This is why Continental was expanding routes even when it could fill only 50 percent of its seats.

In the early 1960s, Continental was able to outperform its competitors by using a secret—the marginal approach to profits. Today, of course, the secret is out, and all airlines use the marginal approach when deciding which flights to offer.[8]

---

[8] For more information about Continental's strategy, see "Airline Takes the Marginal Bone," *Business Week,* April 20, 1963, pp. 111–114.

Summary

In economics, we view the firm as a single economic decision maker with the goal of maximizing the owners' profit. Economic profit is total revenue minus *all* costs of production, explicit and implicit. In their pursuit of maximum profit, firms face two constraints. One is embodied in the demand curve the firm faces; it indicates the maximum price the firm can charge to sell any amount of output. This constraint determines the firm's revenue at each level of production. The other constraint is imposed by costs: More output always means greater costs. In choosing the profit-maximizing output, the firm must consider both revenues and costs.

One approach to choosing the optimal level of output is to measure profit as the difference between total revenue and total cost at each level of output, and then select the output level at which profit is greatest. An alternate approach uses *marginal revenue* (MR), the change in total revenue from producing one more unit of output, and *marginal cost* (MC), the change in total cost from producing one more unit. The firm should increase output whenever $MR > MC$, and lower output when $MR < MC$. The profit-maximizing output level is the one closest to the point where $MR = MC$.

If profit is negative, but total revenue exceeds total variable cost, the firm should continue producing in the short run. Otherwise, it should shut down and suffer a loss equal to its fixed cost. A firm with negative profit in the long run should exit the market.

Key Terms

Accounting profit	Exit	Marginal revenue
Demand curve facing the firm	Loss	Shutdown rule
Economic profit	Marginal approach to profit	Total revenue

Review Questions

Answers to even-numbered Questions and Problems can be found on the text Web site at http://hall-lieb.swlearning.com.

1. What is the difference between accounting profit and economic profit?

2. Can a firm earn an accounting profit at the same time it is suffering an economic loss? If so, give a numerical example. Can a firm earn an economic profit at the same time it is suffering an accounting loss? Again, if this is possible, give a numerical example.

3. Name two contributions to the production process for which profit is a payment. Pick a local business, and briefly explain how the entrepreneur behind it has made each of these contributions.

4. What are the two kinds of demand curves we have discussed in this chapter? What does each tell us?

5. What are the constraints on the firm's ability to earn profit? How does each constraint arise?

6. How does the firm select the level of output where profit is greatest in:
   a. The total revenue and total cost approach?
   b. The marginal revenue and marginal cost approach? How is each approach illustrated graphically?

Problems and Exercises

1. You have a part-time work/study job at the library that pays $10 per hour, 3 hours per day on Saturdays and Sundays. Some friends want you to join them on a weekend ski trip leaving Friday night and returning Monday morning. They estimate your share of the gas, motel, lift tickets, and other expenses to be around $30. What is your total cost (considering both explicit and implicit costs) for the trip?

2. Until recently, you worked for a software development firm at a yearly salary of $35,000. Now, you decide to open your own business. Planning to be the next Bill Gates, you quit your job, cash in a $10,000 savings account (which pays 5 percent interest), and use the money to buy the latest computer hardware to use in your business. You also convert a basement apartment in your house, which you have been renting for $250 a month, into a workspace for your new software firm.

You lease some office equipment for $3,600 a year and hire two part-time programmers, whose combined salary is $25,000 a year. You also figure it costs around $50 a month to provide heat and light for your new office.

a. What are the total annual explicit costs of your new business?

b. What are the total annual implicit costs?

c. At the end of your first year, your accountant cheerily informs you that your total sales for the year amounted to $55,000. She congratulates you on a profitable year. Are her congratulations warranted? Why or why not?

3. The following data are price/quantity/cost combinations for Titan Industry's mainframe computer division:

Quantity	Price per Unit	Total Cost of Production
0	above $225,000	$200,000
1	$225,000	$250,000
2	$175,000	$275,000
3	$150,000	$325,000
4	$125,000	$400,000
5	$90,000	$500,000

a. What is the marginal revenue if output rises from 2 to 3 units? (*Hint:* Calculate total revenue at each output level first.) What is the marginal cost if output rises from 4 to 5 units?

b. What quantity should Titan produce to maximize total revenue? Total profit?

c. What is Titan's fixed cost? How do Titan's marginal costs behave as output increases? Provide a plausible explanation as to why a computer manufacturer's marginal costs might behave in this way.

4. Each entry in this table shows marginal revenue and marginal cost when a firm increases output to the given quantity:

Quantity	MR	MC
10		
	30	25
11		
	29	23
12		
	27	22
13		
	25	25
14		
	23	27
15		
	21	29
16		
	19	31
17		

What is the profit-maximizing level of output?

5. The following tables give information about demand and total cost for two firms. In the short run, how much should each produce?

Firm A

Quantity	Price	Total Cost
0	above $125	$250
1	$125	$400
2	$100	$500
3	$75	$550
4	$50	$600
5	$25	$700

Firm B

Quantity	Price	Total Cost
0	above $500	$500
1	$500	$700
2	$400	$900
3	$300	$1,100
4	$200	$1,300
5	$100	$1,500

6. At its best possible output level, a firm has total revenue of $3,500 per day and total cost of $7,000 per day. What should this firm do in the short run if:

a. the firm has total *fixed* costs of $3,000 per day?

b. the firm has total *variable* costs of $3,000 per day?

7. Suppose you own a restaurant that serves only dinner. You are trying to decide whether or not to rent out your dining room and kitchen during mornings to another firm, The Breakfast Club, Inc., that will serve only breakfast. Your restaurant currently has the following monthly costs:

Rent on building:	$2,000
Electricity:	$1,000
Wages and salaries:	$15,000
Advertising:	$2,000
Purchases of food and supplies:	$8,000
Your foregone labor income:	$4,000
Your foregone interest:	$1,000

a. Which of your current costs are implicit, and which are explicit?

b. Suppose The Breakfast Club, Inc. offers to pay $800 per month to use the building. They promise to use only their own food, and also to leave the place spotless when they leave each day. If you believe them, should you rent out your restaurant to them? Or does it depend? Explain.

8. Suppose that, due to a dramatic rise in real estate taxes, Ned's Beds' total fixed cost rises from $300 to $1,300 per day. Use the data of Table 1 to answer the following:
   a. What does the tax hike do to Ned's *MC* and *MR* curves?
   b. In the short run, how many beds should Ned produce after the rise in taxes?
   c. In the long run, how many beds should Ned produce after the rise in taxes?

9. Suppose Ned's Beds does *not* have to lower the price in order to sell more beds. Specifically, suppose Ned can sell all the beds he wants at a price of $275 per bed.

   a. What will Ned's *MR* curve look like? (*Hint:* How much will his revenue rise for each additional bed he sells?)
   b. In Table 1, how would you change the numbers in the marginal revenue column to reflect the constant price for beds?
   c. Using the marginal cost and *new* marginal revenue numbers in Table 1, find the number of beds Ned should sell.

Challenge Questions

1. A firm's *marginal profit* can be defined as the change in its profit when output increases by one unit.
   a. Compute the marginal profit for each change in Ned's Beds' output in Table 1.
   b. State a complete rule for finding the profit-maximizing output level in terms of marginal profit.

2. Howell Industries specializes in precision plastics. Their latest invention promises to revolutionize the electronics industry, and they have already made and sold 75 of the miracle devices. They have estimated average costs as given in the following table:

Unit	ATC
74	$10,000
75	$12,000
76	$14,000

Backus Electronics has just offered Howell $150,000 if it will produce the 76th unit. Should Howell accept the offer and manufacture the additional device?

 ***Applications***   *These exercises require access to Hall/Lieberman Xtra! If Xtra! did not come with your book, visit http://hallxtra.swlearning.com to purchase.*

1. Use your Xtra! Password at the Hall and Lieberman Web site (http://hallxtra.swlearning.com), select this chapter, and under Economic Applications, click on EconNews. Click on *Microeconomics: Profit Maximization*, and scroll down to find the article, "To Charge or Not to Charge." Is Pitegoff classifying tourism as a variable input, or a fixed input? Why? How does this influence his decision on whether to keep prices constant?

2. Use your Xtra! Password at the Hall and Lieberman Web site (http://hallxtra.swlearning.com), select this chapter, and under Economic Applications, click on EconNews, then on *Microeconomics: Profit Maximization*. Find the article "Money for Nothing." Explain why Sony's decision to buy out Mariah Carey's contract had no impact on its profit (focus solely on the buy-out of the contract, not the secondary effects, such as reduced marketing costs, etc.

Perfect Competition

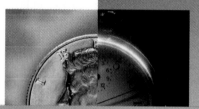

No one knows exactly how many different goods and services are offered for sale in the United States, but the number must be somewhere in the tens of millions. Each of these goods is traded in a market, where buyers and sellers come together, and these markets have several things in common. Sellers want to sell at the *highest* possible price; buyers seek the *lowest* possible price; and all trade is *voluntary*. But here, the similarity ends.

When we observe buyers and sellers in action, we see that different goods and services are sold in vastly different ways. Take advertising, for example. Every day, we are inundated with sales pitches on television, radio, and newspapers for a long list of products: toothpaste, perfume, automobiles, Internet Web sites, cat food, banking services, and more. But have you ever seen a farmer on television, trying to convince you to buy *his* wheat, rather than the wheat of other farmers? Do shareholders of major corporations like General Motors sell their stock by advertising in the newspaper? Why, in a world in which virtually *everything* seems to be advertised, do we not see ads for wheat, shares of stock, corn, crude oil, gold, copper, or foreign currency?

Or consider profits. Anyone starting a business hopes to make as much profit as possible. Yet some companies—Microsoft, Quaker Oats, and PepsiCo, for example—

earn sizable profit for their owners year after year, while at other companies, such as Delta Air Lines and most small businesses, economic profit is generally low.

We could say, "That's just how the cookie crumbles," and attribute all of these observations to pure randomness. But economics is all about *explaining* such things, finding patterns amidst the chaos of everyday economic life. When economists turn their attention to differences in trading, such as these, they think immediately about *market structure,* the subject of this and the next two chapters. We've used this term informally elsewhere in the text, but now it's time for a formal definition:

> By **market structure,** *we mean all the characteristics of a market that influence the behavior of buyers and sellers when they come together to trade.*

Market structure The characteristics of a market that influence how trading takes place.

To determine the structure of any particular market, we begin by asking three simple questions:

1. *How many* buyers and sellers are there in the market?
2. Is each seller offering a *standardized product,* more or less indistinguishable from that offered by other sellers, or are there significant differences between the products of different firms?
3. Are there any *barriers to entry or exit,* or can *outsiders* easily enter and leave this market?

The answers to these questions help us to classify a market into one of four basic types: *perfect competition, monopoly, monopolistic competition,* or *oligopoly.* The subject of this chapter is perfect competition. In the next two chapters, we'll look carefully at the other market structures.

WHAT IS PERFECT COMPETITION?

Does the phrase "perfect competition" sound familiar? It should, because you encountered it earlier, in Chapter 3. There you learned (briefly) that the famous supply and demand model explains how prices are determined in *perfectly competitive markets.* Now we're going to take a much deeper and more comprehensive look at perfectly competitive markets. By the end of this chapter, you will understand very clearly how perfect competition and the supply and demand model are related.

Let's start with the word *competition* itself. When you hear that word, you may think of an intense, personal rivalry, like that between two boxers competing in a ring or two students competing for the best grade in a small class. But there are other, less personal forms of competition. If you took the SAT exam to get into college, you were competing with thousands of other test takers in rooms just like yours, all across the country. But the competition was *impersonal:* You were trying to do the best that you could do, trying to outperform others in general, but not competing with any one individual in the room. In economics, the term "competition" is used in the latter sense. It describes a situation of diffuse, impersonal competition in a highly populated environment. The market structure you will learn about in this chapter—perfect competition—is an example of this notion.

The Three Requirements of Perfect Competition

Perfect competition
A market structure in which there are many buyers and sellers, the product is standardized, and sellers can easily enter or exit the market.

Perfect competition is a market structure with three important characteristics:

1. *There are large numbers of buyers and sellers, and each buys or sells only a tiny fraction of the total quantity in the market.*
2. *Sellers offer a standardized product.*
3. *Sellers can easily enter into or exit from the market.*

These three conditions probably raise more questions than they answer, so let's see what each one really means.

A Large Number of Buyers and Sellers. In perfect competition, there must be many buyers and sellers. How many? It would be nice if we could specify a number—like 32,456—for this requirement. Unfortunately, we cannot, since what constitutes a large number of buyers and sellers can be different under different conditions. What is important is this:

In a perfectly competitive market, the number of buyers and sellers is so large that no individual decision maker can significantly affect the price of the product by changing the quantity it buys or sells.

Think of the world market for wheat. On the selling side, there are hundreds of thousands of individual wheat farmers—more than 250,000 in the United States alone. Each of these farmers produces only a tiny fraction of the total market quantity. If any one of them were to double, triple, or even quadruple its production, the impact on total market quantity and market price would be negligible. The same is true on the buying side: There are so many small buyers that no one of them can affect the market price by increasing or decreasing its quantity demanded.

Most agricultural markets conform to the large-number-of-small-firms requirement, as do markets for precious metals such as gold and silver and markets for the stocks and bonds of large corporations. For example, more than 2 million shares of General Motors stock are bought and sold *every day*, at a price (as this is written) of about $40 per share. A decision by a single stockholder to sell, say, $1 million dollars worth of this stock—about 25,000 shares—would cause only a barely noticeable change in quantity supplied on any given day.

But now think about the U.S. market for athletic shoes. In 2002, four large producers—Nike, Reebok, Adidas, and New Balance—accounted for 72 percent of total sales. If any one of these producers decided to change its output by even 10 percent, the impact on total quantity supplied—and market price—would be *very* noticeable. The market for athletic shoes thus fails the large-number-of-small-firms requirement, so it is not an example of perfect competition.

A Standardized Product Offered by Sellers. In a perfectly competitive market, buyers do not perceive significant differences between the products of one seller and another. For example, buyers of wheat will ordinarily have no preference for one farmer's wheat over another's, so wheat would surely pass the standardized product test. The same is true of many other agricultural products—for example, corn syrup and soybeans. It is also true of commodities like crude oil or pork bellies, precious metals like gold or silver, and financial instruments such as the stocks and bonds of a particular firm. (One share of AT&T stock is indistinguishable from another.)

When buyers *do* notice significant differences in the outputs of different sellers, the market is not perfectly competitive. For example, most consumers perceive differences among the various brands of coffee on the supermarket shelf and may have strong preferences for one particular brand. Coffee, therefore, fails the standardized product test of perfect competition. Other goods and services that would fail this test include personal computers, automobiles, houses, colleges, and medical care.

Easy Entry into and Exit from the Market. Entry into a market is rarely free; a new seller must always incur *some* costs to set up shop, begin production, and establish contacts with customers. But a perfectly competitive market has no *significant* barriers to discourage new entrants: Any firm wishing to enter can do business on the same terms as firms that are already there. For example, anyone who wants to start a wheat farm can do so, facing the same costs for land, farm equipment, seeds, fertilizer, and hired labor as existing farms. The same is true of anyone wishing to open up a dry cleaning shop, restaurant, or dog-walking service. Each of these examples would pass the easy-entry test of perfect competition.

In many markets, however, there are significant barriers to entry. These are often *legal barriers*. An example: For the last 70 years, the number of taxicabs licensed to operate in New York City has been fixed, with only occasional small changes, at around 12,000. Unless the city issues more licenses in the future, true entry into this market will be impossible—the licenses may change hands, but the total number of legally operated taxis cannot increase. Another example of legal barriers to entry is *zoning laws*. These place strict limits on how many businesses such as movie theaters, supermarkets, or hotels can operate in a local area.

Aside from laws, significant barriers to entry can arise simply because existing sellers have an important advantage that new entrants cannot duplicate. The brand loyalty enjoyed by existing producers of breakfast cereals, instant coffee, and soft drinks would require a new entrant to wrest customers away from existing firms—a very costly undertaking. Or as you saw in Chapter 6, significant economies of scale may give existing firms a cost advantage over new entrants. We will discuss these and other barriers to entry in more detail in later chapters.

In addition to easy entry, perfect competition is characterized by easy *exit*: A firm suffering a long-run loss must be able to sell off its plant and equipment and leave the industry for good, without obstacles. Some markets satisfy this requirement, and some do not. Plant-closing laws or union agreements can require lengthy advance notice and high severance pay when workers are laid off. Or capital equipment may be so highly specialized—like an assembly line designed to produce just one type of automobile—that it cannot be sold off if the firm decides to exit the market. These and other barriers to exit do not conform to the assumptions of perfect competition.

Toward the end of this chapter, you'll see that easy entry and exit have important implications for competitive markets in the long run.

Is Perfect Competition Realistic?

The three assumptions a market must satisfy to be perfectly competitive (or just "competitive," for short) are rather restrictive. Do any markets satisfy all these requirements? How broadly can we apply the model of perfect competition when we think about the real world?

First, remember that perfect competition is a *model*—an abstract representation of reality. No model can capture *all* of the details of a real-world market, nor should it. Still, in some cases, the model fits remarkably well. We have seen that the market for wheat, for example, passes all three tests for a competitive market: many buyers and sellers, standardized output, and easy entry and exit. Indeed, most agricultural markets satisfy the strict requirements of perfect competition quite closely, as do many financial markets and some markets for consumer goods and services.

But in the vast majority of markets, one or more of the assumptions of perfect competition will, in a strict sense, be violated. This might suggest that the model can be applied only in a few limited cases. Yet when economists look at real-world markets, they use the perfect competition model more than any other market model. Why is this?

First, the model of perfect competition is powerful. Using simple techniques, it leads to important predictions about a market's response to changes in consumer tastes, technology, and government policies. While other types of market structure models also yield valuable predictions, they are often more cumbersome and their predictions less definitive. Second, many markets, while not strictly perfectly competitive, come *reasonably* close. The more closely a real-world market fits the model, the more accurate our predictions will be when we use it.

We can even, with some caution, use the model to analyze markets that violate all three assumptions. Take the worldwide market for television sets. There are about a dozen major sellers in this market. Each of them knows that its output decisions will have *some* effect on the market price, but no one of them can have a *major* impact on price. Consumers do recognize the difference between one brand and another, but their preferences are not very strong, and most recognize that quality has become so standardized that all brands are actually close substitutes for each other. And there are indeed barriers to entry—existing firms have supply and distribution networks that would be difficult for new entrants to replicate—but these barriers are not *so* great that they would keep out new entrants if they saw the potential for high profit. Thus, although the market for televisions does not strictly satisfy any of the requirements of perfect competition, it is not *too* far off on any one of them. The model will not perform as accurately for televisions as it does for wheat, but, depending on how much accuracy we need, it may do just fine.

In sum, perfect competition can approximate conditions and yield accurate-enough predictions in a wide variety of markets. This is why you will often find economists using the model to analyze the markets for crude oil, consumer electronic goods, fast-food meals, medical care, and higher education, even though in each of these cases one or more of the requirements may not be strictly satisfied.

THE PERFECTLY COMPETITIVE FIRM

When we stand at a distance and look at conditions in a competitive market, we get one view of what is occurring; when we stand close and look at the individual competitive *firm*, we get an entirely different picture. But these two pictures are very closely related. After all, a market is a collection of individual decision makers, much as a human body is a collection of individual cells. In a perfectly competitive market, the individual cells (firms and consumers) and the overall body (the market) affect each other through a variety of feedback mechanisms. This is why, in learning about the competitive firm, we must also discuss the competitive market in which it operates.

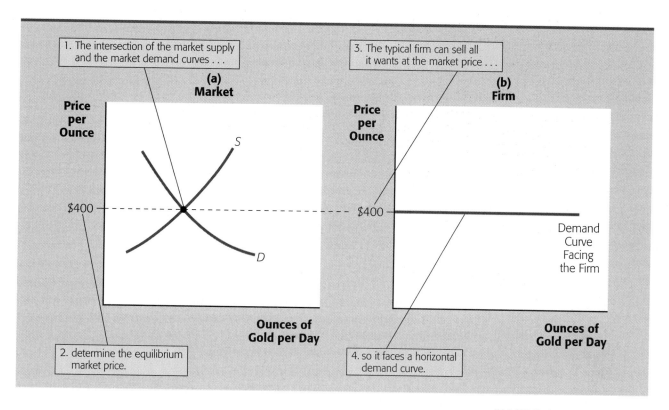

FIGURE 1
**The Competitive Industry
and Firm**

Figure 1(a) applies the tools you have already learned—supply and demand—to the competitive market for gold. The market demand curve slopes downward: As price falls, buyers will want to purchase more. The supply curve slopes upward: As price rises, the total quantity supplied by firms in the market will rise. The intersection of the supply and demand curves determines the equilibrium price of gold, which, in the figure, is $400 per troy ounce.[1] This is all familiar territory. But now let's switch lenses and see how Small Time Gold Mines, an individual mining company, views this market.

Goals and Constraints of the Competitive Firm

Small Time's goal—like that of any business firm—is to *maximize profit*. And, like any firm, it faces constraints. For example, it must use some given production technology to produce its output, and must pay some given prices for its inputs. As a result, Small Time faces a familiar cost constraint; just like Spotless Car Wash in Chapter 6 and Ned's Beds in Chapter 7, Small Time Gold Mines faces a total cost of production for any level of output it might want to produce. In addition to *total* cost, Small Time has *ATC*, *AVC*, and *MC* curves, and these have the familiar shapes you learned about in the previous two chapters.

A perfectly competitive firm faces a cost constraint like any other firm. The cost of producing any given level of output depends on the firm's production technology and the prices it must pay for its inputs.

---

[1] Gold is sold by the troy ounce, which is about 10 percent heavier than a regular ounce.

In addition to a cost constraint, Small Time Gold Mines faces a demand constraint, as does any firm. But there is something different about the demand constraint for a perfectly competitive firm like Small Time.

The Demand Curve Facing a Perfectly Competitive Firm. Panel (b) of Figure 1 shows the demand curve facing Small Time Gold Mines. Notice the special shape of this curve: It is horizontal, or infinitely price elastic. This tells us that no matter how much gold Small Time produces, it will always sell it at the same price—$400 per troy ounce. Why should this be?

First, in perfect competition, output is standardized—buyers do not distinguish the gold of one mine from that of another. If Small Time were to charge a price even a tiny bit higher than other producers, it would lose all of its customers; they would simply buy from Small Time's competitors, whose prices would be lower. The horizontal demand curve captures this effect. It tells us that if Small Time raises its price above $400, it will not just sell *less* output, it will sell *no* output.

Second, Small Time is only a tiny producer relative to the entire gold market. No matter how much it decides to produce, it cannot make a noticeable difference in market quantity supplied and so cannot affect the market price. Once again, the horizontal demand curve describes this effect perfectly: The firm can increase its production without having to lower its price.

All of this means that Small Time has no control over the price of its output—it simply accepts the market price as given:

> *In perfect competition, the firm is a **price taker**: It treats the price of its output as given.*

Price taker Any firm that treats the price of its product as given and beyond its control.

The horizontal demand curve facing the firm and the resulting price-taking behavior of firms are hallmarks of perfect competition. If a manager thinks, "If we produce more output, we will have to lower our price," then the firm faces a *downward-sloping* demand curve and is not a competitive firm. The manager of a competitive firm will always think, "We can sell all the output we want at the going price, so how much should we produce?"

Notice that, since a competitive firm takes the market price as given, its only decision is *how much output to produce and sell*. Once it makes that decision, we can determine the firm's cost of production, as well as the total revenue it will earn (the market price times the quantity of output produced). Let's see how this works in practice with Small Time Gold Mines.

Cost and Revenue Data for a Competitive Firm

Table 1 shows cost and revenue data for Small Time. In the first two columns are different quantities of gold that Small Time could produce each day and the maximum price that it could charge. Because Small Time is a competitive firm, a price taker, the price remains constant at $400 per ounce, no matter *how* much gold it produces.

Run your finger down the total revenue and marginal revenue columns. Since price is always $400, each time the firm produces another ounce of gold, total revenue rises by $400. This is why marginal revenue—the additional revenue from selling one more ounce of gold—remains constant at $400.

Figure 2 plots Small Time's total revenue and marginal revenue. Notice that the total revenue (*TR*) curve in panel (a) is a *straight line* that slopes upward; each time

TABLE 1
Cost and Revenue Data for
Small Time Gold Mines

(1) Output (Troy Ounces of Gold per Day)	(2) Price (per Troy Ounce)	(3) Total Revenue	(4) Marginal Revenue	(5) Total Cost	(6) Marginal Cost	(7) Profit
0	$400	$ 0		$ 550		−$550
			$400		$450	
1	$400	$ 400		$1,000		−$600
			$400		$200	
2	$400	$ 800		$1,200		−$400
			$400		$ 50	
3	$400	$1,200		$1,250		−$ 50
			$400		$100	
4	$400	$1,600		$1,350		$250
			$400		$150	
5	$400	$2,000		$1,500		$500
			$400		$250	
6	$400	$2,400		$1,750		$650
			$400		$350	
7	**$400**	**$2,800**		**$2,100**		**$700**
			$400		$450	
8	$400	$3,200		$2,550		$650
			$400		$550	
9	$400	$3,600		$3,100		$500
			$400		$650	
10	$400	$4,000		$3,750		$250

output increases by one unit, *TR* rises by the same $400. That is, the slope of the *TR* curve is equal to the price of output.

The marginal revenue (*MR*) curve is a *horizontal* line at the market price. In fact, the *MR* curve is the same horizontal line as the demand curve. Why? Remember that marginal revenue is the additional revenue the firm earns from selling an additional unit of output. For a price-taking competitive firm, that additional revenue will always be the price per unit, no matter how many units it is already sells.

> For a competitive firm, marginal revenue at each quantity is the same as the market price. For this reason, the marginal revenue curve and the demand curve facing the firm are the same: a horizontal line at the market price.

In panel (b), we have labeled the horizontal line "*d* = *MR*," since this line is both the firm's demand curve (*d*) *and* its marginal revenue curve (*MR*).[2]

Columns 5 and 6 of Table 1 show total cost and marginal cost for Small Time. There is nothing special about cost data for a competitive firm. In Figure 2, you

[2] In this and later chapters, lowercase letters for quantities and demand curves refer to the individual firm, and uppercase letters to the entire market. For example, the demand curve facing the firm is labeled *d*, while the market demand curve is labeled *D*.

FIGURE 2
**Profit Maximization in
Perfect Competition**

*Panel (a) shows a competitive
firm's total revenue (TR) and total cost (TC) curves. TR is a
straight line with slope equal to
the market price. Profit is maximized at 7 ounces per day,
where the vertical distance between TR and TC is greatest.
Panel (b) shows that profit is
maximized where the marginal
cost (MC) curve intersects the
horizontal demand (d) and marginal revenue (MR) curves.*

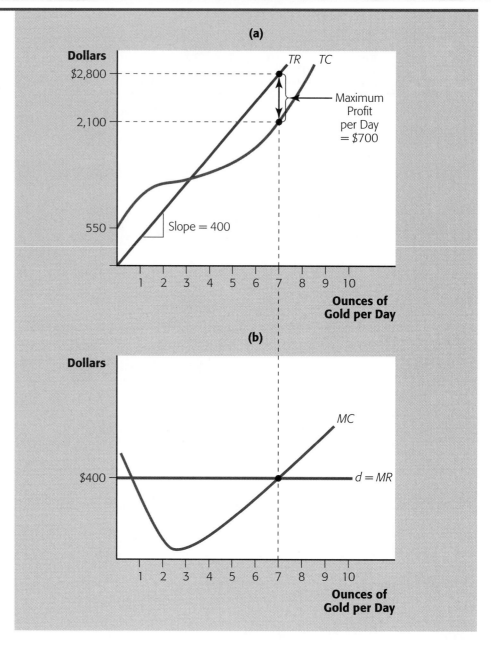

can see that marginal cost (*MC*)—as usual—first falls and then rises. Total cost,
therefore, rises first at a decreasing rate and then at an increasing rate. (You may
want to look at Chapter 6 to review why this cost behavior is so common.)

Finding the Profit-Maximizing Output Level

A competitive firm—like any other firm—wants to earn the highest possible
profit, and to do so, it should use the principles you learned in Chapter 7.
Although the diagrams look a bit different for competitive firms, the ideas behind

them are the same. We can use either Table 1 or Figure 2 to find the profit-maximizing output level. And we can use the techniques you have already learned: the total revenue and total cost approach, or the marginal revenue and marginal cost approach.

The Total Revenue and Total Cost Approach. The *TR* and *TC* approach is the most direct way of viewing the firm's search for the profit-maximizing output level. Quite simply, at each output level, subtract total cost from total revenue to get total profit:

$$\text{Total Profit} = TR - TC$$

Then we just scan the different output levels to see which one gives the highest number for profit.

In Table 1, total profit is shown in the last column. A simple scan of that column tells us that $700 is the highest daily profit that Small Time Gold Mines can earn. Tracing along the row to the first column, we see that to earn this profit, Small Time must produce 7 ounces per day, its profit-maximizing output level.

The same approach to maximizing profit can be seen graphically, in the upper panel of Figure 2. There, total profit at any output level is the distance between the *TR* and *TC* curves. As you can see, this distance is greatest when the firm produces 7 units, verifying what we found in the table.

This approach is simple and straightforward, but it hides the interesting part of the story: the way that *changes* in output cause total revenue and total cost to change. The other approach to finding the profit-maximizing output level focuses on these changes.

The Marginal Revenue and Marginal Cost Approach. In the *MR* and *MC* approach, the firm should continue to increase output as long as marginal revenue is greater than marginal cost. You can verify, using Table 1, that if the firm is initially producing 1, 2, 3, 4, 5, or 6 units, *MR* > *MC*, so producing more will raise profit. Once the firm is producing 7 units, however, *MR* < *MC*, so further increases in output will reduce profit. Alternatively, using the graph in panel (b) of Figure 2, we look for the output level at which *MR* = *MC*. As the graph shows, there are two output levels at which the *MR* and *MC* curves intersect. However, we can rule out the first crossing point because there, the *MC* curve crosses the *MR* curve from above. Remember that the profit-maximizing output is found where the *MC* curve crosses the *MR* curve from *below*. Once again, this occurs at 7 units of output.

You can see that finding the profit-maximizing output level for a competitive firm requires no new concepts or techniques; you have already learned everything you need to know in Chapter 7. In fact, the only difference is one of appearance. Ned's Beds—our firm in Chapter 7—did *not* operate under perfect competition. As a result, both its demand curve and its marginal revenue curve sloped *downward*. Small Time, however, operates under perfect competition, so its demand and *MR* curves are the same horizontal line.

Measuring Total Profit

You have already seen one way to measure a firm's total profit on a graph: the vertical distance between the *TR* and *TC* curves. In this section, you will learn another graphical way to measure profit.

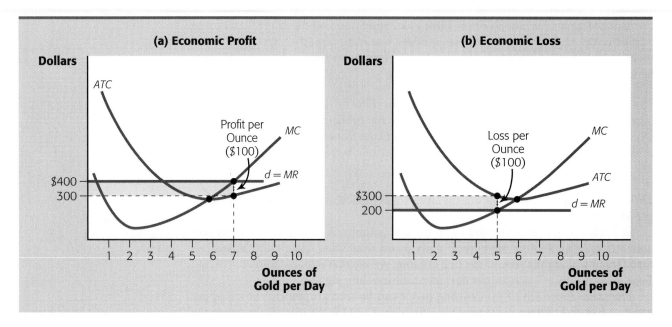

FIGURE 3
Measuring Profit or Loss

The competitive firm in panel (a) produces where marginal cost equals marginal revenue, or 7 units of output per day. Profit per unit at that output level is equal to revenue per unit ($400) minus cost per unit ($300), or $100 per unit. Total profit (indicated by the blue-shaded rectangle) is equal to profit per unit times the number of units sold, $100 × 7 = $700. In panel (b), the firm faces a lower market price of $200 per ounce. The best it can do is to produce 5 ounces per day and suffer a loss shown by the red area. It loses $100 per ounce on each of those 5 ounces produced, so the total loss is $500—the area of the red-shaded rectangle.

To do this, we start with the firm's *profit per unit,* which is the revenue it gets on each unit minus the cost per unit. Revenue per unit is just the price (*P*) of the firm's output, and cost per unit is our familiar *ATC,* so we can write:

$$\text{Profit per unit} = P - ATC.$$

In Figure 3(a), Small Time's *ATC* curve has been plotted from the data in Table 1. When the firm is producing at the profit-maximizing output level, 7 units, its *ATC* is $300. Since the price of output is $400, profit *per unit* = *P* − *ATC* = $400 − $300 = $100. This is just the vertical distance between the firm's demand curve and its *ATC* curve at the profit-maximizing output level.

Once we know Small Time's profit per unit, it is easy to calculate its *total* profit: Just multiply profit per unit by the number of units sold. Small Time is earning $100 profit on each ounce of gold, and it sells 7 ounces in all, so total profit is $100 × 7 = $700.

Now look at the blue-shaded rectangle in Figure 3(a). The height of this rectangle is profit per unit, and the width is the number of units produced. The *area* of the rectangle—height × width—equals Small Time's profit:

> *A firm earns a profit whenever* P > ATC. *Its total profit at the best output level equals the area of a rectangle with height equal to the distance between* P *and* ATC, *and width equal to the level of output.*

In the figure, Small Time is fortunate: At a price of $400, there are several output levels at which it can earn a profit. Its problem is to select the one that makes its profit as large as possible. (We should all have such problems.)

But what if the price had been lower than $400—so low, in fact, that Small Time could not make a profit at *any* output level? Then the best it can do is to choose the smallest possible loss. Just as we did in the case of profit, we can measure the firm's total loss using the *ATC* curve.

Panel (b) of Figure 3 reproduces Small Time's *ATC* and *MC* curves from panel (a). This time, however, we have assumed a lower price for gold—$200—so the firm's $d = MR$ curve is the horizontal line at $200. Since this line lies everywhere below the *ATC* curve, profit per unit ($P - ATC$) is always negative: Small Time cannot make a positive profit at *any* output level.

With a price of $200, the *MC* curve crosses the *MR* curve from below at 5 units of output. Unless Small Time decides to shut down (we'll discuss shutting down for competitive firms later), it should produce 5 units. At that level of output, *ATC* is $300, and profit per unit is $P - ATC = \$200 - \$300 = -\$100$, a *loss* of $100 per unit. The total loss is loss per unit (negative profit per unit) times the number of units produced, or $-\$100 \times 5 = -\$500$. This is the area of the red-shaded rectangle in Figure 3(b), with height of $100 and width of 5 units:

A firm suffers a loss whenever P < ATC *at the best level of output. Its total loss equals the area of a rectangle with height equal to the distance between* P and ATC, *and width equal to the level of output.*

The Firm's Short-Run Supply Curve

A competitive firm is a price taker: It takes the market price as given and then decides how much output it will produce at that price. If the market price changes for any reason, the price taken as given will change as well. The firm will then have to find a new profit-maximizing output level. Let's see how the firm's choice of output changes as the market price rises or falls.

Misusing Profit per Unit It is tempting—but *wrong*—to think that the firm should produce where profit *per unit* ($P - ATC$) is greatest. The firm's goal is to maximize *total* profit, not profit per unit. Using Table 1 or Figure 3(a), you can verify that while Small Time's profit *per unit* is greatest at 6 units of output, its *total* profit is greatest at 7 units.

DANGEROUS CURVES

Figure 4(a) shows *ATC*, *AVC*, and *MC* curves for a competitive producer of wheat. The figure also shows five hypothetical demand curves the firm might face, each corresponding to a different market price for wheat. If the market price were $3.50 per bushel, the firm would face demand curve d_1, and its profit-maximizing output level—where $MC = MR$—would be 7,000 bushels per year. If the price dropped to $2.50 per bushel, the firm would face demand curve d_2, and its profit-maximizing output level would drop to 5,000 bushels. You can see that the profit-maximizing output level is always found by traveling from the price, across to the firm's *MC* curve, and then down to the horizontal axis. In other words,

as the price of output changes, the firm will slide along its MC *curve in deciding how much to produce.*

But there is one problem with this: If the firm is suffering a loss—a loss large enough to justify shutting down—then it will *not* produce along its *MC* curve; it will produce zero units instead. Thus, in order to know for certain how much output the firm will produce, we must bring in the shutdown rule you learned in Chapter 7.

The Shutdown Price. Suppose the price in Figure 4(a) drops down to $2 per bushel. At this price, the best output level is 4,000 bushels, and the firm suffers a loss, since $P < ATC$. Should the firm shut down? Let's see. At 4,000 bushels, it is

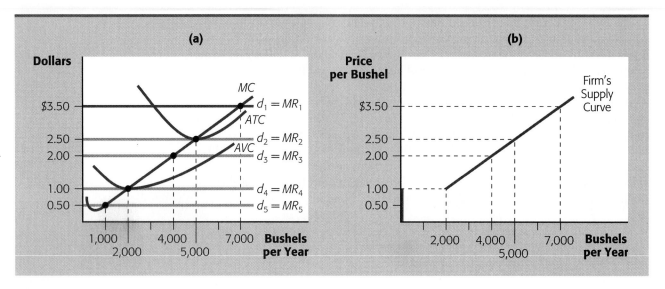

(a)

(b)

FIGURE 4

Short-Run Supply Under Perfect Competition

Panel (a) shows a typical competitive firm facing various market prices. For prices between $1 and $3.50 per bushel, the profit-maximizing quantity is found by sliding along the MC *curve. Below $1 per bushel, the firm is better off shutting down, because* P < AVC, *and so* TR < TVC. *Panel (b) shows that the firm's supply curve consists of two segments. Above the shutdown price of $1 per bushel it follows the* MC *curve; below that price, it is coincident with the vertical axis.*

Shutdown price The price at which a firm is indifferent between producing and shutting down.

also true that $P > AVC$, since the demand curve lies above the AVC curve at this output level. Multiplying both sides of the last inequality by Q gives us

$$P \times Q > AVC \times Q.$$

Since $AVC \times Q$ is just TVC, this inequality is the same as

$$TR > TVC.$$

As we know from Chapter 7, a firm should *never* shut down when $TR > TVC$. Thus, at a price of $2, the firm will stay open and produce 4,000 units of output.

Now, suppose the price drops all the way down to $0.50 per bushel. At this price, $MR = MC$ at 1,000 bushels, but notice that here $P < AVC$. Once again, we multiply both sides by Q to obtain

$$P \times Q < AVC \times Q$$

or

$$TR < TVC.$$

A firm should *always* shut down when $TR < TVC$, so at a price of $0.50, this firm will produce *zero* units of output.

Finally, let's consider a price of $1. At this price, $MR = MC$ at 2,000 bushels, and here we have $P = AVC$ or $TR = TVC$. At $1, therefore, the firm will be indifferent between staying open and shutting down. We call this price the firm's **shutdown price**, since it will shut down at any price lower and stay open at any price higher. The output level at which the firm will shut down must occur at the *minimum* of the AVC curve. Why? Note that as the price of output decreases, the best output level is found by sliding along the MC curve, until MC and AVC cross. At that point, the firm will shut down. But—as you learned in Chapter 6—MC will always cross AVC at its minimum point.

Now let's recapitulate what we've found about the firm's output decision. For all prices above the minimum point on the AVC curve, the firm will stay open and will produce the level of output at which $MR = MC$. For these prices, the firm slides along its *MC* curve in deciding how much output to produce. But for any price below the minimum *AVC*, the firm will shut down and produce zero units. We can summarize all of this information in a single curve—the **firm's supply curve**—which tells us how much output the firm will produce at any price:

> *The competitive firm's supply curve has two parts. For all prices above the minimum point on its* AVC *curve, the supply curve coincides with the* MC *curve. For all prices below the minimum point on the* AVC *curve, the firm will shut down, so its supply curve is a vertical line segment at zero units of output.*

Firm's supply curve A curve that shows the quantity of output a competitive firm will produce at different prices.

In panel (b) of Figure 4, we have drawn the supply curve for our hypothetical wheat farmer. As price declines from $3.50 to $1, output is determined by the firm's *MC* curve. For all prices *below* $1—the shutdown price—output is zero and the supply curve coincides with the vertical axis.

COMPETITIVE MARKETS IN THE SHORT RUN

Recall that the short run is a time period too short for the firm to vary *all* of its inputs: The quantity of at least one input remains fixed. For example, in the short run, a wheat farmer will be stuck with a certain plot of land and a certain number of tractors. Now let's extend the concept of the short run from the firm to the market as a whole. It makes sense that if the short run is insufficient time for a firm to vary its fixed inputs, then it is also insufficient time for a *new* firm to acquire those fixed inputs and *enter* the market. Similarly, it is too short a period for firms to reduce their fixed inputs to zero and *exit* the market. We conclude that

> *in the short run, the number of firms in the industry is fixed.*

The (Short-Run) Market Supply Curve

Once we know how to find the supply curve of each *individual* firm in a market, we can easily determine the short-run **market supply curve,** showing the amount of output that all sellers in the market will offer at each price.

Market supply curve A curve indicating the quantity of output that all sellers in a market will produce at different prices.

> *To obtain the market supply curve, we add up the quantities of output supplied by all firms in the market at each price.*

To keep things simple, suppose there are 100 identical wheat farms and that each one has the supply curve shown in Figure 5(a)—the same supply curve we derived in Figure 4. Then at a price of $3.50, each firm would produce 7,000 bushels. With 100 such firms, the market quantity supplied will be $7,000 \times 100 = 700,000$ bushels. At a price of $2.50, each firm would supply 5,000 bushels, so market supply would be 500,000. Continuing in this way, we can trace out the market supply curve shown in panel (b) of Figure 5. Notice that once the price drops below $1— the shutdown price for each firm—the market supply curve jumps to zero.

The market supply curve in the figure is a *short-run* market supply curve, since it gives us the combined output level of just those firms *already* in the industry. As

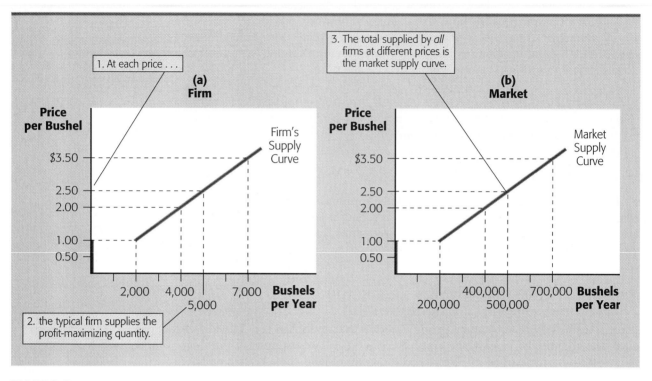

FIGURE 5
Deriving the Market
Supply Curve

we move along this curve, we are assuming that two things are constant: (1) the fixed inputs of each firm and (2) the number of firms in the market.

Short-Run Equilibrium

How does a perfectly competitive market achieve equilibrium? We've already addressed this question in Chapter 3, in our study of supply and demand. But now we'll take a much closer look, paying attention to the individual firm and individual consumer as well as the market.

Figure 6 puts together the pieces we've discussed so far, including those from Chapter 5 on consumer choice, to paint a complete picture of how a competitive market arrives at a short-run equilibrium. On the right side, we add up the quantities supplied by all firms to obtain the market supply curve. On the left side, we add up the quantities demanded by all consumers to obtain the market demand curve. The market supply and demand curves show if/then relationships: *If* the price were such and such, *then* firms would supply this much and consumers would buy that much. Up to this point, the prices and quantities are purely hypothetical. But once we bring the two curves together and find their intersection point, we know the *equilibrium* price: the price at which trading will actually take place. Finally, we confront each firm and each consumer with the equilibrium price to find the actual quantity each consumer will buy and the actual quantity each firm will produce.

Figure 7 gets more specific, illustrating two possible short-run equilibriums in the wheat market. In panel (a), if the market demand curve were D_1, the short-run equilibrium price would be $3.50. Each firm would face the horizontal demand

FIGURE 6
Perfect Competition

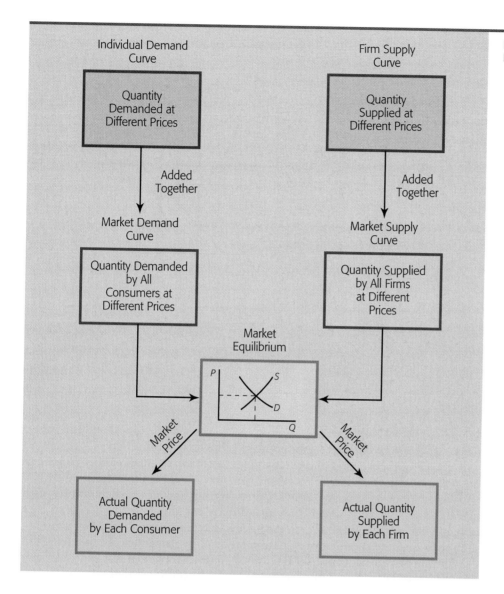

curve d_1 (panel (b)) and decide to produce 7,000 bushels. With 100 such firms, the equilibrium market quantity would be 700,000 bushels. Notice that, at a price of $3.50, each firm is enjoying an economic profit, since $P > ATC$.

If the market demand curve were D_2 instead, the equilibrium price would be $2. Each firm would face demand curve d_2, and produce 4,000 bushels. With 100 firms, the equilibrium market quantity would be 400,000. Here, each firm is suffering an economic loss, since $P < ATC$. These two examples show us that *in short-run equilibrium, competitive firms can earn an economic profit or suffer an economic loss.*

We are about to leave the short run and turn our attention to what happens in a competitive market over the long run. But before we do, let's look once more at how a short-run equilibrium is established. One part of this process—combining supply and demand curves to find the market equilibrium—has been familiar to you

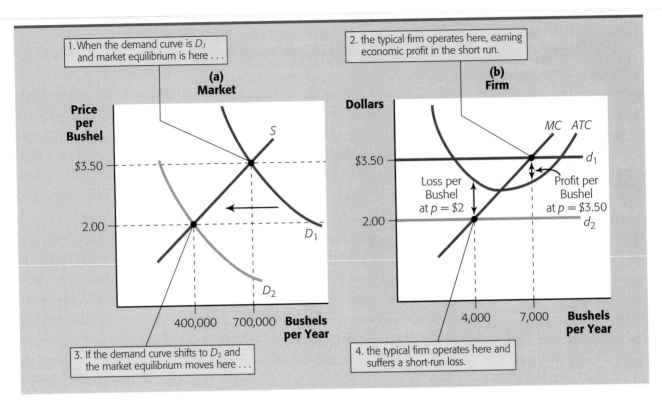

1. When the demand curve is D_1 and market equilibrium is here ...

2. the typical firm operates here, earning economic profit in the short run.

(a) Market

(b) Firm

3. If the demand curve shifts to D_2 and the market equilibrium moves here ...

4. the typical firm operates here and suffers a short-run loss.

FIGURE 7
Short-Run Equilibrium in Perfect Competition

all along. But now you can better appreciate how much information is contained within each of these curves and what an impressive job the market does coordinating millions of decisions made by people who may never even meet each other.

Think about it: So many individual consumers and firms, each with its own agenda, trading in the market. Not one of them has any power to decide or even influence the market price. Rather, the price is determined by *all* of them, adjusting until *total* quantity supplied is equal to *total* quantity demanded. Then, facing this equilibrium price, each consumer buys the quantity he or she wants, each firm produces the output level that it wants, and we can be confident that all of them will be able to realize their plans. Each buyer can find willing sellers, and each seller can find willing buyers.

> *In perfect competition, the market sums up the buying and selling preferences of individual consumers and producers, and determines the market price. Each buyer and seller then takes the market price as given, and each is able to buy or sell the desired quantity.*

This process is, from a certain perspective, a thing of beauty, and it happens each day in markets all across the world—markets for wheat, corn, barley, soybeans, apples, oranges, gold, silver, copper, and more. And something quite similar happens in other markets that do not strictly satisfy our requirements for perfect competition—markets for television sets, books, air conditioners, fast-food meals, oil, natural gas, bottled water, blue jeans. The list is virtually endless.

COMPETITIVE MARKETS IN THE LONG RUN

So far, we've explored the short run only, and assumed that the number of firms in the market is fixed. But perfect competition becomes even *more* interesting in the long run, when entry and exit can occur. After all, the long run is a time horizon long enough for firms to vary *all* of their inputs. It should therefore be long enough for *new* firms to acquire fixed inputs and enter the market, and for firms already in the industry to sell off their fixed inputs and *exit* from the market.

But what makes firms want to enter or exit a market? The driving force behind entry is economic profit, and the force behind exit is economic loss.

Profit and Loss and the Long Run

Recall that economic profit is the amount by which total revenue exceeds *all* costs of doing business. The costs to be deducted include implicit costs like foregone investment income and foregone wages for an owner who devotes money and time to the business. Thus, when a firm earns positive economic profit, we know the owners are earning *more* than they could by devoting their money and time to some other activity.

A temporary episode of positive economic profit will not have much impact on a competitive industry, other than the temporary pleasure it gives the owners of competitive firms. But when positive profit reflects basic conditions in the industry and is expected to continue, major changes are in the works. Outsiders, hungry for profit themselves, will want to enter the market and—since *there are no barriers to entry*—they can do so.

Similarly, if firms in the market are suffering economic losses, they are not earning enough revenue to cover all their costs, so there must be other opportunities that would more adequately compensate owners for their money or time. If this situation is expected to continue over the firm's long-run planning horizon—a period long enough to vary *all* inputs—there is only one thing for the firm to do: exit the market by selling off its plant and equipment, thereby reducing its loss to zero.

In a competitive market, economic profit and loss are the forces driving long-run change. The expectation of continued economic profit causes outsiders to enter the market; the expectation of continued economic losses causes firms in the market to exit.

In the real world of business, entry and exit occur literally every day. In some cases, we see entry occur through the formation of an entirely new firm. For example, in the late 1990s, the high profits of the earliest Internet service providers (ISPs)—such as America Online, CompuServe, and Prodigy—led to the establishment of more than 7,000 new ISPs by the end of the decade. Entry can also occur when an existing firm adds a new product to its line. For example, among the firms that entered the ISP market were many firms that had been established years before there *was* such a thing as an ISP, such as Sprint (which entered with Earthlink), Microsoft (the Microsoft Network), and AT&T. Although these were not *new firms*, they were *new participants* in the market for Internet service.

Exit, too, can occur in different ways. A firm may go out of business entirely, selling off its assets and freeing itself once and for all from all costs. In 2000 and

Kozmo.com—*an Internet-based service that delivered videos and snacks—was one of thousands of online retailers that exited their markets in 2000 and 2001.*

2001, for example, thousands of Internet firms exited their markets in this way, or were purchased by other firms that subsequently exited themselves. These failing firms included the toy seller Toysmart; home delivery services Kozmo.com, Urban-fetch, and Webvan; and pet suppliers pets.com and petstore.com.

But exit can also occur when a firm switches out of a particular product line, even as it continues to produce other things. For example, publishing companies often decide to abandon unsuccessful magazines, yet they continue to thrive by publishing other magazines and books.

Long-Run Equilibrium

Entry and exit—however they occur—are powerful forces in real-world competitive markets. They determine how these markets change over the long run, how much output will ultimately be available to consumers, and the prices they must pay. To explore these issues, let's see how entry and exit move a market to its long-run equilibrium from different starting points.

From Short-Run Profit to Long-Run Equilibrium.

Suppose that the market for wheat is initially in a short-run equilibrium like point A in panel (a) of Figure 8, with market supply curve S_1. The initial equilibrium price is $4.50 per bushel. In panel (b), we see that a typical competitive firm—producing 9,000 bushels—is earning economic profit, since $P > ATC$ at that output level. As long as we remain in the short run, with no new firms entering the market, this situation will not change.

But as we enter the long run, much will change. First, economic profit will attract new entrants, increasing the number of firms in the market. Now remember (from Chapter 3) when we draw a market supply curve like S_1, we draw it for some *given* number of firms, and we hold that number constant. But in the long run, as the number of firms increases, the market supply curve will *shift rightward*; a greater quantity will be supplied at any given price. As the market supply curve shifts rightward, several things happen:

1. The market price begins to fall—from $4.50 to $4.00 to $3.50 and so on.
2. As market price falls, the demand curve facing each firm shifts downward.
3. Each firm—striving as always to maximize profit—will slide down its marginal cost curve, decreasing output.[3]

This process of adjustment, in the market and the firm, continues until . . . well, until when? To answer this question, remember why these adjustments are occurring in the first place: Economic profit is attracting new entrants and shifting the market supply curve rightward. Thus, all of these changes will stop when the *reason* for entry—positive profit—no longer exists. And this, in turn, requires the market supply curve to shift rightward enough, and the price to fall enough, so that *each existing firm is earning zero economic profit.* Panels (c) and (d) in Figure 8 show the final, long-run equilibrium. First, look at panel (c), which shows long-run market equilibrium at point E. The market supply curve has shifted to S_2, and the price has fallen to $2.50 per bushel. Next, look at panel (d), which tells us why the

---

[3] There is one other possible consequence that we ignore here: Entry into the industry, which changes the demand for the industry's inputs, may also change input prices. If this occurs, firms' ATC curves will shift. For now, we will assume that entry (and exit) do not affect input prices, so that the ATC curve does not shift.

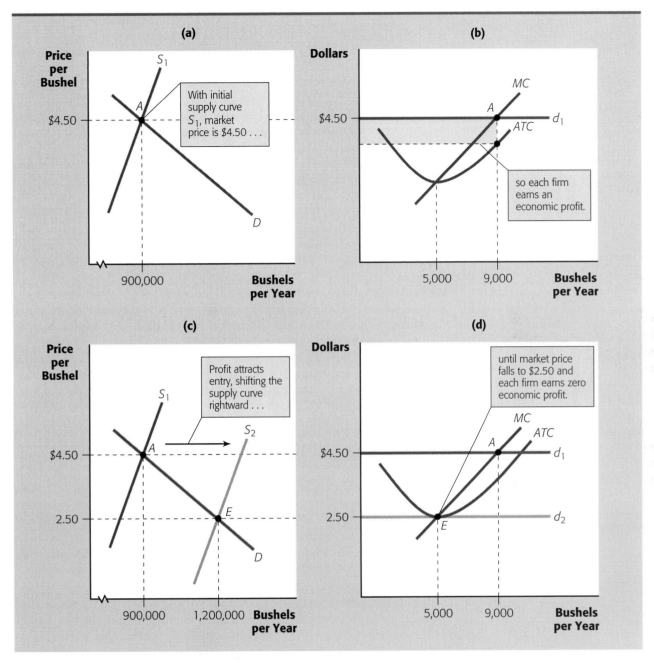

market supply curve stops shifting when it reaches S_2. With that supply curve, each firm is producing at the lowest point of its *ATC* curve, with $P = ATC = \$2.50$, and each is earning zero economic profit. With no economic profit, there is no further reason for entry, and no further shift in the market supply curve.

In a competitive market, positive economic profit continues to attract new entrants until economic profit is reduced to zero.

FIGURE 8
**From Short-Run Profit to
Long-Run Equilibrium**

Now you can see the role played by one of our assumptions about competitive markets: *easy entry.* With no significant barriers to entry, we can be confident that economic profit at the typical firm will attract new firms to the industry, driving down the market price until the economic profit disappears. If a permanent barrier—legal or otherwise—prevented new firms from coming into the market, this mechanism would not work, so long-run economic profit would be possible.

Before proceeding further, take a close look at Figure 8. As the market moves to its long-run equilibrium (point *E* in panels (c) and (d)), output at each firm *decreases* from 9,000 to 5,000 bushels. But in the market as a whole, output *increases* from 900,000 to 1,200,000 bushels. How can this be? (See if you can answer this question yourself. *Hint:* entry!)

From Short-Run Loss to Long-Run Equilibrium. We have just seen how, beginning from a position of short-run profit at the typical firm, a competitive market will adjust until the profit is eliminated. But what if we begin from a position of loss? As you might guess, the same type of adjustments will occur, only in the opposite direction.

This is a good opportunity for you to test your own skill and understanding. Study Figure 8 carefully. Then see if you can draw a similar diagram that illustrates the adjustment from short-run *loss* to long-run equilibrium. Start with a market price of $1.50. Use the same demand curve as in Figure 8, but draw in a new, appropriate market supply curve. Then let the market work. Show what happens in the market, and at each firm, as economic loss causes some firms to exit. If you do this correctly, you'll end up once again at a market price of $2.50, with each firm earning zero economic profit. Your graph will illustrate the following conclusion:

> *In a competitive market, economic losses continue to cause exit until the losses are reduced to zero.*

Notice the role played by our assumption of *easy exit* in competitive markets. When there are no significant barriers to exit, we can be confident that economic loss will eventually drive firms from the industry, raising the market price until the typical firm breaks even again. Significant barriers to exit (such as a local law forbidding a plant from closing down) would prevent this mechanism from working, and economic losses would persist even in the long run.

Distinguishing Short-Run from Long-Run Outcomes. You've seen that the equilibrium in a competitive market can be very different in the short run than in the long run. In short-run equilibrium, competitive firms can earn profits or suffer losses. But in long-run equilibrium, after entry or exit has occurred, economic profit is always zero. The distinction between short-run and long-run equilibrium is important, and not just in competitive markets. In *any* market, our analysis will depend on the time period we are considering, and the correct period depends on the question we are asking. If we want to predict what happens several years after a change in demand, we should ask what the new *long-run* equilibrium will be. If we want to know what happens a few *months* after a change in demand, we'll look for the new *short-run* equilibrium.

When economists look at a market, they automatically think of the short run versus the long run and then choose the period more appropriate for the question at hand. As you'll see, this way of thinking is applied again and again in economics.

The Notion of Zero Profit in Perfect Competition

From the preceding discussion, you may wonder why anyone in his or her right mind would ever want to set up shop in a competitive industry or stay there for any length of time, since—in the long run—they can expect zero economic profit. Indeed, if you want to become a millionaire, you would be well advised not to buy a wheat farm. But most wheat farmers—like most other sellers in competitive markets—do not curse their fate. On the contrary, they are likely to be quite content with the performance of their businesses. How can this be?

Remember that zero *economic* profit is not the same as zero *accounting* profit. When a firm is making zero *economic* profit, it is still making some accounting profit. In fact, the accounting profit is just enough to cover all of the owner's implicit costs, including compensation for any foregone investment income or foregone salary. Suppose, for example, that a wheat farmer paid $100,000 for land and works 40 hours per week. Suppose, too, that the money *could* have been invested in some other way and earned $6,000 per year, and the farmer *could* have worked equally pleasantly elsewhere and earned $40,000 per year. Then the farm's implicit costs will be $46,000, and zero economic profit means that the farm is earning $46,000 in *accounting profit* each year. This won't make a wheat farmer ecstatic, but it will make it worthwhile to keep working the farm. After all, if the farmer quits and takes up the next best alternative, he or she will do no better. To emphasize that zero economic profit is not an unpleasant outcome, economists often replace it with the term **normal profit**, which is a synonym for "zero economic profit," or "just enough accounting profit to cover implicit costs." Using this language, we can summarize long-run conditions at the typical firm this way:

Normal profit Another name for zero economic profit.

> *In the long run, every competitive firm will earn* normal profit—*that is, zero economic profit.*

Perfect Competition and Plant Size

There is one more characteristic of competitive markets in the long run that we have not yet discussed: the plant size of the competitive firm. It turns out that the same forces—entry and exit—that cause all firms to earn zero economic profit *also* ensure that:

> *In long-run equilibrium, every competitive firm will select its plant size and output level so that it operates at the minimum point of its* LRATC *curve.*

To see why, let's consider what would happen if this condition were violated. Figure 9(a) illustrates a firm in a perfectly competitive market. The firm faces a market price of P_1 and produces quantity q_1, where $MC_1 = MR_1$. With its current plant, the firm has average costs given by ATC_1. Note that the firm is earning zero profit, since average cost is equal to P_1 at the best output level.

But panel (a) does *not* show a true long-run equilibrium. How do we know this? First, in the long run, the typical firm will want to expand. Why? Because by increasing its plant size, it could slide down its *LRATC* curve and produce more output at a lower cost per unit. Since it is a perfectly competitive firm—a small participant in the market—it can expand in this way *without* affecting market price. As a result, the

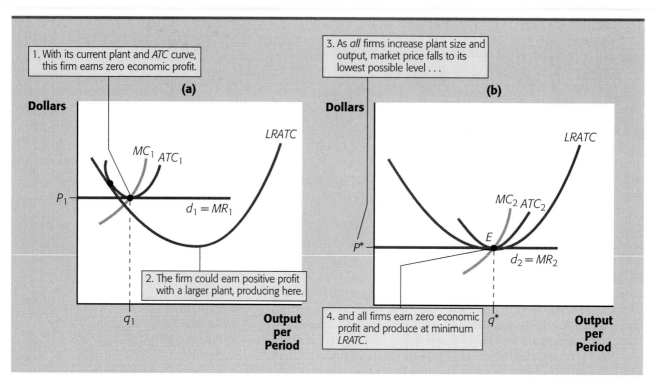

FIGURE 9
Perfect Competition and Plant Size

firm, after expanding, could operate on a new, lower *ATC* curve, so that *ATC* is less than *P*. That is, by expanding, the firm could potentially earn an economic profit.

Second, this same opportunity to earn positive economic profit will attract new entrants that will establish larger plants from the outset. Expansion by existing firms and entry by new ones increase market output and bring down the market price. The process will stop—and a long-run equilibrium will be established—only when there is no potential to earn positive economic profit with *any* plant size. As you can see in panel (b), this condition is satisfied only when each firm is operating at the minimum point on its *LRATC* curve, using the plant represented by ATC_2, and producing output of q^*. Entry and expansion must continue in this market until the price falls to P^*, because only then will each firm—doing the best that it can do—earn zero economic profit. (*Question:* In the long run, what would happen to the firm in panel (a) if it refused to increase its plant size?)

A Summary of the Competitive Firm in the Long Run

Panel (b) of Figure 9 summarizes everything you have learned about the competitive firm in long-run equilibrium. The typical firm, taking the market price P^* as given, produces the profit-maximizing output level q^*, where $MR = MC$. Since this is the long run, each firm will be earning zero economic profit, so we also know that $P^* = ATC$. But since $P^* = MC$ and $P^* = ATC$, it must also be true that $MC = ATC$. As you learned in Chapter 6, MC and ATC are equal only at the minimum point of the *ATC* curve. Thus, we know that each firm must be operating at the lowest possible point on the *ATC* curve for the plant it is operating. Finally, each firm selects the plant that makes its *LRATC* as low as possible, so each operates at the minimum point on its *LRATC* curve.

As you can see, there is a lot going on in Figure 9 (b). But we can put it all together with a very simple statement:

> *At each competitive firm in long-run equilibrium,* P = MC = *minimum* ATC = *minimum* LRATC.

In Figure 9(b), this equality is satisfied when the typical firm produces at point *E*, where its demand, marginal cost, *ATC*, and *LRATC* curves all intersect. This is a figure well worth remembering, since it summarizes so much information about competitive markets in a single picture. (Here is a useful self-test: Close the book, put away your notes, and draw a set of diagrams in which one curve at a time does *not* pass through the common intersection point of the other three. Then explain which principle of firm or market behavior is violated by your diagram. Do this separately for all four curves.)

Figure 9(b) also explains one of the important ways in which perfect competition benefits consumers: In the long run, each firm is driven to the plant size and output level at which its cost per unit is as low as possible. This lowest possible cost per unit is also the price per unit that consumers will pay. If price were any lower than P^*, it would not be worthwhile for firms to continue producing the good in the long run. Thus, given the *LRATC* curve faced by each firm in this industry—a curve that is determined by each firm's production technology and the costs of its inputs—P^* is the lowest possible price that will ensure the continued availability of the good. In perfect competition, consumers are getting the best deal they could possibly get.

WHAT HAPPENS WHEN THINGS CHANGE?

So far, you've learned how competitive firms make decisions, how these decisions lead to a short-run equilibrium in the market, and how the market moves from short- to long-run equilibrium through entry and exit. Now, it's time to ask: *What happens when things change?* In this section, we'll deal with a change in demand for the product and, in the process, learn some important additional features of perfect competition. In the section titled "Using the Theory," we'll look at changes in technology.

A Change in Demand

In Figure 10, panel (a) shows a competitive market that is initially in long-run equilibrium at point *A*, where the market demand curve D_1 and supply curve S_1 intersect. Panel (b) shows conditions at the firm, which faces demand curve d_1 and produces the profit-maximizing quantity q_1.

But now suppose that the market demand curve shifts rightward to D_2 and remains there. (This shift could be caused by any one of several factors. If you can't list some of them, turn back to Chapter 3 and look again at Figure 3.) Panels (c) and (d) show what happens. In the *short run,* the shift in demand moves the market equilibrium to point *B*, with market output Q_{SR} and price P_{SR}. At the same time,

HTTP://

Economists have tried to simulate the behavior of competitive markets through experiments. The University of Arizona's Market. Econ is an Internet-based example **http://market.econ.arizona.edu**.

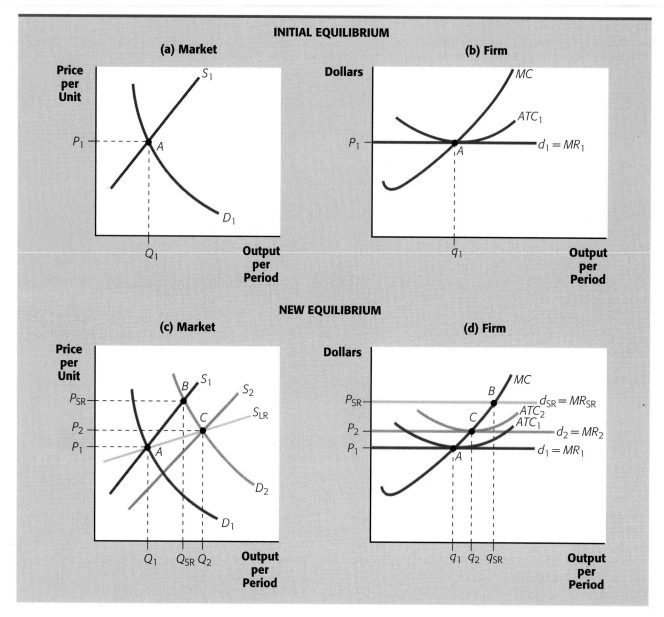

FIGURE 10
An Increasing-Cost Industry

At point A in panel (a), the market is in long-run equilibrium. The typical firm in panel (b) earns zero economic profit. If demand increases, market price rises. Individual firms increase output and earn an economic profit at point B. Profit attracts entry, increasing market supply but also driving up ATC. When long-run equilibrium is reestablished at point C in panel (c), price is higher, but the typical firm again earns zero economic profit. The long-run market supply curve is an upward-sloping line found by connecting points like A and C in panel (c).

the demand curve facing each firm shifts upward, and each firm raises output to the new profit-maximizing level q_{SR}. At this output level, $P > ATC$, so each firm is earning economic profit. Thus, the short-run impact of an increase in demand is (1) a rise in market price, (2) a rise in market quantity, and (3) economic profits.

When we turn to the long run, we know that economic profit will attract the entry of new firms. And, as you learned a few pages ago, an increase in the number of firms shifts the market supply curve rightward, which drives down the price until the economic profit is eliminated. But how far must the price fall in order to bring this about? That is, how far can we expect the market supply curve to shift? In answering this question, we'll add one more detail to our model that we've ignored until now.

Think about what happens as entry occurs in an industry. With more firms, output increases, so the industry will demand more *inputs*—more raw materials, more labor, more capital, and more land. We can usually expect the prices of these inputs to rise.

Misinterpreting the Supply Shift in Figure 10 In Chapter 3, you learned that a rightward shift in demand does *not* cause a rightward shift in supply. Instead, it raises the price and causes *a movement along* the supply curve. But in Figure 10, the demand curve shifts rightward from D_1 to D_2, the price rises, and then . . . the supply curve shifts rightward! So, now you may be wondering whether demand shifts *do* cause supply shifts.

The answer is: They *don't*—not by themselves. In the figure you can see that the shift in demand first raises the price, moving us *along* the supply curve S_1 from point A to point B. This is just as you learned in Chapter 3. But now, we're extending our analysis further, into the long run. The rise in price, if it creates profit for firms already in the market, will cause new firms to enter. It's this *increase in the number of firms* that causes the supply curve to shift.

Now, a rise in input prices will affect a firm's *ATC* curve. Why? Whenever we draw the *ATC* curve, we assume that the firm's production technology and the prices it must pay for its inputs remain constant. But when inputs become more expensive, cost per unit will be greater at *any* level of output. As a result, the *ATC* curve will shift upward. For example, expansion of the artichoke industry would increase the demand for land suitable for growing this crop, cause the price of this land to rise, and force up the *ATC* curve facing each artichoke producer.[4]

Let's sum up what we know so far. After the demand curve shifts, we arrive at point B in panel (c) in the short run. At this point, the price is higher and the typical firm is earning economic profit. Profit attracts entry, so the market supply curve begins to shift rightward, bringing the price back down. At the same time, the expansion of output in the industry raises input prices and shifts the typical firm's *ATC* curve upward. In panel (d), the *ATC* curve shifts upward to the curve ATC_2.

Now comes our important conclusion: Since the *ATC* curve has shifted upward, zero profit will occur at a price *higher* than the initial price P_1. In panel (d), the typical firm will earn zero profit when the price is P_2. Thus, entry will cease, and the market supply curve will *stop* shifting rightward, when the market price reaches P_2. In the figure, this occurs when the market supply curve reaches S_2. The final, long-run equilibrium occurs at point C, with price P_2, industry output at Q_2, and the typical firm producing q_2.

There is a lot going on in Figure 10. But we can make the story simpler if we *skip over* the short-run equilibrium at point B, and just ask: What happens in the *long run* after the demand curve shifts rightward? The answer is: The market equilibrium will move from point A to point C. A line drawn through these two points tells us, in the long run, the market price we can expect for any quantity the market provides. In Figure 10, this is the thin line, which is called the *long-run supply curve* (S_{LR}).

> The **long-run supply curve** shows the relationship between market price and market quantity produced after all long-run adjustments have taken place.

Long-run supply curve A curve indicating the quantity of output that all sellers in a market will produce at different prices, after all long-run adjustments have taken place.

---

[4] Notice that, in Figure 10, we've kept the diagram simple by shifting up the *ATC* curve, but not the *MC* curve. This would be entirely accurate if the inputs whose prices are rising are *lumpy inputs*. Over some range of output, the quantity of these inputs would not vary with output, leaving marginal cost unchanged. But even when both the *MC and* the *ATC* curves shift upward, our conclusions remain the same.

If input prices rise when an industry expands (as in our example), then an increase in market quantity will require an increase in the price. This is why the long-run supply curve S_{LR} has an *upward slope* in Figure 10.

Increasing, Decreasing and Constant Cost Industries. In Figure 10, an increase in demand led to a higher price, after all long-run adjustments in the market were completed. But, things don't *have* to end up as in Figure 10. It depends on what happens to input prices as new firms enter the industry and begin demanding inputs along with the firms already there. In Figure 10, the increase in demand for inputs causes the price of those inputs to *rise*. That's why the *ATC* curve shifts upward, and that's why the long-run supply curve slopes upward. This type of industry—which is the most common—is called an *increasing cost industry*.

Increasing cost industry An industry in which the long-run supply curve slopes upward because each firm's *ATC* curve shifts upward as industry output increases.

> In an ***increasing cost industry***, entry causes input prices to rise, which shifts up the typical firm's *ATC* curve, and raises the market price at which firms earn zero economic profit. As a result, the long-run supply curve slopes upward.

But there are two other possibilities. First, an industry might use such a small percentage of total inputs that, even as new firms enter, there is no noticeable effect on input prices. For example, suppose we want to analyze the effect of an increase in demand for bicycles in the United States. The bicycle industry uses only a tiny fraction of the nation's labor, capital, aluminum, rubber, and almost any other basic input we can think of. This industry could expand considerably without any noticeable rise in input prices. As a result, the *ATC* curve would stay put as new firms entered the industry and—as you are asked to verify in the end-of-chapter challenge question—the long-run supply curve would be horizontal. This type of industry is a *constant cost industry*.

Constant cost industry An industry in which the long-run supply curve is horizontal because each firm's *ATC* curve is unaffected by changes in industry output.

> In a ***constant cost industry***, entry has no effect on input prices, so the typical firm's *ATC* curve stays put and the market price at which firms earn zero economic profit does not change. As a result, the long-run supply curve is horizontal.

DANGEROUS CURVES

Diminishing Marginal Returns vs. Diseconomies of Scale vs. Increasing Cost Industry It's easy to confuse these terms—or their opposites (increasing marginal returns, economies of scale, and decreasing cost industries)—because they all have *something* to do with changes in cost due to changes in production. But they're distinct concepts, so it's useful to see them compared in a way that stresses their difference.

- "Diminishing marginal returns" is a *short-run* concept relating changes in a firm's *output* to changes in a single *input,* holding all other inputs constant. It explains the *upward-sloping portion* of a firm's *marginal cost* (*MC*) curve. (See Chapter 6.)
- "Diseconomies of scale" is a *long-run* concept, describing the *upward-sloping portion* of a firm's *long-run average total cost* (*LRATC*) curve. (See Chapter 6.)
- "Increasing cost industry" is a *long-run* concept, describing an *upward-sloping long-run market supply curve* (S_{LR}) . (See current chapter.)

If you're unclear about any of these terms, this is a good time to refresh your memory. You can also write out a similar set of distinctions for the three *opposite* and often-confused terms: "increasing marginal returns," "economies of scale," and "decreasing cost industry." See if you can distinguish between them without looking at the above.

Another possibility is that of a *decreasing cost industry,* in which entry into an industry by new firms actually *decreases* input prices. For example, suppose that a modest size city has just a few sushi restaurants. Periodically, a partially loaded truck makes a special trip from a distant larger city to deliver raw fish, nori seaweed, wasabi, and other special ingredients to these few restaurants. Transportation costs—part of the price of the ingredients—will be rather high.

Now suppose that demand for sushi meals increases. Profits at the existing restaurants attracts entry.

With more restaurants ordering ingredients, the same delivery truck makes the same trip, but now it is fully loaded and the transportation costs are shared among more restaurants. As a result, transportation costs at *each* restaurant decrease—and each restaurant's *ATC* curve shifts down. Competition among the restaurants then ensures that prices will drop to match the lower *ATC*. As a result, the long-run effect of an increase in demand is a *lower* price for eating sushi at a restaurant—a downward sloping long-run supply curve. (An end-of-chapter problem will ask you to draw the relevant graphs.)

> *In a **decreasing cost industry**, entry causes input prices to* fall, *which causes the typical firm's* ATC *curve to shift* downward, *and* lowers *the market price at which firms earn zero economic profit. As a result, the long-run supply curve slopes* downward.

Decreasing cost industry An industry in which the long-run supply curve slopes downward because each firm's *ATC* curve shifts downward as industry output increases.

Market Signals and the Economy

The previous discussion of changes in demand included a lot of details, so let's take a moment to go over it in broad outline. You've seen that an *increase* in demand always leads to an *increase* in market output in the short run, as existing firms raise their output levels, and an even *greater* increase in output in the long run, as new firms enter the market.

We could also have analyzed what happens when demand *decreases,* but you are encouraged to do this on your own instead, drawing the diagram and tracing through the logic. If you do it correctly, you'll find that the leftward shift of the demand curve will cause a drop in output in the short run and an even greater drop in the long run. The effect on price will depend on the nature of the industry, i.e., whether input prices rise or fall as exit takes place. (Once again, you'll be drawing some of these graphs in end-of chapter questions.)

But now let's step back from these details and see what they really tell us about the economy. We can start with a simple fact: In the real world, the demand curves for different goods and services are constantly shifting. For example, over the last decade, Americans have developed an increased taste for bottled water. The average American gulped down 8 gallons of the stuff in 1990, and more than twice that much—18 gallons—in 2001. As a consequence, the *production* of bottled water has increased dramatically. This seems like magic: Consumers want more bottled water and, presto!, the economy provides it. What our model of perfect competition shows us are the workings behind the magic, the logical sequence of events leading from our desire to consume more bottled water and its appearance on store shelves.

The secret—the trick up the magician's sleeve—is this: As demand increases or decreases in a market, *prices change*. And price changes act as *signals* for firms to enter or exit an industry. How do these signals work? As you've seen, when demand increases, the price tends to initially *overshoot* its long-run equilibrium value during the adjustment process, creating sizable temporary profits for existing firms. Similarly, when demand decreases, the price falls *below* its long-run equilibrium value, creating sizable losses for existing firms. These exaggerated, temporary movements in price, and the profits and losses they cause, are almost irresistible forces, pulling new firms into the market or driving existing firms out. In this way, the economy is driven to produce whatever collection of goods consumers prefer.

For example, as Americans shifted their tastes toward bottled water, the market demand curve for this good shifted rightward and the price rose. Initially, the price rose *above* its new long-run equilibrium value, leading to high profits at existing bottled water firms such as Poland Spring and Arrowhead. High profits, in turn, attracted entry—especially the entry of new brands from established firms not previously selling bottled water, such as Pepsi's Aquafina and Coke's Dasani. As a result, production expanded to match the increase in demand by consumers. More of our land, labor, capital, and entrepreneurial skills are now used to produce bottled water. Where did these resources come from?

In large part, they were freed up from those industries that experienced a *decline* in demand. In these industries, lower prices have caused exit, freeing up land, labor, capital, and entrepreneurship to be used in other, expanding industries, such as the bottled water industry.

Market signals Price changes that cause changes in production to match changes in consumer demand.

*In a market economy, price changes act as **market signals**, ensuring that the pattern of production matches the pattern of consumer demands. When demand increases, a rise in price signals firms to enter the market, increasing industry output. When demand decreases, a fall in price signals firms to exit the market, decreasing industry output.*

Importantly, in a market economy, no single person or government agency directs this process. There is no central command post where information about consumer demand is assembled, and no one tells firms how to respond. Instead, existing firms and new entrants, in their *own* search for higher profits, respond to market signals and help move the overall market in the direction it needs to go. This is what Adam Smith meant when he suggested that individual decision makers act—as if guided by an *invisible hand*—for the overall benefit of society, even though, as individuals, they are merely trying to satisfy their own desires.

USING THE THEORY
Changes in Technology

In this chapter, you've learned that perfectly competitive markets deliver the goods consumers want to buy at the lowest possible price. Moreover, you've seen that production in perfectly competitive markets follows consumer demand. Demand for a good increases, and production rises. Demand decreases, production falls.

But the service of competitive markets extends to other types of changes as well. In this section, we'll explore how competitive markets ensure that the benefits of technological advances are enjoyed by consumers.

One industry that has experienced especially rapid technological changes in the 1990s is farming. By using genetically altered seeds, farmers are able to grow crops that are more resistant to insects and more tolerant of herbicides. This lowers the total—and average—cost of producing any given amount of the crop.

Figure 11 illustrates the market for corn, but it could just as well be the market for soybeans, cotton, or many other crops. In panel (a), the market begins at point A, where the price of corn is $3 per bushel. In panel (b), the typical farm

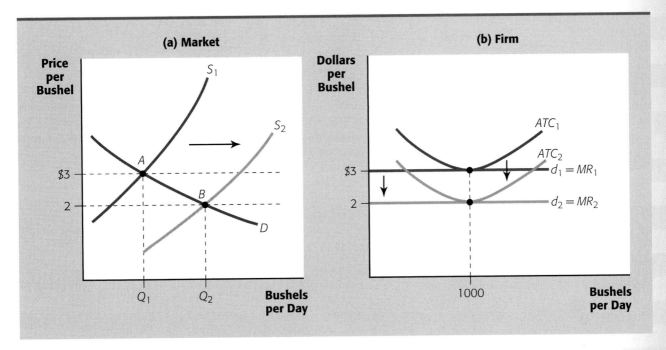

(a) Market

Price per Bushel

S_1

S_2

A

$3

B

D

Q_1 Q_2 Bushels per Day

(b) Firm

Dollars per Bushel

ATC_1

ATC_2

$3 $d_1 = MR_1$

2 $d_2 = MR_2$

1000   Bushels per Day

FIGURE 11

Technological Change in Perfect Competition

Technological change may reduce ATC. In panel (b), any farm that adopts new technology will earn an economic profit if it can produce at the old market price of $3 per bushel. That profit will lead its competitors to adopt the same technology and will also attract new entrants. As market supply increases, price falls until each farm is once again earning zero economic profit.

produces 1,000 bushels per year and—with average cost curve ATC_1—earns zero economic profit.

Now let's see what happens when new, higher-yield corn seeds are made available. Suppose first that only one farm uses the new technology. This farm will enjoy a downward shift in its ATC curve from ATC_1 to ATC_2. Since it is so small relative to the market, it can produce all it wants and continue to sell at $3. Although we have not drawn in the farm's MC curve, you can see that the farm has several output levels from which to choose where $P > ATC$ and it can earn economic profit.

But not for long. In the long run, economic profit at this farm will cause two things to happen. First, all other farmers in the market will have a powerful incentive to adopt the new technology—to plant the new, genetically engineered seed themselves. Under perfect competition, they can do so; there are no barriers that prevent any farmer from using the same technology as any other. As these farms adopt the new seed technology, their ATC curves, too, will drop down to ATC_2.

Second, outsiders will have an incentive to enter this industry with plants utilizing the new technology, shifting the market supply curve rightward (from S_1 to S_2) and driving down the market price. The process will stop only when the market price has reached the level at which *farms using the new technology* earn zero economic profit. In Figure 11, this occurs at a price of $2 per bushel.[5]

From this example, we can draw two conclusions about technological change under perfect competition. First, what will happen to a farmer who is reluctant to change his technology? As *other* farms make the change, and the market price falls from $3 to $2, the reluctant farmer will find himself suffering an economic loss, since his average cost will remain at $3. His competitors will leave him to twist in

---

[5] In this example, we assume that the price of the new technology remains the same as it is adopted throughout the industry. If the price of the new technology were to rise, then—in the long run—the typical firm's ATC curve could still shift downward, but not as far as ATC_2; the market supply curve would then shift rightward, but not as far as S_2; and the price would drop, but not all the way to $2.

the wind, and if he refuses to shape up, he will be forced to exit the industry. In the end, *all* farms in the market must use the new technology.

Second, who benefits from the new technology in the long run? Not the farmers who adopt it. *Some* farmers—the earliest adopters—may enjoy *short-run* profit before the price adjusts completely. But in the long run, all farmers will be right back where they started, earning zero economic profit. The gainers are *consumers* of corn, since they benefit from the lower price.

Although some of the data in this example are hypothetical, the story is not. The average American farmer today feeds 129 people, double the amount fed only a few years ago. And as our example suggests, powerful forces push farmers to adopt new productivity-enhancing technology. From 1995 to 2003, the fraction of U.S. corn acreage planted with genetically modified seeds increased from zero to 38 percent, and is still growing rapidly. For soybeans, the comparable figures are zero to 80 percent.

More generally, we can summarize the impact of technological change as follows:

> *Under perfect competition, a technological advance leads to a rightward shift of the market supply curve, decreasing market price. In the short run, early adopters may enjoy economic profit, but in the long run, all adopters will earn zero economic profit. Firms that refuse to use the new technology will not survive.*

Technological advances in many competitive industries—mining, lumber, communication, entertainment, and others—have indeed spread quickly, shifting market supply curves rapidly and steadily rightward over the past 100 years. While this has often been hard on individual competitive firms, which must continually adapt to new technologies in order to survive, it has led to huge rewards for consumers.

Summary

Perfect competition is a market structure in which (1) there are large numbers of buyers and sellers and each buys or sells only a tiny fraction of the total market quantity; (2) sellers offer a standardized product; and (3) sellers can easily enter or exit from the market. While few real markets satisfy these conditions precisely, the model is still useful in a wide variety of cases.

Each perfectly competitive firm faces a horizontal demand curve; it can sell as much as it wishes at the market price. The firm chooses its profit-maximizing output level by setting marginal cost equal to the market price. Its *short-run supply curve* is that part of its MC curve that lies above the average variable cost curve. Total profit is profit per unit $(P - ATC)$ times the profit-maximizing quantity.

In the short run, market price is determined where the market supply curve—the horizontal sum of all firms' supply curves—crosses the market demand curve. In short-run equilibrium, existing firms can earn a profit (in which case new firms will enter) or suffer a loss (in which case existing firms will exit). Entry or exit will continue until, in the long run, each firm is earning zero economic profit. At each competitive

firm in long-run equilibrium, price = marginal cost = minimum average total cost = minimum long-run average total cost.

When demand curves shift, prices change more in the short run than in the long run. The temporary, exaggerated price movements act as market signals, ensuring that output expands and contracts in each industry to match the pattern of consumer preferences.

In the long run, an increase in demand can result in a higher, lower, or unchanged market price, depending on whether the good is produced, respectively, in an *increasing cost industry*, *decreasing cost industry*, or *constant cost industry*. The long-run supply curve slopes upward in an increasing cost industry and slopes downward for a decreasing cost industry. In a constant cost industry, the long-run supply curve will be horizontal.

A technological advance in a perfectly competitive market causes the equilibrium price to fall and equilibrium quantity to rise. Each competitive firm must use the new technology in order to survive, but consumers reap all the benefits by paying a lower price.

Key Terms

Constant cost industry

Decreasing cost industry

Firm's supply curve

Increasing cost industry

Long-run supply curve

Market signals

Market structure

Market supply curve

Normal profit

Perfect competition

Price taker

Shutdown price

Review Questions *Answers to even-numbered Questions and Problems can be found on the text Web site at http://hall-lieb.swlearning.com.*

1. What are the three characteristics that typify a perfectly competitive market? Explain the importance of each characteristic.

2. How do economists justify using the perfectly competitive model to analyze markets that clearly do not satisfy one or more of the assumptions of that model?

3. On a scale of 1 to 5, with 5 being full satisfaction and 1 being no satisfaction at all, rank the following markets in terms of their satisfaction of the three characteristics of the perfectly competitive model. Assign a score for each characteristic and justify your assignment.
   a. Clothing stores
   b. Restaurants
   c. Book publishing
   d. Home video game production
   e. Jet aircraft production

4. Why is the demand curve facing a perfectly competitive firm infinitely elastic?

5. "To maximize profit, a perfectly competitive firm should produce the level of output at which marginal cost is equal to price." True, false, or uncertain? Explain.

6. To calculate profit (or loss) for a perfectly competitive firm, we look at the difference between *P* and *ATC*, but to determine the profit-maximizing (or loss-minimizing) level of output, we focus on price and marginal cost. Why?

7. Discuss the following statement: "Economists need to pay more attention to the real business world. Their model of perfect competition predicts that firms in a market will end up earning no profit, nothing above costs. As any accountant can tell you, if you look at the balance sheets of most businesses in any industry, their revenue exceeds their costs; they do, in fact, make a profit."

8. True, false, or uncertain? Explain your answer.
   a. A perfectly competitive firm is profitable when price exceeds minimum *AVC*.
   b. A competitive firm's supply curve is just its *MC* curve.

9. What is the fundamental characteristic that distinguishes the short run from the long run in the analysis of a competitive market?

10. True or false? In a perfectly competitive market, an increase in output requires a high price in the short run, but not in the long run. Justify your answer.

Problems and Exercises

1. In 1999, (1) sales of sport utility vehicles (SUVs) skyrocketed, and (2) the price of gasoline rose. Because SUVs get lower gasoline mileage than the automobiles they replaced, their owners ended up buying more gasoline even as the price per gallon rose. Is this a violation of the law of demand?

2. Suppose that a perfectly competitive firm has the following total variable costs (*TVC*):

Quantity:	0	1	2	3	4	5	6
TVC:	$0	$6	$11	$15	$18	$22	$28

It also has fixed costs of $6. If the market price is $5 per unit:
   a. Find the firm's profit-maximizing quantity using the marginal revenue and marginal cost approach.
   b. Check your results by re-solving the problem using the total revenue and total cost approach. Is the firm earning a positive profit, suffering a loss, or breaking even?

3. Assume that the market for cardboard is perfectly competitive (if not very exciting). In each of the following scenarios, should a typical firm continue to produce or

should it shut down in the short run? Draw a diagram that illustrates the firm's situation in each case.

a. Minimum ATC = $2.00
   Minimum AVC = $1.50
   Market price = $1.75
b. MR = $1.00
   Minimum AVC = $1.50
   Minimum ATC = $2.00

4. The following table gives quantity supplied and quantity demanded at various prices in the perfectly competitive meat-packing market:

Price (per lb.)	Q_S (in millions of lbs.)	Q_D (in millions of lbs.)
$1.00	10	100
$1.25	15	90
$1.50	25	75
$1.75	40	63
$2.00	55	55
$2.25	65	40

Assume that each firm in the meat-packing industry faces the following cost structure:

Pounds	TC
60,000	$110,000
61,000	$111,000
62,000	$112,000
63,000	$115,000

a. What is the profit-maximizing output level for the typical firm? (*Hint:* Calculate MC for each change in output, then find the equilibrium price, and calculate MR for each change in output.)
b. Is this market in long-run equilibrium? Why or why not? (*Hint:* Calculate ATC.)
c. What do you expect to happen to the number of meat-packing firms over the long run? Why?

5. Assume that the kitty litter industry is perfectly competitive and is presently in long-run equilibrium:
a. Draw diagrams for both the market and a typical firm, showing equilibrium price and quantity for the market, and MC, ATC, AVC, MR, and the demand curve for the firm.
b. Your friend has always had a passion to get into the kitty litter business. If the market is in long-run equilibrium, will it be profitable for him to jump in head-first (so to speak)? Why or why not?
c. Suppose people begin to prefer dogs as pets, and cat ownership declines. Show on your diagrams from part (a) what happens in the industry and the firm in the long run, assuming that this is a constant cost industry.

6. In a perfect competitive, increasing cost industry, is the long-run supply curve always flatter than the short-run market supply curve? Explain.

7. "A *profit-maximizing* competitive firm will produce the quantity of output at which price *exceeds* cost per unit by the greatest possible amount." True or false? Explain briefly. [*Hint:* see Figure 3(a)]

8. In the "Using the Theory" section of this chapter, you learned that technological advances lead to falling prices, increasing output, and only a temporary burst of profit for early adopters, with long-run profit returning to zero. Would any of these results change if the market demand for the good were completely inelastic? (Draw a diagram similar to Figure 11 to make your case.)

9. "My economics professor must be confused. First he tells us that in perfect competition, the demand curve is completely flat—horizontal. But then he draws a supply and demand diagram that has a downward-sloping demand curve. What gives?" Resolve this confusion in a single sentence.

10. Assume that the firm shown in this table produces output using one fixed input and one variable input.

Output	Price	Total Revenue	Marginal Revenue	Total Cost	Marginal Cost	Profit
0	$50	$0		$5		
					$35	
1	$50					
					$15	
2	$50					
					$35	
3	$50					
					$55	
4	$50					
					$65	

a. Complete this table and use it to find this firm's short-run profit-maximizing quantity of output. How much profit will this firm earn?
b. Redo the table and find the profit-maximizing quantity of output, if the price of the firm's fixed input rose from $5 to $10. How much profit will this firm earn now?
c. Now redo the original table and find the profit-maximizing quantity of output, if the price of the firm's variable input rose so that MC increased by $20 at each level of output. How much profit will this firm earn in this case?

11. Assume that the firm shown in this table produces output using one fixed input and one variable input.
    a. Complete this table and use it to find this firm's short-run profit-maximizing quantity of output. How much profit will this firm earn?
    b. Redo the table and find the profit-maximizing quantity of output, if the price of the firm's fixed input fell from $1,000 to $500. How much profit will this firm earn now?
    c. Now redo the original table and find the profit-maximizing quantity of output, if the price of the firm's variable input fell so that MC fell by half at each level of output. How much profit will the firm earn in this case?

Output	Price	Total Revenue	Marginal Revenue	Total Cost	Marginal Cost	Profit
0	$3500	$0		$1000		
					$4000	
1	$3500					
					$3000	
2	$3500					
					$2000	
3	$3500					
					$1000	
4	$3500					
					$3000	
5	$3500					
					$4000	
6	$3500					
					$9000	
7	$3500					
					$36,000	
8	$3500					

Challenge Questions

1. Figure 10 in the chapter shows the long-run adjustment process after an increase in demand. The figure assumes that input prices *rise* as industry output expands. However, in a *decreasing cost industry*, input prices *fall* as output expands.
    a. Redraw Figure 10 under the assumption that input prices *fall* as industry output expands. Illustrate what happens in the short run and in the long run after the market demand curve shifts rightward.
    b. Trace out the long-run supply curve for this industry. How does it differ from the long-run supply curve in Figure 10?

2. Figure 10 in the chapter shows the long-run adjustment process after an increase in demand. The figure assumes that input prices rise as industry output expands. However, in a *constant cost industry*, input prices *remain constant* as output expands.
    a. Redraw Figure 10 under the assumption that input prices *do not change* as industry output expands. Illustrate what happens in the short run and in the long run after the market demand curve shifts rightward.
    b. Trace out the new long-run supply curve for this industry. How does it differ from the long-run supply curve in Figure 10? How can it be that more output is offered by the market after the increase in demand, when each firm in the industry is producing the same quantity of output as they were at price P_1?

3. Figure 10 in the chapter shows the long-run adjustment process after an increase in demand. In this problem, you will be analyzing the effect of a *decrease* in demand in different types of industries.
    a. Redraw Figure 10 under the assumption that the industry in question is an *increasing cost industry*, and illustrate what happens in the short run and in the long run after the market demand curve shifts *leftward* instead of rightward.
    b. Redraw Figure 10 under the assumption that the industry in question is a *constant cost industry*, and illustrate what happens in the short run and in the long run after the market demand curve shifts *leftward* instead of rightward.
    c. Redraw Figure 10 under the assumption that the industry in question is a *decreasing cost industry*, and illustrate what happens in the short run and in the long run after the market demand curve shifts *leftward* instead of rightward.

4. In rare cases, existing technologies are found to be polluting or physically dangerous, and are banned. Review the "Using the Theory" section of this chapter. Then, show graphically the effects of banning a technology that is in

common use in a competitive industry. (*Hint:* After the technology is banned, what will happen to the average cost curve?)

5. If a firm's demand curve is horizontal, *must* its *MR* curve be horizontal as well? If a firm's *MR* curve is horizontal, *must* its demand curve be horizontal as well? Explain in each case.

 *These exercises require access to Hall/Lieberman Xtra! If Xtra! did not come with your book, visit* http://hallxtra.swlearning.com *to purchase.*

1. Use your Xtra! password at the Hall and Lieberman Web site (http://hallxtra.swlearning.com) and under Economic Applications click on EconNews. Click on *Microeconomics: Production and Costs*, and read the article, "Precision Plowing." Why would a perfectly competitive firm like a farm purchase such expensive equipment if it is producing the same good as its competitors? Carefully explain, making sure to distinguish between the long run and short run in your answer.

2. Use your Xtra! password at the Hall and Lieberman Web site (http://hallxtra.swlearning.com) and under Economic Applications click on EconNews. Select *Microeconomics: Perfect Competition*, and read the article, "One Farmer's Loss Is Another's Grain." Carefully explain, using a diagram with cost and revenue curves, the long-run adjustment that is taking place in this article.

MONOPOLY

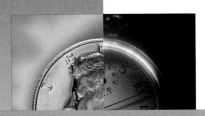

"Monopoly" is as close as economics comes to a dirty word. It is often associated with thoughts of extraordinary power, unfairly high prices, and exploitation. Even in the board game *Monopoly,* when you take over a neighborhood by buying up adjacent properties, you exploit other players by charging them higher rent.

The negative reputation of monopoly is in many ways deserved. A monopoly, as the only firm in its market, has the power to act in ways that a perfectly competitive firm cannot. Adam Smith's "invisible hand"—which channels the behavior of perfectly competitive firms into a socially beneficial outcome—doesn't poke, prod, or even lay a finger on a monopoly firm. Left unchecked, it will *not* create the best of all possible worlds for consumers. Indeed, when a monopoly "takes over" a previously competitive industry, great harm can be done to consumers and society in general. Monopolies, therefore, present a problem that nations around the world address with the very *visible* hand of government policy.

At the same time, a mythology has developed around monopolies. The media often portrays their power as absolute and unlimited, and their behavior as capricious and unpredictable. One sometimes hears suggestions that monopoly, in any form, should be treated like an infectious disease: Try to prevent it from arising in the first place—whenever and wherever it appears—and use every tool at our disposal to

269

destroy it. As you are about to see, this negative characterization goes too far. A monopoly's power may be formidable, but it's far from unlimited. Monopoly behavior—far from capricious—is remarkably predictable. And while monopolies should be avoided in most markets, in some it may be the best way to organize production. In these cases, we do better by *managing* the monopoly problem, rather than eliminating it.

This chapter will help you understand what monopolies are, how they arise, how they behave, and how they respond to changing market conditions. Our focus here will be on *understanding* monopolies and *predicting* their behavior. A fuller assessment of the monopoly problem and the policy options for dealing with it, will be provided in Chapter 14 ("Economic Efficiency and the Role of Government").

WHAT IS A MONOPOLY?

In most of your purchases—a haircut, a meal at a restaurant, a car, a college education—more than one seller is competing for your dollars, and you can choose which one to buy from. But in some markets, you have no choice at all. If you want to mail a letter for normal delivery, you must use the U.S. Postal Service. If you want cable television service, you must use the one cable television company in your area. Many cities have only a single local newspaper. And if you live in a very small town, you may have just one doctor, one gas station, or one movie theater to select from. These are all examples of *monopolies:*

> A *monopoly firm* is the only seller of a good or service with no close substitutes. *The market in which the monopoly firm operates is called a monopoly market.*

Monopoly firm The only seller of a good or service that has no close substitutes.

Monopoly market The market in which a monopoly firm operates.

A key concept in the definition of monopoly is the notion of *substitutability*. There is usually more than one way to satisfy a desire, and a single seller of a good or service is *not* considered a monopoly if other firms sell products—close substitutes—that satisfy that same desire. For example, only one firm in the country—Kellogg—sells Kellogg's Corn Flakes. But other cereal companies sell their own brands of cornflakes, which are close substitutes for Kellogg's. And many other types of flaky cereals—wheat flakes or oat flakes—are also very close substitutes for Kellogg's Corn Flakes. This is why we do not consider Kellogg to be a monopoly firm.

The definition of a monopoly firm or market may seem precise. But in the real world, the definition is not always so clear-cut. Whether a market has one seller, or many sellers, depends on how we define the market itself. Certainly, before declaring a market to be a monopoly, we must define it broadly enough to include sellers of all "close substitutes." But what do we mean by "close"?

Consider, for example, cable television service in the United States. A couple of paragraphs ago, it was one of our examples of a monopoly. But you can also get movies and other entertainment on broadcast television, at your local video store, and even over the Internet. If we include each of these products as part of a broadly defined market for entertainment services, then there are several sellers, and your cable company is *not* a monopoly. But are these other sources of entertainment *close* substitutes? For some people and some purposes, yes. But for many purposes, a cable service has no close substitutes: Using the Internet to download videos requires a special high-speed connection and a home theater that takes computer files; renting videos requires a trip to the video store; and broadcast television is aimed at a broader audience than most cable channels, which tend to target specific viewers. If we define the market more narrowly as that for "reliable, in-home, specialized entertainment services," the local cable company looks like a monopoly again.

Or consider the market for thriller novels. Surely, we might think, this market is not a monopoly. After all, any reasonable definition of the market would include the products of several different publishers, all of them competing for your dollars when you browse the aisles of your local bookstore. But if you really want to read Tom Clancy's latest novel, then as far as you are concerned, there are no close substitutes, and Tom Clancy's publisher is the only seller.

Because we all have different tastes and characteristics, we can have different opinions about what is, and what is not, a "close" substitute. As a result, we can have different ideas about how broadly or how narrowly we should define a market when trying to decide if it is a monopoly. It makes sense, then, to view monopoly as a spectrum rather than a strict category. On one end of this spectrum is *pure monopoly,* where there is just one seller of a good for which very few buyers could find a substitute. The only doctor, attorney, or food market in a small town comes very close to being a pure monopoly. Further along the spectrum, we reach firms that sell a good for which reasonable substitutes do exist—at least for some buyers and for some purposes—but they are not very *close* substitutes for most buyers or most purposes. The local cable company is an example of this middle ground, and most economists would extend the label "monopoly" to this part of the spectrum. But as we go further along the spectrum, we find goods for which so many buyers can find close substitutes that the term *monopoly* no longer makes sense. Penguin Group (USA) Inc, the parent company that publishes most of Tom Clancy's novels in hardcover, is an example of this kind of firm. As stated earlier, suppose you are desperate to read Tom Clancy's latest novel as soon as it comes out. Then for you personally, Penguin might seem like a monopolist. But for most people, other books by other authors are substitutes. As a result, a more reasonable definition of the market would include "all thriller novels" or even "all mass-market fiction." This is why we would not ordinarily characterize Penguin as a monopoly.

THE SOURCES OF MONOPOLY

The mere existence of a monopoly means that *something* is causing other firms to stay out of the market rather than enter and compete with the firm already there. Broadly speaking, there must be some *barrier to entry.* The question, "Why is the market a monopoly?" then becomes, "What *barrier* prevents additional firms from entering the market?" There are several possible answers, and we can organize them into three broad categories: economies of scale, legal barriers, and network externalities.

Economies of Scale

Recall from Chapter 6 that economies of scale in production cause a firm's long-run average cost curve to slope downward. That is, the more output the firm produces, the lower will be its cost per unit. If economies of scale persist to the point where a single firm is producing for the entire market, we call the market a *natural monopoly*:

> *A natural monopoly exists when, due to economies of scale, one firm can produce at a lower cost per unit than can two or more firms.*

The monopoly firm, or the market in which is operates, is called a *natural* monopoly for good reason: Unless the government intervenes, only one seller would survive. The market would *naturally* become a monopoly. Why?

Although we've already discussed the answer (in Chapter 6), let's step through it in a bit more detail here. Figure 1 is a larger and more specific version of panel (b) from Figure 9 in Chapter 6. It shows the *LRATC* curve for a typical dry cleaner operating in a small town. Dry cleaners use several "lumpy inputs"—inputs that must be purchased in some minimum quantities for a wide range of output. For example, whether it cleans 1 article of clothing each week or 300, the dry cleaner will need the same small parcel of land for its shop, a single employee to handle customers, the same amount of electricity for the lights. For all output levels from 0 to 300, it will need either the same amount of machinery (if it cleans the clothes on site) or the same amount of transportation services (if the clothes are cleaned elsewhere). Clearly, the more clothes cleaned, the lower the firm's cost per piece of clothing, creating economies of scale (a downward-sloping *LRATC* curve). As you can see, for any market quantity in our diagram, a single dry cleaning shop could sell it at lower cost per unit than could two or more dry cleaners.

The figure also shows the market demand curve (D_{market}) for dry cleaning in this small town. Notice that it crosses the *LRATC* curve at 300 units, and then drops below it. This tells us that the *maximum* potential market for dry cleaning in this town is 300 pieces per week. Why? In order for quantity demanded in this market to exceed 300 pieces—say, 350—price would have to drop down to $5 per piece (point *C*). But this amount of cleaning wouldn't be offered in the town without driving the cost per unit *above* $5 per piece. For example, a single cleaner servicing all 350 pieces would have a cost per unit of $12 per piece (point *B*) and would go out of business charging the most the market would pay for that quantity, which is $5 per piece. Two firms splitting the market would be in even worse shape: Their cost per unit would be even larger. But in order to get enough customers to clean 350 pieces between them, they could charge only $5.00—less than their cost per unit. Therefore, the maximum amount of dry cleaning that can be done in this market, while permitting the dry cleaning industry to survive in the long run, is 300 pieces per week.

Let's suppose that this town already has such a business—Incumbent Cleaning—and its owner is making a nice profit. (We'll examine how the existing cleaner selects his price to maximize profit in a couple of pages.) Another resident is considering opening a competing firm in the town. Should she do it? Not if she's smart. In order to attract customers, she'd have to at least match, or maybe undercut, the price charged by Incumbent Cleaners. But in any competition over price, Incumbent has an advantage: It's already cleaning more clothes than the newcomer could, even if the newcomer were able to capture half the market. Thus, Incumbent's cost per unit is already lower than the newcomer could hope to achieve. Threatened by the newcomer, Incumbent could always lower its price to just a shade above its low cost per unit and still earn a small profit. But if the newcomer (with fewer initial cus-

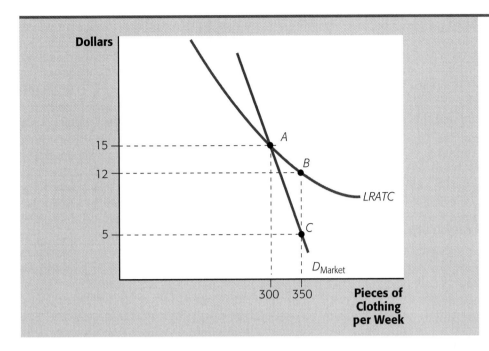

FIGURE 1
A Natural Monopoly
The market quantity of dry cleaning could never be 350 pieces per week because the lowest possible cost per unit of cleaning 350 pieces is $12 (point B), which exceeds the price people would willingly pay. The maximum potential market is 300 pieces. For any quantity up to the maximum potential market, a single firm has a cost advantage over two or more firms that split the market among themselves.

tomers and a much higher cost per unit) tried to match Incumbent's low price, it would suffer a loss.

Since there is time and expense involved in setting up a new dry cleaning shop—and closing it down if it fails—a potential entrant would not want to bear these costs for nothing. She would most likely look for another business, one with *LRATC* and market demand curves that do *not* look like Figure 1.

Small local monopolies are often *natural* monopolies. Think of the sole gas station in a small town. Since it needs a minimum set of certain inputs no matter how little gas it sells (a pump for each type of gas, space for cars to pull up), each additional gallon sold lowers the station's cost per unit. By producing for the entire (small town) market, it achieves the smallest possible cost per unit. Under these circumstances, a potential new entrant would have to think very hard about coming into this market, since it would not be able to survive a price war with the firm already there. The same logic can explain the monopoly position held by the sole food market, attorney, or dentist in a small town. These are all natural monopolies, because they continue to enjoy economies of scale up to the point at which they are serving the entire market.

Legal Barriers

Many monopolies arise because of legal barriers. Of course, since laws are created by human beings, this immediately raises the question: Why would anyone purposely create barriers that lead to monopoly? As you'll see, the answer varies depending on the type of barrier being erected. Here, we'll consider two of the most important legal barriers that give rise to monopolies: protection of intellectual property and government franchise.

Protection of Intellectual Property. The words you are reading right now are an example of *intellectual property*, which includes literary, artistic, and musical works, as well as scientific inventions. Most markets for a specific intellectual property are monopolies: One firm or individual owns the property and is the sole seller of the rights to use it. There is both good and bad in this. As you will learn in this chapter, prices tend to be higher under monopoly than under perfect competition, and monopolies often earn economic profit as a consequence. This is good for the monopoly and bad for everyone else. On the other hand, it is just this promise of monopoly profit that encourages the creation of original products and ideas, which certainly benefits the rest of us. The Palm Pilot personal organizer, the Visex laser for reshaping the eye's cornea, and Internet search engines such as Google, Vivisimo, and Teoma were all launched by innovators who bore considerable costs and risks with an expectation of future profits. The same is true of every compact disc you listen to, every novel you read, and every movie you see.

> *In dealing with intellectual property, government strikes a compromise: It allows the creators of intellectual property to enjoy a monopoly and earn economic profit, but only for a limited period of time. Once the time is up, other sellers are allowed to enter the market, and it is hoped that competition among them will bring down prices.*

The two most important kinds of legal protection for intellectual property are *patents* and *copyrights*. New scientific discoveries and the products that result from them are protected by a **patent** obtained from the federal government. The patent prevents anyone else from selling the same discovery or product for about 20 years. For example, in 1981, the Eli Lilly Company took out a patent on the chemical fluoxetine, the active ingredient in Prozac. As the first antidepressant without serious side effects, Prozac proved enormously profitable for Lilly. The drug earned Lilly as much as $13.5 million in profit *per day* before its patent expired in August 2001. Other pharmaceutical companies, forced to work around Lilly's patent, took much longer to develop their own, similar drugs. In the meantime, Lilly was the sole seller of a product with no close substitutes.

Patent A temporary grant of monopoly rights over a new product or scientific discovery.

Literary, musical, and artistic works are protected by a **copyright,** which grants exclusive rights over the material for at least 50 years. For example, the copyright on this book is owned by South-Western/Thomson Learning. No other company or individual can print copies and sell them to the public, and no one can quote from the book at length without obtaining South-Western's permission.

Copyright A grant of exclusive rights to sell a literary, musical, or artistic work.

Copyrights and patents are often sold to another person or firm, but this does not change the monopoly status of the market, since there is still just one seller. For example, the song "Happy Birthday" was originally written in 1893 but first received copyright protection in 1935. Since then, the copyright has changed hands numerous times and is currently owned by Time Warner. While you are free to sing this song at a private birthday party, anyone who wants to sing it on radio or television—that is, anyone who wants to profit from the song—must obtain a license from Time Warner and pay a small royalty.

Government Franchise. The large firms we usually think of as monopolies—utility, telephone, and cable television companies—have their monopoly status guaranteed through **government franchise,** a grant of exclusive rights over a product. Here, the barrier to entry is quite simple: Any other firm that enters the market will be prosecuted!

Government franchise A government-granted right to be the sole seller of a product or service.

Governments usually grant franchises when they think the market is a *natural monopoly*. In this case, a single large firm enjoying economies of scale would have a lower cost per unit than multiple smaller firms, so government tries to serve the public interest by *ensuring* that there are no competitors. In exchange for its monopoly status, the seller must submit to either government ownership and control or else government regulation over its prices and profits.

This is the logic behind the monopoly status of the U.S. Postal Service. No matter how many letters it delivers, a postal firm must have enough letter carriers to reach every house every day. Two postal companies would need many more carriers to deliver the same total number of letters, raising costs and, ultimately, the price of mailing a letter. Thus, mail delivery is a natural monopoly, one that the federal government has chosen to own and control rather than merely regulate. Federal law prohibits any other firm from offering normal letter delivery service.

Local governments, too, create monopolies by granting exclusive franchises in a variety of industries believed to be natural monopolies. These include utility companies that provide electricity, gas, and water, as well as garbage collection services.

Since ordinary letter delivery is a natural monopoly, the U.S. Postal Service has been granted an exclusive government franchise to deliver the mail.

Network Externalities

Imagine that one day, in a flash of brilliance, you hit upon a simple idea that enables you to create a new, superior operating system for personal computers. You spend the next six months writing the computer code, and you succeed. Compared to Microsoft Windows, your operating system is less vulnerable to viruses, works 10 percent faster, and uses 10 percent less memory. It even allows the user to turn off the caps-lock key, which most people use only by mistake.

Now all you need is a few million dollars to launch your new product. You manage to get appointments with several venture capital firms, specialists in funding new projects. But every time you make your pitch, and the venture capital people realize what you're proposing, you get the same reaction: hysterical laughter. "But really," you say. "It works better than Windows. I can prove it." "We believe you," they always respond. And they do. And then . . . they start laughing again.

Why? Because you're trying to enter a market with significant *network externalities*.[1]

> *Network externalities* exist when an increase in the network's membership (more users of the product) increase its value to current and potential members.

Network externalities A situation in which the value of a good or service to each user increases as more people use it.

When network externalities are present, joining a large network is more beneficial than joining a small network, even if the product in the larger network is somewhat inferior to the product in the smaller one. Once a network reaches a certain size, additional consumers will want to join just because so many others already have. And if joining the network requires you to buy a product produced by only one firm, that firm can rapidly become the leading supplier in the market.

All of this applies to the market for computer operating systems. First, when you buy a Windows computer, you benefit by having a huge number of other computers—owned by friends and coworkers—that you can easily operate, and a

---

[1] The term *externality* will be defined formally in Chapter 14. But if you're curious, an externality is a by-product of a transaction that affects someone other than the buyer or seller (someone external to the transaction). In the case of network externalities, by paying to join the network (e.g., buying a Windows computer), you make the network larger, benefiting others (current and potential members) who weren't involved in your transaction.

large number of people with whom you can easily share documents. And, by buying the Windows machine, you enlarge the network, benefitting your friends and coworkers.

Second, you gain access to many software programs, such as PowerPoint, that are designed for Windows and not for the alternatives (Apple or Linux). Of course, by buying a Windows machine and enlarging the network, you and millions of people like you provide even more incentive to software developers to direct their efforts toward Windows users.

Third, if you've ever had a problem with your computer and tried getting help from a software seller's support line, you've learned the time you can save by just calling a knowledgeable friend or coworker. By joining the huge Windows network, you increase the number of friends who would be able to help you in a pinch. (And you become another person who can help them.)

In addition to the advantages of *joining* a larger network, there is also an advantage in not leaving it once you've joined: avoiding *switching costs*. It takes time to learn to operate and get used to a new operating system. Although the time you've spent mastering Windows is a sunk cost, the time you'd have to spend mastering a new system can be avoided by staying in the network you're in.

Windows, the first operating system to be used by tens of millions of people, has clearly benefited from network externalities, as well as switching costs. And today, with the system installed on more than 80 percent of all personal computers sold in the United States, Windows's leading position in personal computer operating systems would be difficult to overcome. For a new operating system to gain a foothold, the seller would have to incur substantial costs beyond just writing new code. It would have to create a new word processor and spreadsheet, or subsidize sellers of existing software to create versions for the new operating system. It would have to promote its product heavily. And it would have to endure a lengthy period of low prices in order to induce customers to switch.

The reason that venture capitalists would not be willing to bankroll your new operating system is that the costs of all these efforts—beyond your original creation of the operating system—would probably be greater than the revenue that your products would bring in. (If you had designed an operating system for servers instead of PCs, the venture capitalists might have taken you seriously. Network externalities are not nearly as strong for servers. As a result, Linux and other versions of Unix have gained a much larger foothold there.)

Network externalities (and to some extent, switching costs) can also explain the leading positions of eBay in the market for online auctions and Amazon in online retailing. (See if you can identify the sources of these features for eBay and Amazon.)

 ## MONOPOLY GOALS AND CONSTRAINTS

The goal of a monopoly, like that of any firm, is to earn the highest profit possible. And, like other firms, a monopolist faces constraints.

Reread that last sentence because it is important. It is tempting to think that a monopolist—because it faces no direct competitors in its market—is free of constraints. Or that its constraints are special ones, unlike those of any other firm. For example, many people think that the only force preventing a monopolist from charging outrageously high prices is public outrage. In this view, your cable company would charge $200, $500, or even $10,000 per month if only it could "get away with it."

But with a little reflection, it is easy to see that a monopolist faces purely *economic* constraints that limit its behavior—constraints that are similar to those faced by other, nonmonopoly firms. What are these constraints?

First, there is a constraint on the monopoly's *costs:* For any level of output the monopolist might produce, it must pay some total cost to produce it. This cost constraint is determined by the monopolist's production technology—which tells it how much output it can produce with different combinations of inputs—and also by the prices it must pay for those inputs. In other words, the constraints on the monopolist's costs are the same as on any other type of firm, such as the perfectly competitive firm we studied in the previous chapter.

There is also a *demand constraint.* The monopolist's demand curve—which is also the market demand curve—tells us the maximum price the monopolist can charge to sell any given quantity of output.[2]

To sum up:

> *A monopolist, like any firm, strives to maximize profit. And, like any firm, it faces constraints. For any level of output it might produce, total cost is determined by (1) its technology of production and (2) the prices it must pay for its inputs. And for any level of output it might produce, the maximum price it can charge is determined by the market demand curve for its product.*

MONOPOLY PRICE OR OUTPUT DECISION

Notice that the title of this section reads "price *or* output decision," not "price *and* output decision." The reason is that noncompetitive firms—such as monopolies—do *not* make two separate decisions about price and quantity, but rather *one* decision. More specifically, once the firm determines its output level, it has also determined its price (the maximum price it can charge and still sell that output level). Similarly, once the firm determines its price, it has also determined its output level (the maximum output the firm can sell at that price).

Of course, any *change* in output also implies a *change* in price, and vice versa. And these changes will affect both the firm's revenue and its costs. Let's first examine the effect on total revenue.

Output and Total Revenue. Suppose a monopolist is considering selling more output. Then, since it faces a downward-sloping demand curve, it will have to lower its price. However, the new, lower price must be charged *not* just on the new, additional units it wants to sell, but on *all* units of output, including those it was previously selling at a higher price. For example, if your local cable television company wants more subscribers, it will have to lower its rates for everyone, including those who already subscribe at the current rate. Thus, lowering price and increasing output have two offsetting effects on total revenue: On the one hand, more output is sold, tending to *increase* total revenue; on the other hand, *all* units now go for a lower price, tending to *decrease* total revenue. The net effect may be a rise or fall

---

[2] We're currently analyzing the behavior of a *single-price monopoly*—one that charges the same price for every unit it sells. When you see the term *monopoly* by itself, it means *single-price monopoly*. A later section will analyze the case of a *price-discriminating monopoly*, which can charge several different prices simultaneously (for example, by charging different prices to different customers).

FIGURE 2

Demand and Marginal Revenue

A monopoly faces a downward-sloping market demand curve. To sell additional output, the firm must lower its price. Marginal revenue (MR) *shows the change in total revenue that results from a one-unit increase in output.* MR *is less than price; to sell an additional unit, the monopoly must lower the price on that unit* and *on previous units.*

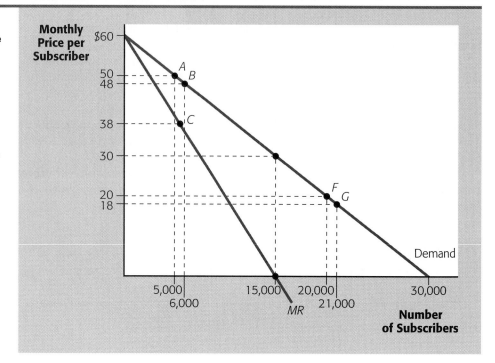

in total revenue, or—another way to say the same thing—the firm's *marginal revenue* may be positive or negative.

This should sound familiar to you. In Chapter 7, Ned's Beds faced a downward-sloping demand curve and had to lower its price on all of its bed frames in order to sell more of them. Although Ned was not necessarily the only seller in his market, his total and marginal revenue behaved in much the same way as we are describing here.

Figure 2 illustrates the demand and marginal revenue curves for Zillion-Channel Cable, a monopoly that sells cable television services to the residents of a town. We will assume that Zillion-Channel is free from government regulation. In the figure, the demand curve shows the number of subscribers at each monthly price for cable. The demand curve is both a *market* demand curve and the demand curve *facing the firm*, since Zillion-Channel is the only firm in its market.

Let's see what happens to Zillion-Channel's revenue as we move from point *A* to point *B* along its demand curve. At point *A*, the firm charges a monthly price of $50 and attracts 5,000 paid subscribers, for a total revenue of 5,000 × $50 = $250,000. If it lowers its price to $48, moving to point *B*, 1,000 more people will subscribe, for a total revenue of 6,000 × $48 = $288,000. Thus, in moving from point *A* to point *B*, total revenue rises by $38,000. The marginal revenue for this move, which tells us the increase in revenue per additional unit of output, can be calculated as follows:

$$MR = \frac{\Delta TR}{\Delta Q} = \frac{(\$288,000 - \$250,000)}{(6,000 - 5,000)} = \frac{\$38,000}{1,000} = \$38$$

This value for marginal revenue—$38—is plotted at point *C*, which is midway between points *A* and *B*. Notice that *MR* is *less* than the new price of output, $48. This follows from the two competing effects just discussed: On the one hand, the monopoly is selling more output and getting $48 on each additional unit; on the other hand, it has to charge a lower price on the previous 5,000 units of output it was selling. In the move from *A* to *B*, it turns out that total revenue rises, and marginal revenue is positive, but less than $48.

> *When any firm, including a monopoly, faces a downward-sloping demand curve, marginal revenue is less than the price of output. Therefore, the marginal revenue curve will lie below the demand curve.*

For other moves along the demand curve, total revenue may decline, so marginal revenue will be negative. (Verify this for the move from point *F* to point *G*.) For such changes, the marginal revenue curve lies below the horizontal axis.

The marginal revenue curve alone tells us something about the monopoly's output decision:

> *A monopoly will always produce at an output level where marginal revenue is positive.*

How can we be sure? Look again at Figure 2. When Zillion-Channel reaches 15,000 subscribers, its marginal revenue is zero. Raising output any further (say, from 15,000 to 16,000 subscribers) pushes *MR* into the negative zone. But negative marginal revenue means that *total* revenue decreases. Thus, by raising output beyond 15,000, total revenue goes down.

What about costs? We know that pushing output higher than 15,000 will increase total costs, just as does *any* rise in output. So, putting this together: Raising output beyond 15,000 causes revenue to decrease and costs to increase. Profit must therefore fall—not a good move. Thus, the firm will not want to push output into the region where marginal revenue is negative. And if it's in that region, it should go into reverse and *decrease* output, since that would *raise* profit. So in the end, it will produce somewhere in the region where *MR* is positive.

The Profit-Maximizing Output Level. Knowing that a monopoly will produce only where marginal revenue is positive narrows down the possibilities somewhat . . . but not enough. Which of the many output levels smaller than 15,000 units will Zillion-Channel choose? To answer, we return to our (now familiar) rule from Chapter 7, which tells us how *any* firm can find its profit-maximizing output level:

> *To maximize profit, a monoply—like any firm—should produce the quantity where* MC = MR *and the* MC *curve crosses the* MR *curve from below.*

Figure 3 adds Zillion-Channel's marginal cost curve to the demand and marginal revenue curves of Figure 2. The greatest profit possible occurs at an output level of 10,000, where the *MC* curve crosses the *MR* curve from below. In order to sell this level of output, the firm will charge a price of $40, locating at point *E* on its demand curve. You can see that for a monopoly, *price and output are not*

FIGURE 3
Monopoly Price and Output Determination

Like any firm, the monopolist maximizes profit by producing where MC *equals* MR. *Here, that quantity is 10,000 units. The price charged ($40) is read off the demand curve. It is the highest price at which the monopolist can sell that level of output.*

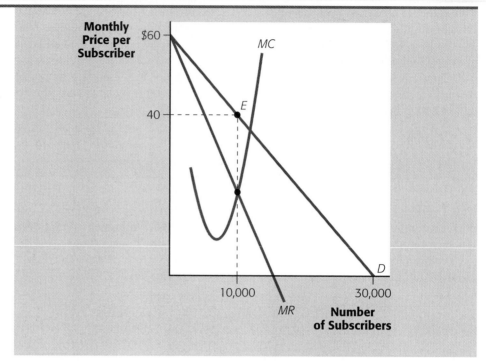

independent decisions, but different ways of expressing the same decision. Once Zillion-Channel determines its profit-maximizing output level (10,000 units), it has also determined its profit-maximizing price ($40), and vice versa.

Profit and Loss

In Figure 3, we can determine Zillion-Channel's price and output level, but we cannot see whether the firm is making an economic profit or loss. This will require one more addition to the diagram—the average cost curve. Remember that

$$\text{Profit per Unit} = P - ATC.$$

A Monopoly Supply Curve? A question may have occurred to you: Where is the monopoly's *supply curve*? The answer is that *there is no supply curve for a monopoly*. A firm's supply curve tells us how much output a firm will want to produce and sell when it is *presented* with different prices. This makes sense for a perfectly competitive firm that takes the market price as given and responds by deciding how much output to produce. A monopoly, by contrast, is *not* a price taker; it *chooses* its price. Since the monopolist is free to choose any price it wants—and it will always choose the *profit-maximizing* price and no other—the notion of a supply curve does not apply to a monopoly.

Now, the price, *P*, at any output level is read off the demand curve. Profit per unit, then, is just the distance between the firm's demand curve and its *ATC* curve.

Figure 4(a) is just like Figure 3 but adds Zillion-Channel's *ATC* curve. As you can see, at the profit-maximizing output level of 10,000, price is $40 and average total cost is $32, so profit per unit is $8.

Now look at the blue rectangle in the figure. The height of this rectangle is profit per unit ($8), and the width is the number of units produced (10,000). The *area* of

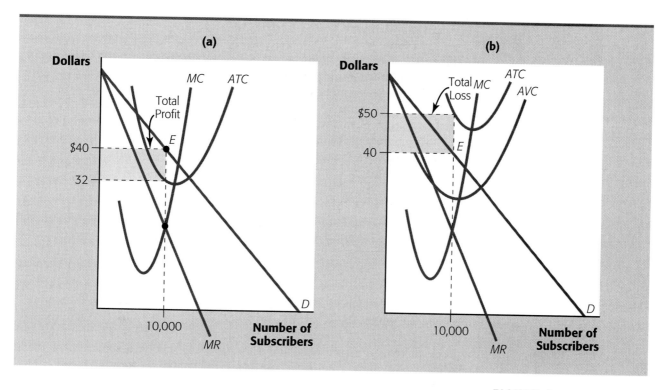

FIGURE 4
Monopoly Profit and Loss

the rectangle—height × width—equals Zillion-Channel's total profit, or $8 × 10,000 = $80,000.

> *A monopoly earns a profit whenever P > ATC. Its total profit at the best output level equals the area of a rectangle with height equal to the distance between P and ATC and width equal to the level of output.*

In panel (a), the monopolist's profit is the difference between price and average total cost (ATC) multiplied by the number of units sold. The blue area indicates a profit of $80,000. Panel (b) shows a monopolist suffering a loss. At the best level of output, ATC exceeds price. The red rectangle shows a loss of $100,000.

This should sound familiar: It is exactly how we represented the profit of a perfectly competitive firm (compare with Figure 3(a) in Chapter 8). The diagram looked different under perfect competition because the firm's demand curve was horizontal, whereas for a monopoly it is downward sloping.

However, a monopoly will not *necessarily* earn economic profit. Figure 4(b) illustrates the case of a monopoly suffering a loss. Here, costs are higher than in panel (a), and the *ATC* curve lies everywhere above the demand curve, so the firm will suffer a loss at any level of output. At the best output level—10,000—*ATC* is $50, so the loss per unit is $10. The total loss ($100,000) is the area of the red rectangle, whose height is the loss per unit ($10) and width is the best output level (10,000). Being a monopolist is no guarantee of profit. If costs are too high, or demand is insufficient, a monopolist may break even or suffer a loss.

> *A monopoly suffers a loss whenever P < ATC. Its total loss at the best output level equals the area of a rectangle with height equal to the distance between ATC and P and width equal to the level of output.*

EQUILIBRIUM IN MONOPOLY MARKETS

A monopoly market is in equilibrium when the only firm in the market, the monopoly firm, is maximizing its profit. After all, once the firm is producing the profit-maximizing quantity—and charging the highest price that will enable it to sell that quantity—it has no incentive to change either price or quantity, unless something in the market changes (which we'll explore later).

But for monopoly, as for perfect competition, we have different expectations about equilibrium in the short run and equilibrium in the long run.

Short-Run Equilibrium

In the short run, a monopoly may earn an economic profit or suffer an economic loss. (It may, of course, break even as well; see if you can draw this case on your own.) A monopoly that is earning an economic profit will, of course, continue to operate in the short run, charging the price and producing the output level at which $MR = MC$, as in Figure 4(a).

But what if a monopoly suffers a loss in the short run? Then it will have to make the same decision as any other firm: to shut down or not to shut down. The rule you learned in Chapter 7—that a firm should shut down if $TR < TVC$ at the output level where marginal revenue and marginal cost are equal—applies to any firm, including a monopoly. And (as you learned in Chapter 8), the statement "$TR < TVC$" is equivalent to the statement "$P < AVC$." Therefore,

any firm—including a monopoly—should shut down if P < AVC *at the output level where* MR = MC.

That is, if the firm's price per unit cannot cover its variable or operating costs per unit at its best output level (where $MR = MC$), then the firm should shut down.

In Figure 3(b), Zillion-Channel is suffering a loss. But since $P = \$40$ and AVC is less than $\$40$ at an output of 10,000, we have $P > AVC$: The firm should keep operating. On your own, draw in an alternative AVC curve in panel (b) that would cause Zillion-Channel to shut down. (*Hint:* It will be higher than the existing AVC curve.)

In some cases, the shutdown rule will accurately and realistically predict when a monopoly will shut down in the short run. In other cases, it will not. Many monopolies produce a vital service, such as transportation or communications, and these monopolies typically operate under government regulation. Suppose the monopoly experiences a temporary upward shift in its AVC curve, say, because the price of a variable input rises. Or suppose it experiences a temporary leftward shift of its demand curve, say, because household income decreases. In either case, if the monopoly suddenly finds that $P < AVC$, government may not allow it to shut down, but instead use tax revenue to make up for the firm's losses.

HTTP://

Macrosoft is a monopoly simulation written by Peter Wilcoxen of the University of Texas. Try it at http://www.eco.utexas.edu/faculty/Wilcoxen/games/macsoft/index.htm.

Long-Run Equilibrium

One of the most important insights of the previous chapter was that perfectly competitive firms *cannot* earn a profit in long-run equilibrium. Profit attracts new firms into the market, and market production increases. This, in turn, causes the market price to fall, eliminating any temporary profit earned by a competitive firm.

But there is no such process at work in a monopoly market, where barriers *prevent* the entry of other firms into the market. Outsiders will *want* to enter an industry when a monopoly is earning above economic profit, but they will be *unable to do so*. Thus, the market provides no mechanism to eliminate monopoly profit.

> *Unlike perfectly competitive firms, monopolies may earn economic profit in the long run.*

What about economic loss? If a monopoly is a government franchise, and it faces the prospect of long-run loss, the government may decide to subsidize it in order to keep it running—especially if it provides a vital service like mail delivery or mass transit. But if the monopoly is privately owned and controlled, it will not tolerate long-run losses. A monopoly suffering an economic loss that it expects to continue indefinitely should always exit the industry, just like any other firm.

> *A privately owned monopoly suffering an economic loss in the long run will exit the industry, just as would any other business firm. In the long run, therefore, we should not find privately owned monopolies suffering economic losses.*

Comparing Monopoly to Perfect Competition

We have already seen one important difference between monopoly and perfectly competitive markets: In perfect competition, economic profit is relentlessly reduced to zero by the entry of other firms; in monopoly, economic profit can continue indefinitely.

But monopoly also differs from perfect competition in another way:

> *We can expect a monopoly market to have a higher price and lower output than an otherwise similar perfectly competitive market.*

To see why this is so, let's explore what would happen if a single firm took over a perfectly competitive market, changing the market to a monopoly. Figure 5 illustrates a competitive market consisting of 100 identical firms. The market is in long-run equilibrium at point *E*, with a market price of $10 and market output of 100,000 units. In panel (b), the typical firm faces a horizontal demand curve at $10, produces output of 1,000 units, and earns zero economic profit.

Now, imagine that a single company buys all 100 firms, to form a monopoly. The new monopoly market is illustrated in panel (c). Under monopoly, the horizontal demand curve facing each firm becomes irrelevant. Instead, the demand curve facing the monolpoly is the downward-sloping *market* demand curve *D*—the same as the market demand curve in panel (a). Since the demand curve slopes downward, marginal revenue will be less than price, and the *MR* curve will lie everywhere below the demand curve. To maximize profit, the monopoly will want to find the output level at which *MC* = *MR*. But what is the new monopoly's *MC* curve?

We'll assume that the monopoly doesn't change the way output is produced: Each previously competitive firm will continue to produce its output with the same technology as before, only now it operates as one of 100 different plants that the monopoly controls. With this assumption, *the monopoly's marginal cost curve will*

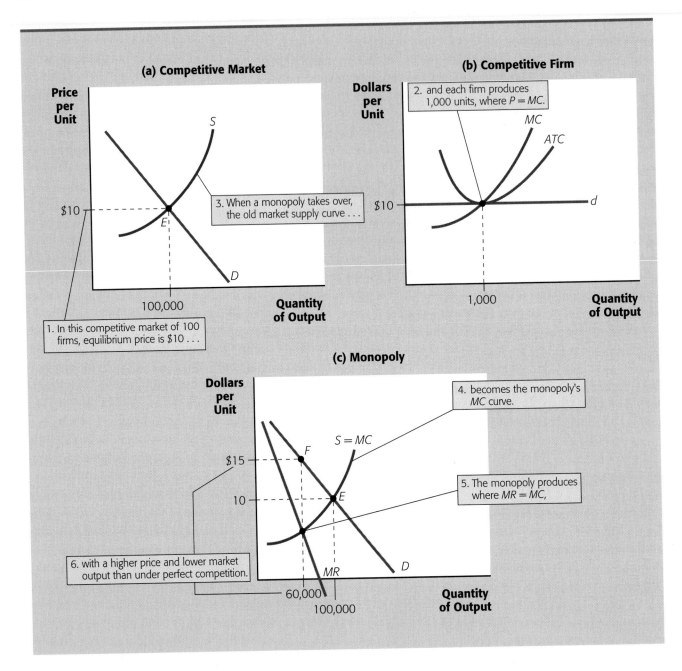

FIGURE 5
Comparing Monopoly and Perfect Competition
Panel (a) shows a competitive market with 100 identical firms. The market price is $10 per unit; at that price, each firm (panel b) sells 1,000 units and earns zero economic profit. A monopolist that buys up all these firms will face the market demand curve D in panel (c). It will produce 60,000 units, where MR = MC. The monopolist produces less than the competitive firms did and charges a higher price ($15 rather than $10).

be the same as the market supply curve in panel (a). Why? First, remember that the market supply curve is obtained by adding up each individual firm's supply curve, that is, each individual firm's marginal cost curve. Therefore, the market supply curve tells us the marginal cost—at *some* firm—of producing another unit of output for the market. When the monopoly takes over each of these individual firms, the market supply curve tells us how much it will cost the monopoly to produce another unit of output at one of its plants. For example, point E on the market supply curve tells us that, when total supply is 100,000, with each plant producing 1,000, increasing output by one more unit will cost the monopoly $10, because that is the marginal cost at each of its plants. The same is true at every other point along the old competitive market supply curve: It will always tell us the monopoly's cost of producing one more unit at one of the plants it now owns. In other words, the upward-sloping curve in panel (c), which is the market supply curve when the market is competitive, becomes the marginal cost curve for a single firm when the market is monopolized. This is why the curve is labeled both S (the old market supply) and MC (the new marginal cost of the monopolist).

Now we have all the information we need to find the monopoly's choice of price and quantity. In panel (c), the monopoly's MC curve crosses the MR curve from below at 60,000 units of output. This will be the monopoly's profit-maximizing output level. To sell this much output, the monopoly will charge $15 per unit—point F on its demand curve.

Notice what has happened in our example: After the monopoly takes over, the price rises from $10 to $15, and market quantity drops from 100,000 to 60,000. The monopoly, compared to a competitive market, would *charge more and produce less.*

Why? Because the monopoly, unlike each competitive firm, faces a downward-sloping demand curve. As a result, for the monopoly, marginal revenue is less than price. (A reminder: When a competitive firm sells another unit of output, it gains the full price as additional revenue. But when a monopoly sells another unit, it must lower the price *not* just on that additional unit, but on *all* units, including those it was previously selling at a higher price. Thus, selling that additional unit will add *less* to the monopoly's revenue than the price of that additional unit.) Therefore, the monopoly will stop increasing its production at a lower level of output than would an industry of perfectly competitive firms. Of course, since the monopoly sells a lower market quantity, it will charge a higher market price.

Now let's see who gains and who loses from the takeover. By raising price and restricting output, the new monopoly earns economic profit. We know this because if the firm were to charge $10—the competitive price—each of its plants would break even, giving it zero economic profit. But we've just seen that $10 is *not* the profit maximizing price—$15 is. So, the firm must make higher profit at $15 than at $10, or higher than zero economic profit. Consumers, however, lose in two ways: They pay more for the output they buy, and, due to higher prices, they buy less output. The changeover from perfect competition to monopoly thus benefits the owners of the monopoly and harms consumers of the product.

Keep in mind, though, an important proviso concerning this result: Comparing monopoly and perfect competition, we see that price is higher and output is lower under monopoly *if all else is equal.* In particular, we have assumed that after the market is monopolized, the technology of production remains unchanged at each previously competitive firm.

But a monopoly may be able to *change* the technology of production, so that all else would *not* remain equal. For example, a monopoly may have each of its new plants *specialize* in some part of the production process, or it may be able to achieve efficiencies in product planning, employee supervision, bookkeeping, or customer relations. If these cost savings enable the monopoly to use a less costly input mix for any given output level, then the monopoly's marginal cost curve in panel (c) would be *lower* than the competitive market supply curve in panel (a). If you add another, lower *MC* curve to panel (c), you'll see that this tends to *decrease* the monopoly's price and *increase* its output level—exactly the reverse of the effects discussed earlier. If the cost savings are great enough, and the *MC* curve drops low enough, a profit-maximizing monopoly could even charge a lower price and produce more output than would a competitive market. (See if you can draw a diagram to demonstrate this case.) The general conclusion is this:

> *The monopolization of a competitive industry leads to two opposing effects. First, for any given technology of production, monopolization leads to higher prices and lower output. Second, changes in the technology of production made possible under monopoly may lead to lower prices and higher output. The ultimate effect on price and quantity depends on the relative strengths of these two effects.*

Why Monopolies Often Earn Zero Economic Profit

The title of this section might puzzle you. We've just seen that in the long run a monopoly can earn economic profit and should never stay in business if it suffers a loss. Then how can it be that monopolies often earn zero profit in the real world? Is it just a coincidence? The answer is no. There are two forces tending to cut monopoly profits.

Government regulation. As discussed earlier, in many cases of natural monopoly, a firm is granted a government franchise to be the sole seller in a market. This has been true of monopolies that provide water service, electricity, and natural gas. In exchange for its franchise, the monopoly must accept government regulation, often including the requirement that it submit its prices to a public commission for approval. The government will want to keep prices high enough to keep the monopoly in business, but no higher. Since the monopoly will stay in business unless it suffers a long-run loss, the ideal pricing strategy for the regulatory commission would be to keep the monopoly's economic profit at zero. Remember, though, that economic profit includes the opportunity cost of the funds invested by the monopoly's owners. If the public commission succeeds, the monopoly's *accounting* profit will be just enough to match what the owners could earn by investing their funds elsewhere—that is, the monopoly will earn zero economic profit. Government regulation of monopoly will be discussed further in Chapter 14.

Rent-seeking activity. Another factor that reduces a monopoly's profit comes from the interplay between politics and economics. As we've seen, many monopolies achieve and maintain their monopoly status due to legal barriers to entry. Even when a monopoly is regulated by government, the regulation may be imperfect, resulting in a higher-than-ideal price.

More important, many monopolies created through government barriers are completely unregulated. For example, a movie theater or miniature golf course may enjoy a monopoly in an area because zoning regulations prevent entry by competitors. Or, especially in less developed countries, a single firm may be granted the exclusive right to sell or produce a particular good even though it is not a natural monopoly. In all of these cases, the monopoly is left free to set its price as it wishes. When regulation is imperfect or when a monopoly is free of regulation, don't we expect it to earn economic profit for its owners?

Not necessarily. Legal barriers to entry—for example, zoning laws—are often controversial because, as you've learned, a monopoly may charge a higher price and produce less output than would a competitive market. Thus, government will be tempted to pull the plug on a monopoly's exclusive status and allow competitors into the market. The monopoly, in turn, will often take action to *preserve* legal barriers to entry. Economists call such actions *rent-seeking activity.*

> *Any costly action a firm undertakes to establish or maintain its monopoly status is called rent-seeking activity.*

Rent-seeking activity Any costly action a firm undertakes to establish or maintain its monopoly status.

In economics, the term *economic rent* refers to any earnings beyond the minimum needed in order for a good or service to be produced. For example, the minimum price to get *land* "produced" is zero, since it's a gift of nature. This is why all the earnings of landowners are called "rent." A monopoly's economic profit is another example of rent, since it represents earnings above the minimum needed in order for the monopoly to stay in business.

In countries with corrupt bureaucracies, rent-seeking activity includes bribes to government officials. In less corrupt governments, it includes the time and money spent lobbying legislators and the public for favorable policies. For example, in 1999, AT&T acquired several cable companies, giving the firm a monopoly on cable television and cable Internet service in millions of homes across the United States. Except for one problem: City governments—before they would approve AT&T as the new operator of their cities' cable service—were demanding that AT&T permit competing Internet service providers, such as AOL and Bell Atlantic, to use their new cable lines. This, of course, would have cut into AT&T's monopoly profits in these cities. As we would predict, AT&T launched a war against these "open access" policies. It spent millions of dollars on lawyers, lobbyists, and public relations firms. It even tried to sway public opinion by helping to fund a lobbying group, "Hands Off the Internet." In Miami for example, AT&T was able to convince 11 of 13 city council members to change their minds and vote against "open access." But as you might guess, AT&T's expenses cut into its monopoly profit.[3]

What is the maximum amount of rent-seeking expenditure a monopoly would be willing to undertake? The answer, as you might guess, is an amount equal to the economic rent the firm is trying to protect. For example, if a firm can preserve $100 million in profit through the passage of a pending bill, it would be willing to pay *up to* $100 million in lobbying expenses. Of course, it may or may not be necessary to pay this much, depending on the nature of the bill and the difficulty in persuading legislators. But we can say this:

> *Rent-seeking activity that helps establish or maintain a firm's monopoly position is part of the firm's costs. As a result, rent-seeking activity can reduce the economic profit of a monpoly and may even reduce it to zero.*

WHAT HAPPENS WHEN THINGS CHANGE?

Once a monopoly is maximizing profit, it has no incentive to change its price or its level of output . . . unless something that affects these decisions changes. In this section, we'll consider two such events: a change in demand for the monopolist's product, and a change in its costs.

---

[3] *Source: Wall Street Journal,* "ATT Used Carrot and Stick Lobbying Efforts in Local Debates over Access to Cable TV Lines," November 24, 1999, p. A20.

An Increase in Demand

Back in Chapter 8, we saw how a competitive market adjusted to a change in demand. In particular, we saw that an increase in demand caused an increase in both market price and market quantity. Does the same general conclusion hold for a monopolist? Let's see.

Panel (a) of Figure 6 shows Zillion-Channel Cable earning a positive profit in the short run. As before, it is producing 10,000 units per month, charging $40 per unit, and earning a monthly profit of $80,000 (not shown). The fact that Zillion-Channel is a monopolist, however, does not mean that it is immune to shifts in demand.

What might cause a monopolist to experience a shift in demand? The list of possible causes is the same as for perfect competition. If you need a reminder of these causes, look back at Figure 3 in Chapter 3. For example, an increase in consumer tastes for the monopolist's good will shift its demand curve rightward, just as it shifts the market demand curve rightward in a competitive market.

Suppose that the demand for local cable service increases because a sitcom shown on one of Zillion-Channel's premium services attracts an enthusiastic following (an increase in tastes for cable services). In panel (b) of Figure 6, this is shown by a rightward shift of the demand curve from D_1 to D_2. Notice that the marginal revenue curve shifts as well, from MR_1 to MR_2. With an unchanged cost structure, the new short-run equilibrium will occur where MR_2 intersects the unchanged MC curve. As you can see, the result is an increase in quantity from 10,000 to 11,000, and a higher price: $47 per month rather than the original $40. In this sense, monopoly markets behave very much like competitive markets (although the *extent* of the rise in price and quantity will generally *not* be the same as in a competitive market). What about the monopolist's profit, though? With both price and quantity now higher, total revenue has clearly increased. But cost is higher as well. So it seems as if profit could either rise or fall.

It turns out, however, that profit *must* be higher in the new equilibrium at point B. We know that because Zillion-Channel has the option of continuing to sell its original quantity, 10,000, at a price higher than before. If, as we assume, it started out earning a profit at that output level, then the higher price would certainly give it an even *higher* profit. But the logic of $MR = MC$ tells us that the greatest profit of all occurs at 11,000 units. We can conclude that:

> *A monopolist will react to an increase in demand by producing more output, charging a higher price, and earning a larger profit. It will react to a decrease in demand by reducing output, lowering price, and suffering a reduction in profit.*

A Cost-Saving Technological Advance

In Chapter 8, we saw that in a perfectly competitive market, all cost savings from a technological advance are passed along to consumers in the form of lower prices. That's not surprising. In the long run, competitive firms always charge a price equal to their minimum possible cost per unit. Therefore, whenever that minimum cost per unit decreases, the price must drop by the same amount.

Now, you've already learned that a monopoly, if it's earning a profit, is charging a price *higher* than its cost per unit. But when a technological advance occurs, will consumers get all the benefits, as they do in perfect competition? Let's see.

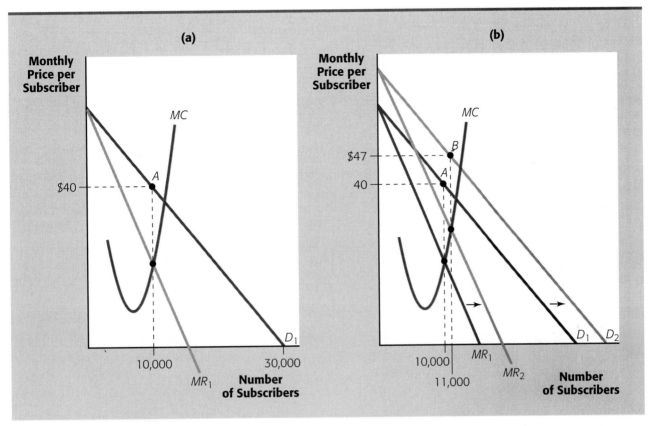

FIGURE 6
A Change in Demand

Panel (a) shows Zillion-Channel in equilibrium. It is providing 10,000 units of cable TV service at a price of $40 per month. Panel (b) shows the same firm following an increase in demand from D_1 to D_2. With the increased demand, MR is higher at each level of output. In the new equilibrium, Zillion-Channel is charging a higher price ($47), providing more TV service (11,000 units), and earning a larger profit.

Suppose a new type of cable box becomes available that breaks down less often, requiring fewer service calls. When Zillion-Channel Cable begins using this equipment, it finds that it gets fewer service calls, so its labor costs decrease by $10 per customer. Figure 7 shows the result. Before the new equipment is used, Zillion-Channel is charging $40 and producing output of 10,000, where its *MR* and *MC* curves cross. The technological advance, when it's distributed to all of Zillion's customers, will lower not only the monthly cost per *current* customer (shifting the *ATC* curve down by $10, which isn't shown), but also the monthly cost of servicing *additional* subscribers. That is, Zillion's *marginal cost* curve will shift down by $10, from MC_1 to MC_2 (which *is* shown). What's the result?

First, Zillion will want to add subscribers, because now, at the original output level of 10,000, *MR* > *MC*. An opportunity to raise profit by increasing output is created. In the figure, the new intersection point between *MC* and *MR* occurs at an output level of 12,000, so that's Zillion's new profit-maximizing output level. The demand curve tells us the price that Zillion will charge at that output level: $38.

So what's happened here? Zillion's cost per subscriber decreased by $10, but its price decreased by only $2 (from $40 to $38). It appears that while consumers do get some benefits from the technological change, they don't get all the benefit. Zillion keeps a chunk of the benefits for itself (the biggest chunk, in our specific example). Further, we know that Zillion's profits have increased. How? Even if it continued producing output of 10,000, the downward shift in its *ATC* curve would

FIGURE 7
Monopoly Profit and Loss

The monopolist's profit is the difference between price and average total cost (ATC) multiplied by the number of units sold. The blue area indicates a profit of $80,000.

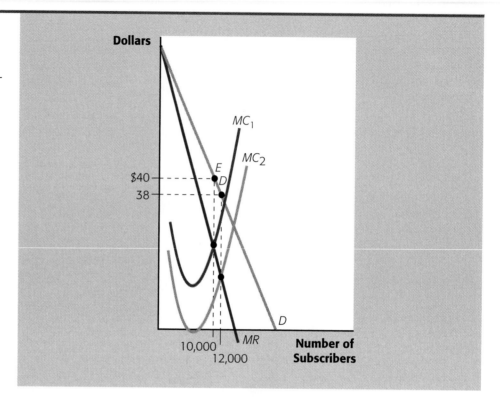

have raised its profit. Then, as output *increases* from 10,000 to 12,000, profit rises further (because *MR > MC* for those moves).

We can summarize our results this way:

> *In general, a monopoly will pass to consumers only part of the benefits from a cost-saving technological change. After the change in technology, the monopoly's profits will be higher.*

This stands in sharp contrast to the impact of technological change in perfectly competitive markets, where—as stated earlier—all of the cost saving is passed along to consumers in the long run.

But there's a silver lining for consumers. Suppose that Zillion's monthly costs *increased* by $10 per subscriber, say, because of a rise in the wage rate needed to maintain its workforce. Figure 7 could be used to analyze this case as well. This time, the *MC* curve would shift *upward* by $10, so we'd view *MC₂* as the initial curve and *MC₁* as the new one. And while the price of cable service would rise, it would rise by *less* than the $10 increase in cost per unit (in our example, price would rise by only $2). Zillion bears part of the burden of the increase in costs, and its profits are reduced.

> *In general, a monopoly will pass only part of a cost increase onto consumers in the form of a higher price. After the cost increase, the monopoly's profits will be lower.*

PRICE DISCRIMINATION

So far, we've analyzed the decisions of a **single-price monopoly**—one that charges the same price on every unit that it sells. But not all monopolies operate this way. For example, local utilities typically charge different rates per kilowatt-hour, depending on whether the energy is used in a home or business. Telephone companies charge different rates for calls made by people on different calling plans. Nor is this multiprice policy limited to monopolies: Movie theaters charge lower prices to senior citizens, airlines charge lower prices to those who book their flights in advance, and supermarkets and food companies charge lower prices to customers who clip coupons from their local newspaper.

Single-price monopoly A monopoly firm that is limited to charging the same price for each unit of output sold.

In some cases, the different prices are due to differences in the firm's costs of production. For example, it may be more expensive to deliver a product a great distance from the factory, so a firm may charge a higher price to customers in outlying areas. But in other cases, the different prices arise not from cost differences, but from the firm's recognition that *some customers are willing to pay more than others:*

> *Price discrimination occurs when a firm charges different prices to different customers for reasons other than differences in costs.*

Price discrimination Charging different prices to different customers for reasons other than differences in cost.

The term *discrimination* in this context requires some getting used to. In everyday language, *discrimination* carries a negative connotation: We think immediately of discrimination against someone because of his or her race, sex, or age. But a price-discriminating monopoly does not discriminate based on prejudice, stereotypes, or ill will toward any person or group; rather, it divides its customers into different categories based on their *willingness to pay* for the good—nothing more and nothing less. By doing so, a monopoly can squeeze even more profit out of the market. Why, then, doesn't *every* firm practice price discrimination?

Requirements for Price Discrimination

Although every firm would *like* to practice price discrimination, not all of them can. To successfully price discriminate, three conditions must be satisfied:

1. *There must be a downward-sloping demand curve for the firm's output.* In order to price discriminate, a firm must be able to raise its price to at least *some* customers without losing their business. A competitive firm cannot price discriminate: If it were to raise its price even slightly to some customers, they would simply buy the identical output from some other firm that is selling at the market price. This is one reason why there is no price discrimination in perfectly competitive markets like those for wheat, soybeans, and silver.

   When a firm faces a downward-sloping demand curve, however, we know that some customers will continue to buy even when the price increases. Monopolies, which face downward-sloping demand curves, always satisfy the downward-sloping demand requirement.

2. *The firm must be able to identify consumers willing to pay more.* In order to determine which prices to charge to which customers, a firm must identify how much different customers are willing to pay. But this is often difficult. Suppose your barber or hairstylist wanted to price discriminate. How would he determine how much you are willing to pay for a haircut? He could *ask* you, but . . . let's be real: You wouldn't tell him the truth, since you know he would only use the

information to charge you more than you've been paying. Price-discriminating firms—in most cases—must be a bit sneaky, relying on more indirect methods to gauge their customers' willingness to pay.

For example, airlines know that business travelers, who must get to their destination quickly, are willing to pay a higher price for air travel than are tourists or vacationers, who can more easily travel by train, bus, or car. Of course, if airlines merely *announced* a higher price for business travel, then no one would admit to being a business traveler when buying a ticket. So the airlines must find some way to identify business travelers without actually asking. Their method is crude but reasonably effective: Business travelers typically plan their trips at the last minute and don't stay over Saturday night, while tourists and vacationers generally plan long in advance and do stay over Saturday. Thus, the airlines give a discount to any customer who books a flight several weeks in advance and stays over, and they charge a higher price to those who book at the last minute and don't stay over. Of course, some business travelers may be able to do advance planning and pay the lower price, and some personal travelers who cannot plan in advance might be priced out of the market. But on the whole, the airlines are able to charge a higher price to a group of people—business travelers—who are willing to pay more.[4]

Catalog retailers—such as Victoria's Secret—have an easily available clue for determining who is willing to pay more: the customer's address. People who live in high-income zip codes are mailed catalogs with higher prices than people who live in lower-income areas. Some Internet retailers have even used software to track customers' past purchases to gauge whether each is a free spender or a careful shopper. Only the careful shoppers get the low prices.[5]

3. *The firm must be able to prevent low-price customers from reselling to high-price customers.* Preventing a product from being resold by low-price customers can be a vexing problem for a would-be discriminator. For example, when airlines began price discriminating, a resale market developed: Business travelers could buy tickets at the last minute from intermediaries, who had booked in advance at the lower price and then advertised their tickets for sale. To counter this, the airlines imposed the additional requirement of a Saturday stayover in order to buy at the lower price. By adding this restriction, the airlines were able to substantially reduce the reselling of low-price tickets to business travelers.

It is often easy to prevent resale of a *service* because of its personal nature. A hairstylist can charge different prices to different customers without fearing that one customer will sell her haircut to another. The same is true of the services provided by physicians, attorneys, and music teachers.

Resale of *goods,* however, is much harder to prevent, since goods can be easily transferred from person to person without losing their usefulness. A classic example of how far a company might have to go to prevent resale of a good is the case of Rohm and Haas, a chemical firm. In the 1940s, Rohm and Haas sold methyl methacrylate powder, used to make durable plastic, at two prices. Indus-

---

[4] It is sometimes argued that airlines' pricing behavior is based entirely on a cost difference to the airline. For example, it is probably more costly for an airline to keep seats available until the last minute, because there is a risk that they will go unsold. The higher price for last-minute bookings would then compensate the airline for the unsold seats. (See, for example, the article by John R. Lott, Jr., and Russell D. Roberts in *Economic Inquiry,* January 1991.) But we know that cost differences are not the only reason for the price differential, or else the airlines would not have added the Saturday stayover requirement, which has nothing to do with their costs.

[5] Woolley, Scott, "I Got It Cheaper than You," *Forbes,* November 2, 1998. For a general discussion of Internet pricing, see Robert E. Hall, *Digital Dealing* (W. W. Norton, 2002).

trial users, who had many other options, paid 85 cents per pound; dental laboratories, which had no other choice of material for making dentures and were willing to pay more, were charged $22 per pound. In spite of Rohm and Haas's diligent efforts to prevent it, this price differential led to a flourishing resale market, in which industrial users were buying methyl methacrylate at 85 cents per pound and selling it for substantially more to dental laboratories. Internal memos at Rohm and Haas revealed that the company, desperate for a solution, considered (but did not finally adopt) a plan to put lead or even arsenic (!) in all powder sold at the lower price so that dental laboratories would be unable to use it.[6]

Effects of Price Discrimination

Price discrimination always benefits the owners of a firm: When the firm can charge different prices to different consumers, it can use this ability to increase its profit. But the effects on consumers can vary. To understand how price discrimination affects the firm and the consumers of its product, let's take a simple example. Imagine that only one company—No-Choice Airlines—offers direct, small-plane flights between Omaha, Nebraska and Salina, Kansas. (What barrier to entry might explain No-Choice's monopoly on this route? If you're stumped, look again at the section on the sources of monopoly in this chapter.)

Figure 8(a) illustrates what No-Choice would do if it could *not* price discriminate and had to operate as a single-price monopoly. Since $MR = MC$ at 30 round-trip tickets per day, No-Choice's profit-maximizing price would be $120 per ticket. The firm's average total cost for 30 round-trips is $80, so its profit per ticket would be $120 − $80 = $40. Total profit is $40 × 30 = $1,200, equal to the area of the shaded rectangle.

Price Discrimination That Harms Consumers. Now suppose that No-Choice discovers that on an average day, 10 of the 30 people buying tickets are business travelers who are willing to pay more, and it can identify them by their *un*willingness to book in advance and stay over on Saturday night. No-Choice could price discriminate by offering two prices: $120 for those who book in advance and stay over on Saturday, and $160 to all others. In effect, No-Choice is raising the price from $120 to $160 for its 10 business customers.

Let's calculate the impact on No-Choice's profit. Since it continues to sell the same 30 round-trip tickets, there is no impact on its costs. Its revenue, however, will rise: It charges $40 more than before on 10 of its round-trip tickets. Thus, No-Choice will earn an additional daily profit of $40 × 10 = $400. This *increase* in profit is identified as the shaded rectangle in Figure 8(b). Total profit is now the sum of two numbers: the profit No-Choice earned *before* price discrimination ($1,200, the area of the shaded rectangle in panel (a)) and the *increase* in profit due to price discrimination ($400, the area of the shaded rectangle in panel (b)). By price discriminating, No-Choice has raised its total profit from $1,200 to $1,600 per day.

What about consumers? Since 10 customers each pay $40 more than before, they lose 10 × $40 = $400 from paying the higher price. Other travelers, who continue to pay $120 for their tickets, are unaffected by the higher price.

[6] From George W. Stocking and Myron W. Watkins, *Cartels in Action: Case Studies in International Business Diplomacy* (New York: The Twentieth Century Fund, 1946), p. 403

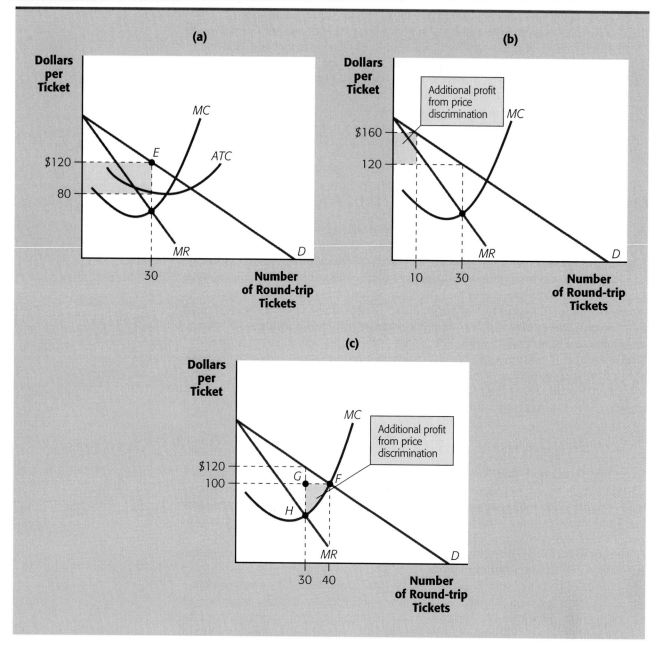

FIGURE 8
Price Discrimination

Panel (a) shows a single-price monopoly airline selling 30 round-trip tickets per day at $120 each and earning a profit of $1,200 per day. Panel (b) shows the same airline if it can charge a higher price to its business travelers. The shaded rectangle shows the additional profit the airline earns by price discriminating; total profit is now $1,600. Panel (c) shows an alternative strategy. In addition to selling 30 regular tickets at $120 each, the airline attracts an additional 10 passengers at a lower student fare of $100. So profit rises by the area of the shaded region.

Summing up, in this case the impact of price discrimination—compared to a single-price policy—is a direct transfer of funds from consumers to the firm. The increase in the firm's profit is equal to the additional payments by consumers. This conclusion applies more generally as well:

> *When price discrimination raises the price for some consumers above the price they would pay under a single-price policy, it harms consumers. The additional profit for the firm is equal to the monetary loss of consumers.*

Price Discrimination That Benefits Consumers. Let's go back to the initial situation facing No-Choice and suppose that, instead of charging a higher price to business travelers, it decides to price discriminate in a different way. No-Choice discovers that students who travel to college in Salina are going by train, because it is cheaper. However, at a price of $100, the airline could sell an average of 10 round-trip tickets per day to the students. No-Choice's new policy is this: $120 for a round-trip ticket, but a special price of $100 for students who show their ID cards. The result is shown in panel (c). Although the decision to sell an additional 10 tickets pushes No-Choice beyond the output level at which *MC = MR,* this is no problem. The *MR* curve was drawn under the assumption that No-Choice charges a single price and must lower the price on all tickets in order to sell more. But this is no longer the case. With price discrimination, the *MR* curve no longer tells us what will happen to No-Choice's revenue when output increases. As you are about to see, the firm will be able to increase its profit by selling the additional tickets.

The reasoning is as follows: No-Choice is now selling 10 *additional* round-trip tickets, so in this case both its cost and its revenue will change. Each additional ticket adds $100 to the firm's revenue; this is the new marginal revenue. Each additional ticket also adds an amount to costs given by the firm's *MC* curve. Thus, the distance between $100 and the *MC* curve gives the *additional profit* earned on each additional ticket, and the total additional profit is the shaded area *HGF* in panel (c) of Figure 8.

What about consumers? The original 30 consumers are unaffected, since their ticket price has not changed. But the new customers—the 10 students—come out ahead: Each is able to take the flight rather than the longer train trip. In this case, price discrimination benefits the monopoly at the same time as it benefits a group of consumers—the students who were not buying the service before, but who *will* buy it at a lower price and gain some benefits by doing so. Since no one's price is raised, no one is harmed by this policy:

> *When price discrimination lowers the price for some consumers below what they would pay under a single-price policy, it benefits consumers as well as the firm.*

Of course, it is possible for a firm to combine *both* types of price discrimination. That is, it could raise the price above what it would charge as a single-price monopoly for some consumers and lower it for others. This kind of price discrimination would increase the firm's profit, while benefiting some consumers and harming others. (For practice, draw a diagram showing the change in total profit if No-Choice were to charge three prices: a basic price of $120, a price of $160 for business travelers, and a price of $100 for students. Who would gain and who would lose?)

Perfect Price Discrimination. Suppose a firm could somehow find out the maximum price customers would be willing to pay for *each* unit of output it sells. Then it could increase its profits even further by practicing *perfect price discrimination:*

Perfect price discrimination
Charging each customer the most he or she would be willing to pay for each unit purchased.

> Under **perfect price discrimination**, a firm charges each customer the most the customer would be willing to pay for each unit he or she buys.

Perfect price discrimination is very difficult to practice in the real world, since it would require the firm to read its customers' minds. However, many real-world situations come rather close to perfect price discrimination. Used-car dealers routinely post a sticker price far higher than the price they think they can actually get and then size up each customer to determine the discount needed to complete the sale. The dealer may look at the customer's clothes and the car the customer is currently driving, inquire about the customer's job, and observe how sophisticated the customer is about cars, all with the aim of determining the maximum price he or she would be willing to pay. A similar sizing up takes place in flea markets, yard sales, and many other situations in which the final price is *negotiated* rather than fixed in advance.

To see how perfect price discrimination works, consider Nancy, who sells Elvis dolls at flea markets. To make our analysis simpler, we'll assume that Nancy has no fixed costs of doing business and that each doll costs her $10 to make, regardless of how many she produces. Thus, Nancy's cost per doll (*ATC*) is $10 at every output level. Further, since each *additional* doll costs $10 to make, her marginal cost (*MC*) is also $10 at any output level. This is why, in Figure 9, both the *MC* and *ATC* curves are the same horizontal line at $10.

Let's first suppose that Nancy is a single-price monopolist, charging a preannounced price on every doll she sells. The figure shows the demand curve she would face on a typical day: At a price of $30 she could sell 20 dolls, at a price of $25 she could sell 30, and so on. Nancy would earn maximum profit by selling 30 dolls per day (why?) and charging $25 each. Her profit per unit would be $25 − $10 = $15—the vertical distance between the *ATC* curve and the demand curve at 30 units. Her total profit would be $15 × 30 dolls = $450 per day, which is equal to the area of the shaded rectangle.

Now, suppose that Nancy becomes especially good at sizing up her customers. She learns how to distinguish true Elvis fanatics (a white, sequined jumpsuit is a dead giveaway) from people who merely want the doll as a gag gift. Moreover, by observing the way people handle the doll and listening to their conversations with their companions, Nancy can discern the exact maximum price each customer would pay. In effect, she knows exactly where on the demand curve each customer would be located. With her new skills, Nancy can increase her profit by becoming a *perfect price discriminator:* For each additional unit along the horizontal axis, she will charge the price indicated by the vertical height of the demand curve.

How many dolls should Nancy sell now? To answer this question, we need to find the new output level at which *MR* = *MC*. But the *MR* curve in the figure is no longer valid: It was based on the assumption that Nancy had to lower the price on *all* units each time she wanted to sell another one. As a perfect price discriminator, she needs to lower the price only on the *additional* unit she sells, and her revenue will rise by the price of that additional unit. For example, if she is currently selling 30 dolls and wants to sell 31, she would lower the price on the additional doll just a tiny bit—say, to $24.50—and in that case, her revenue would rise by $24.50.

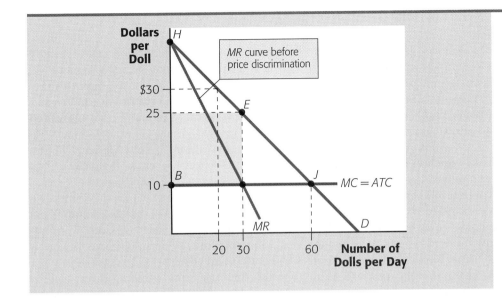

FIGURE 9
Perfect Price Discrimination

The single-price monopolist sells 30 dolls per day at $25 each. With a constant ATC of $10, she earns a profit of $450 per day, as shown by the blue rectangle. However, if she can charge each customer the maximum the customer is willing to pay, shown by the height of the demand curve, she should sell 60 dolls, where MC = P at point J. Her profit would increase to the area of triangle HBJ.

For a perfect price discriminator, marginal revenue is equal to the price of the additional unit sold. Thus, the firm's MR curve is the same as its demand curve.

Now it is easy to see what Nancy should do: Since our requirement for profit maximization is that $MC = MR$, and for a perfect price discriminator, MR is the same as price (P), Nancy should produce where $MC = P$. In Figure 9, this occurs at point J, where the MC curve intersects the demand curve—at 60 units of output. At that point, the only way to increase sales would be to lower the price on an additional doll below $10, but since the marginal cost of a doll is always $10, we would have $P < MC$, and Nancy's profit would decline.

(What is Nancy's profit-maximizing price? Think for a moment. Then see Footnote 7 for the answer.)[7] What about Nancy's total profit? On each unit of output, she charges a price given by the demand curve and bears a cost of $10. Adding up the profit on *all* units gives us the area under the demand curve and above $10, or the area of triangle *HBJ*.

Now we can determine who gains and who loses when Nancy transforms herself from a single-price monopolist to a perfect price discriminator. Nancy clearly gains: Her profit increases, from the shaded rectangle to the larger triangle *HBJ*. Consumers of the product are the clear losers: Since they all pay the most they would willingly pay, no one gets to buy a doll at a price he or she would regard as a "good deal."

A perfect price discriminator increases profit at the expense of consumers, charging each customer the most he or she would willingly pay for the product.

---

[7] Sorry, that's a trick question: There *is* no profit-maximizing price. As a perfect price discriminator, Nancy earns the highest profit by charging *different* prices to different customers.

THE DECLINE OF MONOPOLY?

The past century was not kind to monopolies. In the first half of the century, vigorous antitrust legislation and enforcement broke up many long-standing monopolies, such as Standard Oil in 1911 and Alcoa in 1945. For the rest of the century, many monopolies and would-be monopolies came under the scrutiny of government regulators, and were unable to fully maximize profit. Today, monopolies face a different threat: the relentless advance of technology.

Consider, for example, the natural monopoly of local phone service. The service, which currently takes place over local telephone wires, is characterized by economies of scale: A single company can produce at a lower cost per unit than could several competitors. But soon, cable television companies will have the technology to offer local telephone service over *cable* wires. When this technology is put in place, every household will have two suppliers from which to choose: the existing local phone company *and* the local cable company. At this point, the monopoly status of local telephone companies will come to an end.

Even the old standard of monopolies, the post office, is being threatened by technology. Computerized inventory tracking and fuel-efficient jets have enabled companies such as Federal Express and DHL to offer low-cost overnight letter delivery services, while e-mail and bill paying by phone are cutting into the volume of old-fashioned letters. It is not hard to imagine a time in the future when you will receive all your mail on the Internet, and the notion of *hand-delivered* letters will become a thing of the past, a quaint practice you can tell your children about.

Technology is even threatening the monopolies enjoyed by patent and copyright holders. Almost every college student knows about Napster or its descendants—"sharing services" that enable Internet users to download copyrighted songs from other users, without paying for them. And each time the recording industry defends its intellectual property rights with legal challenges that put one sharing service out of business, another springs up. And the film industry may be next.

Technology is eroding patent protection on physical goods as well. New printing and scanning techniques enable counterfeiters to reproduce exact replicas not only of goods, but also their labels and packaging. The International Chamber of Commerce estimates that 8 percent of all internationally traded goods are counterfeit, and that the percentage is rising rapidly. According to the FBI, U.S. businesses lose more than $200 billion per year from the production and sale of counterfeit products, including clothing, toys, pharmaceuticals, computer hardware, watches, and more. Microsoft alone estimates its losses at about $13 billion per year.[8]

This is not to say that monopolies are taking their last breaths. Just as technological progress weakens some monopolies, it can also help to preserve existing monopolies or create new ones. For example, technology is being called into service to help preserve monopolies created by patents and copyrights, as governments and companies experiment with new techniques for detecting counterfeit products, analogous to those used to detect counterfeit currency.

The latest scientific discoveries may be laying the groundwork for future monopolies in products and services we can't yet imagine. Finally, some small-town

[8] *Source:* "A World of Fakes," *U.S. News and World Report,* July 14, 2003.

monopolies—especially those that provide personal services such as medical care or legal representation—may remain immune to the technological threats. It's safe to say that monopolies in many forms will be with us for some time.

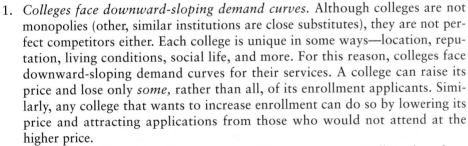

USING THE THEORY
Price Dicrimination at Colleges and Universities

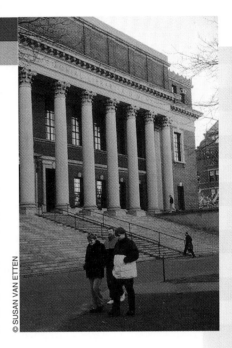

© SUSAN VAN ETTEN

Most colleges and universities give some kind of financial aid to a large proportion of their students. A typical aid package might include outright grants to help pay tuition and room and board, a low-interest loan, and a work-study job on campus. Colleges have many motives for this policy, such as having a more diverse student body and helping to create a better society by making educational services accessible to many who might not otherwise afford them. But increasingly, financial aid has been used as an effective method of price discrimination, designed to increase the revenue of the college. Although colleges are not strictly monopolies, we can use the tools of this chapter to analyze colleges' practice of price discrimination.

How does a college price discriminate? By offering different levels of assistance to different students, financial aid permits the college to charge different *prices* to each one. For example, if full tuition is $12,000 per year, then a student who receives a yearly $5,000 grant pays only $7,000 per year, a student who receives an $8,000 grant pays only $4,000 per year, and so on.

Colleges have long been in an especially good position to benefit from price discrimination, because they satisfy all three requirements:

1. *Colleges face downward-sloping demand curves.* Although colleges are not monopolies (other, similar institutions are close substitutes), they are not perfect competitors either. Each college is unique in some ways—location, reputation, living conditions, social life, and more. For this reason, colleges face downward-sloping demand curves for their services. A college can raise its price and lose only *some,* rather than all, of its enrollment applicants. Similarly, any college that wants to increase enrollment can do so by lowering its price and attracting applications from those who would not attend at the higher price.
2. *Colleges are able to identify consumers willing to pay more.* Colleges have long been in an excellent position to discover how much their customers would be willing to pay for their product. Applicants for financial aid have had to submit data on their families' income and wealth. Admissions officials know that students from poor families are less likely to attend their institutions, unless they are offered a relatively low price, while students from wealthier families are more likely to attend even at higher prices. In recent years, however, colleges have gone even further in their attempts to identify willingness to pay. (See below.)
3. *Colleges are able to prevent low-price customers from reselling to high-price customers.* A college education is much like other personal services: Once you pay for it, you cannot resell it to another person. The result is vastly different prices for different students, highly correlated to their families' willingness to pay.

TABLE 1
Actual Payments for a Year at Williams (2001–2002)

Quintile	Income Range	Actually Paid
Low	$ 0–$23,593	$ 1,683
Lower-Middle	$ 23,594–$40,931	$ 5,186
Middle	$ 40,932–$61,397	$ 7,199
Upper-Middle	$ 61,398–$91,043	$13,764
High	$91,044 and above	$22,013

Note: The offical tuition was equal to $32,470.

A recent study of price differentials at Williams College serves as a good example.[9] Table 1 is based on data for 827 students who received financial aid at Williams during the 2001–2002 academic year, when the "official price" was $32,470 (full tuition, room, board, and fees). The first column identifies the quintile in the U.S. population in which each student would be ranked, by family income. The second column identifies the income range associated with each quintile. The third provides the amount *actually* paid by the average student in each quintile: the official price for a year at Williams *minus* any financial aid provided in the form of outright grants. You can see that those with the highest incomes (and therefore, on average, the greatest willingness to pay) were charged an average of $22,013, while those in the lowest group paid only $1,683 for the year.[10]

Most colleges have been active price discriminators for decades. But many stepped up their efforts in the 1990s when Congress changed the formula used to determine financial need, making most students eligible for assistance. This allowed colleges to allocate financial aid dollars among a wider pool of students. Suddenly, price discrimination could be used even more extensively. But this required new methods of identifying willingness to pay among different students.

The market responded. Specialized consultants, using computer models to predict the likelihood that students would attend college at different prices, began offering their services. One consultant's pamphlet asked admissions officials, "Did you overspend to get students who would have matriculated with lesser aid? Did you underspend and lose students who would have come with more support?"[11]

As a result, during the 1990s the traditional role of financial aid as assistance for those in need has changed. Some colleges have shifted aid dollars toward top-ranked applicants, regardless of financial need, because those students have more options and are less likely to attend any college without financial aid. Drexel University in Philadelphia shifted aid toward those who applied as business majors after a computer model predicted that these students' enrollment decisions were more sensitive to price. Johns Hopkins University shifted aid dollars to humanities majors with SAT scores above 1200 and relatively low financial need, based on a similar model.

[9] Catherine B. Bill and Gordon C. Winston, "Access: Net Prices, Affordability, and Equity at a Highly Selective College," December 2001, *Williams Project on the Economics of Higher Education,* Discussion Paper No. 62.
[10] Notice that none of the groups in the table paid the "full price" of $32,470. But students who were not in the sample (because they did not receive financial aid from Williams) may have paid this price.
[11] "Colleges Manipulate Financial-Aid Offers, Shortchanging Many," *Wall Street Journal,* April 1, 1996, p. 1. The specific examples of price discrimination in the discussion also come from this article. See also "Price Wars on Campus," *Washington Post,* October 15, 2002, p. A1.

Carnegie-Mellon went even further. It determined the effect on student "yield" (the percentage of students with certain characteristics who will actually enroll) of shifting aid dollars from one group to another. In addition, the school asked students who had been admitted to fax the school any better financial aid offers they received, so it could decide whether to match the offer from a special "reaction fund."

Many financial aid consultants have even recommended that colleges shift aid money away from students who come for on-campus interviews, since by doing so, those students reveal a strong desire to attend the college. There are rumors that some institutions have followed this advice, but no college has admitted to the practice.

More effective price discrimination at colleges and universities is certainly changing the traditional view of financial assistance as a program designed primarily to help those in need. And while it has benefited some groups of students, it has harmed others. Under the newer systems, those who can signal a lower willingness to pay have benefited from reduced prices, while those signaling greater willingness to pay have suffered a price increase.

But fully assessing the effects of price discrimination at colleges is complicated by one important fact: Most educational institutions are not private firms striving to maximize profits for their owners. Rather, they are *nonprofit* institutions, *without* private owners. Thus, any additional revenue they gain through price discrimination is likely to be used for educational purposes: to attract better faculty by raising salaries, to improve living conditions for students, to keep tuition from rising even faster, and even to provide increased aid for more students in the future. Each of these alternatives has value to the college and its students, suggesting that increased price discrimination at colleges, like so many other economic issues, is a matter of trade-offs.

Summary

A *monopoly firm* is the only seller of a good or service with no close substitutes. Monopoly arises because of some barrier to entry: economies of scale, legal barriers, or network externalities. As the only seller, the monopoly faces the market demand curve and must decide what price (or prices) to charge in order to maximize profit.

Like other firms, a single-price monopolist will produce where $MR = MC$ and set the maximum price consumers are willing to pay for that quantity. Monopoly profit ($P - ATC$ multiplied by the quantity produced) can persist in the long run because of barriers to entry. However, there are reasons why monopolies often earn zero long-run profit. These reasons include government regulation and rent seeking.

All else equal, a monopoly charges a higher price and produces less output than a perfectly competitive market. When demand for a monopoly's product increases, it will raise prices and increase production. When a monopoly's marginal costs decrease, it will pass only part of the cost savings on to consumers.

Some monopolies can practice *price discrimination* by charging different prices to different customers. Doing so requires the ability to identify customers who are willing to pay more and to prevent low-price customers from reselling to high-price customers. Price discrimination always benefits the monopolist (otherwise, it would charge a single price), but it *may* sometimes benefit some consumers.

Key Terms

Copyright
Government franchise
Monopoly firm
Monopoly market

Network externalities
Patent
Perfect price discrimination
Price discrimination

Rent-seeking activity
Single-price monopoly

Review Questions
Answers to even-numbered Questions and Problems can be found on the text Web site at http://hall-lieb.swlearning.com.

1. Why is it sometimes difficult to decide whether a particular firm is a monopoly? Which U.S. markets are often considered to exemplify monopoly?

2. Why do monopolies arise? Discuss the most common factors that explain the existence of a monopoly.

3. How can the government create a monopoly? Why might the government want to do this?

4. Drunk with power, the CEO of Monolith, Inc., a single-price monopoly, assumes that he can set any price he wants and sell as many units as he wants at that price. Is he correct? Why or why not?

5. True or false? "A firm's marginal cost curve is always its supply curve." Explain.

6. Why might the decision to shut down be different for a monopoly than for a perfectly competitive firm?

7. Why might a monopoly earn an economic profit in the long run? How does this differ from the situation faced by a perfectly competitive firm?

8. Explain why, if a monopoly takes over all the firms in a perfectly competitive industry, its marginal cost curve will be the same as the perfectly competitive industry's supply curve.

9. Firm A maximizes profit at an output of 1,000 units, where Price = 50 and MC = 50. Firm B maximizes profit at an output of 2,000 units, where Price = 5 and MC = 3. Which firm is likely to be a monopoly and which perfectly competitive? Explain your reasoning.

10. How do output and price for a monopoly compare with output and price if the same market were perfectly competitive?

11. In the long run, a monopoly can earn positive economic profit; in the real world, monopolies often don't. Explain this apparent paradox.

12. Explain the difference between a single-price monopoly and a price-discriminating monopoly. What conditions must be present in order for a monopoly to price discriminate? Explain why each condition is necessary.

13. True or false? "Price discrimination by a monopoly always harms consumers." Explain.

Problems and Exercises

1. In a certain large city, hot dog vendors are *perfectly competitive,* and face a market price of $1.00 per hot dog. Each hot dog vendor has the following total cost schedule:

Number of Hot Dogs per Day	Total Cost
0	$63
25	73
50	78
75	88
100	103
125	125
150	153
175	188
200	233

a. Add a *marginal cost* column to the right of the total cost column. (*Hint:* Don't forget to divide by the *change* in quantity when calculating MC.)

b. What is the profit-maximizing quantity of hot dogs for the typical vendor, and what profit (loss) will he earn (suffer)? Give your answer to the nearest 25 hot dogs.

One day, Zeke, a typical vendor, figures out that if he were the only seller in town, he would no longer have to sell his hot dogs at the market price of $1.00. Instead, he'd face the following demand schedule:

Price per Hot Dog	Number of Hot Dogs per Day
> $6.00	0
6.00	25
5.50	50
4.00	75
3.25	100
2.75	125
2.25	150
1.75	175
1.25	200

c. Add *total revenue* and *marginal revenue* columns to the table above. (*Hint:* Once again, don't forget to divide by the *change* in quantity when calculating MR.)

d. As a monopolist with the cost schedule given in the first table, how many hot dogs would Zeke choose to sell each day? What price would he charge?

e. A lobbyist has approached Zeke, proposing to form a new organization called "Citizens to Eliminate Chaos in Hot Dog Sales." The organization will lobby the city council to grant Zeke the only hot dog license in town, and it is guaranteed to succeed. The only problem is, the lobbyist is asking for a payment that amounts to $200 per business day as long as Zeke stays in business. On purely economic grounds, should Zeke go for it? (*Hint:* If you're stumped, re-read the section on rent-seeking activity.)

2. Draw the demand curve for a perfectly competitive firm and for a monopoly, showing the *MR* curve as well as the demand curve on each graph.
   a. In each case, what is the relationship between demand in the market as a whole and demand for an individual firm's output?
   b. For both graphs, explain the position of the *MR* curve in relation to the demand curve.

3. a. Draw demand, *MR*, and *ATC* curves that show a monopoly that is just breaking even.
   b. Redraw your graph from part (a). Show what will happen in the short run if the prices of the firm's variable inputs rise.
   c. Redraw your graph from part (a). Show what will happen in the short run if the prices of the firm's variable inputs fall.

4. Draw the *MR* and demand curves for a perfect price discriminator. How does the *MR* curve for a perfect price discriminator differ from that for a single-price monopoly?

5. Below is demand and cost information for Warmfuzzy Press, which holds the copyright on the new best-seller, *Burping Your Inner Child.*

Q (No. of Copies)	P (per Book)	ATC (per Book)
100,000	$100	$20
200,000	$ 80	$15
300,000	$ 60	$16⅔
400,000	$ 40	$22½
500,000	$ 20	$31

   a. Determine what quantity of the book Warmfuzzy should print, and what price it should charge in order to maximize profit.
   b. What is Warmfuzzy's maximum profit?
   c. Prior to publication, the book's author renegotiates his contract with Warmfuzzy. He will receive a great big hug from the CEO, along with a one-time bonus of $1,000,000, payable when the book is published. This payment was not part of Warmfuzzy's original cost calculations.
   How many copies should Warmfuzzy publish now? Explain your reasoning.

6. Look at Figure 8(c). Clearly, *MR* = *MC* at point *H*. But when the airline sells discount tickets to college students, it is at point *F*, apparently violating the rule that *MR* = *MC*. Does this mean that for a price-discriminating monopoly, *MR* = *MC* doesn't hold? Explain.

7. A doctor in a rural area faces the following demand schedule:

Price per Office Visit	Number of Office Visits per Day
$200	2
$175	3
$150	5
$125	8
$100	12
$ 75	18
$ 50	23
$ 25	25

The doctor's marginal cost of seeing patients is a constant $50 per patient.
   a. If the doctor must charge all patients the same price, what price will she charge, and how many patients will she see each day?
   b. If the doctor can perfectly price discriminate, how many patients will she see each day?

8. You are thinking about tutoring students in economics, and your research has convinced you that you face the following demand curve for your services:

Price per Hour of Tutoring	Number of Students Tutored per Week
> $50	0
$40	1
$35	2
$27	3
$26	4
$20	5
$15	6
< $15	6

Each student who hires you gets one hour of tutoring per week. You have decided that your time and effort is worth $25 per hour and that you will not tutor anyone for less than that.
   a. Suppose you are wary that your students might talk to each other about the price you charge, so you decide to charge them all the same price. Determine (1) how many students you will tutor; (2) what price you will charge; and (3) your weekly earnings from tutoring.
   b. Now suppose you discover that your students don't know each other, and you decide to perfectly price discriminate. Once again, determine (1) how many students you will tutor; (2) what price you will charge; and (3) your weekly earnings from tutoring.

Now suppose that your city requires all tutors to get a license, at a cost of $1,300 per year ($25 per week).
   c. Does it make sense for you to buy this license and be a tutor if you must charge each student the same price? Explain.
   d. Does it make sense for you to buy the license and be a tutor if you can perfectly price discriminate? Explain.

9. Suppose that price discrimination were made illegal, across the board. Who would benefit and who would be harmed? Choose an example with which you are familiar and try to determine both the short-run and long-run effects of banning price discrimination in that case.

10. Draw demand, *MR*, *AVC*, and *ATC* curves that show a monopolist that is operating while incurring an economic loss. Show how a technological change could keep this monopolist from shutting down, first if the change affected only the monopolist's fixed costs, and then if the change affected only its variable costs.

11. Answer the following:
    a. Complete the following table and use it to find this monopolist's short-run profit-maximizing level of output. How much profit will this firm earn?
    b. Redo the table to show what will happen to the short-run profit-maximizing level of output if the monopolist's marginal costs rise by $1 at each level of output. How much profit will the firm earn now?

c. Redo the original table to show what will happen to the short-run profit-maximizing level of output if the monopolist's marginal costs fall by $0.40 at each level of output. How much profit would the firm earn in this case?

d. A change in the price of what kind of input would result in a change in marginal cost?

Output	Price	Total Revenue	Marginal Revenue	Total Cost	Marginal Cost	Profit
0	$5.60			$ 0.50		
1	$5.50			$ 3.50		
2	$5.40			$ 5.45		
3	$5.30			$ 6.45		
4	$5.20			$ 6.90		
5	$5.10			$ 8.90		
6	$5.05			$13.40		
7	$4.90			$20.40		

Challenge Questions

1. Are there any circumstances under which a monopoly will sell at the same price as would a perfectly competitive firm selling the same product? Explain.

2. Let a single-price monopoly's demand curve be given by $P = 20 - 4Q$, where P is price and Q is quantity demanded. Marginal revenue is $MR = 20 - 8Q$. Marginal cost is $MC = Q^2$. How much should this firm produce in order to maximize profit?

3. In the short run, a monopoly uses both fixed and variable inputs to produce its output.

a. Draw a diagram to illustrate why, if the price of using a fixed input rises, there will be no change in the monopoly's equilibrium price or quantity. (*Hint:* Which curves shift if the price of a fixed input rises? Which curves remain unaffected?)

b. Redraw your graph from part (a). Show what will happen in the short run if the prices of the firm's fixed inputs rise.

c. Redraw your graph from part (a). Show what will happen in the short run if the prices of the firm's fixed inputs fall.

 **ECONOMIC** *Applications*   These exercises require access to Hall/Lieberman Xtra! If Xtra! did not come with your book, visit http://hallxtra.swlearning.com to purchase.

1. Use your Xtra! password at the Hall and Lieberman Web site (http://hallxtra.swlearning.com) and under Economic Applications click on EconNews. Select *Microeconomics: Monopoly,* and read the article, "Dentsply Monopoly: A Test of Antitrust Law's Teeth." Then go to EconDebate and again select *Microeconomics: Monopoly.* Find the debate, "Is Microsoft a Monopoly?" Why did the Department of Justice accuse each firm of being a monopoly if they have other competitors in their market? Does this satisfy the definition of monopoly as given in this chapter? Why or why not?

2. Use your Xtra! password at the Hall and Lieberman Web site (http://hallxtra.swlearning.com) and under Economic

Applications click on EconNews. Select *Microeconomics: Monopoly,* and read the article summary "Companies Find Variety of Prices to Be the Spice of Life." Answer the following questions:
   a. Why is a menu of prices for the same good more profitable for a monopolist than a posted "no-haggle" price?
   b. How does this phenomenon of price discrimination relate to elasticity of demand, as discussed in Chapter 5?
   c. How can an online firm like Amazon.com engage in price discrimination if it cannot see you to determine what price to charge you?

Monopolistic Competition and Oligopoly

On any given day, you are probably exposed to hundreds of advertisements. The morning newspaper announces special sales on clothes, computers, and paper towels. On the way to class, you might see numerous billboards competing for your attention, suggesting that you stay at the Holiday Inn, eat at Burger King, or organize your life with a Palm Pilot. You will likely spend more time watching advertisements for breakfast cereals on television than you will spend eating them. And as you search for information on the World Wide Web, ads for video cameras, credit cards, and Internet access providers flash before your eyes. No doubt about it: Advertising is everywhere in the economy.

Yet, so far in this book, not much has been said about advertising. There is a good reason for this: In the two market structures we have studied so far—perfect competition and monopoly—firms do little, if any, advertising. Indeed, perfectly competitive firms *never* advertise, since there is no point to it. Each firm in a competitive industry produces the same product as any other, so what would they advertise? And in any case, each firm can sell all it wants at the market price, so advertising would only raise costs without any benefit to the firm. Monopolists *sometimes* advertise, but—as the only seller of a good with no close substitutes—they are under no pressure to do so.

Where, then, is all the advertising coming from? To answer this question, we must look beyond the market structures we've studied so far and consider firms that are neither perfect competitors nor monopolists. That is what we will do in this chapter. While advertising is one interesting feature we will explore, there are many others as well.

THE CONCEPT OF IMPERFECT COMPETITION

In perfect competition, there are so many firms selling the same product that none of them can affect the market price. In monopoly, there is just *one* seller in the market, so it sets the price as it wishes. Most markets for goods and services, however, are neither perfectly competitive nor perfectly monopolistic. Instead, they lie somewhere *between* these two extremes, with more than one firm, but not enough firms to qualify for perfect competition. We call such markets *imperfectly competitive:*

> Imperfect competition *refers to market structures between perfect competition and monopoly. In imperfectly competitive markets, there is more than one seller, but too few to create a perfectly competitive market. In addition, imperfectly competitive markets often violate other conditions of perfect competition, such as the requirement of a standardized product or free entry and exit.*[1]

Consider the market for automobiles in the United States. It is certainly not a monopoly, since more than a dozen companies sell cars here: General Motors, Ford, DaimlerChrysler, Mazda, Toyota, Honda, Volvo, Nissan, and several more. But neither is this market perfectly competitive: Each of these firms supplies a relatively large part of the market, so each can affect the market price. Moreover, the product of each firm is different from the products of the others: A Toyota is not a Ford, and a Ford is not a Jeep. The market for automobiles, then, falls somewhere between the extremes of monopoly and perfect competition.

Or consider restaurants. Even a modest-size city such as Cincinnati has more than 3,000 different restaurants. This is certainly a large number of competitors, but they are not *perfect* competitors, since each one sells a product that is differentiated in important ways—in the type of food served, the recipes used, the atmosphere, the location, and even the friendliness of the staff.

In this chapter, we study two types of imperfectly competitive markets: *monopolistic competition* and *oligopoly.*

MONOPOLISTIC COMPETITION

Suppose you live in a midsize or large city, and you're embarking on a night out with some friends. As you head out in your car, you notice the gas tank is almost empty. You pass several gas stations, then find one that's not too expensive but doesn't have a line of cars waiting. After filling up, you pick up your friends, and a

---

[1] Imperfect competition is sometimes defined as *any* market structure other than perfect competition, which would include monopoly.

lively discussion ensues because everyone wants to go to a different pizza place. Finally, after some cajoling and compromising, you head across town to your group's choice. Over dinner, you all decide to see a movie. But that leads to another discussion: which multiplex to go to. One has the advantage of being closest, but the good movies there always sell out. A second has better popcorn, but it's impossible to park. And a third has great parking, but it's a 20-minute drive.

Although most people—not taking an economics course—would have no reason to notice, all of your purchases that night would have something in common. The gas station, the restaurant, and the movie theater all operate under a market structure called *monopolistic competition.*

As the name suggests, monopolistic competition is a hybrid of perfect competition and monopoly, sharing some of the features of each. Specifically,

> *a monopolistically competitive market has three fundamental characteristics:*
> 1. *many buyers and sellers;*
> 2. *sellers offer a differentiated product; and*
> 3. *sellers can easily enter or exit the market.*

If you compare this list of characteristics with the list for perfect competition (in Chapter 8), you'll notice that the first and last items are shared by both market structures. The second item is new, but it leads to a feature shared with monopoly. Let's examine each of these characteristics in turn.

Many Buyers and Sellers. In *perfect* competition, the existence of many buyers and sellers played an important role: ensuring that no individual buyer or seller could influence the market price. In monopolistic competition, the "many traders" assumption plays the same role on the buying side: an individual *buyer* has no influence on the price he pays. But an individual seller, in spite of having many competitors, *decides* on what price to charge (as you'll soon see).

Our assumption of many sellers, however, has another purpose: to ensure that no *strategic games* will be played among firms in the market. That is, when a firm under monopolistic competition makes a decision (about price, advertising, product guarantees, etc.), it does *not* take into account how other firms will react. There are so many firms, each supplying such a small part of the market, that no one of them needs to worry that its actions will be noticed—and reacted to—by the others.

Restaurants in most cities satisfy this requirement. With so many other restaurants, when one decides whether to offer an early-bird special, or advertise in the local paper, or put flyers under windshields, it usually doesn't worry how the other restaurants in the city will react.[2]

Sellers Offer a Differentiated Product. In perfect competition, sellers offer a standardized product. In *monopolistic competition,* by contrast, each seller produces a somewhat different product from the others. No two coffeehouses, photocopy

Monopolistic competition A market structure in which there are many firms selling products that are differentiated, and in which there is easy entry and exit.

---

[2] Monopolistic competitors do imitate the successful decisions of others in the market, as you'll see in a few pages. But a monopolistic competitor does not take into account the *potential* for imitation when making a decision. In the second half of this chapter, when we study oligopoly, we'll examine what happens when firms *do* take into account the potential reactions of their rivals.

shops, or food markets are exactly the same. For this reason, a monopolistic competitor can raise its price (up to a point) and lose only *some* of its customers. The others will stay with the firm because they like its product, even when it charges somewhat more than its competitors. Thus, a monopolistic competitor faces a *downward-sloping demand curve* and, in this sense, is more like a monopolist than a perfect competitor:

> *Because it produces a differentiated product, a monopolistic competitor faces a downward-sloping demand curve: When it raises its price a modest amount, quantity demanded will decline—but not all the way to zero.*

What makes a product differentiated? Sometimes, it is the *quality* of the product. By many objective standards—longevity, performance, frequency of repair—a Toyota is a better car than a Volkswagen. Similarly, based on room size and service, the Hilton has better hotel rooms than Motel 6. In other cases, the difference is a matter of taste rather than quality. In terms of measurable characteristics, Colgate toothpaste may be neither better nor worse than Crest, but each has its own flavor and texture, and each appeals to different people.

Another type of differentiation arises from differences in *location*. Two bookstores may be identical in every respect—range of selection, atmosphere, service—but you will often prefer the one closer to your home or office.

Ultimately, though, product differentiation is a subjective matter: A product is different whenever people *think* that it is, whether their perception is accurate or not. You may know, for example, that all bottles of bleach have identical ingredients—5.25 percent sodium hypochlorite and 94.75 percent water. But if *some* buyers think that Clorox bleach is different and would pay a bit more for it, then Clorox bleach is a differentiated product.

Thus, whenever a nonmonopoly firm faces a downward-sloping demand curve, we know buyers perceive its product as differentiated. This perception may be real or illusory, but the economic implications are the same in either case: The firm *chooses* its price.

Easy Entry and Exit. This feature is shared by monopolistic competition and perfect competition, and—as you'll see—it plays the same role in both: ensuring that firms earn zero economic profit in the long run. Remember that "easy entry" does *not* mean that entry is effortless or inexpensive. Rather, it means that you can open up, say, a pizza place if you're willing to bear the same costs that existing pizza places must bear. There are no significant *barriers* to entry that keep out newcomers—no law, for example, that new pizza places must pay higher annual license fees than established ones.

In monopolistic competition, however, our assumption about easy entry goes further: Nothing stops a firm from copying the successful business practices of other firms. If one movie theater finds that offering lower prices for Wednesday-afternoon showings generates economic profit, any other movie theater can do the same. If Circuit City's four-year replacement plan for electronic goods brings it profit, then every other electronic goods retailer can choose to offer the same plan. While it may take time, success will eventually lead to imitation. You'll see that this extended view of entry—specific to monopolistic competition—plays a role in ensuring zero economic profit in the long run.

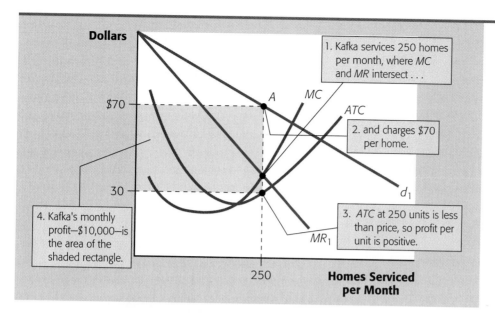

Dollars

1. Kafka services 250 homes per month, where *MC* and *MR* intersect . . .

$70 — — — — — — — — — — A

MC

ATC

2. and charges $70 per home.

30 — — — — — — — — — — — — — — — —

d_1

4. Kafka's monthly profit—$10,000—is the area of the shaded rectangle.

3. *ATC* at 250 units is less than price, so profit per unit is positive.

MR_1

250

Homes Serviced per Month

FIGURE 1
A Monopolistically Competitive Firm in the Short Run

Monopolistic Competition in the Short Run

The individual monopolistic competitor behaves very much like a monopoly. Its constraints are its given production technology, the prices it must pay for its inputs, and the downward-sloping demand curve that it faces. And, like any other firm, its goal is to maximize profit by producing where $MR = MC$. The result may be economic profit or loss in the short run.

The key difference is this: While a monopoly is the *only* seller in its market, a monopolistic competitor is one of many sellers. When a *monopoly* raises its price, its customers must pay up or buy less in the market. When a *monopolistic competitor* raises its price, its customers have one additional option: They can buy a similar good from some other firm. Thus, all else equal, the demand curve facing a firm should be flatter under monopolistic competition than under monopoly. That is, since closer substitutes are available under monopolistic competition than under monopoly, a given rise in price should cause a greater fall in quantity demanded.

Figure 1 illustrates the situation of a monopolistic competitor, Kafka Exterminators. The figure shows the demand curve, d_1, that the firm faces, as well as the marginal revenue, marginal cost, and average total cost curves. As a monopolistic competitor, Kafka Exterminators competes with many other extermination services in its local area. Thus, if it raises its price, it will lose some of its customers to the competition. If Kafka had a *monopoly* on the local extermination business, we would expect the same rise in price to cause a smaller drop in quantity demanded, since customers would have to buy from Kafka or else get rid of their bugs on their own.

Like any other firm, Kafka Exterminators will produce where $MR = MC$. As you can see in Figure 1, when Kafka faces demand curve d_1 and the associated marginal revenue curve MR_1, its profit-maximizing output level is 250 homes served per month, and its profit-maximizing price is $70 per home. In the short run, the firm may earn an economic profit or an economic loss, or it may break

FIGURE 2
A Monopolistically Competitive Firm in the Long Run

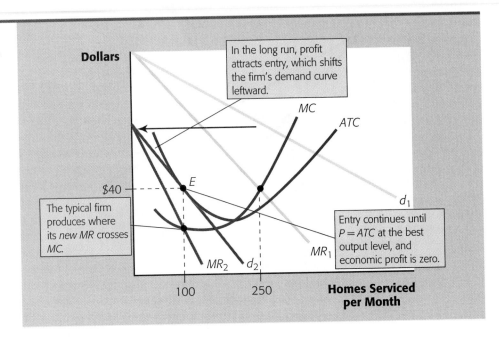

even. In the figure, Kafka is earning an economic profit: Profit per unit is $P - ATC$ = \$70 - \$30 = \$40, and total monthly profit—the area of the blue rectangle—is \$40 × 250 = \$10,000.

Monopolistic Competition in the Long Run

If Kafka Exterminators were a monopoly, Figure 1 might be the end of our story. The firm would continue to earn economic profit forever, since barriers to entry would keep out any potential competitors. But under monopolistic competition—in which there are no barriers to entry and exit—the firm will not enjoy its profit for long. As new sellers enter the market, attracted by the profits that can be earned there, some of Kafka's customers will sign up with the new entrants. At any given price, Kafka will find itself servicing fewer homes than before, and the demand curve it faces will shift leftward. Entry will continue to occur, and the demand curve will continue to shift leftward, until Kafka and other firms are earning zero economic profit. This process of adjustment is shown in Figure 2. As the demand curve shifts leftward (from d_1 to d_2), the marginal revenue curve shifts left as well (from MR_1 to MR_2). Why is this? First, a leftward shift in demand is also a *downward* shift in demand: Now that is has more competitors, Kafka must charge a lower price than before in order to sell any given quantity. But if price is lower, then—starting at any quantity—selling an *additional* unit will *add less* to total revenue than it did before. Thus, at any output level, marginal revenue is lower than before—a downward shift in the MR curve. And, as you can see in the figure, a downward shift in the MR curve is also a leftward shift of that curve.

Kafka's new profit-maximizing output level, 100, is found at the intersection point between its marginal cost curve and its *new* marginal revenue curve. Kafka's new price—found on its demand curve d_2 at 100 units—is \$40. Finally, since ATC is also \$40 at that output level, Kafka is earning zero economic profit—the best it can do in the long run.[3] In long-run equilibrium, the profit-maximizing price, $40, will always equal the average total cost of production.

We can also reverse these steps. If the typical firm is suffering an economic loss (draw this diagram on your own), *exit* will occur. With fewer competitors, those firms that remain in the market will gain customers, so their demand curves will shift *rightward*. Exit will cease only when the typical firm is earning zero economic profit, at point E in Figure 2. Thus, point E represents the long-run equilibrium of the typical firm whether we start from a position of economic profit or economic loss:

> *Under monopolistic competition, firms can earn positive or negative economic profit in the short run. But in the long run, free entry and exit will ensure that each firm earns zero economic profit, just as under perfect competition.*

Is this prediction of our model realistic? Indeed it is: In the real world, monopolistic competitors often earn economic profit or loss in the short run, but, given enough time, profits attract new entrants and losses result in an industry shakeout, until firms are earning zero economic profit. In the long run, restaurants, retail stores, hair salons, and other monopolistically competitive firms earn zero economic profit for their owners. That is, there is just enough accounting profit to cover the implicit costs of doing business, which is just enough to keep the owners from shifting their time and money to some alternative enterprise.

Think of your own city or town. Has a certain kind of business been springing up everywhere? Is another type of business gradually disappearing? If you look around, you will see entry and exit occurring, as monopolistically competitive markets adjust from short-run to long-run equilibrium.

Excess Capacity Under Monopolistic Competition

Look again at Figure 2, which shows Kafka's long-run equilibrium, at point E, after entry has eliminated its profits. When Kafka earns zero economic profit, its demand curve touches, but does not cross, its ATC curve. This will be true for *any* monopolistic competitor in the long run. To see why, draw a diagram right now (you can use the margin of this page) that shows the demand curve actually *crossing* the ATC curve. If you do this correctly, you will find that at *some* output levels, price is greater than ATC, and the firm can earn economic profit by producing there. But such profit would attract entry, so we would not yet be in long-run equilibrium.

In Figure 2, you can see that in long-run equilibrium (point E), the ATC curve has the same slope as the demand curve, a *negative* slope. Thus, in the long run, a monopolistic competitor always produces on the *downward-sloping* portion of its ATC curve and therefore *never produces at minimum average cost*. Indeed, its output level is always *too small* to minimize cost per unit. The firm operates with *excess capacity*. (The output level at which cost per unit is minimized is often called capacity output.) In Figure 2, Kafka Exterminators *would* reach minimum cost per

---

[3] Other things may also happen as the industry expands. For example, the increased demand for inputs may raise or lower the typical firm's ATC and MC curves, depending on whether we are dealing with an increasing- or decreasing-cost industry. (See Chapter 8.) This does not change our result, however: Entry into the market will continue until the typical firm earns zero economic profit, even if its MC and ATC curves have shifted.

unit by servicing about 200 homes per month (the firm's capacity output), but in the long run, it will service only 100 homes per month.

> *In the long run, a monopolistic competitor will operate with excess capacity—that is, it will produce too little output to achieve minimum cost per unit.*

To see why a monopolistic competitor *cannot* minimize average cost in the long run, imagine that Kafka Exterminators wanted to do so, by servicing 200 homes per month. With its current demand curve, it would suffer a loss, since $P < ATC$ at that output level. But there might be another way for Kafka: Perhaps it can buy out one of its competitors and take over its business. Then Kafka's demand and marginal revenue curves would lie farther to the right (you may want to draw this), and the company—by producing more—might be able to achieve minimum (or at least lower) per-unit costs. But while this might work in the short run, it cannot work in the long run. With its new demand curve and its lower cost per unit, Kafka would earn a profit. In the long run, profit would attract entry, and Kafka would be back where it started.

This example gives us another way to view excess capacity: In the long run, there are *too many* firms under monopolistic competition, each one producing too little output, to achieve minimum cost per unit. If there were fewer firms, then each could reduce its cost per unit, but the situation would not last. Each firm would earn a profit, profit would cause entry, entry would force each firm to reduce its output, and in the long run, there would once again be too many firms producing too little output to minimize average cost.

Excess capacity is easy to observe. Think of the suburban shopping mall with a dozen or more clothing stores. Much of the time, one or more of the stores has no customers. Or think of most of the restaurants in your town. How often are they all fully occupied, even at peak hours? In each case, serving more customers would bring down cost per unit, but this would require fewer firms, which—as we know—there cannot be in the long run.

Excess capacity suggests that monopolistic competition is costly to consumers, and indeed it is. Recall that under perfect competition, P = minimum ATC in long-run equilibrium. (Look back at Figure 9 in Chapter 8.) But under monopolistic competition, P > minimum ATC in the long run. Thus, if the ATC curves were the same, price would always be greater under monopolistic competition.

This reasoning may tempt you to leap to a conclusion: Consumers are better off under perfect competition. But don't leap so fast. Remember that in order to get the beneficial results of perfect competition, all firms must produce identical output. It is precisely because monopolistic competitors produce *differentiated* output—and therefore have downward-sloping demand curves—that P > minimum ATC in the long run. And consumers usually *benefit* from product differentiation. (If you don't think so, imagine how you would feel if every restaurant in your town served an identical menu, or if everyone had to wear the same type of clothing, or if every rock group in the country performed the same tunes in exactly the same way.) Seen in this light, we can regard the higher costs and prices under monopolistic competition as the price we pay for product variety. Some may argue that there is too much variety in a market economy—how many different brands of toothpaste do we really need?—but few would want to transform all monopolistically competitive industries into perfectly competitive ones.

HTTP://

For a fascinating analysis of trends in product differentiation see The Federal Reserve Bank of Dallas's 1998 Annual Report, "The Right Stuff: America's Move to Mass Customization." You can find it at the Bank's Web site (http://www.dallasfed.org).

Nonprice Competition

If a monopolistic competitor wants to increase its output, one way is to cut its price. That is, it can move *along* its demand curve. But a price cut is not the only way to increase output. Since the firm produces a differentiated product, it can sell more by convincing people that its own output is better than that of competing firms. Such efforts, if successful, will *shift* the firm's demand curve rightward.

> *Any action a firm takes to increase the demand for its output—other than cutting its price—is called* **nonprice competition.**

Nonprice competition Any action a firm takes to increase the demand for its product, other than cutting its price.

Better service, product guarantees, free home delivery, more attractive packaging, as well as advertising to inform customers about these things, are all examples of nonprice competition. Fast-food restaurants are notorious for nonprice competition. When Burger King says, "Have it your way," the company is saying, "Our hamburgers are better than those at McDonald's because *we* make them to order." When McDonald's responds with an attractive, fresh-faced young woman behind the counter, smiling broadly when you order a Happy Meal, it is saying, in effect, "So what if we don't make your burgers to order; our staff is better looking and more upbeat than Burger King's."

Nonprice competition is another reason why monopolistic competitors earn zero economic profit in the long run. If an innovative firm discovers a way to shift its demand curve rightward—say, by offering better service or more clever advertising—then in the *short run*, it may be able to earn a profit. This means that other, less innovative firms will experience a leftward shift in *their* demand curves, as they lose sales to their more innovative rival.

But not for long. Remember that in monopolistic competition, the "free entry" assumption includes the ability of new entrants, as well as existing firms, to copy the successful business practices of others. If product guarantees are enabling some firms to earn economic profit, then *all* firms will offer product guarantees. If advertising is doing the trick, then *all* firms will start ad campaigns. In the long run, we can expect *all* monopolistic competitors to run advertisements, to be concerned about service, and to take whatever actions have proven profitable for other firms in the industry. All this nonprice competition is costly—one must *pay* for advertising, for product guarantees, for better staff training—and these costs must be included in each firm's *ATC* curve, shifting it upward. But none of this changes our conclusion that monopolistic competitors will earn zero economic profit in the long run.

Indeed, nonprice competition strengthens our conclusions. In the short run, a firm may earn profit because it has relatively few competitors or because it has discovered a new way to attract customers. But in the long run, the profitable firm will find its demand curve shifting leftward due to the entry of new firms, or the imitation of its successful nonprice competition, or both. In the end, each firm will find itself back in the situation depicted in Figure 2. Because of the costs of nonprice competition, each firm's *ATC* curve will be higher than it would otherwise be. However, it will still touch, but not cross, the demand curve, and the firm will still earn zero economic profit. We will take a closer look at one form of nonprice competition, advertising, in the "Using the Theory" section at the end of the chapter.

OLIGOPOLY

A monopolistic competitor enjoys a certain amount of independence. There are so many *other* firms selling in the market—each one such a small fish in such a large pond—that each of them can make decisions about price and quantity without worrying about how the others will react. For example, if a single pharmacy in a large city cuts its prices, it can safely assume that any other pharmacy that could benefit from price cutting has already done so, or will shortly do so, *regardless of its own actions*. Thus, there is no reason for the price-cutting pharmacy to take the reactions of other pharmacies into account when making its own pricing decisions.

But in some markets, most of the output is sold by just a few firms. These markets are not monopolies (there is more than one seller), but they are not monopolistically competitive either. There are so few firms that the actions taken by any one will *very much* affect the others and will likely generate a response. For example, more than 60 percent of the automobiles sold in the United States are made by one of the "Big Three": General Motors, Ford, and DaimlerChrysler. If GM were to lower its price in order to increase its output, then Ford and Chrysler would suffer a significant drop in their own sales. They would not be happy about this and would probably respond with price cuts of their own. GM's output, in turn, would be affected by the price cuts at Ford and Chrysler.

When just a few large firms dominate a market, so that the actions of each one have an important impact on the others, it would be foolish for any one firm to ignore its competitors' reactions. On the contrary, in such a market, each firm recognizes its *strategic interdependence* with the others. Before the management team makes a decision, it must reason as follows: "If we take action *A,* our competitors will do *B,* and then we would do *C,* and they would respond with *D . . . ,*" and so on. This kind of thinking is the hallmark of the market structure we call *oligopoly:*

Oligopoly A market structure in which a small number of firms are strategically interdependent.

> An **oligopoly** is a market dominated by a small number of strategically interdependent firms.

There are many different types of oligopolies. The output may be more or less identical among firms, such as copper wire, or differentiated, such as laptop computers. An oligopoly market may be international, as in the market for automobile tires; mostly national, as in the market for breakfast cereals; or local, as in the market for some daily newspapers. There may be one dominant firm whose share of the market far exceeds all the others, such as Nike, which manufactured 39 percent of all athletic shoes in 2002—more than three times the output of the next largest firm (Reebok). Or there may be two or more large firms of roughly similar size, like Boeing and Airbus in the global market for large passenger aircraft. You can see that oligopoly markets can have different characteristics, but in all cases, *a small number of strategically interdependent firms produce the dominant share of output in the market.*

Oligopoly in the Real World

While defining an oligopoly in theory is straightforward, *applying* the definition to real-world markets raises a host of problems. This is not just a matter of semantics. The extent to which a market follows the oligopoly model—with market dominance by a few firms—is at the heart of public policy toward market structure, a subject we'll examine more closely in Chapter 14.

What's so hard about identifying oligopoly in the real world?

Market Definition. In oligopoly, a few large firms dominate *the market*. But whether a real-world market will satisfy this definition depends on how we define the market itself. With a narrow enough definition, *any* market seems a candidate. For example, "the market for pizza places within a half-mile of the civic center" will have very few firms, so might be considered an oligopoly. But with a broad enough definition, *no* market will fit the oligopoly model. For example, although four firms produce about 70 percent of all athletic shoes sold in the United States, they produce only a small fraction of "all U.S. footwear."

In many cases, common sense provides a sufficient guideline: We should broaden the market definition *just enough* to include all reasonably close substitutes. Thus, we refer to the market for breakfast cereal rather than the market for food, which would be too broad, or the market for cornflakes, which would be too narrow. We refer to the market for steel rather than the market for metal, too broad, or the market for six-inch steel ingots, too narrow.

But in some cases, common sense isn't definitive. Consider what happened in March 2003, when Nestlé (whose product line includes Häagen-Dasz ice cream) announced that it planned to acquire Dreyer's (maker of several premium ice cream brands). In the market for "premium ice cream," Nestlé's acquisition would give it a 60 percent share—a level of dominance by one firm that should raise eyebrows. In the market for "all ice cream," however, Nestlé's share would be significantly smaller, barely enough to elicit a yawn. The question is: Are regular and premium ice cream "close enough" substitutes that our market definition should include both? The government said no: It defined the market as "premium ice cream," and insisted that Dreyer's sell of some of its premium lines as a condition for approving the merger. But the government's view was not the only reasonable one.

Number of Firms. Oligopoly requires that a *few firms* dominate the market. Even if we can agree on a market's definition, what number qualifies as "a few"? Certainly 3 or 4. But is 7 firms too many? How about 12? In theory, we require a number small enough that each firm considers the reactions of its rivals when making decisions, that is, small enough to create strategic interdependence. A market with just 3 large firms will certainly display strong interdependence. As we consider markets with 5, or 10, or 15 firms, interdependence will diminish. At *some* point, the number of firms is so large, and interdependence so weak, that oligopoly becomes a poor description, and monopolistic competition would fit better. But there is no absolute number at which oligopoly ends and monopolistic competition begins.

Market Domination. Strategic interdependence requires that a few firms—whatever their number—*dominate* the market; that is, their share of the market is large. This is needed for strategic interaction among firms. If, for example, the four largest firms together had a 15 percent share of the market, each would be too small to significantly affect the others. But if their combined market share were 90 percent, and all were roughly the same size, then decisions by any one would have huge impacts on the others; strategic interaction would be intense. But what if the combined market share were 70 percent? Or 50 percent? As the number shrinks, strategic interdependence becomes weaker.

* * *

You can see that oligopoly is a matter of degree, not an absolute classification. We can imagine a spectrum: At one end are industries in which a very small number of firms produce a large share of the output. In these industries, there is strong strategic interdependence among firms, so our ideas about oligopoly will fit very closely. As we proceed along the spectrum, market domination by the largest firms decreases, strategic interdependence declines, and oligopoly analysis has less to contribute to our understanding of firm and market behavior.

Why Oligopolies Exist

Oligopoly firms do not always earn economic profit in the long run, but even when they do, entry into the market does not occur—a few large firms continue to dominate the industry. Thus, our search for the origin of oligopolies is really a search for the specific *barriers to entry* that keep out competitors and maintain the dominance of just a few firms. What are these barriers?

Economies of Scale: Natural Oligopolies. In Chapter 6, you learned that economies of scale can limit the number of firms that can survive in a market. (If you need to refresh your memory, look back at panel (c) of Figure 9 in that chapter.) When the minimum efficient scale (MES) for a typical firm is a relatively large percentage of the market, a large firm, supplying a large share of the market, will have lower cost per unit than a small firm. Since small firms can't compete, only a few large firms survive, and the market becomes an oligopoly. And because this tends to happen on its own unless there is government intervention, such a market is often called a **natural oligopoly**, analogous to natural monopoly. Airlines, college textbook publishers, and passenger jet manufacturers are all examples of oligopolies in which economies of scale play a large role.

Natural oligopoly A market that tends naturally toward oligopoly because the minimum efficient scale of the typical firm is large fraction of the market.

Reputation as a Barrier. A new entrant may suffer just from being new. Established oligopolists are likely to have favorable reputations. In many oligopolies—like the markets for soft drinks and breakfast cereals—heavy advertising expenditure has also helped to build and maintain brand loyalty. A new entrant might be able to catch up to those already in the industry, but this may require a substantial period of high advertising costs and low revenues. In some cases, where the potential profits are great, investors may decide it is worth the risk and accept the initial losses in order to enter the industry. Ted Turner took such a risk and sustained several years of losses before his cable ventures (Cable News Network, Turner Network Television, and Turner Broadcasting System) earned a profit. But in other industries, the initial losses may be too great and the probability of success too low for investors to risk their money starting a new firm.

Strategic Barriers. Oligopoly firms often pursue strategies designed to keep out potential competitors. They can maintain excess production capacity as a signal to a potential entrant that, with little advance notice, they could easily saturate the market and leave the new entrant with little or no revenue. They can make special deals with distributors to receive the best shelf space in retail stores or make long-term arrangements with customers to ensure that their products are not displaced quickly by those of a new entrant. And they can spend large amounts on advertising to make it difficult for a new entrant to differentiate its product.

Legal Barriers. Patents and copyrights, which can be responsible for monopoly, can also create oligopolies. For example, all three government-approved drugs commonly prescribed to treat symptoms of Alzheimer's disease are still protected by patents. Until these patents expire, or several new drugs are developed, the market for Alzheimer's drugs will continue to be an oligopoly consisting of just three large pharmaceutical companies.

Like monopolies, oligopolies are not shy about lobbying the government to preserve their market domination. One of the easiest targets is foreign competition. U.S. steel companies are relentless in their efforts to limit the amount of foreign—especially Japanese—steel sold in the U.S. market. In the past, they have succeeded in getting special taxes on imported steel and financial penalties imposed upon successful foreign steel companies. Other U.S. industries, including automobiles, textiles, and lumber, have had similar successes.

Legal barriers can operate against *domestic* entrants, too. Zoning regulations may prohibit the building of a new supermarket, movie theater, or auto repair shop in a local market, preserving the oligopoly status of the few firms already established there. Lobbying by established firms is often the source of these restrictive practices.[4]

Oligopoly Versus Other Market Structures

Of the market structures you have studied in this book, oligopoly presents the greatest challenge to economists. In the other types of markets—perfect competition, monopoly, and monopolistic competition—each firm acts independently, without worrying about the reactions of other firms. The firm's task is a simple one: to select an output level along its demand curve that gives it maximum profit.

But this approach doesn't describe an oligopolist. The essence of oligopoly, remember, is *strategic interdependence,* wherein each firm anticipates the actions of its rivals when making decisions. Thus, we cannot analyze one firm's decisions in isolation from other firms. In order to understand and predict behavior in oligopoly markets, economists have had to modify the tools used to analyze the other market structures and to develop entirely new tools as well.

Let's look at an example of strategic interdependence more closely and see why the tools we've used to analyze the other market structures will not work for oligopoly. Remember Kafka Exterminators? Because it was a monopolistic competitor, it could raise or lower its price, and move along its demand curve, without having to worry that it would cause a change in a *substitute's price.* But what if Kafka had been an oligopolist—say, one of two exterminators in a small town? Then, if Kafka lowered its price, the location of its demand curve would *depend on* the actions of its rival. If the rival chose *not* to change its price, Kafka's demand curve would stay put. But if the rival lowered its price to match Kafka's, Kafka's demand curve would shift leftward—because a substitute good (the services of Kafka's rival) had decreased. Thus, Kafka could not predict whether it would end up on its old demand curve or some new one without taking into account how its competitor would *react* to its decision. Kafka could not use the simple $MR = MC$ rule, because the position of Kafka's MR curve—like the position of its demand curve—would depend on the reaction of its rival. You

---

[4] This kind of lobbying is often disguised. In July 1995, Home Depot, Inc., sued Rickel Home Centers for secretly forming an organization called Concerned Citizens for Community Preservation, whose sole purpose was to prevent Home Depot from opening new stores in towns where Rickel already had its own outlets (*The Wall Street Journal*, August 18, 1995, p. 1).

Game theory An approach to modeling the strategic interaction of oligopolists in terms of moves and countermoves.

can see why oligopoly presents such a challenge, not only to the firms themselves, but also to economists studying them. However, one approach, called **game theory,** has yielded rich insights into oligopoly behavior.

The Game Theory Approach

The word *game* applied to oligopoly decision making might seem out of place. Games—like poker, basketball, or chess—are usually played for fun, and even when money is at stake, the sums are usually small. What do games have in common with important business decisions, where hundreds of millions of dollars and thousands of jobs may be at stake?

In fact, quite a bit. In all games—except those of pure chance, such as roulette—a player's strategy must take account of the strategies followed by other players. This is precisely the situation of the oligopolist. Game theory analyzes oligopoly decisions as if they were games by looking at the rules players must follow, the payoffs they are trying to achieve, and the strategies they can use to achieve them.

HTTP://

The prisoner's dilemma game is the prototype for thinking about game theory in economics. Visit Bryn Mawr College's interactive prisoner's dilemma game at http://serendip.brynmawr.edu/~ann/pd.html to try it out.

The Prisoner's Dilemma. The easiest way to understand how game theory works is to start with a simple, noneconomic example—the prisoner's dilemma—that explains why a technique for obtaining confessions, commonly used by police, is so often successful. Imagine that two partners in crime (let's call them Rose and Colin) have committed a serious offense (say, murder) but have been arrested for a lesser offense (say, robbery). The police have enough evidence to ensure a robbery conviction, but their evidence for murder cannot be used in court. Their only hope for a murder conviction is to get one or both partners to incriminate the other.

The traditional strategy is to separate the partners and explain the following to each one: "Look, you're already facing a five-year sentence for robbery. But we'll offer you a deal: If you confess to the murder and implicate your partner, and your partner does *not* confess, we'll make sure that the D.A. goes easy on you. You'll get three years, tops. If you and your partner *both* confess, we'll send you each away for 20 years. But if your partner confesses, and you do *not,* we'll send *you* away for 30 years."

Payoff matrix A table showing the payoffs to each of two players for each pair of strategies they choose.

Each partner in this situation is a *player* in a *game,* and Figure 3 shows the **payoff matrix** for this game, a listing of the payoffs that each player will receive for each possible combination of strategies the two might select. The payoff matrix presents a lot of information at once, so let's take it step-by-step.

First, notice that each *column* represents a strategy that Colin might choose: confess or not confess. Second, each *row* represents a strategy that Rose might select: confess or not confess. Thus, each of the four boxes in the payoff matrix represents one of four possible strategy combinations that might be selected in this game:

1. Upper left box: Both Rose and Colin confess.
2. Lower left box: Colin confesses and Rose doesn't.
3. Upper right box: Rose confesses and Colin doesn't.
4. Lower right box: Neither Rose nor Colin confesses.

For centuries, police investigators have used the logic of the prisoner's dilemma game to outsmart partners in crime.

Let's now look at the game from Colin's point of view. The green-shaded entries shown in each box are Colin's possible *payoffs:* jail sentences. (Ignore the orange-shaded entries for now.) For example, the lower left square shows that when Colin confesses and Rose does not, Colin will receive just a three-year sentence.

© JAMES SHAFFER/PHOTOEDIT, INC.

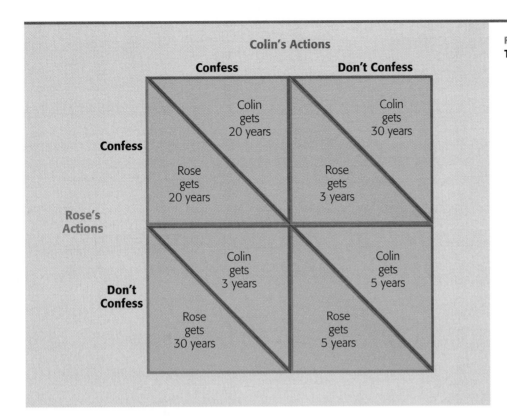

FIGURE 3
The Prisoner's Dilemma

Colin wants the best possible deal for himself, but he is not sure what his partner will do. (Remember, they are in separate rooms.) So Colin first asks himself which strategy would be best *if* his partner were to confess. The *top row* of the matrix guides us through his reasoning: "If Rose decides to confess, my best choice would be to confess, too, because then I'd get 20 years rather than 30." Next, Colin determines the best strategy if Rose does *not* confess. As the *bottom row* shows, he'll reason as follows: "If Rose does not confess, my best choice would be to confess, because then I'd get 3 years rather than 5."

Let's recap: If Rose confesses, Colin's best choice is to confess; if Rose does *not* confess, Colin's best choice is—once again—to confess. Thus, regardless of Rose's strategy, Colin's best choice is to confess. In this game, the strategy "confess" is an example of a *dominant strategy:*

> A ***dominant strategy*** *is a strategy that is best for a player regardless of the strategy of the other player.*

Dominant strategy A strategy that is best for a player no matter what strategy the other player chooses.

If a player has a dominant strategy in a game, we can safely assume that he will follow it.

What about Rose? In another room, she is presented with the *same* set of options and payoffs as her partner, as shown by the orange entries in the payoff matrix. When Rose looks down each *column*, she can see her possible payoffs for each strategy that Colin might follow. As you can see (and make sure that you can, by going through all the possibilities), Rose has the same dominant strategy as Colin: confess. We can now predict that *both* players will follow the strategy of confessing and that the outcome of the game—the upper left-hand corner—is a confession from both partners, with each receiving a 20-year sentence.

The outcome of this game is an example of a *Nash equilibrium,* appropriately named after the mathematician John Nash, who originated the concept. (Nash won the Nobel Prize in economics in 1994, and was the subject of the film *A Beautiful Mind.*)

> **Nash equilibrium** A situation in which every player of a game takes the best action for themselves, given the actions taken by all other players.

> *A **Nash equilibrium** exists when each player is taking the best action for herself, given the actions taken by all other players.*[5]

Note that the Nash equilibrium is not necessarily the best possible outcome for either player. For example, in Figure 3, both Rose and Colin would do even better by moving from the Nash equilibrium to the outcome in the lower right corner. But this outcome—5 years in prison for each of them—requires that each *not* confess. And that is highly unlikely in the situation we're describing. For example, if Rose refuses to confess, hoping Colin will do likewise, she gives Colin an even *greater* incentive to confess: he would get just a 3-year sentence, the best result of all. Rose would know this. She would also know that, if Colin *does* betray her, she'll get 30 years—the *worst* possible for her. So unless each player abandons narrow self-interest *and* has confidence that the other player is doing the same, they cannot move to the lower right corner; the Nash equilibrium will, in fact, be the outcome.

Simple Oligopoly Games. The same method used to understand the behavior of Rose and Colin in the prisoner's dilemma can be applied to a simple oligopoly market. Imagine a town with just two gas stations: Gus's Gas and Filip's Fillup. This is an example of an oligopoly with just two firms, called a **duopoly.** We assume that Gus and Filip, like Rose and Colin in the prisoner's dilemma, must make their decisions independently, without knowing in advance what the other will do.

> **Duopoly** An oligopoly market with only two sellers.

Figure 4 shows the payoff matrix facing each duopolist, where—to keep things simple—each player is limited to two possible actions: charging a high price or a low price for his gas. The columns of the matrix represent Gus's possible strategies, while the rows represent Filip's strategies. Each square shows a possible payoff, yearly profit, for Gus (shaded green) and Filip (shaded orange). (Make sure you can see, for example, that if Gus sets a high price and Filip sets a low price, then Gus will suffer a loss of $10,000 while Filip will enjoy a profit of $75,000.)

The payoffs in the figure follow a logic that we find in many oligopoly markets: Each firm will make greater profit if all firms charge a higher price. But the best situation for any one firm is to have its rivals charge a high price, while *it alone* charges a low price and lures customers from the competition. The worst situation

---

[5] Don't try to connect the concept of a Nash equilibrium to the scene early in *A Beautiful Mind,* in which Russell Crowe explains to his friends at Princeton that if they agree *not* to compete for the same woman, they could all be better off. This speech combined the concept of Nash equilibrium among self-interested players with other concepts Nash wrote about, related to *cooperation.* We'll get to cooperation shortly.

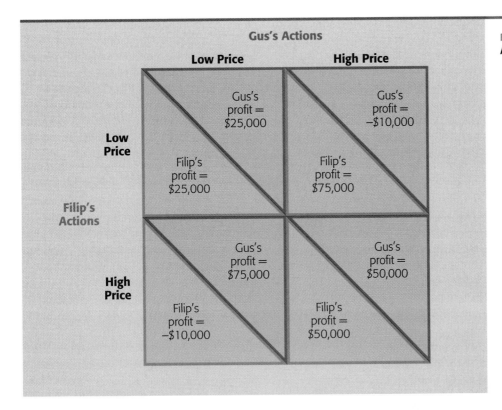

FIGURE 4
A Duopoly Game

for any one firm is to charge a high price while its rivals charge a low one, for then it will lose much of its business to its rivals.

The entries in the payoff matrix in Figure 4 reflect this situation: Profits are higher ($50,000) for both Gus and Filip when they both charge a high price and lower ($25,000) when they both charge a low price. But when the two follow different strategies, the low-price firm gets the best possible payoff ($75,000), while the high-price firm gets the worst possible payoff (−$10,000).

Let's look at the game from Gus's point of view, using the green-shaded entries in the payoff matrix. If Filip chooses a low price (the top row), then Gus should choose a low price, too, since this will get him a $25,000 profit instead of a $10,000 loss. If Filip selects a high price (the bottom row), then, once again, Gus should choose a low price, since this will get him a profit of $75,000 rather than $50,000. Thus, no matter what Filip does, Gus's best move is to charge a low price—his *dominant* strategy.

A similar analysis from Filip's point of view, using the orange-shaded entries, would tell us that his dominant strategy is the same: a low price. Thus, the outcome of this game is the box in the upper left-hand corner, where both players charge a low price and each earns a profit of $25,000.

Notice that our outcome—like the outcome of the prisoner's dilemma—is a Nash equilibrium. Once Gus and Filip reach the upper left-hand corner, each is doing the best that he can do, given what the other is doing. Therefore, as long as each is acting in his own self-interest, neither has any incentive to change. The equilibrium price in the market—where it will come to rest—is the low price.

Oligopoly Games in the Real World. While our simple example helps us understand the basic ideas of game theory, real-world oligopoly situations are seldom so simple. First, there will typically be more than two strategies from which to choose (for example, a variety of different prices or several different amounts to spend on *nonprice* competition such as advertising). Also, there will usually be more than two players, so a two-dimensional payoff matrix like the one in Figure 4 would not suffice. Still, as long as each firm has a dominant strategy, we can predict the outcome of the game—the Nash equilibrium—although we might need the help of a computer in the more complex cases.

Second, in some games, one or more players may *not* have a dominant strategy. For example, if we alter just one entry in the figure, changing Gus's payoff of $75,000 (lower left-hand box) to $40,000, Gus would no longer have a dominant strategy. To see why, draw the revised payoff matrix. (Take a moment to do this before reading on.) If you've drawn the revised matrix correctly, you should be able to verify the following: If Filip charges a low price, Gus should charge a low price; but if Filip charges a high price, Gus should charge a high price. Thus, Gus's best choice depends on Filip's choice. However, since we have not changed any of Filip's payoffs, he still has a dominant strategy: to charge a low price. Since Gus *knows* that Filip will select a low price, Gus will always select a low price, too. We know, therefore, exactly where these two station owners will end up: both charging the low price. This example, and the previous one in which *both* players have a dominant strategy, leads to the following conclusion:

> *A game with two players will have a Nash equilibrium as long as* at least one *player has a dominant strategy, whether the other has a dominant strategy or not.*

But what if we *also* change Filip's payoff of $75,000 (upper right-hand corner) to $40,000? Then, as you can verify, *neither* player will have a dominant strategy, so predicting a competitor's strategy can be more of a challenge. Moreover, we, as outside observers, would need a more sophisticated analysis to predict an outcome to the game.

Finally, in our example, we've limited the players to *one* play of the game. While this might make sense in the prisoner's dilemma—where the players get only one chance to make a decision—it is not realistic for most oligopoly markets. In reality, for gas stations and almost all other oligopolies, there is **repeated play,** where both players select a strategy, observe the outcome of that trial, and play the game again and again, as long as they remain rivals. Repeated play can fundamentally change the way players view a game and lead to new strategies based on long-run considerations. One possible result of repeated trials is *cooperative behavior,* to which we now turn.

Repeated play A situation in which strategically interdependent sellers compete over many time periods.

Cooperative Behavior in Oligopoly

In the real world, oligopolists will usually get more than one chance to choose their prices. Pepsi and Coca-Cola have been rivals in the soft drink market for most of this century, as have Ford, DaimlerChrysler, and GM in the automobile market and Kellogg, Post (Kraft Foods), Quaker, and General Mills in the breakfast cereal market. These firms can change their strategies based on the responses of their rivals.

The equilibrium in a game with repeated plays may be very different from the equilibrium in a game played only once. Often, firms will evolve some form of *cooperation* in the long run.

For example, look again at Figure 4. If this game were played only once, we would expect each player to pursue its dominant strategy, select a low price, and end up with $25,000 in yearly profit. But there is a better outcome for both players. If each were to charge a high price, each would make a profit of $50,000 per year. If Gus and Filip remain competitors year after year, we would expect them to realize that by cooperating, they would both be better off. And there are many ways for the two to cooperate.

Explicit Collusion. The simplest form of cooperation is **explicit collusion**, in which managers meet face to face to decide how to set prices. In our example, Gus and Filip might strike an agreement that each will charge a high price, moving the outcome of the game to the lower right-hand corner in Figure 4, where each earns $50,000 in yearly profit instead of $25,000.

Explicit collusion Cooperation involving direct communication between competing firms about setting prices.

The most extreme form of explicit collusion is the creation of a **cartel**—a group of firms that tries to maximize the total profits of the group as a whole. To do this, the group of firms behaves as if it were a monopoly, treating the market demand curve as the "monopoly's" demand curve. Then, it finds the point on the demand curve—the price and quantity of output—that maximizes total profit. Each member is instructed to charge the agreed-upon price (cartels are often called *price-fixing* agreements), and each is allotted a share of the cartel's total output. This last step is crucial: If any member produces and sells more than its allotted portion, then the group's total *output* rises and the price will fall below the agreed-upon profit maximizing price.

Cartel A group of firms that selects a common price that maximizes total industry profits.

The most famous cartel in recent years has been OPEC—the Organization of Petroleum Exporting Countries—which meets periodically to influence the price of oil by setting the amount that each of its members can produce. In the mid-1970s, OPEC quadrupled its price per barrel in just two years, leading to a huge increase in profits for the cartel's members. In the late 1990s, OPEC exerted its muscle once again, doubling the price of oil over a period of 18 months.

If explicit collusion to raise prices is such a good thing for oligopolists, why don't they all do it? A major reason is that it's usually *illegal*. OPEC was not considered illegal by any of the oil-producing nations, but cartels are against the law in the United States, the European Union, and most of the developed nations. Explicit collusion must therefore be conducted with the utmost secrecy. And the penalties, if the oligopolists are caught, can be severe.

For example, in 2001, a former chairman of Sotheby's auction house was sentenced to jail for his involvement in a price-fixing agreement with competitor Christie's. (The two auction houses together controlled more than 90 percent of the world's live auction market in rare art, jewelry, and other collectibles, and had agreed to cooperate in setting auction commissions.) The same year, a cartel of eight vitamin manufacturers were collectively fined a total of nearly $1 billion by the European Union.[6]

---

[6] Interestingly, the authorities typically use the prisoner's dilemma model to uncover explicit collusion: They treat managers who expose such agreements leniently, and those who don't harshly. In 2003, the European Union went even further, waiving *all* penalties for the first member of a cartel to expose it.

The chances of getting caught, and the severe penalties at stake, are important reasons why *explicit* collusion seems to be rare in the United States and Europe. But as you might guess from the italics on "explicit," oligopolists can collude in other, *implicit* ways.

Tacit Collusion. Any time firms cooperate *without* an explicit agreement, they are engaging in **tacit collusion**. Typically, players adopt strategies along the following lines: "In general, I will set a high price. If my rival also sets a high price, I will go on setting a high price. If my rival sets a low price this time, I will punish him by setting a low price next time." You can see that if both players stick to this strategy, they will both likely set the high price. Each is waiting for the other to go first in setting a low price, so it may never happen.

This type of strategy is often called **tit-for-tat**, defined as doing to the other player what he has just done to you. In our gas station duopoly, for example, Gus will pick the high price whenever Filip has set the high price in the previous play, and Gus will pick the low price if that is what Filip did in the previous play. With enough plays of the game, Filip may eventually catch on that he can get Gus to set the desired high price by setting the high price himself and that he should not exploit the situation by setting the low price, because that will cause Gus to set the low price next time. The result of every play will then be a *cooperative outcome*, rather than the Nash equilibrium: The players move to the lower right-hand corner of Figure 4, with each firm earning the higher $50,000 in profit.

Tit-for-tat strategies are prominent in the airline industry. When one major airline announces special discounted fares, its rivals almost always announce identical fares the next day. The response from the rivals not only helps them remain competitive, but also provides a signal to the price-cutting airline that it will not be able to offer discounts that are unmatched by its rivals.

However, the gentle reminder of tit for tat is not always effective in maintaining tacit collusion, and an oligopolist will sometimes go further, attempting to *punish* a firm that threatens to destroy tacit cooperation. The airline industry is famous for such efforts, which often—to the delight of travelers—lead to price wars.

A typical example occurred during August 2002, when American Airlines, in an effort to gain revenue with a small price cut, quietly began offering 10 percent discounts on tickets sold by certain travel agents. The discounts were not published on American's computer reservation system, where they would have been seen by competitors. But Northwest Airlines found out anyway, and immediately responded with its own 10 percent price cuts on routes it shared with American. This, by itself, would have been a tit-for-tat strategy. But Northwest went one step further by announcing its discounts on its public computer system, thereby applying them to *all* fares on those routes. The next day, American countered by extending *its* discounts to all flights and one day later, Northwest increased its discounts to 20 percent. . . . By the time the price war ended, both airlines had cut their ticket prices by 40 percent, and several other airlines had joined the price war as well.[7]

Another form of tacit collusion is **price leadership**, in which one firm, the *price leader*, sets its price, and other sellers copy that price. The leader may be the dominant firm in the industry (the one with the greatest market share, for example), or the

Tacit collusion Any form of oligopolistic cooperation that does not involve an explicit agreement.

Tit-for-tat A game-theoretic strategy of doing to another player this period what he has done to you in the previous period.

Price leadership A form of tacit collusion in which one firm sets a price that other firms copy.

---

[7] Sources: "U.S. Airlines in Summer Price War," *Airwise News*, August 8, 2002; "Business Fliers Rejoice—Price War!" *Business Week Online*, August 26, 2002; "American Cuts Business Fares," *Aviation News*, August 2002.

position of leader may rotate from firm to firm. During the first half of this century, U.S. Steel typically acted as the price leader in the steel industry: When it changed its prices, other firms would automatically follow. In recent decades, Goodyear has been the acknowledged leader in the tire industry, its price increases virtually always matched within days by Michelin, Bridgestone, and most other tire makers.

With price leadership, there is no formal agreement. Rather, the choice of the leader, the criteria it uses to set its price, and the willingness of other firms to follow come about because the firms realize—without formal discussion—that the system benefits all of them. To keep the price-following firms from cheating—taking large amounts of business by setting a lower price than the price leader—the leader and the firms that choose to follow must be able to punish a cheater. They can do this by setting a low price as quickly as possible after anyone cheats. The expectation of that response may be enough to prevent the cheating in the first place.

The Limits to Collusion. It is tempting to think that collusion—whether explicit or tacit—gives oligopolies absolute power over their markets, leaving them free to jack up prices and exploit the public without limit. But oligopoly power, even with collusion, has its limits.

First, even colluding firms are constrained by the market demand curve: A rise in price will always reduce the quantity demanded from *all* firms together. There is one price—the cartel monopoly price—that maximizes the total profits of all firms in the market, and it will never serve the group's interest to charge any price higher than this.

Second, collusion, even when it is tacit, may be illegal. Although it may be difficult to prove, companies that even *appear* to be colluding may find themselves facing close government scrutiny. Indeed, hardly a month goes by without the announcement of one or more new investigations of collusion by the Justice Department.

Third, collusion is limited by powerful incentives to cheat on any agreement. As the next section shows, cheating is an endemic problem among colluding oligopolists and often leads to the collapse of even the most formal agreements.

The Incentive to Cheat. Let's go back to Gus and Filip for a moment. After repeated plays of the game in Figure 4, with each play ending in the upper left-hand corner ($25,000 in profit for each player), our two gas station owners realize that they can do better with some form of collusion. One way or another—through a formal, explicit agreement, through tit-for-tat behavior, or through an understanding that one of the two will become the price leader—they arrive at the high-price cooperative solution. The outcome of the game then moves to the lower right-hand corner, where each firm earns $50,000 in profit. Will the market stay there?

Maybe. And maybe not. The problem is, each player may conclude that he can do even better by cheating. For example, once Gus commits to a high price, Filip can make even more profit ($75,000) by cheating and selling his gasoline at a lower price. This would reduce Gus's profit to −$10,000, so he, too, would likely switch to the low price, and the two players would be back to the noncooperative outcome based on their dominant strategies.

You might think that in a small-town duopoly of two gas stations such cheating would never occur, since each player can so easily observe what the other is doing, and neither party wants to return to the noncooperative equilibrium. But it may be in each player's interest to cheat *occasionally*. Filip, for example, might think he can enjoy a spell of high profit before Gus has a chance to react, and then—when Gus *does* react—Filip can revert to the cooperative scheme. Gus, by contrast, may try to discourage this with tit-for-tat moves, *punishing* Filip every time he cheats by matching Filip's price or going further and charging an even lower price (not shown on the payoff matrix). By doing so, he is telling Filip: Cheating is not in your interest. Gus, on the other hand, could then set his price still lower, informing Filip, "You better let me cheat occasionally, because punishing me is not in *your* interest."

As you can see, analyzing this sort of behavior requires some rather sophisticated game theory models, and economists are actively engaged in building them. Some of these models predict occasional price wars such as those observed in small-town markets for gasoline and fresh fruit or national markets for air travel.

When Is Cheating Likely? While no firm wants to completely destroy a collusive agreement by cheating—since this would mean a return to the noncooperative equilibrium wherein each firm earns lower profit—some firms may be willing to *risk* destroying the agreement if the benefits are great enough. In any collusive agreement, we can expect each firm to weigh the costs and benefits of cheating. On the cost side is the probability of being detected, bringing about a punitive reaction from other firms or a collapse of the agreement. On the benefit side is the additional profit from charging a lower price than other firms and gaining additional profit.

This logic suggests that cheating is most likely to occur—and collusion will be least successful—under the following conditions:

Difficulty Observing Other Firms' Prices. In markets where prices are negotiated with each customer—as in general contracting or retail auto sales—it is difficult for firms to observe the prices actually charged by their competitors. In such markets, where the probability of being caught cheating is low, we would expect little cooperation or collusion. By contrast, when other firms' prices are easy to observe, cheating is more easily detected and therefore less likely to occur. For example, when the buyers are government agencies or public utilities, competing bids must be made public.

The airlines are an interesting hybrid of observable and unobservable prices. On the one hand, their shared computer system makes it difficult to conceal price cuts from rivals. However, as was seen in our earlier example of American's price war with Northwest, because so many of their tickets are sold through travel agencies, they can sometimes discount secretly—at least for a short time. And the airlines have another opportunity to hide discounts by selling tickets to online travel companies, such as Priceline.com. Since these online companies sell their tickets to individuals at a variety of different prices, other airlines have a harder time detecting price cuts by any one of them.

Unstable Market Demand. Frequent shifts in market demand encourage cheating for a number of reasons. First, any preexisting agreement may no longer make sense once market conditions change. A new arrangement must be established, but this often takes time. In the interim, there may be substantial benefits to cheating on the old agreement. Second, with unstable market demand, it is more difficult for firms to interpret each other's actions. If a firm lowers its price, is it cheating on the arrangement? Or is it merely responding to changing demand conditions and perhaps trying to play the role of price leader itself? With signals less clear the detection of cheating is less likely, so we would expect collusion to break down.

A Large Number of Sellers. The greater the number of firms, the more cheating we expect to occur. That's because with many firms, each may reason that it can cheat—increasing its output beyond its allocated quantity—without having much of an impact on the market price. Thus, its cheating may go undetected. Even if it thinks its cheating *will* be detected, each firm may view itself as a small fish in a big pond, reasoning that its own cheating—having little effect on market price—will be tolerated as a nuisance, rather than a threat.

However, if several firms behave this way—all increasing their output and hoping the other cartel members won't notice—the market price will drop significantly. Cheating will then be noticed. But in this case, the individual firm has even *more* incentive to cheat: otherwise it suffers.

The history of collusion is rife with cheating and the ultimate breakdown of cooperation among firms, suggesting that these three conditions are sufficiently satisfied in many markets. When the benefits to cheating are great and the costs low, we can expect collusive arrangements to collapse.

The Future of Oligopoly

Some people think that the U.S. and other Western economies are moving relentlessly toward oligopoly as the dominant market structure. Technological change is often cited as the reason. For example, in the early part of the century, several dozen U.S. firms manufactured passenger cars. With the development of mass-production technology, the number has steadily fallen to three. Stories like this suggest an economy in which markets are increasingly controlled and manipulated by a few players who, by colluding, exploit the public for their own gain. In 1932, two economists—Adolf Berle and Gardiner Means—noted the trend toward big business and predicted that, unless something were done to stop it, the 200 largest U.S. firms would control the nation's entire economy by 1970.

Berle and Means's prediction has not come true. Today, there are hundreds of thousands of ongoing businesses in the United States. In Chapter 6, we identified one reason: In many markets, the minimum efficient scale of production is so small relative to the size of the market that large firms have no cost advantage over small ones. But the prevalence of oligopoly in the national and world economies is anything but stable. Some forces in our society are helping to keep market dominance in check, while others encourage it. Let's consider some of the major forces affecting the future of oligopoly.

Antitrust Legislation and Enforcement. Antitrust policies in the United States and many other countries are designed to protect the interests of consumers by ensuring adequate competition in the marketplace. In practice, antitrust enforcement has focused on three types of actions: (1) preventing collusive agreements among firms, such as price-fixing agreements; (2) breaking up or limiting the activities of large firms—oligopolists and monopolists—whose market dominance harms consumers; and (3) preventing mergers that would lead to harmful market domination.

The impact of antitrust actions goes far beyond the specific companies called into the courtroom. Managers of firms even *considering* anticompetitive moves have to think long and hard about the consequences of acts that might violate the antitrust laws. For example, many economists believe that in the late 1940s and early 1950s, General Motors would have driven Ford and Chrysler out of business or bought them out were it not for fear of antitrust action. On the other hand, antitrust and other government policies toward business are a part of our *political* system. While the thrust of these policies is always to preserve competition, the type of competition preserved—and the zeal with which the policies are applied—can shift. In Chapter 6, we saw that legislative changes in the 1990s, enabling banks to operate across state lines, led to a merger wave in the banking sector. In mid-2003, a decision by the Federal Communications Commission made it easier for large media companies to acquire local radio and television stations. If this decision holds, then economies of scale may be a driving *economic* force toward market dominance by a few firms, but a change in government policy will have made it possible.

The Globalization of Markets. Recall that when the minimum efficient scale (MES) of the typical firm is large relative to the size of the market, a large firm has a cost advantage over a small one, and the result is a natural oligopoly. But what if the *size of the market* increases? Then an unchanged MES becomes *relatively* smaller, when compared to the market. A larger number of firms can survive there. By enlarging markets from national ones to global ones, international trade can increase the number of firms in a market, thus decreasing market dominance by a few, and increasing competition.

Although oligopolists often try to prevent it, they face increasingly stiff competition from foreign producers. Some economists have argued, for example, that the U.S. market for automobiles now has so many foreign sellers that it resembles monopolistic competition more than oligopoly. Similar changes have occurred in the U.S. markets for color televisions, stereo equipment, computers, beer, and wine. At the same time, the entry of U.S. producers has helped to increase competition in foreign markets for movies, television shows, clothing, household cleaning products, and prepared foods.

On the other hand, globalization also enables firms that have *not* reached their MES (say, because of domestic government restrictions) to become bigger players in the new, global market. And large global firms can force many smaller, national companies out of business. Thus, although globalization may give consumers in each nation access to a greater number of firms, these may be larger and more powerful firms—creating greater likelihood of strategic interaction and the danger of collusion.

Technological Change. One way that technological change works to *increase* competition is by creating new substitute goods. For example, e-mail has provided a substitute for many types of hard copy: personal letters, bills, and some types of documents. The result is tough competition for one of our oldest monopolies—the U.S. Postal Service—as well as competition for a long-standing oligopoly—overnight package delivery services.

Technology can also reduce barriers to entry in much the same way that globalization does: by increasing the size of the market. A small town, for example, might be able to support only a few stores selling, say, luggage, file cabinets, or CDs, because the MES of a brick-and-mortar store is large relative to the small market there. But technology—the Internet—has enabled residents in many smaller towns to choose among a dozen or more online sellers of the same merchandise. By connecting the town's residents to the national market for retail services, the Internet has increased the size of the market in which they are buyers. In that larger, national market, because the MES is smaller relative to the market, several firms can compete.

However, this trend can also be seen as *encouraging* oligopoly. By extending the reach of large national retailers, the Internet enables them to become still larger. And if the small brick-and-mortar stores can't compete in this larger market and go out of business, then the texture of retail service in the country changes. There are more firms competing for the business of residents in any town, but there are fewer of these firms nationwide, and they are larger. The result could be strategic interaction—and possibly collusion—among large national players.

Finally, some technologies actually *increase* the MES of the typical firm, thereby encouraging the formation of oligopolies. For example, producers of digital products—like entertainment, software, and information—have very high up-front costs (lumpy inputs) in creating their goods and services, but almost nonexistent costs of duplicating them to produce and sell another unit. The cost to a software firm of having another buyer download the program, for example, is almost nonexistent. For this reason, a firm in a digital market can continue to experience economies of scale until it serves a relatively large fraction of a national or even global market. Microsoft, Disney, and Time Warner, are examples of companies for which new technology has led to a larger market share.

USING THE THEORY
Advertising in Monopolistic Competition and Oligopoly

© PHOTODISC/GETTY IMAGES

We began this chapter by noting that perfect competitors never advertise and monopolies advertise relatively little. But advertising is almost always found under monopolistic competition and very often in oligopoly. Why? All monopolistic competitors, and many oligopolists, produce differentiated products. In these types of markets, the firm gains customers by convincing them that its product is different and better in some way than that of its competitors. Advertising, whether it merely informs customers about the product ("The new Toyota Corolla gets 45 miles per gallon on the highway") or attempts to influence them more subtly and psychologically ("Our exotic perfume will fill your life with mystery and intrigue"), is one way to sharply differentiate a product in the minds of consumers. Since other firms will take advantage of the opportunity to advertise, any firm that *doesn't* advertise will be lost in the shuffle. In this section, we use the tools we've learned in this chapter to look at some aspects of the economics of advertising.

Advertising and Market Equilibrium Under Monopolistic Competition

A monopolistic competitor advertises for two reasons: to shift its demand curve rightward (greater quantity demanded at each price) and to make demand for its output *less* elastic (so it can raise price and suffer a smaller decrease in quantity demanded). Advertising costs money, so in addition to its impact on the demand curve, it will also affect the firm's *ATC* curve. What is the ultimate impact of advertising on the typical firm?

Figure 5(a) shows demand and *ATC* curves for a company, Narcissus Fragrance, that manufactures and sells perfume. Initially, when there is no advertising at all in

FIGURE 5
Advertising in Monopolistic Competition

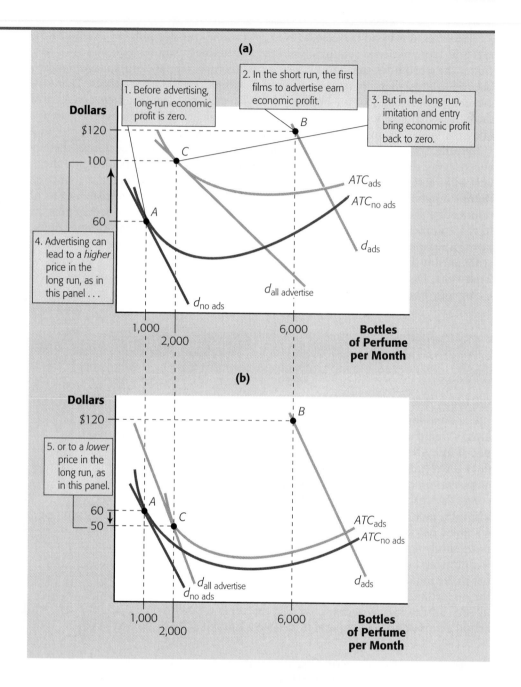

(a)

1. Before advertising, long-run economic profit is zero.

2. In the short run, the first films to advertise earn economic profit.

3. But in the long run, imitation and entry bring economic profit back to zero.

4. Advertising can lead to a *higher* price in the long run, as in this panel . . .

Dollars

$120

100

60

ATC_{ads}

$ATC_{no\ ads}$

d_{ads}

$d_{all\ advertise}$

$d_{no\ ads}$

1,000   2,000   6,000   **Bottles of Perfume per Month**

(b)

5. or to a *lower* price in the long run, as in this panel.

Dollars

$120

60

50

ATC_{ads}

$ATC_{no\ ads}$

$d_{all\ advertise}$

$d_{no\ ads}$

d_{ads}

1,000   2,000   6,000   **Bottles of Perfume per Month**

the industry, Narcissus is in long-run equilibrium at point A, in panel (a), where its demand curve ($d_{no\ ads}$) and ATC curve ($ATC_{no\ ads}$) touch. The firm charges $60 per bottle, sells 1,000 bottles each month, and earns zero economic profit.

Now suppose that Narcissus decides to run a costly television ad campaign and, for now, that no other firm advertises. Then the cost of advertising will shift the company's ATC curve upward, to ATC_{ads}. Cost per unit will be greater at every output level. Notice, however, that the rise is smaller at higher output levels, where the cost of the ad is spread over a larger number of units. In addition to the shift in

ATC, the ad campaign would shift the demand curve rightward and make it steeper. Since Narcissus is the *only* firm advertising, the effect on the demand curve would be substantial, shifting it all the way to d_{ads}. Notice that there are many points along this new demand curve where Narcissus could earn a profit; the greatest profit will be the output level at which its new *MC* and *MR* curves (not shown) intersect. In panel (a), we assume that this occurs at 6,000 bottles per month. The firm will thus operate at point *B* along its new demand curve, charge a price of \$120 per bottle, and earn an economic profit, since $P > ATC$.

Narcissus will not be able to remain at point *B* for long. In the long run, its profit will tempt other firms to initiate ad campaigns of their own. (Remember that under monopolistic competition, we assume that firms can imitate the successful business policies of their competitors.) As other firms advertise, they will take back some of Narcissus's new business, shifting its demand curve leftward. Narcissus's demand curve, however, doesn't shift *all* the way back to its original position; we assume that advertising will increase the overall demand for perfume, so demand for each firm—including Narcissus—will be higher than when no firm advertises. In the end, Narcissus will end up at a point like *C* on demand curve $d_{all\ advertise}$, where $P = ATC = \$100$, and the firm earns zero economic profit.

Notice that, once other firms are advertising, Narcissus *must* advertise as well. Why? If it chooses not to advertise, its *ATC* curve will return to $ATC_{no\ ads}$, but its demand curve will lie somewhere to the *left* of $d_{no\ ads}$. (The demand curve was $d_{no\ ads}$ when *no* firm was advertising. But now, with its competitors running ad campaigns, if Narcissus chooses *not* to advertise, it will sell less output at any price than it did originally.) With average costs given by $ATC_{no\ ads}$, and the demand curve somewhere to the left of $d_{no\ ads}$, Narcissus would suffer a loss at *any* output level. Thus, if it wants to stay in business in the long run, it *must* advertise.

We can summarize the impact of advertising as illustrated in panel (a) this way: The output of the typical firm has increased (from 1,000 to 2,000 units), and thus, advertising has increased the total size of the market: more perfume is being bought than before. But the individual firm does not benefit from this. Since each firm must pay the costs of advertising (and more competitors may have entered the market), Narcissus and its competitors are each earning normal economic profit—just as they were originally.

But what about consumers? We would think that costly advertising will raise the price to consumers, and in panel (a), that is what has happened: Advertising has raised the price from \$60 to \$100 in the long run.

But this is not the *only* possible result. Panel (b) illustrates the somewhat surprising case where advertising leads to *lower* costs per unit and a *lower* price for consumers. As before, we begin with Narcissus at point *A* with no advertising in the market, then move to point *B* when Narcissus is the only firm running ads, and end up at point *C* after imitation by other firms and entry have eliminated Narcissus's economic profit.

Notice that, in panel (b), the ultimate impact of advertising is to decrease both cost per unit and price from \$60 to \$50. How can this be? By advertising, each firm is able to produce and sell more output. This remains true even when *all* firms advertise because total market demand has increased. Since the firm was originally on the downward-sloping portion of its *ATC* curve, we know that its *non*advertising costs per unit will decline as output expands. If this decline is great enough—as in panel (b)—then costs per unit will drop, even when the cost of advertising is included. In other words, because you and I and everyone else is buying more perfume, each producer can operate closer to capacity output, with lower costs per unit. In the long run, entry will force each firm to pass the cost savings on to us.

Our analysis suggests the following conclusion:

> *Under monopolistic competition, advertising may increase the size of the market, so that more units are sold. But in the long run, each firm earns zero economic profit, just as it would if no firm were advertising. The price to the consumer may either rise or fall.*

Advertising and Collusion In Oligopoly

In this chapter, you've learned that oligopolists have a strong incentive to engage in tacit collusion. But such collusion is difficult to detect. When one firm raises its prices and others follow, that may be evidence of price leadership, or it may be that costs in the industry have risen, and *all* firms—affected in the same way—have decided independently to raise their prices. But in some cases, such as strategic decisions about oligopoly, we can use a simple game theory model to show that collusion is almost certainly taking place.

Let's take the airline industry as an example. Polls have shown that passengers have been very concerned about airline safety. This was true before the infamous hijacking of four airliners on September 11, 2001, when thousands died. Since that incident, safety has weighed even more heavily on the minds of those considering flying. Any airline that could convince the public of its superior safety record would profit considerably.

In theory, *any* airline should be able to claim superior safety. After all, there are many different ways to interpret safety data. By searching hard enough, almost any airline could come up with a measure by which it would appear the "safest." And any airline that actually imposed special passenger and baggage screening procedures could tout the changes in its ads, taking business from other airlines. Yet no airline has ever run an advertisement with information about its security policies or attacked those of a competitor. Let's see why.

Figure 6 shows some hypothetical payoffs from this sort of advertising as seen by two firms, United Airlines and American Airlines, competing on a particular route. Focus first on the top, green-shaded entries, which show the payoffs for American. If neither firm ran safety ads, American would earn a level of profit we will call *medium*, as a benchmark. If American ran ads touting its own safety, but United did not, American's profit would certainly increase—to "high" in the payoff matrix. If both firms ran safety ads—especially negative ads that attacked their rival—the public's demand for airline tickets would certainly decline. Reminded of the dangers of flying, more consumers would choose to travel by train, bus, or car. American's profit in this case would be lower than if *neither* firm ran ads, so we have labeled it "low" in the payoff matrix. Finally, the worst possible result for American—"very low" in the figure—occurs when United touts its own safety record, but American does not.

Now consider American's possible strategies. If United decides to run the ads (the top row), American's best action is to run them as well. If United does not run the ads (bottom row), American's best action is still to run the ads. Thus, American has a dominant strategy: Regardless of what United does, it should run the safety ads.

As you can verify, United, whose payoffs are the lower, orange-shaded entries, faces an entirely symmetrical situation, and it, too, has the same dominant strategy: Run the ads. Thus, when each airline acts independently, the outcome of this game

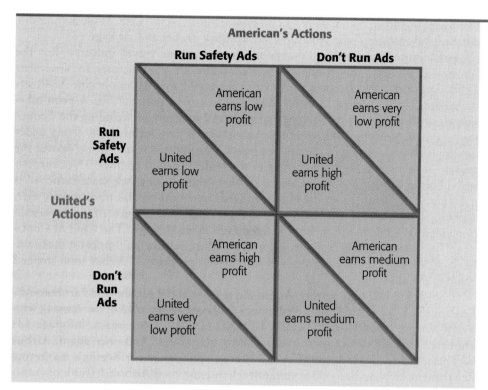

American's Actions

FIGURE 6
An Advertising Game

	Run Safety Ads	**Don't Run Ads**
Run Safety Ads	American earns low profit / United earns low profit	American earns very low profit / United earns high profit
Don't Run Ads	American earns high profit / United earns very low profit	American earns medium profit / United earns medium profit

United's Actions

is shown in the upper left-hand corner, where each airline runs ads and earns a low profit. So why don't we observe that outcome?

The answer is that the airlines are playing against each other repeatedly and reach the kind of cooperative equilibrium we discussed earlier. Each airline can punish its rival next time if it fails to cooperate this time. In the cooperative outcome, each airline plays the strategy that it will *not* run the ads as long as its rival does not. The game's outcome moves to the lower right-hand corner. Here, neither firm runs ads, and each earns medium rather than low profit. This is the result we see in the airline industry.

Should we be surprised at the cooperative outcome in this case? Not really. Recall that the ability to get away with cheating is one of the chief obstacles to cooperation. But when the agreement involves *advertising*, cheating would be instantly detected and would therefore be unlikely to occur. This makes advertising a particularly good opportunity for cooperation.

Until the 1980s, a similar collusive understanding seemed to characterize the automobile industry. As long as the "Big Three" dominated auto sales in the United States, the word *safety* was never heard in their advertising. There seemed to be an understanding that all three would earn greater profits if consumers were *not* reminded of the dangers of driving. Things changed in the 1980s, however, as foreign firms' share of the U.S. market rose dramatically. One of the new players, Volvo, decided that its safety features were so far superior to its competitors that it no longer paid to play by the rules. Volvo began running television advertisements that not only stressed its own safety features, but implied that competing products were dangerous. (On a rainy night, a worried father stops his son at the door, hands him some keys, and says, "Here, son, take the Volvo.") Once Volvo began running ads like these, the other automakers had no choice but to reciprocate. Now, automobile ads routinely mention safety features like antilock brakes and air bags.

Something similar *almost* happened in the airline travel industry. But the "Volvo" in this case was not an airline but an aircraft manufacturer. In November 1999, Airbus ran ads designed to convince the public that its four-engine A340 jets were safer for transatlantic travel than Boeing's twin-engine 777s. A print ad—taken out in more than a dozen newspapers and magazines, including the *Economist, Fortune,* and the *Wall Street Journal*—shows a lone Airbus A340 flying under ominous, dark skies, with a choppy sea below. The caption read, "If you're over the middle of the Pacific, you want to be in the middle of four engines." Not surprisingly, Boeing condemned the ad, declaring that "this not so subtle scare-tactic . . . is a dramatic departure from the high standards our industry has traditionally met. Airbus's actions have, rightfully so, raised a considerable amount of displeasure in our industry." The major airlines reacted even more strongly. The CEO of Continental Airlines, Gordon Bethune, informed Airbus that the ad "makes it more unlikely we would put our confidence in you or your products."[8] Airbus soon stopped running the ads.

Until July 2002, that is, when Airbus did it again at the Air Show in Farnborough, England. This time, Airbus installed a huge billboard at the edge of the runway with a new slogan: "A340—4 ENGINES 4 LONG HAUL." Once again, full-page ads appeared in daily newspapers and air show magazines. And once again, Airbus was attacked by the industry. But this time, a spokesman for Boeing's marketing department launched an odd counterattack against rival Airbus: "Think of it this way. If you have two engines, there are two chances of engine failure. If you have four engines, there are four chances of engine failure. The chance of engine failure doesn't go down with four engines; it goes up."[9] Perhaps the gloves are coming off now.

THE FOUR MARKET STRUCTURES: A POSTSCRIPT

You have now been introduced to the four different market structures: perfect competition, monopoly, monopolistic competition, and oligopoly. Each has different characteristics, and each leads to different predictions about pricing, profit, non-price competition, and firms' responses to changes in their environments.

Table 1 summarizes some of the assumptions and predictions associated with each of the four market structures. While the table is a useful review of the *models* we have studied, it is not a how-to guide for analyzing real-world markets: We cannot simply look at the array of markets we see around us and say, "This one is perfectly competitive," "That one is an oligopoly," and so on. Why not? Because markets in the real world will typically have characteristics of more than one kind of market structure. A barbecue restaurant, for example, may be viewed as a monopolistic competitor in the market for *restaurants* in Memphis, or an oligopolist in

[8] "Competitor's 'scare tactic' vexes Boeing," *Herald Net,* November 6, 1999 (*www.heraldnet.com*); "Airlines Blast New Ads from Airbus . . ." *Wall Street Journal,* November 22, 1999.
[9] Quoted in Kathleen Hanser, "An Airbus Advertising Campaign at the Farnborough Air Show Stoked the Fires in the Debate Between . . . Two Engines & Four Engines," *Boeing Frontiers* (Vol. 1, Issue 5), September 2002 (*http://www.boeing.com/news/frontiers/archive/2002/september/i_ca1.html*)

	Perfect Competition	Monopolistic Competition	Oligopoly	Monopoly
ASSUMPTIONS ABOUT:				
Number of Firms	Very many	Many	Few	One
Output of Different Firms	Identical	Differentiated	Identical or differentiated	—
View of Pricing	Price taker	Price setter	Price setter	Price setter
Barriers to Entry or Exit?	No	No	Yes	Yes
Strategic Interdependence?	No	No	Yes	—
PREDICTIONS:				
Price and Output Decisions	$MC = MR$	$MC = MR$	Through strategic Interdependence	$MC = MR$
Short-Run Profit	Positive, zero, or negative	Positive, zero, or negative	Positive, zero, or negative	Positive, zero,
Long-Run Profit	Zero	Zero	Positive or zero	Positive or zero
Advertising?	Never	Almost always	Yes, if differen-tiated product	Sometimes

TABLE 1
A Summary of Market Structures

the market for *barbecue* restaurants in Memphis, or a monopolist in the market for barbecue restaurants *within walking distance of Graceland.*

You've seen how market structure models help us organize and understand the apparent chaos of real-world markets. But now, it seems, we've ended up with a different type of chaos: We can usually choose among two, three, or even four different models when studying a particular market.

But, as we've seen several times in this text, our choice of model is not really arbitrary; rather, it depends on the *questions we are trying to answer.* Suppose we're interested in barbecue restaurants. To explain why a *particular* barbecue restaurant with no nearby competitors earns economic profit year after year, or why it spends so much of its profit on rent-seeking activity (lobbying the local zoning board), we would most likely use the monopoly model. If we want to explain why *most* barbecue restaurants do *not* earn much economic profit, or why they pay for advertisements in the yellow pages and the local newspapers, or why there is so much excess capacity (empty tables) in the industry, we would use the model of monopolistic competition. To explain a price war among the few restaurants in a neighborhood, or to explore the possibility of explicit or tacit collusion in pricing or advertising, we would use the oligopoly model. And if we're interested in barbecue restaurants as an example of *restaurants in general,* and we want general explanations about restaurant prices, or the expansion or contraction of the restaurant industry in a city or country, we would use the perfectly competitive model, which ignores the distinctions between different restaurants and any barriers to entry that might exist.

We will come back to the four market structures again (in Chapter 14) when we consider the operation of the microeconomy as a whole, the notion of economic efficiency, and the proper role of government in the economy. But first we must explore another type of market, one that, until now, we've ignored.

Summary

Monopolistic competition is a market structure in which there are many small buyers and sellers, easy entry and exit, and firms sell differentiated products. As in monopoly, each firm faces a downward-sloping demand curve, chooses the profit-maximizing quantity where $MR = MC$, and charges the maximum price it can for that quantity. As in perfect competition, short-run profit attracts new entrants. As firms enter the industry, the demand curves facing existing firms shift leftward. Eventually, each firm earns zero economic profit and produces at greater than minimum average cost.

Oligopoly is a market structure dominated by a small number of strategically interdependent firms. New entry is deterred by economies of scale, reputational barriers, strategic barriers, and legal barriers to entry. Because each firm, when making decisions, must anticipate its rivals' reactions, oligopoly behavior is hard to predict. However, one approach, *game theory,* has offered rich insights.

In game theory, a *payoff matrix* indicates the payoff to each firm for each combination of strategies adopted by that firm and its rivals. A *dominant strategy* is a strategy that is best for a particular firm regardless of what its rival does. If there is no cooperation among firms, any firm that has a dominant strategy will play it, and that helps predict the outcome of the game. If no firm has a dominant strategy, it is much harder to predict what will happen—especially for games that are played only once.

Sometimes oligopolists can cooperate to increase profits. *Explicit collusion,* in which managers meet to set prices, is illegal in the United States and many other countries. As a result, other forms of *tacit collusion* have evolved. Still, cheating is a constant threat to collusion. Cheating is most likely when there is difficulty observing prices, when market demand is unstable, and when there are a large number of sellers. Government antitrust enforcement, market globalization, and technological change are forces that can discourage the formation of oligopolies and limit their power. But each can also have the opposite effect: encouraging market dominance by a few large firms.

Key Terms

Cartel
Dominant strategy
Duopoly
Explicit collusion
Game theory

Monopolistic competition
Nash equilibrium
Natural oligopoly
Nonprice competition
Oligopoly

Payoff matrix
Price leadership
Repeated play
Tacit collusion
Tit-for-tat

Review Questions   *Answers to even-numbered Questions and Problems can be found on the text Web site at http://hall-lieb.swlearning.com.*

1. What features does a monopolistically competitive market share with a perfectly competitive market? With a monopoly market?

2. True or false? "In the long run, a monopolistic competitor will produce the level of output that minimizes its average total cost." Explain.

3. True or false? "The only way for a monopolistic competitor to increase its sales is to lower its price." Explain.

4. How does oligopoly differ from monopolistic competition, perfect competition, and monopoly?

5. Classify each of the following business firms as perfectly competitive, monopolistically competitive, oligopolistic, or monopolistic. Justify your answer. That is, discuss what characteristic(s) of the market designation you assign are likely to be present.

a. General Motors
b. An Iowa corn farmer
c. Kinko's copy shop (large city)
d. Kinko's copy shop (the only copy center within a two-mile radius of your campus)
e. Ben & Jerry's ice cream (national)
f. Daily newspaper (one of two in a medium-size city)
g. Spanish-language newspaper (the only one in the Hispanic community of a medium-size southwestern city)

6. What is the difference between a natural oligopoly and a natural monopoly?

7. Discuss some factors that might keep new entrants out of an oligopolistic market.

8. What conditions are likely to lead to cheating on a collusive arrangement? Explain why each makes cheating more probable.

9. The minimum efficient scale in a certain industry is 2,300 units. Exactly what additional information do you need in order to predict whether this industry will be perfectly (or monopolistically) competitive, an oligopoly, or a monopoly?

10. How does technological change limit the degree of concentration in an industry? Give some examples.

11. Discuss how much advertising each of the following will be likely to do and why. In each case where a firm may advertise, explain exactly what it might be trying to accomplish with its advertising.

a. The sole cable-television service provider in a small town
b. A dairy farm in upstate New York
c. Blockbuster video stores
d. Homestake, a gold-mining company
e. Dell Computer Co.

12. Explain why it is difficult to apply the definition of oligopoly to real-world markets.

Problems and Exercises

1. Draw the relevant curves to show a monopolistic competitor suffering a loss in the short run. What will this firm do in the long run if the situation does not improve? How would this action affect *other* firms in this market?

2. Draw the relevant curves to show a monopolistic competitor earning an economic profit in the short run. Graphically show what this firm can expect to happen to this economic profit in the long run.

3. The owner of an optometry practice, in a city with more than a hundred other such practices, has the following demand and cost schedules for eye exams:

Price per Eye Exam	Eye Exams per Week	Total Cost per Week	Total Revenue per Week	Marginal Revenue	Marginal Cost
$100	100	$10,500			
80	140	$10,800			
60	200	$11,300			
40	310	$12,290			
20	550	$14,762			

a. Fill in the columns for total revenue, marginal revenue, and marginal cost. (Remember to put *MR* and *MC between* output levels.)
b. Briefly explain why an optometry practice (like this one) might face a downward-sloping demand curve, even if it is one out of more than a hundred. (*Hint:* What might make this market monopolistically competitive rather than perfectly competitive?)
c. Use the data you filled in for the marginal revenue and marginal cost columns to find the profit-maximizing price and the profit-maximizing number of eye exams per week for this practice.

4. Tino owns a taco stand in Houston, Texas, where there are dozens of other taco stands. He faces the following demand and cost schedules for his taco plates (two tacos and a side of refried beans):

Price per Taco Plate	Taco Plates per Week	Total Cost per Week	Total Revenue per Week	Marginal Revenue	Marginal Cost
$5	50	$30			
4	80	$50			
3	150	$176			
2	800	$1476			
1	1100	$2136			

a. Fill in the columns for total revenue, marginal revenue, and marginal cost and use the table to find the profit-maximizing price and the profit-maximizing number of taco plates per week for Tino's Taco Stand. (Remember to put *MR* and *MC between* output levels.)
b. What will likely happen to Tino's profits if his biggest competitor starts a successful "buy one–get one free" campaign?
c. Redo the table to show what will happen if Tino spends $100 on an advertising campaign that increases the quantity demanded at each output level by 20%. What will happen to his profit-maximizing price and profit-maximizing number of taco plates per week? Do you expect this outcome to persist? Explain.

5. Suppose that the cost data in Problem 3 are for the short run, and that the owner of the practice suddenly realizes that she forgot to include her only fixed cost: her license fee of $2,600 per year (which is $50 per week). Should the practice shut down in the short run? Why or why not?

6. Assume that the plastics business is monopolistically competitive.
a. Draw a graph showing the long-run equilibrium situation for a typical firm in the industry. Clearly label the demand, *MR*, *MC*, and *ATC* curves.
b. One of the major inputs into plastics is oil. Draw a new graph illustrating the short-run position of a plastics company after an increase in oil prices. Again, show all relevant curves.

c. If oil prices remain at the new, higher level, what will happen to get firms in the plastics industry back to a long-run equilibrium?

7. Draw a diagram, including demand, marginal revenue, marginal cost, and any other curves necessary, to illustrate each of the following two situations for a monopolistic competitor:
   a. The firm is suffering a loss, and should shut down in the short run.
   b. The firm is suffering a loss, but should stay open in the short run.

8. In a small Nevada town, Ptomaine Flats, there are only two restaurants, the Road Kill Cafe and, for Italian fare, Sal Monella's. Each restaurant has to decide whether to clean up its act or to continue to ignore health code violations.

   Each restaurant currently makes $7,000 a year in profit. If they both tidy up a bit, they will attract more patrons but must bear the (substantial) cost of the cleanup; so they will both be left with a profit of $5,000. However, if one cleans up and the other doesn't, the influx of diners to the cleaner joint will more than cover the costs of the scrubbing; the more hygienic place ends up with $12,000, and the grubbier establishment incurs a loss of $3,000.
   a. Write out the payoff matrix for this game, clearly labeling strategies and payoffs to each player.
   b. What is each player's dominant strategy?
   c. What will be the outcome of the game? Explain your answer.
   d. Suppose the two restaurants believe they will face the same decision repeatedly. How might the outcome differ? Why?
   e. Assume that if one cleans up and one stays dirty, the cleaner restaurant makes only $6,000 in profit. All other payoffs are the same as before. What will the outcome of the game be now without cooperation? With cooperation?

9. Professor Clemens has two students enrolled in his riverboat pilot course, Huck and Tom. The final exam counts as 100% of the course grade. If one student passes the exam and one student fails, Professor Clemens announces that he will assign the passer an A and the failer an F. If both students pass, he will give them both Bs. If both students fail, he will give them both Cs. When Tom and Huck finish the course, they plan to look for work as riverboat pilots, and their

grades in Professor Clemens's course will determine the salary they can earn. An A in the course is worth $5,000 per year, a B is worth $3,000 per year, a C is worth $2,000 per year, and an F is worth nothing. Assume that if they study, they will pass the exam.
   a. Write out the payoff matrix for Tom and Huck, clearly labeling strategies and payoffs to each player.
   b. What is each player's dominant strategy?
   c. What will be the outcome of the game? Explain your answer.
   d. Suppose that Professor Clemens gives 50 exams instead of one. How might the outcome differ? Why?
   e. Assume that an A is worth only $500 to Huck. All other payoffs are the same as before. What will the outcome of the game be now without collusion? With collusion?

10. Assume that Nike and Adidas are the only sellers of athletic footwear in the United States. They are deciding how much to charge for similar shoes. The two choices are "High" (H) and "Outrageously High" (OH). Nike's payoffs are in the lower left of each cell in the payoff matrix:

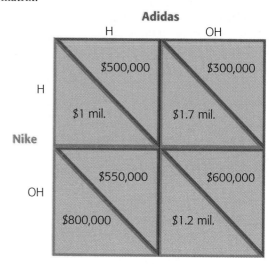

a. Do both companies have dominant strategies? If so, what are they?
b. What will be the outcome of the game?
c. If Nike becomes the acknowledged price leader in the industry, what will be its dominant strategy? What will be the outcome of the game? Why?

Challenge Questions

1. Suppose that the government has decided to tax all the firms in a monopolistically competitive industry. Specifically, suppose it levies a fixed tax on each firm; that is, the amount of the tax is the same regardless of how much output the firm produces. In the short run, how would that tax affect the price, output level, and profit of the typical firm in that industry? What would be the effect in the long run?

2. In the next column you will find the payoff matrix for a two-player game, where each player has three possible strategies: *A*, *B*, and *C*. The payoff for player 1 is listed in the lower left portion of each cell. Assume there is no co-operation among players.
   a. Does either player have a dominant strategy? If so, which player or players, and what is the dominant strategy?
   b. Can we predict the outcome of this game from the payoff matrix? Why or why not?
   c. Suppose that strategy *C* is no longer available to either player. Does either player have a dominant strategy now? Can we now predict the outcome of the game? Explain. (*Hint:* Assume that players know the payoffs—both for themselves and for the other players—for every strategy.)

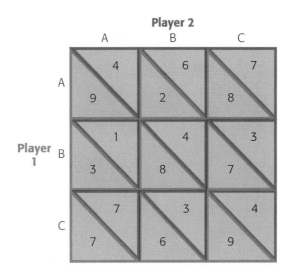

3.  *These exercises require access to Hall/Lieberman Xtra! If Xtra! did not come with your book, visit http://hallxtra.swlearning.com to purchase.*

1. Use your Xtra! password at the Hall and Lieberman Web site (http://hallxtra.swlearning.com) and under Economic Applications click on EconNews. Select *Microeconomics: Monopolistic Competition,* and read the article "Just-in-Time State-of-the-Art Fashion." Explain what form of nonprice competition the firm uses to gain an edge on its rivals.

2. Use your Xtra! password at the Hall and Lieberman Web site (http://hallxtra.swlearning.com) and under Economic Applications click on EconNews. Click on *Microeconomics: Oligopoly* and read the article "Fair Oil Prices," then answer the questions below.
   a. Using a game theory model of cartels, is Venezuela's strategy credible? Why or why not? Would your answer change if the Venezuelan president were visiting only OPEC nations?
   b. Now go to EconDebate. Again select *Microeconomics: Oligopoly* and find the debate, "Should the

Strategic Petroleum Reserve Be Used to Reduce Fluctuations in Oil Prices?" Read the debate. In terms of game theory, would using the Strategic Petroleum Reserve be effective against a cartel like OPEC? Why or why not?
   c. In light of Venezuela's request to increase the price of oil, should we use the SPR to provide additional oil? Why or why not?

3. Use your Xtra! password at the Hall and Lieberman Web site (http://hallxtra.swlearning.com) and under Economic Applications click on EconNews. Select *Microeconomics: Oligopoly* and read "Steel Supply Strategies." The steel industry is arguing that by consolidating firms—that is, becoming more oligopolistic—the resulting firms can be more competitive. Is this notion of increasing competition through consolidation of firms counter-intuitive? Why or why not?

CHAPTER 11

The Labor Market

CHAPTER OUTLINE

If you plan to look for a job when you graduate from college, you'll have a lot of company. Every year from 2005 to 2008, about 1.2 million new college graduates will be seeking work, plus more than a million graduates from earlier years who will be looking for new jobs. You will thus join more than two million others who are offering their college-enhanced labor services to employers expanding their workforce or needing to replace retiring workers. Are you likely to find the kind of job that requires a college degree?

According to the U.S. Bureau of Labor Statistics (BLS), the answer is: *very* likely. The BLS predicts that if the overall economy performs over the next few years as it has over recent decades, about 93 percent of American college-educated job seekers will find the sort of job that typically requires a college degree.[1]

---

[1] Chad Fleetwood and Kristina Shelley, "The Outlook for College Graduates, 1998–2008: A Balancing Act," in *Occupational Outlook Quarterly,* U.S. Bureau of Labor Statistics, Fall 2000. Most college graduates who *don't* get jobs requiring a college education do end up working, but in jobs that don't require a college education.

340

And the job will most likely pay more than one requiring only a high school education. In 2000, for example, average weekly earnings for high school graduates were about $507 per week, while college graduates earned around $834 per week. This earnings differential has been widening for a few decades, and it's expected to widen even more by 2008.

These observations raise some interesting questions. For example, why do such a large fraction of college graduates, year after year, obtain the type of job they are looking for, that is, jobs that typically require a college degree? After all, *your* decision to become, say, a marketing manager trainee, computer systems analyst, or kindergarten teacher is based on your *own* agenda. But those who *hire* college graduates have their own, entirely different agenda—in most cases, to earn the highest possible profit for their firms. Why do these different agendas result in a reasonably good match of job seekers and job offers? Moreover, why do college graduates earn so much more than high school graduates? And why is this earnings differential growing larger, even as more and more workers with college degrees pour into the labor market?

Once you understand how labor markets work—the subject of this chapter—you'll know how to answer these questions.

FACTOR MARKETS IN GENERAL

So far in this book, we have analyzed a variety of markets—for wheat, cable TV service, household exterminators, gasoline, perfume, airline travel, and more. All of these markets had one thing in common: They were **product markets,** in which firms sell goods and services to households or other firms. Of course, products aren't made out of thin air, but rather from the economy's *resources*—labor, capital, land and natural resources, and entrepreneurship. These resources must be purchased from those who own them. Since resources are sometimes called *factors of production,* the markets in which they are traded are called **factor markets.** Labor markets, for example, are a type of factor market.

In this and the next two chapters, we switch our focus from product markets to factor markets. But you will find much that is familiar in our approach. First, just as there are different *market structures* in which products can be traded, the same is true of factor markets. The model of perfectly competitive product markets, for example, has its counterpart in factor markets. Second, many of the *tools* we used to analyze product markets make their appearance in factor markets as well: profit maximization, utility maximization, marginal decision making, equilibrium, and more.

But factor markets also differ from product markets in important ways. Figure 1 illustrates one of the important differences, by showing the role played by each type of market in the economy.[2]

Notice that in product markets, households demand the products, and firms supply them. In factor markets, these roles are typically reversed: Firms demand resources such as labor, land, or capital equipment, while the households who own these resources are the suppliers.

Product markets Markets in which firms sell goods and services to households or other firms.

Factor markets Markets in which resources—labor, capital, land and natural resources, and entrepreneurship—are sold to firms.

---

[2] Notice that Figure 1 uses supply and demand curves to depict the two types of markets. You've already learned that in product markets, we use supply and demand only when viewing the market as *perfectly competitive*. In this chapter, you'll learn that the same applies to factor markets. So, technically, Figure 1 depicts an economy in which both product and factor markets are viewed as perfectly competitive.

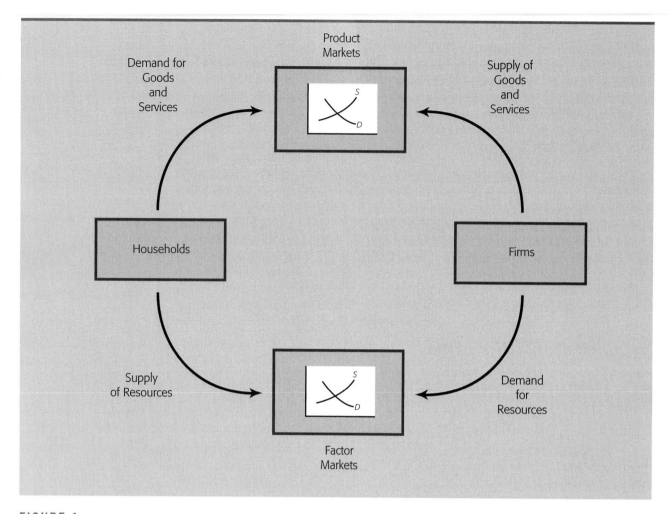

FIGURE 1
**Product Markets and
Factor Markets**

*In product markets, households
demand goods and services, and
firms supply them. In factor
markets, the roles are reversed:
Firms demand resources—such
as labor, capital, land and natural resources, or entrepreneurship. Households supply them.*

Figure 1 also shows an important connection between product and factor markets. Indeed, separating these two types of markets as we've done, while useful for
learning, is highly artificial, since the decision to produce more of any product implies a decision to employ more resources. For example, when Ford decides to produce more automobiles, it must use more labor, more machinery, or more land for
its factories, and perhaps more of all three. It will also need greater quantities of inputs produced by other firms—steel, tires, windshields—and these firms, in turn,
will have to obtain more resources to produce them. You can see that *products* and
the *resources* used to produce them are really two sides of the same coin. What you
learn in these next few chapters will help you understand how these two sides of the
economy—product markets and factor markets—fit together.

LABOR MARKETS IN PARTICULAR

The basic approach we will take in studying the labor market may initially strike
you as a bit heartless: We will treat labor as a commodity—something that is
bought and sold in the marketplace—and regard the wage rate as the price of that

commodity. The wage rate can be defined as an hourly rate (e.g., $20 per hour), a daily rate ($160 per day), or a rate for any other time unit.

As a first approximation, we explain how a worker's wage rate is determined in the same way we'd explain the price of a bushel of wheat. That is, we look at how groups of economic decision makers come together in markets in order to trade. We then look for the equilibrium price determined in those markets and—eventually—explore how various changes affect that equilibrium price. We do this for one simple reason: It works.

Of course, labor *is* different from other things that are traded. First, sellers of wheat do not care who buys their product, as long as they get the market price. Sellers of labor, on the other hand, care about many things besides their wage rate when they look for a job: working conditions, friendly coworkers, commuting distance, possibilities for advancement, prestige, a sense of fulfillment, and more.

A second distinct feature of labor is the special meaning of the price in this market: the wage rate. Most of the income people earn over their lifetimes will come from their jobs, and their hourly, weekly, or yearly wage will determine how well they can feed, clothe, house, and otherwise provide for themselves and their families. This adds a special moral dimension to events in the labor market.

In this chapter, we apply the basic model of supply and demand to explain how wage rates and employment are determined and what causes them to change. Toward the end of the chapter, we'll also discuss some of the special features of the labor market, and continue to explore them in the next chapter.

Defining a Labor Market

When you begin searching for a job after college, you will become a seller in a labor market. But which labor market? As you've seen several times in this book,

> *how broadly or narrowly we define a market depends on the specific questions we wish to answer.*

For example, suppose we are interested in explaining why college graduates, on average, earn more than those with just high school diplomas. Then we would want to define our labor market very broadly: the market for all college-educated labor in the United States. In this market, you would be one of about 131 million suppliers—including all those with college degrees (but not higher degrees) who are already employed. Your employer would be one of hundreds of thousands of buyers. We'd also define another, even larger labor market for workers without college degrees, and the firms that hire them. Then, we'd explore why the equilibrium wage in each of these broadly defined labor markets differs.

On the other hand, we might be interested in finding out how salaries in some profession (say, medicine) are determined. For this purpose, we would use a narrower definition: the market for physicians in the United States. The sellers would be all individuals with medical degrees, and the buyers would be all the hospitals, universities, and private practices that hire them. Or, we could go even narrower, and ask why the wage rates of physicians in Boston are higher than the wage rates of physicians elsewhere. Here, the buyers and sellers would be limited to those already in the Boston area or those who could move there within the period we are considering. In this chapter, we will be asking many different questions about labor markets, and will need to look at both broadly and narrowly defined markets to answer them.

Competitive Labor Markets

Perfectly competitive labor market Market with many indistinguishable sellers of labor and many buyers, and with easy entry and exit of workers.

In most of this chapter, we'll be viewing both product and labor markets are *perfectly competitive.* So let's begin by defining perfect competition in a labor market.

> *A perfectly competitive labor market has the following three characteristics:*
> 1. *There are large numbers of buyers (firms) and sellers (households), and each individual firm or household is only a tiny part of the labor market.*
> 2. *All workers in the labor market appear the same to firms.*
> 3. *Workers can easily enter into or exit from the labor market.*

Do these conditions sound familiar? They should, since they are almost identical to the features of perfect competition in a product market (Chapter 8). The only difference is that here it is labor, rather than a good or service, that is being traded.

Very few labor markets *strictly* satisfy all three of these requirements. But many markets come close enough to make the perfectly competitive model a useful approximation. The more closely a particular labor market satisfies the conditions, the more accurate our analysis will be.

For example, consider the requirement that all workers are the same. We know that no two workers are ever precisely the same, just as no two pocket PCs made by different companies are identical. But in Chapter 3, when we wanted to explain price changes for pocket PCs in general, we ignored the difference between one brand and another and assumed that consumers viewed pocket PCs as a standardized product. Similarly, when we want to explain changes in the wage rate for large groups of workers, it will often make sense to ignore the differences among workers, and assume that employers view all workers in a labor market as essentially the same.

This assumption will be more realistic in some labor markets than in others. A farmer hiring apple pickers may indeed make few distinctions among different job candidates, as long as they meet the minimum requirements for strength and agility. On the other hand, a firm hiring computer programmers may be acutely aware of differences in quality. Still, if our purpose is to analyze changes in pay for computer programmers *in general* (rather than why some computer programmers are paid more than others), our assumption that all workers appear the same to firms is a useful simplification.

We will devote most of this chapter to the competitive model, because it can be applied so broadly and because it serves as a benchmark against which other types of labor markets can be measured. When an economist is asked to analyze the market for computer programmers, attorneys, college professors, nurses, librarians, or stockbrokers, he will reach for the competitive model first, even though in each of these cases one or more of the requirements of perfect competition is not strictly satisfied. We will, however, also look at some important departures from perfect competition in the appendix to this chapter and in the next chapter.[3]

---

[3] More specifically, the appendix to this chapter deals with an important departure from perfect competition called *monopsony,* in which a single firm is a large and important employer in its labor market. Chapter 12 will explore what happens in labor markets when there are *barriers to entry, differences in ability,* and *discrimination.*

Firms in Labor Markets

You might think that firms that compete in the same product market also compete in the same labor market. And this is *sometimes* true. For example, the artichoke farms in Northern California all compete in the same product market (the national market for artichokes) and also in the same labor market (the market for farm labor in Northern California).

But this is not always the case. First, some firms that compete in the same product market operate in entirely *different* labor markets. For example, Volvo and General Motors share several product markets around the world—such as the U.S. market for passenger cars—but they participate in entirely different labor markets. While Volvo hires most of its labor in the Swedish labor market, GM hires most of its labor in the United States.

Second, some firms that operate in entirely different product markets compete in the *same* labor market. For example, airlines operate in entirely different product markets than consulting firms like McKinsey and Company or Boston Consulting. But when the airlines want to hire managers, they must go to the national market for MBAs. In that labor market, the airlines will find themselves in direct competition with the consulting firms, who are also trying to hire MBAs.

> *The demand side of a labor market includes all firms hiring labor in that labor market. These firms may, but do not necessarily, compete in the same product market.*

DEMAND FOR LABOR BY A SINGLE FIRM

A competitive labor market has two sides: buyers and sellers. In this section, we begin our exploration of the buying side of the market—labor demand—by looking at how a typical firm in a labor market decides how much labor to employ. But before we get into the mechanics, let's step back a bit and consider what labor demand—or the demand for any other resource—is all about.

Labor as a Derived Demand

The demand for a resource is unlike the other types of demand you have studied so far in one very important respect: It is a demand for an *input* in production, not a demand for output. When consumers demand outputs—such as perfume, bed frames, or movies—they do so because these things give them pleasure or satisfaction. They are wanted in and of themselves. But General Motors does not demand a resource like labor or capital because its owners (stockholders) get satisfaction from employing people or using more machinery. Rather, GM, facing a demand curve for its cars, chooses to produce and sell the profit-maximizing quantity of them. *As a result,* GM employs a certain number of workers, uses certain quantities of machines, and so on. GM's demand for any resource is therefore *derived from* the public's demand for its cars.

> *The demand for a resource—such as labor—is a **derived demand**; it arises from, and will vary with, the demand for the firm's output.*

Derived demand The demand for a resource that arises from, and varies with, the demand for the product it helps to produce.

The phrase "will vary with" is important: The demand for a resource by a firm will *change* whenever the demand for the firm's product changes. Over the past few decades, as the demand for cars, trucks, and SUVs has grown, the demand for labor by GM, Ford, Toyota, and other automobile companies has grown along with it. By contrast, the demand for dictating machines has decreased, as even the highest-level managers now type their own memos into their computers. The demand for labor and other resources by makers of dictating machines has fallen accordingly.

Resource Demand: A General Rule

In Chapter 7 you learned a general rule for the firm called the *marginal approach to profit:*

> *The marginal approach to profit states that a firm should take any action that adds more to its revenue than it adds to its cost.*

And in several chapters, you've seen this rule applied to one kind of action: increasing production. Our rule in this case translated to: Increase output whenever doing so adds more to revenue than it adds to cost—as long as $MR > MC$.

When we view the firm as a buyer in a resource or factor market, we use the same principle of marginal decision making. Only this time the action under consideration is "increase employment of the resource by another unit." And the rule becomes: *Increase employment of any resource whenever doing so adds more to revenue than it adds to cost.* However, to avoid confusion between decisions about resources and decisions about output, we don't use the terms "marginal revenue" and "marginal cost" when discussing factor markets. But we do use very similar terms.

To track changes on the revenue side, we use the term *marginal revenue product.*

Marginal revenue product (MRP) The change in the firm's total revenue divided by the change in its employment of a resource.

> *A firm's **marginal revenue product** (MRP) for any resource is the change in the firm's total revenue (ΔTR) divided by the change in its employment of the resource (Δ Quantity of Resource):*
>
> $$MR = \frac{\Delta TR}{\Delta \ Quantity \ of \ Resource}$$
>
> *The MRP tells us the change in total revenue per unit increase in the resource.*

In the special case in which the firm thinks about changing the resource by one unit at a time (Δ Quantity of Resource = 1), we can think of the marginal revenue product as the change in the firm's revenue when it employs *one more unit* of the resource.

Why does hiring a resource change revenue? When the firm employs more of any resource, it will produce and sell more output, and this will affect its total revenue.

To track changes on the cost side, we use the term marginal factor cost:

Marginal factor cost (MFC) The change in the firm's total cost divided by the change in its employment of a resource

> *A firm's **marginal factor cost** (MFC) for any resource is the change in the firm's total cost (ΔTC) divided by the change in its employment of the resource (Δ Quantity of Resource):*
>
> $$MFC = \frac{\Delta TC}{\Delta \ Quantity \ of \ Resource}$$
>
> *The MFC tells us the rise in cost per unit increase in the resource.*

Once again, when Δ Quantity of Resource = 1, you can think of *MFC* as the increase in cost from employing *one more unit* of the resource.

Once you are familiar with this special terminology, the marginal approach to profit gives the firm a complete guide to its behavior in a factor market:

> *To maximize profit, the firm should increase its employment of any resource whenever* MRP > MFC, *but not when* MRP < MFC. *Thus, the profit-maximizing quantity of any resource is the quantity at which* MRP = MFC.

The logic of this rule is straightforward: If *MRP* > *MFC*, employing more of the resource increases revenue more than cost, so profit will rise. When *MRP* < *MFC*, using more of the resource adds more to cost than to revenue, so profit falls. When the firm exploits every opportunity to increase profit—that is, using more of the resource whenever *MRP* > *MFC*—it will arrive at the point at which *MRP* = *MFC*.

To see this rule in action, let's now apply it to the firm's decision about how much labor to hire. Until we get to the appendix, we'll analyze labor demand under conditions of *perfect competition*. That is, we'll assume the firm sells its output in a perfectly competitive *product* market, and hires its workers in a perfectly competitive *labor* market. Moreover, to start simply, we'll initially look at a firm for which labor is the *only* variable input.

The Firm's Employment Decision When Only Labor Is Variable

In Table 1, we return to a firm we first met in Chapter 6: Spotless Car Wash. The first two columns in the table are reproduced from Table 3 of that chapter and introduce nothing new. Column 1 shows different numbers of workers that Spotless can hire, column 2 the quantity of output produced each day.

Column 3 shows the marginal product of labor (*MPL*)—the additional output produced when *one more* worker is hired. For example, when the firm hires the third worker, output rises from 90 to 130, so the *MPL* for this change is 40.

The marginal product of labor was discussed in Chapter 6, where it helped us understand the shape of the marginal cost curve. Recall that at very low levels of employment, the *MPL* tends to rise as employment rises, but as more and more workers are added, the *MPL* will eventually decrease. In Table 1, notice that the marginal product of labor *increases* as employment rises from 0 to 1 to 2 workers. This tells us that, from 0 to 2 workers, Spotless has *increasing returns to labor*. Beyond 2 workers, however, additional employment causes the marginal product of labor to *decrease,* and Spotless has *diminishing returns to labor*. (See Chapter 6 if you need a refresher on returns to labor.)

Column 4 shows the price Spotless can charge for each car wash. The price remains constant at $4, no matter how much output is produced, telling us that Spotless is a competitive firm in its product market. It can wash all the cars it wants without decreasing the price. The fifth column lists the firm's total revenue for each number of workers, found by multiplying the quantity of output (column 2) by the price (column 4).

The Firm's *MRP* in a Competitive Product Market. Now look at column 6, which shows the marginal revenue product (*MRP*) of labor. For any change in employment, the *MRP* is the change in total revenue in column 5 divided by the change in employment in column 1. For example, when the firm increases employment from

(1) Quantity of Labor	(2) Total Product (Cars Washed per Day)	(3) Marginal Product of Labor (*MPL*)	(4) Price per Car Wash	(5) Total Revenue	(6) Marginal Revenue Prodcut (*MRP*)	(7) Wage (*W*)
0	0		$4	$0		$60
		30			$120	
1	30		$4	$120		$60
		60			$240	
2	90		$4	$360		$60
		40			$160	
3	130		$4	$520		$60
		31			$124	
4	161		$4	$644		$60
		23			$92	
5	**184**		**$4**	**$736**		**$60**
		12			$48	
6	196		$4	$784		$60
		4			$16	
7	200		$4	$800		$60

TABLE 1
Data for Spotless Car Wash (Perfectly Competitive Product and Labor Markets)

2 to 3 workers (an increase of 1 worker), its daily revenue rises from $360 to $520, an increase of $160. For this change in employment,

$$MRP \text{ of Labor} = \frac{\Delta TR}{\Delta \text{ Quantity of Labor}} = \$160/1 = \$160$$

But we can also calculate Spotless's *MRP* of labor in another way. Since it sells its output (car washes) in a perfectly competitive market, Spotless can increase production without affecting the market price of $4. When Spotless employs one more worker, raising output by the marginal product of labor (*MPL*), each additional unit of output sells for $4. Therefore, revenue will rise by $4 × *MPL*. So now we have another way to calculate the *MRP*: Multiply the market price in column 4 by the *MPL* in column 3. For example, when moving from 2 to 3 workers, Spotless washes 40 more cars (*MPL* = $40), for which it gets $4 each. Its revenue rises by $4 × *MPL* = $4 × 40 = $160. This is the same value for the *MRP* of labor that we obtained above.

In general,

> *When output is sold in a competitive product market, the* MRP *for any change in employment will equal the price of output* (P) *times the marginal product of labor* (MPL):
>
> $$MRP = P \times MPL$$

This explains why the *MRP* values in the table first rise and then fall. As you learned in Chapter 6 (and were recently reminded), we generally expect increasing returns to labor (rising *MPL*) at low levels of employment, and diminishing returns to labor (falling *MPL*) at higher levels of employment. Since *P* remains constant when output is sold competitively, the behavior of $MRP = P \times MPL$ mirrors that of *MPL*, first rising and then falling.[4]

The Firm's *MFC* in a Competitive Labor Market.

We've just looked at Spotless's *MRP*, which tells us how hiring an additional worker changes the firm's *revenue*. But how will it change the firm's *costs*? That is, what is Spotless's *MFC*?

In a competitive labor market, there are so many buyers and sellers of labor and each is such a tiny part of the market, that no buyer or seller can influence the market price of labor: the wage rate. This means that a firm in a competitive market is a **wage taker:** It takes the market wage as a given. In column 7 of the table, we assume that this market wage rate is $60 per day. So for Spotless, no matter what its current level of employment, its marginal factor cost of labor is always $60 per day:

$$MRP \text{ of Labor} = \frac{\Delta TR}{\Delta \text{ Quantity of Labor}} = \$60/1 = \$60$$

More generally,

> *When labor is hired in a competitive labor market, the* MFC *for any change in employment will equal the market wage rate* (W):
>
> $$MFC = W$$

The Profit-Maximizing Employment Level.

How does a firm that operates in competitive product and labor markets find the profit-maximizing level of employment? We can apply the general principle involving *MRP* and *MFC* developed earlier, recognizing that *MFC* in this case is the same as the wage rate, W. This suggests the following simple rule:

> *Hire another worker when* MRP > W, *but not when* MRP < W.

Let's apply the guideline to Spotless Car Wash. When going from 0 to 1 worker, revenue rises by $120 ($MRP = \$120$) and costs rise by $60 ($MFC = W = \$60$).

Don't Take *MPL* Personally Remember that marginal productivity (as well as the marginal revenue product derived from it) is a characteristic of production, not a characteristic of an individual worker. The *MPL* tells us how much a firm's output will increase when one more worker is hired. It is easy to confuse this with an individual's *personal* productivity, which is based on skill and effort. To see the difference, consider this example: Suppose you can type 90 words a minute with no mistakes; your personal productivity as a typist is very high. If a word processing firm hires you, by how much will its output of finished manuscripts increase? That depends. Suppose the firm has just five computers. If you were, say, the fifth worker hired, you would get your own computer, and production would increase considerably. But if you were the twentieth worker hired, you would have to share a computer with perhaps three other workers, and much of your time would be spent waiting for a machine; output would not rise much at all. Even though your own skills are the same in both cases, the output you would *add* to the firm if hired—the marginal productivity of labor at the firm—would be quite different.

DANGEROUS CURVES

Wage taker A firm that takes the market wage rate as a given when making employment decisions.

---

[4] $MRP = P \times MPL$ holds only when output is sold in a perfectly competitive market, in which the firm faces a horizontal demand curve for its product. If the firm faces a *downward-sloping* demand curve for its product, as in monopoly or monopolistic competition, there is a different relationship between *MRP* and *MPL*. Hiring another worker still increases output by the *MPL*, but now the firm must drop its price in order to sell the additional output. In this case, hirinig another worker will increase the firm's revenue by the additional output produced (*MPL*) times the increase in revenue for each unit increase in output (*MR*). Thus, with a downward-sloping demand curve for its product, $MRP = MPL \times MR$.

Although the shape and position of the *MRP* curve is different when the firm faces a downward-sloping demand curve (compared to perfect competition), our conclusions will be unaffected by this difference.

FIGURE 2
**The Profit-Maximizing
Employment Level**

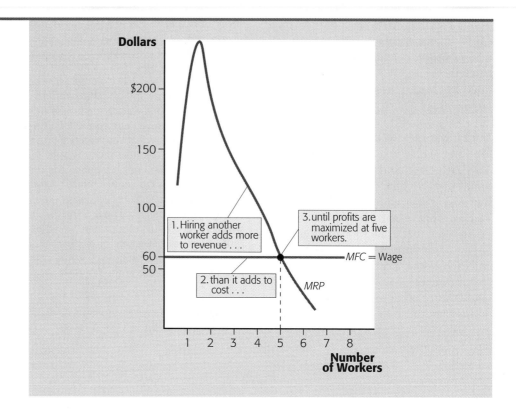

Since revenue rises more than costs ($MRP > W$), hiring this first worker will add to the firm's profit. The same is true when the second, third, fourth, and fifth workers are hired. (Verify this on your own.) But in moving from the fifth to the sixth worker, $MRP = \$48$, while $W = \$60$. Since $MRP < W$, the firm should *not* hire the sixth worker; it should stop at the fifth. We have found the firm's profit-maximizing level of employment: five workers.

We can understand Spotless's employment decision even better by graphing the marginal data from Table 1, as we've done in Figure 2. As usual, marginal values are plotted *between* employment levels, since they tell us what happens as employment changes from one level to another. The value of MRP first rises and then falls as employment changes, so the MRP *curve* in the figure first slopes upward and then downward. The wage rate (the cost per day of hiring the additional worker) is always the same, as shown by the horizontal line at $60.

As long as employment is less than five workers, the MRP curve lies above the wage line ($MRP > W$), so the firm should hire another worker. But suppose the firm has hired five workers and is considering hiring a sixth. For this move, the MRP curve lies *below* the wage line. Since $MRP < W$, increasing employment would *decrease* the firm's profit. The same is true for every increase in employment beyond five workers: In this range, the MRP curve always lies below the wage line, so the firm will decrease its profits by hiring another worker. Using Figure 2, we see that the optimal employment level is five workers, just as we found earlier using Table 1.

The profit-maximizing number of workers, five, is the employment level closest to where $MRP = W$—that is, where the MRP curve crosses the wage line. The reason for this is straightforward: For each change in employment that *increases* profit, the *MRP* curve will lie above the wage line. The first time that hiring a worker *decreases* profit, the *MRP* curve will cross the wage line and dip below it.

This observation allows us to state a simple rule for the firm's employment decision:

> *To maximize profit, the firm should hire the number of workers such that* MRP = W—*that is, where the* MRP *curve intersects the wage line.*[5]

The Two Approaches to Profit Maximization. You've learned two different approaches for the firm to follow to maximize profit. In previous chapters, we used the *MR* and *MC* approach to find profit-maximizing *output*. In this chapter, we've used the *MRP* and *MFC* approach (or *MRP* and *W* approach, in a perfectly competitive labor market) to find profit-maximizing *employment*.

Can these two approaches lead to different decisions? In our example, the *MRP* and *MFC* approach tells Spotless to employ five workers, which (as you can see in Table 1) implies a total output of 184 car washes per day. Could the *MC* and *MR* approach guide Spotless to some *other* level of output, say, 196 car washes?

The answer is: No, because these two "different" approaches are actually the same method viewed in two different ways. To see this, remember that hiring another worker increases the firm's output and therefore changes both its revenue and its cost. For example, in Table 1, increasing employment from four to five workers raises output by 23 units (from 161 to 184 units), and also increases revenue by $92 and cost by $60. Since hiring the fifth worker increases revenue more than it raises cost (i.e., *MRP* > *MFC*), then it must be that increasing output by 23 units raises revenue by more than it raises cost (i.e., *MR* > *MC* for an increase of 23 units).

This applies more generally: Whenever *MRP* > *MFC* for a change in employment, *MR* > *MC* for the associated rise in output. Whenever *MRP* < *MFC* for a change in employment, *MR* < *MC* for the associated rise in output. And if *MRP* = *MFC* for a change in employment, then it must be that *MR* = *MC* for the associated change in output. (To help you see the connection between these two approaches even more clearly, add columns for *MR* and *MC* in Table 1 and find the profit-maximizing output level using the *MR* and *MC* approach. But when calculating *MR* and *MC*, don't forget to divide Δ*TR* and Δ*TC* by the change in *output*, which is *not* one unit in the table.)

The Firm's Labor Demand Curve. In Table 1, the wage rate the firm had to pay was $60 per day. But what if the wage had been different, say, $45 per day? As you can verify on your own, at this lower wage rate, the firm would have hired six workers instead of five. The optimal level of employment will always depend on the wage rate.

---

[5] There is one proviso, however: Profits are maximized only if the *MRP* curve crosses the wage line *from above*—that is, if we are on the *downward-sloping* portion of the *MRP* curve. To prove this to yourself, draw an example in which the upward-sloping portion of the *MRP* curve crosses the wage line from below. Notice that the *MRP* will always be greater than the wage to the right of the crossing point, so it will always pay for the firm to *increase* employment beyond the crossing point. From now on, the diagrams in this chapter will show only the downward-sloping part of the *MRP* curve, since this is the only part used by the firm to make its employment decision.

FIGURE 3
The Firm's Labor Demand Curve

As the wage rate varies, the firm moves along its MRP curve in deciding how many workers to hire. As a result, the downward-sloping portion of the MRP curve is the firm's labor demand curve. It shows how many workers will be demanded at each wage rate.

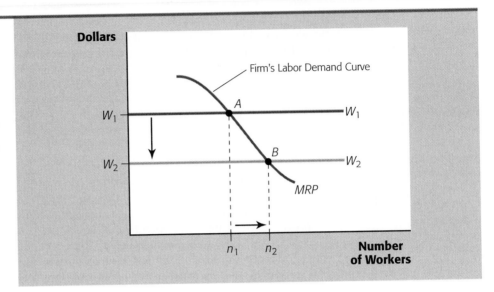

Figure 3 shows what happens at the typical firm as the wage rate varies. For each wage rate, the optimal level of employment, where $MRP = W$, is found by traveling horizontally over to the MRP curve and then down to the horizontal axis. For example, with a wage rate of W_1, the firm will want to hire n_1 workers. If the wage drops to W_2, the optimal level of employment rises to n_2. As the wage rate drops, the firm moves along its MRP curve in deciding how many workers to hire. This is why we call the downward-sloping portion of the MRP curve the *firm's labor demand curve*:

> *When labor is the only variable input, the downward-sloping portion of the MRP curve is the firm's labor demand curve, telling us how much labor the firm will want to employ at each wage rate.*

The Firm's Employment Decision When Several Inputs Are Variable

So far, we've been assuming that labor is the only variable input, and all other inputs were assumed to be fixed in quantity. But it's often important to recognize the firm as choosing quantities of two or more variable inputs. For example, with a long-run planning horizon, a firm will view *all* of its inputs as variable—including its machinery, plant size, and more. Even over the short run, a firm may be able to vary not only its labor, but its use of raw materials, energy, and some types of capital (like hand tools).

When other inputs are variable, the shape of the firm's labor demand curve will be somewhat different. But the key points of our analysis remain the same.

Figure 4 provides an example of what is different—and what remains the same—when inputs other than labor can be varied. The figure shows the situation facing Spotless Car Wash, which uses only two inputs: labor and capital (automated car wash lines). We assume that initially, with wage rate W_1, Spotless employs n_1 workers. This puts us at point A in the figure.

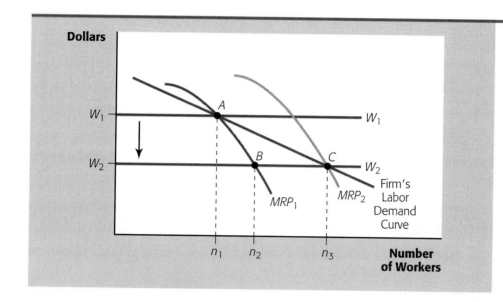

FIGURE 4

The Employment Decision with Several Variable Inputs

When only labor can be varied, a decrease in the wage moves the firm from A to B, increasing employment from n_1 to n_2. But if capital can vary as well, and the lower wage causes the firm to use more capital, the MRP curve could shift upward to MRP_2. In that case, the firm moves from A to C, raising employment for n_1 to n_3.

Now the wage drops to W_2. What will the firm do? If it can vary *only* its labor, it will move along the curve MRP_1 to point B, expanding employment to n_2 workers. This is because, along any MRP curve, the quantities of all other inputs are assumed to remain unchanged. At point B, the firm will use more labor to wash cars, but it will continue to use the same number of automated lines.

But now suppose that Spotless can vary its capital along with its labor. Once again, assume the wage rate drops to W_2, and Spotless decides to use more labor *and* more capital. Assume, also, that the additional capital makes workers *more productive*. Then Spotless's MRP curve will shift upward, to MRP_2 in the figure. As a result, after the drop in the wage rate, Spotless ends up at point C, where its new MRP curve, MRP_2, crosses the new wage line, W_2. The profit-maximizing level of employment is now n_3 workers. And the firm's labor demand curve, showing the best employment level at each wage rate, is the line connecting points A and C. As you can see, when inputs other than labor are variable, the firm's labor demand curve is shaped differently.

We need not worry too much about this difference in shape, though, because the two key conclusions we reached about labor demand in our earlier case (when only labor could be varied) still hold in this case (when several inputs can be varied). First, the optimal level of employment will *still* satisfy the condition that $MRP = W$. After all, if $MRP > W$, the firm can always increase its profit by hiring another worker, whether it varies other inputs at the same time or not.

Second, the labor demand curve still slopes downward: a drop in the wage causes the firm to increase the quantity of labor demanded, whether the firm varies other inputs at the same time or not. *How much* employment rises may depend on whether other inputs can be varied (as in Figure 4) or not (as in Figure 3). But for our analysis, what matters is that a lower wage rate implies a greater quantity of labor demanded.

Whether labor is the only variable input or other inputs can be varied as well, the profit-maximizing level of employment will still satisfy MRP = W, and the labor demand curve will still slope downward.

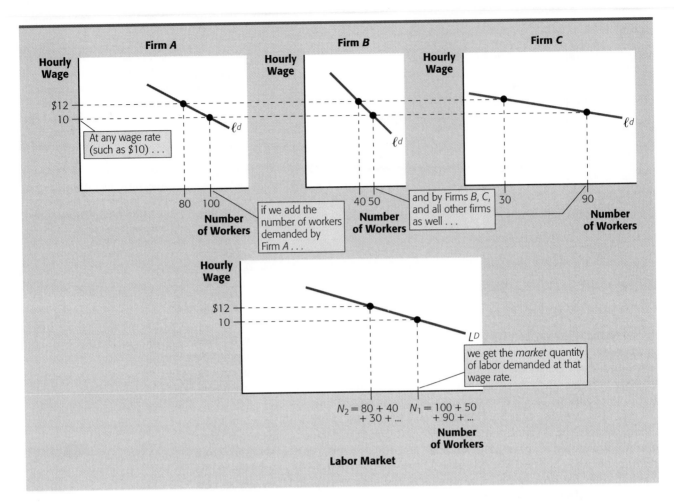

FIGURE 5
The Market Demand for Labor

Each firm participating in a labor market will have its own downward-sloping labor demand curve. The market demand curve is found by adding up the quantity of labor demanded by each firm at each wage rate.

THE MARKET DEMAND FOR LABOR

How many workers will all firms in a labor market want to employ? This question is answered by the *market* labor demand curve. Look at Figure 5, which shows the labor demand curves for three of the many firms in a labor market. At an hourly wage rate of $10, Firm A's labor demand curve, ℓ^d, tells us that it demands 100 workers, while Firm B demands 50 workers, Firm C demands 90, and so on, for all of the other firms in this labor market. By adding up these numbers, we get the market quantity of labor demanded when the wage rate is $10: $N_1 = 100 + 50 + 90 + \ldots$. Now suppose the wage rate rises to $12. Firm A will drop down to 80 workers, Firm B will drop to 40 workers, Firm C to 30 workers, and so on. With fewer workers demanded by each individual firm, the market quantity of labor demanded will shrink to $N_2 = 80 + 40 + 30 + \ldots$.

Market labor demand curve
Curve indicating the total number of workers all firms in a labor market want to employ at each wage rate.

> *The **market labor demand curve** tells us the total number of workers all firms in a labor market want to employ at each wage rate. It is found by horizontally summing across all firms' individual labor demand curves.*

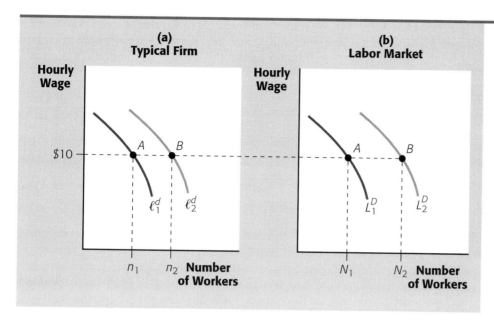

(a)
Typical Firm

Hourly
Wage

$10

A   *B*

ℓ_1^d ℓ_2^d

n_1 n_2 **Number of Workers**

(b)
Labor Market

Hourly
Wage

A   *B*

L_1^D L_2^D

N_1 N_2 **Number of Workers**

FIGURE 6
A Shift in the Labor Demand Curve

An increase in the demand for the product, a change in technology, or a change in the price of another input will cause the individual firm's demand for labor to increase, as from ℓ_1^d to ℓ_2^d in panel (a). In panel (b), the market labor demand curve shifts to the right as well. At any wage rate, more labor is demanded.

Notice that the market labor demand curve slopes downward just like the labor demand curve of each firm. If a drop in the wage rate causes each firm in the market to want to employ more workers, then total quantity demanded will increase as well.

Shifts in the Market Labor Demand Curve

Labor markets, like other markets in the economy, are undergoing constant change, in part caused by *shifts* in labor demand curves. As we'll see in the second half of this chapter, these shifts can have dramatic effects on workers, increasing or decreasing their wage rates, or causing some to lose their jobs entirely.

Figure 6 illustrates a general example. In panel (a), the typical firm experiences a rightward shift of its labor demand curve, from ℓ_1^d to ℓ_2^d. As a result, the market labor demand curve—the horizontal sum of all firms' labor demand curves—shifts rightward as well, from L_1^D to L_2^D in panel (b). After the shift, more labor will be demanded at any wage rate.

But what causes the labor demand curve to *shift?* In general,

a change in any variable that affects the quantity of labor demanded—except for the wage rate—causes the labor demand curve to shift.

Let's consider some of the specific variables that shift the labor demand curve.

A Change in Demand for a Firm's Product. Remember that demand for labor is a *derived* demand: It arises from the demand for the firm's product. If demand for that product increases, its market *price* will rise. Since $MRP = P \times MPL$, the rise in price will cause MRP to be greater at each level of employment; that is, the MRP curve of each affected firm will shift upward. Therefore, its labor demand curve will shift upward (and rightward) as well. Now, *if* many of these firms (the ones whose

Industrial robots are substitutable for less-skilled, assembly-line labor, but complementary with highly skilled labor that programs and repairs the robots.

output price has risen) hire employees in the same labor market, then the *market* demand for labor will increase as well. If very few firms whose price has risen hire in this labor market, there will be no perceptible change in the market labor demand curve. Thus,

> *the effect of a change in product demand on labor demand depends on whether many firms in the same product market also share the same labor market. When they do, a rise in product demand will shift the market labor demand curve rightward; a fall in product demand will shift the market labor demand curve leftward.*

A Change in Technology. Many changes in technology involve the discovery and implementation of an entirely new input to produce a good or service. For example, the development of the Internet in the mid- and late 1990s created an entirely new input for producing many services (retail sales, information, banking, entertainment, and more). The development of new medical diagnostic techniques, cell phones, and genetically modified seeds are other examples of technological advances associated with entirely new inputs. How does the introduction of a new input affect the market demand for labor? That depends on whether the new input is *complementary* with or *substitutable* for the type of labor we're considering.

Complementary input An input whose utilization increases the marginal product of another input.

> *A **complementary input** is one that increases the marginal product of a certain type of labor. Usually, the input is used by this type of labor, making it more productive.*

For example, in Chapter 2 it was pointed out that a doctor can diagnose more patients, and do so more accurately, with a PET scanner than without one. PET scanners are *complementary* inputs for physicians and other diagnostic personnel, increasing their marginal productivity. When a technological advance creates an input that is *complementary* with the labor in a market, increasing the marginal product of labor (MPL), it also increases the $MRP = P \times MPL$ at any level of employment. That is, it will shift each firm's MRP curve (its labor demand curve) upward and *rightward*, and the market labor demand curve will shift to the right. This is shown in Figure 7.

But technological change can have the *opposite* impact on labor demand when the new input is *substitutable* for labor.

Substitutable input An input whose utilization decreases the marginal product of another input.

> *A **substitutable input** is one that decreases the marginal product of a certain type of labor. Usually, the input can be used instead of this type of labor, decreasing its marginal product.*

For example, in 2003 some supermarkets began using sophisticated scanners that enable customers to ring up their own groceries. These scanners are *substitutable* for the labor of supermarket cashiers. At any level of employment, the marginal productivity of these cashiers drops. If this technology becomes widespread, then many supermarkets' MRP curves (their labor demand curves) for cashiers will shift downward and *leftward*, and the market labor demand curve will shift to the left (Figure 7 again).

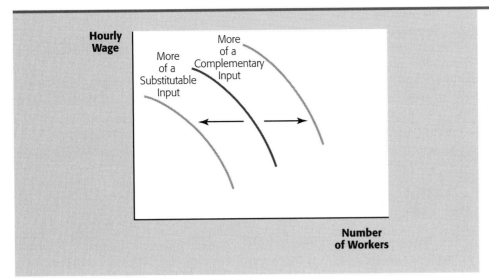

FIGURE 7
Introducing a New Input

If a new input is introduced to the production process, the market demand for labor will shift. If the new input is complementary to labor—if it increases the marginal product of labor at each wage rate—the demand curve will shift rightward. However, if the new input is a substitute for labor, the demand curve for labor will shift leftward.

Once we know whether a new technology is complementary with or substitutable for labor, we can infer how it will affect the market demand for labor:

> *When many firms in a labor market acquire a new technology, the market labor demand curve will shift rightward if the technology is complementary with labor and leftward if the technology is substitutable for labor.*

Determining whether a new technology is complementary with or substitutable for labor can be tricky, since firms often hire more than one type of labor. Think about what happens when retailers such as Macy's or Barnes & Noble acquire the inputs needed to sell over the Internet. Their demand for highly skilled labor—the kind that can operate and maintain hardware, and design and modify Web pages—increases. But their demand for somewhat less skilled labor—salespeople, inventory clerks, and so forth—decreases, because online sales do not require these services to be performed by workers. Thus, the impact of technological progress on labor demand depends crucially on *which* labor market we are looking at—the market for high-tech workers, or the market for salespeople.

A Change in the Price of Another Input. When firms can vary other inputs *besides* labor, their demand for labor will be affected by the prices of other inputs. Not surprisingly, the nature of the effect will depend, in part, on whether the other input is *complementary* with or *substitutable* for the labor in that market.

For example, many factories use automated machinery to package goods with very little human involvement. The automated machinery is a *substitute* for less-skilled product packagers. Let's take a long-run view, regarding this machinery as a variable input. Imagine that its price drops (say, because of technological advances in producing the equipment). Then the least-cost input mix for producing any given level of output will change: The firm will want to use more of the now cheaper machines and fewer less-skilled packagers. Another way of viewing this is that with more of the machines, the marginal productivity of the human packagers decreases.

But this same input—automated packaging machines—is also *complementary* with a different type of factory labor: the higher-skilled workers who program, maintain, and repair the machines. If packaging machines become cheaper, and more of them are used, the marginal productivity of these higher-skilled workers rises, and the firm will tend to employ more of them.

In general,

> *when the price of some other input decreases, the market labor demand curve may shift rightward or leftward. It will* likely *shift rightward if that other input is complementary with labor and leftward if the other input is substitutable for labor.*[6]

Interestingly, one such "other input" can be labor *from a different labor market,* such as foreign workers. Many people oppose free trade agreements with low-wage foreign countries because they fear that it will make it easier and cheaper for U.S. firms to set up factories in those countries. This fear led to fierce political opposition to the North American Free Trade Agreement (NAFTA), which the United States signed with Mexico and Canada in 1993, and contributed to the protests (that led to street riots) when the World Trade Organization met in Seattle in late 1999.

Opponents of free trade claim that as U.S. firms are lured to set up production facilities in Mexico and other poor countries, jobs for American workers disappear. Their argument is that foreign labor is highly substitutable for U.S. labor, so that enabling U.S. firms to hire cheap foreign labor decreases the demand for U.S. labor. (We will dispute this argument—at least in part—in Chapter 15. But here's a hint: Is foreign labor substitutable for American labor *in general* or only in certain labor markets? Are there other labor markets in which foreign labor would be considered *complementary* with American labor?)

A Change in the Number of Firms. Within the United States, firms are continually entering and leaving local labor markets. The entry of new firms will shift the market labor demand curve rightward; exit will shift the curve to the left.

Sometimes, entry is due to the birth of an entirely new industry, as when new Internet firms like Amazon.com, eBay, and Yahoo! were created in the mid-1990s. These new firms caused the demand for labor to shift rightward in several urban areas, especially the area around San Francisco. Other times, entry and exit occur when firms migrate from one local labor market to another. In the mid-1990s, firms in the computer chip industry began relocating to Oregon, shifting the demand for labor rightward in that state and leftward in the areas they abandoned.

---

[6] This effect on labor demand is an example of the *substitution effect* of a change in an input's price. But there is another effect as well: As packaging machines become cheaper, the firm's *marginal cost* curve shifts downward, thereby raising its profit-maximizing output level. When firms produce more, they tend to demand more of *all* inputs—perhaps even less-skilled packagers. This effect on labor demand is called the *output effect* of an input price change. In our discussions of substitutable input prices and substitutable technological change, we've focused only on the substitution effect.

An increase in	Will cause the market labor demand curve to	
Demand for the firm's output	shift rightward	**TABLE 2**
The price of a complementary input	shift leftward	**Shifts in the Labor Demand Curve**
The price of a substitutable input	shift rightward	
The number of firms in the market	shift rightward	
Technology*	shift rightward if a new input is complementary with labor, leftward if the input is substitutable for labor	

*An "increase" in technology here means a technological advance.

Table 2 summarizes what you have learned about shifts in the market labor demand curve. Be careful as you look at the table; it shows only increases in each variable. A decrease in each variable would shift the labor demand curve in the opposite direction.

LABOR SUPPLY

So far, we've considered the demand side of the labor market and the behavior of firms that demand labor. Now we turn our attention to the *supply* side of the labor market and to the *households* that supply labor to firms. We begin with the individual's labor supply decision and then move on to discuss labor supply in the market as a whole.

Individual Labor Supply

In Chapter 5, the individual's problem was to choose the combination of goods and services that maximized satisfaction or utility, subject to the constraints of a limited income and given prices for goods and services. Now we concern ourselves with an individual in the *labor* market who—once again—strives to maximize utility subject to constraints. Let's first look at the constraints that individuals face in a competitive labor market. Then we'll consider how the individual facing those constraints might make choices.

Individuals as Wage Takers. Think of the last time you looked for a job—perhaps a summer job, or a part-time job while going to school. There may have been hundreds—perhaps even thousands—of others looking for similar jobs in your geographic area. Your own decision to sell your labor was a very small drop in a very large bucket: Your decision had no effect on the market wage.

This characteristic—so many sellers that no single one can affect the market wage—is one of our conditions for perfect competition, and it is satisfied in most labor markets.

> *In a competitive labor market, each seller is a wage taker; he or she takes the market wage rate as given.*

This is an important constraint on your job decision. You cannot choose your wage rate; it is determined by conditions in the market.

The Income–Leisure Trade-off. The wage rate you can earn plays an important role in a trade-off that we all face: The more time we spend enjoying leisure activities—talking with friends, going to the movies, reading, exercising, and so on—the less time we spend working and earning income. The wage rate determines the exact nature of this trade-off. For example, if you can earn $10 per hour by working, then each additional hour of leisure time will cost you $10 in foregone income. In a sense, $10 is the *price* of an additional hour of leisure, since that is what you must give up, in money terms, to enjoy it.

Since different people are paid different wage rates, they will face different income–leisure trade-offs. An hour of leisure is "more expensive" to someone who earns $100 per hour than to someone with a wage of $10 per hour.

But in addition to differences in wage rates, there is another way that the income–leisure trade-off can differ among people: Some workers have considerable freedom to vary their weekly hours of work, and some do not.

For example, many self-employed professionals—doctors, lawyers, writers, and others—can adjust their work hours as they please, by increasing or decreasing the number of clients they serve. In addition, hourly workers can sometimes vary their hours of work by choosing to switch between part-time and full-time work or by accepting or refusing overtime. In these cases where hours can be varied, economists think about labor supply using a model of individual choice very similar to the one you learned for consumer theory in Chapter 5. However, instead of choosing the optimal combination of different *goods,* the individual chooses the optimal combination of *income* and *leisure.*

But in most labor markets, you will have relatively little freedom to vary your work hours because your employer will expect you to work a fixed number of hours—typically, eight hours a day, five days a week. In this case, your choice is not *how much* to work but rather *whether to offer your labor in a particular market.* Your choice of work hours in any labor market is constrained to 40 hours per week or zero hours per week. In this chapter, we'll focus on *fixed-hours* labor markets like this, since they are so common in the real world.

The Labor Supply Decision. In a labor market with fixed hours, can we still view an individual as maximizing utility? It might seem that we cannot, at least not in the familiar way. If your hours are fixed, there are no marginal adjustments for you to make. Instead, you make a yes–no decision: to offer your labor services in a market, or *not* to offer them there. But even in this decision, utility maximization plays an important role: In deciding whether or not to work, or in which labor market to supply your labor, you will always select the option that gives you the most utility. Let's explore this choice further.

Reservation Wages. One of the authors of this text, in his youth, spent six months working as an egg cleaner—cleaning the chicken droppings off fertilized eggs for eight hours a day, five days a week. It is not the most pleasant job, and chances are you are not currently planning to enter this line of work. But might you think again and decide that egg cleaning isn't all that bad if the job paid $50 per hour? $100 per hour? What about $200 per hour? Surely there is *some* wage rate that would induce you to take a job as an egg cleaner. Economists call the *lowest wage rate* that would convince you to offer your labor services in a market your **reservation wage** for that labor market. Until you reach this wage rate, you are reserving your time for other uses that give you more utility, either not working at all or working in some other labor market. Whenever the wage rate in a market exceeds your reservation wage for that market, you will decide to work there. When the market wage rate is less than your reservation wage for that market, you will prefer not to work there.[7]

Reservation wage The lowest wage rate at which an individual would supply labor to a particular labor market.

Market Labor Supply

When we speak of the quantity of labor supplied in a market, we mean the number of qualified people who want jobs there. As we've seen, an individual will want to work in a market whenever the wage rate there is greater than his or her reservation wage. But because workers have different preferences over working conditions in different jobs, and different preferences for working at all, they will have different reservation wages for any particular market. For example, if you hate snakes, your reservation wage for a job as assistant snake trainer at a circus would be very high, perhaps $200 per hour or more. If you like snakes, you might jump at the chance to work with them even at a wage of only $10 per hour.

As the wage rate in a market rises, it will exceed more individuals' reservation wages, so more people will offer their labor in that market. Therefore,

the higher the wage rate in a labor market, the greater the quantity of labor supplied in that market.

Panel (a) of Figure 8 illustrates a **labor supply curve** in a hypothetical labor market, telling us the number of people who will want jobs there at each wage rate. In this market, the quantity of labor supplied at an hourly wage of $10 is 1,000 workers, so we know that 1,000 people have reservation wages of $10 per hour or less. At a wage of $12, the quantity of labor supplied is 1,200, so we know that another 200 people have reservation wages between $10 and $12 per hour.

Labor supply curve A curve indicating the number of people who want jobs in a labor market at each wage rate.

Shifts in the Market Labor Supply Curve

A change in the wage rate causes a movement *along* a labor supply curve, as in the move from point C to point D in Figure 8(a). But labor supply curves can (and often do) *shift.* Panel (b) illustrates an increase in labor supply in this market. Notice

---

[7] What happens if the market wage exceeds your reservation wage in more than one market at the same time? As long as preferences are *rational* (see Chapter 5), this cannot happen, for it would mean that you cannot decide which labor market is more attractive; you'd want to enter two labor markets simultaneously. For example, if you say your reservation wage for cleaning eggs is $25 per hour, and the market wage of egg cleaners is $26, then you will become an egg cleaner, giving up all other work opportunities. In other words, at a wage of $26, egg cleaning becomes your most preferred job. In that case, your reservation wage at all other jobs *must* be higher than the market wage in those jobs, or else you wouldn't have been willing to pass them up.

FIGURE 8
The Market Labor Supply Curve

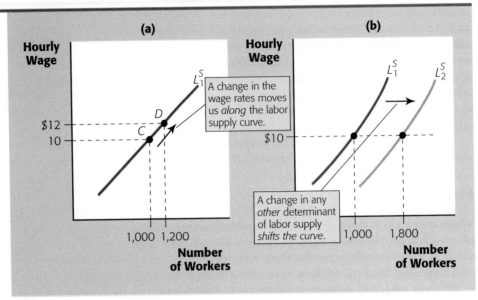

that, *at any given wage rate,* more people want to work in this market after the shift. For example, when the labor supply curve is L_1^S, 1,000 individuals want jobs at an hourly wage rate of $10; after the shift to L_2^S, the number who want jobs at a wage of $10 increases to 1,800.

What makes a labor supply curve shift? At the most general level,

> *a market labor supply curve will shift when something other than a change in the wage rate causes a change in the number of people who want to work in a particular market.*

But let's be more specific. What, exactly, will cause a labor supply curve to shift?

A Change in the Market Wage Rate in Other Labor Markets. Imagine that you've just graduated from law school. You've always dreamed of working for a top-notch law firm. And because you did well in law school, you have good prospects of getting a job in that market, and you expect a first-year salary of $105,000, including bonus. But one day, as you are sending out résumés, a friend calls you up on the phone. "Guess what," he says. "I just heard about an industry that is desperately looking for in-house lawyers, and is willing to pay first-year salaries of $150,000." Upon hearing this news, you decide to go for a job in this other industry, instead of a law firm.

Would your behavior in this story be plausible? Absolutely. Many people will pull out of one labor market (e.g., the market for lawyers at law firms) and enter another (e.g., the market for in-house, corporate lawyers) because of a widening wage differential between them. In our example, your behavior—and the behavior of hundreds of others like you—would cause the labor supply curve in the market for lawyers at top law firms to shift leftward.

And our example is *not* hypothetical. In early 2000, as Internet companies began to offer skyrocketing salaries to just-out-of-school lawyers, the number of applicants for jobs at top law firms decreased dramatically—a leftward shift in the labor supply curve. In order to attract qualified applicants, the top law firms were forced to raise first-year salaries (including bonus) from $105,000 to more than $150,000 in a single year![8] (Note: The ultimate rise in salaries from 1999 to 2000 was determined by the new intersection of the labor supply *and* labor demand curves, as you'll see a bit later in the chapter.)

The moral of the story is that labor supply behavior in *one* labor market may depend importantly on conditions in *other* labor markets. More specifically,

as long as some individuals can choose to supply their labor in two different markets, a rise in the wage rate in one market will cause a leftward shift in the labor supply curve in the other market.

Changes in the Cost of Acquiring Human Capital. To qualify for work in most labor markets, workers need special skills or training, which economists call *human capital*. This is obviously the case for highly paid professionals, like doctors, lawyers, engineers, architects, or business managers. But in most jobs you can think of—computer repair, plumbing, carpentry, language tutoring, and so on—a worker is expected to have specific skills before entering the labor market. Acquiring these skills can be costly—in time, money, or both. A change in the cost of acquiring human capital can affect the number of people who will decide to invest in training at any given wage rate and therefore shift the labor supply curve.

For example, suppose business schools across the country raised their tuition for MBA degrees by 20 percent, and there were no other changes in the economy. What would happen in the market for business managers? Initially, nothing. The suppliers of labor in this market are those who already have MBA degrees, and they would be unaffected by the tuition hike.

But now think about people deciding on careers. At any given wage rate, a career in business will look less attractive than before, now that tuition is higher. And at any given wage rate for MBA holders, fewer people would enroll in MBA programs. Within a few years—the time it takes to get through the program—the labor supply curve in the market for managers with MBA degrees would shift leftward, as retiring managers would not be fully replaced with new entrants.

More generally,

an increase in the cost of acquiring human capital needed to enter a labor market—say, due to an increase in school fees, fewer scholarships, or longer schooling requirements—will shift the labor supply curve leftward; a decrease in the cost of acquiring human capital will shift the labor supply curve rightward.

Number of Qualified People. All else equal, a rise in the number of people qualified to work in a labor market will shift the market labor supply curve rightward. For example, if the number of new economics Ph.D.s exceeds the number retiring each year, the supply of economics professors will increase. Population growth in a country increases labor supply in many markets simultaneously. The U.S. population grows by about 2.5 million every year because births exceed deaths by about 1.6 million, and because immigration exceeds emigration by about 900,000.

---

[8] David Leonhardt, "Law Firms' Pay Soars to Stem Dot-Com Defections," *New York Times* (February 2, 2000).

TABLE 3
Labor Force Participation Rates (Percent of those Over 16 Working or Looking for Work)

	Men	Married Men (Spouse Present)	Women	Married Women (Spouse Present)
1960	83.3	89.2	37.7	31.9
1970	79.7	86.1	43.3	40.5
1980	77.4	80.9	51.5	49.8
1990	76.4	78.6	57.5	58.4
2000	74.7	77.3	60.2	61.3

Source: U.S. Census Bureau, *Statistical Abstract of the United States, 1999* (Tables 657, 658), *2000* (Tables 645 and 651), *and 2001* (Tables 568 and 575).

Labor supply curves can also shift due to migration *within* a country. Often, these shifts are a delayed response to an earlier change in relative wage rates. In the 1990s, higher wage rates in Oregon lured many workers to move there. This led to rightward shifts in labor supply curves in Oregon, and leftward shifts in regions that these workers came from.

Changes in Tastes. In any population, there is a spectrum of tastes for different types of jobs. Some part of the population will like working with numbers and hate working with people; another part will prefer just the reverse. Some like danger and excitement, whereas others like safety and routine. A change in these tastes can change people's reservation wages in a labor market and therefore change the number of people who want to work in a labor market at any given wage rate. That is, a change in tastes can shift the market labor supply curve.

Tastes can also change for working in general. An example is illustrated in Table 3, which shows the change in women's labor force participation from 1960 to 2000. In 1960, only 38 percent of women over 16 were in the labor force (working or looking for work), compared to 83 percent of men. By 2000, women's labor force participation rate had increased to 60 percent. The change was even more dramatic for married women. In 1960, only 32 percent were in the labor force; by 2000, the proportion had almost doubled, to 61 percent.

An important reason for this increase in labor supply appears to be a change in tastes. Many women changed their views of themselves and their economic role in society during this period and decided that they would prefer to work.

Changes in tastes occur in more narrowly defined markets as well. In the midst of the social turmoil of the late 1960s and early 1970s, many college graduates wanted jobs that made a direct, visible contribution to community well-being. Certain careers—teachers, social workers, community organizers—were especially popular. As a result, the labor supply curves shifted rightward. At the same time, traditionally higher paying careers in corporate finance, marketing, and sales became relatively less popular; shifting labor supply curves in these markets leftward.[9] Starting in the early 1980s, and continuing today, tastes have changed back: High-income jobs in business, law, and high-tech fields have become increasingly popular, reversing the labor supply shifts of the 1960s.

HTTP://

Liza Barrow looks at a mother's labor supply decision in her "Child Care Costs and the Return-to-Work Decision of New Mothers" (http://www.chicagofed.org/ publications/workingpapers/ papers/wp98_9.pdf).

[9] Since the number of workers with college degrees rises every year, the labor supply curve in most professional markets shifts rightward each year. The change in tastes discussed here actually caused labor supply curves in high-income jobs to shift rightward *more slowly* than they otherwise would have.

An increase in	Will cause the market labor supply curve to
Tastes for work in a market	shift rightward
Numbers of Qualified People	shift rightward
Human capital costs	shift leftward
The wage rate in an alternative market	shift leftward

TABLE 4

Shifts in the Labor Supply Curve

Table 4 summarizes the causes of shifts in the market labor supply curve. See if you can *explain* each of the entries, rather than merely memorize them.

Short-run Versus Long-run Labor Supply

The quantity of labor supplied to a market depends crucially on the period we are considering. In general, when we adopt a longer time horizon, the quantity of labor supplied will be more sensitive to changes in the wage rate; labor supply will be more *elastic*. Why is this? We know that higher wage rates will increase the quantity of labor supplied to a market. But it often *takes time* for people to acquire the skills needed to qualify in a labor market or to move from one labor market to another.

In some markets, the time needed to acquire skills can be considerable. To qualify as a lawyer requires three full years of postcollege training; a college professor generally needs four years or more; and a physician requires at least seven years, and more in many specialties. Other jobs, such as secretary or construction worker, may have shorter training requirements, but it may still take considerable time before the full response to a wage change occurs.

For example, suppose the wage rate of secretaries increases. Before the full labor supply response occurs, people deciding on careers must *learn* about the change, *decide* to become secretaries, acquire the needed word processing and other skills, prepare their résumés, find out which jobs are available, and, finally, begin looking. It is only at the last stage, where an individual begins *looking* for a job, that he or she becomes part of the total labor supply in a market. The full labor supply response to a wage rate change can take many months or even years, depending on the adjustments required.

When analyzing a *local* labor market, there is another reason to expect a delayed labor supply response: It often takes considerable time to move from one local labor market to another. For example, suppose chefs' wage rates rise in Philadelphia relative to other areas of the country. Would chefs from Austin, Texas, or Seattle, Washington, be on the next flight to Philadelphia? Highly unlikely. Once again, there will be a variety of delays. First, chefs in other cities need to find out about the wage hike in Philadelphia. Second, they need to determine whether the higher wage rate there is permanent or temporary—few people would want to move to another town only to earn higher wage rates for a few weeks or months. Third, they must make the *decision* to move. (If you have ever been faced with this difficult choice, you can appreciate how hard it can be to decide to uproot oneself from friends and family and move to a new town.) Fourth, they need to wrap up affairs in their hometown: to give notice at their current jobs, to let the lease run out on their apartments or sell their homes, perhaps even to wait for their children to finish out the school year. All things considered, it could easily take years before the full labor supply response to the wage increase is completed.

To take account of these delays, it is convenient to define two periods for labor supply behavior. We define the *short run* as a period too short for people to move to a new locality or to acquire new skills. Thus, in the short run, the labor supply response to a change in the wage rate comes from those who *already have the skills and geographic location* needed to work in a market.

The *long run,* by contrast, is enough time to acquire new skills or to change location. In the long run, the labor supply response to a change in the wage rate includes those who will move into or out of the area and those who will acquire the skills needed to qualify in the labor market.

Figure 9 illustrates this distinction on a graph. When the wage rate is $25, 30,000 workers supply labor in the market shown. Now suppose the wage rises to $40. In the short run, the quantity of labor supplied will increase from 30,000 to 60,000 because more of those who *already* have the skills and who *already* live in the area will decide to work in this market at the higher wage rate. These are people whose reservation wage in this market is greater than $25, but no more than $40. Thus, in the short run, we will move along the labor supply curve L_1^S, from point A to point B.

But as we proceed into the long run, the higher wage rate will attract entrants into the labor market. Remember that the number of qualified people in a labor market is a *shift variable* for the labor supply curve—something we hold constant in drawing the short-run labor supply curve L_1^S. But now—as new entrants raise the number of qualified people—the labor supply curve shifts rightward, and continues to shift rightward until the entry of new workers stops. In Figure 9, this occurs when the labor supply curve reaches L_2^S, at which point all those who want to enter this labor market at the wage of $40 have done so. In the end, if the wage rate were to remain at $40, the quantity of labor supplied would rise all the way to 90,000.

If we ask, "What is the *long-run* labor supply response to an increase in the wage rate from $25 to $40?" Our answer is "The amount of labor supplied increases from 30,000 to 90,000." In other words, in the long run, we move from point A to point C in the figure. If we connect these two points with a line, we have the *long-run labor supply curve* labeled L_{LR}^S:

Long-run labor supply curve
Curve indicating how many people will want to work in a labor market after full adjustment to a change in the wage rate.

> The **long-run labor supply curve** tells us how many people will want to work in a labor market at each wage rate, after all adjustments have taken place. That is, after all those who want to acquire new skills or who want to move to another location have done so.

Notice that, for a wage increase from $25 to $40, the long-run labor supply curve (L_{LR}^S) is more wage elastic than the short-run labor supply curve (L_1^S). That is, when the wage rate increases by a given percentage, labor supply rises by a greater percentage in the long run than in the short run. This will always be the case, because when the wage rate increases, the long-run labor supply response includes all those who will enter the labor market in the short run, *plus* the *additional* people who will enter the market in the long run. Thus,

> the long-run labor supply response is more wage elastic than the short-run labor supply response.

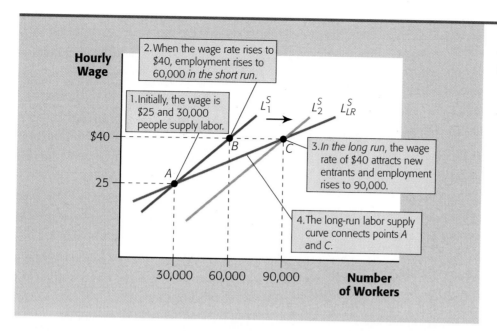

FIGURE 9
The Long-Run Labor Supply Curve

Within the figure:

Hourly Wage

2. When the wage rate rises to $40, employment rises to 60,000 *in the short run.*

1. Initially, the wage is $25 and 30,000 people supply labor.

L_1^S L_2^S L_{LR}^S

$40

B

A

25

3. *In the long run,* the wage rate of $40 attracts new entrants and employment rises to 90,000.

C

4. The long-run labor supply curve connects points *A* and *C.*

30,000   60,000   90,000   **Number of Workers**

Getting It Wrong: Ophthalmologists in Canada. The failure to recognize that labor supply is more elastic in the long run than the short run led to a serious mistake by Canadian policy makers in the mid-1980s. Canada has a national health insurance program that sets fees for medical services. As part of a cost-cutting measure, the system's administrators decided to reduce the fees paid to ophthalmologists for routine eye care, to bring them more in line with optometrists' fees, which were lower.

The reasoning was as follows: If optometrists were willing to provide the service at a low fee, then ophthalmologists should be willing to do the same. After all, ophthalmologists have already paid for their training, so these are *sunk* costs (see Chapter 6), irrelevant to any current decision. The *current* costs for conducting eye exams are the same for both ophthalmologists and optometrists. Therefore, ophthalmologists' eye exam fees could be cut, and there should be very little change in the number of eye exams ophthalmologists offer to perform.

For a while, the policy seemed to work: Ophthalmologists grumbled, but continued to provide routine eye care to their patients. But after several years, a funny thing happened: The number of ophthalmologists declined, rather dramatically, and suddenly Canada's health care administrators became concerned about having too few ophthalmologists.

The administrators' mistake was to view their policy through a short-run lens only, when they should have been worried about the long run as well. From a short-run view, the labor supply response to any change in the wage rate is limited to those who already have the training. Since these doctors' training costs are sunk costs, they would indeed continue to practice with low fees until they retired. In the short run, then, the labor supply curve might resemble L_2^S in Figure 9—not very wage elastic. When the wage rates of ophthalmologists were cut—say, from $40 to $25 as in the figure—the number practicing fell very little, along the curve L_2^S.

But taking a long-run view, we also consider the labor supply response among those who *could* acquire the human capital needed to qualify in the labor market, in this case, those *still deciding on a career.* To become an ophthalmologist, one

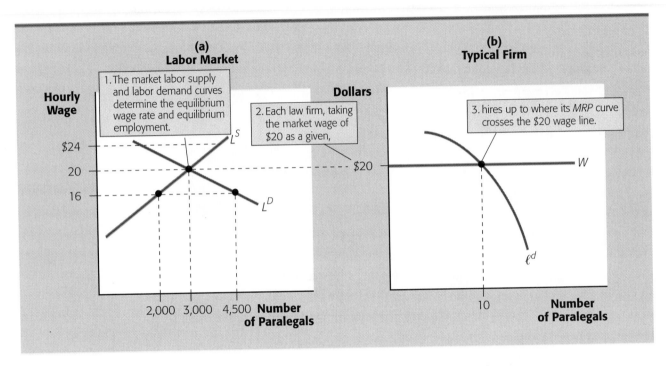

FIGURE 10
Labor Market Equilibrium

must attend medical school for four years, pursue further specialized training in disorders of the eye, and serve a few years of residency. An optometrist, by contrast, needs only two years of postcollege training. Thus, a higher wage rate (higher than optometrists') is needed to attract potential entrants into the ophthalmology labor market. When eye exam fees were equalized, the average income of ophthalmologists declined and, over time, the short-run labor supply curve began shifting leftward. (In Figure 9, imagine a shift from L_2^S to L_1^S.) With the wage still at $25, the number of ophthalmologists dropped further—to 30,000 (point A) in the figure.

Once again, notice that the long-run labor supply curve L_{LR}^S is more wage elastic than the initial short-run supply curve (L_2^S in our story). Accordingly, the labor supply response was much greater in the long run than the administrators, thinking about the short run, had anticipated. Ultimately, the Canadian government was forced to reverse course and restore higher fees for ophthalmologists.

LABOR MARKET EQUILIBRIUM

Figure 10(a) illustrates the market for paralegals in the Chicago metropolitan area. (Paralegals are professionals with legal training, but no law degree, who assist lawyers.) The equilibrium in this market occurs where the supply and demand curves intersect. The equilibrium wage is $20 per hour, and equilibrium employment is 3,000 paralegals. Panel (b) illustrates a typical firm in this market. The firm takes the market wage rate of $20 as given and hires the profit-maximizing number of paralegals, 10, where its labor demand curve cuts the wage line, W.

How do we know that the equilibrium in this market is as we've described it? And how can we have confidence that the market will, indeed, reach this equilibrium? Suppose the wage rate is below $20—say, $16. Then law firms in Chicago would want to hire 4,500 paralegals, but only 2,000 people would want to work in this labor market. Competing with each other to hire paralegals, firms would drive the wage rate up. Therefore, $16 cannot be the equilibrium wage rate in this market, since at that value, it would automatically begin rising. Once the hourly wage hit $20, however, there would be no incentive for any firm to offer a higher wage, since every firm could hire all the paralegals it wanted at $20.

Similarly, suppose the hourly wage were *greater* than $20 (say, $24). As you can see in panel (a) of the figure, at any wage rate greater than $20, more people would want to work as paralegals than firms would want to hire. Firms would discover that they can pay less and still hire all the paralegals they want, so the hourly wage would begin to drop. Once again, when the wage dropped all the way to $20, there would be no reason for any further change.

> *The forces of supply and demand drive a competitive labor market to its equilibrium point—the point where the labor supply and labor demand curves intersect.*

WHAT HAPPENS WHEN THINGS CHANGE?

Labor markets, like product markets, are in continual flux. A variety of events can cause the labor demand curve to shift (see Table 2 of this chapter) or the labor supply curve to shift (see Table 4 of this chapter). In this section, we explore how these shifts affect the equilibrium in a labor market.

A Change in Labor Demand

What happens when a labor demand curve shifts? In Figure 11(a), a labor market is initially in equilibrium at point A, where the demand curve L_1^D intersects the short-run labor supply curve L_1^S. The equilibrium hourly wage is $20, and equilibrium employment is 5,000. Panel (b) shows the typical firm facing the market wage of $20 and maximizing profit by hiring 50 workers.

Now suppose that each firm in this labor market experiences a rightward shift in its labor demand curve. (What might cause this to happen? Look back at Table 2.) Each firm will want to hire more labor at any wage, so the market labor demand curve in panel (a) shifts rightward, driving the market wage up to $40. This is a movement *along* the short-run labor supply curve L_1^S, from point A to point B, with employment rising to 8,000.

Meanwhile, the typical firm takes the new, higher wage of $40 as a given. It decides to employ 80 workers. Who are the additional workers supplying labor in this market? Since this is the short run, they are individuals who are already qualified (in skills or geographic location) to work there and whose reservation wages are greater than $20, but not greater than $40.

But this is not the end of the story. In the long run, the higher wage rate will attract new entrants into the labor market—people who will acquire the needed training or move to a new location. The population of qualified potential workers will increase, shifting the labor supply curve rightward.

This may seem a bit confusing. Aren't we looking at a labor *demand* shift in this section? And didn't you learn—way back in Chapter 3—that a rightward shift in demand does *not* cause a rightward shift in supply? But in Figure 11, the demand curve shifts rightward from D_1 to D_2, the wage rate rises, and then . . . the labor supply curve shifts rightward!

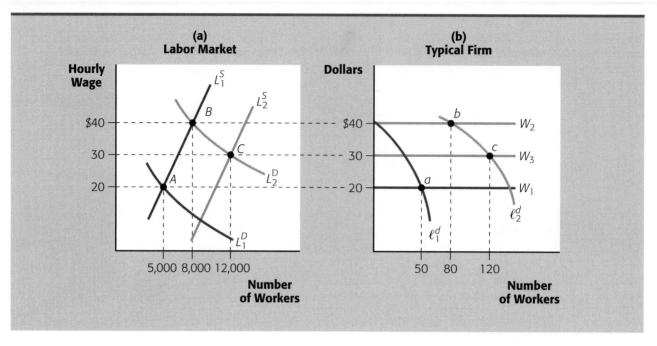

FIGURE 11
A Change In Labor Demand

In panel (a), the market is initially in equilibrium at point A. The wage is $20, and employment is 5,000. This equilibrium is disturbed by a rightward shift of each firm's labor demand curve in panel (b). Each firm will want to hire more workers; as all the firms do, the market demand curve shifts right, driving the wage upward to $40 at point B. Market employment rises to 8,000, and the typical firm hires 80 workers. In the long run, the higher wage will attract additional workers. Their entry shifts the market supply curve to the right; the wage falls to $30 at point C. With the labor market once again in long-run equilibrium, market employment is 12,000, and the typical firm employs 120 workers.

This is not a contradiction. In the figure you can see that the shift in labor demand first raises the wage rate, moving us *along* the labor supply curve L_1^S from point A to point B. But now, from point B, we're extending our analysis further—into the long run. And as you've learned, a rise in the wage—in the long run—causes the *entry of new, qualified people*. It's this *increase in the number of qualified people* (a shift variable for labor supply) that causes the supply curve to shift.

In the short run, a rightward shift in the labor demand curve moves us upward along a short-run labor supply curve, raising the wage rate. Over the long run, the rise in the wage rate entices qualified people to enter the labor market, and then the short-run labor supply curve shifts rightward as well.

The rightward shift in the labor supply curve will move us down along the curve L_2^D. Employment will expand further, and the market wage rate will gradually come down. When will this movement cease? Only when entry into this labor market is no longer attractive. In our diagram, this occurs when the labor supply curve reaches L_2^S, the wage settles at $30, market employment is 12,000, and each firm is hiring 120 workers. Notice that entry stops *before* the wage falls all the way back to its original value, $20. Why is this?

Largely because people have different tastes. In any labor market, those who want to be there the most—who have the lowest reservation wages—will be there *already*, before the wage rate changes. When the wage rate in a market increases, the new entrants are those who would *not* have worked there at the old rate, but who would be willing to work there at a higher rate. In the long run, the wage cannot return to its original value of $20, for at that value, many of the new entrants would leave, causing the wage rate to rise again. When the short-run labor supply curve has stopped shifting, the market wage rate, like $30 in the figure, will be higher than the original wage, $20.

As you can see, the consequences for wage rates are quite different in the short run than in the long run. In the short run, there is a relatively large rise in the wage—from $20 to $40. Indeed, the wage rate actually *overshoots* its long-run equilibrium value. Over time, as more people are attracted into the market and the labor supply curve shifts rightward, the wage rate falls to its long-run equilibrium value.

Wage rates, like the prices of goods and services, act as market signals—leading workers to move to areas where their work is most valued. When the labor demand curve shifts, the wage rate will overshoot its long-run equilibrium value. But as the signal begins to work, the temporary overshooting of the wage rate subsides.

A Change in Labor Supply

Shifts in labor supply typically happen slowly. A look back at Table 4 shows why. While tastes for different jobs can and do change, the changes are usually very gradual. The cost of acquiring human capital can change more rapidly, but this will not shift a labor supply curve until some time later. For example, a drop in the price of going to law school will shift the labor supply curve rightward *three years later*—when those who enter law school now finally get their degrees and begin to enter the job market. Similarly, when the wage rate in some alternative labor market changes, such as the rate in another city, it takes time for people to move from one location to another and enter a new labor market.

Nevertheless, these shifts—as gradual as they may be—are important in understanding labor market changes, especially over the long run. Let's explore an example: a leftward shift in the supply curve for business professors that occurred from 1995 into the early 2000s.

Why did the supply curve for business professors shift leftward? One reason was a decrease in the number of people who were *qualified* to teach business at the college level—that is, a decrease in the number of people with Ph.D.s in business-related subjects. To understand why, we need to go back to the early 1990s, when salaries for individuals with MBA degrees from top universities rose sharply, draining away people who might otherwise have remained in school and obtained their Ph.D.s. The number of new doctorates awarded by accredited business schools declined every year from 1995 to 2000 (falling from about 1,350 in 1995 to under 1,100 in 2000) and remaining more or less stable through 2002.[10] During this period, because the number of new business Ph.D.s fell short of the number retiring, the pool of qualified professors decreased. As you've learned, the number of qualified people is a *shift variable* for the labor supply curve. As this number decreased, the labor supply curve shifted leftward.

But there was more. Those who *did* have their doctorates and *were* qualified to teach in business schools also faced an alternative labor market: the market for private-sector business and financial analysts with Ph.D.s. In this alternative market, wages were rising even more rapidly than in the market for MBAs. In fact, by the year 2000, many Wall Street firms were luring Ph.D.s from universities by offering them salaries two to four times greater than they could earn by teaching. Not surprisingly, at any given wage rate for teaching, fewer people wanted to remain in the university. So for this reason, too, the labor supply curve shifted leftward.

[10] "Number of Business Doctorates Awarded," Association to Advance Collegiate Schools of Business Web site, *http://www.aacsb.edu*, accessed June, 2003.

FIGURE 12
**The Market for Finance
Professors (1995–2002)**

*During the 1990s, the market
supply of new finance professors
fell, as shown by the leftward
shift of the market supply curve.
At the same time, increased demand for finance courses caused
the demand curve to shift rightward. As a result, the equilibrium wage rose from $66,900 to
$102,400.*

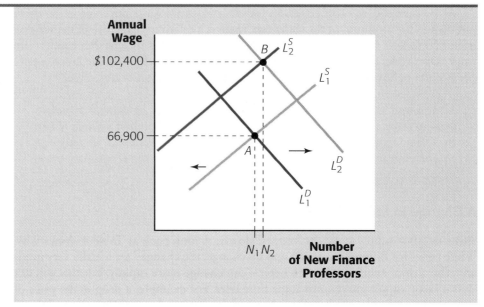

Let's look at a more specific market: the market for new finance professors. In Figure 12, the decrease in supply of these professors is illustrated by the leftward shift of the labor supply curve, from L_1^S to L_2^S. At the same time, there was an increase in demand for finance faculty as MBA enrollments continued to grow. This meant that the *demand* curve for these professors shifted to the right, from L_1^D to L_2^D. The decrease in labor supply and the increase in labor demand combined to move the equilibrium from point *A* to point *B*, causing the equilibrium wage of new finance professors to rise from $66,900 per year in 1995 to $102,400 in 2002.[11]

Labor Shortages and Surpluses

Labor shortage The quantity of labor demanded exceeds the quantity supplied for some period of time.

Labor surplus The quantity of labor supplied exceeds the quantity demanded for some period of time.

We sometimes hear about a shortage or a surplus of labor in some profession or trade: In the early 1990s there was a surplus of scientists, in the mid-1990s a shortage of software developers. Economists define a **labor shortage** as a continuing *excess demand* for labor—a situation in which the quantity of workers demanded in a market is greater than the quantity supplied at the prevailing wage rate. Similarly, a **labor surplus** is a continuing *excess supply* of workers, when the quantity of labor supplied is greater than the quantity demanded.

Look back at Figure 10. When the hourly wage is at its equilibrium value ($20), quantities demanded and supplied are equal—there is neither an excess demand nor an excess supply of paralegals. We've argued that, in a competitive labor market, any excess demand or supply would be self-correcting. Competition for scarce jobs or competition for scarce workers would drive the wage rate to its equilibrium value. Now look back at Figures 11 and 12. There, we saw that changes in labor supply or demand cause changes in the equilibrium wage rate and employment level, but—as long as the wage can adjust—there is no shortage or surplus.

[11] New Doctorate Salaries by Field/Discipline," Association to Advance Collegiate Schools of Business Web site. Figures are mean salary of *new* doctorates in finance taking first-year teaching positions.

These observations suggest that a shortage or surplus can occur only when the wage rate fails to move to its equilibrium value for some reason. This is important because the media often attribute shortages and surpluses to the forces of supply and demand alone.

> *Shortages and surpluses in a labor market are not the natural consequence of shifts in supply and demand curves. A labor shortage will occur only when the wage rate fails to rise to its equilibrium value. Similarly, a labor surplus will occur only when the wage rate fails to fall to its equilibrium value.*

Microeconomists are very interested in shortages and surpluses because they are costly for individuals, for firms, and for society as a whole. A shortage in a labor market makes it harder for firms to find workers and forces them to pay higher recruiting costs to fill job vacancies. In the end, some vacancies must remain unfilled—there are simply not enough workers to go around—which means that valuable output will not be produced.

Similarly, a surplus in a labor market makes it harder for workers to find jobs in that market. Time that could be spent earning income and producing output is instead devoted to sending out résumés, pounding the pavement, or waiting around for good fortune to strike.

Why would a wage rate sometimes fail to adjust to its equilibrium value? Toward the beginning of this chapter, it was pointed out that while the labor market is just like other markets in many respects, it also has some special features. First, the price of labor—the wage rate—is the chief source of most households' incomes. Most of us would not want to work for an employer who changed our wage rate every time there was a shift in labor demand or labor supply, because our income would change rather haphazardly. A firm that developed a reputation for frequent wage cutting would have difficulty attracting workers in the first place. It might have to pay higher wage rates, on average, than a firm with a better reputation. By developing a reputation for wage stability, a firm has an easier time attracting labor and can earn higher profit in the long run.

Moreover, pay cuts can harm employee morale: Many qualified employees may quit, and those who remain may not work as hard. This makes firms reluctant to cut wages, even when the *equilibrium* wage in a labor market falls. But it can *also* create a reluctance to *raise* wages when the equilibrium wage rate rises. If the higher equilibrium is temporary, the firm will face an unpleasant choice later: to continue paying the high wages (even though the equilibrium wage has fallen), or to cut pay back to its old level, with all the negative consequences we've discussed.

With this in mind, consider what happens when shifts in labor demand or supply (as in Figures 11 and 12) increase the equilibrium wage. At the original wage rate, there would be an excess demand for labor, which would ordinarily drive the wage rate up. But if firms resist pay hikes for some time, the result will be a labor shortage. Firms will not be able to hire all the workers they want at the going wage, and there will be unfilled jobs. However, if the change in the equilibrium wage is long-lasting (months? years?), we can eventually expect the market wage to catch up to the equilibrium wage.

The same logic applies for shifts that *decrease* the equilibrium wage. Firms may be slow to cut pay, creating a labor *surplus* in which qualified job applicants exceed the number of openings. Eventually, however, we expect the wage to move down to its new, lower equilibrium value.

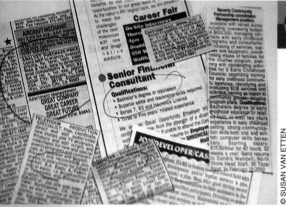

© SUSAN VAN ETTEN

USING THE THEORY
Understanding the Market for College-Educated Labor

Students have many motives for attending college, but one of the most important motives is to invest in their own human capital. Put very simply, going to college will enable you to earn a higher income than you would otherwise be able to earn. How much higher? Economists answer this question by tracking the college *wage premium,* the percentage by which the average college graduate's income exceeds the average high school graduate's income. The wage premium was relatively stable in the 1960s and 1970s, at around 40 to 50 percent. But the premium began to rise sharply in the 1980s and continued its rise through the 1990s. By 2001, the college wage premium reached 76 percent for men and 97 percent for women.[12]

The tools you've learned in this chapter can help you understand why the wage premium has behaved this way. The first step is to realize that, each year, the labor markets for those with college degrees and those with high school degrees experience changes like those shown in Figure 13. That is, each year, in each of these labor markets, both the labor supply curve and the labor demand curve shift rightward. The wage rate, however, may rise or fall in each market, depending on which curve shifts rightward *more*—the labor supply curve, or the labor demand curve.

Let's focus on the market for those with college degrees during the 1980s and 1990s. Why did the labor supply shift rightward each year? First, because there was an increase in the *proportion* of young people attending college. For example, the proportion of recent high school graduates enrolled in college rose from 49 percent in 1980 to 63 percent in 2000.[13] This, in turn, was partly caused by a change in tastes for college education and partly by a delayed, long-run response to the higher wage rates (due to overshooting) earned by college graduates in earlier years.

Second, the population itself increased. This would have increased the number of college graduates and shifted the supply curve rightward even if the *proportion* of young people attending college had remained the same.

Why did the labor demand curve shift rightward each year? In part, because of normal growth in the economy. As firms grow larger, and new firms are born, more labor will be demanded at any wage rate.

But another reason for increases in labor demand has been technological change. Over the last few decades, technological change has increased the skill requirements for many types of work. Routine jobs such as adding up numbers, handling simple requests for information over the phone, or connecting parts on an assembly line are increasingly being performed by computers and other machines. The jobs offered to *people*, meanwhile, have required greater skills than before. Instead of performing routine tasks, firms want to hire people who can write software, who can design and service computers and Web pages, and who know how to use high-tech equipment. As a result, many firms have shifted their hiring efforts toward col-

---

[12] U.S. Census Bureau, *Historical Income Tables*, Tables P-16 and P-17. Based on median earnings for age 25 years and over.
[13] *Statistical Abstract of the United States, 2002*, Table 255.

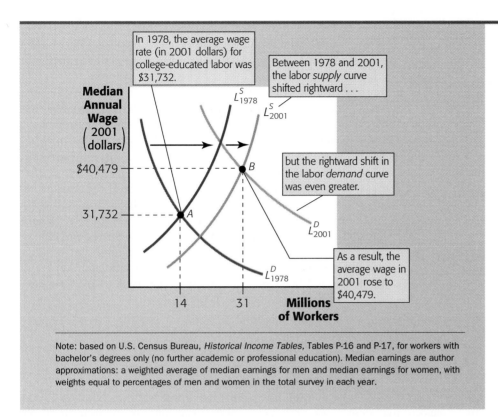

FIGURE 13
**The Market for
College-Educated Labor**

In 1978, the average wage rate (in 2001 dollars) for college-educated labor was $31,732.

Between 1978 and 2001, the labor *supply* curve shifted rightward . . .

but the rightward shift in the labor *demand* curve was even greater.

As a result, the average wage in 2001 rose to $40,479.

Note: based on U.S. Census Bureau, *Historical Income Tables,* Tables P-16 and P-17, for workers with bachelor's degrees only (no further academic or professional education). Median earnings are author approximations: a weighted average of median earnings for men and median earnings for women, with weights equal to percentages of men and women in the total survey in each year.

lege graduates, who are believed to have more skills and to be more capable of acquiring new skills.

Notice that, in Figure 13, the result of the shifts in labor demand and labor supply has been an increase in the yearly wage rate from $31,732 (in 2001 dollars) to $40,479. This is because, over the last two decades, the demand curve for college graduates shifted rightward faster than the supply curve. In the market for those with just high school diplomas (not shown), the opposite was occurring: The labor demand curve shifted rightward at about the same rate, and sometimes more slowly than, the labor supply curve. As a result, the average wage rate (in 2001 dollars) of high school graduates has fallen.

What will happen in the future? There are two competing trends. The first trend is an acceleration in the rightward shift of the labor supply curve for college graduates. This will work to *decrease* the college wage premium. Why the acceleration of labor supply shifts for college graduates? In part, because young people are still responding to the overshooting of the wage rate in previous years. In addition, government subsidies to education—which have grown rapidly in the last decade, from $20 billion in 1990 to about $60 billion in 2002—are expected to grow further in the next decade. These subsidies—in the form of grants, work-study funding, and low-interest student loans—make college more affordable to students, and therefore increase the number who choose to enroll.

But there may also be a countervailing trend: an acceleration in the rightward shift of the labor *demand* curve for college graduates. This is due to further changes in technology. Many of the new technologies currently in the pipeline are complementary with highly skilled labor, but substitutable for low-skilled labor. Students certainly acquire valued skills by going to college. Moreover, studies have shown that business firms invest more formal training in students with college degrees than in students with just high school degrees, further increasing the skill advantage of the college educated.

Most labor market economists predict that, in the market for college-educated labor, the labor demand curve will shift rightward more rapidly than the labor supply curve over the next several years. Thus, the wage rate for college graduates is expected to rise. In the market for high school graduates, however, shifts in the labor supply curve are expected to outpace shifts in the demand curve. As a result, the wage *premium* for college students is expected to increase.

Interestingly, this wage premium for college graduates is one of the reasons behind a trend toward greater income inequality in the 1980s, 1990s, and early 2000s. But it is not the only reason. Studies have shown that inequality has increased even within groups: greater inequality *among* college graduates and *among* high school graduates. What explains this growing income inequality?

To answer that question, we must extend our analysis of labor markets, and also consider economic inequality more generally. We begin to do that in the next chapter.

HTTP://

Jeremy Greenwood explores the link between technology and earnings in "The Third Industrial Revolution" available at http://www.clev.frb.org/ research/review99/third.pdf.

Summary

Firms need *resources*—land, labor, capital, and entrepreneurship—in order to produce output. These resources are traded in *factor markets* in which firms are demanders and households are suppliers. The *labor market* is a key factor market. Most households get most of their income from selling their labor. A *perfectly competitive labor market* is one in which there are many buyers and sellers, all workers appear the same to firms, and there is easy entry and exit.

The demand for labor by a firm is a *derived demand*—derived from the demand for the product the firm produces. In a competitive labor market, each firm faces a market-determined wage rate. The firm hires up to the point at which the *marginal revenue product (MRP)* of labor—the change in total revenue from hiring one more worker—equals the wage rate. If labor is the only variable input, the firm's *labor demand curve* is the negatively sloped portion of its *MRP* curve. If there is more than one variable input, the labor demand curve will have a different shape, because changes in the usage of one input will affect the productivity of other inputs. Still, the firm will hire labor to the point where *MRP* equals the wage rate, and the firm's labor demand curve will still slope downward.

The *market demand for labor* is the horizontal sum of all firms' individual labor demand curves. On the supply side, the upward-sloping *labor supply curve* reflects households' *reservation wages*. A higher wage rate will attract more labor to a particular market. The market labor supply and demand curves intersect to determine the market wage rate and employment for a given category of labor.

Labor market equilibrium can change for a variety of reasons. Shifts in either curve will lead to a new equilibrium wage rate and employment combination. An increase in labor *demand* would result from an increase in the price of firms' output, a technological change that increases the marginal product of labor, a lower price for an input that is complementary with labor, or an increase in the number of firms hiring in that market. In each case, the market labor demand curve would shift rightward, increasing both the wage rate and the level of employment. Market labor *supply* can increase as a result of a decrease in the wage rate in other labor markets, a reduction in the cost of acquiring skills needed for the labor market, an increase in the number of qualified people, or a change in tastes in favor of work in that market. Such increase in labor supply would decrease the wage rate while increasing the level of employment.

It is important to distinguish between a short-run and a long-run change in labor market equilibrium. In the short run, we assume a fixed number of qualified people who are located in the geographic area of the labor market. The long run, by contrast, is a period of time long enough for workers to acquire new job skills or to move to new geographic locations. That is, in the long run outsiders can enter the market and supply labor there. After a shift in labor demand, the wage rate will generally *overshoot* its ultimate value in the short run, and then gradually move back toward its new long-run equilibrium value.

Key Terms

Complementary input
Derived demand
Factor markets
Labor shortage
Labor supply curve

Labor surplus
Long-run labor supply curve
Marginal factor cost
Marginal revenue product
Market labor demand curve

Perfectly competitive labor market
Product markets
Reservation wage
Substitute input
Wage taker

Review Questions
Answers to even-numbered Questions and Problems can be found on the text Web site at http://ball-lieb.swlearning.com.

1. What does it mean when we say that a firm's demand for labor is a *derived demand*?

2. Explain how the introduction of a new input that is complementary with labor will affect labor demand. Do the same for an input that is substitutable for labor.

3. How does a firm in a perfectly competitive labor market decide how many workers to hire? What wage rate does it pay them?

4. What is the difference between marginal revenue, marginal revenue product, and marginal product? What is the difference between marginal cost and marginal factor cost? (Give the formulas for each of these five terms.)

5. Is there a difference between a firm's *MRP* curve and its labor demand curve? If so, what is the difference?

6. Why might a firm's labor demand curve become flatter when other inputs besides labor can be varied (such as in the long run)?

7. Draw a typical market labor supply curve for computer programmers over the next year. Now draw the curve looking over the next decade (the long-run labor supply curve). What explains the principal difference between the two?

8. What is a "reservation" wage? Why would your own reservation wage be different for different jobs? Why will two individuals' reservation wages generally be different when they are thinking about the *same* job?

9. In what sense is the wage rate a *signal*? How does this signal relate to short-run and long-run equilibrium in a labor market?

10. True or false. "When the labor demand curve shifts leftward, the inevitable result is unemployment." Explain.

11. [Appendix] Explain why a monopsonist's *MFC* is greater than the wage it pays at any given level of employment.

12. [Appendix] Compare the employment, output, and wage rates for a firm that operates in a perfectly competitive labor market and a firm that is a monopsonist.

Problems and Exercises

1. In the nation of Barronia, the market for construction workers is perfectly competitive. Explain what would happen to the equilibrium wage rate and equilibrium employment of construction workers under each of the following circumstances:
   a. Young adults in Barronia begin to develop a taste for living in their own homes and apartments, instead of living with their parents until marriage.
   b. Construction firms begin to use newly developed robots that perform many tasks formerly done by construction workers.
   c. Because of a war in neighboring Erronia, Erronian construction workers flee across the border to Barronia.
   d. There is an increased demand for automobiles in Barronia, and Barronian construction workers have the skills necessary to produce automobiles.

2. The following gives employment and daily output information for Your Mama, a perfectly competitive manufacturer of computer motherboards.

Number of Workers	Total Output
10	80
11	88
12	94
13	97
14	99

A motherboard worker at Your Mama earns $80 a day, and motherboards sell for $27.50.
   a. How many workers will be employed? How do you know?
   b. Suppose the market wage for motherboard workers increases by $5 per day per worker, but the market price of motherboards remains unchanged. What will happen to employment at the firm? Why?

3. a. Complete the following table to find how many workers this firm will employ, and how much output it will produce. (Remember to place *MFC* and *MRP between* the rows.)

Price	Quantity of Output	Labor	Total Revenue	MRP	Wage Rate	Total Cost of Labor	MFC
$50	100	6			$400		
$50	200	8			$400		
$50	300	12			$400		
$50	400	18			$400		
$50	500	26			$400		
$50	600	36			$400		
$50	700	51			$400		
$50	800	80			$400		

b. Redo the table in part (a) to show what will happen to employment and production if the price of output falls to $25.

4. You are given the following information about a packaged lunch-meat company, By-products-R-Us:

Number of Workers	Packages per Week
1	100
2	250
3	450
4	600
5	700
6	750
7	775

a. Over what range of output are there increasing returns to labor? . . . diminishing returns to labor?

b. Suppose By-products sells its meat in a perfectly competitive market where the price is $6 per package. Create new columns for Total Revenue and Marginal Revenue Product, and fill them in.

c. Suppose By-products hires its labor in a perfectly competitive labor market, where the wage is $700 per week. How many workers should it hire, and how many packages should it produce each week?

5. Suppose that in the market for finance professors—discussed in the section, "A Change in Labor Supply"—the labor supply curve shifted leftward as discussed, but graduate and undergraduate business classes became less popular instead of more popular. Draw a diagram illustrating what would happen in the market. Would salaries necessarily rise? What would happen to the number of finance professors employed at colleges and universities?

6. Defense-related industries were a major employer of physicists throughout the Cold War. When tensions ended after the fall of the Soviet Union, however, defense cutbacks ensued.

a. Using graphs, illustrate the impact of defense cutbacks on the market for physicists. Assuming the market adjusted to the new equilibrium, what happened to their equilibrium wage rate and the number employed? Would the cutbacks have caused unemployment among physicists? Why or why not?

b. In reality, many defense firms had long-term contracts with their professionals, locking them into specific salaries for years at a time. How does this fact alter your answer to (a)? Could it explain why unemployment occurred among physicists in the early 1990s? Explain.

7. Suppose that dehydrated meat is an inferior good. Discuss the effects on the equilibrium wage rate and level of employment in the dehydrated meat industry of an increase in national income.

8. Look back at Figure 11. When the market wage increased from $20 to $40 in the short run, the typical firm increased the number of workers hired from 50 to 80. How could this be? Common sense dictates that when the wage rate increases, firms will want to hire *fewer*, not more, workers. Resolve the paradox.

9. Reread the section "A Change in the Market Wage in Other Labor Markets." Then, set up two labor market diagrams: one showing the market for attorneys in law firms, and the other showing the market at Internet start-up firms. Show what happened to the wage and employment of lawyers in both markets as many Internet firms exited their industries in 2000 and 2001.

10. In September 2001, the United States declared war on terrorism, and began revamping federal agencies—such as the FBI and the CIA—to closely monitor extremist groups in the United States and abroad. At the same time, these agencies discovered that they had very few agents who could speak Middle Eastern and South Asian languages, and immediately began to correct the deficiency. Economists immediately made two predictions. Draw one or more diagrams to illustrate each of these predictions, and explain briefly.

Prediction #1: Salaries for U.S. residents who knew these languages would rise dramatically over the next year or so, whether they worked for government agencies or not.

Prediction #2: Even though the government's need for these professionals would continue for at least a decade, their salaries would come down after a few years and begin to return toward (but not all the way to) their pre-September 2001 levels.

11. Add MR and MC columns to Table 1 in the chapter and find the profit-maximizing output level using the MR and MC approach. When calculating MR and MC, don't forget to divide ΔTR and ΔTC by the change in *output*, which is not *one* unit in the table.

Challenge Questions

1. Many people think that immigration into the United States, because it causes competition for jobs, will lower the wage rates of U.S. workers. Yet, even though the United States admits hundreds of thousands of immigrants each year, the average U.S. wage has continued to grow. Can you explain why? Are there any groups of workers within the economy for whom the fear of lower wages is justified? Explain.

2. Reread the section "The Two Approaches to Profit Maximization" in the chapter. Then, show that the $MR = MC$ rule and the $MRP = W$ rule give the same result for employment and output for the packaged meat firm, By-products-R-Us, in Problem 4. (*Hint:* Create new columns for MR and MC from the information given.)

3. Suppose a firm sells its output in a market that is *not* perfectly competitive, and can produce five different daily output levels: 300, 400, 500, 600, or 700. The firm has the following daily demand schedule, along with indicated labor requirements for each output level:

P	Q	Labor
$10	300	5
$ 9	400	9
$ 8	500	15
$ 7	600	22
$ 6	700	30

Suppose, too, that the firm hires its labor in a competitive labor market, where workers must be paid $65 per day. Use the $MRP = W$ rule to find the firm's profit-maximizing employment level, price of output, and daily output level.

4. [Appendix] Rework Challenge Question #3, only now assume that the firm is a monopsonist that faces the following labor supply curve.

Labor	Wage Rate
5	$45
9	$55
15	$65
22	$75
30	$85

ECONOMIC *Applications*

These exercises require access to Hall/Lieberman Xtra! If Xtra! did not come with your book, visit http://hallxtra.swlearning.com to purchase.

1. Use your Xtra! password at the Hall and Lieberman Web site (http://hallxtra.swlearning.com), select this chapter, and under Economic Applications, click on EconDebate. Choose *Microeconomics: Labor Markets*, and scroll down to find the debate, "Is a College Education a Good Investment?" Read the debate, and answer the questions below.

   a. What is the main point of Spence's signaling model of college attendance? Do you agree or disagree with this argument? Why?

   b. Now go to EconNews under Economic Applications. Choose *Microeconomics: Labor Markets*, and find the article, "College: To Go or Not to Go—That Is the Question." Read the article summary there. How does this article support, or refute, Spence's signaling theory?

2. Use your Xtra! password at the Hall and Lieberman Web site (http://hallxtra.swlearning.com), select this chapter, and under Economic Applications, click on EconDebate. Choose *Microeconomics: Labor Markets*, and scroll down to find the debate, "Does U.S. Immigration Policy Harm Domestic Workers?" Read the debate, and answer the questions below.

   a. What does the article suggest a rise in immigration will do to wages and hours worked?

   b. Now go to EconData at Economic Applications. Choose *Microeconomics: Labor Markets*, and scroll down to find data for Average Weekly Hours, Manufacturing. Click on Diagrams/Data, and look at the relationship between average weekly hours worked and labor cost per unit. Does the data support the arguments outlined in (a)? Why or why not?

APPENDIX

MONOPSONY

In the body of this chapter, we analyzed perfectly competitive labor markets, in which each firm is an insignificant buyer of labor that takes the market wage it must pay as a given. Perfect competition is a useful assumption in many cases, even when its requirements are not strictly satisfied. But sometimes the departures from the model are so glaring—or the questions we're asking have to do with those departures—that using the perfectly competitive model doesn't makes sense. One such case is a labor market structure called *monopsony*.

> A *pure monopsony*[14] *labor market is one in which a single firm is the only employer.*

While *pure* monopsony is extremely rare, we can use the term monopsony more loosely (without the "pure") for situations in which a single firm is such a *large* employer in a market that its employment decisions affect the market wage. For example, a town with one large hospital may not be the *only* employer of nurses in the area, but it will likely provide jobs to a significant portion of them. When the hospital hires more nurses, its own increase in labor demand can drive up the market wage for nurses. Similarly, staff cutbacks can cause the market wage to drop.

A large university in a small college town is another example. The faculty at the university are often mobile, so the university must compete for them in a national market in which it may be only a small player. But in the markets for administrative staff, maintenance workers, and security guards, workers are more often rooted in the community, with long-standing ties to family and friends. For these workers, the university may be the main option for employment. When the university expands its labor force, it can drive wage rates up in these markets, while contractions in university employment can push wage rates down.

A monopsony employer—pure or not—treats the wage rate as a decision variable, much like a monopolist treats the price of its product. For a monopsonist, each level of employment corresponds to a different wage rate. Therefore, deciding to employ a certain number of workers *implies* paying a certain wage, and vice versa. The wage decision is just the flip side of the employment decision.

How does a monopsonist decide how much labor to employ (or what wage to pay)?

SPOTLESS CAR WASH AS A MONOPSONY

To explore monopsony decisions, let's go back to Spotless Car Wash. But this time, instead of assuming that Spotless hires its labor in a perfectly competitive market, we'll assume that it's a monopsonist. We'll imagine that Spotless is a large car wash in a town whose residents are mostly retired, except for a few small businesses and professionals and about a dozen unskilled teenagers. The retired residents *love* to have their cars washed, but they are not seeking employment. The small businesses and professionals in the town hire only skilled workers at their firms. So the only employment option for the town's teenagers is the car wash.

Table A.1 illustrates the relevant data for Spotless as a monopsonist. Most of the columns are identical to the same numbered columns in Table 1 presented earlier in this chapter. (We've left out column 3—the *MPL*—to make room for some new columns.) Columns 1 and 2—reproduced from Table 1—show various quantities of labor and total product. These numbers come from

---

[14] Key Terms found in this appendix are defined at the end of the appendix and in the glossary.

(1) Quantity of Labor	(2) Total Product (Cars Washed per Day)	(4) Price per Car Wash	(5) Total Revenue	(6) Marginal Revenue Product (*MRP*)	(7) Daily Wage	(8) Total Labor Cost	(9) Marginal Factor Cost (*MFC*)
0	0	$4	$0		<$20	$0	
				$120			$20
1	30	$4	$120		$20	$20	
				$240			$40
2	90	$4	$360		$30	$60	
				$160			$60
3	130	$4	$520		$40	$120	
				$124			$80
4	161	$4	$644		$50	$200	
				$92			$100
5	184	$4	$736		$60	$300	
				$48			$120
6	196	$4	$784		$70	$420	
				$16			$140
7	200	$4	$800		$80	$560	

Spotless's *production* function, and are unaffected by the structure of the labor market. The next three columns—listing the price of a car wash, total revenue, and marginal revenue product—add information about the *product* market (perfectly competitive), but, once again, these numbers have nothing to do with the labor market.

Where Spotless's monopsony status starts to matter is in column 7, which lists the wage at each employment level. When we assumed that Spotless hired labor in a perfectly competitive labor market, it took the wage as given, and paid $60 per day regardless of how many workers it chose to employ. It decided to hire five workers at that wage rate.

But now, with Spotless as a monopsonist, the more teenagers that it hires, the more it will have to pay them. After all, each teenager has a different reservation wage for working. To convince someone who *wasn't* working before to start washing cars, Spotless must make the prospect worthwhile: It must offer a wage higher than that person's reservation wage. For example, if Spotless wants to employ three workers, it must pay a daily wage of $40. But to hire

a fourth worker, it will have to increase the daily wage to $50.

Now we'll make one additional assumption: Spotless must pay the same wage to *all* of its workers. It cannot, for example, increase employment from three to four workers by making a secret offer of $50 to the fourth worker while continuing to pay the other three $40. (Teenagers talk to each other, as do employees of other ages.)

This assumption—that all workers are paid the same wage—is important as we move to column 8, which lists total labor cost for each level of employment. To employ one worker, the firm's total labor cost is just $20—the reservation wage of that worker. But to hire two workers, the firm must pay $30—the reservation wage of the second worker—to *both* workers. This would raise labor cost to 2 × $30 = $60.

The last column lists the *marginal factor cost* (MFC) of labor. As before, the MFC tells us the increase in cost when one more worker is hired. When the firm increases employment from, say, two to three workers, labor cost rises from $20 to $60, an increase of $40. So the MFC for this employment change is $40.

If you look down the *MFC* numbers in column 9, and compare them with the wage rate values in column 7, you'll notice something interesting: For any change in employment (other than hiring the first worker), the *MFC* is larger than the wage that Spotless pays.

> For a monopsonist, MFC *at any level of employment is greater than the wage rate.*

As you're about to see, this will affect both the level of employment at Spotless, and the wage its workers will earn.

THE PROFIT-MAXIMIZING EMPLOYMENT LEVEL

The *general* guideline for profit-maximizing employment is no different for a monopsonist than for any other firm: Increase employment as long as $MRP > MFC$, and stop as soon as $MRP < MFC$, or the two are equal. In the table, the guideline tells us to compare the numbers in column 6 (*MRP*) and column 9 (*MFC*). For all workers up to the fourth, we find that $MRP > MFC$, so Spotless increases its profit by hiring them. For example, going from three to four workers, $MRP = \$124$, while $MFC = \$60$. Hiring the fourth worker adds more to revenue than to cost, so profit rises. But for the fifth worker, $MRP = \$92$, while $MFC = \$100$. This move would add more to Spotless's cost than to its revenue, reducing profit. Thus, Spotless should hire four workers, and no more.

Figure A.1 shows this same decision process graphically. The figure reproduces Spotless's *MRP* curve from Figure 2. It also shows the market *labor supply curve* for unskilled teenage labor, labeled L_S, based on the numbers in column 7. Because Spotless is *the* employer in this labor market, L_S is not only the *market* labor supply curve, but also the labor supply curve *faced by the firm*. It shows the wage rate Spotless must pay to attract different numbers of workers.

The final curve, labeled *MFC*, plots the *MFC* numbers from column 9. Notice that the *MFC* curve lies *above* the labor supply curve. This is a graphical representation of the point made earlier:

> Since MFC *for a monopsonist is greater than the* wage rate, *the* MFC *curve lies* above *the labor supply curve.*

In the figure, to maximize profit, Spotless should increase employment until $MRP = MFC$ (at point *E*), which occurs at four workers. But what *wage* will it pay? The answer—\$50—is found on the labor supply curve L_S at point *F*. After all, it's the labor supply curve, not the *MFC* curve, that tells us what Spotless must pay to attract four workers.

COMPARING MONOPSONY TO PERFECTLY COMPETITIVE LABOR MARKETS

When we compare Spotless as a perfect competitor (Figure 2) with Spotless as a monopsonist (Figure A.1), we come to some disturbing conclusions. First, let's note that nothing has changed from Figure 2 to Figure A.1 *other than* the switch from a perfectly competitive labor market to a monopsony. In both figures, Spotless is the same firm, producing its car washes with the same production function, having the same *MRP* curve, and selling its car washes for \$4 each. Moreover, in both cases, Spotless *could* choose to hire five workers at \$60 each, paying a total labor cost of \$300 per day. In perfect competition, Spotless made just that choice, hiring all five workers and paying each one \$60. As a monopsonist, although Spotless *could* make the same choice (the labor supply curve tells us that five teenagers would work at the firm if they were paid \$60 each), it chooses not to.

Why? Because as a monopsonist, if Spotless employs the fifth worker it must not only pay him \$60 (which, by itself, would be profitable), but must *also* increase the wage of its *other* four workers from \$50 to \$60. When this pay hike for the others is added to the cost of the fifth worker, Spotless would be sacrificing profit if it made the hire. So, as a monopsonist, Spotless employs less labor than it did as a perfect competitor.

Also note that, with four workers instead of five, Spotless washes fewer cars as a monopsonist (161 per day) than it did as a perfectly competitive firm (184 per day). Producing less output is the flip side of hiring fewer workers.

Finally, as a monopsonist, Spotless pays *all* of its workers a lower wage (\$50) than it did as a perfect competitor. This, too, is a direct consequence of lower employment: The fewer workers the firm wants to employ, the lower the wage it can attract them with.

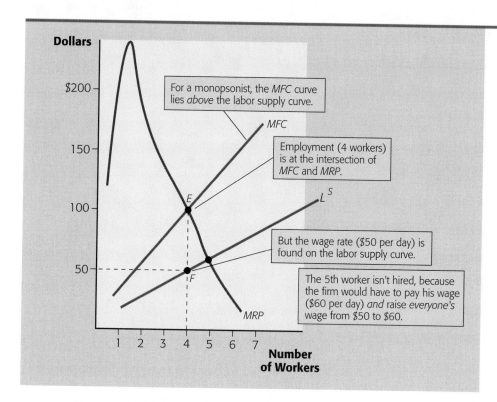

The results for Spotless hold more generally as well:

When all else is the same, firms in monopsony labor markets (1) employ fewer workers, (2) produce less output, and (3) pay lower wages than firms in perfectly competitive labor markets.

As you can see, neither workers nor consumers are well served by monopsony. In this sense, monopsony resembles *monopoly* in a product market, and both market structures present a challenge for public policy. In the next chapter, we'll come back to monopsony in the labor market when we explore wage and income inequality.

Key Terms

Pure monopsony A labor market in which a single firm is the only employer.

Economic Inequality

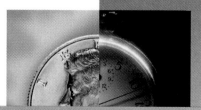

> *When we went to do the deals for* Shrek 2, *they were made in one day. It was that fast and that easy. It was also probably the biggest payday in movie history. They were each paid $10 million for what is in effect 18 hours of work.*
> Jeffrey Katzenberg, cofounder of DreamWorks SKG, referring to payments made to Eddie Murphy, Mike Myers, and Cameron Diaz for voiceovers.[1]

Imagine, for a pleasant moment, that you are Eddie Murphy, Mike Myers, or Cameron Diaz. Your typical workday begins in a limousine, escorting you to the site of the day's recording. There you are doted on by assistants whose sole job is to keep you happy, who look at you respectfully, even worshipfully. Finally, you perform the day's work: a few hours worth of reading from a script. If you make a mistake, everyone laughs good-naturedly, and you get another chance to get it right—as many chances as you need. And after doing this each day for a few weeks, you pick up a check for $10 million.

Now, switch gears and imagine that you have a less-rewarding job, say, as a short-order cook at a coffeehouse. You spend the day sweating over a hot grill, spinning a little metal wheel with an endless supply of orders, each one determining

---

[1] "Question and Answer: Movie Mogul Jeffrey Katzenberg," *Reel West* (Vol. 17, No. 4) July–August 2002.

what you must do for the next three minutes. You cook several hundred meals that day, all the while suffering the short tempers of waiters and waitresses who want you to do it faster, who glare at you if you forget that a customer wanted french fries instead of home fries, and who call you everything but your proper name. At the end of the day, your face is covered with grease, your eyes are red from smoke, and your feet are sore from standing. And for toiling in this way day after day, for an entire year, you earn $20,000.

And some people would consider you lucky: According to the U.S. Census Bureau, almost 35 million people live in poverty, with even smaller incomes—too small to achieve an acceptable standard of living.

We live in a country with extreme differences in wealth and income. One reason for this is a difference in wage rates. In economics, the concept of a *wage rate* is much broader than its official meaning as the rate of pay for people who are officially paid by the hour. In fact, an hourly wage rate can be calculated for *anyone* who works by dividing the earnings over a week, month, or year by the number of hours worked during that period. In this way, we can calculate the hourly wage rate for a sales representative paid on commission, or a movie star with a three-picture deal, or a corporate executive earning a salary and a year-end bonus and other compensation.

The first part of this chapter focuses on differences in these broadly defined wage rates, and why they differ so widely among workers. Here, we'll explore *why* Eddie Murphy earns so much more than a short-order cook. Indeed, you'll learn why most lawyers, doctors, and corporate managers earn more than most teachers, truck drivers, and assembly-line workers, and why these workers, in turn, earn more than farmworkers, store clerks, and waiters. As you'll see, we can explain much about wage differences, using the tools you learned in the previous chapter.

But labor is just one resource that people supply to the market, and labor earnings are just one source of income. Those who possess and supply other resources—such as capital or land—earn income from these as well, beyond any time they spend working. These resource holdings are a major component of household *wealth*. And wealth inequality—especially at the extreme high and low ends—is a major source of economic inequality. To understand income inequality more broadly, we must extend our reach beyond the labor market and look at earnings—or the lack of earnings—from *all* sources. We do this in the second half of the chapter.

WHY DO WAGES DIFFER?

At any time, some of the wage inequality we observe is *short-run* inequality. For example, suppose workers in two labor markets would earn the same wage *if* their markets were in long-run equilibrium. If adjustment to long-run equilibrium takes some time—as it often does (see Chapter 11)—then wages can remain unequal for some time.

But there is also *long-run* wage inequality—differences in wages that persist after all long-run adjustments have taken place. When thinking about income inequality, we are more concerned with long-run differences in wages, since the short-run differences, by definition, will disappear with time.

As a starting point, consider Table 1, which shows hourly earnings in 2001 for full-time workers in selected occupations. Each row of the table lists not only the median wage rate (in bold) for an occupation, but also the wage rate at each percentile. For example, the first row shows that 10 percent of full-time physicians

Occupation	10th Percentile	25th Percentile	Median (50th Percentile)	75th Percentile	90th Percentile
Physicians	$18.56	$36.06	**$62.50**	$102.55	$129.48
Business and Marketing Teachers (College and University)	$21.36	$25.29	**$40.85**	$ 59.81	$ 74.53
Marketing, Advertising, and Public Relations Managers	$19.23	$24.40	**$36.29**	$ 46.18	$ 57.69
Computer Systems Analysts	$20.16	$24.69	**$30.04**	$ 35.91	$ 42.66
Political Science Teachers (College and University)	$20.56	$23.22	**$26.04**	—	$ 38.38
Elevator Installers and Repairers	$21.48	$22.10	**$24.86**	$ 31.76	—
Registered Nurses	$16.82	$18.51	**$21.06**	$ 25.06	$ 29.61
Elementary School Teachers	$12.75	$15.16	**$18.83**	$ 22.02	$ 28.61
Lathe and Turning Machine Operators	$10.50	$12.25	**$14.38**	$ 17.68	$ 22.00
Cabinetmakers	$ 7.50	$ 9.31	**$13.51**	$ 15.00	$ 20.00
Bank Tellers	$ 7.65	$ 8.78	**$ 9.65**	$ 11.14	$ 12.20
Apparel Sales Workers	$ 6.85	$ 7.62	**$ 8.77**	$ 10.40	$ 21.63
Kitchen Workers, Food Preparation	$ 5.86	$ 6.65	**$ 7.97**	$ 9.33	$ 10.65
Cashiers	$ 5.98	$ 6.29	**$ 7.27**	$ 8.50	$ 11.00

Source: Selected data from *National Compensation Survey: Occupational Wages in the United States, January 2001,* (Supplemental Tables), Bureau of Labor Statistics, released January 2003. The BLS data is based on surveys of about 18,000 business establishments employing about 86 million workers.

TABLE 1
Hourly Earnings of Full-time Workers in Selected Occupations, 2001

earned $18.56 per hour or less, while 90 percent earned $129.48 or less (so the top 10 percent earned $129.48 or more). And the bolded middle column tells us that in 2001, half of physicians earned less than $62.50 per hour while the other half earned more.

Note the significant inequality in wage rates among *different* occupations. These sharp differences occur even for jobs in the same industry, in which the work is often similar. Compare, for example, the median hourly wage rate of a business professor ($40.85) and a political science professor ($26.04), or that of a physician ($62.50) and a registered nurse ($21.06).

But you can also see sharp differences in earnings *within* many occupations. For physicians, the wage rate at the 90th percentile is six or seven times higher than at the 10th. Even in the lowest-paying occupations, wage rates at the 90th percentile can be two or three times greater than those at the 10th.

The table tells us that there is substantial wage inequality among and within occupations in the U.S. labor market. Moreover, wage inequality is *persistent*. Both the highest-paid and lowest-paid occupations have been so for decades, and the highest-paid workers within each occupation earned substantially more than the lowest.

Moreover, Table 1—and the Bureau of Labor Statistics data on which it is based—underestimates the full extent of wage inequality in the U.S. labor market. It does not include bonuses, fringe benefits, or other additional labor earnings that are substantially greater for the highest-paying occupations and the highest-paid workers within each job. It also leaves out those at the very top—such as chief executive officers of top corporations, sports celebrities, and movie stars. For example, Eddie Murphy's wage rate on most films is between $10,000 and $20,000 per hour, and—if the quote at the beginning of this chapter is accurate—he earned an astounding $550,000 per hour on *Shrek 2*. Baseball star Alex Rodriguez earns $50,000 each time he steps to the plate.

How can an hour of human labor have such different values in the market?

An Imaginary World

To understand why wages differ in the real world, let's start by imagining an *unreal* world, with three features:

1. Except for differences in wages, all jobs are equally attractive to all workers.
2. All workers are equally able to do any job.
3. All labor markets are perfectly competitive.

In such a world, we would expect every worker to earn an identical wage in the long run. Let's see why.

Figure 1 shows two different labor markets that initially have different wage rates. Panel (a) shows a local market for elementary school teachers, with an initial equilibrium at point A and a wage of $20 per hour. Panel (b) shows the market for computer systems analysts, who, at point B, earn $30 per hour. In our imaginary world, could this diagram describe the *long-run* equilibrium in these markets? Absolutely not.

Imagine that you are an elementary school teacher. By our first assumption, you would find being a systems analyst just as attractive as teaching school. But since systems analysts earn more, you would prefer to be one. By our second assumption, you are *qualified* to be a systems analyst, and by our third assumption, there are no barriers to prevent you from becoming one. Thus, you—and many of your fellow teachers—will begin looking for jobs as systems analysts. In panel (a) the labor supply curve will shift leftward (exit from the market for elementary school teachers), and in panel (b) the labor supply curve will shift rightward (entry into the market for systems analysts). As these shifts occur, the market wage rate of elementary school teachers will rise and that of systems analysts will fall.

When will the entry and exit stop? When there is no longer any reason for an elementary school teacher to want to be a systems analyst—that is, when both labor markets are paying the same wage rate ($25 in our example). In the long run, the market for elementary school teachers reaches equilibrium at point A' and the market for systems analysts at point B'.

Note that these long-run adjustments will occur even if no one actually *switches* jobs. If systems analysts are paid more, then *new* entrants into the labor force—choosing their occupation for the first time—will pick that job over elementary school teaching. As more schoolteachers retire than enter the profession, their number will shrink. Meanwhile, more systems analysts enter the profession than retire, so their number will grow. These changes will continue until, at points A' and B', the long-run wage rate is equal in both markets.

Our conclusion about elementary school teachers and computer systems analysts would apply to *any* pair of labor markets we might choose. In our imaginary world, bank tellers and physicians, kitchen workers and nurses—all would earn the same wage. In this world, different labor markets are like water in the same pool: If

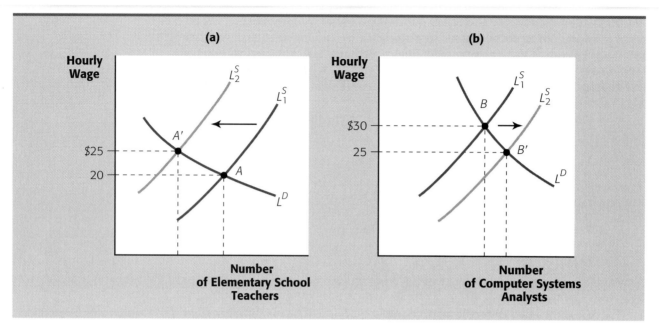

FIGURE 1
Disappearing Wage Differentials

Initially, the supply and demand for elementary school teachers in panel (a), determine an equilibrium wage of $20 per hour— at point A. In panel (b), the equilibrium wage for systems analysts is $30 per hour. If these markets are competitive, if the two jobs are equally attractive, and if all workers are equally able to do both jobs, this wage differential cannot persist. Some elementary school teachers give up that occupation, reducing supply in panel (a), and become systems analysts, increasing supply in panel (b). This migration will continue until the wage in both markets is $25.

the level rises at one end, water will flow into the other end until the level is the same everywhere. In the same way, workers will flow into labor markets with higher wages, evening out the wages in different jobs . . . *if* our three critical assumptions are satisfied.

But take any one of these assumptions away, and the equal-wage result disappears. This tells us where to look for the sources of wage inequality in the real world: a *violation* of one or more of our three assumptions.

Compensating Differentials

In our imaginary world, all jobs were equally attractive to all workers. But in the real world, jobs differ in hundreds of ways that matter to workers. When one job is intrinsically more or less attractive than another, we can expect their wages to differ by a *compensating wage differential:*

> A *compensating wage differential* is the difference in wage rates that makes two jobs equally attractive to workers.

To see how compensating wage differentials come about, let's consider some of the important ways in which jobs can differ.

Compensating wage differential
A difference in wages that makes two jobs equally attractive to a worker.

Nonmonetary job characteristic
Any aspect of a job—other than the wage—that matters to a potential or current employee.

Nonmonetary Job Characteristics. Suppose you clean offices inside a skyscraper, and you find you could earn $1 more per hour washing the building's windows . . . from the *outside.* Would you "flow" to the window washer's labor market, like water in a pool? Probably not. The higher risk of death just wouldn't be worth it.

Danger is an example of a **nonmonetary job characteristic.** It is an aspect of a job—good or bad—that is not easily measured in dollars. When you think about a career, whether you are aware of it or not, you are evaluating hundreds of nonmonetary job characteristics: the risk of death or injury, the cleanliness of the work environment, the prestige you can expect in your community, the amount of physical exertion required, the degree of intellectual stimulation, the potential for advancement . . . the list goes on and on. You will also think about the geographic location of the job and the characteristics of the community in which you would live and work: weather, crime rates, pollution levels, the transportation system, cultural amenities, and so on.

What does all this suggest about differing wages in the long run? Remember that in long-run equilibrium, all adjustments that might affect wage rates have already occurred. This, in turn, requires that people have no incentive to leave one labor market and enter another, for such changes would shift labor supply curves and change the wage in each market. But workers will be satisfied to stay in a job they consider less desirable only if it pays a compensating wage differential. The compensating differential will be just enough to keep workers from migrating from one labor market to another.

Let's see how compensating differentials figure into our example of elementary school teachers and computer systems analysts. Look back at Figure 1. Earlier, we saw that if both jobs were equally attractive, both would pay the same wage rate in the long run. But now let's make an extreme assumption: that everyone in the population has the same tastes for different occupations, and they all prefer the human interaction of school teaching to the abstraction of working with computer systems. Further, suppose it takes a wage differential of $10 in favor of computers to make the two jobs equally attractive. Then the long-run equilibrium would remain at the initial points *A* and *B,* with systems analysts earning a compensating wage differential of $10 per hour to make up for the less desirable features of their job. Even with the higher wage rate for systems analysts, there would be no shift of elementary school teachers to the systems analyst market.

> *The nonmonetary characteristics of different jobs give rise to compensating wage differentials. Jobs considered intrinsically less attractive will tend to pay higher wages, other things being equal.*

What about unusually *attractive* jobs? These jobs will generally pay *negative* compensating differentials. For example, many new college graduates are attracted to careers in the arts or the media. Since entry-level jobs in these industries are so desirable for nonmonetary reasons, they tend, on average, to pay lower wages than similar jobs in other industries. For the same reason, people will accept lower wages when a job offers a high probability of advancement and a higher salary in the future. It comes as no surprise, then, that management trainees at large corporations are often paid relatively low salaries.

Of course, different people have different tastes for working and living conditions. While some prefer a quiet, laid-back work environment like a library or laboratory, others like the commotion of a loading dock or a trading floor. While most people are extremely averse to risking their lives, some actually prefer to live dangerously, as in police work or rescue operations. Therefore, we cannot use our own preferences to declare a job as less attractive or more attractive, or to decide which jobs should pay a positive or negative compensating differential. Rather, when labor markets are perfectly competitive, the entry and exit of workers automatically determines the compensating wage differential in each labor market.

Compensating wage differentials are one reason most economists are skeptical about the idea of *comparable worth,* which holds that a government agency should determine the skills required to perform different jobs and mandate the wage differences needed between them. Although this policy could correct some inequities when labor markets are imperfectly competitive, it could also introduce serious inequities of its own, since no one can know how different workers would value the hundreds of characteristics of each job. Economists generally prefer policies to increase competition and eliminate discrimination, so that the market itself can determine comparable worth.

A Digression: It Pays to Be Unusual. One implication of compensating wage differentials is that workers with unusual tastes often have a monetary advantage in the labor market. For example, only a small fraction of workers *like* dangerous jobs, such as police work. As long as the labor market is competitive, and there is relatively high demand for workers in dangerous jobs, police officers will earn more than those in other, similar jobs that have a lower risk of death or injury. But if you are one of those unusual people who *like* danger, you will earn the same compensating wage differential as all other police officers, even though you would have chosen to be a police officer anyway.

Similarly, if you like the frigid winter weather in Alaska, if you like washing windows on the 90th floor, or if you think it would be fun to defend the cigarette industry in the media, you can earn a higher wage by putting your somewhat unusual tastes to work.

Cost-of-Living Differences. Many people would find living in Cleveland and living in Philadelphia about equally attractive. Yet wages in Philadelphia are about 10 percent higher than in Cleveland. Why? One major reason is that prices in Philadelphia are about 10 percent higher than in Cleveland. If wages were equal in the two cities, many people deciding where to live would prefer Cleveland, where their earnings would have greater purchasing power. The supply of labor in Philadelphia's labor markets would shrink, increasing the wage there, while the supply in Cleveland's labor markets would rise, driving down the wage in Cleveland. In the end, the wage difference would be sufficient to compensate Philadelphians for the higher cost of living in their city.

> *Differences in living costs can cause compensating wage differentials. Areas where living costs are higher than average will tend to have higher-than-average wages.*

Difference in Human Capital Requirements. All else equal, jobs that require more education and training will be less attractive. In order to attract workers, these jobs must offer higher pay than other jobs that are similar in other ways, but require less training.

Let's go back to Figure 1, but this time imagine that we're comparing the market for elementary school teachers in the left panel with the market for *physicians* in the right panel, with an initial equilibrium wage of $62.50. Would we expect labor supply curves in these two markets to shift until wage rates were equal for both? No, because physicians must complete an additional three years of medical school after college, plus a residency and sometimes further training. If these jobs were equally attractive in all other ways, then the point at which the labor supply curves would stop shifting would leave physicians earning substantially more to compensate for the higher costs (such as tuition and foregone income) of becoming a doctor.

> *Differences in human capital requirements can give rise to compensating wage differentials. Jobs that require more costly training will tend to pay higher wages, other things equal.*

Compensating differentials explain much of the wage differential between jobs requiring college degrees and those that require only a high school diploma. In early 2003, the median hourly wage rate of college graduates was $22.57 per hour, but for high school graduates, only $13.72.[2] The especially high earnings of doctors, attorneys, research scientists and college professors reflect—at least in part—compensating differentials for the high human capital requirements—and human capital costs—of entering their professions.

The idea of compensating wage differentials dates back to Adam Smith, who first observed that unpleasant jobs seem to pay more than other jobs that require similar skills and qualifications. It is a powerful concept, and it can explain many of the differences we observe in wages . . . but not all of them.

Differences in Ability

In December 2000, at the age of 26, Alex Rodriguez signed a 10-year contract to play baseball for the Texas Rangers at an average salary of $25 million per year. Was this salary so high because of a compensating differential for the unpleasantness of playing professional baseball? Or was there an unusually high risk of death on this job? Was the cost of living in Dallas hundreds of times greater than in other cities? Had Rodriguez, at the age of 26, spent more years honing his skills than the average attorney, doctor, architect, or engineer—or even more than the average baseball player?

The answer to all of these questions is no. We have overlooked the obvious explanation: Rodriguez is an *outstanding* baseball player, better than 99.999 percent of the population could ever hope to be with *any* amount of practice. This is partly because of his *endowments*—the valuable characteristics he possesses due to birth or childhood experiences but that did not require any opportunity cost on his part. In Rodriguez's case, these would include his natural speed, agility, and coordination. Of course, Rodriguez also had the skill and perseverance to exploit his talent. Together, his endowments of talent and his work at exploiting them have made Rodriguez an outstanding athlete.

While Alex Rodriguez may be an extreme case, the principle applies across the board. Not everyone has the intelligence needed to be a research scientist, the steady hand to be a neurosurgeon, the quick-thinking ability to be a commodities trader, the well-organized mind to be a business manager, or the talent to be an artist or a ballet dancer. This violates our imaginary-world principle that all workers have equal ability to do any job—or at least equal ability to acquire the skills needed. And that explains much of the wage inequality we observe in the real world.

We can understand this in terms of Figure 1 of this chapter. A wage differential between two otherwise equal jobs could persist if those working for lower wages

---

[2] "Usual Weekly Earnings of Wage and Salary Workers: First Quarter 2003," *Bureau of Labor Statistics News*, April 17, 2003.

(point *A* in panel (a)) cannot enter the high-wage market (point *B* in panel (b)) because—regardless of how much human capital they acquire—they can never perform well enough.

Wage rate inequality, and income inequality more generally, increased during the 1990s and early 2000s (see the discussion later in this chapter). Part of the reason may be that differences in abilities have become more important in the labor market. Scientific discoveries and technological advances have increased the skill requirements of many jobs, and the abilities needed to *acquire* those skills. For example, it takes more ability to learn to repair an automatic elevator than to learn how to operate a manual elevator. If significant numbers of workers are unable to master the skills needed for higher-paying jobs, then movement from one labor market to another may be stopped short. This would result in a persistent—and increasing—wage differential between high-skilled and low-skilled workers.

Our discussion so far, centering on Figure 1, explains wage differences *between* occupations. But that is only part of the story. Substantial pay differences also exist *within* each occupation, as you can see by the wage rates at different percentiles in Table 1. Here, too, ability plays an important role. In any job, workers' talents, intelligence, and physical abilities—and their value to firms—vary considerably. For example, suppose two advertising account managers have equal education and training, but manager A, being more talented, can design better ad campaigns and attract twice as many high-paying clients than can manager B. Then, in an otherwise competitive labor market, a firm will be willing to pay manager A twice as much as manager B.

> *In general, those with greater ability to do a job well—based on their talent, intelligence, motivation, or perseverance—will be more valuable to firms. As a result, firms will be willing to pay them a higher wage rate, beyond any compensating differential for their human capital investment.*

Differences in ability also help explain why workers' pay tends to rise with age and experience on the job. Experience not only adds to a worker's human capital, but also provides a signal of ability to employers. Hiring a new, untested worker—even one who seems to have great talent—is always a bit risky, since the worker's ability hasn't yet been proven. By contrast, hiring or continuing to employ someone with a history of advancement and accomplishments reduces this risk. All else equal, firms will typically pay more for a worker with a proven track record. Not surprisingly, when wage rates within an occupation are broken down by age (not shown in the table), those who are older—and have been in their occupation longer—dominate the higher percentiles, while younger and newer entrants are more prevalent in the lower percentiles.

The Economics of Superstars. Why was the owner of the Texas Rangers willing to pay $25 million per year to have Alex Rodriguez play for his team? The immediate answer is: because he is so *good*. Alex Rodriguez is an example of a *superstar*—an individual widely viewed as among the top few in their professions. In recent years, superstars have included actors such as Mel Gibson, Eddie Murphy, and Julia Roberts; talk show hosts Jay Leno and David Letterman; news announcers Dan Rather and Peter Jennings; novelists Stephen King and J. K. Rowling; and film director Stephen Spielberg.

But when we try to explain the extremely high wage rates of these superstars based on their exceptional abilities alone, we confront a puzzle. Clearly Alex Rodriguez has more athletic ability, and more skill in honing it, than almost anyone in the population, including other major-league baseball players. But can this explain a salary that is *25 times* that of the median major-league player? By any measure, is Rodriguez *25 times better*?

Or consider other superstars. ABC news anchor Peter Jennings may deliver the evening news better than most local news anchors. But is he "better enough" to justify a salary estimated to be 100 times higher?[3] And most would agree that Eddie Murphy's voice work for *Shrek 2* was better than, say, the voiceovers on the Saturday morning cartoon shows. But Murphy's hourly pay was about 3,000 times greater than that of the typical cartoon voice actor.[4] Is he *that much better*? Huge wage rate differentials like this are seen in many professions, especially those involving the media. The very top writers, rock stars, comedians, talk show hosts, and movie directors all earn wage premiums that seem vastly out of proportion to their additional abilities. Why?

The explanation in all these cases *is* based on ability—and also the exaggerated rewards the market bestows on those deemed the best or one of the best in a field.[5] Say you like to read one mystery novel a month for entertainment. If you can choose between the best novel published that month or one that is almost—but not quite—as good, you will naturally choose the one you think is best. Only people who read *two* novels each month would choose the best *and* the second best, and only those who read three will choose the top three. If most people rank recent mystery novels in the same order, then the best will sell millions of copies, the second

Two Confusions in Explaining Wage Differentials Two mistakes are commonly made when applying the theory of wage differentials to real-world labor markets. The first is to apply just *one* explanatory factor and ignore others that matter as well. For example, it's tempting to explain college professors' relatively high pay as a compensating differential for high human capital requirements. And that's certainly *part* of the story. But then how do we explain the substantially higher pay of business professors compared to political science professors (see Table 1)? Since human capital investments are about the same in both fields, *other forces* must be at work determining professors' wage rates. These include differing tastes in the population for teaching in general, and for teaching business or political science in particular; differing *abilities* to acquire Ph.D.s in general, and to acquire them in these two fields specifically; and so on. The wage rate in any occupation is always determined by *several* relevant factors.

A second mistake is to attribute a *long-run* wage differential to a factor that can only explain a *short-run* differential. For example, in Chapter 11 we explained the high and rapidly rising salaries of business professors by noting the high *demand* for business professors and their limited *supply* because they can work in high-paying jobs outside of academia. But *neither* of these facts could cause an *indefinite* wage differential in favor of business professors. Why not? Because if these were the only relevant forces, we'd expect a decrease in the supply of political science professors and an increase in the supply of business professors until wages were equal for both. The same applies to those high-paying nonacademic jobs available only to business professors. So to explain a persistent, *long-run* pay difference, we must identify the forces that *stop* these labor supply shifts before wages are equalized. Differences in tastes and differences in abilities are two such explanations.

DANGEROUS CURVES

© MITCHELL GERBER/CORBIS

Although Eddie Murphy's acting talent may not be a thousand times better than the average, he earns more than a thousand times the average actor's salary because he is at the top of his profession.

[3] According to the BLS, the average news anchor earns $83,400 (Bureau of Labor Statistics, U.S. Department of Labor, *Occupational Outlook Handbook, 2002–03 Edition, News Analysts, Reporters, and Correspondents,* on the Internet at *http://www.bls.gov/oco/ocos088.htm*). Peter Jennings's salary is typically reported at $10 million. (See, for example, "Jennings Signs ABC Contract," *Online News Hour,* Public Broadcasting Service, November 18, 2002 (*http://www.pbs.org/newshour/media/media_watch/july-dec02/jennings_11-18-02.html*). Both sites visited July 03, 2003.

[4] Voice actors on Saturday morning cartoons are paid $636 for a four-hour session (not counting time spent rehearsing and auditioning). Patrick Goldstein, "The Big Picture: A Voice Actor Speaks for Herself," *Los Angeles Times,* December 18, 2001.

[5] See, for example, Robert H. Frank and Philip J. Cook, *The Winner Take All Society* (New York: The Free Press, 1995).

best might sell hundreds of thousands, and the third best might sell only thousands. Even though all three novels might be very close in quality, a publisher will earn *10 times* more revenue selling the best novel (compared to the second best), and 10 times more revenue selling the second best (compared to the third best), and so on. Accordingly, a publisher will be willing to pay the same multiples in advances and royalties when bidding for contracts with mystery novelists of different rankings. Even if the top author is viewed as only *slightly* better than the next one down, as long as the vast majority of readers agree on the ranking, she can end up earning 10 times as much.

The same thing happens in markets for athletes, rock concerts, action movies, and news broadcasts. In all these cases, where the service is sold to millions of people and where there is wide agreement about who are the top few superstars, the differences in rewards can be vastly disproportionate to differences in ability. The owner of the Texas Rangers was willing to pay Alex Rodriguez $25 million each year because he believed that Rodriguez, as a superstar, would bring in *at least* that much additional revenue each year—from ticket sales, skybox rentals, TV and radio broadcasting fees, concession sales, parking fees, and more.

But the phenomenon is not limited to media markets or media stars. Suppose you are wealthy and you need a heart transplant. How much more would you be willing to pay to have one of the top 10 surgeons perform your operation, compared to one ranked in the *next* 10? And the same logic can be applied in the business world, in which the chief executive officers of the top corporations have earned huge, and rapidly rising, salaries. Although—as you'll see in the "Using the Theory" section at the end of this chapter—there is much more to the story in *that* labor market.

Barriers to Entry

In our imaginary world, there were no barriers to entering any trade or profession. The absence of barriers is an important element of our assumption that the labor market is competitive. But in some labor markets, barriers keep out would-be entrants, resulting in higher wages in those markets.

In Figure 1 we saw that if systems analysts were paid higher wages than elementary school teachers, entry into the market for systems analysts would help equalize wages in the two jobs. But what if systems analysts were *protected* from competition by a barrier to entry, one that kept newcomers from becoming systems analysts? Then the labor supply curve in panel (b) would *not* shift rightward, and the higher wage for systems analysts could persist. Going back to the analogy of water flowing to equalize the water level at both ends of a pool, a barrier to entry is like a wall in the middle of the pool. It blocks the flow, allowing one end to have a higher water level than the other.

Since barriers to entry help maintain high wages for those protected by the barriers (those who already have jobs in the protected market), we should not be surprised to find that in almost all cases, it is those already employed who are responsible for erecting the barriers. But it is not enough to simply put up a sign, "Newcomers, stay out!" The pull of higher wages is a powerful force, and preventing entry requires a force at least as powerful. What keeps newcomers out of a market, thus maintaining a higher-than-competitive wage for those already working there?

Occupational Licensing. In many labor markets, occupational licensing laws keep out potential entrants. Highly paid professionals such as doctors, lawyers, and dentists, as well as those who practice a trade, like barbers, beauticians, and plumbers,

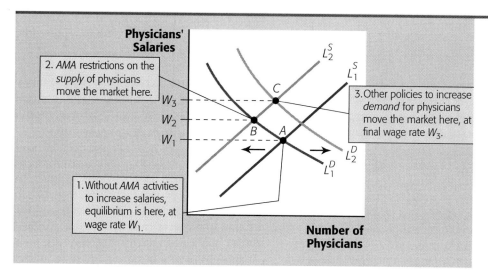

FIGURE 2
The Market for Physicians

Physicians' Salaries

2. *AMA* restrictions on the *supply* of physicians move the market here.

3. Other policies to increase *demand* for physicians move the market here, at final wage rate W_3.

1. Without *AMA* activities to increase salaries, equilibrium is here, at wage rate W_1.

W_3
W_2
W_1

L_2^S
L_1^S
L_2^D
L_1^D

C
B   A

Number of Physicians

cannot legally sell their services without first obtaining a license. In many states you cannot even sell the service of braiding hair without a license. In order to get the license, you must complete a long course in cosmetology and pass an exam.

The American Medical Association (AMA)—a professional organization to which almost half of American physicians belong—is perhaps the strongest example of occupational licensing as a barrier to entry. The AMA portrays itself as a vigilant defender of high standards in health care, through its regulation of medical schools, its certification of specialists, and its government lobbying. Economists tend to have a much different view of the AMA. While not denying that the AMA's efforts do raise the quality of physicians, they see it primarily as an instrument to maintain high incomes for doctors.

Figure 2 shows the market for physicians in the United States. In the absence of any income-raising activity, labor supply curve L_1^S would intersect labor demand curve L_1^D at point *A*, resulting in equilibrium wage W_1. Whether this wage would be relatively high or low is not known; since 1847, when the AMA was founded, this competitive equilibrium has never been attained.

Much of the AMA's activity has been designed to decrease the *supply* of doctors. Immediately after its founding, it imposed strict licensing procedures that increased entry costs for *new* doctors; existing practitioners were exempted from the new requirements. In spite of these restrictions, there was a rapid increase in the number of physicians toward the end of the century. In response, between 1900 and 1920, the AMA closed down almost half of the nation's medical schools.[6] These and other efforts to restrict the supply of doctors have resulted in a supply curve for physicians like L_2^S, lying to the left of L_1^S, moving the equilibrium to point *B*, and raising salaries to W_2.

But this is not the end of the story. The AMA has also increased the *demand* for physicians' services by preventing nonphysicians from competing. Throughout its history, the association has moved aggressively to limit competition from midwives, chiropractors, homeopathists, and other health professionals. By limiting access to these alternative health professionals, the AMA increases the demand for

---

[6] "Doctors Operate to Cut Out Competition," *Business and Society Review,* Summer, 1986, pp. 4–9.

the services of its own members. The impact of these policies has been a rightward shift in the demand curve for doctors, to L_2^D, moving the equilibrium to a point like C and raising salaries further, to W_3.

(If you think maintaining high standards is the main motivation for these policies, consider this: AMA policy allows a physician to practice in *any* area of medicine, even one in which he has no specialized training. For example, a dermatologist with no training or experience in obstetrics can legally deliver a baby; a midwife with extensive experience might be arrested if she delivers a baby without the supervision of an M.D.)

In the late 1980s, rising health care costs led to increased public scrutiny of the AMA, and its anticompetitive practices came under heavy attack. Some restrictions were eased, and the number of doctors per 100,000 people increased from 169 in 1975 to 233 in 1990. At the same time, the Federal Trade Commission and the courts pressured the AMA to remove its ban on physician advertising. For the first time, new entrants could compete with established practices by advertising their prices and services. Not surprisingly, many physicians began to complain about falling incomes.

Union Wage Setting. A labor union represents the collective interests of its members. Unions have many functions, including pressing for better and safer working conditions, operating apprenticeship programs, and administering pension programs. But a major objective of a union is to raise its members' pay. Federal law prohibits a union from creating an overt barrier to entry; it is illegal for a firm to agree to hire only union members. Instead, the union negotiates a higher-than-competitive wage with the firm. But, as we know from the last chapter, at a higher wage, the firm will have a lower profit-maximizing employment level. Thus, many potential workers are kept out of union jobs because the firm will not hire them at the union wage.

The higher union wage is contrary to the interests of the employer, so why does the employer agree? Because the union has the power to strike. During a strike—when the firm's workers refuse to come to work—the firm suffers a loss. Rather than take the risk of a strike, employers will often agree to the higher wage demanded by the union.

Figure 3 illustrates how unions can create wage differences. We assume that jobs in two industries—long-haul trucking and short-haul trucking—are equally attractive in all respects other than the wage rate. With no labor union, these two markets would reach equilibrium at points A and B, respectively, where both pay the same wage, W_1.

Now suppose instead that long-haul truckers are organized into a union, which has negotiated a higher wage, W_2, with employers. At this wage, employment of long-haul truckers drops from 300,000 to 250,000, while the number who would like to work in this market rises to 350,000. Now there is an excess supply of long-haul truckers equal to $350,000 - 250,000 = 100,000$. Ordinarily, we would expect an excess supply of labor to force the wage down, but the union wage agreement prevents this. With fewer jobs available in the unionized sector, some former long-haul truckers will look for work as *nonunion*, short-haul truckers. Thus, in panel (b), the labor supply curve shifts rightward. In equilibrium, the number of short-haul truckers rises from 200,000 to 225,000, and the wage of short-haul truckers drops to W_3. The end result is a union–nonunion wage differential of $W_2 - W_3$.

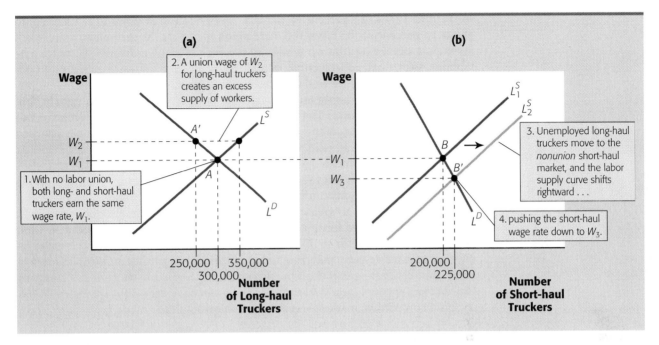

(a)

Wage

2. A union wage of W_2 for long-haul truckers creates an excess supply of workers.

L^S

W_2 — — — — — — A'

W_1 — — — — — —

1. With no labor union, both long- and short-haul truckers earn the same wage rate, W_1.

A

L^D

250,000   350,000
      300,000

Number of Long-haul Truckers

(b)

Wage

L_1^S
L_2^S

B

3. Unemployed long-haul truckers move to the *nonunion* short-haul market, and the labor supply curve shifts rightward . . .

W_1 — — — — — — — — —

W_3 — — — — — — B'

L^D

4. pushing the short-haul wage rate down to W_3.

200,000
      225,000

Number of Short-haul Truckers

FIGURE 3
Union Wage Differentials

Notice that only *part* of the differential $(W_2 - W_1)$ represents an increase in union wages; the other part $(W_1 - W_3)$ comes from a decrease in *nonunion* wages.

In a competitive labor market, a union—by raising the wage firms must pay—decreases total employment in the union sector. This, in turn, causes wages in the nonunion sector to drop. The combined result is a wage differential between union and nonunion wages.

In the end, how big is the union–nonunion wage differential? H. Gregg Lewis[7] reviewed more than 200 studies that asked precisely this question and determined that between 1967 and 1979, union members earned, on average, about 15 percent more than otherwise similar nonunion workers.

Given the conflict that has surrounded many union–management wage negotiations, and the media attention devoted to them, this difference may seem rather small. But keep in mind that a 15 percent differential—about $2.30 per hour at today's average wage rate for hourly production workers—would amount to $4,700 per year, continuing year after year. After 40 years on the job, the average union member would earn about $188,000 more than the average nonunion member, enough to put a down payment on a house *and* put a child through college with no student loans. And if each year's differential were put in the bank at 5 percent interest, it would amount to about $600,000 after 40 years. So a 15 percent wage differential is nothing to sneeze at.

The differential has most likely declined since 1979, however, as unions' bargaining power has weakened. This is partly reflected in a decline in union membership:

[7] H. G. Lewis, *Union Relative Wage Effects: A Survey* (Chicago: University of Chicago Press, 1986).

In the mid-1950s, 25 percent of the U.S. labor force was unionized; today, only about 13 percent of the labor force are union members. Nevertheless, unions still maintain a significant (though declining) presence in many industries, such as automobiles, steel, coal, construction, mining, and trucking, and they are certainly responsible for at least *some* of the higher wages earned in those industries.

Of course, we're viewing unions here from one perspective only: to explain how wage differences can arise. The full effect of unions on labor markets is much more complex. For example, many of the features of modern work that we take for granted today—such as paid vacations and overtime pay—originated in union struggles with management.

Moreover, through grievance procedures and other forms of communications with management, unions can raise worker morale and reduce labor turnover. And if higher morale leads to greater productivity (higher marginal product of labor at each firm), the demand for labor in the union sector could increase, reducing (and possibly reversing) the drop in employment caused by the higher wage. Finally, remember that we've been analyzing union effects on wage rates and employment in labor markets that—other than the presence of the union—are perfectly competitive. In the appendix, you'll learn that unions can have very different effects in *imperfectly* competitive markets—such as a monopsony labor market.

The Minimum Wage. A minimum wage law makes it illegal to hire a worker for less than a specified wage, in any labor market covered by the law. When the federal minimum wage rate was first established in the United States in 1938, the minimum was set at 25 cents per hour, and applied to industries employing only 43 percent of the workforce. In mid-2003, the minimum wage was $5.15 per hour and covered almost 90 percent of the workforce.

Of course, prices rose between 1938 and 2003 as well. When adjusted for inflation, the purchasing power of the minimum wage reached its peak in 1968. But since that year, even though the minimum wage was increased 10 times in *dollars*, its purchasing power has fallen by about 34 percent. As a result, several states now have their own, higher minimum wage rates. In mid-2003, the highest were in Alaska ($7.15) and Washington state ($7.01). In both of these states, the minimum wage automatically rises with the overall level of prices.

When most people think about the minimum wage, they see it as a means to increase living standards for the lowest paid workers, and their analysis stops there. After all, a full-time worker earning the federal minimum wage of $5.15 per hour would earn only $10,712 per year—less than enough to support a single parent and child above the government's official poverty line (discussed later in the chapter). Indeed, the minimum wage *does* raise living standards for some workers above what they would otherwise be. But the minimum wage also serves as a *barrier to entry* in labor markets covered by the law. And this can have paradoxical side effects that hurt some of the people the minimum wage is supposed to help.

To understand the effect of the minimum wage, we'll divide the U.S. labor market into three parts: (1) the market for skilled labor; (2) the market for unskilled labor in industries *covered* by the minimum wage law; and (3) the market for unskilled labor in industries effectively *not covered* by the law, either because it does not apply (waiters, house cleaners, and nannies) or because firms routinely violate it (typically, very small firms that are difficult to monitor).

Figure 4 shows the long-run equilibrium in these markets if *no* minimum were in effect. The wage rate in both unskilled labor markets (panels (a) and (b)) is ini-

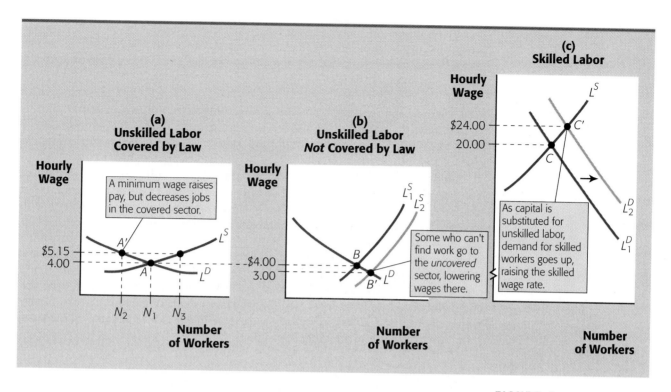

(a)
Unskilled Labor
Covered by Law

Hourly Wage

A minimum wage raises pay, but decreases jobs in the covered sector.

L^S

A'

$5.15
4.00

A

L^D

N_2 N_1 N_3

Number of Workers

(b)
Unskilled Labor
***Not* Covered by Law**

Hourly Wage

L_1^S L_2^S

B

Some who can't find work go to the *uncovered* sector, lowering wages there.

$4.00
3.00

B' L^D

Number of Workers

(c)
Skilled Labor

Hourly Wage

L^S

$24.00
20.00

C'

C

As capital is substituted for unskilled labor, demand for skilled workers goes up, raising the skilled wage rate.

L_2^D

L_1^D

Number of Workers

FIGURE 4
The Minimum Wage

tially $4.00 per hour, at points *A* and *B*. It's the same in both markets because in the absence of a minimum wage law, workers would migrate to whichever market had the higher wage until the wage rates were equal. In the skilled labor market in panel (c), the wage rate is considerably higher at $20, for all the reasons we've discussed in this chapter.

Now let's impose a minimum wage of $5.15 on the *covered unskilled* sector in panel (a), and trace through the effects. First, employment in that sector falls, from N_1 to N_2. Since quantity demanded is less than quantity supplied, and since no firm can be forced to hire more workers than it wants to, there will be an excess supply of labor equal to $N_3 - N_2$. Part of this excess is due to an increase in quantity supplied from N_1 to N_3 (with a higher wage rate, more people want to work in the covered, unskilled sector). But part of it is also due to a *decrease* in quantity *demanded*, from N_1 to N_2. You can already see that while some unskilled workers benefit (those who keep their jobs and are paid more), others are hurt: They lose their jobs.

The job losses in panel (a) can be especially harmful to young workers who are not college bound and who need to establish a job record. A good performance at a first job, even a minimum wage job, can enable an unskilled worker to seek other employment later, at more than the minimum wage. (This is somewhat analogous to the way college students use unpaid internships—which are not covered by minimum wage law—to beef up their résumés and improve their employment prospects.) But the effects in panel (a) are just the beginning.

Some of those who lose their jobs in the covered sector will move to the only sector where jobs are still available—the uncovered sector in panel (b). There the labor supply curve will shift rightward, from L_1^S to L_2^S, and the market wage will fall below its initial value—to $3.00 in our example. Thus the impact of the minimum wage spills over into the sector not covered by it. Increased competition for jobs drives down the wages of *all* workers there, even those who were already employed before the minimum wage was imposed. More specifically, we would expect a decline in the wages of waiters, house cleaners, and unskilled workers who work in law-breaking firms.

> *A minimum wage—by raising wage rates in covered industries, and lowering them in uncovered industries—creates a wage differential among the least-skilled workers, depending on the industry in which they work.*

What about skilled workers? Are they affected by minimum wage legislation? You might think not, since they are already earning more than the minimum. But when the wage of unskilled labor rises in the covered sector, employers there will, to some degree, substitute skilled workers and capital equipment for unskilled labor. For example, a dishwasher might be replaced by a sophisticated dishwashing machine that requires maintenance and repair by skilled workers. An unskilled product packager might be replaced by a high-tech machine designed and maintained by skilled workers. Substitution toward capital that is produced, operated and maintained by skilled labor will shift the labor demand curve in panel (c) rightward, from L_1^D to L_2^D. As a result, the wage rate in the skilled sector will increase, from $20 to $24 in our example.

> *A minimum wage—by causing firms to substitute away from unskilled labor toward capital and skilled labor—can increase the wage differential between skilled and unskilled workers.*

You can see that the minimum wage sets off a chain of events. In the end, some unskilled workers benefit in the form of higher pay. Other unskilled workers are harmed by lower pay or unemployment. There is only one group in which everyone benefits: skilled workers. It should come as no surprise, then, that for many decades the most vocal advocates of raising the minimum wage have been labor unions, whose membership is disproportionately made up of skilled workers.

What do economists think about the minimum wage? There is both agreement and disagreement. Surveys consistently show that a large majority of economists agree with the analysis presented here, as well as its most important conclusion: that the minimum wage law causes unemployment among unskilled workers. For example, in a 1995 survey of economists who specialize in the study of labor markets, 87 percent agreed that "a minimum wage increases unemployment among young and unskilled workers."[8]

Further, most economists regard the minimum wage as an *inefficient* policy for helping poor working families. More than half of those directly affected by the minimum wage are young adults who are not supporting families. Some of these may be teenagers living at home with well-off families, and not in need of help. Others who *do* need help may be harmed, if they are unable to find a job in the covered sector, or if they are unlucky enough to be working in the uncovered sector.

As a rule, economists prefer policies that target assistance directly to those in need and exclude those who are well off. In the United States, the earned income

---

[8] Robert Whaples, "Is There Consensus among American Labor Economists? Survey Results on Forty Propositions," *Journal of Labor Research*, Vol. XVII, No. 4 (Fall 1996) pp. 730–731.

tax credit (EITC)—which supplements the incomes of low-income workers—is an example of such a policy. In 2002, the EITC for a low-income worker supporting two children could reach $4,100 from the federal government, and another $1,000 or so from a state EITC. Unlike the minimum wage, the EITC helps *only* the poor, and it deprives no one of a job. And the funds come out of general tax revenues, most of which is collected from moderate- and high-income taxpayers and profitable corporations. The cost of the minimum wage, by contrast, is paid by business owners and their customers, who may not be well off.

You might think, then, that economists would overwhelmingly *oppose* any increase in the minimum wage. But that is not the case. In the 1995 survey, a majority of labor economists (57 percent) believed that the minimum wage should be increased, in spite of the rise in unemployment it would cause. Similar support was found in another, more recent survey of economists.[9] What explains this support?

First, there is a *positive economic* disagreement—a disagreement about the facts of how the economy works. Those who *favor* an increase in the minimum wage tend to believe the effect on unemployment is much *smaller* than those who oppose an increase.

But there may be other reasons for these survey results. For example, some economists—even if they view an EITC-like program as superior—may feel that the current EITC level is too low. They may favor a hike in the minimum wage because—even with all of its problems—it is more politically achievable than higher EITC benefits. Others may believe that higher unemployment, as a more visible problem than low wages, is more likely to influence public policy in a direction they favor, such as an increase in funding for programs to improve job skills.

You can see that the minimum wage, like most issues of public policy, is not as simple as it appears at first glance, or even at second glance. But as you've seen, it serves as one among many barriers to entry into labor markets. And like occupational licensing and union wage setting, it provides another reason for wage differentials.

DISCRIMINATION AND WAGES

Discrimination occurs when *the members of a group of people have different opportunities because of characteristics that have nothing to do with their abilities.* Throughout American history, discrimination against women and minorities has been widespread in housing, business loans, consumer services, and jobs. The last arena—jobs—is our focus here. While tough laws and government incentive programs have lessened overt job discrimination—such as the help wanted ads that asked for white males as late as the 1950s—less obvious forms of discrimination remain.

Our first step in understanding the economics of discrimination is to distinguish two words that are often confused. *Prejudice* is an emotional dislike for members of a certain group; *discrimination* refers to the restricted opportunities offered to such a group. As you will see, prejudice does not always lead to discrimination, nor is prejudice necessary for discrimination to occur.

Discrimination When a group of people have different opportunities because of personal characteristics that have nothing to do with their abilities.

---

[9] Fuchs, Victor R., Alan B. Krueger, and James M. Poterba, "Economists' Views About Parameters, Values, and Policies: Survey Results in Labor and Public Economics." *The Journal of Economic Literature*, Vol. 36, No. 3 (September, 1998), pp. 1387–1425.

Employer Prejudice

When you think of job discrimination, your first image might be a manager who re-fuses to hire members of some group, such as African-Americans or women, because of pure prejudice. As a result, the victims of prejudice, prevented from working at high-paying jobs, must accept lower wages elsewhere. No doubt, many employers hire according to their personal prejudices. But it may surprise you to learn that economists generally consider employer prejudice one of the *least* important sources of labor market discrimination.

To see why, look at Figure 5, which shows the labor market divided into two broad sectors, A and B. To keep things simple, we'll assume that all workers have the same qualifications and that they find jobs in either sector equally attractive. Under these conditions, if there were *no* discrimination, both sectors would pay the same wage, W_1. (Can you explain why?)

Now suppose the firms in sector A decide they no longer wish to employ mem-bers of some group—say, women. What would happen? Women would begin look-ing for jobs in the *nondiscriminating* sector B, and the labor supply curve there would shift rightward. The equilibrium would move from F to F', decreasing the wage to W_2. At the same time, with women no longer welcome in sector A, the la-bor supply curve there would shift leftward, moving the market from E to E' and driving the wage up to W_3. It appears that employer discrimination would create a gender wage differential equal to $W_3 - W_2$.

But the differential would be only temporary. Why? With the wage rate in sec-tor B now lower, *men* would exit that market and seek jobs in the higher-paying sector A. These movements would reverse the changes in labor supply, and, in the end, both sectors would pay the same wage again. Employer prejudice against women might lead to a permanent change in the *composition* of labor in each sector—with only men working in sector A and both sexes working in sector B—but *no change in wage rates*.

But employer prejudice might not even change the composition of labor in ei-ther sector, because there is another force working to eliminate this form of dis-crimination altogether: the product market. Since biased employers must initially pay higher wages to employ men, they will have higher average costs than unbi-ased employers. If biased firms sell their product in a competitive market, they will suffer losses and ultimately be forced to exit their industries. Over the long run, prejudiced employers should be replaced with unprejudiced ones. Even if the prod-uct market is imperfectly competitive, the firm will still have its stockholders or owners to contend with. Unless *their* prejudice is so strong that they are willing to forego profit, management will be under pressure to hire qualified women rather than pay a premium to hire men. In either case,

> *when prejudice originates with employers, competitive labor markets work to discourage discrimination and reduce or eliminate any wage gap between the favored and the unfavored group.*

Employee and Customer Prejudice

What if *workers*, rather than employers, are prejudiced? Then our conclusions are very different. If, for example, a significant number of male assembly-line work-

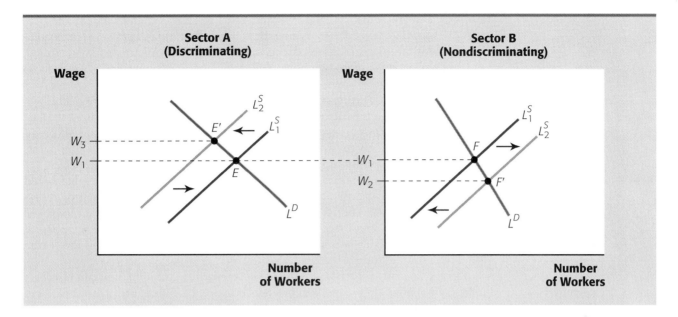

FIGURE 5
Employer Discrimination and Wage Rates

In the absence of discrimination, the wage rate would be W_1 in both sector A and sector B. If firms in sector A discriminate against some group—such as women—the group would seek work in the nondiscriminating sector, B. The increased labor supply in sector B causes the wage there to fall to W_2, while the decreased supply in sector A causes the wage there to rise to W_3. But only temporarily if the discrimination results from employer prejudice. As men migrate from sector B to the now-higher wage sector A, the labor supply changes in both sectors are reversed. The wage returns to W_1 in both sectors.

ers dislike supervision by women, then hiring female supervisors might reduce productivity, raise costs for any level of output, and therefore decrease profit. In a competitive product market, a *nondiscriminating* firm would be forced out of business. And even in imperfectly competitive product markets, stockholders will *want* the firm to discriminate against female supervisors, even if they themselves are not prejudiced. In this case, we cannot count on the market to solve the problem at all.

The same argument applies if the prejudice originates with the firm's *customers*. For example, if many automobile owners distrust female mechanics, then an auto repair shop that hires them would lose some customers and sacrifice profit. True, excluding qualified female mechanics is costly; it means paying higher wages to men and charging higher prices. But customers will be willing to *pay* a higher price, since they prefer male mechanics. Even in the long run, then, women might be excluded from the auto mechanics trade.

More generally, if worker or customer prejudice is common in high-wage industries, then women would be forced into low-wage jobs.

> *When prejudice originates with the firm's employees or its customers, market forces may encourage, rather than discourage, discrimination and can lead to a permanent wage gap between the favored and unfavored groups.*

Statistical Discrimination

Suppose you are in charge of hiring 10 new employees at your firm. Suppose, too, that young, married women in your industry are twice as likely to quit their jobs within two years than men (say, because they decide to have children) and that quits are very costly to your firm: New workers must be recruited and trained, and production is disrupted when there is a temporary gap in staffing. Let's say that 20 people apply for the 10 positions—half men and half women. All are equally qualified, and you have no way of knowing which *individuals* among them are more likely to quit within two years. Whom will you hire?

If your sole goal is to maximize the firm's profit, there is no question: You will hire the men. (If you have goals other than profit maximization, you might not last very long at that firm.) Notice that in this example, there was no mention of prejudice. Indeed, even if there isn't a trace of prejudice in you, in the firm's employees, or in its customers, profit maximization may still dictate hiring the men.

Statistical discrimination—so called because individuals are excluded based on the statistical probability of behavior in their group, rather than their own personal traits—is a case of discrimination without prejudice. It can lead an unbiased profit-maximizing employer to discriminate against an individual member of a group, even though that particular individual might never engage in the feared behavior.

But, as some observers have pointed out, statistical discrimination can also be a cover for prejudice. For example, consider statistical discrimination against women. True, women are more likely to leave work to care for their children. But men are more likely to develop alcohol and drug problems, which can lead to poor judgment and costly accidents on the job. If there were no prejudice, then the risks associated with hiring men would be thrown into the equation. According to critics of the statistical discrimination theory, the negative behavior of a favored group (such as men) is rarely considered by employers.

> **Statistical discrimination** When individuals are excluded from an activity based on the statistical probability of behavior in their group, rather than their personal characteristics.

Dealing with Discrimination

As you've seen, discrimination due to pure employer prejudice is unlikely to have much of an impact on labor markets. As long as some employers are *not* prejudiced, those who *are* prejudiced will be at a competitive disadvantage. In the long run, the market helps to *eliminate* this type of discrimination.

But for other types of discrimination—such as statistical discrimination or discrimination due to worker or consumer prejudice—market incentives work in the opposite way, leading to a permanent and stubborn problem. In these cases, many economists and other policy makers believe that government action is needed. This is especially so when the groups discriminated against are already poor or disadvantaged in some way.

Some favor affirmative action programs, which actively encourage firms to expand opportunities for women and minorities; others favor stricter enforcement of existing antidiscrimination laws and stiffer penalties when discriminatory hiring occurs. Both approaches to policy force *all* firms to bear the costs of nondiscriminatory hiring, so that no single firm is at a disadvantage. For example, by forcing *all* firms to hire women—and to bear the costs of possibly greater quit rates or of alienating workers or customers who might be prejudiced—no single firm is put at a disadvantage by hiring women.

Discrimination and Wage Differentials

How much have the wages of victimized groups been reduced because of discrimination? As you are about to see, this is a very difficult question to answer.

	Median Income	Percent of White Male Income
White Males	$761	100%
Black Males	$582	76%
Hispanic Males	$503	66%
White Females	$590	78%
Black Females	$512	67%
Hispanic Females	$403	53%

Source: Bureau of Labor Statistics News Release, *"Usual Weekly Earnings,"* April 17, 2003. Data are for first quarter of 2003. (*Note:* Persons of Hispanic origin may be of any race.)

TABLE 2
Median Weekly Earnings, 2001 (of Full-time Wage and Salary Workers Over Age 25)

A starting point—but *only* a starting point—is Table 2, which shows median earnings for different groups of full-time workers in the population. Notice the substantial earnings gap between men and women of either race and between whites and blacks of either sex. Doesn't this prove that the impact of discrimination on wages is substantial? Not necessarily.

Consider the black–white differential for men. In 2003, black men earned 24 percent less than white men, on average. But *some* of this difference is due to differences in education, job experience, job choice, and geographic location between whites and blacks. For example, the proportion of black adults with college degrees is a little more than half that of white adults. Even if all firms were completely color-blind in their hiring and wage payments, disproportionately fewer blacks would have higher-paying jobs requiring college degrees, and this would produce an earnings differential in favor of whites. The same would apply if blacks were more likely to live in low-wage areas or, on average, had fewer years of prior experience when applying for jobs.

Several studies suggest that if we limit comparisons to whites and blacks with the same educational background, geographic location, and, in some cases, the same ability (measured by a variety of different tests), 50 percent or more of the earnings difference disappears.[10]

Does this mean that discrimination accounts for half or less of the earnings differential? Not at all: Many of the observed differences in education, geographic location, and ability are the *result* of job market discrimination. Figure 6 illustrates a vicious cycle of discrimination in the labor market. First, job discrimination causes a wage differential between equally qualified whites and blacks. With a lower wage, blacks have less incentive to remain in the labor force or to invest in human capital, since they reap smaller rewards for these activities. The result is that blacks, on average, have less education and less job experience than whites, and even color-blind employers will hire disproportionately fewer blacks in high-paying jobs, perpetuating their lower wages.

In addition to job market discrimination, there is *premarket* discrimination—unequal treatment in education and housing—that occurs *before* an individual enters the labor market. For example, regardless of black families' incomes, housing discrimination may exclude them from neighborhoods with better public schools,

HTTP://

For an update on women's earnings, see Mary Bowler, "Women's Earnings: An Overview," in the *Monthly Labor Review* (12/99) available at http://www.bls.gov/opub/mlr/1999/12/contents.htm.

[10] See, for example, June O'Neill, "The Role of Human Capital in Earnings Differences between Black and White Men," *Journal of Economic Perspectives* (Fall 1990), pp. 25–45.

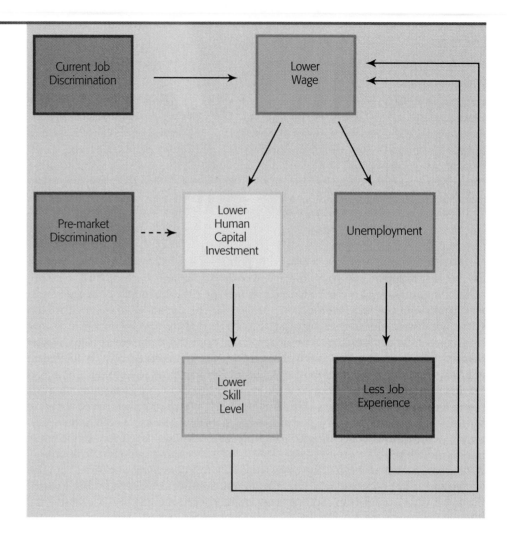

FIGURE 6
The Vicious Cycle of Discrimination

resulting in fewer blacks being admitted to college. Discriminatory treatment by teachers within a school may contribute to lowered aspirations and diminished job-market expectations. All of these contribute to the low-wage syndrome.

Similar reasoning applies to the earnings gap between women and men. On the one hand, we have a large earnings gap. In 2003, for example, the earnings of white female workers were only 78 percent of those of white men. On the other hand, studies suggest that a third or more of the male–female wage gap is due to differences in skills and job experience. But for women, as well as blacks and other minorities, differences in skills and experience can be the *result* of lower wages: Since women know they will earn less than men and will have more trouble advancing on the job, they have less incentive to invest in human capital and to stay in the labor force. Premarket discrimination plays a role, too. Several studies have suggested that different treatment of girls in secondary school may lower their job market aspirations. And even before school, girls may be socialized to prefer different (and lower-paying) career paths than boys, such as nursing rather than medicine.

In the end, we do not know nearly as much about the impact of discrimination on wages as we would like to know, but research is proceeding at a rapid pace. As we've seen, the data must always be interpreted with care:

> *In measuring the impact of job market discrimination on earnings, the wage gap between two groups gives an overestimate, since it fails to account for differences in skills and experience. However, comparing only workers with similar skills and experience leads to an underestimate, since skill and experience are themselves influenced by discrimination—both in the job market and outside of it.*

INCOME INEQUALITY

Wage differentials among households are an important cause of income inequality, but not the only cause. Two people with identical *hourly* wage rates may have vastly different wage or salary *incomes* because one is unemployed more often than the other or because one works more hours each week than the other.

Moreover, wages and salaries are not the only source of income. Some households supply capital or entrepreneurship (earning interest income or profit) or land and natural resources (earning rental income). These forms of income are often called *nonlabor income* or **property income,** to distinguish them from the wage and salary income derived from labor alone. Some of the largest incomes—such as Bill Gates's—are mostly property income. Many households also receive **transfer payments** from the government, such as Social Security, unemployment insurance, or welfare payments.

Property income Income derived from supplying capital, entrepreneurship, land, or natural resources.

Transfer payment Any payment that is not compensation for supplying goods, services, or resources.

When we discuss income inequality, we are ultimately concerned about inequality in *total* income, regardless of source. How much income inequality is there in the United States? Although there are many measures of income inequality, they all leave much to be desired. Here, we consider the two most commonly cited measures.

The Poverty Rate

The **poverty rate** tells us the percentage of families whose incomes fall below a certain minimum, called the **poverty line.** The official poverty rate reported by the U.S. government is calculated as follows: The government determines the cost of feeding families of different types (number and ages of children, rural versus urban families, etc.). Then it is assumed that a family needs at least twice its basic food budget to pay for *other* necessities, such as housing, clothing, and transportation. Accordingly, for each family size, the poverty line is roughly triple the basic food budget (the exact multiple depending on the size of the family). For example, in 2002 the poverty line for a single person was an annual income of $9,359. For a family of two, it was set at $12,047, and for a family of four, $18,244.

Poverty rate The percent of families whose incomes fall below a certain minimum—the poverty line.

Poverty line The income level below which a family is considered to be in poverty.

Finally, the poverty rate is then defined as the percent of U.S. people who fall below their respective poverty lines, given their family status. In 2002, the official U.S. poverty rate was 12.1 percent, telling us that 121 out of every 1,000 people fell below the poverty line defined for their characteristics. During the past two decades, the poverty rate hovered around 13 percent until the end of the 1990s, when it fell rapidly toward 11 percent. It rose again in 2001 and 2002 as the economy went into recession and suffered a slow recovery.

Poverty rates are important because they keep policy makers and the public aware of conditions at the bottom of the economic ladder. Of particular concern is the unequal *distribution* of poverty among different groups in the population. As

TABLE 3
Poverty Rates for U.S. Individuals

Year	All People	White	Black	Hispanic
1970	12.6%	9.9%	33.5%	Not Available
1980	13.0%	10.2%	32.5%	25.7%
1990	13.5%	10.7%	31.9%	28.1%
2000	11.3%	9.4%	22.5%	21.5%
2001	11.7%	9.9%	22.7%	21.4%
2002	12.1%	10.3%	23.9%	21.8%

Source: U.S. Census Bureau (*http://www.census.gov*), "Historical Poverty Tables, Table 2"; and Poverty 2002, Table 1

you can see in Table 3, the poverty rate for black and Hispanic families has remained stubbornly above that for white families.

One reason for the persistently higher incidence of poverty among blacks and Hispanics is the lower wage rates earned by workers in these two groups, and this, in turn, is due to discrimination and differences in education levels (which may result from premarket discrimination). In 2001, for example, 29 percent of the non-Hispanic white population had college degrees, but only 17.5 percent of blacks and 11 percent of Hispanics had graduated from college.[11] In addition to earning lower wage rates, blacks and Hispanics have higher unemployment rates. And they have substantially less wealth, and therefore earn less property income than whites.

The poverty rate gives us important information about the poorest families and how poverty is distributed among different groups within society. As a measure of income inequality, however, the poverty rate suffers from some serious drawbacks.

First, when calculating income, the poverty rate ignores the impact of taxes and some government benefits. On the tax side, few people below the poverty line pay income taxes, but almost all of those who work pay *payroll* taxes (the Social Security tax) on their wages, which reduces spendable income. On the benefits side, many families below the poverty line receive food stamps, Medicaid, rent subsidies, and cash (such as the earned income credit) from the government. The government has alternative measures of poverty that incorporate the effects of taxes and government benefits, but these measures are not widely reported. From 2001 to 2002, the poverty rate—incorporating all taxes and benefits—would have risen from 9.0 to 9.4 percent, instead of the official rise from 11.7 to 12.1 percent.[12]

A second problem with gauging inequality with the poverty rate is that it ignores inequality among those *above* the poverty line. For a more comprehensive picture of inequality, we must turn to other measures, such as the one introduced in the next section.

The Lorenz Curve

Table 4 provides data that we can use to measure inequality across the entire spectrum of the income distribution. The table shows the percentage of total income earned by each fifth of the population, and the top 5 percent, when households are

[11] U.S. Census Bureau *News Release*, March 31, 2003, "Table A. Summary Measures of Educational Attainment of the U.S. Population," (*http://www.census.gov/Press-Release/www/2003/cb03-51.html*).
[12] U.S. Census Bureau (*http://www.census.gov*), "Poverty Estimates Based on Alternative Measures of Income and Deflators, 2002, Table 8."

	Lowest Fifth	Second Fifth	Third Fifth	Fourth Fifth	Highest Fifth	Highest 5 Percent	Gini Coefficient
1970	4.1%	10.8%	17.4%	24.5%	43.3%	16.6%	
1980	4.3%	10.3%	16.9%	24.9%	43.7%	15.8%	.394
1990	3.9%	9.6%	15.9%	24.0%	46.6%	18.6%	.403
2000	3.6%	8.9%	14.8%	23.0%	49.6%	22.1%	.428
2001	3.5%	8.7%	14.6%	23.0%	50.1%	22.4%	.462
							.466
Annual Income Range in 2001	0– $17,970	$17,970– $ 33,314	$33,314– $ 53,000	$53,000– $ 83,500	>$83,500	>$150,499	

Source: U.S. Census Bureau, Table H-2 (*http://www.census.gov/hhes/income/histinc/h02.html*)

TABLE 4
Percent of Total Household Income Earned by Each Fifth and Top 5 Percent of U.S. Households

arranged by their incomes from lowest to highest. For example, the second to last row of the table shows that that in 2001, the 20 percent of households with the lowest incomes (the lowest fifth) earned only 3.5 percent of total income earned by all households that year, while the top fifth earned 50.1 percent of the total. The last row of the table shows the household income range for each income group during 2001. For example, a household that earned $50,000 in income in 2001 would be part of the *third* fifth, falling within the $33,314 to $53,000 range.

If all households had earned identical incomes in a year, then the bottom fifth, and every fifth, would have earned exactly 20 percent of the total income that year. The first five entries would each be 20 percent, and the entry for the highest 5 percent of households would be 5 percent. But notice the high degree of *in*equality, especially at the high and low ends. The bottom fifth earn far less than 20 percent of the total, and the top fifth earn far more—greater than twice their proportional share. And at the very top, the highest 5 percent of households earned 22.4 percent of the total—more than four times their proportion of the population.

To get a clearer picture of what these numbers mean, look at Figure 7. The horizontal axis measures the cumulative percentages of total households, and the vertical axis measures the cumulative percentage of total income. For example, in 2001, the bottom 20 percent of households earned 3.5 percent of the total income, and the next 20 percent earned 8.7 percent, so the bottom 40 percent earned 3.5 percent + 8.7 percent = 12.2 percent of total income. Thus, one of the points in the figure is 40 percent on the horizontal axis and 12.2 percent on the vertical. The curve drawn through all the points obtained in this way is called the **Lorenz curve.**

If all households earned the same income, the Lorenz curve would be the thick straight line with a slope of 1 (marked "Line of Complete Equality"), since the bottom 20 percent would earn 20 percent of the total, the bottom 40 percent would earn 40 percent, and so on, until we reached 100 percent of all households, which—by definition—always earn 100 percent of the income. By contrast, the Lorenz curve in an economy with inequality will always be bowed out in the middle, although it will start and end at the same point as the line of complete equality. This gives us a visual representation of income inequality: The more bowed out the Lorenz curve—or the greater the area marked *A* in the figure—the greater will be the degree of inequality.

Lorenz curve When households are arrayed according to their incomes, a line showing the cumulative percent of income received by each cumulative percent of households.

FIGURE 7
The U.S. Lorenz Curve, 2001

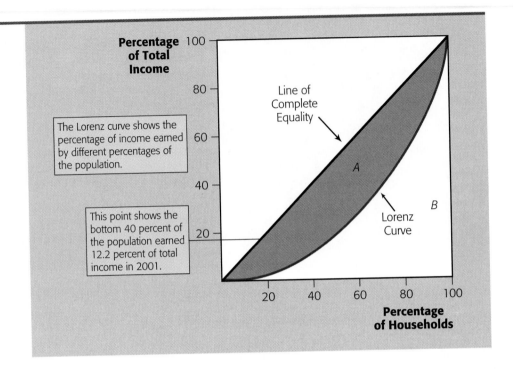

One of the most popular numerical measures of income inequality, the **Gini coefficient,** is obtained from the Lorenz curve in a very simple way: We divide area *A* in Figure 7 by the total area underneath the diagonal (area *A* plus area *B*). The more unequal the income distribution, the larger will be area *A* relative to area *A* + *B*, and the larger the Gini coefficient. If there were complete income equality—where everyone earned the same income—then area *A* would equal zero, so the Gini coefficient, *A*/(*A* + *B*), would equal zero as well. The highest degree of inequality—where one person earned all the income, and the rest earned none—would give a Gini coefficient of 1.0. (Prove this to yourself by drawing the Lorenz curve for this case.) In general:

> *The larger the Gini coefficient—up to a maximum of 1.0—the greater is the degree of income inequality.*

In 2001, the Gini coefficient for U.S. household income was 0.466 (see Table 4).

Growing Income Inequality

Look at the last column of Table 4, which shows how the Gini coefficient has changed from 1970 to 2001. There is a clear trend upward, suggesting that the Lorenz curve has become more "bowed out" (area *A* is getting larger), and inequality is increasing.

The table also shows what is responsible for this trend: In each fifth of the population except for the highest, income shares have been declining. But in the top fifth, there has been a noticeable rise. A closer look shows that the top 5 percent of households are driving the upward trend of the top 20 percent: The share of the top 5 percent rose from 16.6 percent in 1970 to 22.4 percent in 2001—an increase that

Gini coefficient A measure of income inequality; the ratio of the area above a Lorenz curve and under the complete equality line to the area under the diagonal.

HTTP://

For a comprehensive review of recent changes in income distribution, check the Policy Debates page at http://www.swcollege.com/bef/policy_debates/income_inequality.html.

accounts for almost the entire increase of the top 20 percent. This does *not* mean that the incomes in the lower four-fifths are falling; median income (even in purchasing power terms) has actually risen for all quintiles of the population since 1970. But it *does* mean that the top 5 percent of households are earning an ever larger proportion of total earnings, because their incomes are growing at a considerably faster rate than the income of the rest of the population.

Some of what you've learned in this and the previous chapters can help explain this rise in income inequality that has accelerated after 1990. Most of the technological changes of the past decade have been complementary with highly skilled (and high-wage) labor and substitutable for less-skilled (low-wage) labor. This tends to increase income differences. For example, workers who use computers have received much higher wage increases over the past decade than others.

Other forces are at work as well. Increased international trade with low-wage countries—while it has benefited the nation as a whole—may have slowed income growth for the least skilled workers in the United States. At the other end, the very rapid income growth of thousands of superstars—in entertainment, sports, literature, law, business, medicine, and even academia—has played a role.

But what about those at the *very, very* top? Here, our data are not very helpful. In any given year, most of what is reported as income at the very top is *capital gains*—the earnings from selling assets like stocks or real estate at a price higher than their purchase price. Capital gains are counted as income in the year the assets are sold, but such sales are often one-time events. As a result, this form of reported income fluctuates wildly from year to year for any given household. (For example, of the 2,218 households who appeared on the Internal Revenue Service's top-400 income list over nine years from 1992 to 2000, less than a quarter appeared on the list in more than one year, about 13 percent appeared in more than two years, and about 6 percent showed up on the list in five or more of the nine years.[13]

However, even a one-time capital gain that puts someone on this list in one year is significant. In 2000, for example, the *cutoff* point for the IRS's top-400 list was a reported income (including capital gains) of $87 million. But huge capital gains like this are part of an entirely different dimension of economic inequality than we've discussed so far, one having to do with *wealth*.

Wealth Inequality. A household's *wealth* or *net worth* is the total value of all the assets it owns—including real estate, stocks, bonds, and bank accounts—minus the value of its debts. A household that owns more than it owes has positive wealth, and will have negative wealth if it owes more than it owns.

Table 5 shows the percentage of total household net worth in the United States owned by various percentages of the population in three different years. Other than a rise in the share of wealth owned by the wealthiest 400 households, there are no strong trends in wealth inequality over time. But there is still something striking in the table: Wealth is distributed with an astonishing degree of inequality. In 2001, the bottom half of the population (0 to 50th percentile) held just 2.8 percent of total wealth, while the top 1 percent (99th to 100th percentile) held almost a third of the total.

---

[13] See, for example, Tom Herman, "Wealthiest Americans Hold Rising Share of U.S. Income," *Wall Street Journal,* June 26, 2003, and "Those Notorious IRS 400," *Wall Street Journal,* July 8, 2003.

	0 to 50th Percentile	50th to 90th Percentile	90th to 95th Percentile	95th to 99th Percentile	99th to 100th Percentile	Richest 400 People
1989	2.7%	29.9%	13.0%	24.1%	30.3%	1.6%
1995	3.6%	28.6%	11.9%	21.3%	34.6%	1.7%
2001	2.8%	27.4%	12.1%	25.0%	32.7%	2.3%

Source: Arthur Kennickell, "A Rolling Tide: Changes in the Distribution of Wealth in the U.S., 1989–2001," Survey of Consumer Finances, Federal Reserve Board, March 3, 2003 (*http://www.federalreserve.gov/pubs/oss/oss2/papers/concentration.2001.pdf*).

TABLE 5
Percent of Total Household Net Worth Owned by Fractions of U.S. Households

This can be seen even more starkly in Figure 8, which plots a Lorenz curve for wealth in 2001 along with the Lorenz curve for income in that year (reproduced from Figure 7). You can see that the Lorenz curve for wealth is substantially more bowed out than that for income, reflecting considerably more inequality in the distribution of wealth.

Wealth inequality is related to income inequality. First, greater wealth leads to greater income. If you own an apartment building, mini-mall or office tower, you'll receive periodic income in the form of rent. If you own shares of stock in a corporation, you will receive a share of the firm's profit; if you own bonds, you will receive interest payments. Inequality in the distribution of wealth thus contributes to income inequality.

But the causation also runs the other way: Those with the lowest incomes are the least able to save, which is one way a family can build up its wealth. Thus, income inequality contributes to wealth inequality.

Wealth inequality is important for other reasons as well. Wealth provides financial and psychological security beyond its contribution to income. It allows one to pass economic advantage to one's heirs. And it can be a a source of political influence—even a source of funds to run for president, as Steve Forbes did in 1996 and again in 2000. Therefore, wealth inequality raises issues that go far beyond income inequality.

Problems with Inequality Measures

Ideally, we would like our measures of income inequality to tell us something about inequality in *economic well-being* and to use them as a guide for social and economic policy. For these purposes, however, the poverty rate, the Gini coefficient, and other gauges of income inequality—at least the way they are measured in practice—suffer from serious deficiencies.

Earned Income Versus Available Income. Our inequality measures are based on the income *earned* by different groups, not the income *available* for spending. For a variety of reasons, these can be very different.

First, the United States, like virtually all developed countries, has a **progressive income tax** (higher-income households pay a greater percentage of their income in taxes). However, since our inequality measures are based on income before tax, they tend to overstate inequality in available income.

Progressive income tax A tax that collects a higher percentage of total income from higher income households.

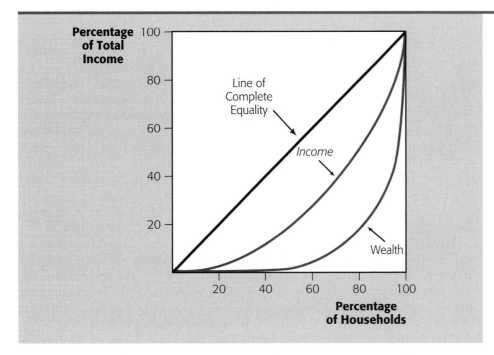

FIGURE 8

U.S. Lorenz Curves for Income and Wealth, 2001

The Lorenz curve for wealth shows even greater inequality in wealth distribution than in income distribution.

Our measures also ignore some government transfers, like free medical care, food stamps, and subsidized housing, which free up income for other uses. While transfer payments will not propel someone from the lowest fifth to the highest, they certainly increase the share of income going to those at the bottom. Ignoring transfers, like ignoring taxes, leads to an *overstatement* of inequality. Sweden's reputation as an egalitarian society, for example, is based on a highly progressive income tax and generous government transfers and programs for those at the bottom. None of this would be reflected in Sweden's Lorenz curve.

On the other hand, our inequality measures ignore fringe benefits, which go mostly to those in the middle. If we included fringes in our measures, they would show a greater proportion of total income going to the middle and the top. For these reasons, our measures may *understate* income inequality.

Income Mobility. It is one thing to say that the bottom 20 percent of households earn only 3.5 percent of the income and quite another to say that, year after year, *the same households remain at the bottom.* The United States has a relatively mobile society: people switch careers, change jobs, and start new businesses more often than in most other countries. These changes, as well as pure chance, will give people good years and bad years. If many of those at the bottom or top are there only temporarily, then over a longer time horizon, there is less inequality than our measures suggest.

Moreover, one's own income tends to change in a predictable pattern over one's lifetime. Most workers start out earning low incomes, which then rise as they acquire more skills and experience, and, finally, fall sharply in retirement. This, too, can distort our measures of income inequality. To take an extreme example, imagine an economy that always has just five workers, each of whom passes through the same five phases of income over their lives: $40,000 per year in the first decade,

$60,000 in the second decade, $80,000 in the third, $100,000 in the fourth, and then $20,000 in the decade of retirement. Suppose, too, that at any point in time, one worker is in each phase. Then total yearly income in the economy will be $20,000 + $40,000 + $60,000 + $80,000 + $100,000 = $300,000. Each year, the bottom fifth (the retired worker) would earn just $20,000/$300,000 = 0.066 of total income. The top fifth (the worker at the height of her earning power) would have $100,000/$300,000 = 0.333 of total income. Even though everyone would have an identical income profile over his or her lifetime—total equality of *lifetime earnings*—the Lorenz curve would show substantial inequality.

The problem is that Lorenz curves, Gini coefficients, poverty rates, and most other measures of inequality give us a snapshot picture of the distribution of income when we would ideally like a moving picture—a picture of the distribution of lifetime earnings. But such information would be very difficult to gather; it would require tracing the incomes of a large sample of people over their entire lifetimes.

However, a few studies have tracked earnings over several years, and the findings are interesting. Table 6 shows the results of one recent study. Each *row* of data represents the individuals in a particular income fifth in *1988*. The entry in each *column* tells us where those families ended up a decade later, in *1998*. For example, the entry in the second row, third column, tells us that 22.6 percent of those who were in the second fifth in 1988 had moved up to the third fifth in 1998.

What do these numbers tell us overall? First, that the U.S. income distribution has been at least somewhat mobile. About half of those in the bottom fifth moved up within 10 years, and half of those in the top fifth moved down. This does not mean that those in the top have switched places with those on the bottom; on the contrary, there was very little movement from one extreme to another. But there was substantial movement from the extremes to the middle three-fifths. For example, over the period studied, 42 percent of those at the bottom and 44 percent of those at the top moved to the middle.

> *The U.S. income distribution exhibits significant mobility between the extremes and the middle. Lorenz curves, poverty rates, Gini ratios, and other measures of income inequality—because they provide only a snapshot of the income distribution at a moment in time—may exaggerate long-run income inequality.*

On the other hand, significant numbers of people seem to stay where they are, as shown by the entries in the upper left and lower right corners, both about 53 percent. This tells us that more than half of those in the bottom fifth, and more than half in the top fifth, ended up in roughly the same place they were 10 years earlier.

And if we compare Table 6 with earlier, similar studies, we find that mobility has *decreased* slightly from earlier decades. In the 1970s, for example, about 4 percent more households in both the lowest fifth and the highest fifth moved toward the middle within a decade, compared to the numbers who made those movements in Table 6. This decrease in mobility—coupled with rising inequality—has caused considerable concern and heated up an ongoing debate about economic inequality in the United States.

Careless Interpretations. Another problem with measures of income distribution is a criticism not of the measures themselves, but of how they are interpreted. So far, we have tried to be entirely descriptive, avoiding value judgments about the words

Where Families Started in 1988	Where Families Ended Up in 1998				
	Lowest Fifth	Second Fifth	Third Fifth	Fourth Fifth	Highest Fifth
Lowest Fifth	53.3%	23.6%	12.4%	6.4%	4.3%
Second Fifth	25.7%	36.3%	22.6%	11.0%	4.3%
Third Fifth	10.9%	20.7%	28.3%	27.5%	12.6%
Fourth Fifth	6.5%	12.9%	23.7%	31.1%	25.8%
Highest Fifth	3.0%	5.7%	14.9%	23.2%	53.2%

Source: Katherine Bradbury and Jane Katz, "Are Lifetime Incomes Growing More Unequal?" *Regional Review,* Federal Reserve Bank of Boston, Fourth Quarter, 2002.

TABLE 6

Income Mobility Between 1988 and 1998

equality and *inequality*. But ask yourself: As you have been reading this chapter, have you made the implicit assumption that more inequality is bad and more equality good? Many people (but few economists) automatically react in this way. They confuse *equality,* which means that everyone gets the same result, with *equity,* which implies *fair and equal treatment.* Even if we had a perfect measure of income inequality—say, one based on the lifetime income actually available to each citizen—extreme caution would be needed in drawing conclusions about equity or fairness. The reasons for this are the subject of the next section.

ECONOMIC INEQUALITY AND FAIRNESS

Fairness is difficult to define, in large part because we all have such different ideas about what it is. Witness the conflicts—which often come to blows—among kids at play, where the accusation "That's not fair" is invariably answered with "Yes, it is." Or think about the conflicts over marital property in divorce proceedings, over business property in the dissolution of a partnership, or over the grades given by teachers. In all of these cases, highly emotional disputes center on entirely different definitions of fair.

Economics often steers clear of the fairness controversy, since most economic research emphasizes positive (descriptive and predictive) issues, rather than normative (prescriptive) ones. But there is no avoiding the problem of fairness when one discusses income inequality. After all, what is the purpose of measuring inequality in the first place, except to compare *what is* to some standard of *what should be*?

Since the controversy over fairness is based on conflicting values, can economics contribute to this debate? To some degree, yes.

First, despite the controversy, there are *some* issues of fairness on which almost everyone agrees. By identifying the many different causes of income inequality—as we've done in this chapter—we can at least pinpoint those types of inequality that almost all of us would regard as fair and those we would regard as unfair. This is no small accomplishment, and it can help us avoid policies that would, when properly understood, actually make the distribution of income more *unfair.*

For example, almost everyone would agree that income inequality due solely to compensating wage differentials is entirely fair. If one worker must put up with longer hours, a greater risk of death, more unpleasant weather, a greater risk of unemployment, or more years of schooling than another, it is only fair that he or she be paid more. Thus, eliminating compensating wage differentials, which would make incomes more *equal,* would also make them less *fair* to most of us.

The same holds for some of the inequality in property income. Remember the fable of the grasshopper, who fiddled all day, and the ant, who prepared for winter? Although many well-to-do Americans have inherited their wealth, many others have acquired theirs through years of working long hours, saving, or bearing risk. If some of us could have chosen to make these sacrifices, but did not, is it really fair for all of us to have the same wealth? Is it fair for the grasshopper to end up as wealthy as the ant? Most of us would say no.

If each of us started in the same place and had the same *options*—to save, to invest in human capital, or to choose among different jobs—then different outcomes resulting from our different choices would not be disturbing to most people. This suggests some *limited* common ground:

> *Inequality that results from equal opportunity, but different choices, is generally regarded as fair.*

By showing how labor markets work, and by identifying sources of inequality, economics can help us identify inequality that results from different choices rather than from different opportunities. In this way, it can help us come to agreement about *some* issues of fairness.

Unfortunately, that doesn't take us very far. Much of the income inequality—especially at the extremes—seems to originate in different *opportunities*. And here, issues of fairness remain contentious. For example, even though we agree that labor market discrimination is unfair, there is disagreement about the solution. Some favor strong affirmative action programs in schools and workplaces; others believe that the government and courts should intervene only in cases where discrimination is clearly occurring.

There is even more disagreement about inherited wealth. While most of us agree that it creates unequal opportunities—with those born into rich families able to make choices that are unavailable to others—there are sharp divisions over the appropriate policy response. Some favor very high estate taxes, with most private wealth going to the government at death, in part to help create a more level playing field. Others believe that the freedom to use one's property as one wishes, including passing it on to one's heirs, is a fundamental human right. Similar disagreements occur over inequality arising from inherited talent, intelligence, beauty, or physical strength that people exploit in superstar markets. And there is disagreement about every change to the tax code proposed in the last hundred years.

One famous effort to form a consensus about fairness was made by philosopher John Rawls, a Harvard philosopher.[14] Rawls maintained that we could discover the rules of a fair and just society by imagining that we had to create them *before knowing* what our opportunities would be in that society. In a sense, we'd make up the rules before we were born, without knowing in advance whether we'd be born into a wealthy family or a poor one, endowed with great talent, intelligence, or beauty, or with very little of these qualities.

---

[14] John Rawls, *A Theory of Justice* (Cambridge, MA: Harvard University Press, 1972).

Rawls argued that we would naturally come to certain conclusions about fairness and equality of opportunity if forced to create them in this way, and that these rules should define our standard of justice. One of Rawls's most famous conclusions was that—because any of us might end up in the worst of all possible situations—we would all agree to create a society in which the least well-off person was made as well-off as possible. In this view, inequality would be justified only if it helped raise the position of the person at the bottom.

Rawls's ideas were highly controversial. And unfortunately for those who agreed with him, issues of fairness in a democracy are ultimately decided in the voting booth by people who *are* already born and already know their relative position. And this is one reason why issues of economic fairness—such as our judgments about the growing economic inequality of the 1990s and early 2000s, and what should be done about it—will remain controversial. The "Using the Theory" section that follows looks at one of the biggest recent controversies relating to economic inequality.

USING THE THEORY
CEOs in the 1990s and Early 2000s

During the 1990s and the early 2000s, payments to chief executive officers (CEOs) of major U.S. corporations rose dramatically. And they were very high to begin with. In 1990, the average total compensation of CEOs at 365 of the largest corporations was about $2 million; by 2000, it had risen to $13.1 million.[15] During the same period, the average American worker's wage rose by only 37 percent, barely keeping ahead of inflation. As a result, the ratio of CEO pay to that of the average worker rose from about 150 to over 500 during the decade. The rise in this ratio received increasing media attention and stirred a divisive political debate during the 1990s—one that grew louder in the early 2000s.

eBay CEO and President, Margaret (Meg) C. Whitman

Table 7 provides an illustration of why. It lists the 12 corporations with the highest-paid CEOs in 2002 (among those for which full data was available). First, look at the middle (bolded) column, which lists total 2002 compensation for the CEO at each firm. As you can see, at all 12 corporations the CEO earned more than $25 million, with two earning more than $100 million. (A year earlier, seven CEOs broke through the $100 million barrier.)

Now, look at the second and third columns, which break total compensation into two categories. Although the numbers in the first category—salary and bonus—are certainly high, most of the earnings are in the form of *additional compensation*. For the top five CEOs, this category accounts for 94 percent or more of the total. Almost all of the additional compensation was in the form of *stock options* or *restricted stock grants* given to the CEO.

Stock options give the person who holds them the automatic right to buy shares in the company at a predetermined price, usually, the market price of shares on the day the options are awarded. If the share price rises *above* that

[15] Information in this section on CEO compensation is from the "Executive Pay" series in various issues of *Business Week* (April 17, 2000; April 16, 2001; April 21, 2003).

Corporation	Ceo Salary and Bonus in 2002	Additional Compensation in 2002	2002 Total CEO Compensation	Three-Year Total CEO Compensation (2000–2002)	Three-Year Percentage Change in Shareholder Wealth (2000–2002)
MBNA	$9.0 million	$185.9 million	**$194.9 million**	$240.7 million	+8%
Tenet Healthcare	$5.5 million	$111.0 million	**$116.6 million**	$124.2 million	+5%
Gap	$2.5 million	$ 88.5 million	**$ 91.0 million**	$108.7 million	−66%
Tyco International	$4.0 million	$ 67.0 million	**$ 71.0 million**	$238.2 million	−56%
Qualcomm	$1.7 million	$ 61.6 million	**$ 63.3 million**	$ 67.4 million	−79%
Comcast	$6.3 million	$ 33.5 million	**$ 39.8 million**	$104.1 million	−53%
First Data	$1.9 million	$ 37.2 million	**$ 39.1 million**	$ 47.2 million	+44%
Starbucks	$2.5 million	$ 36.3 million	**$ 38.8 million**	$ 55.8 million	+68%
Siebel Systems	$0	$ 34.6 million	**$ 34.6 million**	$297.6 million	−82%
Lehman Brothers	$1.8 million	$ 26.9 million	**$ 28.7 million**	$199.9 million	+28%
Sun Microsystems	$0.6 million	$ 25.2 million	**$ 25.9 million**	$ 53.1 million	−92%
Lockheed Martin	$4.4 million	$ 20.9 million	**$ 25.3 million**	$ 47.7 million	+174%

Source: Selected data from "Executive Compensation Scoreboard," *Business Week,* April 21, 2003, pp. 91–101. The table includes only the highest-paid CEOs who were employed at their firms for most of the period 2000–2002.

TABLE 7

Corporations with Highest-Paid CEOs in 2002

predetermined price, they can be purchased for less than their current value, giving the buyer an immediate gain in wealth.[16] Most of the additional CEO compensation in the table was in the form of stock options, used by CEOs to purchase stock after its price had risen.

Restricted stock grants are actual gifts of shares of stock. The restriction is that the shares cannot be immediately sold. Rather, only a portion—typically 20 to 25 percent of the shares granted—can be sold in any one year that a manager is with the company.

Note that although the logic is more complicated, stock options and stock grants—just like a salary—are a *cost* to the corporation. In both cases, shares that the corporation *could* have sold at the higher market price are instead made available to the manager for a lower price (options) or free of charge (grants). So in the end, these are just other ways, but not costless ways, for a corporation to pay its CEO and other managers.

Which brings us to the central question: Why is CEO compensation, especially in these additional stock-based forms, so high? And why has it risen so rapidly over the past decade?

[16] If you're interested, you can see the options contract awarded to Meg Whitman, CEO of eBay, at *http://contracts.corporate.findlaw.com/agreements/ebay/whitman.html*. The options were awarded in February, 1998, at the prevailing price at the time. Within six months, she used them to purchase eBay shares that had risen substantially in price, for a gain of $43.2 million.

The Ability Explanation

Part of the explanation—but only part—can be found in the normal workings of the market for CEOs. Steering a major U.S. corporation is a difficult job. And the job has become even more difficult over the past decade, as corporations have grown larger and as globalization and rapid technological change have dramatically increased the stakes of strategic decision making. Very few people have the ability to do this job, and fewer still have *proven* ability by having successfully managed a large corporation in the past. With such a small number of qualified people, and an increasingly complex business environment, the demand for top candidates is high relative to supply. A major corporation that wants to hire a top CEO will find itself bidding with hundreds of other corporations for this scarce pool of labor.

Second, the market for CEOs shares some of the features of the *superstar* labor markets discussed earlier, like those for movie and sports stars. Suppose that an industry is going through changes, and the firm must make important strategic decisions that will set its course for several years. Then hiring the *slightly* better CEO, who is able to make slightly better decisions, could make a *huge* difference in total profits. It could even make the difference between survival and bankruptcy.

To get an idea of the numbers, suppose that Starbucks must decide whether to hire (or retain) a slightly more able CEO candidate who would make slightly better decisions, or a slightly less able one, who can be hired for a three-year total compensation package of $5 million. Let's suppose that the shareholders are confident that—over the three-year period—the company's share price would be 1 percent higher under the more able CEO. How much *more* would Starbuck's shareholders be willing to pay for the slightly better candidate?

Let's see. In mid-2003, Starbucks shares had a total value of about $10 billion. One percent of that is $100 million, so that is how much the better CEO is expected to increase shareholder wealth. Then Starbucks should be willing to pay any amount up to $105 million to hire the better CEO ($100 million more than the $5 million pay of the less able candidate). Of course, if the stockholders of several other same-size firms have the same opinions, they would *also* be willing to pay a $100 million premium to hire this candidate. The result is a bidding war in which the slightly more able candidate earns an astronomical compensation package, many times greater than the pay of a candidate who is almost as good.

More generally, if there are a hundred or so CEOs perceived as having a slight edge over others, then the largest corporations will bid up their compensation until they are many times higher than the earnings of the average CEO in the economy—and, of course, many *more* times higher than the average worker. In this view, stock options lessen the risk to the shareholders: They provide a way of offering high compensation to CEOs only if these CEOs raise shareholder wealth as predicted.

If this scenario, based on ability, entirely explained high and rising CEO pay, there would be no reason for shareholders to be upset. Moreover, there would be little reason for the government to get involved, other than ensuring that the tax system takes a politically determined fair share of these high incomes, relative to the shares taken from other income groups.

But shareholders and the government *have* been upset about skyrocketing CEO pay—because there is more to the story.

The Market Failure Explanation

The market for CEOs seems to suffer from some serious *market failures*—a term that will be formally defined and discussed later, in Chapter 14. But the general idea is this: A market *fails* when its normal equilibrium does not allocate resources in the best interests of society.

How does the labor market for CEOs *fail*? One problem relates to the *principal–agent relationship* in this market. A *principal* is a person who has an interest at stake, and hires an *agent* to act on his behalf. The agent could be a baby-sitter hired by a parent, or an auto mechanic hired to fix your car, . . . or a CEO hired to maximize profit for a corporation's shareholders.

Principal–agent relationships are a natural consequence of specialization, in which most members of society find it advantageous to specialize in an occupation and perform work for others. The **principal–agent problem**, however, arises when an agent is able to maximize her *own* well-being instead of the well being of the principal who hired her. And this, in turn, occurs when a principal cannot fully *monitor* an agent's performance (such as when you don't have the expertise to know whether your auto mechanic really performed all the work that's on the bill).

The CEO–shareholder relationship is a case in point. Here, shareholders are the principals, and they have neither the expertise nor the information needed to monitor management performance. As a result, shareholders would find it difficult to determine on their own whether high management salaries or generous fringe benefits are in their interests (i.e., necessary to retain top-level managers who are contributing even more than their compensation to the firm's profit) or merely an example of management pursuing its own interests (extracting excessive pay from shareholders).

Large, publicly held corporations use a variety of methods to help solve the principal–agent problem. One of these is a government regulation: The shareholders vote into office a *board of directors* to monitor the firm for them. Board members, who are paid for their work, are supposed to have the expertise, motivation, and power to ensure performance on behalf of the stockholders. Indeed, the board of directors hires, and can fire, the CEO.

Corporations also create incentives to align the interests of managers with those of the shareholders. Stock options and restricted stock grants are examples. Options, for example, benefit managers *only if* they take actions that raise the corporation's profits, make the stock more attractive to buyers, and thereby raise its price. Restricted stock grants, too, benefit managers more when the share price rises than when it falls. In both cases, management is given a stake in raising the price of the shares, and creating wealth for the corporation's owners.

That's all well in theory. But in the view of many economists, these very methods designed to *solve* the principal–agent problem have become part of the problem itself.

Let's first consider the behavior of boards of directors. CEOs control the flow of information to the board, so they can present a biased view of their decisions and outcomes—one that hides actions that are harming shareholders. Also, boards of directors create *another* principal–agent problem: Board members—the agents of the shareholders—may have their own interests, such as collecting their paychecks without doing the hard work of monitoring the firm's performance. Even worse, CEOs frequently sit on *each other's* boards, creating an "I'll scatch your back if

Principal-agent problem A situation in which an agent maximizes her own well-being at the expense of the principal who hired her.

you'll scratch mine" mentality. All of these problems can help CEOs extract greater salaries from their boards—and therefore, from their shareholders—than would be justified by their abilities.

Now let's again consider stock options and grants. Although designed to help *solve* the principal–agent problem, they can also worsen it. Because stock-based compensation seems to be a reward for good performance, it can become a less obvious way for CEOs to extract excessive pay from shareholders.

Indeed, critics have pointed to several practices that seem to contradict options as a reward for good performance. For example, look again at Table 7. The last two columns show total compensation to CEOs (mostly exercise of options) over the three-year period 2000 to 2002, and also the percentage change in the value of shareholder wealth over that period (almost entirely due to changes in each stock's price). While millions of dollars were earned by CEOs who seem to have performed well (such as at Starbucks and Lockheed), millions were also earned by CEOs who seem to have performed poorly (such as at The Gap, Tyco, Siebel Systems, and Sun). Though a change in stock prices does not *prove* a good or bad performance, there are also numerous examples of generous options being awarded to CEOs whose stock performed poorly *relative to other firms in the same industry.*

Another contradiction of options and stock grants as a performance incentive is that they reward CEOs for *any* rise in the stock's price—even one caused by a general boom in the stock market to which the CEO contributed nothing. Indeed, during the 1990s the general rise in share prices rewarded almost all CEOs, regardless of their contribution to the firm. At the same time, when the market falls, CEOs have asked for, and received, new options with a lower exercise price, protecting them (but not their shareholders) from the consequences of a falling market. And restricted stock grants retain most of their value even if the price of the shares falls somewhat.

Beyond stock-based compensation, there have been hefty raises, "good performance" bonuses, and lavish fringe benefits awarded to CEOs who have been outperformed by the market in general, and even by most competitors in their industry. And boards of directors have agreed to contracts guaranteeing CEOs millions of dollars in severance pay, even if they are fired for *poor* performance.

This treatment suggests that CEOs are being rewarded for reasons other than the creation of shareholder wealth. And it helps explain the rapid *growth* in CEO pay in the 1990s: If stock options, for example, are a way to disguise excessive pay, then rising stock prices—such as during the 1990s—enable more pay to be extracted with the same number of options. Also, while there were many other critics of high CEO pay, shareholders—the ones with the ultimate power to stop the speeding train—seemed happy to go along for the ride as long as stock prices were rising, as they were during the 1990s.

In the early 2000s, however, as the stock market tumbled and shareholders grew less complacent, the controversy exploded. In the first half of 2003, groups of shareholders filed more than 800 resolutions to limit their boards' flexibility in designing and awarding stock options, stock grants, bonuses, salaries, severance pay, and more. Many of these resolutions were filed by large institutional investors, such as retirement funds. If approved by the shareholders as a whole, the CEO labor market could see some changes.

But the change may not be as dramatic as the toughest critics might hope. The scarcity of qualified CEOs, and the exaggerated rewards to shareholders from hiring a CEO with a slight edge in ability suggest that—even in a well-functioning market—CEOs of large corporations will continue to earn many times the wage rate of the average worker.

And the need for incentives to deal with the principal–agent problem suggests that stock-based compensation will likely remain important. For example, in July 2003, Microsoft—responding to general shareholder sentiment—announced that it would no longer offer stock options at all. But Microsoft replaced them with restricted stock grants, reflecting its continued belief in the need for management incentives.

Moreover, we will likely continue to see high CEO pay at poorly performing corporations. After all, when a company is in trouble, it most needs the services of a highly qualified chief executive.

Summary

In all nations, incomes vary markedly. Partly, that's because of differences in wages that can be traced to differences in the attractiveness of jobs, differences in ability, and imperfections in labor markets. When the attractiveness of two jobs differs, *compensating wage differentials* will emerge to offset those differences. When the ability of workers differs, the more able workers will earn higher wages. Because of the "superstar" nature of many professions, small differences in ability can create extremely large wage differentials. And in some cases, barriers to entry contribute to higher wages for protected workers.

Another reason for wage differentials is prejudice. When employer prejudice exists, market forces work to discourage discrimination and reduce wage gaps between groups. However, employee and customer prejudice encourage discrimination and can lead to permanent wage gaps.

Incomes also differ because of differences in property income. The *poverty rate* is the fraction of families whose incomes—however measured—fall below a certain minimum poverty line. The *Lorenz curve* and the associated *Gini coefficient* are comprehensive measures of income inequality. In the United States, as in most countries, wealth is less equally distributed than income.

All income measures tell us something about income inequality, but all suffer from deficiencies. A progressive income tax, government transfer programs, and fringe benefits all mean that *earned* income differs from income available for spending. Also, most measures of inequality pertain to a given point in time. But people move in and out of income quintiles over time, so total lifetime income may be distributed more equally than income in any given year.

In recent decades—especially during the 1990s—the income distribution has become more unequal, and income mobility over time has decreased. Most of the rise in inequality has resulted from an increase in the share of income going to the top 5 percent of households.

Key Terms

Compensating wage differential	Nonmonetary job characteristic	Progressive income tax
Discrimination	Poverty line	Property income
Gini coefficient	Poverty rate	Statistical discrimination
Lorenz curve	Principal–agent problem	Transfer payment

Review Questions   *Answers to even-numbered Questions and Problems can be found on the text Web site at http://hall-lieb.swlearning.com.*

1. For each of the following jobs, would you expect the compensating wage differential to be positive or negative? (In each case, compare to a job as a computer programmer.) Describe what nonmonetary job characteristics and human capital requirements might be at work in each case.
   a. Worker in a slaughterhouse
   b. College professor
   c. Attorney
   d. Bartender at a tropical resort
   e. New York City police officer

2. In this chapter, you learned about several explanations for long-run wage inequality. Which explanation (or explanations) best explains each of the following?
   a. A paralegal in New York earns more than a paralegal doing the same work in Keokuk, Iowa.

b. Although they work on the same cases and do many of the same things, an attorney's salary is many times that of a paralegal.

c. Larry King earns more as a talk show host than the morning host of a New York radio show.

d. A professor of philosophy with a Ph.D. earns less than an accountant with only a B.A.

e. Construction workers in Germany, which has strong unions and extensive apprenticeship programs, are paid higher wage rates than American workers in the same trades.

3. Why are earnings not always proportional to ability?

4. True or false? Discrimination does not always arise from prejudice. Explain.

5. Explain how market forces tend to:
   a. Encourage discrimination when the prejudice comes from a firm's employees or customers.
   b. Discourage discrimination when the prejudice comes from employers.

6. What is "statistical discrimination"? What are some possible remedies for it?

7. How did technological advances contribute to increased income inequality in the 1990s?

8. Explain how the union–nonunion wage differential can arise. Illustrate with relevant graphs.

9. List and describe all possible income sources other than wages and salaries.

10. Discuss some of the problems associated with the inequality measures you studied in this chapter.

11. What would the Gini coefficient be if income in a country were equally distributed?

12. Explain how unions can raise worker morale and reduce labor turnover. How could this eliminate the drop in employment caused by higher union wages?

13. Discuss the advantages that the earned income tax credit (EITC) has over the minimum wage as a tool for helping poor working families.

Problems and Exercises

1. The labor markets for factory workers and construction workers are in equilibrium: The wage in both is W_0, and the number employed is N_0. Assume that both labor markets are perfectly competitive, there are no barriers to entry or exit of workers, and workers are equally qualified to do both jobs and find them equally attractive.
   a. Unexpectedly, demand for factory output soars. Using graphs, show the short-run effect on the equilibrium wage and number employed in factories.
   b. Draw graphs that illustrate the long-run equilibrium position in the two industries.

2. The following table lists the annual income of the 10 citizens of the little town of Dismal Seepage.

Joe	$10,000	Dick	$18,000
Jim	$15,000	Ellen	$ 3,000
Sue	$ 4,000	Ann	$30,000
Jack	$25,000	Ralph	$ 8,000
Roy	$ 7,000	Bill	$50,000

   a. Draw the Lorenz curve for this community.
   b. Make a rough estimate of the Gini coefficients.
   c. Assume that all the people in town live alone and that the yearly cost of food for a single person in Dismal Seepage is $3,000. What is the official poverty rate in the town?

3. Refer to question 2.
   a. Dismal Seepage decides to tax 5% of the income of each of the richest 20% of its citizens and divide this tax revenue equally between each of the poorest 40% of its citizens. Make a list showing each citizen's income after taxes and transfer payments and draw the city's new Lorenz curve. How does this Lorenz curve compare with the one found in 2 (a)?
   b. Citizens of Bleak Ooze, located 2 miles from Dismal Seepage, hear about Dismal Seepage's tax and transfer payment plan. What will happen to the average income for each of these two cities? What will happen to the Lorenz curve in Bleak Ooze?
   c. Assume that low income citizens are more geographically mobile than high income ones (because they don't own homes or have stable employment, for instance). How will this change your results in part B?

4. Suppose the demand for unskilled labor were completely inelastic with respect to the wage rate. Using graphs similar to those in Figure 4, but modified to reflect this new assumption, explain how a minimum wage above the equilibrium wage for covered unskilled workers would affect employment and the wage rate among:
   a. covered, unskilled workers;
   b. uncovered, unskilled workers; and
   c. skilled workers.

5. State how each of the following would affect the average wage of college professors relative to other professionals in the long run. In each case, illustrate with a supply and demand diagram.

    a. Requirements to become a college professor are increased from one to two Ph.D. degrees.

    b. Urban colleges around the country relocate to rural areas.

    c. The college-age population decreases.

    d. The number of courses college professors have to teach each year is reduced by 25%. (*Note:* Be sure to state any assumptions you use to arrive at your answer.)

6. Draw the Lorenz curve for an economy in which one person earns all the income and the rest earn nothing. Then, calculate the Gini coefficient for this economy.

7. [Appendix required] Look again at Figure A.1. What would the minimum wage rate have to be set at to get this monopsonist to hire the number of workers and pay the same wage rate as a firm operating in a perfectly competitive labor market? Draw the firm's new *MFC* curve at this minimum wage rate.

Challenge Questions

1. Some advocates of the minimum wage argue that any decrease in the employment of the unskilled will be slight. They assert that an increase in the minimum wage will actually increase the total amount paid to unskilled workers (i.e., wage × number of unskilled workers employed). Discuss what assumptions they are making about the wage elasticity of labor demand.

2. [Appendix Required]

    a. Redraw Figure A.1 Show what will happen when the union wage rate (the wage rate determined through wage bargaining) is set at the wage rate paid if this were a perfectly competitive labor market.

    b. Now assume that the union wage rate is set above the wage rate paid if this were a perfectly competi-

tive labor market, but below the *MRP* of the last worker hired by the monopsonist in the absence of a union. Redraw Figure A.1, drawing the new *MFC* curve, and labeling the union wage rate and *L**, the number of workers hired in this situation.

    c. Redraw Figure A.1 again. Show an example of a union wage rate that will actually reduce employment below what the monopsonist would have chosen if it had not had to bargain with a union. Is it realistic to believe that a union would bargain for such a high wage rate?

    d. Over what range can the union wage rate be set without reducing employment?

 *These exercises require access to Hall/Lieberman Xtra! If Xtra! did not come with your book, visit* http://hallxtra.swlearning.com *to purchase.*

1. Use your Xtra! password at the Hall and Lieberman Web site (http://hallxtra.swlearning.com), select this chapter, and under Economic Applications, click on EconDebate. Choose *Microeconomics: Income Distribution and Poverty*, and scroll down to find the debate, "Does a Gender Wage Gap Still Exist?" Read the debate carefully, and answer the questions below.

    a. What forms of market-based discrimination can explain part of the wage differential between men and women?

    b. Scroll further down the page, and under Primary Sources and Data, find the report by the Council of Economic Advisors, "Explaining Trends in the Gender Wage Gap." Click on this link, and read the Exec-

utive Summary of this report. What arguments does this report give to support the absence of nonmarket gender wage discrimination?

2. Use your Xtra! password at the Hall and Lieberman Web site (http://hallxtra.swlearning.com), select this chapter, and under Economic Applications, click on EconDebate. Choose *Microeconomics, Income Distribution* and *Poverty,* and scroll down to find the debate, "Does an Increase in the Minimum Wage Result in a Higher Unemployment Rate?" Read the debate carefully, and construct a short essay outlining why an increase in the minimum wage might *not* change the unemployment rate.

APPENDIX

THE MINIMUM WAGE AND UNION BARGAINING UNDER MONOPSONY

The body of this chapter analyzed labor markets with specific departures from perfect competition, such as a specific barrier to entry or differences in ability among workers. In the appendix to Chapter 11, however, you learned about an entirely different structure for the labor market: monopsony. A *pure* monopsony (a labor market with only one employer) is extremely rare. But when an employer is large enough for its employment decisions to influence the market wage, we say that it has *monopsony power,* because its behavior is similar to a pure monopsony. In this appendix, we'll see how monopsony power not only changes, but can actually reverse, our most important conclusions about the minimum wage and the impact of labor unions.

Let's first briefly review the employment decision of a monopsony firm, as illustrated in the left panel of Figure A.1. First, the firm faces the *upward-sloping labor* supply curve L^S; it must pay a higher wage each time it wants to hire an additional worker, given by the height of the curve L^S. But the higher wage must be paid not just to the newly hired worker, but to *all* employees, including those previously working for a lower wage. As a result, the monopsony's marginal factor cost (MFC)—the cost of hiring the additional worker—is greater than the wage paid to that worker. This is why, in the figure, the monopsony's MFC curve lies *above* the labor supply curve L^S.

In the absence of a minimum wage or a union, this firm's profit-maximizing employment is found at point *E,* where the marginal revenue product (MRP) and MFC curves intersect. The firm hires 100 workers and pays an hourly wage of $4 at point *F*—on the curve L^S.

MONOPSONY AND THE MINIMUM WAGE

How does a monopsony firm respond to a minimum wage law? Look at the right-hand panel of Figure A.1, in which a minimum wage of $6 per hour—higher than the equilibrium wage of $4—is imposed. Now the firm must immediately raise the wage of all *existing* employees to $6. Moreover, the labor supply curve L^S tells us that $6 per hour is high enough to attract 125 workers. For any employment level *up to* 125 workers, the firm can hire another worker without raising the pay of any of its existing employees, since they're *already* earning $6. So the added cost of a new worker is just $6 per hour.

What if the firm wants to hire a 126th worker? Then it will have to raise the wage *above* $6, not just for that new worker, but for *all* workers, just as it had to do when *no* minimum wage was in effect. So, for the 126th worker and beyond, the MFC is the same as it was before the minimum wage.

This analysis suggests that imposing a minimum wage on a monopsony labor market gives the firm a rather strange-looking MFC curve, which is shown with darker shading in the right panel. For all employment levels up to 125, the MFC curve is a horizontal line at $6. Then it jumps vertically upward to the original (pre–minimum wage) MFC curve for the increase from 125 to 126 workers, and follows along the original curve for all further rises in employment beyond 126.

How many workers should the firm employ now? The answer—as always—is given by the intersection of the MFC and MRP curves. But now this intersection occurs along the vertical part of the MFC curve. As you can see in the figure, for employment *up to* 125, MRP > MFC, so the firm should increase hiring. For employment *beyond* 125, MFC > MRP, so the firm should stop at 125 workers, at point *G*.

Looking at the figure, you can see that with *no* minimum wage the firm pays $4 per hour and employs 100 workers. But with a minimum wage, the firm pays $6 per hour and employs 125 workers. The minimum wage causes the firm to *pay a higher wage rate* and *increase employment.*

This is very different from the minimum wage's effect on a competitive labor market: a rise in pay for those who keep their jobs, but a drop in total employment. And under competition, some of the laid-off workers in the covered minimum wage sector move to the *uncovered* sector, causing wages there to fall. But with monopsony, no one need be laid off; on the contrary, new workers are hired. The firm loses profit because it must pay a higher wage rate. But once confronted with this requirement, the *highest profit it can earn* under the circumstances calls for an increase in hiring.

> *For a firm with monopsony power, a minimum wage law can not only increase the wage rate a firm pays, but also increase employment at the firm.*

Of course, this doesn't mean that *any* minimum wage would have this effect. As the minimum wage rises higher and higher above $6, at some point employment will start to fall again. If you pencil in the horizontal section of the *MFC* curve for different minimum wages in the figure, you'll see that a minimum wage of $8 gives the maximum employment possible: 150 workers. For any minimum wage higher than $8, employment will be less than 150, and if it rises too high, employment could fall below 100 (the original employment level without a minimum wage).

MONOPSONY AND UNION BARGAINING

As you saw in the chapter, a union reduces employment by driving up the wage in a *perfectly competitive labor market*. The union will try to strike the right balance between higher wages and higher employment for its members (and potential members).

But when a union confronts a firm with *monopsony power*, the result can be very different. Figure A.1, once again, can be used to illustrate the situation. The left-hand panel can represent the market without a labor union, in which the firm pays a wage of $4 per hour and employs 100 workers.

Now suppose a union is empowered to negotiate the wage the firm must pay to all its workers. In effect, the union—because of its role in determining the wage the firm will pay—becomes the only *seller* of labor to the firm: a monopoly seller. The firm, however, has monopsony power as a large *buyer* of labor from the union. This situation, in which monopsony confronts monopoly, is often called *bilateral monopoly*. And the

wage will be determined by negotiation between the firm and the union.

What trade-off will the union face now? Surprisingly, over some range of wage rates the answer is: no trade-off at all. Suppose, for example, that we're once again dealing with the firm in Figure A.1, which is initially employing 100 workers and paying a wage rate of $4. Then the union negotiates a wage of $6 (this is much lower than most union wages, but allows us to use the diagram). As was the case in our minimum wage example, the firm will immediately have to raise all of its employees' wage rates to $6. It can then hire another worker at $6 per hour, and not have to raise its existing workers' pay any further—up to 125 workers. To go beyond 125 workers, the firm must offer higher pay to *all* workers, just as it did before there was a union. So—just as in the figure—the monopsony firm's *MFC* curve will be a horizontal line at $6 up to 125 workers, at which point it jumps up to the old *MFC* curve.

The firm reacts to the $6 union wage the same way it reacted to the $6 minimum wage: It raises employment from 100 to 125 workers. And an $8 union wage (not shown) would increase employment to 150. Clearly, in the situation depicted in the right panel of Figure A.1, the union would like *at least* an $8 wage, since it wins on both employment *and* pay. The union will most likely prefer a wage *greater* than $8, which involves some trade-off between employment and pay. The *firm*, however, wants a union wage of only $4, since any higher wage rate reduces its profit.

The inevitable result is *wage bargaining*, with each side using the power at its disposal to move the outcome closer to its own goal. The union can threaten a strike that will temporarily shut down the firm and force the firm to suffer a loss, while the firm can threaten to shut *itself* down and create income losses for union members. In many bargaining situations, both sides can predict which would suffer most from a shutdown, and which would therefore give in first. Often, the more vulnerable side will give up more in bargaining to avoid being harmed, and an agreement will be reached. In some cases, however, the parties may have different views about who will be harmed more—and who will give in first—and an agreement may be impossible without a strike or a plant closure, as each side tries to force the other's hand.

Still, the result of union bargaining—if the wage is not set too high—can be very different from the outcome in a competitive labor market:

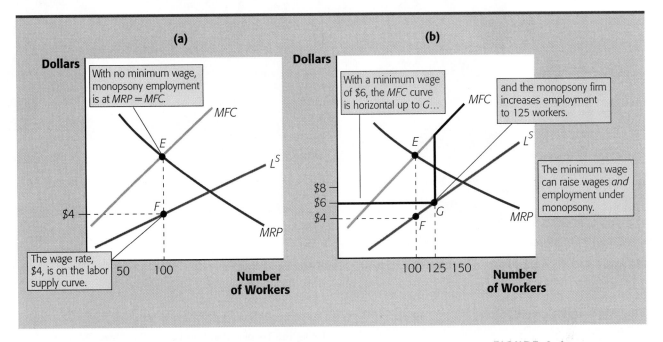

(a)

With no minimum wage, monopsony employment is at *MRP* = *MFC*.

The wage rate, $4, is on the labor supply curve.

(b)

With a minimum wage of $6, the *MFC* curve is horizontal up to *G*…

and the monopsony firm increases employment to 125 workers.

The minimum wage can raise wages *and* employment under monopsony.

FIGURE A.1
The Minimum Wage in a Monopsony Labor Market

In a monopsony labor market, a union that wins a higher wage rate for its members can not only increase their pay, but may be able to increase employment at the firm.

As with the minimum wage, a wage rate of $8 in the figure will maximize employment at 150. As the wage continues to rise beyond that limit, employment falls, eventually dropping below the original, nonunion level of 100.

Capital and Financial Markets

Just about every weekday, each of the following is almost guaranteed to occur in the United States:

- Managers at some corporation launch a new product, covering the costs with funds obtained by issuing new shares of stock or new bonds.
- The owner of a two-story apartment or office building sells it to a real estate developer, who has plans to build a three- or more-story building.
- An experienced registered nurse—earning about $44,000 a year—decides to apply for a costly two-year program to become a nurse practitioner, with starting salaries of around $56,000.
- A new Starbucks opens its doors.
- A college professor goes online and buys a few hundred shares of stock in Amazon.com.
- Another college professor goes online and sells a few hundred shares of stock in Amazon.com.

These events might seem to have little in common. But, in fact, they all share one important feature: in each case, a decision maker—consciously or unconsciously—is putting a value on money to be received *in the future*

In this chapter, we'll study decisions that involve *future payments* and the role these decisions play in the economy. More specifically, we'll focus on decisions about (1) investing in productive capital, such as factory buildings, equipment, or skills and training; and (2) purchasing financial assets, such as stocks and bonds. As you'll see, our analysis will require some new concepts and techniques to help us determine the value of payments to be received in the future.

PHYSICAL CAPITAL AND THE FIRM'S INVESTMENT DECISION

The concept of *capital* was introduced in the first chapter of this book. There, you learned that capital is one of society's *resources,* along with natural resources, labor, and entrepreneurship. More specifically, capital is a produced long-lasting *tool* that is used, in turn, to produce goods and services. You also learned that we can classify capital into two categories: *physical capital,* such as the plant and equipment owned by business firms, and *human capital*—the skills and training of the labor force. In this section, we'll focus on firms' decisions about physical capital, and we'll take up human capital in the next section.

How does a business firm decide how much physical capital to use? In the same way that it makes any other decision. The firm's goal is to maximize its profit—not just this year, but over many years into the future. Are there guidelines the firm should use? Yes, but they depend on the conditions under which the firm obtains and uses its capital. In the next section, we'll make some unrealistic assumptions that will allow us to use a simple and familiar approach. This will help you see what's special about capital, and why, in the end, we'll have to use a more complex method.

A First, Simple Approach

In this section, we'll assume that *one of two* special conditions holds: Either (1) *firms rent their capital at a constant price,* just as they rent labor (by the hour, week, or year); or (2) *firms buy their capital, but it lasts forever.* In either case, as you'll see, we can analyze the firm's decision to use more capital just as we analyzed its decision to employ another worker.

Let's make this more concrete with an example. Imagine you are the fleet manager at Quicksilver Delivery Service. Your firm delivers packages for small retailers in the Chicago metropolitan area. We'll assume this market is perfectly competitive (there are many other, essentially identical firms), so Quicksilver must take the market price of package delivery as a given—$4 per package. You are responsible for determining the number of trucks at the firm's disposal. How many trucks should that be?

Your first step is to remember the *marginal approach to profit,* which you've encountered several times earlier in this book. For reinforcement, here it is again:

> *The marginal approach to profit states that a firm should take any action that adds more to its revenue per period than it adds to its cost per period.*

Here, we regard the action as "add another truck." If the period is a year, the marginal approach says that you should acquire the use of another truck if doing so will increase yearly revenue more than it increases yearly cost. Or, to use the language we

TABLE 1
Additional Annual Revenue of Each Truck for Quicksilver Delivery Service

Number of Trucks	Additional Annual Revenue (*MRP*)
1	$10,000
2	$10,000
3	$8,000
4	$5,500
5	$2,000

Marginal revenue product of capital The increase in revenue due to a one-unit increase in the capital input.

developed in Chapter 11, the firm should use another truck if its **marginal revenue product** (*MRP*) is greater than its marginal factor cost (*MFC*).

Now look at Table 1, which shows the relevant data. The first new truck that you buy would serve the Northern territory, one of the two areas that is best for package delivery business. Buying this truck would enable your firm to deliver 2,500 additional packages each year, thereby generating $4 \times 2,500 = $10,000 in additional yearly revenue.[1] So the *marginal revenue product (MRP)* of that first truck is $10,000 per year, which is listed in the second column.

A second new truck would be used in a new Northeast territory. It turns out that this area is just as good for business, so that truck, too, would generate $10,000 in additional revenue each year. A third truck would be used in the Eastern territory where, in the course of a typical year, it would generate only $8,000 in additional revenue. A fourth truck could generate $5,500 in additional revenue on a new Southern route. And a fifth truck would be used for special deliveries when the other trucks are busy, generating only $2,000 in additional revenue.

Now suppose that you can *rent* a truck (the first of our special assumptions in this section) for $5,000 per year. Then for your firm, the yearly *MFC* is $5,000. You should rent all trucks for which the yearly increase in revenue (*MRP*) is greater than the *MFC* of $5,000. As you can see in the table, this means you should rent the first four trucks, but not the fifth. For the fifth truck, the *MRP* of $2,000 is less than the *MFC* of $5,000.

Suppose instead that you must *buy* your trucks, at a cost of $50,000 each. Then, using our second special assumption that a truck will last forever, once you pay the $50,000 you are done making payments. Except for one thing: As long as you own the truck, you give up investment income—the funds you *could* have earned on that $50,000 by investing them elsewhere. This is a continuing, yearly cost for each truck. If the annual rate of return on alternative investments is 10 percent, then *buying* the truck costs you $0.10 \times $50,000 = $5,000 per year, for as long as you own it. Remember that when maximizing economic profit, an implicit cost is treated just like an explicit cost. So, in this case too, your *MFC* is $5,000 for each additional truck. You should buy the first four trucks, but not the fifth.

> *When firms rent capital, or the capital they buy lasts forever, we can apply the marginal approach to profits just as we apply it for the firm's labor decision: The firm should buy another unit of capital whenever its marginal revenue product is greater than its marginal factor cost.*

Why the Simple Approach Usually Fails. The simple approach, unfortunately, will not help us understand investment decisions, because our special assumptions are problematic. First, our assumption that capital can be *rented*—while it may work for

---

[1] To be more realistic, you can think of revenue as *net* revenue. That is, assume we've already subtracted from revenue any additional costs that automatically go along with *having* another truck, such as the costs of gasoline, maintenance, and paying another driver.

some firms—does not work for the economy in general. That's because every unit of capital in use is *owned* by *someone* or *some firm*. Even if Quicksilver Delivery Service rents its trucks, it will be renting them from a *truck rental firm* that *purchased* them. For any unit of capital employed in the economy, some firm—somewhere along the line—must have made the decision to purchase it. So if we want to understand decisions about capital investment in the economy, we must ultimately account for the decisions of firms that *purchase* the capital before it is used. For that reason, from this point on, we'll focus on the firms that *purchase* their capital.

Second, capital does *not* last forever. Why is this a problem? Imagine—to start with an extreme case—that a truck lasts only one year and then falls apart and becomes worthless. Then you wouldn't want to purchase even the first truck at $50,000, since (see Table 1) it would only generate $10,000 in revenue before it fell apart. (For that matter, no truck *rental* firm would rent out trucks for less than $50,000 per year, and at that yearly rate, you wouldn't want to rent any trucks either.) Even if a truck lasted two years, or even three years, you would not want to buy one. Clearly, the length of time that capital lasts matters when deciding whether to buy it.

But what if a truck lasted 15 years? Then buying it *might* make sense. However, now you have a problem: You'd have to pay $50,000 for each truck *now*, but the revenue from the truck would be spread out over the next 15 years.

"That's easy," you might think. "I'll just add up the revenue each truck will earn in each of those 15 years. The first truck has an *MRP* of $10,000 per year, so over 15 years, the truck will earn 15 × $10,000 = $150,000 in revenue. If it only costs $50,000, I should buy it for the firm. Even the fourth truck, with an *MRP* of $6,000, would earn 15 × $6,000 = $90,000 over its life, so—at a price of $50,000— I should order that one too."

But if you reason this way, you are making a serious error: You're treating each year's revenue as equally valuable, regardless of *when* the revenue is earned. In reality, the value of a future payment depends on *when* that payment is received. To see why, we'll have to take a detour from Quicksilver Delivery and explore the issue of future payments more generally. We'll come back to Quicksilver and its trucks when we're done.

A truck, like most types of physical capital, will increase a firm's revenue for many years. As a result, the firm must calculate the present-dollar equivalent of future receipts.

The Value of Future Dollars

To see why the value of a future payment depends on *when* that payment is received, just run through the following thought experiment. Imagine that you are given the choice between receiving $1,000 now and $1,000 one year from now. Do you have to think hard before making up your mind? Regardless of when you will actually spend the money, it is always better to have the dollars earlier rather than later. For example, say you don't plan to spend the money until next year. Then, if you get the $1,000 now, you could put it in the bank and earn interest for a year, giving you *more* than $1,000 when you finally spend it. On the other hand, say you need to spend the money right away. Then receiving it *now* rather than later saves you the interest you would have to pay to borrow the money for immediate use.

> *Because present dollars can earn interest, and because borrowing dollars requires payment of interest, it is always preferable to receive a given sum of money earlier rather than later. Therefore, a dollar received later has less value than a dollar received now.*

Knowing that dollars received in the future are worth less than dollars received today is an important insight. But when analyzing capital markets, we need to know precisely *how much* less a given payment is worth when its receipt is delayed for some period of time.

To answer that question, we use a concept called *present value*.

Present value The value, in today's dollars, of a sum of money to be received or paid at a specific date in the future.

> The **present value** (PV) *of a future payment is the value of that future payment in today's dollars. Alternatively, it is the most anyone would pay today for the right to receive the future payment.*

To understand this concept better, let's work out a simple example: What is the present value of $1,000 to be received one year in the future? That is, what is the most you would pay *today* in order to receive $1,000 one year from today? The answer is certainly *not* $1,000. Why not? If you paid $1,000 today for a guaranteed $1,000 in one year, you would be giving up $1,000 that you *could* lend to someone else for interest. If you lent the money, you'd end up with *more* than $1,000 one year later. So it never makes sense to pay $1,000 now for $1,000 to be received one year from now.

But would you pay $900 for the guaranteed future payment? Or $800? That depends on how much interest you *could* earn by lending funds to someone else for a year. If you could lend out $900 and, with interest, have *more* than $1,000 in one year, you wouldn't want to pay $900 now to receive just $1,000 a year from now. In fact, the most you'd pay is the amount of money that, if you lent it out for interest, would get you *exactly* $1,000 one year from now. That amount of money is the *present value* (PV) of $1,000 to be received in one year, since that is the most you would part with today in exchange for the future payment.

Suppose the interest rate at which you can lend funds is 10 percent per year. Then the present value of $1,000 to be received one year from today is an amount of money that, if lent out at 10 percent annual interest, would give you precisely $1,000 in one year. At 10 percent interest, each dollar you lend out will give you 1.10 dollars in one year, so the *PV* we seek will satisfy the following equation:

$$PV \times 1.10 = \$1,000.$$

Solving for *PV*, we get

$$PV = \frac{\$1,000}{1.10} = \$909.09$$

In words, if you lent out $909.09 at 10 percent interest, you would have $1,000 one year from today. Therefore, $909.09 is the most you would be willing to give up today for $1,000 in one year, or *$909.09 is the present value of $1,000 received one year from now.*

We can generalize this result by noting that, if the interest rate had been something other than 0.10—we'll call it *r*—or the amount of money had been something other than $1,000—say, Y dollars—then the present value would satisfy the equation

$$PV \times (1 + r) = Y$$

or

$$PV = \frac{Y}{(1 + r)}$$

But what if the payment of $Y were to be received *two* years from now instead of one? Then we can use the same logic to find the present value. In that case, each dollar lent out would become $(1 + r)$ dollars after one year, and then, when the dollar plus the earned interest was lent out again for a second year, it would become $(1 + r)(1 + r) = (1 + r)^2$ dollars at the end of the second year. Thus, the *PV* will satisfy

$$PV \times (1 + r)^2 = Y$$

and solving for *PV*, we obtain

$$PV = \frac{Y}{(1 + r^2)}.$$

Finally, for payments to be received one, two, or any number of years in the future, we can state that

> *the present value of $Y to be received n years in the future is equal to*
>
> $$PV = \frac{Y}{(1 + r)^n}.$$

For example, with an interest rate of 10 percent, the present value of $1,000 to be received three years in the future would be

$$PV = \frac{\$1,000}{(1.10)^3} = \$751.31$$

The process of making dollars of different dates comparable is called **discounting**. Since the interest rate is used to compute the present value of future dollars, the interest rate itself is called the **discount rate**.[2] Table 2 shows the present value of a dollar to be received at different times in the future, at different discount rates (rounded to the nearest penny).

For example, what is the present value of $1 to be received 10 years from today? If the interest rate is 10 percent, the present-day equivalent is $1 *divided by* $(1.10)^{10}$, or $1/2.59 = \$0.39$. This tells us that, when the interest rate (discount rate) is 10 percent, anyone expecting to receive $1 ten years from today might just as well accept $0.39 now. After all, when loaned at 10 percent interest per year, 39 cents will get you $1 in ten years.

From the logic of present-value calculations, and from the entries in Table 2, we can see that

> *the present value of a future payment is smaller if (1) the size of the payment is smaller, (2) the interest rate is larger, or (3) the payment is received later.*

Why does postponing a future payment decrease its value? Because the later you receive your money, the greater the sacrifice of interest you *could* have earned in the meantime. Why do higher interest rates decrease the present value of

Discounting The act of converting a future value into its present-day equivalent.

Discount rate The interest rate used in computing present values.

HTTP://

First Interstate Bank maintains online present and future value calculators. You can find them at http://www.firstinterstatebank.com/calculators.htm.

---

[2] In macroeconomics, the term *discount rate* has a completely different meaning: It's the interest rate that the Federal Reserve charges banks when it lends them reserves. There is no connection between the two different meanings of the term.

TABLE 2
Present Values of
$1 Future Payments

No. of Years in Future	Value of $1 to Be Received at Various Numbers of Years in the Future, at Different Discount Rates		
	5 Percent	10 Percent	15 Percent
0	$1.00	$1.00	$1.00
1	$0.95	$0.91	$0.87
2	$0.91	$0.83	$0.76
3	$0.86	$0.75	$0.66
4	$0.82	$0.68	$0.57
5	$0.78	$0.62	$0.50
10	$0.61	$0.39	$0.25
20	$0.38	$0.15	$0.06

DANGEROUS CURVES

Percentages and Decimals Be careful when working with interest rates: They can be expressed in either percentage form or decimal form. An interest rate of 5 percent (5%) can also be expressed in decimal form as 0.05. This is why the expression "$1 + r$" is equal to 1.05 when the interest rate is 5 percent. Similarly, an interest rate of 0.5% (*one-half* of 1 percent) would translate to 0.005 in decimal form, and "$1 + r$" would then equal 1.005.

a future payment? Because the higher the interest rate, the greater the interest you *could* have earned by lending out your money today and, therefore, the more interest income you *sacrifice* by waiting.

Finally, there is one more way in which we use the formula for present value calculations: to determine the value of a stream of future payments, with each individual payment to be received at a *different* time in the future. Consider the value, in today's dollars, of the following stream of future payments: $1,000 to be received one year from now, $900 to be received two years from now, and $600 to be received three years from now. To get the present value of this stream of payments, we first calculate the present value of each payment, and then we add those present values together:

$$PV = \frac{\$1,000}{(1 + r)} + \frac{\$900}{(1 + r)^2} + \frac{\$600}{(1 + r)^3}$$

With an interest rate of 10 percent, the *total* present value of the entire stream of payments is equal to:

$$PV = \frac{\$1,000}{(1.10)} + \frac{\$900}{(1.10)^2} + \frac{\$600}{(1.10)^3}$$

$$= \$909.09 + \$743.80 + \$450.79$$

$$= \$2,103.68$$

The logic of present value shows us why anyone who expects to receive a stream of future payments must discount each of those payments before adding them together. The next section provides an example of how firms use present value to make decisions about investing in new capital.

Truck	Additional Annual Revenue (*MRP*)	Total Present Value of Additional Revenue over 15 years	
1	$10,000	$\dfrac{\$10,000}{(1.1)} + \dfrac{\$10,000}{(1.1)^2} + \ldots + \dfrac{\$10,000}{(1.1)^{15}} = \$76,060.80$	
2	$10,000	$\dfrac{\$10,000}{(1.1)} + \dfrac{\$10,000}{(1.1)^2} + \ldots + \dfrac{\$10,000}{(1.1)^{15}} = \$76,060.80$	
3	$ 8,000	$\dfrac{\$8,000}{(1.1)} + \dfrac{\$8,000}{(1.1)^2} + \ldots + \dfrac{\$8,000}{(1.1)^{15}} = \$60,848.64$	
4	$ 5,500	$\dfrac{\$5,500}{(1.1)} + \dfrac{\$5,500}{(1.1)^2} + \ldots + \dfrac{\$5,500}{(1.1)^{15}} = \$41,833.44$	
5	$ 2,000	$\dfrac{\$2,000}{(1.1)} + \dfrac{\$2,000}{(1.1)^2} + \ldots + \dfrac{\$2,000}{(1.1)^{15}} = \$15,212.16$	

TABLE 3
The Present Value of Trucks at Quicksilver Delivery Service (with a Discount Rate of 10%)

The Firm's Demand for Capital

Let's return to your problem at Quicksilver Delivery Service. How many trucks should you buy? Table 3 shows the present value calculations you'd need to make, under the following conditions: (1) each truck's yearly *MRP* is the same as it was in Table 1, a few pages earlier; (2) each truck has an expected useful life of 15 years, so that Quicksilver can look forward to 15 years of additional revenue from each truck; and (3) the appropriate discount rate for Quicksilver's present value calculations is 10 percent.

For example, the first truck gives Quicksilver $10,000 per year in additional revenue for 15 years. Since we're assuming for simplicity that each year's revenue is received at the *end* of each year (see the Dangerous Curves feature above), the present value of the first year's revenue is $10,000/ (1.1); the present value of the second year's revenue is $10,000 / (1.1)^2$; and so on. When these present values are added together for all 15 years, we find that the first truck gives the firm $76,060.80 in total additional revenue in present value terms. Similarly, the *PV* of all the revenue from the *fourth* truck is $41,833.44.

Now that we know the total present value that you gain from each truck, do we know how many trucks you should buy? Almost, but not quite. There is still the matter of how much each truck *costs*. But now that we've translated *all* the additional revenue from each truck into a single, present value number, we know the total benefits of the truck to your firm measured in *today's dollars*. That measure can

When Are Future Payments Received? Businesses typically earn revenue every day they are in operation. However, in doing a PDV problem, it would be cumbersome to discount each day's revenue by the appropriate discount factor. (This would require 365 terms to be added for each year's revenue.) As a useful approximation, we can treat each year's revenue as if it is all received in one lump sum at the *end* of the year. This is the convention followed in this book for all future payments. Thus, when we say that a firm or individual receives a payment of $10,000 "in the first year," we mean "at the end of the first year." (Can you see how we've used this assumption in Table 3?)

DANGEROUS CURVES

be compared to the truck's cost, which must *also* be *paid* in today's dollars. If trucks cost $50,000, the firm gains more benefits (in future revenue) than costs for the first three trucks. But the purchase of the fourth truck, whose benefit to the firm is only $41,833.44 in today's dollars, does not make sense, since the cost in today's dollars is $50,000. Quicksilver should buy only three trucks.

Our examples have focused on a special type of capital—delivery trucks. But the same logic works for any other type of physical capital—automated assembly lines, desktop computers, filing cabinets, locomotives, and construction cranes. In each of these cases, the first step in making a decision about a capital purchase is to put a value on an additional unit of capital. This value is the total present value of the future revenue generated by the capital.

This first step—putting a value on physical capital—is so important and so widely applicable that we can refer to it as a general principle:

Principle of asset valuation The idea that the value of an asset is equal to the total present value of all the future benefits it generates.

> The **principle of asset valuation** says that the value of any asset is the sum of the present values of all the future benefits it generates.

The principle of asset valuation tells us how to determine the marginal benefit from buying another unit of capital, such as another truck. Then, as we've done with Quicksilver, we compare this marginal benefit with the cost of the capital itself. As you've seen, the firm should then buy any unit of capital for which the marginal benefit (total present value of future revenue) is greater than the cost.

What Happens When Things Change: The Investment Curve

Investment Firms' purchases of new capital over some period of time.

Investment is the term economists use to describe firms' purchases of new capital over some period of time. In the example above, if trucks cost $50,000 each, Quicksilver should buy three of them. If it bought all three trucks this year, its investment expenditures for the year would be $50,000 × 3 = $150,000.

But this conclusion about investment is based on the assumption that the interest rate, and Quicksilver's discount rate, is 10 percent. With a lower interest rate—say, 5 percent—each year's revenue would have a higher present value, so the total present value of each truck would be higher. Our conclusion about Quicksilver's investment spending might then change. Similarly, a rise in the interest rate—say, to 15 percent—would *lower* the present value of each year's revenue, and *decrease* the total present value of a truck.

Table 4 shows how our total present value calculations for each truck change as the interest rate changes. The table assumes that the other ingredients in the firm's decision making do not change. Each package delivered still generates revenue of $4, and the productivity of each truck is still what it was before. For instance, a truck used on the Northern route would still allow Quicksilver to deliver 2,500 additional packages each year.

The numbers in the last three columns are each calculated just as were the numbers we calculated in Table 3. The only difference is that, instead of always assuming a discount rate of 10 percent, Table 4 shows the total present value for each truck under three different interest rates. Notice what happens as we move from left to right in the table for any particular truck: The interest rate rises, from 5 percent to 10 percent to 15 percent, and the value of the truck to the firm falls.

Truck	Additional Annual Revenue	Total Present Value with a Discount Rate of:		
		5%	10%	15%
1	$10,000	$103,797	$76,061	$58,474
2	$10,000	$103,797	$76,061	$58,474
3	$ 8,000	$ 83,037	$60,849	$46,779
4	$ 5,500	$ 57,088	$41,833	$32,161
5	$ 2,000	$ 20,759	$15,212	$11,695

TABLE 4
Present Value Calculations for Various Interest Rates

Now, if trucks cost $50,000 each, how much will Quicksilver invest (spend on new trucks) at any given interest rate? Let's see. If the interest rate is 5 percent, Quicksilver should buy four trucks, because each of the first four trucks has a total present value greater than $50,000 at that interest rate. The fifth truck, however, has a total present value of only $20,759, so the firm should not buy that one. Thus, if the interest rate is 5 percent, Quicksilver's investment spending will be $50,000 × 4 = $200,000.

If the interest rate rises to 10 percent, we are back to the conclusion we reached in Table 3, which assumed a 10 percent interest rate: Quicksilver should buy three trucks when the interest rate is 10 percent. (You can also verify this using the middle column of Table 3.) Quicksilver's total investment spending would *decrease* to $50,000 × 3 = $150,000. Finally, if the interest rate rises to 15 percent, Quicksilver should buy only two trucks, so its total investment spending is $50,000 × 2 = $100,000.

What is true for Quicksilver is true for every truck-buying firm in the economy: The higher the interest rate, the fewer trucks delivery services and other truck-buying firms will want to purchase, and the smaller will be investment expenditures on trucks during the year.

Take a moment to think about why this happens. The trucks themselves are the same, and they are just as productive as before. But each truck is less valuable to firms in *present-dollar* terms. That's because—with a higher interest rate—the future additional revenue from each truck is worth *less* in today's dollars (delayed earnings impose a greater opportunity cost in lost interest). But the truck is still paid for in today's dollars, whose value is unaffected by the interest rate. So each firm will want fewer trucks at any given price.

Moreover, the same logic applies to other capital purchases. At high interest rates, U.S. firms end up buying less of all different kinds of capital—not just delivery trucks, but also other durable goods such as computers, machine tools, combines, and printing presses. It should be no surprise, then, that we come to the following conclusion:

As the interest rate rises, each business firm in the economy—using the principle of asset valuation—will place a lower value on additional capital, and decide to purchase less of it. Therefore, in the economy as whole, a rise in the interest rate causes a decrease in investment expenditures.

FIGURE 1
The Investment Curve

As the interest rate falls from 10 percent to 5 percent, each firm that buys a particular type of capital will buy more of it. As a result, the economy's total investment in physical capital rises from $1 trillion to $1.5 trillion. This is shown as the movement from point A to point B along the investment curve in the figure.

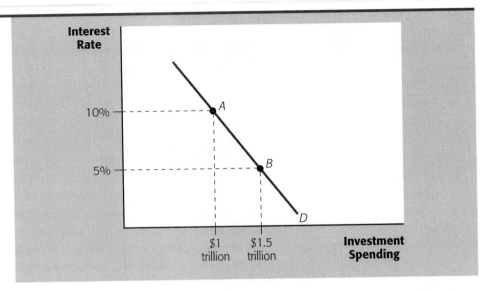

The relationship between the interest rate and investment expenditure is illustrated by the economy's investment curve, shown in Figure 1. The curve slopes downward, indicating that a drop in the interest rate causes investment spending to rise. When you study *macroeconomics*, you'll learn that the investment curve is important for the performance of the overall economy, for several reasons. But here's a hint as to one of them: When the interest rate falls, the increased investment in new capital means that the nation's *capital stock*—the total quantity of installed capital—will grow more rapidly than it otherwise would. With more capital, labor will be more productive, and our standard of living will be higher. This relationship between the interest rate, investment spending, and the ultimate size of our capital stock is one reason that policy makers pay so much attention to the overall level of interest rates in the economy.

To recap:

> *Lower interest rates increase firms' investment in physical capital, causing the capital stock to be larger, and our overall standard of living to be higher.*

INVESTMENT IN HUMAN CAPITAL

So far in this chapter, we've explored investment in *physical* capital. But now let's consider investment in *human* capital—the skills and abilities of the workforce. Like physical capital, these skills and abilities are long-lasting tools that make labor more productive in producing output. But unlike physical capital, which is owned by firms, human capital is ordinarily possessed by individual workers.

Economists are very interested in human capital investment. Here, we will concentrate on just two questions: First, who pays for workers to acquire human capital, the workers themselves or the firms that employ them? We'll see that some types of human capital are usually paid for by firms and other types are paid for by workers. Second, when an individual must pay to acquire human capital on his own, how does he make the decision? That is, how does an individual decide whether or not to acquire skills that would make him more valuable to an employer?

General Versus Specific Human Capital

Economists classify human capital into two categories, according to how broadly it can be applied in the workplace. Human capital that makes you more productive at *many* different firms is called **general human capital.** If you study engineering at college, for example, your knowledge will help you at any of thousands of manufacturing firms across the country, including those that make aircraft, automobiles, and computer chips.

But there is also **specific human capital,** which is chiefly of value at *a specific firm.* For example, suppose you take a job as an engineer working on jet engines at General Electric and you learn specific details about the GE90 engine. That knowledge is specific human capital because it will be useful only if you continue working on GE jet engines. If you move to Pratt & Whitney, the specific details you've learned about the GE90 will be useless because they don't apply to Pratt & Whitney's engines.

Table 5 shows the types of human capital that you might need to be a successful aerospace engineer at General Electric. The entries in the table that are general human capital would be useful not just at GE, but in many other firms as well, including other aircraft engine makers. But the entries that are specific human capital would have no value to any firm other than GE.

There is a very good reason for distinguishing between general and specific human capital. Firms have little incentive to invest in general human capital because they cannot be sure of capturing all the benefits. To see why, suppose that a firm like General Electric were to pay for its employees to get engineering degrees. Once the employees graduate, there is no law requiring them to use their new skills as *General Electric* employees. They might decide to test the job market and find that a rival firm is willing to pay them a higher wage than GE pays. This rival firm, after all, did not bear the cost of educating the GE employees and therefore is better positioned to pay higher wages than is General Electric.

More generally, because firms gain little by investing in their employees' general human capital, few firms do so. Instead, it is left to individuals to acquire general human capital on their own. In fact, you are doing that now as you study economics.

Employers have limited incentives to provide general human capital, since it increases the worker's value to many firms, and the worker will capture the benefits in the form of a higher wage. Therefore, workers must acquire general human capital on their own—or with the help of government subsidies.

General human capital Knowledge, education, or training that is valuable at many different firms.

Specific human capital Knowledge, education, or training that is valuable only at a specific firm.

General	Ability to reason logically
	Mastery of mathematics and physical reasoning
	Knowledge of general engineering design principles
	Courses in thermodynamics, fluid mechanics, and heat transfer
Specific	Experience with General Electric jet engines
	Knowledge of the skills and abilities of other GE engineers
	Familiarity with the kinds of aircraft that use GE jet engines
	Understanding of GE's unique corporate structure and decision-making process

TABLE 5

Types of Human Capital Necessary to Be a Successful Aerospace Engineer at General Electric

Now let's turn our attention to specific human capital, which is of value only to one specific employer. Individual workers are usually *not* willing to pay the cost of specific human capital. Why not? Because unlike general human capital, which ends up benefiting workers, specific human capital ends up benefiting the firm. For example, suppose an engineer at GE develops knowledge about the skills and abilities of *other* GE engineers, an example of specific human capital. Then she is no more valuable to Pratt & Whitney or any other aircraft firm than she was before she acquired this knowledge. These other firms will *not* be willing to pay her any higher wage because of this specific human capital, and therefore, GE will not have to pay her a higher wage in order to keep her. Thus, the specific human capital does not benefit the worker in the form of a higher wage. But it *does* benefit GE, since the worker, although she is paid the same wage as before, is now more productive.

Of course, since both workers and firms know that specific human capital benefits the firm, the firm is the one that ends up paying for it.

> *Individuals have little incentive to pay for specific human capital, since it increases their value to only one firm, and that firm will capture the benefits. Therefore, firms provide their workers with specific human capital at the firms' expense.*

The Decision to Invest in General Human Capital

Now that we've seen that individuals typically pay to acquire their own general human capital, how is the decision made? Let's take a specific example: Suppose an accountant must decide on purely economic grounds whether to take a specialized course in how to handle the books of entertainment companies. It's a costly course: $30,000 in tuition and another $25,000 in foregone income during the three months he is enrolled in the course. But the course will increase his income by $10,000 per year for each of the next eight years, after which he plans to retire.

The principle of asset valuation plays a central role in the accountant's decision. That is,

> *to the worker that possesses it, human capital is an asset that generates higher income in the future. Therefore, the benefit of any given human capital investment is equal to the total present value of the additional future income.*

At an annual interest rate of 10 percent, the total present value of the stream of extra revenue would be $53,349. Since the course costs $55,000, it's not worth it: The total present value of the additional income is *less* than the cost of the course. In purely economic terms, the accountant would be better off not taking the course.

But what if the annual interest rate were lower, say 8 percent? The cost of taking the course—$55,000—would remain the same, because that cost is paid *now*. But the present value of future revenue would change. With a lower interest rate, the total present value of the additional income would be higher: $57,466. Thus, at an interest rate of 8 percent, the investment is worth it, since the benefit (measured in total present value) is now greater than its cost. In general:

> *Investment in human capital, like investment in physical capital, is inversely related to the interest rate. The lower the interest rate, the greater the benefits of any human capital investment, and the more human capital workers will want to acquire.*

Moreover, the consequences of the change in investment are much the same for human capital as for physical capital. Recall what we learned earlier about physical capital: It makes us more productive as workers, and, as firms acquire more of it, the economy and our living standard grows. The same thing is true of human capital. The more we acquire, the more we can produce. Thus:

> *Lower interest rates encourage individuals to invest in general human capital. As a result, the total amount of human capital—and our overall standard of living—will be higher if interest rates are lower.*

FINANCIAL MARKETS

You may be wondering what financial markets, like the markets for stocks and bonds, have to do with the other subject of this chapter: markets for capital. After all, capital—like machines and factories—is something *real*; it enables firms to produce real goods and services. The same is true of human capital: It enables real people to produce more real goods and services.

But in financial markets, the things being traded are just *pieces of paper*, which don't directly help anyone to produce anything. So what do these pieces of paper have to do with capital?

Actually, quite a bit. The pieces of paper being traded in financial markets are **financial assets**—promises to pay future income to their owners. Because capital lasts for many years, most firms fund their capital purchases by issuing and selling these financial assets. For example, the firm might issue and sell shares of stock in the company, obligating it to pay those who hold the shares part of the firm's future profits. Or it might sell bonds, which are promises to pay back a sum of money in the future, along with interest payments. This leaves the firm with long-lasting capital, but also a long-lasting obligation to make future payments. Of course, the more capital a firm purchases, the greater the value of the obligation the firm will take on, and the more financial assets it must issue. So there is a close *economic* connection between a firm's decision to be a demander of capital and its decision to be a supplier of financial assets.

But there is another connection between these two types of markets as well. Because a financial asset gives its holder a stream of future payments, the value of a financial asset is calculated in the same way as the value of any other asset, such as a truck or a computer: We find the *total present value* of the future payments the asset will generate. Thus, our method of valuation is another connection between markets for capital and markets for financial assets.

In the rest of this chapter, we'll explore two types of financial assets: bonds and stocks. We'll also analyze the very well-publicized markets in which these assets are traded.

HTTP://

At South-Western College Publishing's Finance Web site (http://finance.swlearning.com) you can find a wide variety of material on financial markets.

Financial asset A promise to pay future income in some form, such as future profits or future interest payments.

The Bond Market

Bond A promise to pay a specific sum of money at some future date.

Principal (face value) The amount of money a bond promises to pay when it matures.

Maturity date The date at which a bond's principal amount will be paid to the bond's owner.

Pure discount bond A bond that promises no payments except for the principal it pays at maturity.

Coupon payments A series of periodic payments that a bond promises before maturity.

Yield The rate of return a bond earns for its owner.

If a firm wants to buy a new fleet of trucks, build a new factory, or upgrade its computer system, it must decide how to finance that purchase. One way to do this is to sell **bonds**. A bond is simply a promise to pay a certain amount of money, called the **principal** or **face value**, at some future date. Although $10,000 is the most common principal amount, you can also find bonds with face values of $100,000, $5,000, and other amounts.

A bond's **maturity date** is the date on which the principal will be paid to the bond's owner. If a bond has a maturity date 30 years after the date on which it was first sold, we'd call it a 30-year bond. Other bonds have shorter maturities—15 years, 10 years, 1 year, 6 months, or even 3 months.

Some bonds, including many of those sold by the U.S. federal government, are **pure discount bonds**. A discount bond is one that does not make any payments except for the principal it pays at maturity. For example, at some time in your life, you may have gotten a gift of a U.S. savings bond, issued by the federal government and sold at most banks. A $100 savings bond is a promise by the federal government to pay $100 to the bond's owner in, say, 20 years. If the savings bond sells for $38 and pays $100 at maturity, the total interest on the bond is $62, the difference between what the bond originally sold for and what the owner will receive at maturity.

Most bonds, however, promise—in addition to repayment of principal—a series of interim payments called **coupon payments**. For example, a 30-year, $10,000 bond might promise a coupon payment—say, $600—each year for the next 30 years, and then pay $10,000 at maturity.

A bond's **yield** is the effective annual interest rate that the bond earns for its owner. For example, if you buy a 20-year savings bond for $38 that will give you $100 in 20 years, your annual yield is 5 percent. That's because if you put $38 in the bank for 20 years at 5 percent interest, you'd end up with $100 after 20 years—the same as you get with the savings bond. The yield on a bond, as you will see later on, is closely related to the price that someone pays for the bond.

How Much Is a Bond Worth? To determine the value of a bond, let's start with a simple example: a pure discount bond that promises to pay $10,000 when it matures in exactly one year. The $10,000 is a future payment, and our method of calculating its value should not surprise you: It involves *present value*. Let's suppose the interest rate at which you can borrow and lend funds is 10 percent. Then we can determine the present value of the bond with our discounting formula as:

$$PV = \frac{\$Y}{(1 + r)} = \frac{\$10,000}{1.10} = \$9,091.$$

Since the present value of $10,000 to be received in one year is $9,091, that is the most you should pay for the bond. Assuming the bond's current owner can borrow and lend at the same 10 percent interest rate as you, then $9,091 is the lowest price at which she will sell the bond to you. We conclude that this bond will sell for $9,091, no more and no less.

The same principle applies to more complicated types of bonds, such as discount bonds that don't pay off for many years, or coupon bonds. For example, suppose a bond maturing in five years has a principal of $10,000, and also promises a coupon payment of $600 each year until maturity, with the first payment made one year from today. The total present value of this bond would be:

$$PV = \frac{\$600}{(1.10)} + \frac{\$600}{(1.10)^2} + \frac{\$600}{(1.10)^3} + \frac{\$600}{(1.10)^4} + \frac{\$600}{(1.10)^5} + \frac{\$10,000}{(1.10)^5} = \$8,484.$$

Once again, this total present value—$8,484—is what the bond is worth, and this is the price at which it will trade, as long as buyers and sellers use the same discount rate of 10 percent in their calculations.

Bond Prices and Bond Yields. There is an important relationship between the price of a bond and the yield or rate of return the bond earns for its owner. This is easiest to see with a pure discount bond, such as the bond that pays $10,000 in one year in our example above. Suppose you bought this bond for $8,000. Then, at the end of the year, you would earn interest of $10,000 − $8,000 = $2,000 on an asset that cost you $8,000. Your annual yield would be $2,000/$8,000 = 0.25 or 25 percent.

But now suppose you paid $9,000 for that same bond. Then your interest earnings would be $10,000 − $9,000 = $1,000, and your annual yield would be $1,000/$9,000 = 0.111 or 11.1 percent.

As you can see, the yield you earn on a bond depends on the price you pay for it. For each price, there is a different yield. And the greater the price of a bond, the lower the yield on that bond. This applies not only to simple discount bonds, but also to more complicated bonds with coupon payments. And the reasoning is the same in both cases: A bond promises to pay fixed amounts of dollars at fixed dates in the future. The more you end up paying for those promised future payments, the lower your rate of return.

More generally:

> *There is an inverse relationship between bond prices and bond yields. The higher the price of any given bond, the lower the yield on that bond.*

What is true for a single bond is also true for bonds in general: When many bonds' prices are rising together, so that the average price of bonds rises, then the average *yield* on bonds must be falling.

Primary and Secondary Bond Markets. Every type of financial asset is traded in two different types of markets. The **primary market** is where newly issued financial assets are sold for the first time. But once a financial asset is sold in the primary market, the buyer is free to sell it to someone else. When a previously issued asset is sold again, the sale takes place in the **secondary market.** Most of the trading that takes place in financial markets on any given day is *secondary market trading.*

Applying this distinction to bonds, we would say that the *primary bond market* is where newly issued bonds are sold to their original buyers, while the *secondary bond market* is where previously issued bonds change hands.

It is only in the primary market that a firm actually obtains funds for its investment projects. Once a firm has issued and sold a bond, that bond can change hands many times in the secondary market, but the firm will not benefit directly from these sales. Secondary market trading is an exchange between private parties, and the original issuing firm or government agency is not involved.

Primary market The market in which newly issued financial assets are sold for the first time.

Secondary market The market in which previously issued financial assets are sold.

Still, firms and government agencies follow secondary bond markets closely. Why? Because the secondary market affects the primary market, and thus affects firms that want to borrow money by issuing bonds. The link between these two markets arises because most bonds offered for sale in the primary market have very close substitutes available in the secondary market. For example, suppose that IBM wants to borrow funds by issuing 10-year, $10,000 bonds in the primary market. In order to attract buyers, it will have to sell these *new* bonds at the same price as any *old* $10,000 IBM bonds trading in the secondary market that still have 10 years left before maturity. After all, there is no reason for a bond buyer to prefer a new, 10-year bond to an old bond that has 10 years left to run—as long as both are issued by the same corporation and both have the same face value. Thus,

> *while bond issuers are not direct participants in secondary market trading, they are affected by what happens in the secondary market. More specifically, if a bond's price rises in the secondary market, the price one can charge for similar, newly issued bonds in the primary market will rise as well.*

Since there is such a close relationship between bond prices and bond yields, we can also express this idea in terms of yields.

> *If a bond's yield falls in the secondary market, the yield of similar, newly issued bonds in the primary market will fall as well.*

A bond's yield is the interest rate a firm ends up paying when it issues bonds and sells them in the primary market. So a firm would like its bond yield to be as small as possible (its bond price to be as high as possible).

Why Do Bond Prices (and Bond Yields) Differ? Thousands of different kinds of bonds are traded in financial markets every day. There are corporate bonds of various maturities and bonds issued by local, state, and federal governments and government agencies. Bonds issued by foreign firms and governments are also traded in the United States. And each bond has its own unique yield. Why is this? Why don't all bonds give the same yield? That is, why doesn't each bond sell at a price that makes its yield identical to the yield on any other bond?

The answer is found in the principle of asset valuation, which tells us that a bond—like any asset—is worth the total present value of its future payments. Imagine that you are a bond trader and you are trying to determine the maximum price you should offer for a bond. You know the face value of the bond and its maturity date, as well as the values and dates of any coupon payments it might make. Your problem then boils down to determining what discount rate to use in calculating the total present value of those future payments. That is, you must determine which discount rate will accurately reflect the opportunity cost of your funds.

If you were *absolutely certain* that you would receive the promised future payment, then your discount rate should be the interest rate you *could* earn on *other,* absolutely certain investments. The promises made by the U.S. government are generally considered the most reliable, and the interest rate on U.S. government securities is often called the *riskless rate*. So, if you have the same faith in the bond you are considering buying as you would in U.S. government bonds, then you should use the interest rate on government bonds as your discount rate, and calculate the total *PV* accordingly.

However, few bonds are as safe as U.S. government bonds. Indeed, private firms do occasionally go bankrupt and default on their obligations; some recent examples include US Airways, United Airlines, and WorldCom (the parent of the MCI telephone company), all of which filed for bankruptcy in 2002. The bond market is alert to the likelihood of default, and bonds are rated according to this likelihood. Moody's, one of the services that rates bonds, classifies them as Aaa (the least likely to default), followed by Aa, A, Baa, and so on. When a bond has a higher likelihood of default, the opportunity cost of your funds to buy it is greater than just the interest foregone because you are also foregoing safety: You risk losing the entire value of the bond. Therefore, for riskier bonds, your discount rate should include the opportunity cost of foregone interest that you could have earned on U.S. government bonds, *plus* an extra premium reflecting the higher risk. And the riskier the bond, the higher the discount rate you should apply to it, and the lower will be its total present value.

> *To put a value on riskier bonds, market participants use a higher discount rate than on safe bonds. This leads to lower total present values and lower prices for the riskier bonds. With lower prices, riskier bonds have higher yields.*

Table 6 shows that the market does value bonds in this way. In the table, bonds are listed in the order of increasing risk, according to Moody's Investor's Services, a private corporation that analyzes corporations and municipalities that issue bonds and estimates the likelihood that they will default. U.S. Treasury bonds, which are backed by the promise of the U.S. government, have virtually zero probability of default. Aaa is considered "best quality," the highest rating given to the most creditworthy corporations and municipalities. The ratings continue down through Aa (high quality), A (favorable), Baa (medium-grade), and so on. Notice how the yields diverged on July 8, 2003. The difference between the riskless yield of 2.54 percent on U.S. Treasury bonds (which have virtually zero probability of default) and the more risky Baa yield was more than 1.6 percentage points. That difference is the premium that compensates investors for the chance that a Baa bond will go into default in a given year.

The bonds of economically unstable foreign governments often have high risks of default, and these bonds can carry high yields as a result. For example, in mid-2001, the yield on Argentinian government bonds that promised repayment in U.S. dollars was more than eight times the yield on U.S. government bonds. Buyers of Argentinian bonds began to doubt that Argentina's government would be able to obtain the dollars to make good on its promise of repayment. Therefore, they needed to be compensated for the risk of default. Sure enough, in December 2001, the Argentinian government *did* default on its debt, raising the prospect that bondholders could lose billions of dollars.

Riskiness is only one reason that bond prices and bond yields differ. If you go on to study financial economics, you'll learn that two bonds with equal default risk can have different yields for a variety of reasons, including differences in their maturity dates, differences in their frequency of coupon payments, or because one bond is more widely traded (and therefore easier to sell on short notice) than another.

TABLE 6
Interest Rate on 5-Year
Bonds, July 8, 2003

Rating	Interest Rate
U.S. Treasury bond	2.54 percent
Aaa corporate bond	2.67 percent
Aa corporate bond	2.70 percent
A corporate bond	3.01 percent
Baa Corporate bond	4.20 percent
Ba Corporate bond	7.12 percent
B Corporate bond	8.20 percent

Source: http://bonds.yahoo.com/rates.html (accessed on July 9, 2003); Bond rates below A rating are based on sample of individual bond quotes on the same date.

The Stock Market

Share of stock A share of ownership in a corporation.

A **share of stock,** like a bond, is a financial asset that promises its owner future payments. But the nature of the promise is very different for these two types of assets. When a corporation issues a bond, it is *borrowing* funds and promising to pay them back. But when a corporation issues a share of stock, it brings in new ownership of the firm itself. In fact, a share of stock *is,* by definition, *a share of ownership* in the firm. Those who pay for their shares provide the firm with the funds, and in return, the firm owes them, at some future date or dates, a share of the firm's profits.

When a firm wishes to raise money in the stock market, it gets in touch with an investment bank. Investment banks are firms that specialize in assessing the market potential of new stock issues. Together, the firm and its investment banker develop a prospectus that describes the offering—the nature of the firm's business, the number of shares that will be sold, and so on. The purpose of the prospectus is to inform potential investors of the risks involved. It must be reviewed by the *Securities and Exchange Commission,* the principal regulatory agency that oversees financial markets.

Once the prospectus is approved, the firm can sell shares to the public. If it is the first-ever offering of shares by this firm, the sale will be called an *initial public offering (IPO).* The firm's investment banker usually tries to line up buyers for the offering before the securities are actually released for sale. In practice, it's usually large institutional investors, such as mutual funds, who first purchase new shares.

Primary and Secondary Stock Markets. When a corporation issues new shares— as part of an IPO or a secondary offering—they are sold in the *primary stock market.* The only time a corporation receives any income from a trade in its stock is when the corporation itself sells the stock in the primary market. From then on, the stock is traded in the *secondary market*—the market in which previously issued shares are sold and resold.

As in the bond market, the issuing corporation has no *direct* relationship with the secondary market. But the secondary market is very important to firms that raise funds in the primary market, for two reasons. First, because of the secondary market, people who buy shares know they can easily sell them when they want. This makes people more willing to hold stock, including the new shares that firms issue to raise funds.

Second, price changes in the secondary market affect the price a firm can get from selling shares in the primary market. In fact, when a firm's shares are already trading in the secondary market, a small offering of new shares will always sell at the secondary market price. That's because the shares trading in the secondary markets are perfect substitutes for the firm's new shares.

Direct and Indirect Ownership of Stock. Many people own shares of stock directly. You or a family member may have purchased stock for your own account, by calling a broker or going online and ordering, say, 200 shares of Barnes and Noble stock. The stock is then held by your brokerage firm, and you are free to buy more or sell it any time you want, with a phone call or an online order.

But you can also own stock *indirectly*, by purchasing shares of a **mutual fund.** A mutual fund is a corporation that, in turn, buys shares of stock in *other* corporations. There are mutual funds that specialize in Internet companies, in foreign companies located in specific regions like Europe or Asia, and in long-lived companies that have a reputation for stable, slow-growing, profits. Most mutual funds advertise that, by doing careful research into companies and making professional predictions about the future, they can pick stocks within their specialty more wisely than a nonprofessional can. (We'll discuss the accuracy of this claim in the "Using the Theory" section of this chapter.)

Mutual fund A corporation that specializes in owning shares of stock in other corporations.

A final way that households can, indirectly, own stock is through retirement accounts that are managed by their employers. The total funds available for retirement will depend on the performance of the stock and bond markets, but the worker has no ability to buy and sell shares of individual bonds, stocks, or mutual funds on his own. It is not unusual for half or more of the funds in such retirement accounts to be held in stocks, with most of the rest in bonds. There are also 401(k) and 403(b) accounts that employees manage for themselves. In these accounts, which should not be confused with employer-managed accounts, the stock is owned directly or indirectly through mutual fund shares.

Stock ownership in the United States is growing rapidly. In 2002, about half of all American households owned shares of stock or mutual fund shares that they managed themselves, up from about 19 percent of households in 1983.[3]

Why Do People Hold Stock? Why do so many individuals and fund managers choose to put their money into stocks? You already know part of the answer: When you own a share of stock, you own part of the corporation. Indeed, the fraction of the corporation that you own is equal to the fraction of the company's total stock that you own. For example, in July 2003, Starbucks Corporation had 390.5 million shares outstanding. If you owned 4,000 shares of Starbucks stock, then you owned $4,000/390,500,000 = .0000102$, or about one-thousandth of 1 percent of that firm. This means you are, in essence, entitled to a thousandth of a percent of the firm's after-tax profit.

In practice, however, most firms do not pay out *all* of their profit to shareholders. Instead, some of the profit is kept as *retained earnings,* for later use by the firm. The part of profit that is distributed to shareholders is called **dividends.** A firm's dividend payments benefit stockholders in much the same way that interest payments benefit bondholders, providing a source of steady income. Of course, as a

Dividends Part of a firm's current profit that is distributed to shareholders.

---

[3] Securities Industry Association, "Half of American Households Hold Equities," Press Release, September 27, 2002 (*http://www.sia.com/press/html/pr_equity_ownership.html*).

part owner of a firm, you are part owner of any retained earnings as well, even if you will not benefit from them until later.

Aside from dividends, a second—and usually more important—reason that people hold stocks is that they hope to enjoy **capital gains:** the return someone gets when they sell an asset at a higher price than they paid for it. For example, if you buy shares of Hewlett Packard computer at $15 per share, and later sell them at $20 per share, your capital gain is $5 per share. This is in addition to any dividends the firm paid to you while you owned the stock.

Some stocks pay no dividends at all, because the management believes that stockholders are best served by reinvesting all profits within the firm so that *future* profits will be even higher. The idea is to invest profits back into the corporation, enabling it to purchase new capital, develop new products, or purchase other profitable firms. If the firm uses this money well, then future profits (and future dividends) can be even greater. And in the meantime, higher profits raise the price of the stock so that shareholders can get capital gains when they sell it. Until 2003, Microsoft had never paid a dividend. But by plowing its profits back into the company, the firm's shares grew to a total value of almost $300 billion in mid-2003. The company's shareholders had great faith that they would eventually get cash from the firm, and in March 2003, it happened: Microsoft paid its first dividend.

Over the past century, corporate stocks have generally been a good investment. They were especially rewarding during the 1990s, enjoying (on average) a 15 percent annual return. That means that the average $1,000 invested in the stock market on January 1, 1990, would have increased in value to $4,045 by the beginning of 2000. However, the stock market is volatile; over shorter periods of time, one cannot assume that stock prices will rise at all. For example, if you invested $1,000 in the market on January 1, 2000, your stocks would be worth only about $663 by the middle of 2003.

Valuing a Share of Stock. The value of a share of stock, like any other asset, is the total present value of its future payments. For a share of stock, the future payments are all the profits that the share is expected to earn for its owner. But over what time horizon should stocks be valued? Unlike a bond, which has a maturity date, a share of stock is expected to remain an earning asset for some owner for as long as the company exists—forever, unless market participants anticipate the firm will go out of business at some future date. Fortunately, there are formulas to measure the total present value of a firm's future profits under a variety of different assumptions. For example, the simplest formula tells us that,

> *if a firm will earn a constant $Y in profit after taxes each year forever, then the total present value of these future profits is $Y/r, where r is the discount rate.*

So, for example, if a firm is expected to earn $10 million in after-tax profit for its owners per year forever, and the discount rate is 10 percent, then—according to the formula—the total *PV* of those future profits is $10 million/0.10 = $100 million.

What about the value of a single *share* of this firm's stock? If there are 1 million shares of stock outstanding for this firm, then each share should be worth $100 million/1 million = $100.

> *The value of a share of stock in a firm is equal to the total present value of the firm's after-tax profit divided by the number of shares outstanding.*

Capital gain The return someone gets by selling a financial asset at a price higher than they paid for it.

Note that we are valuing a share of stock by future profits, not by dividends. Remember that firms often plow their profits back in the firm in order to increase the firm's growth rate further. What counts is after-tax profits, because these belong to the firm's shareholders, whether they receive them in cash or not.

However, when valuing the shares of real-world companies—companies whose earnings are expected to grow, and companies whose future earnings involve some risk—the simple formula we've just used is too limiting. Other, more complicated formulas have to be used, and you will learn some of them if you go further in your study of economics or business. But even without knowing the detailed formulas, we can come to four important conclusions about the factors that can affect a stock's value.

First, earnings *forecasts* are usually based on the firm's *current* earnings. The total present value of the firm's future profits will be greater if those profits are rising from a higher base of current profit. Thus,

an increase in current profits increases the value of a share of stock.

Second, for any given base value of current profit, a higher anticipated growth rate will raise the profit expected in each future year, which will raise the total present value of the firm's profits. Hence,

an increase in the anticipated growth rate of profits increases the value of a share of stock.

Third, as you've learned, a higher discount rate decreases the present value of any payment to be received in the future. Thus,

a rise in interest rates—or even an anticipated rise in interest rates—decreases the value of a share of stock.

Finally, there is the matter of risk. In making financial decisions, most people prefer a sure thing to a gamble (although there are exceptions). We adjust for risk in our *PV* calculations by applying a higher discount rate to future payments that are more risky. This means that the *PV* of any future year's profits will be lower when the amount of those future profits is less certain. Accordingly,

an increase in the perceived riskiness of future profits decreases the value of a share of stock.

Reading the Stock Pages. In the United States, financial markets are so important that stock and bond prices are monitored on a continuous basis. If you wish to know the value of a stock, you can find out instantly by checking with a broker or logging on to a Web site that reports such information. One such site is Thomson Investors Network (*http://www.thomsoninvest.net/index.sht*) but there are dozens of others. In addition, stock prices and other information is reported daily in local newspapers and in specialized financial publications such as the *Wall Street Journal*.

To some people, the pages that cover the stock market look as impenetrable as Egyptian hieroglyphics. But in fact, the information on the stock pages is very easy to understand, once you decide to learn it.

FIGURE 2
Stock Market Table for Trading on July 8, 2003

Source: The Wall Street Journal (July 9, 2003).

YTD %CHG	52-WEEK HI	LO	STOCK (SYM)	DIV	YLD %	PE	VOL 100s	CLOSE	NET CHG
			Continued From Page C3						
5.8	58.60	43	FPL Gp Corp **FPLB**	4.00	7.1	...	806	56.49	-0.16
8.4	68.08	45	FPL Gp **FPL**	2.40	3.7	16	8915	65.17	-0.41
-11.6	32.45	18.16	FTI Cnsltng **FCN** s		...	18	7828	23.65	0.25
↓ 69.1	47.01	21.15	FactstRsch **FDS**	.24f	.5	34	3765	47.81	1.10
8.0	29.85	19.77	FahnestkVnr **FVH**	.36g	1.3	25	7	27.28	-0.05
22.5	56.75	29.15	Fairlsaac **FIC**	.08	.2	87	3891	52.30	0.50
-16.1	6	3.12	FairchldCp **FA**		...	dd	300	4.16	-0.11
32.0	23.65	6.85	FrchldSemi **FCS**		...	dd	13539	14.14	-0.05
93.3	162.80	46.71	FairfaxFnl **FFH** n	1.50p	...	...	231	148.84	-0.73
-1.7	25.91	19.07	FairmntHtlRt **FHR**	.06	.3	20	2812	23.14	-0.50
2.5	5.85	3.60	FalcnPdt **FCP**		...	59	1006	4.15	0.05
↓ 26.5	39.35	23.75	FamilyDlr **FDO**	.30	.8	28	6972	39.47	0.72
10.9	77.55	58.40	♦FannieMae **FNM**	1.56	2.2	13	30727	71.35	0.45
27.2	3.70	1.90	Fedders **FJC**	.12	3.3	19	1622	3.60	0.25
-11.1	26	15.50	FedAgrMtg A **AGMA**		...	9	11	17.95	0.35
-20.9	36.80	20.10	FedAgri C **AGM**		...	...	138	24.25	0.34
↓ 22.0	34.41	21.83	FedRlty **FRT**	1.94	5.7	27	1718	34.31	-0.10
-4.5	24.40	13.60	FedSgnl **FSS**	.80	4.3	20	1703	18.55	0.25
33.3	40.81	23.51	FedDeptStr **FD**	.13p	...	10	16535	38.33	0.70
14.3	35.04	23.43	FedInv B **FII**	.28f	1.0	17	2998	28.99	0.51
18.6	65.35	42.75	FedExCp **FDX**	.20	.3	23	18274	64.33	1.36
-28.4	18.15	5.80	Felcor **FCH**	.45j	...	dd	1419	8.19	0.06
12.9	24.25	14.25	Ferrellgas **FGP**	2.00	8.7	14	626	23	0.15
-6.3	30.55	19.24	Ferro **FOE**	.58	2.5	13	1731	22.90	-0.11
-15.6	12.80	6	Fiat ADS **FIA**	j	...	...	144	6.71	-0.14
-35.8	9	4.50	♦FiberMark **FMK**		...	dd	31	4.87	0.10
21.3	33	19.08	FidNtlFnl **FNF** s	.48	1.5	7	4926	31.87	0.14
2.9	34.95	17.85	FnlFed **FIF**		...	15	650	25.85	0.10
21.0	28.04	16.14	FstAmCp **FAF**	.40	1.5	8	3638	26.87	0.23
32.3	31.80	21.73	FstBcp **FBP** s	.44	1.5	13	1447	29.90	0.66
16.0	13.45	10.55	FstCmwlthFnl **FCF**	.62	4.6	16	563	13.34	0.15
21.2	44.90	23.75	♦FstData **FDC**	.08	.2	25	31951	42.90	0.50
8.2	33.50	25.75	FstIndRlty **FR**	2.74	9.0	12	9606	30.30	-1.58
↓ 41.4	27.95	18	♦FstRepBnk **FRC**		...	14	430	28.26	0.32
22.3	48.50	29.76	FstTN Ntl **FTN**	1.20	2.7	14	8917	43.94	-0.15
6.1	29.25	25.97	FstUnionCap Carts **KTV**	2.05	7.1	...	10	28.70	...
4.2	27.15	24.55	FstUn ll 7.5Carts **KRD**	1.88	7.1	...	15	26.35	-0.10
0.6	2.30	1.47	FstUnionRE **FUR**	j	...	dd	495	1.79	...

Figure 2 shows an excerpt from the New York Stock Exchange Composite Transactions reported in the July 9, 2003, *Wall Street Journal*. The data refer to the previous trading day: Wednesday, July 8, 2003.

Let's focus on the stock of FedEx Corporation (listed as FedExCp). The first columns show the percentage change in the stock's price from a year ago, and the highest and lowest prices paid during the past 52 weeks. The table tells us that from July 9, 2002, to July 8, 2003, FedEx stock rose 18.6 percent and that its price ranged from a low of $42.75 per share to a high of $65.35 per share during that period.

The next columns show the stock's name, abbreviated to FedExCp, followed by its stock symbol, FDX. You may need to know the stock symbol if you want to find a stock's price online, or on a "ticker tape"—the continuous report of stock trades that runs from wall to wall in many financial institutions or at the bottom of the screen on CNBC television network.

The next two columns report the firm's most recent cash dividend—in this case .20, or 20 cents per share—and the corresponding *dividend yield,* obtained by dividing the most recent year's total dividends by the current stock price. For FedEx, this was .3, meaning that if the entire year's dividends had been paid on July 8, 2003, each share would pay a dividend equal to three-tenths of 1 percent of the stock's current value. The price-earnings (PE) ratio, shown in the next column, is the stock's current price divided by its after-tax profit per share during the previous 12 months. Or, put another way, the PE ratio tells us the cost of each dollar of yearly after-tax profits. The figure of 23 means that FedEx's current stock price was 23 times the size of its most recent annual earnings per share. If you bought this stock, you would be paying $23 for each dollar of yearly profits.

Many people watch PE ratios closely. They theorize that a stock with a low PE ratio is a better deal, since it costs less per dollar of profit. But this strategy can be deceiving. A company's PE ratio might be very low because its future prospects aren't very good. People may not be expecting much growth in the firm's future profits, or they may even be expecting its profits to fall, so they won't pay a very high price for each dollar of *current* earnings. On the other hand, a company whose profits are expected to grow rapidly might command a very *high* PE ratio. People are willing to pay a higher price for this stock because they expect profits to grow, but the PE ratio will be high because it measures the price of a dollar of *current* profits rather than future profits. In general, an unusually high or unusually low PE ratio does not tell people whether the stock is relatively expensive or relatively cheap; one must also consider the stock's future prospects.

The remaining columns tell us about the most recent day's transactions in this stock—July 8, 2003, in this case. The column headed *Vol 100s* indicates how many shares, in hundreds, traded on that day. Multiplying the table figure of 18,274 by 100, we find that about 1.83 million shares changed hands on that day. The next column tells us the last price at which FedEx stock traded on that day. On July 8, 2003, the last person who bought FedEx stock paid $64.33 for each share. The final column—*Net Chg*—tells us that the price of a share of FedEx stock decreased by $1.36 per share, from its price at the end of the *previous* day's trading.

In addition to reporting on individual stocks, the *Wall Street Journal* and other newspapers also report on changes in different stock market averages or indexes. These are meant to represent movements in stock prices as a whole, or movements in particular types of stocks. The most popular average is the **Dow Jones Industrial Average,** which tracks the prices of 30 of the largest companies in the United States, including Boeing, Microsoft, and Wal-Mart. Another popular average is the much broader **Standard & Poor's 500,** which tracks stock prices of 500 large corporations.

Dow Jones Industrial Average An index of the prices of stocks of 30 large U.S. firms.

Standard & Poor's 500 An index of the prices of stocks of 500 large U.S. firms.

Explaining Stock Prices. Glancing at the newspaper clipping in Figure 2, you can see that most stocks experience a price change on any given day. Why? Like all prices, stock prices are determined by supply and demand. However, our supply and demand curves require a bit of reinterpretation.

Figure 3 presents a supply and demand diagram for the shares of FedEx. Unlike most supply curves you've studied in this book—which tell you the quantity of something that suppliers want to *sell* over a given period of time—the supply curve in Figure 3 is somewhat different. It tells us the quantity of shares *in existence* at any moment in time. This is the number of shares that people are *actually* holding.

On any given day, the number of FedEx shares in existence is just the number that FedEx has issued previously, up until that day. Therefore, no matter what happens to the price today, the number of shares remains unchanged. This is why the supply curve in the figure is a vertical line at 298 million, showing that there are 298 million shares in existence regardless of the price.

Now, just because 298 million shares of FedEx stock actually exist, that does not mean that this is the number of shares that people *want* to hold. The desire to hold FedEx shares is given by the downward-sloping demand curve. As you can see, the lower the price of the stock, the more shares of FedEx people will want to hold. Why is this?

As you've learned, the value of a share of stock to any owner is equal to the total present value of its future after-tax profits. However, individuals do not all calculate this total present value in the same way. Some may believe that FedEx's profits will continue to grow as rapidly as they have in the past, while others—more pessimistic—may believe that FedEx's best days are behind it, forecasting a much lower growth rate. Some investors may not mind risk much at all, while others may be especially risk averse, and use a higher discount rate that lowers the present value of each future year's profit.

Thus, at any given moment, there is an array of estimates of a stock's total present value. As the price of the stock comes down, it descends below more and more people's total present value estimates, and so more and more will find the stock to be a bargain and want to hold it. This is what the downward-sloping demand curve tells us.

Now, looking at Figure 3, you can see that at any price other than $64 per share, the number of shares people *are* holding (on the supply curve) will differ

FIGURE 3
The Market for FedEx

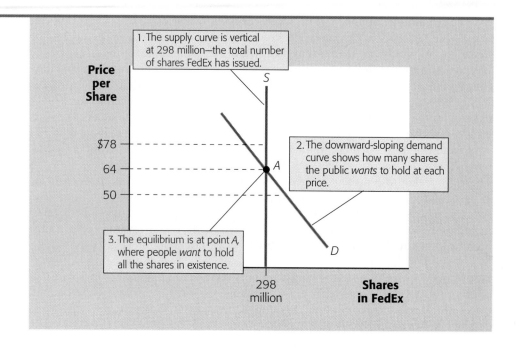

from the number they *want* to hold (on the demand curve). For example, at a price of $50 per share, people would want to hold more shares than they are currently holding. Many would try to buy the stock, and the price would be bid up. At $78 per share, the opposite occurs: People find themselves holding more shares than they want to hold, and they will try to get rid of the excess by selling them. The sudden sales would cause the price to drop. Only at the equilibrium price of $64, where the supply and demand curves intersect, are people satisfied holding the number of shares they are *actually* holding.

Stocks achieve their equilibrium prices almost instantly. Legions of stock traders—both individuals and professional fund managers—sit poised at their computers, ready to buy or sell a particular firm's shares the minute they feel they have an excess supply or a shortage of those shares. Thus, we can have confidence that the price of a share at any time is the equilibrium price.

But why do stock prices *change* so often? Or, since stocks sell at their equilibrium prices at almost every instant, we can ask: Why do shares' *equilibrium* prices change so often?

Since a supply curve, like that in Figure 3, only shifts when there is an initial or secondary public offering, and these happen only occasionally and with great fanfare, the day-to-day changes in equilibrium prices cannot be caused by shifts in the supply curve. So they must be caused by shifts in *demand*. Figure 4 shows how a rightward shift in the demand curve for shares of FedEx could cause the price to rise to $80 per share. Indeed, on rare occasions, the demand curve for a firm's shares has shifted so far rightward in a single day that the share price doubled or even tripled.

But what causes these sudden shifts in demand for a share of stock?

The logic of present value provides the answer. Anything that causes large groups of individuals to change their estimates of the total present value of future

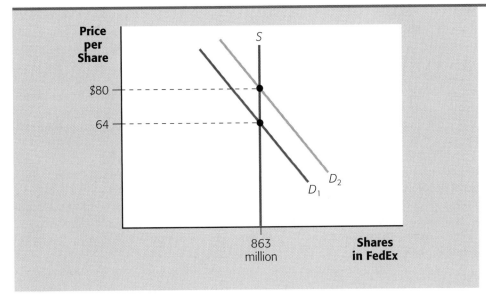

FIGURE 4

An Increase in Demand for Shares of FedEx

Demand for shares of FedEx will increase if (1) interest rates fall; (2) the perceived riskiness of the stock decreases; or (3) the firm's earning prospects brighten. In the figure, the demand curve shifts rightward, from D_1 to D_2, driving up the price from $64 to $80 per share.

profits will shift the demand curve. For example, the discount rate used in *PV* calculations will *decrease* whenever there is a decrease in interest rates in the economy. It will also decrease if future earnings become more certain. By making the discount rate, *d*, smaller, these changes would increase the total present value of a share, and shift the demand curve to the right (people would want to buy more shares at any price). Similarly, an increase in current profit beyond what was expected, or an increase in the expected growth rate of profits, will increase the total present value of shares and shift the demand curve rightward.

When stock prices move dramatically, it is usually because some new information has become available. For example, suppose that jet fuel prices decreased dramatically and were expected to stay low for some time. Since jet fuel is a major cost for FedEx, people would expect higher future profits for the company. Estimates of the present value of profits would rise, shifting the demand curve to the right. As in Figure 4, this would increase the price of the stock.

On the other hand, suppose that United Parcel Service, FedEx's chief competitor, announced a significant price cut for its overnight shipping service. In that case, people would expect UPS sales to increase at the expense of FedEx, or that FedEx would have to lower its own prices in order to keep its market share. Either way, a lower profit per share for FedEx would be forecasted, the demand curve for its shares would shift leftward, and the price would fall (not shown in the figure).

The Economic Role of Financial Markets

Now that we've investigated some of the specific details regarding financial markets, it is worthwhile to back up and take a broader view. What functions do financial markets play? In this section, we will take an economist's viewpoint and try to pinpoint just exactly how financial markets make us all better off.

If there is a single word that resonates throughout this chapter, it is *time*. Markets for physical and human capital as well as financial markets reflect decisions made over time. When a firm purchases a capital asset, it makes an expenditure today in return for a machine or plant that generates benefits many years into the future. When an individual invests in human capital, something similar happens: Costs are incurred today in exchange for future benefits.

In the absence of markets for physical and human capital, we would all be constrained to live as if there were literally no tomorrow. We would have to forego the productivity advances embodied in new capital goods and the conceptual breakthroughs that arise from investment in education and training. Each of us—and society as a whole—would be much poorer.

We would also be poorer if there were no *financial* markets. Firms would be unable to become very large or grow very fast if they were constrained to fund their growth solely through retained earnings. Without capital markets, there would be no AT&T, no IBM, and no Microsoft, and we would not be able to enjoy the products these firms produce. All three of these firms—and indeed, most major corporations—turned to the stock and bond markets to obtain funds for their capital acquisitions.

Moreover, without financial markets, we would be constrained as individuals. We could save for retirement or for our children's education, but not very fruitfully, because we would not earn any interest or dividends on our savings. Without financial markets, banks would be little more than safe houses, storing our cash until we needed it and charging us a fee for the service instead of paying us interest.

All of the markets we have studied in this chapter enable us to save funds and earn a rate of return, and they enable firms to invest and grow. They help relax the economic constraints imposed by scarcity. And they certainly contribute to the high standard of living we enjoy. When savers and borrowers come together in financial markets, both sides benefit. Let's look more closely at some of the economic functions that financial markets play.

1. *Facilitating large-scale production.* The large industrial enterprises that are so common today are only about a century old. In the nineteenth century and earlier, it would have been extremely unusual to find any business employing a hundred workers, much less the thousands of employees that are common in today's firms. But as technology changed and innovations such as rail transportation, electricity, and the gasoline engine were introduced, it suddenly became possible to have firms that served national, rather than local, markets. And as firms grew, so did their need to accumulate large sums of money.

   To take just a single example, think about railroads. As the rail network spread across the United States, the railroads needed to (1) assemble large tracts of land for rail beds, stations, and other facilities; (2) purchase steel rails and hire the labor necessary to lay thousands of miles of track; and (3) invest in locomotives and rolling stock. These were huge tasks, requiring larger sums of money than firms could possibly accumulate from their retained earnings. Therefore, the new railroads turned to the bond market for funding, just as today's large enterprises look to both the stock and bond markets for cash to expand their operations. Without smoothly functioning financial markets, little of the remarkable economic growth of the past century could have occurred.

2. *Reallocating spending across time.* We've seen that financial markets allow firms to invest in new projects today rather than waiting until the necessary

funds accumulate from current operations. Something similar is true for individual households: Financial markets allow them to reallocate their consumption over time. To see this, imagine that you wish to buy a new car. If there were no financial markets, then you would have to wait until you could save up the needed funds. With financial markets, you can take out a loan that enables you to increase your consumption now at the cost of reducing consumption later (as you repay the loan). Or imagine that you are concerned about income during retirement. The markets provide a way for you to accumulate the necessary funds. When you open a savings account, buy a bond, or invest in a mutual fund, you are reducing your consumption today in order to enjoy greater consumption in the future.

More generally, the financial markets reallocate funds from surplus units—mostly individuals who are not consuming their entire incomes today—to deficit units—mostly firms that desire to spend more than their current income today. In so doing, those markets help individuals, firms, and even the government, to achieve the best *intertemporal* utilization of resources.

3. *Reducing risk.* In the absence of financial markets, firms could still invest and households could still save. But doing so would be much riskier. Imagine, for example, that you had some extra money and you wanted it to grow. Then you could get in touch with a local business and offer to lend it money in return for future dividends or interest payments. If you are lucky and the firm thrives, you will come out ahead. But what if the firm encounters hard times, or even goes out of business? With all your eggs in one basket, so to speak, your investment is quite risky.

Now let's replay the scenario—this time with financial markets. Again you have money to invest, but now you have many more options. Rather than putting all your funds into one firm, you can buy shares of stock in a variety of firms, or shares in a mutual fund. As you might imagine, portfolio diversification is a good way to reduce risk. And such diversification is really only possible with well-functioning stock and bond markets.

4. *Disciplining management.* Every market determines a price, and financial markets are no exception. But the prices of stocks and bonds serve several important functions that are not obvious at first glance. One such function is providing instantaneous feedback that allows corporate managers to see how they are doing. The price of a share of Delta Air Lines stock, for example, tells Delta's managers how the market perceives their policies. If the stock price increases and there has been no change in the discount rate, it means that thousands of investors are, collectively, giving a vote of confidence in those policies. They believe that Delta's future earnings will be greater than they thought before the price rose. If the price decreases, that means investors are voting with their dollars against the way the firm is being managed.

Or imagine that you are the chief financial officer at a new software company. Your firm has great prospects for growth, but you need to secure funds in the stock market. What kind of payoff can you expect from selling your stock? By checking the prices of your competitors' shares, you can form at least a rough estimate of what the market is willing to pay for your shares. And once you begin to participate in the stock market, the existing share price will give you an indication of how much money you can raise by selling additional shares.

© GAIL MOONEY/CORBIS

USING THE THEORY
Can Anyone Predict Stock Prices?

Every day, financial news programs, such as *Wall Street Week* or CNBC's *Squawk Box,* offer stock market advice to millions of television viewers. The stock market analysts interviewed on these shows tell us that they have done some careful research, or that they have a secret formula, and that by following their advice, you'll earn more dividends and capital gains than you could hope to earn on your own. Of course, for the *really* good predictions, you'll have to pay a price and subscribe to their private newsletter or use them as your stockbroker.

It may surprise you to hear that the vast majority of economists don't believe them. Economists, as a rule, don't believe that *anyone*—no matter how smart, no matter how much research they do—can do much better than you, an introductory economics student reading this book and finding out about the stock market for the first time. In fact, they don't believe that anyone can predict what will happen to stock prices much better than someone who has *never* taken economics and who chooses which stocks to buy by throwing darts at the stock page.

How can this be? We'll answer this question by first considering the two different methods used by analysts to make their predictions. Both of these methods try to predict shifts in the demand curve for a stock, like the one in Figure 4 of this chapter. But the methods they use to make their predictions are very different.

Predicting Stock Prices: Fundamental Analysis

Fundamental analysis A method of predicting a stock's price based on the fundamental forces driving the firm's future earnings.

One widely practiced method for predicting stock prices is **fundamental analysis.** As its name suggests, fundamental analysis focuses on the *fundamental forces* driving a firm's future earnings, and the value placed on those earnings by stock market participants. Fundamental analysts study data on overall economic conditions, on specific industries, and on individual firms. To try to predict what will happen to share prices for specific firms, they consider the products made by a company, the future demand for these products, and the strategic moves of current or future competitors to the firm in question. They will also study the firm's top management and try to assess how smart and creative they are.

Using these methods, fundamental analysts try to determine whether a stock is undervalued or overvalued relative to the rest of the market. If it is undervalued in their view, they will recommend that their client or employer buy the stock. If it is overvalued, they will recommend that the stock be sold.

Predicting Stock Prices: Technical Analysis

Technical analysis A method of predicting a stock's price based on that stock's past behavior.

Another method for predicting stock prices—which seems to become more popular every year—is **technical analysis.** The basic idea is that you can graph the recent behavior of a stock's price and, based on certain patterns, predict whether the stock is going to increase or decrease in value over the near future. Technical analysts believe that everything you need to know to predict a stock's future price changes is contained in the stock's past behavior. Many technical analysts recommend that their clients or employers buy and sell particular firms' stocks based on past price movements, without even knowing what the firm produces!

Technical analysts believe that stocks move in trends. And they have numerous, colorful names for the patterns they claim to see. For example, there is a pattern called "head and shoulders" that appears when a stock's price hits a high, then falls a little, then rises to a new high, falls again, then rises again. If this last rise—the right shoulder—fails to equal the previous rise, then many technical analysts expect a major decline in value.

Many people find technical analysis appealing because there are, indeed, elements of strategic behavior in stock market investing. When you attempt to forecast what will happen to your 50 shares of General Motors during the next six months, it is not enough to understand GM's prospects and the demographic factors affecting the demand for automobiles. You also need to predict how other GM shareholders see things. If for some reason, many of them think GM shares will plunge in value, then they will sell their shares, thereby driving down the price. Your shares will decline in value as well. So, thinking about the stock market seems akin to the kind of game-theoretic reasoning we encountered in Chapter 10. It seems that each market participant has to determine what other participants are going to do. This is a daunting task that some people think can be handled by looking for patterns in stock prices, and they trust technical analysts to find those patterns.

The Economist's View: Efficient Markets Theory

While economists believe that fundamental and technical analysis can often explain stock price movements in the *past*, they are extremely skeptical about anyone's ability to *predict* stock price changes in the future. This is because economists tend to take the **efficient markets** view of the stock market. According to this view, the stock market digests new information that might affect stock prices *efficiently*, that is, rapidly and thoroughly.

The implications of the efficient markets view are startling. First, it means that you cannot, on average, beat the market by doing research and finding and buying underpriced (or selling overpriced) stocks. You cannot do this because any research that *you* do will also be done by others and is therefore already incorporated into the stock's price. That means—if the goal is to outperform a broad stock market average like the Standard & Poor's 500—both fundamental and technical analysis are largely a waste of time.

For example, fundamental analysis tells us that if a company comes up with a valuable new patent, the total present value of its future profits will rise. As a result, the demand curve for the firm's stock will shift rightward, as in Figure 4 of this chapter, and the equilibrium price will rise. But who benefits from this price rise? If the patent announcement is a surprise, only those lucky enough to be holding the stock when the announcement is made can benefit. That's because the demand shift and the adjustment to the new equilibrium will be virtually instantaneous. All those who hold the stock will immediately adjust their asking price upward, so no one will be able to buy at a price lower than the equilibrium.

But what if the announcement *isn't* a surprise? What if, by doing careful research, you can predict which companies are *about* to come out with valuable new patents? Surely, then, your research would pay off, enabling you to buy a stock when its price is low, then sell it at a higher price when the announcement comes out and surprises everyone else. Right?

Efficient market A market that instantaneously incorporates all available information relevant to a stock's price.

Sorry to say, but according to the efficient markets view, this is dead wrong. Because any research that *you* do can and will also be done by *others*. Therefore, while you may be able to figure out which companies are likely to succeed, that information will already be reflected in the price of the stock. For example, the stock of companies *more likely* to announce valuable patents will already have a higher price than the stock of companies less likely to do so.

> *According to the efficient markets view of the stock market, any information that can be used to predict a stock's future earnings will be incorporated into a stock's price as soon it becomes publicly available. Therefore, by the time a fundamental analyst predicts that a stock's price will rise or fall, it has already risen or fallen. Fundamental analysis cannot help you outperform the market.*

What about technical analysis? After all, it's human beings who buy and sell stocks, and their decisions are based on human psychology. Surely, a brilliant technical analyst, who carefully studies buying and selling decisions of millions of people, and who can discover the secret psychological rules that govern stock trading by divining patterns amidst the chaos . . . surely *he* can outperform the market.

Sorry to say, but the efficient markets view is skeptical about this idea, too. Why? Imagine a very simple pattern: Because of exuberance or fatigue or superstition, people are more likely to buy stocks than to sell them on Friday, so on average, stock prices rise every Friday. Since everyone would anticipate this pattern, they would buy stocks on Thursday, hoping to profit from the Friday runup. But this would cause stocks to rise on Thursday, not Friday, so people would buy on Wednesday, and so on. Soon, there would be no patterns at all; Friday would be like any other day. While this is a very simple example, the logic applies to *any* pattern a technical analyst might uncover.

> *According to the efficient markets view of the stock market, any patterns in stock price movements that can be observed by a good technical analyst will be incorporated into stock prices as soon as they are discernable. Therefore, stock market patterns disappear as soon as anyone can discover them. Technical analysis cannot help you outperform the market.*

Efficient markets theory tells us that the only information that affects the stock market is surprise information—a new announcement of a major technological breakthrough, or even new information that suggests a firm *might* achieve such a breakthrough. And the only people who benefit from this information when it is made public are those who are lucky enough to be holding the stock already, before the information was available at all.[4]

Moreover, efficient markets theory says that there are *no observable patterns* in stock price movements. This, in turn, means that individual stocks, and broad averages like the Dow Jones Industrial Average or the Standard & Poor's 500, will exhibit entirely *random* changes. If a stock—or the Dow Jones Industrial Average—

---

[4] One exception to this rule is *insiders*—those with connections to the firm and access to information *before* it becomes public. They can buy or sell stock early, before information is reflected in the price of the stock. Profiting from insider information is illegal. Those who do so, if they are caught, pay stiff fines and sometimes even go to jail. However, enforcement of insider trading laws is difficult, since it is often hard to detect.

has fallen three days in a row, the likelihood that it will fall again is no different than if it had fallen, risen, and then fallen.

The efficient markets view may at first seem to be a strange theory of prices. Why do we spend so much effort learning how stock prices are determined, only to then learn that their changes are random? The reconciliation lies in understanding that it is *because* so much effort is put into figuring out what price stocks should sell for that price changes are random. Today's price reflects everything known today, by the market as a whole, about the stock. As a result, the price can change only if new information arrives. But information is new only if it was unexpected—that is, random. If we knew that the price would rise, it would already have risen.

The theory of efficient markets is one of the most exhaustively tested theories in all of economics. Thousands of studies have confirmed the efficiency of stock prices with respect to all sorts of information. You can't beat the market by buying stocks only in companies whose presidents went to MIT (or anywhere else). You can't beat the market by buying stock only in companies in growing industries. You can't beat it by buying stocks that have risen. You can't beat the market by buying stocks that have collapsed. You can't beat the market, period!

But wait. Every year, some fundamental and technical analysts seem to do remarkably well, and *do* outperform the market. And if you watch any television program on investing, you will see them being interviewed and making predictions further into the future. Doesn't this contradict efficient markets theory?

Not at all, and here's why. In any large group of people picking stocks, we would always expect some to be unusually lucky, just as we'd expect some to be unusually unlucky. In fact, we'd expect this even if no one in the group knew *anything* about the stock market—even if, say, they chose which stocks to buy by throwing darts at the stock page. Of course, the *unlucky* stock pickers will never be interviewed; only the lucky ones will get the attention. But the evidence shows that outperforming the market in one year—even by a lot—makes an analyst no more or less likely to outperform the market the next year.

It is true that, looking back at the *past* behavior of the market, we can observe periods in which people have overreacted in one direction or another. For example, from 1997 to 2000 the valuation of many companies seemed to project future earnings that were unrealistically high. In retrospect, it was a period of unsupported optimism about the future profits companies could earn, especially those involved in the Internet. However, that does *not* mean that patterns in the market could have been discerned and exploited for above-average profit—at least not with any confidence. Many who thought the market was too high in 1997 or 1998 lost fortunes when it continued to rise through early 2000. Predicting that the market will *eventually* fall is one thing; predicting *when* it will fall is something else.

Although the idea of efficient markets is sweeping and rules out a great many investment strategies as worthless, its implications for the investor who understands it can be quite valuable.

First, just because you can't outperform the market doesn't mean you shouldn't invest in the market at all. The average stock's price, over long periods of time, tends to rise. In fact, if dividends and capital gains are added together, stocks—over the long run—earn their holders a better yield than bonds. This is because stocks are more risky, and investors in the stock market must be compensated for bearing that risk.

Second, if someone asks you to pay for their stock-picking advice, *don't*. You can do just as well by picking stocks on your own, even if you pick them randomly. The stocks you pick will be as likely to rise or fall as stocks chosen by an expert.

Third, because you have to pay commissions when you trade stocks, you should trade as little as possible. By using a "buy and hold" strategy, you can participate in the long-run, higher-than-bonds rate of return at minimum expense.

Finally, choose a diversified portfolio with different stocks that tend not to rise and fall together. Such a portfolio will have less risk than an undiversified portfolio with the same expected rate of return. The investor who follows the implications of the efficient markets hypothesis will assemble a diversified set of stocks and then hold on to them, buying and selling only when new cash comes in or cash needs to be taken out.

Summary

Physical capital, human capital, and financial assets all provide future benefits to their owners that can be obtained by purchasing the asset that generates them. The principle of asset valuation tells us how firms and individuals determine the value of any long-lived asset—the total present value of all the future income the asset will generate.

If a firm's physical capital lasted forever, or could be rented indefinitely at a constant price per period, it would find the profit-maximizing quantity of capital just as it finds the profit-maximizing quantity of labor: increasing its use of capital until its marginal revenue product (MRP) per period equaled its marginal factor cost per period. However, because capital does not last forever, a different decision process must be used. The firm should buy any unit of capital for which the total present value of all future years' MRPs is greater than the purchase price. This total present value will be smaller when interest rates are higher. Therefore, higher interest rates discourage investment in physical capital.

Human capital can be divided between general human capital—valuable at many firms—and specific human capital—mostly valuable at just one firm. While firms will generally pay for their workers to acquire specific human capital, it is up to individual workers to acquire their own general human capital. Higher interest rates discourage investment in human capital, just as they do for physical capital.

There are many types of financial markets, including those for bonds and corporate stock. The price of a bond will equal the total present value of its future payments. The value of a share of corporate stock is the total present value of the future after-tax profits of the firm divided by the number of shares outstanding. This value depends on the firm's current profit, the expected growth rate of profits, the interest rate in the economy, and the risk associated with the firm's future profits. In an efficient market, the price of corporate shares will reflect all available information. There will be no predictable patterns in stock price movements that can be exploited for profit.

Key Terms

Bond
Capital gain
Coupon payments
Discount rate
Discounting
Dividend
Dow Jones Industrial Average
Efficient market
Financial asset

Fundamental analysis
General human capital
Investment
Marginal revenue product of capital
Maturity date
Mutual fund
Present value
Primary market
Principal (face value)

Principle of asset valuation
Pure discount bond
Secondary market
Share of stock
Specific human capital
Standard & Poor's 500
Technical analysis
Yield

Review Questions   *Answers to even-numbered Questions and Problems can be found on the text Web site at http://hall-lieb.swlearning.com.*

1. What is the marginal revenue product of capital? How is it calculated, and how is it related to the demand for capital?

2. Why is $100 received today more valuable than $100 received one year from today?

3. What is the present value of $1,000 to be received two years from today? Assume that the relevant interest rate is 10 percent per year.

4. What is the relationship between the present value of a future payment and (1) the size of that payment, (2) the

interest rate, and (3) the date at which the payment will be received?

5. What is the principle of asset valuation? Give examples of how it would be used to value a piece of physical capital, general human capital, and a bond.

6. Give examples of general and specific human capital (other than those presented in the chapter).

7. Explain the relationship between:
   a. a bond's price and its yield
   b. a bond's price and the riskiness of the firm that issued it
   c. a bond's price and its face value

8. Why would a corporation care about the price of its stock in the secondary market?

9. What are the economic roles played by financial markets? How do they help the economy operate more efficiently and grow more rapidly?

10. What is the efficient markets view of the stock market? What are its main implications?

11. Identify each of the following as either general or specific human capital, and state whether the firm or the employee will pay for each:
   a. a program that introduces newly hired workers to the company's systems, procedures, and policies
   b. a program that teaches workers how to use Excel spreadsheets
   c. a program that teaches workers how to use blow torches
   d. a program that teaches workers how to run the company's ventilation system
   e. a university master's degree program in electrical engineering

Problems and Exercises

1. You are considering buying a new laser printer to use in your part-time desktop publishing business. The printer will cost $380, and you expect it to produce additional revenue of $100 per year for each of the next five years. At the end of the fifth year, it will be worthless. Answer the following questions:
   a. What is the value of the printer to you if the annual interest rate is 10 percent? Is the purchase of the printer justified?
   b. Would your answer to part (a) change if the interest rate were 8 percent? Is the purchase justified in that case? Explain.
   c. Would your answer to part (a) change if the printer cost $350? Is the purchase justified in that case?
   d. Would your answer to part (a) change if the printer could be sold for $500 at the end of the fifth year? Is the purchase justified in that case? Explain.

   What lessons can you derive from your answers to these questions?

2. Your inventory manager has asked you to approve the purchase of a new inventory control software package. The software will cost $200,000 and will last for four years, after which it will become obsolete. If you do not approve this purchase, your company will have to hire two new inventory clerks, at salaries of $30,000 per year. Answer the following questions:
   a. Should you approve the purchase of the inventory control software if the annual interest rate is 7 perceent?
   b. Would your answer to part (a) change if the annual interest rate is 9 percent? Explain.
   c. Would your answer to part (a) change if the software cost $220,000? Explain.

d. Would your answer to part (d) change if the software would not become obsolete until the last day of its sixth year?

3. Ice Age Ice is trying to decide how many $150,000 commercial ice makers to buy. Assume that each machine is expected to last for seven years. Complete the following table if the appropriate discount rate is 5 percent. How many ice makers should Ice Age Ice purchase? How low would the price per machine have to fall before the firm would buy four ice makers?

Ice Machines	Additional Annual Revenue (MRP)	Total Present of Value Additional Revenue over seven years
1	$26,000	
2	$25,000	
3	$16,000	
4	$12,000	
5	$ 6,000	

4. Your firm is considering purchasing some computers. Each computer costs $2,600, and each has an annual marginal revenue product. Because you plan to use the computers for different purposes, you have ranked those purposes in descending order or annual MRP as follows:

Computer	Annual MRP
1	$3,000
2	$2,000
3	$1,000
4	$ 500

a. Assume that each computer has a useful life of three years, and no value thereafter. If the interest rate is 10 percent per year, how many computers should you purchase?

b. If, before you purchased the computers, the interest rate decreased to 5 percent per year, how many computers would you purchase?

5. A drug manufacturer is considering how many of four new drugs to develop. Suppose it takes one year and $10 million to develop a new drug, with the entire cost being paid up front (immediately). The expected yearly profits from the new drugs will begin in the *second* year, and are given in the table below:

Drug	Annual Profit
A	$ 7 million
B	$5.5 million
C	$ 5 million
D	$ 4 million

These profits accrue *only* while the drug is protected by a patent; once the patent runs out, profit is zero.

a. If the interest rate is 10 percent and patents are granted for just two years, which drugs should be developed?

b. If the interest rate is 10 percent and patents are granted for 3 years, which drugs should be developed?

c. Answer (a) and (b) again, this time assuming the interest rate is 5 percent.

d. Based on your answers above, what is the relationship between new drug development and (1) the interest rate; (2) the duration of patent protection?

e. Is there any downside to a change in patent duration designed to speed the development of new drugs? Explain briefly.

6. In each of the following cases, determine what would happen to the amount of human capital that individuals or firms would decide to invest in.

a. State governments invest significant amounts of money in building new colleges and universities.

b. New teaching methods increase the amount of knowledge that students accumulate in each course.

c. The overall interest rate in the economy increases.

d. Because employers are seeking a more skilled workforce, the average wage rate for college graduates increases.

7. Explain in what sense labor markets are similar to capital markets, and in what sense they are different.

8. Good news! Gold has just been discovered in your backyard. Mining engineers tell you that you can expect to extract five ounces of gold per year forever. Gold is currently selling for $400 per ounce, and that price is not expected to change. If the interest rate is 5 percent per year, estimate the total value of your gold mine.

9. One year ago, you bought a two-year bond for $900. The bond has a face value of $1,000 and has one year left until maturity. It promises one additional interest payment of $50 at the maturity date. If the current interest rate is 5 percent per year, what capital gain (or loss) can you expect if you sell the bond today?

10. Suppose a bond has a face value of $100,000 with a maturity date three years from now. The bond also gives coupon payments of $5,000 at the end of each of the next three years. What will this bond sell for if the interest rate is
a. 5 percent?
b. 10 percent?

11. Suppose a bond has a face value of $250,000 with a maturity date four years from now. The bond also gives coupon payments of $8,000 at the end of each of the next four years.

a. What will this bond sell for if the interest rate is 4 percent?

b. What will this bond sell for if the interest rate is 5 percent?

c. What is the relationship between bond price and bond yield in this exercise?

12. Suppose that people are sure that a firm will earn annual profit of $10 per share forever. If the interest rate is 10 percent, how much will people pay for a share of this firm's stock? Suppose that people become uncertain about future profits, causing them to use a discount rate of 15 percent. How much will they pay now?

Challenge Questions

1. Suppose you are thinking about attending medical school. Your medical education will cost $15,000 per year, and you expect to receive your M.D. degree in four years. (The annual costs of $15,000 are the opportunity cost of your education; they include such items as foregone wages and tuition, but do not include food and shelter, which you would consume in any case.) Suppose you expect that, as a result of becoming a physician, your earnings will be $5,000 per year higher than they would have been had you gone to work immediately after earning your bachelor's degree. Assume that the interest rate is 10 percent per year and that your working life expectancy is 20 years. Is the decision to attend medical school justified as an economic investment? Identify the purely economic factors that could change the judgment about medical school as an investment.

2. The asset value formula can be modified to account for variable interest rates over time. For a three-year time horizon, the modified formula would be:

$$\text{Value} = \frac{Y_1}{(1 + r_1)} + \frac{Y_2}{(1 + r_1)(1 + r_2)} + \frac{Y_3}{(1 + r_1)(1 + r_2)(1 + r_3)}$$

where r_1, r_2, and r_3 are the interest rates in years 1, 2, and 3, respectively. Suppose a firm is considering two projects—A and B—with the following costs and revenues:

Project	Cost	Year 1 Revenue	Year 2 Revenue	Year 3 Revenue
A	50	20	20	20
B	33	20	30	40

Use this information to determine which of the projects should be undertaken if:

a. The sequence of interest rates is $r_1 = 0.1$, $r_2 = 0.11$, $r_3 = 0.121$ (i.e., interest rates grow by 10 percent per year starting from an interest rate of 10 percent).

b. The sequence of interest rates is $r_1 = 0.1$, $r_2 = 0.09$, $r_3 = 0.081$ (i.e., interest rates decline by 10 percent per year starting from an interest rate of 10 percent).

c. What lesson can you derive from your answers in parts (a) and (b)?

 *These exercises require access to Hall/Lieberman Xtra! If Xtra! did not come with your book, visit http://hallxtra.swlearning.com to purchase.*

1. Use your Xtra! Password at the Hall and Lieberman Web site (http://hallxtra.swlearning.com), select this chapter, and under Economic Applications, click on EconNews. Choose *Microeconomics: Resource Markets,* and scroll down to find the article, "Sweet and Sour Outlook for U.S. Chip Industry." Read the article summary, and using your understanding of the marginal productivity of capital, draw a graph outlining why firms would be investing much more heavily in China than in other countries such as the United States.

2. Use your Xtra! password at the Hall and Lieberman Web site (http://hallxtra.swlearning.com), select this chapter,

and under Economic Applications, click on EconNews. Choose *Microeconomics: Labor Markets,* and scroll down to find the article "College: To Go or Not to Go—That Is the Question." Read the article summary, and answer the questions below.

a. What is the article's argument about the investment in human capital from going to college?

b. Are unskilled workers in this article receiving general training or specific training as they work? Explain your answer.

c. If this trend continues, what will happen to overall college attendance?

Economic Efficiency
and the Role of Government

In nations around the world, virtually every disagreement about the economy ultimately leads to the government. And some disagreements start there as well.

In the United States, for example, hardly a day goes by without a speech in Congress attacking or applauding the government's spending on defense, education, environmental programs, and more. There are also sharp disagreements about the *role* the government should play in our economic life. Should it help people send their children to private schools by giving them vouchers? Should it discourage the merger of two large airlines? Should local governments be collecting the trash and running the prisons, rather than contracting these services out to private firms? Even events that originate almost entirely in the private economy—such as an accounting scandal at a major corporation, the closing of a large factory, or a drop in stock prices—invariably lead to a sharp disagreement over what government should do. Similar controversies exist in other developed market economies, such as the nations of the European Union or Japan.

But all of these disagreements tend to obscure a remarkable degree of *agreement* about the economy, and the government's role in it. For example, the vast majority of goods and services that you buy in stores, over the Internet, or obtain in other ways are provided by *private firms,* and almost everyone agrees that's how it should be. Hardly anyone proposes that the government should be providing the economy's books, jeans, computers, restaurant meals, entertainment, or soft drinks. At the same time, there is widespread agreement that certain goods and services *should* be provided by government, and government alone, such as general police protection, the court system, and national defense.

Much of this agreement is based on ideas about *economic efficiency*—the organizing theme of this chapter. As you'll see, there is more to the concept of efficiency than appears at first glance. It enables us to understand why markets often perform so well, and why they sometimes don't. And efficiency helps us define a role for government involvement in the economy about which there is broad agreement.

THE MEANING OF EFFICIENCY

What, exactly, do we mean by the word *efficiency*? We all use this word, or its opposite, in our everyday conversation: "I wish I could organize my time more efficiently," "He's such an inefficient worker," "Our office is organized very efficiently," and so on. In each of these cases, we use the word *inefficient* to mean "wasteful" and *efficient* to mean "the absence of waste."

In economics, too, efficiency means the absence of waste, although a very specific kind of waste: *the waste of an opportunity to make someone better off without harming anyone else.* More specifically,

economic efficiency *is achieved when we cannot rearrange the production or allocation of goods to make one person better off without making anybody else worse off.*

Notice that economic efficiency is a limited concept. While it is an important goal for a society, it is not the only goal. Most of us would list fairness as another important social goal. But an economy can be efficient even if most people are extremely poor and a few are extraordinarily rich, a situation that many of us would regard as unfair.

An efficient economy is not necessarily a fair economy.

Why, then, do economists put so much stress on efficiency, rather than on issues of fairness? Largely because it is so much easier for people to agree about efficiency. We all define fairness differently, depending on our different ethical and moral views. Issues of fairness must therefore be resolved politically.

But virtually all of us would agree that if we fail to take actions that would make some people in our society better off *without harming anyone*—that is, if we fail to achieve economic efficiency—we have wasted a valuable opportunity. Economics—by helping us understand the preconditions for economic efficiency and teaching us how we can bring about those preconditions—can make a major contribution to our material well-being.

PARETO IMPROVEMENTS

Imagine the following scenario: A boy and a girl are having lunch in elementary school. The boy frowns at a peanut butter and jelly sandwich, which, on this particular day, makes the girl's mouth water. She says, "Wanna trade?" The boy looks at her chicken sandwich, considers a moment, and says, "Okay."

This little scene, which is played out thousands of times every day in schools around the country, is an example of a trade in which both parties are made better off and no one is harmed. And as simple as it seems, such trading is at the core of the concept of economic efficiency. It is an example of a *Pareto* (pronounced puh-RAY-toe) *improvement,* named after the Italian economist, Vilfredo Pareto (1848–1923), who first systematically explored the issue of economic efficiency.

Pareto improvement An action that makes at least one person better off, and harms no one.

> A *Pareto improvement* is any action that makes at least one person better off, and harms no one.

In a market economy such as that in the United States, where trading is voluntary, literally hundreds of millions of Pareto improvements take place every day. Almost every purchase is an example of a Pareto improvement. If you pay $30 for a pair of jeans, then the jeans must be worth more to you than the $30 that you parted with or you wouldn't have bought them. Thus, you are better off after making the purchase. On the other side, the owner of the store must have valued your $30 more highly than he valued the jeans or he wouldn't have sold them to you. So she is better off, too. Your purchase of the jeans, like virtually every purchase made by every consumer every day, is an example of a Pareto improvement.

The notion of a Pareto improvement helps us arrive at a formal definition of economic efficiency:

> *Economic efficiency is achieved when every possible Pareto improvement is exploited.*

This definition can be applied to an individual market or to the economy as a whole. For example, suppose we look at the market for laser printers and cannot identify a single Pareto improvement in that market that has not already been exploited. No matter how hard we look, we cannot find a change in price or output level, or any other change for that matter, that would make some producer or some consumer better off without harming anyone. Then we would say that the market for laser printers is economically efficient.

Alternatively, we can look at the economy as a whole. If we discover remaining Pareto improvements that are not occurring—say, a change in the price of some good or a change in the quantity of a good produced—then we would deem the economy economically inefficient.

Of course, no economy can exploit *every* Pareto improvement, so no society can ever be completely economically efficient according to our definition. But achieving something close to economic efficiency is an important goal. When we look at real-world markets and real-world economies, it is best to view economic efficiency as a continuum. At one end of the continuum are economies in which, in most markets, most opportunities for Pareto improvements are exploited. At the other end of the continuum are economies in which many markets are economically inefficient—where many opportunities for mutual gain remain unexploited. As you will see in this chapter, perfectly competitive markets tend to be economically efficient, and well-functioning market economies tend to lie close to the economically efficient end of the spectrum.

Side Payments and Pareto Improvements

The examples of Pareto improvements we've considered so far involve easily arranged transactions, in which one person trades with another and both come out ahead. Since both parties benefit, they have every incentive to find each other and trade.

But there are more complicated situations in which a Pareto improvement will come about only if one side makes a special kind of payment to the other, which we call a *side payment*. These are situations in which an action, without the side payment, would benefit one group and harm another.

Here's a simple example. Suppose the owner of an empty lot wants to build a movie theater on her property. Many people might gain from the theater: the owner of the empty lot, moviegoers, the theater's employees, and more. But the residents in the immediate vicinity might be harmed, because the theater will bring noise and traffic congestion.

Imagine that we can measure the dollar value of the gains and losses for each person in the town, and when we sum them up, we find that the total benefits to the gainers are valued at $100,000 while the total harm to the losers is valued at $70,000.

Building the theater—by itself—would *not* be a Pareto improvement, because while some would benefit, others would be hurt. But suppose we could easily arrange for the gainers to pay, say, an $80,000 *side payment* to those harmed. Then, as long as the side payment is made, and distributed properly, *everyone* would come out ahead: Building the theater would be a Pareto improvement.

How do we know that everyone would come out ahead? Because the gainers' benefits of $100,000 are large enough to pay the $80,000 side payment and still have some gains left over. The harm to the losers of $70,000 is small enough so that, when they receive the $80,000 side payment, they actually are better off. These results can be easily seen in the scorecard below:

Action: Build the movie theater (with $80,000 side payment).

Gainers	Effect before side payment:	+$100,000
(theater owner,	Side payment (given):	−$ 80,000
moviegoers, etc.)	Net effect:	+$ 20,000
Losers	Effect before side payment:	−$ 70,000
(nearby residents)	Side payment (received):	+$ 80,000
	Net effect:	+$ 10,000

If you experiment around a bit, you'll see that *any* side payment greater than $70,000 and less than $100,000 would turn this action into a Pareto improvement.

More generally,

if an action creates greater total benefits for gainers than total harm to losers, then a side payment exists which, if transferred from gainers to losers, would make the action a Pareto improvement.

Any side payment with a value between the total benefits to the gainers and the total losses to the losers will do the trick.

This has an important implication for economic efficiency. If there is an action that benefits some more than it harms others, and *if an appropriate side payment can be easily arranged*, then *not* taking the action is a waste of an opportunity to make everyone better off. Economic efficiency requires that we find, and exploit, opportunities that—with side payments—would be Pareto improvements.

But reread the italicized words in the paragraph above. The appropriate side payment—as you'll see later in the chapter—is *not* always easy to arrange. In many instances, arranging a side payment to ensure that everyone benefits has high costs. It may be that, after deducting these costs, too little would be left to adequately compensate the losers while still leaving the gainers better off. When a side payment *cannot* be made—or for any reason is *not* made—then even though the action might create greater gain than harm, it might not be considered fair. Achieving the efficient outcome then becomes *one* consideration, but not the only one. We'll come back to this important issue of side payments later in the chapter and see how it justifies, on efficiency grounds, many instances of government involvement.

MARKETS AND ECONOMIC EFFICIENCY

Now let's turn our attention from the isolated example of a single action—building the movie theater—to consider Pareto improvements and economic efficiency in *markets*. Remember that in a market system, firms and consumers are largely free to produce and consume as they wish, without anyone orchestrating the process from above. Can we expect such unsupervised trading to be economically efficient? That is, will the quantity bought and sold in each market exploit all possible Pareto improvements?

In this section, you'll see that the answer is a conditional yes . . . as long as trading takes place in *perfectly competitive markets*. To demonstrate this, we'll return to the tools we've used to analyze competitive markets: demand and supply curves. But we'll look at them in a slightly different way.

Reinterpreting the Demand Curve

Figure 1 shows a market demand curve for guitar lessons: the quantity demanded per week at each price. It also indicates who would be taking each lesson. For example, at a price of $25, only Flo—who values guitar lessons the most—takes a lesson, so quantity demanded in the market is one. If the price drops to $23, Joe will take one weekly lesson, so quantity demanded is two. At $21, Flo will decide to take a second lesson each week, so quantity demanded rises to three. This is the standard way of thinking about a market demand curve.

But we can also view the curve in a different way: It tells us the maximum price someone would be willing to pay for each unit of the good. Therefore, it tells us how much that unit is *worth* to the person who buys it. In Figure 1, for example, the maximum value of the first lesson to some consumer in the market is just a tiny bit greater than $25. How do we know this? Because Flo, who values this lesson more highly than anyone else, will not buy it at any price greater than $25. But if the price falls to $25, she will buy it. When she decides to buy it, she must be getting at least a tiny bit more in value than the $25 she is giving up. So the value of that first lesson must be just a tiny bit more than $25. Ignoring for the moment the phrase "tiny bit more," we can say that the first lesson in the market is worth $25 to some consumer (Flo), the second is worth $23 to some consumer (Joe), and the third is worth $21 (Flo again).

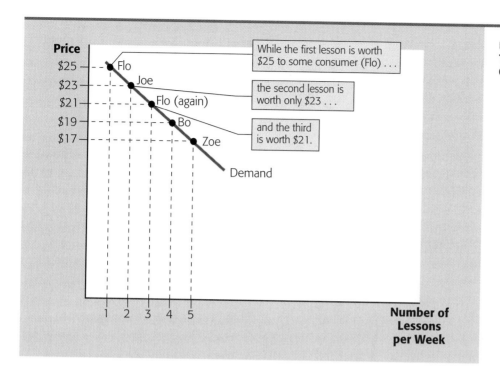

FIGURE 1

The Marginal Benefit from Guitar Lessons

Notice that each guitar lesson in the market has a different value. In part, this is because consumers differ in their incomes and tastes. (For example, based on differences in their incomes or tastes, Flo values one lesson per week more than does Joe.) But also, for each individual, the value of additional lessons declines as more lessons are taken. Flo, for example, values her first weekly lesson at $25, but her second at only $21.

Of course, in Figure 1, we've simplified by assuming there are very few consumers in the market for guitar lessons. This makes the graph easier to read. But the point is the same whether there are 5 consumers in the market, or 500, or 50,000. In general,

the height of the market demand curve at any quantity shows us the value— to someone—of the last unit of the good consumed.

Reinterpreting the Supply Curve

Now let's look at the other side of the market: those who *supply* guitar lessons. Figure 2 shows us a supply curve for guitar lessons: the quantity offered each week at various prices. The figure also indicates who would be supplying each lesson. For example, at a price of $13, Martin would offer one lesson each week. If the price rose to $15, Martin would offer two lessons per week, and at $17, another teacher—Gibson—would enter the market and offer a third.

But this supply curve also tells us the minimum price a seller must get in order to supply that lesson. For example, for the first lesson, the price would have to be at least $13. At any price less than that, no one will offer it. Similarly, $15 is the minimum price it would take to get some producer in this market (Martin again) to supply the second lesson, and $17 is what it would take for the third lesson to be supplied (Gibson this time).

FIGURE 2
The Marginal Cost of Guitar Lessons

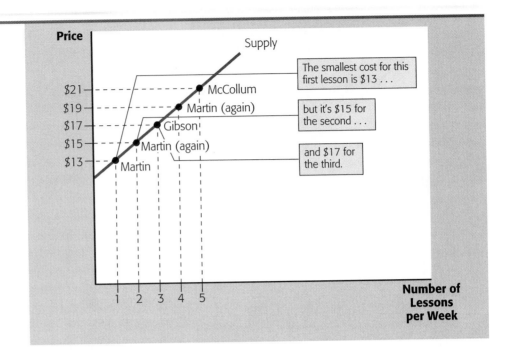

Why does it take higher prices to get more lessons? Because offering lessons is *costly* to guitar teachers. Not only do they have to rent studio space, but they must also use their time, which comes at an opportunity cost. In order to convince a teacher to supply a guitar lesson, the price must *at least* cover the additional costs of giving that lesson. And even if studio rental costs remain the same for all teachers and all lessons, guitar teachers will still value the opportunity cost of their time differently.

The minimum price that would convince Martin, Gibson, or any other teacher to supply a lesson will be the amount that just barely compensates for the additional cost of that lesson—and a tiny bit more. Ignoring the phrase "a tiny bit more," we can say that

> *the height of the market supply curve at any quantity shows us the additional cost—to some producer—of each unit of the good supplied.*[1]

The Efficient Quantity of a Good

Figure 3 combines the supply and demand curves for guitar lessons. Remember that the demand curve shows us the *value* of each lesson to some *consumer* and the supply curve shows us the additional *cost* of each lesson to some producer. We can then find the efficient quantity of weekly guitar lessons by using the following logical principle:

> *Whenever—at some quantity—the demand curve is* higher *than the supply curve, the value of one more unit to some consumer is greater than its additional cost to some producer.*

[1] If you've been reading the chapters in order, you'll recognize *additional cost* as *marginal cost*, first introduced in Chapter 6 and discussed in later chapters. That is, the height of the supply curve tells us the lowest marginal cost at which each unit could be supplied in the market.

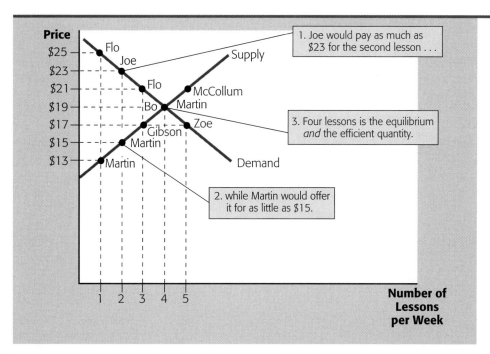

FIGURE 3
Efficiency in the Market for Guitar Lessons

This means that when the supply curve lies above the demand curve, we can always find a price for one more unit that makes both the consumer and the producer better off: a Pareto improvement.

Here's an example: Look at the *second* lesson in the figure. Tracing up vertically, we see that the demand curve (with a height of $23) lies above the supply curve (with a height of $15). That tells us that some consumer—Joe—values this lesson more than it would cost some teacher—Martin—to provide it. If Joe can *buy* the lesson at any price *less than $23*, he comes out ahead; if Martin can *sell* it for any price *greater than $15*, he comes out ahead. So, at any price *between $15 and $23*, both will come out ahead and no one is harmed: a Pareto improvement.

The scorecard below illustrates what would happen at one such price: $17. (In case you're wondering, we're purposely avoiding the equilibrium price in this market, in order to show that these calculations can be made for more than one price.)

Action: Provide the second weekly guitar lesson at a price of $17.

Martin	Effect before payment:	−$15
(sells lesson)	Payment (received):	+$17
	Net effect:	+$ 2
Joe	Effect before payment:	+$23
(buys lesson)	Payment (given):	−$17
	Net effect:	+$ 6

When the price is $17, Joe comes out ahead by $6 and Martin by $2. But if you change the price to any value between $15 and $23, and construct a similar scorecard, you'll see that while the *distribution* of the net gains between Joe and Martin will change, they will both still come out ahead. Moreover, their *total* gain will always be $8—the difference between the value of the lesson to Joe and the cost of producing it to Martin.

Continuing in this way, we find that the third lesson, and even the fourth, could be offered as Pareto improvements. (The fourth would be only a *slight* Pareto improvement, because its value is just a tiny bit greater than $19 and its cost a tiny bit less than $19.)

What about lessons for which the demand curve is *lower* than the supply curve—such as the fifth? Then there is *no* price at which both could come out ahead. To Zoe, the consumer who values the fifth weekly lesson the most, it's worth only $17. And for McCollum, the one who could provide it at the lowest additional cost, that cost would be $21. Producing this lesson could not be a Pareto improvement—no matter what the price—since the lowest cost of providing it is greater than its highest value to anyone in the market. Someone must be harmed: either the buyer or seller, or possibly both. (An end-of-chapter problem asks you to show that, if the fifth lesson *were* being produced, then *not* producing it—along with a possible side payment—would be a Pareto improvement.)

Let's recap: Whenever the demand curve lies *above* the supply curve, producing the lesson is a Pareto improvement. Whenever the demand curve lies *below* the supply curve, producing the lesson can*not* be a Pareto improvement. This tells us that the efficient quantity of guitar lessons—the quantity at which all Pareto improvements are exploited—is where the demand curve and supply curve intersect. At this quantity, the value of the last unit produced will be equal to (or possibly a tiny bit greater than) the cost of providing it.

> *The efficient quantity of a good is the quantity at which the market demand curve and market supply curves intersect.*

Perfect Competition and Efficiency

As you learned in Chapter 3 (and again in Chapter 8), when markets behave as the model of perfect competition predicts, the price adjusts until the market quantity reaches its *equilibrium:* where the market demand curve and market supply curve intersect. But we've just seen that this quantity is also the *economically efficient* quantity—the one that exploits all possible Pareto improvements. This gives us a very important and powerful result:

> *In a well-functioning, perfectly competitive market, the* equilibrium *quantity is also the* efficient *quantity.*

Let's consider this statement carefully. It tells us that, if we leave producers and consumers alone to trade with each other as they wish, then—as long as the market is working well and it's perfectly competitive—the market will exploit every opportunity to make someone better off that doesn't harm anyone else. No special side payments need to be arranged, because the price paid for the good *is itself* the side payment.

Furthermore, we know that the *types* of goods produced in competitive markets will reflect consumer preferences. Goods that are valued by some people greater than the additional cost it would take to provide them *will* be provided in the market. The mutual gain possible for buyers and sellers creates the incentive for trading. But if a good has such low value, relative to its cost, that the demand curve lies below the supply curve at *all* quantities, it will *not* be provided. Mutual gain from

© MICHAEL NEWMAN/PHOTOEDIT, INC.

If the market for guitar lessons is perfectly competitive, the equilibrium quantity will be the efficient quantity.

providing the good is not possible. (You may want to draw the supply and demand graph for such a good to see what it looks like.) This is why you don't find chocolate-covered Brussels sprouts in any store, even though there may be a few people who would pay some small amount for them.

The notion that perfect competition—where many buyers and sellers each try to do the best for themselves—actually delivers efficient markets is one of the most important ideas in economics. The great British economist of the 18th century, Adam Smith, coined the term *invisible hand* to describe the force that leads a competitive economy relentlessly and automatically toward economic efficiency:

> *[The individual] neither intends to promote the public interest, nor knows how much he is promoting it . . . he intends only his own gain, and he is in this, as in many other cases, led by an* invisible hand *to promote an end which was not part of his intention.*[2]

We can recognize the *end* promoted by the invisible hand as the economically efficient outcome.

MEASURING MARKET GAINS

It often proves useful to *measure* the benefits that producers and consumers receive from their economic activities. One reason is that when markets are *not* perfectly competitive, or when they fail to function in other ways, they are *inefficient*. By comparing the benefits in an inefficient market with its *potential* benefits, we can estimate what we lose from the inefficiency. In this section, you'll learn how economists measure the total benefits traders receive in a market—or the potential benefits they *could* receive but don't.

Consumer Surplus

Let's start with the benefits enjoyed by consumers in a market. Consumers rarely have to pay what a unit of a good is actually worth to them. Regardless of how much they value the good, they can buy all they choose at the market price. For example, in panel (a) of Figure 4, the market price of guitar lessons is assumed to be $19. So Flo is able to buy her first lesson at $19, even though that lesson is *worth* $25 to her. By being able to purchase the lesson for less than its value to her, Flo gets a net benefit—called *consumer surplus*—on that lesson.

> *A buyer's **consumer surplus** on a unit of a good is the difference between its value to the buyer and what the buyer* actually *pays for that unit.*

Consumer surplus The difference between the value of a unit of a good to the buyer and what the buyer actually pays for it.

Flo's consumer surplus on the first lesson is equal to $25 − $19 = $6. It can be represented graphically by the *shaded area* of the first (leftmost) rectangle in the upper panel, which has a base of one unit and height of $6 (from $19 to $25).

Continuing down the demand curve, the consumer surplus on the *second* guitar lesson purchased in this market (by Joe) would be what that lesson is worth to him ($23) minus what he actually pays ($19), or $23 − $19 = $4. This is represented by the shaded area of the second, smaller rectangle. In similar fashion, the area of

---

[2] Adam Smith, *The Wealth of Nations* (Modern Library Classics edition, 2000), p. 423.

FIGURE 4
Consumer Surplus in a Small and a Large Market for Guitar Lessons

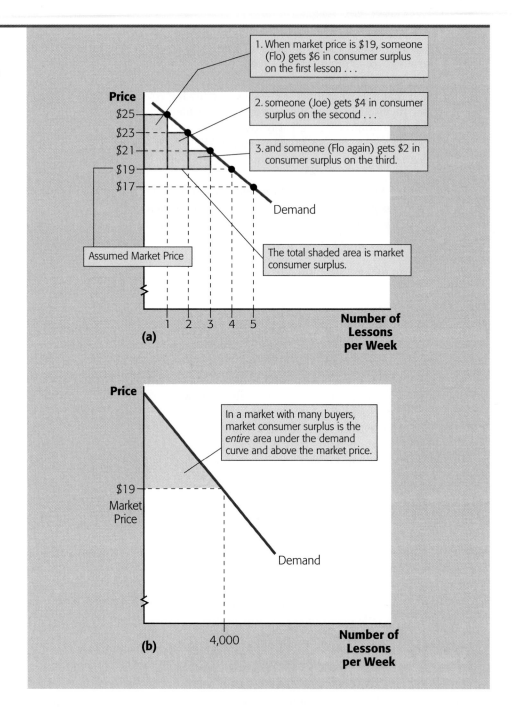

the third rectangle gives us a $2 consumer surplus on the third lesson (Flo again). The fourth lesson is purchased by Bo. Since the most he'd be willing to pay for that lesson is $19, its value to him is at most a tiny bit more than $19—say, $19.01. When the market price is $19, Bo will buy the lesson, but he hardly gets any consumer surplus at all—so little that we can safely ignore it.

The total consumer surplus enjoyed by *all* consumers in a market is called **market consumer surplus,** the sum of the consumer surplus on all units (the areas of the

Market consumer surplus The total consumer surplus enjoyed by all consumers in a market.

shaded rectangles). In the figure, with the price of guitar lessons at $19, market consumer surplus is $6 + $4 + $2 = $12. Notice that this is *roughly* equal to the entire shaded area under the demand curve and above the market price of $19. We say *roughly*, because the shaded area in the upper panel includes some little unshaded triangles. Because our example has only five consumers in the market, these triangles appear rather large.

Panel (b) of Figure 4 shows a larger market—one we might find in a large city, with thousands of potential guitar students. In such a market, a one-unit width for each rectangle would be very small, and the unshaded triangles would be so insignificant that including them as part of consumer surplus hardly makes a difference in our measure. This is why, in the lower panel, we've indicated the market consumer surplus as the *entire* shaded area under the demand curve and above the market price.

> *Market consumer surplus at any price, measured in dollars, is the total area* under *the market demand curve and* above *the market price.*

Producer Surplus

Now let's turn to the supply side of the market. Only in the rarest of situations does a supplier have to sell each unit of a good at the lowest acceptable price—the additional cost of producing that unit. As long as there are *many* sellers and each is too small to influence the market price, each can sell all the units he chooses at that price.

For example, in panel (a) of Figure 5, the market price of guitar lessons is $19. Martin is able to sell the first lesson at $19 even though he'd be *willing* to sell it for as little as $13, which would just barely cover the additional costs of supplying it (studio rental, opportunity cost of time, and so on). By being able to sell the lesson for *more* than $13, Martin gets a net benefit—called *producer surplus*—on that lesson.

> *An individual seller's **producer surplus** on a unit of a good is the difference between what the seller actually gets and the additional cost of providing it.*

Producer surplus The difference between what the seller actually gets for a unit of a good and the cost of providing it.

Martin's producer surplus on the first lesson is equal to $19 − $13 = $6. It can be represented graphically by the *shaded area* of the first (leftmost) rectangle in the upper panel, which has a base of one unit and height of $6 (from $13 to $19).

Continuing up the supply curve, the producer surplus on the *second* guitar lesson (Martin again) is the price for that lesson ($19) minus the lowest amount that would get Martin to supply it ($15), or $19 − $15 = $4. This is represented by the shaded area of the second, smaller rectangle. In similar fashion, the area of the third rectangle gives us the producer surplus on the third lesson (Gibson), equal to $2. The fourth lesson would be provided by Martin once again. Since the lowest price he'd be willing to accept in exchange for that lesson is $19, the additional cost to him is at most a tiny bit less than $19—say, $18.99. When the market price is $19, Martin will sell that lesson, but he hardly gets any producer surplus at all—so little that we can safely ignore it.

The total producer surplus gained by *all* sellers in a market is called **market producer surplus,** found by adding up the producer surplus (the areas of the shaded rectangles) gained by *all* sellers in the market. In the figure, with the market price for guitar lessons at $19, market producer surplus is $6 + $4 + $2 = $12. Notice that this is *roughly* equal to the entire shaded area *above* the supply curve and *below* the market price of $19—except for the little unshaded triangles in panel (a).

Market producer surplus The total producer surplus gained by all sellers in a market.

FIGURE 5
Producer Surplus from Selling Guitar Lessons

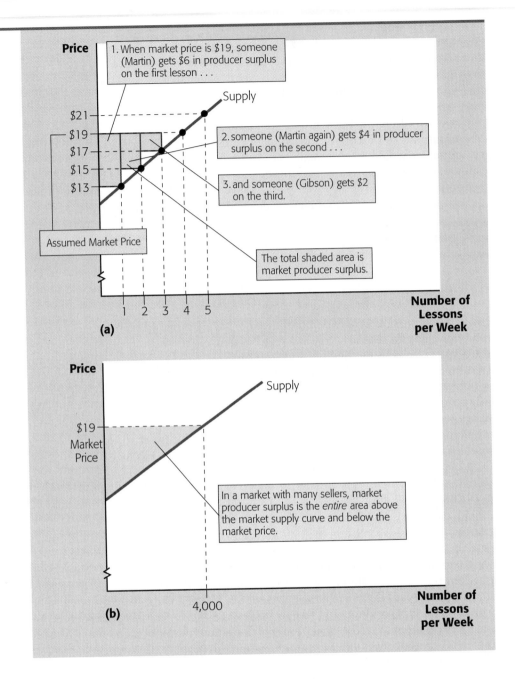

Price

1. When market price is $19, someone (Martin) gets $6 in producer surplus on the first lesson . . .

Supply

$21
$19
$17
$15
$13

2. someone (Martin again) gets $4 in producer surplus on the second . . .

3. and someone (Gibson) gets $2 on the third.

Assumed Market Price

The total shaded area is market producer surplus.

1 2 3 4 5

(a)

Number of Lessons per Week

Price

Supply

$19
Market Price

In a market with many sellers, market producer surplus is the *entire* area above the market supply curve and below the market price.

4,000

(b)

Number of Lessons per Week

Panel (b) of Figure 5 shows a larger market for guitar lessons, which might have hundreds of potential teachers, each capable of offering a dozen or more lessons every week. In such a market, the unshaded triangles are insignificant, so market producer surplus would essentially equal the *entire* shaded area above the supply curve and below the market price.

Market producer surplus at any price, measured in dollars, is the total area above the market supply curve and below the market price.

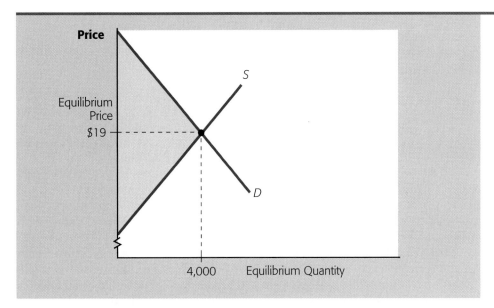

FIGURE 6
**Total Net Benefits in a
Competitive Market for
Guitar Lessons**

*When a competitive market
reaches equilibrium, the sum of
market consumer surplus and
market producer surplus is maximized. At any quantity less
than 4,000 or greater than
4,000, total net benefits will be
smaller.*

Total Net Benefits in a Market

Figure 6 combines the supply and demand curves in the previous figures, for this large-city market for guitar lessons.

The left panel of the figure shows consumer and producer surplus when this perfectly competitive market is in *equilibrium,* with price equal to $19 and quantity equal to 4,000. Market consumer surplus is the area under the demand curve and above the market price, or the blue-shaded area. Market producer surplus is the (red-shaded) area under the market price and above the supply curve. The total shaded area (both blue and red) represents the total net benefits that consumers and producers are receiving from participating in this market.

> *We measure the **total net benefits** gained in a market as the sum of con-
> sumer and producer surplus in that market.*

Total net benefits The sum of
consumer and producer surplus in
a particular market.

Perfect Competition and Efficiency: The Total Benefits View

Each time we make a Pareto improvement in a market, we make at least one party better off and make no one else worse off. Therefore, a Pareto improvement will in-crease the **total net benefits** available in a market—the total of consumer and pro-ducer surplus. But since efficiency requires that all Pareto improvements are ex-ploited in the market, it also requires that the sum of consumer and producer surplus be increased as far as possible. Thus, we have a new way of viewing efficiency:

> *A market is efficient when the sum of producer and consumer surplus is
> maximized in that market.*

Look again at panel (a) of Figure 6. When the market is in equilibrium at 4,000 lessons, the sum of producer and consumer surplus is equal to the shaded area (both blue and red) in the figure. This is also the *maximum* total net benefit achiev-able in this market.

> *In a well-functioning, perfectly competitive market, the* equilibrium *quantity provides the maximum possible benefit to buyers and sellers combined, and is thus the efficient quantity.*

How do we know, in Figure 6, that 4,000 lessons per week provides the maximum possible benefit? If the quantity were *greater* than 4,000, there would be an area of *negative* benefits (an area of losses) that would have to be subtracted from the area of positive net benefits in Figure 6. For example, imagine that the price remained at $19, but guitar teachers were *forced* to offer additional lessons at that price and students were *forced* to take them. Then each lesson beyond 4,000 would harm both guitar teachers (by adding *more* than $19 to costs) and students (because the value is *less* than the $19 they are paying). Of course, in the absence of force, these loss-creating lessons *won't* be provided; the market establishes a price of $19, and buyers and sellers automatically stop at 4,000.

What about a quantity *less* than $4,000? In this case, the area of total net benefit will *not* be maximized: Lessons worth more to buyers than the additional costs to sellers are not being provided, even though there is some price that would create benefits for both. To illustrate this more clearly, let's revisit two policies discussed in Chapter 4 that would reduce market quantity below the equilibrium of 4,000.

A Price Ceiling

In Chapter 4, you learned that a price ceiling imposed on a competitive market creates a *shortage* of the good. You also learned that although some buyers may benefit by being able to buy the good at a lower price, others are harmed by not being able to purchase their quantity demanded and having to go through more trouble and expense to find available supplies. Thus, a price ceiling might help some buyers, but it will harm others. Buyers *as a group* could end up better or worse off.

Here, we'll go further: A price ceiling in a perfectly competitive market—*even if it helps buyers*—creates greater harm for sellers than gains for buyers. That is, the price ceiling reduces the *total* net benefits in the market.

Panel (a) of Figure 7 shows the impact of a $15 price ceiling imposed on the market for guitar lessons. At that price, quantity supplied of 2,000 lessons per week is smaller than quantity demanded of 6,000. Since sellers are the short side of this market, and they can't be forced to offer more than 2,000 lessons, that will be the market quantity bought and sold.

The figure also shows how buyers' and sellers' market benefits are affected by the price ceiling. Producer surplus (shaded in red) is the area above the supply curve and below the new market price of $15, up to 2,000 units. Consumer surplus (in blue) is the area below the demand curve and above $15 also *up to 2000 units.* Even though consumers would like to buy *more* than 2,000 units at a price of $15, we must stop at 2,000 when measuring their surplus: The lessons beyond 2,000 are no longer provided, so no consumer surplus is gained from them.

Comparing the market with the price ceiling (Figure 7) to the market *without* the price ceiling (Figure 6), we find that the blue area measuring consumer surplus (marked B and C) has increased. (It won't always increase, but it does in our example.) But the price floor *decreases* the red area (marked A) measuring producer surplus. (A price ceiling will always reduce producer surplus.)

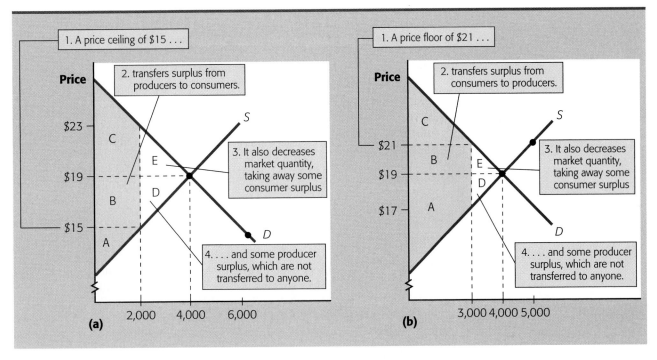

1. A price ceiling of $15 . . .

2. transfers surplus from producers to consumers.

3. It also decreases market quantity, taking away some consumer surplus

4. . . . and some producer surplus, which are not transferred to anyone.

(a)

1. A price floor of $21 . . .

2. transfers surplus from consumers to producers.

3. It also decreases market quantity, taking away some consumer surplus

4. . . . and some producer surplus, which are not transferred to anyone.

(b)

FIGURE 7
Why Price Ceilings and Price Floors Are Inefficient

Moreover, in a perfectly competitive market, the price ceiling will *always* cause total net benefits—the sum of producer and consumer surplus—to fall. The unshaded triangle in Figure 7—the sum of the areas marked D and E—represents the net benefits that *could* be enjoyed in this market, but are *not* enjoyed because the market quantity is 2,000 rather than the efficient quantity of 4,000.

The unshaded areas D and E together are called the *welfare loss* from the price ceiling, because they represent the loss in economic welfare or well-being that *could* be achieved if the market were efficient, but have been lost due to inefficiency.

*The **welfare loss** in a market is the dollar value of potential benefits not achieved due to inefficiency in that market.*

Welfare loss The dollar value of potential benefits not achieved due to inefficiency in a particular market.

Let's take a closer look at how *each* side of the market is affected by the price ceiling, to see where this welfare loss comes from. Compared to the original situation in Figure 6, *buyers* are affected in two ways. On the one hand, they *gain* from a lower price on the 2,000 lessons they still buy. The total value of this gain is represented by the rectangle B. On the other hand, buyers no longer earn *any* consumer surplus on lessons 2,001 to 4,000, which they were previously buying at $19. This loss is the *upper part* of the unshaded triangle, labeled E.

What about *sellers*? Compared to the original situation in Figure 6, sellers are harmed by a lower price on the 2,000 units they sell, represented by the rectangle labeled B—the same rectangle that represents a gain for buyers. Sellers suffer *additional* harm from losing producer surplus on lessons 2,001 to 4,000, which they were previously selling at $19. This loss is the *lower part* of the unshaded triangle, labeled D.

Here's a scorecard summarizing all of these results:

Action: Impose a price ceiling of $17 on the competitive market for guitar lessons.

Buyers	Effect of lower price:	+B
	Effect of fewer lessons:	−E
	Net effect:	B − E
Sellers	Effect of lower price:	−B
	Effect of fewer lessons:	−D
	Net effect:	−(B + D)
Entire Market	Net effect on buyers:	+(B − E)
	Net effect on sellers:	−(B + D)
	Market net effect:	−(E + D)

Notice that, on the first 2,000 lessons, the price ceiling *transfers* surplus area B from sellers to buyers. Total net benefits are not affected by this. But the loss in consumer surplus (E) and producer surplus (D) is not transferred to anyone. This surplus just disappears from the market. Thus, although a price ceiling *may* benefit consumers as a group (as it does in our example), it will always reduce total net benefits in the market.

> *A price ceiling imposed on a perfectly competitive market—by reducing quantity below the efficient level—reduces the total net benefits in the market (causes a welfare loss).*

Calculating the Welfare Loss. To make this more concrete, let's calculate the *dollar value* of the welfare loss caused by the price ceiling—the area of the unshaded triangle formed by areas D and E together. From high school algebra, the area of any triangle is $\frac{1}{2} \times$ base $\times$ height. We can imagine that our triangle has been tipped on its side, so that its *vertical* side is the *base*. This side goes from $15 to $23, so the base has a length of $23 − $15 = $8. Then the horizontal dashed line cutting through the middle of the triangle is its *height*. This line goes from 2,000 to 4,000, so its length is 2,000. Now, applying the formula, we find that the welfare loss = $\frac{1}{2} \times$ base $\times$ height = $\frac{1}{2} \times$ $8 $\times$ 2,000 = $8,000.

In words, when this market is delivering only 2,000 lessons per week instead of the efficient 4,000, guitar teachers and students together lose $8,000 in potential benefits—per *week*. If measured yearly, the welfare loss would be 52 weeks $\times$ $8,000 per week = $416,000 per year.

A Price Floor

Panel (b) of Figure 7 shows the impact of a price *floor* in this market, set at $21 per lesson. At that price, quantity demanded of 3,000 lessons per week is smaller than quantity supplied of 5,000. Now *buyers* are the short side of this market, so 3,000 will be the market quantity.

Producer surplus after the price floor is shaded in red and consumer surplus in blue. Notice that both surpluses are measured only up to 3,000 lessons—the quantity actually provided. Comparing the market with the price floor (Figure 7b) to the market *without* the price floor (Figure 6), we find that the red area measuring producer surplus (marked A and B) has increased. (It won't always decrease, but it does in our example.) But the price floor *decreases* the blue area (marked C) measuring consumer surplus. (A price floor will always reduce consumer surplus.)

Moreover, in a perfectly competitive market, the price floor will *always* shrink total net benefits—the sum of producer and consumer surplus. Using logic analogous to the case of the price ceiling, we see that the price floor *transfers* some surplus (area B) from consumers to producers. But, by eliminating lessons 3,001 to 4,000, the price floor takes away some consumer surplus (area E) and some producer surplus (area D) that is not transferred to anyone.

Here's a scorecard summarizing the results for the price floor:

Action: Impose a price floor of $21 on the competitive market for guitar lessons.

Buyers	Effect of higher price:	−B
	Effect of fewer lessons:	−E
	Net effect:	−(B + E)
Sellers	Effect of higher price:	+B
	Effect of fewer lessons:	−D
	Net effect:	B − D
Entire Market	Net effect on buyers	−(B + E)
	Net effect on sellers	(B − D)
	Market net effect:	−(E + D)

The unshaded triangle in Figure 7—the sum of the areas marked D and E—represents the welfare loss from the price floor, caused by the decrease in quantity to 3,000 from the efficient 4,000.

> *A price floor imposed on a perfectly competitive market—like a price ceiling—reduces quantity below the efficient level. As a result, it reduces the total net benefits in the market (causes a welfare loss).*

An end-of-chapter question asks you to calculate the dollar value of this loss, using the same method described earlier for a price ceiling. (If you want to try it now, keep in mind that we chose a price floor of $21 to make the dollar value of the welfare loss different than in the case of the price ceiling.)

THE EFFICIENCY ROLE OF GOVERNMENT

When a well-functioning, perfectly competitive market is permitted to reach its equilibrium, the outcome is efficient: No opportunities for mutual gain remain unexploited. So it's not surprising that when government intervention *changes* the market quantity (as with a price ceiling or a price floor), the result is *in*efficiency—a welfare loss.

But government can, and does, *contribute* to the economic efficiency of markets, in two crucial ways.

First, the government provides the infrastructure that permits markets to function. Part of the infrastructure is physical—roads, bridges, airports, waterways, and buildings. Equally important is the market system's institutional infrastructure—laws, courts, and regulatory agencies. Although maintaining the institutional infrastructure uses only a small fraction of the nation's resources, the market economy would collapse without it.

The second way government supports market activity is by stepping in when markets are not working properly, that is, when they leave Pareto improvements unexploited.

The rest of this chapter explores these two government contributions to economic efficiency.

THE INSTITUTIONAL INFRASTRUCTURE OF A MARKET ECONOMY

Americans take their institutional infrastructure almost completely for granted. The best way to appreciate the infrastructure of the United States is to visit another country that has a poor one. In many countries, the police are more likely to steal from citizens than to protect them from thievery. In some nations, the people have no effective rights to their own property: Somebody can start building a shack on their land, and the government won't stop him. If a person is injured by a drunk driver, there may be no system for compensating her or punishing the driver. Many nations suffer from powerful mafias that extort protection money by threatening to shut down businesses or physically harm their owners.

For example, a study commissioned by the World Bank estimated that Russian households pay $3 billion in bribes each year, about half the amount they pay in income taxes. Most of the bribes paid by households went to education workers (including teachers!) and traffic police. Russian businesses pay even more in bribes: about $33 billion.[3]

Indonesia has a similar problem. More than half of households and businesses surveyed have been asked for bribes by government officials and others. And almost half of the government officials surveyed acknowledged receiving "unofficial payments."[4] (Teachers—once again—were frequent bribe takers.)

Although these are extreme examples, all too many nations suffer from problems of this type. But in nations with highly developed and stable legal infrastructures, such incidents are the exception rather than the rule. For example, very few students in the United States would even *think* of offering cash to an instructor for a better grade.

Figure 8 shows that when countries are divided into three groups, according to the quality of their institutional infrastructure, there is a strong relation between infrastructure and output per worker. The countries on the left—the ones with the lowest-quality infrastructures—were able to produce only about $3,000 in output per-worker per-year in 1988. These are the nations where property rights are weak, contracts are not enforced, and the government is more often predator than protector of economic activity. In the middle of the figure are countries with medium-quality infrastructures, averaging about $5,500 in output per worker per year. On the right are the best-organized countries, averaging $17,000 in output per worker. In this group, nations with the very best infrastructures—such as the United States—achieved output levels more than double that average.

---

[3] "A Russian Tilts at Graft," *New York Times*, February 10, 2003; and "Report: Russian Society Saturated by Corruption," *Helsingin Sanomat*, International Edition, August 13, 2002 (*http://www.helsinki-hs.net/archive.asp*).

[4] "A Diagnostic Study of Corruption in Indonesia," Partnership for Governance Reform, *Final Report*, February 2002.

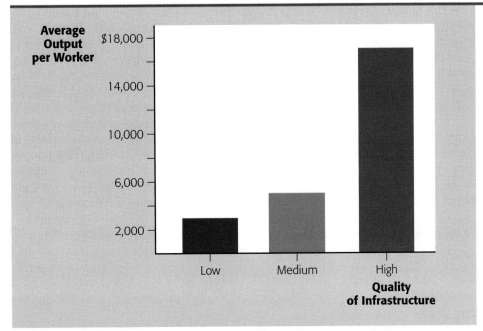

Average Output per Worker

$18,000

14,000

10,000

6,000

2,000

Low   Medium   High

Quality of Infrastructure

FIGURE 8

Government Infrastructure and Output per Worker

Countries with low-quality infrastructures produced an average of only $3,000 per worker per year in 1988. These countries tend to have corrupt governments, poor enforcement of contracts, and weak property rights. Countries with higher-quality infrastructures, including the United States, produced an average of $17,000 per worker per year.

Source: Robert E. Hall and Charles I. Jones, "The Productivity of Nations," Working Paper 5812, National Bureau of Economic Research, November 1997; Robert E. Hall and Charles I. Jones, "Why Do Some Countries Produce So Much More Output per Worker than Others?" *Quarterly Journal of Economics, 114*:83–116, February 1999.

The Legal System

The backbone of a market economy's institutional infrastructure is the legal system. Of course, the legal system is also important for noneconomic reasons. The law protects us from physical and emotional harm, and guarantees us freedom of speech and other vital civil liberties. Here, we will focus on the purely economic role of the legal system—the ways that it supports markets and helps us achieve economic efficiency. We'll look at five very broad categories: criminal law, property law, contract law, tort law, and antitrust law.

Criminal Law. While criminal law has important moral and ethical dimensions, its central economic function is to limit exchanges to voluntary ones. Since both parties agree to a voluntary exchange, they must each benefit from it. Therefore, as long as no third party is harmed, such an exchange will always be a Pareto improvement. But an *involuntary* exchange—robbery, for example—always harms one side.

> *By making most involuntary exchanges illegal, criminal law helps to channel our energies into exchanges and productive activities that benefit all parties involved: Pareto improvements. In this way, criminal law contributes to economic efficiency.*

Of course, to be effective, it's not enough to merely define which activities are harmful; the criminal code must also be enforced, with penalties serious enough and certain enough to dissuade people from committing harmful crimes. In some cases, it has proven much easier to draft a criminal code than to provide for enforcement.

Russia, for example, enacted a sophisticated new criminal code in the mid-1990s, but has been unable to effectively enforce it, due to massive corruption in local governments and police forces. As a result, a disproportionate number of

Russian citizens pursue activities that harm others, such as running protection rackets that victimize small businesses, or eliminating business competitors through threats and even assassinations.

Another example of the inefficiency caused by deficient law enforcement occurred after the U.S. occupation of Iraq in 2003. In the months following the invasion, the country's former government had ceased to operate, but the U.S. military had not exercised control in most of the country. It was not clear what laws were in effect, and no one was enforcing them in any case. As U.S. Army and Iraqi crews desperately tried to restore electric power to the country, they encountered a frequent problem: Looters would remove a length of copper wire from the unguarded power grid to sell on the black market for about $5. Each theft caused thousands of dollars of damage to the power grid and deprived millions of people of electricity for additional days, causing far greater harm to the country than benefits for the thief.[5]

Property Law. Property law gives people precisely defined, enforceable rights over the things they own. Without property law, people would spend a good part of their time dealing with others who claimed to own their house, their farm, or their factory. In the United States and other advanced countries, highly secure systems keep track of who owns land, cars, shares of stock, airplanes, patents, and other important pieces of property.

When property rights are poorly defined, much time and energy are wasted in disputes about ownership, and people spend time trying to capture resources from others—time that could have been spent producing valuable goods and services. As a result, countries with poorly defined property rights do not produce as much output from their resources as they could with better-defined property rights. This is inefficient: Benefits that buyers and sellers *could* gain from the additional output do not occur.

> *Property law—by reducing disputes about property, and channeling resources into production rather than the capture of property belonging to others—contributes to economic efficiency by increasing total production, thus raising the total net benefits that markets can provide.*

Contract Law. In 1995, two 25-year-old Stanford graduate students, Larry Page and Sergey Brin, had an idea for a new Internet search engine, one that would find and organize Web sites according to their likely importance to the searcher. Initially, they funded the enterprise by borrowing money on credit cards and from parents and friends. But by 1998, in order to compete with existing search engines like Yahoo and Alta Vista, they needed more money than these resources could provide. Where could they get it?

Like many entrepreneurs before them, Page and Brin turned to strangers—people with money who were looking for a new company in which to invest. The young entrepreneurs signed contracts promising their investors a portion of the company's future profits.

It turned out that the new search engine—called Google—was indeed a success. Over the next several years, its traffic grew by 20 percent per month, and by the end

---

[5] "Iraq Trip Report," Representative Frank Wolf, May 2003 (*http://www.house.gov/wolf/iraq-report-low.pdf*); Daniel Yergin, "Oil Shortage," CERA Newsroom, May 25, 2003 (*http:// www.cera.com/news/ details/1,1308,5577,00.html*), and various television news broadcasts.

of 2002, Google had about 300 employees and fielded 2,000 searches *per second*. The company had become highly profitable, earning half of its income by selling its search technique to other firms, and the other half from carrying advertising.

But what guaranteed that Page and Brin would honor all their contracts with investors and hand over the appropriate shares of the company's profits? In countries in which contract law is less well defined or less strictly enforced, investors would worry that they would not be able to collect their share. In the United States and other countries with a strong legal system, that worry rarely arises because contracts can be enforced.

A contract is a mutual promise. Often, as in the example of Google, one party does something first (investors provided millions of dollars) and the other party promises to do something later (Page and Brin promised to run the business and pay their investors a share of the profit). As long as no third parties are harmed, the exchange that occurs under a contract is always a Pareto improvement: It's a voluntary deal that won't happen unless both sides are made better off.

Contracts play a special role in a market economy. Without them, only Pareto improvements involving simultaneous exchange could take place: You get a bag of apples from a farmer and simultaneously hand over some money. Contracts enable us to make exchanges in which one person goes first. That person has to be able to rely on the other person to make good on the promise later. Without this assurance, whoever goes first would not be willing to make the deal in the first place. Thus, contracts make it possible to form new companies and to hire the services of experts who specialize in such things as auto repair, plumbing, roof repair, dentistry, and legal services—all cases in which someone goes first.

Contracts enable us to make exchanges that take place over time and in which one person must act first. In this way, contracts help society enjoy the full benefits of specialization and exchange.

Legal enforcement of contracts is not the only force that makes people keep promises. Parents, religious organizations, and schools teach people that keeping a promise is a moral obligation. And a reputation for failing to keep promises would be harmful to a business or a person. Still, contracts and the infrastructure for enforcing them play a vital role in making the economy more efficient. There are enough would-be cheaters to create problems, and contract law provides an effective way to deal with them.

Tort Law. Contract law deals with people or businesses that are economically involved with each other, such as suppliers and their customers, or partners in a business deal. Tort law, on the other hand, deals with interactions among strangers or people not linked by contracts.

More specifically, a **tort** is a wrongful act—such as manufacturing an unsafe product—that causes harm to someone. Tort law defines the types of harm for which someone can seek legal remedy, and what sorts of compensation the injured person can expect.

Tort A wrongful act that harms someone.

When people and businesses are held responsible for injuries they cause, they act more carefully. Tort law in the United States provides incentives for drivers to drive carefully, for doctors to examine their patients more completely, and for manufacturers of products such as power mowers to control hazards through proper design. Tort law also protects against *fraud*, in which a seller of something—a product, a business, shares of stock—lies to the buyer in order to make the sale.

Antitrust Law. Antitrust law is designed to prevent businesses from making agreements or engaging in other behavior that limits competition and harms consumers. More specifically, antitrust law operates in three areas:

1. *Agreements among competitors.* U.S. antitrust law—expressed in Section 1 of the Sherman Act—prohibits "contracts, combinations, or conspiracies" among competing firms that would harm consumers by raising prices. The most flagrant agreements prohibited by this law are those that directly fix prices. But the law also prohibits agreements that raise prices indirectly, by limiting competition among sellers. An agreement by firms to allocate markets among them—so that one seller serves one group of customers exclusively, while other sellers are assigned their own groups of exclusive customers—may violate the law. For example, in the mid-1990s, the only two important sellers of review courses for the bar exam taken by prospective lawyers divided up their territory to avoid competition. The courts outlawed their agreement because it reduced competition.

2. *Monopolization.* Section 2 of the Sherman Act makes it illegal to monopolize or attempt to monopolize a market. As the law is now interpreted, it is illegal for one seller to harm a rival by interfering with its operations or hobbling the rival in certain ways. For example, it is illegal for a company to spread false information about a rival's product as part of an attempt to drive that rival out of the market. But the law does not prohibit monopoly or harm to competitors. Rather, it prohibits *certain steps* to acquire or maintain a monopoly or to harm competitors. A firm that harms its rivals by selling a better product, thus taking business away from them, is not in violation of the law.

3. *Mergers.* In a merger, two firms combine to form one new firm. Mergers can sometimes result in higher prices from oligopoly or monopoly. For example, if the largest firm in a market has a 40 percent share of total sales and the second-largest has a 30 percent share, we can expect that the rivalry between them will benefit consumers. But if they merge to form a single firm with a 70 percent share, the rivalry would disappear and prices would rise. Mergers of this type are often blocked by the U.S. government based on Section 7 of the Clayton Act.

Regulation

Regulation is another important part of the institutional infrastructure that supports a market economy. Under regulation, a government agency—such as the Food and Drug Administration (FDA), the Environmental Protection Agency (EPA), or a state public utilities commission—has the power to direct businesses to take specific actions. The EPA has detailed control over what substances a business can release into the atmosphere or into the water. Public utilities commissions set the prices for electricity, gas, and telephone service. Often, regulators must approve business actions before they are undertaken, as in the case of the FDA's approval of new drugs.

Regulation differs from the use of legal procedures in a fundamental way: Regulators reach deep into the operations of businesses to tell them what to do, while legal procedures typically result in fines or other penalties if businesses do something wrong. To help see the distinction, consider the different ways in which regional and long-distance telephone companies are treated. Because they are regulated, regional telephone companies (such as Bell South or Cincinnati Bell) are *told* what price to charge. Long-distance phone companies, by contrast, are largely unregulated, so they can charge whatever price they wish. But if long-distance companies are caught breaking the law in setting prices (such as, by entering into illegal agreements to restrict competition), they will have to pay fines, and their managers may even have to go to jail.

Law and Regulation in Perspective

The invisible hand of the market system cannot operate on its own. The legal system, along with our regulatory agencies, creates an environment in which the invisible hand can do its job. Almost every Pareto improvement that we can think of relies on the legal and regulatory infrastructure. Recall the last time you bought a meal in a restaurant. If you paid cash, the criminal law against counterfeiting enabled the restaurant to more readily accept your paper currency. If you paid by credit card, contract law assured the restaurant that it would eventually be paid by the credit card company. The restaurant itself couldn't function without contracts with its suppliers, landlord, and employees. You could be reasonably confident that the food was not contaminated, in part because of inspections by local regulatory agencies and also because tort law provides legal disincentives for harmful products.

But what about cases where law and regulation don't seem to be working perfectly? After all, we still have crimes against people and property. Unsafe products like poorly designed automobiles or tainted frozen dinners *are* produced and only sometimes recalled before someone is harmed. Businesses *do* fix prices and are only sometimes caught. Accounting frauds—such as those that occurred at Enron, WorldCom, and some other major corporations in the early 2000s—*do* occur and cause serious harm to employees and stockholders. Do these and countless other examples mean that our institutional infrastructure is failing us?

Yes . . . and no. While instances like these are never welcome, our society has chosen not to eliminate them entirely. We could, if we wanted to, eliminate all crime, all unsafe products, and all other detriments to economic life by enacting more stringent laws and regulations and enforcing them to the hilt. But doing so would require even larger expenditures on legal and regulatory enforcement than we currently make. In deciding whether to make these expenditures, we must balance the benefits—safer products, reduced crime, and the like—against the costs.

For example, in part because of our strong tort law, the United States is one of the safest countries of the world, and is growing safer. Adult on-the-job death rates have fallen dramatically. But even the United States has chosen not to *completely eliminate* safety hazards: Each year, about 30 people out of every 100,000 die from accidents of some kind. Why do we accept this? Because the complete (or almost complete) elimination of fatal accidents would require too many of our resources to be diverted from other uses. Most of us would think it is simply not worth it. For example, to eliminate all preventable fatal accidents, we would have to require that every automobile be inspected dozens of times each month; that drivers enroll in a refresher course each year, perhaps each month, updating and reinforcing their driving skills and safety consciousness; and that all restaurants have laboratories to inspect every meal for *E. coli* contamination before serving it. Moreover, all of these requirements would have to be strictly enforced, requiring more police and inspectors to catch violators and more courts and jails to prosecute and penalize them. In such a world, our standard of living would plummet, and we'd all agree that we'd be better off taking on *some* additional risk of accidents in order to free up resources for increased production.

A legal and regulatory system that ensured the complete elimination of crime, unsafe products, and other unwelcome activities would be less efficient than a system that tolerated some amount of these activities. An efficient infrastructure must consider the costs, as well as the benefits, of achieving our legal and regulatory goals.

MARKET FAILURES

The social infrastructure we've been discussing largely helps to create fertile ground for markets to operate and generate Pareto improvements. But there is another vitally important role for government: to intervene in situations of *market failure.*

Market failure A market that fails to take advantage of every Pareto improvement.

*A **market failure** occurs when a market—even with the proper institutional support—is economically inefficient.*

You've already encountered one specific example of a market failure: the *principal–agent problem* in the market for CEOs (see Chapter 12). Here, we'll focus on three general types of market failures to which economists have devoted a lot of attention: (1) monopoly power; (2) externalities; and (3) public goods. As you'll see, government involvement can often help deal with, and even cure, a market failure. But government involvement has costs as well as benefits, and sometimes government policies create problems of their own. While economists and policy makers agree in theory on what causes a market failure, dealing with real-world market failures remains one of the most controversial aspects of government policy.

MONOPOLY AND MONOPOLY POWER

A firm has *monopoly power* when it can influence the price that it charges for its product. Monopolists, oligopolists, and monopolistic competitors all have some monopoly power, because they *set* their price in order to maximize profit rather than take the price as given. However, competition among monopolistic competitors limits their monopoly power and helps keeps prices low. But a market with just one seller, or a few oligopolists who cooperate and behave as a monopoly, is a more serious market failure.

Why does monopoly power amount to a market failure? Let's consider an example. Imagine that our perfectly competitive market for guitar lessons is taken over by a single firm. We'll assume this new monopoly treats each of the old sellers as an independent operation . . . with one exception: The monopoly owner will now set the price of all lessons in the market, so as to maximize its total profit.

Figure 9 shows the market from the perspective of new monopoly. Each additional lesson is provided by the part of the monopoly's operation that can produce it at the lowest additional cost—that is, by the supplier who provided that lesson before, when the market was perfectly competitive. Thus, the monopoly's *marginal cost* curve—showing the additional cost of another lesson—is the same as the old market supply curve in Figure 6. The demand curve, too, is the same as the old demand curve from Figure 6: At each price, people in the market will still choose to buy the same quantity of lessons they would buy before.

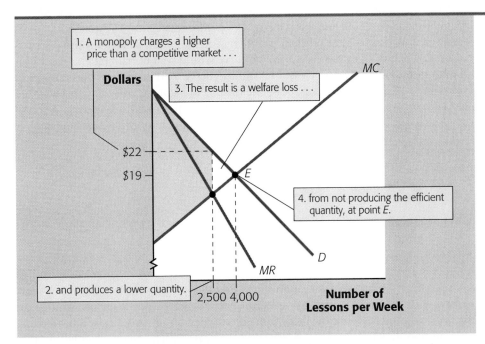

FIGURE 9
**The Welfare Loss from
Monopoly**

1. A monopoly charges a higher
   price than a competitive market . . .

Dollars

3. The result is a welfare loss . . .

MC

$22

$19

E

4. from not producing the efficient
   quantity, at point *E*.

D

MR

2. and produces a lower quantity.

2,500 4,000

**Number of
Lessons per Week**

The monopoly maximizes profit by choosing the number of lessons per week at which marginal revenue and marginal cost are equal. However, the monopoly—unlike the competitive suppliers in Figure 6—must drop the price on *all* lessons in order to sell one more. That's why the monopoly's marginal revenue curve lies below the demand curve: Marginal revenue is less than the price of the last lesson.

In the figure, you can see that the monopoly's profit-maximizing output level is 2,500 lessons per week, and it charges the highest price—$22—at which it can sell that number of lessons. Consumer surplus is the blue-shaded area—below the demand curve, and above the market price of $22. The monopoly's producer surplus is the red-shaded area (above its new marginal cost curve and below the market price of $22). Note that producer surplus on each unit for the monopoly is the difference between the added cost of that unit (given by the *MC* curve) and what it actually gets for it ($22).

If you compare Figure 6 with Figure 9, you'll see that monopolization of this industry has reduced the total net benefits in the market. Or, to put it another way, it has created a welfare loss equal to the unshaded triangle.

To understand the welfare loss caused by monopolization of this market, remember that each unit up to 4,000 *could* be provided at an additional cost (given by the height of the *MC* curve) that is lower than its value to some consumer (given by the height of the demand curve). So 4,000 is the *efficient* quantity, as it was before under perfect competition. But the monopoly does not provide any of the lessons 2,501 through 4,000. Providing these lessons would be Pareto improvements . . . but they aren't provided. Why not? Buyers will only buy lessons whose value is greater than the price. But *the monopoly charges a price that is greater than marginal cost.* Therefore, buyers will choose *not* to buy some lessons even though their value exceeds the additional cost of providing them. For example, in the figure, buyers do not buy the 2,501st lesson because its value is about $22. But the *marginal cost* of the 2,501st lesson is *substantially* below $22, so this lesson *could* increase total net benefits in the market.

Note that if the monopoly could *price discriminate*—continuing to charge $22 on lessons 1 through 2,500, and then charge $19 *just* for lessons 2,501 through 4,000—it *would* choose to supply the efficient quantity. (You may want to review price discrimination in Chapter 9; in this case, the *MR* curve would be a horizontal line at $19 for all quantities between 2,501 to 4,000.) But as you've learned, not all firms can price discriminate. A *single-price* monopoly, like the one in Figure 9, will be inefficient.

Our example generalizes to *any* firm facing a downward-sloping demand curve—that is, any firm with monopoly power—that cannot price discriminate.

> *Monopoly and imperfectly competitive markets—in which firms charge a single price greater than marginal cost—are generally inefficient. Price is too high, and output is too low, to maximize the net benefits in the market.*

What can the government do to make this monopoly market more efficient?

Antitrust Law as a Remedy

In the case of the guitar-lesson monopoly, there may be a solution: Since this market would function very well under competitive conditions, the government could use *antitrust law* to break the monopoly into several competing firms. But breaking up a monopoly would *not* make sense in other cases where the market would perform even worse with more competition.

For example, monopolies that arise from patents and copyrights, as discussed in Chapter 9, provide an incentive for artistic creations and scientific discovery. Breaking up a monopoly in, say, a particular drug—by removing its patent before it expired—would lead to a greater and closer-to-efficient quantity of *that* drug. But it would also reduce incentives to develop *future* drugs. Over a long period of time, the benefits from the drug industry as a whole could be reduced. Drug prices are controversial: There are hot debates about the duration of drug patents and what should qualify as a patentable drug. But no one seriously proposes destroying temporary drug monopolies by eliminating patents and turning the market into anything resembling perfect competition.

Similarly, monopoly power that arises from *network externalities*—discussed in Chapter 9—offers benefits that would be hard to achieve under more competitive conditions. Microsoft, for example, takes advantage of its market power in several ways. But the Windows network, which provides substantial benefits, could not exist unless a single firm produced the operating system used by most personal computers.

Finally, when a monopoly arises as a *natural monopoly,* using antitrust law to break it up or even to prevent its formation in the first place is a poor remedy. Because this type of monopoly presents special challenges, it's worth its own discussion.

The Special Case of Natural Monopoly

In Chapter 6 and again in Chapter 9, you learned that a *natural monopoly* exists when, due to economies of scale, one firm can produce for the entire market at a lower cost per unit than can two or more firms. If the government steps aside, such a market will naturally evolve toward monopoly.

Figure 10 presents an example of a natural monopoly: a local cable company in a small city.

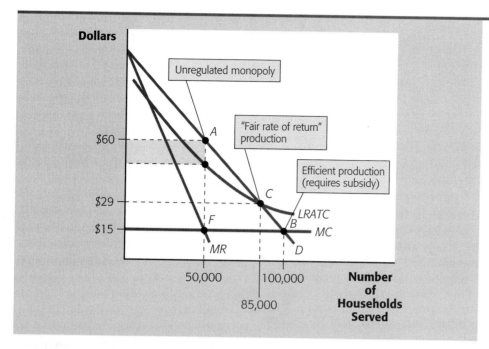

FIGURE 10
Regulating a Natural Monopoly

*Left unregulated, the cable mo-
nopoly would serve 50,000
households, where MC = MR.
This is inefficient, because units
50,001 to 100,000 have value to
some consumer greater than
their marginal cost.*

*By mandating a price of $15,
government regulators could
achieve the efficient outcome—
100,000 households—at point B.
But with price less than LRATC,
the monopoly would suffer a
loss, so would have to be subsidized or go out of business.*

*The alternative, which is typ-
ically chosen, is to set price at
$29—the lowest achievable av-
erage cost in this market, which
includes a "fair rate of return."
At this price, the monopoly
serves 85,000 households. This
is not the efficient quantity of
100,000, but is closer to the efficient outcome than would be
achieved without regulation.*

A cable company has important *lumpy inputs*—inputs needed in fixed amounts over a wide range of output. For example, whether the number of subscribers in the city is 1,000 or 100,000, a cable company must still lay the same, costly, underground cable to every neighborhood, and use up the same resources repairing and maintaining it. Similarly, the company's legal department must negotiate (and periodically renegotiate) contracts with each of its entertainment providers—the same number of contracts whether the company has just a few subscribers or 100,000. Spreading these costs over more subscribers reduces cost per unit. In the figure, these economies of scale continue until the entire market is served: The *LRATC* curve slopes downward through its intersection point with the market demand curve, *D*.

To serve an *additional* household, however, is *not* very costly to a cable company: just the installation appointment, some additional, above-ground cable, periodic replacement of the cable box, and handling the occasional complaint. Therefore, *marginal* cost for a cable company is relatively low. In Figure 10, we assume that marginal cost is a constant $15 per additional household—no matter how many households are served. Accordingly, the marginal cost curve is a horizontal line at $15.

If the market for cable service in the city is left to itself, one firm would become the sole supplier. In the absence of any government intervention, it would then sign up the profit-maximizing number of households, where marginal revenue (*MR*) and marginal cost (*MC*) are equal. In the figure, the *MR* and *MC* curves intersect at point *F*, and the cable monopoly will sign up 50,000 households. The price, at point *A* on the demand curve, is $60 per month and profit is equal to the shaded rectangle.

But point *A*—with an output of 50,000—is *inefficient.* In fact, the efficient level of output in the figure is found at point *B, where the* MC *curve crosses the demand curve* and the firm serves 100,000 households. The 50,001st through the 100,000th households still value cable service more than the additional cost of providing it to them, so total net benefits in the market would rise if they acquired service. Once output has risen to 100,000, further increases are worth less than $15 to consumers but would cost the firm $15 to provide. Thus, serving 100,000 households, and no more, maximizes the total net benefits in this market. Because no household beyond the 50,000th will actually *buy* cable service as long as the monopoly charges $60, the cable monopoly is a market failure. What can the government do?

Using antitrust law to break the natural monopoly into several competing firms would not make sense. With several firms—each supplying to only a part of the market—each firm's cost per unit would be even higher than the monopoly's cost per unit. Therefore, the price in a more competitive market could never be $15 (the price needed to get us to the efficient point *B*). In fact, competition, by raising cost per unit, might result in an even *higher* price than under monopoly, reducing the total net benefits from the market.

But if breaking up a natural monopoly is not advisable, what *can* government do to bring us closer to economic efficiency? One option is public *ownership* and *operation* of cable service, as is done with the post office, another natural monopoly. Public takeover of private business is rare, except when certain conditions are present (to be discussed later in this chapter). That leaves one other option, and the one local governments actually choose for the cable industry: *regulation*.

Regulation of Natural Monopoly

At the beginning of this chapter, you learned that under regulation, a government agency digs deep into the operations of a business and takes some of the firm's decisions under its own control. In the case of a natural monopoly, regulators tell the firm what price it can charge.

At first glance, you might think that natural monopoly regulators have an easy job. For example, in Figure 10, we know that the efficient quantity is 100,000 households—just the number of households that will purchase the service if the price is $15. Therefore, all the regulators have to do is set the official price at $15 and—voila!—an efficient market.

Unfortunately, it's not that easy. First, there is the matter of information: The regulators must be able to trace out the firm's *MC* curve as well as the market demand curve. This job is especially difficult when the monopoly's managers, hoping for a higher price, have an incentive to overstate costs. Even with a cooperative monopoly, the job is extremely complex, and the best regulators can hope for is a crude approximation to the actual curves.

More important, even with perfect information about the monopolist's cost and demand curves, regulators have a serious problem. If you look again at Figure 10, you'll notice that the *MC* curve lies everywhere *below* the *LRATC* curve. This must be the case for a natural monopoly, since economies of scale—the reason for the natural monopoly—means that the *LRATC* curve slopes downward, and this can occur only when marginal cost is less than average cost. (See Chapter 6 on the marginal–average relationship if you've forgotten why. Here, both marginal cost and average cost refer to the long run.)

Now you can see the problem for regulators: If they set the efficient price of $15 so that buyers demand the efficient quantity of 100,000, the firm's cost per unit is *greater* than $15. The firm will suffer a loss. In the long run, it will go out of business.

This problem leaves the regulator with two alternatives. First, it can set price equal to *MC* ($15 in our example) and *subsidize* the monopoly from the general budget, to make up for the loss. But this would require taxpayers in general, rather than just the monopoly's customers, to help pay for the product.

In practice, however, regulators in market economies around the world have usually chosen a different solution. The regulators determine a price that gives owners a "fair rate of return" for funds they've put into the monopoly. This fair rate of return is designed to be the same rate of return they could have earned in a similar, alternative investment. In other words, the fair rate of return should give the monopoly what economists call *normal profit*—a profit just high enough to cover all of the owners' opportunity costs, including the foregone interest on their own funds.

What price will accomplish this? Remember that we've included all costs into our cost curves, including the opportunity cost of owners' funds. Thus, a fair rate of return is already built into the *LRATC* curve in Figure 10. If the firm charges a price equal to average cost, it will cover all the costs of the operation, including the fair rate of return for owners. You can see that at point C—with a price of $29— the firm is charging the lowest possible price that prevents it from suffering a loss. This strategy—called *average cost pricing*—is the most common solution chosen by regulators of natural monopolies. More generally,

> *with average cost pricing, regulators strive to set the price equal to cost per unit where the LRATC curve crosses the demand curve. At this price, the natural monopoly makes zero economic profit, which provides its owners with a fair rate of return and keeps the monopoly in business.*

Average cost pricing is not a perfect solution. For one thing, it does not quite make the market efficient. For example, notice that in Figure 10, only 85,000 units are produced, instead of the efficient quantity of 100,000. Nevertheless, compared to no regulation at all, average cost pricing lowers the price to consumers and increases the quantity they buy, bringing us closer to the efficient level.

Another problem with average cost pricing is that it provides little or no incentive for the natural monopoly to economize on capital. That is, the monopoly can grow larger and larger—taking in more and more new owners by issuing stock and using the proceeds to buy machinery, office buildings, and other forms of capital—confident that the regulators will always ensure that the price will be adjusted to assure normal profit for its stockholders. The tendency of regulated natural monopolies to overinvest in capital is known as the Averch-Johnson effect, after the two economists who first explained it.[6] The Averch–Johnson effect is a specific example of a more general idea: that when a firm is not striving to maximize profit (in this case, because the government is guaranteeing a specific rate of return), the firm need not economize on costs.

EXTERNALITIES

If you live in a dormitory, you have no doubt had the unpleasant experience of trying to study while the stereo in the next room is blasting through your walls—and usually not your choice of music. This may not sound like an economic problem, but it is one. The problem is that your neighbor, in deciding to listen to loud music, is considering only the private costs (the sacrifice of his own time) and private benefits (the enjoyment of music) of his action. He is not considering the harm it causes to you. Indeed, the harm you suffer might be greater than the benefit he gets from

[6] Harvey Averch and Leland Johnson, "Behavior of the Firm Under Regulatory Constraint," *American Economic Review*, December 1962, pp. 1052–1069.

blasting his music. In this case, his turning down the volume could be a Pareto improvement, with an appropriate side payment. And unless he does turn down the volume, the situation remains inefficient.

When a private action has side effects that affect other people in important ways, we have the problem of externalities:

Externality A by-product of a good or activity that affects someone not immediately involved in the transaction.

> *An **externality** is a by-product of a good or activity that affects someone not immediately involved in the transaction.*

For example, the by-product of your neighbor blasting his stereo is the noise coming into your room. We call this a negative externality, because the by-product is harmful. When the by-product is *beneficial* to a third party, it is a positive externality. We'll consider examples of positive externalities a bit later.

The Private Solution to a Negative Externality

Under certain conditions, the inefficiency that would be caused by a negative externality will automatically be resolved by the parties themselves. Remember our example, early in the chapter, of the movie theater that would create benefits for some residents worth $100,000, but $70,000 worth of harm for others?

Imagine that instead of many residents, the harm would be inflicted on only *one* resident: Fernando, the owner of a private Zen mediation center next to the empty lot on which the theater is to be built. Because of the traffic congestion the theater would bring—and the associated engine noise, blaring horns, and pollution—Fernando would have to move his meditation center to another location. Moreover, he has determined that the time, trouble, and expense of moving would bring his total harm to $70,000.

Let's also imagine that the $100,000 in *benefits* would be received by just one person: Grace, the owner of the empty lot, who wants to build the theater on it.

In this situation, there is a negative externality of $70,000 affecting Fernando. Will the theater be built? The answer is: almost certainly *yes*. And—surprisingly—the result remains the same, regardless of who has the *legal rights* in this case.

Suppose Grace, the owner of the empty lot, has the legal right to build whatever she wants there. Then she will do so—and Fernando will move his center and suffer the $70,000 in harm, without compensation. This may or may not be fair, but *the theater will be built.*

Now suppose, instead, that Fernando has the legal right to *block* the sale. (Say, the city zoning law is written to prevent any theaters from being built without approval of those immediately next door.) Would Fernando want the theater to be built? You might think no, since the theater causes him harm. But, in fact, Fernando will almost certainly, in the end, favor the theater and be happy to move. Why?

If Fernando has the power to block the sale, Grace will realize that the only way to come out ahead is to *compensate* Fernando. Any side payment Grace makes under $100,000 still leaves her with a gain. Suppose she offers $80,000. Then by moving, Fernando would come out $10,000 ahead ($80,000 in cash minus the $70,000 in harm). In fact, while we can't predict the exact size of the side payment, we do know that it will end up somewhere between $70,000 and $100,000. We also know that (1) both sides have a powerful incentive to come to an agreement, because they can both gain from it; and (2) with only two parties involved, the costs of arranging the side payment will likely be low. Once again, even though building the theater forces Fernando to move, and he has the legal power to stop it, *the theater will be built.*

Note that building the theater is the *efficient* outcome given our assumptions: It achieves the maximum possible total net benefits in this situation. After all, the gains to the gainers are greater than the losses to the losers.

What if building the theater is *not* efficient, because it causes greater harm than benefits? Then side payments will ensure that it will not be built. (An end-of-chapter problem asks you to show this with a specific example.)

The Coase Theorem. As you've seen in our example, whether the theater will or will not be built depends entirely on whether it is the *efficient* or *in*efficient outcome, regardless of who holds the legal rights. Therefore, in our example, the negative externality is *solved* by the market. No government intervention is required, other than the initial assignment of legal rights.

This rather surprising result is known as the *Coase theorem*, named after the economist Ronald Coase

> The **Coase theorem** states that—*when side payments can be negotiated and arranged without cost*—the private market will solve the externality problem on its own, always arriving at the efficient outcome. While the initial distribution of legal rights will determine the allocation of gains and losses among the parties, it will not affect the action taken.

Coase theorem When a side payment can be arranged without cost, the market will solve an externality problem—and create the efficient outcome—on its own.

Note that the Coase theorem requires that side payments can be arranged *without cost*—or, in practice, that the cost is so low relative to the gains or losses at stake that it doesn't matter. This requirement is most likely to be satisfied when all three of the following conditions are present: (1) legal rights are clearly established; (2) legal rights can be easily transferred; and (3) the number of people involved is very small.

Unfortunately, many-real world situations do not satisfy these conditions. Legal rights are often in dispute. Suppose, for example, that the zoning law makes vague references to prohibiting "businesses known to create serious disturbance." Then, Grace and Fernando are very likely to end up in court, each having a different view about whether a movie theater is that kind of business. Since courts are often more concerned about fairness or legal interpretation than efficiency, the outcome may not be the efficient one. (This is not necessarily bad; fairness, as we've stressed, is a concern as well as efficiency.)

Furthermore, once a court decides the issue, legal rights may not be transferable. For example, if Fernando wins the court case and blocks the sale, the court may not allow Fernando to transfer his court victory to Grace even if she offers him a substantial side payment.

But the biggest problem in applying the Coase theorem to many real-world externalities is the third condition: Often, a large number of people are involved. Earlier in this chapter, we assumed—more realistically—that building the movie theater would affect *many* people in the town, positively and negatively. It would be very costly to determine the gains and losses for each one, get them all together, and then come up with a solution that would please everyone. Moreover, when many people are involved, achieving efficiency with side payments is plagued by an often insoluble problem, to which we turn now.

The Free Rider Problem. Once again, suppose that the efficient outcome is to build the theater. Suppose, too, that those who would be harmed have the legal power to block the sale, and a side payment has, indeed, been negotiated by representatives of the gainers and the losers—one that makes everyone come out ahead. The total side payment is $80,000, with each gainer told to contribute, say, $500. Now, we face another problem: A gainer may try to get a *free ride*, refusing to pay, reasoning that his own part of the payment is so small—just a "drop in the bucket"—that the theater will be built regardless. He may claim that he doesn't receive benefits, or just laugh off anyone who comes to collect. (Remember: the government is not involved at this point.) If *many* of those who should be part of the side payment reason this way and attempt to get a free ride, we have the *free rider problem*.

Free rider problem When the efficient outcome requires a side payment but individual gainers will not contribute.

> *The **free rider problem** occurs when the efficient outcome requires a side payment but individual gainers—each obligated to pay a small share of the side payment—will not contribute.*

The free rider problem, if extensive enough, can shrink the side payment until it isn't large enough to compensate losers and still leave the gainers better off. In that case, the private arrangement—based on voluntary participation rather than government coercion—will break down and the efficient outcome will not be achieved. Indeed, the free rider problem stands in the way of many Pareto improvements. And it is one of the main reasons why we typically turn to government to deal with important externalities that affect many people.

Market Externalities and Government Solutions

A competitive market has, by definition, many buyers and sellers. So when a negative externality affects a *market,* the private (Coase theorem) solution may not work.

Many negative externalities in markets are caused by some form of *pollution.* Cities pollute rivers and lakes with sewage, and industries pollute them with chemicals. Cars and power plants pollute the atmosphere. As you are about to see, the market for a good that creates pollution—like markets with other negative externalities—is inefficient.

Panel (a) of Figure 11 illustrates an inefficiency in the market for gasoline, which pollutes the air with carbon monoxide and soot, dust, and other visible and microscopic solids. In the figure, we assume that the market is perfectly competitive. (Ignore the curve labeled *MSC* for now.) The supply curve *S*—like every market supply curve we've considered so far—reflects the costs of inputs used by *gasoline producers.* The height of the supply curve at any output level tells us the marginal cost (*MC*) of producing the last unit of output.

But the supply curve does *not* reflect any costs to the general public—such as the health and environmental damage caused by pollution—because (before government involvement) the firm does not have to pay them. The market reaches equilibrium at point *A,* where the supply curve *S* and the demand curve *D* intersect. The equilibrium quantity of gasoline is 125 million gallons per period, and the price is $1.00 per gallon.

But if gasoline causes a negative externality, 125 million is *not* the efficient output level. We can see this by incorporating the negative externality into our diagram. Let's suppose that each gallon of gas imposes a cost to the general public of $0.50. When we add this cost to the marginal cost already paid by gasoline producers, we get the **marginal social cost** (*MSC*) of another unit of gasoline. *MSC* includes *all* costs of producing another unit of gas: the resources used up and paid for by the industry, *and* the costs imposed on third parties. Because *MSC* is the fuller concept of costs, whenever there is a negative externality, *MSC* > *MC* at any level of output. This is why the *MSC* curve in Figure 11 lies *above* the market supply curve.

Marginal social cost (*MSC*) The full cost of producing another unit of a good, including the marginal cost to the producer *and* any harm caused to third parties.

Once we draw the *MSC* curve in Figure 11, panel (a), we discover that the *efficient* level of output is 100 million gallons, where the *MSC* curve intersects the de-

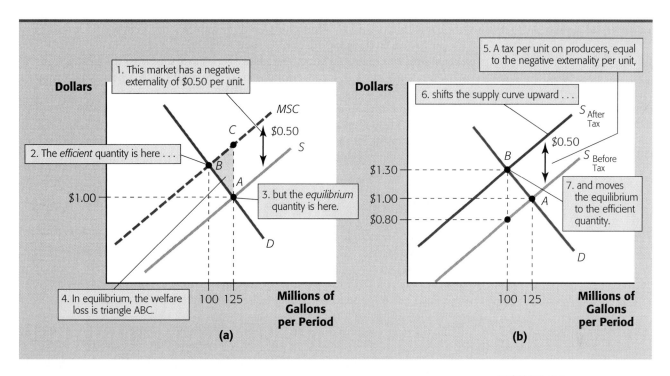

Dollars

1. This market has a negative externality of $0.50 per unit.

2. The *efficient* quantity is here . . .

3. but the *equilibrium* quantity is here.

$1.00

4. In equilibrium, the welfare loss is triangle ABC.

100 125 **Millions of Gallons per Period**

MSC

C

$0.50

S

B

A

D

(a)

Dollars

5. A tax per unit on producers, equal to the negative externality per unit,

6. shifts the supply curve upward . . .

$1.30

$1.00

$0.80

S After Tax

$0.50

B

S Before Tax

7. and moves the equilibrium to the efficient quantity.

A

D

100 125 **Millions of Gallons per Period**

(b)

FIGURE 11
A Tax on Producers to Correct a Negative Externality

mand curve at point *B*. Why? Efficiency requires that the market provide only those units that are valued more highly by consumers than they cost to produce. The *MSC* curve tells us what it *really* costs to produce gas, when *all* costs are considered. For all units up to 100 million, the *MSC* curve lies below the demand curve, so those units are more highly valued than their costs. Net benefits in the market are increased by providing the first 100 million gallons. But for all units *beyond* 100 million, the *MSC* curve lies *above* the demand curve. These units should *not* be produced, because they cost more—in the fullest sense—than their value to consumers. The labeled triangle ABC shows the *welfare loss* for this market in equilibrium—the loss in net benefits from producing too much output.

> *A market with a negative externality associated with producing or consuming a good will produce* more *than the efficient quantity, creating a welfare loss.*

How can we achieve the efficient result of 100 million gallons? One way is to change the *equilibrium* quantity to 100 million. Perhaps we could somehow raise the supply curve to the position of the *MSC* curve in Figure 11, panel (a). Indeed, if the Coase theorem applied—and everyone affected could negotiate and enforce an agreement without cost—the private market could accomplish this on its own.

Unfortunately, with so many people involved, it would take too much time and trouble for individual gasoline producers and consumers to arrange the appropriate side payments and production cutbacks, and in any case, the free rider problem would effectively destroy the arrangement. The efficient outcome, therefore, requires *government intervention* in the market.

Taxing a Negative Externality. One method the government could use to move the gasoline market to point *B* would be a tax on producers. In panel (b) of Figure 11, we show the effect of a tax of $0.50 per gallon, which is the harm caused by each

HTTP://

Jeffrey Frankel's "Greenhouse
Gas Emissions" is an interesting
analysis of an important negative
externality. You can find it at
http://www.brook.edu/comm/
PolicyBriefs/pb052/pb52.htm.

additional gallon of gas. In addition to its other inputs, each firm would have to pay $0.50 per gallon to the government. As each firm's marginal cost rose by $0.50, the market supply curve would shift upward by $0.50, raising it to the position of the *MSC* curve. Once the tax is in place, the market would reach a new equilibrium at point *B*—producing the efficient quantity of 100 million gallons.

Notice that, in the new equilibrium, the price of gasoline to consumers rises from $1.00 to $1.30. Producers, meanwhile, keep only $0.80 of that $1.30, because they have to pay $0.50 to the government on each gallon they sell at $1.30. Thus, the payment of the externality tax is shared between consumers and producers.

> *A tax on each unit of a good, equal to the external harm it causes, can correct a negative externality and bring the market to an efficient output level.*

Let's take a step back and consider the logic of this result. The tax cures the inefficiency because it forces the market to *internalize the externality*—to take account of the harm caused by gasoline. After the tax, the harm caused by gasoline affects the decisions of *both* producers and consumers. The firm receives 20 cents less for each gallon it sells, so it decides to produce less. Consumers pay 30 cents more, so they decide to buy less.

This logic suggests that a tax on *consumers* of gasoline would work just as well as a tax on producers. If a tax of $.50 per gallon were imposed on consumers, the market demand curve would shift *downward* by that amount, and the end result would be the same as in our example: Consumers would pay $1.30 (including the tax), producers would get $0.80, and the market would once again arrive at the same efficient quantity of 100 million. (An end-of-chapter problem asks you to illustrate this.)

Taxes to correct negative externalities have been used in countries around the world: Sweden has imposed a tax on each kilogram of nitrogen oxide emitted by power plants. Denmark imposes taxes on businesses that produce, and households that consume, products that cause carbon dioxide emissions. Malaysia taxes harmful by-products of palm oil mills. And Vietnam has imposed a tax on coal production—largely because of the harm to tourism caused by unsightly coal mines.[7] In the United States, however, negative externalities are more often corrected with other methods.

Regulation and Tradable Permits. A tax is not the only way to correct a negative externality. Government can also use *regulation* to move a market closer to the efficient point. For example, in the gasoline market, regulators could tell car owners how much they could drive, or tell car producers how much pollution their vehicles are allowed to create. Indeed, this last regulation—state pollution restrictions on new automobiles—has been the method of choice for reducing pollution from automobiles in the United States.

But in the last two decades, the U.S. government has also relied increasingly on an innovative technique—called *tradable permits*—to reduce several types of pollution. This method is based on an understanding of Pareto improvements.

Tradable permit A license that allows a company to release a unit of pollution into the environment over some period of time.

A **tradable permit** is a license that allows a company to release a unit of pollution into the environment over some period of time. By issuing a fixed number of permits, the government determines the total level of pollution that can be legally emitted each period. However, firms can sell their government-issued permits to other firms in an organized market.

---

[7] International Institute for Sustainable Development Web page (*http://iisd.ca/susprod/displaydetails.asp?id=74*).

A firm whose technology would make it very costly to reduce pollution generally *buys* permits in the market. By buying a permit at a price lower than its cost of reducing pollution by another unit, the high-cost firm comes out ahead. At the same time, a firm whose technology enables it to reduce pollution rather cheaply will *sell* permits. By giving up permits, the low-cost firm takes on the obligation to reduce its pollution further. But by selling the permit at a price greater than its pollution-control cost, the low-cost firm gains as well.

The trading of permits shifts the costs of any given level of environmental improvement toward those firms who can do so more cheaply. The general public, however, is not affected by the trade, since total pollution remains unchanged. Therefore, for any given level of pollution, allowing firms to buy and sell licenses generates Pareto improvements. Viewed another way, tradable permits—by making it cheaper to lower pollution—has enabled the U.S. government to impose stricter environmental standards with the same total burden on producers.

Tradable permits have been used since the early 1980s to reduce several types of pollution. Permits for adding lead to gasoline virtually eliminated leaded gasoline from the market within five years. And a system of tradable permits begun in 1990 for sulfur dioxide (the pollutant that causes acid rain) cut emissions in half within five years—well ahead of schedule and at much lower cost than anticipated. Tradable permits are catching on in other countries as well, and are being considered, along with other policies, in international efforts to address the problem of global warming.

Left to itself, a market with a negative externality will produce too much output. Taxes, regulation, and tradable permits are examples of government intervention to decrease output toward the efficient level.

Dealing with a Positive Externality. What about the case of a positive externality, in which the by-product of a good or service *benefits* other parties rather than harms them? Once again, the market will not arrive at the economically efficient output level; in this case, output will be *too low*.

To see why, consider the market for a college education. In deciding whether to go to college, each of us takes account of the costs to us (tuition, room and board, what we could have earned instead of going to college) and the benefits to us (a higher-paying and more interesting job in the future, the enjoyment of learning). But by becoming educated, you also benefit other members of society in many ways. For example, you will be a more informed voter and thereby help to steer the government in directions that benefit many people besides you. If you major in chemistry, biology, or mechanical engineering, you may invent something that benefits society at large more than it benefits you. Or you may learn concepts and skills that make you a more responsible member of your community. Thus, the market for college education involves a positive externality.

Let's see why a competitive market in college education, with no government interference, would not produce the economically efficient amount of education.

Figure 12, panel (a), shows the market for bachelor's degrees. The height of the supply curve S reflects the costs of providing each degree at colleges and universities, and the height of the demand curve measures the value of each degree—*to the person who gets it*. But the demand curve does *not* reflect any of the benefits that college provides to the general public. Without government intervention, the market reaches equilibrium at point A, where the supply curve S and the demand curve D intersect. The equilibrium number of degrees is 800,000 per year, and the four-year price of a degree is $100,000.

HTTP://

In "Government's Role in Primary and Secondary Education," (http://www.dallasfed.org/research/er/1999/er9901b.pdf), Lori Taylor explores the rationale for government funding of education.

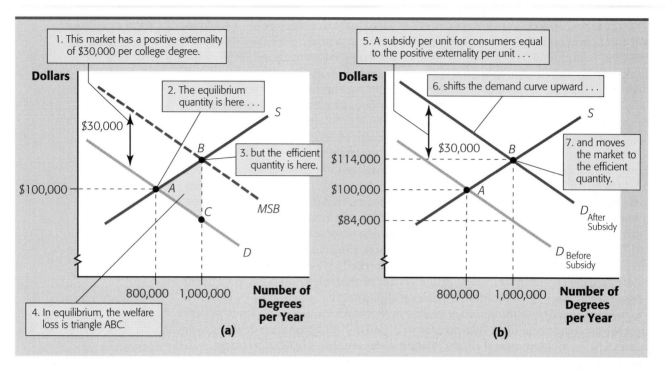

FIGURE 12

A Subsidy for Consumers to Correct a Positive Externality

Marginal social benefit (MSB)
The full benefit of producing another unit of a good, including the benefit to the consumer *and* any benefits enjoyed by third parties.

But since college confers benefits on society at large, 800,000 is *not* the efficient output level. We can see this by incorporating the positive externality into our diagram. Let's suppose that each bachelor's degree gives the general public $30,000 in benefits. When we add this benefit to the benefit for the degree holders themselves, we get the **marginal social benefit** (*MSB*) of another degree. *MSB* includes *all* the benefits of producing another bachelor's degree—the benefits to the holder *and* the benefits to society at large. This is why the *MSB* curve in Figure 12, panel (a), lies *above* the market demand curve. The distance between the curves is $30,000—the value of the positive externality.

Once we draw the *MSB* curve in Figure 12, panel (a), we discover that the *efficient* level of output is 1 million college degrees, where the *MSB* curve intersects the supply curve at point *B*. Why? Efficiency requires that the market provide any unit that has more value than it would cost to produce. The *MSB* curve tells us what the value of each degree *really* is, when *all* benefits are considered. For all units up to 1 million, the *MSB* curve lies above the supply curve, so those units provide greater value than their costs. Net benefits in the market are increased by providing them.

If you ignore the demand curve and look only at the *MSB* curve—which represents the *full* benefits of each degree—you can see that producing less than the efficient level creates a welfare loss. The labeled triangle *ABC* shows the *welfare loss* for this market in equilibrium—the loss in net benefits from producing too few bachelor's degrees each year.

> *A market with a positive externality associated with producing or consuming a good will produce less than the efficient quantity, creating a welfare loss.*

How can we achieve the efficient result of 1 million college degrees each year? One way is to *change* the demand curve so it is the same as the *MSB* curve in panel (a) of Figure 12. If everyone affected could negotiate and enforce an agreement without cost (the Coase theorem, which applies to positive externalities as well as negative), then the private market could solve the problem. People who benefit from *others'* degrees could be asked to give a side payment to those in college. This side payment would be included as part of the value of the degree for those considering college, shifting the demand curve upward. With a side payment of $30,000 per student, the market demand curve would rise to the position of the *MSB* curve and the market would provide 1 million degrees, the efficient level.

Of course, the time, trouble, and expense of arranging such a system privately would be prohibitive. And the free rider problem would be unmanageable. (Imagine someone passing the hat for voluntary contributions to support strangers in college!) Efficiency, once again, requires *government intervention*.

In most countries, the method of choice for government in the education market is *subsidies*—a payment to a producer or consumer for each unit provided. In the figure, we imagine that the subsidy is paid to students. (An end-of-chapter question asks you to explore the case where the subsidy is paid to colleges.) In Figure 12, panel (b), a subsidy of $30,000 per degree causes each student to add $30,000 to the value he or she places on a college education, thereby shifting up the demand curve by that amount. Each student would now be willing to pay $30,000 more than before, because they will receive that sum from the government.

The subsidy causes the market to *internalize* the positive externality of benefits from college degrees. That is, it forces consumers and producers to consider these benefits when making decisions. In the new equilibrium, the price of a degree rises, from $100,000 to $114,000 in the figure. This encourages colleges to increase enrollments. But students, after accounting for the subsidy, pay only $114,000 − $30,000 = $84,000. This is why more of them choose to attend college.

> *A subsidy on each unit of a good, equal to the external benefits it creates, can correct a positive externality and bring the market to an efficient output level.*

PUBLIC GOODS

One of the major roles of government in the economy is to provide *public goods.* These are goods that the market—if left to itself—will not provide at all, or will not provide efficiently even if there is no other market failure. It is left to the government to provide public goods in the efficient quantities, usually free of charge. (A more formal definition of public goods will come a bit later.)

To understand what makes a good public rather than private, let's begin by discussing two important features of *private goods*. First, a private good is characterized by **rivalry** in consumption—if one person consumes it, someone else cannot. If you rent an apartment, then someone else will *not* be able to rent that apartment. The same applies to virtually all goods that you buy in markets—food, computers, air travel, and so on. Rivalry also applies to privately provided services: the time you spend with your doctor, lawyer, or career counselor is time that someone else will *not* spend with that professional.

Rivalry A situation in which one person's consumption of a unit of a good or service means that no one else can consume that unit.

Most of the goods and services we've considered so far in this text are rival goods. By allowing the market to provide rival goods at a *price*, we ensure that people take account of the opportunity costs to society of their decisions to use these goods. If they were provided free of charge, people would tend to use them even if their value were less than the value of the resources used to produce them. Moreover, offering a rival good free of charge enables some people who don't value the good very highly to grab up all available supplies, depriving others who might value the goods even more. Thus, leaving such goods to the market—where a price reflecting marginal cost is charged—tends to promote economic efficiency.

> *If a good is rivalrous, efficiency requires that people pay a price for its use. In the absence of any market failure, private provision will lead to the efficient level of production.*

Excludability The ability to exclude those who do not pay for a good from consuming it.

A second feature of a private good is **excludability,** the ability to exclude those who do not pay for a good from consuming it. When you go to the supermarket, you are not permitted to eat frozen yogurt unless you pay for it. The same is true when you go to the movies or purchase a car. But if firms can*not* prevent nonpayers from consuming a good, the market will be *unable* to provide it, since few consumers would pay if they can consume it without paying. Excludability is what makes it *possible* for private firms to provide a good.

> *If a good is excludable, it* can *be provided by the private market.*

Let's sum up so far: Rivalry means that a price *must* be charged to achieve efficiency. Excludability means that private firms—who *do* charge a price—*can* produce it. If a good has both of these characteristics, it is called a *pure private good.*

Pure private good A good that is both rivalrous and excludable.

> *A good that is both rivalrous and excludable is a **pure private good.** In the absence of any significant market failure, private firms will provide these goods at close to efficient levels.*

But not all goods have these two characteristics. Consider, for example, an urban park located in an area where many people pass by during the day. People will enjoy walking by the park, just because it is pretty to look at. But to provide and maintain it requires many resources and raw materials: the labor of landscape architects and gardeners, gardening tools, fertilizer, flower bulbs, and so on. However, a walk-by park is, essentially, *nonexcludable.* If a private firm provided the park, the firm could not limit the benefits of walking by to those who paid for it. (Yes, it could construct a giant fence, but that would prevent *everyone* who walked by from seeing and enjoying the park.) For this reason, a private firm would have difficulty surviving by creating and maintaining an urban, walk-by park.

"But wait," you may think. "Couldn't the firm *ask* people to contribute according to the importance they place on the park?" Yes, but then each individual would have an incentive to downplay its importance and pay nothing. This is the *free rider problem* mentioned earlier in this chapter: When a good is nonexcludable, people have an incentive to become free riders—to let others pay for the good, so they can enjoy it without paying.

Thus, a private firm is generally unable to provide a nonexcludable good at all; it would not be able to stay in business.

> *When a good is nonexcludable, the private sector will generally be unable to provide it. In most cases, if we want such a good, government must provide it.*

In addition to being nonexcludable, urban parks are *nonrival:* One person can consume or enjoy passing by the park without anyone else consuming or enjoying less of it. Moreover, it uses up *no more of society's resources* when the benefits of the park are extended to an additional person. For this reason, even if the private sector *could* somehow charge us according to our consumption of the view as we walk by the park, it *should not* charge us. Why not? Because by charging a price each time we walk by, it would force each of us to consider a personal cost that does *not* correspond to any opportunity cost for society. Each time an additional person sees the park, a Pareto improvement takes place: That person gains and no one loses. Thus, to be economically efficient, *everyone* who places *any value at all* on seeing the park should be able to see it. But this will only happen if the price of seeing the park is *zero*.

This leads us to an important conclusion: Since the economically efficient price for the park is zero, private firms—which would have to charge a positive price—should not be the ones to provide it. That is, even if a firm *could* exclude those who do not pay, it *should not* do so. By charging a positive price, the number of people deciding to pay and enjoy the park would be below the economically efficient level.

> *When a good or service is nonrival, the market cannot provide it efficiently. Rather, to achieve economic efficiency, the good or service would have to be provided free of charge.*

Now let's combine these features. If a good is nonrival, the private market cannot provide it *efficiently,* since efficiency requires a zero price. If it's nonexcludable, the private market will usually not provide the good *at all*. If a good has both of these characteristics, it is called a *pure public good*.

> *A good that is both nonrivalrous and nonexcludable is a **pure public good**.*

Pure public good A good that is both nonrivalrous and nonexcludable.

A pure public good, if it could provide benefits to some people that are greater than the cost of providing it to them, is a market failure. Producing the good would create net benefits. But because the good is nonexcludable, the private market generally ignores it. This means that if we rely on the private market, we not only don't get the efficient quantity, we generally get *no* quantity. Furthermore, even if the private market *could* provide such a good, it could usually not do so efficiently, because charging *any* positive price for a nonrivalrous good would be inefficient.

Although we've been discussing rivalry and excludability—and their opposites—as absolutes, these characteristics are often murky. Some of the benefits of consuming a good can be rival, and some nonrival. Some of the benefits can be excludable, and some not. Consider a newspaper. Consumption of the paper is mostly rival: The paper I buy at the newsstand and take home can't be bought and taken home by you. It's also partly excludable: You can't buy it from the newsstand unless you pay. But an important aspect of this good is the *information* inside it, which is largely *nonrival* (if I tell you what I've read, you gain knowledge of the news without diminishing my knowledge) and somewhat *nonexcludable* (if I tell you the news, you get the information without having to pay the newspaper company).

Accordingly, it makes sense to view rivalry and excludability as a matter of *degree,* rather than as absolute categories. This is why, in Figure 13, different goods are positioned at different points along a spectrum for rivalry and excludability. Goods that appear farthest toward the upper left corner are the *purest private goods*—those with a very *high degree*

Characterizing Public and Private Goods Public goods and private goods are defined by their characteristics, not by which sector *happens* to be providing it in a particular country. Broadcast television, for example, has the characteristics of a pure public good: nonrivalry and nonexcludability. And in many countries, the government *does* provide the main television channel. But in the United States (other than the Public Broadcasting Corporation's stations) and many other countries, broadcast television is provided by private firms, free of charge. The industry solves the nonexcludabilitiy problem by using a different method for obtaining revenue: heavy advertising.

DANGEROUS CURVES

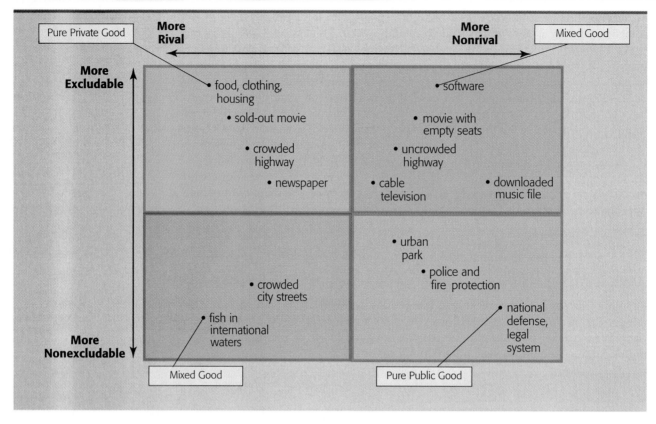

FIGURE 13

Pure Private, Pure Public, and Mixed Goods

of excludability and rivalry. These include most of the goods we've discussed in earlier chapters, such as bed frames, car washes, wheat, extermination services, and so on. The market almost always provides these goods and—with the government's help when necessary to correct for externalities and limit monopoly power—can provide them in close-to-efficient quantities.

Goods that appear farthest toward the lower right corner are the *purest public goods:* almost entirely nonrival and nonexcludable. National defense, for example, has both characteristics: My being defended to any degree doesn't mean you are defended any less. And it is virtually impossible to exclude those who don't pay from the benefits of national defense, as long as they remain in the country.

Many considerations go into the *relative* positions of the goods in Figure 13, and you may disagree with our choices. For example, we've made cable television more nonexludable than highways (it's easier to hook up cable illegally than to bypass a highway tollbooth once it's installed). Similarly, we've positioned cable television as more *rivalrous* than software, because *certain* aspects of cable service—the installation appointment, the cable box, repairs—use up resources that others can't use simultaneously.

Mixed Goods

Goods that appear in the upper right and lower left corners can be called *mixed goods,* because they share features of both public and private goods. These goods are becoming increasingly important in our society, and they are responsible for some growing social tension and controversy.

Excludable but Nonrivalrous Goods. Consider first goods near the upper right-hand corner, which are excludable but nonrivalrous. This category includes most information products. The problem with this type of mixed good is that although the private sector can (and often does) supply it, it does not do so in the efficient quantity. As you've learned, efficiency in the market for a nonrivalrous good is achieved only when additional units are available without charge.

For example, Microsoft and other software companies have considerable power to *exclude* you from using their

Public *Provision* Versus Public *Production* Don't confuse public *provision* of a good with public *production*. The government must *provide* a pure public good in order to correct the market failure problem. But it can provide it by either producing the good itself (public production) or contracting production out to private firms (private production). Many local governments, for example, pay private firms to collect trash or run prisons: private production. These services are purchased by government and *publicly provided* without charge to residents. Similarly, almost all of the *goods* that are used for national defense—tanks, radar equipment, laser-guided munitions—are produced by private firms and purchased by the federal government. However, the government chooses *public production* for the *service* of national defense itself: It hires, trains, and manages U.S. military personnel, and manages defense goods after buying them. It's the government's *provision* of national defense without charge—not the government production—that cures the market failure.

software unless you pay, by encoding discs with copy protection and limiting the number of installations permitted. And although some people can break these codes, most cannot. Yet providing someone with an *additional* copy of its software hardly costs Microsoft anything at all. And if not for the embedded copy protection, people could copy the software from their friends, using up no resource other than the space on their own hard drive. Software, then, is an essentially nonrivalrous good, but an excludable one. It is neither pure public nor pure private.

Digital music files are another example of this type of mixed good. Over the past few years, millions of people have downloaded copyrighted songs from file-sharing servers such as Morpheus, Gnutella, Kazaa, WinMX, and Audiogalaxy. Digital music files are nonrivalrous: The digital code can be recopied endlessly, at almost zero cost. Therefore, it is *efficient* for this good to be provided free of charge. However, unless we want the government to run the music industry, private firms need to charge for music. Currently, music remains somewhat excludable, for two reasons: (1) it is against the law to make copyrighted music available online; and (2) many people—either because of respect for the law, fear of getting caught, lack of technical expertise, or scarce time—still prefer to buy their music from a store or online shopping service.

But by 2003, with an estimated 60 million people downloading music online without paying, excludablility was rapidly breaking down. The easiest solution isn't available: Years ago, the industry adopted common CD audio standards that rule out embedded copy protection. Introducing copy protection now would entail great cost, and risk public alienation, since it would require everyone to buy new stereos and handheld players to listen to the new format. The industry has tried suing the file-sharing companies, but had major success only with the first one—Napster—which it put out of business. In mid-2003, the music industry began threatening lawsuits for individual users, and lobbied for legal changes that would permit the industry to sabotage file-sharing services by flooding them with requests for downloads, redirecting users' queries to their own sites, and posting corrupted files. The music industry in the digital age is desperately looking for ways to achieve greater excludability, but has not yet found a good solution.

Nonexcludable but Rivalrous Goods. Now consider the lower left-hand corner of Figure 13, which shows nonexcludable but rivalrous goods. City streets and some important natural resources fall into this category. Economists use the term *tragedy of the commons* to describe the problem caused by many of these goods. In a traditional English village, the commons was an area freely available to all families for grazing their animals. Grazing rights are a rivalrous good: If one cow eats the grass, another can't. But the commons had no method of exclusion, so it was overgrazed, causing harm to *all* families.

Tragedy of the commons The problem of overuse when a good is rivalrous but nonexcludable.

> *The **tragedy of the commons** occurs when rivalrous but nonexcludable goods are overused, to the detriment of all.*

A current example of the tragedy of the commons is fishing in international waters. No one owns these areas of the ocean and no single government can tell people not to fish in them. And since no one charges for the fish removed, fishing boats use huge nets that catch just about every source of protein (most of which is ground up to be used as cattle feed). A recent study, correcting some inaccuracies in earlier research, has found that world fish landings have been declining steadily since 1980.[8] The decline would be even steeper if not for the efforts of fishers, who have been going farther offshore, fishing deeper, fishing more intensively, and going after smaller and smaller fish. But these very methods are also changing the ocean's ecosystem, threatening species of ocean life further down the food chain. Unless something is done, the decline in the world's supply of fish—and other ocean life—may accelerate, overwhelming the efforts of the fishing industry to forestall the decline in catches. Although scientists have recommended specific limits on national governments since 1987, virtually every country—concerned about the welfare of its *own* fishing industry—has chosen to ignore the recommendations. Each government is a free rider in the international community, reasoning that its own fish catch is just a "drop in the bucket," and that whatever other governments do, it is better off allowing its *own* crews to continue depleting the fish.

EFFICIENCY AND GOVERNMENT IN PERSPECTIVE

In this chapter, you've seen that an economy with *well-functioning, perfectly competitive markets* tends to be economically efficient. But notice the italicized words. As you've seen in this chapter, many types of government involvement are needed to ensure that markets function well and to deal with market failures. The government helps markets to function by providing a legal and regulatory infrastructure. In extreme cases of imperfect competition, government antitrust action or regulation may be needed. The government imposes taxes and subsidies and uses other methods to deal with externalities. And the government often steps in to provide goods and services that are nonrival, nonexcludable, or both.

These cases of government involvement are not without controversy. In fact, most of the controversies that pit Democrats against Republicans in the United States (or Conservatives against Labourites in Britain, or Social Democrats against Christian Democrats in Germany) relate to when, and to what extent, the government should be involved in the economy. Debates about public education, Social Security, international trade, and immigration all center on questions of the proper role for government. Some of the disagreement is over the government's role in bringing about a more fair economy, but there is also debate about the government's role in bringing about economic efficiency.

How could anyone disagree with the government's role in bringing about efficiency with a strong legal structure and corrections for market failure?

While we've been stressing how government *can* improve efficiency, it isn't always easy. First, there are information problems. Just how much damage do nega-

8 Daniel Pauly and Reg Watson, "Counting the Last Fish," *Scientific American*, July 2003 (pp. 42–47).

tive externalities from pollution cause? And how can the harm be valued in dollars? What is the dollar value of the external benefits from a college degree? These questions are not easy to answer with any accuracy, and estimates are always controversial. While government may be able to move us *closer* to efficiency, it can also fall short or overshoot based on inaccurate information.

Second, there are incentive problems for government. Some of these are caused by the *principal–agent problem*, discussed in Chapter 12. Government officials are the agents of the general public and are supposed to serve the public interest. But these officials may have their own incentives, such as expanding the size of their departmental budgets. Although there are checks and balances for monitoring and limiting this type of behavior, their effectiveness is sometimes limited.

Government officials can also be influenced by lobbies for special-interest groups. The benefits from a single, favorable government decision are highly concentrated on a specific firm or industry, but the *costs* of that one decision are widely dispersed among the population. Therefore, firms have great incentive to lobby for favorable policies, while the general public has little incentive to oppose them. For example, from 1997 to 2002, during a period of rapid changes in the health care system that were being shaped by legislation, the pharmaceutical industry spent an estimated $478 million directly lobbying Congress and an additional $172 million on federal campaign contributions, TV ads, and general efforts to sway public opinion.[9] Expenditures of this magnitude can tilt government decision making in favor of a specific industry—which may or not be the efficient policy decision.

Third, in order for government to have the funds it needs to support markets and do other things, it must raise revenue through taxes. These taxes, whether they are imposed on the labor market, goods markets, or capital markets, introduce welfare losses of their own. Just as a tax on airline tickets raises the price and reduces the quantity sold, so the Social Security tax and the income tax—which fall largely on labor income—can raise the price of labor to firms and reduce the number of workers employed.

Finally, there is also an inherent problem with the provision of public goods that almost guarantees *dissatisfaction* about them. With a private good, each of us—facing the market price—buys whatever quantity we choose. We may feel frustrated about the size of our income or wealth, but given those constraints, each of us is free to purchase the quantity of each good that brings us the most satisfaction as individuals. If one person loves Italian food and another loves rock concerts, we'd expect to see them purchasing vastly different amounts of these two goods, based on their differing preferences.

But public goods, by their nature, are provided in a politically determined quantity, and *everyone* must consume the same amount. One person can't consume a strong national defense while another consumes a weak one. So, even if the political process is working *well*, about half the population will feel we are spending too much on a specific public good, and half the population will believe we are spending too little. This does not mean the government is acting inefficiently; but it does explain some of the controversy over government involvement in the economy.

Finally, remember that there are other important roles for the government besides fostering efficiency, such as equity, fairness, justice, and more. As discussed elsewhere in this text, these are not issues over which people easily agree. Taxing gasoline to correct an externality would hit the poor harder than the rich, while taxing airline travel would do the opposite. Eliminating price supports for agricultural goods might move the economy toward efficiency, but it would cause harm to many farmers and their families. Almost every change in the tax code designed to improve either efficiency or equity will raise a firestorm of protest because of the way it might affect the other.

[9] "Drug Industry Sees Increase in Lobbying," *Wall Street Journal*, June 24, 2003.

These controversies are so heated and so varied, that it is easy to forget how much agreement there is about the role of government. Anyone studying the role of government in the economies of the United States, Canada, Mexico, France, Germany, Britain, Japan, and the vast majority of other developed economies, is struck by one glaring fact: Most economic activity is carried out among private individuals. In all of these countries, there is widespread agreement that although government intervention is often necessary, the most powerful forces that exploit Pareto improvements and drive the economy toward efficiency are the actions of individual producers and consumers. And among these countries, there is also substantial commonality in the relatively smaller list of goods and services provided by government.

USING THE THEORY
Traffic as a Market Failure

Almost everyone in the United States has been caught in a traffic jam in some large town or city at some point in their lives. For many, it's a daily experience. Congested streets create even larger problems in some European and Asian cities, and in some developing countries, they can bring economic life to a halt for hours at a time. And the problem in most cities is getting worse.

Consider London. Traffic congestion has worsened dramatically in recent decades, especially in the historic inner city. By 2000, an average of 250,000 cars were entering this eight-square-mile area each day, and average traffic speeds had slowed to nine miles per hour—about the speed of a horse-coach a century earlier. In New York, about 250,000 cars enter central Manhattan, also about eight square miles, in just *three hours* every morning, slowing traffic to an average speed of just seven miles per hour.[10] Urban traffic congestion relates to our use of a good: *city streets*. And we can view the traffic problem as a market failure in two different ways.

First, traffic is an externality problem. When you decide to take your car onto a city street, your decision is based on the costs and benefits to *you*. But if the road is already crowded, your decision creates a negative externality as well: By adding to the traffic, you increase the delay and frustration, gasoline costs, and risk of accident for *others*. Of course, you include the effects of traffic congestion *on yourself* in making your decision to get into your car; but you don't take into account these costs for *others*.

For example, let's suppose that when 1,000 additional cars enter central Manhattan during a one-hour morning period, the result is six minutes ($\frac{1}{10}$ of an hour) of additional delay for the other 250,000 cars in the area for the next *three* hours. (Traffic congestion lasts longer than its original cause, and spreads quickly beyond its point of origin by blocking cross traffic.) Assuming just one person in each car, the total hours of delay would be $250{,}000 \times \frac{1}{10} = 25{,}000$ hours. If this time is valued at just $10 per hour—less than the average hourly wage—the cost is $250,000. Therefore, if you are just *one* of those additional 1,000 entering the area, the costs you impose on others is $250,000 / 1,000 = $250.

Would you take the additional car trip if you had to pay $250 or more? For most people entering the city, the answer would be no. But because they only bear their own direct costs—gas, wear and tear on their *own* car, and their *own* time—

[10] Randy Kennedy, "The Day the Traffic Disappeared," *New York Times Magazine*, April 20, 2003.

the result is inefficiency: People are consuming another unit of a good (the car trip) whose value to them is less than its marginal *social* cost. Total net benefits decrease.

Second, city streets can be viewed as a *mixed good*, in the lower left quadrant of Figure 13. At peak times, city streets are rivalrous: The space occupied by your car can't be occupied by anyone else. On the other hand, streets are not easily excludable. This is why, for the most part, governments *treat* city streets as if they are a pure public good: providing them free of charge to all who want to use them. The result—as in so many other cases of providing a rivalrous good free of charge—is a tragedy of the commons: Consumption increases until everyone is harmed.

Can the government solve the problem? From the externality perspective, the solution would require drivers to *internalize* the externality they impose on others, by making them pay the social costs of their trip. From the rivalry perspective, the solution is similar: People must pay for a rivalrous good in order to avoid the tragedy of the commons. But is this feasible?

Some cities, such as New York, do charge tolls for cars that enter via bridges or tunnels. But entry tolls are problematic, and are rarely set high enough to solve the problem of congestion at peak travel times. One reason is the difficulty of efficiently targeting the entry tolls toward those causing the externality or consuming the rivalrous good. For example, those who live *inside* the city but still contribute to the traffic don't pay the toll at all. And those entering from outside, but who plan to drive to a noncongested (nonrivalrous) area must pay the same toll as people creating more of a problem. New electronic tracking technologies could perhaps solve this problem by imposing fees on each vehicle based on their contribution to congestion. The fees could vary by time of day and the actual locations through which a vehicle travels.

But there is a bigger problem: the political damage to any elected representative who would propose a fee high enough to be efficient on a good that has traditionally been free. Such fees can create resentment among the electorate in general, and also raise serious equity issues. After all, the fee cannot be trivial: It must be high enough to dissuade at least *some* people from driving at certain hours, which is high enough to create hardship for poorer families. True, they could be promised compensation or increased government services from the revenue the fee would provide. But people might not trust the government's promise, given other priorities for city funds.

All of this conventional political wisdom may have changed since early 2003, when Ken Livingstone—the mayor of London—decided to take a chance: His administration established a 5 pound (about $8) *per day* user fee on any automobile that appeared in the eight-square-mile boundary of London's inner city. The fee had to be paid in advance, by 10 P.M. the night before travel, adding to its opportunity cost (the time and trouble of paying the fee)—especially for those who don't plan their travel well in advance. Any car that was seen parked, driving through, or in any way appeared within the eight-square-mile zone would be required to pay the fee. Violators faced fines of 80 pounds (about $130), and were almost certain to be caught: The city positioned more than 700 cameras throughout the zone to record license plate numbers and send the optical data to a central computer, which would instantly determine if the vehicle owner had paid the fee. Livingstone addressed the equity issue as well, using almost all of the additional city revenue for significant expansions in bus service.

On the first day the fee applied, traffic dropped about 25 percent: 60,000 fewer cars entered the area than on a normal day. Traffic speeds doubled to about 20 miles per hour. The political opposition turned out to be manageable. Livingstone—a far-left socialist—has even proposed expanding this market solution to other congested areas of the city. And officials in New York, Paris, Los Angeles, and other large cities around the world have been studying London's success.

Summary

A market or an economy is economically efficient when all Pareto improvements have been exploited, so there is no way to reallocate resources that makes at least one person better off without harming anyone else. In a market, the welfare loss from inefficiency is the potential net benefit (consumer and producer surplus) not achieved due to the inefficiency. The equilibrium in a well-functioning perfectly competitive market is efficient. When markets fail to achieve economic efficiency—when they leave potential Pareto improvements unexploited—government can often step in and help.

The legal system run by governments is a key element of institutional infrastructure to promote efficiency. Criminal law limits exchanges to voluntary ones. Property law contributes to enforceable property rights. Contract law helps improve the efficiency of exchange when one party must go first, while tort law affects interactions among strangers. Finally, antitrust law attempts to prevent harm to consumers from limited competi-

tion. In addition to the legal system, the government's regulatory system affects many aspects of economic life.

A market failure occurs when a market, left to itself, fails to achieve economic efficiency. Monopoly and imperfect competition, externalities, and public goods are examples of market failures. Governments have a variety of tools to correct these failures. Through antitrust action and regulation, governments can sometimes narrow the gap between price and marginal cost in imperfectly competitive markets. Externalities—unpriced by-products of economic transactions that affect outsiders—can be corrected through taxes, subsidies, regulation, or other means. And public goods—those that are nonrival and nonexcludable—can be provided by government itself. Government solutions to market failures are often imperfect and controversial. But there is widespread agreement that government action is needed to prevent the most important market failures.

Key Terms

Coase Theorem
Consumer surplus
Excludability
Externality
Free rider problem
Marginal Social Benefit (MSB)
Marginal Social Cost (MSC)

Market consumer surplus
Market failure
Market producer surplus
Pareto improvement
Producer surplus
Pure private good
Pure public good

Rivalry
Tort
Total net benefits
Tradable Permit
Tragedy of the commons
Welfare loss

Review Questions

Answers to even-numbered Questions and Problems can be found on the text Web site at http://hall-lieb.swlearning.com.

1. What is the relationship between *Pareto improvements* and the concept of *economic efficiency*?

2. Which of the following actions would be a Pareto improvement? Which could become a Pareto improvement if the right side payment were included?
   a. You buy a Coke for $4.50 at an airport restaurant.
   b. You and a friend go to a movie and compromise on which one to see.
   c. An acquaintance, who values your tennis racket more than you do, borrows it, and never returns it.

3. Briefly explain why, in a perfectly competitive market with no market failure, providing *less* than the equilibrium quantity cannot be economically efficient.

4. Briefly explain why, in a perfectly competitive market with no market failure, a quantity *greater than* the equilibrium quantity cannot be economically efficient.

5. "The economically efficient price in a competitive market is the price that maximizes market consumer surplus." True or false? Explain briefly.

6. Explain how each of the following enhances economic efficiency:
   a. Criminal law
   b. Property law
   c. Contract law
   d. Tort law
   e. Antitrust law

7. What are the three major types of market failure discussed in the chapter? For each type, identify a type of government action that could, in theory, correct the failure.

8. Which type of market failure is addressed by the Coase theorem? Under what conditions does the theorem apply?

9. What role does the free rider problem play in understanding the problem posed by *negative externalities*? By *positive externalities*?

10. What is the difference between *marginal cost* and *marginal social cost*?

11. Does the Coase theorem apply to most cases of air pollution? Why or why not?

12. What is a pure public good? How is a pure public good different from a pure private good?

13. State whether the benefits from each of the following goods or services are (1) mostly excludable or mostly nonexcludable; and (2) mostly rival or mostly nonrival.

a. Breakfast at a coffee shop
b. Medical care to treat a highly contagious disease
c. Efforts to maintain homeland security
d. A movie shown in a theater with mostly empty seats
e. Teaching young children not to steal

Problems and Exercises

1. In Figure 3, suppose that, initially, McCollum is providing the fifth guitar lesson to Zoe for a price of $16. Who would gain and who would lose from this lesson? Construct a scorecard, involving a side payment of $2 from McCollum to Zoe, showing that both of them come out ahead by agreeing *not* to provide the fifth lesson.

2. In the chapter, it was stated that a competitive market would not provide goods like chocolate-covered Brussels sprouts because their value—even to those who like them most—would be less than the cost of supplying even a small quantity. Illustrate the market for such a good with supply and demand curves.

3. Figure 7 (b) shows a price floor of $21 in the market for guitar lessons. Calculate the dollar value of the welfare loss caused by the price floor.

4. The following table shows the quantities of bottled water demanded and supplied per week at different prices in a particular city:

Price	Quantity Demanded	Quantity Supplied
$1.10	8,000	0
$1.15	7,000	1,000
$1.20	6,000	2,000
$1.25	5,000	3,000
$1.30	4,000	4,000
$1.35	3,000	5,000
$1.40	2,000	6,000
$1.45	1,000	7,000
$1.50	0	8,000

a. Draw the supply and demand curves for this market, and identify the equilibrium price and quantity.
b. Identify on your graph areas for market consumer surplus and market producer surplus when the market is in equilibrium.
c. Using your graph, calculate the dollar value of market consumer surplus, market producer surplus, and the total net benefits in the market at equilibrium.

5. Suppose the government imposes a price *ceiling* of $1.20 in the market for bottled water in problem 4. Calculate the dollar value of each of the following:
a. market consumer surplus
b. market producer surplus
c. total net benefits in the market
d. the welfare loss from the price ceiling

6. Suppose the government imposes a price *floor* of $1.40 in the market for bottled water in problem 4. Calculate the dollar value of each of the following:
a. market consumer surplus
b. market producer surplus
c. total net benefits in the market
d. the welfare loss from the price floor

7. Review the section of the chapter titled, "The Private Solution to a Negative Externality." Suppose that Grace gains $70,000 from building the theater, but the harm to Fernando is $100,000.
a. Is it efficient to build the theater? Briefly, why or why not?
b. If Fernando has the legal right to *prevent* the theater from being built, would you expect the theater to be built?
c. If Grace has the legal right to *build* the theater, would you expect the theater to be built?

8. Figure 11 shows the market for gasoline with a negative externality from pollution. Using the information in both panels, calculate the dollar value of the welfare loss per period before any government intervention.

9. Figure 12 shows the market for college degrees with a positive externality. Using the information in both panels, calculate the dollar value of the welfare loss per year before any government intervention.

10. Last year, Pat and Chris occupied separate apartments. Each consumed 400 gallons of hot water monthly. This year, they are sharing an apartment. To their surprise, they find that they are using a total of 1,000 gallons per month between them. Why? What concept discussed in this chapter is illustrated by this example?

11. Some have argued that the music industry is by nature inefficient, because once a piece of music is produced, the firm that owns it has a monopoly and charges the monopoly price. Yet, the marginal cost of making the music available to one more member of the public (via the Internet) is zero. Draw a diagram, similar to Figure 10, to represent this situation. Identify on your diagram:
a. the efficient level of production;

b. the level of production a government-regulated music industry would earn if it were permitted to charge just enough for a "fair rate of return";

c. the level of production provided by the (currently unregulated) industry.

12. In Figure 11 (b), a negative externality was corrected with a $0.50 per gallon tax on gasoline producers. Show that the total price paid by consumers, the total price received by firms, and the equilibrium quantity would have been exactly the same if the same tax had been imposed on gasoline consumers instead of producers.

13. In Figure 12 (b), a positive externality was corrected with a $30,000 subsidy paid to college students. Show that the total price paid by students, the total price received by colleges, and the equilibrium quantity of degrees would have been exactly the same if the $30,000 subsidy per student had been given to the colleges.

Challenge Questions

1. The following table shows the quantities of car alarms demanded and supplied per year in a town:

Price	Quantity Demanded	Quantity Supplied
$ 75	800	0
$100	750	150
$125	700	300
$150	650	450
$175	600	600
$200	550	750
$225	500	900
$250	450	1,050

Without drawing a graph, determine the efficient quantity in this market under each of the following assumptions:

a. Each car alarm sold creates a negative externality (noise pollution) that causes $100 in harm to the public.

b. Each car alarm creates a *positive* externality (reduced law enforcement costs) that provides $100 in benefits to the public.

2. Suppose Douglas and Ziffel have properties that adjoin the farm of Mr. Haney. The current zoning law permits Haney to use the farm for any purpose. Haney has decided to raise pigs (the best use of the land). A pig farm will earn $50,000 per year, forever.

a. Assume the interest rate is 10 percent per year. What is Haney's pig farm worth? (*Hint:* Use a special formula from Chapter 13.)

b. Suppose the next best use of Haney's property is residential, where it could earn $20,000 per year. What is the minimum one-time payment Haney would accept to agree to restrict his land for residential use forever?

c. Suppose Douglas is willing to pay $200,000 for an end to pig farming on Haney's land, while Ziffel is willing to pay no more than $150,000. (For some reason, Ziffel does not mind pig farming as much as Douglas does.) If Douglas pays Haney $200,000 and Ziffel pays Haney $150,000, and Haney converts his land to residential use, is this a Pareto improvement? Who benefits, who loses, and by how much?

d. Suppose instead that Douglas pays $150,000 and Ziffel pays $150,000. Is this move a Pareto improvement? Who benefits, who loses, and by how much?

ECONOMIC *Applications*   *These exercises require access to Hall/Lieberman Xtra! If Xtra! did not come with your book, visit http://hallxtra.swlearning.com to purchase.*

1. Use your Xtra! password at the Hall and Lieberman Web site (http://hallxtra.swlearning.com), select this chapter, and under Economic Applications, click on EconDebate. Choose *Microeconomics: Government and the Economy,* and scroll down to find the debate, "Should Anti-pollution Standards Be Strengthened?" The debate argues that most people agree that something must be done to reduce pollution, but are not in agreement as to how much regulation is needed. Suppose the government overregulates production that emits pollution. Show on a graph the welfare loss to society from such overregulation.

2. Use your Xtra! password at the Hall and Lieberman Web site (http://hallxtra.swlearning.com), select this chapter,

and under Economic Applications, click on EconNews. Choose *Microeconomics: Economics and the Environment,* and scroll down to find the summary, "Reducing Airline Emissions: The Future Is the Past." Read the summary, and answer the questions below.

a. Is this an efficient way of reducing emissions? Why or why not?

b. Suppose a tax on fuel is imposed on airlines. Use a graph of marginal benefit and marginal cost to explain how consumer and producer surplus change in the presence of such a tax.

Comparative Advantage and the Gains from International Trade

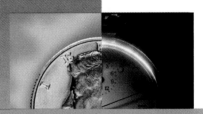

Consumers love bargains. And the rest of the world offers U.S. consumers bargains galore: cars from Japan, computer memory chips from Korea, shoes from China, tomatoes from Mexico, lumber from Canada, and sugar from the Caribbean. But Americans' purchases of foreign-made goods have always been a controversial subject. Should we let these bargain goods into the country? Consumers certainly benefit when we do so. But don't cheap foreign goods threaten the jobs of American workers and the profits of American producers? How do we balance the interests of specific workers and producers on the one hand with the interests of consumers in general? These questions are important not just in the United States, but in every country of the world.

Over the post–World War II period, there has been a worldwide movement toward a policy of *free trade*—the unhindered movement of goods and services across national boundaries. An example of this movement was the creation—in 1995—of a new international body: the World Trade Organization (WTO). The WTO's goal is to help resolve trade disputes among its members, and to reduce obstacles to free trade around the world. And to some extent it has succeeded: Import taxes, import limitations, and all kinds of crafty regulations designed to keep out imports are gradually falling away. By mid-2003, 146 countries had joined the WTO, including China, which was admitted in December 2001. And some 26 other countries, including Russia, Saudi Arabia, and Vietnam, were eager to join the free-trade group.

But while many barriers have come down, others are being put up. Asian governments have been dragging their feet on allowing U.S. firms to sell telecommunications and financial services there. The United States has renewed its long-standing quota on sugar imports and—in 2002—took serious steps to reduce imports of steel from China, Russia, Europe, and Japan. Europeans have restricted the sale of American satellite communications services and American beef. Canada has interfered with the sale of American magazines and television programs within its borders. Poor countries have imposed tariffs on computers, semiconductors, and software exported by rich countries. Rich countries have announced their intention to maintain, at least through the year 2005, existing quotas on textiles and clothing sold by poor countries.

Looking at the contradictory mix of trade policies that exist in the world, we are left to wonder: Is free international trade a good thing that makes us better off, or is it bad for us and something that should be kept in check? In this chapter, you'll learn to apply the tools of economics to issues surrounding international trade. Most important, you'll see how we can extend economic analysis to a global context, in which markets extend across international borders, and the decision makers are households, firms, and government agencies in different nations.

THE LOGIC OF FREE TRADE

Many of us like the idea of being self-reliant. A very few even prefer to live by themselves in a remote region of Alaska or the backcountry of Montana. But consider the defects of self-sufficiency: If you lived all by yourself, you would be poor. You could not *export* or sell to others any part of your own production, nor could you *import* or buy from others anything they have produced. You would be limited to consuming the goods and services that you produced. Undoubtedly, the food, clothing, and housing you would manage to produce by yourself would be small in quantity and poor in quality—nothing like the items you currently enjoy. And there would be many things you could not get at all—electricity, television, cars, airplane trips, or the penicillin that could save your life.

The defects of self-sufficiency explain why most people do not choose it. Rather, people prefer to specialize and trade with each other. In Chapter 2, you learned that specialization and exchange enable us to enjoy greater production and higher living standards than would otherwise be possible.

This principle applies not just to individuals, but also to *groups* of individuals, such as those living within the boundaries that define cities, counties, states, or nations. That is, just as we all benefit when *individuals* specialize and exchange with each other, so, too, we can benefit when *groups* of individuals specialize in producing different goods and services, and exchange them with other *groups*.

Imagine what would happen if the residents of your state switched from a policy of open trading with other states to one of self-sufficiency, refusing to import anything from "foreign states" or to export anything to them. Such an arrangement would be preferable to individual self-sufficiency; at least there would be specialization and trade *within* the state. But the elimination of trading between states would surely result in many sacrifices. Lacking the necessary inputs for their production, for instance, your state might have to do without bananas, cotton, or tires. And the goods that *were* made in your state would likely be produced inefficiently. For example, while residents of Vermont *could* drill for oil, and Texans *could* produce maple syrup, they could do so only at great cost of resources.

Thus, it would make no sense to insist on the economic self-sufficiency of each of the 50 states. And the founders of the United States knew this. They placed prohibitions against tariffs, quotas, and other barriers to interstate commerce right in the U.S. Constitution. The people of Vermont and Texas are vastly better off under free trade among the states than they would be if each state were self-sufficient.

What is true for states is also true for entire nations. The members of the WTO have carried the argument to its ultimate conclusion: National specialization and exchange can expand world living standards through free *international* trade. Such trade involves the movement of goods and services across national boundaries. Goods and services produced domestically, but sold abroad, are called **exports;** those produced abroad, but consumed domestically, are called **imports.** The long-term goal of the WTO is to remove all barriers to exports and imports in order to encourage among nations the specialization and trade that have been so successful within nations.

Exports Goods and services produced domestically, but sold abroad.

Imports Goods and services produced abroad, but consumed domestically.

THE THEORY OF COMPARATIVE ADVANTAGE

Economists who first considered the benefits of international trade focused on a country's *absolute advantage.*

> *A country has an **absolute advantage** in a good when it can produce it using fewer resources than another country.*

Absolute advantage The ability to produce a good or service, using fewer resources than other producers use.

As the early economists saw it, the citizens of every nation could improve their economic welfare by specializing in the production of goods in which they had an absolute advantage and exporting them to other countries. In turn, they would import goods from countries that had an absolute advantage in those goods.

Way back in 1817, however, the British economist David Ricardo disagreed. Absolute advantage, he argued, was not a necessary ingredient for mutually beneficial international trade. The key was *comparative advantage:*

> *A nation has a **comparative advantage** in producing a good if it can produce it at a lower opportunity cost than some other country.*

Comparative advantage The ability to produce a good or service at a lower opportunity cost than other producers.

Notice the difference between the definitions of absolute advantage and comparative advantage. While absolute advantage in a good is defined by the resources used to produce it, comparative advantage is based on the *opportunity cost* of producing it. And we measure the opportunity cost of producing a good not by the resources used to produce it, but rather by the *other goods* that these resources *could* have produced instead.

TABLE 1
Labor Requirements per Unit

Labor Requirements per:	China	United States
Suit	125 hours	50 hours
Computer	625 hours	100 hours

Ricardo argued that a potential trading partner could be absolutely inferior in the production of every single good—requiring more resources per unit of each good than any other country—and still have a comparative advantage in some good. The comparative advantage would arise because the country was *less* inferior at producing some goods than others. Likewise, a country that had an absolute advantage in producing everything could—contrary to common opinion—still benefit from trade. It would have a comparative advantage only in some, but not all, goods.

> *Mutually beneficial trade between any two countries is possible whenever one country is relatively better at producing a good than the other country is. Being relatively better means having the ability to produce a good at a lower opportunity cost—that is, at a lower sacrifice of other goods foregone.*

Opportunity Cost and Comparative Advantage

To illustrate Ricardo's insight, let's consider a hypothetical world of two countries, China and the United States. Both are producing only two goods, men's suits and computers. Could they better themselves by trading with one another? Ricardo would have us look at opportunity costs. But how do we determine the opportunity cost of a computer or a suit?

Let's start out as simply as possible. We'll imagine there is only one resource in each country—labor—and that it takes a constant number of hours to make one computer or one suit no matter how many units of these goods are produced. Table 1 lists the labor hours required. For example, the entry of 125 in the upper left corner tells us that it takes 125 hours of labor to make one suit in China, no matter how many suits are produced there. The upper right corner tells us that it takes 50 hours to make a suit in the United States.

This is all the information we'll need to find the opportunity cost of a computer or a suit in China or the United States.

First, suppose China were to produce one additional computer. Then it would have to divert 625 hours of labor from the suit industry. This, in turn, would require China to produce fewer suits. How many fewer? Since each suit uses up 125 hours of labor, then using 625 hours for one computer would require producing 625/125 = 5 fewer suits. Thus, the opportunity cost of a computer in China is *5 suits*. This opportunity cost is recorded in Table 2; check the table and make sure you can find this entry.

In the United States, producing an additional computer requires diverting 100 hours of labor from suit making. Since each suit requires 50 hours, this means a sac-

Opportunity Costs per:	China	United States	TABLE 2 Opportunity Costs
Suit	$\frac{1}{5}$ computer	$\frac{1}{2}$ computer	
Computer	5 suits	2 suits	

rifice of 2 suits. Thus, in the United States, the opportunity cost of one computer is 2 suits, which can also be found in Table 2.

Summing up, we see that in China, the opportunity cost of a computer is 5 suits; in the United States, it is 2 suits. Therefore, the United States—with the lower opportunity cost of producing computers—*has a comparative advantage in making computers.*

Notice that in Table 2, we do similar calculations for the opportunity cost of making a suit, measuring the opportunity cost in terms of *computers foregone.* These computations are summarized in the first row of the table. Make sure you can use these numbers to verify that China has a comparative advantage in producing suits.

Now we can use our conclusions about comparative advantage to show how both countries can gain from trade. The explanation comes in two steps. First, we show that if China could be persuaded to produce more suits and the United States more computers, the world's total production of goods will increase. Second, we show how each country can come out ahead by trading with the other.

Specialization and World Production

Using the numbers in Table 2, if China produced, say, 10 more suits, it would have to sacrifice the production of 2 computers as resources were shifted between the two industries. If the United States, simultaneously, produced 4 extra computers, it would have to sacrifice 8 suits—again because resources would have to be moved. But note: As a result of even this small change, the world's production of suits increases by 2, and its production of computers also rises by 2—despite the fact that no more labor is used than before. Table 3 summarizes the changes.

The additional production of suits and computers in this example represents the gain from specializing according to comparative advantage—a gain, as the next section will show, that the two trading partners will share. It is also the kind of gain that, multiplied a million times, lies behind the substantial benefits countries enjoy from free trade.

The particular example given here is not the only one that can be derived from our table of opportunity costs. For example, if China produced 20 more suits and, therefore, produced 4 fewer computers, while the United States changed as in Table 3, then world output of suits would increase by 12, while computer production would remain unchanged. And we could come up with other examples in which the world output of computers rises, but suits remain the same. (As an exercise, try to create such an example on your own.)

TABLE 3
A Small Change in Production

	China	United States	World
Suit Production	+10	−8	+2
Computer Production	−2	+4	+2

In all cases, however, the key insight remains the same:

> *If countries specialize according to comparative advantage, a more efficient use of given resources occurs. That is, with the same resources, the world can produce more of at least one good, without decreasing production of any other good.*

How Each Nation Gains from International Trade

Now we proceed to the second step in Ricardo's case, showing that *both* countries can gain from trade. As you've seen (Table 3), when the two countries shift labor hours toward their comparative advantage good, they produce more of that good but less of the other. For example, China produces more suits but fewer computers. However, by *trading* some of its comparative advantage good for the other good, each country can consume more of *both* goods.

Table 4 shows just one example of trading that benefits both countries. The first row of numbers shows the changes in production in each country. These numbers have been taken from Table 3. For example, the first two entries in the first row tell us that when China produces 10 more suits (+10), it sacrifices 2 computers (−2).

The second row shows an example of China's trade with the United States. In this example, China—which has increased suit production by 10—trades 9 of those suits for 3 computers. The entry "−9" means China is giving up or *exporting* 9 suits, and the entry "+3" means it is getting or *importing* 3 computers in exchange for them. The result of these changes in production, as well as exports and imports, is shown in the third row. Since China increases suit production by 10, but exports 9, it is able to consume 1 more suit (+1) than it could before trade. At the same time, since China produces 2 fewer computers but imports 3, it is able to consume 1 more computer (+1) than before trade.

Continuing to the last two columns of the table, we see the numbers for the United States. Because we are dealing with only two countries, China's exports of suits must be the same as U.S. imports of suits, so in the second row, we show +9 for U.S. suit imports. And if China imports 3 computers from the United States, the United States must be exporting them to China, so the table shows −3 to represent U.S. computer exports. In the third row, we see that the United States—like China—gains from trade by being able to consume more of both goods. It produces 4 more computers, but exports only 3, so it gains 1 computer (+1). And it produces 8 fewer suits, but imports 9, so it gains 1 suit (+1).

Let's take a step back and consider what we've discovered. First, look back at Table 1. Note that based on the required labor hours, the United States has an *absolute advantage* in both goods: It can produce both suits and computers using

	China		United States	
	Suits	**Computers**	**Suits**	**Computers**
Change in Production	+10	−2	−8	+4
Exports (−) or Imports (+)	−9	+3	+9	−3
Net Gain	+1	+1	+1	+1

TABLE 4
The Gains from Specialization and Trade

fewer hours of labor than can China. But in Table 2, we saw that the United States has a *comparative advantage* in only *one* of these goods—computers—and China has a comparative advantage in the other—suits. This is because the *opportunity costs* of each good differ in the two countries. Then, in Table 3, we saw how world production of both goods increases when each country shifts its resources toward its comparative advantage good. Finally, in the last row of Table 4, we saw that *international trade* can enable *each* country to end up with more of *both* goods.

Of course, we've only been looking at a *small* change in production toward comparative advantage. But as long as such benefits continue, a country can gain even greater benefits by shifting more and more of its resources toward its comparative advantage good. In our example, China should *specialize* in suit production, and the United States should *specialize* in making computers.

> *As long as opportunity costs differ, specialization and trade can be beneficial to all involved. This remains true regardless of whether the parties are different nations, different states, different counties, or different individuals. It remains true even if one party has an all-round absolute advantage or disadvantage.*

The Terms of Trade

In our ongoing example, China exports 9 suits in exchange for 3 computers. This exchange ratio (9 suits for 3 computers, or 3 suits per computer) is known as the **terms of trade**—the quantity of one good that is exchanged for a unit of the other.

The terms of trade determine how the gains from international trade are *distributed* among countries. Our particular choice of 3 suits to 1 computer for the terms of trade happened to apportion the gains equally between the two countries: Both China and the United States each gain one suit and one computer every time they make the trade shown in Table 4. With *different* terms of trade, however, the benefits would have been distributed differently. For example, an end-of-chapter problem will ask you to calculate the gains for each country when the terms of trade (suits per computer) are 4 to 1 instead of 3 to 1. In that case, while both countries will still gain, the United States gains more than China.

But notice that the terms of trade were not even *used* in our example until we arrived at Table 4. The gains from trade for the *world as a whole* were demonstrated

Terms of trade The ratio at which a country can trade domestically produced products for foreign-produced products.

in Table 3, and were based entirely on the increase in world production when countries specialize according to comparative advantage.

> *For the world as a whole, the gains from international trade are due to increased production as nations specialize according to comparative advantage.* How *those world gains are distributed among specific countries depends on the terms of trade.*

We won't consider here precisely *how* the terms of trade are determined (it's a matter of supply and demand). But we *will* establish the limits within which the terms of trade must fall.

Look again at Table 2. China would never give up *more* than 5 suits to import 1 computer. Why not? Because it could always get 1 computer for 5 suits *domestically,* by shifting resources into computer production.

Similarly, the United States would never export a computer for *fewer than* 2 suits, since it can substitute 1 computer for 2 suits domestically (again, by switching resources between the industries). Therefore, the equilibrium terms of trade must lie *between* 5 suits for 1 computer and 2 suits for 1 computer. Outside of that range, one of the two countries would refuse to trade. Note that in our example, we assume terms of trade of 3 suits for 1 computer—well within the acceptable range.

HOW POTENTIAL GAINS TURN INTO ACTUAL GAINS

So far in this chapter, we have discussed the *potential* advantages of specialization and trade among nations, but one major question remains: How is that potential realized? Who or what causes a country to shift resources from some industries into others and then to trade in the world market?

Do foreign trade ministers at WTO meetings decide who should produce and trade each product? Does some group of omniscient and benevolent people in Washington and other world capitals make all the necessary arrangements? Not at all. Within the framework of the WTO, government officials are supposed to create the environment for free trade, but they do not decide who has a comparative advantage in what, or what should be produced in this or that country. In today's market economies around the world, it is individual consumers and firms who decide to buy things, at home or abroad. By their joint actions, they determine where things are produced and who trades with whom. That is, the promise of Ricardo's theory is achieved through markets. People only have to do what comes naturally: buy products at the lowest price. Without their knowing it, they are promoting Ricardo's vision.

In order to see how this works, we'll have to translate from the labor *hours* required to produce a good into labor *costs*. This is done in Table 5. Because Chinese firms keep books in Chinese yuan (CNY) and American firms in U.S. dollars, our cost data are expressed accordingly.

Going across the first row of the table, we see that one suit requires 125 hours of labor in China (just as it did before, in Table 1). The second column shows the

Countries gain when they shift production toward their comparative advantage goods (such as athletic shoes in China), and trade them for other goods from other countries.

HTTP://

The World Trade Organization's Web page (http://www.wto.org/) is a good source for all kinds of information on international trade.

© AFP/CORBIS

	China			United States			TABLE 5
	(1) Labor Hours per Unit	**(2)** Wage Rate	**(3)** Cost per Unit (1) × (2)	**(4)** Labor Hours per Unit	**(5)** Wage Rate	**(6)** Cost per Unit (4) × (5)	**Costs of Production**
Suits	125 hours	16 CNY per hour	**2,000 CNY**	50 hours	$10 per hour	**$500**	
Computers	625 hours	16 CNY per hour	**10,000 CNY**	100 hours	$10 per hour	**$1,000**	

wage rate in China (assumed to be 16 CNY per hour), so the total labor cost for one suit in China is 125 hours × 16 CNY per hour = 2,000 CNY. In the United States, a suit requires 50 hours of labor, which—at a wage rate of $10 per hour—implies a total labor cost of $500 per suit. The second row shows the same calculations for a computer, which has costs of 10,000 CNY in China, and $1,000 in the United States.

We can use the cost per unit of each good to determine *opportunity cost.* For example, suppose China wants to produce another computer. Then it will have to shift 10,000 CNY worth of resources (labor hours) out of suit production. This will require a sacrifice of 10,000 CNY / 2,000 CNY = 5 suits. So in China, the opportunity cost of one computer is 5 suits—just as it was earlier, in Table 2, before we translated from labor *hours* to labor *cost.* In fact, expressing resource requirements as *costs,* rather than hours, leads to the same opportunity cost numbers, and the same conclusions derived from them. That is, once again, China has a comparative advantage in suits, and the United States in computers.

Now, back to our question: What *makes* China shift resources into its comparative advantage good, suits, and away from computers? And what *makes* the United States shift resources in the other direction? The answer is: *prices.* In the absence of trade, the *price* of a good within a country will generally reflect the cost of the resources needed to produce another unit of that good. That is, if a suit requires 2,000 CNY worth of resources in China, then before trade, the price of a suit in China will be about 2,000 CNY. For the same reason, before trade, the price of a suit will be about $500 in the United States, because that's what it costs to make one there.

Now suppose we allow trade to open up between the two countries. Consider the decision of a U.S. consumer who can choose to purchase computers or suits in either country. To buy goods from Chinese producers (who want to be paid in their own currency) Americans must obtain yuan. Americans can get the needed yuan by going to the *foreign exchange market,* trading their dollars for yuan at the going **exchange rate**—the rate at which one currency can be exchanged for another. Using the exchange rate, we can calculate the *dollar* cost of a suit from China—what it would cost an American. Similarly, we can calculate the dollar

Exchange rate The amount of one currency that is traded for one unit of another currency.

	China		United States	
TABLE 6				
Prices in China and the United States With an Exchange Rate of 8 CNY for $1	**Per Suit**	**2,000 CNY** ($250)	**$500** (4,000 CNY)	
	Per Computer	**10,000 CNY** ($1,250)	**$1,000** (8,000 CNY)	

cost of a computer made in China, or the yuan cost of either good made in the United States.

This is done in Table 6. The bold numbers show the price of each good in each country in *local currency*. The numbers in parentheses show how these numbers translate to the *other country's currency* based on an exchange rate of 8 CNY per dollar.

It's not a big table, but there is a lot going on in it, so let's step carefully through it. Start with the entry in the upper left-hand corner. First, the entry tells us that the price of a suit in China is 2,000 CNY. If an American wants to buy this suit, he can do so—by exchanging dollars for yuan and then buying the suit. With an exchange rate of 8 CNY per dollar, it would take $250 to get 2,000 CNY, since $250 \times 8 = 2,000$. Thus, to the American, the dollar price of a Chinese suit is $250, which appears in parentheses next to the price in yuan. Similarly, the dollar price of a 10,000 CNY Chinese computer is $1,250—also in parentheses.

Looking at Table 6, you can see that, to an American, suits from China at $250 are cheaper than U.S. suits at $500, so *Americans will prefer to buy suits from China.* But when it comes to computers, we reach the opposite conclusion: A U.S. computer at $1,000 is cheaper than a Chinese computer at $1,250, so *Americans will prefer to buy computers in the United States.*

Now take the viewpoint of a Chinese consumer who can buy U.S. or Chinese goods. To buy U.S. goods, China's consumers will need dollars, which they can obtain at the going exchange rate: 8 CNY for $1. The last column of the table shows the prices of U.S. goods in yuan (in parentheses). To a Chinese buyer, Chinese suits at 2,000 CNY are cheaper than U.S. suits at 4,000 CNY, while U.S. computers at 8,000 CNY are cheaper than Chinese computers at 10,000 CNY. Thus, *a Chinese, just like an American, will prefer to buy computers from the United States and suits from China.*

Now suppose that trade in suits and computers had previously been prohibited, but is now opened up. Everyone would buy suits in China and computers in the United States, and the process of specialization according to comparative advantage would begin. Chinese suit makers would expand their production, while Chinese computer makers would suffer losses, lay off workers, and even exit the industry. Unemployed computer workers in China would find jobs in the suit industry. Analogous changes would occur in the United States, as production of computers expanded there. These changes in production patterns would continue until China specialized in suit production and the United States specialized in computer production—that is, until each country produced according to its comparative advantage.

Our example illustrates a general conclusion:

> *When consumers are free to buy at the lowest prices, they will naturally buy a good from the country that has a comparative advantage in producing it. That country's industries respond by producing more of that good and less of other goods. In this way, countries naturally move toward specializing in those goods in which they have a comparative advantage.*[1]

This conclusion applies even beyond the simple example we've been considering. It applies when there are many countries and many goods. And it applies when countries use a *variety* of resources to produce goods, rather than just labor. For example, the prices in Table 6 could come from the cost of *all* resources needed to make a unit of each good in each country—labor, capital equipment, entrepreneurship, and natural resources. The opportunity costs would still be as given in Table 2, and the entire story we've told about the gains from trade, and how they come about, would be the same.

Some Important Provisos

Look back at Tables 3 and 4. There you saw how a small change in production—with China shifting toward suits and the United States shifting toward computers—caused world production of both goods to rise. But if this can happen once, why not again? And again? And again? In fact, our simple example seems to suggest that countries should specialize *completely*, producing *only* the goods in which they have a comparative advantage. In our example, it seems that China should get out of computer production *entirely*, and the United States should get out of suit production *entirely*.

The real world, however, is more complicated than our simplified examples might suggest. Despite divergent opportunity costs, sometimes it does *not* make sense for two countries to trade with each other, or it might make sense to trade, but *not* completely specialize. Following are some real-world considerations that can lead to reduced trade or incomplete specialization.

Costs of Trading. If there are high transportation costs or high costs of making deals across national boundaries, trade may be reduced and even become prohibitively expensive. High transportation costs are especially important for perishable goods, such as ice cream, which must be shipped frozen, and most personal services, such as haircuts, eye exams, and restaurant meals. These goods are less subject to trade according to comparative advantage. (Imagine the travel cost for a U.S. resident to see an optometrist in China, where eye exams are less expensive.)

---

[1] Something may be bothering you about the way we reached this conclusion: We merely *asserted* that the exchange rate was 8 yuan per dollar. What if we had chosen another exchange rate? With a little work, you can verify that at any exchange rate between 4 yuan per dollar and 10 yuan per dollar, our conclusion will still hold: Countries will automatically produce according to their comparative advantage. Further, you can verify that if the exchange rate went *beyond* those bounds, the residents of both countries would want to buy both goods from just one country. This would change the demand for yuan or dollars, and force the exchange rate back between 8 yuan per dollar and 4 yuan per dollar.

The costs of making deals are generally higher for international trade than for trade within domestic borders. For one thing, different laws must be dealt with. In addition, there are different business and marketing customs to be mastered. High transportation costs and high costs of making deals help explain why nations continue to produce some goods in which they do not have a comparative advantage and why there is less than complete specialization in the world.

One final cost of international trade arises from the need to exchange domestic for foreign currency. In international trade, either importers or exporters typically take some risk that the exchange rate might change. For example, suppose a U.S. importer of suits from China agrees in advance to pay 100,000 CNY for a shipment of suits. At the time the agreement is made, the exchange rate is 8 CNY per dollar, so the importer figures the shipment will cost him $12,500. But suppose that, before he pays, the exchange rate changes to 5 CNY per dollar. Then the suit shipment—for which the importer must still pay 100,000 CNY—will cost him $20,000. The rise in costs could cause him to lose money on the shipment.

It is interesting to note that countries can work to reduce the cost of trading. Indeed, this was the primary reason behind the creation of a new, single currency—the *euro*—to be shared by 12 European countries, including France, Germany, Holland, and Italy. The euro was introduced into commerce in early 1999. In 2002, the French franc, the Italian lira, the German mark, and several other national currencies became relics of the past. The move to a single currency has eliminated the costs and risks of foreign exchange transactions from intra-European trade. This should enable these European countries to specialize more completely according to their comparative advantage, and increase the gains from trade even further.

Sizes of Countries. Our earlier example featured two large economies capable of fully satisfying each other's demands. But sometimes a very large country, such as the United States, trades with a very small one, such as the Pacific island nation of Tonga. If the smaller country specialized completely, its output would be insufficient to fully meet the demand of the larger one. While the smaller country would specialize *completely,* the large country would not. Instead, it would continue to produce both goods and would specialize only in the sense of producing *more* of its comparative advantage good after trade than it did before trade. This helps to explain why the United States continues to produce bananas, even though we do so at a much higher opportunity cost than many small Latin American nations.

Increasing Opportunity Cost. In all of our tables, we have assumed that opportunity cost remains constant as production changes. For example, in Table 2, the opportunity cost of a suit in China is $\frac{1}{5}$ of a computer, regardless of how many suits or computers China makes. But more typically, the opportunity cost of a good rises as more of it is produced. (Why? You may want to review the law of increasing opportunity cost in Chapter 2.) In that case, each step on the road to specialization would change the opportunity cost. A point might be reached—before complete specialization—in which opportunity costs became *equal* in the two countries, and there would be no further mutual gains from trading. (Remember: Opportunity costs must *differ* between the two countries in order for trade to be mutually beneficial.) In the end, while trading will occur, there will not be complete specialization. Instead, each country will produce both goods, just as China and the United States each produce suits *and* computers in the real world.

Government Barriers to Trade. Governments can enact barriers to trading. In some cases, these barriers increase trading costs; in other cases, they make trade impossible. Since this is such an important topic, we'll consider government-imposed barriers to trade in a separate section, later in the chapter.

THE SOURCES OF COMPARATIVE ADVANTAGE

We've just seen how nations can benefit from specialization and trade when they have comparative advantages. But what determines comparative advantage in the first place?

In many cases, the answer is the *resources* a country has at its disposal.

A country that has relatively large amounts of a particular resource at its disposal will tend to have a comparative advantage in goods that make heavy use of that resource.

This is most easy to see when the relevant resources are *gifts of nature*, such as a specific natural resource or a climate especially suited to a particular product.

The top part of Table 7 contains some examples. Saudi Arabia has a comparative advantage in the production of oil because it has oil fields with billions of barrels of oil that can be extracted at low cost. Canada is a major exporter of timber because its climate and geography make its land more suitable for growing trees than other crops. Canada is a good example of comparative advantage without absolute advantage: It grows a lot of timber, not because it can do so using fewer resources than other countries, but because its land is even more poorly suited to growing other things.

But now look at the bottom half of Table 7. It shows examples of international specialization that arise from some cause *other* than natural resources. Japan has a huge comparative advantage in making automobiles: More than 40 percent of the world's automobiles are made there. And that number would be even larger, except for laws that limit the import of Japanese cars into Europe. Yet none of the *natural* resources needed to make cars are available in Japan; the iron ore, coal, and oil needed to produce cars are all imported.

What explains the cases of comparative advantage in the bottom half of Table 7? In part, it is due to resources *other* than natural resources or climate. The United States is rich in both physical capital and human capital. As a result, the United States tends to have a comparative advantage in goods and services that make heavy use of computers, tractors, and satellite technology, as well as goods that require highly skilled labor. This, in part, explains the U.S. comparative advantage in the design and production of aircraft, a good that makes heavy use of physical capital (such as computer-based design systems) and human capital (highly trained engineers).

In less-developed countries, by contrast, capital and skilled labor are relatively scarce, but less-skilled labor is plentiful. Accordingly, these countries tend to have a

TABLE 7
Examples of National Specialties in International Trade

Country	Specialization Resulting from Natural Resources or Climate
Saudi Arabia	Oil
Canada	Timber
United States	Grain
Spain	Olive oil
Mexico	Tomatoes
Jamaica	Aluminum ore
Italy	Wine
Israel	Citrus fruit

Country	Specialization *Not* Based on Natural Resources or Climate
Japan	Cars, consumer electronics
United States	Software, movies, music, aircraft
Switzerland	Watches
Korea	Steel, ships
Hong Kong	Textiles
Great Britain	Financial services
Pakistan	Textiles

comparative advantage in products that make heavy use of less-skilled labor, such as textiles and light manufacturing. Note, however, that as a country develops—and acquires more physical and human capital—its pattern of comparative advantage can change. Japan, Korea, and Singapore, after a few decades of very rapid development, acquired a comparative advantage in several goods that, at one time, were specialties of the United States and Europe—including automobiles, steel, and sophisticated consumer electronics.

But another aspect of the bottom half of Table 7 is harder to explain: Why do specific countries develop a *particular* specialty? For example, if you think you know why Japan dominates the world market for VCRs and other consumer electronics—say, some unique capacity to mass-produce precision products—be sure you can explain why Japan is a distant second in computer printers. The company that dominates the market for printers—Hewlett Packard—is a U.S. firm.

Similarly, we take the worldwide dominance of American movies for granted. But if you try to explain it based on the availability of resources like physical capital or highly skilled labor, or cultural traditions that encouraged artists, writers, or actors, then why not Britain or France? At the time the film industry developed in the United States, these two countries had similar endowments of physical and human capital, and much older and stronger theatrical traditions than the United States. Yet their film industries—in spite of massive government subsidies—are a very distant second and third compared to that of the United States.

In even the most remote corner of the world, the cars, cameras, and VCRs will be Japanese, the movies and music American, the clothing from Hong Kong or China, and the bankers from Britain. These specialties are certainly *consistent* with the capital and other resources each nation has at its disposal, but explaining why each *specific* case of comparative advantage arose in the first place is not easy.

We can, however, explain why a country retains its comparative advantage once it gets started. Japan today enjoys a huge comparative advantage in cars and consumer electronics in large part because it has accumulated a capital stock—both physical capital and human capital—well suited to producing those goods. The physical capital stock includes the many manufacturing plants and design facilities that the Japanese have built over the years. But Japan's human capital is no less important. Japanese managers know how to anticipate the features that tomorrow's buyers of cars and electronic products will want around the world. And Japanese workers have developed skills adapted for producing these products. The stocks of physical and human capital in Japan sustain its comparative advantage just as stocks of natural resources lead to comparative advantages in other countries. More likely than not, Japan will continue to have a comparative advantage in cars and electronics, just as the United States will continue to have a comparative advantage in making movies.

HTTP://

The International Trade Administration maintains a Web page that is full of information on U.S. international trade. Find it at http://www.ita.doc.gov/.

Countries often develop strong comparative advantages in the goods they have produced in the past, regardless of why they began producing those goods in the first place.

WHY SOME PEOPLE OBJECT TO FREE TRADE

Given the clear benefits that nations can derive by specializing and trading, why would anyone ever *object* to free international trade? Why do the same governments that join the WTO turn around and create roadblocks to unhindered trade? The answer is not too difficult to find: Despite the benefit to the nation as a whole, some groups within the country, in the short run, are likely to lose from free trade, even while others gain a great deal more. Unfortunately, instead of finding ways to compensate the losers—to make them better off as well—we often allow them to block free-trade policies. The simple model of supply and demand helps illustrate this story.

In our earlier example, after trade opens up, China exports suits and the United States imports them. Figure 1 illustrates the impact on the market for suits in the two countries. To keep things simple, we'll convert the price of suits in China into dollars, so that we can measure dollar prices on the vertical axis of both panels.

Before trade opens up, the Chinese suit market is in equilibrium at point *E*, with a price of $250 and quantity of 200,000 suits per month. The U.S. suit market is in equilibrium at point *F*, with price $500 and quantity 250,000. Notice that before trade opens up, the price is lower in China—the country with a comparative advantage in suits.

Now, when trade opens up, Americans will begin to buy Chinese suits, driving their price upward. As the price in China rises from $250 to $350, Chinese

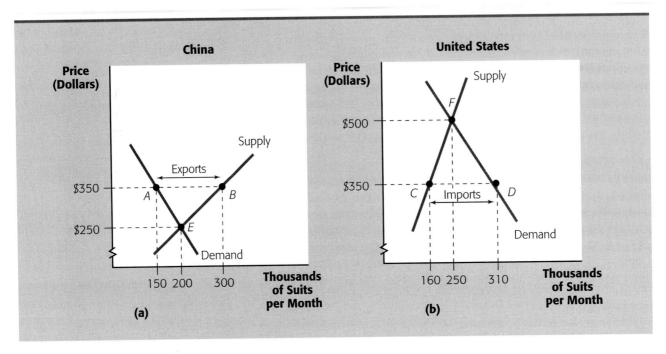

FIGURE 1
The Impact of Trade

Before trade, the Chinese suit market is in equilibrium at point E, and the U.S. market is in equilibrium at point F. When trade begins, Americans buy the cheaper Chinese suits, driving up their price. In response, Chinese manufacturers increase output, and Chinese consumers decrease their purchases. At the world equilibrium price, $350 per suit, Americans buy 150,000 Chinese suits each month (distance CD). China produces 300,000 suits, but Chinese consumers buy only 150,000, with the rest (distance AB) being exported to the United States.

producers increase their output to 300,000, moving from *E* to *B* along the supply curve, and Chinese consumers decrease their purchases to 150,000, moving from *E* to *A* along the demand curve. This seems to create an "excess supply" of suits in China, equal to distance *AB* or 300,000 − 150,000 = 150,000. But it is not *really* an excess supply, because that is precisely the number of suits that are exported to the United States. So, China's entire output of suits, 300,000, is purchased by either Chinese or Americans.

Now let's consider the effects in the United States. There, consumers are switching from suits made in the United States to suits made in China. With less demand for U.S. suits, their price will fall. With free trade, the United States must be able to buy Chinese suits at the same price as the Chinese (ignoring transportation costs), so the price of suits in the United States must fall to $350. As the price falls, U.S. suit producers will decrease their output to 160,000, moving from *F* to *C* along the supply curve, and U.S. consumers will increase their purchases to 310,000 moving from *F* to *D* along the demand curve. This seems to create a shortage of suits in the United States, equal to 310,000 − 160,000 = 150,000, but it is not a shortage: That is precisely the number of suits imported from China.

Now let's see how different groups are affected by the opening up of trade.

The Impact of Trade in the Exporting Country

When trade opens up in suits, China is the exporting country. How are different groups affected there?

- *Chinese suit producers and workers are better off.* Before international trade, producers sold 200,000 suits at $250 each, but with trade, they sell a larger quantity of 300,000 at a higher price of $350. The industry's workers are equally delighted because they undoubtedly share in the bonanza as the number of workers demanded rises along with the level of production. Both management and labor in the Chinese suit industry benefit from free trade.
- *Chinese suit buyers are worse off.* Why? Before trade, they bought 200,000 suits at price $250, and now they must pay the higher price, $350, and consume the smaller quantity 150,000.

When the opening of trade results in increased exports of a good, the producers of the good are made better off. Consumers of the good in the exporting country will be made worse off.

The Impact of Trade in the Importing Country

Now let's consider the impact of free trade in suits on the United States, the importing country. Once again, it is easy to figure out who is happy and who is unhappy with the new arrangement.

- *U.S. suit producers and workers are worse off.* They formerly sold 250,000 at $500 each, but now they sell the lower quantity of 160,000 at the lower price, $350. The industry's workers suffer, too, because the number of workers demanded falls with the level of production.
- *U.S. suit buyers are better off.* They used to buy 250,000 at $500 each, but now they pay the lower price, $350, and consume the larger quantity, 310,000.

When the opening of trade results in increased imports of a product, the domestic producers of the product are made worse off. Consumers of the good in the importing country are better off.

Attitudes and Influence on Trade Policy

In our examples, we've been discussing the impact of free trade in suits. We could tell the same story about free trade in computers. In this case, the United States has the role of exporter and China is the importer. But our conclusions about the impacts on different groups in exporting and importing countries would remain the same. These impacts are summarized in Table 8.

Each group in the table forms a natural constituency for government policies that encourage or discourage free trade. Notice, however, that one of the entries is italicized: producers of a good (and their employees) who would suffer from cheap imports. This group is emphasized because it typically has more influence on trade policy than the others in the table.

An example can help explain why. Imagine that a bill comes before Congress to permit completely free trade in apparel, allowing cheap clothing to enter the United States from Jordan, Pakistan, and several other less-developed countries.

TABLE 8 The Impact of Free Trade		In Export Sectors That Enjoy Comparative Advantage	In Import Sectors That Suffer from Comparative Disadvantage
Gains from Trade		Owners of firms, workers	Consumers
Harm from Trade		Consumers	*Owners of firms, workers*

The benefits to the United States as a whole would be huge, enjoyed mostly by American consumers of clothing—basically, the entire U.S. population. But because the benefits would be spread so widely, the gains for each *individual* consumer would be small. For example, if the benefits to *all* U.S. consumers amounted to $20 billion per year, the annual benefits to any single consumer would be less than $100. As a result, no single consumer has a strong incentive to lobby Congress, or to join a dues-paying organization that would act on his or her behalf.

By contrast, the harm that free trade would do to the owners and employees of domestic apparel firms would be highly concentrated on a much smaller group of people. An individual owner might lose millions of dollars competing with cheap imports, and a worker would face a substantially higher risk of being permanently laid off. These individuals have a powerful incentive to lobby against free trade. Not surprisingly, when it comes to trade policy, the voices raised *against imports* are loud and clear, while those *for imports* are often nonexistent. Since a country has the power to restrict imports from other countries, the lobbying can—and often does—lead to a restriction on free trade. The United States, for example, continues to keep out imports of cheap clothing from low-cost producers, largely due to powerful lobbying by the U.S. textile industry.

What about the export side? Here, as Table 8 suggests, it's the reverse: Individuals involved in the export sector who benefit from trade have the incentive to lobby, while individual consumers who would be harmed by higher prices have little incentive to act. Indeed, in the United States, farmers and cattle ranchers have been active advocates of free-trade policies so they can export corn, rye, soybeans, and beef. This suggests that the forces mounted for and against free trade might be evenly balanced. But notice in Table 8 that this group—firms and workers who benefit from exports—has not been emphasized. Why not?

The Antitrade Bias. While exporters have the incentive to lobby—and do—their effectiveness is limited. After all, it's not the U.S. government that is preventing them from exporting their products; it's some *foreign* government responding to pressure from its *own* producers who would be harmed by U.S. exports. The United States does not have the legal right to *force* another country to import American products. Indeed, European governments have for years used trade barriers to tightly restrict imports of American corn and American beef (officially attributed to environmental and health claims). Despite heavy lobbying from U.S. producers, the U.S. government has been unable to change European policy. Moreover, because the United States has so often given in to pressure from its own producers to restrict imports, it lacks the moral high ground.

> *The distribution of gains and losses creates a policy bias against free trade. Those who benefit from trade in a specific product either have little incentive to lobby for it (consumers of imports) or have limited power to influence policy (producers of exports). But one constituency harmed by trade—domestic producers threatened by imports—has both a powerful incentive to lobby and the ability to influence policy.*

There are, however, three antidotes to this policy bias.

Multilateral Agreements. In a bilateral or multilateral trade agreement, two or more countries agree to trade freely in many goods—or even *all* goods—simultaneously. Producers threatened by imports will lobby against such agreements in each country. But producers of potential exports will lobby just as strongly *for* the agreement. If the agreement is structured as an all-or-nothing proposition, a balance of influence is created that can enable governments to resist antitrade lobbying. An example was the North American Free Trade Agreement (NAFTA) between the United States, Canada, and Mexico, which went into effect in 1994, and, in phases, will eventually apply to virtually all the products produced by the three nations. NAFTA was hotly opposed by many producers and some labor unions in all three countries who stood to lose from imports, but was just as hotly favored by producers and workers that stood to gain from exports. (The biggest gainers—consumers in the three countries—were hardly involved in the debate, for reasons we've discussed.)

The World Trade Organization. Another antidote is the World Trade Organization (WTO). By setting standards for acceptable and unacceptable trade restrictions, and making rulings in specific cases, the WTO has some power to influence nations' trade policies. But its influence is limited because the WTO has no enforcement power. For example, the WTO has ruled several times against European trade barriers against U.S. corn and beef, with little effect. Still, a negative WTO ruling does put some public relations pressure on a country, and it allows a nation harmed by restrictions on its exports to retaliate, in good conscience, with its own trade barriers.

Industries as Consumers. Whenever we use the word *consumer,* we naturally think of a household buying products for its own enjoyment. But the term can apply to *any* buyer of a product, including a firm that uses it as an *input*. If these firms are among the consumers in Table 8 who benefit from cheaper imports, and if the good is an important part of these firms' costs, they have an incentive to lobby for free trade in the good. Moreover, because the issue at stake—import restrictions—is under the control of the *domestic* government, lobbying by industrial consumers can influence policy. For example, in 2001, the steel industry lobbied the Bush administration to restrict imports of steel from Russia, Japan, Korea, and several other countries. But steel *consumers*—including U.S. automobile companies and U.S. appliance manufacturers—lobbied just as strongly *against* the restrictions. While the steel consumers lost the battle, their influence helped to weaken the restrictions on imported steel.

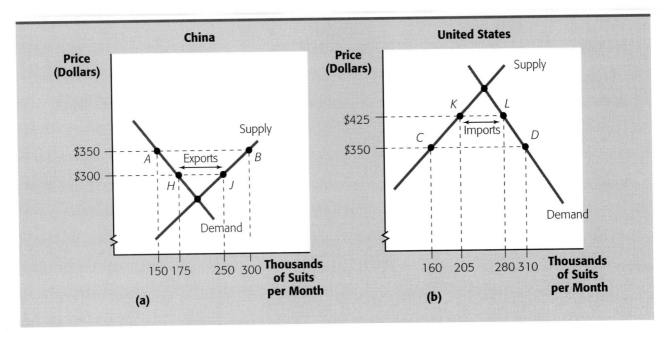

FIGURE 2
The Effects of a Tariff on Suits

A U.S. tariff of $125 on im-ported Chinese suits raises their price in the United States and re-duces U.S. imports. It also low-ers the price in China and re-duces China's exports. In the new equilibrium, the price is $425 in the United States and $300 in China, the prices at which China's exports (distance HJ) are equal to U.S. imports (distance KL). The difference in the two prices—$125—is equal to the U.S. tariff on each imported suit.

Tariff A tax on imports.

HOW FREE TRADE IS RESTRICTED

So far in this chapter, you've learned that specialization and trade according to com-parative advantage can dramatically improve the well-being of entire nations. This is why governments generally favor free trade. Yet international trade can, in the short run, hurt particular groups of people. These groups often lobby their govern-ment to restrict free trade.

When governments decide to accommodate the opponents of free trade, they are apt to use one of two devices to restrict trade: tariffs or quotas.

Tariffs

A **tariff** is a tax on imported goods. It can be a fixed dollar amount per physical unit, or it can be a percentage of the good's value. In either case, the effect in the tariff-imposing country is similar.

Figure 2 illustrates the effects of a U.S. government tariff on Chinese suits. Ini-tially, before the tariff is imposed, the price of suits in both countries is $350, and China exports 150,000, given by the distance *AB*, while the United States imports the same number (represented by the distance *CD* in the U.S. market). Now, sup-pose the United States imposes a tariff of $125 on each suit imported from China. Since it is more costly for Chinese suit makers to sell suits in the United States than before, they will shift some of their output back to the home market in China. In the United States, at the old price of $350, this decrease in the supply of suits *would* create a shortage, but—as we know—shortages force the price up. In our diagram, the United States price rises to $425. As the price rises, the quantity of suits supplied domestically increases, and the quantity demanded domestically decreases. U.S. imports are accordingly cut back to *KL,* or 75,000 per month. In China, the sale of suits formerly exported drives the price there down to $300. Notice that—in the final equilibrium with U.S. price equal to $425 and the price in China equal to $300—U.S. imports (*KL*) and Chinese exports (*HJ*) are equal at 75,000. That is, every Chinese suit that is *not* bought by a Chinese consumer is bought by an American consumer. As you can see, American consumers are worse off: They pay a higher price for fewer suits. U.S. producers, on the other hand, are much better off: They sell more suits at a higher price. In China, the impact is the opposite: The price of suits falls, so Chinese producers lose and Chinese consumers gain.

But we also know this: Since the volume of trade has decreased, the gains from trade according to comparative advantage have been reduced as well. Both countries, as a whole, are worse off as a result of the tariff:

> *Tariffs reduce the volume of trade and raise the domestic prices of imported goods. In the country that imposes the tariff, producers gain and consumers lose. But the world as a whole loses, because tariffs decrease the volume of trade and therefore decrease the gains from trade.*

Quotas

A **quota** is a government decree that limits the imports of a good to a specified maximum physical quantity, such as 75,000 Chinese suits per month. Because the goal is to restrict imports, a quota is set below the level of imports that would occur under free trade. Its general effects are very similar to the effects of a tariff.

Quota A limit on the physical volume of imports.

Figure 2, which we used to illustrate tariffs, can also be used to analyze the impact of a quota. In this case, we suppose that the U.S. government simply decrees that it will allow only 75,000 suits from China into the United States (the distance *KL*), and that it is able to enforce this quota. Once again, the U.S. market price in our example will rise to $425. (Why? Because at any price lower than $425, total imports of 75,000, plus the domestic quantity supplied of 205,000—given by the supply curve—would be smaller than quantity demanded. This would cause the price to rise.) And once again, the decrease in U.S. imports translates into a shrinkage in Chinese exports, down to 75,000, or the distance *HJ*. Both countries' suit markets end up in exactly the same place as if the United States had imposed a tariff that raised the U.S. price to $425.

The previous discussion seems to suggest that tariffs and quotas are pretty much the same. But even though prices in the two countries may end up at the same level with a tariff or a quota, there is one important difference between these two trade-restricting policies. A tariff, after all, is a *tax* on imported goods. Therefore, when a government imposes a tariff, it collects some revenue every time a good is imported. Even though the world loses from a tariff, the country that imposes it loses a bit less (compared to a quota) because at least it collects some revenue from the tariff. This revenue can be used to fund government programs or reduce other taxes, to the benefit of the country as a whole. When a government imposes a quota, however, it typically gains no revenue at all.

Quotas have effects similar to tariffs: They reduce the quantity of imports and raise domestic prices. While both measures help domestic producers, they reduce the benefits of trade to the nation as a whole. However, a tariff has one saving grace: increased government revenue.

Economists, who generally oppose measures such as quotas and tariffs to restrict trade, argue that, if one of these devices must be used, tariffs are the better choice. While both policies reduce the gains that countries can enjoy from specializing and trading with each other, the tariff provides some compensation in the form of additional government revenue.

PROTECTIONISM

Protectionism The belief that a nation's industries should be protected from foreign competition.

This chapter has outlined the *gains* that arise from international trade, but it has also outlined some of the *pain* trade can cause to different groups within a country. While the country as a whole benefits, some citizens in both the exporting and importing countries are harmed. The groups who suffer from trade with other nations have developed a number of arguments against free trade. Together, these arguments form a position known as **protectionism**—the belief that a nation's industries should be *protected* from free trade with other nations.

Myths About International Trade

Some protectionist arguments are rather sophisticated and require careful consideration. We'll consider some of these a bit later. But antitrade groups have also promulgated a number of myths to support their protectionist beliefs. Let's consider some of these myths.

Myth #1: "A HIGH-WAGE COUNTRY CANNOT AFFORD FREE TRADE WITH A LOW-WAGE COUNTRY. THE HIGH-WAGE COUNTRY WILL EITHER BE UNDERSOLD IN EVERYTHING AND LOSE ALL OF ITS INDUSTRIES, OR ELSE ITS WORKERS WILL HAVE TO ACCEPT EQUALLY LOW WAGES AND EQUALLY LOW LIVING STANDARDS."

It's true that some countries have much higher wages than others. Here are 2001 figures for average hourly wages of manufacturing workers, including benefits such as holiday pay and health insurance: Germany, $22.86; United States, $20.32; Japan, $19.59; Italy, $13.76; Korea, $8.09; Singapore, $7.77; Brazil, $3.02; Mexico, $2.34; and less than a dollar in China, India, and Bangladesh. This leads to the fear that the poorer countries will be able to charge lower prices for their goods, putting American workers out of jobs unless they, too, agree to work for low wages.

But this argument is incorrect, for two reasons. First, it is true that American workers are paid more than Chinese workers, but this is because the average American worker is more *productive* than his or her Chinese counterpart. After all, the American workforce is more highly educated, and American firms provide their workers with more sophisticated machinery than do Chinese firms. If an American could produce 25 times as much output as a Chinese worker in an hour, then even though wage rates in the United States may be about 20 times greater, cost *per unit* produced would still be lower in the United States. This is reflected in our example in Tables 5 and 6. If you look closely, you'll see that even though American workers are paid more than their Chinese counterparts, we've assumed that American workers can produce a computer with so much less labor input that labor costs per computer are actually lower in the United States.

But suppose the cost per unit *were* lower in China. Then there is still another, more basic argument against the fear of a general job loss or falling wages in the United States: comparative advantage. Let's take an extreme case. Suppose that labor productivity were the same in the United States and China, so that China—with lower wages—could produce *everything* more cheaply than the United States could. Both countries would still gain if China specialized in products in which its cost advantage was relatively large and the United States specialized in goods in which China's cost advantage was relatively small. That is, even though China would have an absolute advantage in everything, the United States would still have a comparative advantage in some things. The mutual gains from trade arise not from absolute advantage, but from comparative advantage.

Myth #2 "A LOW-PRODUCTIVITY COUNTRY CANNOT AFFORD FREE TRADE WITH A HIGH-PRODUCTIVITY COUNTRY. THE FORMER WILL BE CLOBBERED BY THE LATTER AND LOSE ALL OF ITS INDUSTRIES."

This argument is the flip side of the first myth. Here, it is the poorer, less-developed country that is supposedly harmed by trade with a richer country. But this myth, like the first one, confuses absolute advantage with comparative advantage. Suppose the high-productivity country (say, the United States) could produce *every* good with fewer resources than the low-productivity country (say, China). Once again, the low-productivity country would *still* have a comparative advantage in *some* goods. It would then gain by producing those goods and trading with the high-productivity country. This is the case in our example, where a glance at Table 1 or Table 5 reminds us that that the United States has an absolute advantage in both goods, yet—as we've seen—trade still benefits both countries.

To make the point even clearer, let's bring it closer to home. Suppose there is a small, poor town in the United States where workers are relatively uneducated and work with little capital equipment, so their productivity is very low. Would the residents of this town be better off sealing their borders and not trading with the rest of the United States, which has higher productivity? Before you answer, think what this would mean: The residents of the poor town would have to produce everything on their own: grow their own food, make their own cars and television sets, and even provide their own entertainment. Clearly, they would be worse off in isolation. And what is true *within* a country is also true *between* different countries: Closing off trade will make a nation, as a whole, worse off, regardless of its level of wages or productivity. Even a low-productivity country is made better off by trading with other nations.

Myth #3: "IN RECENT TIMES, AMERICA'S UNSKILLED WORKERS HAVE SUFFERED BECAUSE OF EVER-EXPANDING TRADE BETWEEN THE UNITED STATES AND OTHER COUNTRIES."

True enough, unskilled workers lost ground in the 1980s and 1990s, for *some* reason. College graduates have enjoyed growing purchasing power from their earnings, while those with only a grade school education have lost purchasing power. Rising trade with low-wage countries has been blamed for this adverse trend.

But before we jump to conclusions, let's take a closer look. Our discussion earlier in this chapter tells us where to look for effects that come through trade. If the opening of trade has harmed low-skilled workers in the United States, it would have done so by lowering the prices of products that employ large numbers of those workers. For example, if the United States has been flooded recently with cheap clothes, then we should see a relative decline in U.S. clothing prices and reductions in earnings among clothing workers, who are mostly unskilled. A study taking this approach found almost no change in the relative prices of products in the United States that employ large numbers of unskilled workers. Studies that take other approaches have found only modest effects. In general, economists who have looked at the relation between changes in trade patterns and the depressed earnings of unskilled American workers have concluded that foreign trade is a small contributor.[2]

Sophisticated Arguments for Protection

While most of the protectionist arguments we read in the media are based on a misunderstanding of comparative advantage, some more recent arguments for protecting domestic industries are based on a more sophisticated understanding of how markets work. These arguments have become collectively known as *strategic trade policy*. According to its proponents, a nation can gain in some circumstances by assisting certain *strategic industries* that benefit society as a whole, but that may not thrive in an environment of free trade.

Strategic trade policy is most effective in situations where a market is dominated by a few large firms. With few firms, the forces of competition—which ordinarily reduce profits in an industry to very low levels—will not operate. Therefore, each firm in the industry may earn high profits. These profits benefit not only the owners of the firm, but also the nation more generally, since the government will be able to capture some of the profit with the corporate profits tax. When a government helps an industry compete internationally, it increases the likelihood that high profits—and the resulting general benefits—will be shifted from a foreign country to its own country. Thus, interfering with free trade—through quotas, tariffs, or even a direct subsidy to domestic firms—might actually benefit the country as a whole.

An argument related to strategic trade policy is the **infant industry argument.** This argument begins with a simple observation: In order to enjoy the full benefits of trade, markets must allocate resources toward those goods in which a nation has

Infant industry argument The argument that a new industry in which a country has a comparative advantage might need protection from foreign competition in order to flourish.

---

[2] The studies include Robert Z. Lawrence and Matthew J. Slaughter, "Trade and U.S. Wages: Giant Sucking Sound or Small Hiccup?" *Brookings Papers on Economic Activity: Microeconomics,* 2:1993, pp. 161–210; Jeffrey D. Sachs and Howard J. Shatz, "Trade and Jobs in U.S. Manufacturing," *Brookings Papers on Economic Activity,* 1:1994, pp. 1–84; and Gary Burtless, Robert Lawrence, Robert Litan, and Robert Shapiro, *Globaphobia: Confronting Fears About Free Trade* (1998), The Brookings Institution Press (Washington, DC).

a comparative advantage. This includes not only markets for resources such as labor and land, but also *financial markets,* where firms obtain funds for new products. But in some countries—especially developing countries—financial markets do not work very well. Poor legal systems or incomplete information about firms and products may prevent a new industry from obtaining financing, even though the country would have a comparative advantage in that industry once it was formed. In this case, protecting the infant industry from foreign competition may be warranted until the industry can stand on its own feet.

Strategic trade policy and support for infant industries are controversial. Opponents of these ideas stress three problems:

1. Once the principle of government assistance to an industry is accepted, special-interest groups of all kinds will lobby to get the assistance, whether it benefits the general public or not.
2. When one country provides assistance to an industry by keeping out foreign goods, other nations may respond in kind. If they respond with tariffs and quotas of their own, the result is a shrinking volume of world trade and falling living standards. If subsidies are used to support a strategic industry, and another country responds with its own subsidies, then both governments lose revenue, and neither gains the sought-after profits.
3. Strategic trade policy assumes that the government has the information to determine which industries, infant or otherwise, are truly strategic and which are not.

Still, the arguments related to strategic trade policy suggest that government protection or assistance *may* be warranted in some circumstances, even if putting this support into practice proves difficult. Moreover, the arguments help to remind us of the conditions under which free trade is most beneficial to a nation:

> *Production is most likely to reflect the principle of comparative advantage when firms can obtain funds for investment projects and when they can freely enter industries that are profitable. Thus, free trade, without government intervention, works best when markets are working well.*

This may explain, in part, why the United States, where markets function relatively well, has for decades been among the strongest supporters of the free trade ideal.

Protectionism in the United States

Americans can enjoy the benefits of importing many of the products listed in Table 7: olive oil from Spain, watches from Switzerland, tomatoes from Mexico, cars and VCRs from Japan. But on the other side of the ledger, U.S. consumers have suffered and U.S. producers have gained, from some persistent barriers to trade. Table 9 lists ten examples of American protectionism—through tariffs, quotas, or similar policies—that have continued for years.

As you can see, protection is costly. Quotas and tariffs on apparel and textiles, the most costly U.S. trade barrier, force American consumers to pay $33.6 billion more for clothes each year. And while protection saves an estimated 168,786

TABLE 9
Some Examples of
U.S. Protectionism[3]

Protected Industry	Annual Cost to Consumers	Number of Jobs Saved	Annual Cost per Job Saved
Apparel and Textiles	$33,629 million	168,786	$ 199,241
Maritime Services	$ 2,522 million	4,411	$ 571,668
Sugar	$ 1,868 million	2,261	$ 826,104
Dairy Products	$ 1,630 million	2,378	$ 685,323
Softwood Lumber	$ 632 million	605	$1,044,271
Women's Nonathletic Footwear	$ 518 million	3,702	$ 139,800
Glassware	$ 366 million	1,477	$ 247,889
Luggage	$ 290 million	226	$1,285,078
Peanuts	$ 74 million	397	$ 187,223

workers in this industry from having to make the painful adjustment of finding other work, it does so at an annual cost of $199,241 per worker. Both workers and consumers could be made better off if textile workers were paid any amount up to $199,241 *not* to work and consumers were allowed to buy inexpensive textiles from abroad.

In some cases, the cost per job saved is staggering. The table shows that trade barriers preventing Americans from buying inexpensive luggage save just a couple of hundred jobs, at a yearly cost of more than $1 million each. Trade barriers on sugar are almost as bad: While 2,261 jobs are saved, the annual cost per job is $826,104.

In addition to the dozens of industries in the United States permanently protected from foreign competition, dozens more each year are granted temporary protection when the U.S. government finds a foreign producer or industry guilty of *dumping*—selling their products in the United States at "unfairly" low prices that harm a U.S. industry. Most economists believe that these low prices are most often the result of comparative advantage, and that the United States as a whole would gain from importing the good. Vietnam, for example, has a clear comparative advantage in producing catfish. But based on a complaint by the Catfish Farmers of America, the U.S. government has imposed tariffs of 35 to 65 percent on Vietnamese catfish, starting in August 2003.

In the "Using the Theory" section that follows, we take a closer look at one of the longest-running examples of protectionism in the United States.

[3] *The Fruits of Free Trade,* Federal Reserve Bank of Dallas, Annual Report, 2002, Exhibit 11.

USING THE THEORY
The U.S. Sugar Quota[4]

© RICHARD LORD/PHOTOEDIT, INC.

The United States has protected U.S. sugar producers from foreign competition since the 1930s. Since the 1980s, the protection has been provided in the form of a price guarantee. Essentially, the government has promised U.S. sugar beet and sugar cane producers and processors that they can sell their sugar at a predetermined price—22 cents a pound—regardless of the world price of sugar. The promise is backed by a guarantee: If U.S. sugar prices fall *below* 22 cents, the government will buy the sugar at that price itself.

This may not sound like a high price for sugar. But in the rest of the world, people and businesses can buy sugar for a lot less. Over the last 20 years, the world price of sugar has averaged about 11 cents a pound, while Americans have continued to pay 22 cents. Even in 1985, when the world price of sugar plunged to just 4 cents a pound—a bonanza for sugar buyers around the word—American buyers were not invited to the party: The United States price remained at 22 cents.

Because the world price of sugar is so consistently below the U.S. price, the government cannot keep its promise to support sugar prices while simultaneously allowing free trade in sugar. With free trade, the price of sugar in the United States would plummet and the government would have to spend billions of dollars each year making good on its guarantee to buy the sugar itself. The government's solution is a sugar quota. More accurately, the government decides how much foreign sugar it will allow into the United States each year, free of any tariff; all sugar beyond the allowed amount is hit with a heavy tariff of about 16 cents a pound. Since the tariff is so high, no country exports sugar to the United States beyond the allowed amount. So, in effect, the United States has a sugar quota.

The *primary* effects of the sugar quota are on sugar producers and sugar consumers. As you've learned, an import quota raises the domestic price of sugar (the quota's purpose). Sugar producers benefit. Sugar consumers are hurt.

And the harm is substantial. Table 9 shows that American consumers pay almost $2 billion more each year for sugar and products containing sugar due to the sugar quota. But spread widely over the U.S. population, this amounts to less than $15 per person per year. This probably explains why you haven't bothered to lobby for free trade in sugar.

---

[4] Information in this section is based on: Mark A. Groombridge "America's Bittersweet Sugar Policy," *Trade Briefing Paper No. 13*, Cato Institute, December 4, 2001; John C. Beghin, Barbara El Osta, Jar Y. Cherlow, and Samarendu Mohanty, "The Cost of the U.S. Sugar Program Revisited," *Working Paper 01-WP-273*, March 2001, Center for Agricultural and Rural Development, Iowa State University; Lance Gay, "Soured on Sugar Prices, Candy Makers Leave the U.S." *Scripps Howard News Service*, June 18, 2003; "Closing the 'Stuffed Molasses' Loophole," *White Paper*, United States Sugar Corporation (*http://www.ussugar.com/pressroom/white_papers/stuffed_molasses.html*).

But the costs of the sugar quota go beyond ordinary consumers. Industrial sugar users—such as the ice cream industry—are affected by the higher price too, not all of which can be passed on to consumers. So they try to avoid the quota's harm in other ways. One way is to waste resources buying sugar abroad disguised as other products. In the late 1990s and early 2000s, U.S. firms bought about 125,000 tons of sugar each year mixed with molasses, which was not restricted by the sugar quota. The sugar was then reseparated from the molasses. Even with these additional (and wasteful) processing costs, it was still a better deal to buy the disguised sugar abroad than to buy it through regular channels in the United States.

And sometimes a firm decides it's just not worth it anymore. In June 2003, Lifesavers was added to the list of other candy and baked-goods manufacturers who simply gave up trying to buy sugar in the United States, and moved their production facilities to Canada. In Canada, which doesn't have a quota, sugar can be purchased at the lower, world price.

Taxpayers, too, pay a cost for the sugar quota, because as part of its price support program, the U.S. government must occasionally buy excess sugar from producers. In 2000, the U.S. government was storing about 793,000 tons of sugar at a cost of about $1.6 million per month. The government must also hire special agents to detect and prevent sugar from entering the country illegally.

But perhaps the most significant cost of the sugar quota is indicated by Figure 2 in this chapter. There we saw that a U.S. tariff or quota on Chinese suits raised their price in the United States, but lowered their price in China, the exporting country. The sugar quota has a similar effect: The price in the exporting "country" (in this case, the *rest of the world*) decreases. And since the United States is such a large potential importer of sugar, the quota—by keeping sugar out—causes greater quantities of sugar to be dumped onto the world market, depressing its price. This hurts the poorest countries in the world that rely on sugar as an important source of export revenue. The sugar quota's harm to these countries has been estimated at about $1.5 billion per year.

Why do we bear all of these costs? Because of lobbying by groups who enjoy highly concentrated benefits. There are about 13,000 sugar farms in the United States. When the $2 billion in additional spending by U.S. consumers is spread among this small number of farms, the additional revenue averages out to more than $150,000 per farm per year. Those benefits are sizable enough to mobilize sugar producers each time their protection is threatened.

But there is another group that receives concentrated benefits: producers of high-fructose corn syrup, the closest substitute for sugar. Because of the sugar quota, high-fructose corn syrup can be sold at a substantially higher price.

Not surprisingly, the largest producer of high-fructose corn syrup in the U.S. market—the Archer Daniels Midland (ADM) company—has funded organizations that lobby Congress and try to sway public opinion in the United States. Occasionally, you may see a full-page newspaper advertisement paid for by one of these groups, arguing that sugar in the United States is cheap. And it is . . . until you find out what the country next door is paying.

Summary

International specialization and trade enable people throughout the world to enjoy greater production and higher living standards than would otherwise be possible. The benefits of unrestrained international trade can be traced back to the idea of comparative advantage. Mutually beneficial trade is possible whenever one country can produce a good at a lower opportunity cost than its trading partner can. Whenever opportunity costs differ, countries can specialize according to their comparative advantage, trade with each other, and end up consuming more.

Despite the net benefits to each nation as a whole, some groups within each country lose, while others gain. When trade leads to increased exports, domestic producers gain and domestic consumers are harmed. When imports increase as a result of trade, domestic producers suffer and domestic consumers gain. The losers often encourage government to block or reduce trade through the use of tariffs (taxes on imported goods) and quotas (limits on the volume of imports).

A variety of arguments have been proposed in support of protectionism. Some are clearly invalid and fail to recognize the principle that both sides gain when countries trade according to their comparative advantage. More sophisticated arguments for restricting trade may have merit in certain circumstances. These include strategic trade policy—the notion that governments should assist certain strategic industries—and the idea of protecting "infant" industries when financial markets are imperfect.

Key Terms

Absolute advantage
Comparative advantage
Exchange rate
Exports

Imports
Infant industry argument
Protectionism
Quota

Tariff
Terms of trade

Review Questions

Answers to even-numbered Questions and Problems can be found on the text Web site at http://hall-lieb.swlearning.com.

1. Describe the theory of comparative advantage.

2. What is the difference between absolute advantage and comparative advantage?

3. What are the terms of trade and why are they important?

4. What are the sources of comparative advantage?

5. What makes a country shift resources into its comparative advantage good?

6. Briefly describe the antidotes to the antitrade bias.

7. What is a tariff? What are its main economic effects? How does a quota differ from a tariff?

8. What arguments have been made in support of protectionism? Which of them may be valid, and under what circumstances?

9. List the ways in which a quota on imported coffee would harm the nation that imposes it

Problems and Exercises

1. Suppose that the costs of production of winter hats and wheat in two countries are as follows:

	United States	**Russia**
Per Winter Hat	$10	5,000 rubles
Per Bushel of Wheat	$1	2,500 rubles

a. What is the opportunity cost of producing one more winter hat in the United States? In Russia?

b. What is the opportunity cost of producing one more bushel of wheat in the United States? In Russia?

c. Which country has a comparative advantage in winter hats? In wheat?

d. Construct a table similar to Table 3 that illustrates how a change in production in each country would increase world production.

e. If the exchange rate were 1,000 rubles per dollar, would mutually beneficial trade occur? If yes, explain what mechanism would induce producers to export according to their country's comparative advantage. If no, explain why not, and explain in which direction the exchange rate would change. (*Hint:* Construct a table similar to Table 6.)

f. Answer the same questions for an exchange rate of 100 rubles per dollar.

2. The following table gives information about the supply and demand for beef in Paraguay and Uruguay. (You may wish to draw the supply and demand curves for each country to help you visualize what is happening.)

Paraguay			Uruguay		
Price	Quantity Supplied	Quantity Demanded	Price	Quantity Supplied	Quantity Demanded
0	0	1,200	0	0	1,800
5	200	1,000	5	0	1,600
10	400	800	10	0	1,400
15	600	600	15	0	1,200
20	800	400	20	200	1,000
25	1,000	200	25	400	800
30	1,200	0	30	600	600
35	1,400	0	35	800	400
40	1,600	0	40	1,000	200
45	1,800	0	45	1,200	0

a. In the absence of trade, what is the equilibrium price and quantity in Paraguay? In Uruguay?

b. If the two countries begin to trade, what will happen to the price of beef? How many sides of beef will be purchased in Paraguay and how many in Uruguay at that price?

c. How many sides of beef will be produced in Paraguay and how many in Uruguay? Why is there a difference between quantity purchased and quantity produced in each country?

d. Who benefits and who loses from the opening of trade between these two countries?

3. Use the data on supply and demand given in Question 2 to answer the following questions:

a. Suppose that Uruguay imposed a tariff that raised the price of beef imported from Paraguay to $25 per side. What would happen to beef consumption in Uruguay? To beef production there? How much beef would be imported from Paraguay?

b. How would the tariff affect Paraguay? Specifically, what would happen to the price of beef there after Uruguay imposed its tariff? How would Paraguay's production and consumption be affected?

4. Use the data on supply and demand given in Question 2 to answer the following questions:

a. Suppose that Uruguay imposed a quota on the import of beef from Paraguay—only 200 sides of beef can be imported each year. What would happen to the price of beef in Uruguay? What would happen to beef consumption in Uruguay? To beef production there?

b. How would the quota affect Paraguay? Specifically, what would happen to the price of beef there after Uruguay imposed its quota? How would Paraguay's production and consumption be affected?

5. Refer to Table 4 in the chapter. Calculate the gains for each country when the terms of trade (suits per computer) are 2 to 1, instead of 3 to 1. This time, assume that China increases suit production by 25 suits and exports 20, while the U.S. decreases suit production by 20. Which country gains more under these terms of trade?

6. Refer to Table 4 in the chapter. Calculate the gains for each country when the terms of trade (suits per computer) are 4 to 1, instead of 3 to 1. This time, assume that China increases suit production by 15 suits and exports 12, while the United States increases computer production by 4 computers. Which country gains more under these terms of trade?

7. The following table shows the hypothetical labor requirements per ton of wool and per hand-knotted rug, for New Zealand and for India.

Labor Requirements per Unit

	New Zealand	India
Per Ton of Wool	10 hours	20 hours
Per Hand-Knotted Rug	70 hours	100 hours

a. Use this information to calculate the opportunity cost in each country for each of the two products. Which country has a comparative advantage in each product?

b. Use this information to construct a table similar to Table 3 in the text, showing the overall gain in production if each country produces one unit less of the product for which it does not have a comparative advantage.

c. If India produces one more rug and exports it to New Zealand, what is the lowest price (measured in tons of wool) that it would accept? What is the highest price that New Zealand would pay? Where will the equilibrium terms of trade lie?

8. In Table 6 of this chapter, it was assumed that the exchange rate was 8 yuan per dollar. Recalculate the entries in parentheses in the table assuming that the exchange rate is 6 yuan per dollar. Will trade still take place? Explain briefly.

Challenge Questions

1. Suppose that the Marshall Islands does not trade with the outside world. It has a competitive domestic market for VCRs. The market supply and demand curves are reflected in this table:

Price ($/VCR)	Quantity Demanded	Quantity Supplied
500	0	500
400	100	400
300	200	300
200	300	200
100	400	100
0	500	0

a. Plot the supply and demand curves and determine the domestic equilibrium price and quantity.

b. Suddenly, the islanders discover the virtues of free exchange and begin trading with the outside world. The Marshall Islands is a very small country, and so its trading has no effect on the price established in the world market. It can import as many VCRs as it wishes at the world price of $100 per VCR. In this situation, how many VCRs will be purchased in the Marshall Islands? How many will be produced there? How many will be imported?

c. After protests from domestic producers, the government decides to impose a tariff of $100 per imported VCR. Now how many VCRs will be purchased in the Marshall Islands? How many will be produced there? How many will be imported?

d. What is the government's revenue from the tariff described in part (c)?

e. Compare the effect of the tariff described in part (c) with a quota that limits imports to 100 VCRs per year.

2. a. Use the information in the following table to plot supply and demand curves and determine the domestic equilibrium price and quantity for these two countries.

Country A			Country B		
Price per Unit of Good X (measured in dollars)	Quantity Demanded of Good X	Quantity Supplied of Good X	Price per Unit of Good X (measured in dollars)	Quantity Demanded of Good X	Quantity Supplied of Good X
$10	1	25	$10	5	13
9	2	22	9	6	10
8	3	19	8	7	7
7	4	16	7	8	4
6	5	13	6	9	2
5	6	10	5	10	½
4	7	7	4	11	¼
3	8	4	3	12	⅛

b. Show graphically what will happen if these two countries begin to trade. What will happen to the price of Good X in each country? What will happen to consumption in each country? What will happen to production in each country? Which country has the competitive advantage in the production of Good X? Which country will export Good X? How many units will it export?

 These exercises require access to Hall/Lieberman Xtra! If Xtra! did not come with your book, visit http://hallxtra.swlearning.com to purchase.

1. Use your Xtra! password at the Hall and Lieberman Web site (http://hallxtra.swlearning.com), select this chapter, and under Economic Applications, click on EconDebate. Choose *World Economy: International Trade,* and scroll down to find the debate, "Does the United States economy benefit from the WTO?" Read the debate.

   a. What is the role of the WTO?

   b. Is free trade, as envisioned by the WTO, inconsistent with national sovereignty? That is, will WTO regulations require that nations give up some authority over their own environment, workplace rules, etc, in the name of free trade? Does that really matter? Explain your answer carefully.

2. Use your Xtra! password at the Hall and Lieberman Web site (http://hallxtra.swlearning.com), select this chapter, and under Economic Applications, click on EconDebate. Choose *World Economy: International Trade,* and scroll down to find the debate, "Does the anti-sweatshop movement help or harm workers in low-wage countries?" Read the debate, and write a short essay explaining how the anti-sweatshop movement works in concert with, or in opposition to, the theory of comparative advantage.

The Microeconomics of Domestic Security

© AFP/CORBIS

On September 11, 2001, the United States suffered the most serious terrorist attack in history when hijacked airliners were used to destroy the World Trade Center in New York and a section of the Pentagon in Washington, D.C. More than three thousand people were killed, and thousands more narrowly escaped death by evacuating the twin towers just minutes before they collapsed. The attack left the nation reeling in shock, sadness, and anger. The number of dead was staggering, and the number who had lost a parent, a wife, a husband, or a close friend was many times larger. The nature of the attack—turning passenger aircraft into bombs and crashing them into skyscrapers where people sat working at their desks—was unthinkable. And a chilling realization followed almost immediately: More such attacks, perhaps even more destructive than September 11, were being planned.

The United States, and the world, changed overnight. Vital issues that had dominated U.S. political debates—such as expanding health insurance coverage and bolstering Social Security—suddenly paled in significance as domestic security rose to the top of the national agenda. The United States announced a new war on international terrorism, forged new strategic alliances, and began mobilizing thousands of troops to rout the Al Qaeda terrorist network and the associated Taliban government from Afghanistan. Millions of Americans suddenly knew the geographic and political landscapes of foreign lands that, before September 11, were known only to experts.

There were economic changes as well, some occurring with astonishing speed. The government responded almost immediately: In the weeks following the attacks,

TABLE 1

Corporations' Response
Within Two Months

Changes Since September 11	Already Implemented	Planned Within Three Months
Reviewing disaster plans	90%	0%
Reviewing insurance for adequate disaster coverage	74%	24%
Reviewing business travel policies	64%	11%
Increasing use of videoconferencing	60%	20%
Checking backgrounds of contract personnel	51%	11%
Checking employee backgrounds more thoroughly than before	39%	16%
Contracting for emergency alternative office space	35%	10%
Increasing use of private or corporate planes	22%	7%

Source: Booz Allen Hamilton, "How Corporate Security Is Reshaping the Post-9/11 CEO Agenda," accessed at *http://www.bah.com,* March 23, 2002.

the Bush administration set aside $20 billion to help rebuild lower Manhattan. Billions more were given to the airlines, which were in immediate danger of bankruptcy as the demand for air travel plummeted. Police in cities around the country temporarily stopped worrying about crimes like theft and robbery and focused their attention on possible further attacks.

The private economy, too, responded. Armed security guards appeared at the entrances to corporate headquarters, manufacturing plants, and even university buildings. Package delivery services changed their drop-off deadlines and inspection procedures. And firms that rented out bomb-sniffing dogs were unable to keep up with demand.

To provide some idea of the scope of these changes, and how rapidly they occurred, look at Table 1. It shows the results of a poll of 72 CEOs of large corporations (each with total revenue greater than $1 billion) taken in November and December 2001, just one and two months after the attacks.

As you can see, most of these corporations were reviewing disaster plans, insurance coverage, and travel policies. And a majority had already or were soon planning to substitute videoconferences for business travel and to increase background checks of employees and contractors. Each of these moves requires a reallocation of resources, and so do many other potential changes that were not asked about in the poll, such as the use of security guards or access restrictions.

In subsequent years, the economy has continued to adjust to the new concern for domestic security. The most significant adjustments have been led by the federal government. Table 2 provides some examples of domestic security actions either taken by the federal government or in which it was involved.

In this chapter, you'll be using the tools you've acquired in your study of microeconomics to understand the ongoing adjustments in the economy involving both government and private firms. In the next section, we begin this process by going back to a graph you learned about early in this book.

Bioterror	• Purchased enough smallpox vaccine for every person in the United States
	• Stockpiled enough antibiotics to treat 20 million people for anthrax exposure
	• Increased by sixfold the number of Food and Drug Administration inspectors to monitor security of food supply
Intelligence	• Shifted hundreds of FBI agents to full-time counterterrorism
Airline Security	• Required installation of cockpit doors strong enough to withstand bullets and hand grenades for all passenger planes that fly in the United States.
	• Created new Transportation Security Agency, which hired, trained, and equipped 55,000 airport screeners and oversaw installation of 6,800 screening devices at 429 airports
Borders and Ports	• Increased the screening of large container shipments and introduced early screening abroad
	• Equipped Bureau of Customs and Border Protection agents with portable radiation detectors
	• Mandated face-to-face interviews with almost all visa applicants (about 8 million annually)
Assistance to State and Local Governments	• Granted billions of dollars to states and cities for first responder programs and to increase the security of water and food supplies, airports, and critical infrastructure

TABLE 2

Some Government Actions to Increase Domestic Security: September 2001 to September 2003

Sources: "FBI's New Focus Places Burden on Local Police," *Wall Street Journal,* June 30, 2003; "U.S. Plans to Require Interviews for Almost All Visa Applicants," *Wall Street Journal,* May 16, 2003; "Homeland Security Funding Primer," Center for Arms Control and Non-Proliferation, May 1, 2003 *(http://www.armscontrolcenter. org/terrorism/primer.pdf).*

THE OPPORTUNITY COST OF DOMESTIC SECURITY

In Chapter 2, you learned about the production possibilities frontier (PPF)—a graphical tool that illustrates the opportunity cost of society's choices. The PPF curve in panel (a) of Figure 1 tells a simplified version of the story of the economic response to September 11. It shows the maximum quantity of other goods and services the economy could produce (on the vertical axis) for each different quantity of goods and services devoted to providing security (on the horizontal axis). In this figure, the only way to increase production of security goods is to shift resources like land, labor, capital, and entrepreneurship away from the production of other goods.

Point A represents the position of our economy before September 11, with a relatively small fraction of our resources devoted to security production (Q_1) and the rest being used to produce other things (Q_2). After September 11, there was both

FIGURE 1
Production Possibilities Frontiers for Security Goods and All Other Goods

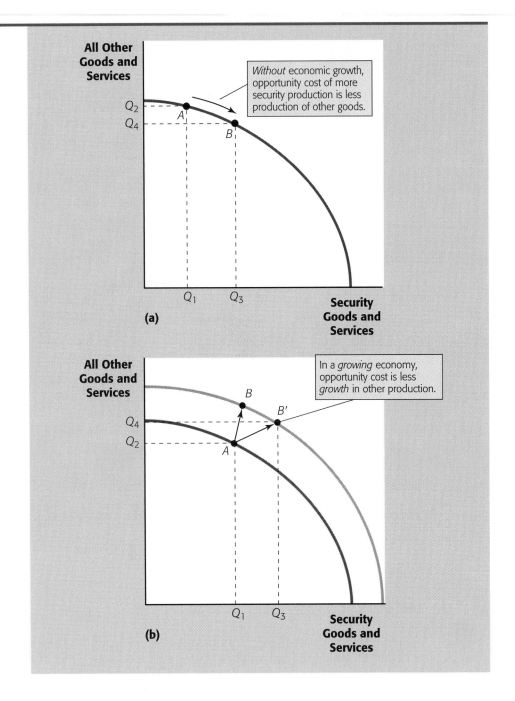

(a)

Without economic growth, opportunity cost of more security production is less production of other goods.

(b)

In a *growing* economy, opportunity cost is less *growth* in other production.

an increased desire for domestic security and a new awareness of the vast quantity of resources that would be needed to provide it. The economy began to move along its PPF, shifting resources out of the production of other things and toward goods and services used to provide domestic security.

But over a longer period of time, the PPF in panel (a) is not realistic enough to describe the ongoing process of adjustment, because it ignores a central fact about the economy: economic growth. Over time the population grows, people acquire new skills, new physical capital is produced and installed, and technology advances. These changes shift out the PPF over time, as in panel (b) of Figure 1. That is, economic growth enables us to produce more goods that provide security, or more of other things, or more of both.

What is the impact of the reallocation of resources in a growing economy, like that depicted in Figure 1, panel (b)? Instead of moving along a fixed PPF, the reallocation forces us to choose a different point on our new PPF.

Let's assume that, before September 11, the economy would have moved in a typical year from point *A* on its original PPF to a point like *B* on its new PPF. That is, in a typical year, we would have had a slight increase in production for security, but most of our growth would have been used to produce other things. Then we can represent the impact of September 11 as a change in our course: Instead of heading from point *A* to point *B,* we're now heading from point *A* to point *B'.* Notice that although we produce more of other things, we don't produce *as much more* of them as we otherwise would have.

Our standard of living depends on how much of these other things—food, medical care, travel, housing, entertainment—we produce *per person.* As long as production of nonsecurity goods grows faster than the population, the average standard of living will rise. If production of these other goods grows more slowly than the population, living standards will fall.

What effect will the ongoing reallocation of resources toward domestic security have on our standard of living? That depends on three things: (1) how much total production grows each year; (2) how much the population grows each year; and (3) how much spending and production for domestic security grows each year. Let's start by considering the last of these three: spending and production for domestic security.

The Ongoing Cost of Domestic Security: The Narrow (Optimistic) Approach

How much more are we spending and producing for domestic security after September 11? Here, we'll use a very narrow definition of domestic security spending: purchases of products or services that are used directly to help prevent or prepare for future terrorist attacks in the United States.

Figure 2 shows the federal government's part of this spending for the three years following the attacks. It includes spending by the new Department of Homeland Security as well as other departments, such as Defense, Justice, and Transportation. However, it includes just expenses directly related to domestic security—not the entire budgets of these departments.

The figure tells us two important facts: First, annual domestic security spending by the federal government has more than tripled from $13 billion in fiscal year 2001 (ending in September 2001) to an average of about $40 billion in the three following years. Second, the figure shows an upward trend for the first two years, and this upward trend is likely to continue through 2004 and beyond. (The figure for 2004 is the initial amount budgeted; supplemental budget requests will likely result in a higher figure.)

Once we leave the federal government, the picture turns a bit murky. State and local governments are spending billions of dollars on first responder programs, protecting food and water supplies, and guarding critical infrastructure. But there is no centralized data source for this spending at the state and local level. However, one

FIGURE 2
Direct Federal Spending for Domestic Security

Sources: Budget of the United States Government, Fiscal Year 2003 (Summary Table 5); *Budget of the United States Government, Fiscal Year 2004* (Summary Table 5); and "Homeland Security Funding Primer," Center for Arms Control and Non Proliferation, May 1, 2003.

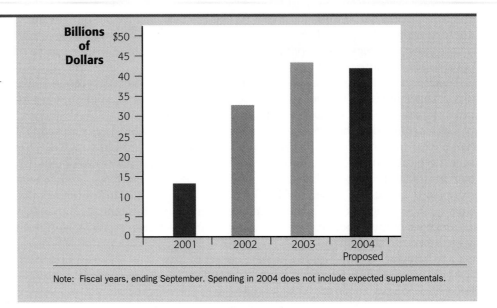

Note: Fiscal years, ending September. Spending in 2004 does not include expected supplementals.

respected study[1] has estimated the *increase* in this spending during 2002 at approximately $6.1 billion—with all but $1.3 billion of this tab picked up by the federal government and, therefore, already included in Figure 2.

Private sector spending for domestic security is even more difficult to estimate. We know that many private firms have hired more security guards, put up security fences and other barriers, and invested in high-tech access and surveillance systems. Economists who study this issue have provided ballpark estimates for the postattack *increase* in such spending that ranges from $10 billion to $25 billion per year.[2]

Table 3 combines all this information, showing a *very* rough estimate of the *increase* in domestic security spending for 2004, compared to the initial, preattack level in the year ending September 2001. The entry for the federal government, for example, is the actual 2004 budget request for domestic security spending ($41.3 billion) minus the initial spending in fiscal year 2001 ($13 billion), giving us $41.3 billion − $13 billion = $28.3 billion. The entry for additional state and local government spending is the 2002 estimate of net additional spending ($1.3 billion), assumed to have increased by 3 percent per year from 2002 to 2004: $1.3 billion × 1.03 × 1.03 = $1.37 billion, or about $1.4 billion. Finally, for additional private sector spending, we'll take the midpoint of $10 billion to $25 billion range of estimates: $17.5 billion.

While this is a lot of money, it is actually tiny in relation to U.S. gross domestic product (GDP), which measures the U.S. economy's total production in a year. Using an estimated GDP for 2004 of $11 *trillion,* increased spending on domestic security in 2004 would amount to less than half of one percent of GDP ($47.1 / $11,000 = .004 or 0.4 percent).

What would this mean for the average standard of living in the United States? Let's see. Suppose that annual growth in real GDP averages 3.1 percent (its aver-

[1] Bart Hobijn, "What Will Homeland Security Cost?" *Federal Reserve Bank of New York Economic Policy Review,* November 2002.
[2] See, for example, Michael O'Hanlon, et. al., *Protecting the American Homeland: A Preliminary Analysis,* Washington, DC: The Brookings Institution, 2002; and Bart Hobijn, "What Will Homeland Security Cost," *Federal Reserve Bank of New York Economic Policy Review,* November 2002. The higher range assumes a doubling of annual security expenses in the wake of the attacks.

age growth rate during the 1980s and 1990s). In this case, increased security spending would reduce annual growth in *nonsecurity* goods and services by 0.4 percent, leaving 3.1 − 0.4 = 2.7 percent. This annual rise in nonsecurity spending is more than enough to keep up with population growth of about 1 percent during the year. Living standards would grow more slowly, but not much more slowly.

Additional Federal Government	$28.3 billion
Additional State and Local Government (not reimbursed by federal government)	$1.3 billion
Additional Private Sector Spending	$17.5 billion
Total	**$47.1 billion**
Reference: Estimated GDP in 2004	$11 trillion

TABLE 3

A Rough Estimate of Increase in Narrowly Defined Domestic Security Spending in 2004 Over 2001

The Ongoing Cost of Domestic Security: The Broad (Pessimistic) Approach

If we consider domestic security costs more broadly—including all opportunity costs that result from our heightened concern for domestic security after September 11—we get a very different picture.

One issue is that, by shifting priorities, the government may be shifting resources away from other valuable activities toward domestic security, even though explicit spending remains unchanged. Here's one example: The total number of FBI special agents—11,633—is actually *smaller* today than in 1999.[3] But after 9/11, the FBI pulled 674 agents off their regular beats (including drug smuggling, violent crime, and white collar crime) and reassigned them to full-time counterterrorism work. With little or no change in the FBI's total spending, we pay an opportunity cost: fewer resources devoted to fighting more traditional types of crime. Not surprisingly, the number of new drug-smuggling cases initiated by the FBI fell from 1,825 in fiscal year 2000 to 944 in 2002, and only 310 in the first half of 2003.[4] At the same time, in cities around the country, the fraction of bank robbers arrested has dropped significantly, no doubt contributing to the rapid rise in the number of bank robberies nationwide.

Another issue is whether to include all or part of the security-related military activities overseas, which are not classified by the government as part of homeland security spending. The U.S. invasion of Afghanistan in late 2001 was widely viewed in the United States and abroad as part of American domestic security policy: The military mission was to overthrow the Taliban regime that had been collaborating with Al Qaeda leaders and sponsoring their training camps. In the broadest sense, the dollar cost of this war—amounting to $10 billion in fiscal year 2002 alone—could rightfully be included as part of the shift of resources toward domestic security.[5]

By contrast, the U.S. invasion of Iraq in early 2003 was highly controversial precisely *because* of differing opinions about its connection to U.S. domestic security. By a small majority, the U.S. population favored the invasion, but larger majorities in the rest of the world opposed it. However, most on both sides of this debate

---

[3] Louis J. Freeh, "A Few Good Men," *Wall Street Journal,* July 25, 2003.

[4] "FBI's New Focus Places Burden on Local Police," *Wall Street Journal,* June 30, 2003.

[5] "Measuring the Costs of the War Against Terrorism," *Budget Monitor,* House Committee on the Budget, Vol. 2, No. 6, June 19, 2002. The $10 billion figure does not include humanitarian or economic assistance to Afghanistan or its neighbors.

would acknowledge that the invasion would not have taken place without the attacks of September 11, and the resulting change in U.S. public attitudes toward aggressive action abroad. Thus, one might include the expense of the U.S. involvement in Iraq—roughly $100 billion in additional military costs alone for the first 12 months—as part of the opportunity cost that the American public has been willing to bear because of the post-9/11 environment.

Moreover, these and other U.S. actions overseas have led to ongoing expenses: billions of dollars each year for reconstruction, development, and humanitarian assistance. And what about the billions of dollars in foreign assistance—for nations such as Colombia, Jordan, Pakistan, Turkey, Egypt, and the Philippines—that has increased, in large part, to ensure continued cooperation in the global war on terrorism? Or the increase in general military spending resulting from a shift in public attitudes toward national defense after September 11? You can see that broadening our definition of domestic security spending radically changes the total cost—and the impact on living standards.

Note that total spending on domestic security may be highly unstable. A future terrorist attack would heighten domestic security concerns, and there is no shortage of projects waiting for funds. Screening all large containers arriving at U.S. ports with radiation detectors, X-rays, or visual inspection would cost $6 billion. (At present, only 4 percent of such containers are checked, because only a tiny fraction of this amount has been spent.) Protecting the nation's 103 nuclear reactors with a single Patriot missile battery each would require another $16.5 billion.[6] The list of such projects—waiting in the wings—is almost endless.

In the broadest and most pessimistic view, the annual cost of domestic security would already have risen much more than the $47.1 billion reported in Table 3— perhaps two or three times as much. And it is not far-fetched to conclude that, with the broadest interpretation of domestic security spending and another attack that heightens concern, living standards could drop. Although the economy would still grow and production of nonsecurity goods *might* still rise, we could move so far rightward and downward along the PPF in Figure 2 that growth in nonsecurity goods would not keep up with the growing population.

Finally, remember that one of the factors that shifts the PPF outward over time is growth in the kind of capital—plant and equipment—that increases our ability to produce goods and services of all kinds. But because of our emphasis on production for security, some of this productivity-enhancing capital that would have been put in place will not be. This will reduce the growth rate of output and reduce the outward shift of the PPF in the figure.

Clearly, with so much uncertainty, the numbers must be considered highly tenuous at best. But our qualitative conclusion remains certain:

The opportunity cost of increased production for security is a sacrifice in the growth of our standard of living. At worst, our living standard could fall. At best, it will rise more slowly than it otherwise would.

Slower growth in living standards is an important (and unpleasant) consequence of the need for more security. But our analysis leaves many questions

[6] Matthew Brzezinski, "Fortress America," *New York Times Magazine*, February 23, 2003.

unanswered. For example, *how* will resources be shifted from other goods and services to the provision of more security? In particular, who actually makes the decisions, and how are these decisions put into effect? Moreover, how will the opportunity cost of increased security be distributed among different groups and individuals?

Remember, from Chapter 2, that societies throughout history have relied primarily on three different systems of resource allocation: command, tradition, and the market. The United States, in spite of some elements of command and tradition, is primarily a market economy: one in which individuals mostly do what they want with the resources at their disposal. This remain largely true even in times of war or national emergency. Thus, it shouldn't surprise you that our efforts to understand the current reallocation of resources will rely heavily on the three-step process we've used to understand the economy throughout this book.

USING THE THREE-STEP PROCESS

Key Step 1: Characterize the Market. The first step in answering almost any question about the economy is to characterize the market. But which markets should we look at? The adjustments taking place in our economy involve many markets, and the ones we choose for our analysis—and how we characterize them—depends on the specific questions we are trying to answer.

For example, if we want to understand how the economy responds when business firms and government agencies demand specific security-oriented goods and services, we'll need to look at the product markets in which these goods and services are produced. To analyze the impacts on wages in different markets, we'd look at labor markets for various types of workers. To help us understand how different industries will expand and contract, we'd look at the financial markets, such as the stock market. And to understand some of the global economic implications, we'd look at markets for internationally traded goods and services.

Key Step 2: Find the Equilibrium. Before we can analyze the economy's response to an event, we must characterize where the economy was before the event took place. Since there are powerful forces pushing markets toward their equilibrium, a natural starting point for our analysis will be the initial equilibrium that markets had achieved before September 11.

Key Step 3: What Happens When Things Change? In most economic analysis, this is the most useful step, and it's why we bother with the others. Here, Step 3 takes center stage, because September 11 created such a huge change in the conditions facing so many economic decision makers.

In the remainder of this chapter, we'll use the three-step process—along with other aspects of the microeconomic theory you've learned in this text—in order to answer a number of questions about the changes our economy is undergoing. That is, we'll be looking at several different types of markets where buyers and sellers come together, each trying to achieve their goals and each facing constraints. We'll be examining the equilibrium in each of these markets, and we'll observe what happens when that equilibrium changes.

CHANGES IN PRODUCT MARKETS

Virtually every product market in the country has been affected in some way by shifting national priorities after September 11. Consumer tastes, production techniques, future investment plans—all have changed, in some cases dramatically. How can we hope to organize our thinking about all of these changes?

First, we'll focus on the types of markets affected most directly. These include industries that have suffered—such as the airline industry, aircraft producers, hotel, and tourism—as well as industries that have benefited, such as the manufacturers of security equipment like concrete barriers, video surveillance systems, hazmat suits, and more.

Second, we'll use the model of perfect competition. True, perfect competition is not an exact fit in many of the markets we'll be looking at. But for the types of broad resource allocation questions we'll be asking, it comes close enough. Especially over long periods of time—and often over shorter time periods—prices and quantities in the markets we'll examine tend to rise and fall with the forces of supply and demand.

Finally, it will be useful to categorize these product markets into two types: those experiencing a significant shift in demand, and those experiencing a significant shift in supply.

Changes in Demand

The most obvious categories of goods experiencing a shift in demand are those used to provide enhanced security. This includes luggage-screening machines, metal detectors, antibiotics, access-pass systems, and some of the new technologies that are likely to be in use soon, such as iris-scanning machines. It also means bomb-sniffing dogs, the market we'll look at here.

An Example: Bomb-Sniffing Dogs. Recall from Chapter 6 that firms (and ideally, government agencies as well) will choose the lowest-cost method of producing any given level of output. This is true of car washes or gold mines, and it is also true of methods of producing a given level of security. As many police departments, federal agencies, and private corporations have discovered, the least-cost method of producing any given level of security often includes dogs.

Why? At first glance, it seems that bomb-sniffing dogs could not compete with bomb-detection machines. The dogs are not cheap. Each one must be trained for around three months, more than five hours each day. The dog must learn to recognize dozens of different scents, and be taught to ignore the scent of food and the distractions of crowds. A training school must have skilled professional instructors, veterinarians, and chemists on its staff, and must maintain supplies of dangerous explosives. The result is that training each bomb-sniffing dog costs between $8,000 and $10,000.

Moreover, once on the job, dogs require handlers who must also be trained, and who generally earn higher salaries than machine operators. Finally, while we fully understand how machines work, and we can accurately measure and control their specifications, we have no such knowledge or control with dogs. Although it has been proven that a dog's sniffing abilities are as good or better than the best machines available today, we don't fully understand why.

Why, then, are dogs so prevalent in the security market?

First, although dogs are expensive, bomb-detection machines are even more expensive. Even the simplest trace-detection machines cost between $25,000 and $50,000 each. The more sophisticated luggage-screening machines that have been installed in airports across the country cost $1 million each.

Second, suspicious material containing explosives must be found and brought to a machine. By contrast, a dog goes to the explosives. It scans a large area rapidly, sniffing here and there and searching for areas where further, closer sniffing might be called for. In this way, a dog can scan a large, underground parking garage in 20 minutes, whereas it would take days using the current, state-of-the-art trace-detection machines. These advantages have led to widespread use of dogs as part of the least-cost input mix in providing security.

How are bomb-sniffing dogs "produced"? Many are trained by the Defense Department at Lackland Air Force Base, or by the Bureau of Alcohol, Tobacco, and Firearms. Although no one knows for sure, there were probably close to a thousand government-trained dogs stationed around the country before September 11. But even more dogs are trained privately. Companies you may never have heard of—United States Bomb Dogs Inc., Washington K–9, Augusta K9 Services, Detection Support Services Bomb Dogs, and dozens of others—train hundreds of dogs each year. Some are sold, while others are rented out by the day or the hour for emergencies.

We'll use Figure 3 to analyze the impact of increased security production in this market. The supply curve in the figure is the short-run supply curve. It tells us the quantity of bomb-sniffing dogs that would be available for sale over the next few months at each price. Note that this supply curve is drawn with very little elasticity: In the short run (too short a time to train a dog), only dogs who are already trained can be supplied. The initial equilibrium occurs at price P_1, with Q_1 dogs sold each month. In panel (b), the typical dog-training firm—facing the market price P_1—is making zero economic profit.

After September 11, there was a dramatic change in this market: Large corporations like Ford Motor Company and Johnson & Johnson, organizers of sporting events like the 2002 winter Olympics, the 2002 Super Bowl, and the 2003 Daytona 500 Nascar races; transportation companies like Amtrak and Carnival Cruise Lines; as well as schools, hospitals, and amusement parks around the country all suddenly wanted to have dogs on hand, just in case. At the same time, federal government agencies and local police forces wanted more dogs. For example, the FAA had only 175 dogs stationed at 30 airports, and wanted to rapidly increase the number of dogs to 300 to protect 80 airports. New York City had only 29 dogs in its City and Port Authority police departments, and suddenly had to spread them among every bridge, tunnel, train station, bus station, government building, and monument in the city. In many cases, government agencies had no choice but to turn to the private market to get them. How did the market respond?

We illustrate the short-run response in the left-hand panel of Figure 3, which shows the market demand curve for bomb-sniffing dogs shifting rightward. The market equilibrium moves to B, with equilibrium price rising to P_2 and quantity of dogs available for sale rising to Q_2.

But how does this increase come about? Because of a quirk in training, it is not possible to switch dogs trained for other purposes to bomb duty. While bomb-sniffing dogs are trained to point their nose at a suspicious area and sit back quietly, those trained to sniff narcotics or currency learn to paw or grab it when they

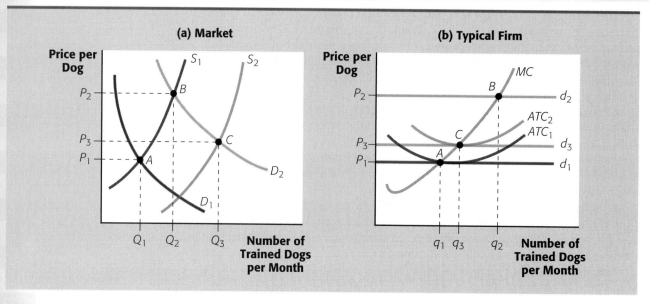

FIGURE 3

An Increase in Demand for Bomb-Sniffing Dogs

In panel (a), the increase in demand for security dogs (from D_1 to D_2) causes the market price of security dogs to rise, with some increase in quantity supplied (to Q_2) in the short run. In panel (b), the typical security dog firm earns economic profit, which leads to entry. In the long run, entry will shift the supply curve in panel (a) from S_1 to S_2, bringing the market price down somewhat. Quantity rises further, to Q_3.

find it, and are rewarded by a game of tug-of-war with their handler. Clearly, dogs trained for narcotics detection would be unsuitable to work with explosives.

However, as often happens in markets, an increase in demand leads to surprising discoveries of new supply. In this case, many dogs that had retired and had been placed in private homes were pressed back into service. Other dogs that were scheduled for retirement had their retirement postponed (just as 10,500 Air Force personnel were temporarily barred from retirement after September 11).

Interestingly, the equilibrium price did not rise fully to P_2 in the weeks following the attack, as owners of training schools, out of a sense of patriotism, chose not to fully exploit opportunities for profit. The result was a modest rise in the price of dogs, and an excess demand. Ordinarily, the shortage would have led to misallocation of dogs: Some would be snapped up for trivial purposes, while other crucial needs would go unsatisfied. In this case, however, the trainers themselves tried to allocate the dogs efficiently, in many cases turning down requests they felt were not vital.

What about the long run? As you can see in panel (b), after the shift in demand, with equilibrium price at P_2, the typical dog-training firm was earning economic profit. This created an incentive to increase capacity in the industry, shifting the supply curve rightward, to S_2 in panel (a). The process was set in motion almost immediately. First, dog handlers at many schools began increasing the number of dogs per "class" and shortened the duration of training. Dog handlers and trainers who were used to working an average of 17 hours per week suddenly found themselves working 60 hours per week.

Second, dog schools began scouring pounds for new recruits, further increasing class size. They also found additional trainers who had retired or moved to other jobs. And within months, owners of existing schools began complaining that too many new competitors were trying to establish dog schools. All of these long-run adjustments worked to bring the price down (to P_3 in the figure), and further increased quantity supplied (to Q_3).

Notice that, in the figure, the price of trained dogs ends up higher than initially. That is, we assume that this is an increasing cost industry. This makes sense: After all, anyone who would have been willing to go into business training dogs at the old price was presumably already doing so before September 11. The only way to induce more entrepreneurs into this business, and to induce more resources like dog trainers and suitable dogs into the industry, is to pay more for them. In panel (b), this increase in input prices is reflected in the upward shift of the *ATC* curve to ATC_2. (The *MC* curve may shift as well, but this is not shown.) Thus, even after all long-run adjustments are completed, we would expect the price of bomb-sniffing dogs to end up higher than initially.

But that may not be the end of the story. The federal government, deciding that bomb-sniffing dogs offer substantial benefits to society, has begun subsidizing research that will change the technology of "producing" them. For example, the Institute of Biological Detection Systems at Auburn University in Alabama is currently conducting federally funded research into dogs' sense of smell, dog learning behavior, and methods of predicting the most trainable dogs: all designed to improve the technology in this market. As you've learned, technological progress shifts a supply curve rightward. If this research proves successful, the supply curve could shift further rightward, and decrease the price of bomb-sniffing dogs in the future.

What we've seen in the market for bomb-sniffing dogs is also occurring in thousands of markets for security-related products throughout the economy. Demand has shifted rightward for the services of security guards, bomb-detection equipment, antibiotics, video cameras, fingerprint recognition software, backup systems for computer data, and more.

> *After September 11, the demand for security-related products has increased. In the short run, the rise in price increases supply to some extent. In the long run, the higher price and the associated profits increase productive capacity in the industry, leading to even greater increases in supply.*

In other markets, the opposite has taken place. After September 11, the demand for air travel decreased by 20 to 30 percent, and was still running 5 percent below normal through April 2003.[7] Prices have dropped, just as we'd expect. And the same has happened at some hotels, cruise lines, and amusement parks. If these decreases in demand turn out to be permanent, we can expect to see continued lower prices, continued economic losses, and finally, exit of some firms from their industries.

> *After September 11, the demand for some products—such as air travel and tourist services—decreased. In the short run, the drop in price decreased quantity supplied to some extent. In the long run, if the decrease in demand persists, the lower price and the associated losses will decrease productive capacity in these industries, leading to even greater decreases in supply.*

Changes in Supply

In our analysis of changes in demand, the supply curve shifts in the long run in response to the change in demand. But there are also markets where the initial impact of the attacks was (and continues to be) a change in supply.

[7] Bureau of Transportation Statistics, "Domestic Airlines Carried 47.4 Million Passengers in April 2003," Press Release, July 7, 2003 (*http://www.bts.gov/press_releases/2003*).

The need for increased security is like the opposite of technological progress. When technology advances, firms discover new ways to produce goods using smaller quantities of some key inputs—such as labor or raw materials—enabling production at lower cost. This causes market supply curves to shift rightward. But increased use of security does the opposite: It requires the use of additional inputs and higher costs to produce any given level of output. This causes market supply curves to shift leftward.

Of course, there are substitutes for direct security expenditures: more insurance, relocation, a change in production methods that is less vulnerable to attack. If these methods provide more security at lower cost than direct security spending, they will be used as part of an alternative input mix. But even these alternative methods still add to the cost of production, shifting supply curves leftward.

An Example: Goods with High Transportation Costs. Every year, U.S. freight carriers move about $10 trillion worth of products, some of this from other countries but most originating and delivered within the United States. (We'll deal with international trade a bit later.) Many changes have been made in the freight industry after September 11, all of which require the use of new inputs or greater quantities of existing inputs, and thus raise costs.

This is especially so for the shipment of hazardous materials. Many of these materials can no longer be shipped by air or by mail. Train transportation of these materials is now prohibited when the tracks go through urban areas. This largely leaves trucks, which may be a more expensive method of shipment.

Further, shipping by truck has itself become more expensive, as hazardous materials (hazmat) trucking companies have come under new scrutiny. They must now run background checks on all drivers, at a cost of $80 per driver. The trucks are frequently held up at weigh stations, where a background check is conducted that can take hours. Trucks carrying hazardous materials are in many cases rerouted around urban areas, or prohibited from using certain tunnels or bridges, adding to total mileage. Insurance rates for companies that ship hazardous goods have skyrocketed. There is more paperwork to perform, and it must be retained for a longer period. There are more frequent safety inspections for trucks. And there are even proposals to equip every hazmat truck with a satellite tracking system so that company management can have 24-hour access to its location.

But lest you think that this applies only to the most hazardous materials, like dynamite, gasoline, or poisonous chemicals, think again: Even shipments of lower risk hazardous materials such as certain food additives, colorings, and flavorings; cleaning materials like ammonia and bleach; and even cooking oils, are subject to the increased security measures. Moreover, trucks not permitted to carry hazardous materials are now more frequently stopped to see if they are carrying them. After all, a terrorist on a mission with hazardous materials would not want to advertise that fact by driving a hazmat truck. The result is that freight transportation in general has become more expensive. This, in turn, shifts supply curves leftward (or upward) especially for goods that are produced using hazardous materials, or for which transportation—especially hazmat transportation—is a major part of the cost.

How do the tools of microeconomics help us understand this?

Figure 4 illustrates the situation for gas stations in a market far removed from sources of crude oil or refineries, which therefore requires heavy use of hazmat transportation. The immediate impact of the additional resources used to transport the gas is a rise in the price of delivered gasoline. In panel (b), the typical gas sta-

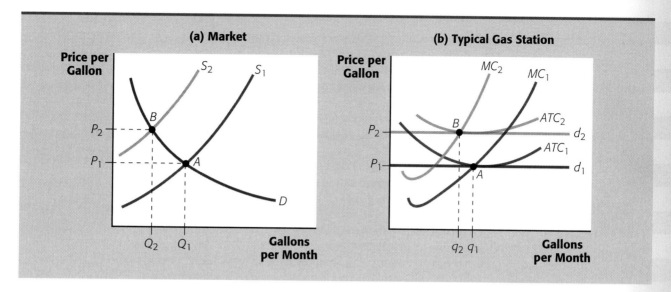

(a) Market

(b) Typical Gas Station

FIGURE 4

A Shift in Supply in a Distant Market for Retail Gasoline

New security procedures have raised the cost of transportation for hazardous materials, like gasoline. In panel (b), the typical gas station's ATC and MC curves shift upward, to ATC_2 and MC_2, respectively. This causes the supply curve in panel (a) to shift leftward, raising market price (from P_1 to P_2) and lowering market quantity (from Q_1 to Q_2).

tion's *ATC and MC* curves shift upward. (The *MC* curve shifts up because greater transportation costs raise the cost to the station of selling *each additional gallon of* gas.) In panel (a), the market supply curve for gasoline shifts leftward (upward). The price rises to P_2, causing a leftward movement along the demand curve.

So much for the mechanics of the graph. But notice what the market accomplishes: Using gasoline in this location now imposes a greater opportunity cost on society than it did before, because of all the additional resources that must be used to limit the now-increased risks of shipping it. The market causes those who produce (and ship) gasoline to pay the additional cost. As a result, they will charge higher prices to the gas stations who, in turn, will charge higher prices to their customers. Thus, those who buy gas are forced to internalize the opportunity costs of the additional resources used to bring it to them. Any gallons of gasoline for which the desire is great enough to justify the greater payment will be produced and purchased. Any gallons for which the opportunity cost is not worth it will not be produced or purchased.

> *After September 11, it will take more resources to produce many goods and services—such as those involving high-risk transportation. Prices of these goods will rise and production will fall, as consumers are forced to take account of the higher opportunity cost of their production.*

Air Travel: A Special Case

The market for air travel stands out among those directly affected by September 11, because of the nature of the attack itself. Air traffic decreased from 40 billion revenue passenger miles in September 2000 to 27 billion in the same month in 2001. Only a small part of the decrease was due to the FAA's decision to shut down air travel for a few days; the rest was caused by cancelled or changed travel plans.

Even in 2003, air travel remained significantly down from 2000 levels. Some industry observers believed that air travel would not regain its former popularity for years, if ever, and all agreed that at best, the growth in air travel will be slower in future years than it otherwise would have been.

What has happened to the airline industry?

It was hit by several of the factors we've discussed above. First, the demand curve has shifted leftward. Business travelers and tourists have become less interested in flying than they were before September 11. To some extent, business has substituted e-mail, videoconferencing, and other forms of communication for traditional, face-to-face business meetings. Tourists are more likely to take vacations closer to home, or to drive even long distances. (Accordingly, Hawaii has been particularly hard hit by the decline in air travel.)

A further leftward shift in demand has been caused by the greater *time cost* of air travel. Since September 11, 2001, airlines have recommended earlier arrival times for passengers, which means a longer wait in the terminal or going through security. Occasional traffic jams at airports, when security alerts lead to rerouting or other delays, make waiting time less predictable. At any given ticket price, the added time costs and uncertainty lead to a decrease in the number of tickets demanded.

In Figure 5, the shift in demand for air travel by itself would move the market from point A to point B along the original supply curve S_1. The price of airline travel would decrease, and so would the number of flights.

But the diagram also shows a shift in the supply curve to S_2. This is the effect of the new tax on air travel to pay part of the costs of the new Transportation Security Administration (TSA), which now runs airport security nationwide. The tax has been set at $2.50 to $10 per ticket, depending on the number of times a passenger boards a plane for a given trip. But the tax may increase, depending on how much of the cost of airport security the government ultimately decides to fund from general tax revenues (to be discussed a bit later). The impact of a tax, as you've learned, is to shift the supply curve upward, moving the market to point C.

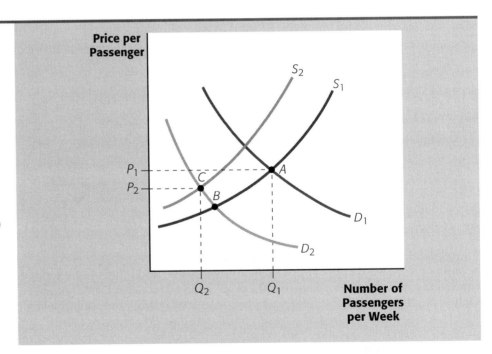

FIGURE 5

Changes in the Market for Air Travel

Safety concerns and greater time requirements have shifted the demand curve for air travel leftward. By itself, this would move the equilibrium from A to B. But at the same time, the security tax on air travel has shifted the supply curve upward (leftward), moving the equilibrium to C. The result—in the short run—has been a lower price (P_2) and lower quantity (Q_2) of air travel. In the long run (not shown in the figure), if the decrease in demand is permanent, exit will shift the supply curve further leftward.

But point C is not the end of the story, because the reduction in demand has created losses at many airlines. The airlines have responded by cutting back on capacity, causing a further leftward shift of the supply curve. Unless the demand for air travel returns to previous levels, we can expect some airlines to exit in the long run. The process may have started in 2002, when two major airlines—U.S. Airways and United Airlines—filed for bankruptcy protection. And in 2003, American Airlines came close to bankruptcy. If exit occurs, it will cause further leftward shifts of the supply curve, further rises in price, and further decreases in the quanity of air travel.

CHANGES IN LABOR MARKETS

Goods and services are ultimately made from resources—land and natural resources, labor, capital, and entrepreneurship. In order to increase production in expanding sectors of the economy (e.g., bomb-sniffing dogs or other security goods), resources must be reallocated from elsewhere in the economy toward the expanding industries. The tools of microeconomics can help explain how the market accomplishes this task.

An Example: Strategic Language Speakers

Let's look at a particular labor market: for people who can speak, read, and write what the federal government has called *strategic languages*. These are languages spoken in areas of the world where the U.S. government believes up-to-date and accurate intelligence is crucial, such as many countries in the Middle East, Africa, and South Asia.

The deterioration in U.S. language capabilities has been well documented for some time. In the early 1990s, the FBI seized documents, recorded phone conversations, and obtained videotapes that pointed directly to the first bombing of the World Trade Center a year later, in 1993, but none of these were translated until after the attack. The reason: not enough agents who could speak and read Arabic. A similar lack of language skills hampered the investigation of the American embassy bombings in Kenya and Tanzania in 1998, and the downing of an Egypt Air flight off Nantucket in 1999. And although there was plenty of evidence that India and Pakistan were planning nuclear tests in 1998, the detonations surprised the American government because the evidence had not been properly translated and analyzed.

September 11 served as a long-delayed wake-up call. While a terrorist threat can come from anywhere—including U.S. citizens, as was proven in Oklahoma City in 1995—the attacks of September 11 suggested that the gravest dangers were from the Middle East, the Asian subcontinent, and North Africa. And as confiscated documents poured in from Afghanistan in late 2001 and early 2002, it became apparent that our national security depended on having large numbers of experts who could translate them.

Moreover, the need to monitor communications and infiltrate foreign organizations would create a continuing need for speakers of Arabic, Farsi (the language of Iran), Hausa (spoken by 22 million people in sub-Saharan Africa), Pashto and Dari (Afghanistan), Tajik, Turkmen or Baluchi (Southwest Asia), and Malay. If you have not heard of some of these languages—or of Tagalog, Uzbek, or Tamil—it is because many of them are not offered in any university in the United States. Courses in most strategic languages are currently offered only at specialized institutions such as the Defense Language Training Institute in Monterey, California. And before September 11, very few people were studying them.

As former Senator Paul Simon wrote in October 2001:

> In every national crisis, our nation has lamented its foreign language short-falls. But then the crisis goes away, and we return to business as usual. One of the messages of Sept. 11 is that business as usual is no longer an acceptable option.[8]

One might think that a country like the United States, with millions of immigrants, should have no such shortage. After all, more than a million U.S. citizens are highly competent in Arabic, several hundred thousand speak Farsi, and tens of thousands of U.S. citizens come from Afghanistan and speak Pashto or Dari. But, ironically, government intelligence agencies have an instinctive mistrust of native speakers, and have discouraged them from seeking jobs. For example, anyone applying for a job with the CIA must list the names of every foreigner with whom they have a close or continuing relationship. For most native speakers—who have spent much of their lives in a foreign country—the list would be rather large, and the investigation of each contact would take months, if not years. Moreover, the more proficient a speaker and the more time spent abroad, the more likely one is to know someone judged "undesirable" or "suspicious" by the CIA. This makes security clearance unlikely. Although these policies make it easier for the CIA and other government agencies to screen and monitor their staff, they have effectively limited employment to native-born Americans who have *learned* a language. For strategic languages, this supply is limited. Although no one knows for sure, several media outlets have reported that before September 2001, the CIA had fewer than a half dozen employees who were fully competent in Arabic, and only a single expert in Farsi.

The U.S. Congress judged this to be a tragic mistake, one of 13 systemic failures in intelligence gathering that made the surprise attack possible. The report released by Congress in July 2003 stated this clearly:

> Finding: Prior to September 11, the Intelligence Community was not prepared to handle the challenge it faced in translating the volumes of foreign language counterterrorism intelligence it collected. Agencies within the Intelligence Community experienced backlogs in material awaiting translation, a shortage of language specialists, and language-qualified field officers, and a readiness level of only 30% in the most critical terrorism-related languages used by terrorists.

Our analysis of labor markets can help us understand the problem, and the economy's adjustment to it after September 11. Figure 6 shows the market for specialists in strategic languages who have the practical qualifications for government agency work—at present, American-born speakers. Notice that we are aggregating all strategic languages together; we are interested here in overall adjustments in the broad market, rather than in explaining why, say, speakers of Pashto might earn higher wages than speakers of Uzbek.

---

[8] Paul Simon, "Beef up the Country's Foreign Language Skills," *The Washington Post*, October 23, 2001.

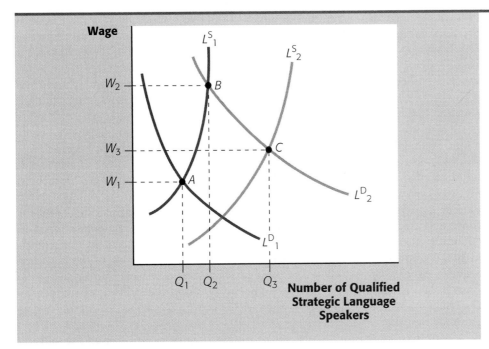

FIGURE 6

Changes in the Market for Strategic Language Speakers

In the short run, an increase in demand for strategic language speakers (from L_1^D to L_2^D) causes their average wage to rise (to W_2), with only a relatively small increase in employment (to Q_2). In the long run, however, the higher wage (as well as shifting tastes) will shift the labor supply curve rightward from L_1^S to L_2^S, bringing the wage down somewhat (to W_3) while increasing quantity further (to Q_3).

The initial demand curve for language experts (L_1^D) slopes downward: The higher the wage, the fewer will be demanded, all else equal. Although the government has a strong need for these speakers, government agencies have budgets and will find ways to economize on experts as their wages rise. Moreover, strategic language speakers are also hired by other employers: universities, international organizations, the media, research organizations, and private firms who conduct business in the regions. These other labor demanders will also respond to wage changes in their hiring decisions.

Now look at the short-run labor supply curve, L_1^S. As the wage rate rises, more people will seek jobs that require their language expertise. However, for reasons already stated, the labor short-run supply curve is very wage inelastic: The number of additional qualified people who would offer their services at higher wages is rather small.

Point *A* represents the initial equilibrium in this market, with Q_1 qualified strategic language speakers working at a wage of W_1. After September 11, the demand curve shifted dramatically rightward, to L_2^D in the figure. Government agencies immediately stepped up their hiring, and the FBI even posted an 800 number on its Web page where speakers of Arabic and Farsi could apply by phone. The short-run equilibrium began moving toward point *B* in the figure, with the wage rising to W_2. Indeed, the FBI found almost immediately that in order to attract qualified translators who spoke Arabic, Farsi, and Pashto, it had to offer as much as $38 per hour, unusually high for this type of work.

What about the long run? Two factors are working to shift the labor supply curve rightward over the next several years, represented by the shift to L_2^S. First, there has been a change in labor market tastes: an increased interest among students to learn the language and culture of a part of the world suddenly very prominent in the news. Before September 11, only 8 percent of U.S. college students studied a foreign language—a fraction that hadn't changed in 25 years. And of these, 90 percent were studying Spanish, French, or German. But when the fall semester began a few weeks after September 11, the media reported that enrollment in Arabic and Farsi classes in U.S. colleges was rising rapidly. For example, class sizes in Arabic at Stanford and Princeton more than doubled.

Second, over the long run, the rising salaries of strategic language speakers is a market signal to people making career decisions. It tells them that expertise in a strategic language is an option worth considering. And the power of this signal will likely be speeded by the government: On December 5, 2001, the Homeland Security Education Act was introduced in the Senate. Among other things, the bill would provide graduate tuition fellowships and stipends of up to $21,500 for those pursuing advanced study in strategic areas (including languages) and who commit to three years of work for the Defense, State, Energy, and Justice departments, or the CIA, the Federal Emergency Management Agency, or the National Security Agency. Ultimately, all of these factors—the increased interest in Middle Eastern languages, the response to higher wages, and the subsidies provided by government—will contribute to a rightward-shifting labor supply curve, such as L_2^S in the figure.

It will take some time before any of these adjustments are seen in the market. Full competency in a language typically takes four years of course work and at least six months of total immersion in a language by living abroad. This means that noticeable shifts in the supply curve will not begin to occur until some time in 2006, and then only slowly. Can the nation wait that long? This is a decision plaguing government officials, who are considering compromises on the barriers to native speakers. Such a change in policy would shift the supply curve rightward much more quickly.

Similar adjustments are taking place in other labor markets as well. Security guards, intelligence agents, aircraft engineers, and biochemists are examples of labor markets that have experienced rightward shifts in labor demand, tending to raise wage rates. In the long run, as more people acquire the human capital to qualify, the labor supply curves in these markets will shift rightward as well.

> *Since September 11, the demand for many types of labor has increased. In the short run, the wage rate has increased, with only limited increase in quantity supplied. In the long run, as people acquire the needed skills, labor supply response will be greater.*

FINANCIAL AND CAPITAL MARKETS

In Chapter 13, you learned that financial markets play an important role in resource allocation: They enable business firms to obtain funds for capital purchases.

The reallocation of resources toward greater domestic security requires new capital purchases in a variety of industries. For example, increasing the production of bomb-sniffing dogs requires more facilities for training the dogs, more on-site laboratories to prepare and calibrate samples of explosives, and so on. Increasing the production of electronic access-pass systems requires new manufacturing plants and new assembly-line tools appropriate for higher levels of output.

After September 11, business firms that produced security-related goods such as bomb-sniffing dogs, access-pass systems, hazmat suits, video monitors, and more wanted to purchase new capital. After all, the market was offering them an opportunity to increase their future profits by expanding productive capacity.

But there is a problem. By increasing production of security goods, these firms would increase their revenue and profits . . . in the future. However, in order to increase production, they needed money for capital purchases in the present. Without financial markets, this would be a classic Catch-22 situation: You can't produce the goods and earn profits until you have the capital, but you can't buy the capital until you produce the goods and earn the profits. This is exactly the problem that is solved by financial markets.

After September 11, security-goods producers went to the stock and bond markets to obtain new funds. At the same time, people were even more willing than before to provide these funds. Why?

Consider the bond market. With the increase in demand for security equipment, the probability that a producer of, say, hazmat suits would go bankrupt and default on its debt had suddenly decreased. Thus, potential buyers of the firm's bonds, now facing a lower default risk, were willing to buy more bonds at any price. Or, looked at another way, they were willing to lend more funds at any given interest rate.

Something similar was happening in the stock market. Since future profits at security-goods firms were expected to rise, their shares became more valuable than before, and people wanted to hold more of them at any given price.

In sum,

after September 11, producers of security-related goods could increase their profits by expanding their plant and equipment, which required the purchase of new capital. At the same time, potential suppliers of funds found the stocks and bonds of these firms more attractive than before. The result has been an increased flow of loanable funds to firms and industries that produce security goods, resulting in an increase in this sector's productive capacity.

Let's consider a specific industry and a financial market that were heavily involved in this process.

An Example: The Defense Industry and the Stock Market

Although national defense is provided by the federal government, it purchases inputs in the private economy. For example, when the Defense Department wants to hire soldiers and other military personnel, it competes with business firms in the private labor market, and must offer a competitive wage and other benefits. Similarly, when the the U.S. military wants to acquire aircraft, radar equipment, infrared goggles, laser-guided bombs, computers, and other needed materials, it purchases them from private, profit-maximizing defense contractors. These private firms, in turn, obtain funds for expanding productive capacity from financial markets, such as the bond and stock markets.

Within days of the terror attacks, it became clear that the U.S. Defense Department was poised for a major increase in orders from its suppliers, both in the short run (the next few months) and the long run (several years or more). In the short run, with a war in Afghanistan likely, American forces would require thousands of bombs. Old-style gravity bombs can be produced for as little as $1,000 each, but the more modern and more accurate laser-guided bombs cost over $100,000 each, and Tomahawk cruise missiles cost a staggering $1 million each. Clearly, with the nation at war, the Defense Department would be spending hundreds of millions of dollars just to replace its depleted inventory of these munitions. Moreover, orders for fighter jets, bombers, helicopters, tanks, and other equipment would be stepped up to replace those damaged and to increase the short-run readiness of the armed forces.

What about the long run? Within weeks of the attacks, it was clear that national defense spending would increase sharply for at least a decade. As if on cue, in late October 2001, the Defense Department announced its largest contract in history: an agreement with Lockheed Martin to build more than 2,000 new Joint Strike Fighters, custom-modified for each branch of the armed services. Delivery would begin 10 years later—in 2011—and Lockheed would eventually be paid about $200 billion for them. Lockheed, in turn, immediately contracted out large portions of the work to other defense producers, and set about acquiring the needed facilities to develop and produce the jets.

All of this additional defense production was sure to generate higher revenues and higher profits for Lockheed Martin and other defense contractors—in the future. But the government needed these contractors to expand production capacity right away. Although the federal government covers some of the research and development costs for national defense (for example, it paid Lockheed $19 billion up front for its development of the Joint Strike Fighter), these firms obtain most of the funds they need for capital purchases in the financial markets. And the financial markets turn out to be a remarkably efficient mechanism for providing them.

The three panels in Figure 7 illustrate this process. Panel (a) shows the behavior of the Standard & Poors 500 index for the two weeks before and the two weeks after the terror attacks. (The gap from September 11 through September 15 represents weekdays when the market was shut down.) As you can see, the S&P 500 plunged when the market reopened on September 17. The following days saw further drops, and by the end of the week, the S&P 500 had dropped a total of about 12 percent.

But now look at panels (b) and (c), which track share prices during the same time period for two major defense companies: Lockheed Martin and Raytheon. Unlike the rest of the market, share prices for these companies—and many other defense contractors—rose. And they rose the instant the market reopened for trading on September 17.

To show how microeconomic theory explains these events, let's focus now on the market for Raytheon shares. Look first at panel (a) of Figure 8. The supply curve S_1 tells us that Raytheon had issued 330 million shares as of September 10. When the market closed that day, the demand curve looked something like $D_{\text{Sept 10}}$,

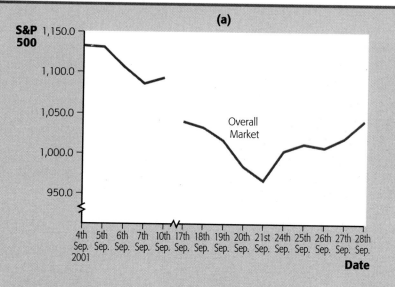

(a)

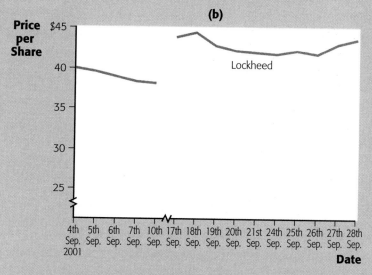

(b)

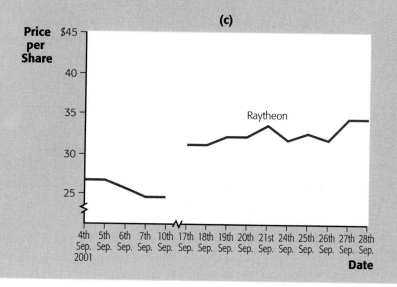

(c)

FIGURE 7

Share Prices for the S&P 500 and Two Defense Contractors in September 2001

When markets reopened after the attacks of September 11, 2001, panel (a) shows that stocks in general dropped sharply. But defense stocks— such as the two pictured in panels (b) and (c)—rose.

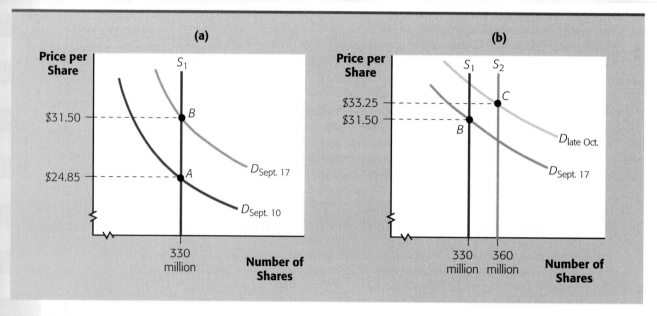

FIGURE 8

Changes in the Market for Raytheon Shares

Panel (a) shows the initial impact of the increase in demand for Raytheon shares on the first day of trading after September 11, 2001. The equilibrium price rose from $24.85 to $31.50. Panel (b) illustrates the effect of Raytheon's public offering of 30 million shares several weeks later, when demand for the stock was even higher. The new shares were sold at a price of $33.25 each.

with the equilibrium price at $24.85 per share. That is, on September 10, based on the public's expectations of Raytheon's future profits, $24.85 was the price per share that made them willing to hold all 330 million shares in existence.

Then came September 11. To see why Raytheon's shares were affected so dramatically, one need only glance at the company's profile as listed on the Yahoo! Finance Web site:

> *Raytheon company is in the business of defense electronics, including missiles; radar; sensors and electro-optics; intelligence, surveillance and reconnaissance; command, control, communication and information systems; naval systems; air traffic control systems; aircraft integration systems; and technical services.*

Not surprisingly, expectations of Raytheon's future profits were revised upward after September 11. And when the stock market reopened six days later, the demand curve had shifted to $D_{\text{Sept. 17}}$. The new equilibrium price rose to $31.50, an increase of 27 percent. Anyone holding Raytheon shares before September 11 was rewarded with a huge capital gain.

But wait . . . all of this trading took place in the secondary market, the market for previously issued shares of stock. While the stock's rise benefited those who owned those shares, it had no direct affect on the company itself. Does this have anything to do with resource allocation?

Plenty. Recall from Chapter 13 that when a company issues new shares, it must sell them at the prevailing price in the secondary market. After all, a share of stock entitles its owner to the same future profits whether it was issued long ago or that very day. The dramatic rise in Raytheon's stock meant that Raytheon could get more funds than before for any new shares it issued, a signal to Raytheon's management that this was a good time to issue them.

Raytheon's managers—who are driven to maximize profits for the firm's owners (see Chapter 7)—did not ignore this signal. About a month after the attacks, the company announced that it would issue about 30 million new shares to raise about $1 billion. The stock sale was completed three days later, at $33.25 per share.[9] Raytheon's public offering is illustrated in panel (b) of Figure 8, where the demand curve has shifted even further rightward (to $D_{\text{late Oct}}$), and the supply curve has shifted rightward to S_2 as a result of the sale.

Like Raytheon, other established defense contractors made public offerings in the months after the terror attacks. In addition, several new defense-related firms decided that, with defense stocks in high demand, it was a good time to "go public" and issue their first shares of corporate stock, collectively raising hundreds of millions of dollars within a few months. In these ways, the stock market played a role in allocating resources toward national defense.

PUBLIC GOODS AND GOVERNMENT INVOLVEMENT

In this book, you've learned that markets are often an efficient engine for bringing about resource allocation. But in Chapter 14 you learned that they don't always work. One example of a market failure is a public good.

To review briefly: When a good is rivalrous (when its use by one consumer prevents its use by another) and excludable (when its use can be restricted to those who pay), private businesses can provide the good, and—in the absence of significant market failures—they will generally charge a price equal to the opportunity cost of the good. For this reason, rivalry and excludability are characteristics of private goods, those that most economists agree should be provided by the market.

But some goods do not have these characteristics and cannot be efficiently provided by business firms. If a good is nonrivalrous, then charging a price would restrict consumption by some, even though their consumption imposes no cost to anyone else. This would be inefficient. If a good is nonexcludable, firms are generally unable to recover their costs by charging a price, since people will be able to enjoy the good without paying.

In most cases, there is widespread agreement about dividing domestic security among public and private goods. National defense, for example, is both nonrivalrous (your use of it doesn't decrease mine) and nonexcludable (we can't prevent those who don't pay from benefiting, since a safer nation benefits all). The same is true of many other aspects of domestic security, such as border patrol and local police and fire protection. But on the issue of airline safety, while there has been some agreement, there has also been strong disagreement. The logic behind public goods can help us understand why.

It might seem, at first glance, that the goods and services needed to provide safe air travel are private goods. After all, they are rivalrous: The special materials American Airlines uses for reinforced cockpit doors or the labor it uses to screen its passenger list cannot be used by anyone else. Thus, it seems that American Airlines, and its customers, should pay for any safety resources they use. Airline safety also seems excludable: The airlines themselves must pay for the resources used to provide it, and their customers must buy tickets in order to get the benefits. This sug-

---

[9] *Boston Business Journal*, "Raytheon Closes Its Common Stock Offering, Raises $1.05 Billion," October 29, 2001, available at *http://boston.bizjournals.com/boston/stories/2001/10/29/daily1.html*.

The government has become involved in both providing and producing airline safety.

gests that the private market *can* provide airline safety in the right amount, by charging those who fly to cover the full cost of the needed resources. The government could still be involved: It could establish regulations that the airlines would have to follow (as it already does), but it would require the airlines to shell out all the funds to abide by the regulations.

A few economists have advocated this solution. They believe that if the true cost of air travel—including disaster prevention—has indeed risen dramatically, then our society should be consuming dramatically less air travel. But is airline safety really a private good? September 11 made clear that a breach of security can kill thousands who have not chosen to fly. When an airline uses resources to prevent another terrorist attack, much of the benefit to the general public is nonrivalrous—similar to the nonrivalrous benefits of national defense. And the airlines, because they have no power to tax, cannot charge the general public for the benefits of protection; these benefits are nonexcludable.

Further, most economists believe that the population as a whole—including those who rarely or never fly—also benefits from the existence of airlines and the interconnected markets they provide. That is, the existence of widespread air travel involves a positive externality. This suggests subsidizing part of the cost of airline safety from general tax revenues. Since the population (including the nonflying public) benefits, the population (including the nonflying public) should pay.

> *Due to significant degrees of nonexcludability and nonrivalry for airline safety, as well as substantial external benefits to the general population from having low-cost air travel, there seems to be a consensus that safe air travel should be partially funded by the government.*

This principle helped to shape the federal government's plan for increasing airport security. On the one hand, those who fly and get many of the direct benefits of increased safety are being asked to pay a part of it: a special security tax of up to $10 per ticket. On the other hand, the new federal government standards are so severe that the new tax does not cover the entire cost. The rest is funded from general tax revenues. This part of the solution has generated little controversy.

But another aspect of airline security has proven controversial. To say that the government should *provide* (i.e., pay for) some part of airline security doesn't necessarily mean the government should *produce* it. Instead, the government can choose to contract out production to private business firms (as the airlines did for decades).

Not surprisingly, once it was decided that the government would *provide* a significant part of airline safety, a heated debate arose over who should *produce* it. Those who favored *government* production argued that control over standards was absolutely vital to airline safety. They pointed out that the United States does not contract out security at points of entry along the nation's borders, so why should it do so at the nation's airports, which are also points of entry? And they worried that competition to keep costs down would lead to compromises in security—as had been documented in airports across the country for more than a decade.

Those who favored *private* production argued that government-imposed standards carried out by private contractors would lead to more efficient, lower-cost production of any given level of security. Public production, they argued, often results in bloated bureaucracies. Moreover, since any new government employees would automatically be unionized, it would be difficult to fire incompetent security workers without long hearings and arbitration procedures. Advocates of private production believed that compromises on security in the past could be remedied by enacting and enforcing stricter standards on the private contractors.

In late 2001, those who favored public production won an almost complete victory. A new government agency was formed—the Transportation Security Agency—and in February 2002, it took official control of passenger and luggage screening across the country. The government would not only be providing a significant part of airline security, it would also be producing it.

However, there were two compromises. First, special rules would make it easier to fire incompetent workers than was possible in other government jobs. Second, starting in 2005 airports would be permitted to return to private contracting if they chose. This may lead to further controversy in 2005.

> *While there is wide agreement that some aspects of airline safety should be funded by government, an unresolved controversy persists over the issue of public versus private* production.

INTERNATIONAL TRADE AND DOMESTIC SECURITY

In Chapter 15, you learned that international trade provides substantial benefits. It enables the world as a whole—and each nation that participates—to produce and consume greater quantities of goods and services than they could possibly produce and consume without trade. Indeed, much of the rise in living standards around the world in the 1990s was made possible by a reduction of tariffs, quotas, and other trade restrictions; and the creation of trade agreements such as the North American Free Trade Agreement between the United States, Mexico, and Canada. You also learned in Chapter 15 that trade restrictions—such as tariffs and quotas—reduce the volume of trade, and tend to reduce living standards as well.

Some trade barriers may actually be reduced as a result of September 11. For example, the new alliance between the United States and Pakistan seems likely to result in some reduction of tariffs on Pakistani textiles. Uzbekistan, another strategic country, may also be given greater access to U.S. markets.

But these effects are likely to be dominated by another, more pervasive impact of September 11: the increased cost of delivering goods across international boundaries due to heightened border security.

Consider, for example, the 5,500-mile border between the United States and Canada. In 2000, more than $1.3 billion in goods and services crossed this border each day, carried in about 18,000 trucks and vans. Another 80,000 tourist or commuter vehicles crossed the border every day. Before September 11 most trucks were simply waved through or were delayed a few minutes. But in the weeks after, the desire for greater security raised the average delay to more than eight hours, as officials of the Customs Service, Border Patrol, and Immigration and Naturalization Service inspected trucks and cars, checked and rechecked documents, and waited for computer confirmations. While the delay has improved since then, by early 2003 it was still taking considerably more time to cross the border than a few years earlier.

Domestic security concerns have raised the costs of transporting goods across the U.S. Canadian border.

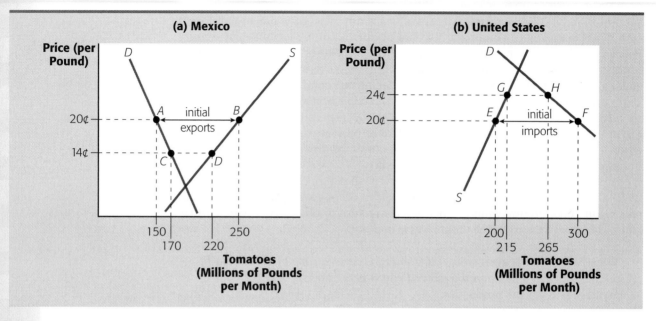

FIGURE 9
Increased Security Concerns and International Trade

Initially, Mexico exports 100 million pounds of tomatoes each month (distance AB), which is equal to U.S. imports (distance EF). The initial price is 20 cents per pound. Then, security concerns result in additional border-crossing costs of 10 cents per pound of tomatoes. As a result, Mexico exports only 50 million pounds (distance CD) and must sell them at the lower price of 14 cents. The U.S. imports the 50 million pounds (distance GH), but pays the higher price of 24 cents. Note that the burden of higher transportation costs is shared between Mexican tomato producers (who get 6 cents less per pound) and American tomato consumers (who pay 4 cents more per pound).

Remember that each hour of delay uses up resources: the time of paid truck drivers, gasoline wasted while idling, and damage to perishable cargo. Something similar happened along the U.S.–Mexican border and along many other borders around the world: Extra resources are now needed to get goods from one country to another.

Figure 9 illustrates the impact of using more resources for international trade. It shows the market for tomatoes in Mexico, panel (a), and the United States, panel (b). Initially, we assume that transportation costs are so insignificant that they can be ignored. Therefore, the selling price of a tomato in Mexico is the same as the buying price in the United States. With free trade, the graph shows us that the price of tomatoes in both countries would settle at 20 cents per pound, because this is the only price at which the excess supply in Mexico (100 million pounds per month) is equal to the excess demand in the United States (100 million pounds per month).

But now suppose an increase in concern for security has led to more thorough vehicle inspections and other significant time delays at the Mexican border. Suppose the value of the additional resources needed to cross the border with a truckload of tomatoes works out to 10 cents per pound shipped. In the new equilibrium after September 11, the cost of tomatoes will have to be 10 cents greater in the United States than in Mexico, to account for the new costs of bringing the tomatoes into the United States.

To find this new equilibrium, we must find a price in the United States and a price in Mexico that differ by exactly 10 cents (to reflect the new transportation costs) and at the same time create an excess supply in Mexico (exports) equal to the excess demand in the United States (imports). In our figure, as you can see, these conditions are satisfied only when the price is 14 cents in Mexico and 24 cents in the United States.

What is the final impact of this increase in transportation costs?

Developed Countries	Exports/GDP	Less-Developed Countries	Exports/GDP
United States	11%	Pakistan	18%
Japan	10%	Mexico	28%
United Kingdom	27%	Ecuador	31%
France	28%	Nigeria	48%
Germany	35%	Thailand	66%
Canada	44%	Congo	84%
Netherlands	65%	Guyana	95%

TABLE 4

Exports of Goods and Services as a Percentage of GDP, 2001

Source: Human Development Report, 2003, Table 14, United Nations Development Programme (UNDP), Oxford University Press, 2003.

First, within each country, there are both gains and losses. In the United States, consumers lose, because they pay more for their tomatoes (24 cents instead of 20 cents) and buy fewer of them (265 million pounds instead of 300 million). But U.S. producers gain: They get more for their tomatoes and produce more of them. In Mexico, it is the reverse: Producers are harmed and consumers gain.

But with all these gains and losses, what is the total effect in each country? You can see that the volume of trade has shrunk. In our example, Mexico's exports (and U.S. imports) decrease from 100 million pounds to 50 million pounds of tomatoes per month. We know (from Chapter 15) that when the volume of trade shrinks, so do the gains from trade. Therefore, both the United States as a whole and Mexico as a whole are harmed.

Does this sound familiar? It should. The effect of using more resources to transport goods is almost exactly like the effect of a tariff, which we explored in Figure 2 of Chapter 15. You may want to glance back at that figure, which illustrates a tariff on exports of suits from China. September 11 has, in effect, imposed a tariff on all internationally traded goods at once. Only it is worse: At least with a tariff the government collects revenue that can enable reductions in other taxes or be used to produce valuable services. In the case of the "September 11 tariff," additional resources are used up without any increase in government revenue.

Ironically, the United States, which suffered the direct consequences of the attack, is among the nations least affected by the increased costs of trade. Only about 16 percent of the value of U.S. GDP comes from abroad, and we export only about 11 percent of our GDP.

But look at Table 4, which shows exports as a fraction of GDP for several developed and less-developed countries. As you can see, international trade plays a much more important role in the economies of our major trading partners—Mexico and Canada—than in the U.S. economy. Trade is more important in Europe as well, where the proportion of exports to GDP is in the 25 to 65 percent range. It is also higher in most less-developed countries, including Ecuador (31 percent), Nigeria (48 percent), the Republic of Congo (84 percent), and Guyana (95 percent). These less-developed countries, highly dependent on international trade to maintain modest and in some cases very low living standards, are especially hard hit by any rise in the cost of trading across borders.

There are also other ways in which the effects on global trade will contribute to slower growth in living standards. Many companies faced with disrupted trade in the immediate aftermath of September 11 are relying less on foreign suppliers and cross-border shipments for critical parts and raw materials. Instead, they are carrying larger inventories, or even switching to less-efficient domestic suppliers. These decisions, even if they avert higher transportation costs, raise the costs of production in other ways.

Thus, we end where we began: with the opportunity cost of greater security. As we saw at the beginning of this chapter, producing greater security requires the sacrifice of other things we value. Now we can add another reason why that is so:

> By increasing the costs of transporting internationally traded goods and changing the patterns of production at home, increased security at our borders will increase resource requirements for a broad array of goods and services, and contribute to slower growth in living standards.

* * *

The last 15 years have seen three major resource reallocations. The first came about due to the end of the cold war, freeing up resources from military to domestic uses. The second was the rapid development and adoption of the Internet, which resulted in huge investments in computers, software, fiber-optic cable, and more. Both of these developments were welcome: They resulted in more rapid gains in living standards than would otherwise have been possible.

In late 2001, the United States—and much of the world—began a third major reallocation of resources: toward the global war on terrorism and the provision of domestic security. Only this time, the development is not welcome, both because of the horrible event that caused it and because of the resulting sacrifice in growth in our own—and the world's—standard of living. We are early in the process—too early to say how long the reallocation will continue or how extensive it will become. Much depends on coming events that are difficult or impossible to predict. But the tools of microeconomics—as you've seen—give us a framework for understanding the role that markets play in the process of adjustment and the likely consequences.

There are other microeconomic changes and tools that we have not addressed here. How will technological change in security goods and services affect the allocation of resources? What changes in the analysis when the market is imperfectly competitive? How might future events alter some of the conclusions reached here? You are invited to think about these and other issues on your own in the end-of-chapter questions.

Problems and Exercises   Answers to even-numbered Questions and Problems can be found on the text Web site at http://hall-lieb.swlearning.com.

1. Suppose that in 2005, increased security spending over the previous year turns out to be as follows:

   Additional Federal Government Spending: $60 billion

   Additional State and Local Government Spending: $10 billion

   Additional Business Spending: $40 billion

   a. What part of our assumed annual 3.1 percent growth rate would be devoted to the production of nonsecurity goods and services?

   b. Would our annual standard of living (output of non-security goods per person) increase or decrease?

   c. Suppose that economic growth in 2004 turns out to be 2 percent instead of the expected 3.1 percent, with security spending as in the table above. Would our standard of living increase or decrease now?

2. Look again at Table 3 and use the information found there to complete the following table. Assume that the population in 2004 was 292 million.

| | Year | |
	2005	**2006**
Additional Federal Government	$80 billion	$88 billion
Additional State and Local Government (net reimbursed by federal government)	$20 billion	$22 billion
Additional Private Sector Spending	$60 billion	$66 billion
Total	$160 billion	$176 billion
Estimated GDP	$11.33 trillion	$11.60 trillion
Population	294.92 million	299 million
Growth Rate in GDP		
Population Growth Rate		
Growth Rate of Non-security Goods and Services		

Does the standard of living rise or fall in 2005? What about 2006?

3. Look at the lower panel of Figure 1. In the chapter it was shown that if the economy were heading to a point like *B* before the increased conern for security, it will now be heading to a point like *B'* with slower growth in living standards.
   a. How would the analysis be affected by more rapid technological progress in the *production* of security goods and services? (Draw a third PPF in the figure that illustrates this).
   b. How would the analysis be affected by a different type of technological progress, one in which we are able to *use* our goods and services more effectively to provide security (i.e., the same production of security goods creates more security)? (*Hint:* In this case, our choice of where to be on the PPF, rather than the PPF itself, would be affected.)

4. Look again at the right panel of Figure 1.
   a. How would the analysis be affected by more rapid technological progress in the production of nonsecurity goods and services?
   b. How would the analysis be affected by a different type of technological progress, one in which we are able to *use* our nonsecurity goods and services more effectively to provide nonsecurity utility?

5. As stated in the chapter, Raytheon Company sold about 30 million new shares in October 2001 at a price of $33.25 each. Use the information provided in the chapter to answer the following:
   a. By what percentage did this public offering dilute the ownership of the firm's previous owners (i.e., as a group, how much did their percentage of ownership of the firm decline?)?
   b. Explain briefly why the previous owners were better off even though their ownership was diluted.

6. Suppose the federal government's subsidies for research into bomb-sniffing dogs results in major technological advances in their training. Show how this would affect the long-run equilibrium in the market, by adding the needed curves to each panel of Figure 3.

7. "If policy changes, and native speakers of strategic languages are hired by government agencies like the CIA, then in the long run, wages for these positions won't rise as high as they otherwise would. That means non-native speakers won't have as much incentive to learn these languages. And that would be disastrous to our national security, because the shortage of these professionals would continue indefinitely." Evaluate this statement.

8. Look back at Figure 5. Can you identify an area that represents the revenue the government will collect in this market from the new security tax? (*Hint:* You will first have to identify another price—call it *P''*—in the diagram.)

9. Suppose an airline has a monopoly on a certain route. Illustrate how the new airport security tax would change the airline's profit-maximizing price and output level. In this case, will the burden of the tax be shared between the airline and the customer? Explain.

10. Look again at Figure 5. Suppose that, in a few years, the public decides it is no longer averse to flying, so that demand returns to its original level. Will the equilibrium ever return to point *A*? Why or why not?

11. Explain how a successful government plan for increasing air safety would affect the market for air travel, assuming that it was fully funded from general tax revenues, and not from a tax on travelers or airlines.

12. In Figure 6, the long-run equilibrium in the market for strategic language speakers ends up at a higher wage (W_3) than initially (W_1). Is this necessarily the case? (*Hint:* Remember that there has been a change in tastes among college students.)

Challenge Question

1. Refer to Problem 11, above. If the (successful) government plan for increasing air safety were funded by air travelers, what would happen to the price and quantity of air travel?

ECONOMIC *Applications*   These exercises require access to Hall/Lieberman Xtra! If Xtra! did not come with your book, visit http://hallxtra.swlearning.com to purchase.

1. Use your Xtra! password at the Hall and Lieberman Web site (http://hallxtra.swlearning.com), select any chapter and under Economic Applications, click on EconDebate. Under *Hot Debates*, click on "Should the US reinstitute a military draft?" Read the debate carefully.

   a. Explain how reinstituting a draft coincides with the emphasis on domestic security.

   b. Using a production possibility frontier (with military spending on one axis, and all other spending on the other axis), explain the impact of a mandatory draft. Does this constitue a shift in the PPF, or a movement along the PPF? Why?

What Macroeconomics
Tries to Explain

You have no doubt seen photographs of the earth taken from satellites thousands of miles away. Viewed from that great distance, the world's vast oceans look like puddles, its continents like mounds of dirt, and its mountain ranges like wrinkles on a bedspread. In contrast to our customary view from the earth's surface—of a car, a tree, a building—this is a view of the big picture.

These two different ways of viewing the earth—from up close or from thousands of miles away—are analogous to two different ways of viewing the economy. When we look through the *microeconomic* lens—from up close—we see the behavior of *individual decision makers* and *individual markets*. When we look through the *macroeconomic* lens—from a distance—these smaller features fade away, and we see only the broad outlines of the economy.

Which view is better? That depends on what we're trying to do. If we want to know why computers are getting better and cheaper each year, or why the earnings of business professors are rising so rapidly, we need the close-up view of microeconomics. But to answer questions about the *overall* economy—about the overall level of economic activity, our standard of living, or the percentage of our potential workforce that is unemployed—we need the more comprehensive view of *macroeconomics*.

MACROECONOMIC GOALS

While there is some disagreement among economists about *how* to make the macroeconomy perform well, there is widespread agreement about the goals we are trying to achieve:

> *Economists—and society at large—agree on three important macroeconomic goals: economic growth, full employment, and stable prices.*

Why is there such universal agreement on these three goals? Because achieving them gives us the opportunity to make *all* of our citizens better off. Let's take a closer look at each of these goals and see why they are so important.

Economic Growth

Imagine that you were a typical American worker living at the beginning of the 20th century. You would work about 60 hours every week, and your yearly salary—about $450—would buy a bit less than $8,000 would buy today. You could expect to die at the age of 47. If you fell seriously ill before then, your doctor wouldn't be able to help much: There were no X-ray machines or blood tests, and little effective medicine for the few diseases that could be diagnosed. You would probably never hear the sounds produced by the best musicians of the day, or see the performances of the best actors, dancers, or singers. And the most exotic travel you'd enjoy would likely be a trip to a nearby state.

Today, the typical worker has it considerably better. He or she works about 35 hours per week and is paid about $34,000 per year, not to mention fringe benefits such as health insurance, retirement benefits, and paid vacation. Thanks to advances in medicine, nutrition, and hygiene, the average worker can expect to live into his or her late 70s. And more of a worker's free time today is really free: There are machines to do laundry and dishes, cars to get to and from work, telephones for quick communication, and personal computers to keep track of finances, appointments, and correspondence. Finally, during their lifetimes, most Americans will have traveled—for enjoyment—to many locations in the United States or abroad.

Economic growth The increase in our production of goods and services that occurs over long periods of time.

What is responsible for these dramatic changes in economic well-being? The answer is: **economic growth**—the increase in our production of goods and services that occurs over long periods of time. In the United States, as in most developed economies, the annual output of goods and services has risen over time, and risen faster than the population. As a result, the average person can consume much more today—more food, clothing, housing, medical care, entertainment, and travel—than in the year 1900.

Economists monitor economic growth by keeping track of *real gross domestic product (real GDP)*: the total quantity of goods and services produced in a country over a year. When real GDP rises faster than the population, output per person rises, and so does the average standard of living.

Figure 1 shows real GDP in the United States from 1929 to 2002, measured in dollars of output at 1996 prices. As you can see, real GDP has increased dramatically over the greater part of the century. Part of the reason for the rise is an increase in population: More workers can produce more goods and services. But real GDP has actually increased *faster* than the population: During this period, while the U.S. population did not quite triple, the quantity of goods and services produced each year has increased more than tenfold. Hence, the remarkable rise in the average American's living standard.

But when we look more closely at the data, we discover something important: Although output has grown, the *rate* of growth has varied over the decades. From

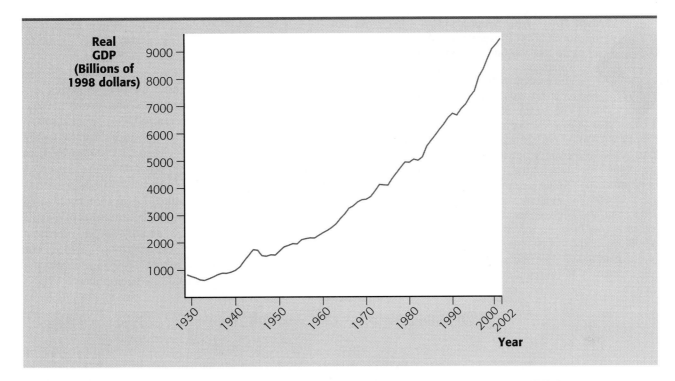

FIGURE 1

U.S. Real Gross Domestic Product, 1929–2002

Real GDP has increased dramatically over the past 73 years. In the figure, real GDP is measured in dollars of output valued at 1996 prices. (The measurement of real GDP will be discussed in more detail in the next two chapters.)

1959 to 1973, real GDP grew, on average, by 4.2 percent per year. But from 1973 to 1991, average annual growth slowed to 2.7 percent. Then, from 1991 to 2002, growth picked up again, averaging 3.7 percent per year. These may seem like slight differences. But over long periods of time, such small differences in growth rates can cause huge differences in living standards. For example, suppose that each year between 1973 and 2000, real GDP had grown by just one percentage point more than its actual rate. Then, over that entire period, the United States would have produced about $27 trillion *more* in goods and services than we *actually* produced over that period (valuing these goods and services at 1996 prices). That amounts to about $75,000 for each person in the population.

Economists and government officials are very concerned when economic growth slows down. Growth increases the size of the economic pie, so it becomes possible—at least in principle—for every citizen to have a larger slice. This is why economists agree that growth is a good thing.

But in practice, growth does *not* benefit everyone. Living standards will always rise more rapidly for some groups than for others, and some may even find their slice of the pie shrinking. For example, since the late 1980s, economic growth has improved the living standards of the highly skilled, while less-skilled workers have benefited very little. Partly, this is due to improvements in technology that have lowered the earnings of workers whose roles can be taken by computers and machines. But very few economists would advocate a halt to growth as a solution to the problems of unskilled workers. Some believe that, in the long run, everyone will indeed benefit from growth. Others see a role for the government in taxing successful people and providing benefits to those left behind by growth. But in either case, economic

DANGEROUS CURVES

Growth Rates from Graphs In Figure 1, it looks like real GDP has not only been growing over time, but growing at a faster and faster rate, since the line becomes steeper over time. But the real GDP line would get steeper even if the growth rate were *constant* over the entire period. That's because as real GDP rises from an increasingly higher and higher level, the same *percentage* growth rate causes greater and greater *absolute* increases in GDP.

For example, when real GDP is $5 trillion, 3 percent growth would cause real GDP to rise by $5 trillion × 0.03 = $0.15 trillion. But when real GDP is $10 trillion, the same 3 percent growth would be $10 trillion × 0.03 = $0.30 trillion. Since the slope of the line depends on the *absolute* rise in real GDP each year rather than its *percentage* rise, the same percentage growth rate would create a steeper line when real GDP is higher.

In fact, the line can become steeper even if the percentage growth rate *decreases* over time. As you've read, real GDP actually grew faster from 1959 to 1973 (where the line is flatter) than during any subsequent period (where the line is steeper). In subsequent chapters, you'll see other graphs that make it easier to see changes in the growth rate of real GDP.

growth, by increasing the size of the overall pie, is seen as an important part of the solution.

Macroeconomics helps us understand a number of issues surrounding economic growth. What makes real GDP grow in the first place? Why does it grow more rapidly in some decades than in others? Why do some countries experience very rapid growth—some much faster than the United States—while others seem unable to grow at all? Can government policy do anything to alter the growth rate? And are there any downsides to such policies?

High Employment (or Low Unemployment)

Economic growth is one of our most important goals, but not the only one. Suppose our real GDP were growing at, say, a 3 percent annual rate, but 10 percent of the workforce was unable to find work. Would the economy be performing well? Not really, for two reasons. First, unemployment affects the distribution of economic well-being among our citizens. People who cannot find jobs suffer a loss of income. And even though many of the jobless receive some unemployment benefits and other assistance from the government, the unemployed typically have lower living standards than the employed. Concern for those without jobs is one reason that consistently high employment—or consistently low *unemployment*—is an important macroeconomic goal.

But in addition to the impact on the unemployed themselves, joblessness affects *all* of us—even those who *have* jobs. A high unemployment rate means that the economy is not achieving its full economic potential: Many people who *want* to work and produce additional goods and services are not able to do so. With the same number of people—but fewer goods and services to distribute among that population—the average standard of living will be lower. This general effect on living standards gives us another reason to strive for consistently high rates of employment and low rates of unemployment.

One measure economists use to keep track of employment is the *unemployment rate*—the percentage of the workforce that is searching for a job but hasn't found one. Figure 2 shows the average unemployment rate during each of the past 80 years. Notice that the unemployment rate is never zero; there are always *some* people looking for work, even when the economy is doing well. But in some years, unemployment is unusually high. The worst example occurred during the Great Depression of the 1930s, when millions of workers lost their jobs and the unemployment rate reached 25 percent. One in four potential workers could not find a job. More recently, in 1982 and 1983, the unemployment rate averaged almost 10 percent.

The nation's commitment to high employment has twice been written into law. With the memory of the Great Depression still fresh, Congress passed the *Employment Act of 1946,* which required the federal government to "promote maximum

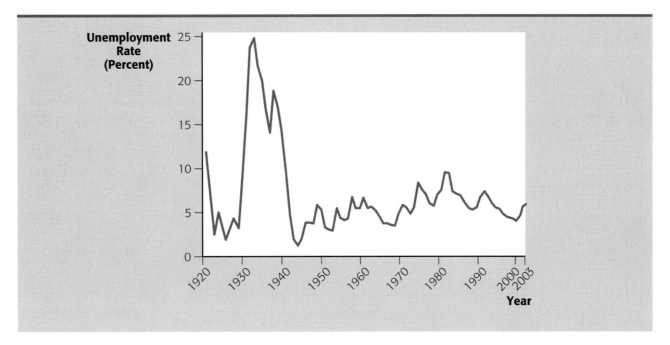

FIGURE 2
**U.S. Unemployment Rate,
1920–2003**

The unemployment rate fluctuates over time. During the Great Depression of the 1930s, unemployment was extremely high, reaching 25 percent in 1933. In the early 1980s, the rate averaged 10 percent. And during the 1990s, it fell rapidly, reaching 4 percent before turning up in the early 2000s.

employment, production, and purchasing power." It did not, however, dictate a target rate of unemployment the government should aim for. A numerical target was added in 1978, when Congress passed the *Full Employment and Balanced Growth Act,* which called for an unemployment rate of 4 percent.

A glance at Figure 2 shows how seldom we have hit this target over the last few decades. In fact, we did not hit it at all through the 1970s and 1980s. But in the 1990s, we came closer and closer and finally, in December 1999, we reached the 4 percent target for the first time since the 1960s. In 2001, the unemployment rate began to creep up again, and continued rising through the first half of 2003, when it averaged 6.0 percent.

Why has the unemployment rate been above its target so often? Why were we able to reach the target at the end of the 1990s, but not maintain it through the early 2000s? And what causes the average unemployment rate to fluctuate from year to year, as shown in Figure 2? These are all questions that your study of macroeconomics will help you answer.

Employment and the Business Cycle. When firms produce more output, they hire more workers; when they produce less output, they tend to lay off workers. We would thus expect real GDP and employment to be closely related, and indeed they are. In recent years, each 1 percent drop in output has been associated with the loss of about half a million jobs. Consistently high employment, then, requires a high, stable level of output. Unfortunately, output has *not* been very stable. If you look back at Figure 1, you will see that while real GDP has climbed upward over time, it has been a bumpy ride. The periodic fluctuations in GDP—the bumps in the figure—are called **business cycles.**

Figure 3 shows a close-up view of a hypothetical business cycle. First, notice the thin upward-sloping line. This shows the long-run upward trend of real GDP, which

Business cycles Fluctuations in real GDP around its long-term growth trend.

FIGURE 3
The Business Cycle

Over time, real GDP fluctuates around an overall upward trend. Such fluctuations are called business cycles. *When output rises, we are in the expansion phase of the cycle; when output falls, we are in a* recession.

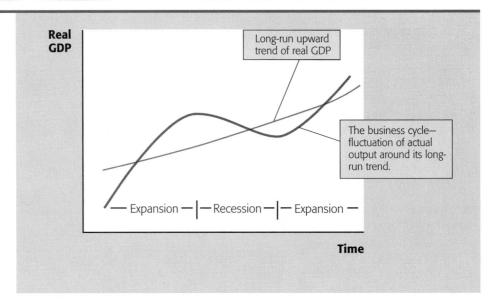

Expansion Versus Economic Growth Although the terms *expansion* and *economic growth* both refer to increases in real GDP, they are not the same. *Economic growth* refers to the long-run upward trend in output over a long period of time, usually more than a decade. It is measured as the *average* annual change in output over the entire period. An *expansion* refers to a usually shorter period of time during which output increases quarter by quarter or year by year.

Here's an example of the difference: From 1973 to 1991, output increased at an *average* rate of 2.7 percent per year over the entire period. This was the rate of economic growth during the period. But during a *part* of this long period—the early 1980s—output *fell* for several quarters. This was a contraction. During another part of this long period—the mid- and late 1980s—output *rose* every quarter. This was an expansion.

Expansion A period of increasing real GDP.

Recession A period of significant decline in real GDP.

Depression An unusually severe recession.

we refer to as *economic growth.* The thicker line shows the business cycle that occurs *around* the long-run trend. When output rises, we are in the **expansion** phase of the cycle; when output falls, we are in the *contraction* or **recession** phase. (Officially, a recession is a contraction considered significant —in terms of depth, breadth, and duration.)

Of course, real-world business cycles never look quite like the smooth, symmetrical cycle in Figure 3, but rather like the jagged, irregular cycles of Figure 1. Recessions can be severe or mild, and they can last several years or less than a single year. When a recession is particularly severe and long lasting, it is called a **depression.** In the 20th century, the United States experienced just one decline in output serious enough to be considered a depression—the worldwide *Great Depression* of the 1930s. From 1929 to 1933, the first four years of the Great Depression, U.S. output dropped by more than 25 percent.

But even during more normal times, the economy has gone through many recessions. Since 1959, we have suffered through two severe recessions (in 1974–75 and 1981–82) and several less severe ones, such as the recession from March to November of 2001.

Why are there business cycles? Is there anything we can do to prevent recessions from occurring, or at least make them milder and shorter? And why—even after a period of severe depression as in the 1930s—does the economy eventually move back toward its long-run growth trend? These are all questions that macroeconomics helps us answer.

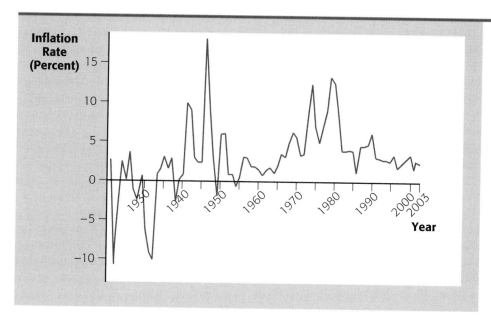

FIGURE 4

U.S. Annual Inflation Rate, 1922–2003

In most years, the inflation rate has been positive. The overall price level increased during those years.

Stable Prices

Figure 4 shows the annual inflation rate—the percentage increase in the average level of prices—from 1922 to 2003.[1] With very few exceptions, the inflation rate has been positive: On average, prices have risen in each of those years. But notice the wide variations in inflation. In 1979 and 1980, we had double-digit inflation: Prices rose by more than 12 percent in both years. During that time, polls showed that people were more concerned about inflation than any other national problem—more than unemployment, crime, poverty, pollution, or anything else. During the 1990s, the inflation rate averaged less than 3 percent per year, and it has averaged about 2½ percent during the early 2000s (through June 2003). As a result, we hardly seem to notice it at all. Pollsters no longer include "rising prices" as a category when asking about the most important problems facing the country.

Other countries have not been so lucky. In the 1980s, several Latin American nations experienced inflation rates of thousands of percent per year. In the early 1990s, some of the newly emerging nations of Central Europe and the former Soviet Union suffered annual inflation rates in the triple digits. An extreme case was the new nation of Serbia, where prices rose by 1,880 percent in the single month of August 1993. If prices had continued to rise at that rate all year, the annual inflation rate would have been 363,000,000,000,000,000 percent.

Why are stable prices—a low inflation rate—an important macroeconomic goal? Because inflation is *costly* to society. With annual inflation rates in the thousands of

---

[1] Figure 4 is based on the Consumer Price Index, the most popular measure of the price level, as well as historical estimates of what this index *would* have been in the early part of the 20th century, before the index existed. We'll discuss the Consumer Price Index and other measures of inflation in more detail in later chapters.

percent, the costs are easy to see: The purchasing power of the currency declines so rapidly that people are no longer willing to hold it. This breakdown of the monetary system forces people to waste valuable time and resources bartering with each other—for example, trading plumbing services for dentistry services. With so much time spent trying to find trading partners, there is little time left for producing goods and services. As a result, the average standard of living falls.

With inflation rates of 12 or 13 percent—such as the United States experienced in the late 1970s—the costs to society are less obvious and less severe. But they are still significant. And when it comes time to bring down the inflation rate, painful corrective actions by government are sometimes required. These actions can cause output to decline and unemployment to rise. For example, in order to bring the inflation rate down from the high levels of the late 1970s (see Figure 4), government policy purposely caused a severe recession in 1981–82, reducing output and increasing unemployment.

Economists regard *some* inflation as good for the economy. In fact, during the early 2000s, policy makers began to worry that the inflation rate might be getting *too low,* and that the economy might be threatened with a harmful *deflation*—a period of *decreasing* prices. Price stabilization requires not only preventing the inflation rate from rising too high, but also preventing it from falling too *low,* where it would be dangerously close to turning negative.

The previous paragraphs may have raised a number of questions in your mind. What causes inflation or deflation? How would a *moderately* high inflation rate of 7 or 8 percent harm society? How does a recession bring down the inflation rate, and how does the government actually *create* a recession? And why might a period of decreasing prices—which sounds so wonderful—be a threat to the economy? Your study of macroeconomics will help you answer all of these questions.

THE MACROECONOMIC APPROACH

If you have already studied microeconomics, you will notice much that is familiar in macroeconomics. The *three-step process* plays an important role in both branches of the field. But the macroeconomic approach is different from the microeconomic approach in significant ways. Most importantly, in *microeconomics,* we typically apply our three steps to *one market at a time*—the market for soybeans, for neurosurgeons, or for car washes. In *macroeconomics,* by contrast, we want to understand how the entire economy behaves. Thus, we apply the steps to *all markets simultaneously.* This includes not only markets for goods and services, but also markets for labor and for financial assets like bonds and foreign currency.

How can we possibly hope to deal with all of these markets at the same time? One way would be to build a gigantic model that included every individual market in the economy. The model would have tens of thousands of supply and demand curves, which could be used to determine tens of thousands of prices and quantities. With today's fast, powerful computers, we could, in principle, build this kind of model.

But it would not be easy. We would need to gather data on every good and service in the economy, every type of labor, every type of financial asset, and so on. As you might guess, this would be a formidable task, requiring thousands of workers just to gather the data alone. And in the end, the model would not prove very useful. We would not learn much about the economy from it: With so many individual trees, we could not see the forest.

Moreover, the model's predictions would be highly suspect: With so much information and so many moving parts, high standards of accuracy would be difficult to maintain. Even the government of the former Soviet Union, which directed production throughout the economy until the 1990s, was unable to keep track of all the markets under its control. In a market economy, where production decisions are made by individual firms, the task would be even harder.

What, then, is a macroeconomist to do? The answer is a word that you will become very familiar with in the chapters to come: **aggregation,** the process of combining different things into a single category and treating them as a whole. Let's take a closer look at how aggregation is used in macroeconomics.

Aggregation The process of combining different things into a single category.

Aggregation in Macroeconomics

Aggregation is a basic tool of reasoning, one that you often use without being aware of it. If you say, "I applied for five jobs last month," you are aggregating five very different workplaces into the single category, *jobs.* Whenever you say, "I'm going out with my friends," you are combining several different people into a single category: people you consider *friends.*

Aggregation plays a key role in both micro- and macroeconomics. Microeconomists will speak of the market for automobiles, lumping Toyotas, Fords, BMWs, and other types of cars into a single category. But in macroeconomics, we take aggregation to the extreme. Because we want to consider the entire economy at once, and yet keep our model as simple as possible, we must aggregate all markets into the broadest possible categories. For example, we lump together all the goods and services that households buy—newspapers, pizza, couches, and personal computers—into the single category *consumption goods.* We combine all the different types of capital purchased by business firms—forklifts, factory buildings, office computers, and trucks—into the single category *investment goods.* Often we go even further, lumping consumption, investment, and all other types of goods into the single category *output* or *real GDP.* And in macroeconomics, we typically combine the thousands of different types of workers in the economy—doctors, construction workers, plumbers, college professors—into the category, *labor.* By aggregating in this way, we can create workable and reasonably accurate models that teach us a great deal about how the overall economy operates.

"Micro" Versus "Macro" In many English words, the prefix *macro* means "large" and *micro* means "small." As a result, you might think that in microeconomics, we study economic units in which small sums of money are involved, while in macroeconomics we study units involving greater sums. But this is not correct: The annual output of General Motors is considerably greater than the total annual output of many small countries, such as Estonia or Guatemala. Yet when we study the behavior of General Motors, we are practicing *microeconomics,* and when we study changes in the unemployment rate in Estonia, we are practicing *macroeconomics.* Why? Microeconomics is concerned with the behavior and interaction of *individual* firms and markets, even if they are very large; macroeconomics is concerned with the behavior of *entire economies,* even if they are very small.

DANGEROUS CURVES

MACROECONOMIC CONTROVERSIES

Macroeconomics is full of disputes and disagreements. Indeed, modern macroeconomics, which began with the publication of *The General Theory of Employment, Interest, and Money* by British economist John Maynard Keynes in 1936, originated in controversy. Keynes was taking on the conventional wisdom of his time, *classical economics,* which held that the macroeconomy worked very well on its own, and the best policy for the government to follow was *laissez faire*—"leave it alone." As he was working on *The General Theory,* Keynes wrote to his friend, the playwright George Bernard Shaw, "I believe myself to be writing a book on economic theory which will largely revolutionize—not, I suppose, at once but in the course of the next ten years—the way the world thinks about economic problems."

Keynes's prediction was on the money. After the publication of his book, economists argued about its merits, but 10 years later, the majority of the profession had been won over: they had become Keynesians. This new school of thought held that the economy does *not* do well on its own (one needed only to look at the Great Depression for evidence) and requires continual guidance from an activist and well-intentioned government.

From the late 1940s until the early 1960s, events seemed to prove the Keynesians correct. Then, beginning in the 1960s, several distinguished economists began to challenge Keynesian ideas. Their counterrevolutionary views, which in many ways mirrored those of the classical economists, were strengthened by events in the 1970s, when the economy's behavior began to contradict some Keynesian ideas. Today, much of this disagreement has been resolved and a modern consensus—incorporating both Keynsian and classical ideas—has emerged. But there are still controversies.

Consider, for example, the controversy over the Bush administration's $350 billion 10-year tax cut. In May 2003, the tax cut was approved by 231 to 200 in the House of Representatives, and passed the Senate only when Vice President Cheney cast his vote to break a 50–50 tie. Within hours of passage, the following appeared on CNN's Web site:

> "This is a great victory for the American people," said Senate Majority Leader Bill Frist, R-Tennessee. "The wonderful thing is it really boils down to greater job security for people."

> "This is a policy of debt, deficits, and decline," said Sen. Kent Conrad, D-North Dakota, adding, "This is a scandal in the making. We're going to read there are perverse results as a result of this tax policy."[2]

Similar opposing views were expressed by economists associated with the Bush administration on the one hand, and those associated with the Democratic Party on the other. What are we to make of macroeconomic policy controversies like these, which occur so often on the political scene?

Remember the distinction between *positive (what is)* and *normative (what should be)*? Some of these disagreements are *positive* in nature. While economists and policy makers often agree on the broad outlines of how the macroeconomy works, they may disagree on some of the details. For example, they may disagree about the economy's current direction or momentum, or the relative effectiveness of

[2] "Congress Approves Tax-Cut Package," CNN.com/Inside Politics, May, 23, 2002.

different policies in altering the economy's course. Indeed, the two opposing senators quoted above were expressing a positive disagreement: a disagreement about the *impact* that tax cuts would have on the economy.

But disagreements that *sound* postive often have *normative* origins. For example in 2003, Democrats in Congress criticized the Bush tax cut as unfair, because it gave the biggest tax reduction to those with the highest incomes. Republicans in Congress countered that the tax cut was fair, because taxpayers with the highest incomes paid higher taxes to begin with. In the competitive and confrontational arena of politics—with each side trying to muster all the arguments it can—positive economics is often enlisted. In 2003, Republicans who began with the view that the Bush tax cut was fair invariably *also* argued that it was the most effective policy to spur the economy into a healthy expansion phase (see Figure 3). And they found a number of economists—who may have had similar normative views—to support that argument. Democrats who began with the view that the tax cut was *un*fair invariably *also* argued that it would cause great harm to the economy. And they found a number of economists—who may have had similar normative views—to support *that* argument.

Because of such political battles, people who follow the news often think that there is little agreement among economists about how the macroeconomy works. In fact, the profession has come to a consensus on many basic principles, and we will stress these as we go. And even when there are disagreements, there is surprising consensus on the approach that should be taken to resolve them.

You won't find this consensus expressed in a hot political debate. But you *will* find it in academic journals and conferences, and in reports issued by certain nonpartisan research organizations or government agencies. And—we hope—you will find it in the chapters to come.

AS YOU STUDY MACROECONOMICS . . .

Macroeconomics is a fascinating and wide-ranging subject. You will find that each piece of the macroeconomic puzzle connects to all of the other pieces in many different ways. Each time one of your questions is answered, 10 more will spring up in your mind, each demanding immediate attention. This presents a problem for a textbook writer, and for your instructor as well: What is the best order to present the principles of macroeconomics? One way is to follow the order of questions as they would occur to a curious reader. For example, learning about unemployment raises questions about international trade, so we could then skip to that topic. But it also raises questions about government spending, economic growth, wages, banking, and much, much more. And each of these topics raises questions about still others. Organizing the material in this way would make you feel like a ball in a pinball machine, bouncing from bumper to bumper. This pinball approach—bouncing from topic to topic—is the one taken by the media when reporting on the economy. If you have ever tried to learn economics from a newspaper, you know how frustrating this approach can be.

In our study of macroeconomics, we will follow a different approach: presenting material as it is *needed* for what follows. In this way, what you learn in one chapter will form the foundation for the material in the next, and your understanding of macroeconomics will deepen as you go.

But be forewarned: This approach requires considerable patience on your part. Many of the questions that will pop into your head will have to be postponed until

Two excellent print sources for news on the U.S. and world economies are The Wall Street Journal *and* The Economist, *a British magazine.*

the proper foundations for answering them have been established. It might help, though, to give you a *brief* indication of what is to come.

In the next two chapters, we will discuss three of the most important aggregates in macroeconomics: output, employment, and the price level. You will see why each of these is important to our economic well-being, how we keep track of them with government statistics, and how to interpret these statistics with a critical eye.

Then, in the remainder of the book, we study how the macroeconomy operates, starting with its behavior in the long run. Here, you will learn what makes an economy grow over long periods of time, and which government policies are likely to help or hinder that growth.

Next, we turn our attention to the short run for several chapters. You will learn why the economy behaves differently in the short run than in the long run, why we have business cycles, and how these cycles may be affected by government policies. We'll also expand our analysis to include the banking system and the money supply, and the special challenges they pose for government policy makers.

Finally, we'll turn our attention to the special problems of a global economy. You'll learn how trade with other nations constrains and expands our macro policy options at home and how economic events abroad influence our own economy. You will also learn why the United States has run persistent trade deficits with the rest of the world and what that means for our citizens.

This sounds like quite a lot of ground to cover, and indeed, it is. But it's not as daunting as it might sound. Remember that the study of macroeconomics—like the macroeconomy itself—is not a series of separate units, but an integrated whole. As you go from chapter to chapter, each principle you learn is a stepping-stone to the next one. Little by little, your knowledge and understanding will accumulate and deepen. Most students are genuinely surprised at how well they understand the macroeconomy after a single introductory course, and find the reward well worth the effort.

Summary

Macroeconomics is the study of the economy as a whole. It deals with issues such as economic growth, unemployment, inflation, and government policies that might influence the overall level of economic activity.

Economists generally agree about the importance of three main macroeconomic goals. The first of these is economic growth. If output, real gross domestic product, grows faster than population, the average person can enjoy an improved standard of living.

High employment is another important goal. In the United States and other market economies, the main source of household incomes is labor earnings. When unemployment is high, many people are without jobs and must cut back their purchases of goods and services.

The third macroeconomic goal is stable prices. This goal is important because inflation imposes costs on society. Keeping the rate of inflation low helps to reduce these costs.

Because an economy like that of the United States is so large and complex, the models we use to analyze the economy must be highly aggregated. For example, we will lump together millions of different goods to create an aggregate called "output" and combine all their prices into a single "price index."

Key Terms

Aggregation	Depression	Expansion
Business cycle	Economic growth	Recession

Review Questions

Answers to even-numbered Questions and Problems can be found on the text Web site at http://hall-lieb.swlearning.com.

1. Discuss the similarities and differences between macroeconomics and microeconomics.

2. What is the basic tool macroeconomists use to deal with the complexity and variety of economic markets and institutions? Give some examples of how they use this tool.

3. List the nation's macroeconomic goals and explain why each is important.

4. Consider an economy whose real GDP is growing at 4 percent per year. What else would you need to know in order to say whether the average standard of living is improving or deteriorating?

5. Explain the difference between a contraction, a recession, and a depression.

Problems and Exercises

1. In 1973, real GDP (at 1996 prices) was $4,123 billion. In 2000, it was $9,191 billion. During the same period, the U.S. population rose from 212 million to 281 million.
   a. What was the total percentage increase in real GDP from 1973 to 2000?
   b. What was the total percentage increase in the U.S. population during this period?
   c. Calculate real GDP per person in 1973 and in 2000. By what percentage did output per person grow over this period?

2. Suppose that real GDP had grown by 8 percent per year from 1973 to 2000. Using the data from Problem 1:
   a. What would real GDP have been in 2000?
   b. How much would output *per person* in 2000 have increased (compared to its actual value in 2000) if annual growth in real GDP over this period had been 8 percent?

3. a. The chapter states that the average growth rate for real GDP in the United States was 3.7 percent from 1991 to 2000. Use the information in the following table (which gives the actual GDP numbers) to calculate how much more we would have produced in 2000 if real GDP had grown by 4.7 percent over that period. [*Hint:* When real GDP grows at 4.7 percent annually, each year it will be 1.047 times its value of the year before.]

Year	Real GDP (measured in billions of dollars)
1991	$6,676.4
1992	$6,880.0
1993	$7,062.6
1994	$7,347.7
1995	$7,543.8
1996	$7,813.2
1997	$8,159.5
1998	$8,508.9
1999	$8,859.0
2000	$9,191.4

b. Calculate, for a 2000 population of 281 million people, how much higher the average output per person would have been in 2000 if the growth rate had been 4.7 percent over this period.

4. Assume that the country of Ziponia produced real GDP equal to $5000 (in billions) in the year 2000.
   a. Calculate Ziponia's output from 2000 to 2006, assuming that it experienced a constant growth rate of 6 percent per year over this period. Use your answers to construct a graph similar to the one in Figure 1. Is the slope of this graph constant? Explain.
   b. Calculate Ziponia's output from 2000 to 2006, assuming that its growth rate was 6 percent from 2000 to 2001, and then that it fell by 1 percent each year. Plot these points onto your graph from part (a). Is the slope of this graph constant? Explain.

5. Assume that the country of Zipinia produced real GDP equal to $5000 (in billions) in the year 2000.
   a. Calculate Zipinia's output from 2000 to 2006, assuming that it experienced a constant growth rate of 10 percent per year over this period. Use your answers to construct a graph similar to the one in Figure 1. Is the slope of this graph constant? Explain.
   b. Calculate Zipinia's output from 2000 to 2006, assuming that its growth rate was 10 percent from 2000 to 2001, and then that it fell by .5 percent each year (to 9.5, 9, 8.5, etc). Plot these points onto your graph from part (a). Is the slope of this graph constant? Explain.

 **ECONOMIC** *Applications* | *These exercises require access to Hall/Lieberman Xtra! If Xtra! did not come with your book, visit http://hallxtra.swlearning.com to purchase.*

1. Use your Xtra! Password at the Hall and Lieberman Web site (http://hallxtra.swlearning.com), select this chapter, and under Economic Applications, click on EconDebate. Choose *Macroeconomics: Productivity and Growth,* and scroll down to find the debate, "Is More Spending on Infrastructure the Key to Economic Growth?" Read the debate and use the information to answer the following questions.

   a. In this chapter it is stated that economic growth, high employment, and stable prices are the main macroeconomic goals. Are these compatible or competing goals? Explain.

   b. What are the most common recommendations for increasing the rate of economic growth? Explain the debate on the appropriate role of government in economic growth.

2. Use your Xtra! Password at the Hall and Lieberman Web site (http://hallxtra.swlearning.com), select this chapter, and under Economic Applications, click on EconNews. Choose *Macroeconomics: Productivity and Growth,* and scroll down to find "Signs of Recovery." Read the full summary.

   a. Answer the three questions posed under the full summary.

   b. Read the article "Deflation" by William Greider http://www.thenation.com/doc.mhtml?i=20030630&s=greider&c=1 and explain why both Greenspan and Greider consider deflation to be an impediment to growth.

Production, Income, and Employment

On the first Friday of every month, at 8:00 A.M., dozens of journalists mill about in a room in the Department of Labor. They are waiting for the arrival of the press officer from the government's Bureau of Labor Statistics. When she enters the room, carrying a stack of papers, the buzz of conversation stops. The papers—which she passes out to the waiting journalists—contain the monthly report on the experience of the American workforce. They summarize everything the government knows about hiring and firing at businesses across the country; about the number of people working, the hours they worked, and the incomes they earned; and about the number of people *not* working and what they did instead. But one number looms large in the journalists' minds as they scan the report and compose their stories: the percentage of the labor force that could not find jobs, or the nation's *unemployment rate*.

Every three months, a similar scene takes place at the Department of Commerce, as reporters wait for the release of the quarterly report on the nation's output of goods and services and the incomes we have earned from producing it. Once again, the report includes tremendous detail. Output is broken down by industry and by the sector that purchased it, and income is broken down into the different types of earners. And once again, the reporters' eyes will focus on a single number, a number that will dominate their stories and create headlines in newspapers across the country: the nation's *gross domestic product*.

The government knows that its reports on employment and production will have a major impact on the American political scene, and on financial markets in the United States and around the world. So it takes great pains to ensure fair and equal access to the information. For example, the Bureau of Labor Statistics allows journalists to look at the employment report at 8:00 A.M. on the day of the release (the first Friday of every month). But they must stay inside a room—appropriately called the lockup room—and cannot contact the outside world until the official release time of 8:30 A.M. At precisely 8:29 A.M., the reporters are permitted to hook up their laptop modems, and then a countdown begins. At precisely 8:30 A.M., the reporters are permitted to transmit their stories. At the same instant, the Bureau posts its report on an Internet Web site (*http://www.bls.gov*).

And the world reacts. Within seconds, wire-service headlines appear on computer screens: "Unemployment Rate up Two-Tenths of a Percent" or "Nation's Production Steady." Within minutes, financial traders, for whom these news flashes provide clues about the economy's future, make snap decisions to buy or sell, moving stock and bond prices. And within the hour, politicians and pundits will respond with sound bites, attacking or defending the administration's economic policies.

In this chapter, we will take our first look at production and employment in the economy, focusing on two key variables: *gross domestic product* and the *unemployment rate*. The purpose here is not to explain what causes these variables to rise or fall. That will come a few chapters later, when we begin to study macroeconomic models. Here, we focus on the reality behind the numbers: what the statistics tell us about the economy, how the government obtains them, and how they are sometimes misused.

PRODUCTION AND GROSS DOMESTIC PRODUCT

You have probably heard the phrase *gross domestic product*—or its more familiar abbreviation, GDP—many times. It is one of those economic terms that is frequently used by the media and by politicians. In the first half of this chapter, we take a close look at GDP.

GDP: A Definition

The U.S. government has been measuring the nation's total production since the 1930s. You might think that this is an easy number to calculate, at least in theory: Simply add up the output of every firm in the country during the year. Unfortunately, measuring total production is not so straightforward, and there are many conceptual traps and pitfalls. This is why economists have come up with a very precise definition of GDP.

Gross domestic product (GDP) The total value of all final goods and services produced for the marketplace during a given year, within the nation's borders.

> The nation's **gross domestic product** (GDP) *is the total value of all final goods and services produced for the marketplace during a given period, within the nation's borders.*

Quite a mouthful. But every part of this definition is absolutely necessary. To see why, let's break the definition down into pieces and look more closely at each one.

The total value . . .

An old expression tells us that "you can't add apples and oranges." But that is just what government statisticians must do when they measure our total output. In a typical day, American firms produce millions of *loaves* of bread, thousands of *pounds* of peanut butter, hundreds of *hours* of television programming, and so on.

These are *different* products, and each is measured in its own type of units. Yet, somehow, we must combine all of them into a single number. But how?

The approach of GDP is to add up the *dollar value* of every good or service—the number of dollars each product is *sold* for. As a result, GDP is measured in dollar units. For example, in 2002, the GDP of the United States was about $10,446,000,000,000—give or take a few billion dollars. (That's about $10.4 trillion.)

Using dollar values to calculate GDP has two important advantages. First, it gives us a common unit of measurement for very different things, thus allowing us to add up "apples and oranges." Second, it ensures that a good that uses more resources to produce (a computer chip) will count more in GDP than a good that uses fewer resources (a tortilla chip).

However, using the dollar prices at which goods and services actually sell also creates a problem: If prices rise, then GDP will rise, even if we are not actually *producing* more. For this reason, when tracking changes in production over time, GDP must be adjusted to take away the effects of inflation. We'll come back to this issue again a bit later in the chapter.

. . . of all final . . .

When measuring production, we do not count *every* good or service produced in the economy, but only those that are sold to their *final users*. An example will illustrate why.

Figure 1 shows a simplified version of the stages of production for a ream (500 sheets) of notebook paper: A lumber company cuts down trees and produces $1.00 worth of wood chips, which it sells to a paper mill for $1.00. The mill cooks, bleaches, and refines the wood chips, turning them into $1.50 worth of paper rolls, which it sells to an office supplies manufacturer for that price. This manufacturer cuts the paper, prints lines and margins on it, and sells its to a wholesaler for $2.25. The wholesaler sells it to a retail store for $3.50, and then, finally, it is sold to a consumer—perhaps you—for $5.00.

Should we add the value of *all* this production, and include $1.00 + $1.50 + $2.25 + $3.50 + $5.00 = $13.25 in GDP each time a ream of notebook paper is produced? No, this would clearly be a mistake, since all of this production ends up creating a good worth only $5 in the end. In fact, the $5 you pay for this good already *includes* the value of all the other production in the process.

In our example, the goods sold by the lumber company, paper mill, office supplies manufacturer, and wholesaler are all **intermediate goods**—goods used up in the process of producing something else. But the retailer (say, your local stationery store) sells a **final good**—a product sold to its *final user* (you). If we separately added in the production of intermediate goods when calculating GDP, we would be counting them more than once, since they are already included in the value of the final good.

Intermediate goods Goods used up in producing final goods.

Final good A good sold to its final user.

> *To avoid overcounting intermediate products when measuring GDP, we add up the value of final goods and services only. The value of all intermediate products is automatically included in the value of the final products they are used to create.*

. . . goods and services . . .

We all know a good when we see one: We can look at it, feel it, weigh it, and, in some cases, eat it, strum it, or swing a bat at it. Not so with a service: When you get a medical checkup, a haircut, or a car wash, the *effects* of·the service may linger, but

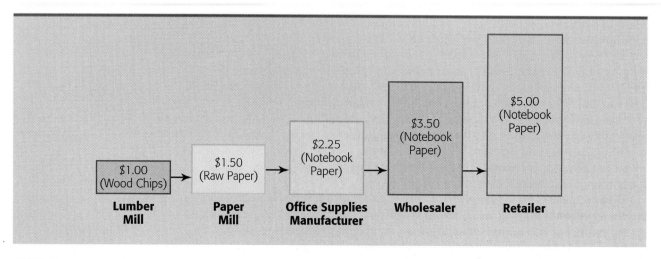

FIGURE 1
Stages of Production

the service itself is used up the moment it is produced. Nonetheless, final services count in GDP in the same way as final goods.

Services have become an increasingly important part of our total output in recent decades. The service sector has grown from about a third of U.S. output in 1950 to well over half of our output in 2002. These include the services produced by Internet providers, the health care industry, the banking industry, the educational system, and the entertainment industry.

. . . produced . . .

In order to contribute to GDP, something must be *produced*. This may sound obvious, but it is easy to forget. Every day, Americans buy billions of dollars worth of things that are *not* produced, or at least not produced during the period being considered, and so are not counted in that period's GDP. For example, people may buy land, or they may buy financial assets such as stocks or bonds. While these things cost money, they are not counted in GDP because they are not "goods and services *produced.*" Land, for example, is not produced at all. Stocks and bonds represent a claim to ownership or to receive future payments, but they are not themselves goods or services.

. . . for the marketplace . . .

GDP does not include *all* final goods and services produced in the economy. Rather, it includes only the ones produced for the marketplace, that is, with the intention of being *sold*. Because of this restriction, we exclude many important goods and services from our measure. For example, when you clean your own home, you have produced a final service—housecleaning—but it is *not* counted in GDP because you are

DANGEROUS CURVES

The Services of Dealers, Brokers, and Other Sellers You've learned that GDP excludes the value of many things that are bought and sold—such as land, financial assets, and used goods—because they are not currently *produced goods and services*. But all of this buying and selling *can* contribute to GDP indirectly. How? If a dealer or broker is involved in the transaction, then that dealer or broker is producing a current service: bringing buyer and seller together. The value of this service is part of current GDP.

For example, suppose you bought a secondhand book at your college bookstore for $25. Suppose, too, that the store had bought the book from another student for $15. Then the purchase of the used book will contribute $10 to this year's GDP. Why? Because $10 is the value of the bookstore's services; it's the premium you pay to buy the book in the store, rather than going through the trouble to find the original seller yourself. The remainder of your purchase—$15—represents the value of the used book itself, and is *not* counted in GDP. The book was already counted when it was newly produced, in this or a previous year.

doing it for yourself, not for the marketplace. If you *hire* a housecleaner to clean your home, however, this final service *is* included in GDP; it has become a market transaction.

The same is true for many services produced in the economy. Taking care of your children, washing your car, mowing your lawn, walking your dog—none of these services are included in GDP if you do them for yourself, but all *are* included if you pay someone else to do them for you.

... *during a given period* ...

GDP measures production during some specific period of time. Only goods produced during that period are counted. But people and businesses spend billions of dollars each year on *used* goods, such as secondhand cars, previously occupied homes, used furniture, or an old photo of Elvis talking to an extraterrestrial. These goods were all *produced,* but not necessarily in the current period. And even if they *were* produced in the current period, they would only count when sold the *first* time, as new goods; to count them again each time they are resold would lead to an overestimate of total production for the period.

What duration of time should we use for GDP? In theory, we could use any duration. In 2002, for example, the United States produced an average of $29 billion worth of output each day, $859 billion each month, and $10,446 billion for the year as a whole. Thus, we could measure daily GDP, monthly GDP, and so on. In practice, however, GDP is measured for *each quarter* and then reported as an *annual rate* for that quarter.

To understand this, look at Table 1, which shows how GDP was actually reported by the government, for six recent quarters. During 2002–I (the first quarter, January through March of 2002), the U.S. economy actually produced about $2,578.25 billion in final goods and services. But you won't see that number in the table. What you *will* see is how much we *would* have produced during an entire year if we produced at that quarter's rate for *four* full quarters (4 × $2,578.28 billion = $10,313.1 billion).[1] Once the fourth-quarter figures are in, the government also reports the official GDP figure for the entire year—what we *actually* produced during the entire year.

... *within the nation's borders.*

U.S. GDP measures output produced *within U.S. borders,* regardless of whether it was produced by Americans. This means we *include* output produced by foreign-owned resources and foreign citizens located in the United States, and we *exclude* output produced by Americans located in other countries. For example, when the rock star Sting, a resident of Britain, gives a concert tour in the United States, the value of his services is counted in U.S. GDP but not in British GDP. Similarly, the services of an American nurse working in an Ethiopian hospital are part of Ethiopian GDP and not U.S. GDP.

The Expenditure Approach to GDP

The Commerce Department's Bureau of Economic Analysis (BEA), the agency responsible for gathering, reporting, and analyzing movements in the nation's output, calculates GDP in several different ways. The most important of these is the

---

[1] There is one other twist to the government's reporting: Before multiplying by 4, each quarter's production is *seasonally adjusted,* raised or lowered to eliminate any changes that usually occur during that time of year.

Quarter	2002–I	2002–II	2002–III	2002–IV	2003–I	2003–II
GDP ($billions)	10,313.1	10,376.9	10,506.2	10,588.8	10,688.4	10,802.7

Source: Bureau of Economic Analysis, "National Income and Product Account Tables," accessed at *http://www.bea.gov.*

TABLE 1
GDP: Recent Quarters

expenditure approach. Because this method of measuring GDP tells us so much about the structure of our economy, we'll spend the next several pages on it.

In the expenditure approach, we divide output into four categories according to which group in the economy purchases it as the final user. The four categories are:

1. *Consumption goods and services (C),* purchased by households;
2. *Private investment goods and services (I),* purchased by businesses;
3. *Government goods and services (G),* purchased by government agencies;
4. *Net exports (NX),* purchased by foreigners.

This is an exhaustive list: Everyone who purchases a good or service included in U.S. GDP must be either a U.S. household, U.S. business, or U.S. government agency (including state and local government), or else is part of the foreign sector. Thus, when we add up the purchases of all four groups, we must get GDP:

Expenditure approach Measuring GDP by adding the value of goods and services purchased by each type of final user.

> In the **expenditure approach** to measuring GDP, *we add up the value of the goods and services purchased by each type of final user:*
>
> $$GDP = C + I + G + NX.$$

Table 2 shows the part of GDP purchased by each sector during the entire year 2002. Ignore the finer details for now and just concentrate on the last number in each column. Applying the expenditure approach to GDP in 2002 gives us GDP = $C + I + G + NX$ = \$7,304 + \$1,593 + \$1,973 + (−\$424) = \$10,446 billion.

Now let's take a closer look at each of the four components of GDP.

Consumption Spending. Consumption (C) is the largest component of GDP—making up about three-quarters of total production in recent years—and the easiest to understand:

Consumption (C) The part of GDP purchased by households as final users.

> **Consumption** *is the part of GDP purchased by households as final users.*

Almost everything that households buy during the year—restaurant meals, gasoline, new clothes, doctors' visits, movies, electricity, and more—is included as part of consumption spending when we calculate GDP.

But notice the word *almost.*

Some of the things that households buy are *not* part of consumption in GDP. First, used goods or assets that households buy during the period are excluded. (Used goods were already counted when first produced, and assets are not goods or services, and therefore not part of GDP at all).

Second, *newly constructed homes*—even though part of GDP and usually purchased directly by households—are included as investment, rather than consumption. We'll discuss the reasons for this in the next section.

Finally, two things *are* included in consumption even though households don't actually buy them: (1) the total value of food products produced on farms that are

Consumption Purchases		Private-Investment Purchases		Government Purchases		Net Exports	
Services	$4,317	Plant, Equipment, and Sofware	$1,117	Government Consumption	$1,621	Exports	$1,015
Nondurable Goods	$2,115	New-Home Construction	$ 472	Government Investment	$ 352	Imports	$1,439
Durable Goods	$ 872	Changes in Business Inventories	$ 4				
Consumption =	**$7,304**	Private Investment =	**$1,593**	Government Purchases =	**$1,973**	Net Exports =	**−$ 424**

$$GDP = C + I + G + NX$$
$$= \$7,304 + \$1,593 + 1,973 + (-424)$$
$$= \$10,446$$

Source: Bureau of Economic Analysis, "National Income and Product Account Tables," accessed at *http://www.bea.gov.*

TABLE 2
GDP in 2002: The Expenditure Approach (Billions of Dollars)

consumed by the farmers and their families themselves; and (2) the total value of housing services provided by owner-occupied homes. The government estimates how much the food consumed on farms *could* have been sold for, and how much owner-occupied homes *could* have been rented for, and then includes these estimates as part of consumption.

Private Investment. What do oil-drilling rigs, cash registers, office telephones, and the house you grew up in all have in common? They are all examples of *capital goods*—goods that will provide useful services in future years. When we sum the value of all of the capital goods in the country, we get our **capital stock.**

Understanding the concept of capital stock helps us understand and define the concept of investment. A rough definition of **private investment** is *capital formation*—the *increase* in the nation's capital stock during the year.

More specifically,

private investment has three components: (1) business purchases of plant, equipment, and software; (2) new-home construction; and (3) changes in business firms' inventory stocks (changes in stocks of unsold goods).

Each of these components requires some explanation.

Business Purchases of Plant, Equipment, and Software. This category might seem confusing at first glance. Why aren't plant, equipment, and software considered intermediate goods? After all, business firms buy these things in order to produce other things. Doesn't the value of their final goods include the value of their plant, equipment, and software as well?

Actually, no, and if you go back to the definition of intermediate goods, you will see why. Intermediate goods are *used up* in producing the current year's GDP. But a firm's plant, equipment, and software are intended to last for many years; only a

Capital stock The total value of all goods that will provide useful services in future years.

Private investment (I) The sum of business plant, equipment, and software purchases, new-home construction, and inventory changes; often referred to as just *investment.*

small part of them is used up to make the current year's output. Thus we regard new plant, equipment, and software as final goods, and we regard the firms that buy them as the final users of those goods.

For example, suppose our paper mill—the firm that turns wood chips into raw paper—buys a new factory building that is expected to last for 50 years. Then only a small fraction of that factory building—one-fiftieth—is used up in any one year's production of raw paper, and only a small part of the factory building's value will be reflected in the value of the firm's current output. But since the entire factory is produced during the year, we must include its full value *somewhere* in our measure of production. We therefore count the whole factory building as investment in GDP.

Plant, equipment, and software purchases are always the largest component of private investment. And 2002 was no exception, as you can see in the second column of Table 2. That year, businesses purchased and installed $1,117 billion worth of plant, equipment, and software, which was about 70 percent of total private investment.

New-Home Construction. As you can see in Table 2, new-home construction made up a significant part of total private investment in 2002. But it may strike you as odd that this category is part of investment spending at all, since most new homes are purchased by households and could reasonably be considered consumption spending instead. Why is new-home construction counted as investment spending in GDP?

Largely because residential housing is an important part of the nation's *capital stock.* Just as an oil-drilling rig will continue to provide oil-drilling services for many years, so, too, a home will continue to provide housing services into the future. If we want our measure of private investment to roughly correspond to the increase in the nation's capital stock, we must include this important category of capital formation as part of private investment.

Changes in Inventories. Inventories are goods that have been produced but not yet sold. They include goods on store shelves, goods making their way through the production process in factories, and raw materials waiting to be used. We count the *change* in firms' inventories as part of investment in measuring GDP. Why? When goods are produced but not sold during the year, they end up in some firm's inventory stocks. If we did *not* count changes in inventories, we would be missing this important part of current production. Remember that GDP is designed to measure total *production,* not just the part of production that is sold during the year.

To understand this more clearly, suppose that in some year, the automobile industry produced $100 billion worth of automobiles, and that $80 billion worth was sold to consumers. Then the other $20 billion remained unsold and was added to the auto companies' inventories. If we counted consumption spending alone ($80 billion), we would underestimate automobile production in GDP. To ensure a proper measure, we must include not only the $80 billion in cars sold (consumption), but also the $20 billion *change* in inventories (private investment). In the end, the contribution to GDP is $80 billion (consumption) + $20 billion (private investment) = $100 billion, which is, indeed, the total value of automobile production during the year.

What if inventory stocks *decline* during the year, so that the change in inventories is negative? Our rule still holds: We include the change in inventories in our measure of GDP. But in this case, we add a *negative* number. For example, if the automobile industry produced $100 billion worth of cars this year, but consumers bought $120 billion, then $20 billion worth must have come from inventory stocks:

Unsold goods, like those pictured in this warehouse, are considered inventories. The change *in these inventories is included as investment when calculating GDP.*

© PHOTODISC/GETTY IMAGES

cars that were produced (and counted) in previous years, but that remained unsold until this year. In this case, the consumption spending of $120 billion *overestimates* automobile production during the year, so subtracting $20 billion corrects for this overcount. In the end, GDP would rise by $120 billion (consumption) − $20 billion (private investment) = $100 billion.

But why are inventory changes included in investment, rather than some other component of GDP? Because unsold goods are part of the nation's capital stock. They will provide services in the future, when they are finally sold and used. An increase in inventories represents capital formation: A decrease in inventories—negative investment—is a decrease in the nation's capital.

Inventory changes are generally the smallest component of private investment, but the most highly volatile in percentage terms. In 2002, for example, inventories rose by $4 billion; one year earlier, they fell by $60 billion, and the year before that they rose by $63 billion. Part of the reason for this volatility is that, while some inventory investment is intended, much of it is *unintended*. As the economy begins to slow, for example, businesses may be unable to sell all of the goods they have produced and had planned to sell. The unsold output is added to inventory stocks—an unintended increase in inventories. During rapid expansions, the opposite may happen: Businesses find themselves selling more than they produced—an unintended decrease in inventories.

Private Investment and the Capital Stock: Some Provisos. A few pages ago, it was pointed out that private investment corresponds only *roughly* to the increase in the nation's capital stock. Why this cautious language? Because changes in the nation's capital stock are somewhat more complicated than we are able to capture with private investment alone.

First, private investment *excludes* some production that adds to the nation's capital stock. Specifically, private investment does not include:

- *Government investment.* An important part of the nation's capital stock is owned and operated not by businesses, but by government—federal, state, and local. Courthouses, police cars, fire stations, schools, weather satellites, military aircraft, highways, and bridges are all examples of government capital. If you look at the third column of Table 2, for example, you'll see that the BEA estimated government investment to be $352 billion in 2002; that was the part of government spending that was devoted to capital formation in 2002.
- *Consumer durables.* Goods such as furniture, automobiles, washing machines, and personal computers for home use can be considered capital goods, since they will continue to provide services for many years. In 2002, households purchased $872 billion worth of consumer durables (see Table 2, first column).
- *Human capital.* Think about a surgeon's skills in performing a heart bypass operation, or a police detective's ability to find clues and solve a murder, or a Web-page designer's mastery of HTML and Java. These types of knowledge will continue to provide valuable services well into the future, just like plant and equipment or new housing. To measure the increase in the capital stock most broadly, then, we *should* include the additional skills and training acquired by the workforce during the year.

In addition to excluding some types of capital formation, private investment also errs in the other direction: It ignores depreciation—the capital that is used up during the year. Fortunately, the BEA estimates depreciation of the private and

Net investment Investment minus depreciation.

public capital stock, allowing us to calculate **net investment** (total investment minus depreciation) for these sectors. For example, for 2002, the BEA estimates that $1,164 billion of the private capital stock depreciated during the year (not shown in Table 2). So net private investment that year was only $1,593 billion − $1,164 billion = $429 billion. Similarly, the BEA estimates that $230 billion in government capital depreciated in 2002, so net government investment that year was $352 billion − $230 billion = $122 billion.

Government Purchases. In 2002, the government bought $1,973 billion worth of goods and services that were part of GDP—about a fifth of the total. This component of GDP is called **government purchases**, although in recent years the Department of Commerce has begun to use the phrase *government consumption and investment purchases*. Government *investment*, as discussed earlier, refers to capital goods purchased by government agencies. The rest of government purchases is considered government *consumption*: spending on goods and services that are used up during the period. This includes the salaries of government workers and military personnel, and raw materials such as computer paper for government offices, gasoline for government vehicles, and the electricity used in government buildings.

Government purchases (G) Spending by federal, state, and local governments on goods and services.

DANGEROUS CURVES

Investment: Economics Versus Ordinary English Be *extremely* careful when using the term *investment* in your economics course. In economics, investment refers to capital formation, such as the building of a new factory, home, or hospital, or the production and installation of new capital equipment, or the accumulation of inventories by business firms. In everyday language, however, *investment* has a very different meaning: a place to put your wealth. Thus, in ordinary English, you invest whenever you buy stocks or bonds or certificates of deposit or when you lend money to a friend who is starting up a business. But in the language of economics, you have not invested but merely changed the form in which you are holding your wealth (say, from checking account balances to stocks or bonds). To avoid confusion, remember that investment takes place only when there is new production of capital goods—that is, only when there is *capital formation*.

There are a few things to keep in mind about government purchases in GDP. First, we include purchases by state and local governments as well as the federal government. In macroeconomics, it makes little difference whether the purchases are made by a local government agency like the parks department of Kalamazoo, Michigan, or a huge federal agency such as the U.S. Department of Defense.

Second, government purchases include *goods*—like fighter jets, police cars, school buildings, and spy satellites—and *services*—such as those performed by police, legislators, and military personnel. The government is considered to be the final purchaser of these things even if it uses them to make other goods or services. For example, if you are taking economics at a public college or university that produces educational services, then your professor is selling teaching services to a state or city government. His or her salary enters into GDP as part of government purchases.

Finally, it's important to distinguish between government *purchases*—which are counted in GDP—and government *outlays* as measured by local, state, and federal budgets and reported in the media. What's the difference? In addition to their purchases of goods and services, government agencies also disburse money for **transfer payments**. These funds are *given* to people or organizations—*not* to buy goods or services from them, but rather to fulfill some social obligation or goal. For example, Social Security payments by the federal government, unemployment insurance and welfare payments by state governments, and money disbursed to homeless shelters and soup kitchens by city governments are all examples of transfer payments. The important thing to remember about transfer payments is this:

Transfer payment Any payment that is not compensation for supplying goods or services.

Transfer payments represent money redistributed from one group of citizens (taxpayers) to another (the poor, the unemployed, the elderly). While transfers are included in government budgets as outlays, they are not purchases of currently produced goods and services, and so are not included in government purchases or in GDP.

Net Exports. There is one more category of buyers of output produced in the United States: *the foreign sector.* Looking back at Table 2, the fourth column tells us that in 2002, purchasers *outside* the nation bought approximately $1,015 billion of U.S. goods and services—about 10 percent of our GDP. These exports are part of U.S. production of goods and services and so are included in GDP.

However, once we recognize dealings with the rest of the world, we must correct an inaccuracy in our measure of GDP the way we've reported it so far. Americans buy many goods and services every year that were produced *outside* the United States (Chinese shoes, Japanese cars, Mexican beer, Costa Rican coffee). When we add up the final purchases of households, businesses, and government agencies, we *overcount* U.S. production because we include goods and services produced abroad. But these are *not* part of U.S. output. To correct for this overcount, we deduct all U.S. *imports* during the year, leaving us with just output produced in the United States. In 2002, these imports amounted to $1,439 billion, an amount equal to about 14 percent of our GDP.

Let's recap: To obtain an accurate measure of GDP, we must include U.S. production that is purchased by foreigners: total exports. But to correct for including goods produced abroad, we must subtract Americans' purchases of goods produced outside of the United States: total imports. In practice, we take both of these steps together by adding **net exports** (*NX*), which are total exports minus total imports.

To properly account for output sold to, and bought from, foreigners, we must include net exports—the difference between exports and imports—as part of expenditure in GDP.

In 2002, when total exports were $1,015 billion and total imports were $1,439 billion, net exports (as you can see in Table 2) were $1,015 - $1,439 = -$424 billion. The negative number indicates that the imports we're subtracting from GDP are greater than the exports we're adding.

Other Approaches to GDP

In addition to the expenditure approach, in which we calculate GDP as $C + I + G + NX$, there are other ways of measuring GDP. You may be wondering: Why bother? Why not just use one method—whichever is best—and stick to it?

Actually, there are two good reasons for measuring GDP in different ways. The first is practical. Each method of measuring GDP is subject to measurement errors. By calculating total output in several different ways and then trying to resolve the differences, the BEA gets a more accurate measure than would be possible with one method alone. The second reason is that the different ways of measuring total output give us different insights into the structure of our economy. Let's take a look at two more ways of measuring—and thinking about—GDP.

HTTP://

The main source of information on U.S. GDP is the Bureau of Economic Analysis. Its Web page can be found at http://www.bea.doc.gov/.

Net exports (*NX*) Total exports minus total imports.

The Value-Added Approach. In the expenditure approach, we record goods and services only when they are sold to their final users—at the end of the production process. But we can also measure GDP by adding up each *firm's* contribution to the product *as it is produced.*

A firm's contribution to a product is called its *value added.* More formally,

Value added The revenue a firm receives minus the cost of the intermediate goods it buys.

> *a firm's **value added** is the revenue it receives for its output, minus the cost of all the intermediate goods that it buys.*

Look back at Figure 1, which traces the production of a ream of notebook paper. The paper mill, for example, buys $1.00 worth of wood chips (an intermediate good) from the lumber company and turns it into raw paper, which it sells for $1.50. The value added by the paper mill is $1.50 − $1.00 = $0.50. Similarly, the office supplies maker buys $1.50 worth of paper (an intermediate good) from the paper mill and sells it for $2.25, so its value added is $2.25 − $1.50 = $0.75. If we total the value added by each firm, we should get the final value of the notebook paper, as shown in Table 3. (Notice that we assume the first producer in this process—the lumber company—uses no intermediate goods.)

The total value added is $1.00 + $0.50 + $0.75 + $1.25 + $1.50 = $5.00, which is equal to the final sales price of the ream of paper. For any good or service, it will always be the case that the sum of the values added by all firms equals the final sales price. This leads to our second method of measuring GDP:

Value-added approach Measuring GDP by summing the value added by all firms in the economy.

> *In the **value-added approach**, GDP is the sum of the values added by all firms in the economy.*

The Factor Payments Approach. If a bakery sells $200,000 worth of bread during the year and buys $25,000 in intermediate goods (flour, eggs, yeast), then its value added (its revenue minus the cost of its intermediate goods) is $200,000 − $25,000 = $175,000. This is also the sum that will be *left over* from its revenue after the bakery pays for its intermediate goods.

Where does this $175,000 go? In addition to its intermediate goods, the bakery must pay for the *resources* it used during the year: the land, labor, capital, and entrepreneurship that enabled it to add value to its intermediate goods.

Factor payments Payments to the owners of resources that are used in production

Payments to owners of resources are called **factor payments,** because resources are also called the factors of production. Owners of capital (the owners of the firm's buildings or machinery, or those who lend funds to the firm so that *it* can buy buildings and machinery) receive *interest payments.* Owners of land and natural resources receive *rent.* And those who provide labor to the firm receive *wages and salaries.*

Finally, there is one additional resource used by the firm: *entrepreneurship.* In every capitalist economy, the entrepreneurs are those who visualize society's needs, mobilize and coordinate the other resources so that production can take place, and gamble that the enterprise will succeed. The people who provide this entrepreneurship (often the owners of the firms) receive a fourth type of factor payment: *profit.*

Now let's go back to our bakery, which received $200,000 in revenue during the year. We've seen that $25,000 of this went to pay for intermediate goods, leaving $175,000 in value added earned by the factors of production. Let's suppose that

Firm	Cost of Intermediate Goods	Revenue	Value Added
Lumber Company	$ 0	$1.00	$1.00
Paper Mill	$1.00	$1.50	$0.50
Office Supplies Manufacturer	$1.50	$2.25	$0.75
Wholesaler	$2.25	$3.50	$1.25
Retailer	$3.50	$5.00	$1.50
			Total: $5.00

TABLE 3

Value Added at Different Stages of Production

$110,000 went to pay the wages of the bakery's employees, $10,000 was paid out as interest on loans, and $15,000 was paid in rent for the land under the bakery. That leaves $175,000 − $110,000 − $10,000 − $15,000 = $40,000. This last sum—since it doesn't go to anyone else—stays with the owner of the bakery. It, too, is a factor payment—profit—for the entrepreneurship she provides. Thus, when all of the factor payments, including profit, are added together, the total will be $110,000 + $10,000 + $15,000 + $40,000 = $175,000—precisely equal to the value added at the bakery. More generally,

> *In any year, the value added by a firm is equal to the total factor payments made by that firm.*

Earlier, we learned that GDP equals the sum of all firms' value added; now we've learned that each firm's value added is equal to its factor payments. Thus, GDP must equal the total factor payments made by all firms in the economy. Since all of these factor payments are received by households in the form of wages and salaries, rent, interest, or profit, we have our *third* method of measuring GDP:

> *In the **factor payments approach**, GDP is measured by adding up all of the income—wages and salaries, rent, interest, and profit—earned by all households in the economy.*[2]

Factor payments approach Measuring GDP by summing the factor payments earned by all households in the economy.

The factor payments approach to GDP gives us one of our most important insights into the marcoeconomy:

> *The total output of the economy (GDP) is equal to the total income earned in the economy.*

This simple idea—output equals income—follows directly from the factor payments approach to GDP. It explains why macroeconomists use the terms "output"

---

[2] Actually, this is just an approximation. Before a firm pays its factors of production, it first deducts a small amount for depreciation of its plant and equipment, and another small amount for the sales taxes it must pay to the government. Thus, GDP and total factor payments are slightly different. We ignore this difference in the text.

and "income" interchangeably: They are one and the same. If output rises, income rises by the same amount; if output falls, income falls by an equal amount. We'll be using this very important insight in several chapters to come.

Measuring GDP: A Summary

You've now learned three different ways to calculate GDP:

$Expenditure\ Approach:$ GDP = $C + I + G + NX$

$Value\text{-}Added\ Approach:$ GDP = Sum of value added by all firms

$Factor\ Payments\ Approach:$ GDP = Sum of factor payments earned by all households

= Wages and salaries + interest + rent + profit

= Total household income

We will use these three approaches to GDP again and again as we study what makes the economy tick. But for now, make sure you understand why each one of them should, in theory, give us the same number for GDP.

Real Versus Nominal GDP

Since GDP is measured in dollars, we have a serious problem when we want to track the change in output over time. The problem is that the value of the dollar—its purchasing power—is itself changing. As prices have risen over the years, the value of the dollar has steadily fallen. Trying to keep track of GDP using dollars in different years is like trying to keep track of a child's height using a ruler whose length changes each year. If we find that the child is three rulers tall in one year and four rulers tall in the next, we cannot know how much the child has grown, if at all, until we adjust for the effects of a changing ruler. The same is true for GDP and for any other economic variable measured in dollars: We usually need to adjust our measurements to reflect changes in the value of the dollar.

Nominal variable A variable measured without adjustment for the dollar's changing value.

Real variable A variable adjusted for changes in the dollar's value.

*When a variable is measured over time with no adjustment for the dollar's changing value, it is called a **nominal variable**. When a variable is adjusted for the dollar's changing value, it is called a **real variable**.*

Most government statistics are reported in both nominal and real terms, but economists focus almost exclusively on real variables. This is because changes in nominal variables don't really tell us much. For example, from the second to the third quarter of 2001 (not shown in earlier tables), nominal GDP increased from $10,050 billion to $10,098 billion, an increase of one-half of one percent. But production as measured by *real GDP* actually *decreased* over that period. The increase in nominal GDP was due entirely to a rise in prices.

The distinction between nominal and real values is crucial in macroeconomics. The public, the media, and sometimes even government officials have been confused by a failure to make this distinction. Whenever we want to track significant changes in key macroeconomic variables—such as the average wage rate, wealth, income, and GDP or any of its components—we always use *real* variables.

> *Since our economic well-being depends, in part, on the goods and services we can buy, it is important to translate nominal values (which are measured in current dollars) to real values (which adjust for the dollar's changing value).*

In the next chapter, you'll learn how economists translate some important nominal variables into real variables.

How GDP Is Used

We've come a long way since 1931. In that year—as the United States plummeted into the worst depression in its history—Congress summoned economists from government agencies, from academia, and from the private sector to testify about the state of the economy. They were asked the most basic questions: How much output was the nation producing, and how much had production fallen since 1929? How much income were Americans earning, how much were they spending? How much profit were businesses earning, and what were they doing with their profits? To the surprise of the members of Congress, no one could answer any of these questions, because *no one was keeping track of our national income and output!* The most recent measurement, which was rather incomplete, had been made in 1929.

Thus began the U.S. system of national income accounts, a system whose value was instantly recognized around the world and rapidly copied by other countries. Today, the government's reports on GDP are used to steer the economy over both the short run and the long run. In the short run, sudden changes in real GDP can alert us to the onset of a recession or a too-rapid expansion that can overheat the economy. Many (but not all) economists believe that, if alerted in time, policies can be designed to help keep the economy on a more balanced course.

GDP is also used to measure the long-run growth rate of the economy's output. Indeed, we typically define the average *standard of living* as *output per capita*: real GDP divided by the population. In order for output per capita to rise, real GDP must grow faster than the population. Since the U.S. population tends to grow by about 1 percent per year, a real GDP growth rate of 1 percent per year is needed just to *maintain* our output per capita; higher growth rates are needed to increase it.

Look at Figure 2, which shows the annual percentage change in real GDP from 1960 through the second quarter of 2003. The lower horizontal line indicates the 1 percent growth needed to just maintain output per capita. You can see that, on average, real GDP has grown by more than this, so that output per capita has steadily increased over time.

Growth in real GDP is also important for another reason: to ensure that the economy is generating sufficient new *jobs* for a workforce that is not only growing in number, but in productivity. Each year, the average worker is capable of producing more output, due to advances in technology, increases in the capital stock, and the greater skills of workers themselves. But if each worker produces more output, then output must increase even *faster* than the population to create enough jobs for everyone who wants to work. If not, the unemployment rate will rise.

In practice, an average annual growth rate of about 3.3 percent—the upper line in Figure 2—seems to prevent the unemployment rate from rising. And over the long run, growth in real GDP has been sufficiently high for this purpose. But you can also see that there are periods of time when GDP growth—even though positive—is too

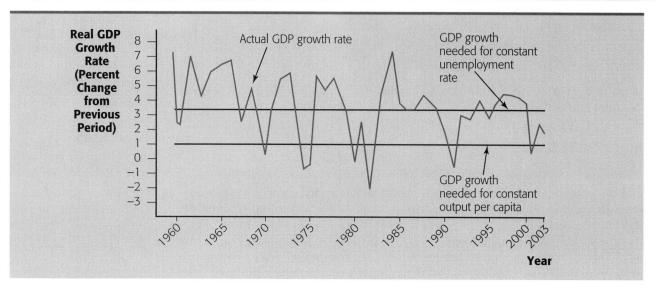

FIGURE 2

Real GDP Growth Rate, 1960–2003

Although the growth rate of real GDP has fluctuated over time, it has rarely dipped below the 1 percent rate needed to maintain output per capita. And although growth has frequently fallen below the 3.3 percent rate needed to prevent a rise in unemployment, it has met that threshold on average.

Source: Bureau of Economic Analysis, *National Economic Accounts,* Table 5.1 (2003 data is for first half of year only).

low to prevent a rise in the unemployment rate. During the recession of 2001 and into the first half of 2003, for example, GDP growth lagged behind the 3.3 percent requirement, and the unemployment rate rose. However, most economists have confidence that over time, real GDP growth will exceed the 3.3 percent requirement by enough to make up for the periods it has fallen behind, and that the economy will continue to generate jobs for a growing and more productive workforce, just as it has in the past. Later, you'll learn the reasons for this confidence.

To sum up: We use GDP to guide the economy in two ways. In the short run, it alerts us to recessions and give us a chance to stabilize the economy. And over long periods it tells us whether our economy is growing fast enough to raise output per capita and our standard of living, and fast enough to generate sufficient jobs for a growing population.

Problems with GDP

You have seen that GDP is an extremely useful concept. But the measurement of GDP is plagued by some serious problems.

Quality Changes. Suppose a new ballpoint pen comes out that lasts four times as long as previous versions. What *should* happen to GDP? Ideally, each new pen should count the same as four old pens, since one new pen offers the same *writing services* as four old ones. But the analysts at the Bureau of Economic Analysis (BEA) would most likely treat this new pen the same as an old pen and record an increase in GDP only if the total number of pens increased. Why? Because the BEA has a limited budget. While it does include the impact of quality changes for many goods and services (such as automobiles and computers), the BEA simply does not have the resources to estimate quality changes for millions of different goods and services. These include many consumer goods (such as razor blades that shave closer and last longer), medical services (increased surgery success rates and shorter recovery periods), and retail services (faster checkout times due to optical scanners). Ignoring these quality improvements causes GDP to understate the true growth in output from year to year.

The Underground Economy.

Some production is hidden from government authorities, either because it is illegal (drugs, prostitution, most gambling) or because those engaged in it are avoiding taxes. Production in these hidden markets, which comprise the *underground economy*, cannot be measured accurately, so the BEA must estimate it. Many economists believe that the BEA's estimates are too low. As a result, GDP may understate total output. However, since the *relative* importance of the underground economy does not change rapidly, the BEA's estimates of *changes* in GDP from year to year should not be seriously affected.

Nonmarket Production.

With a few exceptions, GDP does not include **nonmarket production**: goods and services that are produced but not sold in the marketplace. All of the housecleaning, typing, sewing, lawn mowing, and child rearing that people do themselves, rather than hiring someone else, are excluded from GDP. Whenever a nonmarket transaction (say, cleaning your apartment) becomes a market transaction (hiring a housecleaner to do it for you), GDP will rise, even though total production (cleaning one apartment) has remained the same.

Nonmarket production Goods and services that are produced but not sold in a market.

Over the last half-century, much production has shifted away from the home and to the market. Parenting, which was not counted in past years' GDP, has become day care, which *does* count—currently contributing several billion dollars annually to GDP. Similarly, home-cooked food has been replaced by takeout, talking to a friend has been replaced by therapy, and the neighbor who watches your house while you're away has been replaced by a store-bought alarm system or an increase in police protection. In all of these cases, real GDP increases, even though production has not. This can exaggerate the growth in GDP over long periods of time.

What do all these problems tell us about the value of GDP? That for certain purposes—especially interpreting *long-run* changes in GDP—we must exercise caution. For example, suppose that, over the next 20 years, the growth rate of GDP slows down. Would this mean that something is going wrong with the economy? Would it suggest a need to change course? Not necessarily. It *could* be that the underground economy or unrecorded quality changes are becoming more important. Similarly, if GDP growth accelerates, it could mean that our living standards are rising more rapidly. But it might instead mean that economic activity is shifting out of the home and into the market even more rapidly than in the past.

GDP works much better, however, as a guide to the short-run performance of the economy. Look back at the list of problems with GDP. The distortion in GDP measurement caused by each problem is likely to remain fairly constant from quarter to quarter. If GDP suddenly drops, it is extremely unlikely that the underground economy has suddenly become more important, or that there has been a sudden shift from market to nonmarket activities, or that we are suddenly missing more quality changes than usual. Rather, we can be reasonably certain that output and economic activity are slowing down.

Short-term changes in real GDP are fairly accurate reflections of the state of the economy. A significant quarter-to-quarter change in real GDP indicates a change in actual production, rather than a measurement problem.

This is why policy makers, businesspeople, and the media pay such close attention to GDP as a guide to the economy from quarter to quarter.

EMPLOYMENT AND UNEMPLOYMENT

When you think of unemployment, you may have an image in your mind that goes something like this: As the economy slides into recession, an anxious employee is called into an office and handed a pink slip by a grim-faced manager. "Sorry," the manager says, "I wish there were some other way. . . ." The worker spends the next few months checking the classified ads, pounding the pavement, and sending out résumés in a desperate search for work. And perhaps, after months of trying, the laid-off worker gives up, spending days at the neighborhood bar, drinking away the shame and frustration, and sinking lower and lower into despair and inertia.

For some people, joblessness begins and ends very much like this—a human tragedy, and a needless one. On one side, we have people who want to work and support themselves by producing something; on the other side is the rest of society, which could certainly use more goods and services. Yet somehow, the system isn't working, and the jobless cannot find work. The result is often hardship for the unemployed and their families, and a loss to society in general.

But this is just one face of unemployment, and there are others. Some instances of unemployment, for example, have little to do with macroeconomic conditions. And frequently, unemployment causes a lot less suffering than in our grim story.

Types of Unemployment

In the United States, people are considered unemployed if they are: (1) not working and (2) actively seeking a job. But unemployment can arise for a variety of reasons, each with its own policy implications. This is why economists have found it useful to classify unemployment into four different categories, each arising from a different cause and each having different consequences.

Frictional Unemployment. Short-term joblessness experienced by people who are between jobs or who are entering the labor market for the first time or after an absence is called **frictional unemployment**. In the real world, it takes time to find a job—time to prepare your résumé, to decide where to send it, to wait for responses, and then to investigate job offers so you can make a wise choice. It also takes time for employers to consider your skills and qualifications and to decide whether you are right for their firms. If you are not working during that time, you will be unemployed: searching for work but not working.

Because frictional unemployment is, by definition, short term, it causes little hardship to those affected by it. In most cases, people have enough savings to support themselves through a short spell of joblessness, or else they can borrow on their credit cards or from friends or family to tide them over. Moreover, this kind of unemployment has important benefits: By spending time searching rather than jumping at the first opening that comes their way, people find jobs for which they are better suited and in which they will ultimately be more productive. As a result, workers earn higher incomes, firms have more productive employees, and society has more goods and services.

HTTP://
Employment-related information for the United States can be found at the Bureau of Labor Statistics Web site: http://stats.bls.gov.

Frictional unemployment Joblessness experienced by people who are between jobs or who are just entering or reentering the labor market.

Seasonal Unemployment. Joblessness related to changes in weather, tourist patterns, or other seasonal factors is called **seasonal unemployment**. For example, most ski instructors lose their jobs every April or May, and many construction workers are laid off each winter.

Seasonal unemployment, like frictional unemployment, is rather benign: It is short term and, because it is entirely predictable, workers are often compensated in advance for the unemployment they experience in the off-season. Construction workers, for example, are paid higher-than-average hourly wages, in part to compensate them for their high probability of joblessness in the winter.

However, seasonal unemployment complicates the interpretation of unemployment data. Seasonal factors push the unemployment rate up in certain months of the year and pull it down in others, even when overall conditions in the economy remain unchanged. For example, each June, unemployment rises as millions of high school and college students—who do not want to work during the school year—begin looking for summer jobs. If the government reported the actual rise in unemployment in June, it would *seem* as if labor market conditions were deteriorating, when in fact, the rise would be merely a predictable and temporary seasonal change. To prevent any misunderstandings, the government usually reports the *seasonally adjusted* rate of unemployment, a rate that reflects only those changes beyond normal for the month. For example, if the unemployment rate in June is typically one percentage point higher than during the rest of the year, then the seasonally adjusted rate for June will be the actual rate minus one percentage point.

Seasonal unemployment Joblessness related to changes in weather, tourist patterns, or other seasonal factors.

Structural Unemployment. Sometimes, there are jobs available and workers who would be delighted to have them, but job seekers and employers are mismatched in some way. For example, in 2003, there were plenty of job openings for business professors; for nurses and nurse practitioners; for translators of strategic languages like Arabic, Persian, and Urdu; and in many other professions. Many of the unemployed, however, had been laid off from the airline and hotel industries, or from manufacturing, and did not have the skills and training to work where the jobs were going begging. This is a *skill* mismatch. The mismatch can also be *geographic,* as when construction jobs go begging in Northern California, Oregon, and Washington, but unemployed construction workers live in other states.

Unemployment that results from these kinds of mismatches is called **structural unemployment,** because it arises from *structural change* in the economy: when old, dying industries are replaced with new ones that require different skills and are located in different areas of the country. Structural unemployment is generally a stubborn, *long-term* problem, often lasting several years or more. Why? Because it can take considerable time for the structurally unemployed to find jobs—time to relocate to another part of the country or time to acquire new skills. To make matters worse, the structurally unemployed—who could benefit from financial assistance for job training or relocation—usually cannot get loans because they don't have jobs.

In recent decades, structural unemployment has been a much bigger problem in other countries, especially in Europe, than it is in the United States. Table 4 shows average unemployment rates in the United States and several European countries from 1990 to 2000 as well as in mid-2003. Unemployment rates were consistently higher in continental Europe than in the United States in the late 1990s and, in most of these countries were still high in mid-2003. And the unemployed remain jobless longer in Europe (where half of all the unemployed have been so for more than a year) than in the United States (where only 1 in 10 has been jobless for more than a year).

Structural unemployment Joblessness arising from mismatches between workers' skills and employers' requirements or between workers' locations and employers' locations.

TABLE 4
Average Unemployment Rates in Several Countries, 1990–2000 and 2003

Country	Average Unemployment Rate, 1990–2000	Unemployment Rate, Mid-2003
France	11.1%	9.1%
Italy	10.5%	8.7%
Greece	9.2%	9.6%
Canada	8.6%	7.8%
United Kingdom	8.0%	5.0%
Germany	7.9%	9.4%
Sweden	7.3%	5.4%
United States	5.6%	6.4%

Sources: Constance Sorrentino and Joyanna Moy, "U.S. Labor Market Performance in International Perspective," *Monthly Labor Review,* June 2002, pp. 15–35; *Standardized Unemployment Rates,* Organization for Economic Cooperation and Development, accessed July 30 at *http://www.oecd.org/dataoecd/ 41/13/2752342.pdf.* 2003 unemployment rates are for May 2003 except United Kingdom (March,) Italy (April), the United States (June), and Greece (December 2002). European unemployment rates have been adjusted by the OECD for reasonable comparability with U.S. rate.

And within the United States, some areas have higher structural unemployment than others. For example, in June 2003 when the U.S. unemployment rate was 6.4 percent, the rate in Los Angeles was 6.9 percent; in Detroit, 7.6 percent; in New York and Miami, 7.7 percent; and in Grand Rapids, Michigan, 8.0 percent.

The types of unemployment we've considered so far—frictional, structural, and seasonal—arise largely from *microeconomic* causes; that is, they are attributable to changes in specific industries and specific labor markets, rather than to the overall level of production in the country. This kind of unemployment cannot be entirely eliminated, as people will always spend some time searching for new jobs, there will always be seasonal industries in the economy, and structural changes will, from time to time, require workers to move to new locations or gain new job skills. Some amount of microeconomic unemployment is a sign of a dynamic economy. It allows workers to sort themselves into the best possible jobs, enables us to enjoy seasonal goods and services like winter skiing and summers at the beach, and permits the economy to go through structural changes when needed.

But frictional, structural, and seasonal unemployment rates are not fixed in stone, and government policy may be able to influence them. In the United States, many economists believe that we can continue to enjoy the benefits of a fast-changing and flexible economy with a lower unemployment rate. To achieve this goal, they advocate programs to help match the unemployed with employers and to help the jobless relocate and learn new skills. In Europe, by contrast, most economists believe that government labor and regulatory policies have been a *cause* of the structural unemployment problem. For example, government regulations make it costly or impossible for many European firms to lay off workers once they are hired. While that encourages firms to retain any *currently* employed workers, it also discourages new hiring, since firms regard any newly hired worker as a permanent obligation, even if future production turns down and the new worker is no longer needed. European unemployment benefits may also play a role. They are more generous than in the

United States, and the benefits are given for longer durations with a greater fraction of the potential labor force eligible to receive them. While this certainly helps the unemployed deal with the hardship of job loss, it also means that European workers have less incentive to seek new work once they lose a job.

Note, however, that in both Europe and the United States, the proposed solutions for high seasonal, frictional, or structural unemployment are changes in labor or regulatory policies, rather than changes in macroeconomic policy designed to raise GDP.

Our fourth and last type of unemployment, however, has an entirely *macroeconomic* cause.

Cyclical Unemployment. When the economy goes into a recession and total output falls, the unemployment rate rises. Many previously employed workers lose their jobs and have difficulty finding new ones. At the same time, there are fewer openings, so new entrants to the labor force must spend more than the usual time searching before they are hired. This type of unemployment—because it is caused by the business cycle—is called **cyclical unemployment.**

> **Cyclical unemployment** Joblessness arising from changes in production over the business cycle.

Look at Figure 3, which shows the unemployment rate in the United States for each quarter since 1960, and notice the rises that occurred during periods of recession (shaded). For example, in the recessions of the early 1980s, the unemployment rate rose from about 6 percent to more than 10 percent. And in the more recent recession from March to November of 2001, the unemployment rate rose from 4.2 percent to 5.8 percent; and during the very slow recovery of 2002 and the first half of 2003 the umemployment rate remained entrenched near 6 percent. These were rises in cyclical unemployment.

Since it arises from conditions in the overall economy, cyclical unemployment is a problem for *macroeconomic* policy. This is why macroeconomists focus almost exclusively on cyclical unemployment, rather than the other types of joblessness. Reflecting this emphasis, macroeconomists say we have reached **full employment** when *cyclical unemployment is reduced to zero*, even though substantial amounts of frictional, seasonal, and structural unemployment may remain:

> **Full employment** A situation in which there is no cyclical unemployment.

> *In macroeconomics, full employment means zero cyclical unemployment. But the overall unemployment rate at full employment is greater than zero because there are still positive levels of frictional, seasonal, and structural unemployment.*

How do we tell how much of our unemployment is cyclical? Many economists believe that today, normal amounts of frictional, seasonal, and structural unemployment account for an unemployment rate of between 4.5 and 5.0 percent in the United States. Therefore, any unemployment beyond this is considered cyclical unemployment. For example, when the actual unemployment rate was 6.4 percent in June 2003, we would say that 1.4 to 1.9 percent of the labor force was cyclically unemployed.

The Costs of Unemployment

Why are we so concerned about achieving a low rate of unemployment? What are the *costs* of unemployment to our society? We can identify two different types of costs: economic costs, those that can be readily measured in dollar terms, and

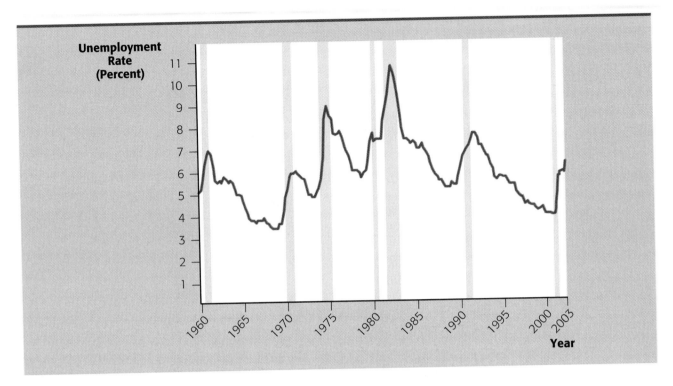

FIGURE 3

U.S. Quarterly Unemployment Rate, 1960–2003

The unemployment rate rises during recessions (shaded) and falls during expansions.

noneconomic costs, those that are difficult or impossible to measure in dollars, but that still affect us in important ways.

Economic Costs. The chief economic cost of unemployment is the *opportunity cost* of lost output: the goods and services the jobless *would* produce if they were working but do not produce because they cannot find work. This cost is borne by our society in general, although the burden may fall more on one group than another. If, for example, the unemployed were simply left to fend for themselves, then *they* would bear most of the cost. In fact, the unemployed are often given government assistance, so that the costs are spread somewhat among citizens in general. But there is no escaping this central fact:

> *When there is cyclical unemployment, the nation* produces *less output, and therefore some group or groups within society must* consume *less output.*

One way of viewing the economic cost of cyclical unemployment is illustrated in Figure 4. The green line shows real GDP over time, while the orange line shows the path of our **potential output**—the output we *could* have produced if the economy were operating at full employment.

Potential output The level of output the economy could produce if operating at full employment.

Notice that actual output is sometimes *above* potential output. At these times, unemployment is *below* the full-employment rate. For example, during the expansion in the late 1960s, cyclical unemployment was eliminated and the sum of frictional, seasonal, and structural unemployment dropped below 4.5 percent, its normal level for those years. At other times, real GDP is *below* potential output, most

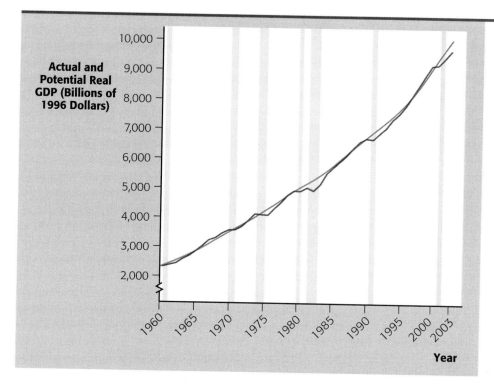

FIGURE 4
Actual And Potential Real GDP, 1960–2003

Sources: Real GDP from Bureau of Economic Analysis, Real Gross Domestic Product, Table 1.2 (http://www.bea.gov). Potential GDP from Congressional Budget Office, "CBO's Method for Estimating Potential Output: An Update," August 2001 (www.cbo.gov), Publications.

often during and following a recession. At these times, unemployment rises above the full-employment rate. In the 2001 recession, the unemployment rate rose from 4.2 percent to 5.8 percent, and stayed near or above 6 percent for the next year and a half.

In the figure, you can see that we have spent more of the last 40 years operating *below* our potential than above it. That is, the cyclical ups and downs of the economy have, on balance, led to lower living standards than we would have had if the economy had always operated just at potential output.

Broader Costs. There are also costs of unemployment that go beyond lost output. Unemployment—especially when it lasts for many months or years—can have serious psychological and physical effects. Some studies have found that increases in unemployment cause noticeable rises in the number of heart attack deaths, suicides, and admissions to state prisons and psychiatric hospitals. The jobless are more likely to suffer a variety of health problems, including high blood pressure, heart disorders, troubled sleep, and back pain. There may be other problems—such as domestic violence, depression, and alcoholism—that are more difficult to document. And, tragically, most of those who lose their job and remain unemployed for long periods also lose their health insurance, increasing the likelihood that these problems will have serious consequences.

Unemployment also causes setbacks in achieving important social goals. For example, most of us want a fair and just society where all people have an equal chance to better themselves. But our citizens do not bear the burden of unemployment equally. In a recession, we do not all suffer a reduction in our work hours;

TABLE 5
Unemployment Rates for Various Groups, June 2003

Group	Unemployment Rate
Whites	5.5%
Hispanics	8.4%
Blacks	11.8%
White Teenagers	16.5%
Black Teenagers	39.3%

Source: The Employment Situation: June 2003, Bureau of Labor Statistics News Release, July 3, 2003 (Tables A-2, A-3; seasonally adjusted data).

instead, some people are laid off entirely, while others continue to work roughly the same hours.

Moreover, the burden of unemployment is not shared equally among different groups in the population, but tends to fall most heavily on minorities, especially minority youth. As a rough rule of thumb, the unemployment rate for blacks is twice that for whites; and the rate for *teenage* blacks is triple the rate for blacks overall. Table 5 shows that the unemployment rates for June 2003 are consistent with this general experience. Notice the extremely high unemployment rate for black teenagers: 39.3 percent. This contributes to a vicious cycle of poverty and discrimination: When minority youths are deprived of that all-important first job, they remain at a disadvantage in the labor market for years to come.

How Unemployment Is Measured

In June 2003, about 150 million Americans were not employed, according to official government statistics. Were all of these people unemployed? Absolutely not. In theory, the unemployed are those who are *willing and able* to work but do not have jobs. Most of the 150 million nonworking Americans were either *unable* or *unwilling* to work. For example, the very old, the very young, and the very ill were unable to work, as were those serving prison terms. Others were able to work, but preferred not to, including millions of college students, homemakers, and retired people. Still others were in the military and are counted in the population, but not counted when calculating civilian employment statistics.

But how, in practice, can we determine who is willing and able? This is a thorny problem, and there is no perfect solution to it. In the United States, we determine whether a person is willing and able to work by his or her *behavior.* More specifically, to be counted as unemployed, you must have recently *searched* for work. But how can we tell who has, and who has not, recently searched for work?

The Census Bureau's Household Survey. Every month, thousands of interviewers from the United States Census Bureau—acting on behalf of the U.S. Bureau of Labor Statistics (BLS)—conduct a survey of 60,000 households across America. This sample of households is carefully selected to give information about the entire population. Household members who are under 16, in the military, or currently residing in an institution like a prison or hospital are excluded from the survey. The interviewer will then ask questions about the remaining household members' activities during the *previous week.*

Figure 5 shows roughly how this works. First, the interviewer asks whether the household member has worked one or more hours for pay or profit. If the answer is yes, the person is considered employed; if no, another question is asked: Has she been *temporarily* laid off from a job from which she is waiting to be recalled? A yes means the person is unemployed whether or not the person searched for a new job; a no leads to one more question: Did the person actively *search* for work during the previous four weeks. If yes, the person is unemployed; if no, she is not in the labor force.

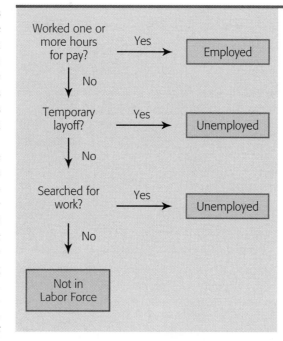

FIGURE 5
How BLS Measures Employment Status

BLS interviewers ask a series of questions to determine whether an individual is employed, unemployed, or not in the labor force.

Figure 6 illustrates how the BLS, extrapolating from its 60,000-household sample, classified the U.S. population in July 2003. First, note that about 70 million people were ruled out from consideration because they were under 16 years of age, living in institutions, or in the military. The remaining 221 million people made up the civilian, noninstitutional population, and of these, 137.7 million were employed and 9.4 million were unemployed. Adding the employed and unemployed together gives us the **labor force,** equal to 137.7 million + 9.4 million = 147.1 million.

Labor force Those people who have a job or who are looking for one.

Finally, we come to the official **unemployment rate,** which is defined as the percentage of the labor force that is unemployed:

Unemployment rate The fraction of the labor force that is without a job.

$$\text{Unemployment rate} = \frac{\text{Unemployed}}{\text{Labor Force}} = \frac{\text{Unemployed}}{(\text{Unemployed} + \text{Employed})}$$

Using the numbers in Figure 6, the U.S. unemployment rate in June 2003 was calculated as 9.4/(9.4 + 137.7) = .064 or 6.4 percent. This was the number released to journalists at 8:00 A.M. on the first Friday of July 2003, and the number that made headlines in your local newspaper the next day.

Problems in Measuring Unemployment

The Census Bureau earns very high marks from economists for both its sample size—60,000 households—and the characteristics of its sample, which very closely match the characteristics of the U.S. population. Still, the official unemployment rate suffers from some important measurement problems.

Many economists believe that our official measure seriously underestimates the extent of unemployment in our society. There are two reasons for this belief: the treatment of *involuntary part-time workers* and the treatment of *discouraged workers.*

As you can see in Figure 5, anyone working one hour or more for pay during the survey week is treated as employed. This includes many people who would like a full-time job—and may even be searching for one—but who did some part-time work during the week. Some economists have suggested that these people, called

FIGURE 6
**Employment Status of the U.S.
Population—June 2003**

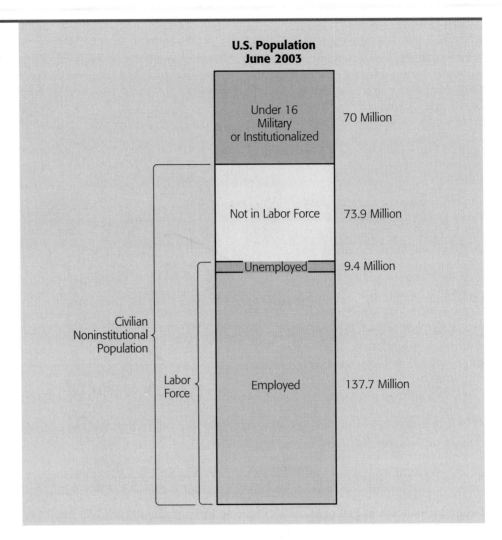

**U.S. Population
June 2003**

Under 16
Military
or Institutionalized — 70 Million

Not in Labor Force — 73.9 Million

Unemployed — 9.4 Million

Employed — 137.7 Million

Civilian
Noninstitutional
Population

Labor
Force

Involuntary part-time workers
Individuals who would like a full-time job, but who are working only part time.

Discouraged workers Individuals who would like a job, but have given up searching for one.

involuntary part-time workers, should be regarded as partially employed and partially unemployed.

How many involuntary part-time workers are there? In June 2003, the BLS estimated that there were about 4.5 million.[3] If each of these workers were considered half-employed and half-unemployed, the unemployment rate in that month would have been 7.9 percent, instead of the officially reported 6.4 percent.

Another problem is the treatment of **discouraged workers,** individuals who would like to work but, because they feel little hope of finding a job, have given up searching. Because they are not taking active steps to find work, they are considered "not in the labor force" (see Figure 5). Some economists feel that discouraged workers should be counted as unemployed. After all, these people are telling us that they are willing and able to work, but they are not working. It seems wrong to exclude them just because they are not actively seeking work. Others argue that counting dis-

---

[3] This and other information about unemployment in June 2003 comes from *The Employment Situation: June 2003*, Bureau of Labor Statistics News Release, July 3, 2003. (All figures are seasonally adjusted except discouraged workers.)

couraged workers as unemployed would reduce the objectivity of our unemployment measure. Talk is cheap, they believe, and people may *say* anything when asked whether they would like a job; the real test is what people *do*. Yet even the staunchest defenders of the current method of measuring employment would agree that *some* discouraged workers are, in fact, willing and able to work and should be considered unemployed. The problem, in their view, is determining which ones.

How many discouraged workers are there? No one knows for sure. The BLS tries to count them, but defining who is genuinely discouraged is yet another thorny problem. Using the BLS's rather strict criteria, there were 478,000 discouraged workers in June 2003. But with a looser, unofficial definition of "discouraged worker"—people who are not working but say they want a job—the count rises to 5.1 million. Including some or all of these people among the unemployed would raise the unemployment rate significantly.

Still, the unemployment rate, as currently measured, tells us something important: the number of people who are *searching* for jobs, but have not yet found them. It is not exactly the same as the percentage of the labor force that is jobless even though willing and able to work. But if we could obtain a perfect measure of the latter, the unemployment rate, as currently measured, would be highly correlated with it.

Moreover, the unemployment rate tells us something unique about conditions in the macroeconomy. When the unemployment rate is relatively low—so that few people are actively seeking work—a firm that wants to hire more workers may be forced to lure them from other firms, by offering a higher wage rate. This puts upward pressure on wages and can lead to future inflation. A high unemployment rate, by contrast, tells us that firms can more easily expand by hiring those who are actively seeking work, without having to lure new workers from another firm and without having to offer higher wages. This suggests little inflationary danger. Later in the book, we will discuss the connection between unemployment and inflation more fully.

USING THE THEORY
GDP After September 11

On September 11, 2001, the United States suffered an unprecedented terrorist attack when four airliners were hijacked and three of them were used to destroy the World Trade Center in New York and a section of the Pentagon in Washington D.C., killing more than 3,000 people. The most profound dimensions of this tragedy were the human lives lost and the continuing bereavement of those left behind—a loss that stunned and disoriented the nation.

But as the nation began to find its balance, it became clear that the events of September 11 would have a significant impact in another way: on the economy. Most economists suspected that the United States was already in recession (a suspicion that was confirmed later when the beginning of the recession was dated to March 2001). But what would happen after September 11? Would the recession deepen? How badly? Could the economy actually tilt into a depression? What was the appropriate economic policy, and how should it be orchestrated? As if the shock of the attacks weren't enough, millions of Americans now began to fear for their jobs.

© ROYALTY-FREE/CORBIS

How an event like September 11 affects the macroeconomy, and how the government responded, are issues you will learn about in later chapters of this book. Here, we look at just one aspect of the problem: the impact of the attacks on U.S. real GDP. By taking a brief look at this now—even before you've learned much about how the macroeconomy works—you'll be able to see how an understanding of GDP and its measurement can help us gauge the effects of September 11.

It will be helpful to distinguish between the *direct* impact on GDP (the direct result of the destruction itself) and the *indirect* impact (resulting from the choices of economic decision makers in the weeks, months, and even years following the attack).

The Direct Impact on GDP

At first, it seems that the direct impact of the attacks on GDP should be huge. For example, compared to the property loss from other recent man-made disasters, September 11 was orders of magnitude more destructive. The property loss from the Los Angeles riots of 1992 amounted to about $775 million; from the first World Trade Center bombing in 1993, $510 million; and from the 1995 bombing of the Federal Building in Oklahoma City, $125 million. By contrast, on September 11, the insured property damage in New York City alone was $16 billion.

But now consider the destruction caused by some recent *natural* disasters. The 1994 earthquake centered in Northridge, California, destroyed about $15 billion in property—almost as much as the direct damage to New York City. And Hurricane Andrew in 1992 caused even more damage—about $27 billion worth—significantly more than the damage to the World Trade Center and the Pentagon combined. The direct national economic impact of both of these natural disasters hardly appeared in the national statistics. And that is not surprising, since these magnitudes amount to only a fraction of a percentage point of our GDP, and an even smaller fraction of our total capital stock.

But as may have already occurred to you, measuring destruction of property—a loss of the capital stock—is beside the point of this section. GDP measures *production,* not the value of our capital stock. So the destruction caused by September 11—while it entered into another, related measure called *net domestic product* (GDP minus depreciation of the capital stock)—had *no direct impact at all* on GDP. Put another way, GDP is not designed to measure the resources at our disposal, but rather the production we get from those resources. While the loss of property did destroy resources capable of producing things, and thus caused production to drop in future quarters, the destroyed resources themselves did *not* count in GDP. Moreover, because our resources are so vast and our production so great, the actual drop in future production from having fewer resources was virtually unnoticeable.

The destruction caused by the terrorist attacks of September 11 had almost no direct impact on U.S. GDP.

Indirect Impacts on GDP

By contrast, the *indirect* losses to GDP—those that resulted from our response to the attacks—were significant. Here, it will be useful to distinguish between the short-run impact (the weeks and months following the attacks) and the long-run impact (which we'll be experiencing for several years).

The Short Run. It did not take long for the aftermath of the attacks to affect economic decision making. First came a decision by the federal government, which immediately shut down airports nationwide for more than 48 hours. Thus, for two days, the number of flights in the United States declined from 30,000 per day to zero—an immediate decrease in airline production and therefore GDP. But the more important impact was the decision made by consumers *after* airports reopened: They no longer wanted to fly. Over the next four weeks, with dramatically reduced bookings, the airlines cut the number of flights offered by more than 20 percent and laid off 80,000 workers.

But that was only the beginning. With fewer people flying, hotel occupancy rates also decreased, by about 20 percent. The hotel industry responded with thousands of layoffs. And then—since there were fewer business travelers and tourists spending money on taxis, restaurants, and amusement parks—there were layoffs in those industries as well. The problem spread further: It wasn't long before the airlines canceled orders for new aircraft and hotels and other businesses halted construction projects, some of which had already started. Thus, the problem spread to the manufacturing and raw materials sectors of the economy.

Consumers made other decisions that affected production. Retail shopping declined dramatically, at first because millions of stunned viewers spent all their free time watching events unfold on television, and then because fears of deepening recession made them worry about their incomes.

There were also instances of *increased* production. On September 11, AT&T, which normally handles 300 million calls on a Tuesday, saw the number of calls spike to 431 million. For several weeks, state and local governments, seeking to beef up security, paid overtime to hundreds of thousands of police and firefighters. And millions of people—looking for emotional escape but not wanting to leave home—created a boom in video and DVD rentals. But these increases in production were swamped by the production cuts already rippling through the economy.

GDP did a good job of capturing all of these changes in spending and production, since that is just what it is designed to do. After taking account of changes in airline flights, hotel bookings, restaurant meals, video rentals, and hundreds of thousands of other changes in production, the Bureau of Economic Analysis reported that production turned southward in the third quarter of 2001, with much of the decline occurring during the three weeks of the quarter that remained after September 11.

The Long Run. What about the long run? Look again at Figure 4. It shows us that GDP can deviate from potential output for several quarters or even several years. But it also shows that, in the long run, GDP tends to rise at about the same rate as potential output. Thus, when we ask about the long-run impact of September 11 on GDP, we are really asking about its long-run impact on *potential* GDP.

What is this long-run impact? In the weeks following the attack, it became clear that the United States was about to start on a course it would follow for many years: a huge reallocation of national resources toward fighting terrorism abroad and achieving greater security at home. These are resources that would otherwise be used to produce other things.

Some of these resources are being purchased by the government. For example, in the first three months of U.S. attacks on terrorist camps and the associated Taliban regime in Afghanistan, the Department of Defense used more than $3.8 billion of additional resources (beyond its normal expenses) for jet fuel, munitions, and additional combat pay for 50,000 troops stationed in the region. Over the next two years, the United States spent billions of additional dollars pursuing a more aggressive foreign policy, including an invasion to overthrow the regime of Saddam Hussein in Iraq, and increased aid to allies—and potential allies—in the war against terrorism. At home, the federal government hired hundreds of air marshals to protect civilian aircraft, and thousands of new airport personnel to screen passengers and luggage.

But private businesses too, have been spending more for security each year than they did before September 11. More armed security guards are stationed at corporate headquarters and manufacturing plants; more sophisticated access-pass equipment and metal detectors have been installed in office buildings; new hires are more carefully screened and investigated; deliveries are more carefully monitored; and bomb-sniffing dogs and increased security have become a routine part of rock concerts and sporting events.

All of these security expenses are slowing the growth of our potential output, and are therefore slowing the growth of real GDP over the long run. Why? Because business security services are *intermediate goods*—things that firms use as inputs to produce final goods and services for sale to others. Just as IBM must use labor, computer chips, plastic, salespeople, and buildings as inputs when it makes computers, it must also hire people to guard its office buildings, to do background checks on employees, and to monitor deliveries to its national headquarters. These are all part of the cost of doing business.

Suppose, for example, that IBM now uses $25 more in security services for each computer it produces. The computer is not faster, lighter, or better in any way than before; it still contributes the same amount to real GDP as it did before. But the additional security uses up resources—land and natural resources, labor, capital, and entrepreneurship—that could otherwise have been used to produce *other* final goods, perhaps by IBM or by *other* firms in the economy. Since these other final goods are *not* being produced, our total output is lower than it would otherwise be.

To see this from another point of view, think about how technological advances normally work to increase our output of goods and services. Personal computers, the Internet, cell phones, assembly-line robots, and new medical devices have all enabled firms in various industries to produce whatever they produce using fewer resources. These freed-up resources are then used to produce other things, so potential output rises and—in the long run—so does our real GDP. But September 11 has had the *opposite* effect of a technological advance. It forces businesses to use *more* resources to produce output—resources that could have been used to make other things.

Of course, while increased security spending tends to reduce potential output, other forces are working to increase it, including technological advances, increases in the capital stock (both human and physical), increases in population. (You'll learn more about this in later chapters.) So increased security spending doesn't necessarily mean that potential output will fall, but it does create a force pulling the growth rate of potential output downward.

> *In the long run, as the nation shifts production away from other goods and services and toward security in the wake of September 11, the impact on our real GDP will be negative. Our potential output—and over the long run, our actual output—will grow more slowly than it otherwise would have.*

Summary

This chapter discusses how some key macroeconomic aggregates are measured and reported. One important economic aggregate is *gross domestic product*—the total value of all final goods and services produced for the marketplace during a given year, within a nation's borders. GDP is a measure of an economy's total production.

In the *expenditure approach,* GDP is calculated as the sum of spending by households, businesses, government agencies, and foreigners on domestically produced goods and services. The *value-added approach* computes GDP by adding up each firm's contributions to the total product as it is being produced. Value added at each stage of production is the revenue a firm receives minus the cost of the intermediate inputs it uses. Finally, the *factor payments approach* sums the wages and salaries, rent, interest and profit earned by all resource owners. The three approaches reflect three different ways of viewing GDP.

Since nominal GDP is measured in current dollars, it changes when either production or prices change. *Real GDP* is nominal GDP adjusted for price changes; it rises only when production rises.

Real GDP is useful in the short run for giving warnings about impending recessions, and in the long run for indicating how fast the economy is growing. Unfortunately, it is plagued by important inaccuracies. It does not fully reflect quality changes or production in the underground economy, and it does not include many types of nonmarket production.

When real GDP grows, employment tends to rise and—if real GDP grows fast enough—the unemployment rate falls. In the United States, a person is considered unemployed if he or she does not have a job but is actively seeking one. Economists have found it useful to classify unemployment into four different categories. *Frictional unemployment* is short-term unemployment experienced by people between jobs or by those who are just entering the job market. *Seasonal unemployment* is related to changes in the weather, tourist patterns, or other predictable seasonal changes. *Structural unemployment* results from mismatches, in skills or location, between jobs and workers. Finally, *cyclical unemployment* occurs because of the business cycle. Unemployment, particularly the structural and cyclical forms, involves costs. From a social perspective, unemployment means lost production. From the individual viewpoint, unemployment often involves financial, psychological, and physical harm.

Key Terms

Capital stock	Government purchases	Private investment
Consumption	Gross domestic product (GDP)	Real variable
Cyclical unemployment	Intermediate goods	Seasonal unemployment
Discouraged workers	Involuntary part-time workers	Structural unemployment
Expenditure approach	Labor force	Transfer payment
Factor payments	Net exports	Unemployment rate
Factor payments approach	Net investment	Value added
Final good	Nominal variable	Value-added approach
Frictional unemployment	Nonmarket production	
Full employment	Potential output	

Review Questions

Answers to even-numbered Questions and Problems can be found on the text Web site at http://hall-lieb.swlearning.com.

1. What is the difference between final goods and intermediate goods? Why is it that only the value of final goods and services is counted in GDP?

2. What is the relationship between private investment and the capital stock? What are the three components of private investment?

3. Describe the different kinds of factor payments.

4. What is the difference between nominal and real variables? What is the main problem with using nominal variables to track the economy?

5. Discuss the value and reliability of GDP statistics in both short-run and long-run analyses of the economy.

6. Real GDP (in 1996 dollars) was measured at around $8.8 trillion in 1999. Was the actual value of goods and services produced in the United States in 1999 likely to have been higher or lower than that? Why?

7. What, if anything, could the government do to reduce frictional and structural unemployment?

8. Categorize each of the following according to the type of unemployment it reflects. Justify your answers.

a. Workers are laid off when a GM factory closes due to a recession.

b. Workers selling software in a store are laid off when the store goes bankrupt due to competition from on-line software dealers.

c. Migrant farm workers' jobs end when the harvest is finished.

d. Lost jobs result from the movement of textile plants from Massachusetts to the South and overseas.

9. Can unemployment ever be good for the economy? Explain.

10. What are some of the different types of costs associated with unemployment?

11. Discuss some of the problems with the way the Bureau of Labor Statistics computes the unemployment rate. In what ways do official criteria lead to an overestimate or underestimate of the actual unemployment figure?

12. Explain this statement: "The Bureau of Economic Analysis reported a 2003 second quarter real GDP figure of $10,802.7 billion."

13. Summarize the three approaches to calculating GDP.

Problems and Exercises

1. Using the expenditure approach, which of the following would be directly counted as part of U.S. GDP in 2005? In each case, state whether the action causes an increase in C, I, G, or NX.

   a. A new personal computer produced by IBM, which remained unsold at the year's end

   b. A physician's services to a household

   c. Produce bought by a restaurant to serve to customers

   d. The purchase of 1,000 shares of Disney stock

   e. The sale of 50 acres of commercial property

   f. A real estate agent's commission from the sale of property

   g. A transaction in which you clean your roommate's apartment in exchange for his working on your car

   h. An Apple iMac computer produced in the United States, and purchased by a French citizen

   i. The government's Social Security payments to retired people

2. Calculate the total change in a year's GDP for each of the following scenarios:

   a. A family sells a home, without using a broker, for $150,000. They could have rented it on the open market for $700 per month. They buy a 10-year-old condominium for $200,000; the broker's fee on the transaction is 6 percent of the selling price. The condo's owner was formerly renting the unit at $500 per month.

   b. General Electric uses $10 million worth of steel, glass, and plastic to produce its dishwashers. Wages and salaries in the dishwasher division are $40 million; the division's only other expense is $15 million in interest that it pays on its bonds. The division's revenue for the year is $75 million.

   c. On March 31, you decide to stop throwing away $50 a month on convenience store nachos. You buy $200 worth of equipment, cornmeal, and cheese, and make your own nachos for the rest of the year.

   d. You win $25,000 in your state's lottery. Ever the entrepreneur, you decide to open a Ping-Pong ball washing service, buying $15,000 worth of equipment from SpiffyBall Ltd. of Hong Kong and $10,000 from Ball-B-Kleen of Toledo, Ohio.

   e. Tone-Deaf Artists, Inc. produces 100,000 new White Snake CDs that it prices at $15 apiece. Ten thousand CDs are sold abroad, but, alas, the rest remain unsold on warehouse shelves.

3. The country of Freedonia uses the same method to calculate the unemployment rate as the U.S. Bureau of Labor Statistics uses. From the data below, compute Freedonia's unemployment rate.

Population	10,000,000
Under 16	3,000,000
Over 16	
In military service	500,000
In hospitals	200,000
In prison	100,000
Worked one hour or more in previous week	4,000,000
Searched for work during previous four weeks	1,000,000

4. Toward the end of this chapter, it was stated that if half of the 4.5 million involuntary part-time workers in June 2003 were counted as unemployed, then the unemployment rate that month would have been 7.9 percent instead of 6.4 percent. Do the necessary calculations to confirm this statement, using the information in Figure 6. [*Hint:* The labor force will not be affected.]

5. Using the information given toward the end of the chapter, what would the unemployment rate have been in June 2003 if it had included among the unemployed:

   a. All officially discouraged workers?

   b. All those who were not working but said they wanted a job? [*Hint:* Don't forget about how these inclusions would affect the labor force.]

6. Ginny asks "If I buy a sweater that was produced in Malaysia, why is its purchase price subtracted from GDP?" How should you answer her question? (You may assume, for simplicity, that there was no value added to the sweater in the United States)

7. Ziponia, which uses the same method to calculate real GDP as the U.S. Bureau of Economic Analysis uses, has made the following calculations for 2004: $C = \$6,000$ million, $I = \$1,500$ million, $G = \$500$ million, and $NX = \$600$ million. Find Ziponia's real GDP for 2004 and explain how it will change for 2005 if the only difference between the two years is that Ziponia's citizens import an additional $5 million worth of DVD players in 2005. Does your answer depend on what Ziponia's firms produce? For instance, will your answer change if part of Ziponia's firms' production was $5 million worth of DVD players that they expected to sell to Ziponians, but were unable to because the Ziponians preferred imported DVD players?

8. a. The country of Ziponia uses the same method to calculate the unemployment rate as the U.S. Bureau of Labor Statistics uses. From the data below, compute Ziponia's unemployment rate.

Population	60,000
Under 16	9,000
Over 16	
In military service	600
In hospitals	60
In prison	200
Worked one hour or more in previous week	46,000
Searched for work during previous four weeks	2,140
Did not work in previous week but would have taken a job if one were offered	200

b. How large is Ziponia's labor force?

c. How many discouraged workers live in Ziponia?

d. Not all of Ziponia's citizens are accounted for in part (a). How are the missing citizens classified? Give some examples of what they may be doing.

e. How many of Ziponia's citizens are not in the labor force?

9. Refer to question 8. The 2,140 Ziponians who searched for work during the previous four weeks included: 54 ski resort employees who lost their winter jobs but expect to get them back in late fall; 200 recent high school graduates; 258 former textile workers who lost their jobs when their employers moved their operations overseas; 143 mothers and 19 fathers who had stayed at home to raise their children but who recently decided to reenter the work force; 394 high school and college students who want summer jobs; 115 people who live in West Ziponia and lost their jobs when their employers moved operations to East Ziponia, but who are not qualified for the remaining jobs in the west; 110 recent college graduates; 12 record-label designers who lost their jobs as consumers substituted CDs for records; and 32 retirees who decided to return to the workforce. The remaining job seekers lost their jobs due to a recession. Use this information to:

   a. Classify the job seekers by their type of unemployment, and calculate how many fell into each category.

   b. Find the frictional, seasonal, structural, and cyclical unemployment rates.

   c. Find how many Ziponians would be unemployed if Ziponia were to achieve full employment.

Challenge Questions

1. Suppose, in a given year, someone buys a General Motors automobile for $30,000. That same year, GM produced the car in Michigan, using $10,000 in parts imported from Japan. However, the parts imported from Japan themselves contained $3,000 in components produced in the United States.
   a. By how much does U.S. GDP rise?
   b. Using the expenditure approach, what is the change in each component (C, I, G, and NX) of U.S. GDP?
   c. What is the change in Japan's GDP and each of its components?

2. In the "Using the Theory" section of this chapter, you learned that business spending on security will work to reduce real GDP over the long run. Is the same true of government expenditures on security? Why or why not?

3. a. Federal Reserve Chairman Alan Greenspan came up with a novel (and facetious) way to measure the United States' output: by weight. Describe some of the problems inherent in measuring output by weight.
   b. What problems might arise if policy makers relied on a weight-based measure of output to determine the health of the U.S. economy?

 ECONOMIC *Applications* *These exercises require access to Hall/Lieberman Xtra! If Xtra! did not come with your book, visit* http://hallxtra.swlearning.com *to purchase.*

1. Use your Xtra! password at the Hall and Lieberman Web site (http://hallxtra.swlearning.com), select this chapter, and click on EconDebate. Choose *Macroeconomics: Employment, Unemployment, and Inflation* and scroll down to find the debate, "Do Technological Advances Result in Higher Unemployment?" Read the debate, and use the information to answer the following questions.
   a. How does technological change alter the composition of the demand for labor? Is the overall effect positive or negative? Why?
   b. What are the effects of technological change on productivity and growth? Explain.

2. Use your Xtra! password at the Hall and Lieberman Web site (http://hallxtra.swlearning.com), select this

chapter, and under Economic Applications, click on EconDebate. Choose *Macroeconomics: Employment, Unemployment, and Inflation* and scroll down to find the *Real GDP*. Read the definition and click on Diagrams/Data and use the information to answer the following questions.
   a. Verify the inverse relationship between the economic growth rate and the unemployment rate. Explain this relationship.
   b. Why is there a direct relationship between real GDP and personal income?
   c. How well does the Index of Leading Economic Indicators perform in forecasting future economic conditions?

The Monetary System, Prices, and Inflation

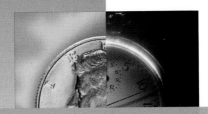

You pull into a gas station deep in the interior of the distant nation of Chaotica. The numbers on the gas pump don't make sense to you, and you can't figure out how much to pay. Luckily, the national language of Chaotica is English, so you can ask the cashier how much the gas costs. He replies, "Here in Chaotica, we don't have any standard system for measuring quantities of gas, and we don't have any standard way to quote prices. My pump here measures in my own unit, called the slurp, and I will sell you 6 slurps of gas for that watch you are wearing, or a dozen slurps of gas for your camera." You spend the next half hour trying to determine how many slurps of gas there are in a gallon and what form of payment you can use besides your watch and camera.

Life in the imaginary nation of Chaotica would be difficult. People would spend a lot of time figuring out how to trade with each other, time that could otherwise be spent producing things or enjoying leisure activities. Fortunately, in the real world, virtually every nation has a *monetary system* that helps to organize and simplify our economic transactions.

THE MONETARY SYSTEM

Unit of value A common unit for measuring how much something is worth.

A monetary system establishes two different types of standardization in the economy. First, it establishes a **unit of value**—a common unit for measuring how much something is worth. A standard unit of value permits us to compare the costs of different goods and services and to communicate these costs when we trade. The dollar is the unit of value in the United States. If a college textbook costs $100, while a round-trip airline ticket from Phoenix to Minneapolis costs $300, we know immediately that the ticket has the same value in the marketplace as three college textbooks.

Means of payment Anything acceptable as payment for goods and services.

The second type of standardization concerns the **means of payment,** the things we can use as payment when we buy goods and services. In the United States, the means of payment include dollar bills, personal checks, money orders, credit cards like Visa and American Express, and, in some experimental locations, prepaid cash cards with magnetic strips.

These two functions of a monetary system—establishing a unit of value and a standard means of payment—are closely related, but they are not the same thing. The unit-of-value function refers to the way we *think* about and record transactions; the means-of-payment function refers to how payment is actually made.

The unit of value works in the same way as units of weight, volume, distance, and time. In fact, the same sentence in Article I of the U.S. Constitution gives Congress the power to create a unit of value along with units of weights and measures. All of these units help us determine clearly and precisely what is being traded for what. Think about buying gas in the United States; you exchange dollars for gallons. The transaction will go smoothly and quickly only if there is clarity about both the unit of fluid volume (gallons) *and* the unit of purchasing power (dollars).

The means of payment can be different from the unit of value. For example, in some countries where local currency prices change very rapidly, it is common to use the U.S. dollar as the unit of value—to specify prices in dollars—while the local currency remains the means of payment. Even in the United States, when you use a check to buy something, the unit of value is the dollar but the means of payment is a piece of paper with your signature on it.

In the United States, the dollar is the centerpiece of our monetary system. It is the unit of value in virtually every economic transaction, and dollar bills are very often the means of payment as well. How did the dollar come to play such an important role in the economy?

History of the Dollar

Prior to 1790, each colony had its own currency. It was named the "pound" in every colony, but it had a different purchasing power in each of them. In 1790, soon after the Constitution went into effect, Congress created a new unit of value called the dollar. Historical documents show that merchants and businesses switched immediately to the new dollar, thereby ending the chaos of the colonial monetary systems. Prices began to be quoted in dollars, and accounts were kept in dollars. The dollar rapidly became the standard unit of value.

But the primary means of payment in the United States until the Civil War was paper currency issued by private banks. Just as the government defined the length of the yard but did not sell yardsticks, the government defined the unit of value but let private organizations provide the means of payment.

During the Civil War, however, the government issued the first federal paper currency, the greenback. It functioned as both the unit of value and the major means of payment until 1879. Then the government got out of the business of money creation for a few decades. During that time, currency was once again issued by private banks. But in 1913, a new institution called the **Federal Reserve System** was created to be the national monetary authority in the United States. The Federal Reserve was charged with creating and regulating the nation's supply of money, and it continues to do so today.

Federal Reserve System
The central bank and national monetary authority of the United States.

Why Paper Currency Is Accepted as a Means of Payment

You may be wondering why people are willing to accept paper dollars—or the promise of paper dollars—as a means of payment. Why should a farmer give up a chicken, or a manufacturer give up a new car, just to receive a bunch of green rectangles with words printed on them? In fact, paper currency is a relatively recent development in the history of the means of payment.

The earliest means of payment were precious metals and other valuable commodities such as furs or jewels. These were called *commodity money* because they had important uses other than as a means of payment. The non-money use is what gave commodity money its ultimate value. For example, people would accept furs as payment because furs could be used to keep warm. Similarly, gold and silver had a variety of uses in industry, as religious artifacts, and for ornamentation.

Precious metals were an especially popular form of commodity money. Eventually, to make it easier to identify the value of precious metals, they were minted into coins whose weight was declared on their faces. Because gold and silver coins could be melted down into pure metal and used in other ways, they were still commodity money.

Commodity money eventually gave way to paper currency. Initially, paper currency was just a certificate representing a certain amount of gold or silver held by a bank. At any time, the holder of a certificate could go to the bank that issued it and trade the certificate for the stated amount of gold or silver. People were willing to accept paper money as a means of payment for two reasons. First, the currency could be exchanged for a valuable commodity like gold or silver. Second, the issuer—either a government or a bank—could print new money only when it acquired additional gold or silver. This put strict limits on money printing, so people had faith that their paper money would retain its value in the marketplace.

But today, paper currency is no longer backed by gold or any other physical commodity. If you have a dollar handy, put this book down and take a close look at the bill. You will not find on it any promise that you can trade your dollar for gold, silver, furs, or anything else. Yet we all accept it as a means of payment. Why?

A clue is provided by the statement in the upper left-hand corner of every bill: *This note is legal tender for all debts, public and private.* The statement affirms that the piece of paper in your hands will be accepted as a means of payment (you can "tender" it to settle any "debt, public or private") by any American because the government says so. This type of currency is called **fiat money**. *Fiat*, in Latin, means "let there be," and fiat money serves as a means of payment by government declaration.

The government need not worry about enforcing this declaration. The real force behind the dollar—and the reason that we are all willing to accept these green pieces of paper as payment—is its long-standing acceptability by *others*. As long as you have confidence that you can use your dollars to buy goods and services, you won't mind giving up goods and services for dollars. And because everyone else feels the same way, the circle of acceptability is completed.

But while the government can declare that paper currency is to be accepted as a means of payment, it cannot declare the terms. Whether 10 gallons of gas will cost you 1 dollar, 10 dollars, or 20 dollars is up to the marketplace. The value of the

© PHOTODISC/GETTY IMAGES

Today, dollars are not backed by gold or silver, but we accept them as payment because we know that others will accept them from us.

Fiat money Anything that serves as a means of payment by government declaration.

dollar—its purchasing power—does change from year to year, as reflected in the changing prices of the things we buy. In the rest of this chapter, we will discuss some of the problems created by the dollar's changing value and the difficulty economists have measuring and monitoring the changes. We postpone until later chapters the question of *why* the value of the dollar changes from year to year.

MEASURING THE PRICE LEVEL AND INFLATION

Price level The average level of prices in the economy.

One hundred years ago, you could buy a pound of coffee for 15 cents, see a Broadway play for 40 cents, buy a new suit for $6, and attend a private college for $200 in yearly tuition.[1] Needless to say, the price of each of these items has gone up considerably since then. Microeconomic causes—changes in individual markets—can explain only a tiny fraction of these price changes. For the most part, these price rises came about because of a continually rising **price level**—the average level of dollar prices in the economy. In this section, we begin to explore how the price level is measured and how this measurement is used.

Index Numbers

Index A series of numbers used to track a variable's rise or fall over time.

Most measures of the price level are reported in the form of an **index**—a series of numbers, each one representing a different period. Index numbers are meaningful only in a *relative* sense: We compare one period's index number with that of another period and can quickly see which one is larger and by what percentage. But the actual value of an index number for a particular period has no meaning in and of itself.

In general, an index number for any measure is calculated as

$$\frac{\text{Value of measure in current period}}{\text{Value of measure in base period}} \times 100.$$

Let's see how index numbers work with a simple example. Suppose we want to measure how violence on TV has changed over time, and we have data on the number of violent acts shown in each of several years. We could then construct a TV-violence index. Our first step would be to choose a *base period*—a period to be used as a benchmark. Let's choose 1996 as our base period, and suppose that there were 10,433 violent acts on television in that year. Then our violence index in any current year would be calculated as

$$\frac{\text{Number of violent acts in current year}}{10,433} \times 100.$$

In 1996, the base year, the index will have the value $(10,433/10,433) \times 100 = 100$. Look again at the general formula for index numbers, and you will see that this is always true: *An index will always equal 100 in the base period.*

Now let's calculate the value of our index in another year. If there were 14,534 violent acts in 2000, then the index that year would have the value

$$\frac{14,534}{10,433} \times 100 = 139.3.$$

Index numbers compress and simplify information so that we can see how things are changing at a glance. Our media violence index, for example, tells us at a glance

[1] Scott Derks, ed., *The Value of the Dollar: Prices and Incomes in the United States: 1860–1989* (Detroit, MI: Gale Research Inc., 1994), various pages.

that the number of violent acts in 2000 was 139.3 percent of the number in 1996. Or, more simply, TV violence grew by 39.3 percent between 1996 and 2000.

The Consumer Price Index

The most widely used measure of the price level in the United States is the **Consumer Price Index (CPI)**. This index, which is designed to track the prices paid by the typical consumer, is compiled and reported by the Bureau of Labor Statistics (BLS).

Consumer Price Index An index of the cost, through time, of a fixed market basket of goods purchased by a typical household in some base period.

Measuring the prices paid by the typical consumer is not easy. Two problems must be solved before we even begin. The first problem is to decide which goods and services we should include in our average. The CPI tracks only *consumer* prices; it excludes goods and services that are not directly purchased by consumers. More specifically, the CPI excludes goods purchased by businesses (such as capital equipment, raw materials, or wholesale goods), goods and services purchased by government agencies (such as fighter-bombers and the services of police officers), and goods and services purchased by foreigners (U.S. exports). The CPI *does* include newly produced consumer goods and services that are part of consumption spending in our GDP—things such as new clothes, new furniture, new cars, haircuts, and restaurant meals. It also includes some things that are *not* part of our GDP but that are part of the typical family's budget. For example, the CPI includes prices for *used* goods such as used cars or used books, and imports from other countries—for example, French cheese, Japanese cars, and Mexican tomatoes.

The second problem is how to combine all the different prices into an average price level. In any given month, different prices will change by different amounts. The average price of doctor's visits might rise by 1 percent, the price of blue jeans might rise by a tenth of a percent, the price of milk might fall by half a percent, and so on. When prices change at different rates, and when some are rising while others are falling, how can we track the change in the *average* price level? It would be a mistake to use a simple average of all prices, adding them up and dividing by the number of goods. A proper measure must recognize that we spend very little of our incomes on some goods—such as Tabasco sauce—and much more on others—like car repairs or rent.

The CPI's approach is to track the cost of the *CPI market basket*—the collection of goods and services that the typical consumer bought in some base period. If the market basket's cost rises by 10 percent over some period, then the price level, as reported by the CPI, will rise by 10 percent. This way, goods and services that are relatively unimportant in the typical consumer's budget will have little weight in the CPI. Tabasco sauce could triple in price and have no noticeable impact on the cost of the complete market basket. Goods that are more important—such as auto repairs or rent—will have more weight.

In recent years, the base year[2] for the CPI has been 1983, so, following our general formula for price indexes, the CPI is calculated as

$$\frac{\text{Cost of market basket in current year}}{\text{Cost of market basket in 1983}} \times 100.$$

The appendix in this chapter discusses the calculation of the CPI in more detail.

[2] To be more specific: The typical consumer's market basket (used to determine the weights to apply to each good) is periodically updated. Currently, for example, the CPI uses information from its 2002 survey of consumer spending habits to determine the proper weights. But the BLS continues to use July 1983 as its official base period; that is, the value of the CPI is still set at 100 for July 1983.

Year	Consumer Price Index (December)
1970	39.8
1975	55.6
1980	86.4
1985	109.5
1990	134.2
1995	153.9
2000	174.6
2001	177.3
2002	181.6

How the CPI Has Behaved

Table 1 shows the actual value of the CPI for December of selected years. Because it is reported in index number form, we can easily see how much the price level has changed over different time intervals. In December 2002, for example, the CPI had a value of 181.6, telling us that the typical market basket in that year cost 81.6 percent more than it would have cost in the July 1983 base period. In December 1970, the CPI was 39.8, so the cost of the market basket in that year was only 39.8 percent of its cost in July 1983. In July 1983 (not shown), the CPI's value was 100.

From Price Index to Inflation Rate

Inflation rate The percent change in the price level from one period to the next.

Deflation A *decrease* in the price level from one period to the next.

The Consumer Price Index is a measure of the price *level* in the economy. The **inflation rate** measures how fast the price level is changing, as a percentage rate. When the price level is rising, as it almost always is, the inflation rate is positive. When the price level is falling, as it did during the Great Depression, we have negative inflation, which is called **deflation.**

Figure 1 shows the U.S. rate of inflation, as measured by the CPI, since 1950. For each year, the inflation rate is calculated as the percentage change in the CPI from December of the previous year to December of that year. For example, the CPI in December 2000 was 174.6, and in December 2001 it was 177.3. The inflation rate for 2001 was $(177.3 - 174.6)/174.6 = 0.015$ or 1.5 percent. Notice that inflation was low in the 1950s and 1960s, was high in the 1970s and early 1980s, and has been low since then. In later chapters, you will learn what causes the inflation rate to rise and fall.

How the CPI Is Used

The CPI is the most important and widely used measure of prices in United States. It is used in three ways:

> *More specifically, as a Policy Target.* In the introductory macroeconomics chapter, we saw that price stability—or a low inflation rate—is one of the nation's important macroeconomic goals. The measure most often used to gauge our success in achieving low inflation is the CPI.

> *To Index Payments.* A payment is **indexed** when it is set by a formula so that it rises and falls proportionally with a price index. An indexed payment makes up for the loss in purchasing power that occurs when the price level rises. It raises the nominal payment by just enough to keep its purchasing power unchanged. In the United States, 52 million Social Security recipients and government retirees have their benefit payments indexed to the CPI. About one-quarter of all union members—more than 2 million workers—have labor contracts that index their wages to the CPI. Since 1985, the U.S. income tax has been indexed as well: the threshold income levels at which tax rates change automatically rise at the same rate as the CPI. And the government now sells

Indexation Adjusting the value of some nominal payment in proportion to a price index, in order to keep the real payment unchanged.

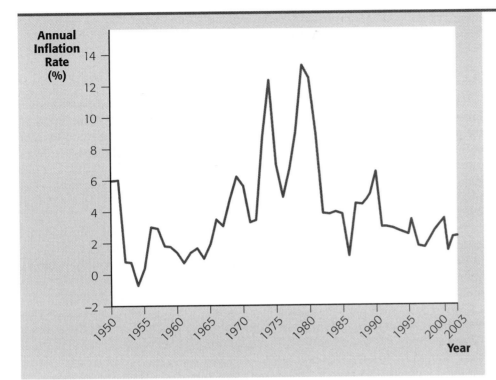

FIGURE 1
The Rate of Inflation Using the Consumer Price Index, 1950–2003

bonds that are indexed to the CPI. The owner of an indexed bond receives a payment each year to make up for the loss of purchasing power when the CPI rises.

To Translate from Nominal to Real Values. In order to compare economic values from different periods, we must translate *nominal variables,* measured in the number of dollars, into *real variables,* which are adjusted for the change in the dollar's purchasing power. The CPI is often used for this translation. Since calculating real variables is one of the most important uses of the CPI, we devote the next section to that topic.

HTTP://

You can find the latest information on the CPI at
http://www.bls.gov/bls/ newsrels.htm—the Bureau of Labor Statistics Web site.

Real Variables and Adjustment for Inflation

Suppose that from December 2004 to December 2005, your nominal wage—what you are paid in dollars—rises from $15 to $30 per hour. Are you better off? That depends. You are earning twice as many dollars. But you should care not about how many green pieces of paper you earn, but how many goods and services you can buy with that paper. How, then, can we tell what happened to your purchasing power? By focusing not on the *nominal wage,* (the number of *dollars* you earn) but on the *real wage,* (the *purchasing power* of your wage). To track your real wage, we need to look at the number of dollars you earn *relative to the price level.*

Since the "typical worker" and the "typical consumer" are pretty

Rising Prices Versus Rising Inflation People often confuse the statement "prices are rising" with the statement "inflation is rising," but they do not mean the same thing. Remember that the inflation rate is the *rate of change* of the price level. To have rising inflation, the price level must be rising by a greater and greater percentage each period. But we can also have rising prices and *falling* inflation. For example, from 1996 to 1998, the CPI rose each year: "Prices were rising." But they rose by a smaller percentage each year than the year before, so "inflation was falling"—from 3.4 percent in 1996 to 1.7 percent in 1997 and to 1.6 percent in 1998.

DANGEROUS CURVES

much the same, the CPI is usually the price index used to calculate the real wage. The real-wage formula is as follows:

$$\text{Real wage in any year} = \frac{\text{Nominal wage in that year}}{\text{CPI in that year}} \times 100.$$

To see that this formula makes sense, let's go back to our fictional example: From 2004 to 2005, your nominal wage doubles from $15 to $30. Now, suppose the price of everything that you buy doubles at the same time. It is easy to see that in this case, your purchasing power would remain unchanged. And that is just what our formula tells us: If prices double, the CPI doubles as well. With 2004 as our base year, the CPI would increase from 100 in 2004 to 200 in the year 2005. The *real* wage would be ($15/100) $\times 100$ = $15 in 2004 and ($30/200) $\times 100$ = $15 in 2005. The real wage would remain unchanged.

Now suppose that prices doubled between 2004 and 2005, but your nominal wage remained unchanged at $15. In this case, your purchasing power would be cut in half. You'd have the same number of dollars, but each one would buy half as much as it did before. Our formula gives us a real wage of ($15/100) $\times 100$ = $15 in 2004 and ($15/200) $\times 100$ = $7.50 in 2005. The real wage falls by half.

Now look at Table 2, which shows the average hourly earnings of wage earners over the past four decades. In the first two columns, you can see that the average American wage earner was paid $4.87 per hour in December 1975, and more than triple that—$15.20—in December 2002. Does this mean the average hourly worker was paid more in 2002 than in 1975? In *dollars,* the answer is clearly yes. But what about in *purchasing power?* Or, using the new terminology you've learned: What happened to the *real wage* over this period?

Let's see. We know that the *nominal wage* rose from $4.87 in 1975 to $15.20 in 2002. But, according to the table, the CPI rose from 55.6 to 181.6 over the same period. Using our formula, we find that

$$\text{Real wage in 1975} = \frac{\$4.87}{55.6} \times 100 = \$8.76.$$

$$\text{Real wage in 2002} = \frac{\$15.20}{181.6} \times 100 = \$8.37.$$

Thus, although the average worker earned more *dollars* in 2002 than in 1975, when we use the CPI as our measure of prices, her purchasing power seems to have fallen over those years. *Why* this apparent decline in purchasing power? This is an interesting and important question, and one we'll begin to answer later in the chapter. The important point to remember here is that

> *when we measure changes in the macroeconomy, we usually care not about the number of dollars we are counting, but the purchasing power those dollars represent. Thus, we translate nominal values into real values using the formula*
>
> $$\text{real value} = \frac{\text{nominal value}}{\text{price index}} \times 100.$$

This formula, usually using the CPI as the price index, is how most real values in the economy are calculated. But there is one important exception: To calculate real GDP, the government uses a different procedure, to which we now turn.

Year	Nominal Wage, Dollars per Hour	CPI	Real Wage in 1983 Dollars per Hour
1970	3.50	39.8	8.79
1975	4.87	55.6	8.76
1980	7.12	86.4	8.24
1985	8.86	109.5	8.09
1990	10.33	134.2	7.70
1995	11.79	153.9	7.66
2000	14.26	174.6	8.17
2001	14.73	177.3	8.31
2002	15.20	181.6	8.37

TABLE 2

Nominal and Real Wages (in December of Each Year)

Source: Bureau of Labor Statistics, Statistical Tables, *http://www.bls.gov/data/*, accessed on July 31, 2003. Wage and CPI data for December of each year. Nominal wage: average hourly earnings of production or nonsupervisory workers in nonfarm private sector CPI: CPI-All Urban Consumers.

Inflation and the Measurement of Real GDP

In the previous chapter, we discussed the difference between nominal GDP and real GDP. After reading this chapter, you might think that real GDP is calculated just like the real wage: dividing nominal GDP by the Consumer Price Index. But the Consumer Price Index is *not* used to calculate real GDP. Instead, a special price index—which we can call the **GDP price index**—is used.

The most important differences between the CPI and the GDP price index are in the types of goods and services covered by each index. First, the GDP price index *includes* some prices that the CPI ignores. In particular, while the CPI tracks only the prices of goods bought by American *consumers*, the GDP price index must also include the prices of goods purchased by the government, investment goods purchased by businesses, and exports, which are purchased by foreigners.

Second, the GDP price index *excludes* some prices that are part of the CPI. In particular, the GDP price index leaves out used goods and imports, both of which are included in the CPI. This makes sense, because while used goods and imports are part of the typical consumer's market basket, they do not contribute to current U.S. GDP.

We can summarize the chief difference between the CPI and the GDP price index this way:

GDP price index An index of the price level for all final goods and services included in GDP.

> *The GDP price index measures the prices of all goods and services that are included in U.S. GDP, while the CPI measures the prices of all goods and services bought by U.S. households.*[3]

THE COSTS OF INFLATION

A high rate of inflation—whether it is measured by the CPI or the GDP price index—is never welcome news. What's so bad about inflation? As we've seen, it certainly

[3] The technical name for the GDP price index is the *chain-type annual weights GDP price index*. It differs from the CPI not only in goods covered, but also in its mathematical formula.

makes your task as an economics student more difficult: Rather than taking nominal variables at face value, you must do those troublesome calculations to convert them into real variables.

But inflation causes much more trouble than this. It can impose costs on society and on each of us individually. Yet when most people are asked *what* the cost of inflation is, they come up with an incorrect answer.

The Inflation Myth

Most people think that inflation, merely by making goods and services more expensive, erodes the average purchasing power of income in the economy. The reason for this belief is easy to see: The higher the price level, the fewer goods and services a given nominal income will buy. It stands to reason, then, that inflation—which raises prices—must be destroying the purchasing power of our incomes. Right?

Actually, this statement is mostly wrong.

To see why, remember that every market transaction involves *two* parties—a buyer and a seller. When a price rises, buyers of that good must pay more but sellers get more revenue when they sell it. The loss in buyers' real income is matched by the rise in sellers' real income. Inflation may *redistribute* purchasing power among the population, but it does not change the *average* purchasing power, when we include both buyers and sellers in the average.

In fact, most people in the economy participate on both sides of the market. On the one hand, they are consumers—as when they shop for food or clothing or furniture. On the other hand, they work in business firms that *sell* products, and may benefit (in the form of higher wages or higher profits) when their firms' revenues rise. Thus, when prices rise, a particular person may find that her purchasing power has either risen or fallen, depending on whether she is affected more as a seller or as a buyer. But regardless of the outcome for individuals, our conclusion remains the same:

> *Inflation can redistribute purchasing power from one group to another, but it does not directly decrease the average real income in the economy.*

Why, then, do people continue to believe that inflation robs the average citizen of real income? Largely because real incomes sometimes do decline—for *other* reasons. Inflation—while not the *cause* of the decline—will often be the *mechanism* that brings it about. Just as we often blame the messenger for bringing bad news, so too, we often blame inflation for lowering our purchasing power when the real cause lies elsewhere.

Let's consider an example. In Table 2, notice the decline in real wages during the late 1970s. The real wage fell from $8.76 in 1975 to $8.24 in 1980, a decline of about 6 percent. During this period, not only wage earners, but also salaried workers, small-business owners, and corporate shareholders all suffered a decline in their real incomes. What caused the decline?

There were several reasons, but one of the most important was the dramatic rise in the price of imported oil—from $3 per barrel in 1973 to $34 in 1981, an increase of more than 1,000 percent. The higher price for oil meant that oil-exporting countries, like Saudi Arabia, Kuwait, and Iraq, got more goods and services for each barrel of oil they supplied to the rest of the world, including the United States. But with these countries claiming more of America's output, less remained for the typical American. That is, the typical American family had to suffer a decline in real income. As always, a rise in price shifted income from buyers to sellers. But in this case, the sellers were *foreigners*, while the buyers were Americans. Thus, the rise in the price of foreign oil caused average purchasing power in the United States to decline.

But what was the mechanism that brought about the decline? Since real income is equal to (nominal income/price index) × 100, it can decrease in one of two ways: a fall in the numerator (nominal income) or a rise in the denominator (the price index). The decline in real income in the 1970s came entirely from an increase in the denominator. (Look back at Figure 1. You can see that this period of declining real wages in the United States was also a period of unusually high inflation; at its peak in 1979, the inflation rate exceeded 13 percent.) As a result, most workers blamed *inflation* for their loss of purchasing power. But inflation was not the cause; it was just the *mechanism*. The cause was a change in the terms of trade between the United States and the oil-exporting countries—a change that resulted in higher oil prices.

To summarize, the common idea that inflation imposes a cost on society by directly decreasing average real income in the economy is incorrect. But inflation *does* impose costs on society, as the next section shows.

The Redistributive Cost of Inflation

One cost of inflation is that it often redistributes purchasing power *within* society. But because the winners and losers are chosen haphazardly—rather than by conscious social policy—the redistribution of purchasing power is not generally desirable. In some cases, the shift in purchasing power is downright perverse—harming the needy and helping those who are already well off.

How does inflation sometimes redistribute real income? An increase in the price level reduces the purchasing power of any payment that is specified in nominal terms. For example, some workers have contracts that set their nominal wage for two or three years, regardless of any future inflation. The nationally set minimum wage, too, is set for several years and specified in nominal dollars. Under these circumstances, inflation can harm ordinary workers, since it erodes the purchasing power of their prespecified nominal wage. Real income is redistributed from these workers to their employers, who benefit by paying a lower real wage.

But the effect can also work the other way: benefiting ordinary households and harming businesses. For example, many homeowners sign fixed-dollar mortgage agreements with a bank. These are promises to pay the bank the same nominal sum each month. Inflation can reduce the *real* value of these payments, thus redistributing purchasing power away from the bank and toward the average homeowner.

In general,

> *inflation can shift purchasing power away from those who are awaiting future payments specified in dollars, and toward those who are obligated to make such payments.*

But does inflation *always* redistribute income from one party in a contract to another? Actually, no; if the inflation is *expected* by both parties, it should not redistribute income. The next section explains why.

Expected Inflation Need *Not* Shift Purchasing Power. Suppose a labor union is negotiating a three-year contract with an employer, and both sides agree that each year, workers should get a 3 percent increase in their *real wage*. Labor contracts, like most other contracts, are usually specified in nominal terms: The firm will agree to give workers so many additional *dollars per hour* each year. If neither side anticipates any inflation, they should simply negotiate a 3 percent *nominal* wage hike. With an unchanged price level, the *real* wage would then also rise by the desired 3 percent.

But suppose instead that both sides anticipate 10 percent inflation each year for the next three years. Then, they must agree to *more* than a 3 percent nominal wage increase in order to raise the real wage by 3 percent. How much more?

We can answer this question with a simple mathematical rule:

> *Over any period, the percentage change in a real value (%∆Real) is approximately equal to the percentage change in the associated nominal value (%∆Nominal) minus the rate of inflation:*
>
> $$\%\Delta\text{Real} = \%\Delta\text{Nominal} - \text{Rate of inflation.}$$

If the inflation rate is 10 percent and the real wage is to rise by 3 percent, then the change in the nominal wage must (approximately) satisfy the equation

$$3 \text{ percent} = \%\Delta\text{Nominal} - 10 \text{ percent} \Rightarrow \%\Delta\text{Nominal} = 13 \text{ percent.}$$

The required nominal wage hike is 13 percent.

You can see that as long as both sides correctly anticipate the inflation, and no one stops them from negotiating a 13 percent nominal wage hike, inflation will *not* affect either party in real terms:

> *If inflation is fully anticipated, and if both parties take it into account, then inflation will not redistribute purchasing power.*

We come to a similar conclusion about contracts between lenders and borrowers. When you lend someone money, you receive a reward—an interest payment—for letting that person use your money instead of spending it yourself. The annual *interest rate* is the interest payment divided by the amount of money you have lent. For example, if you lend someone $1,000 and receive back $1,040 one year later, then your interest is $40, and the interest *rate* on the loan is $40/$1,000 = 0.04, or 4 percent.

Nominal interest rate The annual percent increase in a lender's dollars from making a loan.

Real interest rate The annual percent increase in a lender's purchasing power from making a loan.

But there are actually *two* interest rates associated with every loan. One is the **nominal interest rate**—the percentage increase in the lender's *dollars* from making the loan. The other is the **real interest rate**—the percentage increase in the lender's *purchasing power* from making the loan. It is the *real* rate—the change in purchasing power—that lenders and borrowers should care about.

In the absence of inflation, real and nominal interest rates would always be equal. A 4 percent increase in the lender's *dollars* would always imply a 4 percent increase in her purchasing power. But if there is inflation, it will reduce the purchasing power of the money paid back. Does this mean that inflation redistributes purchasing power? Not if the inflation is correctly anticipated, and if there are no restrictions on making loan contracts.

For example, suppose both parties anticipate inflation of 5 percent and want to arrange a contract whereby the lender will be paid a 4 percent *real* interest rate. What *nominal* interest rate should they choose? Since an interest rate is the *percentage change* in the lender's funds, we can use our approximation rule,

$$\%\Delta\text{Real} = \%\Delta\text{Nominal} - \text{Rate of inflation,}$$

which here becomes

$$\%\Delta \text{ in Lender's purchasing power} = \%\Delta \text{ in Lender's dollars} - \text{Rate of inflation}$$

or

$$\text{Real interest rate} = \text{Nominal interest rate} - \text{Rate of inflation.}$$

In our example, where we want the real interest rate to equal 4 percent when the inflation rate is 5 percent, we must have

$$4 \text{ percent} = \text{Nominal interest rate} - 5 \text{ percent}$$

or

$$\text{Nominal interest rate} = 9 \text{ percent.}$$

Once again, we see that as long as both parties correctly anticipate the inflation rate, and face no restrictions on contracts (that is, they are free to set the nominal interest rate at 9 percent), then no one gains or loses.

When inflation is *not* correctly anticipated, however, our conclusion is very different.

Unexpected Inflation *Does* Shift Purchasing Power. Suppose that, expecting no inflation, you agree to lend money at a 4 percent nominal interest rate for one year. You and the borrower think that this will translate into a 4 percent real rate. But it turns out you are both wrong: The price level actually rises by 3 percent, so the *real* interest rate ends up being 4 percent − 3 percent = 1 percent. As a lender, you have given up the use of your money for the year, expecting to be rewarded with a 4 percent increase in purchasing power. But you get only a 1 percent increase. Your borrower was willing to pay 4 percent in purchasing power, but ends up paying only 1 percent. *Unexpected* inflation has led to a better deal for your borrower and a worse deal for you, the lender.

That will not make you happy. But it could be even worse. Suppose the inflation rate is higher—say, 6 percent. Then your real interest rate ends up at 4 percent − 6 percent = −2 percent, a negative real interest rate. You get back *less* in purchasing power than you lend out—*paying* (in purchasing power) for the privilege of lending out your money. The borrower is *rewarded* (in purchasing power) for borrowing!

Negative real interest rates like this are not just a theoretical possibility. In the late 1970s, when inflation was higher than expected for several years in a row, many borrowers ending up paying negative real interest rates to lenders.

Now, let's consider one more possibility: Expected inflation is 6 percent, so you negotiate a 10 percent nominal rate, thinking this will translate to a 4 percent real rate. But the actual inflation rate turns out to be zero, so the real interest rate is 10 percent − 0 percent = 10 percent. In this case, inflation turns out to be *less* than expected, so the *real* interest rate is higher than either of you anticipated. The borrower is harmed and you (the lender) benefit.

These examples apply, more generally, to any agreement on future payments: to a worker waiting for a wage payment and the employer who has promised to pay it; to a doctor who has sent out a bill and the patient who has not yet paid it; or to a supplier who has delivered goods and his customer who hasn't yet paid for them.

> *When inflationary expectations are inaccurate, purchasing power is shifted between those obliged to make future payments and those waiting to be paid. An inflation rate higher than expected harms those awaiting payment and benefits the payers; an inflation rate lower than expected harms the payers and benefits those awaiting payment.*

The Resource Cost of Inflation

In addition to its possible redistribution of income, inflation imposes another cost upon society. To cope with inflation, we are forced to use up time and other resources as we go about our daily economic activities (shopping, selling, saving) that we could otherwise have devoted to productive activities. Thus, inflation imposes an *opportunity cost* on society as a whole and on each of its members:

> *When people must spend time and other resources coping with inflation, they pay an opportunity cost—they sacrifice the goods and services those resources could have produced instead.*

Let's first consider the resources used up by *consumers* to cope with inflation. Suppose you shop for clothes twice a year. You've discovered that both The Gap and Banana Republic sell clothing of similar quality and have similar service, and you naturally want to shop at the one with the lower prices. If there is no inflation, your task is easy: You shop first at The Gap and then at Banana Republic; thereafter, you rely on your memory to determine which is less expensive.

With inflation, however, things are more difficult. Suppose you find that prices at Banana Republic are higher than you remember them to be at The Gap. It may be that Banana Republic is the more expensive store, or it may be that prices have risen at *both* stores. How can you tell? Only a trip back to The Gap will answer the question—a trip that will cost you extra time and trouble. If prices are rising very rapidly, you may have to visit both stores on the same day to be sure which one is cheaper. Now, multiply this time and trouble by all the different types of shopping you must do on a regular or occasional basis—for groceries, an apartment, a car, concert tickets, compact discs, restaurant meals, and more. Inflation can make you use up valuable time—time you could have spent earning income or enjoying leisure activities. True, if you shop for some of these items on the Internet, you can compare prices in less time, but not zero time. And most shopping is *not* done over the Internet.

Inflation also forces *sellers* to use up resources. First, remember that sellers of goods and services are also buyers of resources and intermediate goods. They, too, must do comparison shopping when there is inflation, which uses up hired labor time. Second, each time sellers raise prices, labor is needed to put new price tags on merchandise, to enter new prices into a computer scanning system, to update the HTML code on a Web page, or to change the prices on advertising brochures, menus, and so on.

Finally, inflation makes us all use up resources managing our financial affairs. When the inflation rate is high, we'll try to keep our funds in accounts that pay high nominal interest rates, in order to preserve our purchasing power. And we'll try to keep as little as possible in cash or in low-interest checking accounts. Of course, this means more frequent trips to the bank or the automatic teller machine, to transfer money into our checking accounts or get cash each time we need it.

All of these additional activities—inspecting prices at several stores or Web sites, changing price tags or price entries, going back and forth to the automatic teller machine—use up not only time, but other resources, too, such as gasoline, paper, or the wear and tear on your computer. From society's point of view, these resources could have been used to produce *other* goods and services that we'd enjoy.

You may not have thought much about the resource cost of inflation, because in recent years, U.S. inflation has been so low—averaging about 3 percent during the 1990s, and about $2\frac{1}{2}$ percent in the early 2000s. Such a low rate of inflation is often called *creeping inflation;* from week to week or month to month, the price level creeps up so slowly that we hardly notice the change. The cost of coping with creeping inflation is negligible. And (as you'll see in a later chapter) low, creeping inflation may actually be good for the economy.

But it has not always been this way. Three times during the last 50 years, we have had double-digit inflation: about 14 percent during 1947–48, 12 percent in 1974, and 13 percent during 1979 and 1980. Going back farther, the annual inflation rate reached almost 20 percent during World War I and rose above 25 percent during the Civil War.

And as serious as these episodes of American inflation have been, they pale in comparison to the experiences of other countries. In Germany in the early 1920s, the inflation rate hit thousands of percent *per month.* And more recently, in the late 1980s, several South American countries experienced inflation rates in excess of 1,000 percent annually. For a few weeks in 1990, Argentina's annual inflation rate even reached 400,000 percent! Under these conditions, the monetary system breaks down almost completely. Economic life is almost as difficult as in the mythical nation of Chaotica, discussed at the very beginning of this chapter.

HTTP://

To learn more about the strengths and weaknesses of the CPI, read Allison Wallace and Brian Motley, "A Better CPI" (http://www.frbsf.org/econrsrch/wklyltr/wklyltr99/el99-05.html).

A Preliminary Word About Deflation

In the early 2000s, as the annual inflation rate approached 2 percent, a new worry appeared on the American political and economic scene: *deflation* (a *negative* inflation rate). In some respects, deflation creates costs for society similar to those of inflation. For example, when the deflation rate is not correctly anticipated, purchasing power will be redistributed between borrowers and lenders. And if the deflation rate is high (prices are *falling* rapidly), resources are used up to cope with it: Prices must be updated more frequently, using up labor and raw materials, and more consumer time will be spent on comparison shopping.

However, deflation has some special costs and risks of its own, entirely different from those of inflation. To understand what's different about deflation, some understanding of macroeconomic models is required. For this reason, we'll postpone our comprehensive discussion of deflation until Chapter 26.

▌ IS THE CPI ACCURATE?

The Bureau of Labor Statistics spends millions of dollars gathering data to ensure that its measure of inflation is accurate. To determine the market basket of the typical consumer, the BLS randomly selects thousands of households and analyzes their spending habits. In the last household survey—completed in 2002—each of about 15,000 families kept diaries of their purchases for two weeks.

But that is just the beginning. Every month, the bureau's shoppers visit 23,000 retail stores and about 50,000 housing units (rental apartments and owner-occupied homes) to record 80,000 different prices. Finally, all of the prices are combined to determine the cost of the typical consumer's market basket for the current month.

The BLS is a highly professional agency, typically headed by an economist. Billions of dollars are at stake for each 1 percent change in the CPI, and the BLS deserves high praise for keeping its measurement honest and free of political manipulation. Nevertheless, conceptual problems and resource limitations make the CPI fall short of the ideal measure of inflation. Economists—even those who work in the BLS—widely agree that the CPI overstates the U.S. inflation rate. By how much?

According to a report by an advisory committee of economists in 1996, the overall bias was at least 1.1 percent during the 1980s and early 1990s.[4] That is, in a typical year, the reported rise in the CPI was about 1 percentage point greater than the true rise in the price level. The BLS has been working hard to reduce this upward bias and—especially in the late 1990s—it made some progress. But significant bias remains.

Sources of Bias in the CPI

There are several reasons for the upward bias in the CPI.

Substitution Bias. Until recently, the CPI almost completely ignored a general principle of consumer behavior: People tend to *substitute* goods that have become relatively cheaper in place of goods that have become relatively more expensive. For example, in the seven years from 1973 to 1980, the retail price of oil-related products—like gasoline and home heating oil—increased by more than 300 percent, while the prices of most other goods and services rose by less than 100 percent. As a result, people found ways to conserve on oil products. They joined carpools, used public transportation, insulated their homes, and in many cases moved closer to their workplaces to shorten their commute. Yet throughout this period, the CPI basket—based on a survey of buying patterns in 1972–73—assumed that consumers were buying unchanged quantities of oil products.

The treatment of oil products is an example of a more general problem that has plagued the CPI for decades. Until recently, the CPI used fixed *quantities* to determine the relative importance of each item. That is, it assumed that households continued to buy each good or service in the same quantities in which they bought it during the most recent household survey—until the next household survey. Compounding the problem, the survey to determine spending patterns—and to update the market basket—was taken only about once every 10 years or so. So by the end of each 10-year period, the CPI's assumptions about spending habits could be far off the mark, as they were in the case of oil in the 1970s.

The BLS has *partially* fixed this problem, in two ways.[5] First, beginning in 2002, it began updating the market basket with a household survey every *two* years instead of every 10 years. This is widely considered an important improvement in CPI measurement.

Second, since January 1999, the CPI has no longer assumed that the typical consumer continues to buy the same *quantity* of each good that he bought in the last household "market basket" survey. Instead, the CPI now assumes that when a good's relative price rises by 10 percent, consumers buy 10 percent less of it, and switch their purchases to other goods whose prices are rising more slowly.

However, this is only a partial fix. The CPI still only recognizes the possibility of such substitution *within* categories of goods and *not among* them. For example, if the price of steak rises relative to the price of hamburger meat, the CPI now assumes that consumers will substitute away from steak and toward hamburger meat, since both are in the same category: *beef*. However, if the price of all beef products

---

[4] See *Toward a More Accurate Measure of the Cost of Living*, Report to the Senate Finance Committee from the Advisory Commission to Study the Consumer Price Index, December 1996.

[5] For a discussion of these and other recent changes in the CPI, see "Planned Change in the Consumer Price Index Formula," Bureau of Labor Statistics, April 16, 1998 (*http://stats.bls.gov/cpigm02.htm*), and "Future Schedule for Expenditure Weight Updates in the Consumer Price Index," Bureau of Labor Statistics, December 18, 1998 (*http://stats.bls.gov/cpiupdt.htm*).

rises relative to chicken and pork, the CPI assumes that there is *no* substitution at all from beef toward chicken and pork. As a result, beef products still would be overweighted in the CPI until the next survey.

Although the BLS has partially fixed the problem, the CPI still suffers from substitution bias. That is, categories of goods whose prices are rising most rapidly tend to be given exaggerated importance in the CPI, and categories of goods whose prices are rising most slowly tend to be given too little importance in the CPI.

New Technologies. Brand-new technologies are another source of upward bias in the CPI. One problem is that goods using new technologies are introduced into the BLS market basket only after a lag. These goods often drop rapidly in price after they are introduced, helping to balance out price rises in other goods. By excluding a category of goods whose prices are dropping, the CPI overstates the rate of inflation. For example, even though many consumers were buying and using cellular phones throughout the 1990s, they were not included in the BLS basket of goods until 1998. As a result, the CPI missed the rapid decline in the price of cell phones. Now that the market basket of the typical consumer is updated every two years instead of every 10, this source of bias has been reduced but not completely eliminated.

But there is another issue with new technologies: They often offer consumers a lower-cost alternative for obtaining the same service. For example, the introduction of cable television lowered the cost of entertainment significantly by offering a new, cheaper alternative to going out to see movies. This should have registered as a drop in the price of "seeing movies." But the CPI does not have any good way to measure this reduction in the cost of living. Instead, it treats cable television as an entirely separate service.

The CPI excludes new products that tend to drop in price when they first come on the market. When included, the CPI regards them as entirely separate from existing goods and services, instead of recognizing that they lower the cost of achieving a given standard of living. The result is an overestimate of the inflation rate.

Changes in Quality. Many products are improving over time. Cars are much more reliable than they used to be and require much less routine maintenance. They have features like air bags and antilock brakes that were unknown in the early 1980s. The BLS struggles to deal with these changes. As far back as 1967, it has recognized that when the price of a car rises, some of that price hike is not really inflation but instead the result of charging more because the consumer was *getting* more. In recent years, the BLS has adopted some routine statistical procedures to automatically adjust price changes for quality improvements for a variety of goods. Table 3 lists some important examples, along with the year that the CPI began measuring and adjusting for quality improvements.

Two things stand out in the table. First, for many of the goods, quality adjustment began very late, *after* huge advances in quality had already taken place. Up until that time, the CPI treated any price hike as pure inflation, thus contributing to an overestimate of the overall inflation rate. Second, while the list of goods in the table is impressive (and growing), most goods do *not* get this special treatment. For

TABLE 3
Goods Adjusted for Quality Changes in the CPI

Prices Adjusted for Quality Changes	Year Adjustment Began
Cars	1967
Used Cars	1987
Clothing	1991
Gasoline	1994
Personal Computers	1998
Televisions	1999
VCRs & DVD Players	2000
Refrigerators, Microwaves, Washing Machines	2000
College Textbooks	2000

Sources: "Program Report," *Monthly Labor Review,* May 2002, p. 47; and various BLS publications.

most goods, improvements in quality are effectively ignored.

Take the Internet. Every year, it offers more information and entertainment content, a greater number of retailers from which to buy things, and faster and more intelligent search engines to help you find it all. Yet, the Internet—which was introduced into the CPI in 1998—has been treated as a good whose quality has not changed. If the price of Internet service rises, the CPI considers it inflation rather than paying more to *get* more. And if the price stays the same, the CPI ignores the *decrease* in the cost per unit of available content and treats the price as unchanged.

The CPI still counts as inflation many cases in which prices rise because of quality improvements. This causes the CPI to overstate the inflation rate.

Growth in Discounting. The CPI treats toothpaste bought at a high-priced drugstore and toothpaste bought at Wal-Mart or Drugstore. com as different products. And it assumes that we continue to buy from high- and low-priced stores in unchanged proportions. But that is not what has been happening. In fact, Americans are buying more and more of their toothpaste and other products from discounters, but the CPI does not consider this in measuring inflation. The purchasing power you have lost from inflation is not as great as the CPI says if you, like most Americans, are stretching your dollar by going more often to discount outlets, warehouse stores, and Web sites with low prices.

© SUSAN VAN ETTEN

USING THE THEORY
The Use and Misuse of an Imperfect CPI

The inaccuracies in measuring the Consumer Price Index discussed in the chapter, as well as an even more important conceptual issue to be discussed below, suggest that the CPI should be used and interpreted with great care. Unfortunately, the CPI is often used for purposes which it cannot handle accurately.

Indexing

Earlier in the chapter, we pointed out that more than 50 million Social Security recipients and other retirees, as well as 2 million workers, have their benefits *indexed* to the CPI: Their nominal (dollar) benefits automatically increase at the same rate as the CPI. The justification for indexing is to protect these people from any deterioration in living standards caused by inflation. But because changes in the CPI *overstate* inflation, these beneficiaries are *over*indexed. That is, their nominal benefit rises by a greater percentage than a more accurately measured price index would rise.

Let's take an example. Suppose that a Social Security recipient who retired in 1980 was promised $1,000 per month in Social Security benefits, indexed to the CPI each year. But suppose that each year from 1980 to 2002 (the period of retirement) the CPI *overstated* the annual rate of inflation by 1 percent. Then every year, the recipient receives 1 percent more in dollars than needed to maintain the *purchasing power* of the benefit, so the real benefit rises by 1 percent every year. At the end of the first year, the real payment is $1,000 \times 1.01 = 1010. For the second year, it's $[$1,000 \times 1.01] \times 1.01 = $1 \times (1.01)^2 = $1,020.10$. And at the end of the 22nd year, it's $1,000 \times (1.01)^{22} = $1,245$. Rather than just maintaining the real Social Security payment over time, indexing to the inaccurate CPI results in a continually rising *real* benefit, one that is 24 percent higher than in the initial period.

This will suit Social Security recipients just fine. And it may suit the rest of us too—when the economy is growing at a rapid pace. After all, why shouldn't retirees get a larger slice of the economic pie when the pie itself is growing rapidly and everyone else's slice is growing as well? But note that the increase in real benefits happens *automatically,* due to overindexing, *regardless* of the rate of economic growth. If the growth rate of real GDP slows down, the average Social Security recipient will *still* get a growing slice of the pie each year, even if everyone else's slice is shrinking. And because Social Security is financed by tax payments from the rest of society, any increase in real benefits shrinks the after-tax real income of nonretirees.

More generally,

when a payment is indexed and the price index overstates inflation, the real payment increases over time. Purchasing power is automatically shifted toward those who are indexed and away from the rest of society.

This general principle applies whether the economy is growing rapidly or slowly, and it applies to anyone who is indexed: Social Security recipients, government pensioners, union workers with indexed wage contracts, or anyone else.

Long-Run Comparisons

If you look back at Table 2, you'll see a rather depressing story: The average hourly worker's real wage in 2002 was just a tiny bit higher than in 1980, and actually *lower* than in 1970. Has the purchasing power of the average wage really behaved this way? Not if the CPI—which was used in the table to calculate the real wage—overstates inflation.

We can get a *somewhat* more accurate view by asking the following question: What story would Table 2 tell if some of the recent improvements in the CPI measurement were applied retroactively? Fortunately, the BLS has attempted to answer this question by constructing an *unofficial* version of the CPI (called the CPI-U-RS, or the CPI for all Urban Consumers—Research Series) going back to 1978. This series is shown in Table 4. The first four columns of the data are selected rows from Table 2. They show the calculation of the wage using the *official* CPI. The fifth column shows the unofficial CPI—what the CPI *would* have been if some recent methodological improvements had been used in earlier years. Finally, the last column shows the recalculation of the real wage based on this somewhat more accurate CPI.

(1) Year	(2) Average Nominal Wage	(3) Official CPI	(4) Official Average Real Wage (1983 dollars) [(2)/(3)] × 100	(5) Partially Corrected CPI	(6) Partially Corrected Real Wage (1983 dollars) [(2)/(5)] × 100
1970	$3.50	39.8	$8.79	(no data available)	—
1980	$7.12	86.4	$8.24	86.0	$8.28
1990	$10.33	134.2	$7.70	130.8	$7.90
2000	$14.26	174.6	$8.17	165.2	$8.63
2002	$15.20	181.6	$8.37	171.7	$8.85

Source: "The Bureau of Labor Statistics' Statement on the Use of the CPI-U-RS," at *http://www.bls.gov/cpi/cpiurstx.htm* (modified April 16, 2003). Base year of CPI-U-RS was converted from 1977 to 1983 by authors.

TABLE 4
**The Official and Partially
Corrected Average Real Wage**

As you can see in the last column, the story looks a bit different. From 1980 to 2002, instead of rising from $8.24 to $8.37 (in 1983 dollars), the partially corrected real wage rose from $8.28 to $8.85. Moreover, instead of falling from 1970 to 2002, the partially corrected real wage actually rose slightly during this period. Keep in mind, too, that Columns 5 and 6 reflect only *some* of the BLS's improved measurement techniques, and these new techniques corrected only *some* of the acknowledged problems. A fuller correction would show an even greater rise in the real wage over the period.

In any case, because the BLS never alters previously published data to reflect later improvements in methodology, the official history of the real wage remains that of Column 4, not Column 6. This is the story you will see on Web sites and press reports that discuss changes in real wages over time.

> *Because the BLS does not correct previously reported CPI numbers to reflect later methodological improvements, long-term comparisons of real variables based on the official CPI will remain inaccurate, even as CPI measurement improves.*

The Bigger, Conceptual Problem

An even more serious problem in using the CPI has to do with the way it is typically viewed: as a measure of the *cost of living*—the cost of maintaining a fixed living standard from purchased goods and services. Indexing, after all, is usually justified as a way to prevent any deterioration in living standards. And discussions about the real wage often end with conclusions about the average worker being better or worse off. These conclusions imply that the CPI—which is used to calculate the real wage— is tracking the cost of achieving a given living standard. However, viewed as a measure of the cost of living, the CPI is even more inaccurate than our discussion so far suggests. This is because of the way it treats new goods—a problem that will not be corrected by any of the BLS's planned improvements.

When a new good comes to market, it is dropped into the CPI market basket at some point, and the CPI tracks changes in its price from that time forward. But the increase in economic well-being made possible by *introducing* the good—and the good's continued availability—is never accounted for. Even if the BLS were able to incorporate the good as soon as it came to market, and even if it accurately adjusted for subsequent quality improvements, it would still be missing the most important factor: the rise in living standards made possible by the new good's availability.

For example, we've already discussed the CPI's failure to account for quality *improvements* in the Internet after it was dropped into the basket in 1998. But in addition to this problem, the CPI has *never* recognized how the Internet has lowered the cost of achieving any given level of economic satisfaction (think of e-mail, online entertainment, online purchases, news, and more). The same is true for new medical procedures or prescription drugs that can treat or cure formerly untreatable diseases. The CPI tracks increases in their prices *after* they appear in the basket, but ignores the impact of these new treatments on our standard of living. In this way, the CPI misses a highly relevant fact: New goods raise the living standard we can achieve at any given dollar cost or, equivalently, they lower the dollar cost of achieving any given living standard.

How serious is this problem? No one knows for sure. But some authors have suggested that the error from ignoring the effect of new goods on living standards could be substantial. This error must be *added* to the combined effects of all the other errors discussed in this chapter.[6]

How might this change the story of the hourly real wage told in Table 2 (or Table 4)? Let's suppose that the ultimate, total overstatement in the cost of living has been 2 percent each year since 1970 to 2002. This would lead the CPI in 2002 to exaggerate the cost of living by about $(1.02)^{32} = 1.88$ or 88 percent. In Table 4, the official CPI over that period rose from 39.8 to 181.6, or a percentage increase of $(181.6 - 39.8)/39.8 = 3.56$ or 356 percent. Deducting the 88 percent error would leave a *true* cost of living increase of $356 - 88 = 268$ percent. Thus, to obtain an accurate CPI in 2002, we would increase 1970's CPI by 268 percent—instead of the official 356 percent. This would give us an accurate CPI in 2002 of $39.8 + (2.68 \times 39.8) = 146.5$. Finally, using this corrected CPI would give us a 2002 hourly real wage of $[\$15.20/146.5] \times 100 = \$10.38$. Comparing with 1970, we see that the real wage increased substantially—from $8.79 to $10.38—rather than falling, as the official story goes.

Of course, this example arbitrarily assumed a 2 percent overstatement of the annual rise in the cost of living. The actual overstatement could be less—or considerably more. But the general point is this:

> Using the CPI as an index of the cost of living *(the cost of achieving a given living standard) creates a further overstatement of inflation, because the CPI ignores the impact of new goods on living standards. Therefore, CPI-based indexing and CPI-based inferences about changes in well-being over time may be highly inaccurate.*

What the CPI Does Well

The CPI has another purpose besides indexing and making inferences about living standards: to measure inflationary tendencies in the economy. For this purpose, the CPI's interpretation as a cost-of-living index is irrelevant: The policy goal is to avoid

[6] See, for example, the suggestions of Jerry Hausman, "Sources of Bias and Solutions to Bias in the CPI," National Bureau of Economic Research, Working Paper 9298, October 2002. Much of the discussion of this subsection is based on Hausman's work.

high costs to society when the price level—however it's interpreted—changes too rapidly. The CPI is one of several useful tools to help achieve this goal.

To see why, suppose the CPI-based inflation rate (or one of its useful variants, which leaves out volatile components like food or energy prices) suddenly jumps up. Because of its measurement errors, the official inflation rate will exaggerate the true rise in prices, but it's unlikely that measurement errors alone would cause the entire increase in reported inflation. (That would require a sudden change in the relative importance of the measurement errors themselves.) Instead, a sudden spike in the CPI would tell policy makers that prices in the economy are, indeed, rising at a faster rate, and that appropriate policy measures should be considered to prevent inflation from getting out of hand. The same might apply to a rapid *decrease* in officially measured inflation to very low levels, creating a danger of deflation.

Also, in times of high inflation—as in the late 1970s—using an imperfect CPI to estimate real wages or to index retirees may be preferable to not accounting for inflation at all. With official annual inflation of 13 percent, for example, indexing Social Security benefits to an exaggerated CPI might raise the living standards of retirees by a few percentage points at the expense of the rest of society. But *not* indexing Social Security benefits at all could cause retirees' living standards to fall by 10 percent or more.

This chapter has raised many questions and left some of them unanswered. What makes the inflation rate rise and fall? Who are these *policy makers* that monitor the inflation rate and often try to alter it? How do they actually change the inflation rate? And why would they worry about an inflation rate that is too *low*? These are all questions we'll address in future chapters, after you've learned about macroeconomic models—the subject we turn to now.

Summary

Money serves two important functions. First, it serves as a *unit of value* that helps us compare the costs of different goods and services. Second, it serves as a *means of payment* by being generally acceptable in exchange for goods and services. Without money, we would be reduced to barter, a very inefficient way of carrying out transactions.

The value of money is its purchasing power, and this changes as the prices of the things we buy change. The overall trend of prices is measured using a price index. Like any index number, a price index is calculated as: (value in current period/value in base period) × 100. The most widely used price index in the United States is the *Consumer Price Index (CPI),* which tracks the prices paid for a typical consumer's "market basket." The percent change in the CPI is the inflation rate.

The most common uses of the CPI are for indexing payments, as a policy target, and to translate from nominal to real variables. Many nominal variables, such as the nominal wage, can be corrected for price changes by dividing by the CPI and then multiplying by 100. The result is a real variable, such as the real wage, that rises and falls only when its purchasing power rises and falls. Another price index in common use is the GDP price index. It tracks prices of all final goods and services included in GDP.

Inflation, a rise over time in a price index, is costly to our society. One of inflation's costs is an arbitrary redistribution of purchasing power. Unanticipated inflation shifts purchasing power away from those awaiting future dollar payments and toward those obligated to make such payments. Another cost of inflation is the resource cost: People use valuable time and other resources trying to cope with inflation.

It is widely agreed that the CPI has overstated inflation in recent decades, probably by more than one percentage point per year. As a result, the official statistics on real variables may contain errors, and people whose incomes are indexed to the CPI have actually been overindexed, enjoying an increase in real income that is paid for by the rest of society. The Bureau of Labor Statistics has been trying to eliminate the upward bias in the CPI. Much progress has been made, but some upward bias remains. The CPI is especially inaccurate as an index of the cost of achieving a given standard of living.

Key Terms

Consumer Price Index	Index	Nominal interest rate
Federal Reserve System	Indexation	Price level
Fiat money	Inflation rate	Real interest rate
GDP price index	Means of payment	Unit of value

Review Questions

Answers to even-numbered Questions and Problems can be found on the text Web site at http://ball-lieb.swlearning.com.

1. Distinguish between the *unit-of-value* function of money and the *means-of-payment* function. Give examples of how the U.S. dollar has played each of these two roles.

2. How does the price level differ from, say, the price of a haircut or a Big Mac?

3. Explain how you might construct an index of bank deposits over time. What steps would be involved?

4. What is the CPI? What does it measure? How can it be used to calculate the inflation rate?

5. Can the inflation rate be decreasing at the same time the price level is rising? Can the inflation rate be increasing at the same time the price level is falling? Explain.

6. What are the main uses of the CPI? Give an example of each use.

7. Explain the logic of the formula that relates real values to nominal values.

8. What are the similarities between the CPI and the GDP price index? What are the differences?

9. What are the costs of inflation?

10. Under what circumstances would inflation redistribute purchasing power? How? When would it *not* redistribute purchasing power?

11. How is a nominal interest rate different from a real interest rate? Which do you think is the better measure of the rate of return on a loan?

12. Explain the common misuses of the CPI.

Problems and Exercises

1. Calculate each of the following from the data in Table 1 in this chapter.
   a. The inflation rate for the year 2002.
   b. *Total* inflation (the total percentage change in the price level) from December 1970 to December 2002.

2. Using the data in Table 2, calculate the following for the period 1995–2000.
   a. The total percentage change in the nominal wage.
   b. The total percentage change in the price level.

3. Calculate the total percentage change in the real wage from 1995 to 2000 in two ways: (a) using your answers in problems 2a and b and the rule given earlier in this chapter; and (b) using the last column of Table 2. Which method is more accurate?

4. Suppose we want to change the base period of the CPI from July 1983 to December 1995. Recalculate December's CPI for each of the years in Table 1, so that the table gives the same information about inflation, but the CPI in December 1995 is now 100 instead of 153.9.

5. Which would be more costly: a steady inflation rate of 5 percent per year, or an inflation rate that was sometimes high and sometimes low, but that averaged 5 percent per year? Justify your answer.

6. Given the following *year-end* data, calculate the inflation rate for years 2, 3, and 4. Calculate the real wage in each year:

Year	CPI	Inflation Rate	Nominal Wage	Real Wage
1	100		$10.00	____
2	110	____	$12.00	____
3	120	____	$13.00	____
4	115	____	$12.75	____

7. Your friend asks for a loan of $100 for one year and offers to pay you 5 percent real interest. Your friend expects the inflation rate over that one-year period to be 6 percent; you expect it to be 4 percent. You agree to make the loan, and the actual inflation rate turns out to be 5 percent. Who benefits and who loses?

8. If there is 5 percent inflation each year for eight years, what is the *total* amount of inflation (i.e., the total percentage rise in the price level) over the entire eight-year period? (*Hint:* The answer is *not* 40 percent.)

9. Given the following data, calculate the real interest rate for years 2, 3, and 4. (Assume that each CPI number tells us the price level at the *end* of each year.)

Year	CPI	Nominal Interest Rate	Real Interest Rate
1	100		
2	110	15%	_____
3	120	13%	_____
4	115	8%	_____

If you lent $200 to a friend at the beginning of year 2 at the prevailing nominal interest rate of 15 percent, and your friend returned the money, with the interest, at the end of year 2, did you benefit from the deal?

10. (Requires appendix) An economy has only two goods, whose prices and typical consumption quantities are as follows:

	Dec. 2005		Dec. 2006	
	Price	Quantity	Price	Quantity
Fruit (lbs)	$1.00	100	$1.00	150
Nuts (lbs)	$3.00	50	$4.00	25

a. Using December 2005 as the base period for calculations and also as the year for measuring the typical consumer's market basket, calculate the CPI in December 2005 and December 2006.

b. What is the annual inflation rate for 2006?

c. Do you think your answer in b. would understate the actual inflation rate in 2006? Briefly, why or why not?

11. a. Use Table 4. For 1990 to 2002, calculate the following:
(i) the total percentage change in the official CPI;

(ii) the total percentage change in the partially corrected CPI;
(iii) the total percentage change in the official real wage; and
(iv) the total percentage change in the partially corrected real wage.

b. Suppose a fully corrected CPI would have increased only 25 percent over this entire period. What would be the percentage change in the fully corrected real wage?

c. Suppose the CPI overstates the cost of living by 2 percent, as discussed at the end of the "Using the Theory" section of this chapter. When this assumed overstatement is corrected, by what percentage would the real wage have increased from 1990 to 2002?

12. Complete the following table. (CPI numbers are for the end of each year).

Year	CPI	Inflation Rate	Nominal Wage	Real Wage
1	37		$ 5.60	
2	48		$ 7	
3		10%	$11.26	
4		19%		$25
5	60		$15	

13. a. Jodie earned $25,000 in year 1, when the CPI was 460. If the CPI in year 2 is 504, what would Jodie have to earn in year 2 to maintain a constant real wage?

b. What would she have to earn in year 2, to obtain a 5 percent increase in her real wage? What percentage increase in the nominal wage is this?

Challenge Questions

1. Inflation is sometimes said to be a tax on nominal money holdings. If you hold $100 and the price level increases by 10 percent, the purchasing power of that $100 falls by about 10 percent. Who benefits from this inflation tax?

2. During the late 19th and early 20th centuries, many U.S. farmers favored inflationary government policies. Why might this have been the case? (*Hint:* Do farmers typically pay for their land in full at the time of purchase?)

 *These exercises require access to Hall/Lieberman Xtra! If Xtra! did not come with your book, visit http://hallxtra.swlearning.com to purchase.*

1. Use your Xtra! password at the Hall and Lieberman Web site (http://hallxtra.swlearning.com), select this chapter, and click on EconDebate. Choose *Macroeconomics: Employment, Unemployment, and Inflation* and scroll down to find the debate, "Should the Federal Reserve Aim at a Zero Inflation Policy?" Read the debate and use the information to answer the following questions.
   a. Explain the "Philips' Curve."
   b. Argue from a new Classical perspective, whether an inflation rate of 0 percent is better or worse than an inflation rate of 3 percent.

2. Use your Xtra! password at the Hall and Lieberman Web site (http://hallxtra.swlearning.com), select this chapter, and under Economic Applications, click on EconData. Choose *Macroeconomics: Employment, Unemployment, and Inflation,* and scroll down to find *Consumer Price Index (CPI).* Read the definition and click on Diagrams/Data and use the information to identify the periods when the relationship described by Philips' curve holds.

APPENDIX

CALCULATING THE CONSUMER PRICE INDEX

The Consumer Price Index (CPI) is the government's most popular measure of inflation. It tracks the cost of the collection of goods, called the *CPI market basket,* bought by a typical consumer in some *base period.* This appendix demonstrates how the Bureau of Labor Statistics (BLS) calculates the CPI. To help you follow the steps clearly, we'll do the calculations for a very simple economy with just two goods: hamburger meat and oranges (not a pleasant world, but a manageable one). Table A.1 shows prices for each good, and the quantities produced and consumed, in two different periods: December 2004 (the base period) and December 2005. The market basket (measured in the base period) is given in the third column of the table: In December 2004, the typical consumer buys 30 pounds of hamburger and 50 pounds of oranges. Our formula for the CPI in any period t is

CPI in period t

$$= \frac{\text{Cost of market basket at prices in period } t}{\text{Cost of market basket at 2004 prices}} \times 100,$$

where each year's prices are measured in December of that year.

TABLE A.1
Prices and Weekly Quantities in a Two-Good Economy

	December 2004		December 2005	
	Price (per lb.)	Quantity (lbs.)	Price (per lb.)	Quantity (lbs.)
Hamburger Meat	$5.00	30	$6.00	10
Oranges	$1.00	50	$1.10	100

Table A.2 shows the calculations we must do to determine the CPI in December 2004 and December 2005. In the table, you can see that the cost of the 2004 market basket at 2004 prices is $200. The cost of the *same* market basket at 2005's higher prices is $235.

TABLE A.2
Calculations for the CPI

	At December 2004 Prices	At December 2005 Prices
Cost of 30 lbs. of Hamburger	$5.00 × 30 = $150	$6.00 × 30 = $180
Cost of 50 lbs. of Oranges	$1.00 × 50 = $50	$1.10 × 50 = $55
Cost of Entire Market Basket	$150 + $50 = $200	$180 + $55 = $235

To determine the CPI in December 2004—the base period—we use the formula with period t equal to 2004, giving us

CPI in 2004

$$= \frac{\text{Cost of 2004 basket at 2004 prices}}{\text{Cost of 2004 basket at 2004 prices}} \times 100$$

$$= \frac{\$200}{\$200} \times 100 = 100.$$

That is, the CPI in December 2004—the base period—is equal to 100. (The formula, as you can see, is set up so that the CPI will always equal 100 in the base period, regardless of which base period we choose.)

Now let's apply the formula again, to get the value of the CPI in December 2005:

CPI in 2005

$$= \frac{\text{Cost of 2004 basket at 2005 prices}}{\text{Cost of 2004 basket at 2004 prices}} \times 100$$

$$= \frac{\$235}{\$200} \times 100 = 117.5.$$

From December 2004 to December 2005, the CPI rises from 100 to 117.5. The rate of inflation over the year 2005 is therefore 17.5 percent.

Notice that the CPI gives more weight to price changes of goods that are more important in the consumer's budget. In our example, the percentage rise in the CPI (17.5 percent) is closer to the percentage rise in the price of hamburger (20 percent) than it is to the percentage price rise of oranges (10 percent). This is because a greater percentage of the budget is *spent* on hamburger than on oranges, so hamburger carries more weight in the CPI.

But one of the CPI's problems, discussed in the body of the chapter, is *substitution bias*. The CPI recognizes that consumers substitute *within* categories of goods. For example, if we had a third good, steak, the CPI would recognize that consumers will buy more steak if the price of hamburger rises faster than the price of steak. But the CPI assumes there is no substitution *among* categories—between beef products and fruit, for example. No matter how much the relative price of beef products like hamburger rises, the CPI assumes that people will continue to buy the same quantity of it,

rather than substitute goods in other categories like oranges. Therefore, as the price of hamburger rises, the CPI assumes that we spend a greater and greater percentage of our budgets on it; hamburger gets *increasing weight* in the CPI. In our example, spending on hamburger is assumed to rise from $150/$200 = 0.75, or 75 percent of the typical weekly budget, to $180/$235 = 0.766, or 76.6 percent. In fact, however, the rapid rise in price would cause people to substitute *away* from hamburger toward other goods whose prices are rising more slowly.

This is what occurs in our two-good example, as you can see in the last column of Table A.1. In 2005, the quantity of hamburger purchased drops to 10, and the quantity of oranges rises to 100. In an ideal measure, the decrease in the quantity of hamburger would reduce its weight in determining the overall rate of inflation. But the CPI ignores the information in the last column of Table A.1, which shows the new quantities purchased in 2005. This failure to correct for substitution bias across categories of goods is one of the reasons the CPI overstates inflation.

The Classical Long-Run Model

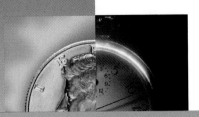

Economists often disagree with each other. In news interviews, class lectures, and editorials, they give differing opinions about even the simplest matters. To the casual observer, it might seem that economics is little more than guesswork, where anyone's opinion is as good as anyone else's. But there is actually much more agreement among economists than there appears to be.

Take the following typical example: At a time when the economy is performing well, two distinguished economists appear on *CNN Moneyline*. In a somber tone, Lou Dobbs—the anchor—asks each of them what should be done to maintain the health of the economy. "We need to cut taxes," replies the first economist. "If individuals can keep more of what they earn, they'll have more incentive to work. And if we lower taxes on business, they'll have more incentive to invest and grow." (Don't worry if this chain of logic isn't clear to you yet; it will be by the end of the next chapter.)

"No, no, no," the second economist might interrupt. "A tax cut would be the *worst* thing we could do right now. The economy is already pumping out just about as many goods and services as it can. A tax cut—which would put more funds into buyers' hands—would only increase spending, overheat the economy, and lead to inflationary dangers that the U.S. Federal Reserve would want to prevent." (You'll begin learning what's behind this argument a few chapters later.)

Which of these economists would be right? Surprisingly, it's entirely possible for *both* of them to be correct. But how can this be? Aren't the two responses contradictory? Not necessarily, because each economist might be hearing—and answering—a different question. The first economist is addressing the likely *long-run* impact of a cut in taxes: the impact we might expect after several years have elapsed. The second economist, by contrast, is focusing on a possible *short-run* impact: the effects we might see over the next year.

Once the distinction between the long run and the short run becomes clear, many apparent disagreements among macroeconomists dissolve. If Lou Dobbs had asked our two economists about the *long-run* impact of cutting taxes, both may well have agreed that it would lead to more jobs and more investment by business firms. If asked about the *short-run* impact, both may have agreed about the potential danger of inflation. If no time horizon is specified, however, an economist is likely to focus on the horizon he or she feels is most important—something about which economists sometimes *do* disagree. The real dispute, though, is less over how the economy *works* and more about what our priorities should be in guiding it.

Ideally, we would like our economy to do well in both the long run and the short run. Unfortunately, there is often a trade-off between these two goals: Doing better in the short run can require some sacrifice of long-run goals, and vice versa. The problem for policy makers is much like that of the captain of a ship sailing through the North Atlantic. On the one hand, he wants to reach his destination (his long-run goal); on the other hand, he must avoid icebergs along the way (his short-run goal). As you might imagine, avoiding icebergs may require the captain to deviate from an ideal long-run course. At the same time, reaching port might require risking the occasional iceberg.

The same is true of the macroeconomy. If you flip back two chapters and look at Figure 4, you will see that there are two types of movements in total output: the long-run trajectory showing the growth of potential output and the short-run movements around that trajectory, which we call economic fluctuations or business cycles. Macroeconomists are concerned with both types of movements. But, as you will see, policies that can help us smooth out economic fluctuations may prove harmful to growth in the long run, while policies that promise a high rate of growth might require us to put up with more severe fluctuations in the short run.

MACROECONOMIC MODELS: CLASSICAL VERSUS KEYNESIAN

Classical model A macroeconomic model that explains the long-run behavior of the economy.

The **classical model**, developed by economists in the 19th and early 20th centuries, was an attempt to explain a key observation about the economy: Over periods of several years or longer, the economy performs rather well. That is, if we step back from current conditions and view the economy over a long stretch of time, we see that it operates reasonably close to its potential output. And even when it deviates, it does not do so for very long. Business cycles may come and go, but the economy eventually returns to full employment. Indeed, if we think in terms of decades rather than years or quarters, the business cycle fades in significance much like the waves in a choppy sea disappear when viewed from a jet plane.

In the classical view, this behavior is no accident: Powerful forces are at work that drive the economy toward full employment. Many of the classical economists went even further, arguing that these forces operated within a reasonably short period of time. And even today, an important group of macroeconomists continues to believe that the classical model is useful even in the shorter run.

Until the Great Depression of the 1930s, there was little reason to question these classical ideas. True, output fluctuated around its trend, and from time to time there were serious recessions, but output always returned to its potential, full-employment level within a few years or less, just as the classical economists predicted. But during the Great Depression, output was stuck far below its potential for many years. For some reason, the economy wasn't working the way the classical model said it should.

In 1936, in the midst of the Great Depression, the British economist John Maynard Keynes offered an explanation for the economy's poor performance. His new model of the economy—soon dubbed the *Keynesian model*—changed many economists' thinking.[1] Keynes and his followers argued that, while the classical model might explain the economy's operation in the long run, the long run could be a very long time in arriving. In the meantime, production could be stuck below its potential, as it seemed to be during the Great Depression.

Keynesian ideas became increasingly popular in universities and government agencies during the 1940s and 1950s. By the mid-1960s, the entire profession had been won over: Macroeconomics *was* Keynesian economics, and the classical model was removed from virtually all introductory economics textbooks. You might be wondering, then, why we are bothering with the classical model here. After all, it's an older model of the economy, one that was largely discredited and replaced, just as the Ptolemaic view that the sun circled the earth was supplanted by the more modern, Copernican view. Right?

Not really. The classical model is still important, for two reasons. First, in recent decades, there has been an active counterrevolution against Keynes's approach to understanding the macroeconomy. Many of the counterrevolutionary new theories are based largely on classical ideas. In some cases, the new theories are just classical economics in modern clothing, but in other cases significant new ideas have been added. By studying classical macroeconomics, you will be better prepared to understand the controversies centering on these newer schools of thought.

The second—and more important—reason for us to study the classical model is its usefulness in understanding the economy over the long run. Even the many economists who find the classical model inadequate for understanding the economy in the short run find it extremely useful in analyzing the economy in the long run.

Keynes's ideas and their further development help us understand economic fluctuations—movements in output around its long-run trend. But the classical model has proven more useful in explaining the long-run trend itself.

This is why we will use the terms "classical view" and "long-run view" interchangeably in the rest of the book; in either case, we mean "the ideas of the classical model used to explain the economy's long-run behavior."

---

[1] Keynes's attack on the classical model was presented in his book *The General Theory of Employment, Interest and Money* (1936). Unfortunately, it's a very difficult book to read, though you may want to try. Keynes's assumptions were not always clear, and some of his text is open to multiple interpretations. As a result, economists have been arguing for decades about what Keynes really meant.

Assumptions of the Classical Model

Remember from Chapter 1 that all models begin with *assumptions* about the world. The classical model is no exception. Many of its assumptions are *simplifying;* they make the model more manageable, enabling us to see the broad outlines of economic behavior without getting lost in the details. Typically, these assumptions involve aggregation, such as ignoring the many different interest rates in the economy and instead referring to a single interest rate, or ignoring the many different types of labor in the economy and analyzing instead a single aggregate labor market. These simplifications are usually harmless: Adding more detail would make our work more difficult, but would not add much insight; nor would it change any of the central conclusions of the classical view.

There is, however, one assumption in the classical model that goes beyond mere simplification. This is an assumption about how the world works, and it is critical to the conclusions we will reach in this and the next chapter. We can state it in two words: *Markets clear.*

Market clearing Adjustment of prices until quantities supplied and demanded are equal.

> *A critical assumption in the classical model is that **markets clear**: The price in every market will adjust until quantity supplied and quantity demanded are equal.*

Does the market-clearing assumption sound familiar? It should: It was the basic idea behind our study of supply and demand. When we look at the economy through the classical lens, we assume that the forces of supply and demand work fairly well throughout the economy and that markets do reach equilibrium. An excess supply of anything traded will lead to a fall in its price; an excess demand will drive the price up.

The market-clearing assumption, which permeates classical thinking about the economy, provides an early hint about why the classical model does a better job over longer time periods (several years or more) than shorter ones. In many markets, prices might not fully adjust to their equilibrium values for many months or even years after some change in the economy. An excess supply or excess demand might persist for some time. Still, if we wait long enough, an excess supply in a market will eventually force the price down, and an excess demand will eventually drive the price up. That is, *eventually,* the market will clear. Therefore, when we are trying to explain the economy's behavior over the long run, market clearing seems to be a reasonable assumption.

In the remainder of the chapter, we'll use the classical model to answer a variety of important questions about the economy in the long run, such as:

- How is total employment determined?
- How much output will we produce?
- What role does total spending play in the economy?
- What happens when things change?

Keep in mind that, in our discussion of the classical model, we will focus on *real* variables: real GDP, the real wage, real saving, and so on. These variables are typically measured in the dollars of some base year, and their numerical values change only when their *purchasing power* changes. While our *actual* measures of the price level are imperfect, you can think of a real variable as one that reflects *true* purchasing power—the value we'd obtain if we used a perfectly accurate price index.

HOW MUCH OUTPUT WILL WE PRODUCE?

Over the last decade, on average, the U.S. economy produced about $8.2 trillion worth of goods and services per year (valued in 1996 dollars). How was this average level of output determined? Why didn't we produce $14 trillion per year? Or just $2 trillion? There are so many things to consider when answering this question, variables you constantly hear about in the news: wages, interest rates, investment spending, government spending, taxes, and more. Each of these concepts plays an important role in determining total output, and our task in this chapter is to show how they all fit together.

But what a task! How can we disentangle the web of economic interactions we see around us? Our starting point will be the first step of our *three-step process*, introduced toward the end of Chapter 3. To review, that first step was to *characterize the market*—to decide which market or markets best suit the problem being analyzed, which means indentifying the buyers and sellers and the type of environment in which they trade.

But which market should we start with?

The classical approach is to start at the beginning, with the *reason* for all this production in the first place: our desire for goods and services, and our need for income in order to buy them. In a market economy, people get their income from supplying labor and other resources to firms. Firms, in turn, use these resources to make the goods and services that people demand. Thus, a logical place to start our analysis is markets for resources: labor, land and natural resources, capital, and entrepreneurship.

For now we'll concentrate our attention on just one type of resource: labor. We'll assume that firms are already using the available quantities of the other resources. Moreover, since we are building a *macroeconomic* model, we'll aggregate all the different types of labor—office workers, construction workers, teachers, taxi drivers, waiters, writers and more—into a single variable, simply called *labor*.

Our question is: How many workers will be employed in the economy?

The Labor Market

The classical labor market is illustrated in Figure 1. The number of workers is measured on the horizontal axis, and the real hourly wage rate is measured on the vertical axis. Remember that the *real wage*—which is measured in the dollars of some base year—tells us the amount of goods that workers can buy with an hour's earnings.

Now look at the two curves in the figure. These are supply and demand curves, similar to the supply and demand curves for maple syrup, but there is one key difference: For a *good* such as maple syrup, households are the demanders and firms the suppliers. But for labor, the roles are reversed: Households supply labor and firms demand it.

The curve labeled L^S is the **labor supply curve** in this market; it tells us how many people will want to work at each wage. The upward slope tells us that the greater the real wage, the greater the number of people who will want to work. Why does the labor supply curve slope upward?

Labor supply curve Indicates how many people will want to work at various real wage rates.

To earn income, you must go to work and give up other activities such as school, parenting, or leisure. Thus, each of us will want to work only if the income we will earn *at least* compensates us for the other activities that we will give up.

FIGURE 1
The Labor Market

The equilibrium wage rate of $15 per hour is determined at point E, where the upward-sloping labor supply curve crosses the downward-sloping labor demand curve. At any other wage, an excess demand or excess supply of labor will cause an adjustment back to equilibrium.

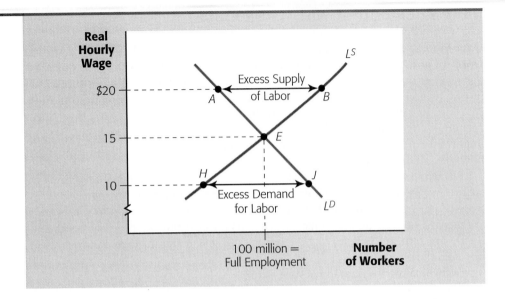

Of course, people value their time differently. Thus, for each of us, there is some critical wage rate above which we would decide that we're better off working. Below that wage, we would be better off not working. Thus, in Figure 1,

> *the labor supply curve slopes upward because, as the wage rate increases, more and more individuals are better off working than not working. Thus, a rise in the wage rate increases the number of people in the economy who want to work—to supply their labor.*

Labor demand curve Indicates how many workers firms will want to hire at various real wage rates.

The curve labeled L^D is the **labor demand curve,** which shows the number of workers firms will want to hire at any real wage. Why does this curve slope downward?

In deciding how much labor to hire, a firm's goal is to earn the greatest possible profit: the difference between sales revenue and costs. A firm will want to keep hiring additional workers as long as the output produced by those workers adds more to the firm's revenue than it adds to costs.

Now think about what happens as the wage rate rises. Some workers that added more to revenue than to cost at the lower wage will now cost more than they add in revenue. Accordingly, the firm will not want to employ these workers at the higher wage.

> *As the wage rate increases, each firm in the economy will find that, to maximize profit, it should employ fewer workers than before. When all firms behave this way together, a rise in the wage rate will decrease the quantity of labor demanded in the economy. This is why the economy's labor demand curve slopes downward.*

Remember that in the classical view, *all markets clear,* and that includes the market for labor. Specifically, the real wage adjusts until the quantities of labor supplied and demanded are equal. In the labor market in Figure 1, the market-clearing wage is $15 per hour, since that is where the labor supply and labor demand curves intersect. While every worker would prefer to earn $20 rather than $15, at $20 there would be an excess supply of labor equal to the distance *AB*. With not enough jobs to go around, competition among workers would drive the wage downward. Similarly, firms might prefer to pay their workers $10 rather than $15, but at $10, the excess demand for labor (equal to the distance *HJ*) would drive the wage upward. When the wage is $15, however, there is neither an excess demand nor an excess supply of labor, so the wage will neither increase nor decrease. Thus, $15 is the equilibrium wage in the economy. Reading along the horizontal axis, we see that at this wage, 100 million people will be working.

Notice that, in the figure, labor is fully employed; that is, the number of workers that firms want to hire is equal to the number of people who want jobs. Therefore, everyone who wants a job at the market wage of $15 should be able to find one. Small amounts of frictional unemployment might exist, since it takes some time for new workers or job switchers to find jobs. And there might be structural unemployment, due to some mismatch between those who want jobs in the market and the types of jobs available. But there is no *cyclical* unemployment of the type we discussed two chapters ago.

Full employment of the labor force is an important feature of the classical model. As long as we can count on markets (including the labor market) to clear, government action is not needed to ensure full employment; it happens automatically:

> *In the classical view, the economy achieves full employment on its own.*

Automatic full employment may strike you as odd, since it contradicts the cyclical unemployment we sometimes see around us. For example, in the recession of 2001, millions of workers around the country, in all kinds of professions and labor markets, were unable to find jobs for many months. Remember, though, that the classical model takes the long-run view, and over long periods of time, full employment is a fairly accurate description of the U.S. labor market. Cyclical unemployment, by definition, lasts only as long as the current business cycle itself; it is not a permanent, long-run problem.

Determining the Economy's Output

So far, we've focused on the labor market to determine the economy's level of employment. In our example, 100 million people will have jobs. Now we ask: How much output (real GDP) will these 100 million workers produce? The answer depends on two things: (1) the amount of other resources available for labor to use; and (2) the state of *technology*, which determines how much output we can produce with those resources.

In this chapter, remember that we're focusing on only one resource—labor—and we're treating the quantities of all other resources firms use as fixed during the period we're analyzing. Now we'll go even further: We'll assume that technology does not change.

Why do we make these assumptions? After all, in the real world technology *does* change, the capital stock *does* grow, new natural resources *can* be discovered, and the number and quality of entrepreneurs *can* change. Isn't it unrealistic to hold all of these things constant?

HTTP://

For the latest on economic output, visit the Economic Statistics Briefing Room at http://www.whitehouse.gov/fsbr/output.html.

Yes, but our assumption is only temporary. The most effective way to master a macroeconomic model is "divide and conquer": Start with a part of the model, understand it well, and then add in other parts. Accordingly, our classical analysis of the economy is divided into two separate questions: (1) What would be the long-run equilibrium of the economy *if* there were a constant state of technology and *if* quantities of all resources besides labor were fixed? And (2) What happens to this long-run equilibrium when technology and the quantities of other resources change? In this chapter, we focus on the first question. In the next chapter on economic growth, we'll address the second question.

The Production Function. With a constant technology, and given quantities of all resources other than labor, there is only one variable left that can affect total output: labor. So it's time to explore the relationship between total employment and total production in the economy. This relationship is given by the economy's *aggregate production function.*

Aggregate production function
The relationship showing how much total output can be produced with different quantities of labor, with quantities of all other resources held constant.

> *The **aggregate production function** (or just **production function**) shows the total output the economy can produce with different quantities of labor, given constant amounts of other resources and the current state of technology.*

The bottom panel of Figure 2 shows what a nation's aggregate production function might look like. The upward slope tells us that an increase in the number of people working will increase the quantity of output produced. But notice the shape of the production function: It flattens out as we move rightward along it.

The declining slope of the aggregate production function is the result of *diminishing returns to labor*: Output rises when another worker is added, but the rise is smaller and smaller with each successive worker. Why does this happen? For one thing, as we keep adding workers, gains from specialization are harder and harder to come by. Moreover, as we continue to add workers, each one will have less and less of the other resources to work with. For example, each time more agricultural workers are added to a fixed amount of farmland, output might rise. But as we continue to add workers and the ratio of workers to acres rises, output will rise by less and less with each new worker. The same is true when more factory workers are added to a fixed amount of factory floor space and machinery, or more professors are added to a fixed number of classrooms: Output continues to rise, but by less and less with each added worker.

Figure 2 also illustrates how the aggregate production function, together with the labor market, determines the economy's total output or real GDP. In our example, the labor market (upper panel) automatically generates full employment of 100 million workers, and the production function (lower panel) tells us that 100 million workers—together with the available amounts of other resources and the current state of technology—can produce $7 trillion worth of output. Since $7 trillion is the output produced by a fully employed labor force, it is also the economy's potential output level.

> *In the classical, long-run view, the economy reaches its potential output automatically.*

This last statement is an important conclusion of the classical model and an important characteristic of the economy in the long run: Output tends toward its poten-

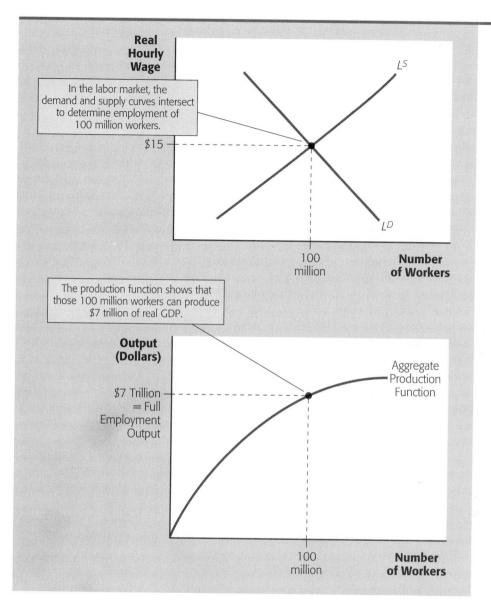

FIGURE 2
Output Determination In the Classical Model

In the labor market, the demand and supply curves intersect to determine employment of 100 million workers.

The production function shows that those 100 million workers can produce $7 trillion of real GDP.

tial, full-employment level *on its own,* with no need for government to steer the economy toward it. And we have arrived at this conclusion merely by assuming that the labor market clears and observing the relationship between employment and output.

THE ROLE OF SPENDING

Something may be bothering you about the classical view of output determination, a potential problem we have so far carefully avoided: What if business firms are unable to sell all the output produced by a fully employed labor force? Then the economy would not be able to sustain full employment for very long. Business firms will not continue to employ workers who produce output that is not being sold. Thus, if

FIGURE 3
The Circular Flow

The outer loop of the diagram shows the flows of goods and resources. Households supply resources to firms, which use them to produce goods. The inner loop shows money flows. Firms' factor payments become income to households. Households use the income to purchase goods from firms.

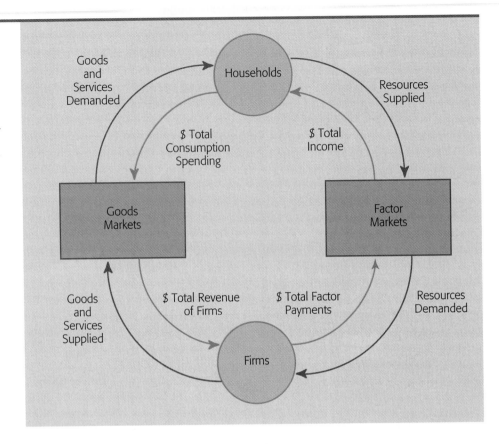

Circular flow A diagram that shows how goods, resources, and dollar payments flow between households and firms.

we are asserting that potential output is an equilibrium for the economy, we had better be sure that *total spending* on output is equal to *total production* during the year. But can we be sure of this?

In the classical view, the answer is, absolutely yes! We'll demonstrate this in two stages: first, in a very simple (but very unrealistic) economy, and then, under more realistic conditions.

Total Spending in a Very Simple Economy

Imagine a world much simpler than our own, a world with just two types of economic units: households and business firms. In this world, households spend all of their income on goods and services. They do not save any of their income, nor do they pay taxes. Such an economy is illustrated in the **circular flow** diagram of Figure 3.

The arrows on the right-hand side show that resources—labor, capital, land and natural resources, and entrepreneurship—are supplied by households, and demanded by firms, in *factor markets*. In return, households receive payments: wages, rent, interest, and profit. For example, if you were working part-time in a restaurant while attending college, you would be supplying a resource (labor) in a factor market (the market for waiters). In exchange, you would earn a wage. Similarly, the owner of the land on which the restaurant sits is a supplier in a factor market (the market for land) and would receive a payment (rent) in return. The payments received by resource owners are called *factor payments*.

On the left side of the diagram, the outer arrows show the flow of goods and services—food, new clothes, books, movies, and more—that firms supply, and households buy, in various *goods* markets. Of course, households must pay for these goods and services, and their payments provide revenue to firms, as shown by the inner arrows.

Now comes an important insight. As you learned two chapters ago, the total output of firms is equal to the total income of households. For example, if the economy is producing $7 trillion worth of output, then it also creates $7 trillion in household income. And in this simple economy—in which households spend all of their income—spending would equal $7 trillion as well.

In general,

> *in a simple economy with just households and firms, in which households spend all of their income, total spending must be equal to total output.*

This simple proposition is called **Say's law**, after the classical economist Jean Baptiste Say (1767–1832), who popularized the idea. Say noted that each time a good or service is produced, an equal amount of income is created. This income is spent, so it comes back to the business sector to purchase its goods and services. In Say's own words:

> A product *is no sooner created than it, from that instant, affords a market for other products to the full extent of its own value. . . . Thus, the mere circumstance of the creation of one product immediately opens a vent for other products.*[2]

For example, each time a shirt manufacturer produces a $25 shirt, it creates $25 in factor payments to households. (Forgot why? Go back two chapters and refresh your memory about the factor payments approach to GDP.) But in the simple economy we're analyzing, that $25 in factor payments will lead to $25 in total spending—just enough to buy the very shirt produced. Of course, the households who receive the $25 in factor payments won't necessarily buy a shirt with it; the shirt manufacturer must still worry about selling its own output. But in the *aggregate*, we needn't worry about there being sufficient demand for the total output produced. Business firms—by producing output—also create a demand for goods and services equal to the value of that output.

> *Say's law states that by producing goods and services, firms create a total demand for goods and services equal to what they have produced. Or, more simply, supply creates its own demand.*

Say's law is crucial to the classical view of the economy. Why? Remember that because the labor market is assumed to clear, firms will hire all the workers who want jobs and produce our *potential* or *full-employment* output level. But firms will only *continue* to produce this level of output if they can *sell* it all. In the simple economy of Figure 3, Say's law assures us that, in the aggregate, spending will be just high enough for firms to sell all the output that a fully employed labor force can produce. As a result, full employment can be maintained.

Say's law The idea that total spending will be sufficient to purchase the total output produced.

[2] J. B. Say, *A Treatise on Political Economy,* 4th ed. (London: Longman, 1821), Vol. I, p. 167.

But the economy in Figure 3 leaves out some important details of economies in the real world. Does Say's law also apply in a more realistic economy? Let's see.

Total Spending in a More Realistic Economy

The real-world economy is more complicated than the imaginary one we've just considered. In the real world,

1. Households don't spend *all* their income. Rather, some of their income is saved or goes to pay taxes.
2. Households are not the only spenders in the economy. Rather, businesses and the government also buy final goods and services.
3. In addition to markets for goods and markets for resources, there is also a *loanable funds* market where household saving is made available to business firms and the government.

All of these details complicate our picture of the economy. Will Say's law still apply?

Let's consider the economy of Classica, a fictional economy that behaves according to the classical model, but one that is more realistic than the economy of Figure 3. Data on Classica's economy in 2004 are given in Table 1. Notice that total output and total income are both equal to $7 trillion in 2004, which is assumed to be Classica's full-employment or potential output level.

Next come three entries that refer to spending by the final users who purchase Classica's GDP. Note that unlike the households in Figure 3, Classica's households spend only *part* of their income: $4 trillion on consumption goods (*C*). Skipping down to government purchases (*G*), we find that Classica's government sector—combining its national, regional, and local government agencies—purchases $2 trillion in goods and services.

Some New Macroeconomic Variables. In addition to consumption and government purchases—with which you are already familiar—Table 1 includes some new variables. Since these will be used throughout the rest of this book, it's worth defining and discussing them here.

Planned Investment Spending (I^P). Two chapters ago, you learned that total investment spending—the component labeled *I* in the expenditure approach to GDP—includes not only business spending on new capital but also *changes in firms' inventories* over a period of time. Inventory changes occur when firms produce more than they sell (an increase in inventories) or sell more than they produce (a decrease in inventories).

Our ultimate goal is to find out if Say's law works in Classica—if total spending exactly matches Classica's total output. Therefore, it would be a mistake to include inventory changes—which represent the mismatch between sales and production—as part of investment spending. When we exclude inventory changes from investment spending, we're left with *planned investment spending*.

Planned investment spending
Business purchases of plant and equipment.

> *Planned investment spending* (I^P) *over a period of time is total investment spending* (I) *minus the change in inventories over the period:*
>
> $$I^P = I - \Delta \text{ inventories.}$$

Here, we're using the Greek letter Δ ("delta") to indicate a change in a variable.

Total Output (GDP)	$7 trillion
Total Income	$7 trillion
Consumption Spending (C)	$4 trillion
Planned Investment Spending (I^P)	$1 trillion
Government Purchases (G)	$2 trillion
Net Taxes (T)	$1.25 trillion
Household Saving (S)	$1.75 trillion

TABLE 1
**Flows in the Economy
of Classica, 2004**

Why do we call this new variable *planned* investment? In the real world, some inventory changes are, in fact, planned by firms. But they can also come as a surprise. For example, suppose Calvin Klein produces $40 million in clothing during a quarter, planning to sell all of it. But during the quarter, it actually ships and sells only $35 million. Then $5 million in unsold output would be an *unplanned increase in inventories*—a surprise, rather than a planned result. On the other hand, if Calvin Klein sold $43 million, then $3 million in sales would come out of inventories. This would be an *unplanned decrease in inventories*—a surprise in the other direction.

Changes in inventories are generally the only component of spending in GDP that is not planned. A firm does not "discover" at the end of a quarter that it has purchased a new factory. This type of investment is intended and planned in advance. And—other than Homer in *The Simpsons*—a consumer doesn't "discover" that he has purchased a new car or a lifetime supply of slurpies; consumption spending is intentional.

In this and future chapters, to keep our discussions simple we'll regard *all* inventory changes as unplanned surprises. This is why, after deducting inventory changes from total investment, we call what is left *planned investment*. In Table 1, you can see that Classica's planned investment spending—which excludes any changes in inventories—is $1 trillion.

Net Tax Revenue (T). Recall (from two chapters ago) that *transfer payments* are government outlays that are *not* spent on goods and services. These transfers—which include unemployment insurance, welfare payments, and Social Security benefits—are just *given* to people, either out of social concern (welfare payments), to keep a promise (Social Security payments), or elements of both (unemployment insurance).

In the macroeconomy, government transfer payments are like negative taxes: They represent the part of tax revenue that the government takes from one set of households (taxpayers) but gives right back to another set of households (such as Social Security recipients), and are not available for government purchases. Since we're interested in the funds that flow from the household sector *as a whole* to the government in any given year, and since transfer payments stay *within* the household sector, we can treat them as if they were never paid to the government at all. We do this by focusing on *net taxes*:

Net taxes (**T**) *are total government tax revenue minus government transfer payments:*

$$T = total \ tax \ revenue - transfers.$$

Net taxes Government tax revenues minus transfer payments.

For example, in 2005 net taxes in Classica are $1.25 trillion. This number might result from total tax revenue of $2 trillion and $0.75 trillion in government transfer payments. It could also result from $3 trillion in tax revenue and $1.75 trillion in transfers. From the macroeconomic perspective, net taxes—what the government has available for purchases—are $1.25 trillion in either case.

Household Saving (S). It's often useful to arrive at household saving in two steps. First, we determine how much income the household sector has left after payment of net taxes. This is the household sector's **disposable income:**

Disposable Income Household income minus net taxes, which is either spent or saved.

$$\text{Disposable Income} = \text{Total Income} - \text{Net Taxes}.$$

The household sector can *dispose* of this disposable (after-tax) income in only two ways: either by spending it (C) or by *not* spending it. The part that is *not* spent is defined as (**household**) **saving** (S):

(Household) saving The portion of after-tax income that households do not spend on consumption.

$$S = \text{Disposable Income} - C.$$

The last entry in Table 1 tells us that in Classica, household saving is $1.75 trillion. Let's check this using disposable income. From the table, total income is $7 trillion and net taxes are $1.25 trillion, so disposable income (not shown in the table) is $7 trillion − $1.25 trillion = $5.75 trillion. Consumption spending is $4 trillion, so:

$$S = \text{Disposable Income} - C = \$5.75 \text{ trillion} - \$4 \text{ trillion} = \$1.75 \text{ trillion}$$

Total Spending in Classica. In Classica, total spending is the sum of the purchases made by the household sector (C), the business sector (I^P), and the government sector (G):[3]

$$\text{Total spending} = C + I^P + G.$$

Or, using the numbers in Table 1:

$$\text{Total spending} = \$4 \text{ trillion} + \$1 \text{ trillion} + \$2 \text{ trillion} = \$7 \text{ trillion}.$$

This may strike you as suspiciously convenient: Total spending is exactly equal to total output, just as we'd like to be if we want Classica to continue producing its potential output of $7 trillion. And just what we needed to illustrate Say's law in this more realistic economy.

But we haven't yet proven anything; we've just cooked up an example that made the numbers come out this way. The question is, do we have any reason to *expect* the economy to give us numbers like these automatically, with total spending precisely equal to total output?

The rectangles in Figure 4 provide some perspective on this question and suggest the way to an answer. Total output (represented by the first rectangle) is, by definition, always equal in value to total income (the second rectangle). As we've seen in Figure 3, if households *spent* all of this income, then consumption spending would equal total output.

But in Classica, households do *not* spend all of their income. Some income goes to pay net taxes ($1.25 trillion), and some is saved ($1.75 trillion). Saving and net

---

[3] Notice that to keep things simple, we've assumed that Classica does not trade with the rest of the world (no exports, no imports). Introducing exports and imports would not change any of our conclusions in important ways, but it would make it harder to see them.

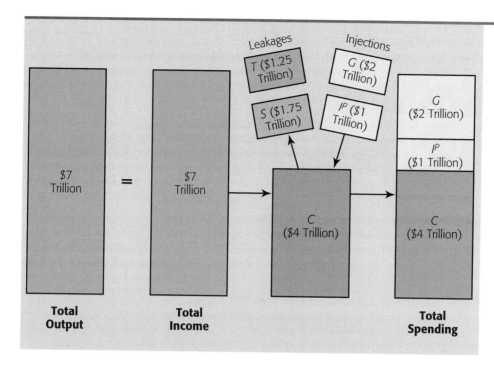

FIGURE 4
Leakages and Injections

By definition, total output equals total income. Leakages—net taxes (T) and saving (S)—reduce consumption spending below total income. Injections—government purchases (G) plus planned investment spending (I^P)—contribute to total spending. When leakages equal injections, total spending equals total output.

taxes are called **leakages** out of spending: the amount of income that households receive, but do not spend. Leakages reduce consumption spending below total income, as you can see in the third, lower rectangle. In Classica, total leakages = $1.75 trillion + $1.25 trillion = $3 trillion, and this must be subtracted from income of $7 trillion to get consumption spending of $4 trillion. Thus, if consumption spending were the only spending in the economy, business firms would be unable to sell their entire potential output of $7 trillion.

Fortunately, in addition to leakages, there are **injections**—spending from sources *other* than households. Injections boost total spending and enable firms to produce and sell a level of output greater than just consumption spending.

There are two types of injections in the economy. First is the government's purchases of goods and services. When government agencies—federal, state, or local—buy aircraft, cleaning supplies, cellular phones, or computers, they are buying a part of the economy's output.

The other injection is planned investment spending *(I^P)*. When business firms purchase new computers, trucks, or machinery, or they build new factories or office buildings, they are buying a part of the GDP along with consumers and the government.

Take another look at the rectangles in Figure 4. Notice that in going from total output to total spending, leakages are subtracted and injections are added. Clearly, total output and total spending will be equal only if leakages and injections are equal as well.

> *Total spending will equal total output if and only if total leakages in the economy are equal to total injections—that is, only if the sum of saving and net taxes is equal to the sum of planned investment spending and government purchases.*

Leakages Income earned, but not spent, by households during a given year.

Injections Spending from sources other than households.

HTTP://

The Census Bureau Web site provides statistics on retail and wholesale sales, national and regional data, and other business and economic data at http://www.census.gov/epcd/www/recent.htm.

And here is a surprising result: In the classical model, this condition will automatically be satisfied. To see why, we must first take a detour through another important market. Then we'll come back to the equality of leakages and injections.

THE LOANABLE FUNDS MARKET

Loanable funds market The market in which households make their saving available to borrowers.

The **loanable funds market** is where households make their saving available to those who need additional funds. When you save—that is, when you have income left over after paying taxes and buying consumption goods—you can put your surplus funds in a bank, buy a bond or a share of stock, or use the funds to buy a variety of other assets. In each of these cases, you would be a supplier in the loanable funds market

Households supply funds because they receive a reward for doing so. But the reward comes in different forms. When the suppliers *lend* out funds, the reward is *interest payments*. When the funds are provided through the stock market, the suppliers become part owners of the firm and their payment is called *dividends*. To keep our discussion simple, we'll assume that all funds made available by households are *loaned* and that the payment is simply *interest*.

> *The total supply of loanable funds is equal to household saving. The funds supplied are loaned out, and households* receive interest *payments on these funds.*

On the other side of the market are those who want to obtain funds—demanders in this market. Business firms are important demanders of funds. When Avis wants to add cars to its automobile rental fleet, when McDonald's wants to build a new beef-processing plant, or when the local dry cleaner wants to buy new dry cleaning machines, it will likely raise the funds in the loanable funds market. It may take out a bank loan, sell bonds, or sell new shares of stock. In each of these cases, a firm's planned investment spending would be equal to the funds it obtains from the loanable funds market. To keep the discussion simple, we'll assume that business firms *borrow* the funds they obtain in the loanable funds market.

> *Businesses' demand for loanable funds is equal to their planned investment spending. The funds obtained are borrowed, and firms pay interest on their loans.*

Aside from households and business firms, the other major player in the loanable funds market is the government sector. Government participates in the market whenever it runs a budget deficit or a budget surplus.

Budget deficit The excess of government purchases over net taxes.

Budget surplus The excess of net taxes over government purchases.

> *When government purchases of goods and services (G) are greater than net taxes (T), the government runs a budget deficit equal to G − T. When government purchases of goods and services (G) are less than net taxes (T), the government runs a budget surplus equal to T − G.*

In our example in Table 1, Classica's government is running a budget deficit: Government purchases are $2 trillion, while net taxes are $1.25 trillion, giving us a deficit of $2 trillion − $1.25 trillion = $0.75 trillion. This deficit is financed by borrowing in the loanable funds market. In any year, the government's demand for funds is equal to its deficit.

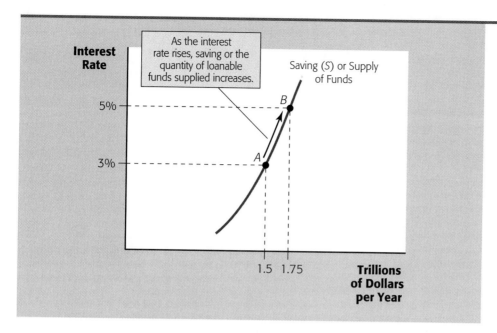

FIGURE 5
Household Supply of Loanable Funds

When the government runs a budget deficit, its demand for loanable funds is equal to its deficit. The funds are borrowed, and the government pays interest on its loans.

(What if Classica's government were running a surplus? We'll consider that toward the end of this chapter.)

We can summarize our view of the loanable funds market so far with these two points:

- The supply of funds is household saving.
- The demand for funds is the sum of the business sector's planned investment spending and the government sector's budget deficit, if any.

Now let's take a closer look at the behavior of each of the key players—households, business firms, and the government—in the market for loanable funds.

The Supply of Funds Curve

Since interest is the reward for saving and supplying funds to the financial market, a rise in the interest rate *increases* the quantity of funds supplied (household saving), while a drop in the interest rate decreases it. This relationship is illustrated by Classica's upward-sloping **supply of funds curve** in Figure 5. If the interest rate is 3 percent, households save $1.5 trillion, and if the interest rate rises to 5 percent, people save more and the quantity of funds supplied rises to $1.75 trillion.

Supply of funds curve Indicates the level of household saving at various interest rates.

The quantity of funds supplied to the financial market depends positively on the interest rate. This is why the saving or supply of funds curve slopes upward.

FIGURE 6
Business Demand for Loanable Funds

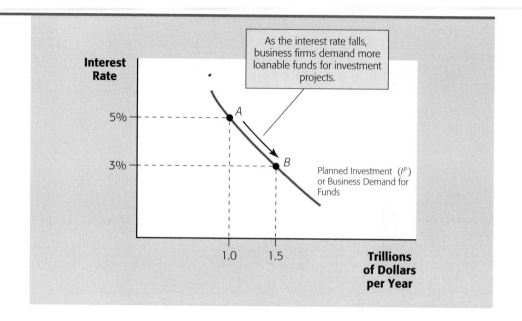

Of course, other things can affect saving besides the interest rate: tax rates, expectations about the future, and the general willingness of households to postpone consumption, to name a few. In drawing the supply of funds curve, we assume each of these variables is constant. In the next chapter, we'll explore what happens when some of these variables change.

The Demand for Funds Curve

Business demand for funds curve Indicates the level of investment spending firms plan at various interest rates.

Businesses buy plant and equipment when the expected benefits exceed the costs. Since businesses obtain the funds for their investment spending from the loanable funds market, a key cost of any investment project is the interest rate that must be paid on borrowed funds. As the interest rate rises and investment costs increase, fewer projects will look attractive, and planned investment spending will decline. This is the logic of the downward-sloping **business demand for funds curve** in Figure 6. At a 5 percent interest rate, firms would borrow $1 trillion and spend it on capital equipment; at an interest rate of 3 percent, business borrowing and investment spending would rise to $1.5 trillion.

> *When the interest rate falls, investment spending and the business borrowing needed to finance it rise. The business demand for funds curve slopes downward.*

What about the government's demand for funds? Will it, too, be influenced by the interest rate? Probably not very much. Government seems to be cushioned from the cost–benefit considerations that haunt business decisions. Any company president who ignored interest rates in deciding how much to borrow would be quickly out of a job. U.S. presidents and legislators have often done so with little political cost.

For this reason, when government is running a budget deficit, our classical model treats government borrowing as independent of the interest rate: No matter

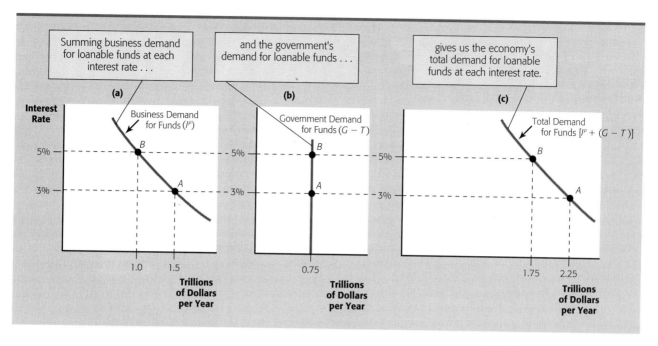

FIGURE 7
The Demand for Funds

what the interest rate, the government sector's deficit—and its borrowing—remain constant. This is why we have graphed the **government's demand for funds curve** as a vertical line in panel (b) of Figure 7.

> *The government sector's deficit and, therefore, its demand for funds are independent of the interest rate.*

In the figure, the government deficit—and hence the government's demand for funds—is equal to $0.75 trillion at any interest rate.

Figure 7 also shows that the **total demand for funds curve** is found by horizontally summing the business demand curve [panel (a)] and the government demand curve [panel (b)]. For example, if the interest rate is 5 percent, firms demand $1 trillion in funds and the government demands $0.75 trillion, so that the total quantity of loanable funds demanded is $1.75 trillion. A drop in the interest rate—to 3 percent—increases business borrowing to $1.5 trillion while the government's borrowing remains at $0.75 trillion, so the total quantity of funds demanded rises to $2.25 trillion.

> *As the interest rate decreases, the quantity of funds demanded by business firms increases, while the quantity demanded by the government remains unchanged. Therefore, the* total *quantity of funds demanded rises.*

Government demand for funds curve Indicates the amount of government borrowing at various interest rates.

Total demand for funds curve Indicates the total amount of borrowing at various interest rates.

Equilibrium in the Loanable Funds Market

In the classical view, the loanable funds market—like all other markets—is assumed to clear: The interest rate will rise or fall until the quantities of funds supplied and demanded are equal. Figure 8 illustrates the loanable funds market of Classica, our fictional economy. Equilibrium occurs at point *E*, with an interest rate of 5 percent and total saving equal to $1.75 trillion. (To convince yourself that 5 percent is the

FIGURE 8
**Loanable Funds Market
Equilibrium**

*Suppliers and demanders of
funds interact to determine the
interest rate in the loanable
funds market. At an interest rate
of 5%, quantity supplied and
quantity demanded are both
equal to $1.75 trillion.*

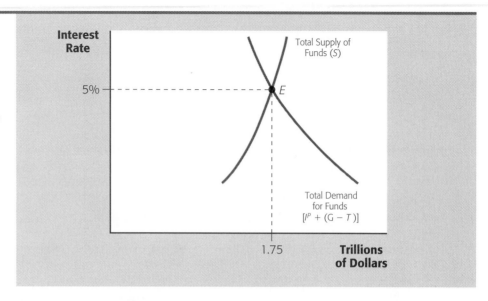

*Borrowing from a bank (such as
First and Ocean) is one way
firms obtain loanable funds for
investment projects.*

equilibrium interest rate, mark an interest rate of 4 percent on the graph. Would
there be an excess demand or an excess supply of loanable funds at this rate? How
would the interest rate change? Then do the same for an interest rate of 6 percent.)

Once we know the equilibrium interest rate (5 percent), we can use the first two
panels of Figure 7 to tell us exactly where the total household saving of $1.75 bil-
lion ends up. Panel (a) tells us that at 5 percent interest, business firms are borrowing $1 trillion of the total, and panel (b) tells us that the government is borrowing
the remaining $0.75 trillion to cover its deficit.

So far, our exploration of the loanable funds market has shown us how three
important variables in the economy are determined: the interest rate, the level of
saving, and the level of investment. But it really tells us more. Remember the question that sent us on this detour into the loanable funds market in the first place:
Can we be sure that all of the output produced at full employment will be purchased? We now have the tools to answer this question.

The Loanable Funds Market and Say's Law

In Figure 4 of this chapter, you saw that total spending will equal total output if and
only if *total leakages* in the economy (saving plus net taxes) are equal to *total injections* (planned investment plus government purchases).Now we can see why this requirement will be satisfied automatically in the classical model. Look at Figure 9,
which duplicates the rectangles from Figure 4. But there is something added: arrows
to indicate the flows between leakages and injections.

Let's follow the arrows to see what happens to all the leakages out of spending.
One arrow shows that the entire leakage of net taxes ($1.25 trillion) flows to the
government, which spends it. Another arrow shows that $1.75 trillion of saving
flows into the loanable funds market. And the last two arrows show that $0.75 tril-
lion of this saving is borrowed by the government, while the rest—$1 trillion—is
borrowed by business firms.

Now let's step back from the numbers, and think about the logic in the diagram.
Remember our question: Will total spending be sufficient to purchase the economy's

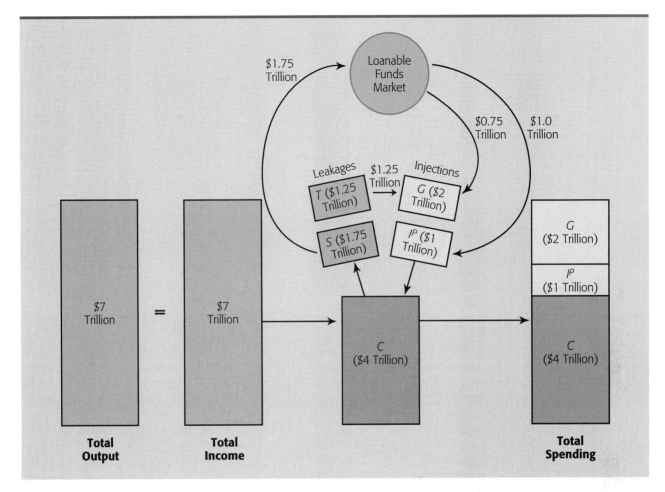

FIGURE 9

How the Loanable Funds Market Ensures that Total Spending = Total Output

Because the loanable funds market clears, we know that total leakages will automatically equal total injections. The leakage of net taxes goes to the government and is spent on government purchases. If the government is running a budget deficit, it will also borrow part of the leakage of household saving and spend that too. Any household saving left over will be borrowed by business firms and spent on capital. Thus, every dollar of leakages turns into spending by either government or private business firms.

total output? And remember what created some doubt about the answer: The household sector spends only *part* of its income, because of the leakages of net taxes and saving.

Now we can see that net taxes and savings don't just disappear from the economy. Net taxes go to the government, which *spends them*. And any funds saved go either to the government—which spends them—or to business firms—which spend them. But wait . . . how do we know that *all* funds that are saved will end up going to either the government or businesses? Because the loanable funds market clears: The interest rate adjusts until the quantity of loanable funds supplied (saving) is equal to the quantity of loanable funds demanded (government and business borrowing).

We can put all this together as follows: Every dollar of output creates a dollar of household income, by definition. And—as long as the loanable funds market clears—every dollar of income will either be spent by households themselves or passed along to some *other* sector of the economy that will spend it in their place.

Or, to put it even more simply,

as long as the loanable funds market clears, Say's law holds: Total spending equals total output. This is true even in a more realistic economy with saving, taxes, investment and a government deficit.

Here's another way to see the same result, in terms of a simple equation. Because the loanable funds market clears, we know that the interest rate—the price in this market—will rise or fall until the quantity of funds supplied (savings, S) is equal to the quantity of funds demanded (planned investment plus the deficit, or $I^P + (G - T)$):

$$\text{Loanable funds market clears} \quad \Rightarrow \quad \underbrace{S}_{\substack{\text{Quantity of} \\ \text{funds supplied}}} = \underbrace{I^P + (G - T)}_{\substack{\text{Quantity of} \\ \text{funds demanded}}}$$

Rearranging this equation by moving T to the left side, we have:

$$\text{Loanable funds market clears} \quad \Rightarrow \quad \underbrace{S + T}_{\text{Leakages}} = \underbrace{I^P + G}_{\text{Injections}}$$

Finally, remember that

$$\text{Leakages} = \text{Injections} \quad \Rightarrow \quad \text{Total spending} = \text{Total output}$$

In other words, market clearing in the loanable funds market *assures us* that total leakages in the economy will equal total injections, which in turn *assures us* that total spending will be just sufficient to purchase total output.

Say's law is a powerful concept. But be careful not to overinterpret it. Say's law shows that the *total* value of spending in the economy will equal the *total* value of output, which rules out a *general* overproduction or underproduction of goods in the economy. It does not promise us that each firm in the economy will be able to sell all of the particular good it produces. It is perfectly consistent with Say's law that there be excess supplies in some markets, as long as they are balanced by excess demands in other markets.

But lest you begin to think that the classical economy might be a chaotic mess, with excess supplies and demands in lots of markets, don't forget about the *market-clearing* assumption. In each market, prices adjust until quantities supplied and demanded are equal. For this reason, the classical, long-run view rules out over- or underproduction in individual markets, as well as the generalized overproduction ruled out by Say's law.

THE CLASSICAL MODEL: A SUMMARY

You've just completed a first tour of the classical model, our framework for understanding the economy in the long run. Before we begin to *use* this model, this is a good time to go back and review what we've done.

We began with a critical assumption: All markets clear. We then used the first two steps of our three-step process to organize our thinking about the economy. First, we focused on an important market—the labor market. We identified the buyers and sellers in that market, and then found the equilibrium by assuming that the market cleared.

We went through a similar process with the loanable funds market, identifying the suppliers and demanders, examining how each would be affected by changes in the interest rate, and finding the equilibrium in that market as well. Finally, we saw how market clearing in the loanable funds market assures us that total spending will be just sufficient to purchase our potential output level.

Our analysis leads us to two important policy conclusions:

In the classical model, the government needn't worry about employment: The economy will achieve full employment on its own;

and

in the classical model, the government needn't worry about total spending: The economy will generate just enough spending on its own to buy the output that a fully employed labor force produces.

But suppose the government wanted to make the economy do even better—to employ even *more* people and produce even *more* output than the classical model suggests. Could the government accomplish this by engineering an *increase* in total spending? We'll answer this question in the "Using the Theory" section.

 U S I N G   T H E   T H E O R Y
Fiscal Policy in the Classical Model

Could the government increase the economy's total employment and total output by raising total spending? It *seems* like an idea that should work. After all, with higher total spending, business firms would sell more output, so they might want to hire more workers and produce more. And two ideas for increasing spending come to mind. First, the government could simply purchase more output: more goods, like tanks and police cars, or more services, like those provided by high school teachers and judges. Second, the government could cut net taxes, letting households keep more of their income, so they would spend more on food, clothing, furniture, new cars, and so on. (Since net taxes are tax revenues minus government transfers, there are two ways to cut net taxes: decrease tax revenues, or increase transfers.)

If the government uses either of these steps, it would be engaging in *fiscal policy:*

© JACQUES M. CHENET/CORBIS

Fiscal policy is a change in government purchases or in net taxes designed to change total spending in the economy and thereby influence the levels of employment and output.

The idea behind fiscal policy sounds sensible enough. But does it work?

Not if the economy behaves according to the classical model. As you are about to see, in the classical model, fiscal policy is completely ineffective. It cannot change total output or employment in the economy, period. It cannot even change total spending. Moreover, fiscal policy is *unnecessary,* since the economy achieves and sustains full employment on its own. Here, we'll demonstrate this conclusion for the case of an increase in government spending. In a challenge question at the end of this chapter, you are invited to demonstrate the same conclusion for the case of a cut in net taxes.

Fiscal policy A change in government purchases or net taxes designed to change total spending and thereby change total output.

Fiscal Policy with a Budget Deficit

Let's first see what would happen if the government of Classica attempted to increase employment and output by increasing government purchases. More specifically, suppose the government raised its spending by $0.5 trillion, hiring people to fix roads and bridges, or hiring more teachers, or increasing its spending on goods and services for homeland security. What would happen?

To answer this, we must first answer another question: Where will Classica's government get the additional $0.5 trillion it spends? If net taxes are unchanged (as we are assuming), then the government deficit will rise, so the government must dip into the loanable funds market to *borrow* the additional funds.

Figure 10 illustrates the effects. Initially, with government purchases equal to $2 trillion, the demand for funds curve is D_1, and equilibrium occurs at point A with the interest rate equal to 5 percent. If government purchases increase by $0.5 trillion, with no change in taxes, the budget deficit increases by $0.5 trillion and so does the government's demand for funds. The demand for funds curve shifts rightward by $0.5 trillion to D_2, since total borrowing will now be $0.5 trillion greater at *any* interest rate. After the shift, there would be an excess demand for funds at the original interest rate of 5 percent. The total quantity of funds demanded would be $2.25 trillion (point H), while the quantity supplied would continue to be $1.75 trillion (point A). Thus, the excess demand for funds would be equal to the distance AH in the figure, or $0.5 trillion. This excess demand drives up the interest rate to 7 percent. As the interest rate rises, two things happen.

First, a higher interest rate chokes off some investment spending, as business firms decide that certain investment projects no longer make sense. For example, the local dry cleaner might wish to borrow funds for a new machine at an interest rate of 5 percent, but not at 7 percent. In the figure, as we move along the new demand for funds curve D_2, from point H to point B, planned investment declines by $0.2 trillion (from $2.25 trillion to $2.05 trillion). (Question: How do we know that only business borrowing, and not also government borrowing, adjusts as we move from point H to point B?) Thus, one consequence of the rise in government purchases is a *decrease in planned investment spending*.

But that's not all: The rise in the interest rate also causes saving to increase. Of course, when people save more of their incomes, they spend less, so another consequence of the rise in government purchases is a *decrease in consumption spending*. In the figure, as we move from point A to point B along the saving curve, saving increases (and consumption decreases) by $0.3 trillion—rising from $1.75 trillion to $2.05 trillion.

Let's recap: As a result of the increase in government purchases, both planned investment spending and consumption spending decline. The government's purchases have *crowded out* the spending of households (C) and businesses (I^P).

Crowding out A decline in one sector's spending caused by an increase in some other sector's spending.

> **Crowding out** *is a decline in one sector's spending caused by an increase in some other sector's spending.*

Complete crowding out A dollar-for-dollar decline in one sector's spending caused by an increase in some other sector's spending.

But we are not quite finished. If we sum the drop in C and the drop in I^P, we find that total private sector spending has fallen by $0.3 trillion + $0.2 trillion = $0.5 trillion. That is, the drop in private sector spending is *precisely equal* to the rise in government purchases, G. Not only is there crowding out, there is **complete crowding out:** Each dollar of government purchases causes private sector spending

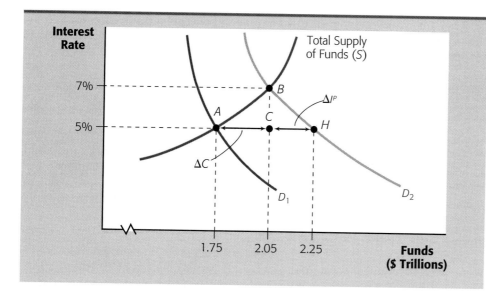

FIGURE 10

Crowding Out with an Initial Budget Deficit

Beginning from equilibrium at point A, an increase in the budget deficit created to finance additional government purchases shifts the demand for funds curve from D₁ to D₂. At point H, the quantity of funds demanded exceeds the quantity supplied, so the interest rate begins to rise. As it rises, households are led to save more, and business firms invest less. In the new equilibrium at point B, both consumption and investment spending have been completely crowded out by the increased government spending.

to decline by a full dollar. The net effect is that total spending ($C + I^P + G$) does not change at all!

> *In the classical model, a rise in government purchases completely crowds out private sector spending, so total spending remains unchanged.*

A closer look at Figure 10 shows that this conclusion always holds, regardless of the particular numbers used or the shapes of the curves. When G increases, the demand for funds curve shifts rightward by the same amount that G rises, or the distance from point A to point H. Then the interest rate rises, moving us along the supply of funds curve from point A to point B. As a result, saving rises (and consumption falls) by the distance AC. But the rise in the interest rate *also* causes a movement along the demand for funds curve, from point H to point B. As a result, investment spending falls by the amount CH.

The final impact can be summarized as follows:

- $G\!\uparrow = AH$
- $C\!\downarrow = AC$
- $I^P\!\downarrow = CH$

And since $AC + CH = AH$, we know that the combined decrease in C and I^P is precisely equal to the increase in G.

Because there is complete crowding out in the classical model, a rise in government purchases cannot change total spending. And the logic behind this result is straightforward. Each additional dollar the government spends is obtained from the loanable funds market, where *it would have been spent by someone else* if the government hadn't borrowed it. How do we know this? Because the loanable funds market funnels every dollar of household saving—no more and no less—to either the government or business firms. If the government borrows more, it just removes funds that would have been spent by businesses (the drop in I^P) or by consumers (the drop in C).

Remember that the goal of this increase in government purchases was to increase output and employment *by increasing total spending*. But now we see that the policy fails to increase spending at all. Therefore,

> *in the classical model, an increase in government purchases has no impact on total spending and no impact on total output or total employment.*

Of course, the opposite sequence of events would happen if government purchases *decreased*: The drop in *G* would *shrink* the deficit. The interest rate would decline, and private sector spending (*C* and I^P) would rise by the same amount that government purchases had fallen. (See if you can draw the graphs to prove this to yourself.) Once again, total spending and total output would remain unchanged.

Fiscal Policy with a Budget Surplus

What if the government were running a budget *surplus* instead of a budget deficit? The classical model works very much the same way and gives us the same conclusions. However, some of the details change.

The government sector runs a budget surplus when its net tax revenue (*T*) is greater than its purchases (*G*):

$$\text{Budget Surplus} = T - G$$

When the government runs a surplus, it pays back debts that it incurred while running deficits in previous years. At the federal level, for example, the federal government's unpaid debt is called the *national debt*. When the federal government runs a surplus (as it did for a few years in the late 1990s), it uses the net tax revenues that it doesn't spend to pay back part of the national debt, buying back government bonds that it issued in previous years when it ran deficits. In this sense, the government becomes a *supplier* of loanable funds, because it is putting funds back into the market, where they can be borrowed by others.

Figure 11 shows the equilibrium in the loanable funds market with a budget surplus. Now, the government *supplies* loanable funds rather than demands them. Therefore, the total demand for loanable funds in Figure 11 is equal to business investment spending alone. The supply of loanable funds, however, now consists of household saving *plus* the budget surplus. So, because of the surplus, the total supply of funds curve S_1 lies farther to the right than it otherwise would, by the amount of the initial surplus.

In the initial equilibrium at point *A*, the interest rate is 5 percent, and the total quantity of funds supplied and demanded are equal, at $1.75 trillion. If government spending rises by $0.5 trillion, with no change in taxes, the budget surplus will shrink by $0.5 trillion, shifting the supply of funds curve leftward by that amount to S_2. In new equilibrium at point *B*, the interest rate is higher (7 percent) and the quantity of funds supplied and demanded is lower ($1.55 trillion).

But that's not all: The rise in the interest rate also causes saving to increase, and consumption spending to decrease. This is represented by the movement from point *H* to point *B* along the new supply of funds curve, which causes saving to rise (consumption to decrease) by $0.3 trillion, or the distance *HC*. The rise in the interest rate also causes investment spending to decrease along the total demand for funds curve, from point *A* to point *B*. Investment spending falls by $0.2 trillion, or the dis-

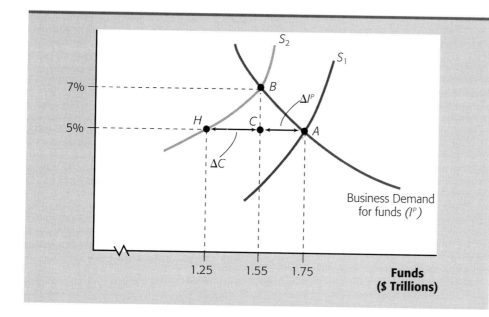

FIGURE 11
Crowding Out with an Initial Budget Surplus

Beginning from equilibrium at point A, an increase in government purchases causes a decrease in the budget surplus, shifting the supply of funds curve from S₁ to S₂. At point H, the quantity of funds demanded exceeds the quantity supplied, so the interest rate begins to rise. As it rises, households are led to save more, and business firms invest less. In the new equilibrium at point B, both consumption and investment spending have been completely crowded out by the increased government spending.

tance *AC*. Once again, we see that the rise in government spending has completely crowded out consumption and investment spending: A $0.5 trillion rise in government spending has caused consumption and investment spending to decrease by a total of $0.5 trillion. Total spending remains unchanged, and the fiscal policy is completely ineffective. This is the same conclusion we reached about fiscal policy in the previous section, with a government budget deficit.

If you look back over the conclusions we've reached in this chapter, you'll see that virtually all of them were preceded by the words, "In the classical model . . ." (Look back, for example, at the last highlighted statement about the effect of an increase in government purchases.) These words have been added for good reason: All of our conclusions followed from a critical assumption of the classical model: *markets clear.*

This assumption is most realistic when we take a very long-run view of the economy. In the labor market, for example, a persistent significant excess supply of labor—in which millions of qualified people are looking for work for long periods of time and not finding jobs—would *eventually* lead to falling wages, more hiring by firms, and the achievement of full employment.

Since the classical model's assumptions are most accurate over the long run, its conclusions, too, will be most accurate when we take the long-run view—when we look at the average performance of the economy over a period of many years.

Our exploration of fiscal policy shows us that, in the long run, government efforts to change total output by changing government spending or taxes are not only unnecessary, but also ineffective. What, then, *should* a government do to help manage the macroeconomy in the long run? And what *can* it do? These are questions we explore in the next chapter, where we use the classical model to analyze how potential output grows over the long run, and how government policy can help or hinder that growth.

Summary

The classical model is an attempt to explain the behavior of the economy over long time periods. Its most critical assumption is that markets clear—that prices adjust in every market to equate quantities demanded and supplied. The labor market is perhaps the most important part of the classical model. When the labor market clears, we have full employment and the economy produces the potential level of output.

Another important concept is the production function. It shows the total output the economy can produce with different quantities of labor and for given amounts of other resources and a given state of technology. When the labor market is at full employment, the production function can be used to determine the economy's potential level of output.

According to Say's law, total spending in the economy will always be just sufficient to purchase the amount of total output produced. By producing and selling goods and services, firms create a total demand equal to what they have produced. If households do not spend their entire incomes, the excess is channeled, as saving, into the loanable funds market, where it is borrowed and spent by businesses and government.

In the loanable funds market, the quantity of funds supplied equals household saving, which depends positively on the interest rate, and the budget surplus (if there is one). The quantity of funds demanded equals business investment, which depends negatively on the interest rate, and any government budget deficit, if there is one. The interest rate adjusts so that the quantity of funds supplied always equals the quantity demanded. Equivalently (with a budget deficit), it adjusts so that saving (S) equals the sum of planned investment spending (^{P}) and the government budget deficit ($G - T$).

Fiscal policy cannot affect total output in the classical model. An increase in government purchases results in complete crowding out of planned investment and consumption spending, leaving total spending and total output unchanged.

Key Terms

Aggregate production function
Budget deficit
Budget surplus
Business demand for funds curve
Circular flow
Classical model
Complete crowding out
Crowding out

Disposable income
Fiscal policy
Government demand for funds curve
(Household) saving
Injections
Labor demand curve
Labor supply curve
Leakages

Loanable funds market
Market clearing
Net taxes
Planned investment spending
Say's law
Supply of funds curve
Total demand for funds curve

Review Questions   *Answers to even-numbered Questions and Problems can be found on the text Web site at http://hall-lieb.swlearning.com.*

1. Discuss the critical assumption on which the classical model is based. How does it relate to the length of time over which we are analyzing the economy?

2. Describe how, in the classical model, the economy reaches full employment automatically. Is this a "realistic" depiction of how the economy behaves?

3. Why does the classical model treat technology and the capital stock as constant?

4. Explain why the slope of the aggregate production function diminishes as more labor is employed.

5. "According to Say's law, all markets always clear." True or false? Explain.

6. What is the difference between net taxes and total tax revenue? Why is the distinction important?

7. Who are the two major groups on the demand side of the loanable funds market? Why does each seek funds there? What is the "price" of these funds?

8. What is the source of funds supplied to the loanable funds market?

9. Explain why the supply of funds curve slopes upward, and why the curve depicting business demand for funds slopes downward.

10. How will the *slope* of the demand for funds curve be affected if the government runs a budget deficit? Why?

11. Why does Say's law hold even after household saving and taxes are taken into account?

12. Explain the implications of the classical model for government economic policy. What are the two consequences

of an increase in government spending that the model predicts?

13. A senator asserts that deficit spending reduces business investment dollar for dollar—every dollar the government borrows means that business investment must fall by a dollar. Is he correct? Why or why not?

14. What is the only type of spending in GDP that is not planned? How does this type of spending occur?

Problems and Exercises

1. Use a diagram similar to Figure 2 to illustrate the effect, on aggregate output and the real hourly wage, of (a) an increase in labor demand, and (b) an increase in labor supply.

2. The following data give a complete picture of the household, business, and government sectors for 2005 in the small nation of Sylvania. (All dollar figures are in billions.)

Consumption spending	$50
Capital stock (end of 2004)	$100
Capital stock (end of 2005)	$103
Change in inventories	$0
Government welfare payments	$5
Government unemployment insurance payments	$2
Government payroll	$3
Government outlays for materials	$2
Depreciation rate	7%
Interest rate	6%

Assuming the government budget for 2005 was in balance, calculate each of the following (in order):
a. government purchases
b. net taxes
c. total investment
d. real GDP
e. total saving
f. total leakages
g. total injections

3. For the economy in Problem 2, suppose that the government had purchased $2 billion more in goods and services than you found in that problem, with no change in taxes.
a. Explain how each of the variables you calculated in Problem 2 would be affected (i.e., state whether it would increase or decrease).
b. Draw a graph illustrating the impact of the $2 billion increase in government purchases on the loanable funds market. Clearly label the equilibrium interest rate, saving, and total quantity of funds demanded at both the original and the new level of government purchases. (Note: You won't be able to find specific numbers.)

4. Once again, as in Problem 3, suppose that Sylvania's government increases its purchases by $2 billion. But this time, suppose Sylvania has a law that prohibits the interest rate from rising above 6 percent. Explain what will happen now in the loanable funds market, and in the economy as a whole. (*Hint:* Will leakages and injections be equal after the increase in government purchases?)

5. Draw a diagram (similar to Figure 10 in this chapter) illustrating the impact of a *decrease* in government purchases. Assume the government is running a budget deficit both before and after the change in government purchases. On your diagram, identify distances that represent:
a. the decrease in government purchases;
b. the increase in consumption spending; and
c. the increase in planned investment spending.

6. Consider the following statement: "In the classical model, just as an *increase* in government purchases causes complete crowding *out*, so a *decrease* in government purchases causes complete crowding *in*."
a. In this statement, explain what is meant by "crowding in" and "complete crowding in."
b. Is the statement true? (*Hint:* Look at the diagram you drew in Problem 5.)

7. Using a three-panel graph similar in style to Figure 7, illustrate how the *supply* of funds curve is obtained when the government is running a budget surplus.

8. Show that Say's law still holds when the government is running a surplus rather than a deficit. (*Hint:* Use a diagram similar to Figure 9.)

9. Use graphs to depict the effect on saving, investment, and the interest rate of a *decrease* in government spending when the government is running a budget *surplus*.

10. Redraw Figure 10 from the chapter, and label
a. the amount of government borrowing that occurs at point B; and
b. the amount of private borrowing that occurs at point B.

How do these amounts compare with the amounts at the original equilibrium at point A?

11.   The following data ($ millions) are for the island nation of
      Pacifica.

Total output	$10
Total income	$10
Consumption	$ 6
Government Spending	$ 3
Total Tax Revenue	$ 2.5
Transfer Payments	$ 0.5

a.   Use this information to find Pacifica's net taxes, dis-
     posable income, and savings.
b.   Determine whether the government is running a sur-
     plus, deficit, or balanced budget.

c.   Find planned investment by calculating how much is
     available in the loanable funds market after the govern-
     ment has borrowed what it might need.
d.   Does total output equal total spending?
e.   Show your answers on a diagram similar to the one in
     Figure 9 in the chapter.

12. Return to Question 11. What will happen if consumption
    spending starts to rise? Assume no change in net taxes.
    Show the effect on the loanable funds market, and tell
    what will happen to C, I^P, and G. (*Note:* You won't be
    able to find specific numbers.)

Challenge Questions

1.   Using an analysis similar to the one in the "Using the
     Theory" section, show that a tax cut (which decreases net
     taxes) cannot increase total spending in the economy, un-
     der each of the following two assumptions:
     a.   Initially (before any change in the interest rate), *none*
          of the tax cut is saved, so that the supply of funds
          curve does not shift at all.
     b.   Initially (before any change in the interest rate), the *en-*
          tire tax cut is saved, causing the supply of funds curve
          to shift rightward by an amount equal to the tax cut.

2.   Assume the loanable funds market is in equilibrium. Influ-
     ential media pundits begin to warn about impending eco-
     nomic doom: recession, layoffs, and so forth. Using
     graphs, discuss what might happen to the equilibrium in-
     terest rate and the equilibrium quantity of loanable funds
     supplied and demanded. Assume that the government bud-
     get is in balance—neither a deficit nor a surplus. (*Hint:*
     How would these warnings separately affect household
     and business behavior in the loanable funds market?)

 **ECONOMIC** *Applications*   *These exercises require access to Hall/Lieberman Xtra! If Xtra! did not come with your book, visit http://hallxtra.swlearning.com to purchase.*

1.   Use your Xtra! password at the Hall and Lieberman Web
     site (http://hallxtra.swlearning.com), select this chapter,
     and under Economic Applications, click on EconDebate.
     Choose *Macroeconomics: Employment, Unemployment,
     and Inflation* and scroll down to find the debate, "Does
     an Increase in the Minimum Wage Result in a Higher Un-
     employment Rate?" Read the debate and use the infor-
     mation to answer the following questions.
     a.   The labor market is one of the most important parts
          of the classical model. What are the ramifications of
          the minimum wage laws on employment and output
          according to the classical model?
     b.   Considering the effects of inflation on the minimum
          wage would you expect the labor markets to clear or

     unemployment to persist in the presence of the mini-
     mum wage laws? Explain.

2.   Use your Xtra! password at the Hall and Lieberman
     Web site (http://hallxtra.swlearning.com), select this
     chapter, and under Economic Applications, click on
     EconDebate. Choose *Macroeconomics: Employment,
     Unemployment, and Inflation* and scroll down to find
     the *Real GDP*, Read the definition and click on Dia-
     grams/Data and use the information to answer the fol-
     lowing question. Does the empirical data on employ-
     ment support the classical assumption that labor
     markets clear? Explain why or why not.

Economic Growth and Rising Living Standards

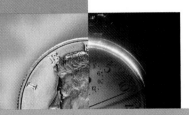

Economist Thomas Malthus, writing in 1798, came to a striking conclusion: "Population, when unchecked, goes on doubling itself every twenty-five years, or increases in a geometrical ratio. . . . The means of subsistence . . . could not possibly be made to increase faster than in an arithmetic ratio."[1] From this simple logic, Malthus forecast a horrible fate for the human race. There would be repeated famines and wars to keep the rapidly growing population in balance with the more slowly growing supply of food and other necessities. The prognosis was so pessimistic that it led Thomas Carlyle, one of Malthus's contemporaries, to label economics "the dismal science."

But history has proven Malthus wrong . . . at least in part. In the industrialized nations, living standards have increased beyond the wildest dreams of anyone alive in Malthus's time. Economists today are optimistic about these nations' long-run material prospects. At the same time, living standards in many of the less-developed countries have remained stubbornly close to survival level and, in some cases, have fallen below it.

What are we to make of this? Why have living standards steadily increased in some nations but not in others? And what, if anything, can governments do to speed the rise in living standards? These are questions about economic growth—the long-run increase in an economy's output of goods and services.

---

[1] Thomas Robert Malthus, *An Essay on the Principle of Population*, 1798.

In this chapter, you will learn what makes economies grow. Our approach will make use of the classical model, focusing on Step 3 of the three-step process: What Happens When Things Change? As you'll see, growth arises from *shifts* of the curves of the classical model. And by the end of this chapter, you will know why increasing the rate of economic growth is not easy. While nations can take measures to speed growth, each measure carries an opportunity cost. More specifically,

> *achieving a higher rate of growth in the long run generally requires some sacrifice in the short run.*

THE IMPORTANCE OF GROWTH

Why should we be concerned about economic growth? For one simple reason:

> When output grows faster than the population, GDP per capita, which we call the **average standard of living**, will rise. When output grows more slowly than the population, the average standard of living will fall.

Average standard of living Total output (real GDP) per person.

Measuring the standard of living by GDP per capita may seem limiting. After all, as we saw two chapters ago, many important aspects of our quality of life are not captured in GDP. Leisure time, workplace safety, good health, a clean environment—we care about all of these. Yet they are not considered in GDP.

Still, many aspects of our quality of life *are* counted in GDP: food, housing, medical care, education, transportation services, and movies and video games, to name a few. It is not surprising, then, that economic growth—measured by increases in GDP—remains a vital concern in every nation.

Economic growth is especially important in countries with income levels far below those of Europe, Japan, and the United States. The average standard of living in some third-world nations is so low that many families can barely acquire the basic necessities of life, and many others perish from disease or starvation. Table 1 lists GDP per capita, infant mortality rates, life expectancies, and adult literacy rates for some of the richest and poorest countries. The statistics for the poor countries are grim enough, but even they capture only part of the story. Unsafe and unclean workplaces, inadequate housing, and other sources of misery are part of daily life for most people in these countries. Other than emigration, economic growth is their only hope.

Growth is a high priority in prosperous nations, too. As we know, resources are scarce, and we cannot produce enough of everything to satisfy all of our desires simultaneously. We want more and better medical care, education, vacations, entertainment . . . the list is endless. When output per capita is growing, it's at least *possible* for everyone to enjoy an increase in material well-being without anyone having to cut back. We can also accomplish important social goals—helping the poor, improving education, cleaning up the environment—by asking those who are doing well to sacrifice part of the rise in their material well-being, rather than suffer a drop.

But when output per capita stagnates, material gains become a fight over a fixed pie: The more purchasing power my neighbor has, the less is left for me. With everyone struggling for a larger piece of this fixed pie, conflict replaces cooperation. Efforts to help the less fortunate, wipe out illiteracy, reduce air pollution—all are seen as threats, rather than opportunities.

Country	Real GDP per Capita	Infant Mortality Rate (per 1,000 Live Births)	Life Expectancy at Birth	Adult Literacy Rate
Rich Countries				
United States	$34,320	7	76.9	Greater than 99%
Japan	$25,130	3	81.3	Greater than 99%
France	$23,990	4	78.7	Greater than 99%
United Kingdom	$24,160	6	77.9	Greater than 99%
Italy	$24,670	4	78.6	98.5%
Poor Countries				
Azerbaijan	$ 3,090	74	71.8	97.0%
Ghana	$ 2,250	57	57.7	72.7%
Pakistan	$ 1,890	84	60.4	44.0%
Cambodia	$ 1,860	97	57.4	68.7%
Sierra Leone	$ 470	182	34.5	36.0%

TABLE 1

Some Indicators of Economic Well-Being in Rich and Poor Countries, 2003

Sources: United Nations Development Programme, *Human Development Report 2003*, pp. 237–240 and 262–265.

In the 1950s and 1960s, economic growth in the wealthier nations seemed to be taking care of itself. Economists and policy makers focused their attention on short-run movements around full-employment output, rather than on the growth of full-employment output itself. The real payoff for government seemed to be in preventing recessions and depressions—in keeping the economy operating as close to its potential as possible.

All of that changed starting in the 1970s, and economic growth became a national and international preoccupation. Like most changes in perception and thought, this one was driven by experience. Table 2 tells the story. It gives the average yearly growth rates of real GDP per capita for the United States and some of our key trading partners.

Over most of the postwar period, output in the more prosperous industrialized countries (such as the United States, the United Kingdom, and Canada) grew by 2 or 3 percent per year, while output in the less wealthy ones—those with some catching up to do—grew even faster. But beginning in the mid-1970s, all of these nations saw their growth rates slip.

In the late 1990s and early 2000s, only the United States and the United Kingdom returned to their previous high rates of growth, while the other industrialized countries continued to grow more slowly than their historical averages.

Looking at the table, you might think that this slowing in growth was rather insignificant. Do the tiny differences between the pre-1972 and the post-1972 growth rates really matter? Indeed, they do. Recall our example a few chapters ago in which an increase in the U.S. growth rate of around 1 percentage point over the past 27 years would mean $27 trillion in additional output over the entire period. Seemingly small differences in growth rates matter a great deal.

TABLE 2
Average Annual Growth Rate of Output per Capita

Country	1948–1972	1972–1988	1988–1995	1995–2001
United States	2.2%	1.7%	1.0%	2.7%
United Kingdom	2.4	2.1	0.9	2.4
Canada	2.9	2.6	0.6	2.3
France	4.3	2.1	1.2	2.1
Italy	4.9	2.8	1.6	1.7
West Germany	5.7	2.2	1.3	1.3
Japan	8.2	3.3	2.1	0.9

Sources: Angus Maddison, *Phases of Capitalist Development* (Oxford: Oxford University Press, 1982); U.S. Census Bureau IDB Summary Demographic Data (*http://www.census.gov/ipc/www/idbsum.html*); and *Economic Report of the President,* 2002, Table B-112, and various World Bank publications. *Note:* Data for Germany includes West Germany only through 1995, and all of Germany from 1995 to 1999.

WHAT MAKES ECONOMIES GROW?

A useful way to start thinking about long-run growth is to look at what determines our potential GDP in any given period. Starting this process is very simple: We can say that real GDP depends on

- The amount of output the average worker can produce in an hour
- The number of hours the average worker spends at the job
- The fraction of the population that wants to work
- The size of the population

If you spend a moment considering each of these variables, you'll see that—all else equal—if any one of them increases, real GDP rises.

Before we start working with these determinants of growth, let's briefly discuss how the first three are measured. The amount of output the average worker produces in an hour is called **labor productivity**, or just **productivity**. It is measured by taking the total output (real GDP) of the economy over a period of time and dividing by the total number of hours that *everyone* worked during that period.

Labor productivity The output produced by the average worker in an hour.

$$\text{Productivity} = \text{Output per hour} = \frac{\text{Total output}}{\text{Total hours worked}}.$$

For example, if during a given month all workers in the United States spent a total of 25 billion hours at their jobs and produced $1 trillion worth of output, then on average, labor productivity would be $1 trillion / 25 billion hours = $40 per hour. Or in words, the average worker would produce $40 worth of output in an hour. As you'll see later in this chapter, increases in productivity are one of the most important contributors to economic growth.

Next, the hours of the average worker can be found by dividing the total hours worked over a period by total employment, the *number* of people who worked during the period. However—since we're ultimately interested in *potential* output rather than actual output in any particular period—we'll assume that, on average, the economy behaves according to the classical model: All those who *want* to work will find a job. Therefore, over the long run, total employment is equal to the number of people who want to work—the *labor force*.

$$\text{Average Hours} = \frac{\text{Total hours}}{\text{Labor Force}}.$$

For example, if the labor force is 200 million people and they would work a total of 25 billion hours per month if all were employed, then average hours per month would be 25 billion hours / 200 million workers = 125 hours per month.

Now let's turn to the fraction of the population working. Once again we'll take a long-run perspective—assuming that all those who want to work will find employment. Then the fraction of the population working is the **labor force participation rate (LFPR)**, and is found by dividing the labor force (all those who want to be working) by the population:[2]

Labor force participation rate (LFPR)
The percentage of the population that wants to be working.

$$\text{LFPR} = \frac{\text{Labor Force}}{\text{Population}}$$

Now that we understand how these variables are measured, let's multiply them together:

$$\frac{\text{Total output}}{\text{Total hours}} \times \frac{\text{Total hours}}{\text{Labor Force}} \times \frac{\text{Labor Force}}{\text{Population}} \times \text{Population}$$

$$= \text{Total output}.$$

Thus, we can write our equation for total output as:

$$\text{Total output} = \text{Productivity} \times \text{Average Hours} \times \text{LFPR} \times \text{Population}.$$

Finally, there is one more step before turning our attention to *explaining* growth. We'll borrow a rule from mathematics that states that if two variables A and B are multiplied together, then the percentage change in their product is approximately equal to the sum of their percentage changes. In symbols:

$$\%\Delta \, (A \times B) \approx \%\Delta A + \%\Delta B.$$

Applying this rule to all four variables in the right side of our equation, as well as to total output on the left, we find that the growth rate of total output over any period of time is

$$\%\Delta \, \text{Total Output} \approx \%\Delta \text{ productivity} + \%\Delta \text{ average hours} +$$
$$\%\Delta \text{ LFPR} + \%\Delta \text{ Population}.$$

Table 3 shows estimates of how each of these variables have contributed to output growth during different periods of recent U.S. history, as well as a six-year future projection. For example, the first column tells us that from 1960 to 1973, real GDP grew, on average, by 4.2 percent per year. Of that growth, 1.8 percentage points were due to a growing population, and 0.2 percentage points were due to a rise in the labor force participation rate. Average hours—which decreased during the period—contributed negatively to growth, reducing it by half of a percentage point. Finally, growth in labor productivity contributed 2.7 percent during this period.

Going across the rows and moving from period to period, you can see that almost all of the growth in real GDP over the last 42 years (and projected for the near

[2] In actual practice in the United States and many other countries, the LFPR is the fraction of the *civilian, noninstitutional population over the age of 16* that is either employed or seeking work. We'll ignore this technical definition in our analysis, and consider LFPR to be the fraction of the entire population that wants to be working.

TABLE 3
Factors Contributing to Growth in Real GDP

Annual Percentage Growth in Real GDP Due to:	1960 to 1973	1973 to 1990	1990 to 2002	2002 to 2008 (projected)
Population	1.8	1.5	1.0	1.1
LFPR	0.2	0.5	0.0	0.0
Average Hours	−0.5	−0.4	−0.1	0.0
Productivity	2.7	1.3	2.0	2.0
Total	4.2	2.9	2.9	3.2

Source: Economic Report of the President, 2003, Table 1–2, p. 66 (*http://w3.access.gpo.gov/eop/*), and author calculations. (The *Economic Report* lists nonfarm business productivity only. In Table 2, annual productivity growth has been reduced by 0.1 to 0.2 percentage points in each period to account for slightly slower output growth in the combined government and farm sectors.)

future) has come from two factors: population growth and productivity growth. Increases in labor force participation have contributed somewhat in the past, and average hours have decreased slightly, slowing growth in real GDP.

Economic Growth and Living Standards

Ultimately, growth in real GDP—by itself—does not guarantee a rising standard of living. Imagine, for example, that real GDP grew by 10 percent over some period while the population doubled. With 10 percent more output divided among twice as many people, the average standard of living would clearly decrease even though real output was growing. What matters for the standard of living is *real GDP per capita*—our total output of goods and services *per person*. Over the long run, since real GDP tends to track along with *potential* output, living standards will depend on *potential* output per person.

To see more clearly what causes potential output per person to rise, let's go back to our basic growth equation:

$$\text{Total Output} = \text{Productivity} \times \text{Average Hours} \times \text{LFPR} \times \text{Population}$$

If we divide both sides of this equation by the population, we get:

$$\frac{\text{Total Output}}{\text{Population}} = \text{Productivity} \times \text{Average Hours} \times \text{LFPR}$$

And, in terms of percentage growth rates:

$$\%\Delta \text{ Total Output per person} \approx \%\Delta \text{ productivity} + \%\Delta \text{ average hours} + \%\Delta \text{ LFPR}.$$

Notice that population drops out of the equation. This tells us that the only way to raise the average standard of living is to increase productivity, increase average hours, or increase the labor force participation rate.

But as we saw in Table 3, average hours in the United States have decreased over the past several decades, and are projected to remain constant for several years. In continental Europe, the decrease in average hours has been even greater. This is why we'll focus our discussion on the remaining two factors in our equation:

Thus,

> *to explain growth in output per person and living standards in the United States and other developed nations, economists look at two factors: increases in the labor force participation rate and growth in productivity.*

Now it's time to look more closely at *how* these two factors raise the average standard of living. And the classical model that you learned in the last chapter is very well suited to helping us understand this. We'll start by considering increases in the labor force participation rate.

GROWTH IN THE LABOR FORCE PARTICIPATION RATE (LFPR)

If the labor force were to grow at the same rate as the population, the labor force participation rate would remain unchanged. For example, if the labor force is 50 million out of a total population of 100 million, then the LFPR = 50 million / 100 million = 0.50. If the labor force and the population each grew by 10 percent, the LFPR would be 55 million / 110 million = 0.50—the same as before the change. In order for the LFPR to grow, the labor force must grow *faster* than the population. In our example, you can verify that if the labor force rose by *more* than 10 percent (say, from 50 million to 57 million) while the population still grew at 10 percent, the LFPR would *rise*.

Over the long run, when the economy operates at full employment, growth in the labor force is the same as growth in total employment. This leads us to the following observation:

> *Over the long run, the labor force participation rate rises when* employment *grows at a faster rate than the* population.

The classical model—which explains how equilibrium employment is determined over the long run—can help us understand long-run changes in the LFPR.

What causes employment to grow?

One possibility is an increase in labor *supply:* a rise in the number of people who would like to work at any given wage. This is illustrated in Figure 1 by a rightward shift in the labor supply curve. We'll discuss *why* the labor supply curve might shift later; here, we'll concentrate on the consequences of the shift.

Before the shift, the labor supply curve is L_1^S, the market clears at a wage of $15 per hour, and the fully employed labor force is 100 million workers. The aggregate production function tells us that, with the given amounts of other resources in the economy, and the given state of technology, 100 million workers can produce $7 trillion in goods and services—the initial value of full-employment output. When the labor supply curve shifts to L_2^S, the market-clearing wage drops to $12. Business firms, finding labor cheaper to hire, increase the number of workers employed along the labor demand curve, from point A to point B. The labor force increases to 120 million workers, and full-employment output rises to $8 trillion.

But growth in employment can also arise from an increase in labor demand: a rise in the number of workers firms would like to hire at any given wage. Once again, we'll consider the *causes* of labor demand changes momentarily; here, we focus on the *consequences*.

FIGURE 1
An Increase in Labor Supply

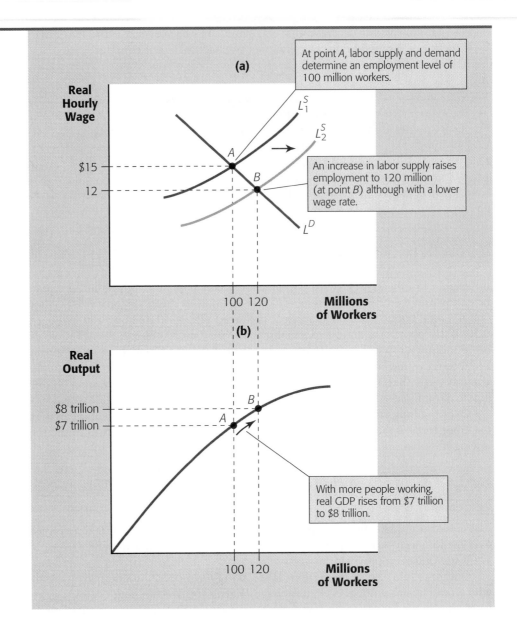

(a)

At point *A*, labor supply and demand determine an employment level of 100 million workers.

Real Hourly Wage

L_1^S

L_2^S

An increase in labor supply raises employment to 120 million (at point *B*) although with a lower wage rate.

L^D

$15
12

100 120   **Millions of Workers**

(b)

Real Output

$8 trillion
$7 trillion

With more people working, real GDP rises from $7 trillion to $8 trillion.

100 120   **Millions of Workers**

Graphically, an increase in labor demand is represented by a rightward shift in the labor demand curve, as in Figure 2. As the wage rate rises from $15 to its new equilibrium of $17, we move along the labor supply curve from point *A* to point *B*. More people decide they want to work as the wage rises. Equilibrium employment once again rises from 100 million to 120 million workers, so full-employment output will rise. Thus,

growth in employment can arise from an increase in labor supply (a rightward shift in the labor supply curve) or an increase in labor demand (a rightward shift of the labor demand curve).

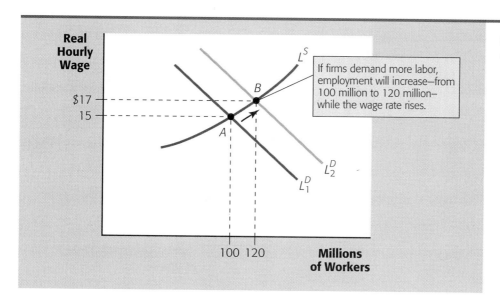

FIGURE 2
An Increase in Labor Demand

You may have noticed one very important difference between the labor market outcomes in Figures 1 and 2: When labor *supply* increases, the wage rate falls (from $15 to $12 in Figure 1); when labor *demand* increases, the wage rate rises (from $15 to $17 in Figure 2). Which of the figures describes the actual experience of the U.S. labor market?

Actually, a combination of both: Over the past 50 years, the U.S. labor supply curve has shifted steadily rightward, sometimes slowly, sometimes more rapidly. Why the shift in labor supply? In part, the reason has been steady population growth: The more people there are, the more will want to work at any wage. But another reason has been an important change in tastes: an increase in the desire of women (especially married women) to work.

Over the past 50 years, as the labor supply curve has shifted rightward, the labor demand curve has shifted rightward as well. Why? Throughout this period, firms have been acquiring more and better capital equipment for their employees to use. Managers and accountants now keep track of inventories and other important accounts with lightning-fast computer software instead of account ledgers. Supermarket clerks use electronic scanners instead of hand-entry cash registers. And college professors or their research assistants now gather data by searching for a few hours on the Web instead of a few weeks in the library. At the same time, workers have become better educated and better trained. These changes have increased the amount of output a worker can produce in any given period, so firms have wanted to hire more of them at any wage.[3]

In fact, over the past century, increases in labor demand have outpaced increases in labor supply, so that, on balance, the average wage rate has risen and employment has increased. This is illustrated in Figure 3, which shows a shift in the labor supply curve from L_1^S to L_2^S, and an even greater shift in the labor demand curve from L_1^D to L_2^D.

---

[3] These changes in physical and human capital have also shifted the economy's production function, but we'll consider that in the next section.

FIGURE 3
The U.S. Labor Market Over a Century

Over the past century, increases in labor demand have outpaced increases in supply. As a result, both the level of employment and the average wage have risen.

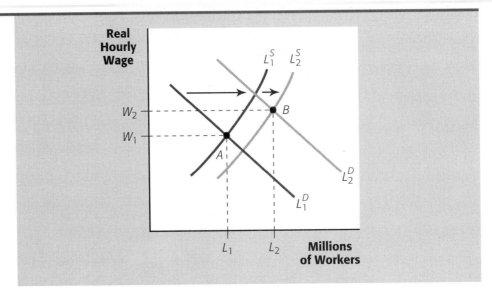

The impact of these changes on total employment has been dramatic. Between 1948 and 2003, the labor force rose from 59 million to 148 million—an increase of about 150 percent. And as the classical model predicts, employment rose by about the same percentage, from 56 million to 139 million. (The rise in employment was only 148 percent, because 2003 was a period of slow recovery from recession—a reflection of the short-run business cycle.)

But what about the labor force participation rate? It did, in fact, rise—from 57 percent to 67 percent of the adult population. This tells us that employment grew *faster* than the population during this period. And as you've learned, this increase in the LFPR causes not just real GDP, but real GDP *per capita*, to grow. However, most of the rise in the LFPR was due to a special factor that is unlikely to be repeated: the greater labor force participation rate of women—especially married women—during the 1960s, 1970s, and 1980s. But in the 1990s—as the female LFPR stabilized—this source of growth disappeared.

Currently, the U.S. Bureau of Labor Statistics predicts employment growth of 1 percent per year until the year 2010—about the same as the growth rate of the population. Thus, the labor force participation rate is not expected to grow at all. Employment growth—while it will raise real GDP, will not increase real GDP per capita, and so will not contribute to a rise in living standards.

Can we do anything about this? Can we speed up the rightward shifts in the labor demand and labor supply curves over the next few years, so that employment grows faster than the 1 percent annual growth rate of the population? Yes, we can. But as you read on, keep in mind that these measures to increase employment are not necessarily socially desirable. They would, most likely, accomplish the goal, but they would also have costs—costs that Americans may or may not be willing to pay. Later, we'll discuss these costs.

How to Increase Employment and the LFPR

One set of policies to speed the rise in employment focuses on changing labor supply. And an often-proposed example of this type of policy is a decrease in income tax rates. Imagine that you have a professional degree in accounting, physical therapy, or some other field, and you are considering whether to take a job. Suppose the going rate for your professional services is $30 per hour. If your average tax rate is 33 percent, then one-third of your income will be taxed away, so your take-home pay would be only $20 per hour. But if your tax rate were cut to 20 percent, you would take home $24 per hour. Since you care about your take-home pay, you will respond to a tax cut in the same way you would respond to a wage increase—even if the wage your potential employer pays does not change at all. If you would be willing to take a job that offers a take-home pay of $24, but not one that offers $20, then the tax cut would be just what was needed to get you to seek work.

When we extend your reaction to the population as a whole, we can see that a cut in the income tax rate can convince more people to seek jobs at any given wage, shifting the labor supply curve rightward. This is why economists and politicians who focus on the economy's long-run growth often recommend lower taxes on labor income to encourage more rapid growth in employment. They point out that many American workers must pay combined federal, state, and local taxes of more than 40 cents out of each additional dollar they earn, and that this may be discouraging work effort in the United States.

Indeed, this was an important part of the logic behind the two tax cuts engineered by President Bush early in his administration. For example, the first tax cut, which Congress passed after much debate in June 2001, called for gradually reduced tax rates over 10 years. It reduced the cumulative tax burden on households by about $1.35 trillion over that period.

In addition to tax rate changes, some economists have advocated changes in government transfer programs to speed the growth in employment. They argue that the current structure of many government programs creates disincentives to work. For example, families receiving welfare payments, food stamps, unemployment benefits, and Social Security retirement payments all face steep losses in their benefits if they go to work or increase their work effort. Redesigning these programs might therefore stimulate growth in labor supply.

This reasoning was an important motive behind the sweeping reforms in the U.S. welfare system passed by Congress, and signed by President Clinton, in August 1996. Among other things, the reforms reduced the number of people who were eligible for benefits, cut the benefit amount for many of those still eligible, and set a maximum coverage period of five years for most welfare recipients. Later in this chapter, we'll discuss some of the *costs* of potentially growth-enhancing measures like this. Here, we only point out that changes in benefit programs have the potential to change labor supply.

A cut in tax rates increases the reward for working, while a cut in benefits to the needy increases the hardship of not working. Either policy can cause a greater rightward shift in the economy's labor supply curve than would otherwise occur, speed the growth in employment, creating growth in labor force participation and output per person.

Government policies can also affect the labor *demand* curve. In recent decades, subsidies for education and training, such as government-guaranteed loans for college students or special training programs for the unemployed, have helped to increase the skills of the labor force and made workers more valuable to potential employers. Government also subsidizes employment more directly—by contributing part of the wage when certain categories of workers are hired—the disabled, college work-study participants, and, in some experimental programs, inner-city youth. By enlarging these programs, government could increase the number of workers hired at any given wage and thus shift the labor demand curve to the right:

> *Government policies that help increase the skills of the workforce or that subsidize employment more directly shift the economy's labor demand curve to the right, increasing labor force participation and output per person.*

Efforts to create growth in labor force participation are controversial. In recent decades, those who prefer an activist government have favored policies to increase labor *demand* through government-sponsored training programs, more aid to college students, employment subsidies to firms, and similar programs. Those who prefer a more *laissez-faire* approach have generally favored policies to increase the labor *supply* by *decreasing* government involvement—lower taxes or a less generous social safety net.

GROWTH IN PRODUCTIVITY

Our analysis of growth began with an equation explaining how total output is determined. Then—one by one—we eliminated variables that could not explain growth in total output—and living standards—over the long run. First, we ruled out population growth, based on the logic of the equation for total output per person. Second, we ruled out growth in average hours, based on the past and projected future behavior of this variable. And in the previous section, we ruled out increases in the labor force participation rate—at least as a source of continual, rapid economic growth in the near future. So only one variable remains: productivity.

HTTP://

Paul Bauer's "Are We in a Productivity Boom?" provides a more in-depth exploration of recent U.S. productivity experience. It's available at http://www.clev.frb.org/research/com99/1015.htm.

If you look back at Table 3, you'll see that growth in productivity has been responsible for most of the growth in real GDP over the last 42 years. (The period from 1973 to 1990, when population growth took the lead, is the exception.) And as you've learned, population growth—while it can raise real GDP—cannot raise real GDP *per capita*. If we restrict ourselves to the three factors in Table 3 that *can* raise real GDP per capita, we see that

> *over the past several decades, and into the near future, virtually all growth in the average standard of living can be attributed to growth in productivity.*

Not surprisingly, when economists analyze rising living standards, they think first and foremost about growth in productivity.

Table 3 shows that productivity is expected to grow at about 2 percent during most of the 2000s. Can we do anything to make it grow even faster?

Growth in the Capital Stock

One key to productivity growth is the nation's capital stock or, more precisely, the amount of capital available for the average worker in the economy. You can dig more ditches with a shovel than with your hands, and even more with a backhoe. And the economy can produce more automobiles, medical services, and education

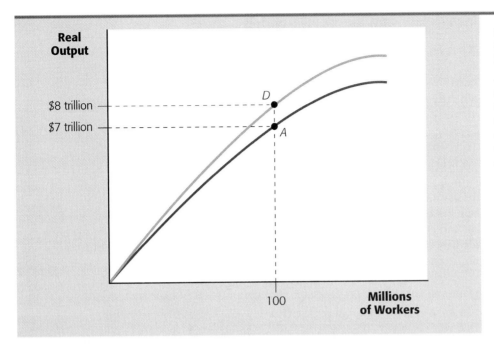

FIGURE 4

Capital Accumulation and the Production Function

An increase in the capital stock shifts the production function upward. At point A, 100 million workers could produce $7 trillion of real GDP. With more capital, those same workers could produce $8 trillion of real GDP.

when the average employee in these industries has more machinery, technical equipment, and computers to work with.

A rise in **capital per worker**—the total capital stock divided by the labor force—results in greater productivity. Figure 4 shows this from the perspective of the classical model. Initially, the economy operates at point *A* on the lower aggregate production function, where 100 million workers produce $7 trillion in output. An increase in the capital stock shifts the production function upward, since any given number of workers can produce more output if there is more capital to work with. Assuming that the labor force remains at 100 million, there will be more capital per worker, greater productivity, and the economy will move to point *D*. At this point, 100 million workers produce $8 trillion in output.

However, in the real world, as the capital stock grows, so does the labor force. While any increase in capital will shift up the production function as in the figure, productivity will rise only if capital *per worker* increases—that is, only if the nation's total capital stock grows *faster* than the labor force.

> *All else equal, if the capital stock grows faster than the labor force, then capital per worker will rise, and labor productivity will increase along with it. But if the capital stock grows more slowly than the labor force, then capital per worker will fall, and labor productivity will fall as well.*

In the United States and most other developed countries, the capital stock has grown more rapidly than the labor force. As a result, labor productivity has risen over time. But in some developing countries, the capital stock has grown at about the same rate as, or even more slowly than the labor force, and labor productivity has remained stagnant or fallen. We will return to this problem in the "Using the Theory" section of this chapter.

Capital per worker The total capital stock divided by total employment.

Investment and the Capital Stock

What determines how fast the capital stock rises, and whether it will rise faster than the labor force? The answer is: the rate of *planned investment spending* in the economy. Investment spending and the capital stock are related to each other, but they are different *kinds* of variables. Specifically, capital is a *stock* variable while investment spending is a *flow* variable.

> A **stock variable** *measures a quantity at a moment in time. A **flow variable** measures a process over a period of time.*

Stock variable a variable measuring a quantity at a moment in time.

Flow variable a variable measuring a *process* over some period of time.

To use an analogy, think of a bathtub being filled with water. The water *in* the tub is a stock variable—so many gallons at any given moment. The water *flowing into* the tub is a flow variable—so many gallons *per minute* or *per hour*. You can always identify a flow variable by the addition of "per period" in its definition. Even when not explicitly stated, some period of time is always implied in a flow variable.

Now let's think about capital again. The capital stock—the total amount of plant and equipment that exists in the economy—is like the quantity of water *in* the tub. It can be measured at any given moment. Investment spending—the amount of *new* capital being installed over some time interval—is like the water flowing *into* the tub. Investment spending is defined *per period*—such as *per quarter* or *per year*. In the simplest terms, investment spending *adds* to the capital stock over time.

But there is one more flow involved in the capital-investment relationship: *depreciation*. Each period, some of the capital stock is used up. If a computer is expected to last only three years, for example, then each year the computer depreciates by about a third of its initial value. Depreciation tends to *reduce* the capital stock over time. (In our tub analogy, depreciation is like the flow of water draining *out* each period.) *As long as investment is greater than depreciation* (more water flows into the tub than drains out), *the capital stock will rise.* Moreover, for any rate of depreciation, the greater the flow of investment spending, the faster the rise in the capital stock.

Pulling all of this together leads us to an important conclusion about investment spending and the capital stock:

> *For a given rate of depreciation and a given growth rate of the labor force, a* higher rate of investment spending *causes faster growth in capital per worker and productivity, and faster growth in the average standard of living.*

This is why when economists think about raising productivity via the capital stock, they focus on raising the rate of investment spending.

How to Increase Investment

A government seeking to spur investment has more than one weapon in its arsenal. It can direct its efforts toward businesses themselves, toward the household sector, or toward its own budget.

Targeting Businesses: Increasing the Incentive to Invest. One kind of policy to increase investment targets the business sector itself, with the goal of increasing planned investment spending. Figure 5 shows how this works. The figure shows a

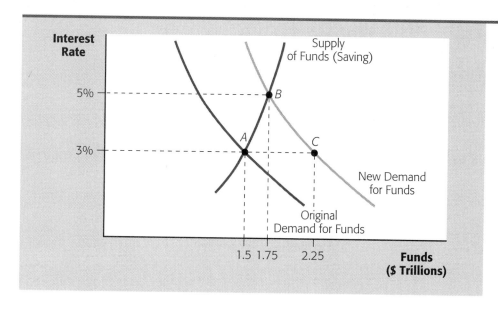

Interest Rate

5%

3%

B

A

C

Supply
of Funds (Saving)

New Demand
for Funds

Original
Demand for Funds

1.5 1.75   2.25

**Funds
($ Trillions)**

FIGURE 5

An Increase in Investment Spending

Government policies that make investment more profitable will increase investment spending at each interest rate. The resulting rightward shift of the investment demand curve leads to a higher level of investment spending, at point B.

simplified view of the loanable funds market where—to focus on investment—we assume that there is no budget deficit, so there is no government demand for funds. The initial equilibrium in the market is at point *A*, where household saving (the supply of funds) and investment (the demand for funds) are both equal to $1.5 trillion and the interest rate is 3 percent. Now suppose that the government takes steps to make investment more profitable, so that—at any interest rate—firms will want to purchase $0.75 trillion more in capital equipment than before. Then the investment curve would shift rightward by $0.75 trillion and the interest rate would rise from 3 percent to 5 percent. Note that, as the interest rate rises, some—but not all—of the original increase in planned investment is choked off. In the end, investment rises from $1.5 trillion to $1.75 trillion, and so each year $0.25 trillion more is added to the capital stock than would otherwise be added.

These are the mechanics of a rightward shift in the investment curve. But what government measures would *cause* such a shift in the first place? That is, how could the government help to make investment spending more profitable for firms?

One such measure would be a reduction in the **corporate profits tax,** which would allow firms to keep more of the profits they earn from investment projects. Another, even more direct, policy is an **investment tax credit,** which subsidizes corporate investment in new capital equipment.

> *Reducing business taxes or providing specific investment incentives can shift the investment curve rightward, thereby speeding growth in physical capital, and increasing the growth rate of living standards.*

Of course, the same reasoning applies in reverse: An *increase* in the corporate profits tax or the *elimination* of an investment tax credit would shift the investment curve to the left, slowing the rate of investment, the growth of the capital stock, and the rise in living standards.

Targeting Households: Increasing the Incentive to Save. While firms make decisions to purchase new capital, it is largely households that supply the funds, via

Corporate profits tax A tax on the profits earned by corporations.

Investment tax credit A reduction in taxes for firms that invest in new capital.

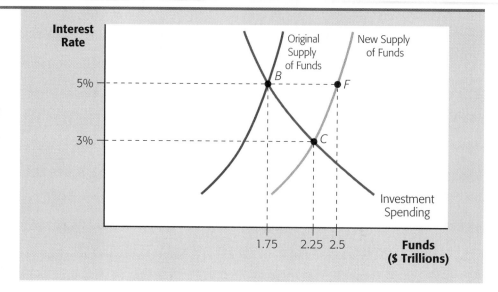

FIGURE 6

An Increase in Saving

If households decide to save more of their incomes, the supply of funds will increase. With more funds available, the interest rate will fall. Businesses will respond by increasing their borrowing, and investment will increase from $1.75 trillion to $2.25 trillion.

personal saving. Thus, an increase in investment spending can originate in the household sector, through an increase in the desire to save. This is illustrated in Figure 6. If households decide to save more of their incomes at any given interest rate, the supply of funds curve will shift rightward. The increase in saving drives down the interest rate, from 5 percent to 3 percent, which, in turn, causes investment to increase. With a lower interest rate, NBC might decide to borrow funds to build another production studio, or the corner grocery store may finally decide to borrow the funds it needs for a new electronic scanner at the checkout stand. In this way, an increase in the desire to save is translated, via the financial market, into an increase in investment and faster growth in the capital stock.

What might cause households to increase their saving? The answer is found in the reasons people save in the first place. And to understand these reasons, you needn't look farther than yourself or your own family. You might currently be saving for a large purchase (a car, a house, a vacation, college tuition) or to build a financial cushion in case of hard times ahead. You might even be saving to support yourself during retirement, though this is a distant thought for most college students.

Given these motives, what would make you save *more*? Several things: greater uncertainty about your economic future, an increase in your life expectancy, anticipation of an earlier retirement, a change in tastes toward big-ticket items, or even just a change in your attitude about saving. Any of these changes—if they occurred in many households simultaneously—would shift the saving curve (the supply of funds curve) to the right, as in Figure 6.

But government policy can increase household saving as well. One way is to decrease the **capital gains tax**. A capital gain is the profit you earn when you sell an asset, such as a share of stock or a bond, at a higher price than you paid for it. By lowering the special tax rate for capital gains, households would be able to keep more of the capital gains they earn. As a result, stocks and bonds would become more rewarding to own, and you might decide to reduce your current spending in order to buy them. If other households react in the same way, total saving would rise, and the supply of funds to the loanable funds market would increase.

Capital gains tax A tax on profits earned when a financial asset is sold at more than its acquisition price.

This was the logic behind a key component of the Bush administration's second tax cut, signed into law in May 2003. The tax cut included a reduction in the capital gains tax, from 20 percent to 15 percent for higher income households, and from 10 percent to 5 percent (and down to 0% in 2008) for lower income households. The lower tax rates applied only to *long-term* capital gains—gains on assets held for a year or longer—to encourage people to put their funds into stocks and other assets and keep them there, rather than engage in short-term speculation.

The 2003 tax cut on capital gains was controversial for two reasons. First, there was an equity issue: since most of the capital gains in the economy are earned by higher income households, this part of the tax cut benefited high-income households more than low-income households. Second, the government was already running a substantial budget deficit in 2003, and the tax cuts threatened to raise it further. As you'll see in the next section, higher budget deficits can work *against* economic growth.

Another frequently proposed measure is to switch from the current U.S. income tax—which taxes all income whether it is spent or saved—to a **consumption tax,** which would tax only the income that households spend. A consumption tax could work just like the current income tax, except that you would deduct your saving from your income and pay taxes on the remainder. This would increase the reward for saving. By saving, you would earn additional interest on the part of your income that would have been taxed away under an income tax. Currently, individual retirement accounts, or IRAs, allow households to deduct limited amounts of saving from their incomes before paying taxes. A general consumption tax would go much further and allow *all* saving to be deducted.

Consumption tax A tax on the part of their income that households spend.

Another proposal to increase household saving is to restructure the U.S. Social Security system, which provides support for retired workers who have contributed funds to the system during their working years. Because Social Security encourages people to rely on the government for income during retirement, they have less incentive to save for retirement themselves. One proposed restructuring would link workers' Social Security benefits to their actual contributions to the system, whereas under the current system some people receive benefits worth far more than the amount they have contributed.

> *Government can alter the tax and transfer system to increase incentives for saving. If successful, these policies would make more funds available for investment, speed growth in the capital stock, and speed the rise in living standards.*

(Do any of these methods of increasing saving disturb you? Remember, we are not advocating any measures here; rather, we are merely noting that such measures would increase saving and promote economic growth. We'll discuss the *costs* of growth-promoting measures later.)

Shrinking the Government's Budget. A final pro-investment measure is directed at the government sector itself. The previous chapter showed that an increase in government purchases, financed by borrowing in the financial market, completely crowds out consumption and investment. A *decrease* in government purchases has the opposite effect: raising consumption and investment.

Figure 7 reintroduces the government to the financial market to show how this works. Initially, the government is running a deficit of $0.75 trillion, equal to the

FIGURE 7
Deficit Reduction and Investment Spending

Eliminating the government's budget deficit will reduce government borrowing in the loanable funds market. As a result, the total demand for funds will fall, as will the interest rate. At a lower interest rate, businesses will increase their investment spending from $1 trillion (point E) to $1.5 trillion (point B).

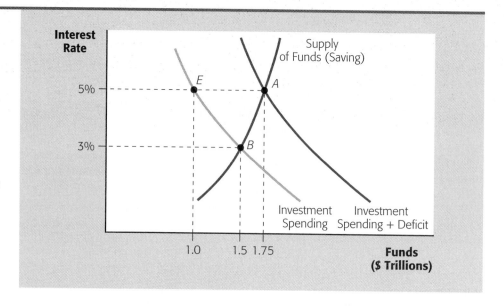

distance *EA*. The total demand for funds is now the sum of investment and the government's budget deficit, given by the curve labeled "Investment Spending + Deficit." The demand for funds curve intersects the supply of funds curve at point *A*, creating an equilibrium interest rate of 5 percent and equilibrium saving of $1.75 trillion. At this interest rate, investment spending is only $1 trillion. The part of saving not going to finance investment spending ($1.75 trillion − $1 trillion = $0.75 trillion) is being used to finance the budget deficit.

Now consider what happens if the government eliminates the deficit—say, by reducing its purchases by $0.75 trillion. The demand for funds would consist of investment spending only. Since there would be no other borrowing, the new equilibrium would be point *B*, with an interest rate of 3 percent and investment equal to $1.5 trillion—greater than before. By balancing its budget, the government no longer needs to borrow in the loanable funds market, which frees up funds to flow to the business sector instead. Initially, this creates an excess supply of funds. But, as the loanable funds market clears, the interest rate drops and the excess supply of funds disappears. (Why does a drop in the interest rate make the excess supply disappear? *Hint:* What happens to saving and to investment as the interest rate declines?)

The link between the government budget, the interest rate, and investment spending is the major reason why the U.S. government, and governments around the world, try to reduce and, if possible, eliminate budget deficits. They have learned that

> *a shrinking deficit or a rising surplus tends to reduce interest rates and increase investment, thus speeding the growth in the capital stock.*

In the 1990s, Congress set strict limits on the growth of government spending, and the budget deficit began shrinking. The restraints on spending, and rapid economic growth during the 1990s, finally turned the federal budget from deficit to surplus in 1998, and continued surpluses were projected for more than a decade.

These surpluses were viewed as positive for economic growth: They would help keep the interest rate low, which in turn would lead to greater business investment spending.

When President George W. Bush took office in 2001, the direction of growth policy shifted away from preserving budget surpluses and toward lower tax rates. The first Bush tax cut in 2001(a total of $1.35 trillion over 10 years) purposely cut into potential future surpluses in order to reduce the tax burden on American households. Shortly afterward, a series of events pushed the budget into deficit. These included a continuing recession that had begun in March 2001 and the attacks of September 11, which resulted in large increases in military and homeland security spending. And a second tax cut in 2003—amounting to $350 billion over 10 years—increased current and projected deficits further.

The tax cuts included some elements (discussed earlier) to increase investment spending, such as a lower tax rate for capital gains and tax incentives for investment by small businesses. Also, you've learned that cutting income tax rates can have some effect on the labor force participation rate by shifting the labor supply curve rightward. But the tax cuts—by raising current and future budget deficits—would ultimately drive the interest rate higher than it would otherwise be, which works in opposition to the growth benefits of the tax cut. We'll discuss budget deficits and their effects on the economy more thoroughly toward the end of this book, in the chapter on fiscal policy.

An Important Proviso About the Government Budget. A reduction in the deficit or an increase in the surplus—even if they stimulate private investment—are not *necessarily* pro-growth measures. It depends on *how* the budget changes. By an increase in taxes? A cut in government spending? And if the latter, which government programs will be cut? Welfare? National defense? Highway repair? The answers can make a big difference to the impact on growth.

For example, in our discussions of the capital stock so far, we've ignored government capital—roads, communication lines, bridges, and dams. To understand the importance of government capital, just imagine what life would be like without it. How would factories obtain their raw materials or distribute their goods if no one repaired the roads? How would contracts between buyers and sellers be enforced if there were no public buildings to house courts and police departments? Government capital supports private economic activity in more ways than we can list here.

> *Government investment in new capital and in the maintenance of existing capital makes an important contribution to economic growth.*

This important observation complicates our view of deficit reduction. It is still true that a decrease in government spending will lower the interest rate and increase private investment. But if the budget cutting falls largely on government investment, the negative effect of smaller public investment will offset some of the positive impact of greater private investment. Shrinking the deficit will then alter the *mix* of capital—more private and less public—and the effect on growth could go either way. A society rife with lawlessness, deteriorating roads and bridges, or an unreliable communications network might benefit from a shift toward public capital. For example, a study of public budgets in African nations—which have poor road conditions—found that each one-dollar-per-year cut in the road-maintenance budget increased vehicle operating costs by between $2 and $3 per year, and in one case, by as much as $22 per year.[4] This is an example of a cut in government spending that, even if it reduces the deficit, probably hinders growth. By contrast, in Sweden—a country with a fully developed and well-maintained public infrastructure—recent governments have decided to shift the mix away from public and toward private capital, in part because they believed this would speed growth.

> *The impact of deficit reduction on economic growth depends on which government programs are cut. Shrinking the deficit by cutting government investment will not stimulate growth as much as would cutting other types of government spending.*

Human Capital and Economic Growth

Human capital Skills and knowledge possessed by workers.

So far, the only type of capital we've discussed is physical capital—the plant and equipment workers use to produce output. But when we think of the capital stock most broadly, we include *human capital* as well. **Human capital**—the skills and knowledge possessed by workers—is as central to economic growth as is physical capital. After all, most types of physical capital—computers, CAT scanners, and even shovels—will contribute little to output unless workers know how to use them. And when more workers gain skills or improve their existing skills, output rises just as it does when workers have more physical capital:

> *An increase in human capital works like an increase in physical capital to increase output: It causes the production function to shift upward, raises productivity, and increases the average standard of living.*

There is another similarity between human and physical capital: Both are *stocks* that are increased by *flows* of investment. The stock of human capital increases whenever investment in new skills during some period, through education and training, exceeds the depreciation of existing skills over the same period, through retirement, death, or disuse. Therefore, greater investment in human capital will speed the growth of the human capital stock, increasing the growth rate of productivity and living standards.

Human capital investments are made by business firms (when they help to train their employees), by government (through public education and subsidized training), and by households (when they pay for general education or professional training). Human capital investments have played an important role in recent U.S. economic growth. Can we do anything to increase our rate of investment in human capital?

In part, we've already answered this question: Some of the same policies that increase investment in *physical* capital also work to raise investment in human capital. For example, a decrease in the budget deficit would lower the interest rate and make it cheaper for households to borrow for college loans and training programs. A change in the tax system that increases the incentive to save would have the same impact, since this, too, would lower interest rates. And an easing of the tax burden on business firms could increase the profitability of *their* human capital investments, leading to more and better worker training programs.

© DOVIC MURIEL/CORBIS SYGMA

College-level courses are one important way that countries increase the stock of human capital and shift up their production function.

---

[4] This World Bank study was cited in *The Economist*, June 10, 1995, p. 72.

But there is more: Human capital, unlike physical capital, cannot be separated from the person who provides it. If you own a building, you can rent it out to one firm and sell your labor to another. But if you have training as a doctor, your labor and your human capital must be sold together, as a package. Moreover, your wage or salary will be payment for both your labor and your human capital. This means that income tax reductions—which we discussed earlier as a means of increasing labor supply—can also increase the profitability of human capital to households, and increase their rate of investment in their own skills and training. For example, suppose an accountant is considering whether to attend a course in corporate financial reporting, which would increase her professional skills. The course costs $4,000, and will increase the accountant's income by $1,000 per year for the rest of her career. With a tax rate of 40 percent, her take-home pay would increase by $600 per year, so her annual rate of return on her investment would be $600/$4,000 = 15 percent. But with a lower tax rate—say, 20 percent—her take-home pay would rise by $800 per year, so her rate of return would be $800/$4,000 = 20 percent. The lower the tax rate, the greater is the rate of return on our accountant's human capital investment, and the more likely she will be to acquire new skills. Thus,

many of the pro-growth policies discussed earlier—policies that increase employment or increase investment in physical capital—are also effective in promoting investment in human capital.

TECHNOLOGICAL CHANGE

So far, we've discussed how economic growth arises from greater quantities of resources—more labor, more physical capital, or more human capital. But another important source of growth is **technological change**—the invention or discovery of new inputs, new outputs, or new methods of production. Indeed, it is largely because of technological change that Malthus's horrible prediction (cited at the beginning of this chapter) has not come true. In the last 60 years, for example, the inventions of synthetic fertilizers, hybrid corn, and chemical pesticides have enabled world food production to increase faster than population.

Technological change The invention or discovery of new inputs, new outputs, or new production methods.

New technology affects the economy in much the same way as do increases in the capital stock. Flip back to Figure 4 of this chapter. There, you saw that an increase in the capital stock would shift the production function upward and increase output. New technology, too, shifts the production function upward, since it enables any given number of workers to produce more output.

In many cases, the new technology requires the acquisition of physical and human capital before it can be used. For example, a new technique for destroying kidney stones with ultrasound, rather than time-consuming surgery, can make doctors more productive—but not until they spend several thousand dollars to buy the ultrasound machine and take a course on how to use it. Similarly, the recent development of the Internet has enabled many businesses—both big and small—to order supplies and market their products using less labor time and other resources than ever before. But they can't take advantage of this technology until they purchase computer equipment and their employees learn how to master the operation of both hardware and software.

In some instances, however, a new technology can be used without any additional equipment or training, as when a factory manager discovers a more efficient way to organize workers on the factory floor. In either case, technological change will shift the production function upward and increase productivity. It follows that

the faster the rate of technological change, the greater the growth rate of productivity, and the faster the rise in living standards.

It might seem that technological change is one of those things that just happens. Thomas Edison invents electricity, or Steve Jobs and Steve Wozniak develop the first practical personal computer in their garage. But the pace of technological change is not as haphazard as it seems. The transistor was invented as part of a massive research and development effort by AT&T to improve the performance of communications electronics. Similarly, the next developments in computer technology, transportation, and more will depend on how much money is spent on research and development (R&D) by the leading technology firms:

The rate of technological change in the economy depends largely on firms' total spending on R&D. Policies that increase R&D spending will increase the pace of technological change.

What can the government do to increase spending on R&D? First, it can increase its own direct support for R&D by carrying out more research in its own laboratories or increasing funding for universities and tax incentives to private research labs.

Patent protection A government grant of exclusive rights to use or sell a new technology.

Second, the government can enhance **patent protection,** which increases rewards for those who create new technology by giving them exclusive rights to use it or sell it. For example, when the DuPont Corporation discovered a unique way to manufacture Spandex, it obtained a patent to prevent other firms from copying its technique. This patent has enabled DuPont to earn millions of dollars from its invention. Without the patent, other firms would have copied the technique, competed with DuPont, and taken much of its profit away. Hundreds of thousands of new patents are issued every year in the United States: to pharmaceutical companies for new prescription drugs, to telecommunications companies for new cellular technologies, and to the producers of a variety of household goods ranging from can openers to microwave ovens.

Since patent protection increases the rewards that developers can expect from new inventions, it encourages them to spend more on R&D. By broadening patent protection—issuing patents on a wider variety of discoveries—or by lengthening patent protection—increasing the number of years during which the developer has exclusive rights to market the invention—the government could increase the expected profits from new technologies. That would increase total spending on R&D and increase the pace of technological change. Currently in the United States, patents give inventors and developers exclusive marketing rights over their products for a period of about 20 years. Increasing patent protection to 30 years would certainly increase R&D spending at many firms.

Finally, R&D spending is in many ways just like other types of investment spending: The funds are drawn from the financial market, and R&D programs require firms to buy something now (laboratories, the services of research scientists, materials to build prototypes) for the uncertain prospect of profits in the future. Therefore, almost any policy that stimulates investment spending in general will also increase spending on R&D. Cutting the tax rate on capital gains or on corporate profits, or lowering interest rates by encouraging greater saving or by reducing the budget deficit, can each help to increase spending on R&D and increase the rate of technological change.

GROWTH POLICIES: A SUMMARY

In this chapter, you've learned about the forces that affect the economy's economic growth, as well as a host of government policies that can speed the economy's growth rate. If you are having trouble keeping it all straight, Table 4—which summarizes all of this information—might help.

As you look at the table, you may notice something interesting: Some of the policies that work to *increase* economic growth through one channel can simultaneously work *against* growth through another channel. For example, in the first row of the table, you can see that a *decrease* in income tax rates contributes to growth by increasing employment. But farther down, you'll see that an *increase* in taxes can aid growth by shrinking a budget deficit (implying that a *decrease* in taxes would have the opposite effect and harm growth). Thus, a decrease in tax rates simultaneously helps growth through one channel and harms growth through another.

The fact that a single policy can have two competing effects on the economy helps us understand one reason for controversy in macroeconomic policy. When we cut income taxes, for example, the ultimate effect on economic growth will depend on which of the two effects is stronger, something over which economists can and do disagree. This is why the Bush tax cut in 2001 was seen by some observers as a growth-enhancing measure (those who stressed the impact on employment) and by others as harmful to economic growth (those who stressed the reduction in the budget surplus and the effects on interest rates and investment).

THE COSTS OF ECONOMIC GROWTH

So far in this chapter, we've discussed a variety of policies that could increase the rate of economic growth and speed the rise in living standards. Why don't all nations pursue these policies and push their rates of economic growth to the maximum? For example, why did the U.S. standard of living (output per capita) grow by 2.7 percent per year between 1995 and 2001? Why not 4 percent per year? Or 6 percent? Or even more?

In this section, you will see that policies to increase a nation's rate of economic growth involve trade-offs.

> *Promoting economic growth involves unavoidable trade-offs: It requires some groups, or the nation as a whole, to give up something else that is valued. In order to decide how fast we want our economy to grow, we must consider growth's costs as well as its benefits.*

Economics is famous for making the public aware of policy trade-offs. One of the most important things you will learn in your introductory economics course is that

TABLE 4
Factors That Influence Growth in Output per Capita

Source of Growth	Method		Examples of Pro-Growth Government Policies
Increase in Labor Force Participation Rate	Rightward shift in labor supply curve		• Lower income tax rates • Less generous transfer payments
	Rightward shift in labor demand curve		• Subsidized college loans • Subsidized training for the unemployed • Programs that target specific types of workers (e.g., disabled, inner-city youth)
Growth in Physical Capital Stock (Productivity Growth)	Rightward shift in investment demand curve		• Investment tax credit • Lower corporate profits tax
	Lower interest rate . . .	via rightward shift in saving curve	• Tax incentives for saving • Changes in Social Security system • Lower capital gains tax
		via decrease in budget deficit (or increase in budget surplus)	• Cuts in government purchases • Cuts in transfer payments • Tax increase
Growth in Human Capital Stock (Productivity Growth)	Lower interest rate . . .	(see above)	• Any policy (above) that lowers the interest rate
	Other methods to make human capital investment more attractive		• Lower income tax rates • Subsidized student loans • Tax incentives for investment in human capital
Technological Progress (Productivity Growth)	Lower interest rate . . .	(see above)	• Any policy (above) that lowers the interest rate
	Other methods to make investment in R & D more profitable		• Investment tax credit for R&D • Lower corporate profits tax • Expansion of patent protection

there are no costless solutions to society's problems. Just as individuals face an opportunity cost when they take an action (they must give up something else that they value), so, too, policy makers face an opportunity cost whenever they pursue a policy: They must compromise on achieving some other social goal.

What are the costs of growth?

Budgetary Costs

If you look again at Table 4, you'll see that many of the pro-growth policies we've analyzed involve some kind of tax cut. Cutting the income tax rate may increase the labor force participation rate. Cutting taxes on capital gains or corporate profits will increase investment directly. And cutting taxes on saving will increase household saving, lower interest rates, and thus increase investment spending indirectly. Unfortunately, implementing any of these tax cuts would force the government to choose among three unpleasant alternatives: increase some other tax to regain the lost revenue, cut government spending, or permit the budget deficit to rise.

Who will bear the burden of this budgetary cost? That depends on which alternative is chosen. Under the first option—increasing some other tax—the burden falls on those who pay the other tax. For example, if income taxes are cut, real estate taxes might be increased. A family might pay lower income taxes, but higher property taxes. Whether it comes out ahead or behind will depend on how much income the family earns relative to how much property it owns.

The second option, cutting government spending, imposes the burden on those who currently benefit from government programs. These include not only those who directly benefit from a program—like welfare recipients or farmers—but also those who benefit from government spending more indirectly. Even though you may earn your income in the private sector, if government spending is cut, you may suffer from a deterioration of public roads, decreased police protection, or poorer schools for your children.

The third option—a larger budget deficit or a smaller budget surplus—is more complicated. Suppose a tax cut causes the government to end up with a larger deficit. Then greater government borrowing will increase the total amount of government debt outstanding—called the national debt—and lead to greater interest payments to be made by future generations, in the form of higher taxes. The same is true even if the government is running a budget surplus. In that case, a tax cut will *reduce* the size of the surplus and reduce the amount of the national debt the government pays back each year. Once again, the tax cut raises the interest payments that future generations must bear.

But that is not all. From the previous chapter, we know that a rise in the budget deficit (by increasing the demand for funds) or a drop in the budget surplus (by decreasing the supply of funds) drives up the interest rate. The higher interest rate will reduce investment in physical capital by businesses, as well as investment in human capital by households, and both effects will work to decrease economic growth. It is even possible that so much private investment will be crowded out that the tax cut, originally designed to boost economic growth, ends up slowing growth instead. At best, the growth-enhancing effects of the tax cut will be weakened. This is why advocates of high growth rates usually propose one of the other options—a rise in some other tax or a cut in government spending—as part of a pro-growth tax cut.

In sum,

> *while properly targeted tax cuts can increase the rate of economic growth, they will force us to either redistribute the tax burden or cut government programs.*

Consumption Costs

Any pro-growth policy that works by increasing investment—in physical capital, human capital, or R&D—requires a sacrifice of current consumption spending. The land, labor, capital and entrepreneurship we use to produce new cloth-cutting machines, oil rigs, assembly lines, training facilities, college classrooms, or research laboratories could have been used instead to produce clothing, automobiles, video games, and other consumer goods. In other words, we face a trade-off: The more capital goods we produce in any given year, the fewer consumption goods we can enjoy in that year.

The role of this trade-off in economic growth can be clearly seen with a familiar tool from Chapter 2: the production possibilities frontier (PPF). Figure 8 shows the PPF for a nation with some given amount of land, labor, capital and entrepreneurship that must be allocated to the production of two types of output: capital goods and consumption goods. At point K, the nation is using all of its resources to produce capital goods and none to produce consumption goods. Point C represents the opposite extreme: all resources used to produce consumption goods and none for capital goods. Ordinarily, a nation will operate at an intermediate point such as A, where it is producing both capital and consumption goods.

Now, as long as capital production at point A is greater than the depreciation of existing capital, the capital stock will grow. In future periods, the economy—with more capital—can produce more output, as shown by the outward shift of the PPF in the figure. If a nation can produce more output, then it can produce more consumption goods for the same quantity of capital goods (moving from point A to point B) or more capital goods for the same quantity of consumption goods (from point A to point D) or more of both (from point A to point E).

Let's take a closer look at how this sacrifice of current consumption goods might come about. Suppose that some change in government policy—an investment tax credit or a lengthening of the patent period for new inventions—successfully shifts the investment curve to the right. (Go back to Figure 5.) What will happen? Businesses—desiring more funds for investment—will drive up the interest rate, and households all over the country will find that saving has become more attractive. As families increase their saving, we move rightward along the economy's supply of funds curve. In this way, firms get the funds they need to purchase new capital. But a decision to *save more* is also a decision to *spend less*. As current saving rises, current consumption spending necessarily falls. By driving up the interest rate, *the increase in investment spending causes a voluntary decrease in consumption spending by households*. Resources are freed from producing consumption goods and diverted to producing capital goods instead.

Although this decrease in consumption spending is voluntary, it is still a cost that we pay. And in some cases, a painful cost: Some of the increase in the household sector's net saving results from a decrease in borrowing by households that—at higher interest rates—can no longer afford to finance purchases of homes, cars, or furniture. In sum,

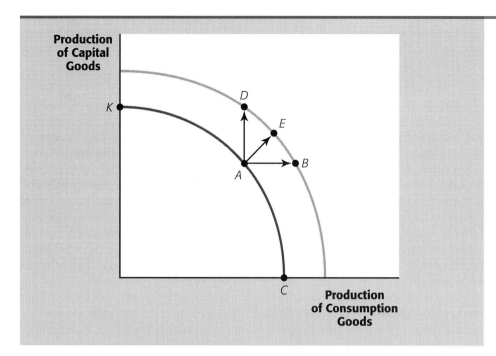

FIGURE 8
Consumption, Investment, and Economic Growth

In the current period, a nation can choose to produce only consumer goods (point C), or it can produce some capital goods by sacrificing some current consumption, as at point A. If investment at point A exceeds capital depreciation, the capital stock will grow, and the production possibilities frontier will shift outward. After it does, the nation can produce more consumption goods (point B), more capital goods (point D), or more of both (point E).

greater investment in physical capital, human capital, or R&D will lead to faster economic growth and higher living standards in the future, but we will have fewer consumer goods to enjoy in the present.

Opportunity Costs of Workers' Time

Living standards will also rise if a greater fraction of the population works or if those who already have jobs begin working longer hours. In either case, there will be more output to divide among the same population. But this increase in living standards comes at a cost: a decrease in time spent in nonmarket activities. For example, with a greater fraction of the population working, a smaller fraction is spending time at home. This might mean that more students have summer jobs, more elderly workers are postponing their retirement, or more previously nonworking spouses are entering the labor force. Similarly, an increase in average working hours would mean that the average worker will have less time for other activities—less time to watch television, read novels, garden, fix up the house, teach his or her children, or do volunteer work.

Thus, when economic growth comes about from increases in the labor force participation rate (or in average hours), we face a trade-off: On the one hand, we can enjoy higher incomes and more goods and services; on the other hand, we will have less time to do things other than work in the market. In a market economy, where choices are voluntary, the value of the income gained must be greater than the value of the time given up. No one forces a worker to reenter the labor force or to increase her working hours. Any worker who takes either of these actions must be better off for doing so. Still, we must recognize that *something* of value is always given up when employment increases:

An increase in the fraction of the population with jobs (or a rise in working hours) will increase output and raise living standards, but also requires us to sacrifice time previously spent in nonmarket activities.

Sacrifice of Other Social Goals

Rapid economic growth is an important social goal, but it's not the only one. Some of the policies that quicken the pace of growth require us to sacrifice other goals that we care about. For example, you've seen that restructuring and even reducing Social Security benefits would increase saving, leading to more investment and faster growth. But such a move would cut the incomes of those who benefit from the current system and increase the burden on other social programs, such as welfare and food stamps. You've learned that extending patent protection would increase incentives for research and development. But it would also extend the monopoly power exercised by patent holders and force consumers to pay higher prices for drugs, electronic equipment, and even packaged foods.

Of course, the argument cuts both ways: Just as government policies to stimulate investment require us to sacrifice other goals, so, too, can the pursuit of other goals impede investment spending and economic growth. Most of us would like to see a cleaner environment and safer workplaces. But safety and environmental regulations have increased in severity, complexity, and cost over time, reducing the rate of profit on new capital and shrinking investment spending.

Does this mean that business taxes and government regulations should be reduced to the absolute minimum? Not at all. As in most matters of economic policy, we face a trade-off:

We can achieve greater worker safety, a cleaner environment, and other social goals, but we may have to sacrifice some economic growth along the way. Alternatively, we can achieve greater economic growth, but we will have to compromise on other things we care about.

When values differ, people will disagree on just how much we should sacrifice for economic growth or how much growth we should sacrifice for other goals.

USING THE THEORY
Economic Growth in the Less-Developed Countries

In most countries, Malthus's dire predictions have not come true. One reason is that increases in the capital stock have raised productivity and increased the average standard of living. Increases in the capital stock are even more important in the less-developed countries (LDCs), which have relatively little capital to begin with. In these countries, even small increases in capital formation can have dramatic effects on living standards.

But how does a nation go about increasing its capital stock? As you've learned, there are a variety of measures, all designed to accomplish the same goal: shifting resources away from consumer-goods production toward capital-goods production. A very simple formula.

Country	Average Annual Growth Rate of Output per Capita	
	1975–2001	1990–2001
Bangladesh	2.3	3.1
Pakistan	2.7	1.2
Ghana	0.2	1.9
Benin	−0.5	1.9
Kenya	0.3	−0.6
Democratic Republic of the Congo	−5.2	−7.7
Sierra Leone	−3.3	−6.6

TABLE 5
Economic Growth in Selected Poor Countries

Source: United Nations Development Programme, *Human Development Report 2003*, pp. 279–281.

Some countries that were once LDCs—like the four Asian tigers (Hong Kong, Singapore, South Korea, and Taiwan)—have applied the formula very effectively. Output per capita in these counties has grown by an average of 6 percent per year over the past two decades. They were able to shift resources from consumption goods into capital goods in part by pursuing many of the growth-enhancing measures discussed in this chapter: large subsidies for human and physical capital investments, pro-growth tax cuts to encourage saving and investment, and the willingness to sacrifice other social goals—especially a clean environment—for growth.[5] These economies gave up large amounts of potential consumption during a period of intensive capital formation.

But other LDCs have had great difficulty raising living standards. Table 5 shows growth rates for several of them. In some cases—such as Pakistan, Bangladesh, and more recently, Ghana and Benin—slow but consistent growth has given cause for optimism. In other cases—such as Kenya—living standards have barely budged over the past few decades. In still other cases—for example, the Democratic Republic of the Congo and Sierra Leone—output per capita has been falling ever more rapidly. Why do some LDCs have such difficulty achieving economic growth?

Much of the explanation for the low growth rates of many LDCs lies with three characteristics that they share:

1. *Very low current output per capita.* Living standards are so low in some LDCs that they cannot take advantage of the trade-off between producing consumption goods and producing capital goods. In these countries, pulling resources out of consumption would threaten the survival of many households. In the individual household, the problem is an inability to save: Incomes are so low that households must spend all they earn on consumption.

2. *High population growth rates.* Low living standards and high population growth rates are linked together in a cruel circle of logic. On the one hand, rapid population growth by itself tends to reduce living standards; on the other hand, a low standard of living tends to increase population growth. Why? First, the poor are often uneducated in matters of family planning. Second, high

---

[5] The Asian tigers also had some special advantages—such as a high level of human capital to start with.

mortality rates among infants and children encourage families to have many off-spring, to ensure the survival of at least a few to care for parents in their old age. As a result, while the average woman in the United States will have fewer than two children in her lifetime, the average woman in Haiti will have about five children, and the average woman in Rwanda will have more than six.

3. *Poor infrastructure.* Political instability, poor law enforcement, corruption, and adverse government regulations make many LDCs unprofitable places to invest. Low rates of investment mean a smaller capital stock and lower productivity. Infrastructure problems also harm worker productivity in another way: Citizens must spend time guarding against thievery and trying to induce the government to let them operate businesses—time they could otherwise spend producing output.

These three characteristics—low current production, high population growth, and poor infrastructure—interact to create a vicious circle of continuing poverty, which we can understand with the help of the familiar PPF between capital goods and consumption goods. Look back at Figure 8, and now imagine that it applies to a poor, developing country. In this case, an outward shift of the PPF does not, in itself, guarantee an increase in the standard of living. In the LDCs, the population growth rate is often very high, and employment grows at the same rate as the population. If employment grows more rapidly than the capital stock, then even though the PPF is shifting outward, capital per worker will decline. Unless some other factor—such as technological change—is raising productivity, then living standards will fall.

> *In order to have rising capital per worker—an important source of growth in productivity and living standards—a nation's stock of capital must not only grow, but grow faster than its population.*

The World Bank Economic Growth Project's Web site is a comprehensive source of information about economic growth (http://www.worldbank.org/programs/macroeconomics).

Point N in Figure 9 shows the minimum amount of investment needed to increase capital per worker, labor productivity, and living standards for a given rate of population growth. For example, if the population is growing at 4 percent per year, then point N indicates the investment needed to increase the total capital stock by 4 percent per year. If investment is just equal to N, then capital per worker—and living standards—remains constant. If investment exceeds N, then capital per worker—and living standards—will rise. Of course, the greater the growth in population, the higher point N will be on the vertical axis, since greater investment will be needed just to keep up with population growth. (We assume throughout this discussion that the labor force and employment are both rising at the same rate as the population.)

The PPF in Figure 9 has an added feature: Point S shows the minimum acceptable level of consumption, the amount of consumer goods the economy *must* produce in a year. For example, S might represent the consumption goods needed to prevent starvation among the least well off, or to prevent unacceptable social consequences, such as violent revolution.

Now we can see the problem faced by the most desperate of the less-developed economies. Output is currently at a point like H in Figure 9, with investment just equal to N. The capital stock is not growing fast enough to increase capital per worker, and so labor productivity and living standards are stagnant. In this situation, the PPF shifts outward each year, but not quickly enough to improve people's lives. It could be even worse: Convince yourself that, at a point like R, the average standard of living declines even though the capital stock is growing—that is, even though the PPF will shift outward in future periods.

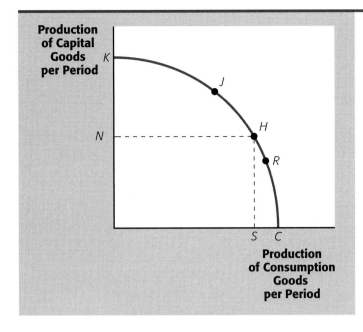

FIGURE 9
LDC Growth and Living Standards

In order to increase capital per worker when population is growing, yearly investment spending must exceed some minimum level N. In any year, there is a minimum level of consumption, S, needed to support the population. If output is currently at point H, capital per worker and living standards are stagnant. But movement to a point like J would require an unacceptably low level of consumption.

The solution to this problem appears to be an increase in capital production beyond point *N*—a movement *along* the PPF from point *H* to a point such as *J*. As investment rises above *N*, capital per worker rises, and the PPF shifts outward rapidly enough over time to raise living standards. In a wealthy country, like the United States, such a move could be engineered by changes in taxes or other government policies. But in the LDCs depicted here, such a move would be intolerable: At point *H*, consumption is already equal to *S*, the lowest acceptable level. Moving to point *J* would require reducing consumption *below S*.

The poorest LDCs are too poor to take advantage of the trade-off between consumption and capital production in order to increase their living standards. Since they cannot reduce consumption below current levels, they cannot produce enough capital to keep up with their rising populations

In recent history, countries have attempted several methods to break out of this vicious circle of poverty. During the 1930s, the dictator Joseph Stalin simply *forced* the Soviet economy from a point like *H* to one like *J*. His goal was to shift the Soviet Union's PPF outward as rapidly as possible. But, as you can see, this reduced consumption below the minimum level *S*, and Stalin resorted to brutal measures to enforce his will. Many farmers were ordered into the city to produce capital equipment. With fewer people working on farms, agricultural production declined and there was not enough food to go around. Stalin's solution was to confiscate food from the remaining farmers and give it to the urban workforce. Of course, this meant starvation for millions of farmers. Millions more who complained too loudly, or who otherwise represented a political threat, were rounded up and executed.

A less-brutal solution to the problem of the LDCs is to make the wealthy bear more of the burden of increasing growth. If the decrease in consumption can be limited to the rich, then *total* consumption can be significantly reduced—freeing up resources for investment—without threatening the survival of the poor. This, however, is not often practical, since the wealthy have the most influence with government in

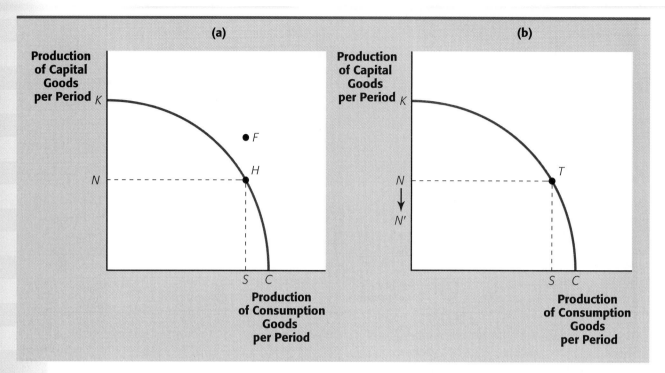

FIGURE 10

Growth Options for LDCs

Panel (a) shows an LDC producing at point H, where the available consumption goods are just sufficient to meet minimum standards (point S). If the nation can obtain goods externally, through foreign investment or foreign assistance, it can make use of capital and consumption goods at a point like F—outside of its PPF.

Panel (b) shows a case where capital production at point T is just sufficient to keep up with a rising population, but not great enough to raise capital per worker and living standards. If this nation can reduce its population growth rate, then the same rate of capital production will increase capital per worker and raise the standard of living.

LDCs. Being more mobile, they can easily relocate to other countries, taking their savings with them. This is why efforts to shift the sacrifice to the wealthy are often combined with restrictions on personal liberties, such as the freedom to travel or to invest abroad. These moves often backfire in the long run, since restrictions on personal and economic freedom are remembered long after they are removed and make the public—especially foreigners—hesitant to invest in that country.

A third alternative—and the one used increasingly since the 1940s—is *foreign investment* or *foreign assistance.* If the wealthier nations—individually or through international organizations such as the World Bank or the International Monetary Fund—provide the LDCs with capital, then the capital *available* to them can increase, with *no* cutbacks in consumption. This permits an LDC to *acquire* capital goods at a point like *F* in Figure 10(a), even though its *production* remains—for the moment—at point *H.*

A variation on this strategy is for foreign nations to provide consumer goods so that the poorer nation can shift its *own* resources out of producing them (and into capital production) without causing consumption levels to fall. Once again, if capital production exceeds point *N* during the year, capital per worker will grow, setting the stage for continual growth to higher standards of living.

Finally, there is a fourth alternative. Consider a nation producing at point *T* in Figure 10(b). Capital production is just sufficient to keep up with a rising population, so the PPF shifts outward each year, but not rapidly enough to raise living standards. If this nation can reduce its population growth rate, however, then less capital production will be needed just to keep up with population growth. In the figure, point *N* will move downward to *N'*. If production remains at point *T*, the PPF will continue to shift outward as before, but now—with slower population growth—productivity and living standards will rise. Slowing the growth in population has been an important (and successful) part of China's growth strategy, although it has required severe restrictions on the rights of individual families to have children. Policy trade-offs, once again.

Summary

The growth rate of real GDP is a key determinant of economic well-being. If output grows faster than the population, then output per person—and the average standard of living—will rise. But in order for output per person to rise, either average working hours, the labor force participation rate (LFPR), or productivity must increase. In developed countries, average hours have been decreasing and are unlikely to rise in the near future. Therefore, higher living standards can be attributed entirely to the last two factors—higher LFPR and higher productivity.

In order for the LFPR to rise, the labor force (and therefore, employment) must grow faster than the population. Employment growth arises from an increase in either labor supply or labor demand. Government tax and transfer policies can influence labor supply, and government subsidy and training programs can influence labor demand.

Productivity increases when capital per worker rises or there are advances in technology. When the flow of investment spending is greater than the flow of depreciation over some period of time, the capital stock will rise. An increase in the capital stock shifts the production upward, enabling any given number of workers to produce more output. If the capital stock rises at a faster rate than the labor force, then capital per worker rises, and so does productivity.

Investment can be encouraged by government policies. If the government reduces its budget deficit, the demand for loanable funds will fall, the interest rate will decline, and investment will increase. Investment can also be stimulated directly through reductions in the corporate profits tax or through subsidies to new capital. Finally, policies that encourage household saving can also lower the interest rate and contribute to capital formation.

Technological change—the application of new inputs or new methods of production—also raises productivity. The rate of technological change depends on spending on research and development, either by government or private firms. Almost any government policy that increases investment spending in general will also increase spending on research and development, and therefore increase the pace of technological change. In addition, patent protection can specifically influence research and development on new, patentable products and technologies.

Economic growth is not costless. Tax cuts that stimulate employment, capital formation, or technological progress require increases in other taxes, cuts in spending programs, or an increase in the national debt. Any increase in employment from a given population requires a sacrifice of leisure time and other nonmarket activities. More broadly, any increase in investment requires the sacrifice of consumption today.

Key Terms

Average standard of living	Flow variable	Patent protection
Capital gains tax	Human capital	Stock variable
Capital per worker	Investment tax credit	Technological change
Consumption tax	Labor force participation rate (LFPR)	
Corporate profits tax	Labor productivity	

Review Questions   *Answers to even-numbered Questions and Problems can be found on the text Web site at http://hall-lieb.swlearning.com.*

1. How do we calculate the average standard of living? Why should economic policy makers be concerned about economic growth?

2. Discuss the three major ways a country can increase its equilibrium level of output.

3. Why can population growth be a mixed blessing in terms of economic growth?

4. Explain how a tax cut could lead to *slower* economic growth.

5. If a country's PPF is shifting outward, is it necessarily the case that the country's standard of living is rising? Why or why not?

6. Why did Malthus's dire prediction fail to materialize? Do you think it could still come true? Explain your reasoning.

7. "Faster economic growth can benefit everyone and need not harm anyone. That is, there is no policy trade-off when it comes to economic growth." True or false? Explain.

8. Explain the following statement: "In some LDCs, it can be said that a significant cause of continued poverty is poverty itself."

9. Compare the effects on the real wage rate and output from an increase in labor demand and an increase in labor supply.

10. Describe four ways in which LDCs might improve their growth performance. Discuss the opportunity cost that must be borne in each case and identify the group that is most likely to bear it.

Problems and Exercises

1. Discuss the effect (holding everything else constant) each of the following would have on full-employment output, productivity, and the average standard of living. Use the appropriate graphs (e.g., labor market, loanable funds market, production function), and state your assumptions when necessary.
   a. Increased immigration
   b. An aging of the population with an increasing proportion of retirees
   c. A baby boom
   d. A decline in the tax rate on corporate profits
   e. Reduction of unemployment compensation benefits
   f. Expanding the scope of the federal student loan program
   g. Easier access to technical information on the Internet

2. Below are GDP and growth data for the United States and four other countries:

	1950 per Capita GDP (in Constant Dollars)	1990 per Capita GDP (in Constant Dollars)	Average Yearly Growth Rate
United States	$9,573	$21,558	2.0%
France	$5,221	$17,959	3.0%
Japan	$1,873	$19,425	5.7%
Kenya	$ 609	$ 1,055	1.3%
India	$ 597	$ 1,348	2.0%

Source: Angus Maddison, *Monitoring the World Economy, 1820–1992.* Paris, OECD, 1995.

   a. For both years, calculate each country's per capita GDP as a percentage of U.S. per capita GDP. Which countries appeared to be catching up to the United States, and which were lagging behind?
   b. If all these countries had continued to grow (from 1990 onward) at the average growth rates given, in what year would France have caught up to the United States? In what years (respectively) would India and Kenya have caught up to the United States?

3. Below are hypothetical data for the country of Barrovia:

	Population (Millions)	Employment (Millions)	Labor Productivity (Output per-Worker per-Year)	Total Yearly Output
1997	100	50	$ 9,500	___
1998	104	51	$ 9,500	___
1999	107	53	$ 9,750	___
2000	108	57	$ 9,750	___
2001	110	57	$10,000	___

   a. Fill in the entries for total output in each of the five years.

   b. Calculate the following for each year (except 1997):
      (1) Population growth rate (from previous year)
      (2) Growth rate of output (from previous year)
      (3) Growth rate of per capita output (from previous year)

4. In addition to shifting the production function upward, an increase in the capital stock will ordinarily make workers more productive and shift the labor demand curve rightward. Graphically illustrate the full impact of an increase in the nation's capital stock under this assumption.

5. Show what would happen to the production function if the capital stock decreased. Suppose, too, that the decrease in the capital stock—because it made workers less productive to firms—shifted the labor demand curve leftward. Graphically illustrate the full impact of a decrease in the nation's capital stock under this assumption. What government policies could cause a decrease in the capital stock?

6. State whether each of the following statements is true or false, and explain your reasoning briefly.
   a. "A permanent increase in employment from a lower to a higher level will cause an increase in real GDP, but not continued growth in real GDP."
   b. "A permanent increase in the nation's capital stock to a new, higher level will cause an increase in real GDP, but not continued growth in real GDP."
   c. "With constant population, work hours, and technology, as long as planned investment spending continues to be greater than depreciation, real GDP will continue to grow year after year."
   d. "All else equal, a permanent increase in an economy's rate of planned investment spending will cause real GDP to grow faster each year than it would at the old, lower level of investment spending."

7. On a diagram, draw an economy's production function. On the same diagram, add curves to illustrate where the production function would be in five years under each of the following assumptions. (Label your additional curves a, b, and c, and assume nothing else affecting economic growth changes.)
   a. Planned investment remains constant at its current level, which exceeds depreciation.
   b. Planned investment remains constant at its current level, which is less than depreciation.
   c. Planned investment rises above its current level, which exceeds depreciation.

8. Complete the following table, then find the growth rate of output from Year 1 to Year 2, from Year 2 to Year 3, and from Year 3 to Year 4, in terms of the percentage change in each of its components.

	Year 1	Year 2	Year 3	Year 4
Total hours worked	192 million	200 million	285 million	368 million
Labor force	1,200,000	1,400,000	1,900,000	2,100,000
Population	2,000,000	2,500,000	2,900,000	3,200,000
Productivity	$50 per hour	$52.50 per hour	$58 per hour	$60 per hour
Average hours per worker				
LFPR				
Total output				

9. Figure 1 in the chapter shows the effects of an increase in labor supply. Redraw both panels and show the effects of (a) an increase in labor demand, (b) a decrease in labor supply and (c) a decrease in labor demand.

10. Redraw Figure 10 from the chapter, and add the new PPF that the country would face in year 2 for each of the following scenarios: (i) the economy produces at point *J* in year 1, (ii) the economy produces at point *H* in year 1.

Challenge Questions

1. Economist Amartya Sen has argued that famines in underdeveloped countries are not simply the result of crop failures or natural disasters. Instead, he suggests that wars, especially civil wars, are linked to most famine episodes in recent history. Using a framework similar to Figure 10, discuss the probable effect of war on a country's PPF. Explain what would happen if the country were initially operating at or near a point like *S*, the minimum acceptable level of consumption.

2. All else equal, why might someone prefer to invest in physical capital in a less-developed country with a small capital stock than in a more-developed country that already has much capital? When wealth holders look for a place to invest and compare prospects in these two types of countries, is all else (other than existing capital stock) really equal? Explain.

These exercises require access to Hall/Lieberman Xtra! If Xtra! did not come with your book, visit http://hallxtra.swlearning.com to purchase.

1. Use your Xtra! password at the Hall and Lieberman Web site (http://hallxtra.swlearning.com), select this chapter, and under Economic Applications, click on EconDebate. Choose *Productivity Growth* and scroll down to find the debate, "Is There a New Economy?" Read the debate, and use the information to answer the following questions.
   a. List and explain the contributing factors to the GDP growth, outlined in this chapter, during the 1980s and 1990s according to the economists who argue in favor of the existence of a "new economy" and those who question it.
   b. Which of the contributing factors, listed in this chapter, are responsible for GDP growth in the manufacturing and agricultural industries? Explain.

2. Use your Xtra! password at the Hall and Lieberman Web site (http://hallxtra.swlearning.com), select this chapter, and under Economic Applications, click on EconData. Choose *Macroeconomics: Employment, Unemployment, and Inflation* and scroll down to find *Labor Productivity*. Read the definition and click on Diagrams/Data for information to answer the following questions.
   a. Do the diagrams confirm the existence of a "new economy"?
   b. Does the relationship between the labor productivity and real compensation per hour indicate a rising living standard for workers? Explain.

Economic Fluctuations

If you are like most college students, you will be looking for a job when you graduate, or you will already have one and want to keep it for a while. In either case, your fate is not entirely in your own hands. Your job prospects will depend, at least in part, on the overall level of economic activity in the country.

If the classical model of the previous two chapters described the economy at every point in time, you'd have nothing to worry about. Full employment would be achieved automatically, so you could be confident of getting a job at the going wage for someone with your skills and characteristics. Unfortunately, this is not always how the world works: Neither output nor employment grows as smoothly and steadily as the classical model predicts. Instead, as far back as we have data, the United States and similar countries have experienced *economic fluctuations*.

Look at panel (a) of Figure 1, which you've seen before in this book. The orange line shows estimated full-employment or potential output since 1960—the level of real GDP predicted by the classical model. As a result of economic growth, full-employment output rises steadily.

But now look at the green line, which shows *actual* output. You can see that actual GDP fluctuates above and below the classical model's predictions. During *recessions,* which are shaded in the figure, output declines, occasionally sharply. During *expansions* (the unshaded periods) output rises quickly, usually faster than potential output is rising. Indeed, in the later stages of an expansion, output often *exceeds* potential output—a situation that economists call a **boom.**

Panel (b) shows another characteristic of expansions and recessions: fluctuations in employment. During expansions, such as the period from 1983 to 1990, employment grows rapidly. During recessions (shaded), such as 1990–91, employment declines.

Figure 1 shows us that employment and output move very closely together. But the figure doesn't tell us anything about the *causal* relationship between them.

Boom A period of time during which real GDP is above potential GDP.

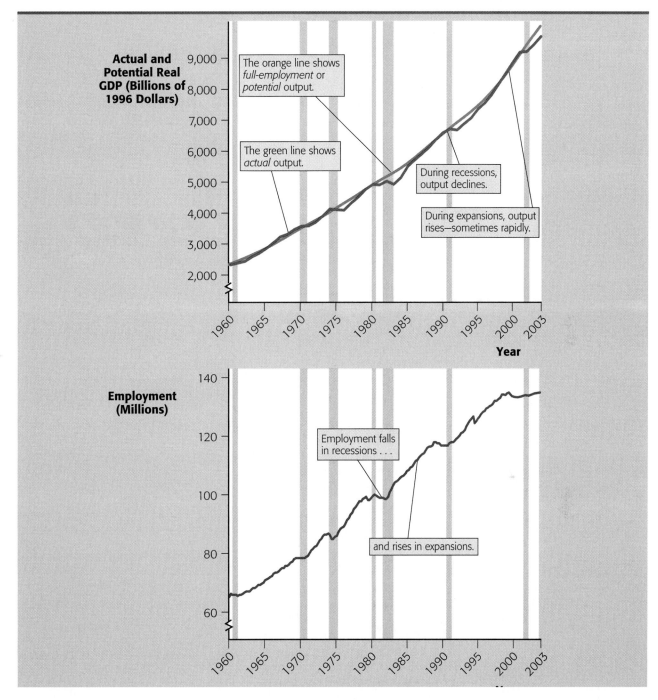

FIGURE 1
Potential and Actual Real GDP and Employment, 1960–2003

However, as you'll see in this chapter, we have good reason to conclude that over the business cycle, it is changes in output that cause firms to change their employment levels. For example, in a recession, many business firms lay off workers. If asked why, they would answer that they are reducing employment *because* they are producing less output.

FIGURE 2
**U.S. Unemployment Rate,
1960–2003**

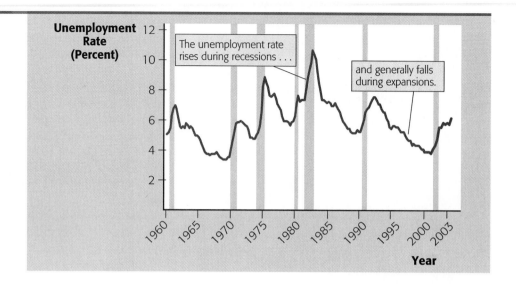

Finally, look at Figure 2, which presents the unemployment rate over the same period as in Figure 1. Figure 2 shows a critical aspect of fluctuations—the bulge of unemployment that occurs during each recession. When GDP falls, the unemployment rate increases. In the last few decades, the worst bulge in unemployment occured in 1982, when more than 10 percent of the labor force was looking for work. In expansions, on the other hand, the unemployment rate falls. In our most recent expansion, which began in March 1991 and ended in March 2001, unemployment dropped to 4 percent. In some expansions, the unemployment rate can drop even lower than the full-employment level. In the sustained expansion of the late 1960s, for example, it reached a low of just over 3 percent. At the same time, output exceeded its potential, as you can verify in Figure 1.

Figure 1 also shows something else: Expansions and recessions don't last forever. Indeed, sometimes they are rather brief. The recession of 1990–91, for example, ended within a year. And the recession that began in March 2001 officially ended in November of that year.

But if you look carefully at the figure, you'll see that the back-to-back recessions of the early 1980s extended over three full years. And during the Great Depression of the 1930s (not shown), it took more than a decade for the economy to return to full employment. Expansions too can last for extended periods. The expansion of the 1980s lasted about seven years, from 1983 to 1990. And the expansion that began in March 1991 turned out to be the longest expansion in U.S. economic history—a duration of 10 years.

The next several chapters deal with economic fluctuations. We have three things to explain: (1) *why* they occur in the first place, (2) why they sometimes last so long, and (3) why they do not last forever. But our first step is to see whether the macroeconomic model you've already studied—the classical, long-run model—can explain why economic fluctuations occur.

CAN THE CLASSICAL MODEL EXPLAIN ECONOMIC FLUCTUATIONS?

The classical model does a good job of explaining why the economy tends to operate near its potential output level, on average, over long periods of time. But can it help

HTTP://

Prakash Loungani and Bharat Trehan discuss the difficulties of forecasting recessions in their March 2002 article, "Predicting When the Economy Will Turn," available at http://www.frbsf.org/ publications/economics/ letter/2002/el2002-07.html.

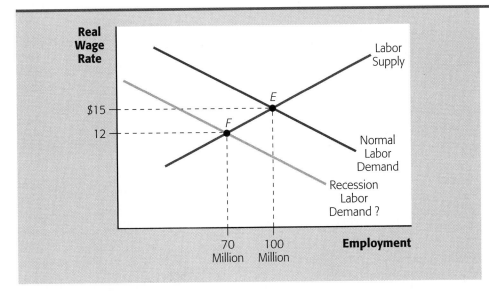

FIGURE 3
A Recession Caused by Declining Labor Demand?

In theory, a recession could be caused by a sudden leftward shift in the labor demand curve, causing employment to fall. In fact, large, sudden shifts in labor demand are an unlikely explanation for real-world fluctuations.

us understand the facts of economic fluctuations, as shown in Figures 1 and 2? More specifically, can the classical model explain why GDP and employment typically fall *below* potential during a recession and often rise above it in an expansion? Let's see.

Shifts in Labor Demand

One idea, studied by a number of economists, is that a recession might be caused by a leftward shift of the labor demand curve. This possibility is illustrated in Figure 3, in which a leftward shift in the labor demand curve would move us down and to the left along the labor supply curve. In the diagram, the labor market equilibrium would move from point *E* to point *F*, employment would fall and so would the real wage rate. Is this a reasonable explanation for recessions? Most economists feel that the answer is no, and for a very good reason.

The labor demand curve tells us the number of workers the nation's firms want to employ at each real wage rate. A leftward shift of this curve would mean that firms want to hire *fewer* workers at any given wage than they wanted to hire before. What could make them come to such a decision? One possibility is that firms are suddenly unable to sell all the output they produce. Therefore, the story would go, they must cut back production and hire fewer workers at any wage.

But as you've learned, in the classical model, total spending is *never* deficient. On the contrary, from the classical viewpoint, total spending is automatically equal to whatever level of output firms decide to produce. As you learned two chapters ago when we analyzed fiscal policy, a decrease in spending by one sector of the economy (such as the government) would cause an equal *increase* in spending by other sectors, with no change in total spending. While it is true that a decrease in output would cause total spending to decrease along with it (because Say's law tells us total spending is always equal to total output), the causation cannot go the other way in the classical model. In that model, changes in total spending cannot arise on their own. Therefore, if we want to explain a leftward shift in the labor demand curve using the classical model, we must look for some explanation other than a sudden change in spending.

Another possibility is that the labor demand curve shifts leftward because workers have become less *productive* and therefore less valuable to firms. This might happen if there were a sudden decrease in the capital stock, so that each worker had less equipment to work with. Or it might happen if workers suddenly forgot how to do things—how to operate a computer or use a screwdriver or fix an oil rig. Short of a major war that destroys plant and equipment, or an epidemic of amnesia, it is highly unlikely that workers would become less productive so suddenly. Thus, a leftward shift of the labor demand curve is an unlikely explanation for recessions.

What about booms? Could a *rightward* shift of the labor demand curve (not shown in Figure 3) explain them? Once again, a change in total spending cannot be the answer. In the classical model, as discussed a few paragraphs ago, changes in spending are caused by changes in employment and output, not the other way around. Nor can we explain a boom by arguing that workers have suddenly become more productive. While it is true that the capital stock grows over time and workers continually gain new skills—and that both of these movements shift the labor demand curve to the right—such shifts take place at a glacial pace. Compared to the amount of machinery already in place, and to the knowledge and skills that the labor force already has, annual increments in physical capital or knowledge are simply too small to have much of an impact on labor demand. Thus, a sudden rightward shift of the labor demand curve is an unlikely explanation for an expansion that pushes us beyond potential output.

> *Because shifts in the labor demand curve are not very large from year to year, the classical model cannot explain real-world economic fluctuations through shifts in labor demand.*

Shifts in Labor Supply

A second way the classical model might explain a recession is through a shift in the labor supply curve. Figure 4 shows how this would work. If the labor supply curve shifted to the left, the equilibrium would move up and to the left along the labor demand curve, from point E to point G. The level of employment would fall, and output would fall with it.

This explanation of recessions has almost no support among economists. First, remember that the labor supply schedule tells us, at each real wage rate, the number of people who *would like to* work. This number reflects millions of families' preferences about working in the market rather than pursuing other activities, such as taking care of children, going to school, or enjoying leisure time. A leftward shift in labor supply would mean that fewer people want to work at any given wage—that preferences have changed toward these other, nonwork activities. But in reality, preferences tend to change very slowly, and certainly not rapidly enough to explain recessions.

Second, even if such a shift in preferences did occur, it could not explain the facts of real-world downturns. Recessions are times when unusually large numbers of people are looking for work (see Figure 2). It would be hard to square that fact with a shift in preferences away from working.

The same arguments could be made about expansions: To explain them with labor supply shifts, we would have to believe that preferences suddenly change *toward* market work and away from other activities—an unlikely occurrence. And, in

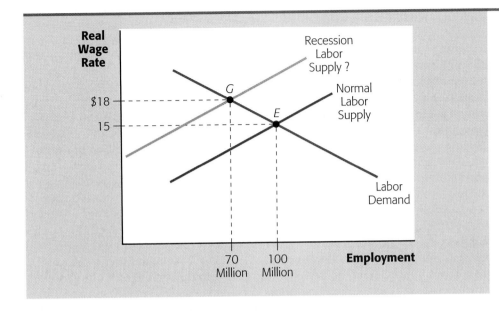

FIGURE 4
**A Recession Caused by
Declining Labor Supply?**

*In theory, a recession could be
caused by a sudden leftward
shift in the labor supply curve,
causing employment to fall. In
fact, shifts in labor supply occur
very slowly, so they cannot explain economic fluctuations.*

any case, expansions are periods when the unemployment rate typically falls to un-usually low levels; *fewer*—not more—people are seeking work.

Because sudden shifts of the labor supply curve are unlikely to occur, and because they could not accurately describe the facts of the economic cycle, the classical model cannot explain fluctuations through shifts in the supply of labor.

Verdict: The Classical Model Cannot Explain Economic Fluctuations

In earlier chapters, we stressed that the classical model works well in explaining the movements of the economy in the longer run. Now we see that it does a rather poor job of explaining the economy in the short run. Why is this? Largely because the classical model involves assumptions about the economy that make sense in the longer run, but not in the short run. Chief among these is the assumption that the labor market clears—that is, that the labor market operates at the point of in-tersection of the labor supply and labor demand curves. As long as this assumption holds, a boom or recession would have to arise from a sudden, significant *move-ment* in that intersection point, caused by a sudden and significant *shift* in either the labor demand curve or the labor supply curve.

But now, we've seen that such sudden shifts are very unlikely. Moreover, even if they did occur, they could not explain the changes in job-seeking activity that we observe in real-world recessions. And this, in a nutshell, is why we must reject the classical model when we turn our attention to the short run.

We cannot explain the facts of short-run economic fluctuations with a model in which the labor market always clears. This is why the classical model, which assumes that the market always clears, does a poor job of ex-plaining the economy in the short run.

WHAT TRIGGERS ECONOMIC FLUCTUATIONS?

Recessions that bring output below potential and expansions that drive output above potential are periods during which the economy is going a bit haywire. In a recession, millions of qualified people *want* to work at the going wage rate, but firms won't hire them. Managers would *like* to hire them, but they aren't selling enough output—in part because so many people are unemployed. The macroeconomy seems to be preventing an opportunity for mutual gain.

In a boom, the economy is going haywire in a different way. The unemployment rate is so low the normal job-search activity—which accounts for frictional unemployment—is short-circuited. Firms, desperate to hire workers because production is so high, are less careful about whom they hire. The result is a poorer-than-normal match between workers and their jobs. Moreover, the overheating of the economy that occurs in a boom can lead to inflation. We'll discuss how this happens a few chapters from now. But the basic outline is this: Because qualified workers are so scarce, firms must compete fiercely with each other to hire them. This drives up wage rates in the economy, raises production costs for firms, and ultimately causes firms to raise their prices.

Booms and recessions are periods during which the economy deviates from the normal, full-employment equilibrium of the classical model. The question is, why do such deviations occur? Let's start to answer this question by looking at a world that is much simpler than our own.

A Very Simple Economy

Imagine an economy with just two people: Yasmin and Pepe. Yasmin is especially good at making popcorn, but she eats only yogurt. Pepe, by contrast, is very good at making yogurt, but eats only popcorn. If things are going well, Yasmin and Pepe will make suitable amounts of popcorn and yogurt and trade with each other. Because of the gains from specialization, their trade will make them both better off than if they tried to function without trading. And under ordinary circumstances, Yasmin and Pepe will take advantage of all mutually beneficial opportunities for trading. Our two-person economy will thus operate at full employment, since both individuals will be fully engaged in making products for the other. You can think of their trading equilibrium as being like the labor market equilibrium in the classical model.

Now, suppose there is a breakdown in communication. For example, Yasmin may get the impression that Pepe is not going to want as much popcorn as before. She would then decide to *make* less popcorn for Pepe. At their next trading session, Pepe will be offered less popcorn, so he will decide to produce less yogurt. The result: Total production in the economy declines, and our two traders will lose some of the benefits of trading. This corresponds to a recession.

Alternatively, suppose Yasmin thinks that Pepe will want *more* popcorn than before. This might lead her to *increase* her production, working more than she normally prefers to work so she can get more yogurt from Pepe before his demand for popcorn returns to normal. Yasmin's production of popcorn—and therefore, total output in the economy—rises even if Yasmin's expectations turn out to be wrong and Pepe does *not* want more popcorn. Temporarily, we are in a boom.

In reading the previous paragraph, you might be thinking, "Wait a minute. If either Yasmin or Pepe got the impression that the other might want less or more of the other's product, wouldn't a simple conversation between them straighten things out?" If these are your thoughts, you are absolutely right. A breakdown in communication and a sudden change in production would be extremely unlikely . . . *in a simple economy with just two people.* And therein lies the problem: The real-world economy is much more complex than the world of Yasmin and Pepe.

The Real-World Economy

Think about the U.S. economy, with its millions of businesses producing goods and services for hundreds of millions of people. In many cases, production must be planned long before goods are actually sold. For example, from inception to final production, it takes nearly a year to build a house and two years to develop a new automobile model or produce a Hollywood film. If one firm—say, General Motors—believes that consumers will buy fewer of its cars next year, it cannot simply call a meeting of all potential customers and find out whether its fears are justified. Nor can it convince people, as Yasmin can convince Pepe, that their own jobs depend on their buying a GM car. Most potential car buyers do *not* work for General Motors and don't perceive any connection between buying a car and keeping their own jobs. Under the circumstances, it may be entirely logical for General Motors to plan for a lower production level and lay off some of its workers.

Of course, this would not be the end of the story. By decreasing its workforce, GM would create further problems for the economy. The workers it has laid off, who will earn less income or none at all, will cut back on *their* spending for a variety of consumer goods—restaurant meals, movies, vacation travel—and they will certainly postpone any large purchases they'd been planning, such as a new large-screen television or that family trip to Disney World. This will cause other firms—the firms producing these consumer goods and services—to cut back on *their* production, laying off *their* workers, and so on. In other words, what began as a perceived decrease in spending in one sector of the economy can work its way through other sectors, causing a full-blown recession.

This example illustrates a theme that we will revisit in the next chapter: the interdependence between production and income. When people spend their incomes, they give firms the revenue they need to hire workers and pay them income! If any link in this chain is broken, output and income may both decline. In our example, the link was broken because of incorrect expectations by firms in one sector of the economy. But there are other causes of recessions as well, also centering on the interdependence between production and income, and a failure to coordinate the decisions of millions of firms and households.

The classical model, however, waves these potential problems aside. It assumes that workers and firms, with the aid of markets, can work things out—like Yasmin and Pepe—and enjoy the benefits of producing and trading. And the classical model is right: People *will* work things out . . . eventually. But in the short run, we need to look carefully at the problems of coordinating production, trade, and consumption in an economy with millions of people and businesses.

A boom can arise in much the same way as a recession. It might start because of an increase in production in one sector of the economy, say, the housing sector. With more production and more workers earning higher incomes, spending increases in other sectors as well, until output rises above the classical, full-employment level.

Shocks That Push the Economy Away from Equilibrium

In our discussion above, General Motors decided to cut back on its production of cars because its managers believed, rightly or wrongly, that the demand for GM cars had decreased. Often, many firms will face a real or predicted drop in spending at the same time. We call this a **spending shock** to the economy—a change in spending that initially affects one or more sectors and ultimately works its way through the entire economy.

Spending shock A change in spending that ultimately affects the entire economy.

In the real world, the economy is constantly buffeted by shocks, and they often cause full-fledged macroeconomic fluctuations. Table 1 lists some of the recessions and notable expansions of the last 50 years, along with the events and spending shocks that are thought to have caused them or at least contributed heavily. You can see that each of these shocks first affected spending and output in one or more sectors of the economy. For example, several recessions have been set off by increases in oil prices, which caused a decrease in spending on products that depend on oil and energy, such as automobiles, trucks, and new factory buildings. Other recessions were precipitated by military cutbacks. Still others came about when the Federal Reserve caused sudden increases in interest rates that led to decreased spending on new homes and other goods. (You'll learn about the Federal Reserve and its policies a few chapters from now.)

Strong expansions, on the other hand, have been caused by military buildups, and by falling oil prices that stimulated spending on energy-related products, or by bursts of planned investment spending. The long expansion of the mid- and late-1990s, for example, began when the development of the Internet, and improvements in computers more generally, led to an increase in investment spending. Once the economy began expanding, it was further spurred by other factors, such as a rise in stock prices and consumer optimism, both of which led to an increase in consumption spending.

Half of our recessions since the early 1950s have been caused, at least in part, by rapid rises in oil prices.

In addition to these identifiable spending shocks, the economy is buffeted by other shocks whose origins are harder to spot. For example, consumption was higher than expected in the late 1980s, contributing to the rapid expansion that occurred in those years. In the early 1990s, consumption fell back to normal, helping to cause the recession of that period. There was no obvious event that caused these changes in consumption.

And each shock has momentum. When a decrease in spending causes production cutbacks, firms will lay off workers. The laid-off workers, suffering decreases in their incomes, cut back their own spending on other products, causing further layoffs in other sectors. The economy can continue sliding downward, and remain below potential output, for a year or longer. The same process works in reverse during an expansion: Higher spending leads to greater production, higher employment, and still greater spending, possibly leading to a boom in which the economy remains overheated for some time.

Booms and recessions do not last forever, however. The economy eventually adjusts back to full-employment output. Often, a change in government macroeconomic policy helps the adjustment process along, speeding the return to full employment. Other times, a policy mistake thwarts the adjustment process, prolonging or deepening a costly recession, or exacerbating a boom and overheating the economy even more.

HTTP://

Katherine Bradbury's "Job Creation and Destruction in Massachusetts" http://www.bos.frb.org/economic/neer/neer1999/neer599c.pdf provides a case study of how the labor market adjusts.

How does this adjustment process work? This is a question we'll be coming back to a few chapters from now, after you've learned some new tools for analyzing the economy's behavior over the short run.

Period		Event	Spending Shock
Early 1950s	Expansion	Korean War	Defense Spending ↑
1953	Recession	End of Korean War	Defense Spending ↓
Late 1960s	Expansion	Vietnam War	Defense Spending ↑
1970	Recession	Change in Federal Reserve Policy	Spending on New Homes ↓
1974	Recession	Dramatic Increase in Oil Prices	Spending on Cars and Other Energy-using Products ↓
1980	Recession	Dramatic Increase in Oil Prices	Spending on Cars and Other Energy-using Products ↓
1981–82	Recession	Change in Federal Reserve Policy	Spending on New Homes, Cars, and Business Investment ↓
Early 1980s	Expansion	Military Buildup	Defense Spending ↑
Late 1980s	Expansion	Huge Decline in Oil Prices	Spending on Energy-using Products ↑
1990	Recession	Large Increase in Oil Prices; Collapse of Soviet Union	Spending on Cars and Other Energy-using Products ↓; Defense Spending ↓
1991–2000	Expansion	Technological Advances in Computers; Development of the Internet; High Wealth Creation	Spending on Capital Equipment ↑; Consumption ↑
2001	Recession	Investment in New Technology Slows; Technology-fueled Bubble of Optimism Bursts; Wealth Destruction	Spending on Capital Equipment ↓

TABLE 1
Expansions, Recessions, and Shocks That Caused Them

WHERE DO WE GO FROM HERE?

The classical model that you've learned in previous chapters is certainly useful: It helps us understand economic growth over time, and how economic events and economic policies affect the economy over the long run. But in trying to understand expansions and recessions—where they come from, and why they can last for one or more years—we've had to depart from the strict framework of the classical model.

One theme of our discussion has been the central role of spending in understanding economic fluctuations. In the classical model, spending could be safely ignored. First, Say's law assured us that total spending would always be sufficient to buy the output produced at full employment. Second, a change in spending—for example, a decrease in military spending by the government—would cause other categories of spending to rise by just the right amount to make up for the lower spending of the government. In the long run, we can have faith in the classical perspective on spending.

But in the short run, we've seen that spending shocks to the economy affect production, usually in one specific sector. When employment changes in that sector, the spending of workers *there* will change as well, affecting demand in still other sectors. Clearly, if we want to understand fluctuations, we need to take a close look at spending. This is what we will do in the next chapter, when we study the *short-run macro model*.

Summary

The classical model does not always do a good job of describing the economy over short time periods. Over periods of a few years, national economies experience economic fluctuations in which output rises above or falls below its long-term growth path. Significant periods of falling output are called recessions, while periods of rapidly rising output are expansions. If an expansion causes output to rise above potential (or full-employment) output, it is called a boom. When real GDP fluctuates, it causes the level of employment and the unemployment rate to fluctuate as well.

The classical model cannot explain economic fluctuations because it assumes that the labor market always clears; that is, it always operates at the point where the labor supply and demand curves intersect. Evidence suggests that this market-clearing assumption is not always valid over short time periods. And when we try to explain economic fluctuations using the classical model, we come up short. Neither shifts in the labor demand curve, nor shifts in the labor supply curve, offer a realistic explanation for what happens during a recession or a boom.

In a simple, two-person economy, decisions about spending and production could be easily coordinated, so economic fluctuations would be easy to avoid. But in a market economy with millions of people and firms, decisions about spending and production cannot be coordinated, making the economy vulnerable to changes in production that are harmful to everyone involved.

Deviations from the full-employment level of output are often caused by *spending shocks*—changes in spending that initially affect one sector and then work their way through the entire economy. Negative shocks can cause recessions, while positive shocks can cause expansions that lead to booms. Eventually, output will return to its long-run equilibrium level, but it does not do so immediately. The origins of economic fluctuations can be understood more fully with the short-run macro model, which we will study in the next chapter.

Key Terms

Boom   Spending shock

Review Questions   *Answers to even-numbered Questions and Problems can be found on the text Web site at http://hall-lieb.swlearning.com.*

1. How does a *recession* differ from an *expansion*? Describe the typical behavior of GDP and the unemployment rate during each of these periods.

2. Why can't a recession be explained in terms of a reduction in labor demand? In terms of a reduction in labor supply?

3. In an economy with just two people, economic fluctuations would be unlikely to occur. Why? What is the key difference in the real-world economy that makes economic fluctuations more likely?

4. "During the last half-century economic fluctuations in the United States have been caused entirely by changes in military spending." True or false? Explain.

5. Suppose the economy is disturbed by a decrease in spending. Describe how this leads to a recession. How would an increase in spending lead to a boom?

Problems and Exercises

1. Using the upper panel of Figure 1, identify two time spans during which the U.S. economy was enjoying an expansion but *not* a boom. [*Hint:* Reread the first page of this chapter.]

2. This chapter explains how a spending shock—such as a decrease in investment spending—could cause a recession. But in the classical model, a decrease in investment spending could *not* causes a recession. Why not? [*Hint:* Use the loanable funds market diagram.]

3. Imagine that you are an unemployed worker. Are you more likely to find a job quickly during a recession or a boom? Once you find a job, explain how your behavior will contribute to the recession or boom that is taking place.

 *These exercises require access to Hall/Lieberman Xtra! If Xtra! did not come with your book, visit http://hallxtra.swlearning.com to purchase.*

1. Use your Xtra! password at the Hall and Lieberman Web site (http://hallxtra.swlearning.com), select this chapter, and under Economic Applications, click on EconDebate. Choose *Macroeconomics: Employment, Unemployment, and Inflation,* and scroll down to find the debate, "Does an Increase in the Minimum Wage Result in a Higher Unemployment Rate?" Read the debate, and use the information to answer the following questions.
   a. The labor market is one of the most important parts of the classical model. What are the ramifications of the minimum wage laws on employment and output according to the classical model?
   b. Considering the effects of inflation on the minimum wage would you expect the labor markets to clear or unemployment to persist in the presence of the minimum wage laws? Explain.

2. Use your Xtra! password at the Hall and Lieberman Web site (http://hallxtra.swlearning.com), select this chapter, and under Economic Applications, click on EconData. Choose *Macroeconomics: Employment, Unemployment, and Inflation,* and scroll down to find *Real GDP.* Read the definition and click on Diagrams/Data and use the information to answer the following question.
   a. Does the real GDP and Personal Income diagram support the interplay of income and spending and their role in explaining short-term fluctuations, as indicated in this chapter? Explain.

The Short-Run Macro Model

Every December, newspapers and television news broadcasts focus their attention on spending. You might see a reporter standing in front of a Circuit City outlet, warning that unless holiday shoppers loosen their wallets and spend big on computers, DVD players, vacation trips, toys, and new cars, the economy is in for trouble.

Of course, spending matters during the rest of the year, too. But holiday spending attracts our attention because the normal forces at work during the rest of the year become more concentrated in late November and December. Factories churn out merchandise and stores stock up at higher than normal rates. If consumers are in Scrooge-like moods, unsold goods will pile up in stores. In the months that follow, these stores will cut back on their orders for new goods. As a result, factories will decrease production and lay off workers.

And the story will not end there. The laid-off workers—even those who collect some unemployment benefits—will see their incomes decline. As a consequence, they will spend less on a variety of consumer goods. This will cause other firms— the ones that produce those consumer goods—to cut back on *their* production.

This hypothetical example reinforces a conclusion we reached in the last chapter: Spending is very important in the short run. And it points out an interesting circularity: The more income households have, the more they will spend. That is, *spending depends on income*. But the more households spend, the more output firms will produce—and the more income they will pay to their workers. Thus, *income depends on spending*.

> *In the short run, spending depends on income, and income depends on spending.*

In this chapter, we will explore this circular connection between spending and income. We will do so with a very simple macroeconomic model, which we'll call the *short-run macro model*. Many of the ideas behind the model were originally developed by the British economist John Maynard Keynes in the 1930s. The **short-run macro model** focuses on the role of spending in explaining economic fluctuations. It explains how shocks that initially affect one sector of the economy quickly influence other sectors, causing changes in total output and employment.

Short-run macro model A macroeconomic model that explains how changes in spending can affect real GDP in the short run.

To keep the model as simple as possible, we will—for the time being—ignore all influences on production *besides* spending. As a result, the short-run model may appear strange to you at first, like a drive along an unfamiliar highway. You may wonder: Where is all the scenery you are used to seeing along the classical road? Where are the labor market, the production function, the loanable funds market, and the market-clearing assumption? Rest assured that many of these concepts are still with us, lurking in the background and waiting to be exposed, and we will come back to them in later chapters. But in this chapter, we assume that spending—and *only* spending—determines how much output the economy will produce.

Thinking About Spending. Before we begin our analysis of spending, we have some choices to make.

First, spending on *what*? People spend on food, clothing, furniture, and vacations. They also spend to buy stocks and bonds, to buy homes, to buy used goods, and to buy things produced in foreign countries.

Remember that our main purpose in building the short-run macro model is to explain fluctuations in real GDP that the long-run, classical model cannot explain. Accordingly, we will ignore spending on things that are *not* part of our GDP, like stocks and bonds and real estate and goods produced abroad. Instead,

> *in the short-run macro model, we focus on spending in markets for currently produced U.S. goods and services—that is, spending on things that are included in U.S. GDP.*

Next, we need to organize our thinking about markets that contribute to GDP. We know who the sellers are: U.S. firms. But there are so many different types of buyers of U.S. goods and services: city dwellers and suburbanites; government agencies like the Department of Defense and the local school board; businesses of all types, ranging from the corner convenience store to a huge corporation such as AT&T; and foreigners from nearby Canada and distant Fiji. What's the best way to categorize all these buyers into larger groups so we can analyze their behavior?

Macroeconomists have found that the most useful approach is to divide those who purchase the GDP into four broad categories:

- Households, whose spending is called consumption spending (C)
- Business firms, whose spending is called planned investment spending (I^P)
- Government agencies, whose spending on goods and services is called government purchases (G)
- Foreigners, whose spending we measure as net exports (NX)

These categories should seem familiar to you. They were the same groups of buyers we used to break down GDP in the expenditure approach. In the first part of this chapter, we'll take another look at each of these types of buyers. Then, we'll add their purchases together to explore the behavior of *total* spending in the economy.

Finally, one more choice: Should we look at *nominal* or *real* spending? (Recall that a nominal variable is measured in current dollars, while a real variable is measured in the constant dollars of some base year.) Ultimately, we care more about real variables, such as real output and real income, because they are the more closely related to our economic well-being. For example, a rise in *nominal* output might mean that we are producing more goods and services, or it might just mean that prices have risen and production has remained the same or fallen. But a rise in *real* output always means that production has increased. For this reason, we will think about real variables right from the beginning. When we discuss "consumption spending," we mean "real consumption spending," "government purchases" means "real government purchases," and so on.

CONSUMPTION SPENDING

A natural place for us to begin our look at spending is with its largest component: *consumption spending*. In all, household spending on consumer goods—groceries, restaurant meals, rent, car repairs, movies, telephone calls, and furniture—averages about two-thirds of total spending in the economy. Total consumption spending in the economy is the sum of spending by over a hundred million U.S. households. What determines the *total* amount of consumption spending?

One way to answer is to start by thinking about yourself or your family. What determines your spending in any given month, quarter, or year?

Disposable Income. The first thing that comes to mind is your income: The more you earn, the more you spend. But in macroeconomics, small differences in language can be crucial. It's not exactly your *income* per period—what you are paid by your employer—that determines your spending, but rather what you get to *keep* from that income after deducting any taxes you have to pay. Moreover, some people receive a flow of transfer payments from the government—such as unemployment insurance benefits or Social Security payments—which they can spend in addition to any income received from an employer. If we start with the income you earn, deduct all tax payments, and then add in any transfer received, we would get your *disposable income*—a term introduced with the classical model. This is the income you are free to spend or save as you wish.

Disposable Income = Income − Tax Payments + Transfers Received.

This can be rewritten as:

Disposable Income = Income − (Taxes − Transfers).

Finally, remember that that the term in parentheses, Taxes − Transfers, is defined as *net taxes*. So the easiest way to think of your disposable income is:

$$\text{Disposable Income} = \text{Income} - \text{Net Taxes}.$$

All else equal, you'd certainly spend more on consumer goods with a disposable income of $50,000 per year than with $20,000 per year. For almost any household, *a rise in disposable income—with no other change—causes a rise in consumption spending.*

Wealth. Given your disposable income, how much of it will you spend and how much will you save? That will depend, in part, on your *wealth*—the total value of your assets (home, stocks, bonds, bank accounts and the like) minus your outstanding liabilities (student loans, mortgage loans, credit card debt, and so on). Even if your disposable income stayed the same, an increase in your wealth—say, because you own stocks or bonds that have risen in value—would probably induce you to spend more. In general, *a rise in wealth, with no other change, causes a rise in consumption spending.*

The Interest Rate. The interest rate is the reward people get for saving, or what they have to pay when they borrow. You would probably save more each year if the interest rate was 10 percent than if it was 2 percent. But when you save more of your disposable income, you spend less. *All else equal, a rise in the interest rate causes a decrease in consumption spending.*

It's worth noting that this relationship between the interest rate and consumption spending applies even for people who aren't "savers" in the common sense of the term. For example, suppose you've been living beyond your means and now you have thousands of dollars in credit card debt. Each month, you have to decide how much of your disposable income to spend and how much to use to pay down your credit card balance. If the interest rate on your unpaid balance is low, you might not worry too much, paying back very little each month. You might even go deeper into debt, continuing to spend *more* than your disposable income.

But at higher interest rates, you'd probably want to pay down more of the balance. To do so, you'd be spending *less* of your disposable income each period. So, whether you are earning interest on funds you've saved, or paying interest on funds you've borrowed, the higher the interest rate, the lower your consumption spending.

Expectations. Expectations about the future can affect your spending as well. If you become more optimistic about your job security or expect a big raise, you might spend more of your income *now*. Similarly, if you become more pessimistic—worried about losing your job or a pay cut—you'd probably spend less now. *All else equal, optimism about future income causes an increase in consumption spending.*

Other variables, too, can influence your consumption spending, including inheritances you expect to receive over your lifetime, and even how long you expect to live. But disposable income, wealth, the interest rate, and expectations are the key variables we'll be coming back to again and again in the short-run macroeconomic model. And just as these variables influence the consumption spending of each individual household, they also influence the consumption spending of the household sector as a whole.

FIGURE 1
**U.S. Consumption and
Disposable Income,
1985–2002**

When real consumption expenditure is plotted against real disposable income, the resulting relationship is almost perfectly linear: As real disposable income rises, so does real consumption spending.

Source: Bureau of Economic Analysis, National Income and Product Accounts Tables, Table 2.1.

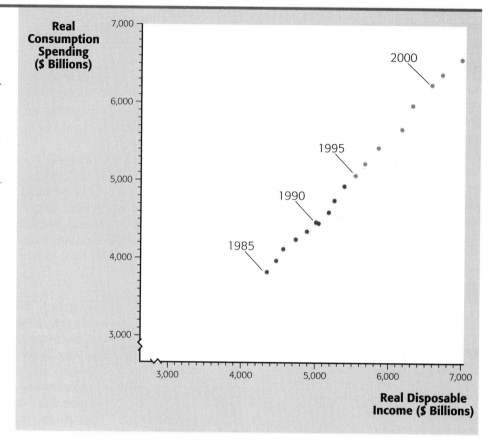

Unless we're focusing on an individual household to make a point (as in the preceding paragraphs), in macroeconomics, we use phrases like "disposable income," "wealth," or "consumption spending" to mean the *total* disposable income, *total* wealth, and *total* consumption spending of all households in the economy combined. So we can state our conclusions this way:

> *All else equal, consumption spending increases when:*
> * *disposable income rises*
> * *wealth rises*
> * *the interest rate falls*
> * *households become more optimistic about the future*

Consumption and Disposable Income

Of all the factors that influence consumption spending, the most important and stable determinant is disposable income. Figure 1 shows the relationship between (real) consumption spending and (real) disposable income in the United States from 1985 to 2002. Each point in the diagram represents a different year. For example, the point labeled "2000" represents a disposable income in that year of $6,630 billion and consumption spending of $6,224 billion. Notice that as disposable income rises, consumption spending rises as well. Indeed, almost all of the variation in con-

Real Disposable Income (Billions of Dollars per Year)	Real Consumption Spending (Billions of Dollars per Year)
0	2,000
1,000	2,600
2,000	3,200
3,000	3,800
4,000	4,400
5,000	5,000
6,000	5,600
7,000	6,200
8,000	6,800

TABLE 1

Hypothetical Data on Disposable Income and Consumption

sumption spending from year to year can be explained by variations in disposable income. Although the other factors we've discussed do affect consumption spending, their impact appears to be relatively minor.

There is something even more interesting about Figure 1: The relationship between consumption and disposable income is almost perfectly *linear*; the points lie remarkably close to a straight line. This almost-linear relationship between consumption and disposable income has been observed in a wide variety of historical periods and a wide variety of nations. This is why, when we represent the relationship between disposable income and consumption with a diagram or an equation, we use a straight line.

Our discussion will be clearer if we move from the actual data in Figure 1 to the hypothetical example in Table 1. Each row in the table represents a combination of (real) disposable income and (real) consumption we might observe in an economy. For example, the table shows us that if disposable income were equal to $7,000 billion in some year, consumption spending would equal $6,200 billion in that year. When we plot this data on a graph, we obtain the straight line in Figure 2. This line is called the **consumption function,** because it illustrates the functional relationship between consumption and disposable income.

Like every straight line, the consumption function in Figure 2 has two main features: a vertical intercept and a slope. Mathematically, the intercept—in this case, $2,000 billion—tells us how much consumption spending there would be in the economy if disposable income were zero. However, the real purpose of the vertical intercept is not to identify what would actually happen at zero disposable income, but rather to help us identify the particular line that represents consumption spending in the diagram. After all, there are many lines we could draw that have the same slope as the one in the figure. But only one of them has a vertical intercept of $2,000.

The vertical intercept in the figure also has a name: **autonomous consumption spending.** It represents the influence on consumption spending of everything *other than* disposable income. For example, if household wealth were to increase, consumption would be greater at any level of disposable income. In that case, the entire consumption function in the figure would shift upward, so its vertical intercept would increase. We would call this *an increase in autonomous consumption spending.* Similarly, a decrease in wealth would cause a *decrease in autonomous consumption spending,* and shift the consumption function downward.

Consumption function A positively sloped relationship between real consumption spending and real disposable income.

Autonomous consumption spending The part of consumption spending that is independent of income; also the vertical intercept of the consumption function.

FIGURE 2
The Consumption Function

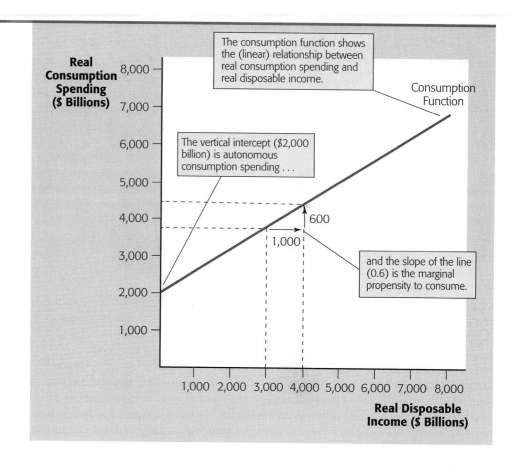

The second important feature of Figure 2 is the slope, which shows the change along the vertical axis divided by the change along the horizontal axis as we go from one point to another on the line:

$$\text{slope} = \frac{\Delta \text{Consumption}}{\Delta \text{Disposable Income}}.$$

As you can see in the table, each time disposable income rises by $1,000 billion, consumption spending rises by $600 billion, so that the slope is

$$\frac{\$600 \text{ billion}}{\$1,000 \text{ billion}} = 0.6$$

The slope in Figure 2 is an important feature not just of the consumption function itself, but also of the macroeconomic analysis we will build from it. This is why economists have given this slope a special name, the *marginal propensity to consume*, abbreviated *MPC*. In our example, the *MPC* is 0.6.

We can think of the *MPC* in three different ways, but each of them has the same meaning:

Marginal propensity to consume
The amount by which consumption spending rises when disposable income rises by one dollar.

> *The **marginal propensity to consume** (MPC) is (1) the slope of the consumption function; (2) the change in consumption divided by the change in disposable income; or (3) the amount by which consumption spending rises when disposable income rises by one dollar.*

Logic suggests that the *MPC* should be larger than zero (when income rises, consumption spending will *rise*), but less than 1 (the rise in consumption will be *smaller* than the rise in disposable income). This is certainly true in our example where *MPC* is 0.6 and each one-dollar rise in disposable income causes spending to rise by 60 cents. It is also observed to be true in economies throughout the world. Accordingly,

we will always assume that $0 < \text{MPC} < 1$.

Representing Consumption with an Equation. Sometimes, we'll want to use an equation to represent the straight-line consumption function. The most general form of the equation is

$$C = a + b \times (\text{Disposable Income})$$

where *C* is consumption spending. The term *a* is the vertical intercept of the consumption function. It represents the theoretical level of consumption spending at disposable income = 0, which you've learned is called *autonomous consumption spending*. In the equation, you can see clearly that autonomous consumption (*a*) is the part of consumption that does *not* depend on disposable income. In our example in Figure 2, *a* is equal to $2,000 billion.

The other term, *b*, is the slope of the consumption function. This is our familiar marginal propensity to consume (*MPC*), telling us how much consumption *increases* each time disposable income rises by a dollar. In our example in Figure 2, *b* is equal to 0.6.

Consumption and Income

The consumption function is an important building block of our analysis. Consumption is the largest component of spending, and disposable income is the most important determinant of consumption. But there is one limitation of the line as we've drawn it in Figure 2: It shows us the value of consumption at each level of *disposable* income, whereas we will need to know the value of consumption spending at each level of *income*. Disposable income, you remember, is the income that the household sector has left after deducting net taxes. How can we convert the line in Figure 2 into a relationship between consumption and income?

Table 2 illustrates the consumption–income relationship when the household sector pays net taxes. In the table, we treat net taxes as a fixed amount—in this case, $2,000 billion. Some taxes are, indeed, fixed in this way, such as the taxes assessed on real estate by local governments. Other taxes, like the personal income tax and the sales tax, rise and fall with income in the economy. Still, treating net taxes as if they are independent of income, as in Table 2, will simplify our discussion without changing our results in any important way.

Notice that the last two columns of the table are identical to the columns in Table 1: In both tables, we assume that the relationship between consumption spending and *disposable* income is the same. For example, both tables show us that, when disposable income is $7,000 billion, consumption spending is $6,200 billion. But in Table 2, we see that disposable income of $7,000 is associated with *income* of $9,000. Thus, when income is $9,000, consumption spending is $6,200. By comparing the first and last columns of Table 2, we can trace out the

TABLE 2
The Relationship Between Consumption and Income

Income or GDP (Billions of Dollars per Year)	Tax Collections (Billions of Dollars per Year)	Disposable Income (Billions of Dollars per Year)	Consumption Spending (Billions of Dollars per Year)
2,000	2,000	0	2,000
3,000	2,000	1,000	2,600
4,000	2,000	2,000	3,200
5,000	2,000	3,000	3,800
6,000	2,000	4,000	4,400
7,000	2,000	5,000	5,000
8,000	2,000	6,000	5,600
9,000	2,000	7,000	6,200
10,000	2,000	8,000	6,800

Consumption–income line A line showing aggregate consumption spending at each level of income or GDP.

relationship between consumption and income. This relationship—which we call the **consumption–income line**—is graphed in Figure 3.

If you compare the consumption–income line in Figure 3 with the line in Figure 2, you will notice that both have the same slope of 0.6, but the consumption–income line is lower by $1,200 billion. Net taxes have lowered the consumption–income line. Why? Because at any level of income, taxes reduce disposable income and therefore reduce consumption spending.

But why is the consumption–income line lower by precisely $1,200 billion? We can reason it out as follows: Any increase in net taxes (T) will cause consumption spending to fall by $MPC \times \Delta T$. In our example, when we impose taxes of $2,000 billion on the population, disposable income will drop by $2,000 billion at any level of income. With an MPC of 0.6, consumption at any level of income falls by $0.6 \times$ $2,000 billion = $1,200 billion.

Finally, we noted earlier that the *slope* of the consumption–income line is unaffected by net taxes. This is because with net taxes held at a fixed amount, disposable income rises dollar-for-dollar with income. With an MPC of 0.6, consumption spending will rise by 60 cents each time income rises by a dollar, just as it rises by 60 cents each time *disposable* income rises by a dollar. You can see this in Table 2: Each time income rises by $1,000 billion, consumption spending rises by $600 billion, giving the consumption–income line a slope of $600 billion / $1,000 billion = 0.6, just as in the case with no taxes. More generally,

when the government collects a fixed amount of taxes from households, the line representing the relationship between consumption and income is shifted downward by the amount of the tax times the marginal propensity to consume (MPC). The slope of this line is unaffected by taxes, and is equal to the MPC.

Shifts in the Consumption–Income Line

As you've learned, consumption spending depends positively on income: If income increases and net taxes remain unchanged, disposable income will rise, and consumption spending will rise along with it. The chain of causation can be represented this way:

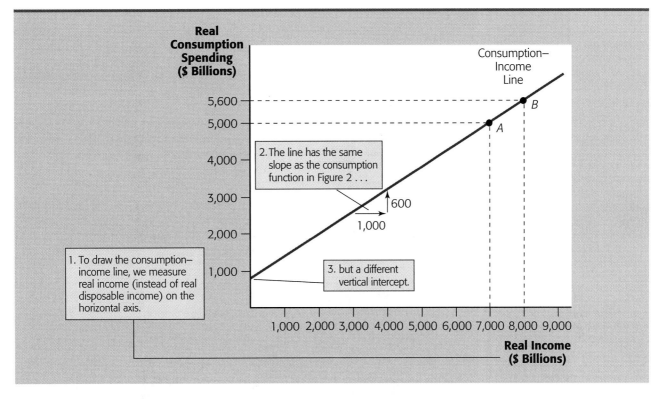

FIGURE 3
The Consumption–Income Line

In Figure 3, this change in consumption spending would be represented by a *movement along* the consumption–income line. For example, a rise in income from $7,000 billion to $8,000 billion would cause consumption spending to increase from $5,000 billion to $5,600 billion, moving us from point *A* to point *B* along the consumption–income line.

But consumption spending can also change for reasons other than a change in income, causing the consumption–income line itself to shift. For example, a decrease in net taxes will increase *disposable* income at each level of income. Consumption spending will then increase at any income level, shifting the entire line upward. The mechanism works like this:

| Taxes ↓ | ⇒ | Disposable income at each income level ↑ | ⇒ | Consumption at each income level ↑ | } | Shift Upward of the Consumption– Income Line |

In Figure 4, a decrease in taxes from $2,000 billion to $500 billion increases disposable income at each income level by $1,500 billion, and causes consumption at each income level to increase by 0.6 × $1,500 billion = $900 billion. This means that the consumption line shifts upward, to the upper line in the figure.

In addition to net taxes, all the other influences on consumption, other than disposable income, shift the consumption–income line as well. But these other shift-variables work by changing the value of *autonomous consumption*, the vertical intercept of the consumption function in Figure 2. By shifting the relationship between

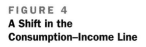

FIGURE 4
**A Shift in the
Consumption–Income Line**

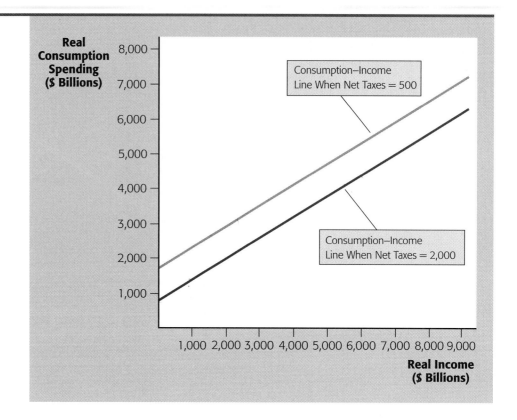

consumption and disposable income, we shift the relationship between consumption and income as well. For example, an increase in household wealth would increase autonomous consumption, and shift the consumption–income line upward, as in Figure 4. Increases in autonomous consumption could also occur if the interest rate decreased, or if households became more optimistic about the future. In general, increases in autonomous consumption work this way:

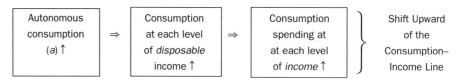

We can summarize our discussion of changes in consumption spending as follows:

> *When a change in income causes consumption spending to change, we move along the consumption–income line. When a change in anything else besides income causes consumption spending to change, the line will shift.*

Table 3 provides a more specific summary of how different types of changes in consumption spending are represented with the consumption–income line. Remember that all of the changes that *shift* the line—other than a change in taxes—work by increasing or decreasing autonomous consumption (*a*).

Rightward Movement Along the Line	Leftward Movement Along the Line	Entire Line Shifts Upward		Entire Line Shifts Downward	
When	When	When		When	
Income ↑	Income ↓	autonomous consumption (*a*) ↑	Taxes ↓ Household wealth ↑ Interest rate ↓ Greater optimism	Taxes ↑ Household wealth ↓ Interest rate ↑ Greater pessimism	autonomous consumption (*a*) ↓

TABLE 3
Changes in Consumption Spending and the Consumption–Income Line

GETTING TO TOTAL SPENDING

In addition to household consumption spending, there are three other types of spending on goods and services produced by American firms: investment, government purchases, and purchases by foreigners. Let's consider each of these types of spending in turn.

Investment Spending

Remember that in the definition of GDP, the word *investment* by itself (represented by the letter *I* by itself) consists of three components: (1) business spending on plant and equipment; (2) purchases of new homes; and (3) accumulation of unsold inventories. In this chapter, as we did when we studied the classical model, we focus not on investment, but on *planned investment* or *investment spending* (we'll use these two terms interchangeably).

Planned investment (I^p) is business purchases of plant and equipment, and construction of new homes.

Why do we focus on planned investment and leave out inventory accumulation? When we look at how spending influences the economy, we are interested in the purchases households, firms, and the government *want* to make. But some inventory changes, as you learned a few chapters ago, are an *unplanned* and *undesired* occurrence that firms try to avoid. While firms want to have *some* inventories on hand, sudden *changes* in inventories are typically not desirable. To keep the model simple, we treat *all* inventory changes as temporary, unplanned occurrences for the firm, and we exclude them when we measure spending in the economy. But even though they are excluded from spending, inventory changes will play an important part in our analysis, as you will see in a few pages.

> *In the short-run macro model, (planned) investment spending* (I^p) *is plant and equipment purchases by business firms, and new home construction. Inventory investment is treated as unintentional and undesired, and is therefore excluded from our definition of investment spending.*

What determines the level of investment spending in a given year? In this chapter, we will regard investment spending as a *fixed value*, determined by forces outside of our analysis. This may seem surprising. After all, aren't there variables that affect investment spending in predictable ways? Indeed, there are.

For example, in the classical model, you learned that planned investment is likely to be affected by the interest rate. Indeed, in the real world, the investment–interest rate relationship is quite strong. Investment is also influenced by the general level of optimism or pessimism about the economy and by new technological developments. But if we introduced all of these other variables into our analysis, we would find ourselves working with a very complex framework, and much too soon. In future chapters, we'll explore some of the determinants of investment spending, but in this chapter, to keep things simple, we assume that investment spending is some given amount. We'll explore what happens when that amount changes, but we will not, in this chapter, try to explain what *causes* investment spending to change.

> *For now, we regard investment spending* (I^P) *as a given value, determined by forces outside of our model.*

Government Purchases

Government purchases include all of the goods and services that government agencies—federal, state, and local—buy during the year. We treat government purchases in the same way as investment spending: as a given value, determined by forces outside of our analysis. Why?

The relationship between government purchases and other macroeconomic variables—particularly income—is rather weak. In recent decades, the biggest changes in government purchases have involved military spending. These changes have been based on world politics rather than macroeconomic conditions. So assuming that government spending is a given value, independent of the other variables in our model, is realistic.

> *In the short-run macro model, government purchases are treated as a given value, determined by forces outside of the model.*

As with investment spending, we'll be exploring what happens when the "given value" of government purchases changes. But we will not try to explain what causes it to change.

Net Exports

If we want to measure total spending on U.S. output, we must also consider the international sector. About 11 percent of U.S.-produced goods are sold to *foreign* consumers, *foreign* businesses, and *foreign* governments. These U.S. *exports* are as much a part of total spending on U.S. output as the other types of spending we've discussed so far. Thus, exports must be included in our measure of total spending.

International trade in goods and services also requires us to make an adjustment to the other components of spending. A portion (about 16 percent) of the output bought by *American* consumers, firms, and government agencies was produced abroad. From the U.S. point of view, these are *imports:* spending on foreign, rather than U.S., output. These imports are included in our measures of consumption, investment, and government spending, giving us an exaggerated measure of spending on *American* output. But we can easily correct for this overcount by simply deducting imported consumption goods from our measure of consumption, deducting imported investment goods from our measure of investment spending, and deducting imported government purchases from our measure of government purchases. Combining all these deductions together, we are actually deducting *total* imports to correct our exaggerated measure of *total* spending.

In sum, to incorporate the international sector into our measure of total spending, we must add U.S. exports and subtract U.S. imports. These two adjustments can be made together by simply including *net exports (NX)* as the foreign sector's contribution to total spending.

$$\text{Net Exports} = \text{Total Exports} - \text{Total Imports}.$$

By including net exports, we simultaneously ensure that we have included U.S. output that is sold to foreigners, and excluded consumption, investment, and government spending on output produced abroad.

Net exports can change for a variety of reasons: changes in tastes toward or away from a particular country's goods, changes in the price of foreign currency on world foreign exchange markets, and more. In a later chapter of this book, we'll discuss in more detail how and why net exports change. But in this chapter, to keep things simple, we assume that net exports—like investment spending and government purchases—are some given amount. We'll explore what happens when that amount changes, but we will not, in this chapter, try to explain what causes net exports to change.

> *For now, we regard net exports as a given value, determined by forces outside of our analysis.*

It is important to remember that net exports can be *negative*; and in the United States, they have been negative since 1982. Negative net exports means that our imports are greater than our exports. Or, equivalently, Americans are buying more foreign goods and services than foreigners are buying of ours. In that case, net exports contribute *negatively* to total spending on U.S. output.

Summing Up: Aggregate Expenditure

Now that we've discussed all of the components of spending in the economy, we can be more precise about measuring total spending. First, we'll use the phrase *aggregate expenditure* to mean total spending on U.S. output over some period of time. More formally,

> *aggregate expenditure is the sum of spending by households, businesses, the government, and the foreign sector on final goods and services produced in the United States.*

Aggregate expenditure (AE) The sum of spending by households, business firms, the government, and foreigners on final goods and services produced in the United States.

Remembering that C stands for household consumption spending, I^p for investment spending, G for government purchases, and NX for net exports, we have

$$\text{Aggregate expenditure} = C + I^p + G + NX.$$

Aggregate expenditure plays a key role in explaining economic fluctuations. Why? Because over several quarters or even a few years, business firms tend to respond to

(1) Income or GDP (Billions of Dollars per Year)	(2) Consumption Spending (Billions of Dollars per Year)	(3) Investment Spending (Billions of Dollars per Year)	(4) Government Purchases (Billions of Dollars per Year)	(5) Net Exports (Billions of Dollars per Year)	(6) Aggregate Expenditure (AE) (Billions of Dollars per Year)	(7) Change in Inventories (Billions of Dollars per Year)
2,000	2,000	700	500	400	3,600	−1,600
3,000	2,600	700	500	400	4,200	−1,200
4,000	3,200	700	500	400	4,800	−800
5,000	3,800	700	500	400	5,400	−400
6,000	**4,400**	**700**	**500**	**400**	**6,000**	**0**
7,000	5,000	700	500	400	6,600	400
8,000	5,600	700	500	400	7,200	800
9,000	6,200	700	500	400	7,800	1,200
10,000	6,800	700	500	400	8,400	1,600

TABLE 4
The Relationship Between Income and Aggregate Expenditure

changes in aggregate expenditure by changing their level of output. That is, a rise in aggregate expenditure leads firms throughout the economy to raise their output level, while a drop in aggregate expenditure causes a decrease in output throughout the economy. While these changes are temporary, they persist long enough to create the kinds of economic fluctuations that you saw in the previous chapter's Figures 1 and 2. In the next section, we'll explore just how changes in spending create these economic fluctuations.

Income and Aggregate Expenditure

As we discussed earlier, the relationship between income and spending is circular: Spending depends on income, and income depends on spending. In Table 4, we take up the first part of that circle: how total spending depends on income. In the table, column 1 lists some possible income levels, and column 2 shows the level of consumption spending we can expect at each income level. These two columns are just the consumption–income relationship we introduced earlier, in Table 2.

DANGEROUS CURVES

GDP Versus Aggregate Expenditure The definition of aggregate expenditure looks very similar to the definition of GDP presented in the chapter entitled "Production, Income, and Employment." Does this mean that aggregate expenditure and total output are always the same number? Not at all. There is a slight—but important—difference in the definitions. GDP is defined as $C + I + G + NX$. Aggregate expenditure, by contrast, is defined as $C + I^p + G + NX$. The difference is that GDP adds actual investment (I), which includes business firms' inventory investment. Aggregate expenditure adds just planned investment (I^p), which *excludes* inventory investment. The two numbers will not be equal unless inventory investment is zero. (We'll use this fact to help us find the equilibrium GDP in the next section.)

Column 3 shows that business firms in this economy buy $700 billion per year in plant and equipment, regardless of the level of income. Government purchases are also fixed in value, as shown by column 4: At every level of income, the government buys $500 billion in goods and services. And net exports, in column 5, are assumed to be $400 billion at each level of income. Finally, if we add together the entries in columns 2, 3, 4, and 5, we get $C + I^p + G + NX$, or aggregate expenditure, shown in column 6. (For now, ignore column 7.)

Notice that aggregate expenditure increases as income rises. But notice also that the rise in aggregate expenditure is *smaller* than the rise in income. For example, you can see that when income rises from $5,000 billion to $6,000 billion (column 1), aggregate expenditure rises from $5,400 billion to $6,000 billion (column 6). Thus, a $1,000 billion increase in income is associated with a $600 billion increase in aggregate expenditure. This is because, in our analysis, consumption is the only component of spending that depends on income, and consumption spending always increases according to the marginal propensity to consume, here equal to 0.6.

> *When income increases, aggregate expenditure* (AE) *will rise by the* MPC *times the change in income:* $\Delta AE = MPC \times \Delta GDP$.

Notice that we've used ΔGDP to indicate the change in total income, because GDP and total income are always the same number.

FINDING EQUILIBRIUM GDP

Table 4 shows how aggregate expenditure depends on income. In this section, you will see how income depends on aggregate expenditure—that is, how spending determines the economy's *equilibrium income* or *equilibrium GDP*. That is, we are about to use Step 2 of our three-step process. As always, the equilibrium will be a point of rest of the economy: a value for GDP that remains the same until something we've been assuming constant begins to change. That part of Step 2 will be familiar to you.

However, be forewarned: Our method of *finding* equilibrium in the short run is very different from anything you've seen before in this text.

Our starting point in finding the economy's short-run equilibrium is to ask ourselves what would happen, hypothetically, if the economy were operating at different levels of output. Let's start with a GDP of $9,000 billion. Could this be the equilibrium GDP we seek? That is, if firms were producing this level of output, would they keep doing so? Let's see.

Table 4 tells us that when GDP, and therefore income, is equal to $9,000 billion, aggregate expenditure is equal to $7,800 billion. Business firms are *producing* $1,200 billion more than they are *selling*. Since firms will certainly not be willing to continue producing output they cannot sell, we can infer that, in future periods, they will slow their production. Thus, if the economy finds itself at a GDP of $9,000 billion, it will not stay there. In other words, $9,000 billion is *not* where the economy will settle in the short run, so it is *not* our equilibrium GDP. More generally,

What About Prices? You may be wondering why, in the short-run macro model, a firm that produces more output than it sells wouldn't just lower the price of its goods. That way, it could sell more of them and not have to lower its output as much. Similarly, a firm whose sales exceeded its production could take advantage of the opportunity to raise its prices rather than increase production.

To some extent, firms *do* change prices—even in the short run. But they change their output levels, too. To keep things as simple as possible, this first version of the short-run macro model assumes that firms adjust *only* their output to match aggregate expenditure. That is, we assume that *prices don't change at all*. In a later chapter, we'll make the model more realistic by assuming that firms adjust both prices and output.

DANGEROUS CURVES

> *when aggregate expenditure is less than GDP, output will decline in the future. Thus, any level of output at which aggregate expenditure is less than GDP cannot be the equilibrium GDP.*

Now let's consider the opposite case: a level of GDP of $3,000 billion. At this level of output. Table 4 shows aggregate expenditure of $4,200 billion; spending is actually *greater* than output by $1,200 billion. What will business firms do in response? Since they are selling more output than they are currently producing, we can expect them to *increase* their production in future months. Thus, if GDP is $3,000 billion, it will tend to rise in the future. So $3,000 billion is *not* our equilibrium GDP.

> *When aggregate expenditure is greater than GDP, output will rise in the future. Thus, any level of output at which aggregate expenditure exceeds GDP cannot be the equilibrium GDP.*

Now consider a GDP of $6,000 billion. At this level of output, our table shows that aggregate expenditure is precisely equal to $6,000 billion: Output and aggregate expenditure are equal. Since firms, on the whole, are selling just what they produce—no more and no less—they should be content to produce that same amount in the future. We have found our equilibrium GDP:

Equilibrium GDP In the short run, the level of output at which output and aggregate expenditure are equal.

> *In the short run, **equilibrium** GDP is the level of output at which output and aggregate expenditure are equal.*

Inventories and Equilibrium GDP

When firms *produce* more goods than they sell, what happens to the unsold output? It is added to their inventory stocks. When firms *sell* more goods than they produce, where do the additional goods come from? They come from firms' inventory stocks. You can see that the gap between output and spending determines what will happen to inventories during the year.

More specifically,

> *the change in inventories during any period will always equal output minus aggregate expenditure.*

For example, Table 4 tells us that if GDP is equal to $9,000 billion, aggregate expenditure is equal to $7,800 billion. In this case, we can find that the change in inventories is

$$\Delta \text{Inventories} = GDP - AE$$

$$= \$9,000 \text{ billion} - \$7,800 \text{ billion}$$

$$= \$1,200 \text{ billion}.$$

When GDP is equal to $3,000 billion, aggregate expenditure is equal to $4,200 billion, so that the change in inventories is

$$\Delta \text{Inventories} = GDP - AE$$

$$= \$3,000 \text{ billion} - \$4,200 \text{ billion}$$

$$= -\$1,200 \text{ billion}.$$

Notice the negative sign in front of the $1,200 billion; if output is $3,000 billion, then inventory stocks will *shrink* by $1,200 billion.

Only when output and total sales are equal—that is, when GDP is at its equilibrium value—will the change in inventories be zero. In our example, when GDP is at its equilibrium value of $6,000 billion, so that aggregate expenditure is also $6,000 billion, the change in inventories is equal to zero. At this output level, we have

$$\Delta \text{Inventories} = GDP - AE$$

$$= \$6,000 \text{ billion} - \$6,000 \text{ billion}$$

$$= \$0.$$

What you have just learned about inventories suggests another way to find the equilibrium GDP in the economy: Find the output level at which the change in inventories is equal to zero. Firms cannot allow their inventories of unsold goods to keep growing for very long (they would go out of business), nor can they continue to sell goods out of inventory for very long (they would run out of goods). Instead, they will desire to keep their production in line with their sales, so that their inventories do not change.

To recap,

$$AE < GDP \Rightarrow \Delta \text{Inventories} > 0 \Rightarrow GDP\downarrow \text{ in future periods.}$$

$$AE > GDP \Rightarrow \Delta \text{Inventories} < 0 \Rightarrow GDP\uparrow \text{ in future periods.}$$

$$AE = GDP \Rightarrow \Delta \text{Inventories} = 0 \Rightarrow \text{No change in } GDP.$$

Now look at the last column in Table 4, which lists the change in inventories at different levels of output. This column is obtained by subtracting column 6 from column 1. The equilibrium output level is the one at which the change in inventories equals zero, which, as we've already found, is $6,000 billion.

Finding Equilibrium GDP with a Graph

To get an even clearer picture of how equilibrium GDP is determined, we'll illustrate it with a graph, although it will take us a few steps to get there. Figure 5 begins the process by showing how we can construct a graph of aggregate expenditure. The lowest line in the figure, labeled C, is our familiar consumption–income line, obtained from the data in the first two columns of Table 4.

The next line, labeled $C + I^p$, shows the *sum* of consumption and investment spending at each income level. Notice that this line is parallel to the C line, which means that the vertical distance between them—$700 billion—is the same at any income level. This vertical difference is investment spending, which remains the same at all income levels.

The next line adds government purchases to consumption and investment spending, giving us $C + I^p + G$. The $C + I^p + G$ line is parallel to the $C + I^p$ line. The vertical distance between them—$500 billion—is government purchases. Like investment spending, government purchases are the same at all income levels.

Finally, the top line adds net exports, giving us $C + I^p + G + NX$, or aggregate expenditure. The distance between the $C + I^p + G + NX$ line and the $C + I^p + G$ line—$400 billion—represents net exports, which are assumed to be the same at any level of income.

Now look just at the aggregate expenditure line—the top line—in Figure 5. Notice that it slopes upward, telling us that as income increases, so does aggregate

FIGURE 5
Deriving the Aggregate Expenditure Line

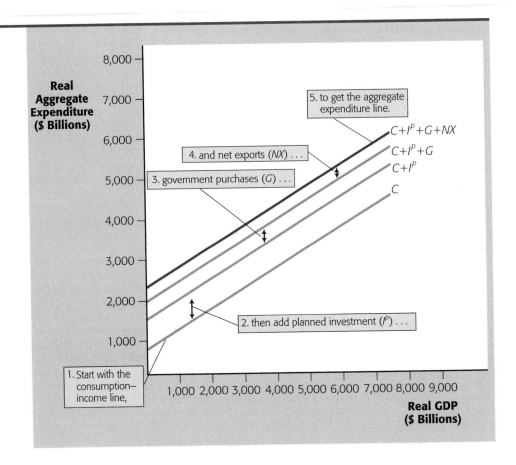

expenditure. And the slope of the aggregate expenditure line is less than 1: When income increases, the rise in aggregate expenditure is *smaller* than the rise in income. In fact, the slope of the aggregate expenditure line is equal to the *MPC*, or 0.6 in this example. This tells us that a one-dollar rise in income causes a 60-cent increase in aggregate expenditure. (Question: In the graph, which of the four components of aggregate expenditure rises when income rises? Which remain the same?)

Now we're almost ready to use a graph like the one in Figure 5 to locate equilibrium GDP, but first we must develop a little geometric trick.

Figure 6 shows a graph in which the horizontal and vertical axes are both measured in the same units, such as dollars. It also shows a line drawn at a 45° angle that begins at the origin. This 45° line has a useful property: Any point along it represents the same value along the vertical axis as it does along the horizontal axis. For example, look at point *A* on the line. Point *A* corresponds to the horizontal distance *0B*, and it also corresponds to the vertical distance *BA*. But because the line is a 45° line, we know that these two distances are equal: *0B* = *BA*. Now we have two choices for measuring the distance *0B*: We can measure it horizontally, or we can measure it as the vertical distance *BA*. In fact, *any* horizontal distance can also be read vertically, merely by going from the horizontal value (point *B* in our example) up to the 45° line.

> *A 45° line is a translator line: It allows us to measure any horizontal distance as a vertical distance instead.*

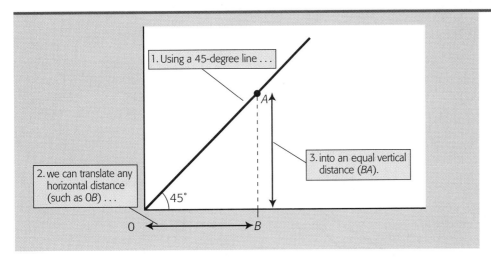

FIGURE 6
Using a 45° to Translate Distances

Now we can apply this geometric trick to help us find the equilibrium GDP. In our aggregate expenditure diagram, we want to compare output with aggregate expenditure. But output is measured horizontally, while aggregate expenditure is measured vertically. Our 45° line, however, enables us to translate output into a vertical distance, and thus permits us to compare output and aggregate expenditure as two vertical distances.

Figure 7 shows how this is done. The blue line is the aggregate expenditure line $(C + I^p + G + NX)$ from Figure 5. (We've dispensed with the other three lines that were drawn in Figure 6 because we no longer need them.) The black line is our 45° translator line. Now, let's search for the equilibrium GDP by considering a number of possibilities.

For example, could the output level $9,000 billion be our sought-after equilibrium? Let's see. We can measure the output level $9,000 billion as the vertical distance from the horizontal axis up to point A on the 45° line. But when output is $9,000 billion, aggregate expenditure is the vertical distance from the horizontal axis to point H on the aggregate expenditure line. Notice that, since point H lies below point A, aggregate expenditure is less than output. If firms *did* produce $9,000 billion worth of output, they would accumulate inventories equal to the vertical distance HA (the excess of output over spending). We conclude graphically (as we did earlier, using our table) that if output is $9,000 billion, firms will accumulate inventories of unsold goods and reduce output in the future. Thus, $9,000 billion is not our equilibrium. In general,

at any output level at which the aggregate expenditure line lies below *the 45° line, aggregate expenditure is less than GDP. If firms produce any of these output levels, their inventories will grow, and they will reduce output in the future.*

Now let's see if an output of $3,000 billion could be our equilibrium. First, we read this output level as the vertical distance up to point J on the 45° line. Next, we note that when output is $3,000 billion, aggregate expenditure is the vertical distance up to point K on the aggregate expenditure line. Point K lies *above* point J,

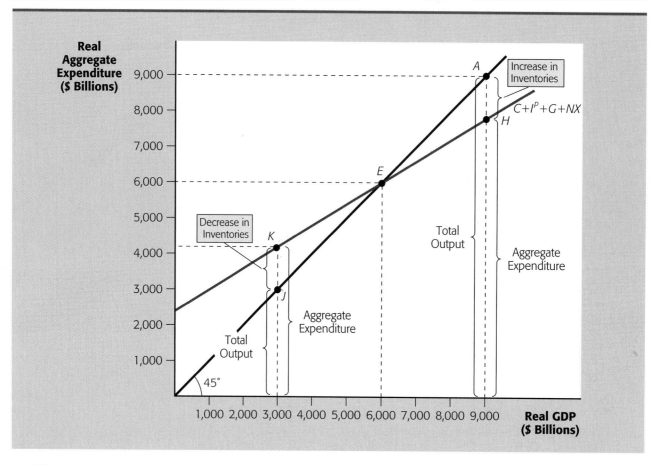

FIGURE 7
Determining Equilibrium Real GDP

At point E, where the aggregate expenditure line crosses the 45° line, the economy is in short-run equilibrium. With real GDP equal to $6,000 billion, aggregate expenditure equals real GDP. At higher levels of real GDP—such as $9,000 billion— total production exceeds aggregate expenditures, and firms will be unable to sell all they produce. Unplanned inventory increases equal to HA will lead them to reduce production. At lower levels of real GDP—such as $3,000 billion—aggregate expenditure exceeds total production. Firms find their inventories falling, and they will respond by increasing production.

so aggregate expenditure is greater than output. If firms *did* produce $3,000 billion in output, inventories would *decrease* by the vertical distance JK. With declining inventories, firms would want to increase their output in the future, so $3,000 billion is not our equilibrium. More generally,

at any output level at which the aggregate expenditure line lies above *the 45° line, aggregate expenditure exceeds GDP. If firms produce any of these output levels, their inventories will decline, and they will increase their output in the future.*

Finally, consider an output of $6,000 billion. At this output level, the aggregate expenditure line and the 45° line cross. As a result, the vertical distance up to point *E* on the 45° line (representing output) is the same as the vertical distance up to point *E* on the aggregate expenditure line. If firms produce an output level of $6,000 billion, aggregate expenditure and output will be precisely equal, inventories will remain unchanged, and firms will have no incentive to increase or decrease output in the future. We have thus found our equilibrium on the graph: $6,000 billion.

> *Equilibrium GDP is the output level at which the aggregate expenditure line intersects the 45° line. If firms produce this output level, their inventories will not change, and they will be content to continue producing the same level of output in the future.*

Equilibrium GDP and Employment

Now that you've learned how to find the economy's equilibrium GDP in the short run, a question may have occurred to you: When the economy operates at equilibrium, will it also be operating at full employment? The answer is: *not necessarily.* Let's see why.

If you look back over the two methods we've employed to find equilibrium GDP—using columns of numbers as in Table 4 and using a graph as in Figure 7, you will see that in both cases we've asked only one question: How much will households, businesses, the government, and foreigners *spend* on goods produced in the United States? We did not ask any questions about the number of people who want to work. Therefore, it would be quite a coincidence if our equilibrium GDP happened to be the output level at which the entire labor force were employed.

Figure 8 illustrates the connection between employment and output in the economy. We'll be going back and forth between the panels, so it's good to make sure you understand each step before going on to the next. Let's start with the right-hand panel, which shows the economy's *aggregate production function*, introduced earlier as part of the classical model. This curve tells us the relationship between any given number of workers and the level of output, with the current state of technology and given quantities of other resources. In this economy, full employment is assumed to be 100 million workers, measured along the horizontal axis. Potential output—$7,000 billion on the vertical axis—is the amount of output a fully-employed labor force of 100 million workers could produce. This is the also the long-run equilibrium output level that the classical model would predict for the economy.

But will $7,000 billion be the economy's equilibrium in the *short run*? Not necessarily. One possible outcome is shown in the left panel. The short-run equilibrium occurs at point *E,* where the aggregate expenditure line crosses the 45° line. At this point, output (on the horizontal axis) is $6,000 billion.

How many people will have jobs? We can answer by using the 45° line to convert the $6,000 billion from a horizontal distance to a vertical distance, then (following the dashed line) carrying that vertical distance across to the right panel. The right panel's production function tells us that to produce $6,000 billion in output, only 75 million workers are needed. In short-run equilibrium, then, only 75 million workers will have jobs. The difference between *full* employment and *actual* employment is 100 million − 75 million = 25 million, which is the amount of cyclical unemployment in the economy.

But why? What prevents firms from hiring the extra people who want jobs? After all, with more people working, producing more output, wouldn't there be more income in the economy and therefore more spending? Indeed, there would be. But not *enough* additional spending to justify the additional employment. To prove this, just look at what would happen if firms *did* hire 100 million workers. Output would rise to $7,000 billion, but at this output level, the aggregate

© CORBIS

During the Great Depression of the 1930s, the economy's short-run equilibrium output fell far below potential, and at least a quarter of the labor force became unemployed.

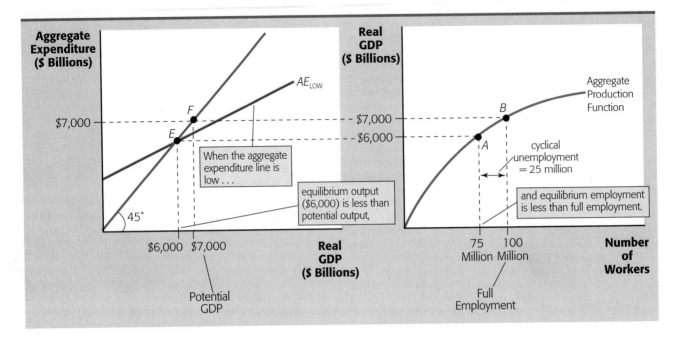

FIGURE 8

Equilibrium GDP Can Be Less than Full-Employment GDP

expenditure line would lie below the 45° line so *firms would be unable to sell all their output.* Unsold goods would pile up in inventories, and firms would cut back on production until output reached $6,000 billion again, with employment back at 75 million.

In sum: Figure 8 shows that we can be in short-run equilibrium and yet have abnormally high unemployment. The reason: The aggregate expenditure line is *too low* to create an intersection at full-employment output.

> *In the short-run macro model, cyclical unemployment is caused by insufficient spending. As long as spending remains low, production will remain low and unemployment will remain high.*

What about the opposite possibility? In the short run, is it possible for spending to be *too high,* causing unemployment to be *too low*? Absolutely. Figure 9 illustrates such a case. Here, the aggregate expenditure line and the 45° line intersect at point *E′*, giving us a short-run equilibrium GDP at $8,000 billion. According to the production function, producing an output of $8,000 billion requires employment of 135 million workers. Since this is greater than the economy's full employment of 100 million, we will have abnormally high employment and abnormally low *un*employment.

> *In the short-run macro model, the economy can overheat because spending is too high. As long as spending remains high, production will exceed potential output, and unemployment will be unusually low.*

In the previous chapter, we concluded that the classical model could not explain economic fluctuations. The short-run macro model, on the other hand, does provide an explanation: The aggregate expenditure line may be low, meaning that in

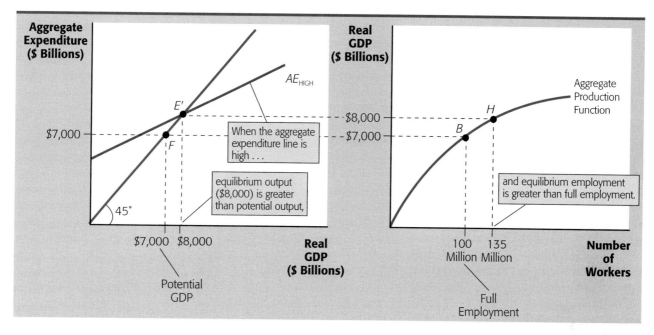

FIGURE 9
**Equilibrium GDP Can Be Greater
than Full-Employment GDP**

the short run, equilibrium GDP is below full employment. Or aggregate expenditure may be high, meaning that in the short run, equilibrium GDP is above the full-employment level. (Of course, this is just a first step in explaining economic fluctuations. In later chapters, we'll add more realism to the model.)

WHAT HAPPENS WHEN THINGS CHANGE?

So far, you've seen how the economy's equilibrium level of output is determined in the short run, and the important role played by spending in determining that equilibrium. But now it's time to use Step 3 and explore how a spending shock—a sudden change in spending—affects equilibrium output.

A Change in Investment Spending

Suppose the equilibrium GDP in an economy is $6,000 billion and then business firms increase their investment spending on plant and equipment. This might happen because business managers feel more optimistic about the economy's future, or because there is a new "must-have" technology (such as the Internet in the late 1990s), or because some new government policy increases the incentive for firms to buy new plant and equipment. Whatever the cause, firms decide to increase yearly planned investment purchases by $1,000 billion above the original level. What will happen?

First, sales revenue at firms that manufacture investment goods—firms like Dell Computer, Caterpillar, and Westinghouse—will increase by $1,000 billion. But remember, each time a dollar in output is produced, a dollar of income (factor payments) is created. Thus, the $1,000 billion in additional sales revenue will become $1,000 billion in additional income. This income will be paid out as wages,

		Additional Spending in Each Round	**Total Additional Spending**
Round		**(Billions of Dollars per Year)**	**(Billions of Dollars per Year)**
Initial Increase in Investment		1,000	1,000
Round 2		600	1,600
Round 3		360	1,960
Round 4		216	2,176
Round 5		130	2,306
Round 6		78	2,384
Round 7		47	2,431
Round 8		28	2,459
Round 9		17	2,476
Round 10		10	2,486
Round 20		0.06	Very close to 2,500

TABLE 5
Cumulative Increases in Spending When Investment Spending Increases by $1,000 Billion

rent, interest, and profit to the households who own the resources these firms have purchased.[1]

What will households do with their $1,000 billion in additional income? Remember that with net taxes fixed at some value, a $1,000 rise in income is also a $1,000 rise in *disposable* income. Households are free to spend or save this additional income as they desire. What they will do depends crucially on the *marginal propensity to consume* (MPC) *in the economy*. If the *MPC* is 0.6, then consumption spending will rise by 0.6 × $1,000 billion = $600 billion. Households will save the remaining $400 billion.

But that is not the end of the story. When households spend an additional $600 billion, firms that produce consumption goods and services—firms such as McDonald's, Coca-Cola, American Airlines, and Disney—will receive an additional $600 billion in sales revenue, which, in turn, will become income for the households that supply resources to these firms. And when *these* households see *their* annual incomes rise by $600 billion, they will spend part of it as well. With an *MPC* of 0.6, consumption spending will rise by 0.6 × $600 billion = $360 billion, creating still more sales revenue for firms, and so on and so on. . . .

As you can see, an increase in investment spending will set off a chain reaction, leading to successive rounds of increased spending and income.

The process is illustrated in Table 5. The second column gives us the additional spending in each round of this chain reaction. The first entry shows the additional spending of $1,000 billion per year from the initial increase in investment. The next entry shows the $600 billion increase in consumption spending, then another $360 billion increase in consumption, and so on. Each successive round of additional spending is 60 percent of the round before. The third column adds up the additional spending created by all preceding rounds, to give the *total* additional spending as this chain reaction continues. For example, total additional spending after the first

[1] Some of the sales revenue will also go to pay for intermediate goods, such as raw materials, electricity, and supplies. But the intermediate-goods suppliers will also pay wages, rent, interest, and profit for the resurces *they* use, so that household income will still rise by the full $1,000 billion.

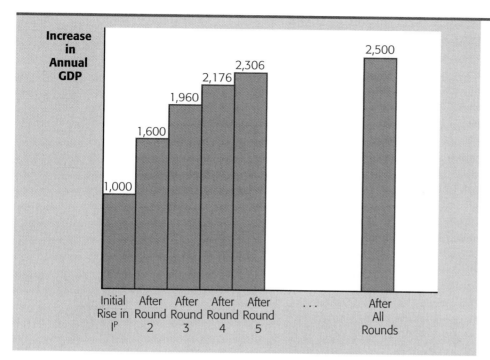

Increase in Annual GDP

1,000 — Initial Rise in I^P
1,600 — After Round 2
1,960 — After Round 3
2,176 — After Round 4
2,306 — After Round 5
. . .
2,500 — After All Rounds

FIGURE 10

The Effect of a Change in Investment Spending

An increase in investment spending sets off a chain reaction, leading to successive rounds of increased spending and income. As shown here, a $1,000 billion increase in investment first causes real GDP to increase by $1,000 billion. Then, with higher incomes, households increase consumption spending by the MPC times the change in disposable income. In round 2, spending and GDP increase by another $600 billion. In succeeding rounds, increases in income lead to further changes in spending, but in each round the increases in income and spending are smaller than in the preceding round.

round is just $1,000 billion, the initial increase in annual investment spending. But after the second round, we add the $600 billion in additional consumption spending, to get $1,600 billion in additional spending per year. After the third round, additional spending rises to $1,960 billion per year.

Remember that each time spending rises, output rises to match it. Figure 10 illustrates what happens to GDP (at an annual rate) after each round of this chain reaction. When we analyze events like this in the U.S. economy, we find that the successive increases in spending and output occur quickly; the process is largely completed within a year. And at the end of the process, when the economy has reached its new equilibrium, total spending and total output are considerably higher.

But how much higher?

If you look at the second column of Table 5, you can see that each successive round adds less to total spending than the round before. And in Figure 10, you see that GDP rises by less and less with each round. Eventually, GDP rises by such a small amount that we can safely ignore it, and the GDP will be so close to its new equilibrium value that we can ignore any difference. In our example, when the chain reaction is virtually completed—equilibrium GDP will be $2,500 billion more than it was initially.

The Expenditure Multiplier

Let's go back and summarize what happened in our example: Business firms increased their investment spending by $1,000 billion, and as a result, spending and output rose by $2,500 billion. Equilibrium GDP increased by *more than* the initial increase in investment spending. In our example, the increase in equilibrium GDP ($2,500 billion) was two-and-a-half times the initial increase in investment spending ($1,000 billion). As you can verify, if investment spending had increased by half as much ($500 billion), GDP would have increased by 2.5 times *that* amount ($1,250 billion). In fact, *whatever* the rise in investment spending, equilibrium GDP would increase by a factor of 2.5, so we can write

$$\Delta GDP = 2.5 \times \Delta I^p.$$

In our example, the change in investment spending was *multiplied by* the number 2.5 in order to get the change in GDP that it causes. For this reason, 2.5 is called the *expenditure multiplier* in this example.

Expenditure multiplier The amount by which equilibrium real GDP changes as a result of a one-dollar change in autonomous consumption, investment spending, government purchases, or net exports.

> The **expenditure multiplier** is the number by which the change in investment spending must be multiplied to get the change in equilibrium GDP.

The value of the expenditure multiplier depends on the value of the *MPC* in the economy. If you look back at Table 5, you will see that each round of additional spending would have been larger if the *MPC* had been larger. For example, with an *MPC* of 0.9 instead of 0.6, spending in round 2 would have risen by $900 billion, in round 3 by $810 billion, and so on. The result would have been a larger ultimate change in GDP, and a larger multiplier.

There is a very simple formula we can use to determine the multiplier for *any* value of the *MPC*. To obtain it, let's start with our numerical example in which the *MPC* is 0.6. When investment spending rises by $1,000 billion, the change in equilibrium GDP can be written as follows:

$$\Delta GDP = \$1,000 \text{ billion} + \$600 \text{ billion} + \$360 \text{ billion} + \$216 \text{ billion} + \ldots$$

Factoring out the $1,000 billion change in planned investment, this becomes

$$\Delta GDP = \$1,000 \text{ billion } [1 + 0.6 + 0.36 + 0.216 + \ldots]$$

$$= \$1,000 \text{ billion } [1 + 0.6 + 0.6^2 + 0.6^3 + \ldots]$$

In this equation, $1,000 billion is the change in investment (ΔI^p), and 0.6 is the *MPC*. To find the change in GDP that applies to *any* ΔI^p and any *MPC*, we can write

$$\Delta GDP = \Delta I^p \times [1 + (MPC) + (MPC)^2 + (MPC)^3 + \ldots]$$

Now we can see that the term in brackets, the infinite sum $1 + MPC + (MPC)^2 + (MPC)^3 + \ldots$, is our multiplier. But what is its value?

We can borrow a rule from the mathematics of sums just like this one. The rule tells us that for any variable *H* that has a value between zero and 1, the infinite sum

$$1 + H + H^2 + H^3 + \ldots$$

always has the value $1/(1 - H)$. So we can replace *H* with the *MPC*, since the *MPC* is always between zero and 1. This gives us a value for the multiplier of $1/(1 - MPC)$.

> For any value of the MPC, *the formula for the expenditure multiplier is* $1/(1 - MPC)$.

In our example, the *MPC* was equal to 0.6, so the expenditure multiplier had the value $1/(1 - 0.6) = 1/0.4 = 2.5$. If the *MPC* had been 0.9 instead, the expenditure multiplier would have been equal to $1/(1 - 0.9) = 1/0.1 = 10$. The formula $1/(1 - MPC)$ can be used to find the multiplier for any value of the *MPC* between zero and one.

Using the general formula for the expenditure multiplier, we can restate what happens when investment spending increases:

$$\Delta GDP = \left[\frac{1}{(1 - MPC)}\right] \times \Delta I^p.$$

The multiplier effect is a rather surprising phenomenon. It tells us that an increase in investment spending ultimately affects GDP by *more* than the initial increase in investment. Further, it tells us that as long as annual investment spending remains $1,000 billion greater than it was previously, yearly GDP will remain higher than previously—$2,500 billion higher in our example. That is, a sustained increase in investment spending will cause a sustained increase in GDP.

By contrast, a one-time increase in investment—followed by a drop in investment back to its original level—will cause only a temporary change in GDP. That's because the multiplier process works in *both* directions, as you're about to see.

The Multiplier in Reverse

Suppose that, in Table 5, investment spending had *decreased* instead of increased. Then the initial change in spending would be −$1,000 billion ($\Delta I^p = -\$1,000$ billion). This would cause a $1,000 billion decrease in revenue for firms that produce investment goods, and they, in turn, would pay out $1,000 billion less in factor payments. In the next round, households, with $1,000 billion less in income, would spend $600 billion less on consumption goods, and so on. The final result would be a $2,500 billion *decrease* in equilibrium GDP.

> *Just as increases in investment spending cause equilibrium GDP to rise by a multiple of the change in spending, decreases in investment spending cause equilibrium GDP to fall by a multiple of the change in spending.*

The multiplier formula we've already established will work whether the initial change in spending is positive or negative.

Other Spending Shocks

Shocks to the economy can come from other sources besides investment spending. In fact, when *any* sector's spending behavior changes, it will set off a chain of events similar to that in our investment example. Let's see how an increase in government spending could set off the same chain of events as an increase in investment spending.

Suppose that government agencies increased their purchases above previous levels. For example, the Department of Defense might raise its spending on new bombers, or state highway departments might hire more road-repair crews, or cities and towns might hire more teachers. If total government purchases rise by $1,000 billion, then, once again, household income will rise by $1,000 billion. As before, households will spend 60 percent of this increase, causing consumption, in the next round, to rise by $600 billion, and so on and so on. The chain of events is exactly like that of Table 5, with one exception: The first line in column 1 would read, "Initial Increase in Government Purchases" instead of "Initial Increase in Investment." Once again, output would increase by $2,500 billion.

Besides planned investment and government purchases, there are two other components of spending that can set off the same process. One is an increase in net exports (NX). Since NX = Exports − Imports, either an increase in the economy's exports or a *decrease* in imports will cause *net* exports to rise. For example, either an increase in exports of $1,000 billion, or a decrease in imports of $1,000 billion, would increase net exports by $1,000 billion and set off the same multiplier process described above.

Finally, a change in *autonomous consumption* can set off the process. For example, after a $1,000 billion increase in autonomous consumption spending we would see further increases in consumption spending of $600 billion, then $360 billion, and so on. This time, the first line in column 1 of Table 5 would read, "Initial Increase in Autonomous Consumption," but every entry in the table would be the same.

> *Changes in planned investment, government purchases, net exports, or autonomous consumption lead to a multiplier effect on GDP. The expenditure multiplier—1/(1 − MPC)—is what we multiply the initial change in spending by in order to get the change in equilibrium GDP.*

The following four equations summarize how we use the expenditure multiplier to determine the effects of different spending shocks in the short-run macro model. Keep in mind that these formulas work whether the initial change in spending is positive or negative.

$$\Delta GDP = \left[\frac{1}{(1 - MPC)} \right] \times \Delta I^p$$

$$\Delta GDP = \left[\frac{1}{(1 - MPC)} \right] \times \Delta G$$

$$\Delta GDP = \left[\frac{1}{(1 - MPC)} \right] \times \Delta NX$$

$$\Delta GDP = \left[\frac{1}{(1 - MPC)} \right] \times \Delta a$$

A Graphical View of the Multiplier

Figure 11 illustrates the multiplier using our aggregate expenditure diagram. The darker line is the aggregate expenditure line from Figure 7. The aggregate expenditure line intersects the 45° line at point *E*, giving us an equilibrium GDP of $6,000 billion.

Now, suppose that either autonomous consumption, investment spending, net exports, or government purchases rises by $1,000 billion. Regardless of which of these types of spending increases, the effect on our aggregate expenditure line is the same: It will *shift upward* by $1,000 billion, to the higher line in the figure. The new aggregate expenditure line intersects the 45° line at point *F*, showing that our new equilibrium GDP is equal to $8,500 billion.

What has happened? An initial spending increase of $1,000 billion has caused equilibrium GDP to increase from $6,000 billion to $8,500 billion, an increase of $2,500 billion. This is just what our multiplier of 2.5 tells us. In general,

$$\Delta GDP = \left[\frac{1}{(1 - MPC)} \right] \times \Delta \text{Spending}$$

and in this case,

$$\$2,500 \text{ billion} = 2.5 \times \$1,000 \text{ billion.}$$

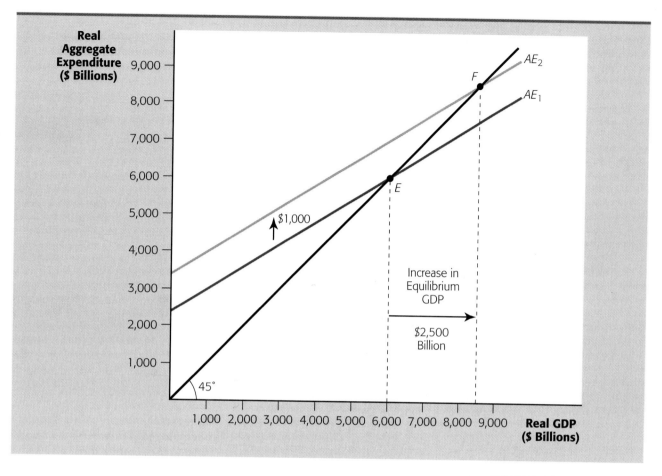

FIGURE 11
A Graphical View of the Multiplier

The economy starts off at point E with equilibrium real GDP of $6,000 billion. A $1,000 billion increase in spending shifts the aggregate expenditure line upward by $1,000 billion, triggering the multiplier process. Eventually, the economy will reach a new equilibrium at point F, where the new, higher aggregate expenditure line crosses the 45° line. At F, real GDP is $8,500, billion, an increase of $2,500 billion.

An increase in autonomous consumption spending, investment spending, government purchases, or net exports will shift the aggregate expenditure line upward by the initial increase in spending, causing equilibrium GDP to rise. The increase in GDP will equal the initial increase in spending times the expenditure multiplier.

Automatic Stabilizers and the Multiplier

In this chapter, we've presented a model to help us focus on the central relationship between spending and output. To keep the model as simple as possible, we've ignored many real-world factors that interfere with, and reduce the size of, the multiplier effect. These forces are called **automatic stabilizers** because, with a smaller multiplier, spending shocks will cause a much smaller change in GDP. As a result, economic fluctuations will be milder.

Automatic stabilizers Forces that reduce the size of the expenditure multiplier and diminish the impact of spending shocks.

Automatic stabilizers reduce the size of the multiplier and therefore reduce the impact of spending shocks on the economy. With milder fluctuations, the economy is more stable.

How do automatic stabilizers work? They shrink the additional spending that occurs in each round of the multiplier, and thereby reduce the final multiplier effect on equilibrium GDP. In Table 5, automatic stabilizers would reduce each of the numerical entries after the first $1,000 billion, and lead to a final change in GDP smaller than $2,500 billion.

Here are some of the real-world automatic stabilizers we've ignored in the simple, short-run macro model of this chapter:

The Two Kinds of Consumption Changes It's easy to become confused about the relationship between consumption spending and the expenditure multiplier. Does a change in consumption spending cause a multiplier effect? Or does the multiplier effect create an increase in consumption spending? Actually, the causation runs in both directions. The key is to recognize that there are two kinds of changes in consumption spending.

DANGEROUS CURVES

One kind is a change in autonomous consumption spending (the term "a" in the consumption function). This change will *shift* the aggregate expenditure line up or down, telling us that total spending will be greater or smaller at *any* level of income. It is the kind of change that *causes* a multiplier effect.

But consumption also changes when something other than autonomous consumption sets off a multiplier effect. This is because consumption depends on income, and income always increases during the successive rounds of the multiplier effect. Such a change in consumption is represented by a movement *along* the aggregate expenditure line, rather than a shift.

Whenever you discuss a change in consumption spending, make sure you know whether it is a change in autonomous consumption (a shift of the *AE* line) or a change in consumption caused by a change in income (a movement along the *AE* line).

Taxes. We've been assuming that taxes remain constant, so that a rise in income causes an equal rise in disposable income. But some taxes (like the personal income tax) rise with income. As a result, in each round of the multiplier, the increase in disposable income will be smaller than the increase in income. With a smaller rise in disposable income, there will be a smaller rise in consumption spending as well.

Transfer Payments. Some government transfer payments fall as income rises. For example, many laid-off workers receive unemployment benefits, which help support them for several months while they are unemployed. But when income and output rise, employment also rises, and newly hired workers must give up their unemployment benefits. As a result, a rise in income will cause a smaller rise in *disposable* income in each round, and a smaller rise in consumption.

Interest Rates. In a later chapter, you'll learn that an increase in output often leads to rising interest rates as well. This will crowd out some consumption and investment spending, making the increase in aggregate expenditure smaller than our simple story suggests.

Imports. Some additional spending is on goods and services imported from abroad. That is, instead of remaining constant as in our example, imports often rise as income rises, and net exports therefore fall as income rises. This helps to counteract any increase in spending caused by a rise in income.

Forward-looking Behavior. Consumers may be *forward-looking.* If they realize that the fluctuations in the economy are temporary, their consumption spending may be less sensitive to changes in their current income. Therefore, any change in income will cause a smaller change in consumption spending, and lead to a smaller multiplier effect.

Remember that each of these automatic stabilizers reduces the size of the multiplier, making it smaller than the simple formulas given in this chapter. For example, the simple formula for the expenditure multiplier is $1/(1 - MPC)$. With an MPC of about 0.9—which is in the ballpark for the United States and many other countries—we would expect the multiplier to be about 10 . . . *if the simple formula were accurate*. In that case, a $1,000 billion increase in government spending would cause output to rise by $10,000 billion—quite a large multiplier effect.

But after we take account of all of the automatic stabilizers, the multiplier is considerably smaller. How much smaller? Most of the forecasting models used by economists in business and government predict that the multiplier effect takes about nine months to a year to work its way through the economy. At the end of the process, the multiplier has a value of about 1.5. This means that a $1,000 billion increase in, say, government spending should cause GDP to increase by only about $1,500 billion in a year. This is much less than the $10,000 billion increase predicted by the simple formula $1/(1 - MPC)$ when the MPC is equal to 0.9.

> *In the real world, due to automatic stabilizers, spending shocks have much weaker impacts on the economy than our simple multiplier formulas would suggest.*

Finally, there is one more automatic stabilizer you should know about, perhaps the most important of all: the *passage of time*. Why is this an automatic stabilizer? Because, as you've learned, the impact of spending shocks on the economy is *temporary*. As time passes, the classical model—lurking in the background—stands ready to take over. And if we wait long enough—a few years or so—we will return to our potential output level. That is, after a shock pulls us away from full-employment GDP, the economy will eventually return to full-employment GDP, right where it started. We thus conclude that

> *in the long run, our multipliers have a value of zero: No matter what the change in spending or taxes, output will return to full employment, so the change in equilibrium GDP will be zero.*

Of course, the year or two we must wait can seem like an eternity to those who are jobless when the economy is operating below its potential. The short run is not to be overlooked. This is why, in the next several chapters, we will continue with our exploration of the short run, building on the macro model you've learned in this chapter. We'll be making the analysis more complete and more realistic by bringing in some of the real-world features that were not fully considered here.

COMPARING MODELS: LONG RUN AND SHORT RUN

Before leaving this chapter, it's important to note some startling differences between the long-run classical model you learned about a few chapters ago and the short-run macro model of this chapter. We've already discussed one of these differences: In the classical model, the economy operates *automatically* at potential GDP. In the short-run macro model, by contrast, the economy can operate above its potential or below its potential. The reason for the difference is that, in the short run, spending affects output: A negative spending shock can cause a recession that pushes output below potential GDP; a positive spending shock can cause a rapid expansion that pushes the economy above potential GDP, a boom.

There are two other important contrasts between the predictions of the two models. One concerns the role of saving in the economy, and the other concerns the effectiveness of fiscal policy. Let's explore each of these issues in turn.

The Role of Saving

In the long run, saving has positive effects on the economy. This was demonstrated two chapters ago, when—using the classical model—we discussed economic growth. Suppose, for example, that households decide to save more at any level of income. In the long run, the extra saving will flow into the loanable funds market, where it will be borrowed by business firms to purchase new plant and equipment. Thus, an increase in saving automatically leads to an increase in planned investment, faster growth in the capital stock, and a faster rise in living standards. Indeed, we can expect an increase in saving to have precisely these effects . . . in the long run.

But in the short run, the automatic mechanisms of the classical model do not keep the economy operating at its potential. On the contrary, *spending* influences output in the short run. If households decide to save more at each income level, they also, by definition, *spend less* at each income level. Or, putting it another way, an increase in saving is the same as a *decrease* in autonomous consumption spending, *a*. As you've learned in this chapter, a decrease in autonomous consumption spending causes a decrease in output through the multiplier process. If the economy is initially operating at full employment, the increase in saving will push output *below* its potential.

In the long run, an increase in the desire to save leads to faster economic growth and rising living standards. In the short run, however, it can cause a recession that pushes output below its potential.

You can see that there are two sides to the "savings coin." The impact of increased saving is positive in the long run and potentially dangerous in the short run. Are you wondering how we get from the potentially harmful short-run effect of higher saving to the beneficial long-run effect? We'll address this question a few chapters later, when we examine how the economy adjusts from its short-run equilibrium to its long-run equilibrium.

The Effect of Fiscal Policy

In the classical model, you learned that fiscal policy—changes in government spending or taxes designed to change equilibrium GDP—is completely ineffective. More specifically, an increase in government purchases *crowds out* an equal amount of household and business spending: The rise in *G* is exactly matched by the decrease in *C* and *I* . . . in the long run.

But in the short run, once again, we cannot rely on the mechanisms of the classical model that are so effective in the long run. In the short run, *an increase in government purchases causes a multiplied increase in equilibrium GDP.* Therefore, in the short run, fiscal policy can actually change equilibrium GDP!

This important observation suggests that fiscal policy could, in principle, play a role in altering the path of the economy. If output begins to dip below potential, couldn't we use fiscal policy to pull us out of it or even prevent the recession entirely? For example, if investment spending decreases by $100 billion, setting off a negative multiplier effect, couldn't we just increase government purchases by $100 billion to set off an equal, positive multiplier effect? Why wait the many months or years it would take for the classical model to "kick in" and bring the economy back to full employment when we have such a powerful tool, fiscal policy, at our disposal?

Indeed, in the 1960s and early 1970s, this was the thinking of many economists. At that time, the popular view was that fiscal policy could effectively smooth out economic fluctuations, perhaps even eliminate them entirely. But very few economists believe this today. Why? In part, because of practical difficulties in executing the right fiscal policy at the right time. But more importantly, the rules of economic policy making have changed: The Federal Reserve now attempts to neutralize fiscal policy changes long before they can affect spending and output in the economy. In later chapters, we'll discuss the practical difficulties of executing fiscal policy and how the Federal Reserve has changed the "rules of the game."

USING THE THEORY
The Recession of 2001

Our most recent recession lasted from March 2001 to November 2001. Table 6 tells the story. Look first at the upper panel. The second column shows real GDP in 1996 dollars in each of several quarters. The figures are stated as *annual rates*. (For example, real GDP in the *second* quarter of 2001 was $9,193 billion. This means that *if* we had continued producing that quarter's GDP for an entire year, we *would* have produced a total of $9,193 billion worth of goods and services in the year 2001.) The other columns show investment spending (also at an annual rate) and the average level of employment for the quarter.

The lower panel, which is derived from the upper panel, gives a somewhat clearer picture of what happened during 2001. For each quarter, it shows the *change* in real GDP, investment spending, and average employment from the quarter before. As you can see, investment spending and real GDP—which were drifting downward before the recession—fell sharply during the second quarter of 2001 and continued to fall throughout the year. Employment mirrored this change, dropping in the second quarter and continuing to drop through the year.

What caused this recession? And can our short-run macro model help us understand it?

The decrease in investment spending is just the sort of spending shock that shifts the aggregate expenditure line downward. Over time, as the multiplier process takes place, a decrease in investment will bring down both GDP and employment, and that is just what happened in 2001.

But what caused these successive decreases in investment spending? In retrospect, we can see there were at least three causes.

First, during much of the late 1990s, there had been a boom in capital equipment spending as existing businesses rushed to incorporate the Internet into factories, offices, and their business practices in general. Firms like Avis, Wal-Mart, and Viacom needed servers and high-speed Internet connections, and the firms that supplied the new technology needed their own new offices, factories, and equipment. But as 2000 ended and 2001 began, firms had begun to catch up to the new technology. The rush ended and investment began to fall.

Another reason for the investment spending shock also had its roots in the 1990s. During this period, the Internet and other new technologies made the public very optimistic about the future profits of American businesses. The public became hungry to own shares of stock in almost any company that had anything to do with the Internet, and share prices rose sky high. The optimism and the high share prices that came along with it encouraged entirely new businesses to start up—businesses that used the Internet to sell pet supplies, prescription drugs, and toys or to deliver

TABLE 6
The Recession of 2001

(a) Real GDP, Investment, and Employment

Quarter	Real GDP (Billions of 1996 Dollars)	Investment Spending (Billions of 1996 Dollars; excludes changes in inventories)	Average Employment (thousands)
	4th quarter, 2000	9,244	1,691	137,329
Recession Quarters	1st quarter, 2001	9,230	1,682	137,752
	2nd quarter, 2001	9,193	1,634	137,086
	3rd quarter, 2001	9,186	1,616	136,707
	4th quarter, 2001	9,248	1,578	136,218
	1st quarter, 2002	9,392	1,576	136,128

(b) Change (from previous quarter) in Real GDP, Investment, and Employment

Quarter	Change in Real GDP (Billions of 1996 Dollars)	Change in Investment Spending (Billions of 1996 Dollars)	Change in Average Employment (thousands)
Recession Quarters	1st quarter, 2001	−14	−9	+423
	2nd quarter, 2001	−37	−48	−666
	3rd quarter, 2001	−7	−18	−379
	4th quarter, 2001	+62	−38	−489
	1st quarter, 2002	+144	−2	−90

videos, groceries, or even fresh hot pizzas. Of course, these new businesses needed their own capital equipment, warehouses, and office buildings, driving investment spending even further skyward in the late 1990s.

Unfortunately, in late 2000 and early 2001, reality set in. Competition was preventing many new firms from earning any profit at all, and many went bankrupt. Optimism shifted to pessimism. Share prices fell, and new business ventures—especially those having something to do with the Internet—came to a halt. And so did the investment spending they had been undertaking. (We'll discuss the stock market in much more detail in the "Using All the Theory" chapter at the end of this book.)

The final reason for the investment shock—more accurately, an exacerbation of the shock already occurring—was the infamous terrorist attacks on the World Trade Center and the Pentagon on September 11, 2001. The nation was traumatized by these events. What little optimism that was left in the future of the U.S. economy turned to uncertainty and fear. Millions of potential airline passengers no longer wanted to fly, forcing the airlines to cancel flights and, of course, cancel any orders for new aircraft. Hotel vacancy rates skyrocketed, causing investment in new hotels and expansion of existing hotels to come to a halt. Similar decisions were being made in other industries, and investment spending fell sharply. (Although the table shows that investment declined only modestly in the third quarter, it is likely that most of the decrease occurred in September.)

One abnormal feature of the recession of 2001 was the behavior of consumption spending. Ordinarily, as income falls in a recession, consumption declines along with it. This is a movement leftward and downward along the consumption–income line (such as the line in Figure 3 of this chapter). Moreover, decreases in wealth from falling stock prices, and a sharp drop in consumer confidence after September 11, would ordinarily have caused a decrease in *autonomous* consumption spending (see Table 3), *shifting* the consumption–income line downward. Yet consumption spending (not shown) actually *rose* during every quarter of 2001. Since income fell during this time, the only way that consumption spending could rise was through an upward shift of the consumption–income line.

> **What Makes It a Recession?** Newspapers and television commentators often state that a recession occurs when real GDP declines for two consecutive quarters. But this is not correct.
>
> Actually, when a U.S recession begins and ends is determined by a committee within the National Bureau of Economic Research, an entirely private, nonprofit research organization headquartered in Boston.[2] The committee makes its decisions by looking at a variety of factors, including employment, industrial production, sales, and personal income, all of which are reported monthly. While it is true that each of these measures tends to move closely with real GDP, the latter is measured only quarterly, and plays only a supporting role in dating recessions.

DANGEROUS CURVES

Part of the reason for the upward shift was a 10-year tax cut that went into effect in June of 2001. But there were other reasons as well—which we'll look at two chapters from now. The increase in consumption spending was not enough to prevent the recession. The decline in investment spending—and the multiplier process it initiated—was too powerful.

The investment spending shock, and the recession it caused, are only half of the story of the recession of 2001. The other half, entirely ignored so far, is the response of government policy makers as they tried to prevent the economic storm from becoming a hurricane. Ultimately, their actions helped to make the recession relatively short and mild by historical standards. But to understand what these policy makers did, why they did it, and why it worked reasonably well, we must expand the short-run macro model. In the next chapter, we begin this process by learning about the banking system, the money supply, and the Federal Reserve.

[2] For the past few decades, the NBER's Business Cycle Dating Committee has been chaired by Robert E. Hall, a coauthor of this textbook.

Summary

In the short run, spending depends on income and income depends on spending. The short-run macro model was developed to explore this circular connection between spending and income.

Total spending is the sum of four aggregates: consumption spending by households, investment spending by firms, government purchases of goods and services, and net exports. Consumption spending (C) depends primarily on disposable income—what households have left over after paying taxes. The consumption function is a linear relationship between disposable income and consumption spending. The slope of the consumption function is the marginal propensity to consume, a number between zero and one. It indicates the fraction of each additional dollar of disposable income that is consumed. The consumption–income line is the linear relationship between consumption and income. It has the same slope as the consumption function, but a different vertical intercept. For a given level of income, consumption spending can change as a result of changes in taxes, the interest rate, wealth, or expectations about the future. Each of these changes will shift the consumption–income line.

Investment spending (I^p), government purchases (G), and net exports (NX) are taken as given values, determined by forces outside our analysis. Aggregate expenditure (AE) is the sum $C + I^p + G + NX$; it varies with income because consumption spending varies with income.

Equilibrium GDP is the level of output at which aggregate expenditure is just equal to GDP (Y). If AE exceeds Y, then firms will experience unplanned decreases in inventories. They will respond by increasing production. If Y exceeds AE, firms will find their inventories increasing and will respond by reducing production. Only when $AE = Y$ will there be no unplanned inventory changes and no reason for firms to change production. Graphically, this occurs at the point where the aggregate expenditure line intersects the 45° line.

Spending shocks will change the economy's short-run equilibrium. An increase in investment spending, for example, shifts the aggregate expenditure line upward and triggers the multiplier process. The initial increase in investment spending causes income to increase. That, in turn, leads to an increase in consumption spending, a further increase in income, more consumption spending, and so on. The economy eventually reaches a new equilibrium with a change in GDP that is a multiple of the original increase in spending. Other spending shocks would have similar effects. The size of the *expenditure multiplier* is determined by the marginal propensity to consume.

There are several important differences between the short-run macro model and the long-run classical model. In the long run, the economy operates at potential output; in the short run, GDP can be above or below potential. In the long run, saving contributes to economic growth by making funds available for firms to invest in new capital. In the short run, increased saving means reduced spending and a lower level of output. Finally, fiscal policy is completely ineffective in the long run, but can have important effects on total demand and output in the short run.

Key Terms

Aggregate expenditure
Automatic stabilizers
Autonomous consumption spending

Consumption function
Consumption–income line
Equilibrium GDP

Expenditure multiplier
Marginal propensity to consume
Short-run macro model

Review Questions   *Answers to even-numbered Questions and Problems can be found on the text Web site at http://hall-lieb.swlearning.com.*

1. Briefly describe the four main categories of spending.

2. There are three different ways to interpret the marginal propensity to consume. What are they?

3. List, and briefly explain, the main determinants of consumption spending. Indicate whether a change in each determinant causes a movement along, or a shift of, the consumption–income line.

4. What are the main components of *planned investment* or *investment spending*? How does the definition of actual investment differ from planned investment?

5. What conditions must be satisfied in order for GDP to be at its equilibrium value? Is this equilibrium GDP the same as the economy's potential GDP? Why or why not?

6. Suppose that an increase in government purchases disturbs the economy's short-run equilibrium. Describe what happens as the economy adjusts to the change in spending.

7. What is the expenditure multiplier? How is it calculated, and how is it used?

8. What is an automatic stabilizer? List some automatic stabilizers for the U.S. economy. Which of these stabilizers do you think have gotten stronger, and which weaker, over the past several decades? Why?

9. Compare the macroeconomic role of saving in the short run and in the long run.

10. Does the short-run macro model reach the same conclusions about fiscal policy as the classical long-run model? Explain.

11. Refer to the relationship between real consumption spending and real disposable income shown in Figure 1. Based on this relationship, what should happen to real consumption spending during a recession? Did we see this behavior during the recession of 2001? Why or why not?

Problems and Exercises

1.

Y	C	I^p	G	NX
3,000	2,500	300	500	200
4,000	3,250	300	500	200
5,000	4,000	300	500	200
6,000	4,750	300	500	200
7,000	5,500	300	500	200
8,000	6,250	300	500	200

a. What is the marginal propensity to consume implicit in this data?

b. Plot a 45° line, and then use the data to draw an aggregate expenditure line.

c. What is the equilibrium level of real GDP? Illustrate it on your diagram.

d. Suppose that investment spending increased by 250 at each level of income. What would happen to equilibrium GDP?

2. a. Complete the following table when autonomous consumption is $30 billion, the marginal propensity to consume is 0.85, and the net taxes are $0.

Real GDP ($ Billions)	Autonomous Consumption	MPC × Disposable Income	Consumption = Autonomous Consumption + (MPC × Disposable Income)
$0			
$100			
$200			
$300			
$400			
$500			
$600			

b. Given your answers in part (a), and given that planned investment is $40 billion, government spending is $20 billion, exports are $20 billion, and imports are $35 billion, complete the following table. (See table at bottom of page.)

c. Plot a 45° line, and then use your data to draw an aggregate expenditure line.

d. What is the equilibrium level of real GDP? Illustrate it on your diagram.

e. What will happen if the actual level of real GDP in this economy is $200 billion?

f. What will happen if the planned investment in this economy falls to $25 billion?

3.

Y	C	I^p	G	NX
7,000	6,100	400	1,000	500
8,000	6,900	400	1,000	500
9,000	7,700	400	1,000	500
10,000	8,500	400	1,000	500
11,000	9,300	400	1,000	500
12,000	10,100	400	1,000	500
13,000	10,900	400	1,000	500

a. What is the marginal propensity to consume implicit in these data?

b. What is the numerical value of the expenditure multiplier for this economy?

c. What is the equilibrium level of real GDP?

d. Suppose that government purchases (G) decreased from 1,000 to 400 at each level of income. What would happen to equilibrium real GDP?

4. Draw a graph showing a 45° line and an aggregate expenditures line.

a. Choose a point where real GDP is less than aggregate expenditures and label it GDP^A. Explain what will happen to inventories if the economy is operating at this point. What signal does this send to firms? Is GDP^A sustainable?

b. Choose a point where real GDP is greater than aggregate expenditures and label it GDP^B. Explain what will happen to inventories if the economy is operating at this point. What signal does this send to firms? Is GDP^B sustainable?

Real GDP ($ Billions)	Consumption Spending	Planned Investment	Government Spending	Net Exports	Aggregate Expenditure
$0					
$100					
$200					
$300					
$400					
$500					
$600					

5. Use an aggregate expenditure diagram to show the effect of each of the following changes:
   a. an increase in autonomous consumption spending due, say, to optimism on the part of consumers
   b. an increase in U.S. exports
   c. a decrease in taxes
   d. an increase in U.S. imports

   In each case, be sure to label the initial equilibrium and the new equilibrium.

6. What would be the effect on real GDP and total employment of each of the following changes?
   a. As a result of restrictions on imports into the United States, net exports (NX) increase.
   b. The federal government launches a new program to improve highways, bridges, and airports.
   c. Banks are offering such high interest rates that consumers decide to save a larger proportion of their incomes.
   d. The growth of Internet retailing leads business firms to purchase more computer hardware and software.

7. Using the data given in Problem 1, construct a table similar to Table 5 in this chapter.
   a. Show what would happen in the first five rounds following an increase in investment spending from 400 to 800.
   b. If investment spending stays at 800, what would be the ultimate effect on real GDP?
   c. How much would households spend on consumption goods in the new equilibrium?

8. Suppose that households become thriftier; that is, they now wish to save a larger proportion of their disposable income and spend a smaller proportion.
   a. In the table in Problem 1, which column of data would be affected?
   b. Draw an aggregate expenditure diagram and show how an increase in saving can be measured in that diagram.

c. Use your aggregate expenditure diagram to show how an economy that is initially in short-run equilibrium will respond to an increase in thriftiness.

9. Calculate the change in real GDP that would result in each of the following cases:
   a. Planned investment spending rises by $100 billion, and the MPC is 0.9.
   b. Autonomous consumption spending decreases by $50 billion, and the MPC is 0.7.
   c. Government purchases rise by $40 billion, while at the same time, investment spending falls by $10 billion. The MPC is 0.6.

10. Calculate the changes in real GDP that would result in each of the following cases:
    a. Government purchases rise by $7,500, and the MPC is 0.95.
    b. Planned investment spending falls by $300,000 and the MPC is 0.65.
    c. Export spending rises by $60 billion at the same time that import spending rises by $65 billion, and the MPC is 0.75.

11. [Requires Appendix 2] Calculate the change in real GDP that would result in each of the following cases:
    a. Taxes fall by $30 billion, and the MPC is 0.8.
    b. Government spending and taxes *both* rise by $100 billion and the MPC is 0.9.

12. [Requires Appendix 2] Calculate the change in real GDP that would result in each of the following cases:
    a. Taxes rise by $400,000, and the MPC is 0.75.
    b. Taxes and government spending both fall by $500,000, and the MPC is 0.60.

13. Reread the last page of the "Using the Theory" section of this chapter. The consumption–income line shifted upward during the recession of 2001. But what happened to the aggregate expenditure line? How do we reconcile the shift in AE with the shift in the consumption–income line?

Challenge Questions

1. [Requires Appendix 1] Suppose that $a = 600$, $b = 0.75$, $T = 400$, $I^P = 600$, $G = 700$, and $NX = 200$. Calculate the equilibrium level of real GDP. Then check that the equilibrium value equals the sum $C + I^P + G + NX$.

2. [Requires Appendix 1] Suppose that $a = 1,000$, $b = 0.65$, $T = 700$, $I^P = 800$, $G = 600$, and $NX = -200$. Calculate the equilibrium level of real GDP. Then check that the equilibrium value equals aggregate expenditures.

3. The short-run equilibrium condition that $Y = C + I^P + G + NX$ can be reinterpreted as follows. First, subtract C from both sides to get $Y - C = I^P + G + NX$. Then note that all income not spent on consumption goods is either taxed or saved, so that $Y - C = S + T$. Now combine the two equations to obtain $S + T = I^P + G + NX$.

   Construct a diagram with real GDP measured on the horizontal axis. Draw two lines, one for $S + T$ and the other for $I^p + G + NX$. How would you interpret the point where the two lines cross? What would happen if investment spending increased?

4. Refer to your answer to Problem 12. Will your answer to part (b) change if the *MPC* is 0.8, rather than 0.60? Use your finding to write a general statement about changes in government spending and taxes, and the resulting change in real GDP.

ECONOMIC *Applications* *These exercises require access to Hall/Lieberman Xtra! If Xtra! did not come with your book, visit http://hallxtra.swlearning.com to purchase.*

1. Use your Xtra! password at the Hall and Lieberman Web site (http://hallxtra.swlearning.com), select this chapter, and under Economic Applications, click on EconData. Choose *Macroeconomics: Employment, Unemployment, and Inflation,* and scroll down to find *Real GDP.* Read the definition and click on Updates and use the information to answer the following questions.

   a. Read the Bureau of Economic Analysis's new release http://www.bea.doc.gov/bea/newsrel/gdp402f.htm and discuss the contributions of each component of the real GDP to growth in the period considered.

   b. Refer to the U.S. GDP and its Components data link http://www.economagic.com/fedstl.htm#GDP. Retrieve the data (in constant dollars), and the percent change of data for the four main components of aggregate expenditure: (1) Personal Consumption Expenditures, (2) Gross Private Domestic Investment, (3) Government Purchases, and (4) Net Exports.

   Which is the largest component? Which is the most volatile component?

   c. Refer to the U.S. GDP and its Components data link http://www.economagic.com/fedstl.htm#GDP. Retrieve the data (in constant dollars), for Personal Consumption and Disposable Income and chart Personal Consumption against Disposable Income. Draw a line to fit the trend and calculate its slope, which represents the marginal propensity to consume. Now calculate the simple multiplier. If spending increases by $1,000 billion, by how much will GDP increase?

   d. Refer to the U.S. GDP and its Components data link http://www.economagic.com/fedstl.htm#GDP. Click on the data series Change in Business Inventories, and then on GIF Chart. From this chart comment on the role of inventory adjustments in arriving at equilibrium, as discussed in this chapter.

APPENDIX 1

FINDING EQUILIBRIUM GDP ALGEBRAICALLY

The chapter showed how we can find equilibrium GDP using tables and graphs. This appendix demonstrates an algebraic way of finding the equilibrium GDP.

Our starting point is the relationship between consumption and disposable income given in the chapter. Letting Y_D represent disposable income:

$$C = a + bY_D$$

where a represents autonomous consumption spending and b represents the marginal propensity to consume. Remember that disposable income (Y_D) is the income that the household sector has left after taxes. Letting T represent net taxes and Y represent total net income or GDP, we have

$$Y_D = Y - T.$$

If we now substitute $Y_D = Y - T$ into $C = a + bY_D$, we get an equation showing consumption at each level of income:

$$C = a + b(Y - T).$$

We can rearrange this equation algebraically to read

$$C = (a - bT) + bY.$$

This is the general equation for the consumption–income line. When graphed, the term in parentheses ($a - bT$) is the vertical intercept, and b is the slope. (Figure 3 shows a specific example of this line in which a = $2,000, b = 0.6, and T = $2,000.)

As you've learned, total spending or aggregate expenditure (AE) is the sum of consumption spending (C), investment spending (I^p), government spending (G), and net exports (NX):

$$AE = C + I^p + G + NX.$$

If we substitute for C the expression $C = (a - bT) + bY$, we get

$$AE = a - bT + bY + I^p + G + NX.$$

Now we can use this expression to find the equilibrium GDP. Equilibrium occurs when output (Y) and aggregate expenditure (AE) are the same. That is,

$$Y = AE$$

or, substituting the equation for AE,

$$Y = a - bT + bY + I^p + G + NX.$$

This last equation will hold true only when Y is at its equilibrium value. We can solve for equilibrium Y by first bringing all terms involving Y to the left-hand side:

$$Y - bY = a - bT + I^p + G + NX.$$

Next, factoring out Y, we get

$$Y(1 - b) = a - bT + I^p + G + NX.$$

Finally, dividing both sides of this equation by $(1 - b)$ yields

$$Y = \frac{a - bT + I^p + G + NX}{1 - b}.$$

This last equation shows how equilibrium GDP depends on a (autonomous consumption), b (the MPC), T (net taxes), I^p (investment spending), G (government purchases), and NX (net exports). These variables are all determined "outside our model." That is, they are given values that we use to determine equilibrium output, but they are not themselves affected by the level of output. If we use actual numbers for these given variables in the equation, we will find the same equilibrium GDP we would find using a table or a graph.

In the example we used throughout the chapter, the given values (found in Tables 1, 2, and 4) are, in billions of dollars, a = 2,000; b = 0.6; T = 2,000; I^p = 700; G = 500; and NX = 400. Plugging these values into the equation for equilibrium GDP, we get

$$Y = \frac{2,000 - (0.6 \times 2,000) + 700 + 500 + 400}{1 - 0.6}$$

$$= \frac{2,400}{0.4}$$

$$= 6,000.$$

This is the same value we found in Table 4 and Figure 7.

APPENDIX 2

THE SPECIAL CASE OF THE TAX MULTIPLIER

You learned in this chapter how changes in autonomous consumption, planned investment, and government purchases affect aggregate expenditure and equilibrium GDP. But there is another type of change that can influence equilibrium GDP: a change in taxes. For this type of change, the formula for the multiplier is slightly different from the one presented in the chapter.

Let's suppose that net taxes (T) *decrease* by $1,000 billion. Since disposable income is equal to total income − net taxes, the immediate impact of the tax cut is to *increase* disposable income by $1,000 billion. As a result, consumption spending will increase by $MPC \times$ $1,000 billion. Using the example in the chapter, with an MPC of 0.6, consumption spending would increase by 0.6 × $1,000 billion = $600 billion. *This is the initial rise in spending caused by the tax cut.* Once consumption spending rises, the multiplier works as with any other change in spending: Consumption rises by another 0.6 × $600 billion = $360 billion in the next round, and by another 0.6 × $360 = $216 billion after that, and so on.

Now let's compare the full multiplier effect from a $1,000 billion cut in net taxes with the effect from a $1,000 billion increase in spending, such as planned investment spending. Look back at Table 5. There you can see that a $1,000 billion rise in investment spending causes a total increase in GDP of $1,000 billion + $600 billion + $360 billion + $216 billion + . . . = $2,500 billion. But when taxes are cut by $1,000 billion, the total increase in GDP is $600 billion + $360 billion + $216 billion + ... These two series of numbers are the same except that for the tax cut, the first $1,000 billion is missing. Therefore, the final rise in GDP from the tax cut must be $1,000 billion less than the final rise in GDP from the increase in investment spending. Since the $1,000 billion rise in investment spending raises GDP by $2,500 billion, a $1,000 billion cut in taxes must raise GDP by $2,500 billion − $1,000 billion = $1,500 billion.

Another way to say this is: For each dollar that taxes are cut, equilibrium GDP will increase by $1.50 rather than $2.50; the increase is one dollar less in the case of the tax cut. This observation tells us that the tax multiplier must have a numerical value *1.0 less than* the spending multiplier of the chapter.

Finally, there is one more difference between the spending multiplier of the chapter and the tax multiplier: While the spending multiplier is a positive number (because an increase in spending causes an increase in equilibrium GDP), the tax multiplier is a negative number, since a tax cut (a negative change in taxes) must be multiplied by a *negative* number to give us a *positive* change in GDP. Putting all this together, we conclude that

Thus, if the MPC is 0.6 (as in the chapter), so that the spending multiplier is 2.5, then the tax multiplier will have a value of $-(2.5 - 1) = -1.5$.

More generally, since the tax multiplier is 1.0 less than the spending multiplier and is also negative, we can write

Tax multiplier = −(spending multiplier − 1).

the tax multiplier is 1.0 less than the spending multiplier, and negative in sign.

Because the expenditure multiplier is $1/(1 - MPC)$, we can substitute to get

$$\text{Tax multiplier} = -\left[\frac{1}{1 - MPC} - 1\right]$$

$$= -\left[\frac{1}{1 - MPC} - \frac{1 - MPC}{1 - MPC}\right]$$

$$= \frac{-MPC}{1 - MPC}.$$

Hence,

> *the general formula for the tax multiplier is*
> $$\frac{-MPC}{(1 - MPC)}.$$

For any change in net taxes, we can use the formula to find the change in net equilibrium GDP as follows:

$$\Delta GDP = \frac{-MPC}{1 - MPC} \times \Delta T.$$

In our example, in which taxes were cut by $1,000 billion, we have $\Delta T = -\$1,000$ billion and $MPC = 0.6$. Plugging these values into the formula, we obtain

$$\Delta GDP = \left[\frac{-0.6}{1 - 0.6}\right] \times -\$1,000 \text{ billion}$$

$$= \$1,500 \text{ billion}.$$

CHAPTER 23

The Banking System and the Money Supply

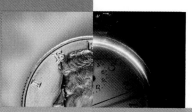

Everyone knows that money doesn't grow on trees. But where does it actually come from? You might think that the answer is simple: The government just prints it. Right?

Sort of. It is true that much of our money supply is, indeed, paper currency, provided by our national monetary authority. But most of our money is *not* paper currency at all. Moreover, the monetary authority in the United States—the Federal Reserve System—is technically not a part of the executive, legislative, or judicial branch of government. Rather, it is a quasi-independent agency that operates *alongside* the government.

In future chapters, we'll make our short-run macro model more realistic by bringing in money and its effects on the economy. This will deepen your understanding of economic fluctuations, and help you understand our policy choices in dealing with them. But in this chapter, we focus on money itself, and the institutions that help create it. We will begin, in the next section, by taking a close look at what money is and how it is measured.

WHAT COUNTS AS MONEY

As discussed several chapters ago, money provides a nation with a *unit of account*, a standardized way of measuring the value of things that are traded. In this and the next chapter, we'll introduce money's function as a *store of value,* one of several ways in which households can hold their wealth. And most importantly, money is a *means of payment:* It can be used to buy things.

But now consider what *is* and what is *not* thought to be money in countries around the world. For example, paper currency, travelers checks, and funds held in checking accounts are all considered to be money in nations with well-established banking systems. That makes sense, because all of these can be used as means of payment. Yet credit cards are *not* considered money, even though you can use them to buy things. Why is this?

A more formal definition of money helps to answer questions like this.

Money An asset widely accepted as a means of payments.

> *Money* *is an asset that is widely accepted as a means of payment in the* *economy.*

Let's consider this definition more closely. First, only *assets*—things of value that people own—can be considered as money. Paper currency, travelers checks, and funds held in checking accounts are all examples of assets that people own, and these are all considered money in the United States. But *the right to borrow* is not an asset, so is not considered money. This is why the credit limit on your credit card, or your ability to go into a bank and borrow funds, is not considered *money* in the economy.

Second, only things that are *widely acceptable* as a means of payment are regarded as money. Coins and paper currency (usually called *cash*), travelers checks, and personal checks can all be used to buy things or pay bills. Other assets—such as stocks and bonds or even gold bars—can*not* generally be used for to pay for goods and services, and so they fail the acceptability test.

MEASURING THE MONEY SUPPLY

As you will learn in the next chapter, the amount of money in circulation can affect the macroeconomy. This is why governments around the world like to know how much money is available to their citizens—the total **money supply.**

Money supply The total amount of money held by the public.

In practice, measuring the money supply is not as straightforward as it might seem, and brings up some conceptual problems. For example, consider funds you might have in a savings account. While you can't use those funds to buy things directly, you can easily *move* the funds *into* your checking account, converting them to money. You might therefore regard your savings account as part of the means of payment that are easily available to you. Should they be included as part of the money supply?

Governments recognize this and other similar sticky questions, and have decided that the best way to deal with them is to have *different* measures of the money supply—in effect, alternative ways of defining what is and what is not money. Each measure includes a selection of *assets* that are *widely acceptable as a means of payment* and, as an additional criterion, *relatively liquid.*

Liquidity The property of being easily converted into cash.

> *An asset is considered **liquid** if it can be converted to cash quickly and at little cost. An illiquid asset, by contrast, can be converted to cash only after a delay, or at considerable cost.*

Checking account balances are highly liquid because you can convert them to cash at the ATM or by cashing a check. Travelers checks are also highly liquid. But stocks and bonds are *not* as liquid as checking accounts or travelers checks. Stock- and bondholders must go to some trouble and pay brokers' fees to convert these assets into cash.

But notice the phrase "*relatively* liquid." This does not sound like a hard-and-fast rule for measuring the money supply, and indeed it is not. This is why there are different measures of the money supply: Each interprets the phrase "relatively liquid" in a different way. To understand this better, let's look at the different kinds of liquid assets that people can hold.

Assets and Their Liquidity

Figure 1 lists a spectrum of assets, ranked according to their liquidity, along with the amounts of each asset in the U.S. public's hands on July 14, 2003. The most liquid asset of all is **cash in the hands of the public.** It takes no time and zero expense to convert this asset into cash, since it's *already* cash. In mid-2003, the public—including residents of other countries—held about $646 billion in U.S. cash.

Next in line are three asset categories of about equal liquidity. **Demand deposits** are the checking accounts held by households and business firms at commercial banks, including huge ones like the Bank of America or Citibank, and smaller ones like Simmons National Bank in Arkansas. These checking accounts are called "demand" deposits because when you write a check to someone, that person can go into a bank and, on demand, be paid in cash. This is one reason that demand deposits are considered very liquid: The person who has your check can convert it into cash quickly and easily. Another reason is that you can withdraw cash from your own checking account very easily—24 hours a day with an ATM card, or during banking hours if you want to speak to a teller. As you can see in the figure, the U.S. public held $314 billion in demand deposits in mid-2003.

Other checkable deposits is a catchall category for several types of checking accounts that work very much like demand deposits. This includes *automatic transfers from savings accounts*, which are interest-paying savings accounts that automatically transfer funds into checking accounts when needed. On July 14, 2003, the U.S. public held $298 billion of these types of checkable deposits.

Travelers checks are specially printed checks that you can buy from banks or other private companies, like American Express. Travelers checks can be easily spent at almost any hotel or store. You can often cash them at a bank. You need only show an I.D. and countersign the check. In mid-2003, the public held about $8 billion in travelers checks.

Savings-type accounts at banks and other financial institutions (such as *savings and loan* institutions) amounted to $3,093 billion in mid-2003. These are less liquid than checking-type accounts, since they do not allow you to write checks. While it is easy to transfer funds from your savings account to your checking account, you must make the transfer yourself.

Next on the list are deposits in *retail money market mutual funds (MMMFs)*, which use customer deposits to buy a variety of financial assets. Depositors can withdraw their money by writing checks. In mid-2003, the general public held about $880 billion in such MMMFs.

Time deposits (sometimes called *certificates of deposit*, or *CDs*) require you to keep your money in the bank for a specified period of time (usually six months or

Cash in the hands of the public Currency and coins held outside of banks.

Demand deposits Checking accounts that do not pay interest.

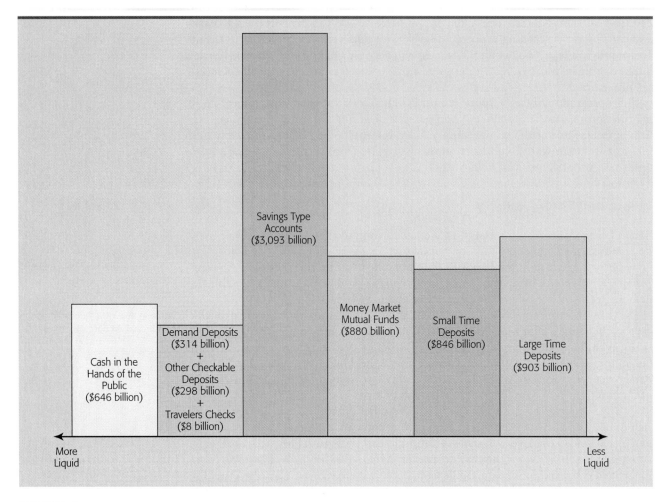

FIGURE 1
Monetary Assets and Their Liquidity (July 14, 2003)

Assets vary according to their liquidity—the ease with which they can be converted into cash. Assets toward the left side of this figure are more liquid than those toward the right side.

Source: http://www.federalreserve.gov, *Money Stock Measures*, H.6, Tables 4 and 5.

M1 A standard measure of the money supply, including cash in the hands of the public, checking account deposits, and travelers checks.

longer), and impose an interest penalty if you withdraw early. In July 2003, the public held $846 billion in *small time deposits* (in amounts under $100,000) and $903 billion in *large time deposits* (in amounts over $100,000).

Now let's see how these assets have been used to define "money" in different ways.

M1 and M2

The standard measure of the money stock is called **M1.** It is the sum of the first four assets in our list: cash in the hands of the public, demand deposits, other checkable deposits, and travelers checks. These are also the four most liquid assets in our list.

$$M1 = \text{cash in the hands of thepublic} + \text{demand deposits} +$$
$$\text{other checking account deposits} + \text{travelers checks.}$$

On July 14, 2003, this amounted to

$$M1 = \$646 \text{ billion} + \$314 \text{ billion} + \$298 \text{ billion} +$$
$$\$8 \text{ billion} = \$1{,}266 \text{ billion.}$$

When economists or government officials speak about "the money supply," they usually mean M1.

But what about the assets left out of M1? While savings accounts are not as liquid as any of the components of M1, for most of us there is hardly a difference. All it takes is an ATM card and, presto, funds in your savings account become cash. Money market funds held by households and businesses are fairly liquid, even though there are sometimes restrictions or special risks involved in converting them into cash. And even time deposits—if they are not too large—can be cashed in early with only a small interest penalty. When you think of how much "means of payment" you have, you are very likely to include the amounts you have in these types of accounts. This is why another common measure of the money supply, **M2**, adds these and some other types of assets to M1:

M2 M1 plus savings account balances, retail money market mutual fund balances, and small time deposits.

$$M2 = M1 + \text{savings-type accounts} + \text{retail MMMF balances} +$$
$$\text{small-denomination time deposits.}$$

Using the numbers for July 14, 2003 in the United States:

$$M2 = \$1{,}266 \text{ billion} + \$3{,}093 \text{ billion} + \$880 \text{ billion} + \$846 \text{ billion}$$
$$= \$6{,}085 \text{ billion.}$$

There are other official measures of the money supply besides M1 and M2 that add in assets that are less liquid than those in M2. But M1 and M2 have been the most popular, and most commonly watched, definitions.

It is important to understand that the M1 and M2 money stock measures exclude many things that people use regularly as a means of payment. Although M1 and M2 give us important information about the activities of the Fed and of banks, they do not measure all the different ways that people hold their wealth or pay for things. Credit cards, for example, are not included in any of the official measures of the money supply (they are not assets). But for most of us, unused credit *is* a means of payment, which we lump together with our cash and our checking accounts. As credit cards were issued to more and more Americans over the last several decades, the available means of payment increased considerably, much more than the increase in M1 and M2 suggests.

HTTP://

For information on electronic money systems around the world, see the "Survey of Electronic Money Developments" at **http://www.bis.org/publ/cpss48.pdf**.

Technological advances—now and in the future—will continue the trend toward new and more varied ways to make payments. For example, at the 1996 Olympics, people used electronic cash to make small transactions—smaller than would make sense with credit cards. You could buy a card worth $5, $10, or $20 and use it in place of cash or checks. In 1999, Citibank began testing similar electronic cash cards in the Upper West Side of Manhattan. In early 2002 electronic cash experiments were being conducted on several college campuses. But in spite of earlier optimistic forecasts, the idea has not yet caught on. Electronic cash is clearly a means of payment, even though it is not yet included in any measure of the money supply. If electronic cash were to become important in the economy, it would no doubt be included in M1.

Cash in Private Banks or the Fed In our definitions of money—whether M1, M2, or some other measure—we include cash (coin and paper currency) only if it is *in the hands of the public.* The italicized words are important. Some of the nation's cash is stored in bank vaults, and is released only when the public withdraws cash from their accounts. Other cash is in the hands of the Federal Reserve, which stores it for future release. But until this cash is released from bank vaults or the Fed, it is not part of the money supply. Only the cash possessed by households, businesses, or government agencies (other than the Fed) is considered part of the money supply.

DANGEROUS CURVES

Fortunately, the details and complexities of measuring money are not important for a basic understanding of the monetary system and monetary policy. For the rest of our discussion, we will make a simplifying assumption:

> *We will assume the money supply consists of just two components: cash in the hands of the public and demand deposits.*
>
> *Money supply = cash in the hands of public + demand deposits.*

As you will see later, our definition of the money supply corresponds closely to the liquid assets that our national monetary authority—the Federal Reserve—can control. While there is not much that the Federal Reserve can do directly about the amount of funds in savings accounts, MMMFs, or time deposits, or about the development of electronic cash or the ability to borrow on credit cards, it can tightly control the sum of cash in the hands of the public and demand deposits.[1]

We will spend the rest of this chapter analyzing how money is created and what makes the money supply change. Our first step is to introduce a key player in the creation of money: the banking system.

THE BANKING SYSTEM

Think about the last time you used the services of a bank. Perhaps you deposited a paycheck in the bank's ATM, or withdrew cash to take care of your shopping needs for the week. We make these kinds of transactions dozens of times every year without ever thinking about what a bank really is, or how our own actions at the bank—and the actions of millions of other bank customers—might contribute to a change in the money supply.

Financial Intermediaries

Financial Intermediary A business firm that specializes in brokering between savers and borrowers.

Let's begin at the beginning: What are banks? They are important examples of **financial intermediaries**: business firms that specialize in assembling loanable funds from households and firms whose revenues exceed their expenditures, and channeling those funds to households and firms (and sometimes the government) whose expenditures exceed revenues. Financial intermediaries make the economy work much more efficiently than would be possible without them.

To understand this more clearly, imagine that Boeing, the U.S. aircraft maker, wants to borrow a billion dollars for three years. If there were no financial intermediaries, Boeing would have to make individual arrangements to borrow small amounts of money from thousands—perhaps millions—of households, each of which wants to lend money for, say, three months at a time. Every three months, Boeing would have to renegotiate the loans, and it would find borrowing money in this way to be quite cumbersome. Lenders, too, would find this arrangement troublesome. All of their funds would be lent to one firm. If that firm encountered difficulties, the funds might not be returned at the end of three months.

An intermediary helps to solve these problems by combining a large number of small savers' funds into custom-designed packages and then lending them to larger

---

[1] The Fed can also control some other types of checkable deposits. To keep our analysis as simple as possible, we consider only demand deposits.

borrowers. The intermediary can do this because it can predict—from experience—the pattern of inflows of funds. While some deposited funds may be withdrawn, the overall total available for lending tends to be quite stable. The intermediary can also reduce the risk to depositors by spreading its loans among a number of different borrowers. If one borrower fails to repay its loan, that will have only a small effect on the intermediary and its depositors.

Of course, intermediaries must earn a profit for providing brokering services. They do so by charging a higher interest rate on the funds they lend than the rate they pay to depositors. But they are so efficient at brokering that both lenders and borrowers benefit. Lenders earn higher interest rates, with lower risk and greater liquidity, than if they had to deal directly with the ultimate users of funds. And borrowers end up paying lower interest rates on loans that are specially designed for their specific purposes.

The United States boasts a wide variety of financial intermediaries, including commercial banks, savings and loan associations, mutual savings banks, credit unions, insurance companies, and some government agencies. Some of these intermediaries—called *depository institutions*—accept deposits from the general public and lend the deposits to borrowers. There are four types of depository institutions:

1. *Savings and loan associations (S&Ls)* obtain funds through their customers' time, savings, and checkable deposits and use them primarily to make mortgage loans.
2. *Mutual savings banks* accept deposits (called *shares*) and use them primarily to make mortgage loans. They differ from S&Ls because they are owned by their depositors rather than outside investors.
3. *Credit unions* specialize in working with particular groups of people, such as members of a labor union or employees in a specific field of business. They acquire funds through their members' deposits and make consumer and mortgage loans to other members.
4. *Commercial banks* are the largest group of depository institutions. They obtain funds mainly by accepting checkable deposits, savings deposits, and time deposits and use the funds to make business, mortgage, and consumer loans.

Since commercial banks will play a central role in the rest of this chapter, let's take a closer look at how they operate.

Commercial Banks

A commercial bank (or just "bank" for short) is a private corporation, owned by its stockholders, that provides services to the public. For our purposes, the most important service is to provide checking accounts, which enable the bank's customers to pay bills and make purchases without holding large amounts of cash that could be lost or stolen. Checks are one of the most important means of payment in the economy. Every year, U.S. households and businesses write trillions of dollars' worth of checks to pay their bills, and many wage and salary earners have their pay deposited directly into their checking accounts. And as you saw in Figure 1, the public holds about as much money in the form of demand deposits and other checking-type accounts as it holds in cash.

Banks provide checking account services in order to earn a profit. Where does a bank's profit come from? Mostly from lending out the funds that people deposit and charging interest on the loans, but also by charging for some services directly, such as check-printing fees or that annoying dollar or so sometimes charged for using an ATM.

TABLE 1
A Typical Commercial Bank's Balance Sheet

Assets		Liabilities and Net Worth	
Property and buildings	$ 5 million	Demand deposit liabilities	$100 million
Government and corporate bonds	$ 25 million	Net worth	$ 5 million
Loans	$ 65 million		
Cash in vault	$ 2 million		
In accounts with the Federal Reserve	$ 8 million		
Total Assets	$105 million	Total Liabilities plus Net Worth	$105 million

A Bank's Balance Sheet

Balance sheet A financial statement showing assets, liabilities, and net worth at a point in time.

We can understand more clearly how a bank works by looking at its *balance sheet*, a tool used by accountants. A **balance sheet** is a two-column list that provides information about the financial condition of a bank at a particular point in time. In one column, the bank's *assets* are listed—everything of value that it *owns*. On the other side, the bank's *liabilities* are listed—the amounts that the bank *owes*.

Table 1 shows a simplified version of a commercial bank's balance sheet.

Why does the bank have these assets and liabilities? Let's start with the assets side. The first item, $5 million, is the value of the bank's real estate—the buildings and the land underneath them. This is the easiest to explain, because a bank must have one or more branch offices in order to do business with the public.

Bond A promise to pay back borrowed funds, issued by a corporation or government agency.

Loan An agreement to pay back borrowed funds, signed by a household or noncorporate business.

Next, comes $25 million in *bonds*, and $65 million in *loans*. A **bond** is a promise to pay funds to the holder of the bond, issued by a corporation or a government agency when it borrows money.[2] A bond promises to pay back the loan either gradually (e.g., each month), or all at once at some future date. **Loans** are promises to pay back funds signed by households or noncorporate businesses. Examples are auto loans, student loans, small-business loans, and home mortgages (where the funds lent out are used to buy a home). Both bonds and loans generate interest income for the bank.

Next come two categories that might seem curious: $2 million in "vault cash," and $8 million in "accounts with the Federal Reserve." Vault cash, just like it sounds, is the coin and currency that the bank has stored in its vault. In addition, banks maintain their own accounts with the Federal Reserve, and they add and subtract to these accounts when they make transactions with other banks. Neither vault cash nor accounts with the Federal Reserve pay interest. Why, then, does the bank hold them? After all, a profit-seeking bank should want to hold as much of its assets as possible in interest-earning form: bonds and loans.

There are two explanations for vault cash and accounts with the Federal Reserve. First, on any given day, some of the bank's customers might want to with-

---

[2] We are using the term "bond" loosely to refer to *all* such promises issued by corporations and government agencies. Technically, a bond must be a long-term obligation to pay back money, 10 years or more from the time the money is first borrowed. Shorter-term obligations are called *notes* (between 1 and 10 years) or *bills* (1 year or less).

draw more cash than other customers are depositing. The bank must always be prepared to honor its obligations for withdrawals, so it must have some cash on hand to meet these requirements. This explains why it holds vault cash.

Second, banks are required by law to hold **reserves**, which are defined as *the sum of cash in the vault and accounts with the Federal Reserve*. The amount of reserves a bank must hold is called **required reserves**. The more funds its customers hold in their checking accounts, the greater the amount of required reserves. The **required reserve ratio**, set by the Federal Reserve, tells banks the fraction of their checking accounts that they must hold as required reserves.

For example, the bank in Table 1 has $100 million in demand deposits. If the required reserve ratio is 0.1, this bank's required reserves are 0.1 × $100 million = $10 million in reserves. The bank must hold *at least* this amount of its assets as reserves. Since our bank has $2 million in vault cash and $8 million in its reserve account with the Federal Reserve, it has a total of $10 million in reserves, the minimum required amount.

Now skip to the right side of the balance sheet. This bank's only liability is its demand deposits. Why are demand deposits a *liability*? Because the bank's customers have the right to withdraw funds from their checking accounts. Until they do, the bank *owes* them these funds.

Finally, the last entry. When we total up both sides of the bank's balance sheet, we find that it has $105 million in assets and only $100 million in liabilities. If the bank were to go out of business—selling all of its assets and using the proceeds to pay off all of its liabilities (its demand deposits)—it would have $5 million left over. Who would get this $5 million? The bank's owners: its stockholders. The $5 million is called the bank's **net worth.** More generally,

$$\text{Net worth} = \text{Total assets} - \text{Total liabilities.}$$

We include net worth on the liabilities side of the balance sheet because it is, in a sense, what the bank would owe to its owners if it went out of business. Notice that, because of the way net worth is defined, both sides of a balance sheet must always have the same total: *A balance sheet always balances.*

Private banks are just one of the players that help determine the money supply. Now we turn our attention to the other key player—the Federal Reserve System.

THE FEDERAL RESERVE SYSTEM

Every large nation controls its money supply with a **central bank**—the nation's principal monetary authority and the institution responsible for controlling its money supply. Most of the developed countries established their central banks long ago. For example, England's central bank—the Bank of England—was created in 1694. France was one of the latest in Europe, waiting until 1800 to establish the Banque de France. But the United States was even later. Although we experimented with central banks at various times in our history, we did not get serious about a central bank until 1913, when Congress established the *Federal Reserve System.*

Why did it take the United States so long to create a central bank? Part of the reason is the suspicion of central authority that has always been part of U.S. politics and culture. Another reason is the large size and extreme diversity of our country, and the fear that a powerful central bank might be dominated by the interests of one region to the detriment of others. These special American characteristics

Reserves Vault cash plus balances held at the Fed.

Required reserves The minimum amount of reserves a bank must hold, depending on the amount of its deposit liabilities.

Required reserve ratio The minimum fraction of checking account balances that banks must hold as reserves.

Net worth The difference between assets and liabilities.

Central bank A nation's principal monetary authority responsible for controlling the money supply.

FIGURE 2

The Geography of the Federal Reserve System

The United States is divided into 12 Federal Reserve districts, each with its own Federal Reserve Bank.

Source: Board of Governors of the Federal Reserve System (1994); *The Federal Reserve System, Purposes and Functions,* Eighth Edition, p. 8.

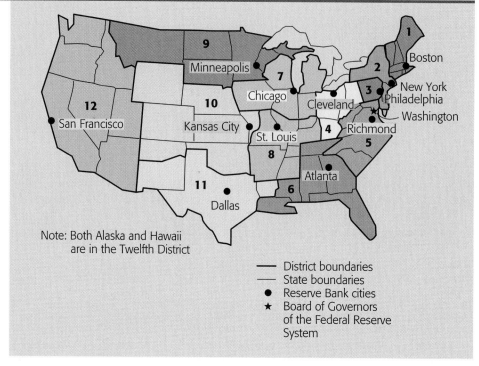

The Federal Open Market Committee meets in this room, inside the Fed's headquarters in Washington DC. The meetings are highly secretive. No one from the media, and no one representing Congress or the president, is permitted in the room during the meetings.

help explain why our own central bank is different in form from its European counterparts.

One major difference is indicated in the very name of the institution: the Federal Reserve System. It does not have the word *central* or *bank* anywhere in its title, making it less suggestive of centralized power.

Another difference is the way the system is organized. Instead of a single central bank, the United States is divided into 12 Federal Reserve districts, each one served by its own Federal Reserve Bank. The 12 districts and the Federal Reserve Banks that serve them are shown in Figure 2. For example, the Federal Reserve Bank of Dallas serves a district consisting of Texas and parts of New Mexico and Louisiana, while the Federal Reserve Bank of Chicago serves a district including Iowa and parts of Illinois, Indiana, Wisconsin, and Michigan.

Another interesting feature of the Federal Reserve System is its peculiar status within the government. Strictly speaking, it is not even a *part* of any branch of government. But the *Fed* (as the system is commonly called) was created by Congress, and could be eliminated by Congress if it so desired. Second, both the president and Congress exert some influence on the Fed through their appointments of key officials in the system.

The Structure of the Fed

Figure 3 shows the organizational structure of the Federal Reserve System. Near the top is the Board of Governors, consisting of seven members who are appointed by the president and confirmed by the Senate for a 14-year term. The most powerful person at the Fed is the *chairman* of the Board of Governors—one of the seven gov-

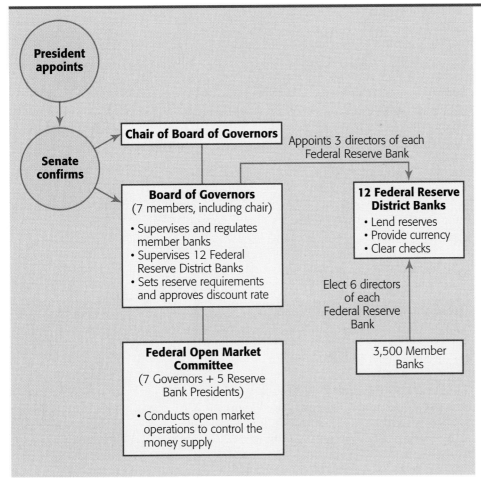

FIGURE 3
The Structure of the Federal Reserve System

Principal decision-making power at the Fed is vested in the Board of Governors, who are appointed by the president and confirmed by the Senate. Monetary policy is set by the Federal Open Market Committee, which consists of the seven governors plus five of the presidents of Federal Reserve Banks.

ernors who is appointed by the president, with Senate approval, to a four-year term as chair. In order to keep any president or Congress from having too much influence over the Fed, the four-year term of the chair is *not* coterminous with the four-year term of the president. As a result, every newly elected president inherits the Fed chair appointed by his predecessor, and may have to wait several years before making an appointment of his own.

Each of the 12 Federal Reserve Banks is supervised by nine directors, three of whom are appointed by the Board of Governors. The other six are elected by private commercial banks, the official stockholders of the system. The directors of each Federal Reserve Bank choose a president of that bank, who manages its day-to-day operations.

Notice that Figure 3 refers to "member banks." Only about a third of the 8,000 or so commercial banks in the United States are members of the Federal Reserve System. But they include all *national banks* (those chartered by the federal government) and about a thousand *state banks* (chartered by their state governments). All of the largest banks in the United States (e.g., Citibank, Bank of America, and Fleet Bank) are nationally chartered banks and therefore member banks as well.

Federal Open Market Committee (FMOC) A committee of Federal Reserve officials that establishes U.S. monetary policy.

The Federal Open Market Committee. Finally, we come to what most economists regard as the most important part of the Fed, the **Federal Open Market Committee (FOMC).** As you can see in Figure 3, the FOMC consists of all seven governors of the Fed, along with 5 of the 12 district bank presidents.[3] The committee meets about eight times a year to discuss current trends in inflation, unemployment, output, interest rates, and international exchange rates. After determining the current state of the economy, the FOMC sets the general course for the nation's money supply.

The word "open" in the FOMC's name is ironic, since the committee's deliberations are private. Summaries of its meetings are published only after a delay of a month or more. In some cases, the committee will release a brief public statement about its decisions on the day they are made. But not even the president of the United States knows the details behind the decisions, or what the FOMC actually discussed at its meeting, until the summary of the meeting is finally released. The reason for the word "open" is that the committee exerts control over the nation's money supply by buying and selling bonds in the public ("open") bond market. Later, we will discuss how and why the FOMC does this.

The Functions of the Federal Reserve

The Federal Reserve, as the overseer of the nation's monetary system, has a variety of important responsibilities. Some of the most important are:

Supervising and Regulating Banks. We've already seen that the Fed sets and enforces reserve requirements, which all banks—not just Fed members—must obey. The Fed also sets standards for establishing new banks, determines what sorts of loans and investments banks are allowed to make, and closely monitors banks' financial activities.

Discount rate The interest rate the Fed charges on loans to banks.

Acting as a "Bank for Banks." Commercial banks use the Fed in much the same way that ordinary citizens use commercial banks. For example, we've already seen that banks hold most of their reserves in reserve accounts with the Fed. In addition, banks can borrow from the Fed, just as we can borrow from our local bank. The Fed charges a special interest rate, called the **discount rate,** on loans that it makes to member banks. In times of financial crisis, the Fed is prepared to act as *lender of last resort,* to make sure that banks have enough reserves to meet their obligations to depositors.

Issuing Paper Currency. The Fed doesn't actually *print* currency; that is done by the government's Bureau of Engraving and Printing. But once printed, it is shipped to the Fed (under *very* heavy guard). The Fed, in turn, puts this currency into circulation. This is why every U.S. bill carries the label *Federal Reserve Note* on the top.

---

[3] Although all Reserve Bank presidents attend FOMC meetings, only 5 of the 12 presidents can vote on FOMC decisions. The president of the Federal Reserve Bank of New York has a permanent vote because New York is such an important financial center. But the remaining four votes rotate among the other district presidents.

Check Clearing. Suppose you write a check for $500 to pay your rent. Your building's owner will deposit the check into *his* checking account, which is probably at a different bank than yours. Somehow, your rent payment must be transferred from your bank account to your landlord's account at the other bank, a process called *check clearing*. In some cases, the services are provided by private clearinghouses. But in many other cases—especially for clearing out-of-town checks—the Federal Reserve system performs the service by transferring funds from one bank's reserve account to another's.

Controlling the Money Supply. The Fed, as the nation's monetary authority, is responsible for controlling the money supply. Since this function is so important in macroeconomics, we explore it in detail in the next section.

THE FED AND THE MONEY SUPPLY

Suppose the Fed wants to change the nation's money supply. (*Why* would the Fed want to do this? The answer will have to wait until the next chapter.) There are many ways this could be done. To increase the money supply, the Fed could print up currency and give it to Fed officials, letting them spend it as they wish. Or it could hold a lottery and give all of the newly printed money to the winner. To decrease the money supply, the Fed could require that all citizens turn over a portion of their cash to Fed officials who would then feed it into paper shredders.

These and other methods would certainly work, but they hardly seem fair or orderly. In practice, the Fed uses a more organized, less haphazard method to change the money supply: *open market operations*.

> *When the Fed wishes to increase or decrease the money supply, it buys or sells government bonds to bond dealers, banks, or other financial institutions. These actions are called* **open market operations.**

Open market operations Purchases or sales of bonds by the Federal Reserve System.

We'll make two special assumptions to keep our analysis of open market operations simple for now:

1. Households and businesses are satisfied holding the amount of cash they are currently holding. Any additional funds they might acquire are deposited in their checking accounts. Any decrease in their funds comes from their checking accounts.
2. Banks never hold reserves in excess of those legally required by law.

Later, we'll discuss what happens when these simplifying assumptions do not hold. We'll also assume that the required reserve ratio is 0.1, so that each time deposits rise by $1,000 at a bank, its required reserves rise by $100.

How the Fed Increases the Money Supply

To increase the money supply, the Fed will *buy* government bonds. This is called an *open market purchase*. Suppose the Fed buys a government bond worth $1,000 from Lehman Brothers, a bond dealer that has a checking account at First

National Bank.[4] The Fed will pay Lehman Brothers with a $1,000 check, which the firm will deposit into its account at First National. First National, in turn, will send the check to the Fed, which will credit First National's reserve account by $1,000.

These actions will change First National's balance sheet as follows:

CHANGES IN FIRST NATIONAL BANK'S BALANCE SHEET

Action	Changes in Assets	Changes in Liabilities
Fed buys $1,000 bond from Lehman Brothers, which deposits $1,000 check from Fed into its checking account.	+$1,000 in reserves	+$1,000 in demand deposits

Notice that here we show only *changes* in First National's balance sheet. Other balance sheet items—such as property and buildings, loans, government bonds, or net worth—are not immediately affected by the open market purchase, so they are not listed here. As you can see, First National gains an asset—reserves—so we enter "+$1,000 in reserves" on the left side of the table. But there are also additional liabilities: the $1,000 that is now in Lehman Brothers' checking account and which First National owes to that firm. The additional liabilities are represented by the entry "+$1,000 in demand deposits" on the right side. Since First National's balance sheet was in balance before Lehman Brothers' deposit, and since assets and liabilities both grew by the same amount ($1,000), we know that the balance sheet is still in balance. Total assets are again equal to total liabilities plus net worth.

Before we go on, let's take note of two important things that have happened. First, the Fed, by conducting an open market purchase, has injected *reserves* into the banking system. So far, these reserves are being held by First National, in its reserve account with the Fed.

The second thing to notice is something that is easy to miss: *The money supply has increased.* How do we know? Because demand deposits are part of the money supply, and they have increased by $1,000. As you are about to see, even more demand deposits will be created before our story ends.

To see what will happen next, let's take the point of view of First National Bank's manager. He might reason as follows: "My demand deposits have just increased by $1,000. Since the required reserve ratio is 0.1, I must now hold 0.1 × $1,000 = $100 in additional reserves. But my *actual* reserves have gone up by more than $100; in fact, they have gone up by $1,000. Therefore, I have **excess reserves**—reserves above those I'm legally required to hold—equal to $1,000 − $100, or $900. Since these excess reserves are earning no interest, I should lend them out." Thus, we can expect First National, in its search for profit, to lend out $900 at the going rate of interest.

How will First National actually make the loan? It could lend out $900 in *cash* from its vault. It would be more typical, however, for the bank to issue a $900 *check* to the borrower. When the borrower deposits the $900 check into his own bank account (at some other bank), the Federal Reserve—which keeps track of these transactions for the banking system—will deduct $900 from First National's

Excess reserves Reserves in excess of required reserves.

---

[4] We'll limit our analysis to commercial banks, which hold demand deposits, although our story would be similar if other types of depository institutions were involved.

reserve account and transfer it to the other bank's reserve account. This will cause a further change in First National's balance sheet, as follows:

CHANGES IN FIRST NATIONAL BANK'S BALANCE SHEET

Action	Changes in Assets	Changes in Liabilities
Fed buys $1,000 bond from Lehman Brothers, which deposits $1,000 check from Fed into its checking account.	+$1,000 in reserves	+$1,000 in demand deposits
First National lends out $900 in excess reserves.	**−$900 in reserves** **+$900 in loans**	
The total effect on First National from beginning to end.	+$100 in reserves +$900 in loans	+$1,000 in demand deposits

Look at the boldface entries in the table. By making the loan, First National has given up an asset: $900 in reserves. This causes assets to change by −$900. But First National also gains an asset of equal value—the $900 loan. (Remember: While loans are liabilities to the borrower, they are assets to banks.) This causes assets to change by +$900. Both of these changes are seen on the assets side of the balance sheet.

Now look at the bottom row of the table. This tells us what has happened to First National from beginning to end. We see that, after making its loan, First National has $100 more in reserves than it started with, and $900 more in loans, for a total of $1,000 more in assets. But it also has $1,000 more in liabilities than it had before: the additional demand deposits that it owes to Lehman Brothers. Both assets and liabilities have gone up by the same amount. Notice, too, that First National is once again holding exactly the reserves it must legally hold. It now has $1,000 more in demand deposits than it had before, and it is holding $0.1 \times \$1,000 = \$100$ more in reserves than before. First National is finished ("loaned up") and cannot lend out any more reserves.

But there is still more to our story. Let's suppose that First National lends the $900 to the owner of a local business, Paula's Pizza, and that Paula deposits her loan check into *her* bank account at Second United Bank. Then, remembering that the Fed will transfer $900 in reserves from First National's reserve account to that of Second United, we'll see the following changes in Second United's balance sheet:

CHANGES IN SECOND UNITED'S BALANCE SHEET

Action	Changes in Assets	Changes in Liabilities
Paula deposits $900 loan check into her checking account.	**+$900 in reserves**	**+$900 in demand deposits**

Second United now has $900 more in assets—the increase in its reserve account with the Federal Reserve—and $900 in additional liabilities—the amount added to Paula's checking account.

Now consider Second United's situation from its manager's viewpoint. He reasons as follows: "My demand deposits have risen by $900, which means my required reserves have risen by $0.1 \times \$900 = \$90$. But my reserves have *actually* increased by $900. Thus, I have *excess reserves* of $\$900 - \$90 = \$810$, which I will lend out." After making the $810 loan, Second United's balance sheet will change once again (look at the boldface entries):

CHANGES IN SECOND UNITED'S BALANCE SHEET

Action	Changes in Assets	Changes in Liabilities
Paula deposits $900 loan check into her checking account.	+$900 in reserves	+$900 in demand deposits
Second United lends out $810 in excess reserves.	**−$810 in reserves** **+$810 in loans**	
The total effect on Second United from beginning to end.	+$ 90 in reserves +$810 in loans	+$900 in demand deposits

In the end, as you can see in the bottom row of the table, Second United has $90 more in reserves than it started with, and $810 more in loans. Its demand deposit liabilities have increased by $900. Notice, too, that the money supply has increased once again—this time, by $900.

Are you starting to see a pattern? Let's carry it through one more step. Whoever borrowed the $810 from Second United will put it into his or her checking account at, say, Third State Bank. This will give Third State excess reserves that it will lend out. As a result, its balance sheet will change as shown.

CHANGES IN THIRD STATE'S BALANCE SHEET

Action	Changes in Assets	Changes in Liabilities
Borrower from Second United deposits $810 loan check into checking account.	+$810 in reserves	+$810 in demand deposits
Third State lends out $729 in excess reserves.	**−$729 in reserves** **+$729 in loans**	
The total effect on Third State from beginning to end.	+$ 81 in reserves +$729 in loans	+$810 in demand deposits

As you can see, demand deposits increase each time a bank lends out excess reserves. In the end, they will increase by a *multiple* of the original $1,000 in reserves injected into the banking system by the open market purchase. Does this process sound familiar? It should. It is very similar to the explanation of the *expenditure multiplier* in the previous chapter, where in each round, an increase in spending led to an increase in income, which caused spending to increase again in the next round. Here, instead of spending, it is the *money supply*—or more specifically, *demand deposits*—that increase in each round.

The Demand Deposit Multiplier

By how much will demand deposits increase in total? If you look back at the balance sheet changes we've analyzed, you'll see that each bank creates less in demand deposits than the bank before. When Lehman Brothers deposited its $1,000 check from the Fed at First National, $1,000 in demand deposits was created. This led to an additional $900 in demand deposits created by Second United, another $810 created by Third State, and so on. In each round, a bank lent 90 percent of the deposit it received. Eventually the additional demand deposits will become so small that we can safely ignore them. When the process is complete, how much in additional demand deposits have been created?

Round	Additional Demand Deposits Created by Each Bank	Additional Demand Deposits Created by *All* Banks
First National Bank	$1,000	$ 1,000
Second United	$ 900	$ 1,900
Third State	$ 810	$ 2,710
Bank 4	$ 729	$ 3,439
Bank 5	$ 656	$ 4,095
Bank 6	$ 590	$ 4,685
. . .		
Bank 10	$ 387	$ 6,511
. . .		
Bank 20	$ 135	$ 8,784
. . .		
Bank 50	very close to zero	very close to $10,000

TABLE 2
Cumulative Increases in Demand Deposits After a $1,000 Cash Deposit

Table 2 provides the answer. Each row of the table shows the additional demand deposits created at each bank, as well as the running total. The last row shows that, in the end, $10,000 in new demand deposits has been created.

Let's go back and summarize what happened in our example. The Fed, through its open market purchase, injected $1,000 of reserves into the banking system. As a result, demand deposits rose by $10,000—10 times the injection in reserves. As you can verify, if the Fed had injected twice this amount of reserves ($2,000), demand deposits would have increased by 10 times *that* amount ($20,000). In fact, *whatever* the injection of reserves, demand deposits will increase by a factor of 10, so we can write

$$\Delta DD = 10 \times \text{reserve injection}$$

where "*DD*" stands for demand deposits. The injection of reserves must be *multiplied by* the number 10 in order to get the change in demand deposits that it causes. For this reason, 10 is called the *demand deposit multiplier* in this example.

> The **demand deposit multiplier** is the number by which we must multiply the injection of reserves to get the total change in demand deposits.

Demand deposit multiplier The number by which a change in reserves is multiplied to determine the resulting change in demand deposits.

The size of the demand deposit multiplier depends on the value of the required reserve ratio set by the Fed. If you look back at Table 2, you will see that each round of additional deposit creation would have been smaller if the required reserve ratio had been larger. For example, with a required reserve ratio of 0.2 instead of 0.1, Second United would have created only $800 in deposits, Third State would have created only $640, and so on. The result would have been a smaller cumulative change in deposits, and a smaller multiplier.

Now let's derive the formula we can use to determine the demand deposit multiplier for *any* required reserve ratio. We'll start with our example in which the required reserve ratio is 0.1. If $1,000 in reserves is injected into the system, the total change in deposits can be written as follows:

$$\Delta DD = \$1{,}000 + \$900 + \$810 + \$729 + \ldots$$

Factoring out $1,000, this becomes

$$\Delta DD = \$1{,}000 \times [1 + 0.9 + 0.9^2 + 0.9^3 + \ldots].$$

In this equation, $1,000 is the initial injection of reserves (Δreserves), and 0.9 is the fraction of reserves that each bank loans out, which is 1 minus the required reserve ratio ($1 - 0.1 = 0.9$). To find the change in deposits that applies to *any* change in reserves and *any* required reserve ratio (RRR), we can write

$$\Delta DD = \Delta\text{Reserves} \times [1 + (1 - RRR) + (1 - RRR)^2 + (1 - RRR)^3 + \ldots].$$

Now we can see that the term in brackets, the infinite sum $1 + (1 - RRR) + (1 - RRR)^2 + (1 - RRR)^3 + \ldots$, is our demand deposit multiplier. But what is its value?

Recall from the last chapter that an infinite sum

$$1 + H + H^2 + H^3 + \ldots$$

always has the value $1/(1 - H)$ as long as H is a fraction between zero and 1. In the last chapter, we replaced H with the MPC to get the expenditure multiplier. But here, we will replace H with $1 - RRR$ (which is always between zero and 1) to obtain a value for the deposit multiplier of $1/[1 - (1 - RRR)] = 1/RRR$.

> *For any value of the required reserve ratio* (RRR), *the formula for the demand deposit multiplier is* 1/RRR.

In our example, the RRR was equal to 0.1, so the deposit multiplier had the value $1/0.1 = 10$. If the RRR had been 0.2 instead, the deposit multiplier would have been equal to $1/0.2 = 5$.

Using our general formula for the demand deposit multiplier, we can restate what happens when the Fed injects reserves into the banking system as follows:

$$\Delta DD = \left(\frac{1}{RRR}\right) \times \Delta\text{Reserves}.$$

Since we've been assuming that the amount of cash in the hands of the public (the other component of the money supply) does not change, we can also write

$$\Delta\text{Money Supply} = \left(\frac{1}{RRR}\right) \times \Delta\text{Reserves}.$$

The Fed's Influence on the Banking System as a Whole

We can also look at what happened to total demand deposits and the money supply from another perspective. When the Fed bought the $1,000 bond from Lehman Brothers, it injected $1,000 of reserves into the banking system. That was the only increase in reserves that occurred in our story. Where did the additional $1,000 in reserves end up? If you go back through the changes in balance sheets, you'll see that First National ended up with $100 in additional reserves, Second United ended up with $90, Third Savings with $81, and so on. Each of these banks is required to hold more reserves than initially, because its demand deposits have increased. In the end, *the additional $1,000 in reserves will be distributed among different banks in the system as required reserves.*

After an injection of reserves, the demand deposit multiplier stops working —and the money supply stops increasing—only when all the reserves injected are being held by banks as required *reserves.*

This observation helps us understand the demand deposit multiplier in another way. In our example, the deposit-creation process will continue until the entire injection of $1,000 in reserves becomes *required* reserves. But with an *RRR* of 0.1, each dollar of reserves entitles a bank to have $10 in demand deposits. Therefore, by injecting $1,000 of reserves into the system, the Fed has enabled banks, in total, to hold $10,000 in additional demand deposits. Only when $10,000 in deposits has been created will the process come to an end.

Just as we've looked at balance sheet changes for each bank, we can also look at the change in the balance sheet of the *entire banking system*. The Fed's open market purchase of $1,000 has caused the following changes:

"Creating Money" Doesn't Mean "Creating Wealth" Demand deposits are a means of payment, and banks create them. This is why we say that banks "create deposits" and "create money." But don't fall into the trap of thinking that banks create wealth. No one gains any additional wealth as a result of money creation.

To see why, think about what happened in our story when Lehman Brothers deposited the $1,000 check from the Fed into its account at First National. *Lehman Brothers* was no wealthier: It gave up a $1,000 check from the Fed and ended up with $1,000 more in its checking account, for a net gain of zero. Similarly, the *bank* gained no additional wealth: It had $1,000 more in cash, but it also *owed* Lehman Brothers $1,000—once again, a net gain of zero.

The same conclusion holds for any other step in the money-creation process. When Paula borrows $900 and deposits it into her checking account at Second United, she is no wealthier: She has $900 more in her account, but owes $900 to First National. And once again, the bank is no wealthier: It has $900 more in demand deposits, but owes this money to Paula.

Always remember that when banks "create money," they do not create wealth.

DANGEROUS CURVES

CHANGES IN THE BALANCE SHEET OF THE ENTIRE BANKING SYSTEM

Changes in Assets	Changes in Liabilities
+$1,000 in reserves +$9,000 in loans	+$10,000 in demand deposits

In the end, total reserves in the system have increased by $1,000—the amount of the open market purchase. Each dollar in reserves supports $10 in demand deposits, so we know that total deposits have increased by $10,000. Finally, we know that a balance sheet always balances. Since liabilities increased by $10,000, loans must have increased by $9,000 to increase total assets (loans and reserves) by $10,000.

How the Fed Decreases the Money Supply

Just as the Fed can increase the money supply by purchasing government bonds, it can also *decrease* the money supply by *selling* government bonds—an *open market sale.*

Where does the Fed get the government bonds to sell? It has trillions of dollars' worth of government bonds from open market *purchases* it has conducted in the past. Since, on average, the Fed tends to increase the money supply each year, it conducts more open market purchases than open market sales, and its bond holdings keep growing. So we needn't worry that the Fed will run out of bonds to sell.

Suppose the Fed sells a $1,000 government bond to a bond dealer, Merrill Lynch, which—like Lehman Brothers in our earlier example—has a checking account at First National Bank. Merrill Lynch pays the Fed for the bond with a $1,000 check drawn on its account at First National. When the Fed gets Merrill

Lynch's check, it will present the check to First National and deduct $1,000 from First National's reserve account. In turn, First National will deduct $1,000 from Merrill Lynch's checking account.

After all of this has taken place, First National's balance sheet will show the following changes:

CHANGES IN FIRST NATIONAL BANK'S BALANCE SHEET

Action	Changes in Assets	Changes in Liabilities
Fed sells $1,000 bond to Merrill Lynch, which pays with a $1,000 check drawn on First National.	−$1,000 in reserves	−$1,000 in demand deposits

Now First National has a problem. Since its demand deposits have decreased by $1,000, it can legally decrease its reserves by 10 percent of that, or $100. But its reserves have *actually* decreased by $1,000, which is $900 more than they are allowed to decrease. First National has *deficient reserves*—reserves smaller than those it is legally required to hold. How can it get the additional reserves it needs?

First National will have to *call in a loan* (ask for repayment) in the amount of $900.[5] A loan is usually repaid with a check drawn on some other bank. When First National gets this check, the Federal Reserve will add $900 to its reserve account, and deduct $900 from the reserve account at the other bank. This is how First National brings its reserves up to the legal requirement. After it calls in the $900 loan, First National's balance sheet will change as follows:

CHANGES IN FIRST NATIONAL BANK'S BALANCE SHEET

Action	Changes in Assets	Changes in Liabilities
Fed sells $1,000 bond to Merrill Lynch, which pays with a $1,000 check drawn on First National.	−$1,000 in reserves	−$1,000 in demand deposits
First National calls in loans worth $900.	**+$ 900 in reserves** **−$ 900 in loans**	
The total effect on First National from beginning to end.	−$ 100 in reserves −$ 900 in loans	−$1,000 in demand deposits

Look at the boldfaced terms. After First National calls in the loan, the composition of its assets will change: $900 more in reserves and $900 less in loans. The last row of the table shows the changes to First National's balance sheet from beginning to end. Compared to its initial situation, First National has $100 less in reserves (it lost $1,000 and then gained $900), $900 less in loans, and $1,000 less in demand deposits.

As you might guess, this is not the end of the story. Remember that whoever paid back the loan to First National did so by a check drawn on another bank. That

---

[5] In reality, bank loans are for specified time periods, and a bank cannot actually demand that a loan be repaid early. But most banks have a large volume of loans outstanding, with some being repaid each day. Typically, the funds will be lent out again the very same day they are repaid. But a bank that needs additional reserves will simply reduce its rate of new lending on that day, thereby reducing its total amount of loans outstanding. This has the same effect as "calling in a loan."

other bank, which we'll assume is Second United Bank, will lose $900 in reserves and experience the following changes in its balance sheet:

CHANGES IN SECOND UNITED BANK'S BALANCE SHEET

Action	Changes in Assets	Changes in Liabilities
Someone with an account at Second United Bank writes a $900 check to First National.	−$900 in reserves	−$900 in demand deposits

Now Second United Bank is in the same fix that First National was in. Its demand deposits have decreased by $900, so its reserves can legally fall by $90. However, its actual reserves have decreased by $900, which is $810 too much. Now it is Second United's turn to call in a loan. (On your own, fill in the rest of the changes in Second United Bank's balance sheet as it successfully brings its reserves up to the legal requirement.)

As you can see, the process of calling in loans will involve many banks. Each time a bank calls in a loan, demand deposits are destroyed—the same amount as were created in our earlier story, in which each bank *made* a new loan. The total decline in demand deposits will be a multiple of the initial withdrawal of reserves. Keeping in mind that a withdrawal of reserves is a *negative change in reserves*, we can still use our demand deposit multiplier—$1/(RRR)$—and our general formula:

$$\Delta DD = \left(\frac{1}{RRR}\right) \times \Delta \text{Reserves}.$$

Applying it to our example, we have

$$\Delta DD = \left[\frac{1}{0.1}\right] \times (-\$1,000) = -\$10,000.$$

In words, the Fed's $1,000 open market sale causes a $10,000 decrease in demand deposits. Since we assume that the public's cash holdings do not change, the money supply decreases by $10,000 as well.

To the banking system as a whole, the Fed's bond sale has done the following:

CHANGES IN BALANCE SHEET FOR THE ENTIRE BANKING SYSTEM

Changes in Assets	Changes in Liabilities
−$1,000 in reserves −$9,000 in loans	−$10,000 in demand deposits

Some Important Provisos About the Demand Deposit Multiplier

Although the process of money creation and destruction as we've described it illustrates the basic ideas, our formula for the demand deposit multiplier—$1/RRR$—is oversimplified. In reality, the multiplier is likely to be smaller than our formula suggests, for two reasons.

First, we've assumed that as the money supply changes, the public does *not* change its holdings of cash. But in reality, as the money supply increases, the public typically will want to hold part of the increase as demand deposits, and part of the increase as cash. As a result, in each round of the deposit-creation process, some

DANGEROUS CURVES

Selling Bonds: Fed Versus Treasury In this section, you learned how the Fed sells government bonds to decrease the money supply. It's easy to confuse this with another type of government bond sale, which is done by the U.S. Treasury.

The U.S. Treasury is the branch of government that collects tax revenue, disburses money for government purchases and transfer payments, and borrows money to finance any government budget deficit. The Treasury borrows funds by issuing *new* government bonds and *selling* them to the public—to banks, other financial institutions, and bond dealers. What the public pays for these bonds is what they are lending the government.

When the Fed conducts open market operations, however, it does not buy or sell *newly* issued bonds, but "secondhand bonds"—those already issued by the Treasury to finance past deficits. Thus, open market sales are *not* government borrowing; they are strictly an operation designed to change the money supply, and they have no direct effect on the government budget.

reserves will be *withdrawn* in the form of cash. This will lead to a smaller increase in demand deposits than in our story.

Second, we've assumed that banks will always lend out all of their excess reserves. In reality, banks often *want* to hold excess reserves, for a variety of reasons. For example, they may want some flexibility to increase their loans in case interest rates—their reward for lending—rise in the near future. Or they may prefer not to lend the maximum legal amount during a recession, because borrowers are more likely to declare bankruptcy and not repay their loans. If banks increase their holdings of excess reserves as the money supply expands, they will make smaller loans than in our story, and in each round, demand deposit creation will be smaller.

Other Tools for Controlling the Money Supply

Open market operations are the Fed's primary means of controlling the money supply. But there are two other tools that the Fed can use to increase or decrease the money supply.

- *Changes in the required reserve ratio.* In principle, the Fed can set off the process of deposit creation, similar to that described earlier, by lowering the required reserve ratio. Look back at Table 1, which showed the balance sheet of a bank facing a required reserve ratio of 0.1 and holding exactly the amount of reserves required by law—$10 million. Now suppose the Fed lowered the required reserve ratio to 0.05. Suddenly, the bank would find that its required reserves were only $5 million; the other $5 million in reserves it holds would become excess reserves. To earn the highest profit possible, the bank would increase its lending by $5 million. At the same time, all other banks in the country would find that some of their formerly required reserves were now excess reserves, and they would increase their lending. The money supply would increase.

  On the other hand, if the Fed *raised* the required reserve ratio, the process would work in reverse: All banks would suddenly have reserve deficiencies and be forced to call in loans. The money supply would decrease.

- *Changes in the discount rate.* The discount rate, mentioned earlier, is the rate the Fed charges banks when it lends them reserves. In principle, a lower discount rate, by enabling banks to borrow reserves from the Fed more cheaply, might encourage banks to borrow more. An increase in borrowed reserves works just like any other injection of reserves into the banking system: It increases the money supply.

  On the other side, a *rise* in the discount rate would make it more expensive for banks to borrow from the Fed, and decrease the amount of borrowed reserves in the system. This withdrawal of reserves from the banking system would lead to a decrease in the money supply.

Changes in either the required reserve ratio or the discount rate *could* set off the process of deposit creation or deposit destruction in much the same way outlined in this chapter. In reality, neither of these policy tools is used very often. The most recent change in the required reserve ratio was in April 1992, when the Fed lowered the required reserve ratio for most demand deposits from 12 percent to 10 percent. Changes in the discount rate are more frequent, but it is not unusual for the Fed to leave the discount rate unchanged for a year or more.

Why are these other tools used so seldom? Part of the reason is that they can have such unpredictable effects. When the required reserve ratio changes, all banks in the system are affected simultaneously. Even a tiny error in predicting how a typical bank will respond can translate into a huge difference for the money supply.

A change in the discount rate may have uncertain effects as well. In the past, many bank managers have preferred *not* to borrow reserves from the Fed, since it would put them under closer Fed scrutiny. And in the past, the Fed discouraged banks from borrowing reserves from it, unless the bank was in difficulty. Thus, a small change in the discount rate was unlikely to have much of an impact on bank borrowing of reserves, and therefore on the money supply.

In January 2003, however, the Fed changed its discount policy, and began to *encourage* banks to borrow. It established two different discount rates—one for banks in excellent financial condition and another, higher rate for banks considered more at risk. Banks in sound condition could borrow freely at the lower rate without Fed scrutiny. As a result, the discount rate may become a more effective, and more frequently used, policy tool in the future.

Still, open market operations will almost certainly remain the Fed's *principal* tool for controlling the money supply. One reason is that they can be so easily fine-tuned to any level desired. Another advantage is that they can be covert. No one knows exactly what the FOMC decided to do to the money supply at its last meeting for several weeks—unless the FOMC chooses to make an earlier announcement. And no one knows whether it is conducting more open market purchases or more open market sales on any given day (it always does a certain amount of both to keep bond traders guessing). By maintaining secrecy, the Fed can often change its policies without destabilizing financial markets, and also avoid the pressure that Congress or the president might bring to bear if its policies are not popular.

> *While other tools can affect the money supply, open market operations have two advantages over them: precision and secrecy. This is why open market operations remain the Fed's primary means of changing the money supply.*

The Fed's ability to conduct its policies in secret—and its independent status in general—is controversial. Some argue that secrecy and independence are needed so that the Fed can do what is best for the country—keeping the price level stable—without undue pressure from Congress or the president. Others argue that there is something fundamentally undemocratic about an independent Federal Reserve, whose governors are not elected and who can, to some extent, ignore the popular will. In recent years, because the Fed has been so successful in guiding the economy, the controversy has largely subsided.

© BETTMANN/CORBIS

A bank failure occurs when a bank cannot meet its obligations to those who have claims on the bank. This includes those who have *lent* money to the bank, as well as those who deposited their money there. For example, if a bank has negative net worth—its total liabilities exceed its total assets—then even if the bank were to sell all of its assets, it could not repay what it borrowed *and* have sufficient assets to back up what it owes to its depositors. Some of the claims on the bank could not be honored.

Historically, many bank failures have occurred when depositors began to worry about a bank's financial health. For example, depositors may believe that their bank has made unsound loans that will not be repaid, so that it does not have enough assets to cover its demand deposit liabilities. In that case, everyone will want to be first in line to withdraw cash, since banks meet requests for withdrawals on a first-come, first-served basis. Those who wait may not be able to get any cash at all. This can lead to a **run on the bank,** with everyone trying to withdraw funds simultaneously.

Ironically, a bank can fail even when in good financial health, with more than enough assets to cover its liabilities, just because people *think* the bank is in trouble. Why should a false rumor be a problem for the bank? Because many of its assets are illiquid, such as long-term loans. A bank may be unable to sell these quickly enough to meet the unusual demands for withdrawal during a run on the bank.

For example, look back at Table 1, which shows a healthy bank with more assets than liabilities. But notice that the bank has only $2 million in vault cash. Under normal circumstances, that would be more than enough to cover a day of heavy withdrawals. But suppose that depositors hear a rumor that the bank has made many bad loans, and they want to withdraw $40 million. The bank would soon exhaust its $2 million in cash. It could then ask the Federal Reserve for more cash, using the $8 million in its reserve account, and the Fed would likely respond quickly, perhaps even delivering the cash the same day. The bank could also sell its $25 million in government bonds and obtain more cash within a few days. But altogether, this will give the bank only $35 million with which to honor requests for withdrawals. What then? Unless the bank is lucky enough to have many of its long-term loans coming due that week, it will be unable to meet its depositors' requests for cash. A false rumor could cause the bank to fail.

A **banking panic** occurs when many banks fail simultaneously. In the past, a typical panic would begin with some unexpected event, such as the failure of a large bank. During recessions, for example, many businesses go bankrupt, so fewer bank loans are repaid. A bank that had an unusual number of "bad loans" would be in trouble, and if the public found out about this, there might be a run on that bank. The bank would fail, and many depositors would find that they had lost their deposits.

But that would not be the end of the story. Hearing that their neighbors' banks were short of cash might lead others to question the health of their own banks. Just to be sure, they might withdraw their own funds, preferring to ride out the storm and keep their cash at home. As we've seen, even healthy banks can fail under the pressure of a bank run. They, too, would have to close their doors, stoking the rumor mill even more, and so on.

Run on the bank An attempt by many of a bank's depositors to withdraw their funds.

Banking panic A situation in which depositors attempt to withdraw funds from many banks simultaneously

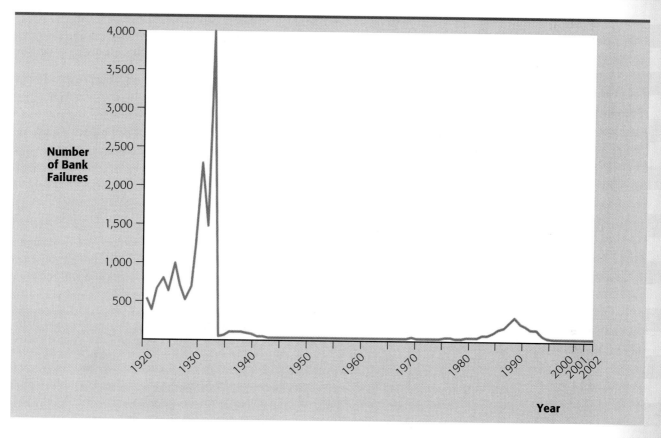

Number of Bank Failures

Year

FIGURE 4

Bank Failures in the United States, 1921–2002

Bank failures continued after the Fed was created in 1913. During the Great Depression, a large number of banks failed. The creation of the Federal Deposit Insurance Corporation in 1933 strengthened faith in the stability of the banking system. Few banks have failed since that time.

Banking panics can cause serious problems for the nation. First, there is the hardship suffered by people who lose their accounts when their bank fails. Second, even when banks do not fail, the withdrawal of cash decreases the banking system's reserves. As we've seen, the withdrawal of reserves leads—through the demand deposit multiplier—to a larger decrease in the money supply. In the next chapter, you will learn that a decrease in the money supply can cause a recession. In a banking panic, the money supply can decrease suddenly and severely, causing a serious recession.

There were five major banking panics in the United States from 1863 to 1907. Indeed, it was the banking panic of 1907 that convinced Congress to establish the Federal Reserve System. From the beginning, one of the Fed's primary functions was to act as a lender of last resort, providing banks with enough cash to meet their obligations to depositors.

But the creation of the Fed did not, in itself, solve the problem. Figure 4 shows the number of bank failures each year since 1921. As you can see, banking panics continued to plague the financial system even after the Fed was created. The Fed did not always act forcefully enough or quickly enough to prevent the panic from spreading.

The Great Depression is a good example of this problem. In late 1929 and 1930, many banks began to fail because of bad loans. Then, from October 1930 until March 1933, more than one-third of all banks failed as frantic depositors stormed bank after bank, demanding to withdraw their funds—even from banks that were in reasonable financial health. Many economists believe that the banking panic of 1930–1933 turned what would have been just a serious recession into the Great Depression. Officials of the Federal Reserve System, not quite grasping the seriousness of the problem, stood by and let it happen.[6]

As you can see in Figure 4, banking panics were largely eliminated after 1933. Indeed, except for the moderate increase in failures during the late 1980s and early 1990s, the system has been almost failure free. In fact, for the five-year period ending in May 2003, a total of 26 banks failed, an average of about 6 per year. Why the dramatic improvement?

Largely for two reasons. First, the Federal Reserve learned an important lesson from the Great Depression, and it now stands ready to inject reserves into the system more quickly in a crisis. Moreover, in 1933 Congress created the Federal Deposit Insurance Corporation (FDIC) to reimburse those who lose their deposits. If your bank is insured by the FDIC (today, accounts are covered in 99 percent of all banks) and cannot honor its obligations for any reason—bad loans, poor management, or even theft—the FDIC will reimburse you up to the first $100,000 you lose in each of your bank accounts. (If you have more than $100,000 in a single bank account, you are not insured for the amount over $100,000.)

The FDIC has had a major impact on the psychology of the banking public. Imagine that you hear your bank is about to go under. As long as you have less than $100,000 in your account, you will not care. Why? Because even if the rumor turns out to be true, you will be reimbursed in full. The resulting calmness on your part, and on the part of other depositors, will prevent a run on the bank. This makes it very unlikely that bank failures will spread throughout the system.

FDIC protection for bank accounts has not been costless. Banks must pay insurance premiums to the FDIC, and they pass this cost on to their depositors and borrowers by charging higher interest rates on loans and higher fees for their services. And there is a more serious cost. If you are thoroughly protected in the event of a bank failure, your bank's managers have little incentive to develop a reputation for prudence in lending funds, since you will be happy to deposit your money there anyway. Without government regulations, banks could act irresponsibly, taking great risks with your money, and you would remain indifferent. Many more banks would fail, the FDIC would have to pay off more depositors, and banks—and their customers—would bear the burden of higher FDIC premiums.

This is the logic behind the Fed's continuing regulation of bank lending. Someone must watch over the banks to keep the failure rate low, and if the public has no incentive to pay attention, the Fed must do so. Most economists believe that if we want the freedom from banking panics provided by the FDIC, we must also accept the strict regulation and close monitoring of banks provided by the Fed and other agencies.

Look again at Figure 4 and notice the temporary rise in bank failures of the late 1980s and the early 1990s. Most of these failures occurred in state-chartered banks. These banks are less closely regulated by the Fed, and are often insured by state agencies instead of the FDIC. When a few banks went bankrupt because highly speculative loans turned sour, insurance funds in several states were drained. Citizens in those states began to fear that insufficient funds were left to insure their own deposits, and the psychology of banking panics took over. To many observers, the experience of the late 1980s and early 1990s was a reminder of the need for a sound insurance system and close monitoring of the banking system.

HTTP://

Fred Furlong and Simon Kwan, in "Rising Bank Risk?" (http://www.frbsf.org/econrsrch/wklyltr/wklyltr99/el99-32.html) explore recent developments in bank behavior.

---

[6] Milton Friedman and Anna Jacobson Schwartz, *A Monetary History of the United States, 1867–1960* (Princeton, NJ: Princeton University Press, 1963), especially p. 358.

Summary

In the United States, the standard measure of money—M1—includes currency, checking account balances, and travelers checks. Each of these assets is liquid and widely acceptable as a means of payment. Other, broader measures go beyond M1 to include funds in savings accounts and other deposits.

The amount of money circulating in the economy is controlled by the Federal Reserve, operating through the banking system. Banks and other financial intermediaries are profit-seeking firms that collect loanable funds from households and businesses, then repackage them to make loans to other households, businesses, and governmental agencies,

The Federal Reserve injects money into the economy by altering banks' balance sheets. In a balance sheet, assets always equal liabilities plus net worth. One important kind of asset is *reserves*—funds that banks are required to hold in proportion to their demand deposit liabilities. When the Fed wants to increase the money supply, it buys bonds in the open market and pays for them with a check. This is called an *open market purchase*. When the Fed's check is deposited in a bank, the bank's balance sheet changes. On the asset side, reserves increase; on the liabilities side, demand deposits (a form of money) also increase. The bank can lend some of the reserves, and the money loaned will end up in some other banks where it supports creation of still more demand deposits. Eventually, demand deposits, and the M1 money supply, increase by some multiple of the original injection of reserves by the Fed. The *demand deposit multiplier*, the inverse of the required reserve ratio, gives us that multiple.

The Fed can decrease the money supply by selling government bonds—an *open market sale*—causing demand deposits to shrink by a multiple of the initial reduction in reserves. The Fed can also change the money supply by changing either the required reserve ratio or the discount rate it charges when it lends reserves to banks.

Key Terms

Balance sheet
Banking panic
Bond
Cash in the hands of the public
Central bank
Demand deposits
Demand deposit multiplier
Discount rate

Excess reserves
Federal Open Market Committee
Financial intermediary
Liquidity
Loan
Net worth
M1
M2

Money
Money supply
Open market operations
Reserves
Required reserves
Required reserve ratio
Run on the bank

Review Questions

Answers to even-numbered Questions and Problems can be found on the text Web site at http://hall-lieb.swlearning.com.

1. Describe the main characteristics of money. What purpose does money serve in present-day economies?

2. Which assets are included when measuring M1? . . . M2?

3. What is a depository institution? Give an example of each of the four types of depository institutions.

4. On a balance sheet, why is net worth listed on the liabilities side, rather than on the assets side?

5. What are reserves? What determines the amount of reserves that a bank holds? Explain the difference between required reserves and excess reserves.

6. What is the difference between the Federal Reserve Board (of Governors) and the Federal Open Market Committee?

7. What are the main functions of the Federal Reserve System?

8. Explain how the Federal Reserve can use open market operations to change the level of bank reserves. How does a change in reserves affect the money supply? (Give answers for both an increase and a decrease in the money supply.)

9. How does a "run on a bank" differ from a "banking panic"? What are their implications for the economy? What steps have been taken to reduce the likelihood of bank runs and bank panics?

10. Why do governments have more than one measure of the money supply?

11. "All U.S. cash is considered part of the U.S. money supply." True or false? Explain briefly.

12. Do banks create wealth when they create money? Explain.

13. Explain why the required reserve ratio and the discount rate have not been used very often, and why the discount rate may be a more frequently used tool in the future.

Problems and Exercises

1. Suppose the required reserve ratio is 0.2. If an extra $20 billion in reserves is injected into the banking system through an open market purchase of bonds, by how much can demand deposits increase? Would your answer be different if the required reserve ratio were 0.1?

2. If the Fed buys $50 million of government securities, by how much can the money supply increase if the required reserve ratio is 0.15? How will your answer be different if the required reserve ratio is 0.18?

3. Which of the following is considered part of the U.S. money supply? (Use the M1 measures.)
   a. A $10 bill you carry in your wallet
   b. A $100 travelers check you bought but did not use
   c. A $100 bill in a bank's vault
   d. The $325.43 balance in your checking account
   e. A share of General Motors stock worth $40

4. Given the following data (in billions of dollars), calculate the value of the M1 money supply and the value of the M2 money supply.

Bank reserves	50
Cash in the hands of the public	400
Demand deposits	400
Retail MMMF balances	880
Other checkable deposits	250
Savings-type account balances	1,300
Small time deposits	950
Travelers checks	10

5. Suppose bank reserves are $100 billion, the required reserve ratio is 0.2, and excess reserves are zero. Calculate how many dollars worth of demand deposits are being supported. Now suppose that the required reserve ratio is lowered to 0.1 and that banks once again become fully "loaned up" with no excess reserves. What is the new level of demand deposits?

6. Suppose bank reserves are $200 billion, the required reserve ratio is 0.2, and excess reserves are zero. Calculate how many dollars worth of demand deposits are being supported. If the Fed wants to decrease demand deposits by $50 billion by changing the required reserve ratio, what will the new required reserve ratio need to be set at?

7. Suppose that the money supply is $1 trillion. Decision makers at the Federal Reserve decide that they wish to reduce the money supply by $100 billion, or by 10 percent. If the required reserve ratio is 0.05, what does the Fed need to do to carry out the planned reduction?

8. Suppose that the money supply is $3.2 trillion. Decision makers at the Federal Reserve decide that they wish to increase the money supply by $500 billion. If the required reserve ratio is 0.10, what does the Fed need to do to carry out the planned increase? What if the required reserve ratio is 0.15?

9. For each of the following situations, determine whether the money supply will increase, decrease, or stay the same.
   a. Depositors become concerned about the safety of depository institutions.
   b. The Fed lowers the required reserve ratio.
   c. The economy enters a recession and banks have a hard time finding creditworthy borrowers.
   d. The Fed sells $100 million of bonds to First National Bank of Ames, Iowa.

10. Suppose that the Fed decides to increase the money supply. It purchases a government bond worth $1,000 from a private citizen. He deposits the check in his account at First National Bank, as in the chapter example. But now, suppose that the required reserve ratio is 0.2, rather than 0.1 as in the chapter.
    a. Trace the effect of this change through three banks—First National, Second United, and Third State. Show the changes to each bank's balance sheet as a result of the Fed's action.
    b. By how much does the money supply change in each of these first three rounds?
    c. What will be the ultimate change in demand deposits in the entire banking system?

11. Suppose accountants at the bank whose balance sheet is depicted in Table 1 discover that they've made an error: Cash in vault is only $1 million, not $2 million.
    a. Which other entries in the bank's balance sheet will change as a consequence of correcting this error?
    b. If the required reserve ratio is 0.10, does this bank now have excess reserves or deficient reserves? Of what value?

12. Assume that the Fed wants to keep the size of the money supply constant by adjusting the required reserve ratio only. How will it have to adjust the required reserve ratio to achieve this goal if
    a. people decide to hold more of their money as cash rather than as demand deposits?
    b. bankers decide to decrease their holdings of excess reserves?

Challenge Questions

1. Sometimes banks wish to hold reserves in excess of the legal minimum. Suppose the Fed makes an open market purchase of $100,000 in government bonds. The required reserve ratio is 0.1, but each bank decides to hold additional reserves equal to 5 percent of its deposits.
   a. Trace the effect of the open market purchase of bonds through the first three banks in the money expansion process. Show the changes to each bank's balance sheet.
   b. Derive the demand deposit multiplier in this case. Is it larger or smaller than when banks hold no excess reserves?
   c. What is the ultimate change in demand deposits in the entire banking system?

2. Suppose the Fed buys $100,000 in government bonds from Jonathan, and that the required reserve ratio is 0.1. Assume that Jonathan and each additional depositor always holds half of their money as cash.
   a. Trace the effect of this open market purchase through the first three banks in the money expansion process. Show the changes to each bank's balance sheet.
   b. Derive the demand deposit multiplier in this case. How does it compare with the demand deposit multiplier when depositors hold no cash?
   c. What is the ultimate change in demand deposits in the entire banking system?

 **ECONOMIC Applications** *These exercises require access to Hall/Lieberman Xtra! If Xtra! did not come with your book, visit http://hallxtra.swlearning.com to purchase.*

1. Use your Xtra! password at the Hall and Lieberman Web site (http://hallxtra.swlearning.com), select this chapter, and under Economic Applications, click on EconDebate. Choose *Macroeconomics: Money and the Financial System,* and scroll down to find the debate, "Should U.S. financial markets be deregulated?" Read the debate, and use the information to answer the following questions.
   a. Explain how the Federal Deposit Insurance Corporation (FDIC) increases the moral hazard problem.
   b. Do you expect the deregulation of U.S. financial markets to increase financial fragility and failures or not? Explain. Can you support your answer with an example from current events?

2. Use your Xtra! password at the Hall and Lieberman Web site (http://hallxtra.swlearning.com), select this chapter, and under Economic Applications, click on EconData. Choose *Macroeconomics: Money and the Fi-*

nancial System, and scroll down to find *Stock Prices S&P 500.* Read the definition and click on Updates and use the information to answer the following questions.
   a. Click on the "review the latest S&P 500 Total Return data," and scroll down to see the percent change from last year for the year 2000 and onward. Describe the trend, and what might have contributed to it.
   b. Scroll down to the article "The Stock Market: Beyond Risk Lies Uncertainty." Read the article. In absence of regulations separating commercial from investment banking, how should the Federal Reserve System intervene to stabilize the financial system? Would Fed intervention exacerbate the moral hazard problem and lead to more instability or alternatively lead to long-term stability of financial markets? Explain.

The Money Market and the Interest Rate

Which of the following two newspsper headlines might you see in your daily paper?

1. **"Motorists Fear Department of Energy Will Raise Gasoline Prices"**
2. **"Wall Street Expects Fed to Raise Interest Rates"**

You probably know the answer: The first headline is entirely unrealistic. The Department of Energy, the government agency that makes energy policy, has no authority to set prices in any market. The Federal Reserve, by contrast, has full authority to influence the interest rate—the price of borrowing money. And it exercises this authority every day. This is why headlines such as the second one appear in newspapers so often.

In this chapter, you will learn how the Fed, through its control of the money supply, also controls the interest rate. We'll continue our focus on the short run, postponing any discussion about longer time horizons until the next chapter.

THE DEMAND FOR MONEY

Reread the title of this section. Does it appear strange to you? Don't people always want as much money as possible?

Indeed, they do. But when we speak about the *demand* for something, we don't mean the amount that people would desire if they could have all they wanted, without having to sacrifice anything for it. Instead, economic decision makers always face constraints: They must sacrifice one thing in order to have more of another. Thus, the *demand for money* does not mean how much money people would *like* to have in the best of all possible worlds. Rather, it means *how much money people would like to hold, given the constraints that they face*. Let's first consider the demand for money by an individual, and then turn our attention to the demand for money in the entire economy.

An Individual's Demand for Money

Money is one of the forms in which people hold their wealth. Unfortunately, at any given moment, the total amount of wealth we have is given; we can't just snap our fingers and have more of it. Therefore, if we want to hold more wealth in the form of money, we must hold less wealth in other forms: savings accounts, money market funds, time deposits, stocks, bonds, and so on. Indeed, people exchange one kind of wealth for another millions of times a day—in banks, stock markets, and bond markets. If you sell shares in the stock market, for example, you give up wealth in the form of corporate stock and acquire money. The buyer of your stock gives up money and acquires the stock.

These two facts—that wealth is given, and that you must give up one kind of wealth in order to acquire more of another—determine an individual's **wealth constraint**. Whenever we speak about the demand for money, the wealth constraint is always in the background, as in the following statement:

Wealth constraint At any point in time, total wealth is fixed.

> *An individual's* quantity of money demanded *is the amount of wealth that the individual chooses to hold as money, rather than as other assets.*

Why do people want to hold some of their wealth in the form of money? The most important reason is that money is a *means of payment;* you can buy things with it. Other forms of wealth, by contrast, are *not* used for purchases. (For example, we don't ordinarily pay for our groceries with shares of stock.) However, the other forms of wealth provide a financial return to their owners. For example, bonds, savings deposits, and time deposits pay interest, while stocks pay dividends and may also rise in value (which is called a *capital gain*). Money, by contrast, pays very little interest (some types of checking accounts) or none at all (cash and most checking accounts). Thus,

> *when you hold money, you bear an opportunity cost—the interest you could have earned by holding other assets instead.*

Each of us must continually decide how to divide our total wealth between money and other assets. The upside to money is that it can be used as a means of payment. The more of our wealth we hold as money, the easier it is to buy things at a moment's notice, and the less often we will have to pay the costs (in time, trouble, and commissions to brokers) to change our other assets into money. The downside to money is that it pays little or no interest.

To keep our analysis as simple as possible, *we'll use bonds as our representative nonmoney asset.* We'll also assume that all assets considered to be money pay no interest at all. In our discussion, therefore, people will choose between two assets that are mirror images of each other. Specifically,

> *individuals choose how to divide wealth between two assets: (1) money, which can be used as a means of payment but earns no interest; and (2) bonds, which earn interest, but cannot be used as a means of payment.*

This choice involves a clear trade-off: The more wealth we hold as money, the less often we will have to go through the inconvenience of changing our bonds into money . . . but the less interest we will earn on our wealth.

What determines how much money an individual will decide to hold? While tastes vary from person to person, three key variables have rather predictable impacts on most of us.

- *The price level.* The greater the number of dollars you spend in a typical week or month, the more money you will want to have on hand to make your purchases. A rise in the price level, which raises the dollar cost of your purchases, should therefore increase the amount of money you want to hold.
- *Real income.* Suppose the price level remains unchanged, but your income increases. Your purchasing power or *real* income will increase, and so will the number of dollars you spend in a typical week or month. Once again, since you are spending more dollars, you will choose to hold more of your wealth in the form of money.
- *The interest rate.* Interest payments are what you give up when you hold money—the *opportunity cost* of money. The greater the interest rate, the greater the opportunity cost of holding money. Thus, a rise in the interest rate *decreases* your quantity of money demanded.

The effect of the interest rate on the quantity of money demanded will play a key role in our analysis. But before we go any further, you may be wondering whether it is realistic to think that changes in the interest rate—which are usually rather small—would have any effect at all. Here, as in many aspects of economic life, you may not consciously think about the interest rate in deciding how to adjust your money-holding habits. Similarly, you may not rethink all your habits about using lights and computers every time the price of electricity changes. But in both cases, you may respond more casually. And when we add up everybody's behavior, we find a noticeable and stable tendency for people to hold less money when it is more expensive to hold it—that is, when the interest rate is higher.

The Demand for Money by Businesses. Our discussion of money demand has focused on the typical individual. But some money (not a lot in comparison to what individuals hold) is held by businesses. Stores keep some currency in their cash registers, and firms generally keep funds in business checking accounts. Businesses face the same types of constraints as individuals: They have only so much wealth, and they must decide how much of it to hold as money rather than other assets. The quantity of money demanded by businesses follows the same principles we have developed for individuals: They want to hold more money when real income or the price level is higher, and less money when the opportunity cost (the interest rate) is higher.

The Economy-Wide Demand for Money

When we use the term *quantity of money demanded* without the word *individual*, we mean the total demand for money by all wealth holders in the economy; businesses

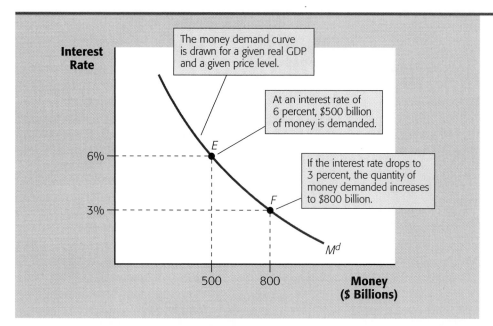

FIGURE 1
The Money Demand Curve

The money demand curve is drawn for a given real GDP and a given price level.

At an interest rate of 6 percent, $500 billion of money is demanded.

If the interest rate drops to 3 percent, the quantity of money demanded increases to $800 billion.

and individuals. And just as each person and each firm in the economy has only so much wealth, so, too, there is a given amount of wealth in the economy as a whole at any given time. In our analysis, this total wealth must be held in one of two forms: money or bonds.

The (economy-wide) quantity of money demanded is the amount of total wealth in the economy that all households and businesses, together, choose to hold as money rather than as bonds.

The demand for money in the economy depends on the same three variables that we discussed for individuals. In particular, (1) a rise in the price level will increase the demand for money; (2) a rise in real income (real GDP) will increase the demand for money; and (3) a rise in the interest rate will *decrease* the quantity of money demanded.

The Money Demand Curve. Figure 1 shows a **money demand curve**, which tells us *the total quantity of money demanded in the economy at each interest rate.* Notice that the curve is downward sloping. As long as the other influences on money demand don't change, a drop in the interest rate—which lowers the opportunity cost of holding money—will increase the quantity of money demanded.

Point *E,* for example, shows that when the interest rate is 6 percent, the quantity of money demanded is $500 billion. If the interest rate falls to 3 percent, we move to point *F,* where the quantity demanded is $800 billion. As we move along the money demand curve, the interest rate changes, but other determinants of money demand (such as the price level and real income) are assumed to remain unchanged.

Shifts in the Money Demand Curve. What happens when something *other* than the interest rate changes the quantity of money demanded? Then the curve shifts. For

Money demand curve A curve indicating how much money will be demanded at each interest rate.

FIGURE 2
A Shift in the Money Demand Curve

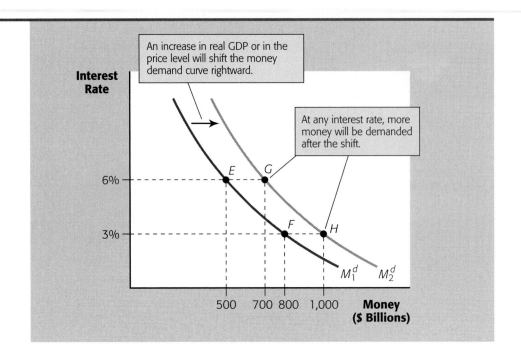

example, suppose that real income increases. Then, at each interest rate, individuals and businesses will want to hold *more* of their wealth in the form of money. The entire money demand curve will shift rightward. This is illustrated in Figure 2, where the money demand curve shifts rightward from M_1^d to M_2^d. At an interest rate of 6 percent, the quantity of money demanded rises from $500 billion to $700 billion; if the interest rate were 3 percent, the amount of money demanded would rise from $800 billion to $1,000 billion.

In general,

> *a change in the interest rate moves us along the money demand curve. A change in money demand caused by something other than the interest rate (such as real income or the price level) will cause the curve to shift.*

Figure 3 summarizes how the key variables we've discussed so far affect the demand for money.

THE SUPPLY OF MONEY

Just as we did for money demand, we would like to draw a curve showing the quantity of money *supplied* at each interest rate. In the previous chapter, you learned how the Fed controls the money supply: It uses open market operations to inject or withdraw reserves from the banking system and then relies on the demand deposit multiplier to do the rest. Since the Fed decides what the money supply will be, we treat it as a fixed amount. That is, the interest rate can rise or fall, but the money supply will remain constant unless and until the Fed decides to change it.

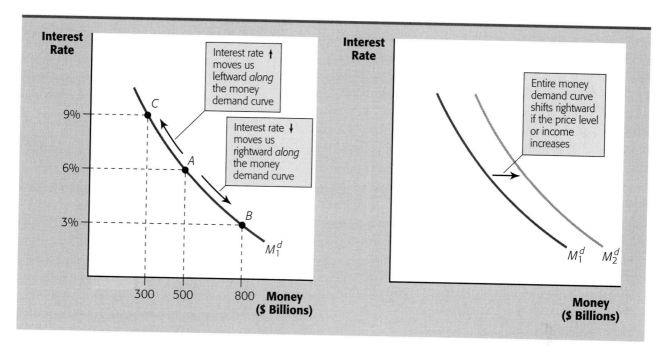

FIGURE 3
**Shifts and Movements
Along the Money Demand
Curve: A Summary**

Money supply curve A line showing the total quantity of money in
the economy at each interest
rate.

Look at the vertical line labeled M_1^S in Figure 4. This is the economy's **money supply curve**, which shows the total amount of money supplied at each interest rate. The line is vertical because once the Fed sets the money supply, it remains constant until the Fed changes it. In the figure, the Fed has chosen to set the money supply at $500 billion. A rise in the interest rate from, say, 3 percent to 6 percent would move us from point J to point E along the money supply curve M_1^S, leaving the money supply unchanged.

Now suppose the Fed, for whatever reason, were to *change* the money supply. Then there would be a *new* vertical line, showing a different quantity of money supplied at each interest rate. Recall from the previous chapter that the Fed raises the money supply by purchasing bonds in an open market operation. For example, if the demand deposit multiplier is 10, and the Fed purchases government bonds worth $20 billion, the money supply increases by 10 × $20 billion = $200 billion. In this case, the money supply curve shifts rightward, to the vertical line labeled M_2^S in the figure.

Open market purchases of bonds inject reserves into the banking system, and shift the money supply curve rightward by a multiple of the reserve injection. Open market sales have the opposite effect: They withdraw reserves from the system and shift the money supply curve leftward by a multiple of the reserve withdrawal.

EQUILIBRIUM IN THE MONEY MARKET

Now let's combine money demand and money supply to find the equilibrium interest rate in the economy (step two in the three-step process). But before we do, a question may have occurred to you. Haven't we already discussed how the interest

FIGURE 4
The Supply of Money

Once the Fed sets the money supply, it remains constant until the Fed changes it. The vertical supply curve labeled M$_1^S$ shows a money supply of $500 billion, regardless of the interest rate. An increase in the money supply to $700 billion is depicted as a rightward shift of the money supply curve to M$_2^S$.

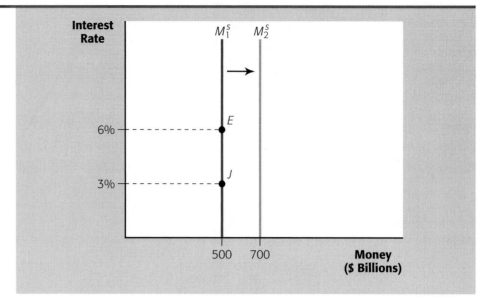

rate is determined? Indeed, we have. The classical model tells us that the interest rate is determined by equilibrium in the *loanable funds market,* where a flow of loanable funds is offered by lenders to borrowers. But remember: The classical model tells us how the economy operates in the *long run.* We can rely on its mechanisms to work only over long periods of time. Here, we are interested in how the interest rate is determined in the *short run,* so we must change our perspective. Toward the end of the chapter, we'll come back to the classical model and explain why its theory of the interest rate does not apply in the short run.

In the short run—our focus here—we look for the equilibrium interest rate in the *money market:* the interest rate at which the quantity of money demanded and the quantity of money supplied are equal. Figure 5 combines the money supply and demand curves. Equilibrium occurs at point *E,* where the two curves intersect. At this point, the quantity of money demanded and the quantity supplied are both equal to $500 billion, and the equilibrium interest rate is 6 percent.

It is important to understand what equilibrium in the money market actually means. First, remember that the money supply curve tells us the quantity of money, determined by the Fed, that *actually exists* in the economy. Every dollar of this money—either in cash or in checking account balances—is held by *someone.* Thus, the money supply curve, in addition to telling us the quantity of money supplied by the Fed, also tells us the quantity of money that people *are actually holding* at any given moment. The money demand curve, on the other hand, tells us how much money people *want* to hold at each interest rate. Thus, when the quantity of money supplied and the quantity demanded are equal, all of the money in the economy is being *willingly held.* That is, people are satisfied holding the money that they are *actually* holding.

> *Equilibrium in the money market occurs when the quantity of money people are* actually *holding (quantity supplied) is equal to the quantity of money they* want *to hold (quantity demanded).*

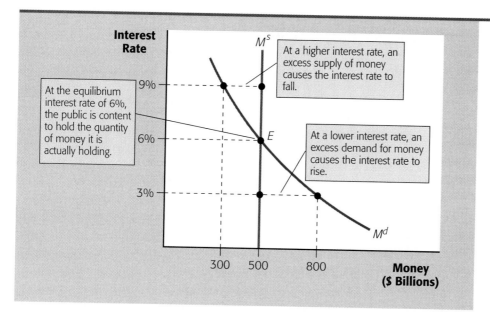

FIGURE 5
Money Market Equilibrium

Within the figure:

Interest Rate

M^S

At a higher interest rate, an excess supply of money causes the interest rate to fall.

At the equilibrium interest rate of 6%, the public is content to hold the quantity of money it is actually holding.

9%

6% E

At a lower interest rate, an excess demand for money causes the interest rate to rise.

3%

M^d

300 500 800

Money ($ Billions)

Can we have faith that the interest rate will reach its equilibrium value in the money market, such as 6 percent in our figure? Indeed we can. In the next section, we explore the forces that drive the money market toward its equilibrium.

How the Money Market Reaches Equilibrium

To understand how the money market reaches its equilibrium, suppose that the interest rate, for some reason, were *not* at its equilibrium value of 6 percent in Figure 5. For example, suppose the interest rate were 9 percent. As the figure shows, at this interest rate the quantity of money demanded would be $300 billion, while the quantity supplied would be $500 billion. Or, put another way, people would *actually* be holding $500 billion of their wealth as money, but they would *want* to hold only $300 billion as money. There would be an **excess supply of money** (the quantity of money supplied would exceed the quantity demanded) equal to $500 billion − $300 billion = $200 billion.

Now comes an important point. Remember that in our analysis, money and bonds are the only two assets available. If people want to hold *less* money than they are currently holding, then, by definition, they must want to hold *more* in bonds than they are currently holding—an **excess demand for bonds.**

> *When there is an excess supply of money in the economy, there is also an excess demand for bonds.*

To understand this more clearly, imagine that instead of the money market, which can seem rather abstract, we were discussing something more concrete: the arrangement of books in a bookcase. Suppose that you have a certain number of books, and you have only two shelves on which to hold all of them: top and bottom. One day, you look at the shelves and decide that, the way you've arranged

Excess supply of money The amount of money supplied exceeds the amount demanded at a particular interest rate.

Excess demand for bonds The amount of bonds demanded exceeds the amount supplied at a particular interest rate.

things, the top shelf has *too many* books. Then, by definition, you must also feel that the bottom shelf has *too few* books. That is, an excess supply of books on the top shelf (it has more books than you want there) is the same as an excess demand for books on the bottom shelf (it has fewer books than you want there).

A similar conclusion applies to the money market. People allocate a given amount of wealth between two different assets: money and bonds. Too much in one asset implies too little in the other.

So far, we've established that if the interest rate were 9 percent, which is higher than its equilibrium value, there would be an excess supply of money, and an excess demand for bonds. What would happen? The public would demand more bonds. Just as there is a market for money, there is also a market for bonds. And as the public begins to demand more bonds, making them scarcer, *the price of bonds will rise*. We can illustrate the steps in our analysis so far as follows:

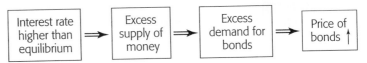

We conclude that, when the interest rate is higher than its equilibrium value, the price of bonds will rise. Why is this important? In order to take our story further, we must first take a detour for a few paragraphs.

An Important Detour: Bond Prices and Interest Rates. A bond, in the simplest terms, is a promise to pay back borrowed funds at a certain date or dates in the future. There are many types of bonds. Some promise to make payments each month or each year for a certain period and then pay back a large sum at the end. Others promise to make just one payment—perhaps 1, 5, 10, or more years from the date the bond is issued. When a large corporation or the government wants to borrow money, it issues a new bond and sells it in the marketplace; the amount borrowed is equal to the price of the bond.

Let's consider a very simple example: a bond that promises to pay to its holder $1,000 exactly one year from today. Suppose that you purchase this bond from the issuer—a firm or government agency—for $800. Then you are lending $800 to the issuer, and you will be paid back $1,000 one year later. What interest rate are you earning on your loan? Let's see: You will be getting back $200 more than you lent, so that is your *interest payment*. The annual interest *rate* is the interest payment over the year divided by the amount of the loan, or $200/$800 = 0.25 or 25 percent.

Now, what if instead of $800, you paid a price of $900 for this very same bond. The bond still promises to pay $1,000 one year from now, so your annual interest payment would now be $100, and your interest rate would be $100/$900 = 0.11 or 11 percent—a considerably lower interest rate. As you can see, the interest rate that you will earn on your bond depends entirely on the *price* of the bond. *The higher the price, the lower the interest rate.*

This general principle applies to virtually all types of bonds, not just the simple one-time-payment bond we've considered here. Bonds promise to pay various sums to their holders at different dates in the future. Therefore, the more you pay for any bond, the lower your overall rate of return, or interest rate, will be. Thus:

When the price of bonds rises, the interest rate falls; when the price of bonds falls, the interest rate rises.[1]

The relationship between bond prices and interest rates helps explain why the government, the press, and the public are so concerned about the *bond market,* where bonds issued in previous periods are bought and sold. This market is sometimes called the *secondary* market for bonds, to distinguish it from the *primary* market where newly issued bonds are bought and sold. When you hear that "the bond market rallied" on a particular day of trading, it means that prices rose in the secondary bond market. This is good news for bond holders. But it is also good news for any person or business that wants to borrow money. When prices rise in the secondary market, they immediately rise in the primary market as well, since newly issued bonds and previously issued bonds are almost perfect substitutes for each other. Therefore, a bond market rally not only means lower interest rates in the secondary market, it also means lower interest rates in the primary market, where firms borrow money by issuing new bonds. Sooner or later, it will also lead to a drop in the interest rate on mortgages, car loans, credit card balances, and even many student loans. This is good news for borrowers. But it is bad news for anyone wishing to lend money, for now they will earn less interest.

Now that you understand the relationship between bond prices and interest rates, let's return to our analysis of the money market.

Back to the Money Market. Look back at Figure 5, and let's recap what you've learned so far. If the interest rate were 9 percent, there would be an excess supply of money, and therefore an excess demand for bonds. The price of bonds would rise. Now we can complete the story. As you've just learned, a rise in the price of bonds means a *decrease* in the interest rate. The complete sequence of events is

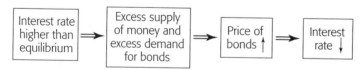

Thus, if the interest is 9 percent in our figure, it will begin to fall. Therefore, 9 percent is *not* the equilibrium interest rate.

How far will the interest rate fall? As long as there continues to be an excess supply of money, and an excess demand for bonds, the public will still be trying to acquire bonds and the interest rate will continue to fall. But notice what happens in the figure as the interest rate falls: The quantity of money demanded *rises.* Finally, when the interest rate reaches 6 percent, the excess supply of money, and therefore the excess demand for bonds, is eliminated. At this point, there is no reason for the interest rate to fall further, so 6 percent is, indeed, our equilibrium interest rate.

---

[1] In our macroeconomic model of the economy, we refer to *the* interest rate. In the real world, there are many types of interest rates: a different one for each type of bond, and still other rates on savings accounts, time deposits, car loans, mortgages, and more. However, all of these interest rates usually move up and down together, even though some may lag behind a few days, weeks, or months. Thus, when bond prices rise, interest rates *generally* will fall, and vice versa.

We can also do the same analysis from the other direction. Suppose the interest rate were *lower* than 6 percent in the figure—say, 3 percent. Then, as you can see in Figure 5, there would be an *excess demand for money,* and an *excess supply of bonds.* In this case, the following would happen:

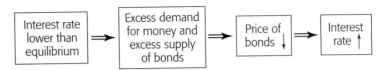

The interest rate would continue to rise until it reached its equilibrium value: 6 percent.

 ## WHAT HAPPENS WHEN THINGS CHANGE?

Now that we have seen how the interest rate is determined in the money market, we turn our attention to *changes* in the interest rate. We'll focus on two questions: (1) What *causes* the equilibrium interest rate to change? and (2) What are the *consequences* of a change in the interest rate? As you are about to see, the Fed can change the interest rate as a matter of policy, or the interest rate can change on its own, as a by-product of other events in the economy. We'll begin with the Fed.

How the Fed Changes the Interest Rate

Changes in the interest rate from day to day, or week to week, are often caused by the Fed. Later in this chapter, you'll learn why the Fed often wants to manipulate the interest rate. For now, we'll focus on how the Fed does this.

Suppose the Fed wants to *lower* the interest rate. Fed officials cannot just declare that the interest rate should be lower. To change the interest rate, the Fed must change the *equilibrium* interest rate in the money market, and it does this by changing the money supply.

Look at Figure 6. Initially, with a money supply of $500 billion, the money market is in equilibrium at point *E,* with an interest rate of 6 percent. To lower the interest rate, the Fed *increases* the money supply through open market purchases of bonds. In the figure, the Fed raises the money supply to $800 billion, shifting the money supply curve rightward. (This is a much greater shift than the Fed would ever actually engineer in practice, but it makes the graph easier to read.) At the old interest rate of 6 percent, there would be an excess supply of money and an excess demand for bonds. This will drive the interest rate down until it reaches its new equilibrium value of 3 percent, at point *F.* The process works like this:

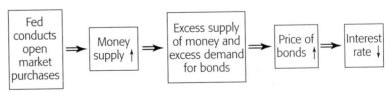

The Fed can *raise* the interest rate as well, through open market *sales* of bonds. In this case, the money supply curve in Figure 6 would shift leftward (not shown), setting off the following sequence of events:

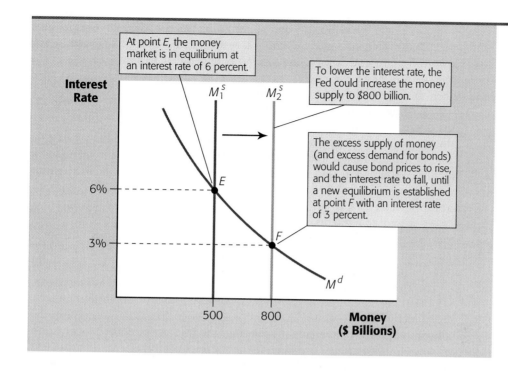

FIGURE 6
An Increase in the Money Supply

At point *E*, the money market is in equilibrium at an interest rate of 6 percent.

To lower the interest rate, the Fed could increase the money supply to $800 billion.

The excess supply of money (and excess demand for bonds) would cause bond prices to rise, and the interest rate to fall, until a new equilibrium is established at point *F* with an interest rate of 3 percent.

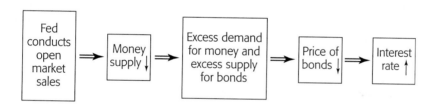

If the Fed increases the money supply by buying government bonds, the interest rate falls. If the Fed decreases the money supply by selling government bonds, the interest rate rises. By controlling the money supply through purchases and sales of bonds, the Fed can also control the interest rate.

HTTP://

You can find recent and historical data on the money supply and interest rates at the Fed's Web site: http://www.federalreserve.gov/rnd.htm.

How Do Interest Rate Changes Affect the Economy?

As you've just learned, if the Fed increases the money supply through open market purchases of bonds, the interest rate will fall. But what then? How is the macroeconomy affected? The answer is: *A drop in the interest rate will boost several different types of spending in the economy.*

How the Interest Rate Affects Spending. First, a lower interest rate stimulates business spending on plant and equipment. This idea came up a few chapters ago in the classical model, but we will go back over it here.

Remember that the interest rate is one of the key costs of any investment project. If a firm must borrow funds, it will have to pay for them at the going rate of interest—for example, by selling a bond at the going price. If the firm uses its *own* funds, so it doesn't have to borrow, the interest rate *still* represents a cost: Each dollar spent on plant and equipment *could* have been lent to someone else at the going interest rate. Thus, the interest rate is the *opportunity cost* of the firm's own funds when they are spent on plant and equipment.

A firm deciding whether to spend on plant and equipment compares the benefits of the project—the increase in future income—with the costs of the project. With a lower interest rate, the costs of funding investment projects are lower, so more projects will get the go-ahead. Other variables affect investment spending as well. But all else equal, a drop in the interest rate will cause an increase in spending on plant and equipment.

Interest rate changes also affect another kind of investment spending: spending on new houses and apartments that are built by developers or individuals. Most people borrow to buy houses or condominiums, and most developers borrow to build apartment buildings. The loan agreement for housing is called a *mortgage*, and mortgage interest rates tend to rise and fall with other interest rates. Thus, when the Fed lowers the interest rate, families find it more affordable to buy homes, and developers find it more profitable to build new apartments. Total investment in new housing increases.

Finally, in addition to investment spending, the interest rate affects consumption spending on big-ticket items such as new cars, furniture, and dishwashers. Economists call these *consumer durables* because they usually last several years. People often borrow to buy consumer durables, and the interest rate they are charged tends to rise and fall with other interest rates in the economy. Spending on new cars, the most expensive durable that most of us buy, is especially sensitive to interest rate changes. Since a lower interest rate causes higher consumption spending at *any* level of disposable income, it causes a *shift* of the consumption function, not a movement along it. Therefore, we consider this impact on consumption to be a rise in autonomous consumption spending, called *a* in our discussion of the consumption function.

We can summarize the impact of money supply changes as follows:

> *When the Fed increases the money supply, the interest rate falls, and spending on three categories of goods increases: plant and equipment, new housing, and consumer durables (especially automobiles). When the Fed decreases the money supply, the interest rate rises, and these categories of spending fall.*

Monetary Policy and the Economy

Two chapters ago ("The Short-Run Macro Model"), you learned that changes in aggregate expenditure cause changes in real GDP through the multiplier process. In this chapter, you've learned that the Federal Reserve, through its control of the money supply, can change the interest rate, and therefore influence aggregate expenditure. Thus, the Fed—through its control of the money supply—has the power to influence real GDP.

When the Fed controls or manipulates the money supply in order to achieve any macroeconomic goal—such as a change in the level of real GDP—it is engaging in **monetary policy.** Let's put all the pieces of our analysis together and see how monetary policy works.

Monetary policy Control or manipulation of the money supply by the Federal Reserve designed to achieve a macroeconomic goal.

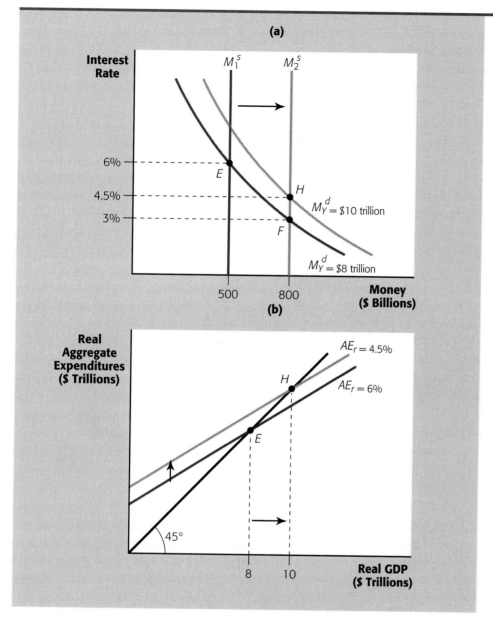

FIGURE 7

Monetary Policy and the Economy

Initially, the Fed has set the money supply at $500 billion, so the interest rate is 6 percent (point E). Given that interest rate, aggregate expenditure is $AE_{r\,=\,6\%}$ in panel (b), and real GDP is $8 trillion (point E).

If the Fed increases the money supply to $800 billion, money market equilibrium moves temporarily to point F in panel (a). The interest rate falls, stimulating interest-sensitive spending and driving aggregate expenditures upward in panel (b). Through the multiplier process, real GDP increases. As it does, the money demand curve shifts rightward in panel (a). In the new equilibrium, real GDP is $10 trillion and the interest rate is 4.5 percent (point H).

In Figure 7, we revisit the short-run macro model, but we now include the money market in our analysis. In panel (a), the Fed has initially set the money supply at $500 billion. Equilibrium is at point *E*, with an interest rate (*r*) of 6 percent. Panel (b) shows the familiar short-run aggregate expenditure diagram, with equilibrium at point *E*, and equilibrium GDP equal to $8 trillion.

But notice the new labels in the figure. The letter *r* stands for the interest rate, and *Y* stands for real GDP and real income. The aggregate expenditure line has the subscript "*r* = 6%," and the money demand curve has the subscript "*Y* = $8 trillion." Why these additional labels?

Recall that the money demand curve will shift if there is a change in real income. Therefore, our particular money demand curve is drawn for a particular level of real income, the level determined in panel (b), or $8 trillion. Similarly, as you are about to see, a change in the interest rate will cause the aggregate expenditure line to shift. Therefore, our aggregate expenditure line is drawn for a particular interest rate, the one determined in the money market, or 6 percent. There is an *interdependence* between these two panels: The equilibrium in each one depends on the equilibrium in the other.

Now we suppose that the Fed increases the money supply to $800 billion. (Again, this is an unrealistically large change in the money supply, but it makes it easier to see the change in the figure.) In the upper panel, the money market equilibrium moves from point *E* toward point *F*, and the interest rate begins to drop. (It won't drop all the way down to 3 percent, because the money demand curve will start shifting before we are finished.) The drop in the interest rate causes planned investment spending on plant and equipment and on new housing to rise. It also causes an increase in consumption spending—especially on consumer durables like automobiles—to rise at any level of income. This is an increase in autonomous consumption spending (*a*). In the lower panel, the rise in spending causes the aggregate expenditure line to shift upward, setting off the multiplier effect and increasing equilibrium GDP. The rise in income causes the money demand curve to shift rightward, since the demand for money is greater when income is higher.

> **Shift Versus Movement Along the *AE* Line** When thinking about the effects of monetary policy, try not to confuse movements *along* the aggregate expenditure line with *shifts* of the line itself. We move *along* the line only when a change in *income* causes spending to change. The line shifts when something *other* than a change in income causes spending to change.
>
> When the Fed changes the interest rate, both types of changes occur, but it's important to keep the order straight. *First,* the drop in the interest rate (something other than income) causes interest-sensitive spending to change, *shifting* the aggregate expenditure line. *Then,* increases in income in each round of the multiplier cause further increases in spending, moving us *along* the new aggregate expenditure line.

DANGEROUS CURVES

To find the final equilibrium in the economy, we would need quite a bit of information about how sensitive spending is to the drop in the interest rate, as well as how changes in income feed back into the money market to affect the interest rate. In Figure 7, we've illustrated just one possibility, in which the new equilibrium is at point *H* in both the money market and the aggregate expenditure diagrams. At this new equilibrium, the interest rate ends up at 4.5 percent, so the higher aggregate expenditure line is labeled "*r* = 4.5%." Equilibrium GDP has risen to $10 trillion, so the new higher money demand curve is labeled "*Y* = $10 trillion." In the end, we see that the Fed, by increasing the money supply and lowering the interest rate, has increased the level of output.

We've covered a lot of ground to reach our conclusion, so let's review the highlights of how monetary policy works. This is what happens when the Fed conducts open market purchases of bonds:

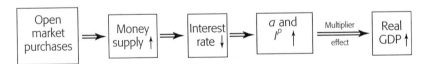

Open market *sales* by the Fed have exactly the opposite effects. In this case, the money supply curve in Figure 7 would shift leftward (not shown), driving the interest rate up. The rise in the interest rate would cause a decrease in interest-sensitive spending (*a* and *I^p*), shifting the aggregate expenditure line downward. Equilibrium GDP would fall by a multiple of the initial decrease in spending.

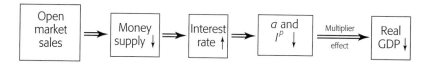

Fiscal Policy (and Other Spending Changes) Revisited

Two chapters ago, we discussed how fiscal policy affects the economy in the short run. For example, an increase in government purchases causes output to rise, and in successive rounds of the multiplier, spending and output rise still more. Now that we've added the money market to our analysis, it's time to revisit fiscal policy. As you'll see, its effects are now a bit more complicated.

Figure 8 shows the money market and the familiar short-run aggregate expenditure diagram. Initially, we have equilibrium in both panels. In panel (a), the money market equilibrium is point E, with the interest rate at 6 percent. In panel (b), the initial aggregate expenditure line, labeled "$r = 6\%$," is consistent with the interest rate we've found in the money market. As you can see, with this aggregate expenditure line, the equilibrium is at point E, with real GDP equal to $10 trillion, just as we assumed when we drew the money demand curve in panel (a).

An Increase in Government Purchases. Now let's see what happens when the government changes its fiscal policy, say, by increasing government purchases (G) by $2 trillion. Panel (b) shows the initial effect: The aggregate expenditure line shifts upward, by $2 trillion, to the topmost aggregate expenditure line. This new aggregate expenditure line is drawn for the same interest rate as the original line: $r = 6\%$. The shift illustrates what *would* happen if there were no change in the interest rate, as in our analysis of fiscal policy two chapters ago.

As you've learned, the increase in government purchases will set off the multiplier process, increasing GDP and income in each round. *If this were the end of the story,* the result would be a rise in real GDP equal to $[1/(1 - MPC)] \times \Delta G$. In our example, with an MPC of 0.6, the multiplier would be $1/(1 - 0.6) = 2.5$. The new equilibrium would be at point F, with GDP equal to $15 trillion—a rise of $5 trillion.

But point F is *not* the end of our story—not when we include effects in the money market. As income increases, the money demand curve in panel (a) will shift rightward, raising the interest rate. As a result, autonomous consumption (a) and investment spending (I) will decrease and shift the aggregate expenditure line downward. That is,

> *an increase in government purchases, which by itself shifts the aggregate expenditure line upward, also sets in motion forces that shift it downward.*

We can outline these forces as follows:

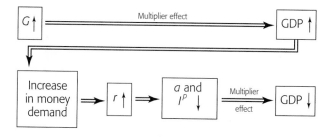

Net Effect: GDP↑, but by less due to effect of r ↑

FIGURE 8
**Fiscal Policy and the
Money Market**

*The economy is initially in equi-
librium with an interest rate of 6
percent in panel (a) and real
GDP of $10 trillion in panel (b).
An increase in government purchases shifts the aggregate expenditure line upward, triggering the
multiplier process. If the interest
rate did not change, equilibrium
would be reestablished at point F
in panel (b) with real GDP of
$15 trillion. But the increase in
GDP increases money demand in
panel (a), driving the interest rate
upward to 8 percent at point L.
That reduces interest-sensitive
spending, lowering aggregate expenditure to* AE$_{r\,=\,8\%}$ *in panel (b)
so that the real GDP at the new
equilibrium is $13.5 trillion
(point* L*).*

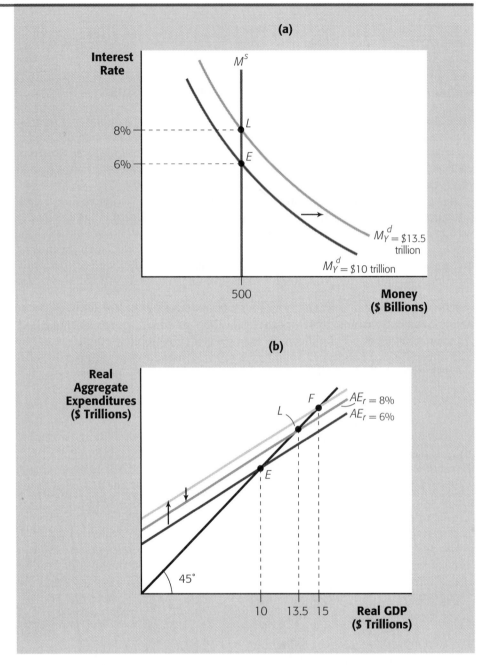

Thus, at the same time as the increase in government purchases has a *positive* multiplier effect on GDP, the decrease in *a* and *I* have *negative* multiplier effects. Which
effect dominates? The positive multiplier effect. Why? Because the only force pulling
GDP down—the higher interest rate—*depends upon* a rise in GDP. (It is the rise in
GDP that shifts the money demand curve and drives up the interest rate.) If the negative effect on GDP were so strong that GDP actually decreased, then the money demand curve would shift leftward, not rightward. Therefore, the interest rate would
be lower, not higher, and there would be no force pulling GDP down at all.

Thus, we know that an increase in government purchases causes GDP to rise. But the rise is smaller than the simple multiplier formula suggests. That's because the simple multiplier ignores the moderating effect of a rise in the interest rate on GDP.

In the short run, an increase in government purchases causes real GDP to rise, but not by as much as if the interest rate had not increased.

Let's sum up the characteristics of the new equilibrium after an increase in government purchases:

- The aggregate expenditure line is higher, but by less than ΔG.
- Real GDP and real income are higher, but the rise is less than $[1/(1 - MPC)] \times \Delta G$.
- The money demand curve has shifted rightward, because real income is higher.
- The interest rate is higher, because money demand has increased.
- Autonomous consumption and investment spending are lower, because the interest rate is higher.

Figure 8 indicates one possible result that is consistent with all of these requirements. In the figure, the new equilibrium occurs at point L in both panels, with the new equilibrium GDP at $13.5 trillion and the new equilibrium interest rate at 8 percent. Notice that real GDP has risen, but by only $3.5 trillion—not the $5 trillion suggested by the simple multiplier formula. Moreover, the two panels of the diagram are consistent with each other. The aggregate expenditure line (labeled "$r = 8\%$") corresponds to the equilibrium interest rate in the money market. The money demand curve (labeled "$Y = \$13.5$ trillion") corresponds to the equilibrium GDP in the aggregate expenditure diagram.

Crowding Out Once Again. Our analysis illustrates an interesting by-product of fiscal policy. Comparing our initial equilibrium (point E in both panels) to the final equilibrium (point L), we see that government purchases increase. But because of the rise in the interest rate, *investment spending has decreased.*

What about consumption spending? It is influenced by two opposing forces. The rise in the interest rate causes *some* types of consumption spending (e.g., on automobiles) to decrease, but the rise in *income* makes other types of consumption spending *increase.* Thus, an increase in government purchases may increase or decrease consumption spending, depending on which effect is stronger.

Summing up:

When effects in the money market are included in the short-run macro model, an increase in government purchases raises the interest rate and crowds out some private investment spending. It may also crowd out consumption spending.

This should sound familiar. In the classical, long-run model, an increase in government purchases also causes crowding out. But there is one important difference between crowding out in the classical model and the effects we are outlining here. In the classical model, there is *complete crowding out*: Investment spending and consumption spending fall by the same amount that government purchases rise. As a result, total spending does not change at all, and neither does real GDP. This is why, in the *long run,* we expect fiscal policy to have no effect on real GDP.

In the short run, however, our conclusion is somewhat different. While we expect *some* crowding out from an increase in government purchases, *it is not complete*. Investment spending falls, and consumption spending *may* fall, but together, they do not drop by as much as the rise in government purchases. In the short run, real GDP rises.

Other Spending Changes. So far, we've focused on the impact on the economy of a change in government purchases. But our analysis extends to *any* shock that shifts the aggregate expenditure line. Positive shocks would shift the aggregate expenditure line upward, just as in Figure 8. More specifically:

> *Increases in government purchases, planned investment, net exports, and autonomous consumption, as well as decreases in taxes, all shift the aggregate expenditure line upward. Real GDP rises, but so does the interest rate. The rise in equilibrium GDP is smaller than if the interest rate remained constant.*

For example, a $2 trillion increase in investment spending shifts the aggregate expenditure line upward by $2 trillion, as in Figure 8. If there were no rise in the interest rate, real GDP would rise according to the simple multiplier of $1/(1 - 0.6) =$ 2.5. Applying this multiplier to a $2 trillion increase in investment tells us that real GDP would rise by a full $5 trillion. But once again, the rise in GDP does drive up the interest rate in the money market, which works to decrease investment and interest-sensitive consumption. And once again, GDP will rise, but not by as much as the simple multiplier suggests.

Negative shocks shift the aggregate expenditure line *downward*. More specifically:

> *Decreases in government purchases, investment, net exports, and autonomous consumption, as well as increases in taxes, all shift the aggregate expenditure line downward. Real GDP falls, but so does the interest rate. The decline in equilibrium GDP is smaller than if the interest rate remained constant.*

What About the Fed? In our analysis of spending shocks, we've made an implicit but important assumption. Look back at Figure 8. Notice that, from beginning to end, the money supply curve never shifted. This implies that the Fed just stands by, not interfering at all with the changes we've been describing. More specifically, we've been assuming that *the Fed does not change the money supply in response to shifts in the aggregate expenditure line.*

While this assumption has helped us focus on the impact of spending shocks, it is not the way the Fed has conducted policy during the past few decades. Instead, the Fed has usually responded to neutralize the impact of spending shocks. That is, it has used monetary policy to prevent spending shocks from changing GDP at all. You'll learn why, and how, the Fed does this when we revisit monetary policy in the chapter after next.

ARE THERE TWO THEORIES OF THE INTEREST RATE?

At the beginning of this chapter, you were reminded that you had already learned a different theory of how the interest rate is determined in the economy. In the classical model, the interest rate is determined in the *market for loanable funds*. In this chapter, you learned that the interest rate is determined in the *money market*, where people make decisions about holding their wealth as money and bonds. Which theory is correct?

The answer is: Both are correct. The classical model, you remember, tells us what happens in the economy in the *long run*. Therefore, when we ask what changes the interest rate over long periods of time—many years or even a decade—we should think about the market for loanable funds. But over shorter time periods—days, weeks, or months—we should use the money market model presented in this chapter.

Why don't we use the classical loanable funds model to determine the interest rate in the short run? Because, as you've seen, the economy behaves differently in the short run than it does in the long run. For example, in the classical model, output is automatically at full employment. But in the short run, output changes as the economy goes through booms and recessions. These changes in output affect the loanable funds market in ways that the classical model does not consider. For example, flip back to the chapter on the classical model and look at Figure 8 there. Recessions, which decrease household income, also decrease household saving at any given interest rate: With less income, households will spend less *and* save less. The supply of loanable funds curve would shift leftward in the diagram, and the interest rate would rise. The classical model—because it ignores recessions—ignores these short-run changes in the supply of loanable funds.

The classical model also ignores an important idea discussed in this chapter: that the public continuously chooses how to divide its wealth between money and bonds. In the short run, the public's preferences over money and bonds can change, and this, in turn, can change the interest rate. This idea does not appear in the classical model.

Of course, in the long run, the classical model gives us an accurate picture of how the economy and the interest rate behave. Recessions and booms don't last forever, so the economy returns to full employment. Thus, in the long run we needn't worry about recessions causing shifts in the supply of loanable funds curve. Also, changes in preferences for holding money and bonds are rather short-lived. We can ignore these changes when we take a long-run view.

> In the long run, we view the interest rate as determined in the market for loanable funds, where household saving is lent to businesses and the government. In the short run, we view the interest rate as determined in the money market, where wealth holders adjust their wealth between money and bonds, and the Fed participates by controlling the money supply.

EXPECTATIONS AND THE MONEY MARKET

One important insight of our money market analysis in this chapter is the inverse relationship between a bond's price and the interest rate it earns for its holder. When the interest rate falls, bond prices rise—and vice versa. Therefore, if people *expect* the interest rate to fall, they *expect* the price of bonds to rise. And this expectation, in turn, will affect the money market.

To see this more clearly, imagine (pleasantly) that you hold a bond promising to pay you $100,000 in exactly one year and that the going annual interest rate is 5 percent. The going price for your bond will be $95,238. Why? If someone bought your bond at that price, she would earn $100,000 − $95,238 = $4,762 in interest. Since the bond cost $95,238, the buyer's rate of return would be $4,762/$95,238 = 0.05, or

FIGURE 9
Interest Rate Expectations

If households and firms expect the interest rate to rise in the future, their demand for money will increase today. Starting from equilibrium at point E, an expected increase in the interest rate from 5 percent to 10 percent will increase money demand to M_2^d. The result is a self-fulfilling prophecy: The interest rate increases to 10 percent today.

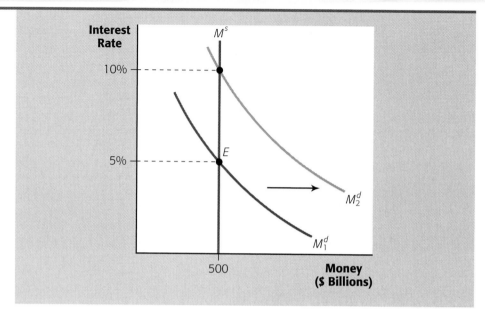

5 percent—the going rate of interest. If you tried to charge more than $95,238 for the bond, its rate of return would be less than 5 percent, so no one would buy it; they could always earn 5 percent by buying another bond that pays the going rate of interest.

Now suppose that you *expect* the interest rate to rise to 10 percent in the near future, say, next week. (This is an unrealistically large change in the interest rate in so short a time, but it makes the point dramatically.) Then you expect the going price for your bond to fall to about $90,909. At that price, a buyer would earn $100,000 − $90,909 = $9,091 in interest, so the buyer's rate of return would be $9,091/$90,909 = 0.10, or 10 percent. Thus, if you believe that the interest rate is about to rise from 5 to 10 percent, you also believe the price of your bond is about to fall from $95,238 to $90,909.

What would you do?

Logically, you would want to sell your bond *now,* before the price drops. If you still want to hold this type of bond later, you can always buy it back next week at the lower price and gain from the transaction. Thus, if you expect the interest rate to rise in the future, you will want to exchange your bonds for money *today.* Your demand for money will increase.

Of course, if *you* expect the interest rate to rise (and the price of bonds to drop), and your expectation is reasonable, others will probably feel the same way. They, too, will want to trade in their bonds for money. Thus, if the expectation is widespread, there will be an increase in the demand for money economy-wide.

> *A general expectation that interest rates will rise (bond prices will fall) in the future will cause the money demand curve to shift rightward in the present.*

Notice that when people expect the interest rate to rise, we *shift* the money demand curve, rather than move along it. People will want to hold more money at any *current* interest rate.

Figure 9 shows what will happen in the money market when people expect the interest rate to rise. Initially, with the money supply equal to $500 billion, the equilibrium is at point *E* and the interest rate is 5 percent. But the expected rise in the interest rate shifts the money demand curve rightward. After the shift, there is an excess demand for money and an excess supply of bonds at the original interest rate of 5 percent. The price of bonds will fall, which means the interest rate will rise.

How far will the interest rate rise? That depends. Imagine a simple case where *everyone* in the economy expected the interest rate to rise to 10 percent next week. Then no one would want to hold bonds at any *current* interest rate less than 10 percent. For example, if the interest rate rose to 9 percent, people would still expect it to rise further (and the price of bonds to fall further), so they would still want to sell their bonds. Therefore, to return the money market to equilibrium, the interest rate would rise to exactly the level that people expected. This is the case we've illustrated in Figure 9, where the money demand curve shifts rightward by just enough to raise the interest rate to 10 percent. More generally:

> *When the public as a whole expects the interest rate to rise in the future, they will drive up the interest rate in the present.*

When information comes along that makes people believe that interest rates will rise and bond prices fall in the near future, the result is an immediate rise in the interest rate and a fall in bond prices. This principle operates even if the information is false and there is ultimately no reason for the interest rate to rise. Thus, a general expectation that interest rates will rise can be a *self-fulfilling prophecy*: Because people believe it, it actually happens. Their expectation alone is enough to drive up the interest rate.

This immediate response to information about the future—and the possibility of a self-fulfilling prophecy—works in the opposite direction as well:

> *When the public expects the interest rate to drop in the future, they will drive down the interest rate in the present.*

In this case, the public expects bond prices to rise, so they try to shift their wealth from money to bonds. In Figure 9, the money demand curve would shift leftward (not shown). The price of bonds would rise, and the interest rate would fall, just as was originally expected.

USING THE THEORY
The Fed and the Recession of 2001

Two chapters ago ("The Short-Run Macro Model"), we began an analysis of our most recent recession, which officially lasted from March to November of 2001. We saw that an investment spending shock caused a decrease in aggregate expenditure, which in turn caused equilibrium GDP and employment to drop. But we left two questions unanswered: (1) What did policy makers do to try to prevent the recession, and to deal with it once it started? and (2) Why did consumption spending behave abnormally, rising as income fell and preventing the recession from becoming a more serious downturn? Now that you've learned about monetary policy, we can begin to answer these questions.

Starting in January 2001—three months before the official start of the recession—the Fed began to worry. Although the economy was operating

© MATT MENDELSOHN/CORBIS

at its potential output (the unemployment rate the previous month was 3.9 percent), there was danger on the horizon: Investment spending had already decreased for two quarters in a row. The decrease in investment spending had started a negative multiplier effect, which was working its way through the economy and could ultimately cause a recession. Other factors made the Fed worry that investment spending could decrease further. And a sharp decrease in stock prices over the previous year—which had destroyed billions of dollars in household wealth—suggested that consumption spending might begin to fall as well.

The upper right panel (b) of Figure 10, which shows the aggregate expenditure diagram, illustrates the situation. Initially, the economy was at point A, with real GDP in the first quarter of 2001 (measured in 1996 dollars) equal to $9,243 billion. The Fed feared that if it did nothing, the investment slowdown would shift the aggregate expenditure line downward, moving the equilibrium to a point like B, with GDP falling (in our diagram) to $9,000 billion.

The Fed decided to take action, indicated by the lower panels of Figure 10. The lower left panel (c) tracks the money supply measure M1 (monthly) from the period before and after January 2001. It shows that beginning in January, the Fed began increasing M1 rapidly. The lower right panel (d) shows changes in the *federal funds rate*—the interest rate that the Fed watches most closely when it conducts monetary policy. The **federal funds rate** is the interest rate that banks with excess reserves charge for lending reserves to other banks. Although it is just an interest rate for lending among banks, many other interest rates in the economy vary with it closely, so it gives us a good idea of how interest rates in general ("the interest rate" in our highly aggregated macro model) were changing during this period. As you can see, the federal funds rate fell continually and dramatically during the year, from 6.4 percent down to 1.75 percent. In September of 2001, during which real GDP probably hit bottom, the federal funds rate averaged about 3.1 percent.

Now look at the upper left panel (a), which shows the effect of the Fed policy in the money market. In January 2001, the money market was in equilibrium at point A, with the M1 measure of the money supply at $1,093 billion and the federal funds rate at 6.4 percent. As the money supply increased to an average of about $1,170 during the third quarter of 2001, the money supply curve shifted rightward and the interest rate fell. In panel (b), this had the effect of making the recession more mild: Instead of falling to point B, the economy ended up at point C, with real GDP hitting bottom at about $9,130 billion in September 2001.[2] Notice that, in panel (a), the final money demand curve ($M^D_{Y = \$9,130 \text{ billion}}$) lies to the left of the initial money demand curve, because it is associated with a lower level of income. The new equilibrium for the money market—point C—is consistent with the new equilibrium in the aggregate expenditure diagram.

Although the Fed's policy did not completely prevent the recession, it no doubt saved the economy from a more severe and longer-lasting one. The lower interest rate was especially helpful in maintaining new-home construction, a category of investment spending that is especially sensitive to the interest rate.

The Fed's policy also helps us understand the other question we raised about the 2001 recession: the continued rise in consumption spending throughout the period. Lower interest rates, as you've now learned, stimulate consumption spending on consumer durables, especially automobiles. Indeed, helped by lower interest rates, auto sales rose in every quarter of 2001.

Federal funds rate The interest rate charged for loans of reserves among banks.

---

[2] Based on monthly real GDP estimates provided by Macroeconomic Advisors, a private consulting firm, to the National Bureau of Economic Research (NBER) (available at *http://www.nber.org/cycles/hall.pdf*).

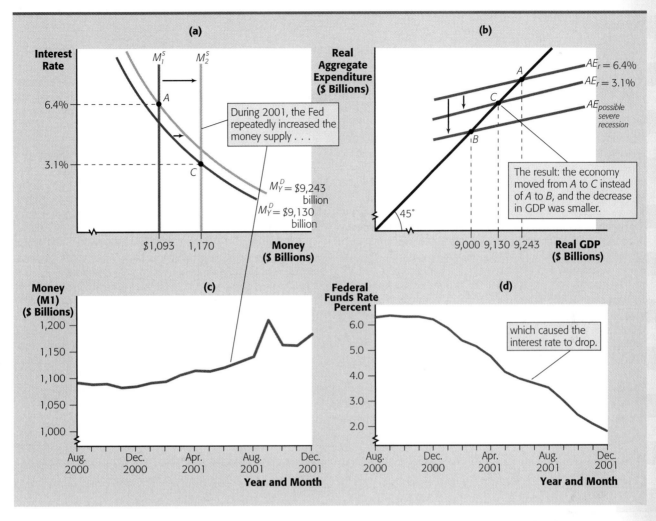

FIGURE 10
The Fed in Action: 2001

Moreover, when interest rates drop dramatically and rapidly—as they did in 2001—a frenzy of *home mortgage refinancing* can occur: Households rush to exchange their existing, higher-interest-rate mortgages for new mortgages at a lower interest rate. After a refinance, monthly mortgage payments are reduced, freeing up disposable income to be spent on goods and services. But many households go further, taking advantage of the refinancing to borrow even more than they owed on their original mortgage. This provides them with a one-time burst of cash to spend. Home refinancing and additional borrowing on homes seemed to play a major role in boosting consumption spending during the recession of 2001.

As you've read these pages, some questions may have formed in your mind. Why wasn't the Fed able to prevent the recession entirely? Couldn't the Fed have reduced the interest rate even more rapidly than it did?

There are, in general, good reasons for the Fed to be somewhat cautious in reducing interest rates. Over the next two chapters, you'll learn some of the reasons for the Fed's caution, and why most economists—despite the recession of 2001—give the Fed high marks for its actions during *that year*.

But you'll also learn that Fed policies during the year or so *before* 2001 may have actually contributed to the recession.

Summary

The interest rate is a key macroeconomic variable. This chapter explores how the supply and demand for money interact to determine the interest rate in the short run, and how the Federal Reserve can adjust the money supply to change the interest rate.

An individual's demand for money indicates the fraction of wealth that person wishes to hold in the form of money, at different interest rates. Money is useful as a means of payment, but holding money means sacrificing the interest that could be earned by holding bonds instead. The higher the interest rate, the larger the fraction of their wealth people will hold in the form of bonds, and the smaller the fraction they will hold as money.

The demand for money is sensitive to the interest rate, but it also depends on the price level, real income, and expectations. An increase in the price level, higher real income, or an increase in the expected future interest rate can each shift the money demand curve to the right.

The money supply is under the control of the Fed and is independent of the interest rate. Equilibrium in the money market occurs at the intersection of the downward-sloping money demand curve and the vertical money supply curve. The interest rate will adjust so that the quantity of money demanded by households and firms just equals the quantity of money supplied by the Fed and the banking system.

Conditions in the money market mirror conditions in the bond market. If the interest rate is above equilibrium in the money market, there will be an excess supply of money there.

People *want to* hold less money than they actually *do* hold, which means that they wish to hold more bonds than they do hold. (An excess supply of money means an excess demand for bonds.) The price of bonds will rise and the interest rate will fall. Thus, an excess supply of money will cause the interest rate to fall. Similarly, an excess demand for money will cause the interest rate to rise.

The Fed can increase the money supply through an open market purchase of bonds, and decrease it through an open market sale. An increase in the money supply creates an excess supply of money. Very quickly, the interest rate will fall so that the public is willing to hold the now-higher money supply. A decrease in the money supply will drive up the interest rate.

Changes in the interest rate affect interest-sensitive forms of spending—firms' spending on plant and equipment, new housing constructions, and households' purchases of "big-ticket" consumer durables. By lowering the interest rate, the Fed can stimulate aggregate expenditures and increase GDP through the multiplier process. Fiscal policy decisions to stimulate the economy, such as an increase in government purchases, raises the interest rate and causes a decrease in investment spending and (possibly) consumption spending. This partial crowding out of spending reduces the multiplier effect of fiscal policy. Finally, expectations of future interest rate changes can become self-fulfilling prophecies.

Key Terms

Excess demand for bonds
Excess supply of money
Federal funds rate

Monetary policy
Money demand curve
Money supply curve

Wealth constraint

Review Questions   *Answers to even-numbered Questions and Problems can be found on the text Web site at http://hall-lieb.swlearning.com.*

1. Why do individuals choose to hold some of their wealth in the form of money? Besides individual tastes, what factors help determine how much money an individual holds?

2. Why does the money demand curve slope downward? Which of the following result in a shift of the money demand curve and which result in a movement along the curve? If there is a shift, in which direction?
   a. The Fed lowers interest rates.
   b. The Fed raises interest rates.
   c. The price level falls.
   d. The price level rises.
   e. Income increases.
   f. Income decreases.

3. Why is the economy's money supply curve vertical? What causes the money supply curve to shift?

4. What sequence of events brings the money market to equilibrium if there is an excess supply of money? An excess demand for money?

5. The text mentions that starting in January 2001, the Fed began buying government bonds, and as a result, the interest rate fell. Explain how the Fed's purchase of bonds led to a lower interest rate.

6. Describe how an increase in the interest rate affects spending on the following:
   a. plant and equipment
   b. new housing
   c. consumer durables

7. Does a change in expectations about the interest rate result in a shift in the money demand curve or a movement

along it? Explain what happens in the money market when people expect the interest rate to fall.

8. Why do we have one theory for how the interest rate is determined in the long run (see the chapter on the classical model), and another theory of how the interest rate is determined in the short run (this chapter)? Briefly, what determines the interest rate in the short run? In the long run?

9. How do people reallocate their wealth holdings if they expect interest rates to fall? What effect do their actions have on the interest rate?

10. What is the *federal funds rate*?

Problems and Exercises

1. Assume the demand deposit multiplier is 10. For each of the following, state the impact on the money supply curve (the direction it will shift, and the amount of the shift).
   a. The Fed purchases bonds worth $10 billion.
   b. The Fed sells bonds worth $5 billion.

2. Assume the demand deposit multiplier is 7. For each of the following, state the impact on the money supply curve (the direction it will shift, and the amount of the shift).
   a. The Fed purchases bonds worth $28 million.
   b. The Fed sells bonds worth $17 million.

3. A bond promises to pay $500 one year from now. For the following prices, find the corresponding interest payments and interest rates that the bond offers.

Price	Amount Paid in One Year	Interest Payment	Interest Rate
$375	$500	____	____
$425	$500	____	____
$450	$500	____	____
$500	$500	____	____

As the price of the bond rises, what happens to the bond's interest rate?

4. A bond promises to pay $20,000 one year from now.
   a. Complete the following chart.

Price	Amount Paid in One Year	Interest Payment	Interest Rate	Quantity of Money Demanded
	$2000			$2300 billion
	$1500			$2600 billion
	$1000			$2900 billion
	$500			$3200 billion
	$0			$3500 billion

   b. Draw a graph of the money market, assuming that it is currently in equilibrium at an interest rate of 5.26 percent. What is the price of this bond? How large is the money supply?
   c. Find the new interest rate and the new bond price if the money supply increases by $300 billion. Show this on your graph.

5. "A general expectation that the interest rate will fall can be a self-fulfilling prophecy." Explain what this means.

6. Suppose that, in an attempt to prevent the economy from overheating, the Fed raises the interest rate. Illustrate graphically, using a diagram similar to Figure 7 in this chapter, the effect on the money supply, interest rate, and GDP.

7. For each of the following events, state (1) the impact on the money demand curve, and (2) whether the Fed should increase or decrease the money supply if it wants to keep the interest rate unchanged. (*Hint:* It will help to draw a diagram of the money market for each case.)
   a. People start making more of their purchases over the Internet, using credit cards.
   b. Greater fear of credit card fraud makes people stop buying goods over the Internet with credit cards, and discourages the use of credit cards in other types of purchases as well.
   c. A new type of electronic account is created in which your funds are held in bonds up to the second you make a purchase. Then—when you buy something—just the right amount of bonds are transferred to the ownership of the seller. (*Hint:* Would you want to increase or decrease the amount of your wealth in the form of money after this new type of account were available?)

8. A fellow student in your economics class stops you in the hallway and says: "An increase in the demand for money causes the interest rate to rise. But a rise in the interest rate causes people to demand *less* money. Therefore, increases in money demand largely cancel themselves out, and have very little effect on the interest rate." Is this correct? Why or why not? (*Hint:* Draw a graph.)

9. In a later chapter, you will learn that a drop in the interest rate has *another* channel of influence on real GDP: It causes a depreciation of the dollar (that is, it makes the dollar cheaper to foreigners), which, in turn, increases our net exports.

a. When we take account of the effect on net exports, does a given change in the money supply have *more* or *less* of an impact on real GDP?

b. Suppose that the Fed wants to stimulate the economy as during 2001. Should the Fed lower the interest rate by more or by less when it takes the impact on net ex-

ports into account (compared to the case of no impact on net exports)? Explain.

10. Figure 10 (c) shows a spike in money growth during September 2001. Using what you know about bonds versus money and the money demand curve, explain why this spike might have occurred.

Challenge Questions

1. Determine whether *fiscal policy* is *more* or *less* effective in changing GDP when autonomous consumption and investment spending are *very sensitive* to changes in the interest rate, and explain your reasoning.

2. In Problem 7, you were asked how the *net export* effect changes the potency of monetary policy. Answer the same question about fiscal policy (that is, does the net export effect make fiscal policy more or less potent in changing GDP?).

3. A fellow student in your economics class is confused again: "Economics makes no sense. On the one hand, we're told that if everyone expects the interest rate to rise, then everyone will sell bonds, and that will cause the price of bonds to fall (and the interest rate to rise). Fair enough. But in the real world, no one can sell a bond unless someone else buys it. And if everyone expects the price of bonds to fall, no one will buy them. Therefore,

no one can *sell* them either, and, therefore, there will be no change in the price of bonds or the interest rate." Can you resolve your friend's confusion?

4. Look back at Figure 10. Notice that from September to October 2001, the Fed actually *decreased* the money supply, and yet the interest rate continued to fall between those two months. Explain how that might be possible, and illustrate with a graph.

5. When the Fed intervenes in the economy it worries not only about how its decisions will affect the interest rate via changes in the money *supply*, but also about how its statements might affect the interest rate via changes in the money *demand*. Explain how statements by the Fed about its intentions can change the demand for money. How this can make the Fed's job in steering the economy more complex?

 *Applications*   *These exercises require access to Hall/Lieberman Xtra! If Xtra! did not come with your book, visit http://hallxtra.swlearning.com to purchase.*

1. Use your Xtra! password at the Hall and Lieberman Web site (http://hallxtra.swlearning.com), select this chapter, and under Economic Applications, click on EconDebate. Choose *Macroeconomics: Money and the Financial System*, and scroll down to find the debate, "Does Dollarization Benefit Developing Economies?" Read the debate, and use the information to answer the following questions.

a. What kind of policies result in high and unstable inflation rate for the developing economies. What is the cost of dollarization to these economies?

b. Under *Primary Resources and Data*, click on the Federal Reserve Board's Web link. Click on the following Web page: http://www.federalreserve.gov/fomc/fundsrate.htm. What is the present intended federal funds rate? Can you explain the trend in this rate? Read the article titled "Open Market Operations in 1990s," *Federal Reserve Bulletin*, http://www.federalreserve.gov/pubs/bulletin/1997/199711lead.pdf, and explain why the Fed relinquished M2 in setting interest rates.

Aggregate Demand and Aggregate Supply

Economic fluctuations are facts of life. If you need a reminder, look back at Figure 1 in the chapter titled "Economic Fluctuations." There you can see that while potential GDP tends to move upward year after year, due to economic growth, *actual* GDP tends to rise above and fall below potential over shorter periods.

But the figure also reveals another important fact about the economy: Deviations from potential output don't last forever. When output dips below or rises above potential, the economy returns to potential output after a few quarters or years. True, in some of these episodes, government policy—either fiscal or monetary—helped the economy return to full employment more quickly. But even without corrective policies—such as during long parts of the Great Depression of the 1930s—the economy shows a remarkable tendency to begin moving back toward potential output. Why? And what, exactly, is the mechanism that brings us back to our potential when we have strayed from it? These are the questions we will address in this chapter. And we'll address them by studying the behavior of a variable that we've put aside for several chapters: the price level.

The chapter begins by exploring the relationship between the price level and output. This is a two-way relationship, as you can see in Figure 1 in *this* chapter. On the one hand, changes in the price level cause changes in real GDP. This causal relationship is illustrated by the *aggregate demand curve*, which we will discuss shortly. On

827

FIGURE 1

The Two-Way Relationship Between Output and the Price Level

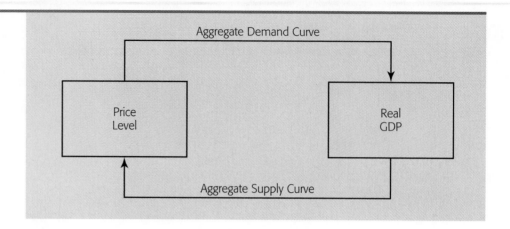

the other hand, changes in real GDP cause changes in the price level. This relationship is summarized by the *aggregate supply curve,* to which we will turn later.

Once we've developed the aggregate demand and supply curves, we'll be able to use them to understand how changes in the price level—sometimes gently, other times more harshly—steer the economy back toward potential output.

THE AGGREGATE DEMAND CURVE

Our first step in understanding how the price level affects the economy is an important fact: When the price level rises, the money demand curve shifts rightward. Why? Remember that the money demand curve tells us how much of their wealth people want to hold as money (as opposed to bonds) at each interest rate. People hold bonds because of the interest they pay; people hold money because of its convenience. Each day, as we make purchases, we need cash or funds in our checking account to pay for them. If the price level rises, so that our purchases become more expensive, we'll need to hold more of our wealth as money just to achieve the same level of convenience. Thus, at any given interest rate, the demand for money increases, and the money demand curve shifts rightward.

The shift in money demand, and its impact on the economy, is illustrated in Figure 2. Panel (a) has our familiar money market diagram. We'll assume that, initially, the price level in the economy is equal to 100. With this price level, the money market is in equilibrium at point *E*, with an interest rate of 6 percent.

In panel (b), equilibrium GDP is at point *E*, with output equal to $10 trillion. The aggregate expenditure line is marked "*r* = 6%," which is the equilibrium interest rate we just found in the money market.

Now let's imagine a rather substantial rise in the price level, from 100 to 140. What will happen in the economy? The initial impact is in the money market. The money demand curve will start to shift rightward, and the interest rate will rise. Next, in panel (b), the higher interest rate decreases interest-sensitive spending—business investment, new housing, and consumer durables. The aggregate expenditure line shifts downward, and equilibrium real GDP decreases. All of these changes continue until we reach a new, consistent equilibrium in both panels. Compared with our initial position, this new equilibrium has the following characteristics:

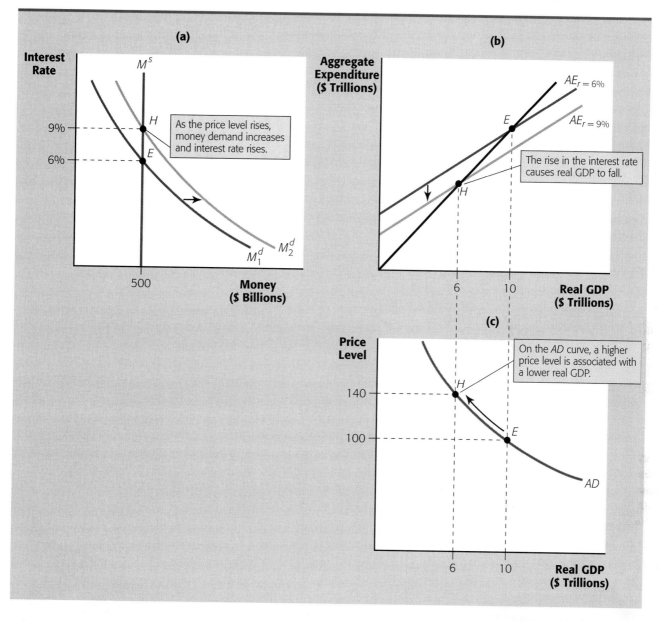

FIGURE 2
Deriving the Aggregate Demand Curve

- The money demand curve has shifted rightward.
- The interest rate is higher.
- The aggregate expenditure line has shifted downward.
- Equilibrium GDP is lower.

Remember that all of these changes are caused by a rise in the price level.

The points labeled H in panels (a) and (b) show one possible new equilibrium that meets these requirements. In panel (a), the money demand curve has shifted to M_2^d. The interest rate has risen to 9 percent. The aggregate expenditure line has shifted downward, to the one marked "$r = 9\%$." Finally, equilibrium output has fallen to $6 trillion.

Now recall the initial event that caused real GDP to fall: a rise in the price level. We've thus established an important principle:

> *A rise in the price level causes a decrease in equilibrium GDP.*

Deriving the Aggregate Demand Curve

In panel (c), we introduce a new curve that directly shows the negative relationship between the price level and equilibrium GDP. In this panel, the price level is measured along the vertical axis, while real GDP is on the horizontal. Point *E* represents our initial equilibrium, with *P* = 100 and equilibrium GDP = $10 trillion. Point *H* represents the new equilibrium, with *P* = 140 and equilibrium GDP = $6 trillion. If we continued to change the price level to other values—raising it further to 150, lowering it to 85, and so on—we would find that each different price level results in a different equilibrium GDP. This is illustrated by the downward-sloping curve in the figure, which we call the *aggregate demand curve*.

Aggregate demand (*AD*) curve A curve indicating equilibrium GDP at each price level.

> *The **aggregate demand** (AD) curve tells us the equilibrium real GDP at any price level.*

Understanding the *AD* Curve

The *AD* curve is unlike any other curve you've encountered in this text. In all other cases, our curves have represented simple behavioral relationships. For example, the demand curve for maple syrup shows us how a change in price affects the behavior of buyers in a market. Similarly, the aggregate expenditure line shows how a change in income affects total spending in the economy.

But the *AD* curve represents more than just a behavioral relationship between two variables. Each point on the curve represents a short-run *equilibrium* in the economy. For example, point *E* on the *AD* curve in Figure 2 tells us that when the price level is 100, *equilibrium* GDP is $10 trillion. Thus, point *E* doesn't just tell us that total spending is $10 trillion; rather, it tells us that when *P* = 100, spending and output are equal to each other only when they *both* are equal to $10 trillion.

As you can see, a better name for the *AD* curve would be the "equilibrium-output-at-each-price-level" curve—not a very catchy name. The *AD* curve gets its name because it *resembles* the demand curve for an individual product. It's a downward-sloping curve, with the price level (instead of the price of a single good) on the ver-

DANGEROUS CURVES

Two Misconceptions About the *AD* Curve Watch out for two very common mistakes about the aggregate demand curve. The first is thinking that it is simply a "total demand" or "total spending" curve for the economy, telling us the total quantity of output that purchasers want to buy at each price level. This is an oversimplification. Rather, the *AD* curve tells us the *equilibrium* real GDP at each price level. Remember that equilibrium GDP is the level of output at which total spending *equals* total output. Thus, total spending is only part of the story behind the *AD* curve: The other part is the requirement that total spending and total output be equal.

A second, related mistake is thinking that the *AD* curve slopes downward for the same reason that a microeconomic demand curve slopes downward. This, too, is wrong: *Microeconomic* demand curves for individual products rely on an entirely different mechanism than the one we've described for the *AD* curve. In the market for maple syrup, for example, a rise in price causes quantity demanded to decrease, mostly because people switch to *other* goods that are now relatively cheaper. But along the *AD* curve, a rise in the price level generally causes the prices of *all* goods to increase *together*. In this case, there are no relatively cheaper goods to switch to!

The *AD* curve works in an entirely different way from microeconomic demand curves. Along the *AD* curve, an increase in the price level raises the interest rate in the money market, which decreases spending on interest-sensitive goods, causing a drop in equilibrium GDP.

tical axis and *equilibrium total output* (instead of the quantity of a single good demanded) on the horizontal axis. But there the similarity ends. The *AD* curve is not a demand curve at all, in spite of its name.

Movements Along the *AD* Curve

As you will see later in this chapter, a variety of events can cause the price level to change, and move us *along* the *AD* curve. It's important to understand what happens in the economy as we make such a move.

Look again at the *AD* curve in panel (c) of Figure 2. Suppose the price level rises, and we move from point *E* to point *H* along this curve. Then the following sequence of events occurs: The rise in the price level increases the demand for money, raises the interest rate, decreases autonomous consumption (*a*) and investment spending (I^P), and works through the multiplier to decrease equilibrium GDP. The process can be summarized as follows:

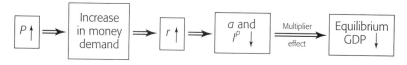

The opposite sequence of events will occur if the price level falls, moving us rightward along the *AD* curve:

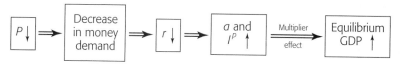

Shifts of the *AD* Curve

When we move along the *AD* curve in Figure 2, we assume that the price level changes but that other influences on equilibrium GDP are constant. When any of these other influences on GDP changes, the *AD* curve will shift. The distinction between movements along the *AD* curve and shifts of the curve itself is very important. Always keep the following rule in mind:

> *When a change in the price level causes equilibrium GDP to change, we move along the* AD *curve. Whenever anything other than the price level causes equilibrium GDP to change, the* AD *curve itself shifts.*

What are these other influences on GDP? They are the very same changes you learned about in previous chapters. Specifically, equilibrium GDP will change whenever there is a change in any of the following:

- government purchases
- taxes
- autonomous consumption spending
- investment spending
- net exports
- the money supply

Let's consider some examples and see how each causes the *AD* curve to shift.

FIGURE 3
A Spending Shock Shifts the
AD Curve

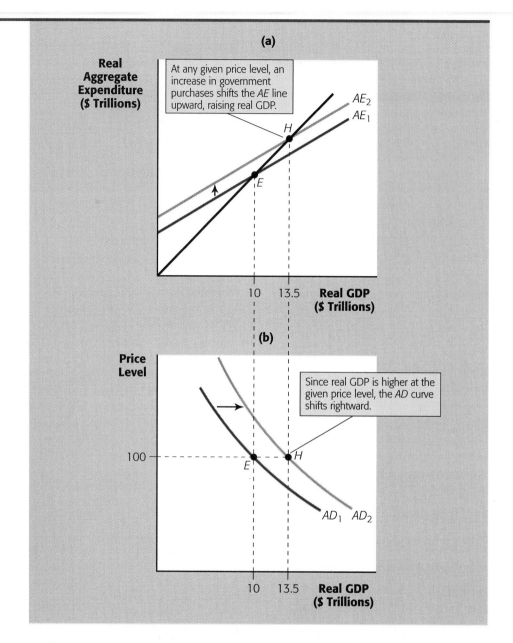

An Increase in Government Purchases. In Figure 3, we assume that the economy begins at a price level of 100. In the money market (not shown), the equilibrium interest rate is 6 percent and equilibrium output—given by point E in panel (a)—is $10 trillion. Panel (b) shows the same equilibrium as represented by point E on AD_1.

Now let's repeat an experiment from the previous chapter: We'll increase government purchases by $2 trillion and ask what happens if the price level remains at 100. If you flip back to Figure 8 in the previous chapter, you'll see that this rise in government purchases caused the AE line to shift upward, but it also caused the equilibrium interest rate to rise to 8 percent, causing the AE line to shift back downward a bit. The result was that equilibrium GDP rose to $13.5 trillion. This new equilibrium is also shown in panel (a) of Figure 3. The aggregate expenditure line shifts upward to AE_2, and the equilibrium moves to point H. With the price level remaining at 100, equilibrium GDP increases.

Now look at panel (b) in Figure 3. There, the new equilibrium is represented by point H ($P = 100$, real GDP = $13.5 trillion). This point lies to the right of our original curve AD_1. Point H, therefore, must lie on a *new AD* curve—a curve that tells us equilibrium GDP at any price level *after the increase in government spending*. The new AD curve is the one labeled AD_2, which goes through point H. What about the other points on AD_2? They tell us that, if we had started at any *other* price level, an increase in government spending would have increased equilibrium GDP at that price level, too. We conclude that *an increase in government purchases shifts the entire AD curve rightward.*

Any other factor that initially shifts the aggregate expenditure line upward will shift the AD curve rightward, just as in Figure 3. More specifically,

the AD curve shifts rightward when government purchases, investment spending, autonomous consumption spending, or net exports increase, or when net taxes decrease.

Our analysis also applies in the other direction. For example, at any given price level, a *decrease* in government spending shifts the aggregate expenditure line *downward*, decreasing equilibrium GDP. This in turn shifts the AD curve leftward.

The AD curve shifts leftward when government purchases, investment spending, autonomous consumption spending, or net exports decrease, or when net taxes increase.

Changes in the Money Supply. Changes in the money supply will also shift the aggregate demand curve. To see why, let's imagine that the Fed conducts open market operations to *increase* the money supply. As you learned in the previous chapter, this will cause the interest rate to decrease, increasing investment spending and autonomous consumption spending. Together, these spending changes will shift the aggregate expenditure line upward, just as in panel (a) of Figure 3, and increase equilibrium GDP. Since this change in equilibrium output is caused by something *other* than a change in the price level, the AD curve shifts. In this case, because the money supply *increased*, the AD curve shifts *rightward*, just as in panel (b) of Figure 3.

A decrease in the money supply would have the opposite effect: The interest rate would rise, the aggregate expenditure line would shift downward, and *equilibrium GDP at any price level would fall*. We conclude that

an increase in the money supply shifts the AD curve rightward. A decrease in the money supply shifts the AD curve leftward.

Shifts Versus Movements Along the *AD* Curve: A Summary. Figure 4 summarizes how some events in the economy cause a movement along the AD curve, and other events shift the AD curve. You can use the figure as an exercise, drawing diagrams similar to Figures 2 and 3 to illustrate why we move along or shift the AD curve in each case.

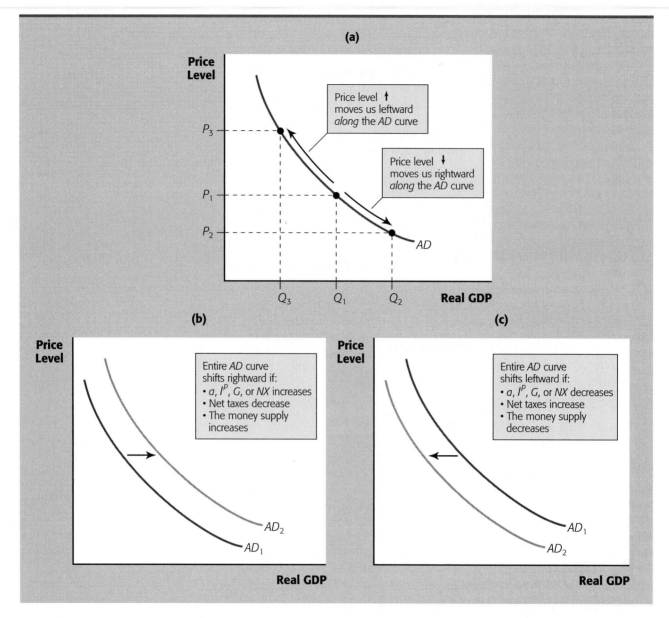

FIGURE 4

Effects of Key Changes on the Aggregate Demand Curve

Notice that panels (b) and (c) of Figure 4 tell us how a variety of events affect the *AD* curve, but *not* how they affect *real GDP*. The reason is that, even if we know which *AD* curve we are on, we could be at *any point* along that curve, depending on where the price level ends up.

But where will the price level end up? Our first step in answering that question is to understand the other side of the relationship between GDP and the price level.

THE AGGREGATE SUPPLY CURVE

Look back at Figure 1, which illustrates the *two-way* relationship between the price level and output. On the one hand, changes in the price level affect output. This is the relationship, summarized by the *AD* curve, that we've just explored in the previous section. On the other hand, changes in output affect the price level. This relationship—summarized by the *aggregate supply curve*—is the focus of this section.

The effect of changes in output on the price level is complex, involving a variety of forces. Current research is helping economists get a clearer picture of this relationship. Here, we will present a simple model of the aggregate supply curve that focuses on the link between prices and costs. Toward the end of the chapter, we'll discuss some additional ideas about the aggregate supply curve.

Costs and Prices

The price *level* in the economy results from the pricing behavior of millions of individual business firms. In any given year, some of these firms will raise their prices, and some will lower them. For example, during the 1990s, personal computers and long-distance telephone calls came down in price, while college tuition and the prices of movies rose. These types of price changes are subjects for *microeconomic* analysis, because they involve individual markets.

But often, all firms in the economy are affected by the same *macroeconomic* event, causing prices to rise or fall throughout the economy. This change in the price *level* is what interests us in macroeconomics.

To understand how macroeconomic events affect the price level, we begin with a very simple assumption:

> *A firm sets the price of its products as a markup over cost per unit.*

Fast-food restaurants, like other firms in the economy, charge a markup over cost per unit. The average markup in the economy is determined by competitive conditions, and tends to change slowly over time.

For example, if it costs Burger King $2.00, on average, to produce a Whopper (cost per unit is $2.00), and Burger King's percentage markup is 10 percent, then it will charge $2.00 + (0.10 × $2.00) = $2.20 per Whopper.[1]

The percentage markup in any particular industry will depend on the degree of competition there. If there are many firms competing for customers in a market, all producing very similar products, then we can expect the markup to be relatively small. Thus, we expect a relatively low markup on fast-food burgers or personal computers. In industries where there is less competition—such as daily newspapers or jet aircraft—we would expect higher percentage markups.

In macroeconomics, we are not concerned with how the markup differs in different industries, but rather with the *average percentage markup* in the economy:

> *The average percentage markup in the economy is determined by competitive conditions in the economy. The competitive structure of the economy changes very slowly, so the average percentage markup should be somewhat stable from year to year.*

But a stable markup does not necessarily mean a stable price level, because unit costs can change. For example, if Burger King's markup remains at 10 percent, but the unit cost of a Whopper rises from $2.00 to $3.00, then the price of a Whopper will rise to $3.00 + (0.10 × $3.00) = $3.30. Extending this example to all firms in the economy, we can say:

---

[1] In microeconomics, you learn more sophisticated theories of how firms' prices are determined. But our simple markup model captures a central conclusion of those theories: that an increase in costs will result in higher prices.

In the short run, the price level rises when there is an economy-wide increase in unit costs, and the price level falls when there is an economy-wide decrease in unit costs.

GDP, Costs, and the Price Level

Our primary concern in this chapter is the impact of *total output or real GDP* on unit costs and, therefore, on the price level. Why should a change in output affect unit costs and the price level? We'll focus on three key reasons.

As total output increases:

Greater amounts of inputs may be needed to produce a unit of output. As output increases, firms hire new, untrained workers who may be less productive than existing workers. Firms also begin using capital and land that are less well suited to their industry. As a result, greater amounts of labor, capital, land, and raw materials are needed to produce each unit of output. Even if the prices of these inputs remain the same, unit costs will rise.

For example, imagine that Intel increases its output of computer chips. Then it will have to be less picky about the workers it employs, hiring some who are less well suited to chip production than those already working there. Thus, more labor hours will be needed to produce each chip. Intel may also have to begin using older, less-efficient production facilities, which require more silicon and other raw materials per chip. Even if the prices of all of these inputs remain unchanged, unit costs will rise.

The prices of nonlabor inputs rise. In addition to needing greater quantities of inputs, firms will also have to pay a higher price for them. This is especially true of inputs like land and natural resources, which may be available only in limited quantities in the short run. An increase in the output of final goods raises the demand for these inputs, causing their prices to rise. Firms that produce final goods experience an increase in unit costs, and raise their own prices accordingly.

The nominal wage rate rises. Greater output means higher employment, leaving fewer unemployed workers looking for jobs. As firms compete to hire increasingly scarce workers, they must offer higher nominal wage rates to attract them. Higher nominal wages increase unit costs, and therefore result in a higher price level. Notice that we use the nominal wage, rather than the real wage we've emphasized elsewhere in this book. That's because we are interested in explaining how firms' prices are determined. Since price is a nominal variable, it will be marked up over *nominal* costs.

A decrease in output affects unit costs through the same three forces, but with the opposite result. As output falls, firms can be more selective in hiring the best, most efficient workers and in choosing other inputs, decreasing their input requirements per unit of output. Decreases in demand for land and natural resources will cause their prices to drop. And as unemployment rises, wages will fall as workers compete for jobs. All of these contribute to a drop in unit costs, and a decrease in the price level.

The Short Run. All three of our reasons are important in explaining why a change in output affects the price level. However, they operate within different time frames.

When total output increases, new, less productive workers will be hired rather quickly. Similarly, the prices of certain key inputs—such as lumber, land, oil, and wheat—may rise within a few weeks or months.

But our third explanation—changes in the nominal wage rate—is a different story. While wages in some lines of work might respond very rapidly, we can expect wages in many industries to change very little or not at all for a year or more after a change in output.

> *For a year or so after a change in output, changes in the average nominal wage are less important than other forces that change unit costs.*

Here are some of the more important reasons why wages in many industries respond so slowly to changes in output:

- Many firms have union contracts that specify wages for up to three years. While wage increases are often built into these contracts, a rise in output will not affect the wage increase. When output rises or falls, these firms continue to abide by the contract.
- Wages in many large corporations are set by slow-moving bureaucracies.
- Wage changes in either direction can be costly to firms. Higher wages to attract new workers must be widely publicized in order to raise the number of job applicants at the firm. Lower wages can reduce the morale of workers—and their productivity. Thus, many firms are reluctant to change wages until they are reasonably sure that any change in their output will be long lasting.
- Firms may benefit from developing reputations for paying stable wages. A firm that raises wages when output is high and labor is scarce may have to lower wages when output is low and labor is plentiful. Such a firm would develop a reputation for paying unstable wages, and have difficulty attracting new workers.

In this section, we focus exclusively on the short run—a time horizon of a year or so after a change in output. Since the average nominal wage rate changes very little over the short run, we'll make the following simplifying assumption: *The nominal wage rate is fixed in the short run.* More specifically,

> *we assume that changes in output have no effect on the nominal wage rate in the short run.*

Keep in mind, though, that our assumption of a constant wage holds only in the *short run*. As you will see later, wage changes play a very important role in the economy's adjustment over the long run.

Since we assume a constant nominal wage in the short run, a change in output will affect unit costs through the other two factors we mentioned earlier. Specifically, in the short run, a rise in real GDP raises firms' unit costs because (1) input requirements per unit of output rise, and (2) the prices of nonlabor inputs rise. With a constant percentage markup, the rise in unit costs translates into a rise in the price level. Thus,

> *in the short run, a rise in real GDP, by causing unit costs to increase, will also cause a rise in the price level.*

FIGURE 5
The Aggregate Supply Curve

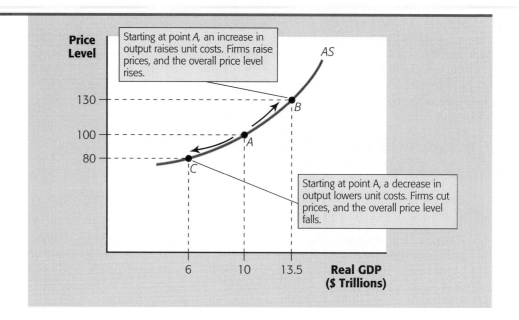

In the other direction, a *drop* in real GDP lowers unit costs because (1) input requirements per unit of output fall, and (2) the prices of nonlabor inputs fall. With a constant percentage markup, the drop in unit costs translates into a drop in the price level.

> *In the short run, a fall in real GDP, by causing unit costs to decrease, will also cause a decrease in the price level.*

Deriving the Aggregate Supply Curve

Figure 5 summarizes our discussion about the effect of output on the price level in the short run. Suppose the economy begins at point *A*, with output at $10 trillion and the price level at 100. Now suppose that output rises to $13.5 trillion. What will happen in the short run? Even though wages are assumed to remain constant, the price level will rise because of the other forces we've discussed. In the figure, the price level rises to 130, indicated by point *B*. If, instead, output *fell* to $6 trillion, the price level would fall—to 80 in the figure, indicated by point *C*.

As you can see, each time we change the level of output, there will be a new price level in the short run, giving us another point on the figure. If we connect all of these points, we obtain the economy's *aggregate supply curve:*

> *The **aggregate supply curve** (or **AS** *curve*) tells us the price level consistent with firms' unit costs and their percentage markups at any level of output over the short run.*

Aggregate supply (AS) curve A curve indicating the price level consistent with firms' unit costs and markups for any level of output over the short run.

A more accurate name for the *AS* curve would be the "short-run-price-level-at-each-output-level" curve, but that is more than a mouthful. The *AS* curve gets its name because it *resembles* a microeconomic market supply curve. Like the supply curve for maple syrup we discussed in Chapter 3, the *AS* curve is upward sloping, and it has a price variable (the price level) on the vertical axis and a quantity variable (total output) on the horizontal axis. But there, the similarity ends.

Movements Along the *AS* Curve

When a change in output causes the price level to change, we *move along* the economy's *AS* curve. But what happens in the economy as we make such a move?

Look again at the *AS* curve in Figure 5. Suppose we move from point *A* to point *B* along this curve in the short run. The increase in output raises the prices of raw materials and other (nonlabor) inputs and also raises input requirements per unit of output at many firms. Both of these changes increase costs per unit. As long as the markup remains somewhat stable, the rise in unit costs will lead firms to raise their prices, and the price level will increase. Thus, as we move upward along the *AS* curve, we can represent what happens as follows:

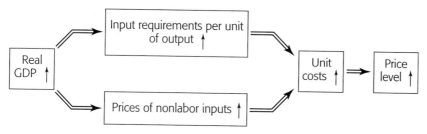

The opposite sequence of events occurs when real GDP falls, moving us downward along the *AS* curve:

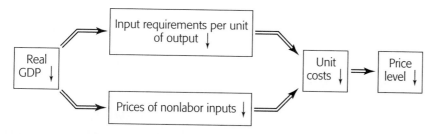

Shifts of the *AS* Curve

When we drew the *AS* curve in Figure 5, we assumed that a number of important variables remained unchanged. In particular, we assumed that the only changes in unit costs were those caused by a change in output. But in the real world, unit costs sometimes change for reasons *other* than a change in output. When this occurs, unit costs—and the price level—will change at *any* level of output, so the *AS* curve will shift.

In general, we distinguish between a movement along the *AS* curve, and a shift of the curve itself, as follows:

> *When a change in real GDP causes the price level to change, we move along the* AS *curve. When anything other than a change in real GDP causes the price level to change, the* AS *curve itself shifts.*

Figure 6 illustrates the logic of a shift in the *AS* curve. Suppose the economy's initial *AS* curve is AS_1. Now suppose that some economic event *other* than a change

FIGURE 6
**Shifts of the Aggregate
Supply Curve**

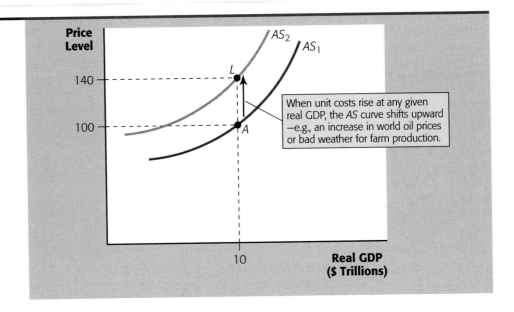

A Misconception About the AS Curve A common mistake about the AS curve is thinking that it describes the same kind of relationship between price and quantity as a microeconomic supply curve. There are two reasons why this is wrong.

First, the direction of causation between price and output is reversed for the AS curve. For example, when we draw the supply curve for maple syrup, we view changes in the price of maple syrup as causing a change in output supplied. But along the AS curve, it's the other way around: A change in *output* causes a change in the *price level*.

Second, the basic assumption behind the AS curve is very different from that behind a single market supply curve. When we draw the supply curve for an individual product, we assume that the prices of inputs used in producing the good remain fixed. This is a sensible thing to do, because an increase in production for a single good is unlikely to have much effect on input prices in the economy as a whole.

But when we draw the AS curve, we imagine an increase in *real GDP*, in which *all* firms are increasing their output. This will significantly raise the demand for inputs, so it is unrealistic to assume that input prices will remain fixed. Indeed, the rise in input prices is one of the important reasons for the AS curve's upward slope.

in output—for the moment, we'll leave the event unnamed—causes firms to raise their prices. Then the price level will be higher at *any* level of output we might imagine, so the AS curve must shift *upward*—for example, to AS_2 in the figure. At an output level of $10 trillion, the price level would rise from 100 to 140. At any other output level, the price level would also rise.

What can cause unit costs to change at any given level of output? The following are some important examples:

- *Changes in world oil prices.* Oil is traded on a world market, where prices can fluctuate even while output in the United States does not. And changes in world oil prices have caused major shifts in the AS curve. Three events over the past few decades—an oil embargo by Arab oil-producing nations in 1973–74, the Iranian revolution in 1978–79, and Iraq's invasion of Kuwait in 1990—all caused large jumps in the price of oil. Each time, costs per unit rose for firms across the country, and they responded by charging higher prices than before for *any* output level they might produce. As in Figure 6, the AS curve shifted upward. Conversely, oil prices fell sharply during 1997 and 1998. This caused unit costs to decrease at many firms, shifting the AS curve downward.

- *Changes in the weather.* Good crop-growing weather increases farmers' yields for any given amounts of land, labor, capital, and other inputs used. This decreases farms' unit costs, and the price of agricultural goods falls. Since many of these goods are final goods (such as fresh fruit and vegetables), the price drop will contribute directly to a drop in the price level and a downward shift of the *AS* curve. Additionally, agricultural products are important inputs in the production of many other goods. (For example, corn is an input in beef production.) Good weather thus leads to a drop in input prices for many other firms in the economy, causing their unit costs, and their prices, to decrease. For these reasons, we can expect good weather to shift the *AS* curve downward. Bad weather, which decreases crop yields, increases unit costs at any level of output and shifts the *AS* curve upward.

- *Technological change.* New technologies can enable firms to produce any given level of output at lower unit costs. In recent years, for example, we've seen revolutions in telecommunications, information processing, and medicine. The result has been steady downward shifts of the *AS* curve.

- *The Nominal Wage.* Remember that in our short-run analysis we're assuming the nominal wage rate does *not* change. As we move along the *AS* curve, we hold the nominal wage rate constant. But later in the chapter—when we extend our time horizon beyond a year or so—you'll see that changes in the nominal wage are an important part of the economy's long-run adjustment process. Here we just point out that, *if* the nominal wage were to increase for any reason, it would raise unit costs for firms at any level of output and therefore *shift* the *AS* curve *upward*. Similarly, *if* the nominal wage rate were to fall for any reason, it would *decrease* unit costs at any level of output and shift the *AS* curve downward. We'll come back to this important fact later.

Figure 7 summarizes how different events in the economy cause a movement along, or a shift in, the *AS* curve. But the *AS* curve tells only half of the economy's story: It shows us the price level *if* we know the level of output. The *AD* curve tells the other half of the story: It shows us the level of output *if* we know the economy's price level. In the next section, we finally put the two halves of the story together, allowing us to determine both the price level and output.

AD AND *AS* TOGETHER: SHORT-RUN EQUILIBRIUM

Short-run macroeconomic equilibrium A combination of price level and GDP consistent with both the *AD* and *AS* curves.

Where will the economy settle in the short run? That is, where is our **short-run macroeconomic equilibrium?** Figure 8 shows how to answer that question, using both the *AS* curve and the *AD* curve. If you suspect that the equilibrium is at point *E,* the intersection of these two curves, you are correct. At that point, the price level is 100 and output is $10 trillion. But it's worth thinking about *why* point *E*—and only point *E*—is our short-run equilibrium.

First, we know that in equilibrium, the economy must be at some point on the *AD* curve. For example, suppose the economy were at point *B,* which lies to the right of the *AD* curve. At this point, the price level is 140 and output is $14 trillion. But the *AD* curve tells us that with a price level of 140, *equilibrium* output is $6 trillion. Thus, at point *B,* real GDP would be greater than its equilibrium value. As you learned several chapters ago, this situation cannot persist for long, since inventories would pile up and firms would be forced to cut back on their production. Thus, point *B* cannot be our short-run equilibrium.

Second, short-run equilibrium requires that the economy be operating on its *AS* curve. Otherwise, firms would not be charging the prices dictated by their unit costs and the average percentage markup in the economy. For example, point *F* lies

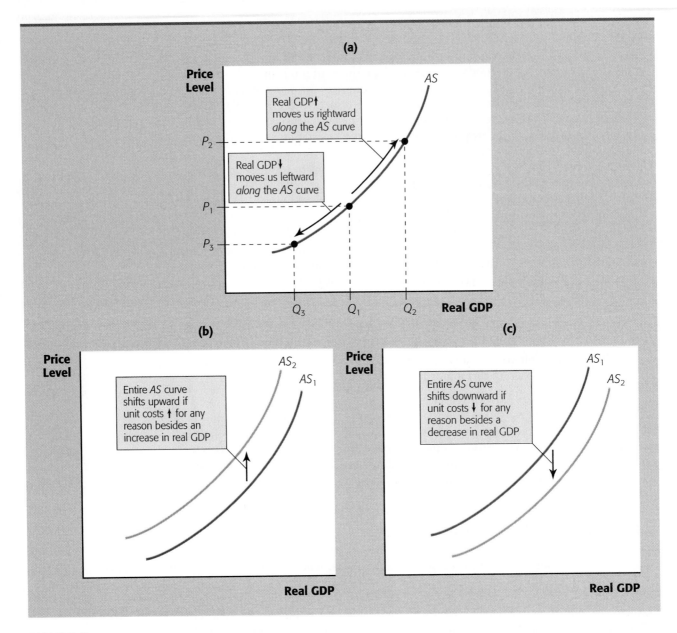

FIGURE 7
Effects of Key Changes on the Aggregate Supply Curve

below the AS curve. But the AS curve tells us that if output is $14 trillion, based on the average percentage markup and unit costs, the price level should be 140 (point B), not something lower. That is, the price level at point F is *too low* for equilibrium. This situation will not last long either, since firms will want to raise prices, causing the overall price level to rise.

We could make a similar argument for any other point that is off the AS curve, off the AD curve, or off of both curves. Our conclusion is always the same: Unless the economy is on *both* the AS and the AD curves, the price level and the level of output will change. Only when the economy is at point E—on *both* curves—can we have a sustainable level of real GDP and the price level.

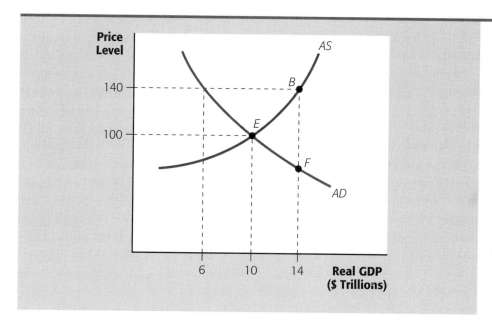

FIGURE 8
Short-Run Macroeconomic Equilibrium

Short-run equilibrium occurs where the AD and AS curves intersect. At point E, the price level of 100 is consistent with an output of $10 trillion along the AD curve. The output level of $10 trillion is consistent with a price level of 100 along the AS curve. At any other combination of price level and output, such as point F or point B, at least one condition for equilibrium will not be satisfied.

WHAT HAPPENS WHEN THINGS CHANGE?

Now that we know how the short-run equilibrium is determined, and armed with our knowledge of the *AD* and *AS* curves, we are ready to put the model through its paces. In this section, we'll explore how different types of events cause the short-run equilibrium to change.

Our short-run equilibrium will change when either the *AD* curve, the *AS* curve, or both, *shift*. Since the consequences for the economy are very different for shifts in the *AD* curve as opposed to shifts in the *AS* curve, economists have developed a shorthand language to distinguish between them:

> *An event that causes the* AD *curve to shift is called a* **demand shock.** *An event that causes the* AS *curve to shift is called a* **supply shock.**

In earlier chapters, we've used the phrase *spending shock*: a change in spending by one or more sectors that ultimately affects the entire economy. As you're about to see, shifts in the aggregate demand curve or the aggregate supply curve both create changes in aggregate expenditure, although in different ways. So *demand shocks* and *supply shocks* are just two *different categories of spending shocks.*

In this section, we'll first explore the effects of demand shocks, both in the short run and during the adjustment process to the long run. Then, we'll take up the issue of supply shocks.

Demand Shocks in the Short Run

Figure 4, which lists the causes of a shift in the *AD* curve, also serves as a list of demand shocks to the economy. Let's consider some examples.

Demand shock Any event that causes the *AD* curve to shift.

Supply shock Any event that causes the *AS* curve to shift.

FIGURE 9

The Effect of a Demand Shock

Starting at point E, *an increase in government purchases would shift the* AD *curve rightward to* AD$_2$. *Point* J *illustrates where the economy would move if the price level remained constant. But as output increases, the price level rises. Thus, the economy moves along the* AS *curve from point* E *to point* H.

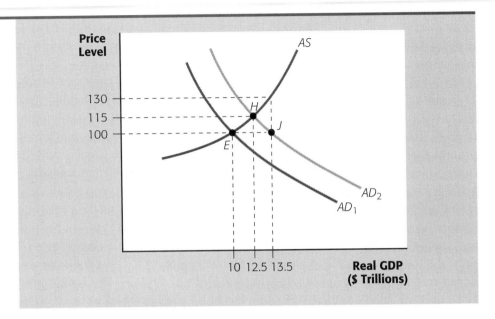

An Increase in Government Purchases. You've learned that an increase in government purchases shifts the *AD* curve rightward. Now we can see how it affects the economy in the short run. Figure 9 shows the initial equilibrium at point *E*, with the price level equal to 100 and output at $10 trillion. Now, suppose that government purchases rise by $2 trillion. Figure 4(b) tells us that the *AD* curve will shift rightward. What will happen to equilibrium GDP?

In our example in the previous chapter, a $2 trillion rise in government purchases increased output to $13.5 trillion, and also raised the interest rate in the money market to 8 percent. (Flip back to Figure 8 in that chapter to refresh your memory.)

But nowhere in our previous analysis did we consider any change in the price level. Thus, the rise in GDP to $13.5 trillion in the previous chapter makes sense *only if the price level does not change.* Here, in Figure 9, this *would* be a movement rightward, from point *E* to point *J*. However, *point* J *does not describe the economy's short-run equilibrium.* Why not? Because it ignores two facts that you've learned about in this chapter: The rise in output will change the price level, and the change in the price level will, in turn, affect equilibrium GDP.

To see this more clearly, let's first suppose that the price level did *not* rise when output increased, so that the economy actually *did* arrive at point *J* after the *AD* shift. Would we stay there? Absolutely not. Point *J* lies below the *AS* curve, telling us that when GDP is $13.5 trillion, the price level consistent with firms' unit costs, and average markup is 130, not 100. Firms would soon raise prices, and this would cause a movement leftward along *AD*$_2$. The price level would keep rising and output would keep falling, until we reached point *H*. At that point, with output at $12.5 trillion, we would be on both the *AS* and *AD* curves, so there would be no reason for a further rise in the price level and no reason for a further fall in output.

However, the process we've just described is not entirely realistic. It assumes that when government purchases rise, *first* output increases (the move to point *J*) and *then* the price level rises (the move to point *H*). In reality, output and the price level tend to rise *together*. Thus, the economy would likely *slide along* the *AS* curve from point *E* to point *H*. As we move along the *AS* curve, output rises, increasing unit costs and the price level. At the same time, the rise in the price level *reduces equilibrium GDP: the level of output toward which the economy is heading on the* AD *curve,* from point *J* to point *H*.

We can summarize the impact of a rise in government purchases this way:

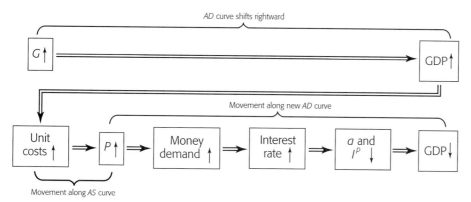

Net Effect: GDP ↑, but by less due to effect of *P* ↑

Let's step back a minute and get some perspective about this example of fiscal policy. This is the third time in this text that we've considered fiscal policy in the short run. Each time, the discussion became more realistic, and we've seen that the effect of fiscal policy becomes weaker. In our first analysis, we ignored any increase in the interest rate, and found that a rise in government purchases increased equilibrium GDP according to the simple multiplier formula $1/(1 - MPC)$. In our second analysis, in the chapter before this one, you learned that a rise in government purchases increases the interest rate, crowding out some interest-sensitive spending, thus making the rise in GDP smaller than it would otherwise be. The multiplier, therefore, was smaller than $1/(1 - MPC)$. Now you've learned that the rise in government purchases *also* increases the price level. This leads to a *further* rise in the interest rate, crowding out still *more* interest-sensitive spending, and making the rise in GDP *smaller still*. The size of the multiplier has been reduced yet again. (In our example, a $2 trillion increase in government purchases increases equilibrium GDP by $2.5 trillion, so the multiplier would be $2.5 trillion/$2 trillion = 1.25.) However, as you can see in Figure 9, the multiplier is still positive: A rise in government purchases—even when we take account of the rise in the price level—still raises GDP in the short run.

We can summarize the impact of price-level changes this way:

> *When government purchases increase, the horizontal shift of the* AD *curve measures how much real GDP would increase if the price level remained constant. But because the price level rises, real GDP rises by less than the horizontal shift in the* AD *curve.*

Now let's switch gears into reverse: How would we illustrate the effects of a *decrease* in government purchases? In this case, the *AD* curve would shift *leftward*, causing the following to happen:

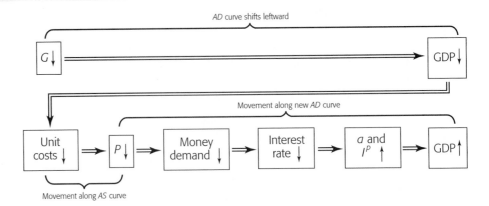

Net Effect: GDP↓, but by less due to effect of P↓

As you can see, the same sequence of events occurs in the same order, but each variable moves in the opposite direction. A decrease in government purchases decreases equilibrium GDP, but the multiplier effect is smaller because the price level falls.

An Increase in the Money Supply. Although monetary policy stimulates the economy through a different channel than fiscal policy, once we arrive at the *AD* and *AS* diagram, the two look very much alike. For example, an increase in the money supply, which reduces the interest rate, will stimulate interest-sensitive consumption and investment spending. Real GDP then increases, and the *AD* curve shifts rightward, just as in Figure 9. Once output begins to rise, we have the same sequence of events as in fiscal policy: The price level rises, so the increase in GDP will be smaller. We can represent the situation as follows:

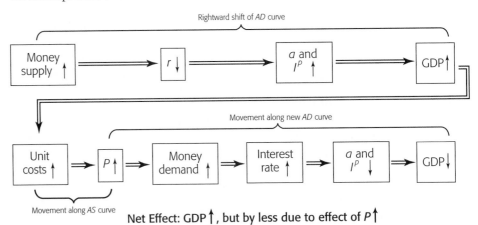

Net Effect: GDP↑, but by less due to effect of P↑

Other Demand Shocks. On your own, try going through examples of different demand shocks (see the list in Figures 4 (b) and (c)) and explain the sequence of events in each case that causes output and the price level to change. This will help you verify the following general conclusion about demand shocks:

> *A positive demand shock—one that shifts the* AD *curve rightward—increases both real GDP and the price level in the short run. A negative demand shock—one that shifts the* AD *curve leftward—decreases both real GDP and the price level in the short run.*

An Example: The Great Depression. As mentioned at the beginning of the chapter, the U.S. economy collapsed far more seriously during the period 1929 through 1933—the onset of the Great Depression—than it did at any other time in the country's history. Because the price level fell during this time, we know that the contraction was caused by an adverse demand shock. (An adverse supply shock would have caused the price level to *rise* as GDP fell.)

What do we know about the demand shocks that caused the depression? This question has been debated by economists almost continuously over the past 70 years. The candidates are numerous, and it appears that a combination of events was responsible. The 1920s were a period of optimism, with high levels of investment by businesses and spending by families on houses and cars. The stock market soared. In the fall of 1929, the bubble of optimism burst. The stock market crashed, and investment and consumption spending plummeted. Similar events occurred in other countries, and the demand for products exported by the United States fell. The Fed—then only 16 years old—reacted by cutting the money supply sharply, which added an adverse monetary shock to all of the cutbacks in spending. Each of these events contributed to a leftward shift of the *AD* curve, causing both output and the price level to fall.

Demand Shocks: Adjusting to the Long Run

In Figure 9, point *H* shows the new equilibrium after a positive demand shock *in the short run*—a year or so after the shock. But point *H* is not necessarily where the economy will end up in the long run. For example, suppose full-employment output is $10 trillion, and point *H*—representing an output of $12.5 trillion—is *above full-employment output*. Then, with employment unusually high and unemployment unusually low, business firms will have to compete to hire scarce workers, driving up the wage rate. It might take a year or more for the wage rate to rise significantly (recall our earlier list of reasons that wages adjust only slowly). But when we extend our horizon to several years or more, we must recognize that if output is above its potential, the wage rate will rise. Since the *AS* curve is drawn for a given wage, a rise in the wage rate will *shift* the curve upward, changing our equilibrium.

Alternatively, we could imagine a situation in which short-run equilibrium GDP was *below* its potential. In this case, with abnormally high unemployment, workers would compete to get scarce jobs, and eventually the wage rate would fall. Then the *AS* curve would shift downward, once again changing our equilibrium GDP.

> *In the short run, we treat the wage rate as given. But in the long run, the wage rate can change. When output is above full employment, the wage rate will rise, shifting the* AS *curve upward. When output is below full employment, the wage rate will fall, shifting the* AS *curve downward.*

Now we are ready to explore what happens over the long run in the aftermath of a demand shock. Figure 10 shows an economy in equilibrium at point *E*. We assume that the initial equilibrium is at full-employment output (Y_{FE}), since—as you are about to see—this is where the economy always ends up after the long-run adjustment process is complete. To make our results as general as possible, we'll use symbols, rather than numbers, to represent output and price levels.

Now suppose the *AD* curve shifts rightward due to, say, an increase in government purchases. In the short run, the equilibrium moves to point *H*, with a higher price level (P_2) and a higher level of output (Y_2). Point *H* tells us where the economy

FIGURE 10
The Long-Run Adjustment Process

Beginning at point E, *a positive demand shock would shift the aggregate demand curve to* AD$_2$, *raising both output and the price level. At point* H, *output is above the full-employment level,* Y$_{FE}$. *Firms will compete to hire scarce workers, thereby driving up the wage rate. The higher wage rate will shift the AS curve to* AS$_2$. *Only when the economy returns to full-employment output at point* K *will there be no further shifts in AS.*

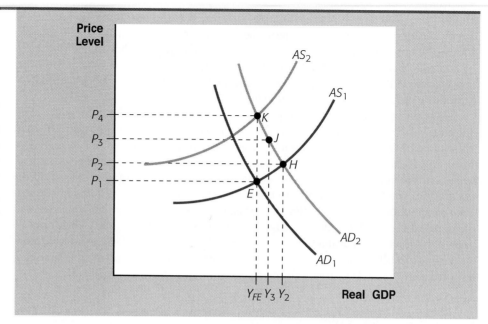

Self-correcting mechanism The adjustment process through which price and wage changes return the economy to full-employment output in the long run.

will be about a year after the increase in government purchases, before the wage rate has a chance to adjust. (Remember, along any given *AS* curve, the wage rate is assumed to be constant.)

But now let's extend our analysis beyond a year. Notice that Y_2 is greater than Y_{FE}. The wage will begin to rise, raising unit costs at any given output level and causing firms to raise prices. In the figure, the *AS* curve would begin shifting upward. Point *J* shows where the shifting aggregate supply curve might be two years after the shock, after the long-run adjustment process has begun. (You might want to pencil this intermediate *AS* curve into the figure, so that it intersects AD_2 at point *J*.) At this point, output would be at Y_3, and the rise in the price level has moved us along the new aggregate demand curve, AD_2.

Now, is point *J* our final, long-run equilibrium? No, it cannot be. At Y_3, output is *still* greater than Y_{FE}, so the wage rate will continue to rise and the *AS* curve will continue to shift upward. At point *J*, the long-run adjustment process is not yet complete. When will the process end? Only when the wage rate stops rising, that is, only when output has returned to Y_{FE}. This occurs when the *AS* curve has shifted all the way to AS_2, moving the economy to point *K*—our new, long-run equilibrium.

As you can see, the increase in government purchases has no effect on equilibrium GDP in the long run: The economy returns to full employment, which is just where it started. This is why the long-run adjustment process is often called the economy's **self-correcting mechanism.** And this mechanism applies to any demand shock, not just an increase in government purchases:

> *If a demand shock pulls the economy away from full employment, changes in the wage rate and the price level will eventually cause the economy to correct itself and return to full-employment output.*

For a positive demand shock that shifts the *AD* curve rightward, the self-correcting mechanism works like this:

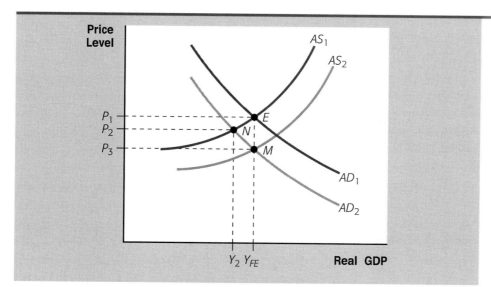

FIGURE 11

Long-Run Adjustment After a Negative Demand Shock

Starting from point E, a negative demand shock shifts the AD curve to AD_2, *lowering GDP and the price level. At point N, output is below the full-employment level. With unemployed labor available, wages will fall, enabling firms to lower their prices. The AS curve shifts downward until full employment is regained at point M, with a lower price level.*

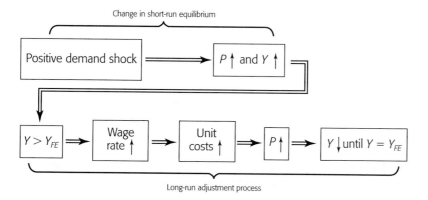

Figure 11 illustrates the case of a negative demand shock, in which the AD curve shifts leftward. Starting at point E, the short-run equilibrium moves to point N with real GDP below Y_{FE}. Over the long run, high unemployment drives the wage rate down, shifting the AS curve down as well. The price level decreases, causing equilibrium GDP to rise along the AD_2 curve. The process comes to a halt only when output returns to Y_{FE}. Thus, in the long run, the economy moves from point E to point M, and the negative demand shock causes no change in equilibrium GDP.

The complete sequence of events after a negative demand shock looks like this:

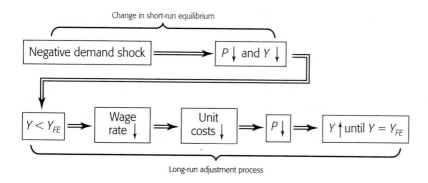

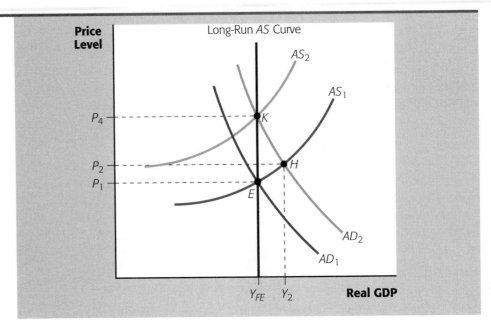

FIGURE 12
**The Long-Run
Adjustment Process**

*This figure, like Figure 10, illus-
trates a positive demand shock,
but focuses on the long-run effects. The initial equilibrium is
at point E, with output at full
employment (Y_{FE}) and price
level P_1. After the positive demand shock and all the long-run
adjustments to it, the economy
ends up at point K with a higher
price level (P_4), but the same
full-employment output level
(Y_{FE}). The long-run AS curve—
a vertical line—shows all possible combinations of price level
and output for the economy,
skipping over the short-run
changes. The vertical, long-run
AS curve shows that in the long
run, demand shocks can affect
the price level but not output.*

Pulling all of our observations together, we can summarize the economy's self-
correcting mechanism as follows:

> *Whenever a demand shock pulls the economy away from full employment,
> the self-correcting mechanism will eventually bring it back. When output ex-
> ceeds its full-employment level, wages will eventually rise, causing a rise in the
> price level and a drop in GDP until full employment is restored. When output
> is less than its full-employment level, wages will eventually fall, causing a drop
> in the price level and a rise in GDP until full employment is restored.*

The Long-Run Aggregate Supply Curve

The self-correcting mechanism provides an important link between the economy's
long-run and short-run behaviors. It helps us understand why deviations from full
employment don't last forever. Often, however, we are primarily interested in the
long-run effects of a demand shock. In these cases, we may want to skip over the
self-correcting mechanism and go straight to its end result. A new version of the *AS*
curve helps us do this.

Now look at Figure 12, which illustrates the impact of a positive demand shock like
the one in Figure 10. The economy begins at full employment at point *E*, then moves
to point *H* in the short run (before the wage rate rises), and then goes to point *K* in the
long run (after the rise in wages). If we skip over the short-run equilibrium, we find that
the positive demand shock has moved the economy from *E* to *K*, which is vertically
above *E*. That is, in the long run, the price level rises but output remains unchanged.

Now look at the vertical line in Figure 12, which shows another way of illustrating this long-run result. In the figure, the vertical line is the economy's **long-run aggregate supply curve**. It summarizes all possible output and price-level combinations
at which the economy could end up in the long run. It is vertical because, in the long
run, GDP will be the same—full-employment output—*regardless* of the position of

Long-run aggregate supply curve
A vertical line indicating all possible output and price-level combinations at which the economy
could end up in the long run.

the *AD* curve. The price level, however, will depend on the position of the *AD* curve. In the long run, a positive demand shock shifts the *AD* curve rightward, moving the economy from *E* to *K*: a higher price level, but the same level of output. Similarly, in Figure 11, a negative demand shock—which shifts the *AD* curve leftward—moves the economy from *E* to *M* in the long run: a lower price level with the same level of output. (You may want to pencil in a vertical long-run aggregate supply curve in Figure 11 to help you see that it is the same curve as the one drawn in Figure 12.)

The long-run aggregate supply curve tells us something very important about the economy: In the long run, after the self-correcting mechanism has done its job, *the economy behaves as the classical model predicts.* In particular, the classical model tells us that demand shocks cannot change equilibrium GDP in the long run. Figure 12 brings us to the same conclusion: While demand shocks shift the *AD* curve, this only moves the economy up or down along a vertical long-run *AS* curve, leaving output unchanged.[2]

The long-run aggregate supply curve also illustrates another classical conclusion. In the classical model, an increase in government purchases causes *complete crowding out*; the rise in government purchases is precisely matched by a drop in consumption and investment spending, leaving total output and total spending unchanged. In Figure 12, the same result holds in the long run. How do we know? The figures tell us that, in the long run, the rise in government purchases causes no change in GDP. But if GDP is the same, and government purchases are higher, then the other components of GDP—consumption and investment—must decrease by the amount that government purchases increased.[3]

> *The self-correcting mechanism shows us that, in the long run, the economy will eventually behave as the classical model predicts.*

But notice the word *eventually* in the previous statement. It can take several years before the economy returns to full employment after a demand shock. This is why governments around the world are reluctant to rely on the self-correcting mechanism alone to keep the economy on track. Instead, they often use fiscal and monetary policies in an attempt to return the economy to full employment more quickly. We'll explore fiscal and monetary policies in more detail in the next two chapters.

Supply Shocks

In recent decades, supply shocks have been important sources of economic fluctuations. The most dramatic supply shocks have resulted from sudden changes in world oil prices. As you are about to see, supply shocks affect the economy differently from demand shocks.

Short-Run Effects of Supply Shocks. Figure 13 shows an example of a supply shock: an increase in world oil prices that shifts the aggregate supply curve upward, from AS_1 to AS_2. As rising oil prices increase unit costs, firms will begin raising prices and the price level will increase. The rise in the price level decreases equilibrium GDP

---

[2] Of course, full-employment output can increase from year to year, as you learned in the chapter on economic growth. When the economy is growing, the long-run *AS* curve will shift rightward. In that case, the level of output at which the economy will eventually settle increases from year to year.

[3] Net exports can be crowded out as well. In a later chapter, you'll learn that a higher interest rate causes a currency's value to increase relative to foreign currencies. This causes exports to fall and imports to rise.

FIGURE 13
The Effect of a Supply Shock

A negative supply shock would shift the AS curve upward from AS_1 to AS_2. In the short-run equilibrium at point R, the price level is higher and output is below Y_{FE}. Eventually, wages will fall, causing unit costs to fall, and the AS curve will shift back to its original position. A positive supply shock would have just the opposite effect.

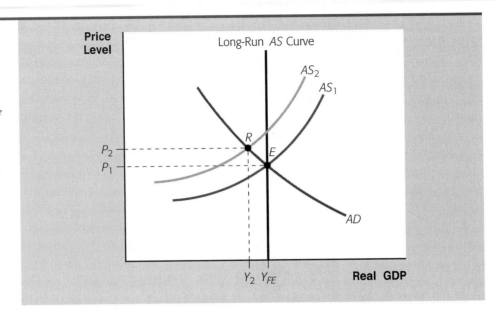

along the *AD* curve. In the short run, the price level will continue to rise, and the economy will continue to slide upward along its *AD* curve, until we reach the AS_2 curve at point R. At this point, the price level is consistent with firms' unit costs and average markup (we are on the *AS* curve), and total output is equal to total spending (we are on the *AD* curve). As you can see, the short-run impact of higher oil prices is a rise in the price level and a fall in output. We call this a *negative* supply shock, because of the negative effect on output.

> *In the short run, a negative supply shock shifts the* AS *curve upward, decreasing output and increasing the price level.*

Notice the sharp contrast between the effects of negative supply shocks and negative demand shocks in the short run. After a negative demand shock (see, for example, Figure 11), both output and the price level fall. After a negative supply shock, output falls but the price level rises. Economists and journalists have coined the term **stagflation** to describe a *stag*nating economy experiencing in*flation*.

Stagflation The combination of falling output and rising prices.

> *A negative supply shock causes* stagflation *in the short run.*

Stagflation caused by increases in oil prices is not just a theoretical possibility. Three of our recessions in the last quarter century—in 1973–74, 1980, and 1990–91—followed increases in world oil prices. And each of these three recessions also saw jumps in the price level.

A *positive supply shock* would increase output by shifting the *AS* curve *downward*. (We call it positive, because of its effect on output.) As you can see if you draw such a shift on your own,

> *a positive supply shock shifts the* AS *curve downward, increasing output and decreasing the price level.*

Examples of positive supply shocks include unusually good weather, a drop in oil prices, and a technological change that lowers unit costs. In addition, a positive supply shock can sometimes be caused by government policy. A few chapters ago, we discussed how the government could use tax incentives and other policies to increase the rate of economic growth. These policies work by shifting the *AS* curve downward, thus increasing output while tending to decrease the price level.

Another type of policy tries to deal directly with negative supply shocks. For example, after the oil price shocks of the 1970s, the federal government built a strategic reserve of oil in huge underground storage areas. The idea was to release oil from the reserve if another oil price shock hit, in order to stabilize the price. The reserve has been used in this way, but not enough to make much difference in world oil prices.

Long-Run Effects of Supply Shocks. What about the effects of supply shocks in the long run? In some cases, we need not concern ourselves with this question, because some supply shocks are temporary. For example, except in unusual cases, periods of rising oil prices are followed by periods of falling oil prices. Similarly, supply shocks caused by unusually good or bad weather, or by natural disasters, are always short-lived. A temporary supply shock causes only a temporary shift in the *AS* curve; over the long run, the curve simply returns to its initial position, and the economy returns to full employment. In Figure 13, the *AS* curve would shift back from AS_2 to AS_1, the price level would fall, and the economy would move from point *R* back to point *E*.

In other cases, however, a supply shock can last for an extended period. One example was the rise in oil prices during the 1970s, which persisted for several years. In cases like this, is there a self-correcting mechanism that brings the economy back to full employment after a long-lasting supply shock? Indeed, there is, and it is the same mechanism that brings the economy back to full employment after a demand shock.

Look again at Figure 13. At point *R*, output is below full-employment output. In the long run, as workers compete for scarce jobs, the wage rate will decline. This will cause the *AS* curve to shift *downward*. The wage will continue to fall until the economy returns to full employment, that is, until we are back at point *E*.

In the long run, the economy self-corrects after a supply shock, just as it does after a demand shock. When output differs from its full-employment level, the wage rate changes and the AS curve shifts until full employment is restored.

SOME IMPORTANT PROVISOS ABOUT THE *AS* CURVE

The upward-sloping aggregate supply curve we've presented in this chapter gives a realistic picture of how the economy behaves after a demand shock. In the short run, positive demand shocks that increase output also raise the price level. Negative demand shocks that decrease output generally put downward pressure on prices.

However, the story we have told about what happens as we move along the *AS* curve is somewhat incomplete.

First, we made the assumption that prices are completely flexible—that they can change freely over short periods of time. In fact, however, some prices take time to adjust, just as wages take time to adjust. Firms print catalogs containing prices that are good for, say, six months. The public utility commission in your state may set the prices of electricity, gas, water, and basic telephone service in advance for a year or more.

Second, we assumed that wages are completely *inflexible* in the short run. But in *some* industries, wages respond quickly. For example, in the construction industry, contractors hire workers for projects lasting a few months. When they can't find the workers they want, they immediately offer higher wages; they don't wait a year.

Third, there is more to the process of recovering from a shock than the adjustment of prices and wages. During a recession, many workers lose their jobs at the same time. It takes time for those workers to become reestablished in new jobs. As time passes, and job losers become job finders, the economy tends to recover. This process, in addition to the changes in wages and prices we've discussed, is part of the long-run adjustment process and helps to bring the economy back to full employment after a shock.

USING THE THEORY

The Story of Two Recessions and "Jobless" Expansions

The aggregate demand and aggregate supply curves are more than just abstract graphs; they're tools to help us understand important economic events. For example, they can help us understand why the economy suffered its two most recent recessions, and also how and why these recessions differed from one another.

The Recession of 1990–91

The story of the 1990–91 recession begins in mid-1990, when Iraq invaded Kuwait, a major oil producer. During this conflict, Kuwait's oil was taken off the world market, and so was Iraq's. The reduction in oil supplies resulted in a rapid and substantial increase in the price of oil, a key input to many industries. From the second to the fourth quarter of 1990, oil prices rose from $14 to $27 per barrel.

The left-hand panel of Figure 14 shows our *AS–AD* analysis of the shock. Initially, the economy was on both AD_{1990} and AS_{1990}. Equilibrium was at point *E*, and output was at the full-employment level. Then, the oil price shock shifted the *AS* curve upward, to AS_{1991}, while leaving the *AD* curve more or less unchanged. As the short-run equilibrium moved to point *R*, real GDP fell and the price level *rose*. Now look at the left side of the next figure (Figure 15). The upper panel shows the behavior of GDP during the period leading up to, and during, the recession. As you can see, consistent with our *AS–AD* analysis, real GDP fell—from a high of $6.73 trillion in the second quarter of 1990 to a low of $6.63 trillion in the first quarter of 1991 (a decrease of 1.5 percent). The lower panel shows the behavior of the Consumer Price Index (CPI). While the CPI was rising modestly before the recession began, it rose more rapidly during the second half of 1990, as the recession took hold. Once again, this is consistent with what our *AS–AD* analysis predicts for a negative supply shock, such as the rise in oil prices in 1990.

What about the recovery that followed this recession? Once you know what the Fed did, you have all the tools to answer this question yourself. Problem 8 at the end of this chapter takes you through the process.

© CHRIS HONDROS/GETTY IMAGES/LIAISON

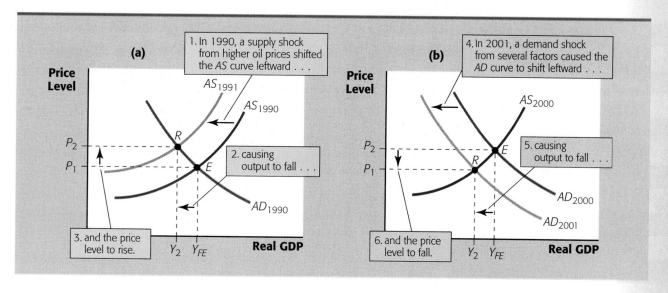

FIGURE 14
An *AD* and *AS* Analysis of
Two Recessions

The Recession of 2001

The story of the 2001 recession was quite different. This time, there was no spike in oil prices and no other significant supply shock to plague the economy. Rather, there was a demand shock, and a Federal Reserve policy during the year before the recession that might have made it a bit worse.

In earlier chapters, you learned that the major cause of the recession was a decrease in investment spending. To review: In the years leading up to 2001, businesses rushed to acquire and develop new equipment needed to exploit new technologies, such as the Internet and wireless communication. By 2001, many firms had sufficiently "caught up" and the flow of investment spending—while still positive and high—began to decrease relative to previous years. This decrease in investment spending was a demand shock to the economy: In 2001, the *AD* curve shifted leftward.

Now we can introduce another force that may have contributed to the recession of 2001: the policy of the Fed. During the late 1990s, the Fed had become concerned that the investment boom and consumer optimism were shifting the *AD* curve rightward too rapidly, creating a danger that we would overshoot potential GDP and set off higher inflation. The Fed responded by tightening up on the money supply and raising the interest rate. From mid-1999 to mid-2000, the Fed raised the federal funds rate six times—a total of almost two full percentage points in less than a year. The Fed then held the rate at a relatively high 6.50 percent for another six months until early 2001. In retrospect, the Fed may have continued raising and holding the rate high a bit too long, even after the *AD* curve stopped moving rightward. And the effects of this policy may have continued into early 2001, exacerbating the decrease in investment that was occurring for other reasons. In this way, the rate hikes themselves may have contributed to a further leftward shift of the *AD* curve.

The right-hand panel of Figure 14 shows our *AS*–*AD* analysis of this period. Initially, the economy was on both AD_{2000} and AS_{2000}, with equilibrium at point *E* and output roughly at the full employment level. Then, the decrease in investment spending—helped along by the Fed—shifted the *AD* curve leftward, to AD_{2001}, while leaving the *AS* curve more or less unchanged. As the short-run equilibrium moved to point *R*, real GDP fell. This is mirrored in Figure 15, where the upper

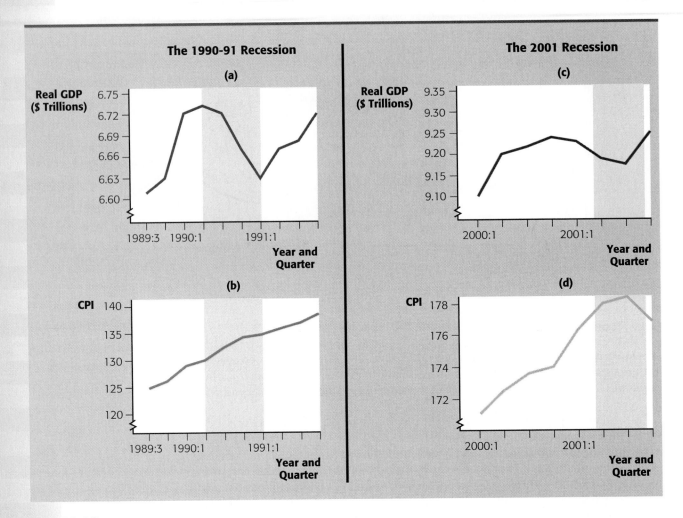

FIGURE 15
GDP and the Price Level in Two Recessions

right-hand panel shows the behavior of GDP during the period leading up to, and during, the 2001 recession. As you can see, consistent with our *AS–AD* analysis, real GDP first slowed and then fell slightly—from a high of $9.24 trillion in the first quarter of 2001 to $9.18 trillion in the third quarter of that year.

But what about the price level? Here, we need to recognize that there is a slight difference between what our *AS–AD* analysis predicts and what actually happened. In the right panel of Figure 14, the price level falls. And indeed, in the lower right panel of Figure 15, you can see that the price level eventually fell—in the fourth quarter of 2001. But for much of the recession, instead of the price level falling we can see that it was rising, but more slowly as 2001 continued. In the next chapter, you will learn that inflation often has some momentum: When it's been rising at a certain rate for some time, then—left alone—it will continue to rise at that rate. The leftward shift in the *AD* curve meant that inflation was *not* left alone in early 2001, so while prices continued to rise, they rose more slowly due to the *AD* shift. And, as you can see, the *AD* shift's downward pressure on prices eventually overcame the inflationary momentum, causing a drop in the price level toward the end of 2001. This is just what we'd expect from our *AS–AD* analysis.

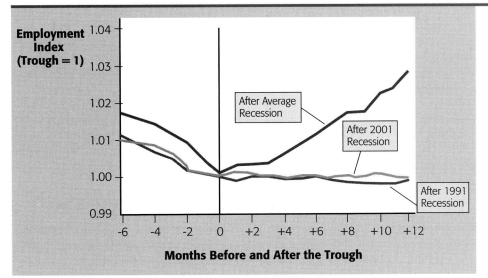

FIGURE 16

The Average Expansion Versus Two Recent Jobless Expansions

Sources: "A Closer Look at Jobless Recoveries," *Economic Review,* Second Quarter 2003, Federal Reserve Bank of Kansas City, p. 48.

Jobless Expansions

After a recession, the economy enters the expansion phase of the business cycle. Typically, because real GDP is starting from such a low level, it grows rapidly in the first year or so of the expansion, as the economy catches back up to potential output. Employment usually grows rapidly during this period as well.

But in our two most recent recessions, the economy experienced abnormal, prolonged periods during which employment did not grow at all. These are *jobless expansions* (often called *jobless recoveries*).

Figure 16 illustrates the behavior of employment during our two most recent recessions, and the average of the six previous recessions. There is a lot going on in the figure, so let's go through it carefully.[4]

The horizontal axis measures the months before and after the *bottom* (or **trough**) of any given recession. For example, the month marked −2 is two months *before* the trough, when we were still in the *contraction* phase of the cycle. The month marked +6 is six months *after* the trough—six months into the expansion phase.

The vertical axis shows an employment index: employment *divided by* employment at the trough. For each recession, the employment index during any month will be higher or lower than 1.0, depending on whether employment is higher than or lower than it was at the trough. For example, an index number of 1.035 in some month would tell us that employment was 3.5 percent higher that month than during the trough of the recession, while an index number of .99 would tell us that employment was 1 percent lower.

Now, look at the blue line, which shows the average of the employment indices for the six business cycles *before* 1990–91. The blue line shows that employment

Trough The bottom point of a recession, when a contraction ends and an expansion begins.

[4] Analysis for this section is based on Stacey L. Schreft and Aarti Singh, "A Closer Look at Jobless Recoveries," *Economic Review,* Federal Reserve Bank of Kansas City, Second Quarter, 2003; Mark Schweitzer, "Another Jobless Recovery," *Economic Commentary,* Federal Reserve Bank of Cleveland, March 1, 2003; and "The NBER's Business Cycle Dating Procedure," July 17, 2003 (*http://www.nber.org/cycles/recessions.html*). Additional data on employment, hours, and real GDP from several tables at the Bureau of Economic Analysis (*www.bea.gov*) and the Bureau of Labor Statistics (*www.bls.gov*).

falls during the contraction phase of the average cycle (the months up to 0), and rises rapidly during the first year of the expansion phase (from months 0 to +12). But the red and pink lines show what happened in the first year of our two most recent expansions—during 1992 and 2002. In both cases, employment drifted slightly *downward*, telling us that the total number of jobs *decreased* during the year. These were jobless expansions. Why?

Explaining Jobless Expansions. Since the story is similar for both of the jobless expansions, we'll focus on the most recent case: the expansion after the recession of 2001. We can start by going back to the equation breaking down *potential* output into its different components, as we did several chapters ago ("Economic Growth and Rising Living Standards"):

$$\text{Total output} = \text{productivity} \times \text{average hours} \times \text{LFPR} \times \text{population}$$

where LFPR stands for the labor force participation rate—the fraction of the population that is either working or seeking work. Note that multiplying the last two terms (LFPR × population) gives us the total labor force, so we can write:

$$\text{Total output} = \text{productivity} \times \text{average hours} \times \text{labor force}$$

It makes sense to include the entire labor force in our calculations when studying economic growth, since—in the long run—the economy tends toward a fully employed labor force. But now we're interested in *deviations* in the economy *away* from full employment in the short run. Accordingly, we need to modify our equation so it explains our *actual* output, rather than our full employment output. The modification is very simple: we'll use *actual* employment (just those actually working) rather than the entire labor force in our equation:

$$\text{Real GDP} = \text{productivity} \times \text{average hours} \times \text{employment}$$

Next, we'll convert this equation into percentage changes (using the same method as in the earlier economic growth chapter):

$$\%\Delta \text{ Real GDP} \approx \%\Delta \text{ productivity} + \%\Delta \text{ average hours} + \%\Delta \text{ Employment}$$

Since average work hours did not change during the first year of our most recent expansion, we'll set %Δ average hours equal to zero, leaving us with

$$\%\Delta \text{ real GDP} \approx \%\Delta \text{ productivity} + \%\Delta \text{ employment}.$$

Finally, rearranging, we end up with:

$$\%\Delta \text{ employment} \approx \%\Delta \text{ real GDP} - \%\Delta \text{ productivity}$$
$$(-0.3\%) \qquad\qquad\qquad (2.9\%) \qquad\quad (3.2\%)$$

We'll get to the numbers in parenthesis in a moment. But notice what this equation tells us: in periods with no significant changes in average hours, the percentage change in total employment is equal to the rate of output growth minus the rate of productivity growth. If output grows faster than productivity, then %Δ employment will be positive: the number of jobs increases. If output grows slower than productivity, then %Δ employment will be negative: the total number of jobs decreases.

Now to the numbers in parenthesis under the last equation: these show the *actual* percentage changes in the first year of the expansion after the 2001 recession. And they show us why that expansion was jobless: *growth in real GDP did not keep up with growth in productivity*. Specifically, real GDP grew at 2.9%, while productivity rose by 3.2 percent. Employment therefore *fell* by 0.3 percent.

But *why* didn't growth in real GDP keep up with productivity growth?

First, because growth in real GDP was unusually low. In the first year of an expansion, output typically grows about 6 percent, but during 2002 it grew by 2.9 percent—less than half its usual rate. Business investment spending gets most of the blame: It usually rises during the first year of an expansion, but in 2002 business investment *decreased*. The reasons for this may include continuing global uncertainty after September 11, 2001, which was followed by the war in Afghanistan and the buildup to war in Iraq. It may also be due to the high levels of investment in information technology and other capital equipment during the 1990s: Once firms caught up with the amount of capital they desired, they had no reason to maintain or return to those previously high rates of annual investment spending.

The second reason for the jobless recovery is productivity, which grew at about the *same* rate as in the average expansion, in spite of the low growth in output. Ordinarily, increases in the capital stock are a major source of productivity growth, but since business investment in new capital *decreased* during 2002, we might expect that productivity growth would slow down that year. But another factor was maintaining high productivity growth: firms' behavior in the labor market. Throughout the first year of the expansion, firms were reluctant to hire full-time, permanent workers, perhaps because the international instability discussed above created uncertainty about the strength and duration of the expansion. Instead, businesses expanded output by hiring part-time and temporary workers.

Why would this boost productivity? Because it enabled firms to adjust their workforce more easily to fluctuations in production. When firms hire regular, full-time employees, they tend to keep them employed at full-time hours even when production dips. But with temporary or part-time workers, firms can adjust employment or hours as production fluctuates. As a result, any given level of output can be produced, on average, with fewer total hours of employed labor. This increases productivity. Firms behaved similarly during the 1990s: Productivity growth exceeded output growth, largely because in 1992—as in 2002—firms relied more heavily on temporary and part-time workers than during a typical expansion.

It might seem odd to think of productivity growth as something harmful. After all, productivity growth is a good thing, the major reason that living standards grow . . . *in the long run.* But in the *short run,* as you've seen, if productivity grows faster than output, it threatens jobs. Keep in mind, though, that the phrase "jobless expansion" refers to just *part* of the expansion phase. Eventually, employment catches up, even to the higher levels of output made possible by productivity growth.

However, the problem can persist for some time. In the early 1990s, even after the expansion finally began to create new jobs after about a year, job creation was so slow that we remained significantly below full employment for another few years, into the mid-1990s. And in mid-2003, a full eighteen months after the trough of the recession, employment was still lower than it was at the trough. Job creation had not yet begun.

It's too early to say if jobless expansions will become the norm in the first year of so after future recessions. Expansions are more likely to be jobless if the early phases of output growth are low—due to uncertainty, abnormally high investment in prior periods, or any other cause. And they are more likely if firms remain wary of hiring regular, full-time workers until the expansion is well under way. But jobless expansions are painful. They leave hundreds of thousands of additional workers without jobs even as the economy expands, and also raise the average *duration* of unemployment. Their mere possibility raises the stakes for the Fed and other government policy makers in trying to prevent future recessions.

Summary

The model of aggregate supply and demand explains how the price level and output are determined in the short run—a period of a year or so following a change in the economy—and how the economy adjusts over longer time periods as well.

The aggregate demand (*AD*) curve shows how changes in the price level affect equilibrium real GDP. A change in the price level shifts the money demand curve and alters the interest rate in the money market. The change in the interest rate, in turn, affects interest-sensitive forms of spending, shifts the aggregate expenditure curve, triggers the multiplier process, and leads to a new level of equilibrium real GDP. A lower price level means a higher equilibrium real GDP, and a higher price level means lower GDP. The downward-sloping AD curve is drawn for given values of government purchases, net taxes, autonomous consumption spending, and the money supply. Changes in any of those variables will cause the AD curve to shift.

The aggregate supply (*AS*) curve summarizes the way changes in output affect the price level. To draw the *AS* curve, we assume that firms set the price of individual products as a markup over their costs per unit, and that the economy's average markup is determined by competitive conditions. We also assume that the nominal wage rate is fixed in the short run. As we move upward along the *AS* curve, a rise in real GDP, by raising unit costs, causes the price level to increase.

When anything other than a change in real GDP causes the price level to change, the entire *AS* curve shifts.

AD and *AS* together determine real GDP and the price level. The economy must be on the *AD* curve, or real GDP would not be at its equilibrium level. It must be on the *AS* curve or firms would not be charging prices dictated by their unit costs and markups. Both conditions are satisfied at the intersection of the two curves.

The *AD—AS* equilibrium can be disturbed by a demand shock. An increase in government purchases, for example, shifts the *AD* curve rightward. As a result, the price level rises, and so does real GDP. In the long run, if GDP is above potential, wages will rise. This causes unit costs to rise and shifts the *AS* curve upward. Eventually, GDP will return to potential and the only long-run result of the demand shock is a higher price level. This implies that the economy's long-run aggregate supply curve is vertical at potential output.

The short-run *AD—AS* equilibrium can also be disturbed by a supply shock, such as an increase in world oil prices. With unit costs higher at each level of output, the *AS* curve shifts upward, decreasing real GDP and increasing the price level. Eventually, the shock will be self-correcting: With output below potential, the wage rate will fall, unit costs will decrease, and the *AS* curve will shift back downward until full employment is restored.

Key Terms

Aggregate demand (*AD*) curve	Long-run aggregate supply curve	Stagflation
Aggregate supply (*AS*) curve	Self-correcting mechanism	Supply shock
Demand shock	Short-run macroeconomic equilibrium	Trough

Review Questions   *Answers to even-numbered Questions and Problems can be found on the text Web site at http://hall-lieb.swlearning.com.*

1. What causal relationship does the aggregate demand curve describe? Why does the *AD* curve slope downward? What does each point on the *AD* curve represent?

2. "Only fiscal policy can shift the aggregate demand curve." True or false? Explain.

3. List three reasons why a change in output affects unit costs and subsequently the price level.

4. What causal relationship does the aggregate supply curve describe? Why does the *AS* curve slope upward?

5. Why does equilibrium occur only where the *AD* and *AS* curves intersect?

6. What is the economy's *self-correcting mechanism,* and how does it work?

7. What is the long-run aggregate supply curve? Why is it vertical?

8. Does the vertical shape of the long-run aggregate supply curve support the predictions of the classical model with regard to the effectiveness of fiscal policy and crowding out? Explain.

9. How does an economy recover from a permanent negative supply shock?

10. Explain why real GDP growth did not keep up with productivity in 2002.

Problems and Exercises

1. Redraw Figure 2, showing how a decrease in the price level will lead to an increase in equilibrium real GDP.

2. With a three-panel diagram—one panel showing the money market, one showing the aggregate expenditure diagram, and one showing the AD curve—show how a *decrease* in the money supply shifts the AD curve leftward.

3. Using a diagram showing the aggregate expenditure line, the money market, and the AD curve, describe how an increase in taxes affects the interest rate, real aggregate expenditure, and the aggregate demand curve. (Assume that the price level does not change.) What other changes would result in these same effects?

4. Suppose firms become pessimistic about the future and consequently investment spending falls. With an AD and AS graph, describe the short-run effects on real GDP and the price level. If the price level were constant, how would your answer change?

5. With an AD and AS diagram, explain the short-run effect of a decrease in the money supply on real GDP and the price level. What is the effect in the long run? Assume the economy begins at full employment.

6. Use an AD and AS graph to explain the short-run and long-run effects on real GDP and the price level of an increase in autonomous consumption spending. Assume the economy begins at full employment.

7. A new government policy successfully lowers firms' unit costs. What are the short-run and the long-run effects of such a policy? (Assume that full-employment output does not change.)

8. Make two copies of Figure 14(a) on a sheet of paper. Add curves to illustrate your answer to (a) on one copy and (b) on the other:
   a. What *would* have happened in the years after 1991 if the Fed had done nothing and the economy had relied solely on the self-correcting mechanism to return to full employment?
   b. What *did* happen as a result of the Fed bringing down the interest rate to end the recession?

   c. Is there a difference in the behavior of the price level during the recovery in these two cases? Explain.

9. Make two copies of Figure 14(b) on a sheet of paper. Add curves to illustrate the impacts of Fed policy for (a) on one copy and (b) on the other:
   a. What *would* have happened in the years following 2001 if the Fed had done nothing and the economy had relied solely on the self-correcting mechanism to return to full employment?
   b. What *did* happen as a result of the Fed's actual policy in 2001 (successive cuts in the interest rate throughout the year)?
   c. Is there a difference in the behavior of the price level during the recovery in these two cases? Explain.

10. Suppose that aggressive antitrust action by the U.S. Justice Department were to successfully increase the degree of competition in many U.S. industries. Use AS and AD curves to illustrate the short-run impact on the economy if, at the same time,
    a. The Fed does nothing.
    b. The Fed pursues a policy that successfully achieves the highest possible level of GDP with no rise in the price level.

11. (a) Use an AD and AS graph to show the effects of a decrease in net exports, assuming that the Fed intervenes to keep the economy at full employment. Assume the economy begins at full employment. (b) What would be the short-run and long-run effects if the Fed does not intervene?

12. a. Graphically show the effects of a temporary decrease in nonlabor input prices.
    b. How will your results change if this decrease lasts for an extended period?
    c. How would your results differ if the Fed intervened to keep the economy at full employment?

13. What will happen if real GDP grows by 4 percent while productivity grows by 4.6 percent?

Challenge Questions

1. Suppose that wages are slow to adjust downward but rapidly adjust upward. What would the AS curve look like? How would this affect the economy's adjustment to demand shocks (compared to the analysis given in the chapter)?

2. During the 1990s, because of technological change, the AS curve was shifting downward, but—except for a few months—the price level did not fall. Why not? (*Hint:* What was the Fed doing?)

ECONOMIC *Applications* | *These exercises require access to Hall/Lieberman Xtra! If Xtra! did not come with your book, visit http://hallxtra.swlearning.com to purchase.*

1. Use your Xtra! password at the Hall and Lieberman Web site (http://hallxtra.swlearning.com), select this chapter, and under Economic Applications, click on EconDebate. Choose *Monetary Policy,* and scroll down to find the debate, "Will the European Monetary Union Succeed?" Read the debate, and use the information to answer the following questions.

   a. This debate emphasizes the relationship between monetary and fiscal policy. Use the AD–AS framework to explain what would happen to the output and inflation rate of a country at full employment, if the European Central Bank engages in expansionary monetary policy and reduces interest rates.

   b. Use the AD–AS framework to explain what would happen to the output and inflation rate of a country

in recession, if another (larger) country increases government borrowing to finance fiscal expenditures, and in the process raises the interest rates in all participating countries.

2. Use your Xtra! password at the Hall and Lieberman Web site (http://hallxtra.swlearning.com), select this chapter, and under Economic Applications, click on EconData. Choose *Monetary Policy,* and scroll down to find *Civilian Unemployment Rate.* Read the definition, then click on Diagrams/Data. The CPI Inflation Rate and the Unemployment Rate diagram illustrates the pattern of inflation and unemployment during the business cycle. Confirm that during recessions inflation rates fall while unemployment rates rise.

CHAPTER 26

Inflation and Monetary Policy

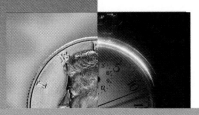

In the late 1970s, the annual inflation rate in the United States reached 13 percent. At the time, polls showed that the public considered inflation the most serious economic problem facing the country. In the 11 years after 1990, however, the annual inflation rate never exceeded 3.5 percent, and the problem receded as a matter of public concern. Bringing the inflation rate down, and keeping it low, was one of the solid victories of national economic policy.

But in late 2002 and early 2003, a new worry arose: that the inflation rate might be *too* low and the nation was in danger of experiencing *deflation*—an ongoing *decrease* in the price level.

Why was the inflation rate so high in the 1970s? How did the Fed bring the rate down? Why did the possibility of deflation keep some Fed officials awake at night? And finally, how should the Fed respond to future economic disturbances?

In this chapter, we'll be addressing these and other questions as we take a closer look at the Fed's conduct of monetary policy. Our earlier discussions of monetary policy were somewhat limited, because we lacked the tools—aggregate demand and aggregate supply—to explain changes in the price level. In this chapter, we'll explore monetary policy more fully, making extensive use of the *AD* and *AS* curves.

THE OBJECTIVES OF MONETARY POLICY

The Fed's objectives have changed over the years. When the Fed was first established in 1913, its chief responsibility was to ensure the stability of the banking system. By acting as a *lender of last resort*—injecting reserves into the banking system in times of crisis—the Fed was supposed to alleviate financial panics.

By the 1950s, the stability of the banking system was no longer a major concern, largely because the United States had not had a banking panic in decades. (Deposit insurance programs had effectively eliminated panics.) Accordingly, the Fed's objective in the 1950s and 1960s changed to keeping the interest rate low and stable. In the 1970s, the Fed's objectives shifted once again. As stated in the Federal Reserve Banking Act of 1978, which is still in force, the Fed is now responsible for achieving a low, stable rate of inflation, and full employment of the labor force. Let's consider each of these goals in turn.

Low, Stable Inflation

Why is a low rate of inflation important? Several chapters ago, we reviewed the social costs of inflation. When the inflation rate is high, society uses up resources coping with it—resources that could have been used to produce goods and services. Among these resources are the labor needed to update prices at stores and factories, as well as the additional time spent by households and businesses to manage their wealth and protect it from a loss of purchasing power.

In addition to keeping the inflation rate low, the Fed tries to keep it *stable* from year to year. For example, the Fed would prefer a steady yearly inflation rate of 3 percent to an inflation rate of 5 percent half the time, and 1 percent the other half, even though the average inflation rate would be 3 percent in both cases. The reason is that unstable inflation is difficult to predict accurately; it will often turn out higher or lower than people expected. As you learned several chapters ago, an inflation rate higher than expected redistributes real income from lenders to borrowers, while an inflation rate lower than expected has the opposite effect. Thus, unstable inflation adds to the risk of lending and borrowing, and interferes with long-run financial planning.

The Fed, as a public agency, chooses its policies with the costs of inflation in mind. And the Fed has another concern: Inflation is very unpopular with the public. Surveys show that most people associate high rates of inflation with a general breakdown of government and the economy.[1] A Fed chairman who delivers low rates of inflation is seen as popular and competent, while one who tolerates high inflation goes down in history as a failure.

Full Employment

"Full employment" means that unemployment is at normal levels. But what, exactly, is a *normal* amount of employment?

Recall that there are different types of unemployment. Some of the unemployed in any given month will find jobs after only a short time of searching. This *frictional* unemployment is part of the normal workings of the labor market and is not a seri-

---

[1] Robert J. Shiller, "Public Resistance to Inflation: A Puzzle," *Brookings Papers on Economic Activity,* 1997.

ous social problem. Other job seekers will spend many months or years out of work because they lack the skills that employers require, or because they lack information about available jobs. While this *structural* unemployment is a serious social problem, it is best solved with *micro*economic policies, such as job-training programs or improved information flows.

Cyclical unemployment, by contrast, is a *macro*economic problem. It occurs during a recession, in which millions of workers lose their jobs and remain unemployed as they seek new ones. This is why macroeconomists use the term "full employment" to mean *the absence of cyclical employment.* When the economy achieves full employment according to this definition, macroeconomic policy has done all that it can do.

The Fed is concerned about cyclical unemployment for two reasons. First is its *opportunity cost*: the output that the unemployed could have produced if they were working. Part of this opportunity cost is paid by the unemployed themselves, in the form of lost earnings, and part is paid by people who remain employed but pay higher taxes to provide unemployment benefits to job losers. By maintaining full employment, the Fed can help society avoid this cost.

Second, cyclical unemployment represents a social failure. In a recession, people who have the right skills and who could be working actually *lose* their jobs. Excess unemployment lingers for several years after a recession strikes. Thus, cyclical unemployment caused by a recession is a partial breakdown of the system. The economy is not doing what it should do: provide a job for anyone who wants to work and who has the needed skills.

But why should the Fed try to eliminate only *cyclical* unemployment? Why not go further and push output above its full-employment level? After all, at higher levels of output, business firms would be more willing to hire *any* available workers. The frictionally unemployed would find jobs more easily, and some of the structurally unemployed would be hired as well. If unemployment is a bad thing, shouldn't the Fed aim for the lowest possible unemployment rate?

The answer is no. If the unemployment rate falls too low, GDP rises beyond its potential, full-employment level. As you learned in the last chapter, this causes the economy's self-correcting mechanism to kick in: The *AS* curve shifts upward, increasing the price level. Thus, unemployment that is too low compromises the Fed's other chief goal by creating inflation. And, as you will see later in the chapter, the Fed cannot keep the economy operating above full employment for more than a short time anyway. In the long run, its attempts to push the economy too hard would only create more inflation and would not succeed in lowering unemployment.

The unemployment rate at which GDP is at its full-employment level—that is, with no cyclical unemployment—is sometimes called the **natural rate of unemployment.**

Natural rate of unemployment
The unemployment rate when there is no cyclical unemployment.

> *When the unemployment rate is below the natural rate, GDP is greater than potential output. The economy's self-correcting mechanism will then create inflation. When the unemployment rate is above the natural rate, GDP is below potential output. The self-correcting mechanism will then put downward pressure on the price level.*

The word *natural* must be interpreted with care. The natural unemployment rate is not etched in stone, nor is it the outcome of purely natural forces that can't be influenced by public policy. But it is determined by rather slow-moving forces in the economy: how frequently workers move from job to job, how efficiently the unemployed can search for jobs and firms can search for new workers, and how well the skills of the unemployed match the skills needed by employers.

Still, the natural rate can change when any of these underlying conditions change. And it can also be influenced by government policies that provide incentives or disincentives for workers to find jobs quickly, or for employers to hire them. Indeed, economists generally believe that over the past decade, the natural rate has decreased in the United States—from 6 or 6.5 percent in the mid-1980s to perhaps as low as 4.5 percent today. Meanwhile, in many European countries, the natural rate of unemployment has increased over the last decade. In the late 1990s, the natural rate reached 10 percent in France and close to 20 percent in Spain. The causes of these changes in the natural rate, as well as the *extent* of the changes, are hotly debated by economists. But there is general agreement about the direction: down in the United States, up in continental Europe.

Why use the term *natural* for such a changeable feature of the economy? The term makes sense only from the perspective of *macroeconomic* policy. Simply put, there isn't much that macroeconomic policy can do about the natural rate. Stimulating the economy with fiscal or monetary policy may bring the *actual* unemployment rate down for a time, but it will not change the natural rate itself. And pushing unemployment below the natural rate would cause inflation. Thus, the natural rate of unemployment can be seen as a kind of goalpost for the Fed. The location of the goalpost may change over the years, but during any given year, it tells us where the Fed is aiming.

THE FED'S PERFORMANCE

How well has the Fed achieved its goals? Panel (a) of Figure 1 shows the annual inflation rate since 1950, as measured by the Consumer Price Index. You can see that monetary policy permitted extended periods of high inflation in the 1970s and early 1980s. You can also see, as noted at the beginning of the chapter, that the Fed has achieved great success in controlling inflation since then. Indeed, in the 20 years leading up to 2003, the annual inflation rate exceeded 4.6 percent only once—in 1990, during the supply shock caused by higher oil prices. And in recent years, inflation at or below 2.5 percent has become the norm.

Panel (b) shows the quarterly rate of unemployment since 1950. Over the last 20 years—a period during which the Fed has succeeded in keeping inflation in check—the Fed's performance on unemployment has been somewhat mixed. From 1983 through the end of 2003, the unemployment rate was 7 percent or greater—significantly above its natural rate—more than one-fourth of the time. But notice the remarkable improvement from mid-1992 and after, as the Fed slowly inched the unemployment rate down to 4 percent *without* heating up inflation. The Fed even managed to keep the unemployment rate hovering near 4 percent for more than two years until it began to rise during the recession of 2001.

As you can see, the Fed has mostly had a good—and improving—record in recent years. The inflation rate has been kept low and relatively stable, and—except for our most recent recession—unemployment has been near and even below most estimates of the natural rate. How has the Fed done it? Are there any general conclusions we can reach about how a central bank should operate to achieve the twin goals of full employment and a stable, low inflation rate? Indeed there are, as you'll see in the next section.

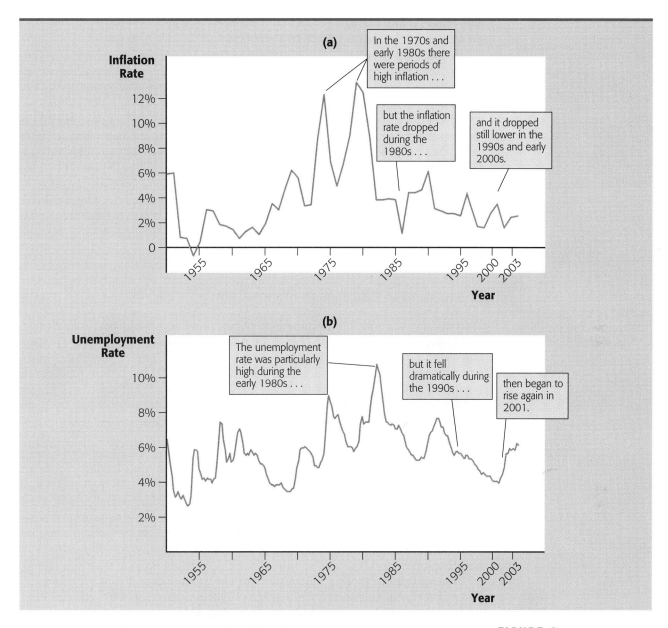

FIGURE 1
**The Fed's Performance
Since 1950**

FEDERAL RESERVE POLICY: THEORY AND PRACTICE

So far in this text, we've assumed that the Fed's response to demand shocks or supply shocks is a **passive monetary policy.** That is, in the face of these shocks, the Fed conducts neither open market purchases nor open market sales of bonds, and just keeps the money supply constant. While this was useful for understanding how different events can affect the economy, it is not a realistic description of the Fed's actions. In recent years, the Fed has tried to maintain a stable level of real GDP, rather than a stable money supply. Ideally, the Fed would like to keep the economy operating as close to its potential output as possible. If output falls

Passive monetary policy When the Fed keeps the money supply constant regardless of shocks to the economy.

below potential, there is painful and wasteful unemployment; if output rises above potential, there is a danger of inflation.

Active monetary policy When the Fed changes the money supply in response to economic shocks.

In order to keep real GDP as close as possible to its potential, the Fed must pursue an **active monetary policy,** in which it responds to events in the economy by *changing* the money supply. As you'll see, the required change in the money supply depends on what type of event the Fed is responding to.

In some cases, the proper response is easy to determine, because the same action that maintains full employment also helps maintain low inflation. But in other cases, the Fed must trade off one goal for another: Responses that maintain full employment will worsen inflation, and responses that alleviate inflation will create more unemployment.

We'll make a temporary simplifying assumption in this section: that the Fed's goal for the inflation rate is *zero*. In reality, the Fed's goal is *low,* but not zero, inflation. Later, we'll discuss why the Fed prefers a low inflation rate to a zero rate, and how this modifies our analysis.

Responding to Changes in Money Demand

Potential disturbances to the economy sometimes arise from a shift in the money demand curve. For example, two chapters ago, you learned about the effects of expectations on money demand. If people expect the interest rate to rise (the price of bonds to fall) in the near future, they will want to hold less wealth in the form of bonds and more in money, so the money demand curve will shift rightward. Larger and longer-lasting shifts in the money demand curve may occur for reasons that are not well understood, although leading suspects are the development of new types of financial assets and new methods of making payments.

How should the Fed respond to shifts in the money demand curve? Figure 2 shows the effect of a rightward shift of the money demand curve. Look first at panel (a). Initially, the money market is in equilibrium at point E, with the interest rate equal to r_1. When the money demand curve shifts rightward, to M_2^d, the equilibrium moves to point F, with the higher interest rate r_2. With a passive monetary policy—leaving the money supply unchanged—the rise in the interest rate would cause interest-sensitive spending to fall. This, in turn, would decrease equilibrium GDP at any given price level.

Panel (b) shows another way to view the effect of the change in money demand: The AD curve shifts leftward, from AD_1 to AD_2—a demand shock to the economy. With a passive monetary policy, the economy would slide down the AS curve from point E to point F, causing a recession. Since the economy began at full-employment output (Y_{FE}), the passive monetary policy would cause unemployment to rise above the natural rate and the price level would decrease.

If the Fed wants to maintain full employment with zero inflation (an unchanged price level) then a passive monetary policy is clearly the wrong response. Is there a better policy?

Indeed there is: an *active* monetary policy. By increasing the money stock—shifting the money supply curve rightward (indicated by the dashed arrow in panel (a))—the Fed can move the money market to a new equilibrium (directly to the right of point E), *preventing any rise in the interest rate*. If the Fed acts quickly enough, there will be no decrease in interest-sensitive spending and no shift in the AD curve.

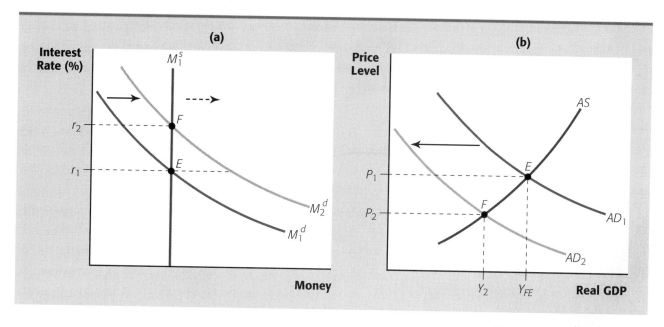

(a)

Interest Rate (%)

M_1^s

r_2 — — — F

r_1 — — — E

M_2^d

M_1^d

Money

(b)

Price Level

AS

P_1 — — — — — — — E

P_2 — — — — F

AD_1

AD_2

Y_2 Y_{FE} **Real GDP**

In panel (b), the economy remains at point E, and the Fed maintains full employment with zero inflation.[2]

As you can see, shifts in the money demand curve present the Fed with a no-lose situation: By adjusting the money supply to prevent changes in the interest rate, the Fed can achieve both price stability and full employment. During most periods, when the economy is not affected by any shocks other than money demand shifts, the constant interest rate policy will keep the economy on an even keel. This is why, in its day-to-day operations, the Fed sets and maintains an **interest rate target** and then adjusts the money supply to achieve that target.

> *To deal with money demand shocks, the Fed sets an interest rate target and changes the money supply as needed to maintain the target. In this way, the Fed can achieve its goals of price stability and full employment simultaneously.*

How the Fed Keeps the Interest Rate on Target. A quick review of the day-to-day mechanics of Fed policy making shows how it sets and maintains its interest rate target in practice. Fed officials meet each morning to determine that day's monetary policy, based on information gathered the previous afternoon and earlier that morning. A key piece of information is what actually happened to the interest rate since the morning before. A rise in the interest rate means that the money demand curve has shifted rightward; a drop in the interest rate means the curve has shifted leftward.

Using this and other information about the banking system and the economy, the Fed decides what to do. At 11:30 A.M., if the interest rate is above target, the Fed buys government bonds. This increases the money supply and brings the interest rate back down to its target level, as in Figure 2. If, instead, the interest rate is

FIGURE 2
Responding to Shifts in Money Demand

Beginning at point E in panel (a), an increase in money demand drives the interest rate up to r_2 (point F). Under a passive monetary policy, interest-sensitive spending would decrease, and the aggregate demand curve would shift leftward in panel (b). GDP falls from Y_{FE} to Y_2. The economy would suffer a recession. To maintain full employment, the Fed could increase the money supply (indicated by the dashed arrow), preventing any change in the interest rate and any shift in AD.

Interest rate target The interest rate the Federal Reserve aims to achieve by adjusting the money supply.

---

[2] Where will the money market end up in Figure 2 (a)? See Challenge Question #3 at the end of this chapter.

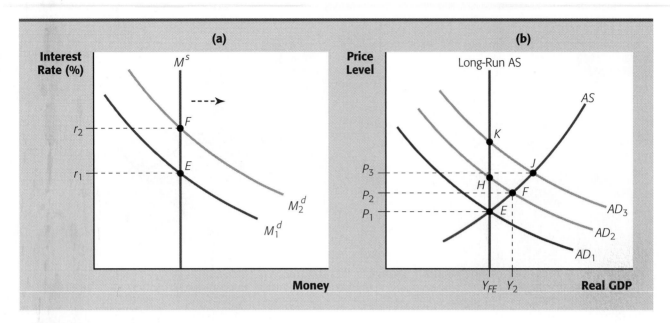

FIGURE 3

Responding to Demand Shocks that Originate with Aggregate Expenditure

A positive spending shock would shift the AD curve rightward to AD$_2$ in panel (b), causing both the price level and output to rise. Under a passive monetary policy, that rise in income would cause the money demand curve to shift to M$_2^d$ in panel (a), driving the interest rate upward from r$_1$ to r$_2$.

An active policy of maintaining the interest rate at r$_1$ would make matters worse. To maintain the interest rate target, the Fed would have to increase the money supply (shown by the dashed arrow), causing an additional rightward shift of the AD curve to AD$_3$ and pushing the economy even further above full employment. The price level would increase to P$_3$ in the short run and even higher (at point K) in the long run.

below target, the Fed sells government bonds, decreasing the money supply and raising the interest rate back up to its target level.[3]

Responding to Other Demand Shocks

You've just seen that changes in money demand shift the *AD* curve, so they are one kind of demand shock. But there are *other* demand shocks that originate with a shift in the aggregate expenditure line. The Fed has a more difficult time responding to this kind of demand shock than to shifts in money demand.

Figure 3 illustrates why. In panel (a) the money market is initially in equilibrium at point *E*, with the interest rate at its initial target level of r_1. In panel (b) the economy's short-run equilibrium is at point *E*, with output at full employment.

Now suppose that there is a positive demand shock that originates with an increase in aggregate expenditure. The shock might come from government policy—an increase in government purchases or a decrease in taxes—or in the private sector—an increase in investment or autonomous consumption or net exports. Whatever the source, the impact in panel (b) is the same: The *AD* curve will shift rightward—from AD_1 to AD_2—and output will rise. Back in panel (a), the rise in output will shift the money demand curve rightward to M$_2^d$, raising the interest rate. Now let's consider three possible responses by the Fed.

First, the Fed could follow a *passive* monetary policy, leaving the money supply unchanged. In this case, the interest rate would be allowed to rise above its target. In panel (b), the economy would slide upward along the *AS* curve, moving to point *F*. Both output and the price level would rise.

---

[3] In an earlier chapter, you learned that the interest rate targeted most directly by the Fed is the *federal funds rate*—the rate that banks charge when lending reserves to other banks. But the Fed knows that changes in the federal funds rate cause *other* interest rates to change—those that directly affect investment and consumption spending—and influencing these rates is the ultimate goal of the Fed.

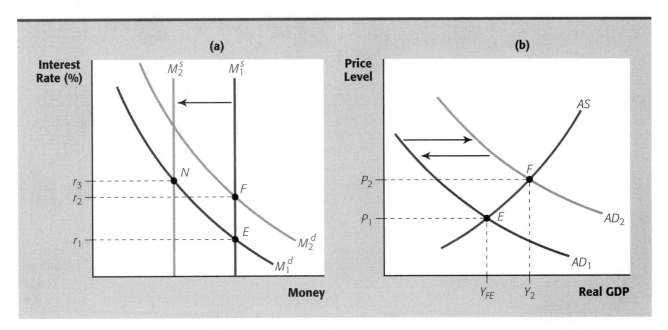

FIGURE 4
**The Best Response to a
Demand Shock Originating
with Aggregate Expenditure**

*A demand shock that shifts the
AD curve to AD$_2$ threatens to
raise output beyond its full-
employment level, and increase
the price level as well. The Fed
can neutralize that shift by raising its interest rate target to r$_3$
and decreasing the money supply to M$_2^s$ in order to achieve
that target. The result is a decrease in interest-sensitive
spending and a return of
the AD curve to AD$_1$.*

As you can see, the Fed would not want to respond to a demand shock with a passive monetary policy. Output would rise, bringing the unemployment rate below the natural rate. The price level would rise as well—to P_2. And in the long run, the price level would rise further as the self-correcting mechanism returned the economy to full employment at point H.

Would the active policy described earlier—maintaining an interest rate target—be an improvement? Actually, no; it would be even worse. To maintain the interest rate at r_1, the Fed would have to *increase* the money supply. But with no rise in the interest rate to crowd out some consumption and investment spending, the demand shock would shift the AD curve rightward even further—say, to AD_3. The new short-run equilibrium would then be at point J. As you can see, maintaining the interest rate target would push the economy even further beyond its potential output, and increase the price level even more, both in the short run (to P_3) and in the long run (to the higher price level at point K).

How, then, should the Fed respond to the demand shock? To maintain full employment and a stable price level, the Fed must pursue an active policy, but one that shifts the AD curve back to AD_1. And it can, indeed, do so. Look at Figure 4. Once again, the figure shows a demand shock that shifts the AD curve rightward to AD_2, increasing both output and the price level. In the money market, the higher price level and higher income shift the money demand curve rightward, raising the interest rate to r_2. But, as you saw in Figure 3, the rise to r_2 is not enough to choke off the increase in spending; it causes *some* crowding out of consumption and investment but not *complete* crowding out. In order to shift the AD curve back to AD_1, the Fed must raise the interest rate *further*, enough to cause *complete* crowding out. That is, it must raise the interest rate by just enough so that consumption and investment spending decline by an amount equal to the initial increase in aggregate expenditure. In the figure, we assume that an interest rate of r_3 will do the trick (point N). The Fed must decrease the money supply to M_2^s.

If the Fed acts quickly enough, it can prevent the demand shock from shifting the *AD* curve at all.[4]

> *To maintain full employment and price stability after a demand shock (other than a change in money demand), the Fed must change its interest rate target. A positive demand shock requires an increase in the target; a negative demand shock requires a decrease in the target.*

In recent years, the Fed has changed its interest rate target as frequently as needed to keep the economy on track. If the Fed observes that the economy is overheating—and that the unemployment rate has fallen below its natural rate—it will raise its target. The Fed, believing that the *AD* curve was shifting rightward too rapidly, reacted this way from mid-1999 to mid-2000, raising its interest rate target six times in one year. When the Fed raises its target, it responds to forces that shift the *AD* curve rightward by creating an opposing force—a higher interest rate—to shift it leftward again.

When the Fed observes that the economy is sluggish—and the unemployment rate has risen above its natural rate—the Fed will lower its target. The Fed did this aggressively throughout 2001, dropping its interest rate target 12 times that year. In this way, the Fed created a force opposing the leftward shift of the *AD* curve.

As you can see, demand shocks that originate with a shift of the aggregate expenditure line present the Fed with another no-lose situation: The same policy that helps to keep unemployment at its natural rate also helps to maintain a stable price level. However, these shocks present a challenge to the Fed that it doesn't face during other, less-eventful periods. To change the interest rate target by just the right amount, the Fed needs accurate information about how the economy operates. We'll return to this and other problems in conducting monetary policy in the "Using the Theory" section of this chapter.

The Interest Rate Target and the Financial Markets. The members of the Open Market Committee think very hard before they vote to change the interest rate target. In addition to its effects on the level of output and the price level, changes in the interest rate target can create turmoil in the stock and bond markets.

Why? Recall that the interest rate and the price of bonds are negatively related. Thus, when the Fed moves the interest rate to a higher target level, the price of bonds drops. Because the public holds trillions of dollars in government and corporate bonds, even a small rise in the interest rate—say, a quarter of a percentage point—causes the value of the public's bond holdings to drop by billions of dollars.

The stock market is often affected in a similar way. People hold stocks because they entitle the owner to a share of a firm's profits, and because stock prices are usually expected to rise as the economy grows and firms become more profitable. But stocks must remain competitive with bonds, or else no one would hold them. The lower the price of a stock, the more attractive the stock is to a potential buyer.

When the Fed raises the interest rate, the rate of return on bonds increases, so bonds become more attractive. As a result, stock prices must fall, so that stocks, too, will become more attractive. And that is typically what happens. Unless other changes are affecting the stock market, a rise in the interest rate causes people to try to sell their stocks in order to acquire the suddenly-more-attractive bonds. This

---

[4] Notice that the new money market equilibrium is along the original money demand curve M_1^d. Since this policy returns both the price level and income to their original values, the money demand curve returns to its original position.

causes stock prices to fall, until stocks are once again as attractive as bonds. Thus, a rise in the interest rate causes stock prices, as well as bond prices, to fall:

> *The stock and bond markets move in the opposite direction to the Fed's interest rate target: When the Fed raises its target, stock and bond prices fall; when it lowers its target, stock and bond prices rise.*

The destabilizing effect on stock and bond markets is one reason that, as a rule, the Fed prefers not to change its interest rate target very often. Frequent changes in the target would make financial markets less stable and the public more hesitant to supply funds to business firms by buying stocks and bonds.

Importantly, financial markets are also affected by *expected* changes in the interest rate target—whether or not they occur. If you expect the Fed to raise its target, you also expect stock and bond prices to fall. Therefore, you would want to dump these assets *now*, before their price drops. Similarly, an expectation of a drop in the interest rate target would make you want to buy stocks and bonds now, before their prices rise. Thus, *changes in expectations* about the Fed's future actions can be as destabilizing as the actions themselves.

This is why the financial press speculates constantly about the likelihood of changes in the interest rate target. Most of the time, the news is of the dog that didn't bark—the Federal Open Market Committee meets and decides to keep the target unchanged. Still, interest rates and stock prices often jump around in the days leading up to meetings of the Open Market Committee.

Once you understand the Fed's logic in changing its interest rate target, you can understand a phenomenon that—at first glance—appears mystifying: Stock and bond prices sometimes fall when good news about the economy is released, and rise when bad news is released. For example, if the Bureau of Labor Statistics announces that jobs are plentiful and the unemployment rate has dropped, or the Commerce Department announces that real GDP has grown rapidly in the previous quarter, the stock and bond markets may plummet. Why? Because owners of stocks and bonds believe that the Open Market Committee might interpret the good news as evidence that the economy is overheating. They would then expect the Committee to raise its interest rate target, so they try to sell their stocks and bonds before the committee even meets.

HTTP://

Some income-distributional aspects of monetary policy are explored by Christina and David Romer in "Monetary Policy and the Well-Being of the Poor." It is available at http:// www.kc.frb.org/PUBLICAT/ SYMPOS/1998/S98romer.pdf.

> *Good news about the economy sometimes leads to expectations that the Fed, fearing inflation, will raise its interest rate target. This is why good economic news sometimes causes stock and bond prices to fall. Similarly, bad news about the economy sometimes leads to expectations that the Fed, fearing recession, will lower its interest rate target. This is why bad economic news sometimes causes stock and bond prices to rise.[5]*

Responding to Supply Shocks

So far in this chapter, you've seen that demand shocks, in general, present the Fed with easy policy choices. By sticking to its interest rate target, it can neutralize any demand shocks that arise from shifts in money demand. And by changing its interest

[5] For a more complete discussion of the stock market, see the "Using All the Theory" chapter at the end of this book.

FIGURE 5
Responding to Supply Shocks

Starting at point E, *a negative supply shock shifts the AS curve upward to AS₂. Under a passive monetary policy, a new short-run equilibrium would be established at point R, with a higher price level (P₂) and a lower level of output (Y₂). The Fed could prevent inflation by decreasing the money supply and shifting AD to AD_{no inflation}, but output would fall to Y₃. At the other extreme, it could increase the money supply and shift the AD curve to AD_{no recession}. This would keep output at the full-employment level, but at the cost of a higher price level, P₃.*

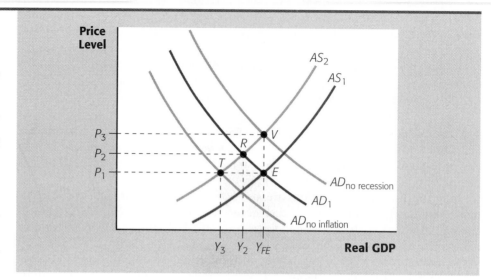

HTTP://

For more information about supply shocks, download Bharat Trehan's "Supply Shocks and the Conduct of Monetary Policy," available at **http://www.frbsf.org/econrsrch/ wklyltr/wklyltr99/el99-21.html.**

rate target from time to time, it can deal with demand shocks caused by changes that originate with aggregate expenditure. In each of these cases, the very policy that maintains a stable price level also helps to maintain full employment.

But adverse or negative *supply* shocks present the Fed with a true dilemma: If the Fed tries to preserve price stability, it will worsen unemployment; if it tries to maintain high employment, it will worsen inflation. And even though supply shocks are usually temporary, the shocks themselves—and the Fed's response—can affect the economy for several quarters or even years.

Figure 5 illustrates the Fed's dilemma when confronting an adverse supply shock. Initially, the economy is at point *E* (full employment). Then, a supply shock—say, a rise in world oil prices—shifts the *AS* curve up to AS_2. Under a passive monetary policy, the Fed would not change the money stock, keeping the *AD* curve at AD_1. The short-run equilibrium would then move from point *E* to point *R*, and the economy would experience *stagflation*—both inflation and a recession—with output falling to Y_2 and the price level rising to P_2.

But the Fed can instead respond with an active monetary policy, changing the money supply in order to alter the short-run equilibrium. Which policy should it choose? The answer will depend on whether it is mostly concerned about rising prices or rising unemployment. Let's start by imagining two extreme positions.

First, the Fed could prevent inflation entirely by decreasing the money supply, shifting the *AD* curve leftward to the curve labeled $AD_{\text{no inflation}}$. This would move the short-run equilibrium to point *T*. Notice, though, that while the price level remains at P_1, output decreases to Y_3—even lower than under the passive policy.

At the other extreme, the Fed could prevent any fall in output. To accomplish this, the Fed would *increase* the money supply and shift the *AD* curve rightward, to $AD_{\text{no recession}}$. The equilibrium would then move to point *V*, keeping output at its full-employment level. But this policy causes more inflation, raising the price level all the way to P_3.

In practice, the Fed is unlikely to choose either of these two extremes to deal with a supply shock, preferring instead some intermediate policy. But the extreme positions help illustrate the Fed's dilemma:

> *A negative supply shock presents the Fed with a short-run trade-off: It can limit the recession, but only at the cost of more inflation; and it can limit inflation, but only at the cost of a deeper recession.*

The choice between the two policies is a hard one. After supply shocks, there are often debates within the Fed—and in the public arena—about how best to respond. Inflation *hawks* lean in the direction of price stability, and are willing to tolerate more unemployment in order to achieve it. In the face of an adverse supply shock, hawks would prefer a response that shifts the *AD* curve closer to $AD_{no\ inflation}$, even though it means higher unemployment. Inflation *doves* lean in the direction of a milder recession, and are more willing to tolerate the cost of higher inflation. They would prefer a response that brings the *AD* curve closer to $AD_{no\ recession}$.

Choosing Between Hawk and Dove Policies. When a supply shock hits, should the Fed use a hawk policy, should it employ a dove policy, or should it keep the *AD* curve unchanged? That depends. Over time, as the economy is hit by supply shocks, the hawk policy maintains more stability in the price level but less stability in output and employment. The dove policy gives the opposite result: more stability in output and less stability in the price level. The Fed should choose a hawkish policy if it cares more about price stability, and a dovish policy if it cares more about the stability of output and employment. Or it can pick an intermediate policy—one that balances price and employment stability more evenly.

The proper choice depends on how the Fed weights the harm caused by unemployment against the harm caused by inflation. And since the Fed is a public institution, its views should reflect the assessment of society as a whole. This is why supply shocks present such a challenge to the Fed: The public itself is divided between hawks and doves. Both inflation and unemployment cause harm, but of very different kinds. Inflation imposes a more general cost on society: the resources used up to cope with it. If the inflation is unexpected, it will also redistribute income between borrowers and lenders. The costs of unemployment are borne largely by the unemployed themselves—who suffer the harm of job loss—but partly by taxpayers, who provide funds for unemployment insurance. Balancing the gains and losses from hawk and dove policies is no easy task.

In recent years, some officials at the Fed have argued that having two objectives—stable prices *and* full employment—is unrealistic when there are supply shocks. The current chair of the Board of Governors, Alan Greenspan, has asked Congress to change the Fed's mandate to one of controlling inflation, period. But it would be difficult for the Fed to ignore the costs of higher unemployment, even if it were legally permitted to do so. Others have proposed that the Fed follow a predetermined rule, spelling out just how hawkish or dovish its response to supply shocks will be. We'll come back to this controversial idea in the "Using the Theory" section of this chapter.

© SUSAN VAN ETTEN

Significant supply shocks—which have often been caused by higher oil prices—force the Fed to choose between a recession or a higher inflation rate.

EXPECTATIONS AND ONGOING INFLATION

So far in this chapter, we've assumed that the Fed strives to maintain *zero* inflation, and that the price level remains constant when the economy reaches its long-run, full-employment equilibrium. But as we discussed earlier, this is not entirely realistic. Look again at panel (a) of Figure 1. There you can see that the U.S. economy has been characterized by *ongoing inflation*. Even in the 1990s and into early 2001—with unemployment at its natural rate—the annual inflation rate hovered around 2 to 3 percent. This means that, even though the economy was at full employment so the economy's self-correcting mechanism was not operating, prices were *continually rising*.

Why should the price level continue to rise when unemployment is at its natural rate? And how does ongoing inflation change our analysis of the effects of monetary policy or the guidelines that the Fed should follow? We'll consider these questions next.

How Ongoing Inflation Arises

The best way to begin our analysis of ongoing inflation is to explore how it arises in an economy. We can do this by revisiting the 1960s, when the inflation rate rose steadily, and ongoing inflation first became a public concern.

What was special about the economy in the 1960s? First, it was a period of exuberance and optimism, for both businesses and households. Business spending on plant and equipment rose, and household spending on new homes and automobiles rose as well. At the same time, government spending rose—both military spending for the war in Vietnam and social spending on programs to help alleviate poverty. These increases in spending all contributed to rightward shifts of the AD curve; they were positive demand shocks. The unemployment rate fell below the natural rate—hovering around 3 percent in the late 1960s. And, as expected, the economy's self-correcting mechanism kicked in: Higher wages shifted the AS curve upward, causing the price level to rise.

As you've learned in this chapter, the Fed could have neutralized the positive demand shocks by raising its interest rate target (as in Figure 4), shifting the AD curve back to its original position. Alternatively, the Fed could have done nothing, allowing the self-correcting mechanism to bring the economy back to full employment with a higher—but stable—price level (as in the move from point F to point H in Figure 3). But in the late 1960s, the Fed made a different choice: It maintained its low interest rate target. This required the Fed to increase the money supply, thus adding its *own* positive demand shock to the spending shocks already hitting the economy. In Figure 3, this was the equivalent of moving the AD curve all the way out to AD_3, preventing any rise in interest rates but overheating the economy even more.

Why did the Fed act in this way? No one knows for sure, but one likely reason is that, in the 1960s, the Fed saw its job differently than it does today. The Fed's goal was to keep the interest rate stable and low, both to maintain high investment spending and to avoid instability in the financial markets. This is what it had been doing for years, with good effect: Americans had prospered in the previous decade, the 1950s, and financial markets were, indeed, stable.

But while this policy worked well in the 1950s, it did not serve the economy well during and after the demand shocks of the 1960s. That's because the Fed's policy—year after year—prevented the self-correcting mechanism from bringing the economy back to full employment. Instead, each time the price level began rising, and the economy began to self-correct, the Fed would increase the money supply *again*, causing output to remain *continually* above its potential output. And that, in turn, meant that the price level would continue to rise, year after year.

Now comes a crucial part of the story: As the price level continued to rise in the 1960s, the public began to *expect* it to rise at a similar rate in the future. This illustrates a more general principle:

When inflation continues for some time, the public develops expectations that the inflation rate in the future will be similar to the inflation rates of the recent past.

Why are expectations of inflation so important? Because when managers and workers expect inflation, it gets built into their decision-making process. Union contracts that set wages for the next three years will include automatic increases to compensate for the anticipated loss of purchasing power caused by future inflation. Nonunion wages will tend to rise each year as well, to match the wages in the unionized sector. And contracts for future delivery of inputs—like lumber, cement, and unfinished goods—will incorporate the higher prices everyone expects by the date of delivery.

A continuing, stable rate of inflation gets built into the economy. The built-in rate is usually the rate that has existed for the past few years.

Once there is built-in inflation, the economy continues to generate inflation even *after* the self-correcting mechanism has finally been allowed to do its job and bring us back to potential output. To see why, look at Figure 6. It shows what might happen over three years in an economy with built-in inflation. In the figure, output is at its full-employment level. Each year, the *AS* curve shifts upward and the *AD* curve shifts rightward, so the price level rises from P_1 to P_2 to P_3. Why does all this happen when there is built-in inflation?

Let's start with the reason for the upward shift of the *AS* curve. Unemployment is at its natural rate, so the self-correction mechanism is no longer contributing to any rise in wages or unit costs. But something else is causing unit costs to increase: inflationary expectations. Based on recent experience, the public expects the price level to rise as it has been rising in the past, so wages (and other input prices) will continue to increase, *even though output remains unchanged at full employment.* Thus,

in an economy with built-in inflation, the AS *curve will shift upward each year, even when output is at full employment and unemployment is at its natural rate. The upward shift of the* AS *curve will equal the built-in rate of inflation.*

For example, if the public expects inflation of 3 percent per year, then contracts will call for wages and input prices to rise by 3 percent per year. This means that unit costs will increase by 3 percent. Firms—marking up prices over unit costs—will raise their prices by 3 percent as well, and the *AS* curve will shift upward by 3 percent each year.

Explaining why the *AS* curve shifts upward is only half the story of the long-run equilibrium in Figure 6. We must also explain why the *AD* curve continues to shift rightward. The simple answer is: The *AD* curve shifts rightward because the Fed continues to increase the money supply. But *why* does the Fed shift the *AD* curve rightward, when it knows that doing so only prolongs inflation? One reason is that reducing inflation would be *costly* to the economy.

Imagine what would happen if, one year, the Fed decided *not* to shift the *AD* curve rightward as it had done in the past. During the year, the *AS* curve will shift upward anyway, by a percentage shift equal to the built-in rate of inflation. This will happen *no matter what the Fed does,* because the shift is based on expected inflation, which, in turn, is based on past experiences of inflation. There is nothing

FIGURE 6
**Long-Run Equilibrium
with Built-In Inflation**

*Each year, the aggregate supply
curve shifts upward by the built-
in rate of inflation. To keep the
economy at full employment,
the Fed shifts the AD curve
rightward each year by increasing the money supply.*

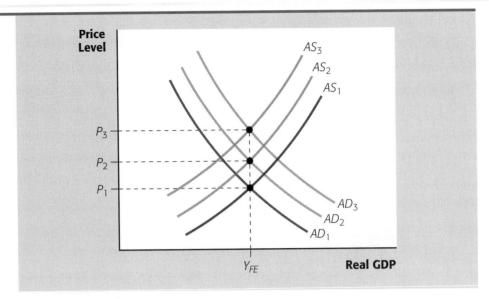

the Fed can do today to affect what has happened in the past, so each year, it must accept the upward shift of the AS curve as a given.

But now suppose the Fed decides to reduce inflation by *not* shifting the AD curve as it has in the past. Instead, it will just leave the AD curve where it was the year before. For example, as the AS curve shifts from AS_2 to AS_3, the Fed might keep the AD curve at AD_2. See if you can pinpoint the new, temporary equilibrium that the Fed will achieve for the economy. (*Strong hint:* It's at the intersection of AD_2 and AS_3.) If you've identified the point correctly, you'll see that the Fed would achieve its goal of reducing the inflation rate that year. The price level would rise from P_2 to something less than P_3, instead of all the way to P_3. But the reduction in inflation is not without cost: The economy's output will decline—a recession.

> *In the short run, the Fed can bring down the rate of inflation by reducing the rightward shift of the AD curve, but only at the cost of creating a recession.*

Would the Fed ever purposely create a recession to reduce inflation? Indeed it would, and it has—more than once. By far the most important episode occurred during the early 1980s. As Figure 1 shows, annual inflation reached the extraordinary level of 13.3 percent in 1979. Soon after, with some support from the newly elected President Reagan, the Fed embarked on an aggressive campaign to bring inflation down. The Fed stopped increasing the money supply, stopped shifting the AD curve rightward, and a recession began in July of 1981. Unemployment peaked, as shown earlier in in Figure 1, at 10.7 percent at the end of 1982. With tremendous slack in the economy, the inflation rate fell rapidly, to below 4 percent in 1982. The Fed deliberately created a serious recession, but it brought down the rate of inflation.

Creating a recession is not a decision that the Fed takes lightly. Recessions are costly to the economy and painful to those who lose their jobs. The desire to avoid a recession is one reason that the Fed tolerated ongoing inflation for years and continued to play its role by shifting the AD curve rightward. We'll discuss other reasons for the Fed's tolerance of ongoing inflation a bit later.

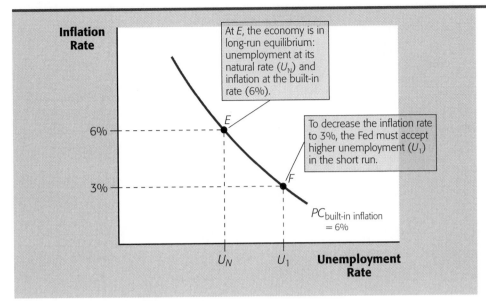

At *E*, the economy is in long-run equilibrium: unemployment at its natural rate (U_N) and inflation at the built-in rate (6%).

To decrease the inflation rate to 3%, the Fed must accept higher unemployment (U_1) in the short run.

$PC_{\text{built-in inflation} = 6\%}$

FIGURE 7
The Phillips Curve

Ongoing Inflation and the Phillips Curve

Ongoing inflation changes our analysis of monetary policy. For one thing, it forces us to recognize a subtle, but important, change in the Fed's objectives: While the Fed still desires full employment, its other goal—price stability—is not zero inflation, but rather a *low and stable inflation rate*.

Another difference is in the graphs we use to illustrate the Fed's policy choices. Instead of continuing to analyze the economy with *AS* and *AD* graphs, when there is ongoing inflation, we usually use another powerful tool.

This tool is the *Phillips curve*—named after the late economist A. W. Phillips, who did early research on the relationship between inflation and unemployment. The **Phillips curve** illustrates the Fed's choices between inflation and unemployment in the short run, for a given built-in inflation rate.

Figure 7 shows a Phillips curve for the U.S. economy. The inflation rate is measured on the vertical axis, the unemployment rate on the horizontal. Point *E* shows the long-run equilibrium in the economy when the built-in inflation rate is 6 percent. At point *E*, unemployment is at its natural rate—U_N—and inflation remains constant from year to year at the built-in rate of 6 percent.

Notice that the Phillips curve is downward sloping. Why? Because it tells the same story we told earlier—with *AD* and *AS* curves—about the Fed's options in the short run. If the Fed wants to decrease the rate of inflation from 6 percent to 3 percent, it must slow the rightward shifts of the *AD* curve. This would cause a movement *along* the Phillips curve from point *E* to point *F*. As you can see, in moving to point *F*, the economy experiences a recession: Since output falls, unemployment rises above the natural rate.

> In the short run, the Fed can move along the Phillips curve by adjusting the rate at which the AD curve shifts rightward. When the Fed moves the economy downward and rightward along the Phillips curve, the unemployment rate increases, and the inflation rate decreases.

Phillips curve A curve indicating the Fed's choice between inflation and unemployment in the short run.

FIGURE 8

The Shifting Phillips Curve

Initially, the economy is at point E, with inflation equal to the built-in rate of 6%. If the Fed moves the economy to point F and keeps it there, the public will eventually come to expect 3% inflation in the future. At that point, the built-in inflation rate will fall and the curve will shift down to $PC_{built-in\ inflation\ =\ 3\%}$. The economy will move to point G in the long run, with unemployment at the natural rate and an actual inflation rate equal to the built-in rate of 3%.

Starting again at point E, suppose the Fed moved the economy to point H. The inflation rate would rise to 9 percent, and the unemployment rate would fall to U_2. If the Fed then held the economy at point H, the built-in inflation rate would rise to 9%, and the Phillips curve would shift up to $PC_{built-in\ inflation\ =\ 9\%}$. Eventually, the economy would move to point J. The vertical line connecting points E, G, and J is the long-run Phillips curve.

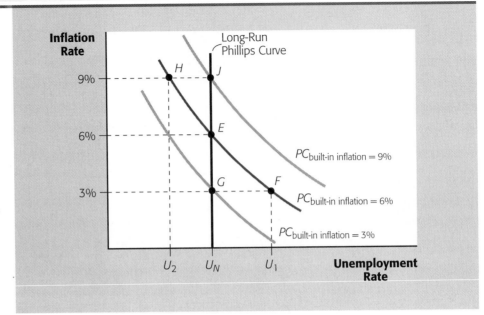

Now suppose the Fed keeps the economy at point *F*. In the long run, the public—observing a 3 percent inflation rate—will come to expect 3 percent inflation in the future. Thus, in the long run, 3 percent will become the economy's built-in rate of inflation. Figure 8 shows the effect on the Phillips curve (ignore the vertical line for now). When the economy's built-in inflation rate drops from 6 percent to 3 percent, the Phillips curve shifts downward, to the lower curve. At any unemployment rate, the inflation rate will be lower, now that the public expects inflation of only 3 percent rather than 6 percent.

> *In the long run, a decrease in the actual inflation rate leads to a lower built-in inflation rate, and the Phillips curve shifts downward.*

Once the Fed has reduced the built-in inflation rate, it can locate anywhere on the new Phillips curve by adjusting how rapidly it lets the money supply grow (and therefore, how rapidly the *AD* curve shifts rightward each year). Therefore, the Fed can choose to bring the economy back to full employment (point *G*), with a new, lower inflation rate of 3 percent rather than the previous 6 percent.

Riding Up the Phillips Curve. The process we've described—moving down the Phillips curve and thereby causing it to shift downward—also works in reverse: Moving *up* the Phillips curve will cause it to shift *upward*. Figure 8 also illustrates this case. Once again, assume the economy begins at point *E*, with a built-in inflation rate of 6 percent and unemployment at its natural rate. Now suppose the Fed begins to increase the money supply *more rapidly* than in the past, and begins shifting the *AD* curve further rightward than in Figure 6. In the short run, the economy would move *along* the Phillips curve from point *E* to point *H* in Figure 8. The inflation rate would rise to 9 percent, and the unemployment rate would fall below its natural rate—in the short run.

But suppose the Fed keeps the economy at point *H* for some time, continuing to shift the *AD* curve rightward at a faster rate than before. Then, in the long run, the public will begin to expect 9 percent inflation, and that will become the new built-in rate of inflation. The Phillips curve will then shift upward. At this point, if the Fed returns the economy to full employment, we end up at point *J*. The economy will be back in long-run equilibrium—but with a higher built-in inflation rate.

Long-Run Equilibrium. In Figure 8, you can see that the Fed's policy choices are different in the short run and in the long run. In the short run, the Fed can move along the Phillips curve, exploiting the trade-off between unemployment and inflation. But in the long run—once the public's expectations of inflation adjust to the new reality—the built-in inflation rate will change, and the Phillips curve will shift. Indeed, the Phillips curve will *keep* shifting whenever the unemployment rate is kept above or below the natural rate. (To see why, ask yourself what would happen in the future if the Fed tried to keep the unemployment rate *permanently* at a level like U_2—below the natural rate.) Thus, the economy cannot be in long-run equilibrium until the unemployment rate returns to its natural rate, and output is back to its potential level. In the long run, when we are at the natural rate of unemployment, the Fed can only choose *which* Phillips curve the economy will be on.

> *In the short run, there is a trade-off between inflation and unemployment: The Fed can choose lower unemployment at the cost of higher inflation, or lower inflation at the cost of higher unemployment. But in the long run, since unemployment always returns to its natural rate, there is no such trade-off.*

The Long-Run Phillips Curve. Let's reconsider what we've learned about the Fed's options in the long run. Figure 8 shows us that, when the Fed slows the rightward shifts of the *AD* curve, unemployment returns to the natural rate but the inflation rate is lower. The figure also shows us that, when the Fed allows the *AD* curve to shift rightward more rapidly than in the past, unemployment returns once again to the natural rate but the inflation rate is higher. As you can see,

> *in the long run, monetary policy can change the rate of inflation, but not the rate of unemployment.*

Now look at the vertical line in Figure 8. It tells us how monetary policy affects the economy in the long run, without the distractions of the short-run story. The vertical line is the economy's **long-run Phillips curve**, which tells us the combinations of unemployment and inflation that the Fed can choose in the long run. No matter what the Fed does, unemployment will always return to the natural rate, U_N, in the long run. However, the Fed can use monetary policy to select any rate of inflation it wants:

Long-run Phillips curve A vertical line indicating that in the long run, unemployment must equal its natural rate, regardless of the rate of inflation.

> *The long-run Phillips curve is a vertical line at the natural rate of unemployment. The Fed can select any point along this line in the long run, by using monetary policy to speed or slow the rate at which the AD curve shifts rightward.*

Why the Fed Allows Ongoing Inflation

Since the Fed can choose any rate of inflation it wants, and since inflation is costly to society, we might think that the Fed would aim for an inflation rate of zero. But a look back at panel (a) of Figure 1 shows that this is not what the Fed has chosen to do. In recent years, with unemployment very close to its natural rate, the Fed has maintained annual inflation at around 2 or 3 percent. Why doesn't the Fed eliminate inflation from the economy entirely?

One reason is a widespread belief that the Consumer Price Index (CPI) and other measures of inflation actually *overstate* the true rate of inflation in the economy. As you've learned, many economists believe that the CPI has overstated the true annual inflation rate by 1 to 2 percent—or more—in recent decades. Although the Bureau of Labor Statistics has been working hard to correct the problem, some significant upward bias remains. If the Fed forced the *measured* rate of inflation down to zero, the result would be an *actual* rate of inflation that was negative—*deflation*. In the "Using the Theory" section of this chapter, we'll discuss the special problems deflation would cause for the Fed and the economy.

Some economists have offered another explanation for the Fed's behavior: Low, stable inflation makes the labor market work more smoothly. The argument goes as follows: While no one wants a cut in their real wage rate, people seem to react differently, depending on *how* the real wage is decreased. For example, suppose there is an excess supply of workers in some industry, and a real wage cut of 3 percent would bring that labor market back to equilibrium. Workers would strongly resist a 3 percent cut in the nominal wage. But they would more easily tolerate a freeze in the nominal wage while the price level rises by 3 percent, even though in both scenarios, the real wage falls by 3 percent.

If this argument is correct, then a low or modest inflation rate would help wages adjust in different markets, helping to ensure that workers move to industries where they would be most productive as the structure of the economy changes over time. In some labor markets, real wages can be raised by increasing nominal wages faster than prices. In other labor markets, real wages can be cut by increasing nominal wages more slowly than prices, or not at all.

> *The Fed has tolerated measured inflation at 2 to 3 percent per year because it knows that the true rate of inflation is lower, and because low rates of inflation may help labor markets adjust more easily.*

© AFP/CORBIS

USING THE THEORY
Challenges for Monetary Policy

So far in this chapter, we've described some clear-cut guidelines the Fed *can* and *does* follow in conducting monetary policy. We've seen that the proper policy for dealing with day-to-day changes in money demand is to set and *maintain* an interest rate target. The proper response to demand shocks that originate with aggregate expenditure is a *change* in the interest rate target. Dealing with a supply shock is more problematic, since it requires the Fed to balance its goal of low, stable inflation with its goal of full employment. But even here, once the Fed decides on the proper balance, its policy choice is straightforward: Shift the *AD* curve to achieve the desired combination of inflation and unemployment in the short run, and then guide the economy back to full employment in the long run.

One might almost conclude from this chapter that monetary policy is akin to operating a giant machine—adjusting this or that knob, and making the occasional repair by consulting the manual. And policy making might appear rather uncontroversial, other than the occasional debate between those who favor hawkish and dovish policies toward inflation after a supply shock.

But the truth is very much the opposite. First, the Fed faces frequent criticism from members of Congress, the business community, the media and some academic economists—not just over its policy choices, but also the *way* it arrives at them. Second, the Fed, rather than operating a well-understood machine, must conduct monetary policy with highly imperfect information about the economy's course and precisely how its policies will alter it. Finally, in the early 2000s, the Fed found itself facing a new economic challenge—the possibility of deflation—requiring it to develop some new, untested tools for monetary policy . . . just in case. Let's consider each of these challenges facing the Fed.

Information Problems

The Federal Reserve has hundreds of economists carrying out research and gathering data to improve its understanding of how the economy works, and how monetary policy affects the economy. Research at the Fed is widely respected, and has made great progress. But because the economy is complex and constantly changing, serious gaps remain. Two of the most important gaps concern the time lag before monetary policy affects the economy, and knowledge of the natural rate of unemployment (or—equivalently—the economy's potential output).

Uncertain and Changing Time Lags. Suppose that we are in the midst of an expansion, and Fed officials begin to worry that the economy is about to overheat. They respond by raising their interest rate target. Eventually, the higher interest rate will dampen planned investment and consumption spending and cool the economy off. But when?

Monetary policy works with a time lag. Even after a rise in the interest rate, business firms will likely continue to build the new plants and new homes they've already started constructing. The most powerful effects on investment spending will be the cancellation of *new* projects currently being planned—projects that *would* have entered the pipeline of new spending many months later. The same applies in the other direction: When the Fed lowers the interest rate to stimulate additional spending, the full effects will be felt many months later, after new investment projects are planned and firms begin making the associated purchases.

The time lag in the effectiveness of monetary policy can have serious consequences. For example, by the time a higher interest rate target has its maximum effect, the economy may already be returning to full employment on its own, or it may be hit by a negative demand shock. In this case, the Fed—by raising its interest rate target—will be reining in the economy at just the wrong time, causing a recession.

Economists often use an analogy to describe this problem. Imagine that you are trying to drive a car with a special problem: When you step on the gas, the car will go forward . . . but not until five minutes later. Similarly, when you step on the brake, the car will slow, but also with a five-minute lag. It would be very difficult to maintain an even speed with this car: You'd step on the gas, and when nothing happened, you'd be tempted to step on it harder. By the time the car begins to move, you will have given too much gas and find yourself speeding down the road. So you try to slow down, but once again, hitting the brakes makes nothing happen. So you brake harder, and when the car finally responds, you come to a dead halt.

The Fed can make—and, in the past, has made—similar mistakes. When it tries to cool off an overheated economy, it may find that nothing is happening. Is it just a long time lag, or has the Fed not hit the brakes hard enough? If it hits the brakes harder, it runs the risk of braking the economy too much; if it doesn't, it runs the risk of continuing to allow the economy to overheat. Even worse, the time lag before monetary policy affects prices and output can change over the years: Just when the Fed may think it has mastered the rules of the game, the rules change.

The Natural Rate of Unemployment

In the Phillips curve diagram (Figure 8), we've assumed that the economy's natural rate of unemployment is known and remains constant, signified by the vertical long-run Phillips curve at some value U_N. In this case, once the economy achieved a long-run equilibrium, the Fed's job would be relatively straightforward: to shift the *AD* curve rightward by just the right amount each period to maintain the natural rate of unemployment with an acceptable rate of inflation.

But even though there is wide agreement that the natural rate rose in the 1970s and has fallen since the late 1980s, economists remain uncertain about its value during any given period. Many economists believe that today the natural rate is between 4.5 and 5 percent, but no one is really sure.

Why is this a problem? It's very much like the two mountain climbers who become lost. One of them pulls out a map. "Do you see that big mountain over there," he says, pointing off into the distance. "Yes," says the other. "Well," says the first, "according to the map, we're standing on top of it." In order to achieve its twin goals of full employment. And a stable, low rate of inflation, the Fed tries to maintain the unemployment rate as close to the natural rate as possible. If its estimate of the natural rate is wrong, it may believe it has succeeded when, in fact, it has not.

For example, suppose the Fed believes the natural rate of unemployment is 5 percent, but the rate is really 4.5 percent. Then—at least for a time—the Fed will be steering the economy toward an unemployment rate that is unnecessarily high and an output level that is unnecessarily low. We've already discussed the costs of cyclical unemployment. An overestimate of the natural rate makes society bear these costs needlessly. On the other hand, if the Fed believes the natural rate is 4.5 percent when it is really 5 percent, it will overheat the economy. This will raise the inflation rate—and a costly recession may be needed later in order to reduce it.

Trial and error can help the Fed determine the true natural rate. If the Fed raises unemployment above the true natural rate, the inflation rate will drop. If unemployment falls below the true natural rate, the inflation rate will rise. But (as we discussed earlier) trial and error works best when there is continual and rapid feedback. It can take some time for the inflation rate to change—six months, a year, or even longer. In the meantime, the Fed might believe it has been successful, even while causing avoidable unemployment, or planting the seeds for a future rise in the inflation rate.

Estimating the natural rate of unemployment is made even more difficult because the economy is constantly buffeted by shocks of one kind or another. If the Fed observes that the inflation rate is rising, does that mean that unemployment is below the natural rate? Or is the higher inflation being caused by a negative supply shock? Or by the Fed's response to an earlier, negative demand shock? This information is difficult to sort out, although the Fed has become increasingly sophisticated in its efforts to do so.

Rules Versus Discretion and the "Taylor Rule"

Over the last several decades, the Federal Reserve has formulated monetary policy using *discretion*: responding to demand and supply shocks in the way that Fed officials thought best at the time. In some cases, this seems to have helped the economy's performance, as when the Fed aggressively cut interest rates during 2001 and helped to make the recession of that year shorter and milder than it would otherwise have been. In other cases, discretion has worked less well. A notable example is during the late 1970s, when frequent changes in monetary policy contributed to wide fluctuations in output and a rapidly rising inflation rate that reached 13.3 percent in 1979. A more recent example is the Fed's policy in 2000: raising its interest rate target and, in retrospect, waiting too long before bringing it down again, missing an opportunity to begin an early fight against the recession of 2001.

Should the Federal Reserve have complete discretion to change its interest rate target in response to demand and supply shocks as it sees fit? Or should it stick to rules or guidelines in making monetary policy—rules that it announces in advance, with a justification required for any departure?

Some economists have suggested that the Fed's performance on average would be better with less discretion and more deference to predetermined rules. Currently, the most often-discussed rule is the **Taylor rule**, originally proposed in 1993 by economist John Taylor (currently Undersecretary of Treasury for International Affairs).

Taylor rule A proposed rule that would require the Fed to change the interest-rate by a specified amount whenever real GDP or inflation deviate from their pre-announced targets.

According to the Taylor rule, the Fed would announce a target for the inflation rate (say 2 percent per year) and another target for real GDP (equal to its estimate of potential GDP in that period). Then, the Fed would obligate itself to change its interest rate target by some predetermined amount for each percentage point that either output or inflation deviated from its respective target.

For example, suppose the economy began to overheat from a positive demand shock. Then either the inflation rate would begin to rise above its target rate, or real GDP would rise above potential, or both would occur. The Fed would then be obligated to raise its interest rate target by an amount that everyone knew in advance, depending on the changes observed in output and inflation. On the other side, if a negative demand shock started to threaten a recession, changes in inflation and/or output would commit the Fed to *lower* its interest rate target, and stimulate the economy back toward full employment.

What about a negative supply shock—such as a rise in oil prices—that causes the inflation rate to rise and output to fall? In this case, inflation would rise *higher* than its target, and output would fall *below* it. But the rule would identify in advance just how the Fed would respond. It would raise or lower the interest rate target depending on which variable—output or inflation—deviated the most, and depending on the response to each variable that the rule calls for. Thus, the hawk–dove debate that follows every supply shock would be settled—publically—in advance.

What would be the advantage of such a rule? First, if the Federal Reserve were committed to respond to the first signs of a boom, the public would know that the Fed would *not* allow the economy to continue overheating. This would discourage the formation of inflationary expectations. In effect, the Fed would be saying to the public, "Even though the inflation rate just rose, you know the rules. We have to bring the inflation rate back down, so don't get any ideas that we're going to let this continue." Similarly, if a negative demand shock sends the economy into a recession, and the Fed begins to stimulate the economy, the public needn't wonder whether the Fed will go too far and create ongoing, higher inflation. The rule says that the Fed will stimulate the economy only until we are back at potential output, and then maintain its original inflation rate target.

Second, the Taylor rule would give the Fed ammunition to fight inflation with a higher interest rate even when doing so might prove unpopular at the time. The Fed would only be following the rule that everyone understood in advance. This would help discourage the sort of discretion, and political pressure, that contributed to the high inflation rates of the late 1970s.

The Taylor rule is controversial. Opponents argue that it implies more advanced knowledge about the economy—and what an appropriate future response should be—than is realistically possible. And unless the rule were written into law—which only a few economists would advocate—the Fed would not be obligated to follow it. Since the public would know this, the existence of the rule might not be a strong deterrent to inflationary expectations.

Interestingly, the Fed's behavior under Alan Greenspan has followed reasonably close to the specific numerical rule that Taylor originally proposed. Whether the economy performed better or worse due to Greenspan's *deviations* from the rule remains controversial.

Deflation

During the first four years of the Great Depression, the price level fell an average of 10 percent per year—a very serious episode of deflation. Since then, episodes of deflation have been mild and short lived. In early 2003, however, deflation was back in the news. Not because the economy was experiencing it, but rather because of the fear that it would limit the Fed's ability to do its job. People pointed to Japan as an example. During the late 1990s and early 2000s, Japan's price level fell modestly, while the economy languished in recession. And Japan seemed unable to use monetary policy to stimulate its economy out of its recession.

Why does deflation create difficulties for monetary policy? To answer, we need to go back to the distinction between nominal and real interest rates you learned about several chapters ago. Recall that the nominal interest rate is the percentage rate in *dollars* that a borrower pays on a loan. The real interest rate, by contrast, is the percentage rate in *purchasing power* a borrower pays.

You also learned that the *real* rate that people expect to pay (or receive) over the life of a loan is what matters for decisions about borrowing and lending. Now we can extend this notion further: The expected *real* rate is what matters for decisions about consumption and investment spending. Businesses and households—in deciding whether to borrow for investment projects or consumer durables like automobiles—will base their decision on how much *purchasing power* they are giving up by taking out the loan.

The Federal Reserve, however, sets the *nominal* interest rate with its open market operations: the percentage paid in *dollars* when money is borrowed. The problem for the Fed—and for the central bank of Japan or any other country—is that the *nominal* interest rate cannot go below zero. After all, a nominal interest rate below zero would mean that borrowers would pay back fewer *dollars* than they borrowed. Under those circumstances, no one would ever lend money!

Now recall the relationship between the real and nominal interest rates:

$$\text{Real interest rate} = \text{Nominal interest rate} - \text{Rate of inflation.}$$

We can also write this in terms of the real interest rate that people *expect* to pay (or receive) on a loan:

Expected real interest rate = Nominal intererst rate − Expected rate of inflation.

This means that, when the expected inflation rate is positive, the expected real interest rate will be *less* than the nominal rate. For example, with annual inflation expected to be 4 percent, a nominal interest rate of 6 percent per year translates to an expected real interest rate of 2 percent. Under these circumstances, if the economy is in the midst of a recession, and the Fed lowers the nominal interest rate without creating expectations of higher inflation, the real interest rate will drop as well and spending will rise.

But suppose there is *deflation*—a *negative* rate of inflation—and suppose that people begin to expect continuing deflation. Then our equation tells us that the expected real interest rate will be *higher* than the nominal interest rate. For example, with expected deflation of 5 percent per year (expected inflation of −5 percent per year), a nominal interest rate of 4 percent translates to an expected real interest rate of 4 percent − (−5 percent) = 9 percent. And even if the nominal interest rate fell to 0 percent—the lowest it can go—the expected real interest rate would still be 5 percent—the negative of the rate of deflation. Thus,

ongoing, expected deflation puts a positive floor under the expected real interest rate. Once this floor is reached, the Fed cannot reduce the expected real interest rate—or stimulate aggregate expenditure—using the traditional tools of monetary policy.

In 2003—with the annual federal funds rate set at 1 percent and annual inflation running at about 2 percent—the *real* federal funds rate was −1 percent. This negative *real* interest rate was certainly helping to stimulate the economy, by encouraging borrowing for investment projects and consumer durables. But if the inflation rate dropped to zero—or turned negative—the real interest rate would rise. And if people expected deflation to continue, the *expected* real interest rate would rise. The Fed would then have only one percentage point left by which to cut the nominal interest rate. After that, any further deflation would automatically cause the real interest rate to *rise*, *decreasing* planned investment and consumption spending.

Deflation could then create a vicious cycle. The decreased spending—a negative demand shock—would further decrease the inflation rate (a greater *deflation* rate), which in turn would push the real interest rate even higher. And the Fed would be unable to fight the negative demand shock: With the nominal interest rate at zero, its normal tools—designed to lower the nominal interest rate—would be useless.

Fed officials have been aware of this problem, and in the early 2000s, they began to plan for the contingency of deflation. Part of their planning involved public announcements to reassure the public. First, they pointed out that while deflation of 5 or 10 percent a year would be a serious threat, a *modest* deflation rate was unlikely to create a downward spiral for the economy. (Japan's deflation rate, for example, had remained relatively stable for about a decade at 1 percent per year.) And a deflation perceived as temporary need not affect the economy significantly. What matters for spending is the real interest rate that people *expect* to pay over the life of a loan. As long as their expectations of future inflation remained positive and stable, an actual deflation needn't raise the expected real interest rate.

Second, the Fed announced that it was prepared to change the way it conducts monetary policy should the need arise. Instead of limiting its open market operations to injecting reserves into the federal funds market, it was prepared to start buying long-term government bonds.

Why would this help? The nominal interest rate on long-term bonds is generally higher than on short-term obligations, and higher than the very-short-term federal funds rate. This is mostly due to a greater risk that inflation will rise over a longer period, which would erode the *real* interest rate on the bond. In mid-2003, the interest rate on longer-term government bonds was about 4 percent—substantially higher than the federal funds rate. By buying large quantities of long-term government bonds directly—thus adding to the demand for them and raising their price—the Fed would cause the interest rate on these bonds to drop. Thus, even if the Fed could not reduce the federal funds rate any further once it hit zero, it could still reduce *other* interest rates—not just on long-term government bonds, but also on long-term corporate bonds whose rates tend to move closely with their government counterparts.

Finally, the Fed has one other tool: its ability to influence expectations. By announcing that it would follow credible policies to raise the inflation rate to a modest, positive level, the Fed could create positive inflationary expectations *even in the midst of deflation.* Look again at the equation for the real interest rate. For a given nominal interest rate, every *rise* in the *expected* inflation rate causes a *decrease* in the real rate. Thus, even if all nominal interest rates in the economy hit zero, the Fed could try to convince the public that it would raise the inflation rate in the near future. If successful, it could continue to lower real interest rates merely by raising expected inflation. Most economists believed that the Fed would be able to convince the public, should the need arise.

Finally (although Fed officials did not stress this), even if *all* monetary policy tools were unable to stimulate spending, fiscal policy could be used: The government could increase purchases itself, or reduce taxes even further to raise disposable income. It might take time for the government to do this. But eventually, fiscal policy would work through the normal multiplier process to raise spending and output—a completely separate channel of influence over the economy from monetary policy. Indeed, modest increases in government purchases during the Great Depression helped to stop the economy's downward spiral. And what finally ended the last stages of the depression—very rapidly—was the huge increase in military purchases as the United States entered World War II.

As you can see, conducting monetary policy is not easy. The Fed has hundreds of economists carrying out research and gathering data to improve its information about the status of the economy and its understanding of how the economy works. And the effort seemed to have paid off during the decade leading up to 2001. But some economists believe that the Fed, in retrospect, could have done more to offset the forces that caused the recession that began in March 2001. They believe that the Fed raised the interest rate too high in 2000 and waited too long before starting to lower the interest rate in January 2001. This is an easy conclusion to come to with hindsight. But given the uncertainties faced by the Fed in conducting monetary policy, many economists continue to give the Fed high marks.

Will the Fed *continue* to be as successful as it has been in recent years? That is difficult to say. Since we don't know what kinds of shocks will hit the economy in the future (oil price shocks came out of the blue in the 1970s) or how the Fed will respond to them, we cannot be certain that monetary policy will continue to work well in the future.

Summary

As the nation's central bank, the Federal Reserve bears primary responsibility for maintaining a low, stable rate of inflation and for maintaining full employment of the labor force as the economy is buffeted by a variety of shocks. The money demand curve, for example, may shift, causing a change in the interest rate, a shift in the AD curve, and a change in output and employment. The Fed can neutralize such money demand shocks by setting an interest rate target. To maintain the target, it increases the money supply whenever money demand increases, and decreases the money supply when money demand decreases. This policy enables the Fed to stabilize both inflation and unemployment.

Demand shocks from spontaneous shifts in aggregate expenditure can also shift the AD curve, causing output to deviate from its full-employment level. The Fed can neutralize these shocks by adjusting its interest rate target—changing the money supply to shift the AD curve back to its original position.

The Fed's most difficult problem is responding to supply shocks. A negative supply shock—an upward shift of the AS curve—presents the Fed with a dilemma. In the short run, it must choose a point along that new AS curve. If it wishes to maintain price stability, it must shift the AD curve to the left and accept higher unemployment. If the Fed wishes to maintain full employment, it must shift the AD curve to the right and accept a higher rate of inflation. A "hawk" policy puts greater emphasis on price stability, while a "dove" policy emphasizes lower unemployment.

If Fed policy leads to ongoing inflation, then businesses and households come to expect the prevailing inflation rate to continue. As a result, the AS curve continues to shift upward at that built-in expected inflation rate. To maintain full employment, the Fed must shift the AD curve rightward, creating an inflation rate equal to the expected rate.

If the Fed wishes to change the built-in inflation rate, it must first change the expected inflation rate. For example, to lower the expected inflation rate, the Fed will slow down the rightward shifts of the AD curve. The actual inflation rate will fall, and expectations will eventually adjust downward. While they do so, however, the economy will experience a recession. The Fed's short-run choices between inflation and unemployment can be illustrated with the Phillips curve. In the short run, the Fed can move the economy along the downward-sloping Phillips curve by adjusting the rate at which the AD curve shifts. If the Fed moves the economy to a new point on the Phillips curve and holds it there, the built-in inflation rate will eventually adjust and the Phillips curve will shift. In the long run, the economy will return to the natural rate of unemployment with a different inflation rate. The long-run Phillips curve is a vertical line at the natural rate of unemployment.

In conducting monetary policy, the Fed faces several challenges. It has imperfect information about the time required for its policies to affect the economy, and also about the economy's potential GDP (or its natural rate of unemployment) during any given period. The Fed often faces criticism for using discretion rather than following rigid rules, especially when the economy does not perform well. And, in recent years, the Fed has had to worry about deflation and the need to develop new (and less tested) tools for conducting monetary policy.

Key Terms

Active monetary policy
Interest rate target
Long-run Phillips curve

Natural rate of unemployment
Passive monetary policy
Phillips curve

Taylor rule

Review Questions

Answers to even-numbered Questions and Problems can be found on the text Web site at http://hall-lieb.swlearning.com.

1. "The Fed should aim for the lowest possible unemployment rate." True or false? Explain.

2. What effect does a change in the Fed's interest rate target have on financial markets? How do changes in expectations regarding the Fed's position on the interest rate target affect financial markets?

3. "The Fed should respond to any shift in the AD curve by maintaining its interest rate target." True or false? Explain.

4. Explain the trade-off that the Fed faces with regard to negative supply shocks. What do "hawks" and "doves" have to do with this trade-off?

5. Why do expectations of inflation have a significant impact on the economy? What is the impact?

6. What relationship does the Phillips curve illustrate? How does the Fed control movements along the Phillips curve? Why is the long-run Phillips curve vertical?

7. List and explain two reasons why the Fed tolerates some ongoing inflation.

8. What are the biggest information problems faced by the Fed?

9. Describe the Taylor rule. What are the advantages of following it? Why is it controversial?

10. How did the Fed plan for the contingency of deflation in the early 2000s?

Problems and Exercises

1. Suppose that a law required the Fed to do everything possible to keep the inflation rate equal to zero. Using AD and AS curves, illustrate and explain how the Fed would deal with (a) a rightward shift of the money demand curve, (b) a negative demand shock from a decrease in investment spending, and (c) an adverse aggregate supply shock. What would the costs and benefits of such a law be?

2. Suppose that, in a world with *no* ongoing inflation, the government raises taxes. Using AD and AS curves, describe the effects on the economy if the Fed decides to practice a passive monetary policy. Alternatively, how could the Fed use active policy to neutralize the demand shock?

3. Suppose that initially the price level is P_1 and GDP is Y_1, with no built-in inflation. The Fed reacts to a negative demand shock by shifting the aggregate demand curve in the appropriate direction. The next time the Fed receives data on GDP and the price level, it finds that the price level is above P_1 and GDP is above Y_1. Give a possible explanation for this finding.

4. Suppose the economy has been experiencing a low inflation rate. A new chair of the Federal Reserve is named, and he or she is known to be sympathetic to dove policies. Explain the possible effects on the Phillips curve.

5. "The idea of the Fed having to choose between hawk and dove policies in Figure 5 is silly. All the Fed has to do is shift the AS curve back to its original position, which would prevent *both* recession *and* inflation." Do you agree? Why or why not?

6. Using a graph similar to Figure 8, show what will happen in the future if the Fed tried to keep the unemployment rate permanently at a level like U_2—below the natural rate.

7. What would the Fed have to do to reduce the built-in inflation in our economy? Would it be likely to take this action if it was most concerned about achieving a lower unemployment rate, or if it was most concerned about preventing a loss of purchasing power?

8. One of your classmates stops you in the hall and says, "I was reading a statement from the Fed's Federal Open Market Committee (FOMC) meeting. It stated that the members were concerned that an already low rate of inflation might become lower. Why do they want to keep inflation rates high? I thought inflation was a bad thing." How should you explain to your classmate why the FOMC is worried about inflation becoming too low?

Challenge Questions

1. Suppose the economy is experiencing ongoing inflation. The Fed wants to reduce expected inflation, so it announces that in the future it will tolerate less inflation. How does the Fed's credibility affect the success of the reduction? How can the Fed build its credibility? Are there costs to building credibility? If so, what are they?

2. This chapter mentioned what would happen if the Fed over- or underestimated the natural rate of unemployment. Using the AD–AS model, suppose the economy is at the true natural rate of unemployment, so that GDP is at its potential level. Suppose, too, that the Fed wrongly believes that the natural rate of unemployment is higher (potential GDP is lower) and acts to bring the economy back to its supposed potential. What will the Fed do? What will happen in the short run? If the Fed continues to maintain output below potential, what will happen over the long run?

3. Look again at Figure 2. Suppose that the rightward money demand shift in the figure results from a permanent, one-time increase in tastes for holding money. Suppose, too, that the Fed wishes to pursue an active monetary policy to neutralize the impact of the shift. The Fed must increase the money supply by just enough to bring the interest rate back to r_1. However, as it does so, and as income increases in panel (b), the money demand curve will move rightward as well. (Why?) Identify the new, final equilibrium point in panel (a). (*Note:* This is not as easy as it seems. M_2^D is the money demand curve after the increase in tastes for holding money *and* the change in output to Y_2. You will have to draw in a *third* money demand curve that is consistent with the new tastes for holding money, but also consistent with output and income back at full employment.)

4. Given your answer to Problem 6, would you expect the short-run Phillips curve to shift by equal amounts in successive years?

5. The slope of the money demand curve helps to determine the effectiveness of Fed policy. Draw a graph to illustrate the concept that the steeper the money demand curve is, the more effective an increase in the money supply will be. Does this conclusion also hold for a decrease in the money supply?

ECONOMIC Applications

These exercises require access to Hall/Lieberman Xtra! If Xtra! did not come with your book, visit http://hallxtra.swlearning.com to purchase.

1. Use your Xtra! password at the Hall and Lieberman Web site (http://hallxtra.swlearning.com), select this chapter, and under Economic Applications, click on EconDebate. Choose *Monetary Policy*, and scroll down to find the debate, "Should the Fed Pursue a Fixed Policy Rule?" Read the debate, and use the information to answer the following questions.
   a. Why did Milton Friedman and other monetarists argue that the government should rely on fixed policy rules and avoid discretionary policies?
   b. What are the views of new-classical and new-Keynesian economists on discretionary monetary and fiscal policies?

2. Use your Xtra! password at the Hall and Lieberman Web site (http://hallxtra.swlearning.com), select this chapter, and under Economic Applications, click on EconData. Choose *Monetary Policy*, and scroll down to find *Money Supply (M2)*. Read the definition, click on Diagrams/Data, then use the information to answer the following questions.
   a. Considering the diagrams in this section, discuss the Fed's behavior with regard to monetary policy.
   b. Click on the Updates and read Governor Ben S. Bernanke's remarks titled: "Constrained Discretion" and Monetary Policy at http://www.federalreserve.gov/boarddocs/speeches/2003/20030203/default.htm. What are his views on monetary rules and discretion?

Fiscal Policy: Taxes, Spending, and the Federal Budget

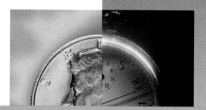

Almost every year throughout the 1980s and early 1990s, a best-selling book would be published that predicted economic disaster for the United States and the world. In most of these books, the U.S. federal government played a central role. Arguments and statistics were offered to show that federal government spending—which was growing by leaps and bounds—was out of control, causing us to run budget deficits year after year. As a result, the United States was facing a growing debt burden that would soon swallow up all of our incomes, sink the United States economy, and bring about a worldwide depression.

During the late 1990s, as the federal budget picture improved, these disaster books quietly disappeared. Now, the federal government was running *surpluses*—raising more funds in tax revenues than it was spending. Moreover, the surpluses were projected to continue for at least a decade. News articles and public statements described a bright economic future in which our most pressing problem would be: What shall we do with our mounting budget surpluses?

Then, in 2002, another flip-flop: The government was again running a deficit, and more deficits were projected through the end of the 2000s and beyond. Once again, concern over the budget and growing U.S. debt saturated the media, and the word *disaster* reappeared in the media.

What caused these flip-flops in the government's budget? And why should we care?

In this chapter, we'll take a close look at the government's role in the macroeconomy. You'll learn how to interpret trends in the government's budget, and how to identify the causes and effects of those trends. You'll also learn to distinguish between fiscal policy's long-run effects on the economy and its short-run effects.

THINKING ABOUT SPENDING, TAXES, AND THE BUDGET

Let's start with some simple numbers. In 1959, the federal government's total outlays for goods and services, transfer payments, and interest on its debt was $92 billion. By 2003, the total had grown to $2,140 billion, an increase of more than 2,200 percent. Does this show that government spending is out of control?

Or consider the national debt—the total amount that the government owes to the general public from past borrowing in years in which it ran a budget deficit. In 1959, the national debt was $235 billion; by late 2003, it had grown to $3,876 billion. Is this evidence that debt is crushing the economy?

Actually, these figures don't tell us much of anything. First, prices rose during that period, so *real* government outlays and the *real* national debt rose considerably less than these nominal figures suggest. In addition, from 1959 to 2003, the U.S. population grew, the labor force grew, and the average worker became more productive. As a result, real GDP and real income roughly quadrupled during this period. Why is that important? Because *spending and debt should be viewed in relation to income.*

We automatically recognize this principle when we think about an individual family or business. Suppose you are told that a family is spending $50,000 each year on goods and services, and has a total debt—a combination of mortgage debt, car loans, student loans, and credit card balances—of $200,000. Is this family acting responsibly? Or is its spending and borrowing out of control? That depends. If the income of the household is less than its spending—say, $40,000—and is expected to remain so, then there is serious trouble. A family that spends more than it earns would see its debt grow every year until it could not handle the monthly interest payments.

But what if the family's income is $800,000 per year? Then our conclusion would change dramatically: We'd wonder why this family spends so *little*. And if it owed $200,000, we would not think it irresponsible at all. After all, the family could pay the interest on its debt—with a tiny fraction of its income.

What is true for an individual family is also true for the nation. Spending and debt are *relative* concepts. As a country's total income grows, it will want more of the things that government can provide—education, high environmental standards, domestic security, programs to help the needy, and more. Therefore, we expect government spending to rise as a nation becomes richer. Moreover, as its income grows, a country can *handle* higher interest payments on its debt. Government spending and the total national debt, considered in isolation, tell us nothing about how responsibly or irresponsibly the government is behaving.

Budget-related figures such as government outlays, tax revenues, or government debt should be considered relative to a nation's total income—as percentages of GDP.

Viewing budget-related figures relative to GDP helps to put things in perspective. In 1959, the federal government's total outlays were 19 percent of GDP. In 2003, they were about 20 percent—reflecting a slight upward drift, but far from out of control. And the national debt in the hands of the public was lower in 2003 than in 1959, shrinking from about 48 percent to 36 percent of GDP. This doesn't suggest that everything is fine with the federal budget, and we'll discuss some causes for concern in this chapter. But our concerns should be based on, and expressed with, the proper perspective.

In the rest of this chapter, as we explore recent trends in fiscal behavior and their effects on the economy, we'll do so with these lessons in mind. Accordingly, we'll look at fiscal variables as *percentages of GDP*.[1]

SPENDING, TAXES, AND THE BUDGET: SOME BACKGROUND

Our ultimate goal in this chapter is to understand how fiscal changes have affected, and continue to affect, the macroeconomy. But before we do this, some background will help. What has happened to the *composition* of government spending in recent decades? How does the U.S. tax system work, and what has happened to the government's tax revenues? Why has the national debt decreased in some years, risen slowly in other years, and risen very rapidly in still others? This section provides answers to these and other questions about the government's finances. Although state and local spending also play an important role in the macroeconomy, most of the significant macroeconomic changes in recent decades have involved the *federal* government. This is why we'll focus on spending, taxing, and borrowing at the federal level.

Government Outlays

The federal government's *outlays*—the total amount spent or disbursed by the federal government in all of its activities—can be divided into three categories:

- *government purchases*—the total value of the goods and services that the government buys (corresponding to "G" in GDP = C + I + G + NX)
- *transfer payments*—income supplements the government provides to people, such as Social Security benefits, unemployment compensation, and welfare payments
- *interest on the national debt*—the interest payments the government must make to those who hold government bonds

Government Purchases. Until the mid 1970s, government purchases of goods and services were the largest component of government spending. To understand how these purchases have changed over time, it's essential to divide them into two categories: military and nonmilitary. Figure 1 shows total federal purchases, as well as federal military and nonmilitary purchases, from 1959 to 2003.

One fact stands out from the figure: The federal government uses up only a tiny fraction of our national resources for nonmilitary purposes. These nonmilitary pur-

---

[1] It makes no difference whether we divide *nominal* government outlays by *nominal* GDP, or *real* government outlays by *real* GDP; we get the same answer for government outlays as a percentage of GDP. When we measure a variable as a percentage of GDP, we adjust for inflation *and* for growth in real income at the same time.

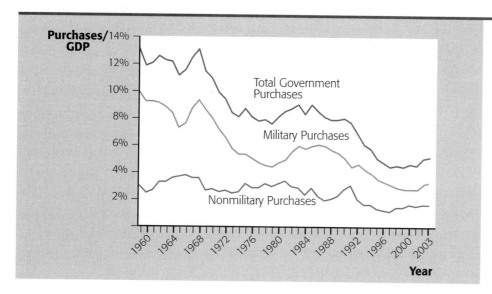

FIGURE 1

Federal Government Purchases as a Percentage of GDP

Over the last several decades, total government purchases have trended downward largely because nonmilitary purchases remained a stable, small percentage of GDP while military purchases have steadily decreased. Exceptions were the late 1960s (Vietnam War), 1980s (Reagan defense buildup) and the early 2000s (Bush defense buildup after September 11, 2001).

Source for this and most of the other figures in this chapter: Office of Management and Budget, *The Budget for Fiscal Year 2004, Historical Tables* (especially Tables 1.1, 1.3, 2.1, 2.3, 6.1, and 7.1).

chases include the salaries paid to all government workers outside the Defense Department (for example, federal judges, legislators, and the people who run federal agencies), as well as purchases of buildings, equipment, and supplies. Added together, all the different kinds of nonmilitary government purchases account for a stable, low fraction of GDP—about 2 percent.

This strongly contradicts a commonly held notion: that government spending is growing by leaps and bounds because of bloated federal bureaucracies. Those who believe that the government's budget is a growing concern must look somewhere besides nonmilitary purchases for the reason.

> *As a percentage of GDP, nonmilitary government purchases have remained very low and stable. They have not contributed to growth in total government outlays.*

What about military purchases? Here, we come to an even stronger conclusion:

> *As a percentage of GDP, military purchases have declined dramatically over the past several decades. Like nonmilitary purchases, they have not contributed to the upward drift in government outlays.*

The decline in military purchases is shown by the middle line in Figure 1. They were around 10 percent of GDP in 1959, fell almost continuously to about 3 percent in the late 1990s, and started to rise again in the early 2000s. In between, there were two large military buildups—one associated with the Vietnam War in the late 1960s and the other during the Reagan administration in the 1980s. But both of these buildups were temporary. The decline of military spending freed up resources amounting to 6½ to 7 percent of GDP over the span shown in Figure 1.

FIGURE 2

Major Federal Transfer Programs, 2003

Retirement benefits are the largest component of federal transfers, followed closely by health care programs, and then income security.

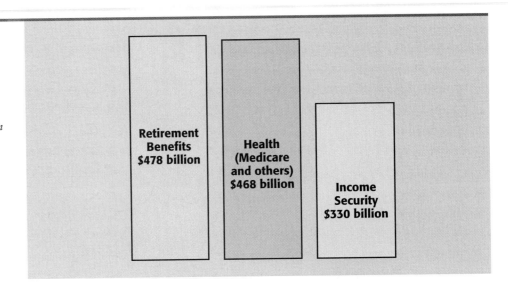

It is too early to say whether the current rise in military purchases will be temporary, or how large it will become. But given the current U.S. role in global politics, significant future cuts seem highly unlikely. The implications are tremendously important for thinking about the recent past and the future of the federal government's role in the economy:

> *The decline in military spending in relation to GDP since the early 1960s has made huge amounts of resources available for other purposes. Because military spending has little room to fall further and is likely to rise over the next decade, there will not be any similar freeing up of resources in coming years.*

The resources released from military spending eased many otherwise tough decisions about resource allocation in the economy. In particular, they made it easy for the federal government to provide increases in resources to some parts of the population, through transfer payments. The likelihood of continued increases in military spending will have the opposite implication: the government will be presented with difficult budget choices.

Social Security and Other Transfers. Transfer programs provide cash and in-kind benefits to people whom the federal government designates as needing help. Figure 2 shows the three major categories of transfers.

The largest category is retirement benefits—the payments made by the Social Security system to retired people. Although the benefits are loosely related to past contributions to the Social Security system, workers whose earnings are low receive benefits that are worth far more than their contributions. And after age 72, even someone with no history of contributions receives the minimum benefit. Social Security outlays have grown rapidly over the last few decades, and are expected to rise even more rapidly as the baby-boom generation begins retiring and collecting benefits in the late 2000s.

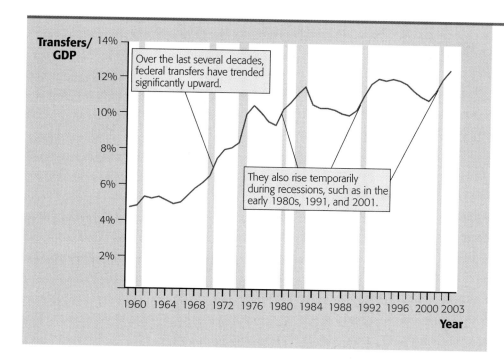

Transfers/ GDP

Over the last several decades, federal transfers have trended significantly upward.

They also rise temporarily during recessions, such as in the early 1980s, 1991, and 2001.

1960 1964 1968 1972 1976 1980 1984 1988 1992 1996 2000 2003

Year

FIGURE 3

Federal Transfer Payments as a Percentage of GDP

Note: Federal transfers in this chapter include grants to state and local governments that are used for health and income security assistance.

The second-largest category of transfers—and the fastest-growing—occurs in health programs. The Social Security system provides health-related benefits to everyone aged 62 and over through Medicare. This is a health insurance plan in which, until recently, people would go to any doctor they chose, as often as they wanted, and Medicare would pay 80 percent of the bills. Over the last several years, some efforts have been made to control Medicare's rapidly rising costs, but they have continued to rise as a percentage of GDP. They are expected to rise even more rapidly over the next decade for two reasons: (1) the retirement of the baby boomers in the late 2000s, and (2) the likely addition of coverage for prescription drugs, which until 2003 had not been covered by the program. And in addition to funding Medicare, the federal government helps finance state-operated health plans for the poor, through a program called Medicaid. The costs of these programs have been rising rapidly as well.

Government "Outlays" Versus Government "Purchases" Don't confuse government outlays with government purchases, which are just one component of the government's outlays. The other components are transfer payments and interest on the debt.

DANGEROUS CURVES

The third and smallest of the three categories of transfers is *income security*—programs to help poor families. Within this category, the largest component is the food stamp program, which gives coupons or special credit cards—good only for buying food—to qualified families. Welfare payments to poor families are also in this category, but these payments are much smaller than outlays on food stamps.

Have transfer payments been growing as a fraction of GDP? Indeed, they have. All three categories of transfer programs have grown rapidly in recent decades. Figure 3 shows how *total* transfer payments as a percentage of GDP have trended upward.

FIGURE 4
Federal Government Interest Payments as a Percentage of GDP

Federal interest payments relative to GDP rose rapidly during the 1980s as the national debt grew relative to GDP, then fell rapidly during the 1990s, as national debt fell relative to GDP. In spite of a rising debt-to-GDP ratio, interest payments relative to GDP did not rise in the early 2000s, because interest rates had dropped.

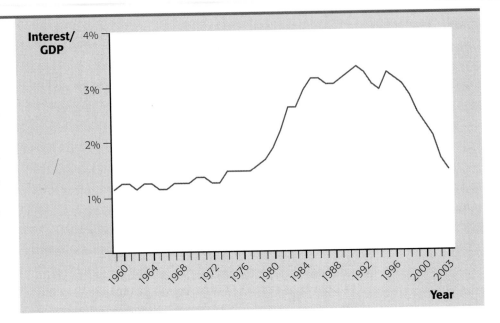

In recent decades, transfers have been the fastest-growing part of federal government outlays and are currently equal to about 12.5 percent of GDP.

Growth in transfers relative to GDP was most rapid in the 1970s during the Nixon administration. During this period, government-financed retirement benefits became much more generous, food stamps were introduced, and Medicare expanded. Since then, transfers have continued to rise modestly but are projected to soar as baby boomers retire and receive Social Security and Medicare benefits.

Notice, too, that transfers are sensitive to the ups and downs of the economy. Transfers as a fraction of GDP rise during recessions, as in 1974, 1981, 1991, and 2001. This is for two reasons. First, the number of needy recipients rises in a recession, so transfer payments—the numerator of the fraction—increase. Second, GDP—the denominator—falls in a recession. Similarly, transfers as a fraction of GDP tend to fall during expansions, such as the long expansion that ran from 1991 through early 2001. During expansions, the numerator of this fraction falls (why?), and the denominator rises. We will come back to these movements in transfers toward the end of the chapter.

Interest on the National Debt. Figure 4 shows the behavior of the third and smallest category of government spending: interest on the national debt. As you can see, interest as a percentage of GDP grew rapidly in the early 1980s, when the debt was growing and interest rates were rising. In the 1990s, interest as a fraction of GDP fell slowly at first, as growth in the debt slowed, and then fell dramatically as the national debt dropped from 1998 to 2001. Interest relative to GDP continued to decline in the early 2000s even though the national debt was rising, because the Federal Reserve repeatedly lowered interest rates in 2001 and kept them very low well into 2003.

Total Government Outlays. Figure 5 shows total outlays in relation to GDP over the past several decades. There are two important things to notice in the figure. The

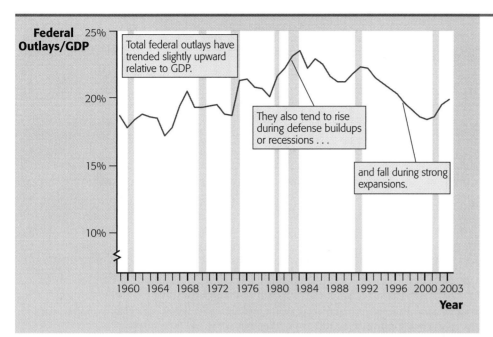

FIGURE 5

Total Federal Outlays as a Percentage of GDP

first is the *fluctuations* in government outlays over the period. There was a sharp increase in outlays in each recession (shaded) due to the jump in transfers that we saw in Figure 3. The recession of 1981–82 is a striking example. Also visible is the increase in military spending for the Vietnam War in the late 1960s.

The second thing to notice is the *upward trend* of federal outlays as a percentage of GDP:

For several decades up to the early 1990s, federal government outlays as a percentage of GDP drifted upward. The main causes were increases in transfer payments and increases in interest on the national debt that exceeded the decreases in military spending.

Finally, notice the important *downward* trend in the mid- and late 1990s:

From 1992 to 2000, federal government spending as a percentage of GDP fell steadily, although it remained a higher percentage of GDP than in 1959. The main causes of the decline were sharp decreases in military spending, and more modest decreases in transfer payments relative to GDP during a long expansion.

However, Figure 5 also shows the appearance of a likely new trend:

In the early 2000s, due to a rise in military and domestic security purchases and continued increases in transfers, federal government outlays as a percentage of GDP began rising, and seem likely to continue rising through the decade.

TABLE 1
Sources of Federal Revenue, 2003 (Estimated)

Source	Revenue (Billions of Dollars)	Percentage of Total Revenue
Personal income taxes	849	46%
Social Security taxes	727	40%
Corporate income taxes	143	8%
Excise taxes	68	4%
Other sources	49	3%
Total	1,836	

Source: Office of Management and Budget, *Budget of the United States Government, Fiscal Year 2004,* Historical Tables (Table 2.1).

These trends in government outlays have important implications, but they are only half of the story. In order to understand their impact on the budget and the macro-economy, we must look at the other side of the budget: tax revenue.

Federal Tax Revenues

The federal government obtains most of its revenue from two sources: the personal income tax and the Social Security tax. Table 1 breaks down the revenue from these and other less-important sources.

The Personal Income Tax. The personal income tax is the most important source of revenue for the federal government and also the most conspicuous and painful. Almost every adult has to file Form 1040 or one of its shorter cousins. One of the signs of success as an American is seeing your federal tax return swell to the size of a magazine. Proposals to reduce both the amount of taxes people pay and the complexity of the tax forms are immensely popular.

Progressive tax A tax whose rate increases as income increases.

The personal income tax is designed to be **progressive**, to tax those at the higher end of the income scale at higher rates than those at the lower end of the scale, and to excuse the poorest families from paying any tax at all. Table 2 shows how the income tax works, in theory, by computing the amount of tax a family of four should have paid on its 2002 income if it took the standard deduction.[2] The table also shows the **average tax rate**—the fraction of total income a family pays in taxes—and the **marginal tax rate**—the tax rate paid on *each additional dollar* of income.

Average tax rate The fraction of a given income paid in taxes.

Marginal tax rate The fraction of an additional dollar of income paid in taxes.

We can see from Table 2 that the income tax is designed to be quite progressive. In principle, a family in the middle of the income distribution, earning $50,000 per year, should have paid 7.9 percent of its income in taxes, while a family at the top should have paid 30.5 percent of its income in taxes. The table also shows that marginal tax rates on families with the highest income are in the range of 30 to 39 percent.

[2] The federal government allows households to deduct certain expenses (like medical care or the costs of moving to a new job) from their income before calculating the tax that they owe. Alternatively, they may deduct a standard amount (the *standard deduction*) from their income, regardless of their spending patterns.

TABLE 2

The 2002 Personal Income Tax for a Married Couple with Two Children

Income	Tax	Average Tax Rate	Marginal Tax Rate
$ 10,000	$ 0	0%	0%
20,000	16	.08	10
30,000	1,103	3.4	15
50,000	3,926	7.9	15
75,000	8,693	11.6	27
150,000	30,895	20.6	30
250,000	66,565	26.6	35
400,000	122,129	30.5	38.6

Source: Calculated from the 2002 Form 1040 tax table with the standard deduction of $7,850. First column shows income before standard deduction or deduction for dependents.

But the tax system shown in the table does not reflect the ways that people can avoid tax. Many people have deductions far above the standard deduction. Some people earn income that they never report to the government, thereby evading taxes entirely. And people can shelter income in their employer's retirement plan or in a plan of their own. Studies have shown that higher-income households avoid more taxes than poorer families and that the federal tax system—while still progressive—is much less progressive than suggested by Table 2.

Also, remember that we are looking at the *federal personal income* tax only. Households pay other taxes related to their income, some of which are **regressive**—taking a lower percentage in taxes as household income rises. For example, state and local sales taxes are regressive: Lower-income households *spend* a larger fraction of their incomes, so they pay a higher percentage of that income in sales taxes. Another example of a regressive tax is the federal payroll tax, earmarked to fund Social Security and Medicare, which we'll turn to now.

Regressive tax A tax that collects a lower percentage of income as income rises.

The Social Security Tax. The Social Security tax applies to wage and salary income only. It was put in place in 1936, to finance the Social Security system created in that year. Whereas the personal income tax is a nightmare of complex forms and rules, the Social Security tax is remarkably simple. The current tax rate (including the Medicare part of the tax) is a flat 15.3 percent,[3] except for one complication: Most of the tax is applied only on earnings below a certain amount ($87,000 in 2003, although the cap rises each year).

Because the payroll tax applies only to earnings below a certain level, it is regressive. For example, employees earning $87,000 or below in 2003 paid the full 15.3 percent of their income in taxes, while someone who earned twice that amount—$174,000—paid only 7.65 percent (since the tax applied to only half of their earnings). The Social Security tax is actually the largest tax paid by many

HTTP://

The Congressional Budget Office maintains historical data on the U.S. federal budget. You can find it at http://www.cbo.gov/showdoc.cfm?index=1821&sequence=0&from=7#1.

[3] If you look at your own paycheck, it may seem that the Social Security tax (including Medicare) is only 7.65 percent instead of the 15.3 percent we've just mentioned. The reason is that your employer pays half the tax and you pay the other half. But the amount paid on your earnings is the sum, 15.3 percent.

Americans, especially those with lower incomes. These families pay little or no income tax, but pay the Social Security tax on all of their wage earnings. For example, a family with $30,000 of earnings in Table 2 would pay $1,013 in federal income tax, but Social Security taxes on those earnings would be $4,590.

Other Federal Taxes. Table 1 shows that the federal government also collects around $260 billion annually from other taxes. The most important of these is the *corporate profits tax,* which raised $143 billion in 2003 by taxing the profits earned by corporations at a rate of 35 percent.

The corporate profits tax is often criticized by economists because of two important problems. First, it applies only to corporations. Thus, a business owner can avoid it completely by setting up a sole proprietorship or partnership instead of a corporation. As a result, the tax causes many businesses to forego the benefits of being corporations because of the extra tax they would have to pay.

Second, the corporation tax results in *double taxation* on the portion of corporate profits that corporations pay to their owners. This portion of profits is taxed once when the corporation is taxed and again when the profits are included as part of the owners' personal income. The corporation tax is thus a prime target for tax reform. Almost all reform proposals put forward by economists involve integrating the taxation of corporations into the tax system in a way that avoids these two distortions.

The federal government also taxes the consumption of certain products, such as gasoline, alcohol, tobacco, and air travel. These are called *excise taxes.* Excise taxes raise additional revenue for the government, but they are usually put in place for other, nonrevenue reasons as well. The excise tax on gasoline is seen, in part, as a fee on drivers for the use of federal highways. The taxes on alcohol and tobacco are intended to discourage consumption of these harmful products.

Trends in Federal Tax Revenue. The top line in Figure 6 shows total federal government revenue, as a percentage of GDP, from all of the taxes we've discussed. Until recently, there was an upward trend. More specifically,

> *federal revenue trended upward from around 18 percent of GDP in the early 1960s to around 20 percent in the late 1990s.*

But notice the sharp drop in the early 2000s. This was partly a short-run change (due to the very slow recovery from the 2001 recession) and partly the beginning of a new downward trend (due to significant long-term reductions in tax rates proposed by the Bush administration, and passed by Congress, in 2001 and 2003.)

> *In the early 2000s, federal tax revenues began a projected downward trend due to long-term reductions in tax rates.*

We'll have much more to say about these tax cuts in the "Using the Theory" section of this chapter.

While the trends in total federal revenue as a fraction of GDP have been rather mild, its *composition* has changed dramatically. The lower two lines in Figure 6 show the part of federal revenue that comes from Social Security taxes and all

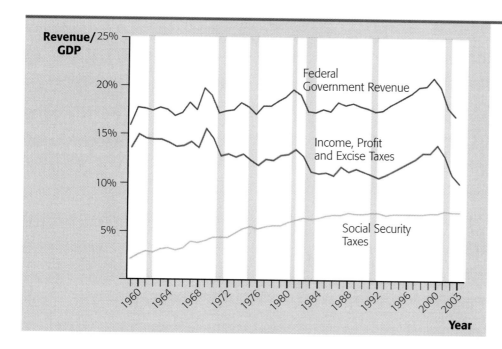

FIGURE 6

Federal Government Revenue as a Percentage of GDP

Over the last several decades, total federal revenue relative to GDP has trended upward somewhat. But its composition has changed. All sources other than Social Security taxes have fallen relative to GDP while Social Security taxes have more than doubled relative to GDP.

other taxes. Notice the steady upward trend in Social Security tax revenue. Also notice that all other sources of revenue have trended slightly downward over the same period.

Why have Social Security taxes grown in importance? First, a little background. The Social Security system operates on a pay-as-you-go principle: It taxes people who are working now in order to pay benefits to those who worked earlier and are now retired. But it also pays more benefits to those who have worked longer.

Over the years, the system has benefited from a number of favorable circumstances. In its early decades, most retirees who received benefits had started working before the system began, so their benefits were small in relation to the earnings of those at work. Then, for the past several decades, the system benefited from two favorable demographic factors: first, a relatively small number of retirees (due to very low birth rates during the 1930s); and second, a large number of taxpayers (due to the baby boomers of the 1950s entering and remaining in the labor force).

But now, some demographic trends are working against the system. First, improved health is allowing people to spend a larger fraction of their lives in retirement. That is good from a human perspective, but from an accounting point of view, it means that the average retiree is drawing more benefits. At the same time, the baby boomers will begin retiring en masse in the late 2000s, which means greater *numbers* of people drawing benefits. Finally, these increased benefits will be funded by a smaller number of working taxpayers. As a result of these trends, *the government has been raising Social Security tax rates* not just to keep the system solvent, but to go further—building up reserves in a separate government account (called the Social Security Trust Fund) for retiring baby boomers.

Note that keeping Social Security reserves in a separate trust fund makes little difference for policy. Its main importance is psychological and political: making retirees and future retirees feel confident that the money is being held for them, and creating a political disincentive to use the funds for any other purpose. But Social Security benefits are considered an obligation of the federal government, whether held in a separate trust account or not. If the trust fund should turn negative, the government would be obliged to pay benefits out of general tax revenues. And if the government decided to scale back this obligation somewhat because of other fiscal pressures, a positive trust fund balance would not protect retirees from any cutback. Ironically, though, the focus on keeping the trust fund solvent has had a side-effect: it has caused the government to continually raise the regressive payroll tax rate over the past few decades, rather than rely on the progressive personal income tax to fund future benefits.

HTTP://

Try your hand at managing the budget by using the National Budget Simulation at www. budgetsim.org/NBS.

The Federal Budget and the National Debt

Finally, we can bring together what we've learned about the government's tax revenue (from the Social Security tax, personal income tax, corporate profits tax, and other sources) with what we've learned about the government's outlays (on purchases, transfers, and net interest). Look first at the upper panel in Figure 7. This shows total federal outlays (from Figure 5) and total federal revenue (from the top line in Figure 6). The difference between these two lines in any year is the federal budget deficit (when outlays exceed revenue) or surplus (when revenue exceeds outlays).

$$\text{Budget Surplus} = \text{Tax Revenue} - \text{Outlays}$$

$$\text{Budget Deficit} = \text{Outlays} - \text{Tax Revenue}^4$$

The bottom panel shows the history of the budget in recent decades, with surpluses as positive values and deficits as negative values.[5] The lower panel looks much choppier because the scale of the diagram is different there. But you can see that there was a dramatic change in the behavior of the budget around 1975. Until that year, the government mostly ran deficits, but rarely more than 2 percent of GDP. But from 1975 until 1993, the deficit grew significantly. During that period, it was usually greater than 3 percent of GDP, and often more than 4 percent. Notice, for example, the especially large rise in the deficit that occurred in the

---

[4] Other than our current inclusion of interest payments as a category of government outlays, these are the same definitions given earlier in the text. To see this, just ignore interest payments in this chapter's definition of the deficit:

Budget Deficit = Outlays − Tax Revenue
= (Government Purchases + Transfers) − Tax Revenue
= Government Purchases − (Tax Revenue − Transfers)
= $G - T$

The last line is the definition for the deficit given in the chapter on the classical model, where G is government purchases in GDP and T is net taxes.

[5] To measure the deficit or surplus, we have included all sources of revenue and all types of federal spending, whether they are part of the official federal budget or not. In particular, we've included Social Security taxes and Social Security payments even though they are officially considered "off budget" in U.S. government statistics.

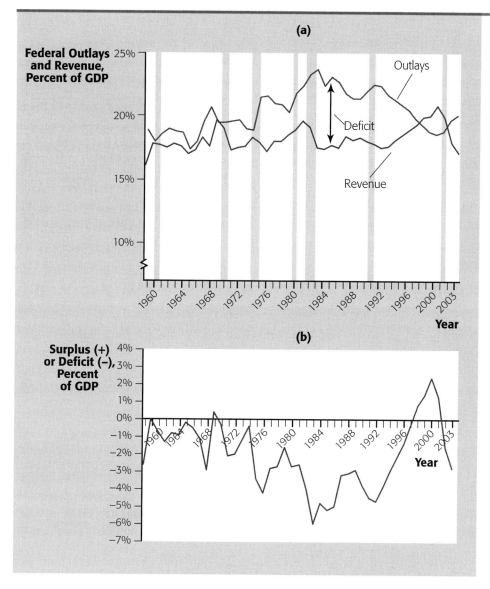

FIGURE 7
The Federal Budget Deficit or Surplus as a Percentage of GDP

In any given year, the federal deficit (relative to GDP) is the difference between total federal revenue and total federal outlays relative to GDP. The deficit rises in recessions and after large tax cuts. Both occurred in the early 1980s and again in the early 2000s.

early 1980s. This was the combined result of a severe recession, which caused transfers to rise as shown in Figure 3, the buildup in military spending shown in Figure 1, and a large cut in income taxes during President Reagan's first term in office.

In the mid-1990s, the deficit began to come down, and finally, in the late 1990s, the federal government began running budget surpluses for a few years. But in 2002, the budget was back into deficit, and the deficits were projected to continue through the end of the decade. Even though the world has changed much since the 1980s, the reasons for the deficits of the early 2000s seem like a repeat of history: a recession, increased military spending, and a sizable, multi-year tax cut.

The National Debt. Before we consider the government's budget further, we need to address some common confusion among three related, but very different, terms: the federal *deficit*, the federal *surplus*, and the national *debt*. The federal deficit and surplus are *flow* variables: They measure the difference between government spending and tax revenue *over a given period*, usually a year. The national debt, by contrast, is a *stock* variable: It measures the total amount that the federal government owes *at a given point in time*. (See the chapter "Economic Growth and Rising Living Standards" if you need a refresher on stocks and flows.)

The relationship between these terms is this: Each year that the government runs a deficit, it must borrow funds to finance it, *adding to the national debt*. For example, in 1996, the federal government ran a deficit of $107 billion. During that year, it issued about $107 billion in new government bonds, adding that much to the national debt. On the other hand, if the government runs a surplus, it uses the surplus to *pay back* some of the national debt. For example, in 2000, the federal government ran a surplus of about $236 billion. That year, it purchased about that much in government bonds it had issued in the past, thus reducing the national debt.[6]

We can measure the national debt as the total value of government bonds held by the public. Thus,

> *deficits—which add to the public's holdings of government bonds—add to the national debt. Surpluses—which decrease the public's bond holdings—subtract from the national debt.*

Since the cumulative total of the government's deficits has been greater than its surpluses, the national debt has grown over the past several decades. For most of this period, it has also grown relative to GDP, as shown in Figure 8.

The rise and fall in the national debt also explains another trend we discussed earlier: the rise and fall in *interest payments* the government must make to those who hold government bonds. All else equal, the larger the national debt, the greater will be the government's yearly interest payments on the debt. As you saw in Figure 4, total interest payments rose rapidly during the 1980s—the same period in which the national debt zoomed upward. In the 1990s, as the national debt decreased relative to GDP, so did interest payments on the debt. If you compare Figure 4 with Figure 8, however, you'll see that, as a percentage of GDP, the national debt rose in the early 2000s while yearly interest payments fell. That's because all else was *not* equal during this period: As mentioned earlier, the Federal Reserve dramatically lowered interest rates in the early 2000s, which reduced the government's interest payments on each dollar of newly issued debt.

Now that we've outlined the recent history of federal government spending, taxes, and debt, we turn our attention to the relationship between fiscal changes and the economy.

THE EFFECTS OF FISCAL CHANGES IN THE SHORT RUN

In the short run, there is a two-way relationship between the government's budget and the macroeconomy. On the one hand, changes in the economy affect the gov-

---

[6] The increase or decrease in the national debt is never exactly the same as the annual deficit or surplus, because of accounting details.

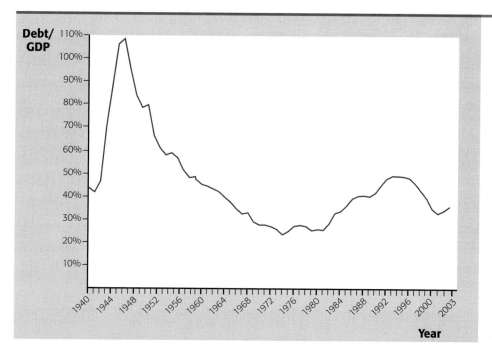

FIGURE 8
Federal Debt as a Percentage of GDP

Federal debt (the national debt) relative to GDP soared during World War II then fell steadily for several decades. It rose during the 1980s due to a combination of tax cuts and defense buildups during the Reagan administration, then fell during the shrinking deficits and expansion of the 1990s. In the early 2000s, a combination of recession and slow recovery, tax cuts and defense spending caused the debt-GDP ratio to begin rising.

Source: Office of Management and Budget (*http://www.whitehouse.gov/omb*) *Historical Tables, Budget of the United States Government, Fiscal Year 2003,* Table 7.1.

ernment's outlays and taxes; on the other hand, changes in outlays and taxes affect the economy. Let's begin by considering how economic fluctuations affect the government's budget.

How Economic Fluctuations Affect the Federal Budget

Economic fluctuations affect both transfer payments and tax revenues. In a recession, in which many people lose their jobs, the federal government contributes larger amounts to state-run unemployment insurance systems and pays more in transfers to the poor, since more families qualify for these types of assistance. Thus, a recession causes transfer payments to rise. Recessions also cause a drop in tax revenue, because household income and corporate profits—two important sources of tax revenue—decrease during recessions.

In a recession, because transfers rise and tax revenue falls, the federal budget deficit increases (or the surplus decreases).

An expansion has the opposite effect on the federal budget: With lower unemployment and higher levels of output and income, federal transfers decrease and tax revenues increase. Thus,

in an expansion, because transfers decrease and tax revenue rises, the budget deficit decreases (or the surplus increases).

Because the business cycle has systematic effects on spending and revenue, economists find it useful to divide the deficit into two components. The **cyclical deficit** is

Cyclical deficit The part of the federal budget deficit that varies with the business cycle.

the part that can be attributed to the current state of the economy. We have a cyclical deficit when output is below potential GDP, and a cyclical surplus when output is above potential. When the economy is operating just at full employment, the cyclical deficit is, by definition, zero.

Structural deficit The part of the federal budget deficit that is independent of the business cycle.

The **structural deficit** is the part of the deficit that is *not* caused by economic fluctuations. As the economy recovers from a recession, for example, the cyclical deficit goes away, but any structural deficit in the budget will remain.

Cyclical changes in the budget are not a cause for concern, because they average out to about zero, as output fluctuates above and below potential output. Thus, the cyclical deficit should not contribute to a long-run rise in the national debt.

How the Budget Affects Economic Fluctuations

Budget changes that occur automatically during expansions and recessions—that is, changes in the cyclical deficit or surplus—have an important impact: They help to make economic fluctuations milder than they would otherwise be. Recall that spending shocks have a multiplier effect on output. The larger the multiplier, the greater will be the fluctuations in output caused by any given spending shock. But changes in the cyclical deficit make the multiplier *smaller,* and thus act as an *automatic stabilizer.* How?

Let's use unemployment insurance as an example. In normal times, with the unemployment rate at around, say, 4.5 percent or lower, federal transfers for unemployment insurance are modest. But when a negative spending shock hits the economy, and output and income begin to fall, the unemployment rate rises. Federal transfers for unemployment insurance rise *automatically.* Without assistance from the government, many of the newly unemployed would have to cut back their consumption spending substantially. But unemployment insurance cushions the blow for many such families—at least for six months or sometimes longer—allowing them to make smaller cutbacks in consumption during that time. As a result, the total decline in consumption is smaller and GDP declines by less. Unemployment insurance thus reduces the multiplier.

Other transfer programs have a similar stabilizing effect on output. More people receive food stamps during recessions. Consequently, their consumption falls by less than it would if they did not have this help. And the tax system contributes to economic stability in a similar way. Income tax payments, for example, fall during a recession. With the government siphoning off a smaller amount of income from the household sector, the drop in consumption is smaller than it would be if tax revenues remained constant.

The same principle applies when a positive spending shock hits the economy. Transfer payments automatically decline, as the unemployed find jobs and fewer families qualify for government assistance. And tax revenues automatically rise, since income rises. As a result, the positive spending shock causes a smaller rise in GDP than would otherwise occur.

> *Many features of the federal tax and transfer systems act as automatic stabilizers. As the economy goes into a recession, these features help to reduce the decline in consumption spending, and they also cause the cyclical deficit to rise. As the economy goes into an expansion, these features help to reduce the rise in consumption spending, and they also cause the cyclical deficit to fall.*

This immediately raises a question: If *automatic* changes in the budget help to stabilize the economy, can the government *purposely* change its spending or tax policy to make the economy even more stable?

Countercyclical Fiscal Policy

When the government uses fiscal policy to keep the economy closer to potential GDP in the short run, it is engaging in **countercyclical fiscal policy.** The government's tools in this effort are changes in government purchases, or changes in policy toward taxes or transfers. Notice the phrase "changes in policy"; the automatic changes in taxes or transfers that occur during the business cycle are not considered countercyclical fiscal policy because these occur without any government action.

Countercyclical fiscal policy
Changes in taxes or government spending designed to counteract economic fluctuations.

Figure 9 illustrates the idea behind countercyclical fiscal policy. It shows the aggregate expenditure line for an economy that is initially operating at point *A*, with full-employment output of $10 trillion. Now suppose that investment spending decreases. The aggregate expenditure line will start to shift downward, and the economy will begin heading toward point *B*, where—in the absence of government action—output would settle at $9 trillion. Note that, even if the government does nothing, automatic stabilizers will be at work: As output heads toward its new equilibrium of $9 trillion, tax revenue falls and transfers rise. In fact, without these stabilizers, output would decline further.[7]

But in theory, the government could try to *prevent* the recession with countercyclical fiscal policy. At the first signs of a contraction, it could increase government purchases (say, hiring more people to work with children in after-school programs). Alternatively, the government could increase transfers (further than they are rising automatically) with a change in policy—say, increasing the amount of unemployment insurance benefits paid to each unemployed worker. Or the government could decrease tax revenue (further than it is falling already) with a change in tax policy—say, an across-the-board decrease in everyone's income tax rate. Any of these actions would work to shift up the aggregate expenditure line. If taken early enough, the government could even stop the downward shift in its tracks and keep the economy close to full employment.

In the 1960s and 1970s, many economists and government officials believed that countercyclical fiscal policy could be an effective tool to counteract the business cycle. Today, however, economists tend to be more skeptical. Instead, they would put the Fed in charge of stabilizing the economy and reserve fiscal policy for addressing long-run issues of resource allocation. Why? Because countercyclical fiscal policy is plagued with several problems.

Timing Problems. It takes many months or even longer for most fiscal changes to be enacted. Consider, for example, a decision to decrease taxes in the United States. A tax bill originates in the House of Representatives and then goes to the Senate, where it is usually modified. Then a conference committee irons out the differences between the House and Senate versions, and the tax bill goes back to each chamber

---

[7] We've been drawing the aggregate expenditure line with a slope equal to the marginal propensity to consume. In more advanced treatments, automatic stabilizers are built into the slope of the aggregate expenditure line, making it flatter (a slope *less* than the MPC). With some experimentation, you can show that the flatter the line, the less any given decrease in investment spending will decrease equilibrium GDP.

FIGURE 9
Countercyclical Fiscal Policy

Initially, the economy's equilibrium is at full-employment output of $10,000 billion (point A). Then a decrease in investment spending shifts the aggregate expenditure line down to AE$_2$, and the economy starts heading toward point B—a recession. The government could shift the AE line back to its original position by increasing its own purchases, or by decreasing net taxes with a change in tax or transfer policies. If the change were enacted quickly enough, the government could prevent the recession.

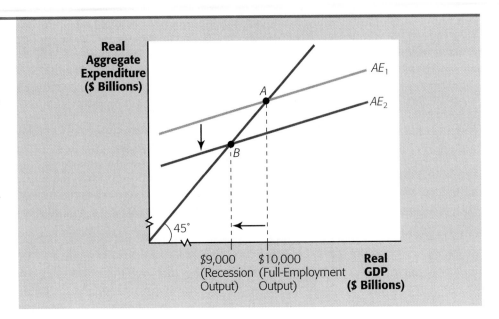

for a vote. Once the legislation has passed, the president must sign it. Even if all goes smoothly, this process can take many months.

But in most cases, it will *not* go smoothly. First, there is the thorny question of *distributing* the benefits of any total tax cut among different groups within the country—an issue about which Democrats and Republicans rarely agree. And some senators and representatives will see the bill as an opportunity to change the tax system in more fundamental ways, causing further political debate. All of these problems create the danger that the tax cut will take effect long after it is needed—stimulating the economy after it has recovered from recession and is beginning to overheat.

The same timing problem occurs in the opposite situation—when a tax hike is needed to counteract a boom—or when the fiscal policy is implemented through changes in government purchases or transfers. Because of delays, regular use of fiscal policy would be a *destabilizing* force in the economy—stepping on the gas when we should be hitting the brakes, or vice versa.

The Fed, by contrast, can increase or decrease the money supply *on the very day it decides that the change is necessary*. While there are time lags in the *effectiveness* of monetary policy (see the previous chapter), the ability to execute the policy in short order gives monetary policy an important advantage over fiscal policy for stabilizing the economy.

Irreversibility. To be effective, countercyclical fiscal policy must be reversible. In our example in Figure 9, a fiscal change is needed to counteract a decrease in investment spending. Therefore, once investment spending returns to normal levels, the fiscal stimulation should be reversed as well, so as not to overheat the economy. But reversing changes in government purchases or taxes is difficult. Spending programs that create new government departments or expand existing ones tend to become permanent, or at least difficult to terminate. Many temporary tax changes become permanent as well; the public is never happy to see a tax cut reversed, and the government is often reluctant to reverse a tax hike that has provided additional revenue for government programs.

Reversing monetary policy, while not painless, is easier to do. Fed governors are appointed to long terms and never have to stand for reelection. Thus, the Fed is at least somewhat insulated from the political process as it makes its decisions. Moreover, the public and Congress have largely accepted the Fed's role in stabilizing the economy, and expect that the interest rate will be adjusted as the condition of the economy changes.

The Fed's Reaction. Even if the government attempted to stabilize the economy with fiscal policy, it could usually not do so very effectively, because—to put it simply—the Fed would not allow it. The Fed views most changes in fiscal policy just as it views other changes in aggregate expenditure: as a change to be neutralized. In Figure 9, if the Fed had perceived that the aggregate expenditure line was beginning to shift downward, it would have *already* lowered its interest rate target, long before any fiscal change was enacted. The fiscal stimulus, when it finally took effect, would be counteracted with an offsetting rise in the interest rate target. As long as the Fed remains free to set its own course, and sees its goal as stabilizing the economy at full employment with low inflation, there is generally no opportunity—and no need—for countercyclical fiscal policy. (An exception discussed in the previous chapter is the very special circumstance in which the Fed has pushed the federal funds rate to zero, and exhausted all other tools to stimulate the economy out of a recession. In that case, fiscal policy would be an effective backup.)

THE EFFECTS OF FISCAL CHANGES IN THE LONG RUN

Fiscal changes have important effects on the economy over the long run. And, as you've learned, the classical model—which focuses on the determinants of potential output—provides a useful framework for analyzing these long-run effects.

Let's first list three important conclusions about fiscal policy in the classical model that you learned in earlier chapters:

- The government's tax and transfer policies can influence the rate of labor force participation. For example, higher tax rates on labor income (or household income, generally) or more generous transfers can reduce the labor force participation rate, and *decrease* the average standard of living. Lower tax rates or less generous transfers can raise the labor force participation rate and raise the standard of living.

- The government's tax policies can directly influence the rate of investment spending on new capital and R&D. Higher tax rates on the profits from investment projects will

Deficits and Growth: A Proviso This section has argued that rising deficits over the long run will come at the cost of lower investment spending and therefore reduce the rate of economic growth. But this is not *always* the case. It depends on what causes the deficit to increase. If the rise in the deficit results from a long-run rise in, say, transfer payments, the effects on growth will be negative. But suppose the deficit arises from an increase in government spending to improve the legal, financial, and physical infrastructure of the economy, or to improve education. All of these types of spending contribute to economic growth themselves. Thus, even if the deficits caused by this higher government spending crowd out private investment, their net effect on growth could be favorable.

DANGEROUS CURVES

lower investment spending and lead to slower growth in the average standard of living. Lower tax rates or other investment incentives will increase investment spending and lead to faster growth in living standards.

- The government's budget deficit can influence investment spending as well. An increase in the budget deficit causes the government to demand more loanable funds. This raises the interest rate, lowers investment spending, and slows the growth in living standards. Lower budget deficits reduce the government's demand for loanable funds, resulting in a lower interest rate, greater investment spending, and faster growth in living standards.

And, from this chapter, you've learned the following:

- Budget deficits add to the national debt.

But what are the *consequences* of adding to the national debt? Because there are so many widely held myths about this subject, it deserves a section of its own.

The National Debt

On a billboard in midtown Manhattan, a giant clocklike digital display tracks the U.S. national debt and how it changes each minute. Through the mid-1990s, as the publicly held debt soared beyond $3 trillion and headed toward $4 trillion, the clock showed the debt growing by about $240,000 per minute. The last four digits on the display changed so rapidly that they appeared as a blur.

The national debt clock was one of several public relations campaigns that spread fear among the American public. How could we ever hope to repay all of this debt? Surely, we were speeding toward a debt disaster.

Economists do have concerns about the national debt. But they are very different from the concerns suggested by the national debt clock or other similar gimmicks.

Mythical Concerns About the National Debt. What bothers many people about a growing national debt is the belief that one day we will have to pay it all back. But although we might *choose* to repay the national debt, we do not have to. *Ever.* Moreover, there is nothing automatically wrong with a national debt that *grows* every year. That may sound surprising. How could a government keep borrowing funds without ever paying them back? Surely, no business could behave that way.

But actually, many successful businesses *do* behave that way, and continue to prosper. For example, the debt of many major corporations—like AT&T and General Motors—continues to grow, year after year. While they continue to pay interest on their debt, they have no plans to pay back the amount originally borrowed in the foreseeable future. As these companies' bonds become due, they simply *roll them over*; they issue new bonds to pay back the old ones.

Why don't these firms pay back their debt? Because they believe they have a better use for their funds: investing in new capital equipment and research and development to expand their businesses. This will lead to higher future profits. And as long as their profits continue to grow, they can continue to increase their debt.

Of course, this does not mean that *any* size debt would be prudent. Recall the important principle we discussed earlier in the chapter: *Debt and interest payments have meaning only in relation to income.* If a firm's income is growing by 5 percent each year, but its interest payments are growing by 10 percent per year, it would eventually find itself in trouble. Each year, its interest payments would take a larger and larger fraction of its income, and at some point interest payments would exceed total income. But even *before* this occurred, the firm would find itself in trouble. Lenders, anticipating the firm's eventual inability to pay interest, would cut the firm off. At that point, the firm would reach its *credit limit*—the maximum amount it can borrow based on lenders' willingness to lend. Since it could no longer roll over its existing debt with further borrowing, it would have to pay back any bonds coming due until its debt was comfortably below its credit limit.

All of these observations apply to the federal government as well. As long as the nation's total income is rising, the government can safely take on more debt. More specifically, if the nation's income is growing at least as fast as total interest payments, the debt can continue to grow indefinitely, without putting the government in danger.

The federal government *could* pay back the national debt—by running budget surpluses for many years. But the government could also choose to behave like most corporations and *not* pay back its debt. In fact, the government would better serve the public by not paying down the debt if it has better uses for its revenue than debt repayment.

But how rapidly could the government continue to accumulate debt? Or, equivalently, how large could annual deficits be without making the national debt a looming danger?

Let's see. As long as total national income grows at least as fast as interest payments on the debt, the ratio of interest payments to income will not grow. In that case, we could continue to pay interest without increasing the average tax rate on U.S. citizens. Let's use some round numbers to make this clearer. Suppose that the nominal GDP is $10 trillion and the national debt is $5 trillion. And suppose that annual interest payments average out to 7 percent of the national debt, or $350 billion. Then the ratio of interest payments to nominal GDP would be $350 billion/$10 trillion = 0.035 or 3.5 percent of GDP. Now suppose that, over some period of time, both nominal GDP and the national debt double, to $20 trillion and $10 trillion, respectively. Then interest payments would double as well, to $700 billion. But the ratio of interest payments to nominal GDP would remain constant, at $700 billion/$20 trillion = 0.035.

More generally,

as long as the debt grows by the same percentage as nominal GDP, the ratios of debt to GDP and interest payments to GDP will remain constant. In this case, the government can continue to pay interest on its rising debt without increasing the average tax rate in the economy.

Genuine Concerns About the National Debt. When *should* we be concerned about a growing national debt? Our previous discussion has hinted at three scenarios that should cause concern.

A National Debt That Is Growing Too Rapidly. An important *minimal guideline* for responsible government is that the debt should grow no faster than nominal GDP. Whenever that guideline is violated, interest payments as a fraction of GDP rise, and the average tax burden on the public—taxes relative to GDP—grows. The violation cannot go on forever, because the tax burden has a mathematical upper limit of 100 percent of GDP. And even before that limit was reached, tax rates would become oppressive, harming growth and—if pushed too high—actually reducing living standards. However, if the violation of the guideline is temporary, and the debt begins growing at the same rate as nominal GDP again, tax payments as a fraction of GDP stop rising.

This has two important implications. First, to prevent a long-term disaster after too-rapid growth in the debt, we do not have to run budget surpluses. A surplus is only necessary if the goal is to reduce the *total* debt. But all that is required to put the economy on a *responsible path* is a reduction of the growth rate of the debt back to the growth rate of nominal GDP. After that, we can keep running deficits and the debt can keep rising indefinitely, as long as it rises no faster than nominal GDP.

But there is a second implication as well: Even a temporary violation of the guideline is costly. During the time that debt grows faster than nominal GDP, the tax burden rises. Then, after the debt starts growing at the same rate as nominal GDP again, the tax burden stops rising—but *the burden remains at its new, higher level.* Thus, while a temporary violation of the guideline does not mean a disaster, it *does* leave us with a permanently elevated tax burden . . . at least, until we do something about it.

How can the tax burden be brought back down after a temporary violation of the guideline? There are only two basic ways: (1) raise the growth rate of nominal GDP *above* the growth rate of the debt for some time; or (2) lower the growth rate of the debt below the growth rate of nominal GDP for some time. Either of these solutions could return the debt-to-GDP ratio back to its original level, so that interest payments relative to GDP and the tax burden could return to their original levels as well.

But these solutions are costly to society. Let's consider (1): raising the growth rate of nominal GDP. Since policy has only limited ability to influence the growth rate of *real* GDP over long periods, the only practical method to ensure a higher growth rate of *nominal* GDP is faster growth in the price level. This means allowing the inflation rate to rise for some time. But we've already seen that allowing the inflation rate to rise can be costly for society in numerous ways—including the buildup of inflationary expectations that would be difficult to reverse.

Now let's consider (2): slowing down the growth rate of the debt below the growth rate of nominal GDP. The only way to do this is to run *smaller deficits* as a fraction of GDP than we would otherwise be able to run. And the only way to reduce the deficit for some length of time is to raise tax rates or reduce government outlays during that period.

Thus,

> *a debt that rises too fast—faster than nominal GDP—for some period of time will impose an opportunity cost in the future. The cost will be either a permanently higher tax burden, a period of inflation, or a temporary period of reduced government outlays or higher taxes relative to GDP.*

This is not just theoretical, as the U.S. experience during the 1970s and 1980s demonstrates. During this time, nominal GDP was growing at about 9 percent per year—mostly due to increases in the price level. But the debt grew by an average of 11 percent per year, beyond the minimal guidelines for responsible government. The debt-to-GDP ratio was therefore rising (see Figure 8) and so were interest payments relative to GDP (see Figure 4). This could not go on indefinitely, or interest payments on the debt would require a larger and larger share of GDP. How did we solve the problem? As we entered the 1990s, we gradually shrunk the budget deficit with higher tax rates and strict limits on the growth of government spending. Indeed, we went further than necessary: turning the budget into surplus territory. The result was a rapidly declining debt and interest burden relative to GDP during the 1990s. Fortunately, the 1990s was a period of prolonged expansion and reduced military purchases, so the opportunity cost of lower deficits was not as painful as it might otherwise have been.

A Debt Approaching the National Credit Limit. If debt were to rise *too* rapidly relative to GDP, for *too* long, there is a theoretical danger of reaching the nation's credit limit—the amount of debt that would make lenders worry about the government's ability to continue paying interest. If this credit limit is approached, a nation is truly flirting with disaster: a tiny increase in the ratio of debt to GDP would lead to a cutoff of further lending and require that the budget be balanced immediately. It could also cause a financial panic, with everyone trying to sell their government bonds at the same time, causing bond prices to fall and household wealth to plummet. This was a common scenario in the disaster books discussed at the beginning of this chapter.

While approaching a credit limit is a *theoretically* sound danger of a rapidly rising debt, it is doubtful the United States has been anywhere near that limit during recent decades. If you flip back to Figure 8, you'll see that the federal debt reached as high as 50 percent of GDP in 1993. But you can also see that at the conclusion of World War II, the debt was much higher—109 percent of GDP. At that time, there was little concern that the government would not honor its debt obligations. And, in fact, the debt-to-GDP ratio was brought down dramatically—to 24 percent of GDP by 1974.

> *The notion of an absolute credit limit leading to a cutoff of funding and a financial panic—while theoretically possible—is not realistic for the levels of national debt the United States has experienced in recent decades.*

Failing to Account for Future Obligations. Many students reading this book are getting financial help from parents to pay the costs of college. Planning for this obligation may have begun very early—perhaps even before you knew what college was. This makes sense: If a family wants to avoid a drastic decrease in its standard of living in the future, it should start accounting for future obligations in the present.

The federal government is in an analogous situation. It has effectively promised to provide Medicare and Social Security payments to millions of people at some time in the future. Based on demographic and other trends, Social Security, Medicare, and Medicaid benefits are projected to rise significantly and continually over the next 75 years—from 7.6 percent of GDP in 2000 to 21.1 percent in 2075. If the federal government is to act like a responsible household, it should take these future obligations into account in its planning process. Otherwise, we may have to dramatically decrease *other* government outlays, dramatically increase taxes, or have an ever-rising debt-to-GDP ratio, leading to the dangers discussed earlier.

Of course, trying to project total federal revenues and outlays over the next 75 years, 50 years, or even 15 years would be guesswork at best. Even official forecasts of *10-year* projections are typically widely off the mark. In 1989, for example, when the government made its fiscal projections for 1990–1999, no one could have predicted the development of the Internet and other technologies, and the rapid economic growth that would accompany them. And in 1999, when projections for 2000–2009 were completed, who could have predicted the events of September 11, 2001, and how it would change our spending on national defense and homeland security?

This uncertainty over future projections has led to divergent views about policy. Some argue that a responsible government should be exceedingly cautious, running budget surpluses now, paying down the national debt, and leaving us better prepared for any dramatic future rise in government outlays. Others argue that preparing for the worst would require huge sacrifices in the present—sacrifices that might be completely unnecessary in hindsight.

These divergent views formed part of the background for the controversy over the Bush tax cuts.

© WWW.OMB.GOV

USING THE THEORY
The Bush Tax Cuts of 2001 and 2003

In 2001, the Bush administration cut taxes over 10 years by $1.35 trillion, and in 2003, by another $350 billion. Marginal tax rates were reduced on all income brackets, as were tax rates on capital gains and dividends. There were additional reductions for taxpayers with children, and a reduction of the "marriage penalty" that taxed married couples at higher rates than if they were single. Also, the tax cuts in 2003 accelerated some of the 2001 reductions that had originally been postponed until 2006 and beyond.

Much of the debate over the tax reductions had to do with distribution: whether the cuts were apportioned fairly among different income groups. But they also raised two important macroeconomic issues that we've discussed in this chapter.

The Short Run: Countercyclical Fiscal Policy?

The tax cuts of 2001 and 2003 seem, at first glance, like perfect examples of well-timed countercyclical fiscal policy. After all, the first cuts were put in place in June 2001—in the middle of a recession that began just three months earlier. And the cuts in May 2003 took effect as the economy was still struggling with the weak expansion and joblessness of 2002 and 2003 (see the chapter "Aggregate Demand and Aggregate Supply") Does this show that countercyclical fiscal policy works?

Not really, because a closer look suggests that neither tax cut was really designed for that purpose. The tax cut of June 2001 had actually been proposed more than 18 months earlier by presidential candidate Bush as a long-run policy measure, to promote growth in potential output. At the time, the economy was in a boom, and the Federal Reserve was actively trying to slow it down. The fact that the tax cut was enacted during a recession was a stroke of luck, not an example of well-timed short-run fiscal policy.

Moreover, remember that countercyclical fiscal policy requires that changes in taxes be reversible when economic conditions change. But both of the Bush tax cuts were *long-term* policy changes: Some of their provisions applied through the end of the decade, and the others were expected to be extended at least that long, and probably beyond.

As so often happens in macroeconomic debates, however, politics took over. As the economy entered the recession of 2001, the debate over the 2001 tax cut quickly shifted to its short-run stimulus potential. And the 2003 cut—weighted heavily toward long-run reforms in the tax code—was both touted and opposed almost entirely on the basis of its ability to create jobs in the short run, during a slow recovery.

In between these two cuts, however, the Bush administration proposed a purely countercyclical, $60 billion tax cut. This was formulated and designed as an emergency measure, shortly after September 11, 2001, to prevent the economy from sliding further into recession. Timing was crucial, and the administration urged quick passage by Congress. If there was ever an opportunity to showcase the effectiveness of countercyclical fiscal policy, this was it. But the tax bill was debated for a full six months in the House and Senate, and was not signed by the president until March 2002. During these six months of debate, the Fed reduced its interest rate target four times, illustrating the greater flexibility of monetary policy as a countercyclical tool.

The Long Run: The Tax Cuts and the National Debt

Now let's consider the **long-run** macroeconomic issue raised by the tax cuts. Table 3 shows two different projections of budget deficits and the national debt. Let's start with the upper half of the table, which shows numbers released by the administration's Office of Management and Budget (OMB) as part of its midyear budget update in July 2003. The second column shows the projected deficit in each fiscal year, ending in September of the year indicated. The deficit is approximately equal to the rise in the debt from the end of the previous year to the end of the current year. For example, in 2005, the projected deficit is $304 billion, and the debt is expected to rise from $4,473 billion at the end of 2004 to $4,789 billion at the end of 2005, a rise of $4,789 − $4,473 = $316 billion. (The difference between the deficit and the annual rise in the debt is due to technical factors in measuring the official debt.)

Judging by the OMB's numbers, it appears that the administration's fiscal policy is an example of a temporary violation of the guideline for responsible government: Debt is rising faster than GDP through 2006, and then stabilizing

TABLE 3
Projected Budget Deficits and the Rising National Debt

(a) Office of Management and Budget (White House) Projections

	Deficit: ($billion)	Debt (End of year) ($billion)	Nominal GDP ($billion)	Debt as Percentage of GDP
2002 (actual)	$158	$3,540	$10,446	33.8%
2003	$455	$4,036	$10,757	37.5%
2004	$475	$4,473	$11,303	39.6%
2005	$304	$4,789	$11,884	40.3%
2006	$238	$5,043	$12,483	40.4%
2007	$213	$5,272	$13,104	40.2%
2008	$226	$5,516	$13,752	40.1%

(b) House Budget Committee—Democratic Caucus Projections

	Deficit ($billion)	Debt (End of year) ($billion)	Nominal GDP ($billion)	Debt as Percentage of GDP
2002 (actual)	$158	$3,540	$10,446	33.8%
2003	$416	$3,956	$10,757	36.8%
2004	$489	$4,455	$11,303	39.4%
2005	$364	$4,809	$11,884	40.0%
2006	$345	$5,154	$12,483	41.3%
2007	$329	$5,483	$13,104	41.8%
2008	$343	$5,826	$13,752	42.4%
. . .				
2013	$2,090 (cumulative, 2009–2013)	$7,915	$17,505	45.2%

Sources: Office of Management and Budget, *Fiscal Year Budget, 2004*, Table 20, "Federal Government Financing and Debt," and House Budget Committee, Democratic Caucus, "Deficits Hit Record Levels," Press Release, July 16, 2003.

and descending. (In 2003, the government issued only a 5-year projection, instead of the usual 10 years, citing uncertainties over the military occupation of Iraq and the war on terrorism.)

What do these numbers tell us? Certainly not a debt disaster. But a fiscal policy with future costs. By raising the national debt as a percentage of GDP, interest payments relative to GDP and the tax burden will rise. Afterward, the debt-to-GDP ratio comes down a bit, but not enough to bring the tax burden back to where it was originally.

Where does this rise in the debt come from? Some of the early rise comes from *cyclical* deficits. Because of the economy's slow recovery after the recession in 2001, it is still assumed to be operating below potential even in 2004, with lower tax revenues and higher transfers than would occur at full employment. But the continued deficits in 2006 and beyond—when the economy is assumed to have recovered—are mostly *structural* deficits. According to the OMB's estimates, the two Bush tax cuts account for about 25 percent of the total rise in the national debt over the projection period.

Now look at the lower table. It shows the numbers put out by the Democratic Caucus of the House Budget Committee in a press release, within days of the OMB document's release. It shows a more sharply rising deficit, and what looks like a *long-run* violation of the guideline for responsible government. The debt-to-GDP ratio rises continually, with no end in sight. Note that the Democratic Caucus projects 10 years forward instead of 5. But that accounts for only part of the dramatic difference in the fiscal story each side tells. What accounts for the rest?

The answer is: the assumptions behind the numbers. The OMB deficit numbers leave out estimates of government outlays for military operations in Iraq or Afghanistan beyond 2003. It also assumes that any provisions of the two tax cuts that are legally set to expire between 2004 and 2008 will, in fact, expire, thereby boosting tax revenues.

The Democrats make different assumptions. On the outlays side, they included the estimated cost of Iraq and Afghanistan from 2004 through 2006, and projected greater increases in national defense through 2008 and beyond (compared to the administration estimates). They also added the expenses of a proposed prescription drug benefit plan for Medicare, starting in 2006. And on the revenue side, the Democrats not only assumed that expiring provisions of the tax cuts would be renewed, but that further changes in the tax code the administration has favored in the past would also be enacted.

Using the Democratic numbers, virtually *all* of the rise in the debt during their 11-year projection period can be attributed to tax cuts of some form—either the original cuts in 2001 and 2003, or the expected extensions and further reductions the administration has discussed.

Note that, based on *either* set of numbers, we are entering a period of rising debt that will entail the kinds of future costs we've discussed in the chapter. Under the Democrats' assumptions, the path is unsustainable in the long run: Debt and interest payments are rising faster than GDP for 10 years and perhaps beyond. Under the Bush administration's assumptions, the path is costly, but sustainable, with debt and interest payments topping out in 2006.

Ultimately, our conclusions about any economic policy must compare its costs with its *benefits*. And views about the benefits associated with the administration's fiscal plan diverge even more widely than views about its costs. Was the tax cut distributed in the right way? Should the United States have gone to war with Iraq? How much should the current generation of younger workers sacrifice to care for retiring baby boomers? How one answers questions like these ultimately determines whether the costs of higher debt—under either set of numbers—are justified. But this is where economics leaves off and politics and ideology begins.

Summary

The U.S. federal government finances its spending through a combination of taxes and borrowing. When government outlays exceed tax revenue, the government runs a budget deficit. It finances that deficit by selling bonds, thereby adding to the national debt. When government outlays are less than tax revenue, the government runs a budget surplus. It uses that surplus to buy back bonds it has issued in the past, thus shrinking the national debt.

Federal government outlays consists of three broad categories: government purchases of goods and services, transfer payments, and interest on the national debt. Nonmilitary government purchases have traditionally accounted for a stable, low 2 percent of real GDP. Military purchases vary according to global politics; in recent years, they have declined dramatically relative to GDP, but seem likely to rise in 2002 and beyond. Transfer programs—such as Social Security, Medicare, and welfare—have been the fastest-growing part of government spending. They currently equal about 12.5 percent of GDP.

On the revenue side, the government relies on personal and corporate income taxes, Social Security taxes, and some smaller excise taxes and user fees. Federal revenue was trending mildly upward until the early 2000s.

From 1970 through the mid-1990s, federal spending exceeded federal revenues every year, so that the government ran budget deficits. Particularly large deficits occurred in the early 1980s. But in the 1990s, the deficit declined, and in 1998 the government began running yearly budget surpluses. In 2002, the budget picture flip-flopped again, as deficits were projected for several years.

In the short run, there is a two-way relationship between government outlays and taxes on the one hand and the level of output on the other. Changes in output affect government outlays and taxes. In recessions, for example, government tax revenues fall and transfer payments rise. In this way, the tax and transfer system acts as an automatic stabilizer, helping to smooth out fluctuations in output.

In principle, the government could use countercyclical fiscal policy—changing tax and transfer policies or government purchases in order to offset economic fluctuations. However, because of practical problems, most economists are skeptical about its effectiveness.

In the long run, fiscal changes have important effects. All else equal, we can expect larger budget deficits to slow growth in living standards, and smaller budget deficits or surpluses to speed the growth of living standards.

Over the 1970s and, especially, the 1980s, the average federal budget deficit was so large, and the national debt growing so rapidly, that interest payments were rising relative to GDP. While we were not on the brink of disaster, the deficits and the growing national debt did require a future sacrifice, which we paid in the 1990s by reducing the deficit through tight fiscal policy. The same scenario of high deficits and rising national debt relative to GDP is now projected for the coming decade. The rising debt-to-GDP ratio—even if temporary—will require future sacrifices.

Key Terms

Average tax rate
Countercyclical fiscal policy

Cyclical deficit
Marginal tax rate
Progressive tax

Regressive tax
Structural deficit

Review Questions

Answers to even-numbered Questions and Problems can be found on the text Web site at http://ball-lieb.swlearning.com.

1. Why is it misleading to compare the national debt of $235 billion in 1959 with the national debt of $3,878 billion in 2003?

2. List the three broad categories of federal government outlays. According to the most recent data in the chapter, which is the largest category? How have these types of spending changed relative to GDP over the past few years?

3. What is a *progressive* income tax?

4. List the main sources of federal revenue. How and why has the composition changed recently?

5. Explain the difference between the federal deficit and the national debt. Explain the relationship between the federal budget surplus and the national debt.

6. Define the cyclical deficit and the structural deficit. Why are changes in the cyclical deficit not a major long-run concern?

7. What is countercyclical fiscal policy? Is it an effective tool? Explain.

8. "A decrease in the national debt as a fraction of GDP requires the federal government to run budget surpluses." True or false? Explain.

9. While the national debt has been an important concern, most economists don't believe we were truly headed for disaster in the 1980s. Explain.

10. Judging from the Office of Management and Budget (OMB) numbers, explain whether or not the Bush administration is running a sustainable budget policy. Judge the same situation using the Democratic Caucus of the House Budget Committee's numbers. What accounts for the difference?

11. Explain why Medicare costs are expected to rise rapidly over the next two decades.

Problems and Exercises

1. Use the following statistics, in billions of units, to calculate the real national debt and the debt relative to GDP in 1990 and 2000 for this hypothetical country. Which figures would you use to compare the national debt in the two years?

National Debt in 1990:	1.2
National Debt in 2000:	13.8
Nominal GDP in 1990:	101.7
Nominal GDP in 2000:	552.2
Price Index in 1990:	35.2
Price Index in 2000:	113.3

2. You are running for president of the small nation of Utopia. You promise to cut tax rates, increase transfers and government purchases, reduce the government's budget deficit, and reduce the government's debt as a fraction of GDP. If elected, is it possible for you to keep all of your campaign promises in the short run? What about in the long run?

3. You are running for reelection as president of the nation of Utopia. Your opponents have criticized you for allowing the national debt to grow by almost 50 percent over the last four years. Use the following statistics, measured in millions of dollars, to defend yourself to Utopia's voters:

National debt in year 1 of your presidency:	$152
National debt in year 4 of your presidency:	$200
Nominal GDP in year 1 of your presidency:	$3042
Nominal GDP in year 4 of your presidency:	$4098
Price index in year 1 of your presidency:	45
Price index in year 4 of your presidency:	72

4. Suppose there is a country with 30 households divided into three categories (A, B, and C), with 10 households of each type. If a household earns 20,000 zips (the country's currency) or more in a year, it must pay 15 percent of its income in taxes. If the household earns less than 20,000 zips, it doesn't pay any tax. When the economy is operating at full employment, household income is 250,000 zips per year for each type A household, 50,000 zips for type B households, and 20,000 zips for type C households.

   a. If the economy is operating at full employment, how much revenue does the government collect in taxes for the year?

   b. Suppose a recession hits and household income falls for each type of household. Type A households now earn 150,000 zips, type B households earn 30,000 zips, and type C households earn 10,000 zips for the year. How much does the government collect in tax revenue for the year? Assume the government spends all of the revenue it would have collected if the economy had been operating at full employment. Under this assumption, what is the effect of the recession on the government budget deficit (i.e., the effect on the cyclical deficit)?

   c. Suppose instead that the economy expanded and household incomes rose to 400,000 zips, 75,000 zips, and 30,000 zips, respectively, for the year. How much tax would the government collect for the year? What is the effect on the cyclical deficit (assume again that the government spends exactly the amount of revenue it collects when household income is at the values in part (a))? What does this problem tell you about the relationship between shocks to the economy and the budget deficit? structural deficit?

5. Suppose a nation's government purchases are equal to $2 trillion, regardless of the state of the economy. However, its taxes and transfers depend on economic conditions. When the economy is at potential output, net taxes (taxes minus transfers) equal $2.2 trillion. However, for each 1 percent GDP falls below potential output, net taxes fall by 5 percent.

   a. Suppose the economy was operating at potential output. What would be the structural deficit? The cyclical deficit?

   b. Suppose that real GDP was 5 percent below potential output. What would be the cyclical deficit? The structural deficit?

6. Are either of the following countries violating the minimal guidelines for responsible government as outlined in this text?

   Country A
   (Figures in Billions of $)

	Debt	GDP
1999	1	100
2000	2	110
2001	3	150

   Country B
   (Figures in Billions of $)

	Debt	GDP
1999	1236	1400
2000	1346	1550
2001	1406	1707

7. At the end of this chapter, you learned that in March 2002, a three-year fiscal stimulus package was put into effect. Suppose that when the stimulus began to have an impact, the economy had already returned to full employment.
   a. Show the likely effect of this policy on an AS–AD diagram, assuming that the Fed did nothing.
   b. What would be the Fed's normal response to such a fiscal stimulus? Why? Illustrate the effect of the Fed's policy on your AS–AD diagram.
   c. What can you conclude about the ultimate impact of an ill-timed fiscal stimulus on GDP and the price level when the Fed reacts as expected? Should the Fed be indifferent about such stimulus? Why or why not?

8. Assume that the unemployment rate in the small country of Economica is currently 6 percent, and that in this country government purchases = $10 million, tax revenue = $17 million, transfers and interest payments = $5 million, and the current unemployment rate is 6 percent.
   a. Find the size of the Economica's budget deficit.
   b. What can you tell about Economica's cyclical deficit and its structural deficit?

9. Complete this table for the small country of Microland. Assume that Microland started year one with no federal debt. What is the relationship between the deficit and the debt? How can the real national debt fall in the absence of a change in government outlays and tax revenue?

	Year						
	1	2	3	4	5	6	7
Price Index	100	103	105	110	118	133	140
Nominal GDP	$400	$500	$600	$700	$800	$900	$1000
Outlays	$100	$120	$125	$135	$133	$130	$ 130
Tax Revenue	$105	$126	$130	$132	$134	$138	$ 130
Deficit/Surplus							
Debt							
Real National Debt							
Debt to GDP							

Challenge Question

Suppose the United States were running a budget surplus and decided to eliminate it by either cutting taxes or increasing government spending.

a. Compared to a policy of just accruing surpluses and paying down the national debt, what will this policy do to U.S. real GDP and interest rates in the *short run*? Illustrate your answer graphically. (*Hint*: Which macro model, and which graphs, should you use to illustrate effects on output and interest rates in the short run?)

b. Compared to a policy of just accruing surpluses and paying down the national debt, what will this policy do to U.S. real GDP and interest rates in the *long run*? Illustrate your answer graphically.

c. Going back to the short run, suppose the Fed responds by neutralizing the impact of the fiscal change in part (a) above. What will happen to real GDP and interest rates in the short run?

These exercises require access to Hall/Lieberman Xtra! If Xtra! did not come with your book, visit http://hallxtra.swlearning.com to purchase.

1. Use your Xtra! password at the Hall and Lieberman Web site (http://hallxtra.swlearning.com), select this chapter, and under Economic Applications, click on EconDebate. Choose *Fiscal Policy,* and scroll down to find the debate, "How Should the U.S. Budget Surplus Be Used?" Read the debate, and use the information to answer the following questions.
   a. Explain the liberal and conservative views on budget deficit/surplus.
   b. Is the 2001 (and 2003) tax cut legislation, sponsored by the Bush administration, an example of counter-cyclical fiscal policy in light of recessions in these periods? Explain.

2. Use your Xtra! password at the Hall and Lieberman Web site (http://hallxtra.swlearning.com), select this chapter, and under Economic Applications, click on EconData. Choose *Taxes, Spending, and Deficits,* and scroll down to find *Real per-Capita Disposable Income.* Read the definition, click on Diagrams/Data.

   Disposable personal income is the portion of personal income that is available for consumption spending or saving after personal taxes are taken out. Confirm that in the short run, the increase in real per-capita disposable personal income is inversely related to personal tax rates, or directly related to personal consumption.

CHAPTER 28

Exchange Rates and Macroeconomic Policy

If you've ever traveled to a foreign country, you were a direct participant in the **foreign exchange market**—a market in which one country's currency is traded for that of another. For example, if you traveled to Mexico, you might have stopped near the border to exchange some dollars for Mexican pesos.

Even if you have never traveled abroad, you've been involved, at least indirectly, in all kinds of foreign exchange dealings. For example, suppose you buy some Mexican- grown tomatoes at a store in the United States, where you pay with dollars. Except for shipping and retailing services, the resources used to produce those tomatoes were Mexican. A Mexican farmer grew the tomatoes; Mexican truckers transported them to the distribution center in the nearest large city; and Mexican workers, machinery, and raw materials were used to package them. All of these people want to be paid in Mexican pesos, regardless of who buys the final product. After all, they live in Mexico, so they need pesos to buy things there. But you, as an American, want to pay for your tomatoes with dollars.

Foreign exchange market
The market in which one country's currency is traded for another country's.

Let's think about this for a moment. You want to pay for the tomatoes in dollars, but the Mexicans who produced them want to be paid in pesos. How can this happen?

The answer: *Someone*, here or abroad, must use the foreign exchange market to exchange dollars for pesos. For example, it might work like this: You pay dollars to your supermarket, which pays dollars to a U.S. importer, who pays dollars to the distributor in Mexico, who—finally—turns the dollars over to a Mexican bank in exchange for pesos. Finally, the Mexican distributor pays the Mexican farmer in pesos. In this case, the actual changing of dollars into pesos takes place in a Mexican bank. But why is the Mexican bank willing to trade pesos for dollars? Because the bank is a participant in the market for foreign exchange, and it also trades dollars for pesos.

In this chapter, we'll look at the markets in which dollars are exchanged for foreign currency. We'll also expand our macroeconomic analysis to consider the effects of changes in exchange rates. As you'll see, what happens in the foreign exchange market affects the economy, and changes in the economy affect the foreign exchange market. This has implications for the Fed as it tries to use monetary policy to steer the economy and keep it growing smoothly. Finally, in the "Using the Theory" section, you'll see how the tools of the chapter can help us understand why the United States has such a large and persistent trade deficit.

FOREIGN EXCHANGE MARKETS AND EXCHANGE RATES

Every day, all over the world, more than a hundred different national currencies are exchanged for one another in banks, hotels, stores, and kiosks in airports and train stations. Traders exchange dollars for Mexican pesos, Japanese yen, European euros, Indian rupees, Chinese yuan, and so on. In addition, traders exchange each of these foreign currencies for one another: pesos for euros, yen for yuan, euros for yen. . . . There are literally thousands of combinations. How can we hope to make sense of these markets—how they operate and how they affect us?

Our basic approach is to treat each pair of currencies as a separate market. That is, there is one market in which dollars are exchanged for euros, another in which Angolan kwanzas trade for yen, and so on. The physical locations where the trading takes place do not matter: Whether you exchange your dollars for yen in France, Germany, the United States, or even in Ecuador, you are a trader in the same dollar–yen market.

Exchange rate The amount of one country's currency that is traded for one unit of another country's currency.

In any foreign exchange market, the rate at which one currency is traded for another is called the **exchange rate** between those two currencies. For example, if you happened to trade dollars for British pounds on August 8, 2003, each British pound would have cost you $1.60. On that day, the exchange rate was $1.60 per pound.

Dollars per Pound or Pounds per Dollar?

Table 1 lists exchange rates between the dollar and various foreign currencies on a particular day in 2003. But notice that we can think of any exchange rate in two ways: as so many units of foreign currency per dollar, or so many dollars per unit of

Country	Name of Currency	Symbol	Units of Foreign Currency per Dollar	Dollars per Unit of Foreign Currency
Brazil	real	R	2.9869	$0.3348
China	yuan	Y	8.2781	0.1208
European Monetary Union Countries	euro	€	1.1304	0.8584
Great Britain	pound	£	0.6239	1.6028
India	rupee	R	45.977	0.02175
Japan	yen	¥	119.05	0.0084
Mexico	peso	P	10.665	0.09376
Russia	ruble	R	30.414	0.03288

TABLE 1

Foreign Exchange Rates, August 8, 2003

foreign currency. For example, the table shows the exchange rate between the British pound and the dollar as 0.6239 pounds per dollar, or 1.6028 dollars per pound. We can always obtain one form of the exchange rate from the other by taking its reciprocal: $1/0.6239 = 1.6028$, and $1/1.6028 = 0.6239$.

In this chapter, we'll always define the exchange rate as "dollars per unit of foreign currency," as in the last column of the table. That way, from the American point of view, the exchange rate is just another *price*. The same way you pay a certain number of dollars for a gallon of gasoline (the price of gas), so, too, you pay a certain number of dollars for a British pound (the price of pounds).

The exchange rate is the price of foreign currency in dollars.

Table 1 raises some important questions: Why, in mid-2003, did a pound cost $1.60? Why not $1? Or $5? Why did one Japanese yen cost less than a penny? And a Russian ruble about three cents?

The answers to these questions certainly affect Americans who travel abroad. Suppose you are staying in a hotel in London that costs 100 pounds per night. If the price of the pound is $1, the hotel room will cost you $100, but if the price is $5, the room will cost you $500. And exchange rates affect Americans who stay at home, too. They influence the prices of many goods we buy in the United States, they help determine which of our industries will expand and which will contract, and they affect the wages and salaries that we earn from our jobs.

How are all these exchange rates determined? In most cases, they are determined by the familiar forces of supply and demand. As in other markets, each foreign exchange market reaches an equilibrium at which the quantity of foreign exchange demanded is equal to the quantity supplied.

In the next several sections, we'll build a model of supply and demand for a representative foreign exchange market: the one in which U.S. dollars are exchanged for British pounds. Taking the American point of view, we'll call this simply "the market for pounds." The other currency being traded—the dollar—will always be implicit.

THE DEMAND FOR BRITISH POUNDS

To analyze the demand for pounds, we start with a very basic question: *Who is demanding them?* The simple answer is, anyone who has dollars and wants to exchange them for pounds. But the most important buyers of pounds in the pound–dollar market will be American households and businesses. When Americans want to buy things from Britain, they will need to acquire pounds. To acquire them, they will need to offer U.S. dollars. To keep our analysis simple, we'll focus on just these American buyers. We'll also—for now—ignore any demand for pounds by the U.S. government.

> *In our model of the market for pounds, we assume that American households and businesses are the only buyers.*

Why do Americans want to buy pounds? There are two reasons:

- *To buy goods and services from British firms.* Americans buy sweaters knit in Edinburgh, airline tickets sold by Virgin Airways, and insurance services offered by Lloyd's. American tourists also stay in British hotels, use British taxis, and eat at British restaurants. To buy goods and services from British firms, Americans need to acquire pounds in order to pay for them.
- *To buy British assets.* Americans buy British stocks, British corporate or government bonds, and British real estate. In each case, the British seller will want to be paid in pounds, so the American buyer will have to acquire them.

The Demand for Pounds Curve

Demand curve for foreign currency A curve indicating the quantity of a specific foreign currency that Americans will want to buy, during a given period, at each different exchange rate.

Panel (a) of Figure 1 shows an example of a **demand curve for foreign currency,** in this case, the demand curve for pounds. The curve tells us *the quantity of pounds Americans will want to buy in any given period, at each different exchange rate.* Notice that the curve slopes downward: The lower the exchange rate, the greater the quantity of pounds demanded. For example, at an exchange rate of $2.25 per pound, Americans would want to purchase £200 million (point *A*). If the exchange rate fell to $1.50 per pound, Americans would want to buy £300 million (point *E*).

Why does a lower exchange rate—a lower price for the pound—make Americans want to buy more of them? Because the lower the price of the pound, the less expensive British goods are to American buyers. Remember that Americans think of prices in dollar terms. A British compact disc that sells for £8 will cost an American $18 at an exchange rate of $2.25 per pound, but only $12 if the exchange rate is $1.50 per pound.

Thus, as we move rightward *along* the demand for pounds curve, as in the move from point *A* to point *E*:

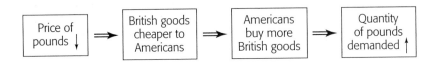

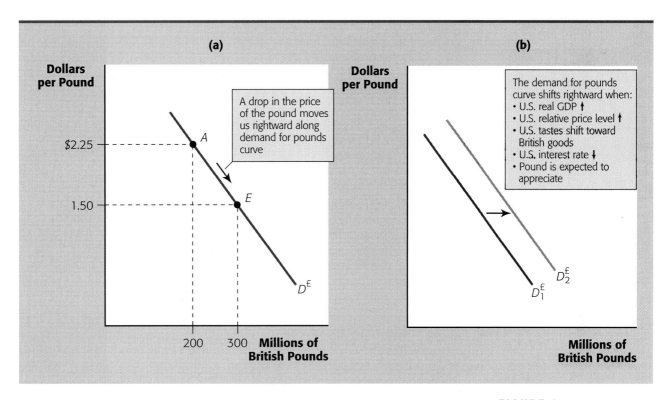

(a)

Dollars
per Pound

A drop in the price
of the pound moves
us rightward along
demand for pounds
curve

$2.25 ---- A

1.50 ---- E

$D^£$

200   300 **Millions of
British Pounds**

(b)

Dollars
per Pound

The demand for pounds
curve shifts rightward when:
• U.S. real GDP ↑
• U.S. relative price level ↑
• U.S. tastes shift toward
  British goods
• U.S. interest rate ↓
• Pound is expected to
  appreciate

$D_2^£$

$D_1^£$

**Millions of
British Pounds**

FIGURE 1
The Demand for British Pounds

Shifts in the Demand for Pounds Curve

In panel (a), you saw that a change in the exchange rate moves us *along* the demand for pounds curve. But other variables besides the exchange rate influence the demand for pounds. If any of these other variables changes, the entire curve will shift. As we consider each of these variables, keep in mind that we are assuming that only one of them changes at a time; we suppose the rest to remain constant.

U.S. Real GDP. Suppose real GDP and real income in the United States rise—say, because of continuing economic growth or a recovery from a recession. Then, Americans will buy more of everything, including goods and services from Britain. Thus, at any given exchange rate, Americans will demand more pounds. This is illustrated, in panel (b), as a rightward shift of the demand curve from $D_1^£$ to $D_2^£$.

Relative Price Levels. Suppose that the U.S. price level rises by 8 percent, while that in Britain rises by 5 percent. Then U.S. prices will rise *relative* to British prices. Americans will shift from buying their own goods toward buying the relatively cheaper British goods, so their demand for pounds will rise. That is, the demand for pounds curve will shift rightward.

Americans' Tastes for British Goods. All else being equal, would you prefer to drive a General Motors Aurora or a Jaguar? Do you prefer British-made films, like

Mansfield Park or *Hillary and Jackie,* or America's offerings, such as *American Beauty* or *Galaxy Quest*? These are matters of taste, and tastes can change. If Americans develop an increased taste for British cars, films, tea, or music, their demand for these goods will increase, and the demand for pounds curve will shift rightward.

Relative Interest Rates. Because financial assets must remain competitive in order to attract buyers, the rates of return on different financial assets—such as stocks and bonds—tend to rise and fall together. Thus, when one country's interest rate is high relative to that of another country, the first country's assets, *in general,* will have higher rates of return.

Now, suppose you're an American trying to decide whether to hold some of your wealth in British financial assets or in American financial assets. You will look very carefully at the rate of return you expect to earn in each country. All else being equal, a lower U.S. interest rate, relative to the British rate, will make British assets more attractive to you. Accordingly, as you and other Americans demand more British assets, you will need more pounds to buy them. The demand for pounds curve will shift rightward.

Expected Changes in the Exchange Rate. Once again, imagine you are an American deciding whether to buy an American or a British bond. Suppose British bonds pay 10 percent interest per year, while U.S. bonds pay 5 percent. All else equal, you would prefer the British bond, since it pays the higher rate of return. You would then exchange dollars for pounds at the going exchange rate and buy the bond.

But what if the price of the pound falls before the British bond becomes due? Then, when you cash in your British bond for pounds, and convert the pounds back into dollars, you'll be *selling your pounds at a lower price* than you bought them for. While you'd benefit from the higher interest rate on the British bond, you'd lose on the foreign currency transaction—buying pounds when their price is high and selling them when their price is low. If the foreign currency loss is great enough, you would be better off with U.S. bonds, even though they pay a lower interest rate.

As you can see, it is not just relative interest rates that matter to wealth holders; it is also *expected changes in the exchange rate.* An expectation that the price of the pound will fall will make British assets less appealing to Americans, since they will expect a foreign currency loss. In this case, the demand for pounds curve will shift leftward.

The opposite holds as well. If Americans expect the price of the pound to *rise,* they will expect a foreign currency *gain* from buying British assets. This will cause the *demand for pounds curve to shift rightward.*

THE SUPPLY OF BRITISH POUNDS

The demand for pounds is one side of the market for pounds. Now we turn our attention to the other side: the supply of pounds. And we'll begin with our basic question: *Who* is supplying them?

In the real world, pounds are supplied from many sources. Anyone who has pounds and wants to exchange them for dollars can come to the market and supply pounds. But the most important sellers of pounds are British households and businesses, who naturally have pounds and need dollars in order to make purchases from Americans. To keep our analysis simple, we'll focus on just these British sellers, and we'll ignore—for now—any pounds supplied by the British government:

In our model of the market for pounds, we assume that British households and firms are the only sellers.

The British supply pounds in the dollar–pound market for only one reason: because they want dollars. Thus, to ask why the British supply pounds is to ask why they want dollars. We can identify two separate reasons:

- *To buy goods and services from American firms.* The British buy airline tickets on United Airlines, computers made by IBM and Apple, and the rights to show films made in Hollywood. British tourists stay in American hotels and eat at American restaurants. The British demand dollars—and supply pounds—for all of these purchases.
- *To buy American assets.* The British buy American stocks, American corporate or government bonds, and American real estate. In each case, the American seller will want to be paid in dollars, and the British buyer will acquire dollars by offering pounds.

The Supply of Pounds Curve

Panel (a) of Figure 2 shows an example of a **supply curve for foreign currency**— here, British pounds. The curve tells us *the quantity of pounds the British will want to sell in any given period, at each different exchange rate.* Notice that the curve slopes upward: The higher the exchange rate, the greater is the quantity of pounds supplied. For example, at an exchange rate of $1.50 per pound, the British would want to supply £300 million (point *E*). If the exchange rate rose to $2.25 per pound, they would supply £400 million (point *F*).

Why does a higher exchange rate—a higher price for the pound—make the British want to sell more of them? Because the higher the price for the pound, the more dollars someone gets for each pound sold. This makes U.S. goods and services less expensive to British buyers, who will want to buy more of them—and who will therefore need more dollars.[1]

To summarize, as we move rightward *along* the supply of pounds curve, such as the move from point *E* to point *F*:

Supply curve for foreign currency
A curve indicating the quantity of a specific foreign currency that will be supplied, during a given period, at each different exchange rate.

---

[1] Actually, it is not a logical necessity for the supply of pounds curve to slope upward. Why not? When the price of the pound rises, it is true that the British will buy more U.S. goods and need more dollars to buy them. However, each dollar they buy costs *fewer pounds*. It might be that, even though the British obtain more dollars, they actually supply fewer pounds to get them at the higher exchange rate. In this case, the supply of pounds curve would slope downward. Economists believe, however, that a downward-sloping supply curve for foreign currency—while theoretically possible—is very rare.

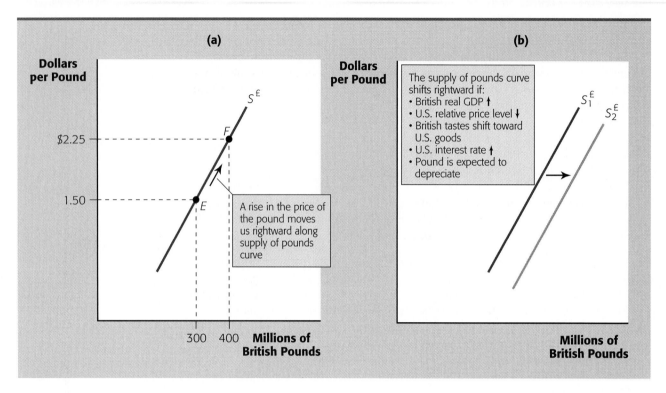

FIGURE 2
The Supply of British Pounds

Shifts in the Supply of Pounds Curve

When the exchange rate changes, we *move along* the supply curve for pounds, as in panel (a) of Figure 2. But other variables can affect the supply of pounds besides the exchange rate. When any of these variables change, the supply of pounds curve will shift, as shown in panel (b). What are these variables?

Real GDP in Britain. If real GDP and real income rise in Britain, British residents will buy more goods and services, including those produced in the United States. Since they will need more dollars to buy U.S. goods, they will supply more pounds. In panel (b) this causes a rightward shift of the supply curve, from $S_1^£$ to $S_2^£$.

Relative Price Levels. Earlier, you learned that a rise in the relative price level in the United States makes British goods more attractive to Americans. But it also makes *American* goods *less* attractive to the British. Since the British will want to buy fewer U.S. goods, they will want fewer dollars and will supply fewer pounds. Thus, a rise in the relative U.S. price level shifts the supply of pounds curve leftward.

British Tastes for U.S. Goods. Recall our earlier discussion about the effect of American tastes on the demand for pounds. The same reasoning applies to the effect of British tastes on the *supply* of pounds. The British could begin to crave things American—or recoil from them. A shift in British tastes toward American goods will shift the supply of pounds curve rightward. A shift in tastes *away* from American goods will shift the curve leftward.

Relative Interest Rates. You've already learned that a rise in the relative U.S. interest rate makes U.S. assets more attractive to Americans. It has exactly the same effect on the British. As the U.S. interest rate rises, and the British buy more U.S. assets, they will need more dollars and will supply more pounds. The supply of pounds curve will shift rightward.

Expected Change in the Exchange Rate. In deciding where to hold their assets, the British have the same concerns as Americans. They will look, in part, at rates of return; but they will *also* think about possible gains or losses on foreign currency transactions. Suppose the British *expect the price of the pound to fall.* Then, by holding U.S. assets, they can anticipate a foreign currency gain—selling pounds at a relatively high price and buying them back again when their price is relatively low. The prospect of foreign currency gain will make U.S. assets more attractive, and the British will buy more of them. *The supply of pounds curve will shift rightward.*

THE EQUILIBRIUM EXCHANGE RATE

Now we will make an important—and in most cases, realistic—assumption: that the exchange rate between the dollar and the pound *floats*. A **floating exchange rate** is one that is freely determined by the forces of supply and demand, without government intervention to change it or keep it from changing. Indeed, many of the world's leading currencies, including the Japanese yen, the British pound, the 11-nation euro, and the Mexican peso, do float freely against the dollar most of the time.

Floating exchange rate An exchange rate that is freely determined by the forces of supply and demand.

In some cases, however, governments do not allow the exchange rate to float freely, but instead manipulate its value by intervening in the market, or even *fix* it at a particular value. We'll discuss government intervention in foreign exchange markets later. In this section, we assume that both the British and U.S. governments leave the dollar–pound market alone.

When the exchange rate floats, the price will settle at the level where quantity supplied and quantity demanded are equal. Here, buyers and sellers are trading British pounds, and the price is the exchange rate—the *price of the pound.*

Look at panel (a) of Figure 3. The equilibrium in the market for pounds occurs at point *E,* where the supply and demand curves intersect. The equilibrium price is $1.50 per pound. As you can verify, if the exchange rate were higher, say, $2.25 per pound, there would be an *excess supply* of pounds, forcing the price of the pound back down to $1.50. If the exchange rate were *lower* than the equilibrium price of $1.50, there would be an *excess demand* for pounds, driving the price back up to $1.50.

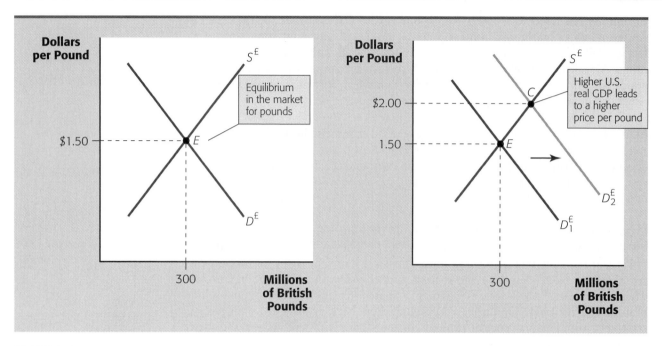

FIGURE 3
The Equilibrium Exchange Rate

When the exchange rate floats—that is, when the government does not intervene in the foreign currency market—the equilibrium exchange rate is determined at the intersection of the demand curve and the supply curve.

WHAT HAPPENS WHEN THINGS CHANGE?

What would cause the price of the pound to rise or fall? The simple answer to this question is, anything that shifts the demand for pounds curve, or the supply of pounds curve, or both curves together. Have another look at the right-hand panels of Figures 1 and 2. They summarize the major factors that can shift the demand and supply curves for pounds and therefore change the floating exchange rate.

Let's illustrate with a simple example. In panel (b) of Figure 3, the initial equilibrium in the market for pounds is at point E, with an exchange rate of $1.50 per pound. Now suppose that real GDP rises in the United States. As you've learned (see Figure 1), this rise in U.S. GDP will shift the demand for pounds curve rightward, from $D_1^{\pounds}$ to $D_2^{\pounds}$ in the figure. At the old exchange rate of $1.50 per pound, there would be an excess demand for pounds, which would drive the price of the pound higher. The new equilibrium—where the quantities of pounds supplied and demanded are equal—occurs at point C, and the new equilibrium exchange rate is $2.00 per pound.

To recap, the increase in American GDP causes the price of the pound to rise from $1.50 to $2.00. When the price of any floating foreign currency rises because

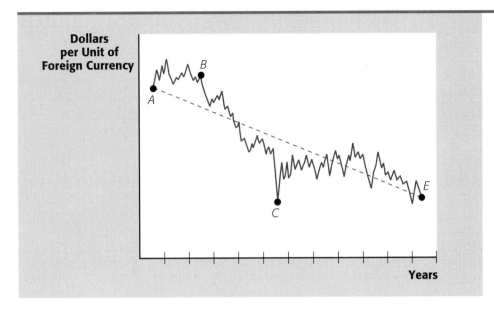

Dollars per Unit of Foreign Currency

Years

FIGURE 4
Hypothetical Exchange Rate Data Over Time

These hypothetical data show typical patterns of exchange rate fluctuations. Over the course of a few minutes, days, or weeks, the exchange rate can experience sharp up-and-down spikes. Over several months or a year or two, the exchange rate may rise or fall, as in the appreciation of the foreign currency from points A to B and the depreciation from B to C. Over the long run, there may be a general upward or downward trend, like the depreciation of the foreign currency illustrated by the dashed line connecting points A and E.

of a shift in the demand curve, the supply curve, or both, we call it an **appreciation** of the currency. In our example, the pound appreciates against the dollar. At the same time, there has been a **depreciation** of the dollar—a fall in its price in terms of pounds. (To see this, calculate the price of the dollar in terms of pounds before and after the shift in demand.)

> *When a floating exchange rates changes, one country's currency will appreciate (rise in price) and the other country's currency will depreciate (fall in price).*

As you've learned, there are many other variables besides U.S. GDP that can change and affect the exchange rate. We could analyze each of these changes, using diagrams similar to panel (b) of Figure 3. However, we'll organize our discussion of exchange rate changes in a slightly different way.

How Exchange Rates Change Over Time

When we examine the actual behavior of exchange rates over time, we find three different kinds of movements. Look at Figure 4, which graphs hypothetical exchange rate data between the U.S. dollar and some other currency. We're using hypothetical data to make these three kinds of movements stand out more clearly than they usually do in practice.

Notice first the sharp up-and-down spikes. These fluctuations in exchange rates occur over the course of a few weeks, a few days, or even a few minutes—periods of time that we call the *very short run.*

Second, we see a gradual rise and fall of the exchange rate over the course of several months or a year or two. An example is the appreciation of the foreign currency from point *A* to *B* and its depreciation from point *B* to *C*. These are *short-run* movements in the exchange rate.

Appreciation An increase in the price of a currency in a floating-rate system.

Depreciation A decrease in the price of a currency in a floating-rate system.

Finally, notice that while the price of the foreign currency fluctuates in the very short run and the short run, we can also discern a general *long-run* trend: This nation's currency seems to be depreciating in the figure. This long-run trend is illustrated by the dashed line connecting points A and E.

In this section, we'll explore the causes of movements in the exchange rate over all three periods: the very short run, the short run, and the long run.

The Very Short Run: "Hot Money"

Banks and other large financial institutions collectively have trillions of dollars worth of funds that they can move from one type of investment to another at very short notice. These funds are often called "hot money." If those who manage hot money perceive even a tiny advantage in moving funds to a different country's assets—say, because its interest rate is slightly higher—they will do so. Often, decisions to move billions of dollars are made in split seconds, by traders watching computer screens showing the latest data on exchange rates and interest rates around the world. Because these traders move such large volumes of funds, they have immediate effects on exchange rates.

Let's consider an example. Suppose that the relative interest rate in the United States suddenly rises. Then, as you've learned, U.S. assets will suddenly be more attractive to residents of both the United States and England, including managers of hot-money accounts in both countries. As these managers shift their funds from British to United States assets, they will be dumping billions of pounds on the foreign exchange market in order to acquire dollars to buy U.S. assets. This will cause a significant rightward shift of the supply of pounds curve.

In addition to affecting managers of hot-money accounts, the higher relative interest rate in the United States will affect ordinary investors. British investors will want to buy more American assets, helping to shift the supply of pounds curve further rightward. And American investors will want to buy fewer British assets than before, causing some decrease in the *demand* for pounds. Thus, in addition to the very large rightward shift in the supply of pounds, there will be a more moderate leftward shift in the demand for pounds.

Both of these shifts are illustrated in Figure 5: The supply of pounds curve shifts from $S_1^\pounds$ to $S_2^\pounds$, and the demand for pounds curve shifts from $D_1^\pounds$ to $D_2^\pounds$. The result is easy to see: The equilibrium in the market for pounds moves from point E to point G, and the price of the pound *falls* from $1.50 to $1.00. The pound depreciates and the dollar appreciates.

Expectations about future exchange rates can also trigger huge shifts of hot money, and Figure 5 also illustrates what would happen if American and British residents suddenly *expect* the pound to depreciate against the dollar. In this case, it would be the anticipation of foreign currency gains from holding U.S. assets, rather than a higher U.S. interest rate, that would cause the supply and demand curves to shift. As you can see in Figure 5, the expectation that the pound will depreciate actually *causes* the pound to depreciate—a self-fulfilling prophecy.

Sudden changes in relative interest rates, as well as sudden expectations of an appreciation or depreciation of a nation's currency, occur frequently in foreign exchange markets. They can cause massive shifts of hot money from the assets of one country to those of another in very short periods of time. For this reason,

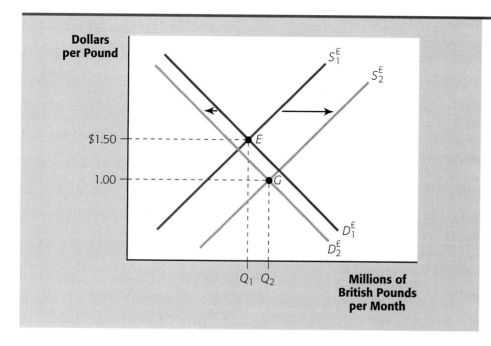

FIGURE 5
Hot Money in the Very Short Run

The market for pounds is initially in equilibrium at point E, with an exchange rate of $1.50 per pound. A rise in the U.S. interest rate relative to the British rate will make U.S. assets more attractive to both Americans and Britons. Hot-money managers in both countries will shift funds from British to U.S. assets, causing a rightward shift of the supply of pounds curve. American investors will want to buy fewer British assets, causing a decrease in the demand for pounds. The net effect is a lower exchange rate—$1.00 per pound at point G.

relative interest rates and expectations of future exchange rates are the dominant forces moving exchange rates in the very short run.

The Short Run: Macroeconomic Fluctuations

Look again at Figure 4. What explains the movements in the *short-run* rate—the changes that occur over several months or a few years? In most cases, the causes are economic fluctuations taking place in one or more countries.

Suppose, for example, that both Britain and the United States are in a recession, and the U.S. economy begins to recover while the British slump continues. As real GDP rises in the United States, so does Americans' demand for foreign goods and services, including those from Britain. The demand for pounds curve will shift rightward, and—as shown in panel (a) of Figure 6—the pound will appreciate.

A year or so later, when Britain recovers from *its* recession, its real GDP will rise. British residents will begin to buy more U.S. goods and services, and supply more pounds so they can acquire more dollars. The supply of pounds curve will shift rightward, and—as shown in panel (b) of Figure 6—the pound will depreciate. Thus,

in the short run, movements in exchange rates are caused largely by economic fluctuations. All else equal, a country whose GDP rises relatively rapidly will experience a depreciation of its currency. A country whose GDP falls more rapidly will experience an appreciation of its currency.

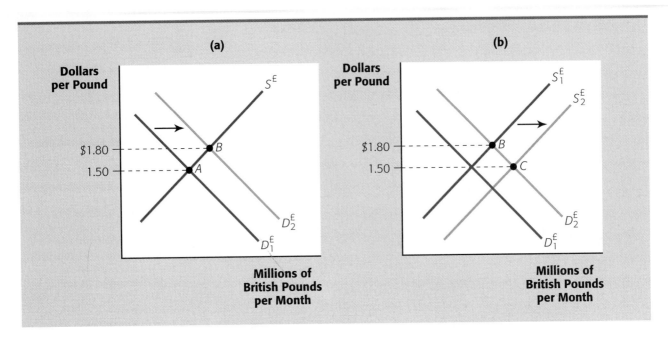

FIGURE 6
Exchange Rates in the Short Run

Panel (a) shows a situation in which the United States recovers from a recession first. U.S. demand for foreign goods and services increases, shifting the demand for pounds curve to the right. The result is an appreciation of the pound. Panel (b) shows Britain's subsequent recovery from its recession. As the British begin to buy more U.S. goods and services, the supply of pounds curve shifts rightward, causing the pound to depreciate.

This observation contradicts a commonly held myth: that a strong (appreciating) currency is a sign of economic health and a weak (depreciating) currency denotes a sick economy. The truth may easily be the opposite. Over the course of several quarters or a few years, the dollar could appreciate because the U.S. economy is *weakening*—entering a serious recession. This would cause Americans to cut back spending on domestic *and* foreign goods, and decrease the demand for foreign currency. Similarly, a *strengthening* U.S. economy—in which Americans are earning and spending more—would increase the U.S. demand for foreign currency and (all else equal) cause the dollar to depreciate.

Keep in mind, though, that other variables can change over the business cycle besides real GDP, including interest rates and price levels in the two countries. For example, a recession can be caused by a monetary contraction that raises the relative interest rate in a country. Or a monetary stimulus in the midst of a recession could result in a relatively low interest rate. These changes, too, will influence exchange rates over the business cycle.

The Long Run: Purchasing Power Parity

In mid-1992, you could buy about 100 Russian rubles for one dollar. In mid-1998, that same dollar would get you more than 6,000 rubles—so many that the Russian government that year created a new ruble that was worth 1,000 of the old rubles. (The ruble exchange rate in Table 1 is for the new ruble.) What caused the ruble to depreciate so much against the dollar during those six years?

This is a question about exchange rates over many years—the long run. Movements of hot money—which explain sudden, temporary movements of exchange rates—cannot explain this kind of long-run trend. Nor can business cycles, which are, by nature, temporary. What, then, causes exchange rates to change over the long run?

In general, long-run trends in exchange rates are determined by *relative price levels* in two countries. We can be even more specific:

> According to the **purchasing power parity (PPP) theory,** the exchange rate between two countries will adjust in the long run until the average price of goods is roughly the same in both countries.

Purchasing power parity (PPP) theory The idea that the exchange rate will adjust in the long run so that the average price of goods in two countries will be roughly the same.

To see why the PPP theory makes sense, imagine a basket of goods that costs $750 in the United States and £500 in Britain. If the prices of the goods themselves do not change, then, according to the PPP theory, the exchange rate will adjust to $750/£500 = $1.5 dollars per pound. Why? Because at this exchange rate, $750 can be exchanged for £500, so the price of the basket is the same to residents of either country—$750 for Americans and £500 for the British.

Now, suppose the exchange rate was *below* its PPP rate of $1.50 per pound—say, $1 per pound. Then a trader could take $500 to the bank, exchange it for £500, buy the basket of goods in Great Britain, and sell it in the United States for $750. She would earn a profit of $250 on each basket of goods traded. In the process, however, traders would be increasing the demand for pounds and raising the exchange rate. When the price of the pound reached $1.50, purchasing power parity would hold, and special trading opportunities would be gone. As you can see, trading activity will tend to drive the exchange rate toward the PPP rate. (An end-of-chapter review question asks you to explain the adjustment process when the exchange rate starts *higher* than the PPP rate.)

The PPP theory has an important implication:

> In the long run, the currency of a country with a higher inflation rate will depreciate against the currency of a country whose inflation rate is lower.

Why? Because in the country with the higher inflation rate, the relative price level will be rising. As that country's basket of goods becomes relatively more expensive, only a depreciation of its currency can restore purchasing power parity. And traders—taking advantage of opportunities like those just described—would cause the currency to depreciate.

Purchasing Power Parity: Some Important Caveats. While purchasing power parity is a good general guideline for predicting long-run trends in exchange rates, it does not work perfectly. For a variety of reasons, exchange rates can deviate from their PPP values for many years.

First, some goods—by their very nature—are difficult to trade. Suppose a haircut costs £5 in London and $30 in New York, and the exchange rate is $1.50 per pound. Then British haircuts are cheaper for residents of both countries. Could traders take advantage of this? Not really. They cannot take $30 to the bank in exchange for £20, buy four haircuts in London, ship them to New York, and sell them for a total of $120 there. Haircuts and most other personal services are nontradable.

Second, high transportation costs can reduce trading possibilities even for goods that *can* be traded. Our earlier numerical example would have quite a different ending if moving the basket of goods between Great Britain and the United States involved $500 of freight and insurance costs.

Third, artificial barriers to trade, such as special taxes or quotas on imports, can hamper traders' ability to move exchange rates toward purchasing power parity.

Still, the purchasing power parity theory is useful in many circumstances. Under floating exchange rates, a country whose relative price level is rising rapidly will almost always find that the price of its currency is falling rapidly. If not, all of its tradeable goods would soon be priced out of the world market.

Indeed, we often observe that countries with very high inflation rates have currencies depreciating against the dollar by roughly the amount needed to preserve purchasing power parity. For example, we've already mentioned the sharp depreciation of the Russian ruble from 1992 to 1998. During those six years, the number of rubles that exchanged for a dollar rose from around 100 to about 6,000. Over the same period, the annual inflation rate averaged about 200 percent in Russia, but only about 3 percent in the United States. As a result, the relative price level in Russia skyrocketed, leading to a dramatic depreciation of the ruble against the dollar. Another example is Turkey: From mid-1996 to mid-1997, its price level almost doubled, while the dollar price of its currency was cut in half.

GOVERNMENT INTERVENTION IN FOREIGN EXCHANGE MARKETS

As you've seen, when exchange rates float, they can rise and fall for a variety of reasons. But a government may not be content to let the forces of supply and demand change its exchange rate. If the exchange rate rises, the country's goods will become much more expensive to foreigners, causing harm to its export-oriented industries. If the exchange rate falls, goods purchased from other countries will rise in price. Since many imported goods are used as inputs by U.S. firms (such as oil from the Middle East and Mexico, or computer screens from Japan), a drop in the exchange rate will cause a rise in the U.S. price level. Finally, if the exchange rate is too volatile, it can make trading riskier or require traders to acquire special insurance against foreign currency losses, which costs them money, time, and trouble. For all of these reasons, governments sometime *intervene* in foreign exchange markets involving their currency.

Managed Float

Many governments let their exchange rate float *most of the time,* but will intervene on occasion when the floating exchange rate moves in an undesired direction or becomes too volatile. For example, look back at Figure 5, where the price of the British pound falls to $1 as hot money is shifted out of British assets. Suppose the British government does not want the pound to depreciate. Then its central bank—the Bank of England—could begin trading in the dollar–pound market itself. It would buy British pounds with dollars, thereby shifting the demand for pounds curve rightward. If it buys just the right amount of pounds, it can prevent the pound from depreciating at all. Alternatively, the U.S. government might not be happy with the *appreciation* of the dollar in Figure 5. In that case, the Federal Reserve can enter the market and buy British pounds with dollars, once again shifting the demand for pounds curve rightward.

The central banks of many countries—including the Federal Reserve—will sometimes intervene in this way in foreign exchange markets. When a government buys or sells its own currency or that of a trading partner to influence exchange rates, it is engaging in a "managed float" or a "dirty float."

> *Under a **managed float**, a country's central bank actively manages its exchange rate, buying its own currency to prevent depreciations, and selling its own currency to prevent appreciations.*

Managed float A policy of frequent central bank intervention to move the exchange rate.

Managed floats are used most often in the very short run, to prevent large, sudden changes in exchange rates. For example, during the week after the terror attacks of September 2001, the Bank of Japan (Japan's central bank) sold 2 trillion yen (about $17 billion worth) in order to stop a rapid *appreciation* of the yen against the dollar. On the other side—and on a smaller scale—Argentina's central bank purchased 15 million Argentinian pesos (about $9 million worth at the time) on January 15, 2002, in order to slow the *depreciation* of the peso against the dollar.

That last example raises a question. When a country—such as Argentina—wants to prevent or slow a depreciation against the dollar, it has to buy its own currency with dollars. Where does it get those dollars? Unfortunately for Argentina, it cannot print dollars; only the U.S. Federal Reserve can do that. Instead, Argentina must use its *reserves* of dollars—the dollars its central bank keeps on hand specifically to intervene in the dollar–peso market.

Almost every nation holds reserves of dollars—as well as euros, yen, and other key currencies—just so it can enter the foreign exchange market and sell them for its own currency when necessary. Under a managed float, periods of selling dollars are usually short-lived, and alternate with periods of buying dollars. Thus, countries rarely use up all of their dollar reserves when they engage in managed floats.

Managed floats are controversial. Some economists believe they help to avoid wide swings in exchange rates, and thus reduce the risks for international traders and investors. But others are critical of how managed floats often work out in practice. They point out that countries often intervene when the forces behind an appreciation or depreciation are strong. In these cases, the intervention only serves to delay inevitable changes in the exchange rate—sometimes, at great cost to a country's reserves of dollars and other key currencies.

HTTP://

If you are interested in learning more about exchange rate systems, read "The International Financial Architecture" by Jeffrey Frankel at http://www.brook.edu/comm/PolicyBriefs/pb051/pb51.htm.

Fixed Exchange Rates

A more extreme form of intervention is a **fixed exchange rate**, in which a government declares a particular value for its exchange rate with another currency. The government, through its central bank, then commits itself to intervene in the foreign exchange market any time the *equilibrium* exchange rate differs from the *fixed* rate.

Fixed exchange rate A government-declared exchange rate maintained by central bank intervention in the foreign exchange market.

For example, from 1987 to 1997, the government of Thailand fixed the value of its currency—the *baht*—at $0.04 per baht. The two panels of Figure 7 show the different types of intervention that might be necessary in the baht–dollar market to maintain this fixed exchange rate. Each panel shows a different set of supply and demand curves—and a different equilibrium exchange rate that might exist

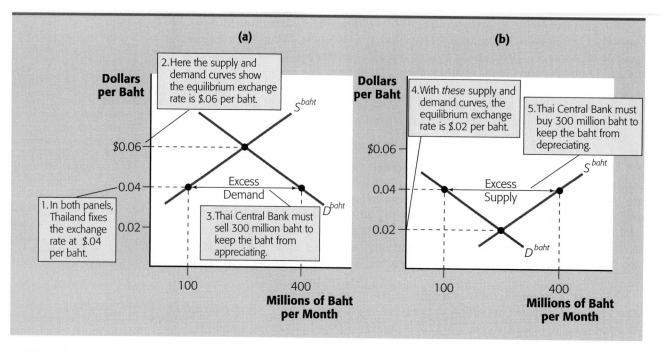

FIGURE 7
A Fixed Exchange Rate for the Baht

for the baht. Look first at panel (a). Here, we assume that the equilibrium exchange rate is $0.06 per baht, so that the fixed rate is *lower* than the equilibrium rate. At the fixed rate of $0.04 per baht, 400 million baht would be demanded each month, but only 100 million would be supplied. There would be an *excess demand* of 300 million baht, which would ordinarily drive the exchange rate back up to its equilibrium value of $0.06. But the Thai government prevents this by entering the market and *selling* just enough baht to cover the excess demand. In panel (a), the Central Bank of Thailand would sell 300 million baht per month to maintain the fixed rate.

> *When a country fixes its exchange rate below the equilibrium value, the result is an excess demand for the country's currency. To maintain the fixed rate, the country's central bank must sell enough of its own currency to eliminate the excess demand.*

Panel (b) shows another possibility, where the equilibrium exchange rate is $0.02, so that the same fixed exchange rate of $0.04 per baht is now *above* the equilibrium rate. There is an excess *supply* of 300 million baht. In this case, to prevent the excess supply from driving the exchange rate down, the Central Bank of Thailand must *buy* the excess baht.

> *When a country fixes its exchange rate above the equilibrium value, the result is an excess supply of the country's currency. To maintain the fixed rate, the country's central bank must buy enough of its own currency to eliminate the excess supply.*

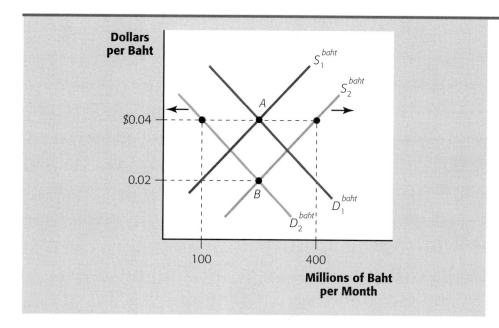

FIGURE 8
A Foreign Currency Crisis

Initially, the baht is fixed at the equilibrium rate of $0.04. When the supply and demand curves shift to D$_2$ and S$_2$, the equilibrium exchange rate falls to $0.02. If Thailand continues to fix the rate at $0.04, it will have to buy up the excess supply of 300 million baht per month, using dollars. As its dollar reserves dwindle, traders will anticipate a drop in the value of the baht, shifting the curves out further, as indicated by the arrows.

Fixed exchange rates present little problem for a country as long as the exchange rate is fixed at or very close to its equilibrium rate. But when the equilibrium exchange rate moves away from the fixed rate—as in the two panels of Figure 7—governments often try to maintain their fixed rate anyway, sometimes for long periods. This can create problems, especially when the exchange rate is fixed *above* the equilibrium rate.

Foreign Currency Crises, the IMF, and Moral Hazard

To see how a fixed exchange rate can be problematic, look at Figure 8. Initially, the supply and demand curves for baht are given by S_1 and D_1, respectively, so that the equilibrium exchange rate, $0.04, is equal to the fixed exchange rate. At this point, the central bank is neither selling nor buying baht. Now, suppose that, for some reason (we'll be more specific in a few paragraphs), the supply and demand curves shift to S_2 and D_2, respectively. The equilibrium rate falls, so the fixed rate of $0.04 is above the equilibrium rate of $0.02. The Central Bank of Thailand must now *buy* its own currency with dollars—at the rate of 300 million baht per month. Each baht costs the central bank 4 cents, so as the months go by, its dollar reserves are being depleted at the rate of 300 million × $0.04 = $12 million per month. Once those reserves are gone, Thailand will have only two choices: to let its currency float (which means an immediate depreciation to the lower, equilibrium rate) or to declare a new, lower fixed rate—a **devaluation** of its currency.

Of course, at a certain point, foreign exchange speculators and traders would see that Thailand doesn't have many dollars left. (Most countries' central banks regularly report their holdings of key currencies, and economists can estimate the holdings of countries that don't.) Looking ahead, these speculators and traders will

Devaluation A change in the exchange rate from a higher fixed rate to a lower fixed rate.

begin to *anticipate* a drop in the baht. And—as you've learned in this chapter—expected changes in the exchange rate *shift* supply and demand curves for foreign currency. In this case, an expected fall in the baht causes the supply curve for baht to shift further rightward and the demand curve to shift further leftward, as indicated by the heavy arrows in the diagram. In Figure 8, these shifts will *decrease* the equilibrium value of the baht, increase the *excess supply* of baht, and make the fixed rate of $0.04 even harder to maintain. The country is now experiencing a *foreign currency crisis*.

Foreign currency crisis A loss of faith that a country can prevent a drop in its exchange rate, leading to a rapid depletion of its foreign currency (e.g., dollar) reserves.

> A *foreign currency crisis* arises when people no longer believe that a country can maintain a fixed exchange rate above the equilibrium rate. As a consequence, the supply of the currency increases, demand for it decreases, and the country must use up its reserves of dollars and other key currencies even faster in order to maintain the fixed rate.

Once a foreign currency crisis arises, a country typically has no choice but to devalue its currency or let it float and watch it depreciate. And ironically, because the country waited for the crisis to develop, the exchange rate may for a time drop even lower than the original equilibrium rate. For example, in Figure 8, an early devaluation to $0.02 per dollar might prevent a crisis from occurring at all. But once the crisis begins, and the supply and demand curves shift out further than S_2 and D_2, the currency will have to drop *below* $0.02 to end the rapid depletion of dollar reserves.

Our analysis of a foreign currency crisis used the example of the Thai baht for good reason. In 1997 and 1998, Thailand was at the center of a financial crisis that rocked the world.

The crisis began when a lack of confidence in Thailand's financial system led to dramatic shifts in the supply and demand curves for baht—just as in Figure 8. While the *equilibrium* exchange rate fell, Thailand continued to fix the *actual* exchange rate at $0.04 per baht, above the equilibrium rate. As a result, Thailand's central bank was depleting its reserves of dollars and other foreign currencies. This, of course, led currency traders to anticipate a devaluation, shifting the supply and demand curves even further. Finally, in July 1997, the Thai central bank simply ran out of foreign currency reserves, and was forced to let its currency float. The baht immediately depreciated from $0.04 to $0.02.

But this was only the beginning of the story. Many of Thailand's banks—counting on the fixed exchange rate—had borrowed heavily in dollars, yen, and other foreign currencies, but then lent funds to Thai businesses in baht. Once the baht depreciated, these banks were obligated to make unchanged dollar and yen payments on their debts, while continuing to receive unchanged baht payments on the funds they had lent. The problem was that, after the depreciation, the baht coming in would no longer cover the dollars going out. Thailand's banks were in trouble.

And the trouble spread. Investors began to wonder if banks in *other* nearby countries were similarly vulnerable, and began to dump the foreign exchange of Indonesia, South Korea, Malaysia, and the Philippines. Before the crisis ended, it had even spread to several Latin American countries.

What ended the crisis? In large part, the crisis was resolved by the **International Monetary Fund (IMF)**, an international organization formed in 1945 in large part

HTTP://

Professor Nouriel Roubini of New York University maintains an excellent Web page devoted to global financial crises. You can find it at http://www.stern.nyu.edu/~nroubini/asia/AsiaHomepage.html.

International Monetary Fund (IMF) An international organization founded in 1945 to help stabilize the world monetary system.

to help nations avoid such foreign currency crises and help them recover when crises occur. In 1998, the IMF—in cooperation with the U.S. government—orchestrated a rescue package of more than $100 billion to cover the Asian economies' foreign debt.

The rescue was controversial, however. Why? Helping a troubled country leads other countries to expect that they, too, will get help if they pursue untenable policies and get themselves into trouble. This is an example of a more general problem which economists call *moral hazard.*

> *Moral hazard occurs when a decision maker (such as an individual, firm, or government) expects to be rescued in the event of an unfavorable outcome, and then changes its behavior so that the unfavorable outcome is more likely.*

Moral hazard When decision makers—expecting assistance in the event of an unfavorable outcome—change their behavior so that the unfavorable outcome is more likely.

Moral hazard plagues the insurance industry (are you as likely to lock your car if you're insured against theft?), efforts to care for the unemployed (will you look as hard for a new job after being laid off if you are collecting unemployment insurance?), and troubled business firms (will mega-corporations be careful not to take risks if they expect the government to rescue them in the event of a disaster?).

But here, our focus is on the international financial system. The problem of moral hazard helps explain the very different response of the IMF when, in late 2001 and early 2002, Argentina faced a somewhat similar foreign currency crisis. Like the Asian countries a few years earlier, Argentina needed billions of dollars of help to prevent it from devaluing its currency and defaulting on its foreign debt. This time, however, it was felt that Argentina's problems were unique, and so its foreign currency crisis—unlike the Asian crisis a few years earlier—was unlikely to spread to other countries. Accordingly, the Bush administration—concerned about the moral hazard problem—encouraged the IMF to take a tough stand. There was no rescue, and Argentina was forced into devaluation *and* default in January 2002.

The Euro

One answer to the problems that countries have encountered in managing their own currencies is to adopt another country's currency or an international currency. In 2001, both Ecuador and El Salvador scrapped their own national currencies and adopted the U.S. dollar as their official money. That same year, Guatemala passed legislation permitting the U.S. dollar and other foreign currency to circulate alongside the Guatemalan quetzal. And on January 1, 2002, 12 European countries—including Germany, France, Italy, and Spain—introduced their new common currency: the euro.

The European Central Bank has sole authority for changing the supply of euros. It determines a single monetary policy for all of Euroland, replacing the separate monetary policies of the different countries.

Why did these 12 European countries decide to do away with their national currencies?

There are several advantages. First, a single currency means that European firms—when they buy or sell across borders—no longer have to pay commissions

Euro coins and paper money became the official currency of 12 European countries in 2002.

on the exchange of currency, or face the risk that exchange rates might change before accounts are settled. This will increase the volume of trade among the Euroland nations.

Second, the elimination of exchange rate risk makes it easier for European firms to sell stocks and bonds to residents anywhere in Euroland. This will help ensure that funds are channeled to the most profitable firms throughout the area. Third, adopting a single currency makes cross-country comparison shopping easier. This will help increase competition among firms, and help keep prices down to European consumers.

Finally, some of these countries—such as Italy—have had a history of loose monetary policy that has generated high rates of inflation and high expected inflation. By giving up the right to run an independent monetary policy, and leaving it to the (presumably stricter) European Central Bank, the high-inflation countries of Europe will benefit from lower inflation rates.

There are, however, downsides to the euro. In fact, some economists believe that—at least for a while—the euro will create significant problems for the Euroland countries. Why? With a single currency, there must be a single monetary policy, making it impossible to adjust the money supply and interest rates to the problems of individual nations. For example, suppose Spain goes into a recession. In the old days before the euro, its central bank would increase the Spanish money supply and lower interest rates. But now, what if while Spain is in recession, the rest of Europe has full employment or even a boom? Then, the European central bank will be tightening the money supply and raising interest rates, which will worsen conditions in Spain. Spain could always use fiscal policy. But, as you've learned, countercyclical fiscal policy is fraught with problems. Moreover, membership in Euroland requires countries to maintain strict fiscal discipline that might prevent them from using a fiscal stimulus when it is needed.

Optimum currency area A region whose economies perform better with a single currency than with separate national currencies.

Optimum Currency Areas. The economists who worry about these problems question whether Europe is an **optimum currency area**—a region whose economies will perform better with a single currency rather than separate national currencies. To be an optimum currency area, the different nations in a region should face common, rather than national, shocks, so that they tend to go into booms and recessions together. In that case, a single monetary policy will be appropriate, because all nations will need stimulus or restraint at the same time. In Europe, unfortunately, the shocks are often national: Different countries are dominated by different industries, face different types of labor unions, and have different institutional frameworks and laws. They are therefore susceptible to national as well as regional shocks.

Another requirement for an optimum currency area is that labor is highly mobile from one country to another. That way, if one country is experiencing a negative shock and goes into a recession that can't be addressed with monetary or fiscal policy (for the reasons discussed earlier), at least its unemployed workers can find work in other countries whose economies are performing better. Indeed, this is what happens in the United States, where labor is highly mobile among states.

But at present, labor is much less mobile across European borders than across the American states. And if unemployed workers stay within a country, its government may feel pressure to abandon the euro so that it can use expansionary fiscal and monetary policy.

In the very long run, the abolition of national currencies—and the creation of the euro—may work to increase labor mobility across Europe, especially if it changes the attitudes of European firms and workers toward cross-national employment. This would help make Europe more of an optimum currency area, and help make the euro a more workable common currency in the future.

EXCHANGE RATES AND THE MACROECONOMY

Exchange rates can have important effects on the macroeconomy—largely through their effect on net exports. And although we've included net exports in our short-run macro model, we haven't yet asked how exchange rates affect them. That's what we'll do now.

Exchange Rates and Demand Shocks

Suppose that the dollar depreciates against the foreign currencies of its major trading partners. (We'll discuss *why* that might happen in a later section.) Then U.S. goods would become cheaper to foreigners, and net exports would rise at each level of output. This increase in net exports is a positive demand shock to the economy—it increases aggregate expenditure and shifts the aggregate demand curve to the right. And, as you've learned, positive demand shocks increase GDP in the short run.

> *A depreciation of the dollar causes net exports to rise—a positive demand shock that increases real GDP in the short run. An appreciation of the dollar causes net exports to drop—a negative demand shock that decreases real GDP in the short run.*

The impact of net exports on equilibrium GDP—often caused by changes in the exchange rate—helps us understand one reason why governments are often concerned about their exchange rates. An unstable exchange rate can result in repeated shocks to the economy. At worst, this can cause fluctuations in GDP; at best, it makes the central bank's job more difficult as it tries to keep the economy on an even keel.

Exchange Rates and Monetary Policy

In several earlier chapters, we've explored how the Fed tries to keep the U.S. economy on an even keel with monetary policy. The central banks around the world are engaged in a similar struggle, and face many of the same challenges as the Fed. One challenge to central banks is that monetary policy causes changes in exchange rates, and thus has additional effects on real GDP that we have not yet considered.

To understand this, let's run through an example. Suppose the United States is in a recession, and the Fed decides to increase equilibrium GDP. As you've learned, the Fed—by increasing the money supply—brings down the interest rate.

Interest-sensitive spending rises, and so does aggregate expenditure. When we consider the foreign exchange market, however, there is an additional effect on aggregate expenditure.

By lowering the U.S. interest rate, the Fed makes *foreign* financial assets more attractive to Americans, which raises their demand for foreign currency. In the market for pounds, for example, this will shift the demand for pounds curve rightward. At the same time, U.S. financial assets become less attractive to foreigners, which decreases the supply of foreign exchange (in the market for pounds, a leftward shift in the supply of pounds curve). If you sketch out these shifts right now, you'll see that, as long as the exchange rate floats, the result is a *depreciation of the dollar* against the pound.

Now let's see how the depreciation of the dollar affects the economy. With dollars now cheaper to foreigners, they will buy more U.S. goods, raising U.S. exports. At the same time, with foreign goods and services more expensive to Americans, U.S. imports will decrease. Both the increase in exports and the decrease in imports contribute to a rise in net exports, *NX*. This, in turn, increases aggregate expenditure.

Thus, as you can see, the expansionary monetary policy causes aggregate expenditures to rise in two ways: first, by increasing interest-sensitive spending, and second, by increasing net exports. As a result, equilibrium GDP rises by more—and monetary policy is more effective—when the effects on exchange rates are included.

The channels through which monetary policy works are summarized in the following schematic:

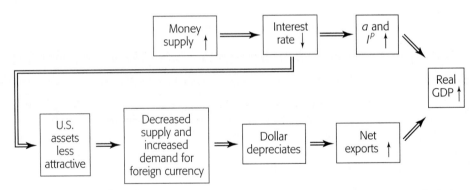

Net Effect: GDP ↑ by more when the exchange rate's effect on net exports is included

The top line shows the familiar effect on interest-sensitive spending: An increase in the money supply causes a drop in the interest rate, which increases autonomous consumption spending (*a*) and investment spending (I^P). The bottom line shows the *additional* effect on net exports through changes in the exchange rate—the effects we've been discussing.

The analysis of contractionary monetary policy is the same, but in reverse. A decrease in the money supply will not only decrease interest-sensitive spending, it will also cause the dollar to appreciate and net exports to drop. Thus, it will cause equilibrium GDP to fall by more than in earlier chapters, where we ignored the foreign exchange market.

The channel of monetary influence through exchange rates and the volume of trade is an important part of the full story of monetary policy in the United States. And in countries where exports are relatively large fractions of GDP—such as those of Europe—the trade channel is even more important. It is the main channel through which monetary policy affects the economy.

> *Monetary policy has a stronger effect when we include the impact on exchange rates and net exports, rather than just the impact on interest-sensitive consumption and investment spending.*

U S I N G   T H E   T H E O R Y
The Stubborn U.S. Trade Deficit

The U.S. trade deficit is often in the news. But what, exactly, is it?

The trade deficit is the extent to which a country's imports exceed its exports:

$$\text{Trade deficit} = \text{imports} - \text{exports}.$$

On the other hand, when exports exceed imports, a nation has a trade surplus:

$$\text{Trade surplus} = \text{exports} - \text{imports}.$$

As you can see, the trade surplus is nothing more than a nation's net exports (NX). And when net exports are negative, we have a trade deficit.

The United States has had large trade deficits with the rest of the world since the early 1980s. In 2002, the trade deficit was $424 billion. Simply put, Americans bought $424 billion more goods and services from other countries than their residents bought from the United States.

Why does the United States have a trade deficit with the rest of the world? A variety of explanations have been offered in the media, including poor U.S. marketing savvy in selling to foreigners, and a greater degree of protectionism in foreign markets.

But economists believe that there is a much more important reason. In this section, we'll use what you've learned about exchange rates to show how the U.S. trade deficit arose and why it continues. To keep our analysis simple, we'll start by looking at the U.S. trade deficit with just one country—Japan—but our results will hold more generally to the trade deficit with other countries as well.

Before we analyze the causes of the trade deficit, we need to do a little math. Let's begin by breaking down the total quantity of yen demanded by Americans $(D^{¥})$ into two components: the yen demanded to purchase Japanese goods and

Trade deficit The excess of a nation's imports over its exports during a given period.

Trade surplus The excess of a nation's exports over its imports during a given period.

services (U.S. imports from Japan) and the yen demanded to buy Japanese assets:

$$D^{¥} = \text{U.S. imports from Japan} + \text{U.S. purchases of Japanese assets.}$$

Similarly, we can divide the total quantity of yen supplied by the Japanese ($S^{¥}$) into two components: the yen exchanged for dollars to purchase American goods (U.S. exports to Japan) and the yen exchanged for dollars to purchase American assets like stocks, bonds, or real estate:

$$S^{¥} = \text{U.S. exports to Japan} + \text{Japanese purchases of U.S. assets.}$$

As long as the yen floats against the dollar without government intervention—which it does during most periods—we know that the exchange rate will adjust until the quantities of yen supplied and demanded are equal, or $D^{¥} = S^{¥}$. Substituting the foregoing breakdowns into this equation, we have

$$\left\{ \begin{array}{l} \text{U.S. imports from Japan} \\ + \text{ U.S. purchases of Japanese assets} \end{array} \right\} = \left\{ \begin{array}{l} \text{U.S. exports to Japan} \\ + \text{ Japanese purchases of U.S. assets.} \end{array} \right\}$$

Now let's rearrange this equation—subtracting U.S. exports from both sides—and subtracting American purchases of Japanese assets from both sides—to get

$$\left\{ \begin{array}{l} \text{U.S. imports from Japan} \\ - \text{ U.S exports to Japan} \end{array} \right\} = \left\{ \begin{array}{l} \text{Japanese purchases of U.S. assets} \\ - \text{ U.S. purchases of Japanese assets.} \end{array} \right\}$$

The term on the left should look familiar: It is the U.S. trade deficit with Japan. And since a similar equation must hold for every country, we can generalize it this way:

$$\left\{ \begin{array}{l} \text{U.S imports from other countries} \\ - \text{ U.S. exports to other countries} \end{array} \right\} = \left\{ \begin{array}{l} \text{foreign purchases of U.S. assets} \\ - \text{ U.S. purchases of foreign assets.} \end{array} \right\}$$

But what is the expression on the right? It tells us the extent to which foreigners are buying more of our assets than we are buying of theirs. It is often called the **net financial inflow** into the United States, because when the residents of other countries buy U.S. assets, funds flow into the U.S. financial market, where they are made available to U.S. firms and the U.S. government. Thus, the equation we've derived—which must hold true when exchange rates float—can also be expressed as

Net financial inflow An inflow of funds equal to a nation's trade deficit.

$$\textbf{U.S. trade deficit} = \textbf{U.S. net financial inflow.}$$

Why have we bothered to derive this equation? Because it tells us two very important things about the U.S. trade deficit. First, it tells us how the trade deficit is *financed*. Think about it: If the United States is running a trade deficit with, say, Japan, it means that the Japanese are providing more goods and services to Americans—more automobiles, VCRs, memory chips, and other goods—than Americans are providing to them. The Japanese are not doing this out of kindness. They must be getting *something* in return for the extra goods we are getting, and the equation tells us just what that is: U.S. assets. This is one reason why the trade deficit concerns U.S. policy makers: It results in a transfer of wealth from Americans to foreign residents.

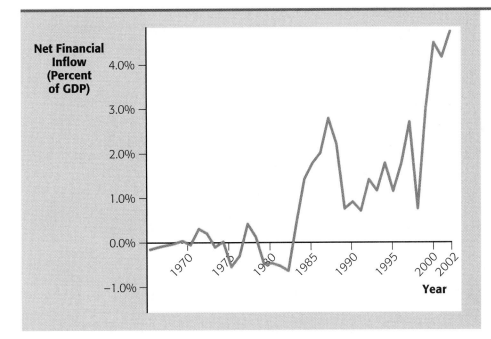

Net Financial Inflow (Percent of GDP)

Year

FIGURE 9
Net Financial Flows into the United States as a Percent of GDP

Beginning in the early 1980s, and continuing today, a massive financial inflow has caused a U.S. trade deficit. The financial inflow was originally caused by high U.S. interest rates relative to interest rates abroad. But in the 1990s and early 2000s, the financial inflow has been sustained by the favorable investment climate in the United States.

The second important insight provided by the equation is that a trade deficit can arise *because* of forces that cause a financial inflow. That is, if forces in the global economy make the right side of the equation positive, then the left side must be positive as well, and we will have a trade deficit.

Indeed, economists believe this is just what has happened to the United States: that the U.S. trade deficit has been caused by the desire of foreigners to invest in the United States. The result was a massive financial inflow and trade deficit that arose in the early 1980s, as illustrated in Figure 9. This financial inflow was unprecedented in size and duration, and it reversed a long-standing pattern of ownership between the United States and other countries. For decades, American holdings of foreign assets far exceeded foreign holdings of U.S. assets. But the financial inflows of the 1980s changed that: By 1988, foreigners held about $500 billion more in U.S. assets than Americans held in foreign assets. By the end of 2002, the difference in asset holdings increased more than fivefold, and exceeded $2.5 trillion.

But how do the forces that create a financial inflow also *cause* a trade deficit?

From a Financial Inflow to a Trade Deficit

Figure 10 illustrates this process, using the yen–dollar market. We'll assume that initially, neither the Japanese nor the Americans are buying *assets* from the other country. Only goods and services are traded. Point *A* shows the initial equilibrium under this special assumption. Under these circumstances, the demand curve for yen would reflect U.S. *imports* of goods and services from Japan, and

FIGURE 10
How a U.S. Financial Inflow
Creates a U.S. Trade Deficit

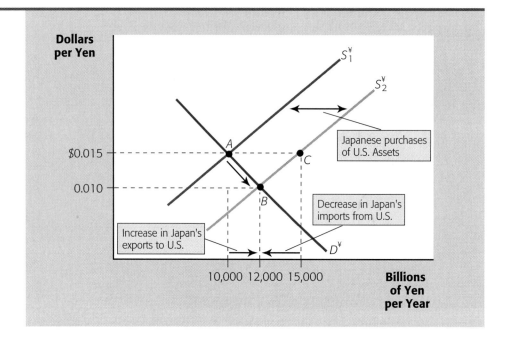

the supply curve would reflect U.S. *exports* of goods and services to Japan. The exchange rate would be $0.015 per yen (one-and-a-half cents per yen), and each year, 10,000 billion yen would be traded in exchange for 10,000 × .015 = 150 billion dollars. Since the quantity of yen demanded and supplied are equal in equilibrium, there is no trade deficit: The United States buys $150 billion in goods from Japan, and Japan buys $150 billion in goods from the United States.

Now suppose that the Japanese start to buy U.S. stocks, bonds, and real estate. Specifically, they want to purchase 5,000 billion yen worth of these assets from Americans each year. To do so, they need dollars, so they must supply additional yen to the foreign exchange market to get them. Accordingly, the supply of yen curve shifts rightward by 5,000 billion yen. The market equilibrium moves from point *A* to point *B*, and the new exchange rate is $.01 per yen. The yen depreciates against the dollar, and the dollar appreciates against the yen.

But something interesting happens in the market as the exchange rate changes. First, there is a *movement along the demand curve* for yen, from point *A* to point *B*. Why? The yen is now cheaper, so Americans—finding Japanese goods and services cheaper—buy more of them. Thus, the movement along the demand curve represents an *increase in Japan's exports to the U.S.* (valued in yen, the units on the horizontal axis). In the figure, Japan's exports—the quantity of yen demanded—rise by 2,000 billion yen as we move from *A* to *B*.

But there is a second movement as well. After the shift in the supply curve, *and at the old exchange rate of $0.015*, the Japanese want to supply 15,000 billion yen to the market (point *C*). But as the exchange rate falls, there is a movement from point *C* to point *B*—the quantity of yen supplied decreases. Why does this happen? Because as the yen depreciates (the dollar appreciates), U.S. goods and services become more expensive to the Japanese. Accordingly, they purchase fewer U.S. goods. Assuming that the Japanese still want to purchase the same 5,000 billion yen in U.S. *assets*, the entire decrease in the quantity of yen supplied as we move from *C* to *B* represents a *decrease in Japan's imports from the U.S.* (valued in yen). In the figure, Japan's imports decrease by 3,000 billion yen.

Let's recap: Because the Japanese wanted to purchase 5,000 billion yen in U.S. assets (a net financial inflow to the United States of 5,000 billion yen), the yen depreciated. This, in turn, made Japanese goods cheaper for Americans—increasing Japan's exports (U.S. imports) by 2,000 billion yen per year. It also made U.S. goods more expensive in Japan, decreasing Japan's imports (U.S. exports) by 3,000 billion yen per year. Since U.S. imports have risen by 2,000 billion ¥ and U.S. exports have fallen by 3,000 billion ¥, the United States—which initially had no trade deficit with Japan at point *A*—now has a trade deficit equal to 5,000 billion yen. This is exactly equal to the financial inflow—Japan's purchases of U.S. assets.

More generally,

> *an increase in the desire of foreigners to invest in the United States contributes to an appreciation of the dollar. As a result, U.S. exports—which become more expensive for foreigners—decline. Imports—which become cheaper to Americans—increase. The result is a rise in the U.S. trade deficit.*

What explains the huge financial inflow that began in the 1980s, and has grown larger over the past decade? In the 1980s, an important part of the story was *a rise in U.S. interest rates relative to interest rates abroad*, which made U.S. assets more attractive to foreigners, and foreign assets less attractive to Americans. In the 1990s, however, U.S. interest rates were low relative to rates in other countries, yet the inflow continued. Why?

Even when U.S. interest rates are the same or lower than abroad, it seems that residents of other countries have a strong preference for holding American assets. In part, this is because of a favorable investment climate. The United States is a stable country with a long history of protecting individual property rights. People know that if they buy American stocks or bonds, unless there is a violation of U.S. criminal law, the U.S. government is very unlikely to confiscate foreign-owned assets in the United States or suddenly impose punitive taxes when foreigners want to repatriate the funds to their home countries.

And in the late 1990s, there was another reason for the growing financial inflow: American companies took the lead in exploiting the Internet. New businesses—with the prospect of high future profits—sprang up daily, issuing shares of stock to anyone in the world who wanted to buy them. Thus, an asymmetry developed: The United States was offering assets that foreigners found attractive, while no foreign country was offering assets that Americans found nearly as attractive.

Remember that, under floating exchange rates, the financial inflow equals the trade deficit. Thus, the story of the U.S. financial inflow of the 1980s, 1990s, and early 2000s is also the story of the U.S. trade deficit:

FIGURE 11
The Growing U.S. Trade Deficit with China

Source: Wayne M. Morrison, "China-U.S. Trade Issues," Congressional Research Service, Library of Congress, Updated May 16, 2003.

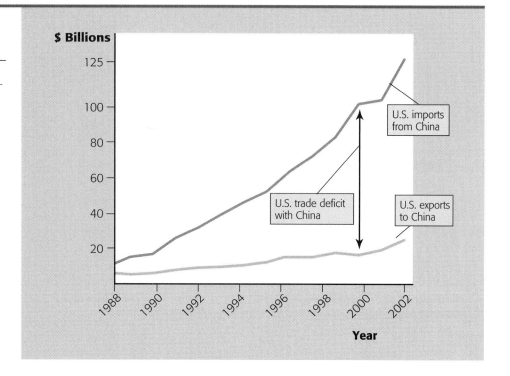

We can trace the rise in the trade deficit during recent decades to two important sources: first, relatively high interest rates in the 1980s, and second, a long-held preference for American assets that grew stronger in the 1990s. Each of these contributed to a large financial inflow, a higher value for the dollar, and a trade deficit.

The Growing Trade Deficit with China

In addition to a strong desire to buy U.S. assets, a trade deficit can arise from another cause: a foreign currency fixed at an artificially low value. In the minds of many economists, this has contributed to the United States' growing trade deficit with China.

Figure 11 shows United States imports to, and exports from, China from 1988 to 2002. Notice that while United States exports to China slightly more than quadrupled, United States *imports* from China increased almost 15-fold, from $8.5 billion in 1988 to $125.2 billion in 2002. During this period, China went from being a relatively unimportant trading partner of the United States to the fourth-largest trading partner. In the figure, the growing trade deficit is the increasing distance between the (higher) imports line and the (lower) exports line. In 2002, the United States had a larger trade deficit with China—$103 billion—than with any other country.

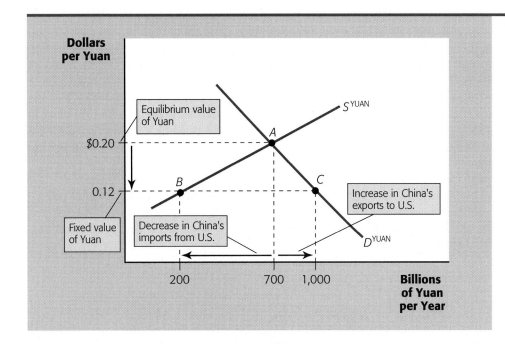

FIGURE 12
How an Undervalued Chinese Yuan Can Create a U.S. Trade Deficit

The U.S. trade deficit with China has been soaring for a variety of reasons, including special trade agreements during this period that gave China new access to U.S. markets, and Chinese trade policies that have encouraged exports and discouraged imports. But another factor, as mentioned above, is China's undervalued exchange rate. Since 1994, China has fixed the value of its currency (the yuan) against the dollar—first at 8.7 yuan per dollar, and since 1997, at a steady 8.27–8.28 yuan per dollar (about $.12 per yuan). This is widely believed to be lower than the equilibrium value of the yuan. (China's controls on trading the yuan make its equilibrium value difficult to determine.)

Figure 12 illustrates how an undervalued yuan can create a trade deficit for the United States. We'll assume that if the exchange rate were floating, the market equilibrium would be at point *A*, with an exchange rate of $0.20 per yuan. In this case, 700 billion yuan would be exchanged for 700 × .02 = 140 billion dollars each year.

Now we introduce the lower, fixed exchange rate of $.12 per yuan. Compared to the equilibrium exchange rate, the fixed exchange rate causes a movement along the *demand* for yuan curve, from point *A* to point *C*. The yuan is now cheaper, which makes Chinese goods and services cheaper to Americans, who buy more of them. Measured along the horizontal axis, *China's exports to the U.S. increase* by 300 billion yuan per year.

There is also a move from point *A* to point *B* along the *supply* curve; the quantity of yuan supplied decreases. A lower-valued yuan makes U.S. goods and services more expensive to Chinese households and businesses, so they purchase fewer of them. Along the horizontal axis, *China's imports from the U.S. decrease* by 500 billion yuan.

Since the fixed exchange rate has caused *China's imports from the U.S. to decrease* by 500 billion yuan, and *China's exports to the U.S. to increase* by 300 billion yuan, the U.S. trade deficit with China—valued in yuan—rises by 500 + 300 or 800 billion yuan per year. (If you convert the U.S. trade deficit to dollars, you'll see that our example comes close to the actual U.S. trade deficit with China.)

But wait . . . doesn't the rise in the U.S. trade deficit have to equal the rise in the net financial inflow? Indeed it does. Figure 11 shows an *excess demand for yuan* of 1,000 − 200 = 800 billion at the fixed exchange rate. The Chinese government must supply these yuan, selling them for U.S. dollars. These dollars are then used to purchase U.S. assets, contributing to the U.S. net financial inflow.

> *When a U.S. trading partner fixes the dollar price of its currency below its equilibrium value, U.S exports—which become more expensive to foreigners—decline. U.S. imports—which become cheaper to Americans—increase. The result is a rise in the U.S. trade deficit.*

China's fixed exchange rate with the dollar is the source of considerable tension between the two countries. On the one hand, it enables Americans to purchase cheap goods from China. And for most of the goods China exports, it would have a cost advantage over the United States even *without* the artificially low yuan, since China enjoys a comparative advantage in producing them (see the chapter on *Comparative Advantage and the Gains from International Trade*).

But trade with China also disrupts production in the U.S. economy, as U.S. businesses that produce sandals, shoes, suits, electronic goods, toys, and textiles find they are unable to compete with cheaper goods from China. The fixed exchange exacerbates their problem. By giving China an even *greater* cost advantage than it would otherwise have, U.S. firms and workers that compete in these markets must adjust more rapidly—and painfully—to the new pattern of international trade.

Summary

When residents of two countries trade with one another, one party ordinarily makes use of the foreign exchange market to trade one national currency for another. In this market, suppliers of a currency interact with demanders to determine an exchange rate—the price of one currency in terms of another.

In the market for U.S. dollars and British pounds, for example, demanders are mostly Americans who wish to obtain pounds in order to buy goods and services from British firms, or to buy British assets. A higher dollar price for the pound will lead Americans to demand fewer pounds—the demand curve slopes downward. Changes in U.S. real GDP, the U.S. price level relative to the British price level, Americans' tastes for British goods, interest rates in the United States relative to Britain, or expectations regarding the exchange rate can each cause the demand curve to shift.

Suppliers of pounds are mostly British residents who wish to buy American goods, services, or assets. A higher dollar price for the pound will lead Britons to supply more pounds—the supply curve slopes upward. The supply curve will shift in response to changes in British real GDP, prices in Britain relative to the United States, British tastes for U.S. goods, the British interest rate relative to the U.S. rate, and expectations regarding the exchange rate.

When the exchange rate floats, the equilibrium rate is determined where the supply and demand curves cross. If the equilibrium is disturbed by, say, a rightward shift of the demand curve, then the currency being demanded will appreciate—the exchange rate will rise. (The other country's currency will depreciate.) In a similar way, a rightward shift of the supply curve will cause the currency being supplied to depreciate.

Governments often intervene in foreign exchange markets. Many countries manage their float, buying and selling their own currency to alter the exchange rate. Some countries fix their exchange rate to the dollar or the currency of a major trading partner. And in Europe, 12 national governments have eliminated their national currencies and replaced them with the euro. Although these 12 nations may not yet be an optimum currency area, they are moving closer to one.

When a currency depreciates, its net exports rise—a positive demand shock. Monetary policy, in addition to its impact on interest-sensitive spending, also changes the exchange rate and net exports, adding to changes in output. This monetary policy is more effective in changing GDP when its effects on net exports are included.

The U.S. has had a persistent—and growing trade deficit—with the rest of the world. Much of this trade deficit can be explained by the growing U.S. financial inflow from the rest of the world. U.S. assets have been consistently more attractive to foreigners than foreign assets have been to Americans. The U.S. financial inflow causes the dollar to appreciate, which decreases U.S. exports and increases U.S. imports. In addition, an undervalued foreign currency can create a trade deficit. By making the U.S. dollar artificially more expensive to residents of the foreign country, it causes U.S. exports to decline and U.S. imports to rise.

Key Terms

Appreciation
Demand curve for foreign currency
Depreciation
Devaluation
Exchange rate
Fixed exchange rate

Floating exchange rate
Foreign currency crisis
Foreign exchange market
International Monetary Fund
Managed float
Moral hazard

Net financial inflow
Optimum currency area
Purchasing power parity (PPP) theory
Supply curve for foreign currency
Trade deficit
Trade surplus

Review Questions
Answers to even-numbered Questions and Problems can be found on the text Web site at http://hall-lieb.swlearning.com.

1. Why do Americans demand foreign currency? Why does the demand curve for foreign currency slope downward? What factors shift the demand curve for foreign currency to the right? What factors shift it to the left?

2. Why do foreigners supply foreign currency? Why does the supply of foreign currency curve slope upward? What factors shift the supply curve for foreign currency to the right? What factors shift it to the left?

3. Explain how an expected appreciation of a foreign currency can become a self-fulfilling prophecy.

4. What forces move exchange rates in the very short run? In the short run?

5. "A weak currency is a sign of a sick economy." True or false? Explain.

6. What is purchasing power parity? Why might exchange rates deviate from purchasing power parity?

7. Suppose the purchasing power parity exchange rate between the dollar and the pound is $1.50 per pound but the actual exchange rate is $2 per pound. Explain how a trader could profit by buying a basket of goods in one country (which country?) and selling it in the other. How would such actions by traders affect the exchange rate?

8. What is a managed float and why would a government use it?

9. How does an appreciation of the dollar affect U.S. real GDP?

10. According to economists, what caused the U.S. trade deficit in the 1980s? Why does the trade deficit persist?

11. Some nations might not be well suited to join together to use a common currency. What requirements are necessary for nations to be an optimum currency area?

12. Explain why managed floats are controversial.

Problems and Exercises

1. Do the following events cause the dollar to appreciate against the euro or to depreciate?
   a. Health experts discover that red wine, especially French and Italian red wine, lowers cholesterol.
   b. GDP in nations across Europe falls.
   c. The United States experiences a higher inflation rate than Europe does.
   d. The United States runs a large budget deficit.

2. Let the monthly demand for British pounds and the monthly supply of British pounds be described by the following equations:

$$\text{Demand for pounds} = 10 - 2e$$
$$\text{Supply of pounds} = 4 + 3e,$$

where the quantities are in millions of pounds and e is dollars per pound.

a. Find the equilibrium exchange rate.

b. Suppose the U.S. government intervenes in the foreign currency market and uses U.S. dollars to buy 2 million pounds each month. What happens to the exchange rate? Why might the U.S. government do this?

3. Let the demand and supply of Philippine pesos each month be described by the following equations:

$$\text{Demand for pesos} = 100 - 2,000e$$
$$\text{Supply of pesos} = 20 + 3,000e,$$

where the quantities are millions of pesos, and e is dollars per peso.

a. Find the equilibrium exchange rate.

b. Suppose the Philippine central bank wants to fix the exchange rate at 50 pesos per dollar and keep it there. Should the Philippine central bank buy or sell its own currency? How much per month?

4. Suppose the United States and Mexico are each other's sole trading partners. The Fed, afraid that the economy is about to overheat, decreases the U.S. money supply.

a. Will the dollar appreciate or depreciate against the Mexican peso? Illustrate with a diagram of the dollar–peso foreign exchange market.

b. What will happen to equilibrium GDP in the United States?

c. How would your analyses in (a) and (b) change if, at the same time that the Fed was increasing the U.S. interest rate, the Mexican central bank increased the Mexican interest rate by an equivalent amount?

5. Jordan fixes its national currency—the dinar—against the dollar. In June, 2003, the fixed rate was 1.41 dinars per dollar.

a. Draw a diagram illustrating the market in which Jordanian dinars are traded for U.S. dollars, assuming that the equilibrium exchange rate is 1.00 dinar per dollar. (In your diagram, put the number of dinars per month on the horizontal axis.)

b. Under the assumption in (a) above, would Jordan's central bank be buying or selling Jordanian dinars in this market? Indicate the number of dinars per month that the central bank must buy or sell as a distance on your graph.

c. Based on your diagram and your answers so far, could Jordan continue to fix its currency at 1.41 dinars per dollar forever? Why or why not?

d. Suppose that foreign currency traders believe that Jordan will soon allow the dinar to float. How would this affect the current supply and demand curves for dinars? (Draw new curves to indicate the impact.)

e. How would the events in (d) above affect the number of dinars that Jordan's central bank must buy or sell?

6. As in problem 5, note that Jordan fixes its national currency—the dinar—against the dollar at 1.41 dinars per dollar.

a. Draw a diagram illustrating the market in which Jordanian dinars are traded for U.S. dollars, assuming that the equilibrium exchange rate is 2.00 dinars per dollar. (Put the number of dinars per month on the horizontal axis.)

b. Under the assumption in (a) above, would Jordan's central bank be buying or selling Jordanian dinars in this market? Indicate the number of dinars per month that the central bank must buy or sell as a distance on your graph.

c. Based on your diagram and your answers so far, could Jordan continue to fix its currency at 1.41 dinars per dollar forever? Why or why not?

d. Suppose that foreign currency traders believe that Jordan will soon allow the dinar to float. How would this affect the current supply and demand curves for dinars? (Draw new curves to indicate the impact.)

e. How would the events in (d) above affect the number of dinars that Jordan's central bank must buy or sell?

7. Some nations that fix their exchange rates make their currency more expensive for foreigners (an overvalued currency), while others make their currency artificially cheap to foreigners (an undervalued currency).

a. Why would a country want an overvalued currency? How, specifically, would the country benefit? Would the policy cause harm to anyone in the country? Explain briefly.

b. Why would a country want an undervalued currency? How, specifically, would the country benefit? Would the policy cause harm to anyone in the country? Explain briefly.

8. If the inflation rate in Country A is 4 percent and the inflation rate in Country B is 6 percent, explain what will happen to the relative value of each country's currency.

9. a. Use the information in the table below to find the exchange rate if the euro and the U.S. dollar are allowed to float freely.

Dollars per Euro	Quantity of Euros Demanded	Quantity of Euros Supplied
$1.20	500 million	2,600 million
$1.10	1,000 million	2,400 million
$1.00	1,500 million	2,200 million
$0.90	2,000 million	2,000 million
$0.80	2,500 million	1,800 million

b. What will happen to the exchange rate if the demand for euros rises by 700 million at each price if there is no intervention?

c. Assume that the European central bank currently owns 400 million dollars and the Fed currently owns 300 million euros. If the demand for Euros rises by 700 million at each price, what would the European central bank have to do to maintain a fixed exchange rate equal to the exchange rate you found in part (a)? Is this possible?

10. Use a diagram showing the market for British pounds, a money market diagram, and an AD–AS graph for the U.S. to show all the effects of an increase in the U.S. money supply on U.S. real GDP.

11. Refer to Figure 10 in the chapter. Remember that there was no trade deficit at point *A*. What is the U.S. trade deficit with Japan in *dollars* at point *B*?

Challenge Questions

1. It is often stated that the U.S. trade deficit with Japan results from Japanese trade barriers against U.S. goods.

   a. Suppose that Japan and the United States trade goods but not assets. Show—with a diagram of the dollar–yen market—that a U.S. trade deficit is impossible as long as the exchange rate floats. (*Hint:* With no trading in assets, the quantity of yen demanded at each exchange rate is equal in value to U.S. imports, and the quantity of yen supplied at each exchange rate is equal in value to U.S. exports.)

   b. In the diagram, illustrate the impact of a reduction in Japanese trade barriers. Would the dollar appreciate or depreciate against the yen? What would be the impact on U.S. net exports?

   c. Now suppose that the United States and Japan also trade assets, but that the Japanese buy more U.S. assets than we buy of theirs. Could the elimination of Japanese trade barriers wipe out the U.S. trade deficit with Japan? Why, or why not? (*Hint:* What is the relationship between the U.S. trade deficit and U.S. net financial inflow?)

2. Suppose that the U.S. government raises spending without increasing taxes. Will there be any effects on the foreign exchange market? (*Hint:* What does this policy do to U.S. interest rates?) When we add in the effects from the foreign exchange market and net exports, is fiscal policy more effective or less effective in changing equilibrium GDP in the short run?

 *These exercises require access to Hall/Lieberman Xtra! If Xtra! did not come with your book, visit http://hallxtra.swlearning.com to purchase.*

1. Use your Xtra! password at the Hall and Lieberman Web site (http://hallxtra.swlearning.com), select this chapter, and under Economic Applications, click on EconDebate. Choose *International Trade*, and scroll down to find the debate, "What Are the Pros and Cons of IMF Involvement with Global Economies?" Read the debate, and use the information to answer the following questions.

   a. What is the effect of volatility of exchange rates on international trade? Explain.

   b. Explain the debate over the austerity measures required for IMF loans in the case of the Asian crisis.

2. Use your Xtra! password at the Hall and Lieberman Web site (http://hallxtra.swlearning.com), select this chapter, and under Economic Applications, click on EconDebates Online. Choose *International Trade*, and scroll down to find the debate, "Does the U.S. Economy Benefit from the WTO?" Read the debate,

and use the information and explain the views of the proponents of the WTO. Which side of the debate do you find to have more plausible arguments? Explain why.

3. Use your Xtra! password at the Hall and Lieberman Web site (http://hallxtra.swlearning.com), select this chapter, and under Economic Applications, click on EconData. Choose *International Trade*, and scroll down to find *Current Account*. Read the definition and click on Diagrams/Data and use the information to answer the following questions.

   a. Consider the current account balance and the yen per dollar exchange rate diagram and explain what would happen to the current account balance if the dollar depreciates.

   b. Consider the current account balance and real personal income diagram and explain what happens to the current account balance during an economic recession.

The Stock Market and the Macroeconomy

In December 1996, Alan Greenspan, the chair of the Federal Reserve Board, uttered two sentences that caught the world's attention. Speaking to a Washington research organization, he asked, "How do we know when irrational exuberance has unduly escalated asset values which then become the subject of unexpected and prolonged contractions . . . ? And how do we factor that assessment into monetary policy?"

Greenspan was referring to the rapid rise in stock prices that had occurred over the previous several years. By one broad measure, the average stock's price had doubled over this period—a very rapid rise by historical standards. But when the markets opened for trading at 9:30 A.M. on the morning after Greenspan's speech, stock prices dropped by about 2 percent almost immediately.

Everyone agreed that Greenspan's remarks had been designed to bring down stock prices and that he had succeeded somewhat. But this effort to "talk down the market" brought a wave of criticism in business and media circles. Who was Alan Greenspan to decide when stock prices are too high or too low? And what right did he have to try to bring stock prices down?

Flash forward to September 17, 2001. It was the first day of trading after the stock market had been closed for a week in the wake of the terrorist attacks of September 11. And it was not a good day. Stock prices

© SUSAN VAN ETTEN

fell on average more than 5 percent, with some airline and travel industry stocks plunging 40 to 50 percent. The next several days were little better, and by September 20, stocks had fallen more than 13 percent.

Alan Greenspan—still chair of the Federal Reserve—watched the market with deep concern that week. And when Congress called him to testify, they hoped he would have something encouraging to say. He did. In highly technical language, he reassured the nation that the Fed had responded appropriately and that, although the economy faced short-term uncertainty, there was no reason for long-run pessimism.

In the following days, the market began to rise—slowly at first, then more rapidly. And within a few weeks, stocks had regained all that they had lost after September 11. While there were many influences on the market during this time, no one doubted that Greenspan's reassuring words had helped to turn the tide and that he was once again trying to influence stock prices. Only this time, no one complained.

The events of 1996 and 2001 raise a number of important questions. *Why* does the stock market matter? What is its role in the economy? Why should public officials worry when stock prices are too high or too low? And why do stock prices sometimes fluctuate so widely? In this chapter—after providing some basic background about the stock market—we'll answer all these questions.

BASIC BACKGROUND

Let's start with the most basic question of all: What is a share of stock?

First, a share of stock is a private financial asset, like a corporate bond. In fact, stocks and corporate bonds are alike in two ways. Both are issued by corporations to raise funds for investment projects, and both offer future payments to their owners.

But there is also an important difference between these two types of assets. When a corporation issues a bond, it is *borrowing* funds; the bond is just a promise to pay back the loan. A share of stock, by contrast, is a share of *ownership* in a corporation. When a firm issues new shares of stock, those who pay for those shares provide the firm with new funds, and in return, the firm owes them—at some future date or dates—a share of the firm's profits.

When a firm issues new shares of stock—in what is called a *public offering*—the sale of stock generates funds for the firm. Once the newly issued shares are sold, however, the buyer is free to sell them to someone else. Indeed, virtually all of the shares traded in the stock market are previously issued shares, and this trading does not involve the firm that issued the stock.

But a firm is still *concerned* about the price of its previously issued shares for two reasons. First, the firm's owners—its stockholders—want high share prices because that is the price they can sell at. A management team that ignores the desires of stockholders for too long might find itself replaced by other managers who will pay more attention.

Moreover, the price of previously issued shares has an important impact on firms that are planning new public offerings. That's because previously issued shares are perfect substitutes for the firm's new shares, so the firm cannot expect to receive a higher price for its new shares than the going price on its old shares.

The higher the price for previously issued shares, the higher the price the firm will receive for *new* shares and the more funds it will obtain from any given public offering.

Why Do People Hold Stock?

Stock ownership in the United States is growing rapidly. In 1983, only 19 percent of Americans owned shares of stock either directly or through mutual funds—companies that invest in a variety of stocks for their clients. In 2003, almost half of all Americans owned stock in these two ways. If we included stocks in employer-managed retirement accounts, the percentage of Americans with a stake in the stock market would be much higher. And the stakes are significant.

Why do so many individuals choose to hold their wealth in stocks? You already know part of the answer: When you own a share of stock, you own part of the corporation. The fraction of the corporation that you own is equal to the fraction of the company's total stock that you own. For example, in July 2003, there were 298,500,000 shares outstanding in FedEx Corporation, which runs the overnight package delivery service Federal Express. If you owned 10,000 shares of FedEx stock, then you owned 10,000/298,500,000 = 0.000033, or about three-thousandths of a percent of the company. That means that you are, in a sense, entitled to three-thousandths of a percent of the firm's after-tax profits.

In practice, however, most firms do not pay out *all* of their profit to shareholders. Instead, some is kept as *retained earnings,* for later use by the firm. The part of profit that is distributed to shareholders is called *dividends.* A firm's dividend payments benefit stockholders in much the same way that interest payments benefit bondholders, providing a source of steady income. Of course, as part owner of a firm, you are part owner of any retained earnings as well, even if you will not benefit from them until later.

Aside from dividends, a second—and usually more important—reason that people hold stocks is that they hope to enjoy *capital gains.* A capital gain is the return someone gets when they sell an asset at a higher price than they paid for it. For example, if you buy shares of FedEx at $60 per share, and later sell them at $65 per share, your capital gain is $5 per share. This is in addition to any dividends you earned while you owned the stock.

Some stocks pay no dividends at all, because the management believes that stockholders are best served by reinvesting all profits within the firm so that *future* profits will be even higher. The idea is to increase the value of the stock and create capital gains for the shareholders when the stock is finally sold. New or fast-growing companies—such as Yahoo! and Time Warner—typically pay no dividends at all.

Over the past century, corporate stocks have generally been a good investment. Holding stocks was especially rewarding during the 1990s, as you'll see in the next section.

Tracking the Stock Market

In the United States, financial markets are so important that stock and bond prices are monitored on a continuous basis. If you wish to know the value of a

TABLE 1

The Performance of Three Stock Market Indexes

Index	Increase, 1 Year Ending June 30, 2003	Average Annual Increase, 3 Years Ending June 30, 2003	Average Annual Increase, 5 Years Ending June 30, 2003	Average Annual Increase, 10 Years Ending June 30, 2003
Dow Jones Industrial Average	−3.2%	−5.2%	0.1%	10.0%
Standard & Poor's 500	−0.3%	−12.6%	−7.6%	8.3%
NASDAQ	14.8%	−25.5%	−2.6%	9.0%

Source: http://www.yahoo.com, and author's calculations.

stock, you can find out instantly by checking with a broker or logging onto a Web site (such as Yahoo.com, Morningstar.com, or thomsoninvest.com). In addition, stock prices and other information are reported daily in local newspapers and in specialized financial publications such as the *Wall Street Journal* and the *Financial Times*.

In addition to monitoring individual stocks, the media keep a close watch on many stock market indices or averages. These averages track movements in stock prices as a whole, or movements in particular types of stocks. The oldest and most popular average is the *Dow Jones Industrial Average (DJIA)*, which tracks the prices of 30 of the largest companies in the United States, including AT&T, IBM, and Wal-Mart. Another popular average is the much broader *Standard & Poor's 500 (S&P 500)*, which tracks stock prices of 500 corporations chosen to represent all stocks in the market. Finally, the *NASDAQ* index tracks share prices of about 5,000 mostly newer companies whose shares are traded on the Nasdaq stock exchange, an association of stockbrokers who execute trades electronically. The companies in the NASDAQ include most of the new high-tech companies that are closely connected to the Internet sector.

Often, the three stock market averages will rise and fall at the same time, sometimes by the same percentage. That's because many of the shocks that hit the stock market affect most share prices *together*. But the indices can and do behave differently—sometimes very differently. For example, in 2000, Internet stocks fluctuated wildly from day to day, as new information changed public opinion about the future of the industry. There were many days on which the NASDAQ rose substantially while the Dow and the Standard & Poor's 500 fell, and vice versa.

Table 1 shows how the three averages performed over different lengths of time ending in June 30, 2003. The entries in the table tell us the average annual increase in each index over the period. For example, the entry 8.3 percent in the table (be sure you can find it) tells us that—over the period June 30, 1993, to June 30, 2003—the S&P 500 rose an average of 8.3 percent per year.

In spite of falling stock prices in 2000 and 2001, the last decade was good for stocks. Someone who invested $10,000 in a typical group of S&P 500 stocks on June 30, 1993, would have been able to sell them for $22,196 on June 30, 2003.

And someone who had invested $10,000 in a typical collection of NASDAQ stocks would have $23,674 at the end of the period. However, you can also see that even a broad portfolio of stocks is risky in the short run. An investor who put $10,000 into NASDAQ stocks in mid-2000 would have found them worth only $4,135 at the end of the year.

EXPLAINING STOCK PRICES

Why do stock prices change? And why do they change so often?

We can answer these questions—as we answer most questions about the economy—by using our three-step process.

Step 1: Characterize the Market

The price of a share of stock—like any other price—is determined in a market. But which market? Initially, we'll be focusing on price changes for shares of a particular stock, so the most useful way to organize our thinking is to look at the market for a single corporation's shares. That is, we'll view the "stock market" as a collection of *individual* markets, one for shares of stock in Time Warner, another for shares in FedEx, another for shares in Starbucks, and so on.

Further, we'll characterize the market for a company's shares as perfectly competitive. Indeed, markets for shares *do* satisfy the three requirements of perfect competition rather closely. There are many buyers and sellers (so many that no one of them can do much to change the market price of the stock).[1] There is a standardized product (it makes no difference to the buyer whether her FedEx shares are being sold to her by Smith or by Jones). And there is easy entry (virtually anyone with funds to invest can open up a brokerage account and buy or sell any publicly traded stock).

In sum,

> *we'll view the stock market as a collection of individual, perfectly competitive markets for particular corporations' shares.*

Step 2: Find the Equilibrium

Like all prices in competitive markets, stock prices are determined by supply and demand. However, in stock markets, our supply and demand curves require careful interpretations.

Figure 1 presents a supply and demand diagram for the shares of FedEx Corporation. Unlike most supply curves you've studied in this book—which show the quantity of something that suppliers want to *sell* over a given period of time—the supply curve in Figure 1 is somewhat different. It tells us the quantity of shares of FedEx stock *in existence* at any moment in time. This is the number of shares that people are *actually* holding.

---

[1] In some cases, a single buyer or seller holds such a large fraction of a company's shares that his or her decisions have a significant impact on market price. But these exceptions are rare for publicly traded shares.

FIGURE 1

The Market for Shares of FedEx Corporation

The supply curve shows the number of shares of FedEx stock people are holding. The curve is vertical at the number of shares outstanding—which was about 298 million in early 2002. The demand curve tells us how many shares people want to hold. It slopes downward— the lower the price, the more shares people want to hold. At any price other than the equilibrium price of $60, there would be either an excess supply or an excess demand for shares.

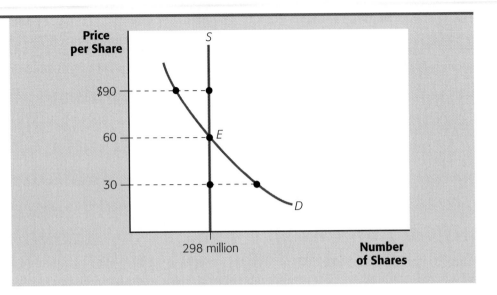

On any given day, the number of FedEx shares in existence is just the number that the firm has issued previously. By mid-2003, FedEx had issued about 298 million shares since the corporation began. Therefore, no matter what happens to the price of the stock on any particular day, the number of shares will remain unchanged, and so will the quantity supplied. This is why the supply curve in the figure is a vertical line at 298 million: We assume that over the time period we're analyzing, FedEx will not issue any new shares.

Now, just because 298 million shares of FedEx stock exist, that does not mean that this is the number of shares that people will *want* to hold. The desire to hold FedEx shares is given by the downward-sloping demand curve. As you can see, all else equal, the lower the price of the stock, the more shares of FedEx that people will want to hold. Why is this?

First, people have different expectations about the firm's future profits. Some may believe that FedEx will continue to grow as it has in the past. Others will think it is poised for a spurt of higher growth, while still others—more pessimistic—may believe that FedEx's best days are behind it. There will also be different opinions about the *risk* of those future profits. Thus, at any given moment, with an array of opinions about the company's future, each person will have a different price in mind that would make the stock an attractive buy. As the price per share falls, more and more people will find the stock to be a bargain, and want to hold it. This is what the downward-sloping demand curve tells us.

In the figure, you can see that at any price other than $60 per share, the number of shares people *are* holding (on the supply curve) will differ from the number they *want* to hold (on the demand curve). For example, at a price of $30 per share, people would want to hold more shares than they are currently holding. Many would try to buy the stock, bidding the price up. At $90 per share, the opposite occurs: People find themselves holding more shares than they want to hold, and they will try to get rid of the excess by selling them. The sudden sales would cause the price to drop. Only at the *equilibrium price* of $60—where the supply and demand curves intersect—are people satisfied holding the number of shares they are *actually* holding.

Stocks achieve their equilibrium prices almost instantly. There are so many stock traders—both individuals and professional fund managers—poised at their computers, ready to buy or sell a particular firm's shares at a moment's notice, that any excess supply or excess demand will cause the price to move within seconds. Thus, we can have confidence that the price of a share at any time is the equilibrium price.

But why do stock prices *change* so often? To answer that question, we need Step 3.

Step 3: What Happens When Things Change?

The *supply* curve for a corporation's shares, like the one in Figure 1, shifts rightward whenever there is a public offering. Can this explain changes in share prices? Not really. Public offerings occur only occasionally and with great fanfare. Moreover, most public offerings by existing companies are for a relatively small number of shares. They shift the supply curve only a little, and therefore have little impact on the market price of the stock. Thus, the changes in equilibrium prices we observe for most stocks are *not* caused by shifts of the supply curve.

That leaves only one explanation: shifts in *demand*.

> *The changes we observe in a stock's price—over a few minutes, a few days, or a few years—are virtually always caused by shifts in the demand curve.*

Panel (a) of Figure 2 shows how a rightward shift of the demand curve for shares of FedEx could cause the equilibrium price to rise to $75 per share. Indeed, on rare occasions, the demand curve for a firm's shares has shifted so far rightward in a single day that the share price doubled or even tripled.

But what causes these sudden changes in demand for a share of stock?

In almost all cases, it is one or more of the following three factors:

1. *Changes in expected future profits of the firm.* At any given time, people have an idea about the expected profits of every firm. But these ideas can change as new information becomes available. The new information can pertain to a scientific discovery, a corporate takeover or merger with another company, or a new government policy. Even information that suggests that one of these events *might* occur can change the attractiveness of stocks. After all, a stock in a company that has a 50 percent chance of making huge profits from a new invention is more attractive than a stock that has only a 20 percent chance of such profits.

   New information can be positive, shifting the demand curve rightward and increasing the price of the stock. But it can also be negative, shifting the demand curve leftward. A dramatic example was the plunge in passenger airline stocks when the market reopened on September 17, 2001. After the attacks of September 11, it was clear to everyone that fewer people would want to fly and that the cost of providing airline safety would soon rise. With fewer passengers and higher safety costs, profits were sure to fall; thus fewer people wanted to hold airline stocks at any given price.

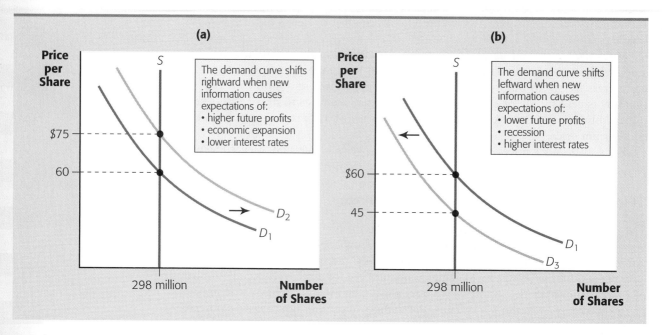

FIGURE 2

Shifts in the Demand for Shares Curve

Any new information that increases expectations of firms' future profits—including announcements of new scientific discoveries, business developments, or changes in government policy—will shift the demand curves of the affected stocks rightward. New information that decreases expectations of future profits will shift the demand curves leftward.

2. *Macroeconomic fluctuations.* When the economy is expanding, and real GDP is rising, firms *in general* tend to earn higher profits, and these profits are less risky. By contrast, in a recession, sales and profits decrease. For this reason,

any news that suggests the economy will enter an expansion, or that an expansion will continue, will shift the demand curves for most stocks rightward. Any news that suggests an economic slowdown or a coming recession shifts the demand curves for most stocks leftward.

3. *Changes in the interest rate.* Stocks are not the only way that people can hold their wealth. They can also hold money and—more importantly—they can hold interest-earning assets like certificates of deposit or bonds. If the interest rate rises, these other assets become more attractive, and many people will want to shift their wealth *out* of stocks so they can buy them. Thus,

a rise in interest rates will shift the demand curves for most stocks to the left. Similarly, a drop in interest rates will shift the demand curves for most stocks to the right.[2]

---

[2] If you've studied *microeconomics*, you've learned another way to view the impact of interest rate changes on stock prices: Higher interest rates reduce the *present value* of any given stream of future profits.

Even *expectations* of a future interest rate change can shift demand curves for stocks. This can create some rather convoluted—but logical—explanations for movements in stock prices. For example, suppose that a report comes out suggesting that real GDP is growing very rapidly. All else equal, this makes stocks more attractive. But . . . all else may *not* remain equal. In fact, you may surmise that the U.S. Federal Reserve and its influential chair—currently Alan Greenspan—will want to prevent inflation at almost any cost. You might then *anticipate* that the Fed—concerned about the economy overheating—will raise interest rates in the near future to slow down the growth in real GDP. You also know that—if the interest rate *does* rise—stock prices will fall, for the reasons we've just discussed. What should you do? *Dump your stocks now,* to avoid a capital loss later. Since you and many others will have access to the same information and feel the same way, the announcement of rapid economic growth could lead—almost immediately—to a *decrease* in stock prices.

Such an event occured on February 27, 2002, when Fed Chair Greenspan announced that it appeared the economy was recovering from its recession. Market participants felt that with this perception, the Fed was more likely to raise interest rates in the near future than lower them, and the Dow Jones Industrial Average dropped 200 points (about 2 percent).

Similarly, bad news about economic growth—if it leads to an expected decrease in interest rates—can cause stock prices to rise.

News that causes people to anticipate *a rise in the interest rate will shift the demand curves for stocks leftward. Similarly, news that suggests a future drop in the interest rate will shift the demand curves for stocks rightward.*

Panels (a) and (b) of Figure 2 summarize the different forces that cause the demand curve for a stock to shift rightward or leftward.

THE STOCK MARKET AND THE MACROECONOMY

As you can see in Figure 3, there is a *two-way* relationship between the stock market and the economy. That is, the performance of the stock market affects the performance of the economy, and vice versa. In the next two sections of this chapter, we'll look at this two-way relationship. Let's start with the impact of the stock market on the economy, as illustrated by the upper arrow in the figure.

How the Stock Market Affects the Economy

On October 19, 1987, there was a dramatic drop in the stock market, one that made the decline on September 17, 2001 seem small by comparison. That day, the Dow Jones Industrial Average fell by 508 points—a drop of 23 percent—and about $500 billion in household wealth disappeared. That same evening, as President Reagan boarded his helicopter, a breathless Sam Donaldson of ABC News thrust a microphone in front of him and asked, "Mr. President, are you concerned about the drop in the Dow?" As Reagan entered his helicopter, he smiled calmly and replied, "Why, no, Sam. I don't own any stocks."

FIGURE 3

The Two-Way Relationship Between the Stock Market and the Economy

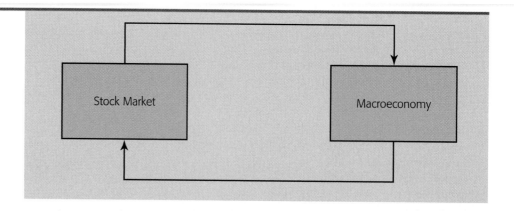

It was a curious exchange. Reagan was probably kidding—perhaps trying to calm a worried nation with his trademark humor. Or perhaps he was annoyed at a frantic reporter invading his personal space. Or he might have been caught off guard and said the first thing that popped into his head.

Whatever Reagan's intent, the statement was startling because, in fact, the stock market *does* matter to all Americans, whether they own stocks or not. As you are about to see, the ups and downs of stock prices—if they are big enough and sustained enough—can cause ups and downs in the overall economy.

The Wealth Effect. To understand how the market affects the economy, let's run through the following mental experiment: We'll suppose that, for *some* reason (we'll discuss specific reasons later), stock prices rise. As a result, those who own stock will feel wealthier. In fact, they *are* wealthier. After all, just as you measure the value of your house by the price at which you could sell it, the same is true of your financial assets, like stocks. When stock prices rise, so does household wealth.

What do households do when their wealth increases? Typically, they increase their spending. In our short-run macro model, we would classify this as an increase in *autonomous consumption*—an increase in consumption spending at *any* level of disposable income.

The link between stock prices and consumer spending is an important one, so economists have given it a name: the *wealth effect*. And the wealth effect works in both directions: Just as an increase in stock prices increases autonomous consumption, so will a drop in stock prices—which decreases household wealth—cause autonomous consumption spending to fall.

More generally,

> *the wealth effect tells us that autonomous consumption spending tends to move in the same direction as stock prices. When stock prices rise, autonomous consumption spending rises; when stock prices fall, autonomous consumption spending falls with it.*

The Wealth Effect and Equilibrium GDP. As you learned when you studied the short-run macroeconomic model, autonomous consumption is a component of to-

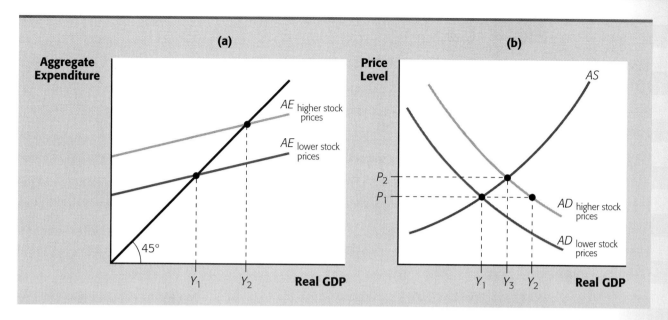

FIGURE 4

The Effect of Higher Stock Prices on the Economy

Higher stock prices have a wealth effect on spending, increasing consumption spending at any level of real GDP. In panel (a), the wealth effect of higher stock prices shifts the aggregate expenditure line upward, raising equilibrium GDP from Y_1 to Y_2. Panel (b) shows a more complete way of illustrating the wealth effect: Higher stock prices shift the aggregate demand curve rightward, increasing both equilibrium real GDP and the price level.

tal spending. And an increase in total spending tends to increase equilibrium real GDP, as shown in panel (a) of Figure 4. There, when stock prices rise, the increase in real wealth causes the aggregate expenditure line to shift upward, and increases the economy's equilibrium GDP from Y_1 to Y_2.

Panel (b) of Figure 4 shows a more complete way to view the impact of rising stock prices. In this panel, the increase in equilibrium GDP at any given price level is shown as a rightward shift in the economy's *AD* curve. And—in the absence of any change in government policy—this shift of the *AD* curve will increase both equilibrium GDP (to Y_3) and the price level (to P_2). (Why does equilibrium GDP increase by less in panel (b) than in panel (a)?)

We can summarize the logic of the wealth effect as follows:

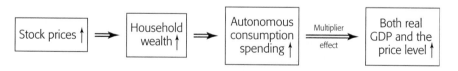

In words:

Changes in stock prices—through the wealth effect—cause both equilibrium GDP and the price level to move in the same direction. That is, an increase in stock prices will raise equilibrium GDP and the price level, while a decrease in stock prices will decrease both equilibrium GDP and the price level.

How important is the wealth effect? Economic research shows that the *marginal propensity to consume out of wealth*—the change in consumption spending for each one-dollar rise in wealth—is between 0.03 and 0.05. In other words, when household wealth rises by a dollar, all else remaining the same, consumption spending tends to rise by between 3 and 5 cents. Moreover, recent research suggests that virtually *all* of the increase in consumption comes rather quickly—within one quarter (3 months) after the quarter in which stock prices rise.[3] Let's translate this into some practical numbers.

First, as a rule of thumb, a 100-point rise in the DJIA—which generally means a rise in stock prices in general—causes household wealth to rise by about $100 billion. This rise in household wealth, we've now learned, will increase autonomous consumption spending by between $3 billion and $5 billion—we'll say $4 billion. As you learned several chapters ago, the multiplier in the real world—after we take account of all the automatic stabilizers that reduce its value—is equal to about 1.5, with most of its impact in the first nine months to a year after a shock. Thus, a 100-point rise in the DJIA, which causes consumption spending to rise by about $4 billion, will cause real GDP to increase by about $4 billion × 1.5 = $6 billion. Extrapolating from these results, a 6,000- or so point rise in the Dow—as occurred in the second half of the 1990s—would generate about $240 billion in additional consumption spending and drive up real GDP by about $360 billion—an increase of about 4 percent. This is in addition to the normal rise in real GDP that would be occurring anyway, as income grows and spending grows with it. Thus,

> *rapid increases in stock prices can cause significant positive demand shocks to the economy, shocks that policy makers cannot ignore. Similarly, rapid decreases in stock prices can cause significant negative demand shocks to the economy, which would be a major concern for policy makers.*

How the Economy Affects the Stock Market

Now that we've explored how the stock market affects the economy, let's look at the other side of the two-way relationship: how the economy affects stock prices.

Actually, many different types of changes in the overall economy can affect the stock market. Some—like the revolution in telecommunications that took place in the 1990s—are rare, happening once or twice a century. Others—like the impact of macroeconomic fluctuations—happen much more frequently. In this section, we'll focus on the more frequent scenario: how the stock market responds as the economy goes through expansions and recessions in the short run.

Let's start by looking at the typical expansion, in which real GDP rises rapidly over several years. In the typical expansion, profits will rise along with GDP. Higher profits are themselves enough to make stocks look more attractive. But the process is further helped by another factor: an improvement in investor psychology. In an expansion, not only are corporate profits rising, but also the unemployment rate falls and household incomes rise. Memories of the last recession are dim, and it

[3] Sydney Ludvigson and Charles Steindel, "How Important Is the Stock Market Effect on Consumption?" New York Federal Reserve Bank *Policy Review*, July 1999. (Also available at *http://www.ny.frb.org/rmaghome/econ_pol/799lud.htm.*) For a study that shows a somewhat larger effect of stockholder wealth on consumption, see Karen E. Dynan and Dean M. Maki, "Does Stock Market Wealth Matter for Consumption?" *Finance and Economics Discussion Series*, Board of Governors of the Federal Reserve System, May 2001.

looks as if the economy will continue to grow and grow, perhaps forever. This optimistic outlook raises estimates of future profits—sometimes dramatically. The demand curves for stocks will shift rightward and stock prices will rise.

We can summarize the impact of an *expansion* on the market as follows:

Of course, the process also works in reverse. When a *recession* strikes—such as the one from March through November 2001—corporate profits drop, unemployment rises, and the economy begins to look bleak. Stockholders turn pessimistic and expect lower profits in the future. The demand curves for stocks shift leftward, driving stock prices down:

In sum,

in the typical expansion, higher profits and stockholder optimism cause stock prices to rise. In the typical recession, lower profits and stockholder pessimism cause stock prices to fall.

WHAT HAPPENS WHEN THINGS CHANGE?

Now that you understand how stock prices affect the overall economy—and how the economy can affect stock prices—it's time to apply Step 3 one more time. But this time, we'll apply it very broadly: We'll observe how *both* the stock market and the macroeconomy are affected when *something* changes.

But . . . *what* changes?

Figure 5 illustrates three different types of changes we might explore. A change might have most of its initial impact on the overall economy rather than the stock market. For example, a change in government spending or taxes—with an unchanged interest rate target by the Fed—would initially affect real GDP rather than the stock market. Ultimately, stock prices would be affected, but primarily *through* the change in real GDP.

Alternatively, there might be a shock that initially affects the stock market. An example would be a change in the duration of patent protection for intellectual property, which would change the expected profits of firms and shift the demand curves for stocks. Direct shocks to the market—without simultaneously affecting the economy—are rare.

Finally, a shock could have powerful, initial impacts on *both* the stock market *and* the overall economy. Examples are the technological revolution of the late

FIGURE 5
Three Types of Shocks

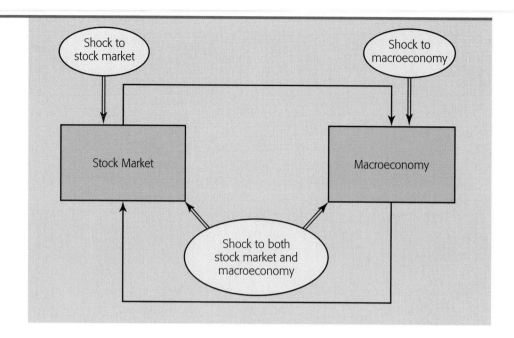

1990s and early 2000s and the collapse of dot-com shares in late 2000 and 2001. Each of these events rocked both the economy and the market simultaneously.

In the next section, we'll explore the consequences of an initial shock to the *economy*. Then, we'll turn our attention to shocks that simultaneously hit the market and the economy, as occurred during the 1990s and again in the early 2000s. Finally, in the end-of-chapter questions, you'll be asked to address the remaining case: a shock that initially hits just the stock market.

A Shock to the Economy

Imagine that new legislation greatly increases government purchases—say, to equip public schools with more sophisticated telecommunications equipment, or to increase the strength of our armed forces. This demand shock—and increase in government purchases—will have its primary initial impact on the overall economy, rather than the stock market. Let's suppose, too, that the Fed maintains its interest rate target, so there is no direct impact on the stock market from changes in the interest rate. What will happen?

As you've learned in your study of macroeconomics, the rise in government purchases will first increase real GDP through the expenditure multiplier:

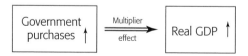

In previous chapters, the multiplier process was a simple one: Increases in output and income cause increases in consumption, which cause further increases in output and income and then further increases in consumption, and so on. But now, there is a *new* contributor to the multiplier process: the stock market.

First, remember that increases in real GDP cause corporate profits to rise. This, in turn, leads to investor optimism about *future* profits, shifting the demand curves for stocks rightward and increasing the average price of stocks.

But the story doesn't end there. The increase in stock prices will—through the wealth effect—cause an increase in autonomous consumption spending. Note that this is *in addition* to the increase in consumption spending caused by the normal multiplier process. Indeed, the increase in autonomous consumption spending caused by the wealth effect sets off its *own* multiplier process, further increasing real GDP:

Now, look back at the three cause-and-effect chains just presented. You can see that an increase in government purchases will cause a *larger* rise in real GDP when we include the effects of the stock market. Another way of saying this is that,

when we include the effects of the stock market, the expenditure multiplier is larger. An increase in spending that increases real GDP will also cause stock prices to rise, causing still greater increases in real GDP. Similarly, a decrease in spending that causes real GDP to fall will also cause stock prices to fall, causing still greater decreases in real GDP.

When you first learned about the multiplier, you learned about automatic stabilizers: features of the economy, such as the income tax or unemployment insurance payments, that make the expenditure multiplier smaller and thus help to stabilize real GDP. Now you can see that the normal behavior of the stock market—which makes the expenditure multiplier larger—works as an *automatic destabilizer*. This is one reason why stock prices are so carefully watched by policy makers, and matter for everyone—whether they own stocks themselves or not.

A Shock to the Economy *and* the Stock Market: The High-Tech Boom of the 1990s

The 1990s—especially the second half of the 1990s—saw a dramatic rise in stock prices. Both the Dow Jones Industrial Average and the Standard & Poor's 500 more than quadrupled over the period, and the NASDAQ increased almost ninefold.

The 1990s were also a period of rapid expansion, especially the period from 1995 to 2000, in which growth in real GDP averaged 4.2 percent per year—much faster than in previous decades.

In part, the economic expansion and the rise in stock prices were reinforcing: Each contributed to the other, as we've seen in this chapter. But the expansion and the climb in stocks were *initiated* by a common shock: a technological revolution, led by the Internet.

The Internet had a direct impact on the stock market through its effect on expected future profits of U.S. firms. In particular, stockholders (and potential stockholders) believed that the new technology would enable firms to produce goods and services at much lower costs than before, and that this reduction in costs would translate into an increase in profit. The increase in expected future profits translated into a rightward shift of the demand curve for stocks at virtually any firm that had the potential to exploit the new technology, or help other firms exploit it.

For example, during this period, AT&T positioned itself to be a major supplier of information and voice communication using the Internet and other new technologies. As a result, the demand curve for AT&T stock shifted rightward—enough to drive the price of AT&T stock from $28 per share in early 1997 to $60 in early 2000.

At the same time, the technological revolution was having a huge impact on the overall economy. Investment spending rose, as business firms—in order to take advantage of the new technology—invested in new plants and equipment. Autonomous consumption spending also rose: Consumers wanted new gadgets that would enable them to enjoy new types of services—new cellular phones, new computers, Palm Pilots, high-speed Internet connections, and more.

Faced with these demand shocks, the Federal Reserve would ordinarily have raised its interest rate target to prevent real GDP from exceeding potential output. But the technological revolution of the 1990s was having *another* effect on the economy: It *increased* potential output more rapidly than before. New computers, new software, and other forms of new capital equipment—along with the increased skills and training of the workforce—raised the typical worker's hourly output by about 22 percent over the decade.

The technological changes of the 1990s were an example of a shock to both the stock market *and* the economy. But remember that each of these also influences the other. As the expansion gained steam and real GDP was growing steadily and rapidly, profits and expected profits soared, pushing stock prices up further. And as stock prices rose, the wealth effect worked to propel consumer spending still higher. The result was a market and an economy that were feeding on each other, sending both to new performance heights. Was this a good thing?

Yes, and no. Higher stock prices certainly make stockholders happy. And a rapid expansion is good for workers, since it makes it easy to find jobs and forces firms to compete for workers by offering higher wages and better fringe benefits. Indeed, from a high of almost 8 percent in 1991, the unemployment rate dropped steadily during the 1990s, reaching 4 percent at the end of the decade.

But in spite of all this good news, there were dark clouds on the horizon. . . .

A Shock to the Economy *and* the Stock Market: The High-Tech Bust of 2000 and 2001

The market—especially high-tech NASDAQ stocks—began to decline in early 2000. By September 2001—even *before* September 11—the NASDAQ was down about 65 percent from its high. At the same time, a wave of pessimism was infecting the economy. The high-tech boom of the 1990s had become the high-tech bust of the early 2000s. What happened?

Both the economy and the market were being affected by several events discussed in earlier chapters of this book. Now let's bring these events together to understand what happened to the market and the economy.

First, during the 1990s, there had been an investment boom, as businesses rushed to incorporate the Internet into factories, offices, and their business practices in general. Firms across the country needed servers and high-speed Internet connections, and the high-tech firms that supplied these high-tech goods and services needed to expand, in order to meet the high demand of their clients. But as 2000 came to a close, firms had begun to catch up to the new technology. The rush had ended. Investment remained positive, but it was smaller than in previous periods. Of course, when investment is positive but smaller, this translates to a decrease in investment spending—a negative demand shock that set the stage for the recession that would begin a few months later.

The Fed may have played a role as well. Concerned about the economy overheating, the Fed raised interest rates throughout 2000. Some observers believe the Fed kept rates high for too long—into January 2001—and that this pulled investment spending down faster and further than it otherwise would have gone.

In any case, the decline in investment—and the recession it caused—can be regarded as a shock to the economy. As you've learned, though, shocks to the economy feed back to the market: Stock prices tend to fall during recessions. This was a part of the reason stock prices fell in 2001.

But in addition, there was a direct shock to the market: a change in expectations about the future. The late 1990s were a period of high optimimsm. The Internet and other new technologies seemed capable of increasing business profits to unprecedented heights. The public became hungry to own shares of stock in almost any company that had anything to do with the Internet, driving up share prices and encouraging the formation of many new businesses through public offerings.

Unfortunately, in late 2000 and early 2001, reality set in. Competition was preventing many new firms from earning any profit at all, and many went bankrupt. Optimism about future profits shifted rapidly to pessimism. Share prices fell. Ordinarily the drop in share prices would be expected to bring down consumption spending through the wealth effect. Surprisingly, though, consumption spending remained strong during the recession of 2001. Does this mean that there was no feedback effect from the market to the economy? Not really. A declining market *did* decrease real wealth, and this no doubt had some negative effect on consumption spending. But other forces (such as interest rate reductions by the Fed in 2001) helped to buoy consumption spending and keep it steady *in spite of* the negative wealth effect.

The Fed and the Stock Market

The experience of the late 1990s and early 2000s raised some important questions about the relationship between the Federal Reserve and the stock market—questions that have not been entirely resolved.

In 1995 and 1996, Greenspan began to worry that share prices might be rising out of proportion to the future profits corporations would be able to deliver to their owners. The Fed was worried that the market was experiencing a speculative *bubble*—a frenzy of buying that encouraged people to buy stocks and drive up their price because . . . well, just because their prices were rising.

In this view, the market in the late 1990s resembled the stock market in the 1920s, which is also often considered a bubble. While there were indeed reasons for optimism in the 1920s, there also seemed to be a speculative frenzy: Many investors borrowed money to buy stocks in companies they knew nothing about, just because of an anonymous tip or because they were watching the price of the stock go up. Indeed, the Dow Jones Industrial Average almost quadrupled from early 1920 to September 1929—just as it did during the 1990s. But when the bubble burst, it burst hard. From September 3, 1929, to July 8, 1932, the Dow fell from 381 to 41—about a 90 percent decline.[4] Many stocks of the most reliable and successful corporations (the so-called "blue chip" corporations) fell to only tiny fractions of their highs. General Electric stock, for example, fell from a high of $396\frac{1}{4}$ in 1929 to $8\frac{1}{2}$ in 1932; Bethlehem Steel from $140\frac{3}{8}$ to $7\frac{1}{4}$; and RCA from 101 to $2\frac{1}{2}$. Millions of people were financially wiped out—in itself, a human tragedy.

In 1996, when Alan Greenspan first made his "irrational exuberance" speech, he seemed to side with those who believed that the stock market was in the midst of a speculative bubble. His fear was that when the bubble burst—when people realized that there weren't sufficient buyers to keep propping up stock prices out of proportion to their future profits—then stock prices would come plummeting down to earth. And a burst bubble would be painful—millions of people would lose substantial amounts of wealth. Moreover, the Fed would be forced to intervene to prevent the wealth effect—this time in a negative direction—from creating a recession.

Could the Fed do so? Probably. We understand how the economy works much better today than we did in 1929, when—in retrospect—the Fed made several mistakes after the stock market crashed. But the Fed's knowledge isn't perfect and—as you've learned—Fed intervention is still fraught with uncertainty. There is always a chance the Fed will react too strongly, or not enough. From the Fed's point of view in the mid-1990s, the best economy would be one that hummed along without needing any policy intervention: That is, an economy with stock prices rising steadily and *slowly*, rather than a bubble that might burst and require a big policy shift.

In the mid-1990s, Greenspan seemed to be trying to "talk the market down" by letting stockholders know that he thought share prices were too high. The implied threat: If stocks rose any higher, the Fed would raise interest rates and bring them down. Indeed, according to many observers, merely hinting that the Fed *might* raise interest rates was designed to keep stock prices from rising too rapidly, and perhaps bring them down gently.

Only it didn't work. While Greenspan's irrational exuberance speech did bring the market down for a day or so, the relentless rise in stock prices continued. In October 1996, just before Greenpan's speech, the DJIA stood at about 6,500. By March 1999—less than three years later—it had reached 10,000.

---

[4] The Dow Jones Industrial Average measures *nominal* stock prices. Since the price level decreased over this period, the decline in *real* stock prices was less than 90 percent, but still a substantial loss.

Not only were Greenspan's efforts to "talk the market down" unsuccessful, they were also widely criticized. In the view of his critics, the value of stocks should be based on the decisions of those who buy and sell them. If people believe that a company is onto something good and that its future profits justify a doubling or tripling of its stock price within a short time, what business is it of the Fed to say they are wrong? After all, stock buying—and the funds it has made available to American corporations—is partly responsible for the remarkable rise in U.S. living standards over the past century. Moreover, the stock market has been especially effective in funneling funds to good ideas and away from bad ones because it relies on *decentralized* decision making. Those who put their money at risk decide for themselves what is and is not a good idea.

Greenspan himself seemed to change his tune as the 1990s continued. By 1998, he had stopped referring to exuberance—rational or irrational. Instead, he began to stress the remarkable changes in the economy, the rapid rise in productivity and potential output, and the fact that the American people—who buy and sell stocks— have a certain wisdom that should not be second-guessed by government officials. It was almost a complete reversal.

But as the 1990s came to a close, and the stock market continued to soar, the Fed faced a new problem: *the wealth effect.* Justified or not, share prices had continued to rise—and they rose a lot. In the two and a half years after Greenspan's famous irrational exuberance remarks in 1996, about $3 trillion in new wealth was created. Consumer spending was rising dramatically, and the Fed began to worry that the economy might be exceeding—or would soon exceed—its potential output.

Figure 6 shows one way we can view the Fed's problem: with aggregate demand and supply curves. In panel (a), the wealth effect of rising stock prices shifts the aggregate demand curve from AD_1 to AD_2, causing an increase in real GDP from Y_1 to Y_2 along with a rise in the price level. The question is: What happens next? That depends on where our potential output is relative to Y_2. If Y_2 is greater than potential output, the self-correcting mechanism will begin to work: The price level will rise further, bringing the economy back to potential output (assumed to be Y_1 in the figure). This is something the Fed has worked hard to avoid. As you've learned, inflation—once it begins—tends to be self-perpetuating. People begin to expect it. And once the inflation is embedded in the economy, eradicating it is painful: The Fed would have to raise interest rates and slow the economy by more than would have been necessary to prevent the inflation in the first place. Moreover, in the past, efforts to bring the inflation rate down have triggered deep recessions. From the Fed's point of view, preventing inflation in the first place is always the preferred alternative.

Figure 6 is useful, but it has a serious limitation: It doesn't take account of the rise in potential output. Each year, potential output increases because the population is growing, and because productivity—output per worker—is growing. In the 1990s and through early 2000, potential output was growing even more rapidly than in previous decades. We could illustrate this on an *AS–AD* diagram by shifting the *AS* curve rightward and downward over time. That is, due to changes in population and productivity, we could produce more output at any given price level, or have a lower price level at any given level of output. With a shifting *AS* curve, the Fed's goal is to shift the *AD* curve rightward each year by just enough to prevent inflation.

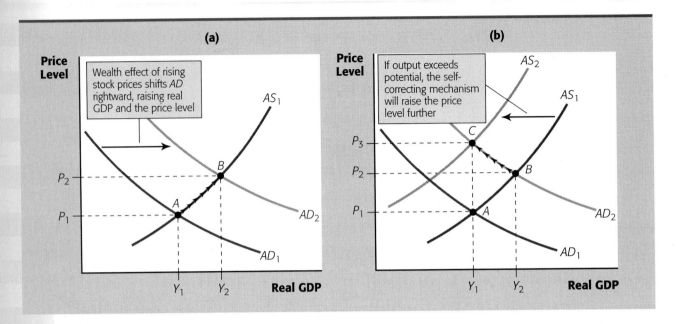

FIGURE 6
The Fed's Problem in 2000:
An *AS–AD* View

But the Phillips curve can illustrate the Fed's goal more easily. Look first at panel (a) of Figure 7, where the position of the economy in late 1999 and early 2000 is represented by point *A* on the Phillips curve PC_1: 4 percent unemployment and a 2.5 percent annual inflation rate. As you learned a few chapters ago ("Inflation and Monetary Policy"), the Fed can *keep* the economy at point *A* only if the actual unemployment rate, 4 percent, is also the *natural* rate of unemployment. In that case, the Fed—by keeping the economy at point *A*—would be allowing actual output to rise each year by just enough to keep it equal to potential output.

But what if the natural rate of unemployment is *greater* than 4 percent—say, 5 percent? Then, as you can see in panel (b), the economy would need to operate at point *B* to be at the natural rate. Point *A* now represents an overheated economy, with output greater than potential output. If we remain at point *A*, then over time the entire Phillips curve would shift upward, to the curve labeled PC_2, and point *A* would no longer be an option. If the Fed tried to maintain a 4 percent unemployment rate, the economy would then be at point *C*, with a rise in the inflation rate to 5 percent. To prevent any rise in inflation, the Fed would have to engineer a recession, bringing the economy to point *D* with unemployment above the natural rate.

To keep inflation low and stable without needing corrective recessions, the Fed strives to maintain unemployment at its natural rate. But no one—including the Fed—knows what the natural rate of unemployment *is* during any given year. We know that it is lower today than in the early 1990s—when it was believed to be about 5.5 or 6 percent. But no one knows how far it has fallen since then.

You might think that the Fed can estimate the natural rate by a process of trial and error, bringing the unemployment rate to a certain level (such as 4 percent) and seeing what happens to inflation. Then, if the inflation rate rises, the Fed would

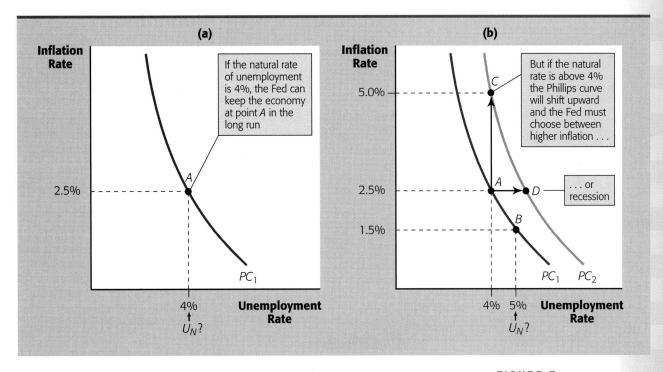

(a)

Inflation Rate

If the natural rate of unemployment is 4%, the Fed can keep the economy at point *A* in the long run

2.5%

A

PC_1

4% **Unemployment Rate**

$U_N?$

(b)

Inflation Rate

But if the natural rate is above 4% the Phillips curve will shift upward and the Fed must choose between higher inflation . . .

5.0% — *C*

. . . or recession

2.5% — *A* — *D*

1.5% — *B*

PC_1 PC_2

4% 5% **Unemployment Rate**

$U_N?$

FIGURE 7
The Fed's Problem In 2000: A Phillips Curve View

know that it had underestimated the natural rate. It could then slow the economy and bring unemployment back up to the natural rate.

Unfortunately, things are not so simple. In the real world, when the economy overheats, the inflation rate begins to rise only after a lag of several quarters or longer. By the time the Fed notices a rise in the inflation rate, the economy may have been overheated for months, and the Fed may have to take even more drastic action to bring us back to potential output. For this reason, the Fed looks ahead and determines whether *current* economic conditions are likely to raise the inflation rate in the *future*.

And that is just what the Fed did beginning in mid-1999. With the unemployment rate near 4 percent, the economy growing at a rapid 3.8 percent clip for a year, and the stock market continuing to rise to record levels, Fed officials believed that the wealth effect would overheat the economy if nothing were done. So the Fed took action, even though inflation was still low and stable. From June 1999 through May 2000, the Fed raised its target for the federal funds rate six times: from 4.75 percent to 6.5 percent.

Of course, by raising interest rates to rein in the economy, the Fed *also* brought down stock prices—both by slowing economic growth and the growth in profits *and* through the direct effect of higher interest rates on stocks. Thus the Fed, in trying to steer the economy, was accused of trying to regulate stock prices. Indeed, the Fed itself continued to regard stock prices as one of its tools for steering the economy: Higher interest rates decrease (or slow the rise in) stock prices, and thus slow spending through the wealth effect.

By 2001, the high-tech bust, the recession of 2001, and the attacks of September 11 brought the criticism to an end. It was not that the Fed stopped paying attention to the stock market in making policy. Rather, now the Fed was concerned about a *falling* market and an economy slowing *too* much. The Fed's moves—dropping interest rates rapidly throughout 2001—were popular: They helped to prop up the economy and the market at the same time, with each feeding back to the other.

As the economy began a slow expansion in 2002 and early 2003, the Fed kept the interest rate low. But most observers believed it was only a matter of time before the Fed began raising rates again. In that case, the unresolved question will surface again: Who should be setting the general level of share prices—the millions of stockholders who buy and sell shares, or the Federal Reserve?

Problems and Exercises
Answers to even-numbered Questions and Problems can be found on the text Web site at http://hall-lieb.swlearning.com.

1. The chapter contains the following statement: "The last decade was good for stocks. Someone who invested $10,000 in a typical group of S&P 500 stocks on January 30, 1993, would have been able to sell them for $22,196 on June 30, 2003." Using information in Table 1, demonstrate that this statement is correct. [*Hint:* Don't forget to compound the annual percentage changes.]

2. Use Table 1 to determine how much a $10,000 investment on June 30, in a typical group of Standard and Poor's 500 stocks would be worth three years later.

3. Use Table 1 to determine how much a $5,000 investment on June 30, 1993, in a typical group of Dow Jones industrial stocks, would be worth 10 years later.

4. Use Table 1 to answer the following questions.
   a. What was the *cumulative* percentage change in NASDAQ stocks from June 30, 1998 to June 30, 2003?
   b. What was the *cumulative* percentage change in the Standard and Poor's 500 from June 30, 2000 to June 30, 2003?

5. Use Table 1 to answer the following questions.
   a. What was the *cumulative* percentage change in the Dow Jones Industrial Average from June 30, 1993 to June 30, 2003?
   b. What was the *cumulative* percentage change in NASDAQ stocks from June 30, 2000 to June 30, 2003?

6. Suppose the corporate profits tax rate is reduced, and other taxes in the economy are increased by just enough to leave total tax revenue unchanged. Thus, the economy's equilibrium real GDP is unaffected, at least initially.
   a. Would this event have any impact on the stock market? Illustrate, using supply and demand curves for the typical stock. What will happen to the price of the typical stock?

   b. Using cause-and-effect diagrams like the ones in this chapter, show how this change in tax policy would first affect the stock market, then affect the economy, and then create feedback effects in the stock market.
   c. When we include feedback effects from the macroeconomy, is the ultimate effect on stock prices greater or smaller than the initial impact in (a) above? Explain.

7. Sometimes corporations will use their profits to buy back their own shares.
   a. Explain why this action—using funds that could have been given to shareholders as dividends—might actually benefit shareholders. (*Hint:* Draw a supply and demand diagram for the corporation's shares. Which curve is affected by a stock buyback?)
   b. In the United States, the tax rate on long-term capital gains (capital gains on assets held longer than one year) is lower than the tax rate on ordinary income, including income from dividends. Does this help explain why corporations sometimes buy back their own shares? Explain.

8. Suppose that, over time, people become more sophisticated about changes in stock prices. Specifically, they realize that while stock prices go down in a recession, they tend to rise when the recession ends. Would this change the way the economy affects stock prices? Would it change our view of the stock market as an automatic destabilizer over the business cycle? Explain.

9. Classify each of the following events as a shock that initially affects (a) primarily the economy; (b) primarily the stock market; (c) both the stock market and the economy. Justify your answer in each case.
   a. Government spending increases, while the Fed leaves its interest rate target unchanged.
   b. The Fed—beginning to worry about inflation—increases its interest rate target.

09/28/2004　　01:06 PM
RECEIPT EXPIRES ON 12/27/04

A receipt dated within 90 days is
required for ALL returns & exchanges
Giving a gift? Include a gift receipt!

RETURN

ORIG RCPT ID# 5 4265 0029 0079 1630 1
058160295　　STAR WARS TR　　T　44.99-
　　　　　　RETURN SUBTOTAL　44.99-
T = IA TAX 6.0000% on　44.99　2.70-
　　　　　　RETURN TOTAL　47.69-

PURCHASE

058160296　　STAR WARS TR　　T　44.99
　　　　SAME ITEM ONLY IF OPEN
　　　　Regular Price $49.99
　　　　PURCHASE SUBTOTAL　44.99
T = IA TAX 6.0000% on　44.99　2.70
　　　　PURCHASE TOTAL　47.69

　　　　EXCHANGE TOTAL　+0.00

RECEIPT ID# 2 4212 0029 0121 5258 6
VCD#759215547　　TM0xxxx1475

* INDICATES SALE PRICE

Save ALL Receipts
Give Gift Receipts & Gift Cards
Ask about Receipt Lookup

Return & Exchange Policy

A receipt dated within 90 days is required for all returns & exchanges.

All returns and exchanges must be new, unused, and contain all original packaging and accessories. Some items cannot be returned if opened, including music, movies, video games, software, & collectibles. Some items are subject to a 15% restocking fee, including camcorders, digital cameras, portable DVD and portable electronics. Other restrictions may apply.

Holiday and seasonal merchandise on clearance at time of return will be refunded at the current clearance price. Any purchase made by check may be refunded as a merchandise voucher.

All other returns or exchanges—including those without receipt—will be offered manufacturers' warranty & repair assistance at 1-800-303-0308.

For a gift receipt, bring this receipt back to any Target store within 90 days.

Return & Exchange Policy

A receipt dated within 90 days is required for all returns & exchanges.

All returns and exchanges must be new, unused, and contain all original packaging and accessories. Some items cannot be returned if opened, including music, movies, video games, software, & collectibles. Some items are subject to a 15% restocking fee, including camcorders, digital cameras, portable DVD and portable electronics. Other restrictions may apply.

10. In the section "A Shock to the Economy," we explored the impact of an increase in government purchases with an unchanged interest rate target by the Fed.
    a. In order to maintain an unchanged interest rate target, will the Fed have to increase or decrease the money supply? Illustrate with a diagram of the money market.
    b. Suppose the Fed instead decides to pursue a completely passive monetary policy—leaving the *money supply* unchanged. What will happen to the interest rate? (Illustrate with another diagram of the money market.)
    c. Under a passive monetary policy, does the change in government spending have more or less of an initial impact on the stock market (compared to the policy of maintaining an unchanged interest rate target)?

11. When population and productivity are increasing, potential output increases each year. One way to illustrate this is to shift the economy's *AS* curve rightward (and downward) each year. Assume that there is no expected inflation embedded in the economy, so that the ongoing inflation rate is zero. Using *AS–AD* diagrams, illustrate each of the following scenarios.

    a. Potential output is increasing, and the Fed allows actual output to rise just enough to keep up with potential.
    b. Potential output is increasing, and the Fed allows actual output to rise above potential.
    c. Potential output is increasing, and the Fed allows so little growth that output falls below potential.

12. Using a diagram similar to panel (b) of Figure 7, show what happens over time if the Fed maintains an unemployment rate of 4 percent when the *natural* rate of unemployment is actually 3.5 percent.

13. Figure 6 illustrates how a rise in stock prices can affect the economy in the short run (panel (a)) and the long run (panel (b)). Draw a diagram to illustrate the effect of a *drop* in stock prices (such as occured in 2000 and 2001) in the short run and the long run under two assumptions:
    a. The Fed stands by and does nothing.
    b. The Fed takes action (as it did in 2001) to fight the impact of the fall in stock prices.

Challenge Question

1. In addition to its short-run effects on the economy via the wealth effect, the stock market affects the economy in another way: It is part of the loanable funds market in which households make their saving available to firms. Thus, the *existence* of a stock market should affect the economy in the long run.
    a. Do stocks have any advantages for households over other forms of saving? If so, what are they? (Think of yourself or your family. Why might you want to hold some of your wealth in the form of stocks, rather than hold all of it in other forms such as bonds or cash?)
    b. Using a loanable funds diagram, and your answer in part (a), show what happens—in an economy that is initially without a stock market—when a viable

   stock market is introduced. In particular, which curve will shift?
    c. Using your graph from part (b), how does introducing a stock market into the economy affect the level of investment spending and the standard of living over the long run?
    d. Do stocks have any advantages for business firms over other ways of obtaining funds for investment projects? If so, what are they?
    e. On your loanable funds diagram, and using your answer from part (d), illustrate the impact of the stock market on the investment demand curve. Does this contribute to, or work against, the impact of the stock market on the economy that you found in part (c)?

 These exercises require access to Hall/Lieberman Xtra! If Xtra! did not come with your book, visit http://hallxtra.swlearning.com to purchase.

1. Use your Xtra! password at the Hall and Lieberman Web site (http://hallxtra.swlearning.com), select "Using *All* the Theory": The Stock Market and the Macroeconomy, and under Economic Applications, click on Econ-Data. Under *Hot Data,* scroll down to click on *Stock Prices: S&P 500.* Read the definition and click on Diagrams/Data, and use the information to answer the following questions.

    a. In the "Using *All* the Theory" section, changes in expected future profits of the firm is listed as a determinant of demand for a share of stock. Consider the S&P 500 and after-tax corporate profit diagram and confirm this relationship in aggregate. Why are these two graphs out of phase, i.e., why do the changes in the S&P 500 tend to be a leading indicator of corporate after-tax profits.

    b. In the "Using *All* the Theory" section, changes in the interest rate are listed as a determinant of demand for a share of stock. Consider the S&P 500 and the 10-year treasury bond yield diagram and explain the strong inverse relationship between interest rates—such as the yield on the prominent 10-year U.S. treasury bond, and stock prices, as indicated by the S&P 500 index.

    c. Consider the S&P 500 and the index of leading economic indicators diagram. Given that the S&P 500 is an element of the index of leading economic indicators, and that they tend to move together, what could be some of the possible reasons behind the decline in the indicator prior to each of the U.S. recessions since 1980, and the decline of the S&P 500 during these recessions?

Glossary

A

Absolute advantage The ability to produce a good or service, using fewer resources than other producers use.

Accounting profit Total revenue minus accounting costs.

Active monetary policy When the Fed changes the money supply in response to economic shocks.

Aggregate demand (*AD*) curve A curve indicating equilibrium GDP at each price level.

Aggregate expenditure (*AE*) The sum of spending by households, business firms, the government, and foreigners on final goods and services produced in the United States.

Aggregate production function The relationship showing how much total output can be produced with different quantities of labor, with quantities of all other resources held constant.

Aggregate supply (*AS*) curve A curve indicating the price level consistent with firms' unit costs and markups for any level of output over the short run.

Aggregation The process of combining different things into a single category.

Alternate goods Other goods that a firm could produce, using some of the same types of inputs as the good in question.

Appreciation An increase in the price of a currency in a floating-rate system.

Automatic stabilizers Forces that reduce the size of the expenditure multiplier and diminish the impact of spending shocks.

Autonomous consumption spending The part of consumption spending that is independent of income; also the vertical intercept of the consumption function.

Average fixed cost Total fixed cost divided by the quantity of output produced.

Average standard of living Total output (real GDP) per person.

Average tax rate The fraction of a given income paid in taxes.

Average total cost Total cost divided by the quantity of output produced.

Average variable cost Total variable cost divided by the quantity of output produced.

B

Balance sheet A financial statement showing assets, liabilities, and net worth at a point in time.

Banking panic A situation in which depositors attempt to withdraw funds from many banks simultaneously

Behavioral economics A subfield of economics focusing on behavior that deviates from the standard assumptions of economic models.

Black market A market in which goods are sold illegally at a price above the legal ceiling.

Bond A promise to pay a specific sum of money at some future date.

Boom A period of time during which real GDP is above potential GDP.

Budget constraint The different combinations of goods a consumer can afford with a limited budget, at given prices.

Budget deficit The excess of government purchases over net taxes.

Budget line The graphical representation of a budget constraint, showing the maximum affordable quantity of one good for given amounts of another good.

Budget surplus The excess of net taxes over government purchases.

Business cycles Fluctuations in real GDP around its long-term growth trend.

Business demand for funds curve Indicates the level of investment spending firms plan at various interest rates.

Business firm An organization, owned and operated by private individuals, that specializes in production.

C

Capital Something produced that is long-lasting and used to produce other goods.

Capital gain The return someone gets by selling a financial asset at a price higher than they paid for it.

Capital gains tax A tax on profits earned when a financial asset is sold at more than its acquisition price.

Capital per worker The total capital stock divided by total employment.

Capital stock The total amount of capital in a nation that is productively useful at a particular point in time.

Capitalism A type of economic system in which most resources are owned privately.

Cartel A group of firms that selects a common price that maximizes total industry profits.

Cash in the hands of the public Currency and coins held outside of banks.

Central bank A nation's principal monetary authority responsible for controlling the money supply.

Change in demand A shift of a demand curve in response to a change in some variable other than price.

Change in quantity demanded A movement along a demand curve in response to a change in price.

Change in quantity supplied A movement along a supply curve in response to a change in price.

Change in supply A shift of a supply curve in response to some variable other than price.

Circular flow A diagram that shows how goods, resources, and dollar payments flow between households and firms.

Classical model A macroeconomic model that explains the long-run behavior of the economy.

Coase theorem When a side payment can be arranged without cost, the market will solve an externality problem-and create the efficient outcome-on its own.

Command or centrally planned economy An economic system in which resources are allocated according to explicit instructions from a central authority.

Communism A type of economic system in which most resources are owned in common.

Comparative advantage The ability to produce a good or service at a lower opportunity cost than other producers.

Compensating wage differential A difference in wages that makes two jobs equally attractive to a worker.

Complement A good that is used together with some other good.

Complementary input An input whose utilization increases the marginal product of another input.

Complete crowding out A dollar-for-dollar decline in one sector's spending caused by an increase in some other sector's spending.

Constant cost industry An industry in which the long-run supply curve is horizontal because each firm's *ATC* curve is unaffected by changes in industry output.

Constant returns to scale Long-run average total cost is unchanged as output increases.

Consumer Price Index An index of the cost, through time, of a fixed market basket of goods purchased by a typical household in some base period.

Consumer surplus The difference between the value of a unit of a good to the buyer and what the buyer actually pays for it.

Consumption (C) The part of GDP purchased by households as final users.

Consumption function A positively sloped relationship between real consumption spending and real disposable income.

Consumption tax A tax on the part of their income that households spend.

Consumption-income line A line showing aggregate consumption spending at each level of income or GDP.

Copyright A grant of exclusive rights to sell a literary, musical, or artistic work.

Corporate profits tax A tax on the profits earned by corporations.

Corporation A firm owned by those who buy shares of stock and whose liability is limited to the amount of their investment in the firm.

Coupon payments A series of periodic payments that a bond promises before maturity.

Critical assumption Any assumption that affects the conclusions of a model in an important way.

Cross-price elasticity of demand The percentage change in the quantity demanded of one good caused by a 1-percent change in the price of another good.

Crowding out A decline in one sector's spending caused by an increase in some other sector's spending.

Cyclical deficit The part of the federal budget deficit that varies with the business cycle.

Cyclical unemployment Joblessness arising from changes in production over the business cycle.

D

Decreasing cost industry An industry in which the long-run supply curve slopes downward because each firm's *ATC* curve shifts downward as industry output increases.

Deflation A decrease in the price level from one period to the next.

Demand curve facing the firm A curve that indicates, for different prices, the quantity of output that customers will purchase from a particular firm.

Demand curve for foreign currency A curve indicating the quantity of a specific foreign currency that Americans will want to buy, during a given period, at each different exchange rate.

Demand deposit multiplier The number by which a change in reserves is multiplied to determine the resulting change in demand deposits.

Demand deposits Checking accounts that do not pay interest.

Demand schedule A list showing the quantities of a good that consumers would choose to purchase at different prices, with all other variables held constant.

Demand shock Any event that causes the *AD* curve to shift.

Depreciation A decrease in the price of a currency in a floating-rate system.

Depression An unusually severe recession.

Derived demand The demand for a resource that arises from, and varies with, the demand for the product it helps to produce.

Devaluation A change in the exchange rate from a higher fixed rate to a lower fixed rate.

Diminishing marginal returns to labor The marginal product of labor decreases as more labor is hired.

Discount rate The interest rate used in computing present values.

Discounting The act of converting a future value into its present-day equivalent.

Discouraged workers Individuals who would like a job, but have given up searching for one.

Discrimination When a group of people have different opportunities because of personal characteristics that have nothing to do with their abilities.

Diseconomies of scale Long-run average total cost increases as output increases.

Disposable income Household income minus net taxes, which is either spent or saved.

Diversification The process of reducing risk by spreading sources of income among different alternatives.

Dividends Part of a firm's current profit that is distributed to shareholders.

Dominant strategy A strategy that is best for a player no matter what strategy the other player chooses.

Dow Jones Industrial Average An index of the prices of stocks of 30 large U.S. firms.

Duopoly An oligopoly market with only two sellers.

E

Economic growth The increase in our production of goods and services that occurs over long periods of time.

Economic luxury A good with an income elasticity of demand greater than 1.

Economic necessity A good with an income elasticity of demand between 0 and 1.

Economic profit Total revenue minus all costs of production.

Economic system A system of resource allocation and resource ownership.

Economics The study of choice under conditions of scarcity.

Economies of scale Long-run average total cost decreases as output increases.

Efficient market A market that instantaneously incorporates all available information relevant to a stock's price.

Elastic demand A price elasticity of demand with absolute value greater than 1.

Entrepreneurship The ability and willingness to combine the other resources—labor, capital, and natural resources—into a productive enterprise.

Equilibrium GDP In the short run, the level of output at which output and aggregate expenditure are equal.

Equilibrium price The market price that, once achieved, remains constant until either the demand curve or supply curve shifts.

Equilibrium quantity The market quantity bought and sold per period that, once achieved, remains constant until either the demand curve or supply curve shifts.

Excess demand At a given price, the excess of quantity demanded over quantity supplied.

Excess demand for bonds The amount of bonds demanded exceeds the amount supplied at a particular interest rate.

Excess reserves Reserves in excess of required reserves.

Excess supply At a given price, the excess of quantity supplied over quantity demanded.

Excess supply of money The amount of money supplied exceeds the amount demanded at a particular interest rate.

Exchange The act of trading with others to obtain what we desire.

Exchange rate The amount of one currency that is traded for one unit of another currency.

Excise tax A tax on a specific good or service.

Excludability The ability to exclude those who do not pay for a good from consuming it.

Exit A permanent cessation of production when a firm leaves an industry.

Expansion A period of increasing real GDP.

Expenditure approach Measuring GDP by adding the value of goods and services purchased by each type of final user.

Expenditure multiplier The amount by which equilibrium real GDP changes as a result of a one-dollar change in autonomous consumption, investment spending, government purchases, or net exports.

Explicit collusion Cooperation involving direct communication between competing firms about setting prices.

Explicit cost The dollars sacrificed—and actually paid out—for a choice.

Exports Goods and services produced domestically, but sold abroad.

Externality A by-product of a good or activity that affects someone not immediately involved in the transaction.

F

Factor markets Markets in which resources—labor, capital, land and natural resources, and entrepreneurship—are sold to firms.

Factor payments Payments to the owners of resources that are used in production

Factor payments approach Measuring GDP by summing the factor payments earned by all households in the economy.

Federal funds rate The interest rate charged for loans of reserves among banks.

Federal Open Market Committee A committee of Federal Reserve officials that established U.S. monetary policy.

Federal Reserve System The central bank and national monetary authority of the United States.

Fiat money Anything that serves as a means of payment by government declaration.

Final good A good sold to its final user.

Financial asset A promise to pay future income in some form, such as future profits or future interest payments.

Financial intermediary A business firm that specializes in brokening between savers and borrowers.

Firm's quantity supplied The specific amount a firm would choose to sell over some time period, given (1) a particular price for the good; (2) all other constraints on the firm.

Firm's supply curve A curve that shows the quantity of output a competitive firm will produce at different prices.

Fiscal policy A change in government purchases or net taxes designed to change total spending and thereby change total output.

Fixed costs Costs of fixed inputs.

Fixed exchange rate A government-declared exchange rate maintained by central bank intervention in the foreign exchange market.

Fixed input An input whose quantity must remain constant, regardless of how much output is produced.

Floating exchange rate An exchange rate that is freely determined by the forces of supply and demand.

Flow variable a variable measuring a process over some period

Foreign currency crisis A loss of faith that a country can prevent a drop in its exchange rate, leading to a rapid depletion of its foreign currency (e.g., dollar) reserves.

Foreign exchange market The market in which one country's currency is traded for another country's.

Free rider problem When the efficient outcome requires a side payment but individual gainers will not contribute.

Frictional unemployment Joblessness experienced by people who are between jobs or who are just entering or reentering the labor market.

Full employment A situation in which there is no cyclical unemployment.

Fundamental analysis A method of predicting a stock's price based on the fundamental forces driving the firm's future earnings.

G

Game theory An approach to modeling the strategic interaction of oligopolists in terms of moves and countermoves.

GDP price index An index of the price level for all final goods and services included in GDP.

General human capital Knowledge, education, or training that is valuable at many different firms.

Gini coefficient A measure of income inequality; the ratio of the area above a Lorenz curve and under the complete equality line to the area under the diagonal.

Government demand for funds curve Indicates the amount of government borrowing at various interest rates.

Government franchise A government-granted right to be the sole seller of a product or service.

Government purchases (G) Spending by federal, state, and local governments on goods and services.

Gross domestic product (GDP) The total value of all final goods and services produced for the marketplace during a given year, within the nation's borders.

H

(Household) saving The portion of after-tax income that households do not spend on consumption.

Household's quantity demanded The specific amount a household would choose to buy over some time period, given (1) a particular price, (2) all other constraints on the household.

Human capital The skills and training of the labor force.

I

Imperfectly competitive market A market in which a single buyer or seller has the power to influence the price of the product.

Implicit cost The value of something sacrificed when no direct payment is made.

Imports Goods and services produced abroad, but consumed domestically.

Incidence The division of a tax payment between buyers and sellers, determined by comparing the new (after tax) and old (pretax) market equilibriums.

Income The amount that a person or firm earns over a particular period.

Income effect As the price of a good decreases, the consumer's purchasing power increases, causing a change in quantity demanded for the good.

Income elasticity of demand The percentage change in quantity demanded caused by a 1-percent change in income.

Increasing cost industry An industry in which the long-run supply curve slopes upward because each firm's *ATC* curve shifts upward as industry output increases.

Increasing marginal returns to labor The marginal product of labor increases as more labor is hired.

Index A series of numbers used to track a variable's rise or fall over time.

Indexation Adjusting the value of some nominal payment in proportion to a price index, in order to keep the real payment unchanged.

Indifference curve A curve representing all combinations of two goods that make the consumer equally well off.

Indifference map A set of indifference curves that represent an individual's preferences.

Individual demand curve A curve showing the quantity of a good or service demanded by a particular individual at each different price.

Inelastic demand A price elasticity of demand with absolute value between 0 and 1.

Infant industry argument The argument that an industry in which a country has a comparative advantage might need protection from foreign competition in order to flourish.

Inferior good A good that people demand less of as their income rises.

Inflation rate The percent change in the price level from one period to the next.

Injections Spending from sources other than households.

Input Anything (including a resource) used to produce a good or service.

Interest rate target The interest rate the Federal Reserve aims to achieve by adjusting the money supply.

Intermediate goods Goods used up in producing final goods.

International Monetary Fund (IMF) An international organization founded in 1945 to help stabilize the world monetary system.

Investment Firms' purchases of new capital over some period of time.

Investment tax credit A reduction in taxes for firms that invest in capital.

Involuntary part-time workers Individuals who would like a full-time job, but who are working only part time.

L

Labor The time human beings spend producing goods and services.

Labor demand curve Indicates how many workers firms will want to hire at various real wage rates.

Labor force Those people who have a job or who are looking for one.

Labor force participation rate (LFPR) The percentage of the population that wants to be working.

Labor productivity The output produced by the average worker in an hour.

Labor shortage The quantity of labor demanded exceeds the quantity supplied for some period of time.

Labor supply curve A curve indicating the number of people who want jobs in a labor market at each wage rate.

Labor surplus The quantity of labor supplied exceeds the quantity demanded for some period of time.

Law of demand As the price of a good increases, the quantity demanded decreases.

Law of diminishing marginal returns As more and more of any input is added to a fixed amount of other inputs, its marginal product will eventually decline.

Law of diminishing marginal utility As consumption of a good or service increases, marginal utility decreases.

Law of increasing opportunity cost The more of something that is produced, the greater the opportunity cost of producing one more unit.

Law of supply As the price of a good increases, the quantity supplied increases.

Leakages Income earned, but not spent, by households during a given year.

Liquidity The property of being easily converted into cash.

Loan An agreement to pay back borrowed funds, signed by a household or noncorporate business.

Loanable funds market The market in which households make their saving available to borrowers.

Long run A time horizon long enough for a firm to vary all of its inputs.

Long-run aggregate supply curve A vertical line indicating all possible output and price-level combinations at which the economy could end up in the long run.

Long-run average total cost The cost of producing each quantity

Long-run elasticity An elasticity measured a year or more after a price change.

Long-run labor supply curve Curve indicating how many people will want to work in a labor market after full adjustment to a change in the wage rate.

Long-run Phillips curve A vertical line indicating that in the long run, unemployment must eqal its natural rate, regardless of the rate of inflation.

Long-run supply curve A curve indicating the quantity of output that all sellers in a market will produce at different prices, after all long-run adjustments have taken place.

Long-run total cost The cost of producing each quantity of output when all inputs are variable and the least-cost input mix is chosen.

Lorenz curve When households are arrayed according to their incomes, a line showing the cumulative percent of income received by each cumulative percent of households.

Loss The difference between total cost (TC) and total revenue (TR), when $TC > TR$.

Lumpy input An input whose quantity cannot be increased gradually as output increases, but must instead be adjusted in large jumps.

M

M1 A standard measure of the money supply, including cash in the hands of the public, checking account deposits, and travelers checks.

M2 M1 plus savings account balances, noninstitutional money market mutual fund balances, and small time deposits.

Macroeconomics The study of the behavior of the overall economy.

Managed float A policy of frequent central bank intervention to move the exchange rate.

Marginal approach to profit A firm maximizes its profit by taking any action that adds more to its revenue than to its cost.

Marginal cost The increase in total cost from producing one more unit of output.

Marginal factor cost (MFC) The change in the firm's total cost divided by the change in its employment of a resource

Marginal product of labor The additional output produced when one more worker is hired.

Marginal propensity to consume The amount by which consumption spending rises when disposable income rises by one dollar.

Marginal rate of substitution (MRSy,x) The maximum amount of good *y* a consumer would willingly trade for one more unit of good *x*. Also, the slope of a segment of an indifference curve.

Marginal revenue The change in total revenue from producing one more unit of output.

Marginal revenue product (MRP) The change in the firm's total revenue divided by the change in its employment of a resource.

Marginal revenue product of capital The increase in revenue due to a one-unit increase in the capital input.

Marginal social benefit (MSB) The full benefit of producing another unit of a good, including the benefit to the consumer and any benefits enjoyed by third parties.

Marginal social cost (MSC) The full cost of producing another unit of a good, including the marginal cost to the producer and any harm caused to third parties.

Marginal tax rate The fraction of an additional dollar of income paid in taxes.

Marginal utility The change in total utility an individual obtains from consuming an additional unit of a good or service.

Market A group of buyers and sellers with the potential to trade with each other.

Market clearing Adjustment of prices until quantities supplied and demanded are equal.

Market consumer surplus The total consumer surplus enjoyed by all consumers in a market.

Market economy An economic system in which resources are allocated through individual decision making.

Market failure A market that fails to take advantage of every Pareto improvement.

Market labor demand curve Curve indicating the total number of workers all firms in a labor market want to employ at each wage rate.

Market producer surplus The total producer surplus gained by all sellers in a market.

Market quantity demanded The specific amount of a good that all buyers in the market would choose to buy over some time period, given (1) a particular price, (2) all other constraints they face.

Market quantity supplied The specific amount of a good that all sellers in the market would choose to sell over some time period, given (1) a particular price for the good; (2) all other constraints on firms.

Market signals Price changes that cause changes in production to match changes in consumer demand.

Market structure The characteristics of a market that influence how trading takes place.

Market supply curve A curve indicating the quantity of output that all sellers in a market will produce at different prices.

Maturity date The date at which a bond's principal amount will be paid to the bond's owner.

Means of payment Anything acceptable as payment for goods and services.

Microeconomics The study of the behavior of individual households, firms, and governments; the choices they make; and their interaction in specific markets.

Minimum efficient scale The lowest output level at which the firm's *LRATC* curve hits bottom.

Model An astract representation of reality.

Monetary policy Control or manipulation of the money supply by the Federal Reserve designed to achieve a macroeconomic goal.

Money An asset widely accepted as a means of payments.

Money demand curve A curve indicating how much money will be willingly held at each interest rate.

Money supply The total amount of money held by the public.

Money supply curve A line showing the total quantity of money in the economy at each interest rate.

Monopolistic competition A market structure in which there are many firms selling products that are differentiated, and in which there is easy entry and exit.

Monopoly firm The only seller of a good or service that has no close substitutes.

Monopoly market The market in which a monopoly firm operates.

Moral hazard When decision makers-expecting assistance in the event of an unfavorable outcome-change their behavior so that the unfavorable outcome is more likely.

Mutual fund A corporation that specializes in owning shares of stock in other corporations.

N

Nash equilibrium A situation in which every player of a game takes the best action for themselves, given the actions taken by all other players.

Natural monopoly A market in which a single firm's production is characterized by economies of scale, even when its output expands to serve the entire market.

Natural oligopoly A market that tends naturally toward oligopoly because the minimum efficient scale of the typical firm is large fraction of the market.

Natural rate of unemployment The unemployment rate when there is no cyclical unemployment.

Natural resources Land as well as the naturally occurring materials that come with it.

Net exports (NX) Total exports minus total imports.

Net financial inflow An inflow of funds equal to a nation's trade deficit.

Net investment Investment minus depreciation.

Net taxes Government tax revenues minus transfer payments.

Net worth The difference between assets and liabilities.

Network externalities A situation in which the value of a good or service to each user increases as more people use it.

Nominal interest rate The annual percent increase in a lender's dollars from making a loan.

Nominal variable A variable measured without adjustment for the dollar's changing value.

Nonmarket production Goods and services that are produced but not sold in a market.

Nonmonetary job characteristic Any aspect of a job—other than the wage—that matters to a potential or current employee.

Nonprice competition Any action a firm takes to increase the demand for its product, other than cutting its price.

Normal good A good that people demand more of as their income rises.

Normal profit Another name for zero economic profit.

Normative economics The study of what should be; it is used to make value judgments, identify problems, and prescribe solutions.

O

Oligopoly A market structure in which a small number of firms are strategically interdependent.

Open market operations Purchases or sales of bonds by the Federal Reserve System.

Opportunity cost What is given up when taking an action or making a choice.

Optimum currency area A region whose economies perform better with a single currency than with separate national currencies.

P

Pareto improvement An action that makes at least one person better off, and harms no one.

Partnership A firm owned and usually operated by several individuals who share in the profits and bear personal responsibility for any losses.

Passive monetary policy When the Fed keeps the money supply constant regardless of shocks to the economy.

Patent A temporary grant of monopoly rights over a new product or scientific discovery.

Patent protection A government grant of exclusive rights to use or sell a new technology.

Payoff matrix A table showing the payoffs to each of two players for each pair of strategies they choose.

Perfect competition A market structure in which there are many buyers and sellers, the product is standardized, and sellers can easily enter or exit the market.

Perfect price discrimination Charging each customer the most he or she would be willing to pay for each unit purchased.

Perfectly (infinitely) elastic demand A price elasticity of demand approaching minus infinity.

Perfectly competitive labor market Market with many indistinguishable sellers of labor and many buyers, and with easy entry and exit of workers.

Perfectly competitive market A market in which no buyer or seller has the power to influence the price.

Perfectly inelastic demand A price elasticity of demand equal to 0.

Phillips curve A curve indicating the Fed's choice between inflation and unemployment in the short run.

Physical capital The part of the capital stock consisting of physical goods, such as machinery, equipment, and factories.

Planned investment spending Business purchases of plant and equipment.

Plant The collection of fixed inputs at a firm's disposal.

Positive economics The study of how the economy works.

Potential output The level of output the economy could produce if operating at full employment.

Poverty line The income level below which a family is considered to be in poverty.

Poverty rate The percent of families whose incomes fall below a certain minimum—the poverty line.

Present value The value, in today's dollars, of a sum of money to be received or paid at a specific date in the future.

Price The amount of money that must be paid to a seller to obtain a good or service.

Price ceiling A government-imposed maximum price in a market.

Price discrimination Charging different prices to different customers for reasons other than differences in cost.

Price elasticity of demand The sensitivity of quantity demanded to price; the percentage change in quantity demanded caused by a 1-percent change in price.

Price elasticity of supply The percentage change in quantity supplied of a good or service caused by a 1-percent change in its price.

Price floor A government-imposed minimum price in a market.

Price leadership A form of tacit collusion in which one firm sets a price that other firms copy.

Price level The average level of dollar prices in the economy.

Price taker Any firm that treats the price of its product as given and beyond its control.

Primary market The market in which newly issued financial assets are sold for the first time.

Principal (face value) The amount of money a bond promises to pay when it matures.

Principal-agent problem A situation in which an agent maximizes her own well-being at the expense of the principal who hired her.

Principle of asset valuation The idea that the value of an asset is equal to the total present value of all the future benefits it generates.

Private investment (I) The sum of business plant, equipment, and software purchases, new- home construction, and inventory changes; often referred to as just investment.

Producer surplus The difference between what the seller actually gets for a unit of a good and the cost of providing it.

Product markets Markets in which firms sell goods and services to households or other firms.

Production function A function that indicates the maximum amount of output a firm can produce over some period of time from each combination of inputs.

Production possibilities frontier (PPF) A curve showing all combinations of two goods that can be produced with the resources and technology currently available.

Productive inefficiency A situation in which more of at least one good can be produced without sacrificing the production of any other good.

Profit Total revenue minus total cost.

Progressive income tax A tax that collects a higher percentage of total income from higher income households.

Progressive tax A tax whose rate increases as income increases.

Property income Income derived from supplying capital, entrepreneurship, land, or natural resources.

Protectionism The belief that a nation's industries should be protected from foreign competition.

Purchasing power parity (PPP) theory The idea that the exchange rate will adjust in the long run so that the average price of goods in two countries will be roughly the same.

Pure discount bond A bond that promises no payments except for the principal it pays at maturity.

Pure private good A good that is both rivalrous and excludable.

Pure public good A good that is both nonrivalrous and nonexcludable.

Q

Quota A limit on the physical volume of imports.

R

Rational preferences Preferences that satisfy two conditions: (1) Any two alternatives can be compared, and one is preferred or else the two are valued equally, and (2) the comparisons are logically consistent or transitive.

Real interest rate The annual percent increase in a lender's purchasing power from making a loan.

Real variable A variable adjusted for changes in the dollar's value.

Recession A period of significant decline in real GDP.

Regressive tax A tax for which the percentage of income taxed falls as income rises.

Relative price The price of one good relative to the price of another.

Rent controls Government-imposed maximum rents on apartments and homes.

Rent-seeking activity Any costly action a firm undertakes to establish or maintain its monopoly status.

Repeated play A situation in which strategically interdependent sellers compete over many time periods.

Required reserve ratio The minimum fraction of checking account balances that banks must hold as reserves.

Required reserves The minimum amount of reserves a bank must hold, depending on the amount of its deposit liabilities.

Reservation wage The lowest wage rate at which an individual would supply labor to a particular labor market.

Reserves Vault cash plus balances held at the Fed.

Resource allocation A method of determining which goods and services will be produced, how they will be produced, and who will get them.

Resources The labor, capital, land and natural resources, and entrepreneurship that are used to produce goods and services.

Rivalry A situation in which one person's consumption of a unit of a good or service means that no one else can consume that unit.

Run on the bank An attempt by many of a bank's depositors to withdraw their funds.

S

Say's law The idea that total spending will be sufficient to purchase the total output produced.

Scarcity A situation in which the amount of something available is insufficient to satisfy the desire for it.

Seasonal unemployment Joblessness related to changes in weather, tourist patterns, or other seasonal factors.

Secondary market The market in which previously issued financial assets are sold.

Self-correcting mechanism The adjustment process through which price and wage changes return the economy to full-employment output in the long run.

Share of stock A share of ownership in a corporation.

Short run A time horizon during which at least one of the firm's inputs cannot be varied.

Short side of the market The smaller of quantity supplied and quantity demanded at a particular price.

Shortage An excess demand not eliminated by a rise in price, so that quantity demanded continues to exceed quantity supplied.

Short-run elasticity An elasticity measured just a short time after a price change.

Short-run macro model A macroeconomic model that explains how changes in spending can affect real GDP in the short run.

Short-run macroeconomic equilibrium A combination of price level and GDP consistent with both the *AD* and *AS* curves.

Shutdown price The price at which a firm is indifferent between producing and shutting down.

Shutdown rule In the short run, the firm should continue to produce if total revenue exceeds total variable costs; otherwise, it should shut down.

Simplifying assumption Any assumption that makes a model simpler without affecting any of its important conclusions.

Single-price monopoly A monopoly firm that is limited to charging the same price for each unit of output sold.

Socialism A type of economic system in which most resources are owned by the state.

Sole proprietorship A firm owned by a single individual.

Specialization A method of production in which each person concentrates on a limited number of activities.

Specific human capital Knowledge, education, or training that is valuable only at a specific firm.

Spending shock A change in spending that ultimately affects the entire economy.

Stagflation The combination of falling output and rising prices.

Standard & Poor's 500 An index of the prices of stocks of 500 large U.S. firms.

Statistical discrimination When individuals are excluded from an activity based on the statistical probability of behavior in their group, rather than their personal characteristics.

Stock variable a variable measuring a quantity at a moment in time.

Structural deficit The part of the federal budget deficit that is independent of the business cycle.

Structural unemployment Joblessness arising from mismatches between workers' skills and employers' requirements or between workers' locations and employers' locations.

Substitutable input An input whose utilization decreases the marginal product of another input.

Substitute A good that can be used in place of some other good and that fulfills more or less the same purpose.

Substitution effect As the price of a good falls, the consumer substitutes that good in place of other goods whose prices have not changed.

Sunk cost A cost that has been paid or must be paid, regardless of any future action being considered.

Supply curve A graphical depiction of a supply schedule; a curve showing the quantity of a good or service supplied at various prices, with all other variables held constant.

Supply curve for foreign currency A curve indicating the quantity of a specific foreign currency that will be supplied, during a given period, at each different exchange rate.

Supply of funds curve Indicates the level of household saving at various interest rates.

Supply schedule A list showing the quantities of a good or service that firms would choose to produce and sell at different prices, with all other variables held constant.

Supply shock Any event that causes the *AS* curve to shift.

Surplus An excess supply not eliminated by a fall in price, so that quantity supplied continues to exceed quantity demanded.

T

Tacit collusion Any form of oligopolistic cooperation that does not involve an explicit agreement.

Tariff A tax on imports.

Tax shifting The process by which some or all of a tax imposed on one side of a market ends up being paid by the other side of the market.

Taylor rule A proposed rule that would require the Fed to change the interest-rate by a specified amount whenever real GDP or inflation deviate from their preannounced targets.

Technical analysis A method of predicting a stock's price based on that stock's past behavior.

Technological change The invention or discovery of new inputs, new outputs, or new production methods.

Technology A method by which inputs are combined to produce a good or service.

Terms of trade The ratio at which a country can trade domestically produced products for foreign-produced products.

Tit-for-tat A game-theoretic strategy of doing to another player this period what he has done to you in the previous period.

Tort A wrongful act that harms someone.

Total cost The costs of all inputs-fixed and variable.

Total demand for funds curve Indicates the total amount of borrowing at various interest rates.

Total fixed cost The cost of all inputs that are fixed in the short run.

Total net benefits The sum of consumer and producer surplus in a particular market.

Total product The maximum quantity of output that can be produced from a given combination of inputs.

Total revenue The total inflow of receipts from selling a given amount of output.

Total variable cost The cost of all variable inputs used in producing a particular level of output.

Tradable permit A license that allows a company to release a unit of pollution into the environment over some period of time.

Trade deficit The excess of a nation's imports over its exports during a given period.

Trade surplus The excess of a nation's exports over its imports during a given period.

Traditional economy An economy in which resources are allocated according to long-lived practices from the past.

Tragedy of the commons The problem of overuse when a good is rivalrous but nonexcludable.

Transaction costs The time costs and other costs required to carry out market exchanges.

Transfer payment Any payment that is not compensation for supplying goods, services, or resources.

Trough The bottom point of a recession, when a contraction ends and an expansion begins.

U

Unemployment rate The fraction of the labor force that is without a job.

Unit of value A common unit for measuring how much something is worth.

Unitary elastic demand A price elasticity of demand equal to 21.

Utility A quantitative measure of pleasure or satisfaction obtained from consuming goods and services.

V

Value added The revenue a firm receives minus the cost of the intermediate goods it buys.

Value-added approach Measuring GDP by summing the value added by all firms in the economy.

Variable costs Costs of variable inputs.

Variable input An input whose usage can change as the level of output changes.

W

Wealth constraint At any point in time, wealth is fixed.

Wealth The total value of everything a person or firm owns, at a point in time, minus the total value of everything owed.

Welfare loss The dollar value of potential benefits not achieved due to inefficiency in a particular market.

Y

Yield The rate of return a bond earns for its owner.

Index